Praise for previous editio[ns of]

SAD MACs, BOMBS, AND OTHER DISASTERS

"… the *only* book that Apple recommends as reading for its [Support Techs]."
— Rachel Rowe, Apple Support Technician

Main selection.
— Mac Professional's Book Club

"…the hardware- and software-troubleshooting guide that ought to ship with every Mac."
— Andy Ihnatko, *MacUser*

"I know of no other resource, book, or software that explains system errors, what causes them, and what to do about them as completely and cogently as *Sad Macs, Bombs, and Other Disasters*. Having saved my bacon several times over, it has earned a permanent place of honor on my bookshelf. It's worth every penny…"
— Bob LeVitus, Mac book author and *MacUser* Help Folder columnist

"I agree that Ted's sage advice is well worth the investment."
— Christopher Breen, Help Folder, *MacUser*

"Ted Landau is a true expert in Macintosh troubleshooting, and his book, *Sad Macs, Bombs, and Other Disasters*, is an excellent reference."
— Ric Ford, MacInTouch, *MacWEEK*

"I recommend Ted Landau's excellent book, *Sad Macs, Bombs, and Other Disasters.*"
— Lon Poole, Quick Tips, *Macworld*

"Whether you're still operating with System 6.1 or are in charge of a workgroup, this book gives you the background needed to diagnose a problem and take steps to prevent its recurrence."
— *Macworld*

"The best book for finding out what is wrong with your Mac and dealing with it. Using a non-technical, step-by-step approach, this book provides disaster relief at its finest. Whether you are a new or seasoned user, this book is crammed full of updated and vital fix-it information you can't survive without."
A Choice Product since 1994.
— BMUG

"With *Sad Macs,* you'll be well-prepared when trouble hits. This book is like a wise uncle who has seen it all before. A keeper."
— Charles Haddad, *Mac News, Atlanta Journal/Constitution*

"If you buy no other book for your Mac, buy this one!"
— Dennis Walls, MacBooks Web site

Ted Landau

AND WHAT TO DO ABOUT THEM

Third Edition

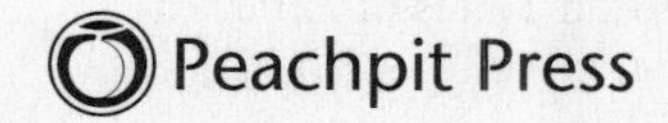

Sad Macs, Bombs, and Other Disasters
Ted Landau

Peachpit Press
2414 Sixth Street
Berkeley, CA 94710
510/548-4393
510/548-5991 (fax)

Find us on the World Wide Web at: *http://www.peachpit.com*

Peachpit Press is a division of Addison Wesley Longman

Editor: Jeremy Judson
Copyeditor: Chris Kelly
Production: David Van Ness
Cover design: Profile Design

ISBN 0-201-68810-7

9 8 7 6 5 4 3

Printed and bound in the United States of America

To Naomi and Brian
and
To Ruthe

Acknowledgments

The support and encouragement that I get from my wife, Naomi, and my son, Brian, seem to get greater with each new edition of this book. Given how difficult I can be, especially as deadlines loom, I don't know how they do it! But I am sure glad they do. Thank you, thank you, thank you.

The biggest behind-the-scenes change for this edition is that I have changed publishers. After several successful years of working with Addison-Wesley, I have moved over to their "subsidiary," Peachpit Press. The reason for this move is simple. Addison-Wesley has shifted the focus of their publishing line to concentrate on books for developers. As a book for a more general audience, *Sad Macs* no longer fit. All parties agreed that a shift to Peachpit was the obvious solution. Still, I will miss Keith Wollman and all the folks at Addison-Wesley. They were there for me when my book was still mostly in my imagination and no one knew whether or not it would be a success. I won't soon forget that.

On the other hand, I very much welcome the move to Peachpit. They have a great reputation as a publisher of Macintosh books and they have been every bit as wonderful as their reputation suggests. A special nod of thanks goes to my editor, Jeremy Judson (who I first got to know when I was working on my chapter for *The Macintosh Bible*). I also want to acknowledge my gratitude to Ted Nace, former publisher of Peachpit. Agreeing to a contract for my book was one of his last official acts before he left for his Bali vacation!

Speaking of gratitude, I have plenty left over for David Rogelberg. He was my editor at Addison-Wesley for the first edition of this book and is now my agent. His friendship and advice over these past years—and his willingness to listen whenever I needed to talk—have helped me through many difficult decisions. Thanks also to Carole McClendon, who negotiated all three contracts for *Sad Macs'* three editions.

A special thanks to Owen Linzmayer. It was because of his dedication—much more than mine—that there was a Sad Macs Utilities Disk for the previous edition of *Sad Macs*. Rain, snow, sleet, or hail, he mailed out the disks on time and graciously handled every request I made for changes to the disk.

In previous editions of this book, I've mentioned my debt to the magazine editors at *MacUser,* with whom I have worked over the years. This time, I want to single out a new addition to the list: Nancy Peterson. She has worked with me on a series of troubleshooting articles (information from some of them have found their way into this book). I have especially enjoyed writing these articles. A good part of the reason for this is that I have enjoyed working with Nancy. It also helps that her editing has always made the articles better than they otherwise would have been.

Then there is my *MacFixIt* site on the World Wide Web. Keeping this Web site going has been more fun (and more work!) than I ever imagined. But I could have never gotten it off the ground without the help of others. Most especially, I want to thank Ric Ford. The time and energy he spent answering my questions and generally giving me support is way beyond what I had any reason to expect. Also thanks to several other webmasters (especially Eric Belsley, Steve Tannehill, and Dan Frakes) who have been unhesitantly willing to help me out whenever I asked.

A warm thanks to all of the public relations people and product managers for the various products that are mentioned in this book. They answered my technical questions and sent me the software when I needed it.

The sleeker Mac OS 8 look of many of the screen shots in this edition were the result of Greg Landweber's and Edward Voas' *Aaron* extension. Thanks guys!

And of course, a special thanks to all of the readers of the previous editions of *Sad Macs* and to the many visitors to my Web site. Your enthusiastic support was an essential morale booster as I worked on this third edition. It was the spark that kept me going when I might have otherwise given up.

Finally, most of you know that 1996 was far from the best year that Apple has ever had. Still, I remain an optimist. I fully expect that Apple will rebound in the years ahead. But whatever happens, my gratitude goes out to all of those that created the Macintosh and have helped make it a success over the past dozen years. My life is richer (in all meanings of the word) for your efforts.

Ted Landau
January 1997

Contents

Acknowledgments vi
What's New in This Edition? xxi
Preface xxiii

Part I Background and Basics 1

Chapter 1 Macintosh Basics: Hardware and Software 3
Exactly How Did I Get Here? 4
Macintosh Models and Computer Systems 4
Computing and Storage Hardware 5
The CPU and ROM 5
RAM: Electronic Storage 7
Disks: Physical Storage 10
Types of Disks and Disk Drives 12
System Software 15
System Software Versions 15
The System and the Finder 16
The Special Subfolders 18
The Rest of the System Folder Files 22
Getting Help 23

Chapter 2 Be Prepared: Preventing Problems 27
Tooling Up 29
Damage Control 29
Damaged Files and Disks 29
Software Bugs and Conflicts 30
A Troubleshooter's Toolkit 31
Toolkit Essentials 34
Troubleshooting with the Finder 36
Preventative Maintenance 45
Have an Emergency Startup Disk Ready 45
Save and Back Up Your Work 49
Prune Your Hard Drive 52
Install Protection Utilities 55
Give Your Macintosh a Tune-up 62

Chapter 3 Problem Solving: General Strategies 67
Uh-Oh... 68
Five Steps to Solving Macintosh Problems 68
1. Read Alert Box Messages 68
2. Check If the Problem Repeats 69
3. Isolate the Cause 70
4. Go for Help 71
5. Fix the Problem 73

Avoiding Problems 74
Get to Know Shortcuts 74
Go Exploring 74

Part II Symptoms, Causes, and Cures 77

Chapter 4 System Errors: Living with the Bomb 79
The Mac's Worst-Kept Secret 81
Solve It! A Catalog of System Errors 82
System Crashes 81
System Freezes 99
Endless Loops 105
Unexpected Quits 106
The Finder Disappears 108
Solve It! Recurring System Errors 109
Seek the Cause of a Recurring System Error 109
Fix It So That the System Error Does Not Recur 111

Chapter 5 Startup and Disk Problems: Stuck at the Starting Gate 119
Unpleasant Topics 123
Understanding the Startup Sequence 123
What Is a Normal Startup Sequence? 123
What Is a Startup Disk? 124
What Determines Which Disk Is the Startup Disk? 125
Starting with an Alternate Startup Disk 128
Solve It! When Your Macintosh Won't Start Up 131
The Macintosh Is Dead 131
Sad Macs and Unusual Startup Tones 133
The "?" Disk Icon or a Reappearing Happy Mac 140
The "X" Disk Icon Appears 145
A System Error Occurs Just Prior to or While "Welcome to Macintosh" Appears on the Screen 146
Problems While Launching the Finder and the Desktop 151
Solve It! Generic Problems with Disks 157
A Hard Disk Won't Mount 157
A Floppy Disk Won't Mount 163
A Floppy Disk Won't Eject or Unmount 166
Repeated Requests to Reinsert a Floppy Disk 170
A CD-ROM Disc Won't Mount 172
A CD-ROM Disc or Removable Cartridge Won't Eject 174
A Hard Disk Gets Unmounted 177
Problems with Restart, Shut Down, or Sleep 179
Files Missing from the Desktop 182
The Macintosh's Speed Is Unexpectedly Slow 183
Frequent System Crashes and Other Disk-Related Quirks 187

Chapter 6 When You Can't Find, Open, or Otherwise Use a File 189
It's the Little Things 191
Understanding Opening and Saving 191
Open and Save Dialog Boxes 191
Opening Files from the Finder 192
Using Save versus Save As 192
Solve It! Problems with Files 193
When You Can't Locate a File 193
When You Can't Launch an Application or Control Panel 203
When You Can't Open a Document 213
When You Can't Delete a File or Folder 225
When You Can't Rename a File or Folder or Volume 232
When You Can't Save or Copy a File 233
When the Going Gets Weird 238

Chapter 7 When You Can't Print 245
The Paperless Office? 247
Your Dialog Boxes May Vary 248
LaserWriter versus LaserWriter 8 248
Desktop Printers 249
QuickDraw versus QuickDraw GX 249
And So 250
When Things Go Right 251
Step 1: Select the Chooser 251
Step 2: Select Page Setup 259
Step 3: Use the Print Command 261
What Happens Next 263
Special Case: Background Printing and PrintMonitor 264
Special Case: Desktop Printers 267
Solve It! When Things Go Wrong 274
The Macintosh Can't Find the Printer 275
Printing Halts with No Error Message 281
Printing Halts Due to a System Crash, PostScript Error, or Other Printing-Related Error 284

Chapter 8 Getting Under the Hood: The Invisible Macintosh 299
Peeking Under the Hood 301
File Type and File Creator 301
How Kind 301
Type and Creator Code Problems 303
TEXT and PICT Formats: Type and Creator Code Issues 310
Five More Good Reasons to View or Change a File's Type/Creator Code 311
Finder Flags (Attributes) 315
What Are Finder Flags (Attributes)? 315
Viewing and Editing Finder Flags 317

Invisible Files and Folders 318
Viewing and Editing Invisible Files and Folders 318
Viewing and Editing *Really* Invisible Files and Folders 321

Chapter 9 Fonts and Text: Write and Wrong 325
The Write Stuff 329
Font Basics 330
Font Files versus Font Suitcases 330
Where the Fonts Are 330
Locating, Adding, and Removing Fonts from Your System Folder 331
The Different Types of Fonts 334
Bitmapped Fonts 334
Outline Fonts: TrueType and PostScript 336
TrueType Fonts 337
PostScript Fonts 338
Combining TrueType, PostScript, and/or Bitmapped Versions of the Same Font 345
Which Font Format Should You Use? 347
Summing Up 349
Solve It! Text and Font Problems 350
A Document Displays the Wrong Font 350
A Document Prints with a Different Font from the One Displayed 355
A Document Displays or Prints with the Wrong Formatting 357
The Text Is Clipped at the Margins When Printed 363
PostScript Fonts Do Not Print Using PostScript 364
The Jaggies Appear Unexpectedly 365
A Paragraph Unexpectedly Shifts Its Formatting 367
Problems Copying and Pasting Text Across Applications 369
Text Turns into Bitmapped Graphics 373
Solve It! Font File Problems 375
Damaged Font Files 375
Damaged Font Suitcase Files 379
Solve It! Font Menu Problems 380
Fonts Unexpectedly Appear or Disappear from Font Menus 380
Font Menu Clutter 383

Chapter 10 Graphics: What's Wrong with This Picture? 387
Picture This 390
Resolution and Display Depth 390
Understanding Resolution 390
Understanding Display Depth: Color and Grayscale 393
Setting the Depth and Resolution of the Display 395
Types of Graphics, Programs, and Files 399
Bitmapped versus Object-Oriented Graphics 399
Paint versus Draw versus PostScript Programs 402
Graphics File Formats 404

Movies, Video, and More 408
QuickTime and Beyond 408
Mini-Solve It! Problems with Movies and Video 411
Solve It! Problems Transferring Graphics Across Applications 414
You Are Unable to Paste a Graphic Across Applications 414
File Format Shifts When Transferring Graphics Across Applications 418
Solve It! Problems Displaying Color/Grayscale 420
Color Shift Problems 420
Problems Displaying at Different Color Depths 423
Solve It! Problems Printing Graphics 426
Problems Printing Color/Grayscale to a Black-and-White Printer 426
Problems Printing Color/Grayscale to a Color Printer 429
Problems Printing PostScript Graphics 432
Problems Printing Bitmapped Graphics 433
Special Case: Problems with ImageWriter Printers 436

Chapter 11 Trouble To Go: Not Just PowerBooks **439**
You *Can* Take It with You 442
Basics for PowerBooks and Beyond 443
PowerBook Models 443
PowerBook Control Panels (and Control Strip) 444
PowerBook Battery Conservation 446
Using RAM Disks 452
Using an External Monitor 456
Solve It! Basic PowerBook Problems 458
Restarting a PowerBook After a System Error 458
Problems Running on Battery Power 463
PowerBook Appears Dead 468
Sleep Problems 469
PowerBook Quick Fixes 472
Transfer Files to and from a PowerBook 476
Transfer Files Via the SCSI Port 477
Transfer Files Via File Sharing 479
Transfer Files Via a Modem (Apple Remote Access) 486
Solve It! File Transfer Problems 488
Can't Get File Sharing to Work 488
You Can't Get a PowerBook Modem to Work 496
Problems Using Apple Remote Access 498

Chapter 12 Powerful Problems: Power Macs, PCI-Based Macs & AppleVision Monitors **505**
New Technology, New Problems 507
Power Macintosh Basics 507
What Makes a Power Mac Different from Other Macs? 507
Running in Emulation Mode versus Native Mode 510
Power Macintosh Native Software 511
PCI-Based Power Macintoshes 514

Solve It! Power Macintosh Problems 515
Compatibility and Memory Problems 515
System Error and Related Problems 520
Monitor Problems 522
PCI-Based Macintosh Quick Fixes 523
AppleVision Monitors 529
AppleVision Software 530
Solve It!: AppleVision Problems 531

Chapter 13 Mac OS System 7.5/7.6 and Beyond **539**
System 7.5/7.6 Basics 542
Why This Chapter? 542
Apple's Mac OS Release Strategy 542
Getting Help from Apple 543
Solve It! System 7.5/7.6 Problems 544
Installation Problems 545
Compatibility and Memory Problems 554
Apple Guide Does Not Work 562
OpenDoc and Live Objects 564
What Is OpenDoc? 564
Installing and Using OpenDoc 567
QuickDraw GX 572
Installing and Using QuickDraw GX 572
QuickDraw GX and Printing 573
QuickDraw GX and Fonts 583
QuickDraw GX and Graphics 588
Solve It! QuickDraw GX Problems 589
Memory Problems 589
Printing and Printing-Related Problems 590
Font Problems 595
On the Horizon 596
Software 596
Hardware 597

Chapter 14 Road Service for the Infobahn: The Internet, the Web, and the Online World **599**
No Mac is an Island ... Anymore 602
Understanding Modems 603
Modem Speed 693
Flow Control 607
Modem Initialization Strings 608
Understanding Open Transport, TCP, & PPP 609
Why Open Transport, Anyway? 609
What Files Are Needed For Open Transport (vs. Classic AppleTalk)? 610
Choosing Between Open Transport and Classic AppleTalk 610
Memory Requirements 612
Making a TCP (and PPP) Connection 612

Solve-It! Open Transport Problems 622
Compatibility Problems 622
Modem and PPP Connection Problems 623
The Internet (especially the World Wide Web) 629
Understanding Internet Addresses 629
Working with Downloaded and Uploaded Files 632
Solve-It! Web Browser Problems 637
Web Pages Won't Load or Load Slowly 637
System Freezes, Crashes, and Directory Damage 642
Pages Display Incorrectly or Have Features Missing 648
Helper Problems 650
Web Pages Do Not Get Updated as Expected 653
Ethernet Quick Fixes 655
Ethernet Extensions Solve Problems 655
Cables and Hardware for Ethernet Mini-Networks 656

Part III: Disaster Relief: The Fix-Its 657

Fix-It #1 Check for Incompatibilities Between Hardware and Software . . . 665
Application Software Is Too New or Too Powerful for the Hardware 666
Hardware Is Too New for the Application Software 666
Hardware Is Too New for the System Software 666
General Strategies 666
A Few Common Hardware Incompatibilities 668
Monitor Incompatibilities 668
Card Incompatibilities 669
Peripheral Hardware Incompatibilities 669
No Math Coprocessor 669
Insufficient RAM 670

Fix-It #2 Check for Problems with Preferences Files 671
Loss of Customized Settings 672
Corrupted and Upgraded Preferences Files 672

Fix-It #3 Check for Mislocated or Missing Accessory Files 678

Fix-It #4 Check for Problems with Extensions and Control Panels (Startup Extensions) 682
Startup Extension Conflicts 683
Startup Extensions That Do Not Load or Run 684
Disable Startup Extensions to Determine If You Have a Startup Extension Conflict 685
Method #1: Disable Startup Extensions by Holding Down the Shift Key at Startup 686
Method #2: Disable Startup Extensions by Using a Startup Management Utility 686
Method #3: Disable Startup Extensions by Removing Startup Extensions from Your System Folder 692

Identify the Problem Startup Extension 693
Check Recently Added Startup Extensions 693
Check Suspicious Startup Extensions 693
Check for Known Incompatibilities and Bugs 693
Disable and Re-enable Individual Startup Extensions 694
Special Case: Conflict Between Two Startup Extensions 696
Special Case: Conflict Occurs Only When Using a Startup Extension 697
Special Case: If a Startup Extension Causes a System Crash at Startup 697
Resolve the Conflict 699
Rearrange the Loading Order of Startup Extensions 699
Upgrade the Problem Startup Extension or Other Software 702
Replace Potentially Damaged Files 702
Check for Memory-Related Problems 703
Delete the Problem Startup Extension 703
If the Startup Extension Does Not Load or Run 704
Is It a Codependent Startup Extension Problem (or Other Startup Extension Conflict)? 704
Did You Restart After Installing the Startup Extension? 704
Is the Startup Extension in the System Folder? 704
Is the Startup Extension in Its Proper Location in the System Folder? 705
Was the Startup Extension Disabled by Your Startup Manager? 705
Is the Startup Extension Turned On? 706
Special Case: Startup Icons Appear with an "X" Over Them or Disappear 706

Fix-It #5 Check for Problems with System Software **708**
Complete Install/Reinstall of System Software 710
Doing a Clean Reinstall of System Software 710
Using the System Software Installer 716
Selective Install/Reinstall/Deletion of System Software 724
Basis for a Selective Install/Reinstall 724
Install/Reinstall Selected System Software Files 725
Special Case: Delete Multiple System Folders 727

Fix-It #6 Check for Problems with Memory Management **729**
Memory Problems When Trying to Open an Application 732
Check the Advice, If Any, in the Alert Message 732
Quit One or More Other Open Applications 732
Reduce the Size of a Large Clipboard 732
Check for Fragmented Memory Space 733
Check for Memory Leaks (A Step Beyond Memory Fragmentation!) 734
Reduce the Minimum/Current Memory Size 736
Remove Plug-in Modules and Other Accessory Files 737
If None of the Preceding Steps Work 738

Memory Problems When Using an Open Application 738
Close Any Open Documents That Do Not Need to Be Open 739
Reduce the Size of the Clipboard 739
Do Not Try to Open the Document from the Finder 739
Quit the Application and Relaunch It, Restarting If Needed 739
Increase the Preferred/Current Memory Size 740
Special Case: Finder-Related Memory Problems 741
Quit Applications and Close Windows 741
Increase the Finder's Memory Size 742
How to Increase Overall Memory Availability 742
Reduce Applications' Preferred/Current Memory Size 742
Reduce the Memory Size Needed by System Software 746
Increase the Size of the System Heap 749
Increase the Total Available Memory 750

Fix-It #7 Check for Viruses 756
Use an Anti-Virus Utility 760
Install an Anti-Virus Utility 760
Keep Your Anti-Virus Utility Updated 761
Customize Your Anti-Virus Utility 762
Prevent a Virus Attack from Infecting Your Disk 763
A Virus Is Detected 763
A Suspicious Activity Is Detected 763
Suspicious-Activity False Alarms 764
Eradicate an Existing Virus 764
Scan for and Delete Infected Files 765
Repair an Infected File? 767
If the Anti-Virus Utility Didn't Solve Your Problem 767
Determine the Source of Your Virus Infection 767

Fix-It #8 Defragment/Optimize the Disk 768
Optimizing/Defragmenting Basics 769
Before You Optimize 770
Optimize the Disk 770
Beyond the Basics 771
Check for Fragmentation of Individual Files 771
Make Sure Files Are Free to Defragment (Startup Disk Problems and More) . . . 772
Create Free Space 772
Don't Optimize Floppy Disks 772
A Disk Is Optimized When You Reformat and Restore It 773
The Downside of Optimizing and Defragmenting 773
Defragmenting Takes Time 773
Defragmenting Can Erase Files That Otherwise Could Have Been Undeleted . . 773
Defragmenting Can Cause Disk Damage 774

Fix-It #9 Rebuild the Desktop 775
The Desktop File Can Become Bloated 776
The Desktop File Can Become Corrupted or Incorrectly Updated 776
Generic Icon Problems 776
Rebuilding Basics 777
Beyond the Basics 778
Fixing Generic Icon Problems 778
Losing (and Saving) Get Info Comments After Rebuilding the Desktop 782
Minor Repairs Alert Message 782
Don't Bother to Rebuild the Desktop After Initializing a Disk 783
Desktop Files and Reusing Floppy Disks 783
The Desktop Rebuilds Every Time You Start Up 783
Keep Extensions Off When You Rebuild? 784
Really Rebuild the Desktop 785

Fix-It #10 Run Disk First Aid 787
Using Disk First Aid 788
Getting Started 788
Verify or Repair a Disk 789
Further Damage Checks 792

Fix-It #11 Zap the Parameter RAM 793
Zapping Basics 795
For All Macs Running System 7 (except PCI-based Macs) 795
For PCI-based Macs (PRAM and NVRAM) 795
Optional: Remove the battery 796
After Zapping the PRAM 796
Really Zap the PRAM: Use TechTool 798

Fix-It #12 Update the Disk Device Driver 801
Update to Accommodate New System Software 802
Update to Accommodate New Hardware 802
Update to Repair Damage to the Driver 803
Get the Latest Version of the Formatting Utility 804
Update the Driver 807

Fix-It #13 Check for Damaged Disks: Repair, Restore, or Recover 810
Repair 811
Restore 811
Recover 812
Repair a Damaged Disk 812
Before Using Your Repair Utility 812
Make Repairs 815
Restore a Damaged or Accidentally Erased Disk 821
Before Attempting to Restore a Disk 821
Restore the Disk 822
Recover Selected Files from a Damaged Disk 823

Fix-It #14 Check for Damaged Files: Replace or Recover 827
Damaged Files Due to Miscopied Information 828
Damaged Files Due to Bad Blocks 828
Caveats 828
Replace the Damaged File 829
For Applications 829
For Documents 830
Recover the Damaged File 830
Make a Copy of the Damaged File 830
Try to Open the Damaged Document 831
File Recovery Via CanOpener 831
File Recovery with MacTools or Norton Utilities 832
Resolve Problems with Bad Blocks 833
Recover Damaged Files and Repair Bad Blocks 833
Repairing Bad Blocks: Recovery Utilities versus Reformatting 835
Special Case: Recovering Files from Floppy Disks with Bad Blocks 836

Fix-It #15 Format, Initialize, and Verify Disks 838
Floppy Disks 839
Formatting an Unformatted Disk 840
Reformatting an Already Formatted Disk 841
Reformatting versus Deleting 842
Unreadable or Damaged Disks That Really Aren't 842
Macintosh PC Exchange and PC-Formatted Disks 843
Damaged Disks 843
Hard Disks 844
Formatting and Reformatting in General 844
Apple HD Setup Vs. Drive Setup: Which One Do You Use? 845
Reformatting Using Apple HD SC Setup 847
Reformatting Using Drive Setup 848
Reformatting Using Other Formatting Utilities 850
Reformatting versus Erasing versus Deleting 851
Partition the Disk 852
Verifying Disks and Media Damage 855
For Floppy Disks 855
For Hard Disks 856

Fix-It #16 Check for Problems with SCSI Devices and Connections 858
What's a SCSI Chain? 859
What's the Problem? 859
Using a SCSI Utility 862
Mounting SCSI Devices with SCSIProbe 862
If SCSIProbe Lists a Device, But Doesn't Mount It 864
If SCSIProbe Doesn't List or Mount the Device 867
Special Case: Disk Drives That Don't Automatically Mount at Startup 868

SCSI-Related Problems 869
Make Sure the SCSI Port Is Functioning 871
Check If All SCSI Devices in the Chain Are Turned On 871
Be Careful When Turning Off a Non-Startup Drive 871
Disconnect All SCSI Devices 872
Make Sure No Two SCSI Devices Have the Same ID Number 872
Make Sure All SCSI Devices Are Properly Terminated 873
Reconnect and Rearrange the Connection Order of SCSI Devices 873
Confront Cable Connection Confusion 875
Running with Devices Disconnected 876
Check for Damage 876

Fix-It #17 Check If Hardware Repairs or Replacements Are Needed **877**
Diagnose Hardware Problems 879
Preliminary Checks 879
Use Hardware Diagnostic Utilities 879
Repair Selected Hardware Problems 881
Hard Drives and Other SCSI Devices 882
Floppy Drives 882
Keyboard and Mouse/Trackball/TrackPad 884
Monitor I: No Display or Dimmed Display 886
Monitor II: Quality of Display Problems 889
Serial Port Devices: Printers, Modems, and Networks 891
The Macintosh 893
Memory I: Adding or Replacing Memory 894
Memory II: Getting the Correct Modules for Your Machine 898

Fix-It #18 Seek Technical Support or Other Outside Help **903**
Product Technical Support 904
When to Call Technical Support 904
When to Seek Other Types of Technical Support 905
Be Prepared Before You Call 905
Using Utilities to Help Get Prepared 906
Make the Call 907
Seeking Other Outside Help 909
Online Information Services 909
The Internet (especially the World Wide Web) 910
User Groups 913
Magazines 913
Books 913
Other Options 914

Appendix: Stocking Your Troubleshooter's Toolkit **915**

Symptom Index **921**

Index **937**

What's New in This Edition?

"Since the publication of the previous edition of this book, the Macintosh landscape has changed substantially." Those were the opening words of this section of the second edition. If anything, they ring even more true for this edition. Change in the world of computers is nothing if not rapid and constant. This third edition does its best to keep pace with these changes.

Once again, I have retained the basic structure of previous editions. This means that a cursory glance at the table of contents hardly hints at all of the changes that lie just beneath the surface. To give you a better idea of what's new, here's a list of the more noteworthy additions:

- Chapter 2: includes a major revision to the section on emergency startup disks.
- Chapter 4: has expanded material on Type 10 and 11 errors.
- Chapter 7: has been almost completely rewritten. It describes all of the new features of LaserWriter 8.4 and Desktop Printing 2.x, plus additional coverage of StyleWriters. These revisions also extend to printing-related information covered in Chapters 9 and 10.
- Chapter 10: has a new section on Movie and Video problems, plus coverage of the new Monitors & Sound control panel.
- Chapter 11: has new material on the PowerPC PowerBooks, as well as updates on features such as the Control Strip, RAM disks, and Sleep (features that are increasingly common in all Macs, not just PowerBooks). There are also more details on using Apple Remote Access.
- Chapter 12: What was Chapter 12 in the second edition has now been split into two new chapters (12 and 13). This first one focuses on hardware and includes new information about PCI-based Power Macs and about AppleVision monitors (among its other Power Mac-related updates). Also look for new information on shared libraries.
- Chapter 13: This chapter focuses on software and includes a *completely* rewritten and much expanded coverage of System 7.5/7.6 issues, focusing on System 7.5.3, System 7.5.5, Mac OS 7.6, and beyond. It features a new section on OpenDoc.
- Chapter 14: This chapter features material that is entirely new to this edition. Recognizing the explosive growth of the Internet (and online communications in general), this chapter covers such matters as Open Transport, PPP, Web browsers, and more. The emphasis, as always, is on problems and solutions.
- Fix-It #5: has updated and expanded information regarding installing system software (including what's new in Mac OS 7.6).
- Fix-It #6: adds new information on several memory-related topics, including memory leaks.
- Fix-It #9: has an entirely new section on generic icon problems.

- Fix-It #11: includes information on new procedures for zapping the PRAM in PCI-based Macs, and explains even more exotic PRAM-related procedures.
- Fix-It #12 and #15: have been revised to include coverage of Apple's new Drive Setup formatting utility. Fix-It #12 also adds new information about driver-related problems.
- Fix-It #16: has expanded information on dual-bus SCSI systems and other new SCSI-related features.
- Fix-It #17: has a revised discussion of diagnostic utilities, new information on multiscan monitor problems, plus almost completely rewritten coverage of memory problems, including new material on DIMMs and L2 caches.
- Fix-It #18: has revised coverage of where to go for technical support, with much greater emphasis on using World Wide Web resources.

This list is far from complete. Every chapter and Fix-It has at least some changes. Summarizing all of this, I once again find that what I said here in the second edition still applies:

"Overall, I am quite pleased with the results of all these changes. I believe you hold in your hands the most comprehensive book on Macintosh troubleshooting that is available anywhere.

"If there is a downside to all of this change, it is how it affects the simplicity of this book. As a book designed to appeal to users of all Macintoshes, it benefits from an ability to make generalizations that are generally accurate—no matter what Macintosh you own and what system software you use. This effort is stymied by Apple's recent proliferation of hardware and software variations. These days, the chasm between users of an ancient relic like the Mac Plus and the latest Power Macintosh, while not yet the size of the Grand Canyon, is still uncomfortably large. And that doesn't even consider the special problems of PowerBook (of which there are several types) users. Add to this the complexities of figuring out exactly what is in today's overstuffed System Folders, and you clearly have your work cut out for you (or at least I do!).

"And still more is on the way. Apple plans major enhancements to its system software over the next months. It may already be on the shelves by the time you read this. New hardware, as always, is on its way as well.

"The bottom line for writing this book is what you might expect: It ain't getting any easier. Increasingly, I am forced to give several separate explanations for a particular problem, each one specific to a different hardware or software variation. It would be almost funny if it wasn't serious.

"Anyway, I don't mean to sound too complaining. I enjoy learning about and writing about this stuff. That's why I wrote this book in the first place. And that's why I came back to do it again."

Preface

Who's in Charge Here?

Every Macintosh user has had this uneasy feeling at some time or other. Some rarely have it anymore; others have it every day. It's the feeling that working with your Macintosh is akin to being an apprentice lion trainer. You're never sure who is in charge. Rather than feeling in control of your computer, you feel controlled by it.

Nowhere is this more apparent than when something goes wrong—when a problem occurs that you can't figure out how to fix, when even your collection of manuals doesn't seem to have the answer. That's where this book comes in. Its goal is to put you back in charge, providing you with the information you need to diagnose and solve whatever problems you may confront.

At this point, you may be saying, "Fix *any* problem? And fix it *myself?* You must be kidding!" No, I'm not. You *can* solve most Macintosh problems yourself, regardless of your level of technical skill. Here's why I say this with such confidence:

- You don't need to know how to make hardware repairs to solve most of the common Macintosh problems. This is because most things that go wrong with your Macintosh are not hardware problems. They are primarily software problems and can be repaired directly from your keyboard, using a relatively small assortment of software tools and techniques. At most, you may need to check a few cables and switches, but that's it.
- Solving these Macintosh problems does not require any advanced technical knowledge. You do not have to be—or learn to become—a Macintosh expert. Neither do you need any programming skills. What tools and techniques you do need to know about are all designed with nonexpert users in mind.
- For many problems, everything is working fine and as it should be. The apparent problem is one of understanding. When you learn more about how your application (or the Macintosh in general) works, the unexpected will transform into the expected, and the problem is "solved." It's like discovering that the reason you are getting no sound from your TV is because someone pressed the mute button. Nothing's really wrong. That's the way it is supposed to work!
- Though this book does not specifically mention every possible problem you might have (no book could do that!), it does teach you the general skills needed to diagnose and solve even those problems that are not mentioned.
- If you follow the advice given in this book, there is virtually no risk that anything you do will harm the computer. There is certainly no key that you can press or button that you can click that will break the computer hardware.

Computer Problem Solving, Cookbooks, and Fishing

For quick answers to specific problems, you can use this book as you might use a cookbook. That is, a cookbook recipe tells you to add a teaspoon of baking powder, but doesn't tell you why the baking powder is required or why a teaspoon of baking soda would or would not be an acceptable substitute. Such an approach has an undeniable value. With a well-written cookbook, you can make very good meals even if you have no idea why the recipes work.

Similarly, this book offers "recipes" for problem solving on your Macintosh. With this book, you can solve most problems without understanding why the solutions work.

However, I want this book to do more than that. I hope to take some of the mysticism out of using computers—eliminating the feeling that what is going on either makes no sense or is beyond your ability to make sense of it.

This book offers you the opportunity to learn why problems occur and why the solutions work. With this information, you can go beyond the limits of the pages of this book and begin to solve most problems entirely on your own.

This is where fishing comes in. An old saying goes, "Give a person a fish and feed him for a day. Teach a person to fish and feed him for a lifetime." The cookbook explanations are the "fish" that this book gives you. The more general explanations will teach you "how to fish."

You can limit yourself to eating the "fish" if you wish. My hope is that you will want to take the next step and learn "how to fish" as well.

What This Book Is and Is Not

Perhaps you are browsing through this introduction at a bookstore, trying to decide whether this book is for you. Or perhaps you want to make sure that you clearly understand what this book does and does not cover. Fair enough. Here is an overview of what this book is and is not:

What This Book Is

- This book is designed to help you solve the common problems that occur when working with the Macintosh. Other more general information about the Macintosh is included only when relevant to problem solving.
- This book is about many more problems than just the disasters suggested by the title. Many of the problems discussed do not even qualify as disasters. Whether it is an inability to eject a disk, empty the Trash, copy a selection to the Clipboard, or get text to print in the correct font, rest assured that these types of problems are also covered here.
- This book explains the material in as nontechnical, plain English as possible. Where it uses technical jargon, it clearly explains what it means and why you should know about it.

- This book is appropriate for everyone from near-beginners to almost-experts. In fact, it is targeted primarily for users with only minimal technical skills. It makes few assumptions about your level of expertise. However, it does assume that you are currently using a Macintosh and are at least vaguely familiar with some basic terms and concepts. For example, if I say that you need to "close a window" or "double-click that icon," or "pull down the File menu and select Save," this ideally should not sound to you as if I am talking in a foreign language.

What This Book Is Not

- This book is not a general introduction to the Macintosh. If that's all you want, check out the documentation that came with your Macintosh or any number of other excellent introductory books available in bookstores.
- This book is not designed to be a comprehensive encyclopedia of tips and hints that, while helpful and interesting, are not directly relevant to problem solving.
- This book does not cover hardware repairs, other than to indicate how to tell if such a repair is needed. Rather, the book focuses on software-based problems and solutions.
- This book does not cover problems that occur only in conjunction with optional hardware peripherals such as scanners. Instead, it limits discussions to those problems that occur with a minimum standard hardware configuration: computer, mouse, keyboard, monitor, storage devices, and printer.
- This book does not generally cover problems specific only to a single application. For example, if there is a problem specific to Microsoft Word, you are not likely to find out about it here. However, you should still be able to solve most such problems, using the more general techniques that are described.

How This Book Is Organized

This book has three main parts:

- *Part I: Background and Basics* deals with general background information and some problem-solving basics. This is designed to bring all users up to speed so that any relevant gaps in your knowledge get filled before you proceed.
- *Part II: Symptoms, Causes, and Cures* covers the whole range of Macintosh problems, what their symptoms are, what causes them, and what you can do to solve them.
- *Part III: Disaster Relief* focuses on specific problem-solving tools, called Fix-Its, rather than on symptoms. Each Fix-It contains all the necessary information about how and when to use it and why it works.

These three sections are followed by an appendix, called "Stocking Your Troubleshooter's Toolkit," that provides the information needed to obtain any of the troubleshooting software mentioned in this book. This is followed by two separate indexes: a symptom index and a general subject index.

On a Related Note

Throughout this book, you will find three types of text set off from the main text. Each of these has a different purpose:

> **TAKE NOTE ▶**
>
> **AN EXAMPLE**
>
> These notes contain important information directly relevant to the topic under discussion. For example, they may include definitions or explanations of terms used in the main text.

> **BY THE WAY ▶**
>
> **AN EXAMPLE**
>
> These notes contain more tangential information than you will find in the Take Note boxes. For example, they may list changes expected in a forthcoming version of the software under discussion.

> **TECHNICALLY SPEAKING ▶**
>
> **AN EXAMPLE**
>
> These notes contain supplementary information that is more technical than the rest of the book. Less technically inclined readers may choose to skip them.

See: What I Mean

This book contains numerous cross-references: Some of these references direct you to a continuation of the steps needed to solve a problem, such as, "If the system error continues to recur, see 'Solve It! Recurring System Errors,' later in this chapter." Others inform you where you can find more information about a subject, such as:

SEE: • Chapter 8 for more details on invisible files

Still others point to the location of the initial description of a term or item.

On the one hand, the sheer number of these references may seem disconcerting at first, especially if you are in a hurry to solve a problem. However, not all of these references demand immediate attention. Many of them are only suggestions. Thus, if you can solve your current problem without needing to know more about invisible files, for example, you need not bother with that particular cross-reference.

See Also: The Fix-Its

If you have just started browsing through this book and have come across a reference such as

SEE: • Fix-It #6 for more on rebuilding the desktop

you may be a bit mystified. What's a Fix-It? Where is it? The Fix-Its, as just mentioned, make up Part III (Disaster Relief) of this book. This book is deliberately designed so that the chapters make frequent reference to them. Each Fix-It covers a different troubleshooting topic, such as rebuilding the desktop or solving extension conflicts. They are the central location for all information on their given topic.

If a particular chapter section includes a long list of Fix-It references, you probably won't wind up needing all of them. As soon as one of them fixes your problem, you can stop. If the length of a particular list seems daunting, remember that the longest lists cover the most general cases, when the information at hand provides little or no guidance on which direction to go. Usually, if you can describe your problem more specifically, you can find more specific advice, with a narrower range of Fix-It choices, elsewhere in the book.

TAKE NOTE ▶

ARE YOU STILL USING SYSTEM 6?

If you are still using System 6, this book may disappoint you. While much of the advice here is relevant to all system software versions, the focus of the book is clearly on System 7 (especially System 7.5 or later). No problems specific to System 6 are covered. This is a change from previous editions of the book.

If you are unsure what version you are using, look at the top item in the Apple menu when you are in the Finder. If it reads *About This Macintosh* or *About This Computer*, you are using System 7. If it reads *About the Finder*, you are using System 6 (or earlier!). To know exactly what version of System 7 you are using, select the *About This Macintosh* item. The box that appears will contain the answer.

On the Web: *MacFixIt*

The *Sad Macs Utilities Disk*, introduced in the second edition, contained a collection of most of the freeware and shareware utilities mentioned in this book. It also included a text file with updated information about topics covered in *Sad Macs*. It was available by mail order.

With this third edition, the Sad Macs Utilities Disk is gone. But don't worry. A much more extensive and timely resource has replaced it: *MacFixIt* (formerly the *Sad Macs Update Site*). It's on the World Wide Web.

This Web site includes a much larger collection of software than I could fit on the disk, and it is constantly being updated. Even better, unlike with the disk, you can always come back later and check if any newer versions of programs have come along. And it's all free.

But that's only the beginning of what you will find at *MacFixIt*. The other part of the site contains the latest news, tips, and information about anything and everything related to troubleshooting your Macintosh. While it is designed to be useful to all Mac users, whether they own this book or not, it serves especially well as a means of getting updated information about topics covered in *Sad Macs*. Check it out at:
MacFixIt: <*http://www.macfixit.com*>

A Final Note: Feedback

I've tried to create a book that was not too technical for novices yet not too elementary for everyone else. As to whether I succeeded in this goal, you are the final judge.

I encourage you to send me your comments about this book. Did you find the book helpful? Was the information easily accessible? Were you disappointed that certain topics were omitted? Were some topics covered in too little or too much detail? Or were you impressed with the breadth and depth of the coverage? Were you pleased to find just what you were seeking in just the right amount of detail? Any suggestions, criticisms, or compliments are welcome. This third edition was, in part, shaped by comments from readers of the first two editions. Your comments can play a role in determining the direction of the next edition.

Here's how to reach me:

- **email:** landau@macfixit.com or landau@oakland.edu
- **regular mail:** Ted Landau, Department of Psychology, Oakland University, Rochester, MI 48309

Part I: Background and Basics

These first three chapters lay the groundwork for the material in the remainder of the book. If you are already familiar with the basics of using a Mac as well as with troubleshooting fundamentals, you can probably skip these three chapters (or maybe just skim through them). You can always return to them later, if necessary. Users just getting started with troubleshooting should definitely start here, however.

Chapter 1 is an overview of basic computer terms, concepts, and operations. I explain the essentials of the different types of memory that your Macintosh uses and the different methods used to store data, as well as some specifics about other common hardware, especially monitors and printers. I also delve into the mysteries of the System Folder.

Chapter 2 covers preventative maintenance. It begins with an overview of the causes of Macintosh problems. The next part describes the important software tools you need to make your repairs. The final part describes a general set of routine maintenance procedures designed to keep your Macintosh out of trouble.

Chapter 3 provides a set of general strategies for solving problems. With these skills, you will be ready to tackle almost any problem that comes your way, even if it is not specifically covered in this book.

Chapter 1

Macintosh Basics: Hardware and Software

Exactly How Did I Get Here? 5

Macintosh Models and Computer Systems 5

Computing and Storage Hardware 6

The CPU and ROM 6

- The Processor Is the Computer 7
- The Macintosh User Interface Is Largely in ROM 7
- Different Processors and ROMs in Different Macs 7

RAM: Electronic Storage 8

- Measuring RAM 9
- RAM Is Fast 9
- RAM Is Electrical 9
- Information in RAM Is Not Read-Only 10
- RAM Is Expensive 11
- RAM Is Temporary 11

Disks: Physical Storage 11

- Measuring Storage Capacity 11
- Disk Storage Is Temporarily Permanent 12

Types of Disks and Disk Drives 13

- Floppy Disks 13
- Hard Disks 14
- Other Storage Devices 15

System Software 16
System Software Versions 16
The System and the Finder 17
The System File 17
The Finder (and the Desktop) 18
The Special Subfolders 19
Which Item Goes Where? 19
Apple Menu Items Folder 20
Extensions Folder 20
Contol Panels Folder 21
Startup Items Folder 21
Shutdown Items Folder 22
Preferences Folder 23
Fonts Folder 23
Still More Folders 23
The Rest of the System Folder Files 23
Getting Help 24
Balloon Help 24
Apple Guide 25

Exactly How Did I Get Here?

You turn on your Macintosh. The smiling Macintosh icon appears briefly and is soon replaced by the Mac OS display. Eventually, this too disappears and is replaced by the *desktop*—a display where your disk icon appears in the upper right corner of the screen, and the various files on your disk are listed in any number of windows. In one of these windows, you find the program icon for your word processor. You double-click on the icon and the application opens. You create a new document and save it. You quit the application and shut off the machine.

That's a typical brief session with your Macintosh.

If you are relatively new to using computers (and even if you are not), you have probably wondered exactly how all this happens. Where does the Mac OS display come from? How does the computer know what to do next? What happens when you open an application? Where was the application information stored before you opened it, and where is it now? What exactly happens when you save something, and why isn't it saved automatically as you create it (by typing, in this case)?

These are big questions, and they can be answered on many levels. Sometimes the desired answer is simpler than the question seems to imply. It is a bit like the little child who asked his parent, "Where do I come from?" After the mother made several uncomfortable attempts at answering the question, the boy blurted out, "But Billy said he comes from Cleveland. I want to know where I come from."

It is with this in mind that I attempt to answer these "big" questions. As in the rest of this book, my focus is limited to what you need to know to understand the problem-solving material in the chapters to come. I will make no pretense of being comprehensive.

The Macintosh's ability to strut its stuff—whether that "stuff" is creating sophisticated page layouts or displaying incredibly detailed color graphics—is the result of an intricate interplay between hardware and software. If you are going to solve the problems that will confront you in your day-to-day life with the Macintosh, you need some minimal understanding of how all that interplay works. That's what this chapter is all about.

Macintosh Models and Computer Systems

Dozens of different models of Macintosh now exist, but they can be divided into four main categories:

- *Compact Macintoshes* These include all of the models based on the original design of the Macintosh: the all-in-one box with a built-in 9-inch monitor. These range from the Macintosh Plus to the Macintosh Classics. There are no compact Macintoshes in Apple's current lineup.

- *Modular Macintoshes* These Macintoshes are simply a box, in either a flat or tower design. All other components, including the monitor, are purchased and added separately. Most Macintoshes sold today are modular. Historically, they range from the Macintosh II series, most LCs, and the Quadras to the latest Power Macintoshes.
- *Hybrid Macintoshes* This term describes a few Macintoshes where the computer and monitor are combined into a single unit, as in compact Macintoshes, but the overall design more closely mimics that of modular Macintoshes. The Power Macintosh 5400 is an example.
- *Notebook Macintoshes* These are all battery-powered portable Macintoshes, of which there are two main types: the all-in-one PowerBooks (which contain a built-in floppy drive and have ports to connect to most external peripherals, such as an external monitor) and the PowerBook Duos (which don't have a floppy drive or external ports, but can access them via an optional "docking" accessory).

The term *computer system* typically refers to the essential combination of hardware components necessary to use the computer. For a modular Macintosh, this typically includes the computer "box" itself, a monitor, input devices such as a keyboard and mouse, and any disk drives. A printer is an almost essential additional component.

Apple's Performa line of Macintoshes are special versions of standard Mac systems, usually bundled with additional software. They are primarily marketed to home users.

Recent years have seen the arrival of Macintosh *clones,* most notably those made by Power Computing. These are fully compatible machines that should run all software that an Apple Macintosh will run.

Computing and Storage Hardware

The CPU and ROM

If you opened up any model of Macintosh, the most distinctive object you would see is a board full of soldered circuits; it looks sort of like the electronic equivalent of an aerial view of New York City. This is called the *main logic board* (or *motherboard*).

Many items are on this board, but for now I'll focus on two of them: the *central processing unit* (CPU, or *processor*) and the *read-only memory* (ROM) module. The expression *read-only* means that the information stored there cannot be altered in any way—as with a compact disc, for example. (In contrast, a cassette tape is read-write).

Simply put, the CPU is what makes a Macintosh a computer, and ROM is what makes it a Macintosh.

What you need to know:

The Processor Is the Computer

The processor is where most computations take place. Essentially, any program is simply a set of instructions that are executed by the processor to produce the desired result.

The Macintosh User Interface Is Largely in ROM

The ROM contains the essential instructions needed to create the windows, menu bars, scroll boxes, dialog boxes, and graphics that make up what is commonly called the *Macintosh user interface.* All other programs can be designed to access this information. This common availability ensures that all programs have a similar look and feel; it's a great time-saver for programmers, since they don't have to keep reinventing the wheel (or the interface, to be more precise).

TAKE NOTE ▶

MACS WITHOUT MAC ROMS

The Mac user interface may not be in the ROM much longer. Starting in 1997, a joint venture between Apple and IBM will produce a common computer that can run a variety of operating systems, including the Mac OS. For these Power PC Reference Platform (PPRP) computers, as they are called, the Mac OS will be a software application rather than part of ROM. The next version of the Mac operating system (Mac OS 8) will likely move in this direction as well.

One advantage of this change is that it will allow clone makers to develop Macs much more easily, because they will be freed from having to build the Mac OS into their hardware.

Different Processors and ROMs in Different Macs

All Macintoshes have one of two types (680x0 or Power PC) of processors and similar ROMs. This is the main reason that all Macintoshes behave, look, and feel in such similar ways and can mostly run the same software.

Different models of Macintosh, however, may have different versions of the same basic processor. The most important consequence of differences in these processors is differences in performance speed; Macintoshes with faster processors do *everything* faster. The fastest processors, of course, are found in the most expensive Macs, but even a rock-bottom Mac today has a faster processor than the priciest Macs of just a few years ago.

Similarly, newer Macintosh models often have improved and expanded versions of the basic ROM. The most important consequence of these differences is that older Mac models may be unable to match certain features of newer models. For example, older models of Macintosh have limits on how many colors they can display—limits that no longer apply to the newer models.

TECHNICALLY SPEAKING ▶

POWER MACINTOSHES VS. 680X0 MACS—WHAT DOES IT ALL MEAN?

All Macintosh processors are developed by the Motorola corporation. Until recently, all Macintoshes were based on a numbered series of processors with names like Motorola 68030 and 68040 (collectively referred to as "680X0" processors). Generally, the higher the number of the CPU, the newer and faster it was. More recently, Apple introduced its line of Power Macintoshes. These are based on an entirely new processor, the PowerPC chip, and different variations of these processors have names like 601 and 604. With PowerPC processors, though, the processor number is *not* a reliable way to tell which processor is faster (some 601s are faster than some 603s, for example).

Despite this radical shift to a new processor, the Power Macintoshes can still emulate (that is, imitate) a 68040 Macintosh, and so a Power Mac is able to run software designed for the older machines.

SEE: • Chapter 12 for more on Power Macintoshes

For problem solving:

The most important thing to know is that the existence of different processors and ROMs across different models of Macintoshes may lead to incompatibilities. For example, certain programs may work fine with some models of Macintosh, but not others.

RAM: Electronic Storage

RAM stands for *random access memory.* When you hear people talking about how much memory their Macintosh has, they are talking about RAM. When a manual says that a program needs a certain amount of memory to run, it is referring to RAM.

When you first turn your computer on, the RAM contains nothing at all. Indeed, the startup process consists largely of *loading* the needed information into RAM. This is because almost all program instructions must be loaded into RAM before they can be carried out.

Similarly, when you open an application, you are transferring the instructions contained within that file from its normal storage location (usually a disk) to RAM.

The hardware that determines the amount of RAM in your machine is located on the main logic board inside your computer. These hardware components are often referred to as *memory chips* or *memory modules.*

By the way, some Macs have separate RAM just for creating the monitor's display, called video RAM or just VRAM. I'll have more to say about this in Chapter 10.

What you need to know:

Measuring RAM

RAM is usually measured in megabytes (MB): the more RAM is in your machine, the more megabytes of memory you have. Older Macintoshes came with as little as 1MB of RAM (the original Macintosh had only 128K!). In contrast, the minimum amount of RAM shipped with Macintoshes today is 12MB, and it may be larger by the time you read this.

This RAM measurement has nothing directly to do with the physical size of the memory chip. Instead, it refers to the capacity of the chip to hold information.

Though some Macs come with memory chips soldered to the logic board, virtually all Macs have at least one RAM slot where memory chips can be snapped in or removed. Adding RAM here (or replacing a smaller-capacity chip with a larger one) is how you increase your Mac's memory.

See: • Fix-It #17 for more on adding and replacing RAM

TECHNICALLY SPEAKING ▶

BYTING OFF MORE THAN YOU CAN CHEW

The byte is the basic unit of measurement for computer memory and storage. In particular, 1 megabyte is equal to 1,024 kilobytes (K), just as 1 kilobyte is equal to 1,024 bytes. As a rough guideline, a page of single-spaced text requires about 5K.

These days, the most popular hard disks exceed 1 gigabyte (1,000 megabytes) in size.

The most common memory (RAM) chips in use today (such as on Apple's PCI-based Macs) are 8MB in size; even 16MB is fairly common.

These "average" sizes get larger every year. You can never have too much disk space or memory!

RAM Is Fast

The term *random access,* as used in random access memory, means that you can almost instantly get to any portion of what is stored in RAM. Most storage mechanisms that you are familiar with are *not* random access. For example, with a cassette tape, you must fast-forward or rewind to get where you want, which can take considerable time. Even a compact disc, which has a much faster access time, technically still works on the same principle.

Thus, RAM access speed far exceeds that of any other alternative method the computer could use. This speed advantage is the main rationale for using RAM. Without it, all computer operations would slow down immensely, if they could be done at all.

RAM Is Electrical

One reason RAM can achieve such a speed advantage is that information is stored in RAM in a purely electronic manner. Theoretically, information in RAM can be accessed at the speed at which electricity travels—which, of course, is quite fast.

Information in RAM Is Not Read-Only

Information in RAM can be easily modified or erased. It's just a matter of altering the path of electrical current flow in the memory chip.

With all of these advantages, you might wonder why anyone would use something other than RAM to store data. Actually, there are two very good reasons, as you'll see in the next two paragraphs.

RAM Is Expensive

Memory chips are expensive. The amount of RAM needed to store all the information on just one floppy disk could cost $50, maybe more. As I write this, RAM prices have plummeted to all-time lows, but it is still more expensive than any other storage alternative (and most people feel that prices will rise again).

RAM Is Temporary

Because RAM is electrical in nature, anything in RAM is lost forever when you turn the computer off, restart it, or interrupt the flow of electricity in any way. (If you use RAM disks, as described more in Chapter 11, you may know that they are a partial exception to this generalization). Thus, an unexpected power failure could result in the loss of several hours of work if it was stored only in RAM. To save your information permanently, you need another form of storage, typically disks (as described in the next section).

For problem solving:

The most important thing to know is whether you have enough memory for what you want to do—and what to do about it if you don't.

RAM is generally the bottleneck that limits how much you can do at one time. Whenever you open an application, the RAM that it occupies becomes temporarily unavailable for any other use. Since everything you want to use needs to load into RAM, you can only work with as many applications and/or files as can fit into the available RAM.

Of course, information in RAM can be removed. That information is then no longer available for immediate use, but the RAM is freed up. For example, quitting an application removes it from RAM and leaves that RAM available for another program.

Some programs may not run at all on your machine because you do not have sufficient RAM to open them, even if nothing else is running already. When that happens, it's time to buy more memory!

The minimum amount of RAM you need to run the latest software effectively keeps increasing as the software evolves. If you have an older Mac model and still run older software, you may be able to get by with as little as 4 or 8MB. For everyone else, double-digit RAM is a necessity. Without enough RAM, you will keep getting "out of memory" messages throughout your work day. That's why adding more RAM is one of the best investments you can make.

Disks: Physical Storage

Disks are used to store information permanently—that is, even after the computer is turned off. The information stored on disks is commonly referred to as *software.*

Most Macintosh models have a *hard disk* built into the computer box itself. This disk is *not* in any way part of the main logic board (which holds the processor, ROM, and memory chips); in fact, it is only a matter of convenience that it is inside the box at all. The Macintosh could work just as well by accessing a separate hard disk unit connected to the Macintosh on an outlet in the rear of the machine. Still, many users lump all of these components together as the "internal hardware" of the Macintosh. Whether in RAM, ROM, or on a hard disk, information is viewed as being stored somewhere inside the machine.

The other most common type of disk is the floppy disk. Information on the *floppy disk* is accessed by first inserting the disk into a *floppy disk drive.* Again, almost all Macintoshes (except for some notebook models) come with at least one such drive built into the machine.

SEE: • **Next section, "Types of Disks and Disk Drives," for more details**

As mentioned in the section on RAM, when you *open* an application stored on a disk, you are copying its information from the disk to RAM. From here, its instructions can be sent to the processor as needed, which essentially means that the program will *run.*

Conversely, when you use an application's Save command to *save* a document, you are taking a copy of the document's information, which at that moment is at least partially in RAM, and transferring it to a disk.

What you need to know:

Measuring Storage Capacity

If RAM is normally referred to as memory, disk space is normally referred to as *storage capacity.* Thus, you may be asked, "What is the storage capacity of your hard drive?" or simply, "How large is your hard drive?" Like RAM, storage capacity is measured in *kilobytes* (K) and *megabytes* (MB). This can be a source of confusion. For example, when someone is talking about megabytes, it may not be immediately clear whether he or she is referring to RAM (memory) capacity or disk (storage) capacity. Once you understand the context, however, it is usually clear how to distinguish between these two alternatives.

By the way, don't expect the amount of space a file occupies on a disk to be the same as the amount of space it needs when it loads into RAM—for various reasons, the numbers may be different. A program may load only part of its instructions into RAM at one time, thus requiring less RAM than you might expect. Alternatively, a program may need a lot more space than the storage size of the file to accommodate documents that you may open with the application.

Disk Storage Is Temporarily Permanent

Disks work in a way that is metaphorically similar to cassette tape. You can write to a computer disk, just as you can record to a cassette tape. When you turn off your cassette recorder, the information remains on tape; you can play back the tape later, or erase it and record something else. You can do the same thing with most types of computer disks.

Thus, disk storage is "temporarily permanent": information you have saved remains on the disk until you change it. Unlike with RAM, information on a disk is not stored electronically. Instead, as with cassette tape, an actual physical change to the disk occurs when you write new information to it. This is why the information is retained even after you turn the computer off.

For problem solving:

The most important thing to know is that as you go through a typical computer session, a frequent two-way flow of information takes place from disk to RAM and back again. Understanding the distinctions between these two ways of holding information is often critical to isolating the causes of a problem and thus to solving it.

For example, if an application cannot open because of insufficient memory, that is basically a RAM-related problem. If it cannot open because the instructions stored on the disk have been damaged in some way, that is essentially a disk-related problem. The methods used to solve these different types of problems are, as you will see, quite different.

TECHNICALLY SPEAKING ▶

PUTTING IT ALL TOGETHER

With this information now digested, you can answer the questions that began this chapter (see "Exactly How Did I Get Here?") with more clarity.

When you turn on your machine, the processor and the ROM kick in immediately. They continue to play an essential role in all operations until the moment you shut down. Everything your computer does ultimately depends on instructions being sent to and carried out by the processor.

Almost immediately after this initial step, information stored on disk (most likely the hard disk inside your machine, and particularly from the System Folder files that I talk about later in this chapter) begins to load into RAM. As all this occurs, the smiling Macintosh icon appears briefly to indicate a problem-free start, followed by the "Welcome to Macintosh" or "Mac OS" display. Eventually, the desktop appears, as the program, called the Finder, opens.

When you launch your word processor or any other software, this too is transferred from its disk storage location to RAM so that you can use it (assuming you have enough RAM for that program to run). The menu bars, windows, and dialog boxes that appear are produced by information from the application itself in combination with standard information accessed from the ROM (and, in some cases, from system software, as described later in this chapter).

When you work on your document and save it, the information is transferred out of RAM to disk storage, so it remains there even after you turn your Macintosh off. When you quit your application, the RAM it occupied is freed up to be used by some other program.

Types of Disks and Disk Drives

The term *disk* refers to the actual medium that stores the information used by the computer. It is the metaphorical equivalent of the tape in a cassette tape player. The term *drive* refers to the mechanism used to read and write information to and from the disk. That is, the drive is like the tape deck or CD player in a component stereo system. To hear the tape, you must connect the deck to a receiver and speakers; similarly, to use information on a disk, the disk drive must be connected to the Macintosh.

Four basic categories of disks are considered here: floppy disks, hard disks, CD-ROM disks, and removable cartridges.

Floppy Disks

Floppy disks are the common denominator of Macintosh storage. Every Macintosh (except the Duos) comes with at least one floppy drive built into it. Until recently, all software that you purchased came on floppy disks, although CD-ROM discs are increasingly popular now.

What's Floppy About Them? Looking at the hard-shell plastic case of a floppy disk, it may seem that the disk does not live up to its name—it's not floppy. This is because the term *floppy* refers to the truly flexible, thin plastic disk encased inside the hard plastic shell. Visible when you slide the metal shutter back, this floppy part actually stores the information.

The metal shutter, incidentally, is pulled back automatically when you insert the disk into a disk drive. This gives the disk drive access to the actual floppy media.

Types of Floppy Disks The standard capacity of floppy disks in use today is 1.44MB; these are referred to as high-density (HD) disks. The other storage size you are likely to see is 800K.

As the front of the disk faces you with the metal slide on the bottom (see Figure 1-1), 800K and HD disks have a small square hole visible in the upper right-hand corner. On the rear side of this hole is a slide tab. When the tab is up—so that you can see through the hole—the disk is locked, which means that you cannot modify its contents in any way (see Chapter 6 for more on locked disks). HD disks include an extra hole on the upper left-hand side. There is no slide tab here; this hole is simply used by the floppy disk drive to identify the disk as an HD disk. For those of us who are humans instead of computers, HD disks also have the HD symbol to the side of the metal slide. Otherwise, the two types of disks look virtually identical.

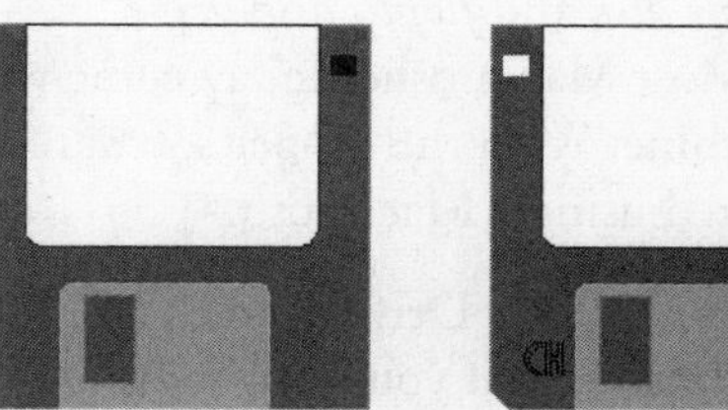

Figure 1-1 *An 800K floppy disk (left) and a HD floppy disk (right; the HD symbol is upside down). The lock tab on both disks is in the unlocked position, meaning that you cannot see through the hole.*

HD and 800K disks are both *double-sided* disks. This means they store information on both sides of the inner plastic disk.

A third type of floppy disk is a 400K or *single-sided* disk, which is identical to an 800K disk but is designed to store information on only one side of the disk. Single-sided disks are almost never used anymore.

Types of Floppy Disk Drives The floppy disk drive shipped with Macintoshes today is the SuperDrive, which distinguishes HD disks from 800K disks by the extra hole on the HD disk. Even so, due to restrictions placed by the system software, 400K disks do not work with most new models of Mac.

Older Macintoshes may have 800K drives; you cannot use HD disks with these drives. If you have an ancient Mac, it may have a 400K drive. These drives recognize only single-sided disks.

Hard Disks

A hard disk, like its floppy counterpart, is simply a means of storing information—except that it can hold a lot more information than a floppy disk. These days, drives of 1 gigabyte (GB, or 1,000MB) or more are common. To put this in perspective, a 1GB hard disk can hold the equivalent of more than 700 high-density floppy disks.

Amazingly, drive prices keep getting cheaper. You can buy a 1GB drive today for less money that you could buy a 20MB drive a decade ago! As with memory, get the largest hard drive you can afford; you won't regret it.

Types of Hard Disk Drives Basically, a hard disk drive (usually referred to as simply a *hard drive*) is a mechanism that has a hard disk permanently encased inside it. You cannot remove the disk or insert another one. Thus, for many people the terms *hard disk* and *hard drive* seem synonymous, though technically they are as different as the terms *floppy disk* and *floppy disk drive.*

Most Macintoshes today come with an internal hard disk drive located inside the machine. With the proper software installed on this disk, no other disk is needed to get started using a Macintosh.

External Hard Drives and the SCSI Port If your Macintosh does not have an internal hard drive, or if you want to have more than one hard drive, you can add one externally. External hard drives are attached to the Macintosh via a special connection in the back of the machine called the *SCSI* (pronounced "scuzzy") port, which is described further in Fix-It #16.

Why You Must Have a Hard Drive The original Macs did not come with a hard drive; they only had floppy disk drives. In contrast, all Macintoshes sold today come with an internal hard drive. You can no longer effectively run a Macintosh from just floppy disks.

Other Storage Devices

CD-ROM Discs These discs (the word *disk* often becomes *disc* when referring to CD-ROMs) have become quite common in recent years. All current models of desktop Macintoshes come with an internal CD-ROM drive. Alternatively, or if you have an older model, you can hook one up separately via the SCSI port.

Basically, CD-ROM discs look just like the compact discs that are now standard in the music industry. The big advantage of CD-ROM discs is that they can hold a great deal of information for their small size—exceeding that of many hard drives—yet at much less cost than other storage media.

This plus is offset, however, by two major disadvantages: CD-ROM drives are significantly slower than hard drives, and you *cannot* write to a CD-ROM disc. Except in some special cases (such as Photo CD discs), you cannot add to, modify, or delete the information contained on the disc when you purchased it.

Removable Cartridges Removable-media cartridges, as their name implies, can be inserted into and ejected from a drive, much like how floppy disks work. Once the cartridge is inserted, however, the Mac treats it more like a fixed hard disk.

Incredibly popular these days are a new generation of removable drives from Iomega and SyQuest, especially Iomega's *Zip* and *Jaz* drives. Because of their much larger capacity, faster speed, and dropping costs, these drives are threatening to replace floppy disk drives as the common denominator of storage. Some Mac clones come with internal Zip or Jaz drives preinstalled.

Optical drives, a less popular alternative so far, work on a principle similar to how a CD-ROM drive works, except that you can write to an optical cartridge as well as read from it. Capacities of cartridges vary depending on the type and exact model of drive. The Zip drive cartridge has a capacity of 100MB, while the Jaz cartridge has a 1GB maximum; optical discs are also in the 1GB range. Expect newer models to exceed even these limits.

TAKE NOTE ▶

WHAT ABOUT MONITORS AND PRINTERS?

In addition to the basic components described here, virtually all computer systems include some type of a monitor and a printer. For now, however, I'll defer any description of these components. Check out Chapters 7, 9, and 10 for more information.

System Software

The term *system software* most commonly refers to the basic set of files included with each Macintosh. These files come preinstalled on your hard drive. They are also typically included on a set of floppy disks or a CD-ROM disc that comes with your Macintosh. Finally, you can buy system software upgrade kits (independent of any hardware purchase) in order to make sure you've got the latest version of the operating system.

A few system software files are essential for the use of your Macintosh—namely, the System and Finder. Without access to them, your Macintosh typically will not even start up. Others are nearly as essential, needed for routine operations such as printing. In most cases, these and related files are contained in a special folder called the *System Folder.* A disk that contains such a folder is called a *startup disk* (a topic discussed more in Chapter 5).

Many users are not familiar with what is inside a System Folder; some may not even be aware they have one. If this describes you, things are about to change. To solve problems effectively on the Macintosh, however, understanding the basics of the System Folder and its contents is essential.

BY THE WAY ▶

SYSTEM SOFTWARE OR OPERATING SYSTEM?

In the fall of 1994, Apple introduced the term Mac OS (Macintosh Operating System) as the new official name of its system software. This was done mainly because Apple was, for the first time, licensing its operating system to run on non-Apple computers. The Mac OS name and logo will identify that a computer runs Macintosh system software, whether it is an Apple Macintosh or not.

System Software Versions

Apple periodically releases new versions, or upgrades, to its system software. Often, rather than releasing a complete new version of the system software, it may release a special subset of files typically called System Updates. In either case, there are at least three reasons for doing this:

- To fix problems with the previous version of the software
- To provide support for new models of Macintosh that have been released
- To add new features that improve on the previous version

What you need to know:

Understanding the differences in features across versions is highly relevant to the problem-solving issues in this book. These differences affect what problems you may have and what problem-solving tools are at your disposal.

Every time a significant revision occurs, Apple assigns it a new numerical name. People therefore refer to system software by its version number, such as version 7.1 or version 7.5.3. The version number indicates the extent of the difference of the new version from its predecessor, with added digits representing less significant revisions. Thus, changes in the number after the second decimal indicate the most minor changes. Really major upgrades call for a change in the first digit.

Because the first digit is the most important, all version numbers that begin with a 6 are usually referred to together as simply System 6. Similarly, versions that begin with a 7 are referred to as System 7. Almost every Macintosh user today should be using some version System 7 (most likely some version of System 7.5 or later). If you are using an earlier version, wake up—you're about to be left behind.

By some time in late 1997 or 1998, a totally new Mac OS will arrive, based on the NeXT OS (which Apple recently acquired).

SEE:
- **"Macintosh System Software" in Chapter 2, for how to tell exactly what system version you are using**
- **Chapter 13 for more on the latest system software**
- **Fix-It #5 for more on installing and upgrading system software**

BY THE WAY ▶

THE PERFORMA MACINTOSHES AND SYSTEM SOFTWARE

Originally, Apple's Performa series of Macintoshes was shipped with a special version of system software designed specifically for these models (for example, System 7.1P rather than 7.1).

Starting with System 7.5, however, the Performas come with the same system software as all other Macs. The one remaining difference, as of this writing, is that Performas do not come with the same system software CD-ROM disc included with other Macs, particularly, the traditional Installer-based files (see Fix-It #5, "By the Way: Reinstalling System Software on Performas," for more details).

The System and the Finder

The System File

The System file is the most critical file in your System Folder. The System file consists largely of instructions that complement and extend what is found in the Macintosh ROM. The information in the System file tends to be those things that are more likely to need frequent revision than what is contained in the ROM.

In some cases, certain types of files (such as fonts, sounds, or keyboard layout files) can be installed directly in the System file. These will be described more in later chapters.

What you need to know:

- First and foremost, your Macintosh will not run without the System file.
- Compatibility problems can occur between the system software and other software you use. Older programs may not work well with newer versions of the system software, and vice versa.

System

Figure 1-2 *The System "suitcase" file icon.*

- Files (such as sounds or fonts) that are installed in the System file are potentially accessible by any and all other applications.

TAKE NOTE ▶

SYSTEM ENABLERS AND UPDATES

Starting with System 7.1, when Apple introduced a new model of Macintosh, a matching System Enabler file for that model was also introduced. This file was required in order to start up that model of Macintosh. More recently, Apple has shifted to using a single file, called an Update file, that combines the new information needed for all Mac models. Depending upon what version of the system software you are using, and what kind of Macintosh you have, you may or may not have one of these Update or Enabler files. If your system software does include such a file, it is essential—the Mac will not start up without it. For more information on this, see Chapter 2 (on creating an emergency startup disk, Chapter 5 (on startup problems), Chapter 13 (on System 7.5 problems), and Fix-It #5 (on reinstalling system software).

The Finder (and the Desktop)

The Finder is the second most critical file in the System Folder, because it creates the Macintosh *desktop.* The desktop is where you find the disk icons, the Trash, and the various windows that display the contents of all mounted disks. (In fact, the words *Finder* and *desktop* are often used interchangeably.) When you are in the Finder, the menu bar contains the familiar File, Edit, View, and Special menus.

BY THE WAY ▶

ICON VIEWS

You probably already know what an icon is, even if you are not familiar with the term itself. Icons are small graphic images; their most prevalent use is for files on the Finder's desktop.

You use the Finder's View menu to determine how files on the desktop are displayed. File icons are most easily viewed by selecting By Icon or By Small Icon from this menu. Other views display files in a more traditional text-list format. In these other views, however, you can still see icons down the leftmost column. To change the size of icons in list views, select the Views control panel (see "Control Panels Folder" later in this chapter) and select one of the other sizes of icon displays available for list views. If you use the smallest size, you will see only a bland generic icon rather than each file's custom icon.

For the figures in this book, I generally use the By Icon view.

What you need to know:

- The Finder is an essential component of system software. Your Macintosh will not start up without it, except under very unusual circumstances.
- The Finder is your main way of navigating around your disks. It is from here that you locate, open, copy, and delete files. In general, you would not want to do without it, even if you could.
- The Finder is also a great problem-solving tool. Starting in the next chapter and continuing throughout this book, I describe numerous Finder features—such as the Get Info command in the File menu—that can be used for fixing problems.

The Special Subfolders

The System Folder depends heavily on the use of several special subfolders that now contain most of the Macintosh system software. These folders, together with the standard files that Apple places in them, are all installed automatically when you first create the System Folder with Apple's Installer.

Which Item Goes Where?

When you put a new item in your System Folder, you generally don't need to know which special subfolder it goes into, if any. Simply place the file destined for the System Folder on the System Folder icon (*not* in the System Folder window). When you see the System Folder icon highlighted, release the mouse. The Macintosh then checks if it knows where the file should go. If it does, you get a dialog box informing you of the file's intended destination and asking you to confirm that this is correct. Click OK, and you are done.

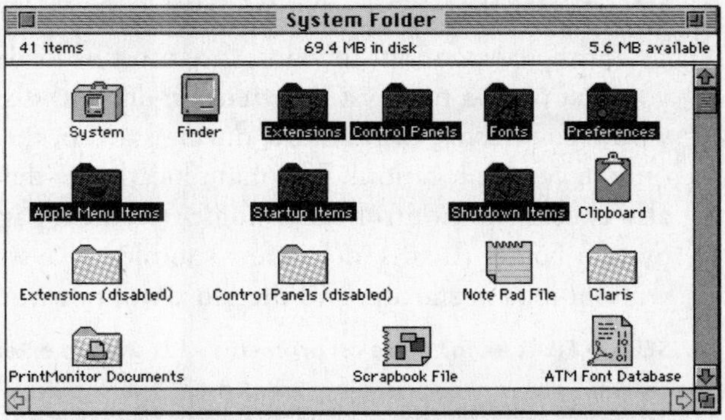

Figure 1-3 *The inside of a System Folder. The highlighted folders include the special subfolders described in this chapter.*

Helpful Hint: Watch out for some newer files that are supposed to be in the Control Panels folder but are really ordinary applications in disguise. When you drag these to the System Folder icon, no dialog box will appear and the "control panels" will *not* be placed in the Control Panels folder. Instead, they will be left in the top (or root) level of the System Folder. If this happens, you will have to drag them to the Control Panels folder yourself (of course, they will work okay whether or not they are in the Control Panels folder; you just won't see them listed in the folder if they are not placed there).

SEE: • **Fix-It #4 for more on extensions and control panels**

The main System Folder subfolders are named Apple Menu Items, Extensions, Control Panels, Startup Items, Shutdown Items (System 7.5 or later only), Preferences, and Fonts.

Apple Menu Items Folder

Any file placed in the Apple Menu Items folder appears in the Apple menu. This menu, located on the left side of the menu bar and denoted by an Apple logo, is available in almost all applications.

In System 6, this menu was reserved for a special type of file called a *desk accessory* (or *DA*). These DAs needed to be installed directly in the System file. At one time, using DAs was the only way to have more than one program open at a time.

With System 7, the distinction between DAs and ordinary applications has blurred. In most cases, they work the same way. For example, you can now launch DAs from any location on the desktop (by double-clicking them), just as you can do with an ordinary application.

Extensions Folder

The Extensions folder now contains several types of files. The most common are *System extensions* and *Chooser extensions.*

System Extensions System extensions accomplish a variety of specialized tasks, mostly by working in the background the entire time the Macintosh is on.

SEE: • "Take Note: What's an INIT?," later in this chapter

For these extensions to work, they must be loaded into memory at startup. Thus, when you first place a new system extension on your disk, it has no effect until you restart your Macintosh. Furthermore, during startup, the Macintosh looks for these extensions only in certain locations. The main location is the Extensions folder, of course, but it also checks the Control Panels folder (see next page) as well as the top level of the System Folder (that is, not in any subfolder). System extensions in any other location will not load at startup, and therefore will not work.

SEE: • Fix-It #4 for more on problems with startup extensions

Chooser Extensions To understand the meaning of Chooser extensions, you first have to understand the Chooser itself. The Chooser is a desk accessory found in the Apple Menu Items folder. Its primary function, as its name implies, is to let you *choose* which printer (or networking server) you intend to use.

When you select the Chooser, a selection of icons (such as LaserWriter, ImageWriter, or AppleShare) is displayed on the left side of the Chooser window. Each icon represents a Chooser extension located in your Extensions folder.

The most common type of Chooser extension is called a printer driver. These files are necessary so that the Macintosh and the printer can talk to each other. Printer drivers for all of Apple's printers come with the Macintosh system software; printers from other companies may require their own drivers.

AppleShare is a Chooser extension that has functions related to networking and file sharing (a topic I discuss more in Chapter 11). By the way, unlike most Chooser extensions, AppleShare loads into memory at startup together with system extensions.

SEE: • **Chapter 7 for more on the Chooser and printing in general**
• **Chapters 9 and 10 for more details on the Page Setup and Print dialog boxes**
• **Chapter 13 on how all of this is different if you are using QuickDraw GX**

Other "Extensions" The Extensions folder, especially in System 7.5.x or later, may also contain files besides those in the two previous categories, even if they would not technically be considered a "true" extension. Examples of these include communications tools and Apple Guide documents.

Control Panels Folder

As its name implies, the Control Panels folder holds special files called *control panels.* (They are sometimes referred to more technically as *control panel devices,* or *cdev's.)*

Many of the control panels that come with the system software—such as General Controls, Mouse, and Sound—set basic preferences for the operation of the Macintosh, including the cursor blinking rate, mouse tracking speed, and sound volume. Most remaining control panels are similar to System extensions: they perform some task(s) while working in the background, and they must be loaded into memory at startup before they can perform their task. In these cases, each control panel's window is primarily used to select among options that modify how its background activity works.

SEE: • **"Take Note: What's an INIT?" later in this chapter**

Several control panels that are particularly relevant to problem solving are described in more detail in the next chapter.

In System 7, control panels (like DAs) open like ordinary applications. That is, you can open a control panel by double-clicking its icon, no matter where on the desktop it is located. If you do not keep control panels in the Control Panels folder, however, the ones that function like system extensions may not load at startup. Also, for convenience, System 7 creates an alias of the Control Panels folder (see the following sections for more on aliases) and places it in the Apple Menu Items folder. This makes it easy to access control panels from the Apple menu.

Startup Items Folder

Any application or document file that you place in the Startup Items folder automatically opens as part of the startup process. So, if you want your word processor to be opened automatically each time you turn on your Macintosh, place the word processor file (or its alias) in this folder.

These files are distinctly different from the system extensions and control panels that load into memory at startup. Placing an item in the Startup Items folder is simply a shortcut method for getting the file to open; this folder confers no special properties on the file. In contrast, System extensions, as described previously, are special types of files that must be loaded into memory at startup in order to work at all.

TAKE NOTE ▶

WHAT'S AN INIT?

The term INIT is generally used to describe programs that, when correctly located in a System Folder, load into memory during the Macintosh's initial startup process. Usually, they remain in memory until you select Shut Down. In particular, virtually all system extensions and the majority of control panels fall into this category.

INITs typically perform functions that require a constant presence and availability throughout a session. For example, a given INIT may place a digital clock on the menu bar. The clock continues to work in the background, remaining on the screen no matter what application is active, as long as the menu bar is visible. Similarly, Apple's QuickTime extension is an INIT. Unless it is present in the background, no application can run QuickTime movies. Other INITs act to modify particular components of the Macintosh interface. For example, an INIT may add new features to the Macintosh's Open and Save As dialog boxes. (SuperBoomerang, part of a software package called Now Utilities, is a popular example of this type of INIT.)

The term INIT, though, has fallen into some disfavor. Apple currently prefers to refer to these programs simply as *extensions*, but there is a good deal of potential confusion here. Not all extensions function by loading into memory at startup. System extensions do; Chooser extensions generally do not. Conversely, not all programs that load into memory at startup are technically called extensions; some control panels also work this way. The only real difference between these startup control panels and system extensions is that the control panels provide a dialog box (the actual control panel) for selecting various options, while System extensions typically do not. Since you could say that a System extension component is contained within the control panel, I find it preferable to group all of the files that load into memory at startup (system extensions or control panels) under the umbrella term of INITs. This is the convention I used in previous editions of this book. The term INIT has now become so rarely used elsewhere, however, that I will refer to these files as *(startup) extensions* (some more technical aspects of this terminology are described in Chapter 8).

By the way, there is no way to immediately identify which control panels function as extensions and which do not. You can usually tell what's going on because most System extensions, and most control panels that function like System extensions, place a small icon along the bottom of the "Welcome to Macintosh" screen as the file loads into memory. Not all of these files do this, however, and even those that do usually have an option to turn this feature off. A possibly more reliable alternative is to check the listing of a startup management utility (see Fix-It #4); most of these utilities only list those extensions and control panels that are truly startup extensions, though exceptions exist. Perhaps the most reliable method is to check something called a file's Finder flags (a method that I describe in Chapter 8).

Shutdown Items Folder

This feature is new in System 7.5. Complementary in function to the Startup Items folder, any applications in this folder are launched just after you select Shut Down but before the Mac actually shuts down. Personally, I don't imagine there will be much practical use for this folder (though experienced users might like to set up some AppleScript files to run just before they shut down). Note that the Shut Down item in the Apple menu may not launch items in the Shutdown Items folder; if this is the case, select Restart or Shut Down from the Finder's Special menu instead.

Preferences Folder

Many programs, including the Finder, allow you to change the default settings of the program—that is, these changes are remembered even after you quit the application, and they are still in effect the next time you use it. For example, a word processor may normally open with its text ruler visible; however, you can usually select a Hide Ruler command to get rid of it. In some cases, you may even be able to set a Preferences option so that the ruler is automatically hidden from view whenever the program opens (eliminating the need to select the Hide Ruler command each time). This is a change from the *default* setting.

Generally, the program remembers these settings by placing the information in a special *preferences* file, which the program accesses whenever it is opened. These preferences files, together with miscellaneous other accessory files, are typically located in the Preferences folder. They can also sometimes be found at the root level of the System Folder, however, or even within the same folder as the application to which it is linked.

System 7.5 adds a dizzying array of new preferences files that work with its new system software enhancements. For example, Apple Menu Options, WindowShade, Find File, and Control Strip (to name a few) all now have matching preferences files.

Fonts Folder

Fonts placed in this folder are used by applications and thus appear in Fonts menus. Prior to System 7.1, fonts were stored directly in the System file itself. The folder provides a simpler and quicker alternative to having to add and delete font files from the System file.

Still More Folders

Other system software folders you may see in your System Folder include Launcher Items (used with the Launcher utility), Control Strip Modules (used by the new Control Strip utility found on PowerBooks) and Editors (used by OpenDoc). These, and other possible folders, will be described more later in the book. Of course, you may also have folders, such as Claris, that are not part of the system software at all; these are created by other applications on your disk.

The Rest of the System Folder Files

The rest of the System Folder contains items of varying degrees of significance. Some of these are part of the Macintosh system software and are installed at the same time that the System and Finder are installed. The Scrapbook File, which is used in conjunction with the Scrapbook desk accessory, is an example of this.

Is It Apple or Not Apple? You can generally use the Finder to tell whether a particular item in the System Folder comes from Apple by clicking once on the item and then selecting Get Info from the File menu. If the item is part of the system software, this is usually indicated at the top of the window (where it says something like "System Software 7.5") and/or at the bottom next to the word *Version* (where it says that the file is copyrighted by Apple).

The remaining items in your System Folder come from other companies. They can be virtually any type of file, most commonly control panels and extensions. Some you may have placed there directly, while others were placed there by some Installer utility (similar to the Installer used by the system software) when you installed a particular piece of software. Still other files, such as some preferences files, may have been created automatically by an application the first time you launched it.

With so many possible files, if you open your System Folder now, you will almost certainly find some files that are unfamiliar to you—that is, you have no idea what they do. For now, leave them alone. Later on in this book, especially in Chapter 2, I'll discuss how to decide whether you need them or not.

SEE: • Chapter 2, on using Get Info and on pruning your hard drive

TAKE NOTE ▶

ALIASES

For every file mentioned in this chapter, you could create an alias of it. Here's the what, how, and why of aliases.

In the File menu of the Finder is a command called Make Alias. When you select a file (or folder) and then select this command, the Finder creates a new file that superficially is identical to the original file. Its name is in italics rather than plain text, however, and the word *alias* is attached to the end of the name. More important, the file is as small as 1K in size. It does not contain any of the information of the original file; it is simply used to point to that file. You can move this alias anywhere on your disk, and whenever you double-click on it, the Macintosh will locate the original file (even if it is now in a different folder) and launch it.

Figure 1-4 *A Microsoft Word document and its alias.*

Among other uses, placing a collection of aliases together in a single folder is a convenient way of having access to a variety of applications that may be scattered in different locations on your hard drive.

Of course, if you delete the original file, the alias becomes useless, and double-clicking the alias does not open anything. (Instead, you get an error message that says the original item could not be found.) Renaming the original file, however, does not break the connection.

SEE: • Chapter 6 for more on problems using aliases

Getting Help

When you need an answer to a basic question about your Macintosh, your first thought may be to look it up in the manuals that came with your computer. Unfortunately, Apple's printed documentation seems to get skimpier with each new version of the system software. In contrast, Apple's digital (that is, on-disk) help keeps expanding. Aside from special tutorial and demo files that may come with your computer, there are two basic ways to get help from Apple's system software.

Balloon Help

In the upper right-hand corner of the menu bar, immediately to the left of the Application menu icon, is a question-mark (?) icon. This is the Guide/Balloon Help menu. To see what it does, select Show Balloons from the menu (with the Finder as the active application). Now move the cursor to various locations. You will find that balloons periodically appear, each containing a brief description of the purpose and use of the item underneath the cursor. By selecting Hide Balloons from the Balloon Help menu, you can turn this function off again.

9:13 AM
About Apple Guide
Hide Balloons
Turns Balloon help off.
Macintosh Guide ⌘?
Shortcuts

Figure 1-5 *The Guide/Balloon Help menu, showing the balloon for the Hide Balloon command.*

Whether this feature works for applications other than the Finder depends on whether the application has been designed to support Balloon Help. As a result, Balloon Help is not available in all applications.

Apple Guide

Apple Guide, a new feature introduced in System 7.5, is the equivalent of Balloon Help on steroids. You access it from the Guide menu (formerly the Balloon Help menu), where Balloon Help still remains available.

Apple Guide is an interactive help system. From a list in the main Guide window, you select the topic for which you want help. The Guide then uses a series of HyperCard-like windows to take you step by step through the process of answering your question. In many cases, if it tells you to do something (such as "Select the Apple menu"), it further assists you by indicating on the screen exactly what to do (for example, by actually "circling" the Apple menu icon). You carry out the suggested steps while Apple Guide remains active; this is what is meant by "interactive help."

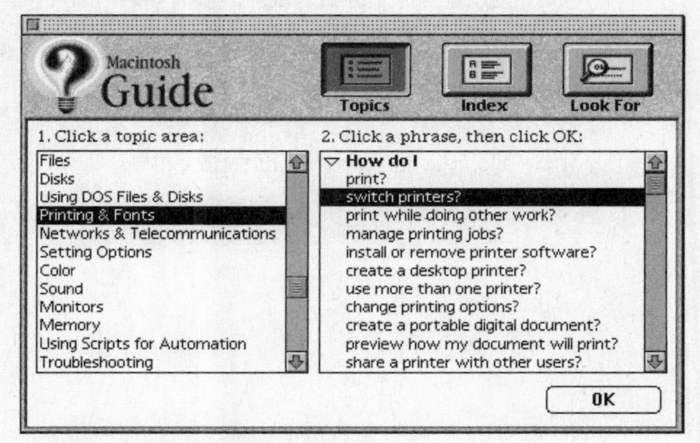

Figure 1-6 *An Apple Guide window.*

Exactly what help topics are available from Apple Guide depends on where you are. If you are in the Finder, the Guide menu will list Macintosh Guide as a selection. This is Apple's general help Guide (included as part of System 7.5). It provides information that supplements what is found in the System 7.5 printed documentation, offering advice on how to do most basic tasks on the Mac as well as a selection of troubleshooting help.

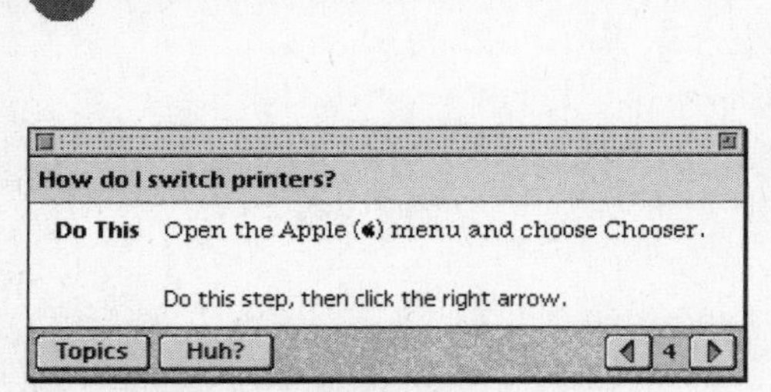

Figure 1-7 *Apple Guide in action.*

As with Balloon Help, application developers can write Apple Guide documents specific to their application. If so, these Guides will only be listed in the Guide menu when the relevant application is active.

Overall, Apple Guide is better than any other help system I have seen. Try it out!

SEE: • **Chapter 12 for more information on Apple Guide, especially what to do if you cannot get Apple Guide to work**

TAKE NOTE ▶

APPLICATIONS AND DOCUMENTS

In addition to the software categories already described in this chapter, there are two other major types of files: applications and documents. Typically, *applications* are the programs that are used to create *documents*. For example, ClarisWorks is an application, while a letter that you create with ClarisWorks is called a ClarisWorks document.

This distinction can get blurry around the edges. For example, some applications never create documents (for instance, a utility application that is used just to check whether a disk is damaged). Further, many applications use accessory files (such as translator files and plug-in modules) that are a special type of document file, even though they are not created by the application.

Finally, with Apple's new OpenDoc technology, this whole application-centered approach changes. The document becomes the focus, as a document may contain "parts" that belong to several different "applications."

SEE: • **Chapter 13 for more on OpenDoc**

Chapter 2

Be Prepared: Preventing Problems

Tooling Up 29

Damage Control 29

Damaged Files and Disks 29

Software Bugs and Conflicts 30

A Troubleshooter's Toolkit 31

Toolkit Essentials 34

System Software 34

Data Recovery Package 34

System Enhancement Package 35

The Best of the Rest 35

Troubleshooting with the Finder 36

Get Info 36

About This Macintosh 40

Window Headers 41

The Find Command 42

The Erase Disk and Empty Trash Commands 44

The Restart and Shut Down Commands 44

Preventative Maintenance 45

Have an Emergency Startup Disk Ready 45

Apple's Disk Tools Startup Floppy Disk 45

A Finder-Less Startup Floppy Disk 47

Data Recovery Utility Startup Floppy Disks 48

CD-ROM Startup Discs 48

Secondary Hard Drives or Partitions as Startup Disks 49

Universal Startup Disks 49

Preventative Maintenance (continued)

Save and Back Up Your Work 49
Save Your Work ... Often 50
Make Regular Backups 50
Devise a Good Backup Strategy 51
Prune Your Hard Drive 52
Delete Unneeded Data and Application Files 52
Delete Items from the System Folder 52
Delete Mystery Files 53
Other Ways to Save or Get More Space 54
Install Protection Utilities 55
Protect Against Virus Infections 55
Protect Against Accidentally Deleted Files 56
Protect Against Crashed or Accidentally Erased Hard Disks 59
Protect Against Disk Damage 60
Protect Against Loss of Data Due to System Crashes 61
Give Your Macintosh a Tune-Up 62
Defragment Your Disk 62
Rebuild Your Desktop File 63
Run Disk First Aid 63
Check or Replace the System File 63
Stay Up-to-Date 64

Tooling Up

For hardware repairs of any sort, you can't do much without the proper tools. Whether the hardware is a computer, a television, a refrigerator, or a car, you need screwdrivers, pliers, and more. The same is true for software repairs on the Macintosh—except that in this case, your main tools are electronic rather than metal. Once again, you need to gather the relevant tools and become familiar with how to use them.

Being prepared to solve problems also means trying to avoid the problem in the first place: preventative maintenance. Regularly changing the oil filter in your car can prevent the problems caused by using dirty oil, and the same logic is true again for computers.

That's what this chapter is all about: troubleshooting tools and preventative maintenance.

Damage Control

I talk about many different types of problems in this book, but certain themes keep recurring. For example, I make frequent references to terms such as *damaged disks*, *corrupted files*, *bugs*, and *software conflicts*.

If these terms are not familiar to you, it can all seem a bit confusing. What exactly gets damaged? How does this damage even occur? Where do bugs come from? Here are the answers.

Damaged Files and Disks

A *damaged* (or *corrupted) file* means that the data contained in the file have, at least partially, been lost or incorrectly altered. The result is that the Macintosh can no longer correctly "understand" the file. This usually means that the file either will not open at all or will not function properly if it does open. In some cases, trying to use such a file may result in the Mac abruptly coming to a halt—an event typically referred to as a *system crash.*

Certain special invisible files on your disk are responsible for informing the Macintosh computer about everything else that is on the disk and how it is organized. If these files get damaged, the result is often referred to as a *damaged disk.* A variety of symptoms are possible. In the worst cases, the Mac may react as if the entire disk is unreadable; if the disk is your startup disk, you may not be able to start up.

In most cases, damage to files and disks is essentially *software damage.* No physical damage to the disk itself has occurred. A reasonable analogy is a videotape of a movie that somehow has had a few seconds of the film erased. The videotape machine is still fine, and so is the actual videotape, but the movie is not—when you view it, the erased scene is missing. With computers, however, damaged files (the equivalent of an erased scene) can have effects beyond the "missing" portion itself. Also, in some cases, special software can be used to "fix" damaged files.

Software damage can occur if a file is being saved (or even accessed) at the time of some unexpected interruption, such as a power failure or a system crash. The result is that the file is saved incorrectly, as the wrong data are written to the file. Software damage can also occur because of seemingly random and unpredictable changes that happen, as a result of various causes, over the lifetime of a disk. For example, the stored information is vulnerable to almost any sort of electromagnetic interference, and even a minor alteration can have serious consequences.

Defects in the physical disk itself are referred to as *media damage* (often considered synonymous to *bad blocks*). If a part of the surface of the disk gets marred, any file that occupies that area would be damaged as well. It takes only the smallest amount of damage to cause total loss of access to a file. Like software damage, media damage can also result in system crashes and disk crashes.

Media damage often occurs if part of the magnetic surface of the disk is scratched or flakes off. This damage may be present from the first time you use a disk, occur following a specific event (such as an accidental bumping of the drive while it is in use), or happen simply as a consequence of normal use and/or aging of the disk.

Returning to the videotape analogy, imagine a scene in a movie suddenly appearing blurry or distorted because the tape had been stretched or crumpled in that area. The movie scene is probably irrecoverably damaged, and you can no longer use that section of the tape for future recordings (you may choose to splice it out). If the damage is severe enough, you may even have to discard the tape altogether. Still, you do not need to bring the recorder itself in for repairs. In this respect, tape damage is clearly distinct from damage to the mechanical or electronic components of the recorder.

Although it is technically a hardware problem, media damage is separate from problems with the mechanisms of the disk drive itself. As with videotape damage, media damage problems can usually be resolved without a trip to the repair shop. Only software tools are needed. If the software techniques fail to work, however, media damage to a fixed hard drive will require repair or replacement of the entire drive.

Finally, a damaged disk may in fact be due to actual *hardware damage* to some component of the disk drive. This will almost certainly require repair or replacement of the drive.

SEE:
- **Chapter 8 for more on invisible files**
- **Fix-Its #13 and #14 for more on file and disk damage**

Software Bugs and Conflicts

A software *bug* is simply an error made by the programmer when the application was written. Because it is caused by the people who created the program, not by you, there is no way that you can repair a bug yourself. The only permanent solution is to get a new version of the software (when one is available) that has fixed the problem. In the meantime, you may find some acceptable work-around solutions.

Bugs vary in their level of seriousness. Minor bugs may have only a cosmetic effect on the display and can often be ignored (be careful, though, since these bugs may be harbingers of serious problems). More serious bugs may entirely prevent you from using the program.

A *software conflict* is a bug where one program's instructions fail to take into account something that another program may do. If both of these programs are in use at the same time, they conflict with each other, often causing a system crash. A conflict may also occur between a software program and a hardware component (such as a particular type of monitor). In such cases, the program may not work when that hardware is in use.

If all software was written perfectly, none of these bugs or conflicts would occur. Since this is admittedly very difficult if not impossible to do, bugs and conflicts do occur—all too frequently.

A Troubleshooter's Toolkit

In days of yore, you could only solve computer problems if you were a programmer and developed your own problem-solving tools. Thankfully, these days, the tools have already been designed for you. Many of them are free, and a few require only a relatively inexpensive purchase. These tools cannot solve every problem, but there aren't many problems you can solve without them.

The problem-solving tools (or *utilities*) described here are designed for nonexpert users who have little or no technical skills. Some are so easy to use that they practically run themselves, while others may take a bit more effort to learn.

TAKE NOTE ▶

WHAT'S A UTILITY?

Most applications that you use probably fall in the productivity category—that is, they allow you to do something on the computer faster, easier, and better than you could do it without the computer. Word processors and spreadsheet programs are typical examples.

Utilities, however, exist only to accomplish tasks that you would never need to do if you did not use a computer. For example, you can get utilities to help you back up your software (that is, to make a second copy that you keep in the event something goes wrong with the first copy). Unless you used a computer, you would obviously have no reason to make backups of computer disks.

Utilities are available to assist in almost every imaginable task, from backing up files to undeleting them to recovering damaged files. Some are designed to make your computer life easier while others are designed to help solve problems. I describe many of them in this chapter.

Many beginning users balk at using these utilities, feeling that they are primarily for power users who have the time and interest to learn how to master them. This is not true. Every user, regardless of skill level, can learn how to use—and benefit from using—the utilities described in this chapter.

Table 2-1 gives a summary of useful troubleshooting tools. It is not complete; other utilities will be mentioned throughout the book.

Make sure that your personal toolkit includes at least one data repair and recovery package, an anti-virus utility, a back-up utility, a disk formatting utility, an extension manager, and a SCSI control panel (such as SCSIProbe). A diagnostic utility, while not as essential, is desirable.

You don't need the other utilities right away. In fact, there are some you may never need. But the time to start stocking your toolkit is now.

Table 2-1 A Catalog of Troubleshooting Utilities

NAME(S)	USE IT TO...	FOR MORE INFO, SEE ...
Macintosh System Software		
Balloon Help and Apple Guide	Display interactive help for problem solving	Chapter 1
Functions built into System file and ROM	Rebuild desktop, zap parameter RAM, reset Power Manager (on PowerBooks), and more	This chapter, Fix-It #9, Fix-It #11
Finder	Determine pertinent information about files (such as version number), locate files, copy files, delete files, set memory allocations for files, erase floppy disks, restart, shut down, and more	This chapter, Chapter 4, Chapter 5, Chapter 6, Fix-It #6, Fix-It #15
Installer	Reinstall system software from scratch	Fix-It #5
Memory control panel	Access disk cache, virtual memory, 32-bit addressing, and RAM disk settings	Fix-It #6
Startup Disk control panel	Select which disk is to be the startup disk, if more than one potential startup disk is available	Chapter 5
Monitors and Monitors & Sound control panels, and related Control Strip options	Adjust the depth of the display (that is, how many colors or grays are displayed)	Chapter 10
General Controls control panel	Automatically lock application and System Folder files, hide the Finder when it is in the background (new features in System 7.5), and more	Chapter 6, Chapter 12
Chooser desk accessory	Turn on AppleTalk, select printer, access AppleShare, and related functions	Chapter 7
Disk First Aid	Check for and possibly repair damaged disks	This chapter, Fix-It #10
Apple HD SC Setup and Drive Setup	Update disk driver, check for media damage, reformat disk	Fix-It #12, Fix-It #15
Extensions Manager	Manage extensions (that is, which ones are on or off at startup)	Fix-It #4
Disk Copy	Create exact copies of floppy disks (also needed to convert disk image files to a usable floppy disk format)	This chapter, Chapter 6, Fix-It #5, Fix-It #14
Apple Printer Utility	Check on and/or adjust the status of a LaserWriter, download fonts, and more	Chapter 9
PowerBook control panel, and related Control Strip options	Access settings that affect battery conservation and related PowerBook-specific features	Chapter 11
Apple System Profiler	Profiles contents of your disk and characteristics of your hardware	Fix-It #17
Macintosh Easy Open and PC Exchange	Helps in opening files that otherwise could not be opened, especially PC-formatted files (included with System 7.5)	Chapter 6
Data Protection, Repair, and Recovery Packages		
Norton Utilities for Macintosh, or MacTools	Check for and repair damaged files and disks, undelete files, optimize disks, back up files, and make exact copies of floppy disks (plus virus protection, in MacTools only)	This chapter, Chapter 6, Chapter 8, Fix-It #8, Fix-It #13, Fix-It #14

Table 2-1 A Catalog of Troubleshooting Utilities *(continued)*

NAME(S)	USE IT TO...	FOR MORE INFO, SEE ...
Anti-Virus Utilities		
SAM, Virex, Disinfectant, or MacTools Anti-Virus	Detect and eradicate viruses	This chapter, Fix-It #7
General System Enhancement Packages		
Now Utilities	Manage extensions, assist in locating and launching files (plus several other functions)	This chapter, Chapter 6, Fix-It #4
Extension Managers		
Conflict Catcher II and Now Startup Manager	Manage extensions (these have more features than Apple's Extension Manager)	Fix-It #4
Diagnostic Utilities		
TechTool Pro	Determine whether hardware components are functioning properly (also has some limited software checks)	Fix-It #17
MacEKG , Peace of Mind, Gauge Series	Determine whether hardware components are functioning properly	Fix-It #17
Help!	Determine whether there are any known software conflicts, bugs, or related incompatibilities	Fix-It #4, Fix-It #5, Fix-It #17
Backup Utilities		
Retrospect, Redux, DiskFit Pro, Norton Utilities, or MacTools	Back up the data on a hard disk	This chapter
Disk Format Utilities		
Drive7, Hard Disk ToolKit, Silverlining (or whatever custom utility came with your hard drive)	Update disk driver, check for media damage, reformat disk, partition disk (use instead of Apple HD Setup for non-Apple drives)	Fix-It #12, Fix-It #15
Selected List of Other Troubleshooting Utilities		
Last Resort, SpellCatcher GhostWriter, Now Utilities NowSave	Recover text unsaved at the time of a system crash	This chapter, Chapter 4
Bomb Shelter or System Error Patch	Recover (if possible) from a system crash without having to restart	This chapter, Chapter 4
Spring Cleaning, Yank, CleanSweep, Preferences Cleaner	Clean up unneeded files in System Folder, uninstall files, and more	This Chapter, Fix-It #2
SCSIProbe control panel	Conveniently list and mount SCSI devices	Chapter 5, Fix-It #16
Alias Dragon and Alias Zoo	Fix broken alias links and related alias problems	Chapter 6
HellFolderFix, Rename Rescue, Unlock Folder	Fix problems with renaming or deleting files	Chapter 6
DiskTop, Snitch, InvisiFile Save A BNDL	Work with invisible files and file attributes	Chapter 8
Font Box and FONDler	Fix damaged fonts and related font problems	Chapter 9
ResetPwrMgr	Reset Power Manager in PowerBooks	Chapter 11
Finder Fixer, MacOS Purge, FixHeap	Fix certain system heap memory problems and/or give more memory to the Finder	Fix-It #6
Disk Express II	Optimize disks in background	Fix-It #8
TechTool	Rebuild desktop and zap Parameter RAM (it's better than using Apple's methods)	Fix-It #9, Fix-It #11
Can Opener	Recover text and graphics from damaged and unopenable files	Fix-It #14

Toolkit Essentials

System Software

All it takes is a glance at Table 2-1 to discover that system software is the single biggest collection of troubleshooting tools at your disposal. And with System 7.5, Apple gives you more of these tools than ever before. All of which is great news to the cost-conscious, because everyone gets system software free when they purchase their Macintosh (though you will have to pay to upgrade to any later versions).

Data Recovery Package

By far the next most important item on your list of acquisitions should be a data protection, repair, and recovery package. Owning at least one of these packages is essential; each is a collection of several separate utilities that share a common goal of preventing or fixing problems. At the moment, you have two main choices here: Norton Utilities for Macintosh, and MacTools Pro. Which one of these should you get? The answer depends on whom you ask, exactly what problem you have, and which package just came out with its latest upgrade. You won't go far wrong with either of them. If your finances permit, in fact, I would actually recommend getting both of these packages. Often, one of them can detect or fix a problem that the other cannot (though neither

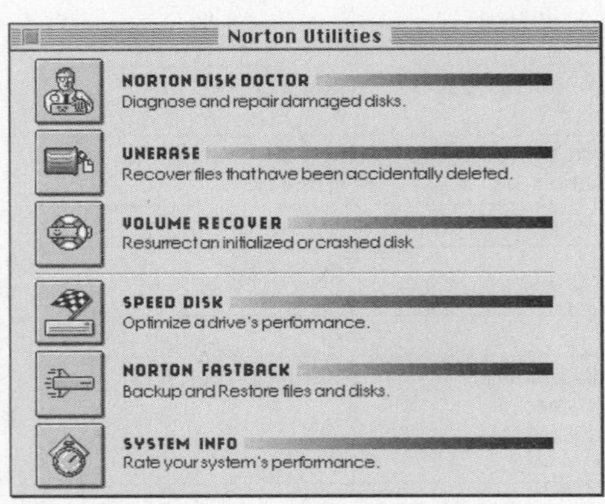

Figure 2-1 *The Norton Utilities main window.*

BY THE WAY ▶

SHAKEUP IN THE DATA RECOVERY UTILITIES MARKET

When I wrote the first edition of this book, there were three data recovery packages I could unequivocally recommend: Norton Utilities for Macintosh, MacTools, and Public Utilities. Since then, Symantec (the publisher of Norton Utilities) purchased Fifth Generation (the publisher of Public Utilities). As a result, Public Utilities is now gone, with some of its unique features incorporated into version 3.0 of Norton Utilities. More recently, Symantec also purchased Central Point, the publisher of MacTools. Symantec has now announced that it no longer intends to maintain MacTools Pro.

This continues a Symantec tradition begun several years ago when Norton Utilities itself was purchased by Symantec and combined with its then-competing product, called SUM (Symantec Utilities for Macintosh). The result of all this is that Symantec has now virtually eliminated any competition in the data-recovery utilities market—Norton Utilities is the only option left.

On a related note, prior to itself being taken over by Symantec, Central Point bought out Maxa (a company that made two excellent diagnostic utilities, Snooper and Alert). Symantec thus appears to have the rights to these programs as well; they, too, have been discontinued.

Because of all the MacTools Pro users still out there, I will continue to refer to the program in this edition of *Sad Macs*. Unless things change yet again, however, MacTools will be gone from the next edition.

program consistently outperforms the other). I provide more details on the use of these packages later in this chapter and in several other locations in this book, especially Chapter 8, Fix-It #13, and Fix-It #14.

System Enhancement Package

I also strongly recommend getting a system enhancement package. My current favorite is Now Utilities (currently at version 6.5), a kitchen-sink collection of programs that assist in troubleshooting and simply make using your Mac more pleasant: a utility that helps locate and launch applications (Now Menus, SuperBoomerang), a startup management utility (Startup Manager), a utility that can recover text not saved at the time of a system crash (Now Save), and more. In the past, you would have had to buy several single-purpose programs, at a much higher total cost, to come close to duplicating the features of Now Utilities.

Apple's System 7.5 incorporates several of the features that previously led people to purchase these packages (including some key features of NowMenus). I expect Now Utilities to stay ahead of the curve, however, and so it remains a worthwhile investment.

Other system enhancement packages, such as screen savers, are not directly relevant to troubleshooting and thus will not be mentioned much in this book.

The Best of the Rest

Yes, you should have backup utility software (such as Retrospect or Redux) and an anti-virus program (such as SAM or Virex). You may also want a separate disk formatting utility, such as Drive7 or Hard Disk ToolKit, though some sort of disk formatting utility certainly came with your hard drive.

Similarly, don't forget that your system software already includes utilities that compete with many of these third-party single-purpose products. Examples of these utilities include Drive Setup, Extensions Manager, and Disk First Aid. Third-party single-purpose utilities often include features and conveniences not available with either the system software or the general packages, however, so don't automatically rule them out.

TAKE NOTE ▶

SYSTEM 7.6: A SLIGHTLY DIFFERENT LOOK

There are several, largely cosmetic, changes introduced in System 7.6 that affect some of the generalizations made in *Sad Macs*. In particular:

- "About This Macintosh" now reads "About This Computer."
- The traditional "Welcome to Macintosh" screen is gone. Instead, you immediately go to a Mac OS splash screen, where the words "Welcome to Mac OS" appear.
- If you hold down the Shift key at startup, the phrase "Extensions Disabled," rather than the previous "Extensions Off," appears.
- The Disk Tools disk has been changed somewhat. You will likely find something called "Emergency Disk 1" and "Emergency Disk 2." Only Disk 2 will have a Finder.

SEE: • Chapter 13, especially "Take Note: System 7.6: A Closer Look," for a more complete list of these types of changes

Also, some shareware and freeware programs (such as SCSIProbe and TechTool) have features unmatched by any commercial software. For instance, Apple makes a freeware utility called ResEdit. Though it was designed primarily for programmers, it can sometimes be useful as a more general troubleshooting tool. I won't go into details of its use in this book, since I'd rather focus on more end-user-oriented tools. Because some readers are already familiar with this utility, however, I will occasionally refer to it.

See Table 2-1 for other recommendations. Details on how to get any of the products mentioned are described in the Appendix.

Troubleshooting with the Finder

As indicated in Table 2-1, the majority of system software troubleshooting-related files are described in more detail in the other parts of this book. Because of how often I refer to its features in the pages ahead, though, I will describe the basic troubleshooting features of the Finder right now.

Get Info

From the Finder, select any file on your disk (that is, click its icon once). Then select the Get Info command from the File menu—or type its keyboard shortcut, Command-I. This brings up the appropriately named Get Info window, which is filled with important information about that file. You can also view some of the same information directly in the Finder's folder windows, if you select a non-icon view (such as By Name) from the View menu.

The first part of the Get Info window displays the name of the file and its icon. If the file selected is part of Macintosh system software—for example, the Finder—the name should also include the version of the system software to which the file belongs (such as "System Software 7.5").

The next line in the Get Info window is called Kind; most commonly, it says either "application program" or "document." If the file is a document, and the Finder recognizes it as belonging to a particular application, this line probably says so (such as "ClarisWorks document"). If you don't know what application created a particular document, this can be a quick way to find out. (Alternatively, turning on Balloon Help and moving the cursor over the document file's icon on the desktop also tells you the name of the creating application.)

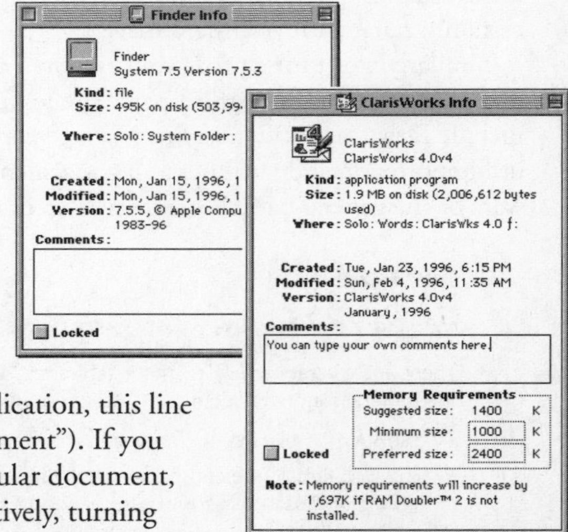

Figure 2-2 *Two examples of Get Info windows.*

For system software, all sorts of additional Kind names are possible, such as "desk accessory," "control panel," or "system extension. "The System file itself is listed as a "suitcase" in System 7.

The Size and Where lines in the Get Info window refer to how much disk space the file occupies and where on the disk the file is located.

The Created and Modified lines tell you when the file was first created and the last time that it was modified (that is, changed in any way). Every time you save a document, its modification date changes. Because sometimes even applications get modified, the modification date for an application on your hard drive may be different from the date on your backup copy of that same application. This may be just fine and normal, but unexpected changes in the modification date may also be a warning sign of trouble, such as damage to the file.

The Version number is usually relevant only for applications and system software. It identifies the particular version of a program. This information can be essential when you are trying to determine incompatibilities. For example, suppose you are told that version 2.0 of BusyWorks (a fictitious application I'll use in some examples) is incompatible with System 7. The Version line of the Get Info window is where you can find out if you are using the problematic version 2.0.

BY THE WAY ▶

FINDING THE VERSION NUMBER

Sometimes, the programmers forget to include the version information in the Get Info window. In that case, if you need to know the version, you should be able to find it by launching the application and then selecting About BusyWorks (or whatever the name of the program is) from the top of the Apple menu. The window that then appears usually indicates the version number.

The Comments box may contain any text, including whatever you care to type there. Most often, it is empty.

The Locked check box is used to lock the file. This simply prevents the file from being deleted when you place it in the Trash and select Empty Trash. You can still delete a locked file either by unlocking it first (by unchecking the check box) or by holding down the Option key when you attempt to empty the Trash that contains the locked file.

TAKE NOTE ▶

LOCKING FLOPPY DISKS

On floppy disks, you can lock the entire disk; this prevents you from adding, deleting, or even modifying any of the files on the disk. Even holding down the Option key while you select Empty Trash does not allow you to delete a file from a locked disk. The *only* way to delete a file from a locked disk is to unlock it first.

To lock a floppy disk, slide up the tab that is located in the upper right-hand corner of the disk (as the front of the disk faces you), so that you can see through the hole. Sliding the tab back down unlocks it again.

SEE: • Chapter 6 for more on deleting locked files

For an application, the lower right-hand corner of its Get Info window has an area called Memory Requirements. It includes three numbers: Suggested size, Minimum size, and Preferred size. These numbers refer to the amount of memory (that is, RAM) that the program occupies when it is opened.

The default values of all three numbers are initially set by the application itself. The Suggested size can never be altered; this is the recommended amount of memory needed to run the program under normal conditions.

The user can alter the remaining two values simply by typing a new number in the appropriate box. You can increase or decrease these values at any time, as long as the application itself is not currently open. (If it is open, just quit the application and then make the change.)

The Minimum size is the smallest amount of memory the program must be able to access in order to open. If you need to conserve memory, this number can be set to less than the Suggested size, but consider yourself warned—some of the program's features may not work, or serious problems (such as system crashes) may develop. If the program's default Minimum size is already set lower than the Suggested size, certainly don't set the Minimum size any lower.

You can set the Preferred size for considerably more than the Suggested size. Whenever a program opens, it uses the Preferred memory size if that much free memory is available. Applications such as graphics and multimedia programs generally run faster or can work with larger documents when they have additional memory available.

If the available free memory when you open an application is less than the application's Preferred size (as might happen, for example, if other applications are already open), the application uses whatever free memory is left. If the free memory is less than the Minimum size, however, the program does not open at all. And once an application launches, its memory allocation cannot change until the next time you use it, even if more memory is freed up while you are running the application.

So, the amount of memory occupied by an application can vary anywhere between the Minimum and the Preferred size, depending on the available memory at the time you launch the application. If you don't like this degree of uncertainty, you can guarantee that the program always uses the same amount of memory by setting the Minimum size and Preferred size to the same number. Otherwise, to find out exactly how much memory an open application is using, you have to check in the About This Macintosh window (as described in the next section).

In most cases, you will probably do just fine if you leave the memory values the way they were initially set by the program's publisher. Some adjustments, however, may occasionally be required. For example, an application's memory allocation includes the amount available to the application *plus* all its open documents. For some programs, you may need to increase the Preferred size in order to be able to open several documents at once or to open a single large, complex document.

On the other hand, if you plan to have several applications open at the same time, you may want to use a smaller value for any one application's Preferred size. Doing so increases the amount of memory left over for the other applications to use. Of course, the greater the amount of memory hardware inside your machine, the more leeway you have in making these adjustments. Deciding on the best settings may take some experimentation.

Overall, knowing how to work with these settings is an important technique for solving numerous memory-related problems.

SEE: • **Chapter 6 and Fix-It #6 for more on memory management**

In System 7.0, this memory area of the Get Info window is designed a bit differently than in System 7.1 or 7.5. The area is simply called Memory and there are only two settings: Suggested size and Current size. Often, the default values of these two numbers are identical. The Suggested size works the same as in System 7.1/7.5, while the Current size is how much memory the program actually occupies when you launch it. To shift from a minimum to a preferred maximum value (or anywhere in between), you must change the Current size as desired. System 7.1/7.5 provides greater flexibility by essentially splitting the Current size setting into two separate settings: Minimum and Preferred.

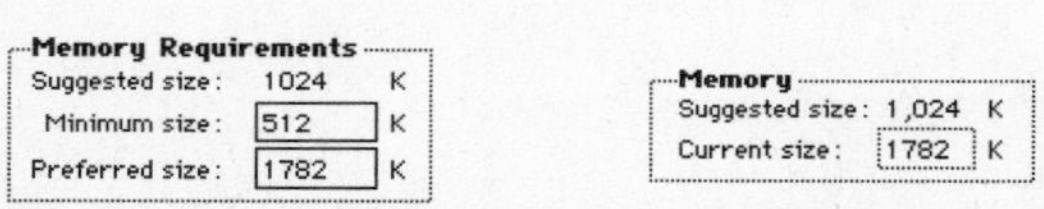

Figure 2-3 *The Memory Requirements section of an application's Get Info window in System 7.5 (left); the similar Memory section in System 7.0 (right).*

Power Macintosh Alert: If you have a Power Macintosh, you may also see a note at the bottom of the screen concerning virtual memory. The significance of this is explained in Chapter 12 and Fix-It #6.

You may find other items in a Get Info window. For example, if the file is an alias, a button called Find Original locates the original file that the alias represents. If the file is a document, you are likely to see a check box for a Stationery pad. If checked, this means that if you launch the file from the Finder, it opens to an untitled copy of the file, rather than the original file itself. However, this System 7 feature does not work with all applications. If it doesn't work, it will open a document in its ordinary format.

BY THE WAY ▶

YOUR FINDER MODIFICATION DATE DID NOT UPDATE

There is a known bug in System 7 whereby the modification date of a file may not be immediately updated in Finder windows, including the Get Info window. If this happens to you, the solution is simple: just close and reopen the window.

About This Macintosh ...

If the Finder is the active application, the first item in the Apple menu is About This Macintosh (or About This Computer). Select this item, and the window that appears should tell you the general name of the Macintosh model you are using (in case you didn't already know it). It is also another location where you can get the exact version number of the system software you are using.

More important, it tells you the settings for Total Memory and Largest Unused Block. The Total Memory is equivalent to the amount of RAM you have installed in your computer.

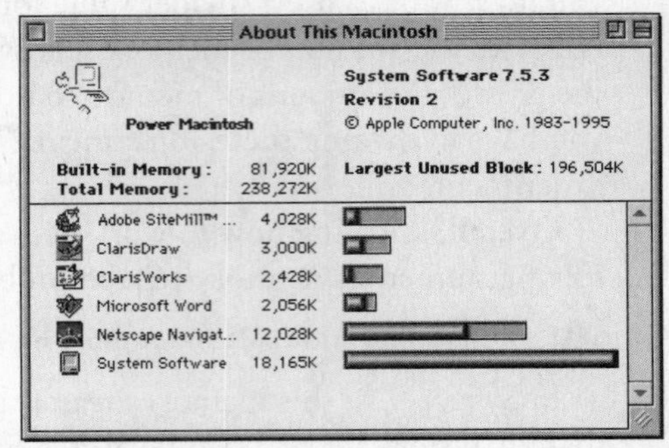

Figure 2-4 *The About This Macintosh window shows the amount of memory allocated to all open programs.*

TECHNICALLY SPEAKING ▶

BUILT-IN MEMORY AND VIRTUAL MEMORY

If you are using virtual memory (set in the Memory control panel, as described in Fix-It #6), another line above the Total Memory line reads Built-in Memory. In this case, the Built-In Memory refers to the amount of RAM installed in your computer. Total Memory then refers to the sum of the Built-in Memory plus virtual memory or RAM Doubler-extended memory. If you are using a Power Macintosh and virtual memory, the Total Memory may be larger than the sum of your built-in memory and virtual memory setting. This is normal (and is explained more in Chapter 12).

The Largest Unused Block is essentially how much of that RAM currently is not in use and therefore is available for use by other applications. Sometimes, however, the Largest Unused Block size may be less than the total amount of unused memory (as explained in Fix-It #6).

The remainder of this window contains a series of bar graphs that indicate the memory usage of every currently open application plus the system software. In System 7.1 or higher, this value can range from the application's Minimum size to Preferred size, as listed in the Memory Requirements area of the application's Get Info window. For example, ClarisWorks may open with a memory allocation of 1,850K, larger than its Minimum size (1,000K) and smaller than its Preferred size (2,400K). This could be because ClarisWorks was the last of all the programs listed to be opened and this was all the memory left at that time. (If 2,400K or more of memory were available, ClarisWorks would have used the full 2,400K.) In System 7.0, the situation is simpler: the memory allocation is always equal to the Current size for that application, as set in its Get Info window.

The last line of the bar graph is always for the system software. It lists the combined amount of memory currently used by the System file, the Finder, and various other system software (as well as third-party extensions and control panels). Its size varies depending on what system software version you are using, and how many extensions/control panels you have installed.

By the way, you might think that the size of the Largest Unused Block plus the sum of the memory allocation of any items listed in the display should be approximately equal to the Total Memory value. Although this is often the case, there are some exceptions (for reasons described more in Fix-it #6).

The bar graphs also indicate how the memory is currently allocated within each application. The total length of the bar represents the total amount of memory assigned to that application (also shown as a number to the left of the bar). The dark-shaded portion of the bar represents how much of that memory is currently in use by the application.

For example, every time you open an additional document within an application, you use more of the memory allocation for that application. This means that the dark-shaded area gets larger, while the light area of the bar graph gets smaller.

When the light-shaded portion of the bar gets very small, you are approaching the memory limits of the program. At this time, you may be unable to open any more documents (without first closing other currently open ones). Further attempts to tax the application's use of memory in this (or any other) way result in "out of memory" alert messages.

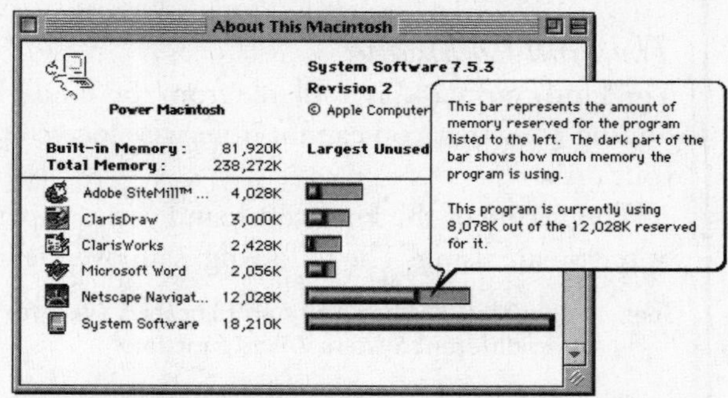

Figure 2-5 *Using Show Balloons to find out exactly how much of Netscape Navigator's memory allocation is actually in use.*

Also, be aware that even if a program is not using most of its assigned memory at the moment, that memory cannot be used by any other program. It sits there waiting for the program to use it, until you quit the application.

If you want to know precisely how much memory the shaded and unshaded areas of each bar represent, select Show Balloons from the Balloon Help menu and then move the cursor over a bar. A balloon appears that gives you the size of the darker-shaded area.

Window Headers

Underneath the title of each window in the Finder is a line that lists three items: the number of *items* in the window, the amount of space currently occupied *in disk,* and the amount of disk space currently *available*. The number of items listed varies depending on how many items are in the selected folder, since the other numbers refer to the entire disk, they are the same no matter what folder is selected. The last two items, if added together, should yield the total storage capacity of the disk (give or take a few megabytes). This information is useful when

Figure 2-6 *The top of a window, showing the window header information just below the title.*

you are trying to determine whether you have sufficient space available for an operation such as copying files to the disk.

This header information is initially missing when you are using a non-icon view. In System 7, however, you can still get this information to appear, by selecting the Show Disk Info in Header option from the Views control panel.

By the way, hidden within the window title is a feature you can use to locate where you are on the disk and navigate quickly to a related location. To access it, hold down the Command key when you click the name of the window in the header. This brings up a pop-up menu showing the hierarchy of folders, starting from the current folder and working backward to the root level. Selecting any folder from this menu immediately takes you there. (Another tip for easier navigation and preventing screen clutter: If you hold down the Option key when opening a folder, the window that contains the folder will close as the new one opens.)

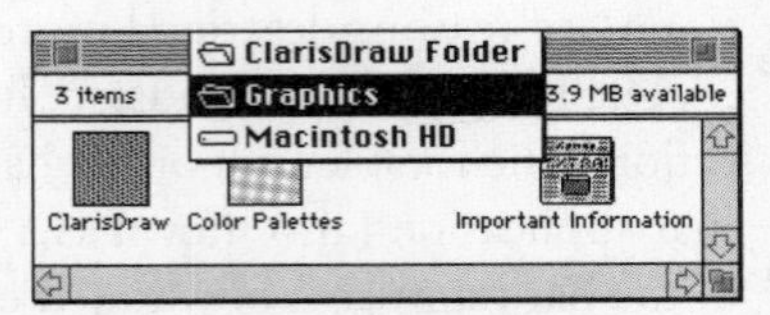

Figure 2-7 *The pop-up menu that appears when you click on a window title while holding down the Command key.*

The Find Command

The Find command is available from the Finder's File menu. It is an essential tool for finding a file that you cannot otherwise locate or to check if a certain file even exists on your disk.

The nature of the Find command varies depending on the level of the system software you are using. The following is an overview of each version.

See: • **Chapter 6, "When You Can't Locate a File," for a step-by-step example of using each of the two different System 7 Find functions**

- System 7.0/7.1

  When you select Find (Command-F) from the Finder's File menu, the Macintosh will bring up the Find window. Simply type the name of the file you are searching for and click the Find button. Remember, you do not have to type the entire name; a search for any portion of the name (such as BusyW for BusyWorks) will eventually find all files that contain that portion.

  When the computer locates its first matching file (or folder), it opens the window containing that file, and the file itself is highlighted. If this is not the file you want, select Find Again (Command-G). The Macintosh will continue to search for matching files, displaying each in turn, until all have been found.

  For more extensive search criteria, select the More Choices button to open up an expanded window. From here you can search on criteria other

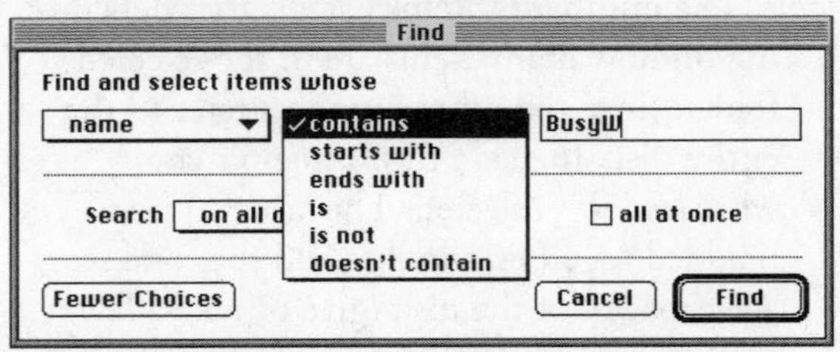

Figure 2-8 *Two views of the Finder's Find window (System 7.0/7.1), accessed by selecting Find from the File menu.*

than name (such as date created, kind, and size) as well as specifying more specific limits on a criteria (such as name starts with, name ends with, or name contains). You can also limit the search to specified volumes. If you select the "all at once" button, you get a listing of all searched files with the ones that match the criteria highlighted.

- **System 7.5**
  An expanded Find capability is included with System 7.5 as a desk accessory called Find File, available from the Apple menu. If you have the Find File extension installed in the Extensions Folder, however, selecting Find (Command-F) from the Finder's File menu will also bring up this desk accessory. Otherwise, selecting Find brings up the same window as in System 7.0/7.1. (Actually, even with this extension installed, you can still get the old Find function by holding down the Shift key when you select Find or Find Again.)

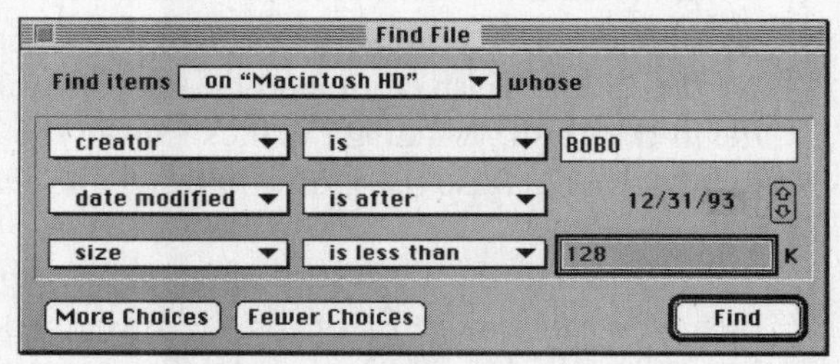

Figure 2-9 *The Find File desk accessory in System 7.5 or later.*

  The new Find File accessory is somewhat similar to the More Choices view of the previous version, but behind this similarity are significant new features. First, it has two important new search criteria: File Type, and Creator (the meaning of these criteria is explained more in Chapter 8, and an example of using them is described in Fix-It #2). Second, the function of the More Choices button has changed. It now opens up as many as eight selection criteria rows, allowing you to search using multiple criteria at one time (such as all files less than 128K that were last modified after December 31, 1996).

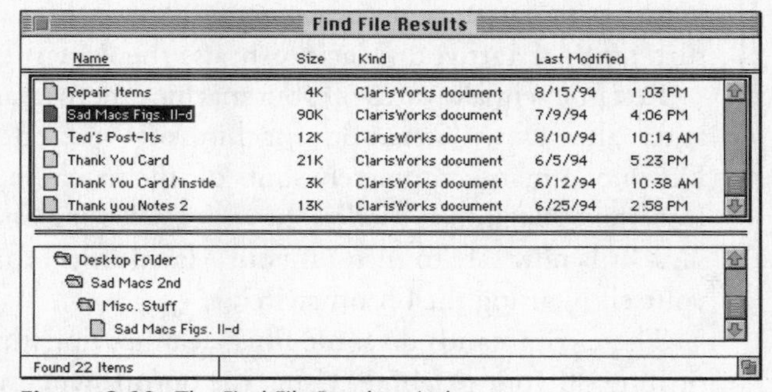

Figure 2-10 *The Find File Results window.*

  A more dramatic change is that, after you select Find, the search results are displayed in a Find File Results window (no more need for Find Again!). The top part of this window lists every file and folder that matches the selected criteria. Double-click on any given listing, and the Finder will launch

BY THE WAY ▶

HIDDEN SEARCH OPTIONS IN FIND FILE

Hold down the Option key while accessing the Name pop-up menu. If you do, you will get four additional attributes that you can select as search criteria: name/icon lock (searches for locked files and icons); custom icon (searches for files that have a custom icon); visibility (can search for invisible files); and contents (searches for text within a file, up to 30 characters).

the file or open the folder. With System 7.5's drag-and-drop capabilities, you can even directly drag the name from the Results window to any location on your disk (such as the Desktop or the Trash), and the file will be immediately moved there. The bottom of the Results window lists the hierarchical location of the currently selected file; again, double-clicking any folder directly opens that folder. Personally, the advantages of the Results window have sold me on using this new Find File over the previous version.

The Erase Disk and Empty Trash Commands

These commands are found in the Finder's Special menu. The Erase Disk command is primarily used to reformat floppy disks; that is, the entire disk is erased and re-created as if you had started with an unformatted disk.

The Empty Trash command deletes only the files currently in the Trash. To place a file in the Trash, you drag the file's icon to the Trash icon until the Trash icon is highlighted, then release the mouse button. The Trash can icon bulges to show that it contains the file(s).

In System 7, the Trash is never actually emptied until you select Empty Trash. Until then, you can remove files from the Trash by double-clicking the Trash icon to open up its window, and then dragging the file out again.

By the way, if you want to bypass the message that appears each time you empty the Trash, select Get Info for the Trash and then uncheck "Warn before emptying."

SEE: • **"Protect Against Accidentally Deleted Files," later in this chapter**
• **Fix-It #15 for more on erasing disks**

The Restart and Shut Down Commands

Under most circumstances, do *not* use the on/off switch in the back of your machine to turn off or restart your Macintosh; use the Restart or Shut Down command instead.

Restart essentially turns off your machine momentarily and then immediately restarts it again. Shut Down turns your machine off—period. In most Macintoshes, the Shut Down command completely shuts off the machine. No further action is necessary. In certain Macintosh models, however, selecting Shut Down results in a message that says "It is now safe to turn off your Macintosh." You then have to turn off the machine yourself by using the on/off switch.

These commands do some final cleanup, updating, and proper closing of files before turning off your machine. Using the on/off switch without first selecting Shut Down bypasses these actions and may result in the loss of data and possible damage to files.

SEE: • **Chapter 4 for more on restarting and shutting down**

Preventative Maintenance

As is often the case, you can avoid big headaches later on by enduring some small headaches now. This is what preventative maintenance is all about: solving problems before they happen.

I am certainly sympathetic to those who abhor routine maintenance; I do, too. Whenever I purchase a piece of equipment, such as an air conditioner or a microwave oven, one of the first things I check out is how long I can happily ignore cleaning it, replacing any of its parts, or anything else that might take up more than five seconds of my time.

Thankfully, there isn't much cleaning maintenance necessary with your Macintosh, aside from occasionally cleaning dust and dirt out of your mouse or floppy disk drive (as described in Fix-It #17). The rest is either common sense (don't spill coffee on your keyboard) or more for aesthetics than to prevent any real problem (such as wiping dust off the monitor screen).

There is, however, another form of maintenance—electronic maintenance. This is the focus of the remainder of this chapter. It can be just as tedious as any other kind of maintenance, but ignoring these procedures can seriously hamper the performance of your computer and (without wanting to sound too alarmist) possibly result in the irrecoverable loss of valuable data.

Have an Emergency Startup Disk Ready

If your one and only hard drive is your startup disk and it develops a serious problem, you will not be able to use it to start your Macintosh. Similarly, several troubleshooting utilities cannot make alterations or repairs to the current startup disk—which, of course, will be a problem if your current startup disk is the one that needs repairing. For these reasons, you need to have a special emergency startup floppy disk (or disks). Having one of these ready *before* trouble strikes is wise preventative maintenance.

In previous editions of this book, I went into considerable detail on how to set up startup floppy disks and maximize how much you can fit on them. This time around, I am skipping over most of this, as it is not really needed any more. Most people no longer need to depend on a floppy disk as a startup disk, because they can use a CD-ROM startup disk or a removable cartridge instead. Briefly, then, here is a summary of your options.

Apple's Disk Tools Startup Floppy Disk

With the possible exception of some Performas, every Macintosh is shipped with a Disk Tools disk, or at least a disk image of it (see: "Take Note: To Make an Exact Copy of an Entire Floppy Disk") on a CD-ROM disc. This disk can serve as a startup disk and already contains two of the most needed utilities: a formatting utility (such as Drive Setup) and Disk First Aid. Note: System 7.6 includes some changes in the Disk Tools disk, as described in Chapter 13.

TAKE NOTE ▶

TO MAKE AN EXACT COPY OF AN ENTIRE FLOPPY DISK

Most times, you copy a file by dragging the file's icon to the disk icon (or any folder window) of the destination disk. There is a special method, however, for copying an entire floppy disk from the Finder. Simply drag the icon of the disk you wish to copy to the icon of your desired destination disk. When the prompt asks you whether you want to replace the contents of the destination disk with that of the source disk, click OK.

In System 7, however, this procedure does not make an exact duplicate of the original disk. The name of the disk isn't replaced, the location of the files and folders on the new disk do not match those on the original disk, and any invisible files are not copied.

To truly make an exact duplicate copy of a floppy disk, you need to use a copy utility. Apple makes such a utility, called Disk Copy. Although it is free (and available from the usual sources, as described in the Appendix, "Stocking Your Troubleshooter's Toolkit"), it is not included with all versions of the Macintosh system software (it does come with the CD-ROM disc versions of System 7.5). Norton Utilities and MacTools include utilities with a similar ability, called Floppier and FastCopy, respectively.

Use these utilities whenever you want to make a copy of a disk and be certain that is an exact duplicate of your original disk.

Also note, if your Mac came with a CD-ROM disc, it typically has all of the system software floppy disks on it in what is called *disk image* format (Performas are an exception here). You can use these image files, in conjunction with Disk Copy, to create an exact duplicate of the Disk Tools disk.

SEE • Fix-It #5, "Take Note: "Why Can't I Open the System Software I Just Downloaded?," and Chapter 15 for more details on all of this

If you update to a newer version of the system software than the one that came with your Mac, it may come with updated versions of these basic utilities. If so, you can copy them to your existing Disk Tools disk. Otherwise, the software update may include a new Disk Tools disk (perhaps in a disk image format) that you can use instead.

SEE ALSO: • "Take Note: System 7.6: A Slightly Different Look," earlier in this chapter.

If you need a startup disk with additional utilities, simply make a copy of the Disk Tools disk, delete everything on it but the System Folder, and add what utilities you want. Of course, you won't have too much space to spare, so don't expect to add much.

Helpful hint: If you choose the Custom Install option with the Installer software that came with your Mac, you will likely find an option to install a "minimal" System Folder. This may or may not create a System Folder small enough to fit on a HD floppy disk. You are best off ignoring this option for creating a startup floppy disk.

Another helpful hint: Don't try to make a startup disk by dragging the System and Finder and Enabler files from your hard drive to a floppy disk. They won't fit. Similarly, don't ever drag the System Folder files from a startup floppy disk to use on a hard drive. The System Folder files on a floppy disk are usually special versions designed just to work on floppy disks, and they should not be used on a hard drive.

Yet another helpful hint: A Disk Tools disk that came with a different Macintosh model may not work with your Mac. There are several possible reasons for this. One is that your Mac needs a specific Enabler file (as described more in Fix-It #5), and the Disk Tools disk you are trying to use does not have it. Also, it is possible that the system software on the other disk is too old a version to be used on your (newer) Mac.

A Finder-Less Startup Floppy Disk

You can squeeze even more utilities onto a single startup floppy disk by getting rid of the Finder. This is how some commercial utilities make their startup emergency disks. While there are several ways to set up Finder-less startup disks, what follows here are two of the simplest and best. The idea in both cases is to "fool" the Macintosh into thinking that a substitute application is the Finder. Otherwise, the Mac will look for the real Finder at startup and, failing to find it, refuse to start.

Both methods assume you are starting with a floppy disk that has a System Folder on it already (created by using one of the methods described in the previous section).

Method #1: Renaming an Application as the Finder

This works well if you only need to run a single application from the startup disk.

1. Start with a copy of your Disk Tools disk. Move the System file from the System Folder to the root level of your floppy disk (that is, not in any folder). Also move any Enabler or Update file that you find. Discard the rest of the System Folder.
2. Copy any single application you want to your disk and rename it Finder. This file should also be at the root level of the disk.
3. Restart with the floppy disk inserted; it should directly launch the application you renamed as Finder. You won't be able to quit from it or go to other applications, and you will need to restart again when you are done. Otherwise, it should work fine.

System 7.5 Alert This method may not work with System 7.5. If it doesn't, you should still be able to accomplish this trick by also changing the type and creator codes of the application to match that of the Finder (I'll explain this more in Chapter 8, "By the Way: Other Types of Finder-Less Startup Disks").

Helpful Hint: Boot Blocks This technique may not work if you simply copy a System file to a floppy disk that was never used as a startup disk and therefore does not have the needed startup *boot blocks* on it (as explained more in Chapter 5 and in "Take Note: To Make an Exact Copy of an Entire Floppy Disk"). The simplest way to get a floppy disk to have the startup boot blocks is to make an *exact* copy of an existing startup floppy disk (such as a Disk Tools disk) by using a program such as Disk Copy (as I suggest in Step 1 above). You can then delete files from the copy as needed. There are also some freeware programs that write boot blocks, but most of them are quite old and may not work with current system software.

Method #2: Using ShortFinder

This method requires using a shareware utility called ShortFinder. The main advantage of ShortFinder is that it takes up hundreds of kilobytes less disk space than the real Finder.

1. Start with a copy of your Disk Tools disk. Move the System file from the System Folder to the root level of your floppy disk (that is, not in any folder). Also move any Enabler or Update file that you find. Discard the rest of the System Folder.
2. Copy ShortFinder to the floppy disk and rename it "Finder." Copy to the floppy disk any other applications you wish to use, until you run out of room. All files should be at the root level of the disk.
3. Restart with the floppy disk inserted. It should directly launch ShortFinder. From there, you should be able to launch other applications by selecting Launch Application from its File menu.

TECHNICALLY SPEAKING ▶

GETTING FANCY WITH SHORTFINDER

With ShortFinder, you can even set up a floppy disk so that you can leave the System and Enabler/Update files (and any other system software files you wish, such as extensions and control panels) in the System Folder, starting up almost as if you were using the real Finder. As with the Finder itself, you can access multiple applications with ShortFinder set up this way. To do this, however, you have to change ShortFinder's type and creator to match that of the real Finder. I describe exactly how to do this in Chapter 8.

Data Recovery Utility Startup Floppy Disks

Both Norton Utilities and MacTools Pro come with floppy disks that can be used as startup disks to run their software. These disks may not work on all Macs, especially models that were released after the software came out (primarily because they may be missing needed Enabler/Update files). For these cases, the programs come with special utilities—such as Norton Utilities' Startup Disk Builder—that can create a startup disk for you. MacTools even has a feature to automatically set up a RAM disk as a startup disk.

SEE:
- **Fix-It #5 for more on Enabler/Update files needed for specific Mac models**
- **Fix-It #13 for more on startup disks from data recovery utilities**

CD-ROM Startup Disc

If your Mac came with an internal CD-ROM drive, it also came with a CD-ROM disc that contains system software and other related files. In most cases, you can use this disc as a startup disk by holding down the "C" key at startup; the Mac will boot from the CD-ROM rather than the internal hard drive (see Chapter 5, "Understanding the Startup Sequence," for more details).

You can use this CD-ROM disc, instead of a floppy disk, as your emergency startup disk. It contains the same essential files (such as Disk First Aid) that are on the Disk Tools disk. As a bonus, if you need something that is not on the CD-ROM, you still have the floppy drive free to run the desired program from a floppy disk.

Secondary Hard Drives or Partitions as Startup Disks

If you have two hard drives, you can always set up System Folders on both of them (using the System Software Installer disks). You can then use one as an emergency startup disk when the other fails to work. Using a removable cartridge (such as with a Zip or Jaz drive) as an emergency startup disk is especially popular these days. With this method, you don't have to worry about how to squeeze everything you need onto one disk.

If you have only one hard drive, you can do almost as well by dividing your drive into two partitions and setting up a System Folder on each. This won't help you if your drive fails altogether, but if you just need to run from a different startup volume (such as to do repairs with Disk First Aid), this will work fine.

See: • **Chapter 5, "Understanding the Startup Sequence," for more details on starting up with alternate hard drives and partitions**
• **Fix-It #5 for more on installing system software**

Universal Startup Disks

Finally, if you work with more than one model of Macintosh, you may wish to have one emergency startup disk (perhaps on a Zip or Jaz drive cartridge) that can work with all Mac models (that is, one that includes all model-specific Enablers, Updates, and related software, as explained more in Fix-It #5). At least, you may want one that can work with all models that were out at the time that your latest version of the System Software was released. You *can* do this; it's called creating a Universal System Folder. To do this from a System 7.5 or later CD, for example, select Custom Install and then select the "System for Any Macintosh" option.

BY THE WAY ▶

IF THE INSTALLER WILL NOT LAUNCH SUCCESSFULLY

If the Installer will not open because it says that your Macintosh model does not support that version of the system software, just hold down the Option key while launching the Installer. You will now get the Custom Install window and should be able to select the Any Macintosh option. Such a solution is needed, for example, when trying to run the System 7.5.0 Installer on a PCI-based Mac. In this case, the resulting "universal" System Folder would still not work on a PCI-based Mac, although it would work on all Macs that can run System 7.5.0. To get it to run on a PCI-based Mac, additionally use the "universal" Custom Install option of the System 7.5 Update 2.0 Installer to update to System 7.5.3.

Save and Back Up Your Work

Saving your work simply means using the Save command to save a file to disk. Backing up your work means making a copy of the file to a separate disk location.

Regularly saving and backing up your work is Preventative Maintenance Rule #1. It supersedes every other rule by a wide margin. It cannot be emphasized enough. It is critically important. Save often. Back up *everything* regularly. Am I making myself clear? The dire consequences of almost every type of disaster that could possibly befall you can be avoided if you frequently save your files while you work and back everything up when you are through.

Almost everyone has a horror story about how their only copy of an important document, representing weeks of work, was lost or destroyed just before it needed to be printed out. Don't add your name to that roster. Save the document, and back it up. It *can* happen to you.

I wouldn't have to emphasize this advice so vigorously if it weren't ignored so routinely—even by people who should know better. Why is this? The usual culprits are time and money. People complain that it takes too much time to back everything up, or that it costs too much money to buy the equipment needed to do it at a reasonable speed.

But ask anyone who has ever lost any critical files (maybe it's happened to you already) about the time and/or money it cost to replace those files. Then reconsider your attitude.

Save Your Work … Often

The simplest of all methods of preventing disaster is to make generous use of the Save command (found in the File menu of almost all applications). Remember that because unsaved information exists only in RAM (that is, electronic memory), it disappears into hyperspace if there is a sudden system crash or power failure. Yes, hours of unsaved work could vanish in an instant—unless you have already saved it.

When you are working on a file, save it frequently—at least every ten minutes. Alternatively, if your program has an *autosave* feature, you can use it. An autosave function saves documents, without any prompting or input from the user, at any specified interval. Some people like this idea. Personally, I prefer to do my saving the old-fashioned way. If I'm experimenting with some strange formatting, I don't want it to be saved automatically before I can decide whether to keep it or revert to the previous format. Still, for some people, autosaving could be just the ticket.

If your program does not include an autosave function, some utilities (such as NowSave from Now Utilities) allow you to include this function in virtually any program.

SEE: • **Chapter 6 for more on the use of the Save and Save As commands**
• **"Protect Against Loss of Data Due to System Crashes," later in this chapter**

Make Regular Backups

Don't Depend on Just the Finder and Floppy Disks Copying files from one disk to another (such as from your hard disk to a floppy disk) via the Finder is a quick and easy backup method. However, it is not an effective way to back up an entire hard disk (what is called a *global* backup). There are several reasons for this:

- At least some files on your hard disk are too large to fit on a single floppy disk. The Finder cannot split a file across more than one disk.
- The Finder is not an efficient mechanism to locate a single file (if that's all you want) that may be stored on any one of several dozen backup floppy disks.
- Your disk probably contains important invisible files that the Finder does not copy.

Use Special Backup Software and Hardware Software utilities specifically designed for backing up your files can overcome the limitations of the Finder. They make global backups relatively easy, keeping track of what goes where so that you don't have to. They can split large files across disks and can quickly identify what disk contains a particular file you are seeking.

The utility workhorses mentioned earlier, MacTools and Norton Utilities, both contain decent backup utilities. Other popular alternatives include Retrospect, Redux, and DiskFit. For global backups, using one of these utilities should be considered essential.

Backing up to floppy disks is far less manageable (not to mention more time-consuming) than using a special backup device. These devices include an additional fixed hard drive, a removable cartridge drive, or a tape drive.

Devise a Good Backup Strategy

How, how thoroughly, and how often should you back up your files? Everyone has their own recommendation for the best way to accomplish the most with the least amount of hassle. Here are the two most important things to do.

Back Up All Personal Document Files Your personal files, such as manuscripts and illustrations, are your unique creations and thus are irreplaceable. Back them up frequently (that is, every time you modify them) and maintain multiple backups if feasible. This *can* be done by just using the Finder and floppy disks, if the files are not too large or numerous. You should be doing this in addition to any global backups.

Maintain a Global Backup of Your Hard Drive(s) Ideally, you want to use special backup software that can create a *mirror image* global backup. This can be used to re-create your entire hard drive, down to every customized preference file and every invisible file, with all files and folders in their original hierarchical location. This will be a tremendous time-saver if you ever have to reformat your hard drive. If you work on your computer almost every day, update this backup at least once a week—more often if you make frequent major changes to the contents of the drive.

After doing an initial global backup, your backup software/hardware may provide the option to do either an incremental or archival backup on subsequent updates. An *incremental* backup backs up only newly added and modified files (deleting the old version of any modified files). *Archival* backups work similarly except that they never delete anything, not even files that have been modified or deleted since the last backup. This allows you to revert to versions prior to the most recent version, if desired.

Helpful hint: Try a restore *before* you have a problem. Try restoring some files to your hard disk using your specialized backup software. If you can, get a spare hard disk or cartridge and try a global restore. Doing so may reveal that the restore fails because of procedural problems that you can now easily address and fix. If you wait until the crisis occurs, however, it may be too late.

Prune Your Hard Drive

Delete Unneeded Data and Application Files

As you back up your hard drive, you won't want to keep useless and outdated files. That's why you should periodically go through your hard drive and remove these unneeded files.

If you never delete anything, you probably still have that 1988 letter to your Aunt Millie sitting in some folder somewhere. Get rid of it. In fact, throw out any applications and documents that you rarely use, or haven't used at all for the last six months or more. Maintain a copy of them on floppy disks, if you want, but get them off of your hard drive.

Why bother with all this cleaning? First, it will be easier to locate files you want, since you won't have to wade through old "garbage." Second, depending on your work habits, you'll also free up a surprising amount of space. If your disk is nearly full, the extra space can allow you to add more important files, as well as to avoid all sorts of minor problems. For example, certain activities (such as printing) may create temporary files in order to work and there needs to be enough free disk space to hold these files. I'm getting ahead of myself a bit here, but too little empty disk space hastens fragmentation of the files on your disk, which can slow down your Mac. Conversely, discarding unneeded files prior to rebuilding your desktop leads to a more compact Desktop file, which will speed things up.

SEE: • **"Give Your Macintosh a Tune-Up," later in this chapter, for more on fragmented files and rebuilding the desktop**

Overall, for hard drives of 100MB or less, at least 5 percent—and preferably 10 percent—of your hard drive should remain unused. For larger-capacity hard drives, try to keep at least 5MB to 10MB of unused space at all times. Need to know how much free space you have left? Remember, the current amount is usually visible in the upper right corner of any open Finder window on your disk.

Delete Items from the System Folder

Extraneous files in the System Folder can be a huge waste of space. Here's what to look for in cleaning out the folder.

Application-Related Files For example, suppose you decide to discard a word processor you have been using in favor of another one. You may forget that your old word processor included a special dictionary file (for use with its built-in spelling checker) that is still buried somewhere in your System Folder. After a while, you can build up quite a collection of these unneeded files. Because you probably also have preferences files for deleted applications, the Preferences Folder is often a rich source of files that can be deleted. Two utilities, Clean Sweep and Prefs Cleaner, can assist in this effort.

If the initial placement of an application on your disk required an Installer utility, your System Folder may have many application-related files that you did not even know existed. Once the application is deleted, these can all be removed as well.

Some application installers may have a Custom Remove option that will assist in making sure that most associated software gets deleted when you remove the application. Otherwise, there are several utilities that can help out here (such as Yank).

SEE ALSO: • **"Take Note: Cleaning Up Unneeded Preferences Files (and More)," in Fix-It #2**

System Software Files Similarly, when your system software was installed on your hard drive, it probably installed many files that you never use. For example, if you find a printer driver (such as StyleWriter or ImageWriter) for a printer that you do not have or use, delete it. If you are not on a network with other users and don't intend to use file sharing, you can delete any control panels or extensions that deal with file sharing (such as Network, Network Extension, File Sharing Extension, File Sharing Monitor, or Sharing Setup). If you are on a LocalTalk network and don't use Ethernet, you can get rid of any Ethernet-related software. If you don't load non-Macintosh CD-ROMs, you can delete all of the CD files that end in the word "Access," and so on.

The same thing is true for any extensions, control panels, fonts, and Apple menu items that you no longer use: *get rid of them.* This often has the side benefit of reducing the amount of memory occupied by the system software, freeing up more RAM for other uses.

Delete Mystery Files

What if you don't even know what a particular file is? How do you know if it is safe to delete it? For applications and documents, this problem is usually easy to solve—just open them and see what they are. If a data document cannot be opened, it probably belongs to an application that is no longer on your drive.

Many System Folder files, though, cannot be opened from the Finder under any circumstances. You may have trouble identifying the purpose of these files.

In these cases, select Get Info for the mysterious file. The information there might give you a hint about the source and purpose of the file, which may be enough for you to make a decision about deleting it. If Get Info at least identifies the origin of the file, you can presumably go to the relevant documentation for more help.

Also try turning on Balloon Help and placing the cursor over the mystery item. This is particularly useful for System extensions. If you are unlucky, you will get the generic message that simply says the file in question is an extension. If you are lucky, you may learn exactly what the extension does.

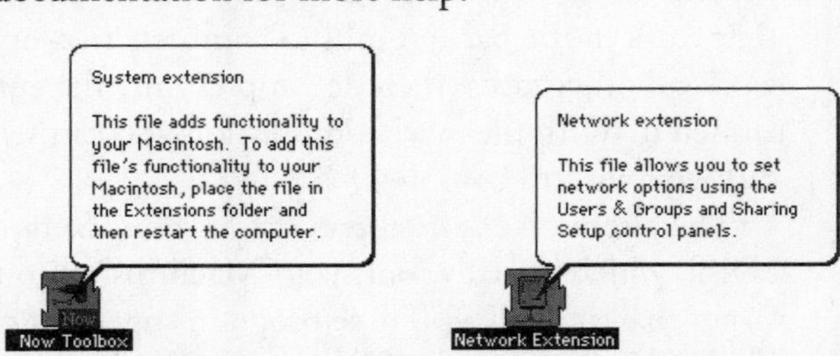

Figure 2-11 *Balloon help messages may not (left) or may (right) help you identify a mystery file.*

BY THE WAY ▶

WHAT'S WITH FOLDERS WITH NAMES LIKE DUPLICATE ITEMS AND DEINSTALLED?

Occasionally, in your System Folder, you may find folders with names like Duplicate Items or Deinstalled 4/10/97. These folders were created at the time you ran an Installer utility of some sort (for example, when you upgraded your system software). In many cases, Installers replace existing older versions of software with the newer versions. Sometimes, though (as a protection to you in case you still want to preserve the older version), it will move the older version to a new folder it names Duplicate Items or something similar. In general, you can probably delete this folder, because you already have other versions of its contents somewhere else (such as in the Control Panels folder). This is another way to free up some disk space.

Similarly, if you find a file called Installer Cleanup, you can delete it. It is a temporary file that should have been deleted automatically when you quit the Installer and restarted.

SEE: • Chapter 6 for more on opening and identifying files

Other Ways to Save or Get More Space

If you discard all unneeded files and there is still not enough free space on your hard drive, you have two alternatives:

- Replace your hard drive with a larger one (or just add another one)
- Use an automatic compression utility

The rationale behind increasing your hard drive space is obvious—and with drive prices falling faster than a two-ton rock in water, it is definitely something to consider if you have an older low-capacity drive. Compression utilities may require a bit more explanation.

Compression utilities reduce the size of files stored on your disk by eliminating "redundancy" in the file's data. When you really need to use the file, the compression utility uncompresses it to its normal state, without any data loss. There are currently two main types of compression utilities. One is *file-level compression,* exemplified by programs like AutoDoubler or StuffIt SpaceSaver. These utilities are system extensions that work in the background to compress files on your disk automatically, while you work on other tasks, then decompress any file automatically when you attempt to launch it. With file-level compression you can select which files and/or folders on your disk you wish to compress.

The alternative is *disk-level compression,* exemplified by programs such as Stacker or eDisk, which actually fools your Macintosh into thinking that your disk drive is much larger than it really is. These programs operate at the disk driver level (described more in Fix-It #12) to compress files even before they are written to the disk, decompressing them when you use them. It. You have no option to select which files to compress; the utility always compresses everything. Many users claim disk-level compression is more subject to compatibility problems than file-level compression, but other users find them reliable. (Personally, I would not trust disk-level compression and never use it. Among other things, it can become a problem if and when you have to upgrade your disk driver.

Actually, with the prices of large capacity hard disks being as low as they are, I suspect that these utilities will vanish from the market altogether.)

With either method, the utility's operation is quite transparent—that is, it happens without your issuing any commands or even being directly aware that it is taking place. Because these compressed files can take up as little as 50 percent of their original size, these utilities can free up a lot of space on the disk.

Still, automatic compression is not for everyone. The compression and decompression procedures, although fast, do take up extra time. In particular, disk-level compressors always compress a file as soon as you close it, a habit that can introduce a substantial time lag. In contrast, file-level compressors usually wait to compress a closed file until the Macintosh is idle, making the wait less noticeable. Finally, should you lose access to the decompressing program for any reason, the compressed files may be rendered useless.

BY THE WAY ▶

ARCHIVAL COMPRESSION UTILITIES

For occasional compression of a few infrequently used files, for archival storage of files, or for transmitting files across networks and modems (where reduced size means less transmission time), consider manual archival compression utilities such as DiskDoubler Pro, StuffIt Deluxe, or Compact Pro. These are really a variation on file-level compression, but they compress files only when you launch the application and specifically issue a command from within the utility itself. In some cases, you can also make self-extracting compressed files that can be decompressed even without the utility. Archival compression and decompression times are typically much slower than with the automatic utilities, which is one reason why you wouldn't want them for files you use regularly. On the plus side, they manage to compress files down to a smaller size than the automatic utilities.

By the way, StuffIt includes a neat feature, called DropStuff and Expander, that allows you to automatically compress or decompress a file simply by dragging the file's icon over the relevant StuffIt icon. These programs are also available as freeware/shareware.

Install Protection Utilities

Most protection utilities are control panels and system extensions that can do their intended job only if they are installed on your startup disk before a problem occurs. Thus, getting them installed is part of preventative maintenance. None of these utilities is essential, but all are worth considering, depending on your work situation.

Protect Against Virus Infections

To protect yourself against computer viruses, you need to use an anti-virus utility. The most popular ones are Symantec Anti-Virus for Macintosh (SAM) and Virex. They are all good.

Of course, these utilities can be used at any time to check for and eradicate an existing virus infection. When properly set up, however, they can also monitor your disk and block a virus infection before it occurs. That's why I mention it here as part of preventative maintenance.

SEE: • **Fix-It #7 for more details on checking for viruses**

Protect Against Accidentally Deleted Files

Have you ever unintentionally deleted a file or deliberately deleted a file that you subsequently wished you had back? Sure you have. Luckily, utility packages such as the Norton Utilities and MacTools provide a means of recovering files that have been deleted via the Finder's Empty Trash command.

These utilities can recover deleted files because when you empty the Trash, you do not really immediately remove the file from the disk. Only its name is removed from a special area of the disk (where the computer looks to find out what is on your drive). The file data remain on the disk, intact, until it is overwritten by a new file. Undelete utilities can find these deleted files, even though the Finder cannot, and restore them to their undeleted condition.

Eventually, of course, you will write new information over that area of the hard drive, and then the file will be unrecoverable. Thus, these utilities work best if you use them as soon as possible after deleting the file. You should not depend on this method as a guaranteed method of recovering deleted files!

While these utility packages have some ability to recover deleted files even if you don't install their special protection features first, they work best with these features installed. So do it.

Norton Utilities Norton Utilities uses a control panel called FileSaver. It operates according to the following steps:

1. To set FileSaver in motion, place it in the Control Panels folder.
2. Open the control panel and click the On button (if it isn't already on).
3. Select Fewer Choices (if it is not already selected). Advanced users may want the greater customization control possible with the More Choices option; if so, check out the Norton Utilities manual for details.
4. Click the check box next to the name of each mounted volume that you wish to protect.
5. Close the control panel and restart.
6. When you need to undelete files, launch Open UnErase from the Finder (or select UnErase either from the Norton Utilities main menu window or from the Utilities menu). Details on using UnErase are given in Chapter 6.

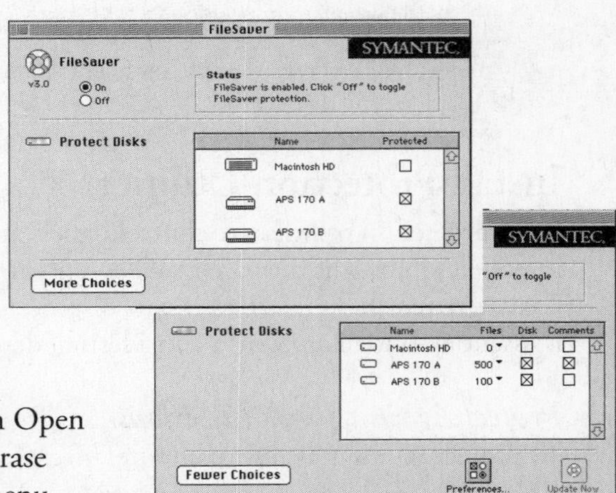

Figure 2-12 *Norton Utilities' FileSaver control panel. Left: the Fewer Choices display. Right: the More Choices display.*

MacTools Pro MacTools Pro uses an extension called MacTools TrashBack. Here's how it works:

1. To set TrashBack in motion, place the extension in the Extensions folder and restart the Macintosh. This was most likely done automatically when you first installed MacTools Pro; if not, the extension may be in a folder called "Move these to System Folder" located in your MacTools Pro folder. In the latter case, move the extension to the System Folder, as the folder's name suggests. Otherwise, you will need to return to the MacTools Pro Installer to install TrashBack.
2. Launch MacTools Pro's Clinic application. From the top row of buttons in the Clinic window, click the Undelete button. From the dialog box that appears next, click the TrashBack button. This finally results in the opening of the TrashBack window.

   Alternatively, assuming the TrashBack extension is installed and active, a TrashBack item is added to the bottom of the Finder's Special menu. If you select it, you are taken directly to the TrashBack window. Actually, selecting this command takes you to a separate TrashBack application (called MacTools TrashBack App) stored in a folder called Support Files, which is located in the MacTools Pro folder. If you delete this application, the Special menu's TrashBack command will not work. When the application is present, though, you can also choose to directly launch TrashBack from the App, rather than from the Finder menu command.

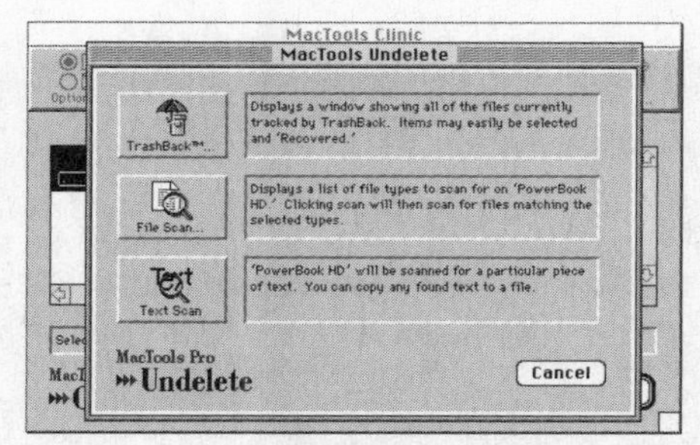

Figure 2-13 *Left: the dialog box that appears after selecting Undelete from MacTools Clinic. Right: MacTools Pro's TrashBack command in the Finder's Special menu.*

3. Click the Options button from the row of buttons along the top of the TrashBack window. From the list of TrashBack options, make sure you have selected "Enable TrashBack protection." If you want TrashBack to protect removable hard drive cartridges, uncheck the item that says "Don't protect files on removable drive." TrashBack will now automatically enable protection for all hard disks, even ones that get mounted at some later time (but not floppy or RAM disks).

   If you click the Recover Options button next, you will be presented with choices as to where you want recovered items to be placed. In particular, you can choose between having all items stored in a folder called Recovered Items or having all items returned to their original location.

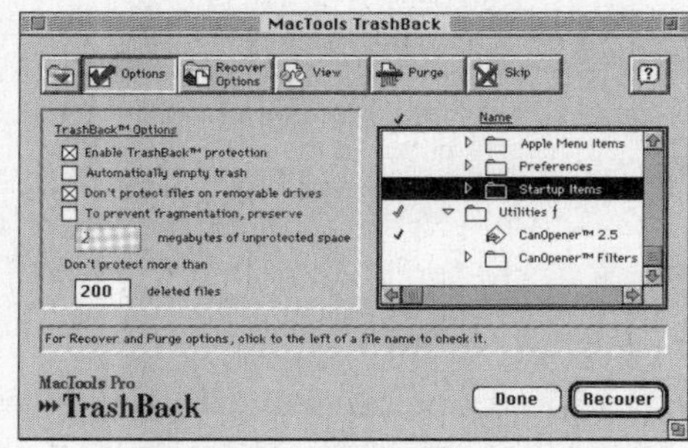

Figure 2-14 *The TrashBack window as seen with the Options button selected.*

4. To undelete files, locate the items you want to undelete in the directory listing of the TrashBack window. Click to the left of each item's name to place a check mark in front of it; checking a folder automatically checks all items contained in the folder. Finally, click the Recover button at the bottom of the window.

   If you did not have TrashBack turned on when you deleted a file you now want to recover, you still have a chance to undelete it. In this case, you must use MacTools Pro Clinic and, after clicking the Undelete button (as described in Step 2), select one of the other two options (File Scan or Text Scan) listed in the dialog box that next appears, rather than the TrashBack option.

   All of this is described more in Chapter 6, as part of a general discussion of how to undelete files. Otherwise, check the MacTools Pro manual for explanations of the remaining buttons and options.

TAKE NOTE ▶

TRASHBACK'S INVISIBLE FOLDER

TrashBack stores deleted files in a special invisible folder. Normally you have no access to this folder, but it becomes visible if you start up with the TrashBack extension off. If you have done this, look for a folder called CPS TrashBack (or some similar name), at the root level of each protected disk (inside the folder will be other folders, with names such as TrashBack Temporary Items and Deleted Files). This is where "deleted" files are stored.

Files deleted while the TrashBack extension is off are not placed in the CPS TrashBack folder. Also, when TrashBack is off, all files in the CPS TrashBack folder contribute to your occupied disk space, just as if the files were not deleted (which, in fact, is technically true). The result is that you will probably have significantly fewer megabytes listed as available on your disk when TrashBack is off. Don't worry; if necessary, you can go to the TrashBack folder and directly delete files by moving them to the Trash (this is functionally similar to using TrashBack's Purge option). While this will eliminate TrashBack's ability to recover these files later, it will make your available disk space listing more accurate. Otherwise, you will have to wait until you restart with TrashBack on once again.

Occasionally, I have found that deleting files this way is needed for problem files that TrashBack refused to remove when I clicked its "Remove" button.

Some applications may list the invisible TrashBack folder (and its deleted files) in their Open dialog box, just as if the files had not been deleted. This can happen even when TrashBack is on, though it seems to be less likely with the current version of the utility; you may even be able to open such "deleted" files. If you think you may be viewing the TrashBack folder, just click the Desktop button in the Open dialog box to take you out of there. Some Find utilities (including the Finder's Find command) may also list these invisible folders/files, though surprisingly most do not.

By the way, this invisible folder is a bit unusual in that most utilities that list invisible files (such as DiskTop or Norton Utilities or MacTools Pro or even ResEdit) do not list this folder. The only program I found that works is the DiskEdit program that was included in older versions of MacTools.

Oddly, System 7.5's Find File function will list the Deleted Files subfolder, which is inside the CPS TrashBack folder, but it will not list the CPS TrashBack folder name itself.

TrashBack can retrieve undeleted files even after a disk has been optimized (a process described in Fix-It #8), and it does so more reliably than Norton Utilities. This is because TrashBack works by maintaining an invisible folder that essentially contains all of the supposedly undeleted files (see "Take Note: TrashBack's Invisible Folder").

They are only really deleted when there is no other free space available for whatever other activity you are trying to do; undeleted files in the TrashBack folder are not overwritten when a disk is optimized. In contrast, FileSaver from Norton Utilities creates a special invisible file that essentially keeps a record of the location of files that have been deleted but does not protect them from being overwritten during a disk optimization.

Two final important points to remember: First, if you wait until you need to recover a file before you install FileSaver or TrashBack, it will be too late. The critical point here is prevention. The undelete features of Norton Utilities and MacTools work best if their associated control panel or extension is installed *before* you need to use it! While you still may be able to recover files even without this prior installation, you are severely hurting your chances. Second, only files that have been saved can be undeleted. These utilities are not useful for recovering work that was lost because of a system crash that occurred before you saved the file.

SEE: • **"Protect Against Loss of Data Due to System Crashes," later in this chapter**
• **Chapter 6 for more on undeleting files**

Protect Against Crashed or Accidentally Erased Hard Disks

Disk Crash A disk crash is when you have lost all access to your disk and its contents. Usually, the disk does not even appear on the desktop. If the disk is your startup disk, you may even be temporarily unable to start up your Macintosh.

Accidentally Erased Hard Disk An event almost as traumatic as a crashed disk would be to erase your hard drive accidentally. It's hard for me to imagine how this could occur by accident. You would first have to select Erase Disk inadvertently from the Finder's Special menu, then click OK to the prompt asking if you really want to do this. Not only that, the Macintosh prohibits you from erasing the current startup disk (which is often your one and only hard drive). Still, I suppose it may happen to some poor soul somewhere.

Installing FileSaver or TrashBack (as described in the previous section) prior to the crash or accidental disk erasure will facilitate any recovery.

FileSaver, however, includes a special recovery feature that is not available with MacTools: Norton Utilities can quickly restore an entire disk in one step, rather than via a file-by-file selection. This feature is similar to restoring a disk from a global backup, except it's much faster and you don't need the separately stored backup files. The effectiveness of this recovery feature depends on having the relevant invisible files (maintained by FileSaver) periodically updated—the more recently they have been updated, the better the recovery. This updating is done automatically at certain predetermined times. To modify the default update options (such as "At Restart/Shut Down"), select More Choices, then click the Preferences button and select "Protection Preferences" from the pop-up menu. You can also update the files at any time by clicking the "Update Now" button (or select "Update FileSaver Files" from the Options menu of the Norton Utilities main menu window).

Older versions of MacTools included a similarly functioning utility called Mirror, but it was dropped from version 3.0 and hasn't resurfaced. This was done because Central Point contended that this type of recovery was only a rarely needed option, likely to cause more problems than it could solve (for reasons explained more in Fix-It #13, "Take Note: Use Backups Instead of Restore or Recover"). So if you insist on having this type of volume recovery protection, you will have to go with Norton Utilities.

SEE:
- **Chapter 5 for more on disk crashes**
- **Fix-It #13 for more on repairing and restoring disks**
- **Fix-It #14 for more on file recovery**
- **Fix-It #15 for details on formatting disks**

Protect Against Disk Damage

The most critical use of MacTools and Norton Utilities is to repair a damaged disk. In some cases, damage to a disk at first causes few, if any, symptoms. Eventually symptoms worsen, though, and a disk crash may ultimately occur. To prevent the more serious symptoms from developing, both of these packages have options to scan disks periodically for potential problems automatically and in the background. If a problem is spotted, an alert message appears on the screen informing you of the problem and typically suggesting a course of action (such as "There is a problem on the disk. … Run Norton Disk Doctor"). These background scans only scan during idle activity, so as not to slow down your other work.

These automatic scans are far from essential as a preventative measure; personally, I don't use them anymore. Others have found them useful, however. I'll explain how to set them up.

Norton Utilities Simply install FileSaver (as explained in Steps 1 through 5 of "Protect Against Accidentally Deleted Files"). That's all you really need to do. With the More Choices option selected, however, you can modify when a scan is initiated and exactly what it scans for.

MacTools Pro To accomplish a similar sort of protection with MacTools, you need to place its AutoCheck application in the Startup Items folder. You then select the timing of the automatic background scans by setting AutoCheck options (accessed by clicking the Options button from MacTools Pro's Clinic window and then clicking the AutoCheck button). AutoCheck checks for most but not all of what DiskFix checks, so it is not a total substitute for DiskFix. New to MacTools Pro, AutoCheck can now "auto-repair" problems that it detects, eliminating the need to access DiskFix separately.

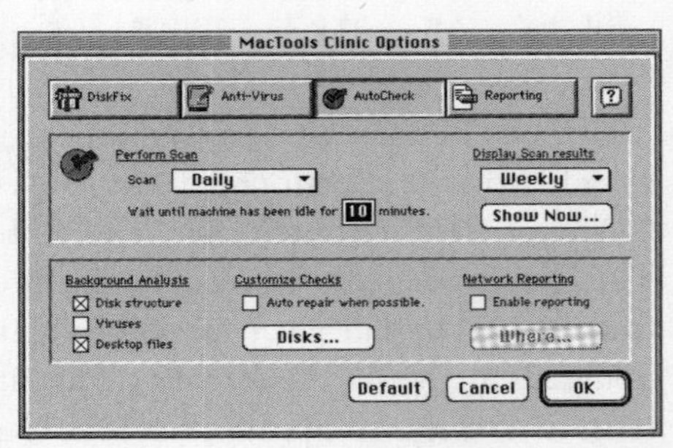

Figure 2-15 *MacTools Pro's AutoCheck settings.*

Protect Against Loss of Data Due to System Crashes

Following some sadistic logic, a system crash or bomb seems to occur most often when you are in the middle of some important task.

Even if you take all the previous precautions, the day will probably come when you have been working for an hour or so on some important document, so engrossed in what you were doing that you forgot to save your work. Suddenly, you remember and reach for your mouse to select Save, when wham!—the infamous system bomb appears. Or maybe there is just a brief power failure. Whatever the case, all your work is lost.

Recovering from a system crash is usually as simple as restarting your computer. This gets you up and running again, but it does not resurrect any data that were unsaved at the time of the crash. The probability of recovering this unsaved work is almost zero, unless you have previously installed certain protection utilities (and even then, the probabilities may not be all that good!).

Saving Text Data After a System Crash NowSave is a control panel included as part of Now Utilities. With version 4.0 or a later version of Now Utilities, you can set NowSave so that it saves all text input to a special continually updated file, no matter what application you are using to type the text. If a system crash or power failure occurs, this file has a copy of all of your work up to (or almost up to) the point of the interruption.

This feature has its limits: for example, text is saved in the order you typed it, which may not be the order it appears in the document. In times of crisis, however, whatever is saved may be worthwhile.

Other similar alternatives include Last Resort and the GhostWriter option of SpellCatcher, a spelling checker.

Recovering from a Crash Without Loss of Data Two freeware utilities, Bomb Shelter and System Error Patch, are startup extensions that supposedly increase your chances of recovering from a system crash. If they succeed, they ideally return you to where you were just prior to the crash, and you then have a chance to save your data before proceeding further. Crash Barrier, a commercial product along these lines with much-enhanced features, appears to be no longer on the market.

How often do these utilities really allow you to recover from a crash and save your unsaved data? Some say only very rarely, but others claim to find them helpful. Personally, I don't use any of these utilities. Even if they work only once or twice a year, though, they may be worth getting. Don't expect miracles, and you won't be disappointed.

Another possibility here is to install Apple's MacsBug debugger (available from Apple's public online software libraries). While this is really designed for programmers trying to debug their work, it may allow you to recover from a system crash without having to restart.

SEE: • **"By The Way: Recover From a System Crash Without Restarting (Maybe): Resume, Continue, MacsBug, and More," in Chapter 4, for more details**

Using an Autosave Function An autosave function, which is another feature of NowSave, can be viewed as a means of protecting you against loss of data after a system crash. This view assumes that the feature automatically saves your data just prior to a crash and that you ordinarily would not have manually saved the data at that point.

SEE: • Chapter 4 for more details on system errors, including more on all of these utilities

Give Your Macintosh a Tune-Up

The following quintet of procedures should be done on a regular basis, even if your machine seems to be running smoothly:

- Defragment your disk
- Rebuild your desktop
- Run Disk First Aid
- Check and/or Replace the System file
- Stay up-to-date

Think of these as the equivalent of giving your car a tune-up. I do these operations at least three or four times a year, more often if it seems warranted. While I am sure many people have merrily gone along without ever having done any of these things, I don't recommend doing so. As the saying goes, better safe than sorry.

These procedures are more than preventative measures; you can also use them to solve problems after they happen. For this reason, I discuss these procedures again, from a more detailed problem-solving perspective, in Part III, especially Fix-Its #1, #5, #8, #9, and #10. For now, I simply present an overview.

Defragment Your Disk

It may surprise you to learn that when you save a file to your hard drive, the file may be split in several sections, scattered across your drive. This situation typically occurs when there is not enough disk space in a single unused chunk to hold the entire file. While fragmentation is not a problem by itself, if too much exists you may see a slowdown in performance or an inability to open a file. At the very least, less file fragmentation tends to improve chances of recovering files after a disk crash.

You usually defragment a disk by using a special disk-optimizing utility. In Norton Utilities and MacTools, the optimizing utilities are called Speed Disk and Optimizer, respectively. Another such utility is called Disk Express. The advantage of Disk Express is that it can be set to defragment your disk automatically in the background by bits and pieces, whenever your computer is idle, rather than waiting for you to do it manually all at once.

By the way, whenever you reformat your hard drive and restore files from your backup copies, you have also defragmented the files on your disk.

SEE: • Fix-It #8 for details on how to defragment a disk

Rebuild Your Desktop File

Rebuild your desktop. Rebuild your desktop. This is almost a mantra of Macintosh problem solving. It is usually one of the first things recommended, no matter what your problem is, with the general attitude of, "Well, even if it doesn't do anything, it can't hurt to try."

So what does it really mean to rebuild your desktop? The Desktop files are invisible files that the Finder uses to keep track of information required to create the Finder's desktop display. Basically, rebuilding your desktop means to update or replace your existing Desktop files. This can correct problems due to an improperly updated or corrupted Desktop file.

Rebuilding the desktop is a useful tool for solving a variety of problems, especially those related to the functioning of the Finder (such as an inability to launch files). It is also useful as a maintenance measure, however, even if you don't suspect anything is wrong at the moment.

The basic way to rebuild the desktop is to hold down the Command and Option keys just prior to the mounting of a disk (hold them down at startup for the startup disk) until an alert box appears asking if you want to rebuild the desktop. Click OK.

SEE • **Fix-It #9 for more on how to rebuild the desktop**
• **Chapter 8 for more on invisible files, including the Desktop files**

Run Disk First Aid

Disk First Aid is included with all versions of the system software and with every Macintosh that is sold (it's on your Disk Tools disk). It's a repair utility designed primarily to detect and fix problems caused by corruption of the Directory files, special invisible files that keep track of the overall organization of your hard drive.

Though there are competing utilities that detect and fix more problems, Disk First Aid has the distinct advantage of being free. Also, since it comes from Apple and is frequently upgraded, it sometimes gets the scoop on fixing a newly discovered problem. Thus it is a good place to start, even if it does not turn out to be your last stop.

Although Disk First Aid is most often used after a problem has been discovered, I also recommend using it periodically even if nothing appears to be wrong. When I run Disk First Aid for a maintenance check, I have been surprised by how often it reports that a repair is needed—even though I did not suspect a problem existed.

SEE • **Fix-It #10 for how to use Disk First Aid**
• **Fix-It #13 for more on using other utilities to check and repair disks**
• **Chapter 8 for more on invisible files, including the Directory files**

Check and/or Replace the System File

The System file is the most essential and probably the most complicated file on your disk. Unfortunately, it is also one of the most frequently modified. The Macintosh alters the System file quite often as part of its normal operation; since you get no special notification that this has happened, you may not even be aware of it. With every modification, though, there is a chance that an error will occur and that the System file will be corrupted. This can lead to a variety of problems whose cause may not be easily diagnosed as a corrupted System file. Sometimes, in fact, these problems may not even appear until weeks after the damage first occurred.

Thus it is usually a good idea to replace the System file every three or four months, even if you are not yet experiencing any symptoms. The easiest way to do this is if you keep a special backup copy of your System file (one that you are confident is not damaged) maintained for just this purpose. Otherwise, you will have to reinstall the System file from your system software disks, using the Installer utility—a less than ideal solution if you have customized the System file from its original state.

If you are reluctant to replace a System file as a preventative measure, especially since the file may be perfectly fine, at least check it out. The freeware program TechTool can check the integrity of the System file, although you should make sure your version of TechTool is newer than the version of the system software you are using. Otherwise, the utility may be unable to check the System file.

SEE: • **Fix-It #5 for how to reinstall system software and more about checking for damaged system software**

Stay Up-to-Date

Periodically check sources such as those described in Fix-It #18 to find out if Apple has recently released any new or upgraded system software files that you should install. If so, install them. These upgrades can solve problems whose cause you couldn't figure out, or help you to avoid other problems before they ever show up on your machine.

In particular, Apple periodically releases software, typically called System Updates, that fix bugs known to exist in its system software. Read Me files that come with these utilities describe precisely what problems are fixed; if you have any of the symptoms described, be certain to install the update. Most updates incorporate all the enhancements of their predecessors, (exceptions will be noted in the documentation that comes with the Update).

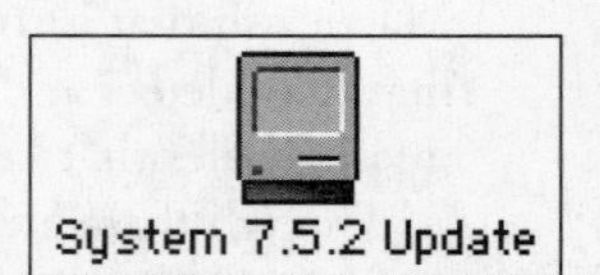

Figure 2-16 *The System 7.5 Update file; it took earlier versions of System 7.5 (System 7.5.2 in this case) to System 7.5.3.*

A major component of these updates is often an Update file that gets installed in the root level of your System Folder. The Update package will also likely install other software and make numerous changes to other system software files, however, including the System and Finder. Sometimes, when a new *reference release* (a full set of system software, as opposed to just an update) comes out, the need for the Update file is eliminated. So don't count on seeing one in your System Folder, even if you have the latest possible software.

As a rule, also stay current with your non-Apple software, especially by checking for maintenance releases that fix bugs uncovered in previous versions.

SEE: • **Chapter 13 for more on the latest system software**
• **Fix-It #5 for more details on installing System Updates and Enablers**
• **Fix-It #18 for more on how to keep up to date with the latest software**

BY THE WAY ▶

WHAT EXACTLY GETS UPDATED BY A SYSTEM UPDATE?

There are four updates to System 7.5: System 7.5 Update 1.0 (released in March 1995, upgrading users to System 7.5.1), System 7.5 Update 2.0 (released in March 1996, upgrading to System 7.5.3), System 7.5.3 Revision 2 (released in June 1996 to fix some lingering problems from the previous update) and System 7.5.5 (released in the fall of 1996 with several additional bug fixes and enhancements, primarily improving the performance of virtual memory). Ending this 7.5 Update cycle, System 7.6 was released in early 1997.

These updates often add new features and interface changes. For example, System 7.5 Update 1.0 replaced the "Welcome to Macintosh" startup screen with the "Mac OS" screen. System 7.5 Update 2.0 added translucent icons (which appear when you drag an icon in the Finder, at least on Power Macs).

Beyond that, most of the changes in the Updates are bug fixes. Some may fix things that you probably knew needed fixing, but others may correct problems you haven't confronted yet, or errors that you may not have thought were caused by system software bugs. So even if you don't think you have any problems that an Update will fix, it's a good idea to install it anyway. System 7.5 Update 2.0, fixed so many things that it took three separate Read Me files to list them all! To give you some feel for what you might expect an update to correct, here is the much smaller list of fixes handled by System 7.5.3 Revision 2:

1. **Type 8 errors on PowerBooks:** Fixes problem that caused Type 8 errors only on PowerBooks, especially if RAM Doubler was also installed.
2. **Floppy driver problem**: If a PC floppy is inserted into a Macintosh prior to ever being inserted in a PC, the floppy becomes unreadable on PCs, though it is still readable on all Macintoshes. The revision fixes this.
3. **Drive spin up problem**: When a Power Macintosh is powered on, it may not boot from the hard drive selected in the Startup Disk control panel. This problem only occurs with Virtual Memory turned off. If this problem occurs, it will happen on every boot thereafter, even if Virtual Memory is turned back on. A new Startup Tuner extension is included to fix this problem.
4. **SCSI problem:** Eliminates a possible cause of data loss and corruption on 7200, 7500, 8500, and 9500 systems with 1GB IBM drives.
5. **Cache Flush problem**: A performance patch is included that affects all PowerPC PowerBooks.
6. **Emulator problem**: Fixes a variety of problems with the 680X0 emulator that affected all 7200, 7500, 8500, and 9500 systems.

Chapter 3

Problem Solving: General Strategies

Uh-Oh 68

Five Steps to Solving Macintosh Problems 68

1. Read Alert Box Messages 68
2. Check If the Problem Repeats 69
3. Isolate the Cause 70
    - Look for Recent Changes or Unusual Circumstances 70
    - Assess the Specificity of the Problem 71
4. Go for Help 71
    - Check an Application's Built-In Help 71
    - Check the Manual! 72
    - Get Outside Help 72
    - Consult This Book 72
5. Fix the Problem 73
    - The Troubleshooter's Cure-Alls 73

Avoiding Problems 74

Get to Know Shortcuts 74

Go Exploring 74
- Work Only with Duplicates 75
- Use Undo 75
- Use Cancel 75

Uh-Oh…

Something has gone wrong with your Macintosh. You are sitting and staring at your screen, trying to figure out what has happened and, more important, what you can do to fix it. That's exactly what you are about to find out.

Five Steps to Solving Macintosh Problems

1. Read Alert Box Messages

After something unexpected has occurred with your Macintosh, an alert box error message often appears. These messages frequently contain valuable information.

The alert box may inform you of an action you need to take ("Please select Page Setup before printing your document"). It may also inform you why you cannot perform a command you requested ("The disk cannot be erased because the disk is locked"), or it may tell you what has just gone wrong ("The application unexpectedly quit"). In any case, it can also provide advice on how to carry out the command successfully or fix the problem.

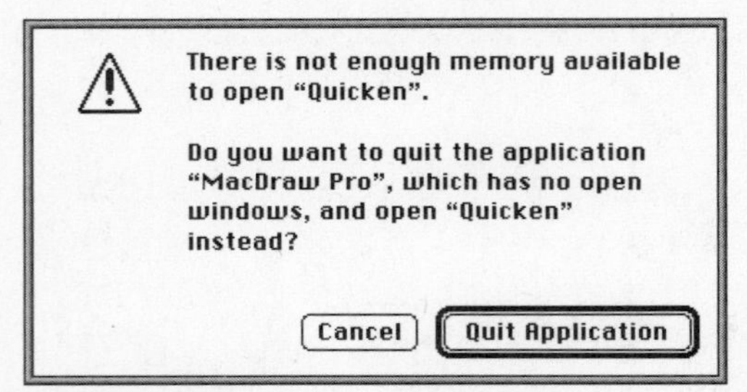

Figure 3-1 *An alert box indicating that there is insufficient memory available to open Quicken. It offers a work-around solution.*

For example, let's suppose you have an application that does not open when you try to launch it, and you get an alert box message that says there is "Not enough memory available." The alert box may offer a suggested solution to the problem and even provide a button for enacting that solution ("Quit Application").

For another example, consider a message that tells you that the Trash cannot be emptied. It may not only tell you why you could not empty the Trash but give you a *keyboard shortcut* needed to solve the problem quickly. This keyboard shortcut works faster than having to go to the Get Info window of each locked file and unlock it.

The Trash cannot be emptied, because all of the items in it (other than folders) are locked. To delete locked items, hold down the Option key while you choose Empty Trash.

OK

Figure 3-2 *An alert box that may appear when you try to empty the Trash. It not only tells you the problem but provides a solution.*

What if you don't understand the meaning of the alert box message or if it doesn't offer any useful advice? This is where the rest of this book can help. I'll describe dozens of alert box messages and how to deal with them; you can look up any particular error message in the Symptom Index at the back of this book. I will not list every possible alert message you might get, because no single book could do that. But I will describe and explain the most important and most common alert messages you are likely to encounter.

TECHNICALLY SPEAKING

WHAT'S AN ALERT BOX?

An *alert box* pops up on your screen to warn you or inform you about the consequences of what you have just done ("Your file has been successfully transferred") or what you are about to do ("Erasing the disk will permanently erase all data on it. Do you still want to erase it?"). It is usually accompanied by either an exclamation-mark icon (which means "Caution") or the hand-in-a-stop-sign icon (which is more serious and means "Stop and read this before proceeding").

Usually, you cannot do much in response to an alert box message other than click an OK or Cancel button.

Alert boxes are a normal and expected part of the Macintosh's operation. Their appearance doesn't necessarily mean that you have any problem; however, when you do have a problem, they are particularly likely to appear. In such cases, they are often referred to as error messages.

A terminology note: A cousin to the alert box is the *dialog box*. A dialog box usually appears after you've selected a command from a menu. For example, the box that appears after you select Print from the File menu is a dialog box. Dialog boxes are distinguished from alert boxes both by the different functions and by the fact that dialog boxes usually have many more options than the one or two choices typical of an alert box.

One final note: Alert boxes that accompany serious problems such as a system crash or an unexpected quit often include esoteric information about the cause of the problem (such as "An error of Type 11 occurred"). While I generally recommend ignoring this information, as it is rarely helpful for most users, I do describe its meaning in some detail in Chapter 4.

2. Check If the Problem Repeats

Clearly, not all problems can be solved by reading error messages (especially if your problem did not result in an error message!). Still, the solution may be close at hand, often just a few mouse clicks away.

First off, many Macintosh problems are unique occurrences. They happen for reasons that may never again be exactly duplicated and that no one will ever fully understand. So, before you run off and spend hours trying to solve a problem, see if you can get it to recur.

If the problem involves an application, quit and relaunch it. If the problem involves a floppy disk, eject and then reinsert it, and so on.

If your problem is a system crash or other equally debilitating event, you will have to restart the Macintosh before you can check if the problem recurs. Even for less serious errors, it is usually good advice to restart before checking for a recurrence; a restart solves a surprising array of problems all by itself. Beware, though, since sometimes a restart may only appear to solve a problem. The symptoms may return again the next day or the next week.

If the problem does not recur, be happy! You probably had one of those once-in-a-lifetime unknown glitches. Chalk it up as one of life's cosmic mysteries. If it does recur, you have more work to do.

3. Isolate the Cause

From a general perspective, there are relatively few types of Macintosh problems. System crashes and system freezes alone probably account for more than half of what people complain about. The problem is that figuring out the exact cause of a particular crash is not always easy, since there are many causes that can produce the same symptom.

On the other hand, I continue to be surprised by how often a seemingly inexplicable problem turns out to have a common, simple-to-fix cause. For example, you may get a symptom that is so rare that no one has ever heard of it happening before. Yet the cause could be something quite basic, perhaps even a lack of proper termination on your SCSI chain (as described in Fix-It #16). No one knows all of the many symptoms that this SCSI cause could produce.

To take another example, someone may ask me for advice on why they have suddenly started to get a system freeze when selecting Print from their favorite word processor. After checking my "database" of troubleshooting notes and failing to find any mention of this specific problem, I am unsure what to suggest. But a little basic experimenting soon uncovers the cause: a previously unknown (at least to me) conflict with an extension that the user had recently added to their System Folder. It had nothing to do with the printer, the printer driver, the application in use, damaged software, or any other cause that I might have thought to be more likely. So before searching for odd explanations for odd symptoms, make sure you have covered the basics.

In any case, your job is to progressively narrow the range of possible causes of your problem until you succeed in isolating the right one. While the general problem-solving strategies described here are useful to apply no matter what the specific nature of your problem, they are most critical for those times when you are trying to diagnose and solve problems on your own, on those occasions when seeking help did not provide the answer.

SEE: • **Chapter 4, "Solve It! Recurring System Errors," for more detailed strategies on diagnosing recurring system errors**

Look for Recent Changes or Unusual Circumstances

Suppose that while you are trying to save a BusyWorks word processing document, a system crash occurs. You have saved many documents with BusyWorks before and have never had a system crash. What's going on? Usually, some recent change to your software or hardware is precipitating the crash. The culprit may be a newly added system extension or a recently connected hardware peripheral. The problem may even be due to a change you recently made in existing software, such as changing an application's default preference setting or turning on a new option in a control panel. So, if you are aware of any recent changes to your computer system, focus your search on them.

If you don't know of any such changes, consider whether any unusual circumstances could have caused the problem. For example, perhaps you were trying to save a particularly long BusyWorks document when the crash occurred—a document longer than any you'd tried to save before. If so, the size of the document might be the problem.

Assess the Specificity of the Problem

Suppose you cannot open a particular document file currently stored on a floppy disk. What's the cause? The problem could be with the particular file, the application you used to open the file, some related file stored in the System Folder, the floppy disk, or even the disk drive hardware.

Often, the exact symptom or error message (if one appears) helps you choose among these possibilities. Otherwise, you need to isolate the source of the problem. To see if the problem is specific to that file, try opening another file. To see if it is specific to that application, try opening files in other applications. To see if it is specific to that disk, try using other disks. I think you get the point by now; there are no exact rules here. In the end, determining the precise cause of a problem is often more of an art than a science.

TAKE NOTE ▶

RISK MANAGEMENT

Whenever you try to fix a problem, there is at least a small risk that what you do will somehow succeed only in making matters worse. Always look for ways to minimize this risk. For example, as stressed in Chapter 2, always back up your files *before* you attempt to fix a problem.

In general, try the simplest, easiest, and most-likely-to-work techniques first, then proceed gradually to those that are more powerful, difficult to use, or time-consuming and/or have a lower probability of success, if necessary. This not only saves you time and hassle, it is also generally safer. The more powerful techniques tend to be the riskier ones.

4. Go for Help

Don't think you have to exhaust all possible attempts to isolate the cause before skipping to this step. Similarly, you don't always need to go for help before you can go on to the next step and solve the problem. These last two steps can be thought of as more parallel than sequential; move from one to the other in whatever order gets you to the fastest solution.

Check an Application's Built-In Help

If the problem is specific to a particular application, and the application has built-in help, check it out. The location of the help file will vary from application to application. Sometimes it is a separate program; sometimes it is accessed from within the application, under the Apple menu; and other times it may be found in the Balloon Help menu. Check if there is a special Apple Guide document for the application.

Also be sure to check both your hard drive and the application's original disks for any Read Me files. These often contain important late-breaking troubleshooting information.

Check the Manual!

I know, I know. Many Macintosh users are proud of how much they can accomplish without *ever* looking at the manual. At best, people use the manual for a while when they first start using a new program and then they never glance at it again. Whole sections of the book remain untouched by human hands.

And I know that most manuals are not fun to read. They are reference books, after all, not science fiction adventures.

Despite all of this, I am telling you to read the manual—whatever manuals, for hardware or software, seem potentially relevant to your problem. No, you don't have to read the whole thing cover to cover; just check for the part relevant to the problem you are having. Check the opening pages of the manual, the ones that discuss how to install the program. Vital details about where files should be located and possible incompatibilities are found here. Check the troubleshooting section, if there is one. Use the index, if necessary. You will be amazed how many problems you can solve this way. Sometimes you will even discover helpful tips that make it easier to use the program, regardless of any problems you may be experiencing.

If some feature doesn't work the first time you try it, don't immediately assume there is a problem with the application. Often the problem is that you did not correctly understand how to use the program. Reading the manual will almost invariably solve this type of problem.

Get Outside Help

Almost all software and hardware companies maintain a phone number to help answer your technical questions. The number should have been included somewhere in the documentation that came with the program or equipment.

These days, if you have Internet access, checking on a vendor's web site is probably the best place to start. Commercial online services (such as America Online) also offer a wealth of help available via bulletin boards and/or update libraries.

Technical support should not be used as a substitute for reading manuals or generally developing your own problem-solving skills. It can be helpful, however, in providing information about undocumented features or recently discovered bugs in software—information not readily available anywhere else. The company may even be able to supply an updated version of the software that fixes the bug.

SEE: • **Fix-It #18 for more on technical support and seeking outside help**

Consult This Book

This is an obvious bit of advice. After all, solving problems is the purpose of this book.

5. Fix the Problem

Oftentimes, the most difficult and time-consuming step in this whole procedure is identifying the cause of a recurring problem. It obviously, however, is not the last step: you next need to fix the problem so that it no longer recurs.

Problems unique to a particular application are usually solved by replacing or upgrading the application and/or its preferences file(s). Otherwise, they are probably due to a conflict with an extension or some aspect of the system software. Symptoms that span across most applications are usually caused by system software, especially if the problem involves activities (such as printing) that depend heavily on system software files. Solutions to these problems often involve replacing or upgrading the system software files; conflicts with extensions and control panels are also common causes.

Problems that affect the entire disk or affect basic system operations (such as an inability to empty the Trash) are usually due to damage to special invisible files on the disk. You should try to repair this damage, if possible, using special repair utilities. If they can't be repaired, you will probably have to reformat the entire disk.

The Troubleshooter's Cure-Alls

As an alternative to searching for the precise cause of and solution to a given problem, many experts suggest working your way through a familiar list of cures likely to fix almost any problem you might encounter: rebuild the desktop, do a clean reinstall of your system software, turn off all your extensions, run Disk First Aid, and so on. It can't hurt to try at least some of these procedures. Indeed, I've already advised you (in Step 3) not to ignore these "basics," even for apparently rare problems.

Still, following these procedures blindly will often result in your wasting time trying things that have little or no hope of helping you. Instead, this book helps you to figure out when certain "cures" might or might not be useful. This book also presents a series of specific diagnoses and treatments for a broad range of Macintosh problems. Finally, it shows how to understand what went wrong, so that you can solve future problems on your own more intelligently.

BY THE WAY ▶

IF YOU CAN'T FIX IT, MAYBE YOU CAN WORK AROUND IT

If the exact circumstances that must be repeated to get the problem to recur are sufficiently unusual, you may be able to live without ever repeating those circumstances. For example, maybe the problem occurs only when you have Word, Excel, and Canvas all open at the same time and you try to open an Excel document immediately after trying to print a Word document.

If necessary, you can probably avoid this problem without having to find the cause; just don't duplicate those events in the future. This type of solution is often called a *work-around* because you have worked around the problem rather than actually fixing it.

Avoiding Problems

Get to Know Shortcuts

Almost anything you can do with the Macintosh can be done in more than one way. For example, do you want to close a window on the desktop? Simply select the Close command from the Finder's File menu, or click the close box in the upper left corner of the window, or use the Command-W keyboard shortcut (listed in the File menu next to the word Close; other shortcuts are more obscure and can be found only by consulting an application's manual). The Command (⌘), Option, Control, Shift, and Escape keys, in combination with other keys, often produce a variety of strange and wonderful results and shortcuts, depending on which application you are using.

Familiarity with these shortcuts—or at least the more common of them—is invaluable in negotiating many problem-solving tasks, not to mention making your daily work with the Macintosh considerably more pleasant. For starters, go to the Apple Guide menu when you are in the Finder and select the Shortcuts item. Beyond this, check the manuals of your applications for details, or simply explore on your own and see what happens.

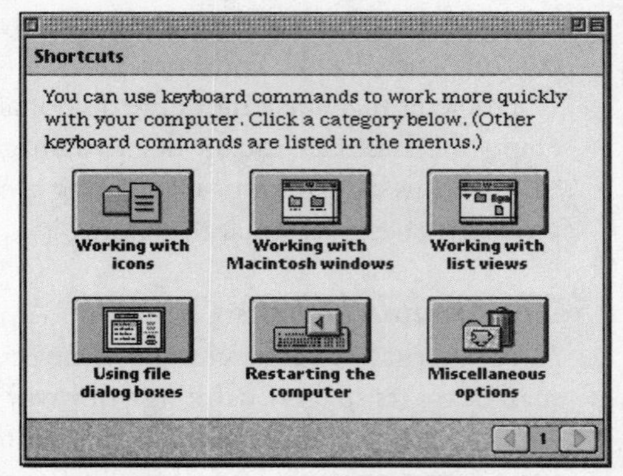

Figure 3-3 *Did you forget the key combination to zap your PRAM? Don't despair. The Macintosh's Shortcuts Apple Guide file gives you the low-down on all of the "secret" key combinations built-in to the Mac system.*

Go Exploring

The design of the Macintosh, with its pull-down menus and point-and-click approach, encourages exploring—in part because it minimizes the need to memorize anything or type in long and obscure commands. Take advantage of this. Even if you never look at an application's manual, spend some time exploring its menus and dialog boxes. Try out potential shortcut commands.

You may feel like you do not have the time to spend on this sort of frivolity. Time spent exploring, however, can be an investment repaid several times over in avoiding future frustrations. Often the biggest benefit of exploring is the pleasant surprise of discovering that there is a way—often an easy way—to do something that you thought was impossible. This "I didn't know you could do that" reaction in itself can be considered a form of problem solving.

Still, if you are a relatively inexperienced user, this may sound like dangerous advice—like advising a novice tightrope walker to practice without a net. With a little common sense, however, the risks are minimal. Here's some practical advice to use while exploring.

Work Only with Duplicates

Work only with a duplicate copy of any important document, or use a document that you don't mind losing. That way, even if the document gets deleted or corrupted in some way, it does not matter. Even if your entire machine crashes and you have to start all over again, no harm is done.

Use Undo

Remember that most actions can be reversed by the Undo command and that (usually!) no changes are saved until you select Save from the File menu. When in doubt, undo.

Use Cancel

Almost all potentially "dangerous" operations on the Macintosh, such as erasing a disk, are preceded by a warning and an opportunity to cancel. If you get too anxious about what you might be about to do, just select Cancel.

PART II:

SYMPTOMS, CAUSES, AND CURES

This section of the book is the one to turn to when preventative measures are not enough and a problem occurs anyway. Here you will find a listing of symptoms that cover a broad range of both the most common and the most serious problems you are likely to confront, together with step-by-step instructions for what to do to solve them. Again, the solutions require only a few simple software tools and no particular expertise on your part.

Chapters 4 and 5 cover those problems that are the most disruptive to your use of the Macintosh.

Chapter 4 covers system errors (also called system crashes), typified by the infamous bomb alert box. Chapter 4 walks you through exactly what to do after specific system errors. It may surprise you to learn that you can often do more than simply give up and restart your Macintosh.

Chapter 5 covers what is probably the most anxiety-provoking problem to confront any computer user: a total inability to start up the machine, where the power is turned on but the startup sequence never begins or never reaches a successful conclusion. Chapter 5 also describes what to do for any crashed disk, whether it is a startup disk or not. The chapter concludes with a look at a few other general disk-related problems, such as problems with ejecting floppy disks or shutting down the Macintosh.

From launching applications to printing documents, Chapters 6 through 8 explain what can go wrong and how you can make it right again.

Chapter 6 covers the most common and yet most frustrating file-related problems: Are you having trouble locating a particular file? Or if you do locate it, do you find that it refuses to open? Maybe there is insufficient memory to use the Clipboard. Perhaps you want to copy or delete a file, but the Macintosh refuses to let you do it. If you are having any of these problems, Chapter 6 guides you to a solution.

Even after you have successfully completed and saved your masterpiece, your problems may not be over: you probably want to print out your work. This introduces a new host of potential problems. **Chapter 7** is devoted to what to do when you cannot get a document to print.

Chapter 8 is a more technical look at some of the Macintosh's more esoteric, yet still comprehensible and certainly useful topics: file types, creators, and attributes. As always, the focus remains on how you can apply this knowledge to solve problems.

Chapters 9 and 10 are devoted to problems specific to the two most common categories of document files: text and graphics. Whether it's dashing off a memo or writing a novel, creating a chart in a spreadsheet, or creating a full-page ad for a magazine, virtually every Macintosh user spends most of his or her time with these two prime functions.

Chapter 9 covers text problems. Although they are most likely to crop up when using a word processor, text problems can appear when you are using any application that contains text, including spreadsheets and databases. The chapter begins with an overview of the different categories of fonts and how they determine the appearance of your text. It concludes with a description of common text-related problems and their solutions.

Chapter 10 deals with graphic-related problems that can confront even the most nongraphic of Macintosh users. It begins with an explanation of the different types of graphics files and the basics of how your computer displays grayscale and color documents. The chapter concludes with a collection of common graphics-related problems and how to solve them. New material in this edition includes coverage of video- and movie-related problems.

Chapters 11 through 13 cover problems that are specific to PowerBooks, Power Macintoshes, and the latest versions of the system software.

Chapter 11 deals with issues that are unique to PowerBooks or have a special relevance to them (such as RAM disks and the Control Strip). Finally, it covers problems related to transferring files from one Mac to another, with a focus on file sharing between a PowerBook and a desktop Macintosh.

Chapter 12 describes the problems unique to Power Macintoshes, including the special problems of PCI-based Macintoshes. Problems unique to Performas and to Macintosh clones are briefly addressed. It concludes with a section on AppleVision monitors.

Chapter 13 covers problems specific to the latest versions of System 7.5, including System 7.5.3, 7.5.4, and beyond. It also features troubleshooting coverage of OpenDoc and QuickDraw GX, then concludes with a look at the future of the Mac world.

Chapter 14 is a unit unto itself, dealing with online and networking problems (beyond the file-sharing issues covered in Chapter 11).

Chapter 14 covers problems with setting up and using Open Transport and PPP software. It offers troubleshooting advice on successfully connecting online via a modem, and it explores a variety of Internet-related issues, such as problems in downloading files and troubleshooting your Web browser. More general LocalTalk and Ethernet networking issues are also briefly covered.

As you go through these chapters, you will find frequent references to other parts of the book, particularly the Fix-Its from Part III. Part II emphasizes the diagnosis of a problem and, in general, how to go about solving it. The Fix-Its more specifically describe the tools used to solve these problems. If this were a book on home repairs, Part II might tell you that the squeak in your flooring is caused by a loose floorboard and that you have to hammer in some nails to fix it. Part III, in contrast, would explain what hammers are and the general techniques for using them. So, if any explanations in these chapters seem less than complete, check out the Fix-Its for the rest of the story.

Chapter 4

System Errors: Living with the Bomb

The Mac's Worst-Kept Secret . . . 81

Solve It! A Catalog of System Errors . . . 82

System Crashes . . . 81

- The Bomb Alert Box Appears . . . 82
- Breakup of Screen Display . . . 83
- Understanding System Error Alert Box Messages (Or, What the Heck Is a "Bad F Line Instruction" Anyway?) . . . 84
- Positive versus Negative Error Codes . . . 85
- Special Case: Type 11 and "No FPU Installed" errors . . . 85
- Restart the Macintosh . . . 90
- Recover Unsaved Data After a Restart . . . 96
- What If the System Error Keeps Recurring? . . . 99

System Freezes . . . 99

- Try to Save Your Work (Press Command-S) . . . 100
- Try a Force Quit (Press Command-Option-Escape) . . . 100
- If the Force Quit Succeeds 101
- If the Force Quit Fails to Work ... Restart . . . 102
- If the Freeze Recurs . . . 102

Endless Loops . . . 105

- Break Out of the Loop with Command-Period . . . 105
- Retry the Procedure . . . 106
- Otherwise 106

Unexpected Quits . . . 106

- Interpreting System Error Codes ... Again . . . 107
- Save Data in Open Applications . . . 107
- Restart the Macintosh . . . 107
- Increase Preferred Size of Memory Requirements . . . 107
- If the Unexpected Quit Occurs During Launch . . . 108
- Otherwise 108

Solve It! A Catalog of System Errors (continued)

The Finder Disappears 108

Wait a Minute 108

Try a Force Quit (Press Command-Option-Escape) and Restart 108

Replace the Finder and Its Preferences File 109

Otherwise 109

Solve It! Recurring System Errors 109

Seek the Cause of a Recurring System Error 109

What Circumstances, If Any, Reliably Cause the System Error? 109

What Variations in Circumstances, If Any, Will Eliminate the System Error? 110

What If the System Error Recurs at Unpredictable Intervals and Situations? 110

Fix It So That the System Error Does Not Recur 111

Check for Hardware and/or System Software That Is Incompatible with the Application in Use 111

Install the Latest System Update (Fixes System Software Bugs) 112

Check for Software Bugs in the Application 112

Turn Off Selected Options from Memory and Turn Off Sharing Setup Control Panels 113

Check for Startup Extension Conflicts 113

Check for Memory Allocation Problems 113

Zap the PRAM 113

Check for Damaged Document Files 114

Check for Other Damage 114

Check for More Than One System Folder on the Startup Disk 115

Check for Multiple Copies of Applications and Related Files 116

Check for Viruses 116

Check for Problems with the Hard Disk's Device Driver 116

Check for Hardware Problems: Cable Connections, Peripheral Devices, SIMMs, and Logic Board 116

Seek Outside Help 117

The Mac's Worst-Kept Secret

If you are new to the world of computers, you may think that a *system crash* is the sound your computer makes after you have thrown it to the floor in frustration. That's not exactly right—though a series of system crashes can certainly get you thinking about sending your Macintosh into free fall. Actually, a system crash refers to any time your computer's processing gets so messed up that it simply stops and no longer responds to further user input.

What to do when you have this type of system crash, or any other of several related *system errors,* is the subject of this chapter. System errors are the Macintosh's worst-kept secret. Many software manuals barely mention the possibility that system errors can occur. Yet they do occur, all too frequently.

If—or, more realistically, *when*—you get any sort of system error, it is the equivalent of seeing a "Road Closed" sign at the end of a long stretch of highway. There's no going forward, and you will have to spend some time heading back before you can make progress again.

I am not going to delve much into what causes these system errors; my goal is simply to explain how to rid yourself of them. Still, it may make you feel better to know that system crashes are not the result of some mistake on your part. It is either the result of faulty hardware or (much more likely) damaged or imperfectly designed software. Your freedom from guilt, though, is small consolation when a system error does occur. This knowledge doesn't save any of your data or eliminate any of the frustration.

Helpful hint: No software is perfectly designed. Therefore all software is potentially a source of a system error. Trust no one. But wait! Don't get overly alarmed by this warning. Programming for the Macintosh is not the easiest thing in the world to do, and it is almost impossible to anticipate every potential circumstance that might lead to a system crash—especially when the programmer has to contend with the ever-growing number of Macintosh models, a dizzying assortment of potential peripherals, and a seemingly endless variety of software, all of which may be combined in a nearly infinite number of permutations. The real surprise is that, most of the time, things work just as expected.

Your immediate concerns are probably the following:

- What permanent damage has been done to the machine, if any?
- What data have I lost, if any?
- How do I get the Macintosh working again?
- How do I prevent the system error from occurring again?

The answer to the first question is good news: system errors never cause any permanent damage to your hardware. A system crash can result from damaged hardware but it will never cause it. And while a system crash may damage your software (particularly anything you were using at the time of the crash), it is much more likely that everything on your disks is still okay. In general, you should be able to get your Macintosh up and running again in a matter of minutes.

The answer to the second question is potentially bad news. Barring a few exceptions to be discussed shortly, everything you were working on at the time of the crash that had not been previously saved to a disk is lost in space, never to be seen again. If you spent the last hour writing the opening chapter of your next novel and never saved it, it is probably gone forever. Actually, any file open at the time of the crash—saved or unsaved—is at some risk of damage.

Helpful hint: Save frequently. Saving is your greatest protection against the worst-case scenarios of a system crash. If you are planning to spend the day working on your Great American Novel, don't forget to use the Save command every few minutes.

The answers to the remaining two questions depend on the cause of the system error. The main thing you will do after most system crashes is to restart the Macintosh. Happily, in many cases the system error does *not* recur, because the specific combination of events that led to the system error are not repeated. Even if you think you are doing exactly what you did prior to the system error, the Macintosh may see it differently. Sometimes, however, a system error occurs repeatedly. In these cases, you must track down the cause of the error, so you can find a way to prevent its recurrence.

Solve It! A Catalog of System Errors

System Crashes

Symptoms:

The Bomb Alert Box Appears

The bomb alert box is the best-known of all system errors. The alert box includes an icon of a bomb, as well as a text message apologizing for what has just occurred ("Sorry, a system error has occurred."). Users typically refer to this unhappy event by saying, "My computer crashed" or "My Mac just bombed."

Sometimes, a bomb alert box may appear with no text at all in it. It's still a crash.

This alert is not a warning that your computer may explode. But it does mean that your Mac's activity has come to a grinding halt.

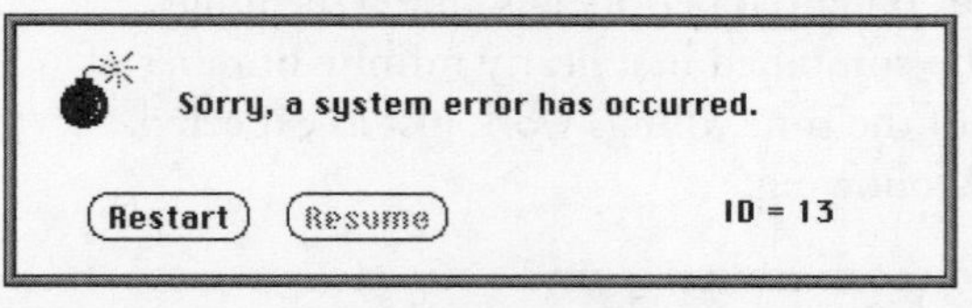

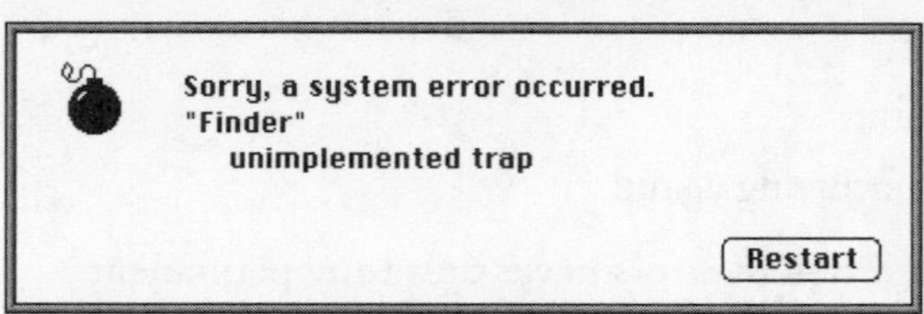

Figure 4-1 *Two examples of system bomb alert boxes.*

TAKE NOTE ▶

SOLVING SYSTEM ERRORS IN A HURRY

This chapter provides extensive details about what to do in the event of a system error—more details than you are likely to find in any other single source. Still, if you have a system error right now and want quick advice on what to do, you don't have to wade through this whole chapter to find it. So here's a quick summary of what to do:

1. If you get any system error dialog box, jot down any error code that appears in it, just in case it proves to be useful later on.
2. Regain control of your machine. Try a Force Quit (press Command-Option-Escape). If this does not work, restart your Macintosh either by clicking the Restart button in the system error dialog box, pressing the Reset button (or using an equivalent keyboard command, usually Command-Control-Power, if your model supports this feature), or by simply turning the Macintosh off and then back on again.
3. If the Mac restarts successfully, check the Trash for recovered files that may contain unsaved data.
4. Return to what you were doing prior to the error. If the error does not recur, forget about it for now; it may not happen again. Resume your work.
5. If the error does recur, and it is limited to the use of a specific application or document, the software may be damaged. Replace the software from your backups. In replacing a program, you may also want to delete any preferences files related to that program, as reinstalling does not typically create a new preferences file.
6. If the error still recurs, you probably have a software bug in the application or a conflict between the application and a system extension, control panel, system software, or hardware. Contact the manufacturer of the application for advice. Otherwise, try to resolve the conflict yourself. For example, check for startup extension conflicts by restarting with extensions disabled (hold down the Shift key during startup); disk damage by using Disk First Aid; and system software problems by reinstalling the system software.
7. If none of this helps, or you are uncertain about how to do any of the previous steps, then you need to wade through the rest of this chapter. Even if the preceding advice did help, browse through this chapter at some later point. What you learn will better prepare you for your next system error.

Breakup of Screen Display

The other type of system crash is so severe that the Macintosh cannot even muster the strength to put up the bomb alert message. Instead, the screen display may break up into an unintelligible mess, complete with flashes of light and crackling noises. (This is less common on the newer Macintosh models.) Despite the pyrotechnics, it is still a system crash, and no permanent harm has been done to your machine.

Causes:

Most crashes are due to a software bug or conflict between two active programs. Bad memory management is the likely immediate culprit in most of these cases.

System crashes can also have some hardware-related causes. These include defective memory chips, defective power supply, and SCSI device problems.

What to do:

Understanding System Error Alert Box Messages (Or, What the Heck Is a "Bad F Line Instruction" Anyway?)

Besides offering its apologies, the bomb-box error message typically provides a description of the cause of your crash. You are not likely to be impressed with these descriptions, which define the problem either by name (such as "bad F line instruction" or "unimplemented trap") or by number (such as "ID = 02" or "an error of Type 1"). Not very informative, is it? On a scale of understandability, it ranks slightly lower than the instructions for how to calculate depreciation on your tax return.

The truth is, this information was not meant to be easily understood by the masses. It was meant to help programmers figure out why their programs are crashing. Most of the time, the numbers simply mean that there is a bug in the program that needs to be fixed (for example, this is what typically causes a "bad F-line instruction" or "unimplemented trap" message). Since correcting a program's instruction code is not something you can do yourself, the ID information is almost always of little value to you.

If you are still curious about what the error code numbers mean, though, there are several places that list their translation. Unfortunately, the translation usually is not much more illuminating than the error code itself. For example, you will learn that an error of ID 1 is a "bus error" and an error of ID 2 is an "address error." Coming to the rescue here, Table 4-1 lists several common error codes, together with a more non-jargonese explanation of what they mean and what you might do about them. Otherwise, check out any one of several shareware utilities, such as MacErrors, for a more complete listing.

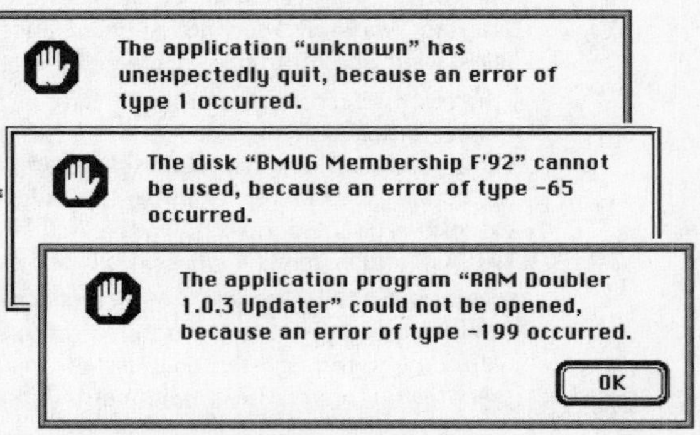

Figure 4-2 *System error ID numbers as they appear in a variety of different types of alert messages. In case you are curious, Type 1 means a "bus error," –65 means "read/write requested for an offline drive," and –199 means "map inconsistent with operation." Aren't you glad you asked?*

Theoretically, understanding these error codes might sometimes help you track down the cause of a repeating system error. But even this assumes that you can trust the error code to be accurate. Unfortunately, a system crash can so mess things up that the Macintosh may put up a code that doesn't really describe the true cause of the problem—in which case the information is once again useless.

Helpful hint: Don't waste much time trying to interpret the error message. Understanding these messages *never* helps in the immediate crisis of recovering from the crash, and it only rarely helps in diagnosing the ultimate cause of the crash. At most, jot down the number for later reference.

Positive versus Negative Error Codes

Actually, error codes come in two basic varieties: positive and negative. Positive error codes most often accompany system crashes or unexpected quits.

Negative error codes occur after a variety of less disruptive problems, such as a failure to copy or delete a file. These codes, ironically, are more likely to point you in a useful direction for solving the problem than a positive error code. In the most benign cases, the message may inform you why you can't do what you are trying to do (such as copy a file or open an application) but will otherwise let you proceed with using your Mac. Table 4-1 gives a few examples of common negative error codes; file system errors (–33 to –61) are probably the most common category. Upcoming sections of this chapter (as well as other chapters, especially Chapters 5 and 6) include more examples of negative error codes.

There are literally dozens more negative codes; some are undocumented, and even calling Apple's technical support for help may not lead to an explanation of what they mean. Utilities such as MacErrors, however, list most of them. If you want to know what a given negative error code means, keep this utility (or one like it) handy.

SEE ALSO: • **"Take Note: System Errors Due to Purgeable WDEF Resources," later in this chapter**

Special Case: Type 11 and "No FPU Installed" errors

Type 11 and "No FPU Installed" system errors have become surprisingly common for Power Mac users (especially after upgrading to System 7.5.1 or later), making it one of the most asked-about problems today. The ultimate cause of these errors is almost always a bug in application software, so you cannot really "fix" these errors yourself. Still, there are a number of quasi-fixes that can help eliminate or reduce the chances of getting these errors. In particular, here's a complete list of things to try:

- Restart. The error may not occur again any time soon.
- If the error occurs only or mainly with one application, and especially if you can reproduce it consistently, a bug in that program is the likely cause. Contact the vendor for compatibility information.

  One special note: Power Mac versions of Microsoft Office applications (Word 6 and Excel 5) can lead to Type 11 errors, most often when also using virtual memory and/or QuickDraw GX. To fix this, you should install the Office4.2x Update for Power Mac extension (version 1.0.1 or later). If you use System 7.5.2, also get Microsoft's Office Manager Patch for 7.5.2; however, you will be better off simply upgrading to System 7.5.3 or later and skipping the patch. In general, Microsoft Office 4.2.1b (or later) incorporates these fixes, making the separate updates unnecessary. Still, due to all of this confusion about what is and is not needed, you may want to experiment here.

  If problems persist, consider dumping the MOM control panel altogether. It has been especially implicated in problems with shutting down the Mac.

Table 4-1 Some Common System Error Codes*

ID/ERROR NAME	WHAT IT MEANS	WHAT TO DO**
Positive Error Codes		
01/Bus error and 02/Address error	Most often a software bug, extension conflict, or insufficient memory assigned to an application; the exact cause varies with when the error occurs. (1) Immediately at startup: probably a problem with an externally connected SCSI device (possibly an incompatible disk driver). (2) While the extensions are loading: probably an extension conflict. (3) While in the Finder: probably corrupted system software. (4) In any other application: a bug in the application. These errors are most common on 680X0 Macs.	If problem is specific to one application, try increasing its memory size (Fix-It #6). Otherwise, call manufacturer to find out about a possible bug. If error happens across many applications, replace system software (Fix-It #5). See Fix-Its # 4, #16, and #17 for more on extension conflicts, SCSI problems, and logic board problems, respectively.
03/Illegal instruction	Most likely a software bug. Technically, the Macintosh is trying to execute an instruction not in its processor's vocabulary.	Problem is usually specific to a single application. Contact manufacturer for information about a bug-fixed upgrade.
04/Divide by zero error	A mistake in the program code has caused the program to attempt to divide a number by zero. Since this is impossible, the system error results.	Problem is almost assuredly specific to the program in use. Contact manufacturer for information about a bug-fixed upgrade. Also, see Fix-It #4 to check for possible extension conflicts.
08/Trace Mode Error	Definitely a software bug. A debugger (such as MacsBug) isn't installed, and the processor is accidentally placed in Trace mode (a mode that should ordinarily only be used by programmers when debugging a program).	Installing MacsBug (see "By The Way:Recover From a System Crash Without Restarting (Maybe)" in this chapter) can work around the error. Otherwise, upgrade the software (for example, a Type 8 error that occurred on PowerBooks after waking from sleep was fixed by upgrades to RAM Doubler and/or to System 7.5.3 Revision 2).
09/Line trap (A-line) error and 10/F-line instruction error and 12/Unimplemented trap of core routine (operating system)	Typically an extension conflict or a software bug. For example, a program may assume that the Mac's ROM contains information that is only found in newer Macs, and thus it bombs when run on an older model. Technically, it typically means a call was made to the Macintosh's ROM for an entry that doesn't exist. Type 10 errors are essentially the same as "No FPU Installed" errors.	Problem is usually specific to a single application. Contact manufacturer for information about a bug-fixed upgrade. Otherwise, see "Special Case: Type 11 and 'No FPU Installed' errors" for much more advice. Also see Fix-It #1, "No Math Coprocessor."
11/Miscellaneous hardware exception error	An error generated by the processor and not covered by IDs 1 to 10; the exact cause is unknown. This error is much more common on Power Macintoshes than 680X0 Macs.	Problem is usually specific to a single application. Contact manufacturer for information about a bug-fixed upgrade. Otherwise, see "Special Case: Type 11 and 'No FPU Installed' errors," for much more advice.
15/Segment Loader Error	Macintosh programs can be broken up into segments that may be separately loaded, so as to minimize RAM usage. The system software's Segment Loader, in conjunction with instructions from the program, determines how this is done. A bug in the system software and/or the program can cause this error.	Upgrade the program or system software. If an extension is the cause, disabling the extension is a work-around.

Table 4-1 Some Common System Error Codes* *(continued)*

ID/ERROR NAME	WHAT IT MEANS	WHAT TO DO**
25/Out of memory and 28/Stack ran into heap	While this should be caused by an application running out of memory, the Macintosh may be "fooled" by some other cause into thinking there is a memory problem.	Increase the application's memory allocation (see Fix-It #6). Otherwise, seek more general solutions as described in this chapter.
Negative Error Codes		
–34/Disk is full	Not enough room on the disk (typically occurring when trying to save a file to a disk). Otherwise, disk may be damaged.	Delete or transfer files on the disk to free up more room for what you are trying to do. Otherwise, try to repair the disk (see Fix-Its #10 and #13).
–39/End of file	Indicates a discrepancy between the actual and expected size of a file. Usually means the file is hopelessly corrupted.	If it is an application, replace it and its preferences file (if any). See Chapter 6 (on deleting files) and Fix-Its #2 and #3. For a data file, recover data, if possible, then delete it (see Fix-It #14). Otherwise, try replacing the System and Finder (see Fix-It #5) and/or check for disk damage (see Fix-Its #10 and #13).
–43/File not found	A file you are trying to use could not be located.	Unless the file is really missing, it probably means you have disk damage (see Fix-Its #10 and #13).
–97/Port in use	Most likely a problem with a serial port (printer or modem) connection. Possibly a problem with a SCSI device.	Turn off the serial port peripheral device and turn it back on again. Restart the Mac and try whatever caused the error again. If the problem persists, zap Parameter RAM (see Fix-It #11). Otherwise, check for disk driver (Fix-It #12) or other SCSI problems (Fix-It #16).
–108/Out of memory	While this should be caused by an application running out of memory, the Macintosh may be "fooled" by some other cause into thinking there is a memory problem.	Increase the application's memory allocation (see Fix-It #6). Otherwise, seek more general solutions as described in this chapter.
–127/Internal file system error	Usually due to a corrupted Directory file.	Try repairing the disk with Disk First Aid (Fix-It #10) or other repair utilities (Fix-It #13). Otherwise, reformatting the disk will probably be required (Fix-It #15).
–192/Resource not found	Usually due to a corrupted application.	If it only happens with one application, that program is probably corrupted. Replace it. A bug in an extension or control panel can also cause this error.

**Most other positive number error codes imply either a bug in an application (especially likely with IDs 5–7, 16, or 26) or a damaged file, particularly the System file (especially likely with IDs 17–24 or 27). Negative number error codes have a variety of specific, usually technical meanings. See a utility such as MacErrors for a more complete list.*

***Refer to main text for more complete explanations of suggested actions.*

TAKE NOTE ▶

SYSTEM CRASHES AT STARTUP

If a system error occurs during startup, skip the rest of this chapter for now. Instead, go immediately to Chapter 5, which deals with startup problems.

- Upgrade to System 7.5.3 (or later). These recent versions have numerous bug fixes, and Apple reports that several of them will reduce the number of Type 11 errors you should get (though some unfortunate users have reported that it increases their error rate!).

  SEE: • Chapter 13

- Zap the PRAM. Some Type 11 errors may be caused by corrupted PRAM.

  SEE: • Fix-It #11

- Update the disk driver to the latest available version (especially because some older drivers are incompatible with SCSI Manager 4.3, which is used by System 7.5). Be sure to use Drive Setup (rather than HD SC Setup) if your Mac model is one that can use it.

  SEE: • Fix-Its #12 and #15

- Turn off Modern Memory Manager, which may trigger Type 11 errors in situations that would be ignored by the "old" Memory Manager. Be aware, though, that keeping Modern Memory Manager on (especially on PCI-based Macs) reportedly eliminates some Type 11 errors that would otherwise occur.

  SEE: • Chapter 12 and Fix-It #6

- Check for extension conflicts, and turn off conflicting extensions (or get an upgrade that fixes the problem, if such an upgrade exists). Some known conflict possibilities include QuickDraw GX and some versions of ATM.

  SEE: • Fix-It #4

- Too many fonts in the Fonts folder can cause Type 11 errors. To check for this, remove the Fonts folder from the System Folder temporarily and see if the error disappears.
- Corrupted fonts can also cause Type 11 errors. If removing the Fonts folder eliminates the problem, use a utility like Font Box to check for corrupted fonts.

  SEE: • Chapter 9

- Incompatible 680X0 software may be a cause on a Power Mac. Upgrade to Power Mac native versions if possible.

  SEE: • Chapter 12

- Do a clean install of your system software. The software may have become corrupted.

  SEE: • Fix-It #5

- Consider increasing the size of your system heap via options available in utilities such as Now Startup Manager or Conflict Catcher 3. For example, if you don't have enough heap space to load a shared library, a Type 11 error may occur. Increasing the memory size of the Finder itself may also help.

  Also, try increasing the Preferred Memory size of the applications you are using (if you have enough available RAM to do so).

  SEE: • Fix-It #6 for details on how to make these adjustments

TECHNICALLY SPEAKING ▶

WHY HAVE TYPE 10 AND 11 ERRORS BECOME SO COMMON RECENTLY?

On Power Macintoshes, it turns out that Type 11 errors can occur after almost any type of system error (bus error, address error, and so on), as long as the error occurs while the Mac is running Power PC native code (see Chapter 12 for an explanation of native code).

No FPU Installed errors (which are functionally the same as Type 10 errors) occur under two main conditions:

- The Power Mac is running in emulation mode. Essentially, since the Power Mac's emulator does not have a FPU (floating point unit), an error occurs if any 680X0 program includes instructions to call the FPU. This can also happen if a program somehow mistakenly executes data and interprets it as a call for the FPU.
- The Mac can't determine the correct error situation, when running either in emulation or native mode. More specifically, Apple has stated: "A number of errors are occurring simultaneously. They eventually percolate out as an 'FPU not installed' error. An error did occur, but it has nothing whatsoever to do with the need for a floating point unit."

Overall, errors that would have resulted in an address error (Type 1 error) or even no error at all on a 680X0 Mac, will more likely cause Type 11 or "No FPU Installed" errors on Power Macs.

Type 11 errors may also be indirectly due to corruption of the 680X0 emulator as it loads in to RAM. I had originally gotten this tidbit from an Apple TechNote, but Apple doesn't seem to emphasize this as a cause anymore.

- Some Type 11 errors only occur when you are connected online and use software such as Netscape Navigator. Increasing the memory of problem applications may help.

  SEE: • Chapter 14 for more suggestions

- If you are still desperate for a cure, disconnect any external SCSI devices to see if that helps. If it does, there may be a problem or incompatibility with the external hardware or cables.

  SEE: • Fix-It #16

- Defective memory (SIMMs/DIMMs) can cause seemingly random Type 11 errors.

  SEE: • Fix-It #17

- Defective RAM cache cards are a known source of Type 11 errors in Power Macs. This is especially a problem for RAM cache cards that shipped with early Power Mac 8100/80s. There have also been problems with RAM cache in PCI-based Macs, particularly the 7500.

  SEE: • Fix-It #17

- If the errors continue after all of this, particularly if they occur while in the Finder, there may be a hardware problem with the logic board itself. Call Apple or take it in for service.

Restart the Macintosh

There is no way to completely undo the effects of a system crash or other serious system error! It would be wonderful if you could simply select an Undo command and return your Macintosh to exactly where it was prior to the crash, with all your data still intact, but this is not possible. Even if it were, the crash might recur a few moments later.

What you can do, though, is to restart the Macintosh through one of the following solutions. If one doesn't work or is not applicable, try the next one until you are successful.

- **Click the Restart button in the System error alert box**
  System bomb alert boxes usually include a Restart button. Clicking this button, as its name implies, should restart the Macintosh just as if you had selected Restart from the Finder's Special menu. However, this button works at best only about half the time.
  If the Restart button does work, you will probably notice that it takes longer for the Welcome to Macintosh screen to appear than after using the Finder's normal Restart command. This is largely because the startup sequence is partially compensating for the lack of cleaning up (including saving and closing all files, updating Directory files,

BY THE WAY ▶

RECOVER FROM A SYSTEM CRASH WITHOUT RESTARTING (MAYBE): RESUME, CONTINUE, MACSBUG, AND MORE

In System 6, bomb alert boxes typically included two buttons: Restart and Resume. The Resume button, if it works, is designed to return your computer back to normal. I suspect that the Resume button was largely there only for humor value, though, since it almost never worked to resume anything. In recognition of this fact, the Resume button has faded from view in System 7. Occasionally I have gotten a System 7 bomb alert box that contained a Continue button, but it usually has about the same lack of effect as the Resume button.

Actually, if these buttons do anything at all, it is usually only to make the situation slightly worse. In particular, the cursor is likely to freeze up so that you no longer can even click the button again.

Then there are the special extensions first described in Chapter 2. A freeware extension called Bomb Shelter increases the odds that a Resume or Continue button will appear in a system error box and actually work, but not by much. Another extension, System Error Patch, bypasses the error box altogether, sounding three beeps and directly quitting the offending application. It seems marginally more reliable than Bomb Shelter, though the current version of System Error Patch has a minor bug that causes the Mac to bypass the dialog box that appears after you select Shut Down in certain mostly older Mac models (the box that tells you that you can safely shut off your machine). The best of these extensions was Crash Barrier—but this commercial product is no longer on the market.

A last alternative is to install Apple's free MacsBug utility (a utility primarily designed to assist programmers in debugging their software). To install it, just place it in your System Folder and restart. Now, when you get a system crash, instead of whatever message would ordinarily appear, you get a screen full of what appears to nonprogrammers as gibberish. At the bottom of the screen, though, is a place where you can enter keyboard input. Type "ea" (for "exit application"). With some luck, you will be returned to the Finder, from where you should at least be able to save data in open applications other than the one that crashed. Otherwise, typing "rs" will typically force a restart of your Mac.

In the unlikely case that you actually do return your computer to active duty, my recommendation is to save any unsaved work immediately and select Restart from the Finder's Special menu. Otherwise, you are at imminent risk of having a second system crash.

BY THE WAY ▶

SYSTEM 7.5 AND THE SHUT DOWN WARNING MESSAGE

If you restart after a system crash with System 7.5 (or, really, any time you shut down other than by using the Shut Down command), you will probably get a message during your next startup sequence telling you what you already know: that you did not restart your Mac last time in the normal fashion. If you don't want to keep seeing this message every time you have a system crash, you can turn it off by unchecking Shut Down Warning in the newly designed General Controls control panel.

By the way, here's how the Mac knows that you crashed: There is an invisible file of size 0 bytes called "Shutdown Check" at the root level of the startup volume. The presence or absence of this file determines whether the warning message appears on your next startup. The file normally gets deleted at shutdown. In such cases, the warning message does not appear. If you restart after a system crash, however, the file is not deleted, and so the warning message appears.

This computer may not have been shut down properly the last time it was used.

To turn off this computer, always choose Shut Down from the Apple menu, or press the Power key on the keyboard.

File Edit
About This Macintosh...
Automated Tasks
Calculator
Stickies
• Shut Down

or

Press the Return key on the keyboard to continue. OK

Figure 4-3 *In System 7.5, this message may appear after restarting following a system crash.*

Note that this also means the warning message will appear the first time you start up with a disk after it has crashed, even if you have started up successfully with other disks in the meantime.

As a new feature in System 7.5.3, the Shut Down warning dismisses itself after two minutes, rather remaining on the screen until dismissed by the user.

and so on) that would have normally been done after you selected Restart or Shut Down from the Finder. With recent versions of the Mac software, however, I have noted a trend toward the Restart button resulting in a "proper" shut down that *does* avoid the long disk access time at the beginning of the next startup.

- **Press the Reset button (not the Interrupt button)**

The (physical) Reset button The Reset button in older Mac models is an actual physical button located somewhere on the case of your Macintosh (as opposed to the onscreen buttons described in the previous section). It is identified by a triangle symbol (though on my old Macintosh Plus, it was identified by the word "Reset").

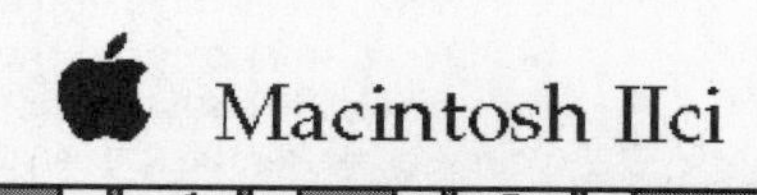

Figure 4-4 *The Reset and Interrupt buttons on the front of a Macintosh IIci. The Reset button is the one with the triangle symbol, while the Interrupt button has the circle symbol.*

Pressing the Reset button restarts the Macintosh in almost the same way as if you had clicked the bomb box's Restart button. Unlike the Restart button, however, the Reset button always works (at least, it has never failed for me). Press it and you have restarted your Macintosh.

The (physical) Interrupt button Next to the Reset button is the Interrupt button (identified by a circle symbol). In most cases, just ignore the Interrupt button, since it is rarely if ever useful to you. If you press it by accident instead of the Reset button after a system crash, don't fret; just press the Reset button next. Alternatively, if you should press the Interrupt switch when nothing is actually wrong with the Macintosh, you should be able to return to where you were—with no data lost—by typing "G," immediately followed by pressing Return. (Note: If you have MacsBug installed, pressing the Interrupt button will invoke MacsBug.)

One notable problem you may have with using the Reset or Interrupt buttons is finding them. The hardware designers at Apple apparently amuse themselves by devising new ways to hide the location of these buttons. In some cases, there may be no Reset and Interrupt buttons at all (as described next).

SEE ALSO: • **"Oh Where, Oh Where Did My Reset Button Go?"**

The keyboard Reset and Interrupt commands On most newer Mac models, the Reset and Interrupt buttons have been replaced by keyboard commands that do the same thing as their physical equivalents. The Command-Control-Power key combination acts as a Reset button, and at least on some models, Command-Power

BY THE WAY

OH WHERE, OH WHERE DID MY RESET BUTTON GO?

Oh, for the good old days of, say, four or five years ago—when there were only a half dozen or so Macintosh models and they all were designed fairly similarly. Now, explaining even the most simple of features can be a daunting task. The location of the Reset and Interrupt buttons is a case in point.

In the oldest Macintoshes, these buttons came as a separate piece of plastic (referred to as the Programmer's Switch) that you installed on the side of the case. In subsequent modular Macintoshes (such as the IIci), the switch was similar but was installed on the front of the unit. If you have any of these models, though, you may not find this switch installed at all, because you—or whoever first set up the Macintosh—never bothered to install it. If you can no longer find it stashed away somewhere, your only recourse is to call Apple to see if you can order a replacement. If you do eventually find the missing switch or get a new one, follow the instructions in your manual as to how to install it (or get some outside help, if needed).

On more recent desktop models, the two buttons typically came preinstalled on the front of the unit—that is, unless they aren't. On some models (such as the Power Mac 6100/60), they are on the back of the machine. If you don't find them anywhere, it is probably because your model uses the special keyboard commands to serve the same function.

Oh, I almost forgot: PowerBooks of the 100 series (except the PowerBook 100) have their buttons recessed on the back panel. You need something like an unbent paper clip to get in there and press these buttons, which is hardly convenient. For the PowerBook 100, the buttons are on the side of the machine. As far as I am aware, PowerBook Duos and 500 series PowerBooks have no Reset or Interrupt buttons; for these models, you must use the keyboard command equivalents.

The PowerBook 190 and 5300 series have the rough equivalent of a Reset button (but no Interrupt button) on the rear of the machine, underneath the video-out connector. Actually, although it is often referred to as a Reset button, it is not quite a "real" Reset button. Press it and it turns the PowerBook off instantly; press it again to turn the Mac back on (see also: Take Note: Power On, Power Off," for more on this button). For a typical reset, the Command-Control-Power keys work.

If you are still having a problem finding your Reset button, check with the manual that came with your machine.

SEE: • **Chapter 11, "Restarting a PowerBook After a System Error," for more on PowerBooks**

TAKE NOTE ▶

POWER ON, POWER OFF

There are two types of Power buttons on Macintoshes: some Macs have only one of these buttons, while some have both. One is usually on the rear of the machine (though sometimes it is on the front) and can turn the Mac both on and off. The other one is on the keyboard in either the upper right-hand corner or the top middle area and usually has a triangle symbol on it (yes, it's similar to the symbol on the Reset button). The keyboard button does not work on all Mac models; if it does work, using it will turn on the Mac.

This can get a bit confusing as both the button on the Mac and the button on the keyboard are referred to as the Power button. I usually try to distinguish them by referring to the keyboard button as the "Power key" and the other button as the "Power button."

Starting with System 7.5.1, pressing the Power key when the Mac is already on brings up an alert box with the option to shut down the Mac (you can also select Sleep or Restart from here). System 7.5 also includes a Shut Down desk accessory in the Apple menu. Selecting this also allows you to shut down a Mac from within any application, without having to return to the Finder's Special menu.

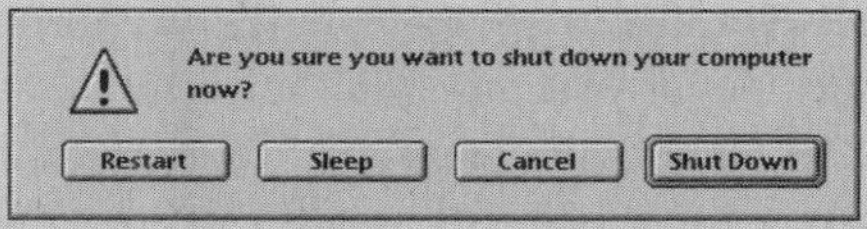

Figure 4-5 *This alert box appears when you press the Power key on the keyboard of most recent Macs running System 7.5.1 or later.*

For those who need to know, here are some more specifics:

Most older compact Macs have a rocker on/off switch in the back. When you select Shut Down, you are soon greeted with a message that says to turn off that switch. This message may also appear on some newer Macs (such as the Power Mac 6100).

On most Macintosh II, Quadra, and Power Mac models of Macintosh, selecting Shut Down turns off the Macintosh without any further action needed. The Power key turns the Mac back on again. In most cases, however, these Macintoshes also have an on/off push button somewhere on the Mac itself. On the Mac IIci, for example, it is in the rear; on the Power Mac 7600, it is in the front.

On some models, the on/off button may have a slot in it. The slot should be horizontal. If it is vertical, this means that the Macintosh automatically restarts itself after any loss of power. This is great if your Macintosh is an unattended file server on a network, but it is less than ideal for anyone else. If you seem to have this problem, use a screwdriver to turn the slot to the horizontal direction. By the way, if your Mac does not have this button option, and you want it to have automatic restarts, some Macs can be set to do this via software (such as via the Preferences settings in the latest versions of Apple's Energy Saver control panel).

The PowerBooks have their own special attributes. The 100 series PowerBooks and the Duos have a Power button on the rear of the machine, and the Duos also have a Power key on the keyboard. If your Duo is in a Duo Dock or MiniDock, there is also an on/off button on the rear of the dock. For the 500 series PowerBooks, there is a Power key on the keyboard, identified by a circle symbol with a vertical bar inside it. These PowerBooks do not have a separate on/off button.

PowerBook 190 and 5300s have a Power on key on the keyboard that works much the same as the one on desktop Macs. There is also a small so-called Reset button on the rear of the machine; pressing it turns the Mac on (just in case the keyboard key fails to work). Holding it in for a few seconds and then letting go may even clear up a startup problem now and then (such as a SCSI mode appearing when you are not connected to another Mac). Do not use it, however, for a normal shutdown; pressing it when the Mac is on shuts the computer off without the normal saving and closing of files that occurs with a typical shutdown.

SEE: • **Chapter 11, "Restarting a PowerBook After a System Error," for more on PowerBooks**

(or Control-Power, or Command-Control-Shift-Power) acts as an Interrupt button. (If none of these Interrupt key combinations work, you can still add this capability via a freeware extension called Programmer's Key). On some Mac models, these keyboard equivalents work even if the Mac does have separate physical buttons. Try it out.

By the way, a system crash might mess things up so much that the keyboard Reset command won't work, but this happens only very rarely. If it does happen, you'll have to turn the Mac off, as described in the next section.

Helpful hint: The Reset button/command is designed to be used after system crashes. It is not the ideal way to routinely restart your Macintosh. Use the Finder's Restart command for routine restarts. Not only does it have the advantage of prompting you to save all unsaved work before it restarts, there is a small chance that restarting with the Reset button instead may cause some software damage to files on your disk (especially if you press the button while something is being written to a disk). This has never actually happened to me, and I have used a Reset button quite often, so the risk must be quite small. But why take it at all, unless you must?

BY THE WAY ▶

ENERGY SAVERS

Depending upon what version of the system software you have and what Macintosh model you have, Apple also makes various Energy Saver (or similarly named) control panels. These allow you to put your monitor to sleep, shut the monitor completely off, spin down your hard disk, and/or shut your Mac off entirely, all on an automatic schedule or after specified periods of inactivity. If all of these choices get confusing, a shareware utility called Sleeper is a good alternative. It works with virtually all Mac models.

By the way, the Energy Saver 2.0 "control panel" that ships with PCI-based Macs (and possibly other models) is actually an ordinary application, not a true control panel (cdev). It works in conjunction with a separate Energy Saver extension. To disable it, set the control panel's settings to "Never" and restart, then disable the extension.

SEE: • **Chapter 12 on AppleVision monitors, for more on the Energy Saver control panel**

- **Turn the Macintosh off and then back on**

If the Reset button should ever fail to work, locate the Power button for your Macintosh (see: "Take Note: Power On, Power Off," for its location) and turn off the computer altogether. Wait about ten seconds, to make sure that everything has really shut down. Then, depending on your model of Macintosh, either press the Power button again or press the Power key on your keyboard. Doing this will initiate a restart that is similar to using the Reset button—that is, it does not do the cleanup (such as saving and closing all open files) that is done after using the Finder's Restart command.

At this point, you may well wonder: why bother with the Reset button at all? Why not always use the alternative of turning the Macintosh off and then back on again? Won't this do pretty much the same thing as the Reset button? The short answer is yes, so go ahead and turn the Macintosh off and on again to restart it after a system crash if you want.

Still, the official view is that using the Reset button is preferred because by not actually shutting down the system, it places less strain on the computer's electronic circuitry, thereby prolonging the life of the components. It may also extend the life of the on/off switch (though you would have to be having a lot of system crashes for this to be relevant). Personally, I believe that this threat is highly exaggerated, but I still use the Reset switch whenever possible. Why take chances, especially when the Reset button on most models is more conveniently located than the on/off switch?

Finally, if the on/off switch should fail to initiate a restart (an extremely unlikely possibility), unplug the Macintosh from the wall outlet, wait a few seconds (or minutes), and plug it back in.

See if you can start normally now. If not, you probably have a hardware problem. Start by checking Chapter 5 for how to deal with startup problems. Otherwise, contact Apple or an authorized Apple dealer for what to do.

BY THE WAY ▶

WHEN NOT TO TURN ON OR OFF YOUR MACINTOSH

- Don't turn the Mac on during a thunderstorm. If a power failure occurs during the storm, the Macintosh may restart itself when power returns; this is the equivalent of using the on/off switch under normal power conditions. During a storm, however, the return of power may be accompanied by a power surge that could damage your hardware (even if you are using a surge-protected outlet). Since a power failure may be only momentary (too short for you to react to it by turning the Macintosh off), your safest action is to turn off and unplug the Macintosh until the storm is over. (Note: I have ignored this advice myself many times, and nothing has ever happened. You'll have to make your own decision on what risks you wish to take.)
- Never turn the machine off (or hit the Reset or Interrupt buttons) while the Macintosh is reading from or writing to a disk. You may damage the data files currently in use.

- **Special case: PowerBooks and restarting after a system error**

  For most 100 series and Duo PowerBooks, you are likely to use the Power button to restart your PowerBook after a system crash, especially with the 100s because of their difficult-to-access Reset button. If so, hold in the Power button (on the rear of the machine) for around five seconds before letting it go; this is called a *hard shutdown.* If you let go of the button too soon, pressing the button may have no effect. After the PowerBook turns off, press the Power button again to restart.

  On these PowerBooks, a brief press of the Power button initiates what is called a *soft shutdown,* which is equivalent to selecting the Shut Down command from the Finder's Special menu—an option that will not work after a system crash.

  Since the 500 series PowerBooks have no on/off button, if you can't get a 500 series PowerBook to reset after a system crash, try pressing Command-Option-Control-Power On. If this fails, your only alternative is to remove the batteries and disconnect AC power temporarily.

SEE: • Chapter 11, "Restarting a PowerBook After a System Error," for more details

- **Special case: RAM disks and restarting after a system crash**
  There is an important exception to the just-described cavalier attitude about using a hard shutdown to restart a PowerBook after a system crash: Doing this may result in the loss of the contents of a RAM disk. You may think that any type of restart would have the same result, but you would be wrong. Surprisingly, selecting the Restart command or using the Reset button preserves the contents of the RAM disk (though you still lose your unsaved work in the rest of RAM). After any type of shutdown, however, the RAM disk's contents are lost.

  You can increase your odds of saving a RAM disk's contents, even after a shutdown, by using software such as Apple's Assistant Toolbox (included with System 7.5) or Connectix's Maxima RAM disk utility.

  Finally, note that a RAM disk's contents are now typically saved after a restart on most desktop Macintoshes that have the RAM disk option, not just on PowerBooks.

  SEE: • Chapter 11 and Fix-It #6 for more on RAM disks and these related utilities

Recover Unsaved Data After a Restart

Okay, you're back in the saddle again. You've successfully restarted your Macintosh and returned to the Finder's desktop. What now? If you didn't lose any unsaved data or don't care about what you did lose, just return to whatever you were doing before the crash and hope that it doesn't happen again. In the meantime, be careful to save your work frequently.

You can also try to recover any data that weren't saved prior to the crash. I know, this sounds almost impossible. It also seems to contradict my previous statements that unsaved work cannot be recovered after a system crash because it is present only in RAM, and information in RAM evaporates when you restart the Macintosh. Despite this, you may yet be able to recover some "unsaved" data.

A word to the wise before you start trying the options I'm about to describe: They are really only good for rescuing text data, and even then they are often unsuccessful. Even if they do work, they typically only save part of your information or save it in a form that requires deleting unwanted text, rearranging paragraphs, and reformatting (fonts and margins and so on) before it resembles how it appeared originally. This all takes time. If you only lost a small amount of work, you are often better off simply starting from scratch and redoing it. For those times when you really are desperate, however, try the following techniques.

Check for Temporary Files Many (but far from all!) programs create temporary files, sometimes called *work files,* that hold part or all of a document's data while the document is open. Ordinarily, you are unaware of the existence of these files; the software manual may not even refer to them. This is usually okay, because these temporary files should be automatically deleted when you quit the program. After an unexpected quit, a Force Quit, or a reset after a system crash, however, these temporary files typically do not get deleted and remain somewhere on your hard drive.

These temporary files may contain data from the document you were last working on before the crash, even if you had not yet saved the data. More often, though, these temporary files will be useless, containing virtually no data at all. Still, it can't hurt to check them.

Temporary files are not shown on the Finder's desktop or in most Open or Save dialog boxes so you won't use them inadvertently during normal operation of the Macintosh. For example, deleting a temporary file while the application that created it is still open (assuming the Macintosh lets you do this) could cause a system crash! The downside, however, is that their invisibility makes these files more difficult to find when you do want to use them.

Some temporary files on your disk may be left over from system errors that are now ancient history. These will obviously be of no value to you in recovering data from your current system error. Ideally, you are looking for the one temporary file that contains data from the document you were working on at the time of the crash. Often you can figure this out by the name of the file, which tends to give away its origin and nature (such as Word Work File for Microsoft Word 6.0 temporary files). To be certain that you ferreted out all of these files, look for both visible and invisible temporary files.

SEE: • **Chapter 8 for more on invisible files and folders**

- **Look for visible temporary files (check the Trash!)**
After a system crash, the first place to look for visible temporary files is in the Trash. If you are using System 7, the system software creates a special folder called Temporary Items. Any programs that are written to utilize this folder place their temporary files into it. This folder, and the files within it, are normally invisible.

  After a system crash and a subsequent restart, however, the Macintosh automatically places all the items in the Temporary Items folder into a new folder called "Rescued items from [the name of your disk]." This folder is visible and is placed in the Trash. It contains the files that were in the invisible Temporary Items folder at the time of the system error. On Power Macintoshes, the folder may simply be named Temporary Items.

  The Macintosh places the Rescued Items folder in the Trash for a good reason; deleting these files is usually the best way to deal with them. Still, the point of all this discussion is that these rescued files may contain some of your unsaved data. So, if you find the Trash can bulging immediately after a restart, double-click the Trash icon to open its window. If you find a Rescued Items folder in the Trash, remove it and place it in any other location. The temporary files in the folder should all be from applications that were open at the time of the system error, so it should be relatively easy to check for the ones that are useful to you.

  Occasionally, there may be visible temporary files on your disk that do not make it to the Trash. They are typically in your System Folder, in the same folder as the application that was active at the time of the crash, or at the root level of your disk. You can use the Finder's Find command to help locate these temporary files, if necessary. If you are unsure of what the name of the temporary file might be, try search words such as "Temp" or the name of the application itself. Even better, search by creator (as explained in Chapter 8).

- **Look for invisible temporary files**
If you are having trouble locating the temporary file you want, it may be because it is invisible. These files can still appear in the Open dialog boxes of some applications; for example, Microsoft Word can do this (as described in the following paragraphs). Otherwise, your main hope of finding invisible temporary files is to use a special utility that lists them, such as Norton Utilities or MacTools. For text data files, these utilities may be able to extract and save the text to a separate visible file, using the same technique you would use to recover text from a damaged file. Alternatively, these utilities can change the invisible file to a visible file. The probability of successfully recovering any data from these files is fairly low, however, so don't feel compelled to try this unless the lost data are important.

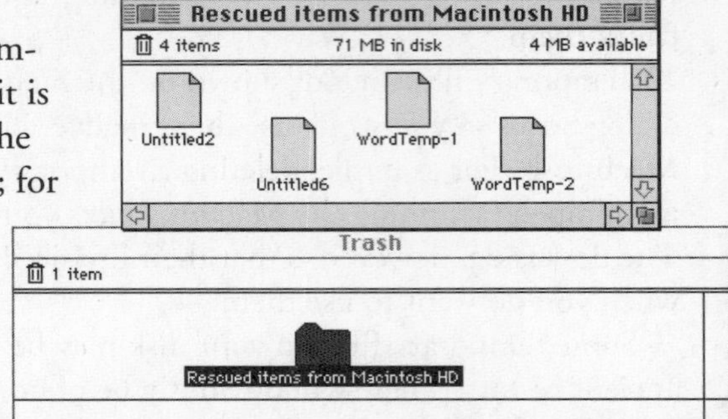

Figure 4-6 *A Rescued Items folder, normally found in the Trash following a restart after a system crash.*

SEE: • **Fix-It #14 on extracting data from damaged files**
• **Chapter 8 on changing an invisible file to a visible one**

- **Recover data from temporary files**
Once you have located the appropriate temporary file by any method, you'll want to open it to view its contents. To do this, your best bet is to open the application that was in use at the time of the crash. See if it lists the relevant temporary file in its Open dialog box; if so, open it.

Some applications may not list their temporary files as openable. Others may do so, but only after a bit of fiddling. For example, to see temporary files listed with Microsoft Word, select the All Files option from the List Files of Type pop-up menu in the Open dialog box. Otherwise, for text files, try any other application you have that can read text files. In general, select the option that shows the broadest range of file types.

If you are successful in opening the temporary file, you may find some useful data in it (primarily text data), even if it is only a partial recovery. If so, edit and save the data as with any other file. If there is any garbage data along with the real data, you can cut them.

Temporary files that remain on your disk after a system error are not used again as temporary files. Rather, the program creates a new temporary file the next time one is needed. Thus, if there is nothing worth saving in these recovered temporary files (which, unfortunately, is all too often the case), delete them so they don't take up space on your disk. And as long as you are doing this, you might as well delete any other old temporary files that you find.

Delete these temporary files, however, only when the program that created them is *not* open. This way you can be sure that you do not accidentally delete a temporary file that is currently in use, which (as mentioned above) can lead to a system crash.

Use Special Recovery Utilities You can recover text by using utilities such as NowSave from Now or SpellCatcher's GhostWriter feature. As described in Chapter 2, these utilities record each keystroke that you make as you type. The resulting text is automatically saved every minute or so in a special file, typically stored in your System Folder. Unlike any auto-save function you might have, which saves the actual file you are using, these utilities save data even if the file itself was not saved. After a system crash, locate these special data files and open them in a word processor. With luck, you will find your unsaved text. The recovered data may not be in perfect shape (some text may be missing or garbled), but it should be far preferable to having nothing at all. If you remember to use the ordinary Save command fairly often, though, these utilities will probably not be of much extra benefit.

Helpful hint: These extension utilities only work if you install them prior to a system crash.

SEE: • **Chapter 2 for more details on these recovery utilities**

What If the System Error Keeps Recurring?

After completing all the previous advice, you can typically return to what you were doing prior to the system crash and continue your work. Most often, another crash will not occur. But what if it does? What, most especially, if it keeps recurring every time you get back to the same point? If this unfortunate event happens to you, you will have to spend some time trying to determine the source of the problem—or stop doing whatever caused the system error.

To solve recurring system error problems, skip to the last section of this chapter.

SEE: • **"Solve It! Recurring System Errors," later in this chapter**

System Freezes

 **Symptoms:**

The Macintosh appears to lock up. Without warning, everything on the screen display comes to a complete halt. If you had an animated cursor, like the watch cursor, all animation has stopped. At best, the cursor may continue to respond to the mouse, but you can't get it to do anything. Menus do not drop down, applications do not open, and typically keyboard input has no effect either. At worst, everything, including the cursor, refuses to move or respond to any input. For the moment, your computer screen has become little more than an expensive paperweight.

When any of this happens, you have a system *freeze* (also called a *hang*).

Causes:

A freeze is almost always caused by a software bug. Identifying the program that contains the bug, though, can be tricky: it can be in the application, or in the system software, or a conflict between two programs that are active at the same time. Most often, the bug is related to problems with the way a program is trying to access RAM.

Damaged files, particularly if they are System, Finder, or font files, may cause a freeze. A damaged Directory may similarly lead to a system freeze, and so can trying to defragment a disk with a damaged Directory. A loosened and disconnected cable can cause the same symptoms as a freeze, although no system error has occurred. A multitude of other causes remain, including low memory and SCSI problems.

What to do:

Try to Save Your Work (Press Command-S)

Despite the system freeze, you may still be able to save your unsaved work. Presumably, you cannot actually select the Save command from the File menu because of the freeze. Sometimes, however, the Macintosh will respond to certain keyboard input. By pressing Command-S (the keyboard shortcut for Save), you may be able to save whatever document you were using at the time of the freeze; otherwise, it is almost certain to be lost. In either case, you still have a (semi-)frozen Macintosh that needs to be remedied.

Try a Force Quit (Press Command-Option-Escape)

To do a Force Quit, press the Command-Option-Escape keys all at the same time. An alert box should appear at this point, asking if you want to do a Force Quit of the active application and telling you that any unsaved changes in that application will be lost. Since you have few other alternatives at this point, go ahead and do it.

This should return you to the Finder's desktop. The Macintosh should be functioning fairly normally now, except that the application you were using has been closed and any unsaved work is lost. Still, if you had other applications open at the time, you should be able to return to them and save any previously unsaved documents in these other applications.

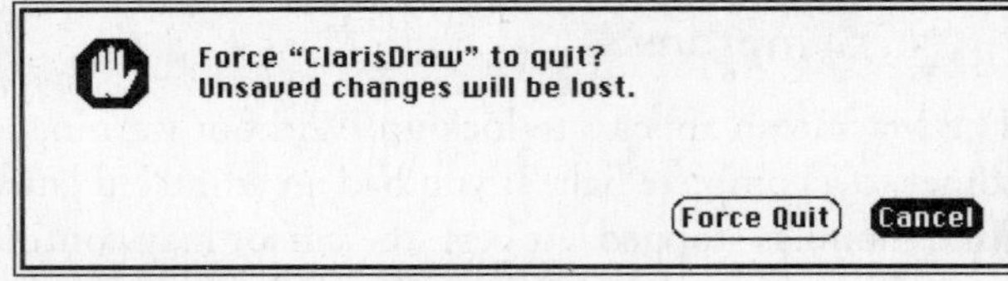

Figure 4-7 *The "Force Quit" alert box.*

By the way, a Force Quit is designed to work primarily after either a system freeze or an endless loop (as described in the next section). I have never seen it work following a system crash (where the bomb alert box appears), but it can't hurt to try.

TECHNICALLY SPEAKING ▶

FORCE QUIT FROM THE FINDER

If you do a Force Quit when you are already at the Finder level, the alert box normally asks whether you wish to quit one of your other open applications, rather than letting you quit the Finder itself. If the Finder is the only open application at the time of a Force Quit, however, you are offered the chance to quit the Finder itself. Since, under most circumstances, the Finder must be running at all times, the result of this action is to quit and then immediately relaunch the Finder. (Note: In the latest versions of the system software—System 7.5.3 or later—you can force quit from the Finder even when other applications are open. The previous restriction no longer seems to hold.)

Normally, there is little reason to do this. Simply restarting your Macintosh accomplishes the same thing and is more reliable. If you are having problems with the Finder short of a system freeze or crash, though, quitting the Finder sometimes eliminates the problem without requiring you to restart.

There are also several shareware/freeware utilities that allow you to quit the Finder directly. The one I currently use is called Terminator, and it works as a Control Strip module. As a bonus, quitting the Finder this way (rather than doing a Force Quit) reduces the chances of problems recurring if you do not also restart the Mac. Of course, these utilities only work if you want to quit the Finder before you get a freeze.

If the Force Quit Succeeds ...

- **Try (again) to save your work**
  Assuming the Force Quit succeeds in bringing your Macintosh back to life, immediately save any unsaved work still open in other applications. Otherwise, the danger is that another error may occur again soon, because you have not fixed whatever caused the first error to occur. You may even be able to recover unsaved data from the application that led to the freeze, either by searching for temporary files or by using other special recovery utilities.

  SEE: • **"Recover Unsaved Data After a Restart," in the section on System Crashes earlier in this chapter**

- **Select Restart from the Finder's Special menu**
  To be honest, I have recovered from a freeze with a Force Quit and then continued using my Macintosh for several more hours without any problem. You can risk it too, but don't blame me if it soon leads to another freeze or crash. Problems are especially likely to recur if you were online at the time of the freeze and attempt to reconnect immediately after a Force Quit.

  Instead, restart the Macintosh; this usually "corrects" the problem that led to the system freeze. The best way to restart is simply to select the Restart command from the Finder's Special menu. This ensures that all files are properly updated, saved, and closed before the actual restart occurs, thus preventing any accidental loss of data and minimizing the (admittedly unlikely) chance of damaging files.

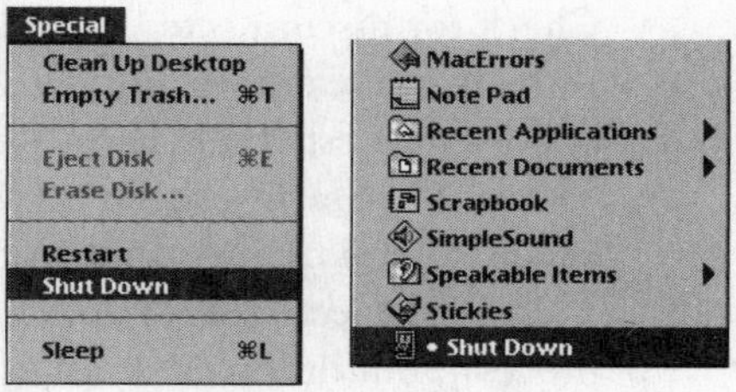

Figure 4-8 *The Restart and Shut Down commands in the Finder's Special menu (left); the Shut Down item in the Apple Menu (right).*

TECHNICALLY SPEAKING ▶

TO SLEEP ... PERCHANCE TO POWER DOWN

If you have a PowerBook, and you select Sleep from the Special menu, the computer appears to shut down—but it hasn't. Power to the hard drive is essentially cut off (to preserve battery power), but enough current is maintained so that the information in memory is preserved. On most PowerBooks, pressing any key (except Caps Lock) will awaken the PowerBook; on some models, you must press the Power On key. The hard drive then spins up, the screen brightens, and all returns to normal.

On some PowerBooks, such as the 190 and 5300s, just closing the lid puts the PowerBook to sleep. A small blinking light lets you know that the PowerBook is sleeping. Pressing the reset button on the rear of the machine will turn it off completely.

Some desktop Macs, primarily PCI-based Macs, have a similar Sleep capability.

SEE: • Chapter 11, on PowerBooks, for more details
SEE: • Chapter 12 on PCI-based Macs

Some other utility programs may contain a similar Restart command. If this command is more convenient, you can use it instead of the Finder's command. If you select Shut Down from the Finder (or from the Shut Down desk accessory) and then turn your Macintosh back on, this is virtually identical to selecting Restart.

If the Force Quit Fails to Work ... Restart

Unfortunately, sometimes the Force-Quit trick fails to work. Instead, when you click the Force Quit button, your system freeze worsens to where now even the cursor is frozen, or it may develop into a system crash. In some cases, the Force-Quit dialog box never even appears. In any of these cases, your main recourse is to restart the Macintosh, as previously described for a system crash: hit the reset button or the Power (on/off) switch.

SEE: • "Restart the Macintosh" and "Recover Unsaved Data After a Restart," in the section on System Crashes earlier in this chapter

If the Freeze Recurs

After restarting, you will usually be able to continue your work without another freeze occurring. If the freeze recurs after restarting, however, you will need to try to figure out the cause. As you will see, knowing exactly when the freeze occurs (such as during startup or when you try to launch an application) is useful in diagnosing the cause.

- **Check for disconnected cables**

  If the freeze reappears immediately upon startup, your best bet is to check the keyboard cable, especially if your mouse is connected to the keyboard rather than to the back of the Macintosh. In this case, a loose or defective keyboard cable prevents both keyboard and mouse input from having any effect. I call this a *false freeze.*

  A disconnected cable does not halt any operation in progress (such as a printing process), but otherwise mimics a true system freeze. It is not a true freeze because the processing of information has not been disrupted. If other cables, such as a printer cable or the SCSI cable (most commonly used for connecting an external hard drive), become disconnected, this can precipitate a true freeze.

Always turn off the Macintosh before reconnecting any disconnected cables you may find. This is especially true for the keyboard and SCSI cables. Although the threat is generally conceded to be minimal at best, reconnecting the cable may cause permanent damage to the Macintosh's circuitry.

Even if you do reconnect a cable while the computer is running and nothing adverse happens, it may not by itself restore the Mac to normal. You still probably have to restart the computer.

- **Check whether a cable, keyboard, and/or mouse may need a repair**
  It is always possible that a cable, mouse, and/or the keyboard have suddenly gone belly up. This, too, may mimic a freeze that appears immediately upon startup. If this is the case, try to swap your keyboard and cables for other ones, if alternatives are available (remembering to turn off your Macintosh before removing or connecting any cables). If replacing components eliminates the freeze, you need to replace the defective components.
- **Check for SCSI and disk drive problems**
  If a freeze occurs before extensions start to load, it may be a SCSI-related problem. To check for this, disconnect external SCSI devices from the Mac, try to restart the computer, and see if the problem goes away.

  If a system freeze occurs whenever you try to mount an external hard drive, try to repair the disk with software repair utilities. If that fails, reformat the disk.

SEE: • **Chapter 5 on startup problems**
• **Fix-It #13 on disk repairs**
• **Fix-It #15 on reformatting a disk**
• **Fix-It #16 for more on dealing with SCSI problems**

BY THE WAY ▶

INTERNAL HARDWARE PROBLEMS CAN CAUSE SYSTEM FREEZES

Problems with the internal hardware of the Macintosh—typically faulty components on the logic board—can cause repeated system freezes. Defective RAM can also be a cause of frequent freezes.

In some cases, problems are specific to a particular model of Macintosh:

- In early versions of the PowerBook 540c, a flawed chip on the logic board would cause intermittent freezes. Call Apple at 1-800-SOS-APPL to get a free fix for this.
- Macintosh 630s have a hardware problem that can result in periodic freezes during long SCSI transfers (such as when copying large files from one hard disk to another). Apple has released an extension (available on online services), called 630 SCSI Update, that fixes this.
- In 1996, Apple announced what is essentially a free extended warranty program to fix certain problems with 5200, 5300, 6200, and 6300 series Macs as well as 190 and 5300 series PowerBooks (that is, primarily those that use a 603 processor). Problems that qualify for this repair include recurring system freezes caused by specific, known component issues that have been identified by Apple (in other words, not every cause of a system freeze is covered!). Replacing the motherboard seems to be the required solution. Contact 1-800-SOS-APPL for more details.

SEE: • **Fix-It #16 on SCSI devices**
• **Fix-It #17 on hardware repairs and for more on the Repair Extension Program**

- **Give the application more memory**
  Freezes that occur when you launch or quit an application are sometimes due to insufficient memory for the application. To solve this, go to the program's Get Info window, increase its Preferred Memory size by at least several hundred kilobytes, and try again. Repeat this process several more times if needed, assuming that you have sufficient free RAM. Use virtual memory or RAM Doubler to make more memory available (but watch out for the next item in this list).

  SEE: • **Fix-It #6 on memory problems**

- **Turn off virtual memory or other memory-enhancing utilities**
  Freezes are often due to problems with memory-enhancement software. If you are using virtual memory or a utility such as RAM Doubler, turn it off. RAM Doubler is especially known as a possible cause of freezes while running communication and/or networking software.

  Turning off Modern Memory Manager or 32-bit addressing may also help.

- **Replace damaged font files**
  If a freeze occurs whenever you try to launch a particular application, a damaged font file may be the cause. Claris Corporation specifically mentions this as a potential cause for freezes with its software (ClarisWorks, FileMaker, MacWrite Pro, and so on). Damaged font files may also cause a freeze to occur when printing. The solution is to identify the damaged font and replace it from your backups.

  SEE: • **Chapter 9 for more on identifying and replacing damaged font files**

- **For freezes that occur when printing, turn off background printing**
  Freezes that occur when printing are often memory related; turning off background printing is a useful first step. Try printing again. If this doesn't work, you also may have an incompatible printer driver.

  SEE: • **Chapter 7 for more on printing problems**

- **Replace the System, the Finder, Finder Preferences, and/or Enabler/Update files**
  This is particularly likely to work if the freeze only occurs in the Finder or when you are doing system-related activities (for example, whenever a floppy disk is inserted into a disk drive). Similar situations include freezes that occur when copying files or emptying the Trash.

  Replace the System, the Finder, Finder Preferences, and/or Enabler files to attempt to correct these problems.

  SEE: • **Fix-It #2 on replacing Preferences files**
  • **Fix-It #5 for more on replacing system software**

- **Extensions conflicts and other causes**

If none of these suggestions solves the problem, it's time to look elsewhere. Extensions conflicts are the most likely cause at this point.

SEE: • **Fix-It #4 on extensions conflicts**
• **"Solve It! Recurring System Errors," later in this chapter, for a longer laundry list of things to try**

Endless Loops

Symptoms:

The symptoms of an endless loop appear, at first, not to be symptoms at all. Everything looks perfectly normal. As usual, when a process promises to take more than a few seconds to complete (such as a complex transformation in a graphics program), the cursor changes to a watch cursor with rotating clock hands, or a spinning beach ball. This is perfectly normal. It is the Macintosh's way of telling you to wait a minute.

During this time, the cursor continues to move across the screen in response to movement of the mouse, but all other activity is temporarily disabled. You wait for the task to be completed, at which time the regular cursor (usually an arrow) will reappear.

The signal that you have a problem is that the task never seems to reach completion. The watch or spinning-ball cursor appears destined to remain on the screen until at least the turn of the century. Welcome to an endless loop! Be especially suspicious of an endless loop anytime a task is taking much longer to complete than expected (for example, saving a document should almost never take more than a few seconds).

A similar situation occurs when the computer's activity is monitored by a progress bar on the screen (as occurs when copying disks from the Finder). The dark part of the bar continues to grow as the activity moves to completion. If the movement in the bar seems to stop, no longer showing any sign of progress, you may be caught in an endless loop.

At a practical level, the endless loop is a first cousin to the system freeze. Your course of action will be similar in both cases.

Causes:

Before taking any action, consider that you may not be in an endless loop. The Macintosh may just be doing something that takes a very long time to complete. For example, depending on your printer, it can take more than ten minutes to print one page of a complex PostScript graphics document.

The other alternative is that you *are* in an endless loop. This is typically due to a software bug that causes the program to attempt the same action repeatedly—and indefinitely.

What to do:

Break Out of the Loop with Command-Period

To check whether you really do have a freeze, press Command-period (holding both keys down together). This is an almost universal command for canceling an operation in progress. Hold the keys down for several seconds before letting go, then wait a few more seconds to see if the operation halts, as should be indicated by the progress bar (if any) disappearing and/or the animated cursor being replaced by the arrow cursor. If nothing seems to happen, try again. Continue retrying for at least a minute before giving up.

If canceling does work, you either halted a normal but slow process, or (less likely) you have a forgiving program that was able to break out of an endless loop with this technique.

BY THE WAY ▶

CANCELING A COMMAND

This Command-period technique is useful anytime you wish to halt an operation that you no longer want to finish, even if there is no suspected endless loop. It does not always work, but it is worth a try whenever you need it. Depending on the operation in progress, it may take as long as a minute or so before the operation is canceled.

Retry the Procedure

If you were able to break out of the loop, try the procedure a second time. Wait even longer before resorting to Command-period.

If it is just a slow process, it may reach completion this time. If the problem was an endless loop, it may have been a fluke that will not repeat itself.

Otherwise ...

If you cannot break out of the endless loop, treat this exactly as if it were a system freeze. In particular, try a Force Quit (hold down the Command-Option-Escape keys). If this doesn't work, restart the Macintosh.

SEE: • **"System Freeze," earlier in this chapter, for more details**

Whether or not you can break out of the endless loop, if it continues to recur, you will have to figure out the cause.

SEE: • **"Solve It! Recurring System Errors," later in this chapter**

Unexpected Quits

Symptoms:

An application abruptly and inexplicably quits, returning you to the Finder. Often, you will see an alert message informing you that the application unexpectedly quit. (I guess unless the Mac detects that you selected the Quit command, it treats the quit as "unexpected.") This is the most benign of system errors described in this chapter, because the system almost always continues to function after the unexpected quit.

Causes:

Unexpected quits are usually due to software bugs that affect memory management. Typically, less memory is available than the program needs. Ideally, the program should detect this and warn you of the problem. When the program is not written carefully enough, however, an unexpected quit happens instead.

If this happens, you can consider yourself lucky in a way. The alternative is usually a system crash that would immediately require a restart of the computer.

What to do:

Interpreting System Error Codes . . . Again

An unexpected-quit alert box often indicates the type of error that led to the unexpected quit (such as an error of "Type 4"). These numbers refer to the same codes as used for system crashes. While trying to figure out exactly what these mean is not likely to be helpful, you can check Table 4-1 for guidance. Sometimes the alert box often says the cause of the quit is of a type "unknown," making it irrelevant to look up the meaning of the error code.

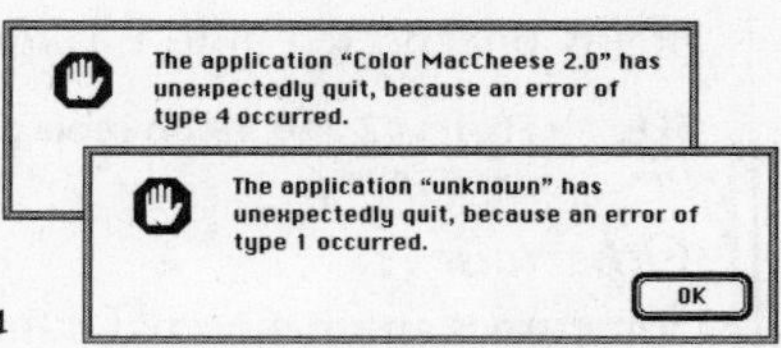

Figure 4-9 *Two examples of the "Unexpected Quit" alert box.*

Save Data in Open Applications

As with almost all system errors, any unsaved information in files that were open when the application unexpectedly quit is almost certainly lost. You should, however, still be able to save any data in other applications that remain open. You may even be able to recover unsaved data from the application that led to the unexpected quit, either by searching for temporary files or using other special recovery utilities.

SEE: • **"Recover Unsaved Data After a Restart," in the section on System Crashes earlier in this chapter**

Restart the Macintosh

To restart, select Restart from the Finder's Special menu. You can probably continue using your Macintosh without restarting. To be safe, however, you should restart first because once this problem occurs, the probability that it will recur increases until you restart.

Actually, if you want to return to the problem program, it may be necessary to restart. For example, I have occasionally had a program that would no longer relaunch immediately after an unexpected quit; it simply quit again whenever I tried to launch it. Restarting the Macintosh cleared up this problem.

Increase Preferred Size of Memory Requirements

The immediate cause of some unexpected quits is insufficient memory assigned to the application. This can be the case even if you are using the default assignments given to the application. If the unexpected quit persists after a restart, try increasing the Preferred Size of the application's memory from the file's Get Info window.

If increasing the application's Preferred Memory Size does not work, you may have to increase overall memory availability, as described in Fix-It #6.

Finally, make sure that there is adequate memory in the Font Cache of Adobe Type Manager. This is set from its control panel. Adobe recommends 50K to 80K for every font that needs to be rendered on screen at one time (including italics, bold, and so on).

SEE: • **Chapter 2 on Get Info window and Fix-It #6 on memory problems, for more details**

If the Unexpected Quit Occurs During Launch

Unexpected quits often occur in the middle of using an application. Sometimes they occur as a program is first launched, preventing you from successfully opening the program. If this happens, and the previous solutions have been unable to solve the problem, try removing the application's preferences file from the Preferences folder—and, if that fails, replacing the application itself. While a damaged application file may be the cause of any unexpected quit, it is more likely to be involved if the quit occurs during launch.

SEE: • Fix-Its #2 and #3 on replacing applications and their related files

Otherwise ...

Sometimes an unexpected quit will develop into a system freeze or a system crash before you can successfully restart. If so, refer to the previous sections on those topics for what to do.

Finally, if the unexpected quit continues to recur despite all the previous attempts at a solution, you need to track down what else may be the cause.

SEE: • "Solve It! Recurring System Errors," later in this chapter

The Finder Disappears

Symptoms:

The desktop seems to vanish. All disk icons and folder windows disappear; sometimes the menu bars on the top of the screen disappear as well. At the same time, the Macintosh appears to freeze.

Causes:

Basically, this is still another variation on the freeze or endless loop, and it has similar underlying causes. In this case, however, it is more likely that something is amiss with the Finder and/or System files.

What to do:

Wait a Minute

Occasionally, the Finder will reappear by itself if you wait a minute or two. If this happens, I would still be suspicious that a more serious error could occur soon. Restart the computer, just to be safe.

Try a Force Quit (Press Command-Option-Escape) and Restart

If the Finder does not return on its own, try a Force Quit. Occasionally, as with a generic system freeze, a Force Quit may return you to a fully functional desktop.

If the Force Quit does succeed, rather than immediately resume your work, you should save any unsaved work and restart the Macintosh by selecting the Restart command from the Finder's Special menu. If the Force Quit does not succeed, use the Reset button to restart. In either case, the Macintosh should return to normal following the restart.

SEE: • "System Freezes," earlier in this chapter, for more details

Replace the Finder and Its Preferences File

If the problem keeps recurring, replace the Finder and its preferences file.

SEE: • Fix-It #2 on problems with the Finder preferences file

Otherwise ...

If the Finder continues to vanish, replace or upgrade the system software. If even that doesn't work, it's time to look for more esoteric causes.

SEE: • Fix-It #5 on replacing system software
• "Solve It! Recurring System Errors," later in this chapter

Solve It! Recurring System Errors

If you have been directed to this section, you presumably have a recurring system error. If the error does recur, you probably want to eliminate it. This requires using the diagnostic guidelines that follow:

Seek the Cause of a Recurring System Error

Recent changes to the contents of your disk (such as a new system extension added, or an upgrade to the system software) are the most likely culprits for a recurring system error. In general, the most common causes of system errors are software conflicts or incompatibilities, software bugs, or damaged software.

What Circumstances, If Any, Reliably Cause the System Error?

To see if a system error recurs, first try to *exactly* duplicate the precipitating situation (for example, reopen all applications and documents that were open at the time of the error).

System errors can be quite finicky about when they will or will not recur. For example, perhaps the error occurs only when you select Check Spelling immediately after you select Save, or maybe it happens only when you select the command while a specific graphics application is also open. Or it may occur only when a specific startup extension is in use, or only when many applications are open and memory is running low. You don't really know for sure whether a system error will recur until you repeat the exact circumstances.

More generally, note what process is typically taking place when the error occurs. Does it occur only at startup, when launching an application, when printing, or at some other time? This, too, is an important diagnostic cue. For example, errors that occur while extensions are loading at startup are almost certainly due to an extensions conflict.

What Variations in Circumstances, If Any, Will Eliminate the System Error?

If you do get the system error to recur reliably under a specific set of circumstances, your next step is to determine how altering those circumstances affects the error. For example, suppose a crash occurs after you select Check Spelling from your word processor. Does it happen regardless of what documents, other applications, and other extensions are open and/or in use at the same time? Are there other commands that will also result in the same type of system error? Does the error recur when you are working with other documents and/or trying similar procedures with other applications?

An error that recurs only whenever a specific document is open suggests a problem with the document. If the error happens across all documents within an application, the problem is most likely with the application. If the error keeps recurring during the launch of the program, it usually means damage to the application (or one of its accessory files). If it happens across several applications, it is most likely an extension conflict or a bug or incompatibility in the system software.

Whatever happens, hopefully you can narrow down or isolate the cause of the system error via this approach.

What If the System Error Recurs at Unpredictable Intervals and Situations?

System errors that occur at unpredictable intervals or in apparently unrelated situations are the worst possible scenario. If nothing else, it is hard to know if and when the problem has gone away.

The single most likely cause of these types of system errors is a startup extension conflict. The second most likely cause is corrupted system software, particularly the System file or the Finder. A corrupted font file can also cause system errors. Damage to the Directory, the Desktop, or the disk driver is also a possible cause. SCSI connection or other hardware-related problems may similarly lead to system errors. Computer viruses are yet another cause of widespread system errors. Check out the next section of this chapter ("Fix It So That the System Error Does Not Recur") for a complete list of possible causes and how to find out what to do about them.

SEE: • **Chapter 3 for more on general problem-solving strategies**

BY THE WAY ▶

SLOW DOWN

Some system crashes occur because you are trying to do too much too fast. If this seems to be a possibility, slow down. Simply trying everything again, but at a slower pace, may solve the problem. In particular, don't select several commands in rapid succession, especially from across different applications (such as printing in one application and then quickly opening a large graphic document in another). Also, don't have too many background activities going on at one time (such as background printing and copying files).

Fix It So That the System Error Does Not Recur

Once you have narrowed down the cause as much as possible, it's time to do something to fix the problem. A list of suggestions is given in this section. Don't worry if you do not entirely understand all of the terminology (such as *device driver* or *SCSI*). The terms are explained in more detail in the indicated Fix-Its.

TAKE NOTE ▶

BEFORE YOU TAKE ANOTHER STEP

It would take time and effort to carry out all of the Fix-Its listed on the following pages, and most of them—perhaps all but one of them—will have little benefit for your particular problem.

If you have followed all the steps in this chapter up to now, however, you may have narrowed down the likely cause to just a few of these. So, if a damaged document seems likely, go right to the most promising step. You don't have to try the strategies that follow in any specific order.

Otherwise, bear in mind that system-error problems are mentioned in different contexts throughout this book. You may want to look in other chapters for more specifics before checking here.

Still, this section serves as a last resort for the most general case, when you have little or no insight as to the cause of the system error and therefore no basis for limiting the scope of your search. Since the first few causes account for almost all system error problems, you are unlikely to have to go too far down the list.

SEE:
- **Chapter 5 for system errors at startup**
- **Chapter 6 for system errors when launching an application or when copying or deleting files**
- **Chapter 7 for more on system errors specific to printing**
- **Chapter 11 for more on system errors specific to PowerBooks**
- **Chapter 12 for more on system errors specific to Power Macintoshes**
- **Chapter 13 for more on system errors specific to System 7.5 or later**
- **Chapter 14 for more on system errors specific to online connections**

Check for Hardware and/or System Software That Is Incompatible with the Application in Use

If the system error is specific to a particular application, check its manual for any troubleshooting advice. In particular, check for any mention of incompatibilities between the application and either the particular hardware or any version of the system software you are using. For example, an application may crash when launched on a Power Macintosh, but not a 680X0 Mac. Or a game may crash if you try to run it with virtual memory turned on. In general, new versions of an application sometimes do not work with older versions of the system software. Similarly, older versions of the application sometimes do not work with newer versions of the system software.

SEE:
- **Fix-It #1 on incompatibilities between software and hardware**
- **Fix-It #5 on system software problems**

Install the Latest System Update (Fixes System Software Bugs)

Apple now releases system software updates on a regular basis (it claims that it expected to release one at least every three months). Updates to specific components of its software, such as QuickTime, may get released separately. Apple literally comes out with some sort of update almost every week. Try to stay up to date, as difficult as this may sound; checking online is the best way to do it.

SEE: • **Chapter 2, "By the Way: What Exactly Does a System Update Update?," for more specific information about System Updates**
• **Fix-It #18 for more on getting online help and technical support**

Check for Software Bugs in the Application

If you suspect a bug in the application, your only recourses are to find some work-around solution, avoid using the offending software, or get a bug-fixed upgrade (if one is available). Call the software vendor, or check on their web site, to find out about known work-arounds and upgrades. Publishers often release minor maintenance updates just designed to fix bugs. Sometimes, they will only send you these updates if you call to complain, though, so call and complain. Remember, you cannot fix buggy software yourself.

SEE: • **Fix-It #18 for more on getting online help and technical support**

TAKE NOTE ▶

SYSTEM ERRORS DUE TO PURGEABLE WDEF RESOURCES

Do you ever get system errors of ID numbers 84, 87, 88, or 89? Does it happen especially when you are moving windows around? If so, the likely cause is that the WDEF (window definition) resource of one of your currently open applications is set to be "purgeable." You probably have no idea what this means. That's okay. You don't need to know what it means to fix it. There are several utilities that fix the problem for you. My favorite is an extension called WDEF Leopard. Just put it in your System Folder, restart, and the problem should be fixed.

For those of you who want to know a bit more about what is going on here, read this:

A resource is a section of an application's code. To say that a resource is "purgeable" means that after the resource loads into memory, it can later be cleared from memory (for example, if the memory space is needed for something else) even though the application is still open. Nonpurgeable resources must stay in memory until the appliation quits. Generally, it is a good idea for a programmer to make resources purgeable. It gives the Mac more flexibility in dealing with memory problems. If a program later needs a purged resource, it can always call it up again (purging something else if necessary). At least that's the idea. Until recently, however, it was a little known fact that if you set the WDEF resource to be purgeable, system crashes could result. Essentially, this was because the WDEF resource, used to draw certain types of windows (notably floating mini-windows), was not available in RAM when it was needed. This situation may not occur often, but it is a risk. The end-user solution is to change the WDEF resource settings of all applications to be nonpurgeable. WDEF Leopard does this for you "on the fly" as each application loads. It makes no permanent change to the application file itself (unlike some other utilities that are also designed to solve this problem).

Despite the fact that there are very few reports of new problems created by using WDEF-fixing utilities, I would still be cautious about using one unless you believe you have WDEF-generated system crashes.

Turn Off Selected Options from Memory and Turn Off Sharing Setup Control Panels

Turn off File Sharing from the Sharing Setup control panel. Similarly, turn off 32-bit Addressing (for Macs that have this as an option). Turn off the Modern Memory Manager (for Power Macintoshes) from the Memory control panel, or try turning it on if it is currently off. While you're in the Memory control panel, turn virtual memory off or reduce its size. For example, Apple reports that setting virtual memory to larger than 20MB can result in an error of type –250.

SEE: • **Fix-It #6 on the Memory control panel**

Check for Startup Extension Conflicts

Turn off all your startup extensions (files that load into memory at startup). To do this, restart the Macintosh while holding down the Shift key. Continue to hold down the key until the desktop appears. If this procedure eliminates your system error, you have a startup extension problem.

Be especially wary of extensions that actively process information in the background, such as Disk Express II. Similarly, be wary of the prevention checking features of MacTools and Norton Utilities (see Chapter 2).

Be especially careful never to use two extensions that do essentially the same thing, such as two screen savers. This is almost a sure way to cause problems.

SEE: • **Fix-It #4 on resolving startup extension problems**

Check for Memory Allocation Problems

Whether a software bug is the ultimate cause or not, the immediate cause of many system errors is a memory problem. Usually this means that an application or extension is trying to grab some memory that, for one reason or another, it can't have. Memory problems are the most common cause of an unexpected quit.

Some recurring system errors can be solved simply by allocating more memory to the application via its Get Info window (to access this, select the application icon and hold down Command-I). For starters, try increasing the Preferred size by several hundred kilobytes, assuming you have the memory to do so. Other related solutions are covered in the relevant Fix-Its.

If the problem occurs while trying to print, try turning off background printing.

SEE:
- **Chapter 7 for more on printing-related problems**
- **Chapter 12 on Power Macintosh problems and memory**
- **Fix It #4 on problems with startup extensions**
- **Fix It #6 on memory management problems**

Zap the PRAM

Zapping the PRAM may eliminate certain system crash problems, or at least make them go away for awhile. This has been especially recommended for Type 11 errors with Power Macs.

SEE: • **Fix-It #11 for details on how to zap your PRAM**

Check for Damaged Document Files

If a crash occurred while a document file was open, you may find that your entire document is now corrupted—either it does not open at all, or it just displays gibberish.

If these problems occur, the crash may have been the cause of the damage to the file. Alternatively, the damage may be the cause of the crash, in which case trying to open the document will surely cause the crash to recur.

In either case, the preferred solution is to delete the damaged file and replace it with a copy from your backups. This, by itself, may solve the system error problem. If you do not have a backup of the file, you can try to repair the file or at least recover data from it before you discard it. For starters, if you can open the file (most often you cannot), try copying the document to a new file by using the Save As command. Otherwise, you will probably want help from a recovery utility.

SEE: • Fix-It #14 for more on recovering data from damaged files

Check for Other Damage

A mixed bag of related causes fall into this area. Check each one below to see if it applies.

- **System software (System, Finder, Enablers, Updates Finder preferences, and so on)** If you have TechTool Pro, use it to see if your System file, Finder, Update and/or Enabler files are damaged (just make sure you have the latest version of the software if you have a new model Mac). The freeware version of TechTool does a similar check, but only for the System file.

  If you have an extensions manager such as Conflict Catcher, it can check for possibly damaged startup extensions (from Apple system software as well as from third parties).

  Otherwise, replace the System, Finder, and Enabler/Update files if you have backups. Delete the Finder Preferences file (drag the file to the Trash, restart, then empty the Trash). Make sure you are using matching and most recent versions of all system software files and that they are designed for your model of Macintosh. If there is any doubt, do a clean reinstall of the entire system software.

  By the way, if a freeze occurs while using the Scrapbook desk accessory, this is more likely due to damage to the Scrapbook File (located in the root level of the System Folder) than to the Scrapbook desk accessory itself (located in the Apple Menu Items folder). Delete the file after recovering items from it, if needed (using a utility such as Can Opener, as described in Fix-It #14). Similarly, for problems with the Clipboard, delete the Clipboard file if you find one in the System Folder. In either case, the Mac will create a new replacement file when one is needed.

  SEE: • Fix-It #5 on selective system software damage
  • Fix-It #17 on TechTool Pro

- **Program preferences**
  A program's preferences file may be damaged. To fix this, locate and delete the file. Go to the Preferences folder, located in the System Folder, and locate the Preferences file that appears to match the problem application (such as Panorama Prefs for Panorama, or Word Settings for Microsoft Word). Delete this file, making sure first that the application is closed. Do this after starting up with extensions off, if you are doing it for a control panel.

  The program will automatically make a new preferences file the next time you use it. You may have to reselect any customized preference settings you may have made previously.

- **Font files**
  A font file may be damaged. Claris particularly cites this as a reason that you may have trouble launching its applications. Also suspect font-related problems, among other possible causes, if system errors occur only when you are trying to print.

- **Directory**
  Check for damage to the Directory files on your disk. If you find Directory damage and it cannot be repaired, you will have to reformat the disk.

  Check for a damaged Desktop file by rebuilding the desktop.

- **Media damage**
  With any type of damaged file, there is the possibility of associated media damage. If so, the disk will probably have to be reformatted.

SEE: • Chapter 7 on printing problems
• Chapter 9, "Damaged Font Files," for how to detect and replace a damaged/corrupted font
• Fix-It #2 for problems with preferences files
• Fix-It #3 for replacing application and accessory files
• Fix-It #5 for replacing system software
• Fix-It #9 to rebuild the desktop
• Fix-It #10 to run Disk First Aid, checking for damaged disks
• Fix-It #14 for more on damaged files
• Fix-It #13 to do more checks for damaged disks
• Fix-It #15 for reformatting the disk

Check for More Than One System Folder on the Startup Disk

Though opinions on this issue remain divided, some people believe that the presence of two or more System Folders on the same startup disk could cause system crashes. Personally, I think the potential for this to cause problems is highly exaggerated. Still, to be safe, if you find more than one System Folder on your startup disk, delete all but one of them. (By the way, the one that is currently considered the active System Folder is the one that has a mini-icon of a Macintosh on its folder icon.) You can't entirely delete this folder from a disk while it is currently the active System Folder. Should this be the folder you want to delete, the easiest solution is to restart from another disk, then delete the undesired System Folder.

SEE: • Chapter 5 and Fix-It #5 for more on multiple System Folder problems

Check for Multiple Copies of Applications and Related Files

Though it is only rarely a source of system error problems, make sure there are not two different versions of the same application on your disk. If possible, check for files related to the application that may have two versions in the System Folder (such as two preference files with slightly different names). If you find any out-of-date files, delete them; use only your newest version.

Check for Viruses

A virus becomes more likely if you are having frequently recurring system errors that show no predictable pattern. It is especially likely if the problem begins immediately after you've added a potentially infected file to your disk.

SEE: • **Fix-It #7 to check for viruses**

Check for Problems with the Hard Disk's Device Driver

The device driver is software, contained on a hard disk, that is needed for the Macintosh to recognize and interact with the disk. It is contained in an area of the drive that is normally inaccessible to the user. It may become damaged, or an older version of the driver may be incompatible with newer versions of the system software and newer models of Macintosh. In such cases, the driver needs to be replaced or updated.

SEE: • **Fix-It #12 to update the disk device driver**

Check for Hardware Problems: Cable Connections, Peripheral Devices, SIMMs, and Logic Board

This is an especially likely cause if you are having frequent system crashes and/or ones that occur at apparently random and unpredictable intervals. A system error does not create a hardware problem, but it may be the symptom of an existing hardware problem.

Defective SIMMs/DIMMs are a prime cause of frequent system crashes (assuming that you can start your Macintosh at all!). Persistent "Type 1" and "Bad F line" errors are sometimes caused by nondefective but dirty SIMMs/DIMMs. If you have the skill, remove the SIMMs (or DIMMs) and clean them; otherwise, seek outside assistance for doing this.

If you are having frequently recurring system errors that seem to occur only when a specific external hard disk (or other peripheral device connected via the SCSI port) is in use, this signals a problem with how these devices are connected. Start by disconnecting the SCSI chain to see if the problem goes away.

Crashes that occur in a variety of contexts (such as whenever you launch an application or try to empty the Trash) may indicate a defective logic board.

Hardware problems tend to cause system freezes more often than they cause system crashes. Especially consider, as mentioned previously, whether you might have a "false freeze" (that is, an apparent freeze due to a defective keyboard, mouse, or keyboard cable).

Also note that some hardware-related causes of persistent freezes have been identified by Apple, and you may qualify for a free repair or replacement of your Mac's logic board.

See: • **"By The Way: Internal Hardware Problems Can Cause System Freezes," earlier in this chapter**

While some hardware-related problems can be fixed easily by even an unskilled user, others will require a trip to the repair shop.

SEE: • **Fix-It #16 to check for problems with SCSI devices and connections**
• **Fix-It #17 to check if hardware repairs or replacements are needed**

Seek Outside Help

If none of the preceding suggestions has helped, and you haven't already done so, it's time to seek outside help.

SEE: • **Fix-It #18 for more information on getting outside help**

Chapter 5

Startup and Disk Problems: Stuck at the Starting Gate

Unpleasant Topics 123

Understanding the Startup Sequence 123

What Is a Normal Startup Sequence? 123

What Is a Startup Disk? 124

What Determines Which Disk Is the Startup Disk? 125

Default Rules for Selecting a Startup Disk 125

The Startup Disk Control Panel: Changing the Default Startup Selection 126

Starting with an Alternate Startup Disk 128

Start Up with an Alternate Hard Disk 128

Start Up with an Emergency Floppy Disk 130

Solve It! When Your Macintosh Won't Start Up 131

The Macintosh Is Dead 131

Are All Cables Plugged In and All Switches Turned On? 132

Check the Battery 132

Substitute Cables and Components 132

Is It Just the Monitor? 133

Visit the Repair Shop 133

Sad Macs and Unusual Startup Tones 133

The Sad Mac Icon 133

Unusual Startup Tones 133

Decode the Message 134

Restart the Macintosh 136

If the Macintosh Successfully Restarts from an Alternate Startup Disk 137

If the Macintosh Does Not Restart from an Alternate Startup Disk 138

Solve It! When Your Macintosh Won't Start Up (continued)
The "?" Disk Icon or a Reappearing Happy Mac 140
If Your Startup Disk Is an External Hard Drive: Check Connections 140
If Your Startup Disk Is an Internal Drive: Disconnect Any External SCSI Devices and Restart .. 141
Check Indicator Lights 141
Restart the Macintosh 141
Check for System Folder Problems 141
Check for Startup Partition Problems 143
Zap the PRAM 144
Battery Problems 144
Make Disk Repairs 144
The "X" Disk Icon Appears 145
Do Nothing ... At First 145
A System Error Occurs Just Prior to or While "Welcome to Macintosh" Appears on the Screen 146
Do You Have the Correct and Latest Version of the System Software? 147
Test for a Startup Extension Problem 148
Determine the Problem Startup Extension 149
Not Enough Memory 149
Zap the PRAM 150
Replace or Reduce System Software 150
Check for Other Problems 150
Problems While Launching the Finder and the Desktop 151
Can't Load the Finder 151
The Disk Needs Minor Repairs 152
The Desktop File Could Not Be Created 153
Other Unusual Messages at Startup 153
Unreadable or Damaged Disk 153
Cursor Alternates Between a Watch and an Arrow (or All Icons in a Window Are Missing) ... 154
For Any Other Symptom, Including System Errors 154

Solve It! Generic Problems with Disks 157
A Hard Disk Won't Mount 157
Check Power and Connections 157
Restart or Try to Mount the Drive Manually 158
Check for SCSI-Related Problems 158

Special Case: Problems Mounting Removable Media Cartridges 159
Check for Damaged Files and Disks (Disk Is "Unreadable" or "Not a Macintosh Disk") 160
Reformat 161
Hardware Problems: Stiction and Beyond 162

A Floppy Disk Won't Mount 163
For the "Disk Needs Minor Repairs" Message 163
For the "Disk Is Unreadable" or "Is Not a Macintosh Disk" Messages 163
If No Error Message Appears 164
After You Eject the Disk 164

A Floppy Disk Won't Eject or Unmount 166
Standard Methods for Ejecting a Disk 166
Nonstandard Methods for Ejecting a Disk 167
The Low-Tech Approach 168
Reinserting the Disk 168
Special Cases 168

Repeated Requests to Reinsert a Floppy Disk 170
Make Sure You Are Inserting the Requested Disk 171
To Break out of the Cycle, Try Pressing Command-Period 171
Unmount the Disk or Close Windows 171
Restart (Possibly with Extensions Off) 171

A CD-ROM Disc Won't Mount 172
Make Sure the Disc Is Inserted Correctly 172
Make Sure the Drive Is Turned On Before You Start Up 172
Make Sure the CD-ROM Driver Is Installed in the System Folder and Enabled at Startup 173
Make Sure You Have Foreign File Access and Other Related Extensions as Needed 173
You May Have Damaged CD-ROM Files or an Extension Conflict 173
Otherwise, Check for Miscellaneous SCSI and Related Hardware-Related Problems 173
Special Case: Problems Mounting Multi-Session CD-ROM Discs 174

A CD-ROM Disc or Removable Cartridge Won't Eject 174
Use the Put Away Command 175
Eject Instead of Put Away 175
If a File on the Disk Is "In Use," Quit the Relevant Application(s) 175
Turn Off Virtual Memory 175
Turn Off File Sharing 176
Other Ways to Eject a CD-ROM Disc 176
Other Ways to Eject a Removable Cartridge 177

***Solve It! Generic Problems with Disks** (continued)*

A Hard Disk Gets Unmounted 177

Removing a Disk Icon 177

Dimmed Hard Disk Icons 177

Turning the Power Off 178

Drag the Disk Icon to the Trash 178

Drag a Shadow Icon to the Trash 178

Remount Any Unmounted Disk 178

Problems with Restart, Shut Down, or Sleep 179

Save Documents, Quit Any Open Applications (and Related Issues) 179

Check for Background Application Problems 180

Check for Startup Extension Problems 180

Restart (by Using the Reset Button If Needed) 180

Replace the Finder Preferences File 181

Zap the Parameter RAM 181

Replace the Open Application and/or the System Software 181

Check for Disk Directory or Hardware Problems 181

Files Missing from the Desktop 182

Close and Reopen the Window 182

Use Find 182

Rebuild the Desktop 183

Use Disk First Aid 183

Upgrade 183

The Macintosh's Speed Is Unexpectedly Slow 183

Frequent System Crashes and Other Disk-Related Quirks 187

Check for Damage 187

Check for Viruses 187

System Software and Application Problems 187

Startup Disk Problems 188

Hard Disk Problems 188

If All Else Fails 188

Unpleasant Topics

Sad Macs. Dead Macs. Crashed disks. Unreadable disks. Damaged disks. These are the unpleasant topics of discussion for this chapter. Although the emphasis is on those times when you can't even start your Macintosh, I'll also tell you about disk-related problems that can happen at any time.

These problems tend to fall into one of three categories. Some problems are specific to the startup process; disks with these problems cannot act as startup disks but may otherwise function normally. More generic problems, such as an inability to mount a disk, cause problems whether the disk is used as a startup disk or not. Finally, some fairly serious problems have little or nothing to do with startup; for example, files and folders may begin to vanish from your disk.

Inevitably, some of these problems are caused by damaged hardware. Once again, however, many of these problems are entirely due to software-related causes. And even some hardware problems, such as those related to SCSI connections, can be remedied without requiring any repairs. The point is that there's a lot of simple stuff you can do to solve these problems on your own. So let's get going.

Understanding the Startup Sequence

What Is a Normal Startup Sequence?

For most users, the startup disk is usually an internal hard drive. Assuming this is the case for you, here's how a normal startup sequence proceeds:

1. Turn on your Macintosh. I am assuming you already know how to do this—if you have any questions, check the section in Chapter 4 on turning your Mac on and off.
2. The Macintosh immediately begins a series of diagnostic tests that check the condition of the hardware. Since we are describing a normal startup, I will assume no problems are found.

   In this case, the Macintosh plays its normal startup tone—the sound you hear every time you turn on your Macintosh. These days, the tone may be a single note or a chord, depending on what type of Macintosh you are using (this is yet another example of how Apple makes life difficult for those of us who would like to be able to describe these matters without citing numerous exceptions and variations!). The Power Macs have added an entirely new startup sound not heard on any previous models.
3. You may or may not briefly see the appearance of a disk icon with a ? inside it.
4. The Macintosh checks all available disks (in a prescribed order, to be described shortly) to see if any of them are startup disks (typically, this means a disk with a valid System Folder on it). If it finds one, you briefly see the smiling happy-Mac icon. The Macintosh has now passed all of its initial diagnostic tests.

Figure 5-1 *The smiling Happy Mac icon—a sign of a successful startup.*

5. Eventually, the "Welcome to Macintosh" screen (or other custom startup screen, if you use one) appears. With System 7.5.1 or later, this is quickly replaced by the Mac OS "splash" screen. In System 7.6, the "Welcome to Macintosh" screen is gone; the Mac OS screen appears directly.
6. Startup extensions (and related files) load. You can usually identify this activity by the sequential appearance of small icons along the bottom of the screen. These are the icons of the startup extensions being loaded (see Chapter 1 and Fix-It #4). Not all extensions show an icon here, but you will almost certainly have at least a few that do.
7. Finally, the Finder's desktop appears. The startup disk icon appears in the upper right-hand corner. This means the disk has mounted (in other words, is recognized and usable by the Macintosh).

   The term *mounted* is used to describe all volumes, not just the startup disk, that appear along the right border of the desktop. For example, you can have both a floppy disk and your internal hard disk mounted at the same time; the icons for both disks would then appear on the desktop.

   The icons for other disks, if there are any, appear beneath the startup disk icon. The startup disk is *always* the disk that is—initially, at least—at the top of the stack of disk icons. You can change the icon's location with the mouse, though this does not affect which disk is the startup disk.

Figure 5-2 *When you reach the desktop, the topmost disk icon displayed on the right border of the desktop (Macintosh HD, in this case) represents the startup disk.*

8. If you have placed any files in the Startup Items folder, these are launched next, and the startup sequence concludes.

What Is a Startup Disk?

To qualify as a startup disk, the disk typically needs a valid System Folder. While there are ways to create startup disks without a true System Folder (a few such methods are described in Chapters 2 and 8), I will be ignoring these unusual exceptions in this chapter.

A valid System Folder is one that contains at least a System and a Finder (and an Enabler or Update file, if needed for your Mac model). Usually, a valid System Folder can be identified on the desktop by a miniature Macintosh symbol on its folder icon. A folder with this icon is called a *blessed System Folder*.

Figure 5-3 *A blessed System Folder has a miniature Macintosh icon on it.*

The contents of the blessed System Folder on the current startup disk determines what fonts, sounds, system extensions, control panels, and Apple menu items are in menus and available for use. The Macintosh ignores information from any other System Folders that may be present.

A working startup disk also needs a valid set of *boot blocks.* This refers to a special invisible (to you, anyway) area of the disk containing information that the Macintosh checks at startup to determine the status of a disk. The boot blocks get their name from the fact that the startup process is sometimes referred to as "booting your computer" (which in turn comes from the expression "pulling yourself up by your own bootstraps").

Most of the time, you can be blissfully unaware of the boot blocks; creating and writing to them are tasks that normally are handled automatically. Boot blocks are created when you first initialize a disk. Whenever you change the startup status of a disk—by adding a System and Finder, for example—the Macintosh modifies the disk's boot blocks accordingly. It's only when things go wrong that you may need to be aware of boot blocks.

What Determines Which Disk Is the Startup Disk?

Suppose you have two hard drives connected to your Macintosh, each with a valid System Folder on it—and you start the computer with both hard drives running. How does the Mac decide which disk to use as the startup disk?

Default Rules for Selecting a Startup Disk

The Macintosh will check the following locations, in the order listed, until it finds an appropriate startup disk.

Floppy Drive(s) The Macintosh first tries to start up from an internal floppy drive; if it fails to find a startup disk there, it will check any external floppy drives.

CD-ROM Drive Apparently, automatically only certain Macintosh models check the CD-ROM drive for a possible startup disk at this point. Even then, it may not work unless you also hold down the "C" key at startup (see "Take Note: CD-ROM Startup Discs").

Startup Disk Control Panel Selection A choice here overrides what would otherwise be the default choice (as explained in the next section).

Internal Hard Drive This is the normal default startup device. The Macintosh looks here first for a valid System Folder if no floppy disks or CD-ROM discs are present at startup and no changes have been made in the Startup Disk control panel.

External Hard Drive(s) This is the default choice only if there is no internal hard drive in your Macintosh. If there is more than one external hard drive—all with System Folders on them—the Macintosh will select one to be the startup disk, based on the SCSI ID numbers of the drives. The drive with the highest ID number (starting from 6 and working down to 0) becomes the default startup disk.

If, by this point, the Macintosh has failed to find a startup disk anywhere, it will return to the beginning and try again.

SEE: • **Fix-It #16 for information about SCSI device ID numbers**

TAKE NOTE ▶

CD-ROM STARTUP DISCS

System software CD-ROM discs (such as those that ship with most recent models of Mac) can be used as startup disks (assuming, of course, that they are present in a CD-ROM drive at startup). There are qualifications and limitations, however, to getting this to work beyond the need for a blessed System Folder on the CD-ROM startup disc.

One problem is that you normally cannot access a CD-ROM drive until after the CD-ROM driver extension has loaded. CD-ROM startup discs include special instructions that allow them to get around this problem. Initially, in fact, CD-ROM startup discs could only be made by Apple because the needed special instructions involve a technique that Apple kept secret. Now, however, CD-ROM system software discs that come with Macintosh clones (such as from Power Computing) can also act as startup discs.

Similarly, CD-ROM startup discs may not work with all CD-ROM drives. They should work with all Apple-brand drives (especially internal drives) on all Macintosh models released with the last few years. They may or may not work, however, with third-party drives (although, again, it appears that they will work in the drives that come with Power Computing clones, for example). In any case, these discs can still be mounted as a non-startup disc on any Macintosh with a CD-ROM drive (Apple brand or not, internal or external).

To test a CD-ROM disc as a startup disk with 680X0 Macs, either select it as the startup disk from the Startup Disk control panel (and restart) or hold down the Command-Option-Shift-Delete keys at startup. In either case, if the method is successful, the internal drive should still automatically mount as a secondary disk (see "By The Way: The Internal Drive May Still Mount When Using Command-Option-Shift-Delete," later in this main section). I have found that these techniques may fail to work, however, if you have an external hard drive with a System Folder on it; in this case, the external drive becomes the startup disk. To work around this (assuming that you must start up from the CD-ROM disc), you will need to start up with the external drive off or disconnected from the SCSI port.

With Power Macs the situation is improved, but not entirely foolproof. Apple initially claimed that these machines should start up from a CD-ROM disc as long as the latter is in the drive at startup (similar to how startup floppy disks work), regardless of the control panel selection or external hard drive. Apparently this does work in some instances (especially with Power Computing's Mac clones), but Apple now says you should hold down the "C" key immediately at startup to get a Power Mac (or 630 series Mac) to recognize a CD-ROM startup disc. In either case, with this technique, it is much easier to use these discs as startup disks in emergencies, such as when your startup hard drive crashes.

Power Book 1400s are an exception. The "C" key technique does not work. You must use the Command-Option-Shift-Delete method instead.

There are other potential problems with using a CD-ROM startup disc on a Power Mac. The CD-ROM may not eject when you shut down the Mac, perhaps causing it to be the startup disk again when you restart. If this happens, you can get the disk to eject by holding down the mouse at startup, just like for floppy disks. You can also press the eject button immediately at startup. If you have any problems restarting a Power Mac that had just previously used a CD-ROM as a startup disk, doing a soft restart (by holding down Command-Control-Power) or pressing the Reset button should cure the problem.

The Startup Disk Control Panel: Changing the Default Startup Selection

You can change the Macintosh's default startup disk by using the Startup Disk control panel. After opening the control panel, simply click on the icon for the disk you want to assign as the startup disk—you could use this, for example, to switch the default from your internal to your external drive. The selected disk will be used as the startup disk the next time you restart (assuming that there is a valid System Folder on the selected disk).

This control panel lists all mounted hard disks and CD-ROM discs. Thus you can use it to select a CD-ROM startup disc to be the startup disk on almost any Mac, not just Power Macs (but see "Take Note: CD-ROM Startup Discs," for some possible problems here).

If the selected disk is not present at startup (for example, if it is an external drive that is no longer connected, or a CD-ROM disc that is not reinserted at startup), the Macintosh will return to its default search procedures.

Finally, don't confuse this control panel with the Startup Items folder, which contains *files* that you want to be automatically opened at startup. The Startup Disk control panel is used to select a particular *disk* to be the startup disk.

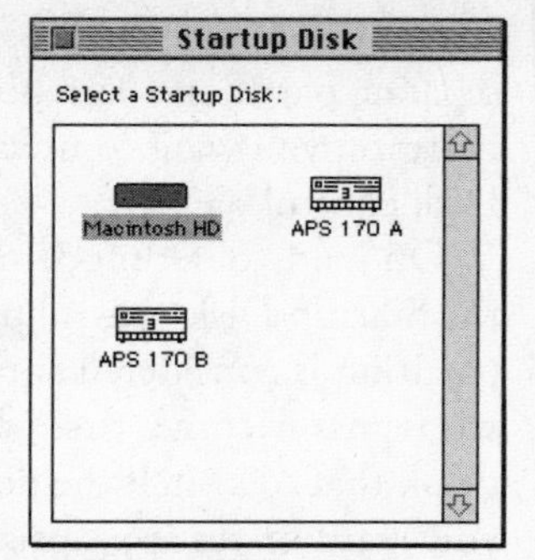

Figure 5-4 *The Startup Disk control panel.*

TAKE NOTE ▶

WHERE IS MY EXTERNAL HARD DRIVE?

A common use of the Startup Disk control panel is to switch the startup disk from an internal hard disk to an external one. I suppose it is obvious that the external drive must be turned on before you can make this switch. Unlike internal drives, however, external drives usually have a power supply that is separate from the Macintosh, and so they typically need to be turned on separately.

Ideally, an external drive should be turned on at least a few seconds before you start up the Macintosh itself. Otherwise, the drive may not have warmed up enough for the Macintosh to recognize its presence when the computer checks for startup disks. If your only possible startup drive is the external drive, the Macintosh will eventually locate it and start up from it. If the drive is not warmed up, however, the Macintosh recycles its search for a startup disk, stopping at the first one it finds and uses it as the startup disk. If you have an internal drive that has a valid System Folder on it, it will start up from that drive instead, despite what you have selected from the Startup Disk control panel. In such a case, the external drive probably will not even appear on the desktop when the startup sequence is over.

If this happens, just restart the Macintosh, and it should start up from the external drive as expected.

By the way, there is a converse situation where the internal drive does not mount when the external drive is the startup disk (see "Starting with an Alternate Startup Disk").

The Startup Disk control panel cannot be used to assign a floppy disk as the default startup disk. If a floppy startup disk is present, though, it is selected as the startup disk in preference to any hard disk, regardless of the setting in the Startup Disk control panel. The Startup Disk setting is retained and will be used the next time you start up without a floppy disk present.

System 7.5.3 Alert: There was a bug in the initial release of System 7.5.3 that could result in the Macintosh not recognizing the selection you made from the Startup Disk control panel. To fix this, Apple created the Startup Tuner extension, included as part of the System 7.5.3 Revision 2 (and later built into System 7.5.5 and later revisions).

Partition Alert: On most recent Mac models, if you have divided a hard disk into separate partitions (and both partitions contain System Folders), you can select which partition you want to use as your "startup disk" by making the selection in the Startup Disk control panel.

On many older models (and maybe even some newer ones), however, you cannot use the Startup Disk control panel to select which partition is used as the startup disk. One partition is considered automatically to be the default startup partition, usually, the one whose name comes first when the partitions are listed in alphabetical order. You might think that to switch the default startup partition, all you would need to do is rename your hard drives appropriately, but I have found this to be unreliable. In general, you can assume that the preferred partition is the one that appears at the top of the stack of icons on your desktop, regardless of their names.

If you want to start up from a non-default partition and the Startup Disk control panel doesn't let you do it, there are a number of things you can try. The most reliable method is available if your disk formatting utility has an option to let you assign which partition is to be the startup partition; Apple HD SC Setup and Drive Setup do *not* have such an option. A quicker method, which almost always works, is to select the desired startup partition via a freeware utility from Apple called System Picker. Just launch it and select which partition you want to use. (By the way, System Picker modifies your boot blocks. If you have used any other utility to change your boot block data, as is discussed occasionally in other parts of this book, System Picker will erase those changes.)

If you still are unsuccessful, go to the partition that you want to remove as the startup disk and place the Finder in another folder (such as in the Control Panels folder). This "unblesses" the System Folder. Now, when you select the disk from the Startup Disk control panel, the remaining "blessed" partition should act as the startup disk. If you really don't care to save the System Folder, you can even delete it entirely. (If you have more than two partitions, you may have more work of this sort to do.)

None of these methods is guaranteed to work, but I have had success with them. Much of the variation in success seems to depend on differences among different disk drivers (see Fix-It #12). You'll have to experiment a bit to see what works for you.

Starting with an Alternate Startup Disk

If you are having any problems starting up your Macintosh, you should try to restart the Macintosh using an alternate startup disk. If the problem is specific to the original startup disk rather than the Macintosh hardware, you should be able to start up successfully with the alternate disk. I'm assuming here that your normal startup disk is a hard disk, either internal or external.

Start Up with an Alternate Hard Disk

If you have two or more hard disks (including any removable cartridge drive, such as a Zip drive) connected to your Macintosh, and you are unable to start with the one you normally use as the startup disk, you can try to switch to one of the other ones (assuming it has a valid System Folder).

There is one problem, though, with using an alternate startup disk. Since the Macintosh will not start up with your current settings, you cannot access the Startup Disk control panel to change the default startup disk.

What to do:

Bypass the Internal Drive If your current startup disk is your internal hard drive, and you have at least one external hard drive, you can bypass the internal drive at startup and attempt to start up from an external hard drive instead. To do this:

1. Restart your Macintosh, typically by using the Reset button (I'm assuming here that a system error is preventing a normal restart).

   SEE: • Chapter 4 for more details on restarting

2. Hold down the Command-Option-Shift-Delete key combination immediately after restarting. Hold these keys down until the "Welcome to Macintosh" screen appears, then release the keys. The Macintosh should now start up from the external drive (assuming it has a System Folder on it). If you have partitions on the disk that each have separate System Folders, see the "Partition Alert" in the previous section of this chapter for more information.

Note: Using Removable Cartridge Drives With removable cartridges, you may also have problems with the cartridge automatically ejecting when you restart (such problems are more likely if you use the Restart command rather than Reset). If the cartridge does eject, you may be able to re-insert it quickly enough for the Mac to recognize it as a potential startup disk.

Otherwise, consult your drive's documentation for specific advice on what to do. For example, with the APS SyQuest drive that I have, I can use the APS PowerTools software to define whether the cartridge will eject at Restart and/or at Shutdown.

Bypass the External Drive If your default startup disk is an external hard disk and you also have an internal hard disk, bypassing a default disk that won't start up is even simpler. If you restart the Macintosh with the external drive turned off, The Macintosh should start up from the internal drive. When startup is complete, turn the external drive back on.

Mounting the Problem Drive With either of the above methods, the bypassed disk will not appear on the desktop when startup is finished (though see "By the Way: The Internal Drive May Still Mount When Using Command-Option-Shift-Delete"). To get it to appear, you have to mount it manually. There are several control panel utilities you can use to do this.

One popular such utility is a control panel called SCSIProbe. To mount disks manually with it is usually as simple as clicking a Mount button. If SCSIProbe fails to work, you will probably have to use a repair utility to mount the disk.

SEE: • "A Hard Disk Won't Mount," later in this chapter, for more details
• Fix-It #16 for more on SCSIProbe, especially on using it to mount disks at startup

BY THE WAY ▶

THE INTERNAL DRIVE MAY STILL MOUNT WHEN USING COMMAND-OPTION-SHIFT-DELETE

Typically, when you use the Command-Option-Shift-Delete (COSD) technique to bypass an internal drive at startup, the internal drive does not mount. If you try this with System 7.0.1 or later, though, the internal drive may mount. This is because a patch in the system software causes the Macintosh to do a second check for connected SCSI devices later in the startup sequence, mounting any devices that it finds. (This patch was intended to prevent large-capacity, slow-starting drives from being bypassed during a normal startup.) When you use the COSD shortcut, the result is that the drive mounts at the second check. Whether or not this happens to you depends on which Macintosh model you are using and the size of your hard disk. (There is also a way to accomplish a similar effect with any Macintosh by using SCSIProbe, as described in Fix-It #16.)

Normally, if this happens to you, it is not a problem, as you would just as soon have the internal drive mount anyway. However, if it is important not to have the internal drive mount at startup (because it precipitates a crash, for example), you can still bypass the internal drive altogether. The way to do this is to both reset (or "zap") the Parameter RAM (PRAM) and use the COSD shortcut. This works because the second check uses information about connected SCSI devices that is stored in the PRAM; if it is zapped, the Macintosh does not find the information needed to get it to load at startup.

Specifically, hold down the Command-Option-P-R keys at startup until you hear the startup tone for a second time (this resets the PRAM), then immediately hold down the Command-Option-Shift-Delete keys. This technique supposedly does not work on the Quadra 700.

SEE: • Fix-It #11 for more on zapping the Parameter RAM

Start Up with an Emergency Floppy Disk

For many users, their startup hard disk is their only hard disk. If it fails to start, the alternative is to use a startup floppy disk (or a startup CD-ROM disc, if available). Actually, though, in emergencies you may prefer to use a startup floppy disk (containing needed repair utilities) regardless of your hardware setup.

Here is where the default rules for selecting a startup disk help. Recall that the Macintosh uses a floppy disk as a startup disk if one is present, regardless of what hard disks are also present and what default rules are in effect. This automatically allows you to use a floppy disk as the startup disk simply by inserting it into your floppy disk drive at startup (with Power Macs, you can usually do this with CD-ROM startup discs if you hold down the "C" key at startup).

What to do:

Start Up from Your Emergency Disk Hopefully, you have already obtained or created such a disk. You obviously cannot create one on a Macintosh that won't start up!

SEE: • Chapter 2 for how to prepare or obtain an emergency startup floppy disk

1. Restart your Macintosh, typically by using the Reset button.

   SEE: • Chapter 4 for more details on restarting, if needed

2. *Immediately* after restarting, insert your emergency disk; the Macintosh should recognize it as the startup disk. If you wait too long to insert the floppy disk, the Mac will try again to start up from the problem hard disk—and you may have to begin all over again.

Bypass Hard Drives at Startup Even when you use a floppy disk as the startup disk, the Macintosh will still try to mount any hard drives that it finds during the startup sequence. Sometimes, the same problem that prevents a hard drive from acting as the startup disk will cause similar trouble when the Mac attempts to mount it as a secondary drive. In these cases, you need to bypass the hard drive entirely to prevent it from mounting.

To do this, use essentially the same techniques as described in the previous section. If you are using an external hard drive, turn it off before restarting with a floppy disk; after startup has completed, turn the external drive back on. For an internal hard drive, hold down the Command-Option-Shift-Delete keys while restarting.

Assuming the startup is now successful, you will find that the bypassed drive is not mounted on the desktop (that was the idea, after all). So you now need to mount it in order to try to fix the problem. Again, as described in the previous section, you can try to mount the disk manually. If this causes problems, other solutions, including using repair utilities to mount the disk, are detailed later.

SEE: • **"A Hard Disk Won't Mount," later in this chapter**

Solve It! When Your Macintosh Won't Start Up

Welcome to every Macintosh user's worst nightmare: you turn on your Macintosh, and nothing happens. Or maybe all that happens is that your screen turns dark except for a ominous-looking "sad Mac" icon. Or maybe you keep getting system crashes before the startup sequence is over.

If any of these things happens to you, don't panic. All is not lost—at least not yet. You are about to go on a tour of the startup sequence, stopping at every place where something can go wrong and learning what to do in each case. You will soon see that the vast majority of startup problems can be completely and easily fixed right from your keyboard.

The Macintosh Is Dead

Symptoms:

You turn on the Macintosh and absolutely nothing happens. There is no "bong," no whirring of the hard drive, no status lights going on, no nothing.

Causes:

This is such an unlikely occurrence that it often means something embarrassingly simple to fix is the cause (for example, your Macintosh is not plugged in). Otherwise, it does imply a major hardware failure, such as a dead power supply.

What to do:

Are All Cables Plugged In and All Switches Turned On?

Make sure all cords are securely plugged into their respective receptacles. I know, this seems almost too elementary to include, but check just the same. If you are using an outlet that is controlled by a wall switch, make sure the switch is on. If you are using a separate power strip, press its reset button.

If you are starting the Macintosh from the keyboard Power key, make sure that the keyboard cable is actually connected to the Macintosh (to be safe, though, turn off the Macintosh before attempting to reconnect any cables). If your model of Macintosh requires that an on/off switch be on before the keyboard button will work, make sure the switch is on.

Check the Battery

I discuss PowerBooks more specifically in Chapter 11. Obviously, though, one possible reason you can't start up from battery power is that your battery is dead. Plug the PowerBook into an AC outlet to see if it starts. If it does, your problem is specific to the battery; you will need to recharge it, or, if it won't hold a charge, replace it. If it is a relatively new battery and it won't hold a charge, check Chapter 11 for some other things to try.

For all Macs, check the internal battery on the Mac's logic board (see Fix-It #11 and #17). A dead battery can cause these symptoms.

Substitute Cables and Components

If you can start the Macintosh from the Power button in the rear of the unit, but not from the Power key on the keyboard, you should suspect a defective keyboard or keyboard cable. Try swapping the keyboard or keyboard cable (if you have a second one available) to see if that gets things moving. If it works, you have isolated the problem—

TAKE NOTE ▶

ADB PORTS

The keyboard is connected to the Macintosh via a port in the back of the machine called an ADB (Apple Desktop Bus) port. Most Mac models have two of these ports, although some PowerBooks have only one. If you are unable to get a response from the keyboard, try switching to the other ADB port. If it works, at least you can use the computer until you have time to get the broken port fixed.

SEE: • Fix-It #17 for more on ADB ports

be thankful it is not inside the Macintosh itself. The solution is to repair or replace the faulty component.

Is It Just the Monitor?

Sometimes, your Mac appears to turn on okay, but your monitor stays black. This obviously suggests a broken monitor, but some other possibilities exist.

SEE: • **Chapter 12 on AppleVision monitors**
• **Fix-It #17 on hardware problems**

Visit the Repair Shop

If nothing works, or if you have already determined that you have a hardware problem, take your Macintosh to an authorized service location to have it checked out. Sometimes professional help is the only answer.

SEE: • **Fix-It #17 for more on diagnosing hardware repairs**

Sad Macs and Unusual Startup Tones

 **Symptoms:**

The Sad Mac Icon

When you start up, the screen turns black except for the (frowning) sad-Mac icon in the center. It is the inverse of the happy Mac that normally appears.

Figure 5-5 *The sad-Mac icon appears above a sequence of numbers (and/or letters A through F; it's hexadecimal code)—sort of an "Unwelcome to Macintosh" greeting.*

Unusual Startup Tones

A sad-Mac icon is typically accompanied by unusual startup tones (that is, tones other than the ones you normally hear almost immediately after turning on or restarting your Mac). These tones have various pessimistic-sounding names, such as "Chimes of Death" or "Chords of Doom." It may be a single note, a chord, a progression of as many as four notes, or the sound of a car crash (new to Power Macs).

A Sad Mac may occur without unusual startup tones, just as these tones may appear without a Sad Mac occurring. In any of these cases, though, all progress comes to a halt. The startup process stops.

 **Causes:**

These symptoms occur when the Macintosh's initial diagnostic tests discover a problem that prevents the startup from continuing.

You may have heard that a sad Mac only happens if you have a serious hardware problem. This is a myth. The truth is that the vast majority of sad-Mac problems are either software problems or minor hardware problems (such as replacing a cable) that you can fix yourself.

Sometimes, though, a sad Mac does signal a serious hardware problem with your Macintosh. The damage could be to the Macintosh itself (that is, to a component of the main logic board), a card or memory chip plugged into the main logic board, a disk drive (especially if it is your startup hard disk), or any other peripheral SCSI device. In rare cases, a stuck Interrupt switch may be the cause.

Software damage to the Directory area of the disk could also lead to a sad Mac. Other, less ominous causes include a non-system disk in the default startup drive or an incompatible System file on the startup disk.

In general, if the Macintosh can start up from another disk than the one that first caused the sad Mac, you probably do not have a hardware problem. Conversely, if the sad Mac appears immediately after turning on the power—in other words, even before the Macintosh tries to access a disk—you most likely *do* have a hardware problem.

What to do:

Decode the Message

Sad-Mac Codes Decoded If you have already read the chapter on system errors, you know that I don't recommend wasting much time trying to interpret the error ID messages. The same is generally true for the string of letters and numbers that you find underneath the sad-Mac icon, although there are a couple of exceptions.

Beneath the Sad Mac should be two rows of eight digits (the code is in hexadecimal format, which means that the digits can range from 0 to 9 and A to F). Check out the last digit of the first row. If it's an F, it almost certainly means that your problem is software related. Sad Macs caused by software problems are most often accompanied by an arpeggio-like four-note startup tone. These are all good signs because, as you will see shortly, they suggest that you can probably fix the problem yourself. If you have a Mac Plus or older model, there will be only one row of six digits. In this case, a likely software problem is indicated if the first two digits are 0F.

Otherwise, the problem probably involves your hardware. In particular, the most common hardware cause for the appearance of the sad-Mac icon is a problem with memory chips (SIMMs or DIMMs). This is especially likely if the sad Mac first appeared soon after you added memory to your machine. Some error codes specifically indicate a memory module problem; in some cases, they even suggest in which slot the problem memory module is located (though I won't be going into this level of detail here). Table 5-1 lists a few of the more common or more easily interpreted codes.

How Soon After Startup Does the Sad Mac Appear? In addition to the sad-Mac code itself, you can sometimes glean useful information by noting the exact moment that the sad Mac appears, which can indicate what diagnostic test failed. For instance, the Macintosh's logic board and the SIMM/DIMMs are among the first items tested, so if a sad Mac appears almost as soon as you turn the Macintosh on, a problem with one of them is the likely cause. On the other hand, if the sad Mac appears shortly after the hard drive begins to start working, a problem with the hard drive or with the SCSI connections is more probable (though software causes are possible here, too). If the sad Mac appears even later in the startup sequence (such as after the "Welcome to Macintosh" or "Mac OS" message appears), software problems are by far the most likely cause. These problems are also the ones most likely to have the error codes that end with an F on the first row.

Table 5-1 Some Common Sad-Mac Error Codes*

ERROR CODE**	WHAT IT MEANS	WHAT TO DO
xxxx0001 xxxxxxxx	ROM test failed. The Macintosh ROM has a problem.	Take the Macintosh in for repair.
xxxx0002 or xxxx0003 or xxxxxxxx xxxxxxxx xxxx0004 or xxxx0005 xxxxxxxx xxxxxxxx	RAM test failed. At least one SIMM/DIMM is defective or not seated properly.	Check if SIMM/DIMMs are inserted correctly. Otherwise, if possible, get a replacement SIMM/DIMM and use it to replace existing modules to determine which one is defective. Replace the defective module if you find it. Otherwise, take the Macintosh in for repair.
xxxx0008 xxxxxxxx	ADB failed. ADB refers to Apple Desktop Bus; these are the ports where the mouse and the keyboard connect to the Macintosh. Either an ADB device or the ADB section of the logic board is defective.	Check if ADB devices are correctly plugged in. Otherwise, take the Macintosh and all ADB devices in for repair.
xxxx000A xxxxxxxx	NuBus failed. This refers to the special NuBus cards (such as graphics cards) and the NuBus slots on the logic board that hold these cards. A NuBus card or a NuBus slot is defective. [Note: I am not sure how this error code might apply to PCI cards.]	If you can, try removing the NuBus cards one at a time to see if that solves the problem. If so, the faulty NuBus card needs to be replaced. Otherwise, take the Mac in for repair.
xxxx000B xxxxxxxx	SCSI chip failed. The section of the main logic board (that controls the SCSI port and the devices connected to it) is defective.	Take the Mac in for repair.
xxxx000C xxxxxxxx	Floppy drive chip (called IWM chip) failed.	This is more likely a problem with the chip on the logic board that controls the floppy drive than with the floppy drive itself. You can check Fix-It #17 for some suggestions on fixing floppy drives, but most likely the Mac will need repair.
xxxx000D xxxxxxxx	Chip controlling the serial and modem ports (called SCC chip) failed.	Guess what? You will most likely need a hardware repair.
xxxx000F 00000001	Bus error. Most likely a software error.	Try solutions indicated in text.
xxxx000F 00000002	Address error. Most likely a software error.	Try solutions indicated in text.
xxxx000F 00000003	Illegal instruction. Most likely a software error.	Try solutions indicated in text.
xxxx000F xxxxxxxx	Most likely a software error.	Try solutions indicated in text.

* *Codes are different for Mac Plus and older models and for the Macintosh Portable; other special codes exist for PowerBooks and Power Macintoshes. Apple Tech Info Library files are available that give more details (see Fix-It #18 for how to access these files).*

** *An "x" in the codes listed here means any digit from 0 to 9 or A to F.*

Error Tones Decoded The exact notes and pattern of unusual startup tones are often indicative of the cause of the problem. Trying to learn how to make use of this information, however, is probably more trouble than it is worth. This is because Apple keeps changing both the startup tones as it comes out with different models, making useful generalizations practically impossible. First, for example, the sound that means a memory problem on AV Macs is not what you will hear if you have a memory problem on a Macintosh IIci. Even the normal startup sound varies widely on different Macintoshes. Second, interpreting some of the tones requires that you identify the note (such as whether it is a C or an F), which you may not be able to do. Finally, older Macintoshes (Macintosh SE and earlier models) do not have error tones. I don't recommend bothering to learn about the different tones.

Here's my best rough guide to interpreting these tones. A single note of a different pitch from the usual tone or any two-note sequence generally means defective SIMM/DIMMs. A four-note chord (or other unusual sound, such as a car crash) indicates an unknown problem that most often turns out to be software related (though a hardware cause remains possible).

If you have a PowerBook, an eight-note tone typically means a problem with a memory expansion card.

Helpful hint: Unless you are the type of person who enjoys memorizing the names of every episode of "Gilligan's Island," don't waste time trying to figure out what the different sounds mean. In the unlikely event that you confront this symptom, try the simple tests and possible fixes regardless of what sound you get. If they don't work, you're going to be taking your Macintosh in for repair anyway.

Restart the Macintosh

Restart Again with the Same Disk as a Startup Disk Maybe the sad Mac will vanish when you restart (but don't bet on it!). To find out, press the Reset button. If the sad Mac goes away, you can probably forget about it for now. If you really have a problem, it will return soon enough.

SEE: • **Chapter 4 for more details about restarting**

Restart with an Alternate Startup Disk If you do get the sad-Mac icon after your initial restart, it's time to try to restart with an alternate startup disk.

SEE: • **"Starting with an Alternate Startup Disk," earlier in this chapter, for more details**

By the way, if you were already trying to use a floppy disk as the startup disk, it may appear to be stuck in the drive (that is, it does not come out when you restart). If this happens, hold down the mouse button before you restart; continue to hold it down until the floppy disk ejects. If you also have a connected hard drive, your Mac should now try to start from this drive. If the software on the floppy disk was the problem, this may cure your sad Mac all by itself.

If the Macintosh Successfully Restarts from an Alternate Startup Disk

You probably have a software problem. As stated earlier, this is especially likely if the first line of the sad-Mac error code ended in an F. Fortunately, there are a number of solutions to try. The first three listed below only work if the problem disk appears as a secondary disk on the Finder's desktop after restarting; the remaining solutions are worth trying whether or not the problem disk mounts.

After each attempted solution, restart the Macintosh with the original startup disk to see if the problem is solved. Continue until one solution succeeds.

Reinstall the System Software You may have a corrupted System file. To check for this, reinstall a fresh copy of the System file or (even better) do a clean reinstall of the entire system software.

Upgrade the System Software If the version of the system software on your emergency startup disk is different from the version on the disk that generated the sad Mac, the problem may be specific to the system software version on your problem disk. In particular, you probably have an incompatibility between an out-of-date version of the system software and your current (presumably newer) hardware. In this case, the solution is to upgrade to a more recent version of the system software.

Most newer Macs will not run older versions of system software; for example, PCI-based Macs will only run on System 7.5.2 or later.

SEE: • Fix-It #1 on incompatibilities between hardware and software

Rebuild the Desktop Apple says this is worth trying, but I have never seen it work.

Zap the Parameter RAM I have actually seen this work, especially for problems with external drives.

Update the Disk Driver A sad Mac could also be caused by a corrupted or out-of-date disk driver. Try reinstalling the driver by using your disk formatting utility (such as Apple HD SC Setup). Upgrade to the latest version of the disk driver available.

Repair the Directory Your Directory files or boot blocks on the problem startup disk may have become corrupted. To repair this, use the appropriate utilities on your emergency startup disk(s). Start with Disk First Aid, and then try Norton Utilities, MacTools, or whatever comparable utility you have.

Even if the disk did not mount from the Finder, the more heavy-duty repair utilities, such as MacTools or Norton Utilities, may be able to mount it. If repairs fail, these utilities may still be able to recover files from the disk.

Check for SCSI Problems If the problem disk is an external SCSI-connected disk, you may have a problem with its connection to the Macintosh. The trouble may be with conflicting SCSI ID numbers, improper termination, or defective cables, or the SCSI device may need to be repaired. SCSI problems are particularly likely if the problem first appears just after you've added a new SCSI device to your computer.

In one special case, Apple reports that a sad Mac may occur if a removable-media drive is on at startup and a cartridge is present in the drive (this problem would seem to preclude using such a cartridge as a startup disk!). This is especially likely if you are using Macintosh PC Exchange.

SEE: • **"Technically Speaking: The Sad Mac Makes a Visit," later in the chapter**

Reformat the Disk If all else fails, this is your almost-always-successful last resort.

SEE:
- **Fix-It #1 hardware and software incompatibilities**
- **Fix-It #5 on reinstalling system software**
- **Fix-It #9 on rebuilding the desktop**
- **Fix-Its #10 and #13 on repairing damaged disks**
- **Fix-It #11 on zapping the Parameter RAM**
- **Fix-It #12 on updating the disk device driver**
- **Fix-It #15 on reformatting**
- **Fix-It #16 on SCSI problems**

BY THE WAY ▶

A SAD MAC WHEN USING AT EASE

Apple reports that a sad Mac might occur at startup if you are using At Ease for Workgroups 3.0 or 3.0.1 and the following conditions are true: (1) the At Ease administrator has set the "Lock startup volume" option, and (2) the Macintosh is equipped with an IDE internal hard drive and a recent version of the driver software. (This includes the PowerBook 190, PowerBook 2300, and PowerBook 5300 series computers.) If you attempt to start up from the internal hard disk, a Sad Mac will appear, you will not be able to get to the At Ease logon screen or to the Finder, and corruption of data is possible. This problem was fixed in version 3.0.2 of At Ease.

If the Macintosh Does Not Restart from an Alternate Startup Disk

This symptom is more likely to mean a hardware problem, but don't despair quite yet. Try the following steps.

Check for System Software Problems You may have an outdated version of the system software that is incompatible with your current hardware. Perhaps the software on your emergency startup disk is the same out-of-date version as on your normal startup disk, which is why you could not start up with either disk. (This is an unlikely possibility, but I mention it just for the sake of completeness.) In this case, you will need to obtain a set of system software disks for the most recent version and use them to update your system software.

SEE:
- **Fix-It #5 on updating system software**
- **"Technically Speaking: The Sad Mac Makes a Visit," later in the chapter**

Check for SCSI Problems You may have a problem with your SCSI devices and/or connections. Turn off your Mac, disconnect the SCSI cable from the back of the machine, and restart. If you restart successfully now (presumably from your internal drive or startup floppy disk), you have a SCSI-related problem. You may be able to fix this yourself, though ultimately it may require something as extreme as reformatting your external drive.

In one special case, Apple reports that a Sad Mac may occur if a removable-media drive is on at startup and a cartridge is present in the drive (which would seem to preclude using such a cartridge as a startup disk!). This is especially likely if you are using Macintosh PC Exchange.

SEE: • **Fix-It #16 for SCSI problems**

Check for Hardware Problems If all of the preceding efforts fail, you probably have a hardware problem. The most likely hardware cause is an improperly mounted or defective SIMM/DIMM (including L2 Cache memory). This is almost certain to be the case if the sad-Mac error code or startup tones indicate a SIMM/DIMM problem.

If the problem is a loose or improperly mounted SIMM/DIMM, you may be able to solve this yourself by reseating the SIMM/DIMM chip in its respective slot on the main logic board inside the Macintosh. If the small clip that holds the SIMM/DIMM in place (on some models of Macintosh) is broken, this clip will need to be replaced. Otherwise, you probably have a defective SIMM/DIMM that itself will need to be replaced.

TECHNICALLY SPEAKING ▶

THE SAD MAC MAKES A VISIT

Here are two cases of Sad Mac problems I have had. Neither involved hardware problems. The first was solved almost immediately; the second took more effort.

- I once tried to start up my Macintosh IIci with a 400K floppy disk that had an ancient System Folder on it. I didn't use my hard drive as a startup disk because I knew that the game on the floppy disk was incompatible with the system software on my hard drive. Unfortunately, the sad-Mac icon appeared rather than my game. After my initial shock, I noticed the "F" in the sad-Mac code, indicating a probable software problem. I assumed (correctly, as it turned out) that the System Folder on the game disk was incompatible with my hardware. Reluctantly, I accepted that the game was destined to be unusable on my machine.

  I gave up and hit the Reset button on the programmer's switch, intending to return to my hard drive as a startup disk, but the floppy disk did not eject. Instead, the Macintosh again tried to start from the floppy disk, and the sad Mac reappeared. To solve this problem, I held down the mouse button immediately after restarting, keeping it down until the floppy disk ejected. At last the Macintosh started up normally, using my internal hard drive as the startup disk.
- A sad Mac appeared the first time I started up my Macintosh after connecting a new external hard drive. The exact code was uninformative, other than suggesting a non-hardware cause (code = 0000000F; 00000001). Obviously suspecting the newly added hard drive as the root cause, I restarted with it off; sure enough, everything worked fine. I then turned the drive on and tried to mount it using SCSIProbe (as described later in this chapter and in Fix-It #16)—this led to a system freeze. Next I tried to mount it using MacTools (see Fix-It #13), which eventually succeeded, but only when I used its Load Emergency Driver option. At this point, the utility inexplicably rebuilt the desktop and then finally mounted the drive. I now used MacTools to recover whatever files I had on the disk that had not been previously backed up. MacTools finally identified the problem not as a damaged disk driver (see Fix-It #12) but as a bad partition map (a related "low-level" area of the disk). Reformatting the drive was necessary (as explained in Fix-It #15). After that the disk was fine, and the sad Mac never reappeared.

If you have a modular Macintosh, you can usually do most of this yourself by removing the lid of the Macintosh and directly examining the SIMM/DIMMs. Of course, I am aware that some readers of this book might not recognize SIMM/DIMMs if they saw them, and many others would not feel inclined to open up their Macintosh and start fiddling with the SIMM/DIMMs in any event. Many Macintosh users seek the help of others here. The most surefire alternative is to take your Macintosh to a qualified service technician to have it checked out.

SEE: • **Fix-It #17 for more on SIMM/DIMM-related and other hardware problems**

The "?" Disk Icon or a Reappearing Happy Mac

Symptoms:

The ? disk icon remains on the screen indefinitely, or the happy Mac icon appears, disappears, and reappears in an endless loop.

Figure 5-6 *The blinking ? icon—a sign of trouble if it does not quickly go away.*

Causes:

The most common cause is that the Macintosh cannot locate a valid startup disk. If so, the computer sits and stares at you with the blinking question-mark (?) disk icon, asking you to insert a startup disk and waiting until you do so. For example, this would happen if you turned on your Macintosh without a floppy disk inserted and with no hard drive connected.

If the ? disk icon persists even when a supposed startup disk is available, you have a more serious problem. Usually, the problem is with the startup hard drive. Either the disk is not connected properly (which can easily happen with an external hard drive), the software on the disk is damaged, or a hardware repair is needed.

A cycling happy-Mac icon indicates similar causes, especially damaged software. Other possible causes include incorrect SCSI connections or corrupted Parameter RAM.

What to do:

Try each of the following items, in turn, until one is successful in getting your Macintosh to start up. Remember to turn off all the devices before disconnecting or reconnecting any cables.

If Your Startup Disk Is an External Hard Drive: Check Connections

Make sure that the external drive is connected properly to the Macintosh. Make sure the drive is on and plugged in to a power outlet. Check that all cables are firmly connected. Restart.

SEE: • **Fix-It #16 on SCSI problems**

If Your Startup Disk Is an Internal Drive: Disconnect Any External SCSI Devices and Restart

Disconnect the SCSI cable from the back of your Mac. If this succeeds in getting your Mac to start up, you probably have either a SCSI connection problem or a hardware problem with one or more of your external SCSI devices.

SEE: • **Fix-It #16 on SCSI problems**

Check Indicator Lights

Most hard drives have one or two indicator lights on the front of the unit (the light is built into the front panel of the Macintosh if it is an internal drive). If there are two lights, one usually indicates that the drive is on, while the other only goes on if the drive is being accessed (reading or writing). If there is only one light, it is usually an access light. In either case, the light should go on—at least intermittently—at startup. If it does not, it means that the drive is not functioning (assuming that the light bulb itself is working okay!), and a likely hardware repair looms ahead.

Restart the Macintosh

Restart Again with the Same Disk as a Startup Disk Hopefully, the problem will disappear, in which case your troubles may be over. If it returns later, however, you may have an intermittent problem, such as *stiction.*

SEE: • **"A Hard Disk Won't Mount," later in this chapter**

Restart with an Alternate Startup Disk If the previous restart did not work, try restarting with an alternate disk, preferably a floppy disk. If this succeeds, continue to the next step.

By the way, if you are starting up from a floppy disk, you can still change settings of some control panels on your hard disk. For example, you could change the Startup Disk setting from an external drive (if that is its current setting) back to an internal drive for your next restart.

SEE: • **"Starting with an Alternate Startup Disk," earlier in this chapter**

Check for System Folder Problems

If you can get the Macintosh to start up with an alternate startup disk, check to see if the problem disk has mounted and is now present as a secondary disk (that is, its icon is shown below the startup disk icon on the Finder's desktop). Most likely it will be there. If so, check for the following problems (using the problem disk as the startup disk, restart the Macintosh after each attempted solution to see if the problem is solved).

Make Sure a System Folder Is on the Problem Disk Okay, presumably you already know that a System Folder is there. But just in case, check anyway. If there isn't one already there, install a System Folder and start again.

SEE: • **Fix-It #5 on installing system software**

Make Sure There Is Only One System Folder on the Disk Multiple System Folders (or, more technically, more than one copy of the System file and/or Finder) on your startup disk are not likely to cause startup problems, especially if you are using System 6.0.7 or later. Still, to be safe, it is good practice to delete all but the intended startup System Folder from your disk. If you are unsure whether additional System Folders are present, you can use the Finder's Find command and search for "Finder" or "System."

SEE: • Fix-It #5 on system software problems for more details

Bless the System Folder If Necessary Using the Icon View in the Finder, check to see if the System Folder has the mini-icon of a Macintosh on it; this is the indication that you have a blessed System Folder. The Macintosh typically does not accept a disk as a startup disk, even if it appears to have a valid System Folder on it, unless the latter is shown as a blessed System Folder.

SEE: • "Understanding the Startup Sequence," earlier in this chapter

Normally, all System Folders are blessed folders unless there is more than one on the same volume, as described just below. Occasionally, however, a problem may develop where an apparently valid System Folder is not blessed. For example, the utility System Picker unblesses otherwise valid System Folders. Similarly, if you remove the Finder or System file from a blessed System Folder, it will become unblessed; replacing these files will "rebless" the folder.

Also, an unblessed System Folder may be a warning signal that there is more than one System Folder on your disk. This is because a disk can have *only* one blessed System Folder on it, which is the one that the Macintosh actually uses when it starts up from that disk.

If the System Folder isn't blessed, open the System Folder to check if the essential files (System, Finder and possibly an Update file) are really there. If they are, remove the System file from the System Folder, then close the folder. Now open it again, replace the System file, and close the System Folder once more. This usually reblesses the System Folder. You should now see the mini-icon of the Macintosh on the folder.

Whether the mini-icon appears immediately or not, try restarting with this disk as the startup disk. The disk will most likely start up without further problems.

TECHNICALLY SPEAKING ▶

BOOT BLOCK PROBLEMS

Corrupted or incorrect data in a disk's boot blocks are the technical reason why an apparently valid System Folder may appear as unblessed. Such a disk does not start up properly.

In some cases, the procedure described here for blessing the System Folder fixes a boot block problem. Otherwise, you may have to resort to special utilities (such as Norton Utilities and MacTools) that repair boot blocks. If there is a boot block problem, these utilities find it, report the problem to you, and fix it. If they cannot fix the problem, your last resort is to reformat the disk.

SEE: • Chapter 8 on boot blocks and Fix-It #13 on disk damage for more details

Replace the System and the Finder If the previous steps have not worked, the System file, the Finder and/or the Update file may be damaged. TechTool and TechTool Pro are useful for checking for damage to these files. Otherwise, to be safe, just replace the files. You might also try replacing the Finder Preferences file.

SEE: • **Fix-It #5 for replacing system software**

Check for Startup Partition Problems

If your startup disk is divided into partitions, only one of those partitions can normally act as the startup disk. If you place a System Folder on another partition and try to select it as the startup disk (via the Startup Disk control panel), it will not work. In some cases (depending on your particular disk driver and especially if the only available System Folder is on the partition that cannot act as the startup disk), the result may be that you get the cycling happy Mac. If this happens, follow the steps listed here.

Select a Different Startup Disk First, start up from a floppy startup disk. Then, if needed, install a System Folder on the partition that *can* act as a startup disk. Next, select that disk (or any other valid startup volume) as the startup disk from the Startup Disk control panel. (If you had used System Picker originally, you may need to use it again to select a new startup disk.) Restart.

Update Your Disk Driver Switching to a different disk driver may eliminate this cycling happy-Mac problem altogether, allowing you to start up from the previously problematic partition. In general, however, you will keep these and other related problems to a minimum by using the disk driver from the utility that was used to format your disk and by using the same utility for all of your mounted volumes.

An incorrect or out-of-date driver can prevent startup even if the driver is on a secondary hard drive rather than the startup drive itself! All mounted drives should have correct drivers.

SEE: • **"The Startup Disk Control Panel: Changing the Default Startup Selection," earlier in this chapter, for more details**
• **Fix-It #12 on disk drivers**

PowerBook 150 alert: If you replace the hard drive that comes with a PowerBook 150 with another IDE hard drive, you will likely find that you cannot use this drive as a startup disk. The reason is that the PowerBook 150 reads the disk driver from its ROM and will not start up if there is another driver on the disk itself. To get things to work, you must format the disk with the Internal HD Format utility that came with the 150. Unfortunately, if your new disk is already formatted, Internal HD Format will refuse to work. So any new hard drive you purchase must be completely unformatted, or you can use a utility such as Norton Utilities to zero out the boot blocks and partition map. Either solution will allow the disk to be reformatted.

SEE: • **Fix-It #15, on formatting your disk, for more details**

Zap the PRAM

Parameter RAM (or PRAM) is a special type of memory that is preserved by a battery inside the Macintosh even after the computer is shut off. Some of the data stored in PRAM relate especially to SCSI connections. If the data stored in PRAM become corrupted, they can prevent a hard disk from mounting properly. Zapping the PRAM restores the data to their default value and should solve this problem.

SEE: • **Fix-It #11 on zapping the Parameter RAM**

Battery Problems

There have been reports that if the battery installed on the logic board of your Mac (the one that maintains the PRAM settings etc.) goes dead, you may lose not only your PRAM settings but the ability to start up your Mac at all. Fortunately, replacing the battery fixes the problem, so no major repair is needed.

On some Macs, a dead battery may result in a normal startup except that the monitor display remains black. If this happens, try zapping your PRAM. If the video comes back, you probably need to replace the battery.

See: • **Fix-It #11 for more on zapping the PRAM and replacing batteries**
• **Chapter 12 for related issues specific to AppleVision monitors**

Make Disk Repairs

If none of the preceding solutions worked, or if the problem disk did not mount when starting up with the alternate disk—or if you could not start up at all when using an alternate disk—try the following steps.

"Repair" and Defragment the Disk If you get the blinking question-mark icon as soon as you restart after a system crash (or some other improper shutdown), you may have something called the Disk Check bug. What is happening is that the Macintosh's startup diagnostics are mistakenly reporting a damaged disk, even though the disk is fine.

To fix this, use a repair utility, such as Disk Doctor (Norton Utilities), to "repair" and mount the disk. This disk will now work normally.

To prevent this from happening in the future, defragment your disk. Continue to defragment it on a regular basis.

To see if you are even susceptible to this particular bug, run a freeware utility called Disk Bug Checker. Supposedly, this problem has been fixed altogether in System 7.5 and subsequent revisions.

SEE: • **Fix-It #8 on defragmenting disks**
• **Fix-It #13 on repairing disks**

Last Resort If none of the previous solutions worked, check for other disk damage, corrupted data, or a hardware problem. For starters, try running Disk First Aid.

SEE: • **"A Hard Disk Won't Mount," later in this chapter**

The "X" Disk Icon Appears

Symptoms:

At the beginning of the startup process, the floppy disk is ejected, and a disk icon with an "X" in the center appears. You should see this icon only if you are trying to start up from a floppy disk.

If you do not have any startup hard disk connected to the Macintosh (a rarity these days), the blinking "?" disk icon returns, and the startup process halts.

Figure 5-7 *The "X" disk icon usually means that there is no System Folder on a floppy disk.*

Causes:

This is usually no cause for concern. It simply means that the Macintosh did not find a valid System Folder on the floppy disk and so could not start up. The disk is otherwise likely to be a normal, undamaged Macintosh disk.

This has become a relatively rare problem, since few people use a floppy disk as a startup disk anymore (except in emergency or other special situations). Normally, if you do get this icon, it is because a floppy disk was unintentionally present in a drive at startup.

What to do:

Do Nothing ... At First

If you have a startup internal or external hard disk connected to your Macintosh, the Mac will start up normally from the hard disk after ejecting the floppy disk.

If you do not have a hard disk connected, you need to start up with an alternate startup floppy disk.

SEE: • **"Starting with an Alternate Startup Disk," earlier in this chapter**

Check the Problem Floppy Disk Once startup is complete, reinsert the problem floppy disk, ejecting the alternate startup floppy disk if necessary.

Check for a System Folder There almost certainly isn't one, but check anyway. If there is no System Folder and you want one on the disk, install one. Try to start up from the disk again; it should work.

SEE: • **Fix-It #5 on installing system software**

Make Sure the System Folder Is Blessed If there is a System Folder, you do have some problem with the disk. Assuming that the System Folder is a recent enough version to work on your Mac, it may simply be that the System Folder is not blessed. To check for this, follow the guidelines described previously for blessing System Folders. Most of the time, if it is a valid System Folder with no damaged files, simply opening and closing the folder should get it blessed.

SEE: • **"The "?" Disk Icon or a Reappearing Happy Mac," earlier in this chapter**

Check for Disk Damage For more general advice on problems with floppy disks, including dealing with a possibly damaged disk, see "A Floppy Disk Won't Mount," later in this chapter

A System Error Occurs Just Prior to or While "Welcome to Macintosh" Appears on the Screen

Symptoms:

A system error occurs while the "Welcome to Macintosh" (or "MacOS") screen—or any substitute startup screen you may use instead—is visible. The system error may be a freeze (where everything just stops dead), a crash (with the bomb message perhaps appearing), or a spontaneous restart (where the whole process begins again and crashes again at the same spot). A variety of other error messages are also possible.

If you get the system bomb error message at this point, the message may offer advice on how to proceed next (for example, "To temporarily turn off extensions, restart and hold down the Shift key").

Certain startup management utilities, such as Now Utilities Startup Manager (as described more in Fix-It #4), will sometimes provide a special message alerting you to the problem when you restart after a startup crash caused by a startup extension conflict.

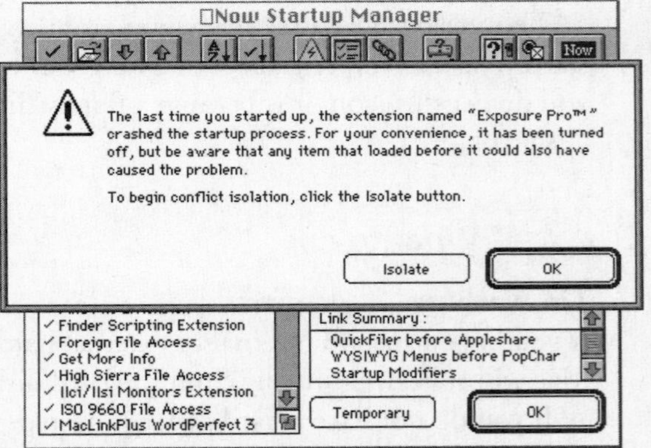

Figure 5-8 *A message at startup from the Now Utilities Startup Manager.*

Causes:

This almost always means a problem with a system extension or control panel that loads at startup (previously referred to as startup extensions). The loading of these files corresponds to the appearance of their icons along the bottom of the screen. Some problems may be caused by not having enough RAM to load all extensions and panels successfully (these may also lead to symptoms when the Finder is loading, as covered in the next section).

Otherwise, the problem is probably with the system software. In some cases, the PRAM may be corrupted. Occasionally, improper SCSI connections may be the cause.

A spontaneous restart at startup is most likely due to a startup extension problem. Otherwise, it may be due to more general causes as described later in this chapter.

SEE: • **"Problems with Restart, Shut Down, or Sleep," later in this chapter**

A Macintosh that requires a system Update or Enabler file will not start up successfully if it does not have the required file in the startup disk's System Folder. Actually, any time you try to start up with a version of software incompatible with your current hardware, you should get an error message informing you of this (in worse cases, you may get a system crash or a sad Mac instead).

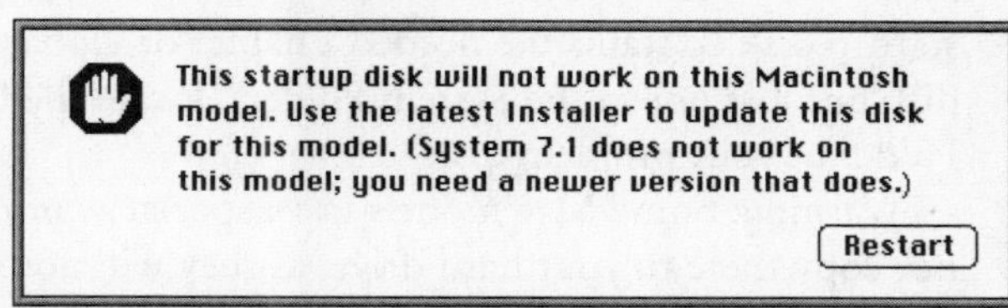

Figure 5-9 *This message, or one like it, may or may not mean exactly what it says. In this case, this message could appear even if you are using System 7.1 or later (see the main text for details).*

What to do:

Try each of the following solutions until you find one that works.

Do You Have the Correct and Latest Version of the System Software?

Suppose you get a message that seems to imply that you need to upgrade your system software: "This startup disk will not work on this Macintosh model. Use the latest Installer to update this disk for this model."

If you are using out-of-date system software (such as System 6 on a Macintosh that requires System 7), the obvious solution is to update it, as the message suggests.

A message like this, however, may also mean that your version of the system software is customized for a different Macintosh model than the one you are now using. For example, if you have an external drive with system software customized for a Quadra and then attach it to a PCI-based Power Macintosh, you will have problems. Once again, the solution is to reinstall the system software, using a version compatible with your current model (creating either a version just for the current Mac or a universal "any Macintosh" option).

SEE: • **Fix-It #5 on installing system software**

Oddly enough, you may get this message even when you are using the correct and latest version of the system software. If so, the appropriate Enabler or Update file is probably missing from your System Folder. You may not require an Update or Enabler file. It depends upon the specific Mac model and system software version you are using (as described in Fix-It #5). If you do need one of these files and it is missing, however, your Mac will not start up even if the remaining System and Finder software is correct.

In order to fix this, you need only to reinstall the needed Enabler/Update file itself. Here's what to do:

1. Press the Restart button in the alert box.
2. Restart from another startup disk (ideally, one with a System and Finder) that is known to work with your Mac, such as your Emergency Toolkit disk. If the alternate startup disk contains the needed Enabler or Update file (or if it is on your problem disk but just not in the System Folder), locate the file and copy it to the System Folder of your problem disk.

   Warning: Some Mac models use a special *minimal* Enabler on floppy disks. Do not copy these to your hard drive, as they will not work properly; skip to the next step instead.
3. If you do not have a handy copy of a needed Update or Enabler file for your system, you will have to go back and reinstall it from the appropriate system software (or System Update) floppy disks or CD.

   In some older versions of the system software, you may have a Custom Install option such as "Update Universal System" or "Updates System Software for Any Macintosh." Select this option. It will install the correct Enabler, as well as some additional control panels, but will not replace your System and Finder. Similarly, System 7.5 Update 2.0 has a special option just to install the Update file. Otherwise, you will have to do a complete update of the system software.

   SEE: • Fix-It #5 on installing system software

Test for a Startup Extension Problem

If missing or outdated system software does not seem to be the cause of your problem, restart with your startup extensions off (by holding down the Shift key at startup). When the "Welcome to Macintosh" screen appears, the words "Extensions Off" should appear as well. This means that you have bypassed the startup extensions, and you can now release the Shift key. If an startup extension was the source of the problem, you should now start up successfully.

BY THE WAY ▶

AN EXTENSION REFUSES TO LOAD IF YOU HAVE A NETWORK CONNECTION. WHY?

Though it is not actually a system error, you may have the following problem at startup: An extension (such as Now Toolbox from Now Utilities) may refuse to load because your Mac is connected to a network and it detects another copy of the program with the same serial number installed on another machine. This problem can occur even if AppleTalk is "not active"; it only requires that the LocalTalk cable be plugged into your Mac. While I am not recommending that you illegally try to defeat this form of copy protection, you can prevent these problems (assuming you have a legitimate reason for doing so) by restarting with the LocalTalk cable pulled out. You can safely reconnect the cable after the Mac has loaded the extension.

Determine the Problem Startup Extension

If the previous step indicated an startup extension problem, you'll now want to determine which extension is to blame. If you have several startup extensions, this may not be at all obvious.

SEE: • Fix-It #4 for more details on how to solve startup extension problems

Once you isolate the problem startup extension, just about the only solution is to stop using it (by removing it from your System Folder). You should then be able to restart successfully using the original startup disk. As explained in Fix-It #4, another possible solution may be to rearrange the loading order of the extensions. There may also be a newer version that corrects the problem.

Not Enough Memory

Not Enough Memory to Load All Extensions With the amount of memory that the latest versions of the basic system software require (and the growing number of extensions that are commonly used), even if you have 12MB or more installed in your Mac you may not have enough memory to load all of your startup extensions.

If this does happen, you may get a message such as this: "There is not enough memory to load all of your extensions... .To make more memory available, remove one or more extensions from the Extensions folder or reduce the size of the RAM disk and/or Disk Cache in the Memory Control panel, then restart your Macintosh." The advice here is sound. There is no specific startup extension that must be removed in this case; you should remove extensions from the System Folder one at a time until you no longer get this message. The amount of memory needed by startup extensions varies from one to the next, though, so be aware that one startup extension may require as much memory as three or four others combined. As a help here, some startup management utilities (see Fix-It #4 again) list the RAM usage of each startup extension.

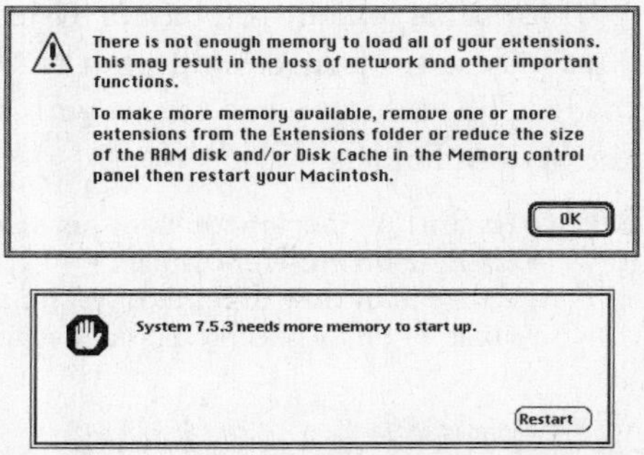

Of course, adding more physical memory—or using virtual memory, or a program such as RAM Doubler—may also solve this problem (see Fix-It #6).

Figure 5-10 *These messages may appear if you don't have enough memory to load all of your enabled startup extensions (or perhaps not even enough to load essential system software). If this happens, only those extensions that could load before you ran out of room will be active when startup is over—or you may not be able to start up at all!*

Note: The "There is not enough memory..." message has been reported to occur as a result of damaged preferences files for Apple Menu Options 1.0.2. The solution here is to delete the preferences file (which is located in the Preferences folder) and restart.

Not Enough Memory, Period In the most extreme cases, you may not have enough memory to start up successfully even with all extensions off. You may see a message at startup such as "System 7.5 needs more memory to start up."

In this case, especially if you have less than 12MB of RAM installed, you will almost certainly have to add more memory to your Mac to get things working. Using RAM Doubler or virtual memory might help in a pinch.

Otherwise, your only choice is to go back to an older version of the system software that requires less memory. Occasionally, reducing the number of sounds in your System file or fonts in your Fonts folder may help (you will need to start up from another disk first), but don't bet on it.

Zap the PRAM

Some of the data stored in PRAM relates especially to SCSI connections. If the data stored in PRAM become corrupted, it can cause problems with a hard disk mounting. Zapping the PRAM restores the data to its default value and should solve this problem.

SEE: • **Fix-It #11 on zapping the Parameter RAM**

Replace or Reduce System Software

If there is no startup extension or PRAM problem, and you seem to have enough memory, the system software may be damaged. Be especially wary of a System file that has suddenly increased substantially in size for no apparent reason. In this case, reinstall your system software; you can also use TechTool or TechTool Pro to check for System file damage.

If for some reason, you have a System Folder with a System file but no Finder, the Mac may start up successfully, but crash at the point that the Finder would normally be loaded. The solution is to restart with another disk and install a copy of the Finder into the System Folder.

SEE:
- **Fix-It #1 on incompatibilities between hardware and software**
- **Fix-It #2 on Preferences files**
- **Fix-It #5 for how to replace system software**
- **Fix-It #6 on increasing memory availability**

BY THE WAY ▶

CD-ROM DISKS THAT CAUSE STARTUP PROBLEMS

Some CD-ROM discs contain information on their first few tracks that make them appear to the Macintosh to be startup disks, even though they are not. If you start up with these discs inserted in the CD-ROM drive, a crash may occur. If this happens, manually eject the disc (by inserting a paper clip in the pinhole on the front of the drive) and then restart.

Check for Other Problems

If none of the preceding steps is effective, check for other file or disk damage, SCSI connection problems, or a hardware problem.

SEE:
- **"A Hard Disk Won't Mount," later in this chapter**
- **"By the Way: The Iomega Driver Extension could not load...," later in this chapter**

Problems While Launching the Finder and the Desktop

Symptoms:

The loading of startup extensions has completed, the "Welcome to Macintosh" screen has disappeared, and the Macintosh is now ready to launch the Finder and create the desktop. Just when you thought it was safe to start using your Macintosh, though, something goes wrong.

Typically, problems here are signaled by the appearance of an error message. The message may appear at any time from just prior to the appearance of the desktop to just before the end of the entire startup sequence (as the disk icons appear on the right side of the screen).

If the error occurs before the icon for the startup disk appears, the startup disk is the likely source of the problem. If it occurs after the appearance of the startup disk's icon but before you see the icon of any other disk that may be mounting (such as a second hard drive), the problem is probably with the secondary disk.

Possible error messages include: "Can't load the Finder," "The desktop file could not be created," "The disk is damaged," and "The disk <name of disk> needs minor repairs." More rarely, you may get a message that says that the disk is "unreadable" or "is not a Macintosh disk."

Occasionally, rather than an error message, a system freeze or system crash may occur, typically just before the startup disk icon would appear on the screen.

Causes:

Usually, the "Can't load the Finder" error message is a one-time glitch; the exact reason it happened may never be clear. If it recurs, you most likely have a defective Finder and/or System file.

The other messages may simply mean a problem with an extension that may be solved by reinstalling software or (conversely) deleting an extension. Otherwise, they typically signal damage to system software (including Preferences files) or to the Desktop and/or Directory files (the critical invisible files that allow the Macintosh to interact with the disk). Sometimes it is a SCSI-related problem.

SEE: • Chapters 2 and 8 for more details on these invisible files

What to do:

Can't Load the Finder

A message that says "Can't load the Finder" may appear near the end of a startup sequence (sometimes with a –41 system error ID code). Here are four potential solutions to this problem.

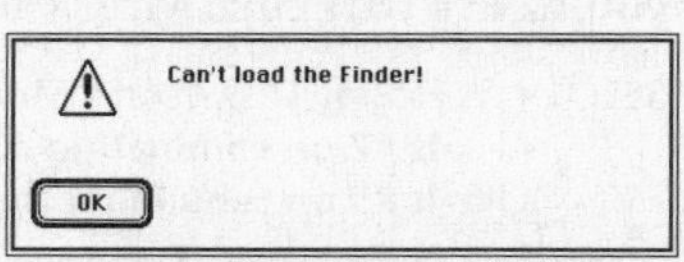

Figure 5-11 *If you get this error message, simply restarting the Macintosh usually solves the problem.*

Restart Restart the Macintosh (typically by using the Reset button), and wait to see if the Finder loads correctly on the next startup sequence. If the startup is successful, the problem may not recur. Otherwise, try restarting again with extensions off. This may succeed because it reduces the amount of memory needed by the system software, leaving more memory for the Finder.The bad news is that it may mean that you cannot use so many extensions without adding more RAM. If the problem still recurs even with extensions turned off, you need to start up using an alternate startup disk and proceed to the next potential solution.

Replace the Finder, System, and Update/Enabler Files Replace the Finder and the System file. Also, to be safe, replace or reinstall any Enabler or Update file (if one is needed).

SEE: • **Fix-It #5 on replacing the Finder and the System file**

Check for Disk Damage Use utilities such as Norton Utilities or MacTools. In particular, there may be a problem with the boot blocks, since they contain information that tells the Macintosh which file on the disk is considered the Finder.

SEE: • **Fix-It #13 on using Norton Utilities and MacTools**

Wrong Boot Block? If the problem disk is a copy of a floppy disk you made using the Finder, use a utility such as Disk Copy to make another copy. The Finder does not copy customized boot blocks to new disks, but Disk Copy will.

SEE: • **Chapter 2, "Take Note: To Make an Exact Copy of an Entire Floppy Disk"**

The Disk Needs Minor Repairs

A message saying "the disk needs minor repairs" doesn't occur often—in fact, it's so rare these days that I suspect it may have disappeared from current system software altogether. Just in case it does occur (usually with a floppy disk), though, here's what to do.

Click OK Clicking OK usually repairs the problem. If all goes well, the startup sequence is successfully completed, and your problem is over.

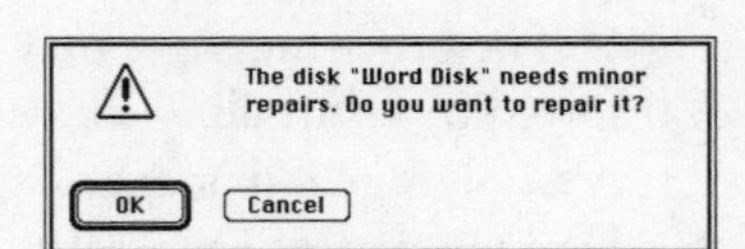

Figure 5-12 *Choosing "OK" here usually remedies the minor repair problem.*

Rebuild the Desktop Clicking OK to this message appears to fix minor damage to the Directory files, as well as make repairs to the Desktop file(s). So, if clicking OK failed to work, try rebuilding the desktop.

Check for Viruses If the minor repairs message keeps recurring, it may indicate that you have a particular virus called INIT-29. Run an anti-virus utility to check for this.

SEE: • **"A Floppy Disk Won't Mount," later in this chapter**
• **Fix-It #7 on eliminating a virus**
• **Fix-It #9 on rebuilding the desktop**

The Desktop File Could Not Be Created

Rebuild the Desktop If you get this message, the Desktop file may be damaged. Rebuilding it should fix the problem.

Note, however, that the Desktop cannot be rebuilt on a locked floppy disk; occasionally, this may prevent a locked disk from even mounting. The solution is to unlock the disk.

Check for Other Damage There may be damage to the Directory files or SCSI problems.

SEE: • **Fix-It #13 on repairing damaged disks**
• **"A Hard Disk Won't Mount" and "A Floppy Disk Won't Mount," in the following sections, for more general advice**

Other Unusual Messages at Startup

Sometimes when you try to open any window in the Finder immediately after startup you will get a message that says the window could not be opened because you are "out of memory." This can happen even if you seem to have plenty of free RAM available. While the long-term cause of this is not always clear (and it may ultimately involve damaged system software), a short-term cure is to use a utility, such as Conflict Catcher or Now Utilities, to increase the size of the system heap (as discussed more in Fix-It #6).

Here are some other error messages that may appear at startup. What to do about them follows each message in the list (although the solution is often self-evident from the message itself):

"*This disk must be unlocked in order to perform one-time housekeeping.*" Unlock the disk.

"*The 'System' file on the startup disk may be damaged. The Installer can be used to repair this disk.*" Replace the System file from your backups or do a clean reinstall of the system software (as described in Fix-It #5).

"*The System file on this startup device does not contain the resources necessary to boot this Macintosh. Please use the Installer to update the System file.*" Somehow, the System file in use was not created for use on your current hardware. You should do a clean reinstall; an ordinary install may not fix this problem.

Unreadable or Damaged Disk

A message that a disk is unreadable, not a Macintosh disk, or is damaged usually refers to a secondary disk mounted during the startup, not the startup disk itself. If the problem had been with the startup disk, something probably would have gone wrong earlier in the startup process.

For Unformatted Disks If one of these messages appears when you use a disk for the first time, the disk may never have been formatted. If so, format it. If it is a floppy disk, accept the alert box's offer to initialize it.

SEE: • **Fix-It #15 on formatting disks**

For Formatted Disks If the disk has been formatted previously, *don't* reinitialize the disk. If it's a floppy disk, you may simply be using the wrong type of disk drive for the disk. If so, the disk itself is still fine. Otherwise, for floppy or hard disks, try repair utilities to remedy the problem. Reformatting may ultimately be necessary.

SEE: • "A Hard Disk Won't Mount" and "A Floppy Disk Won't Mount," in the following sections
• Fix-It #15 on formatting disks

For RAM Disks This unusual situation is described in Chapter 11.

SEE: • "Technically Speaking: An 'Unreadable' RAM disk," in Chapter 11

Cursor Alternates Between a Watch and an Arrow (or All Icons in a Window Are Missing)

An alternating cursor usually happens when the Finder having a problem trying to display the contents of windows that are automatically opened at startup. Most of the time, the end result is a system freeze.

To solve this problem, restart and hold down the Option key until the Finder mounts (if you want, you can wait to press the key until just after the "Welcome to Macintosh" message disappears). Doing this forces the Finder to close all open windows; when startup is over, you should be able to reopen the windows without further symptoms.

A related symptom, basically due to the same cause, is if all the icons are missing from the display of an open window at startup. Sometimes just closing and reopening the window will solve the problem; if it doesn't, close the window again and restart the Macintosh.

For Any Other Symptom, Including System Errors

Try Restarting a Few Times See if the problem fixes itself. If the Macintosh restarts and things now seem normal, run Disk First Aid just to be safe. The utility may spot damage that was causing the problem.

SEE: • Chapter 4 for more on system errors
• Fix-It #10 on Disk First Aid

Rebuild the Desktop Restart the Macintosh and hold down the Command-Option keys until a message appears asking whether you want to rebuild the desktop. You will get a separate message for each disk to be mounted; click OK for the suspected problem disk(s).

SEE: • Fix-It #9 for more details on rebuilding the desktop

Insufficient Finder Memory Many of these symptoms can result from the Finder having too little memory. This has become a more common problem in System 7.5.5 or later. The solution is to increase the Finder's memory size (to at least 256K) using a utility such as Finder Heap Fix (as detailed in Fix-It #6).

A Problem with a Corrupted System and/or Finder One symptom that may result from a corrupted System and/or Finder is an empty alert box that appears and "shimmers," freezing your Mac. You are probably looking at a clean reinstall of system software to fix this (or at least a replacement of the System and Finder).

SEE: • Fix-It #5 on reinstalling system software

Delete the Finder Preferences File This file (located in the Preferences folder) may get corrupted and cause a variety of serious problems, including system freezes and crashes. Deleting the file will cause a new one to be created automatically, although you will have to redo customized changes you may have made (such as in the Views control panel).

SEE: • Fix-It #2 for more on how and why to delete the Finder Preferences file

Delete Other Possibly Corrupted Preferences Files I personally had a problem once where startup halted prior to the appearance of the Finder's menus and icons—only a blank menu bar and the desktop pattern appeared. A Force Quit (Command-Option-Escape) succeeded in getting the Finder to load, but the problem kept recurring unless I restarted with extensions off as well. Ultimately, I discovered that the problem was due to a corrupted Now Toolbox Prefs file (needed for Now Utilities); deleting the Prefs file (after starting up with extensions off) fixed the problem. Now Utilities is especially notorious for this sort of problems.

More generally, if you check for extension conflicts (using procedures as described in Fix-It #4) and isolate the conflicting extension, you may find that deleting the extension's preferences file (rather than replacing or disabling the extension itself) solves the problem.

A Problem with a Control Strip Module I had one case where a third-party Control Strip module, called Control PPP, caused a system freeze at startup. The true cause was somewhat hard to identify; my Startup Manager initially identified the problem as a triple conflict involving ATM, MacTCP, and Control Strip. When I saw Control Strip listed as a conflict, though, it occurred to me that a Control Strip module might actually be the cause. As I had recently added the Control PPP module, this seemed like a likely candidate to try. Sure enough, deleting it eliminated the problem.

Did You Deinstall At Ease Improperly? If you use Apple's At Ease program, it is important that you use its Installer utility to deinstall it. To do this, select the Installer's Remove option and click to remove the software. If you remove the At Ease extension any other way—such as by simply dragging it out of the System Folder—your disk will crash at startup. The other main solution at this point is to do a clean reinstall of your system software.

SEE: • Fix-It #5 on removing software and reinstalling system software

BY THE WAY ▶

AT EASE IS NOT ALWAYS THAT EASY

Why does removing At Ease without using the Installer cause a system crash at startup? Because At Ease modifies the boot blocks so that the Mac looks for At Ease rather than the Finder at startup. With At Ease gone, the Mac doesn't know what to start up with. Using the Installer to deinstall At Ease prevents this problem by altering the boot blocks appropriately.

On a related front, if you have password-protected your disk with At Ease and you forget your password, you can still start up with a floppy disk, then delete the At Ease Preferences file (in the Preferences Folder of the System Folder). This eliminates the password protection, allowing you to start up from the hard disk again. With the enhanced security options used by At Ease for Workgroups (a special version of At Ease for large multiuser environments), however, you can be prevented from accessing the At Ease startup drive even if you start up from a floppy disk.

Because At Ease accomplishes this feat by modifying the disk driver (similar to how most dedicated security utilities work), updating the disk driver used to eliminate this password protection. With current versions of At Ease for Workgroups, however, you need a special program called Unlock (which is included with the At Ease package) to gain access to the disk again. You will also have to call Apple to get a special password to unlock Unlock. If all of this should fail to work, you will need to reformat the disk to use it again.

There are numerous other problems associated with At Ease. Especially common are problems making copies of floppy disks from the Finder while At Ease is on; the program can also cause improper rebuilding of the desktop. If you are having such problems, disabling At Ease is a good way to begin looking for a solution.

More recently, Apple has reported several problems with At Ease for Workgroups on Macs that use IDE drives. Problems include possible sad Macs at startup and an inability to get At Ease's security features to work on Macs that have unpartitioned IDE drives.

Another issue of concern is that, with all versions of At Ease up to 3.0.2, you cannot prevent access to removable media (such as CD-ROM discs) from the Restricted Finder. If this is important, you need to upgrade to At Ease 4.0.

More generally, many problems with At Ease can be solved by throwing away the At Ease Preferences, At Ease Setups, and/or At Ease Users files. Deleting all of these files, though, will require that you re-create your custom settings. Otherwise, check the Read Me file that comes with At Ease (or its updater) for the latest information.

SEE: • **"By the Way: A Sad Mac When Using At Ease," earlier in this chapter**
• **Fix-It #12 on disk device drivers**

Check for Damage If these techniques do not work, you have to start up with an alternate startup disk. Then check for other disk damage (including media damage), corrupted data, or a hardware problem.

SEE: • **"A Hard Disk Won't Mount" and "A Floppy Disk Won't Mount," in the following sections**

Solve It! Generic Problems with Disks

A Hard Disk Won't Mount

Symptoms:

- A hard disk won't mount, even when it is not the startup disk. This is typically referred to as a *crashed disk*. Most often, no error message or any other indication of a problem occurs; the disk's icon simply does not appear on the desktop. The operation of the Macintosh otherwise proceeds normally.
- In some cases, an error message appears, indicating why the disk cannot mount. Most commonly, the error message appears that says the disk is damaged, is unreadable, or is not a Macintosh disk.
- In the worst cases, you may get a system crash.

Note: If the problem disk you are trying to mount is your current startup disk, thereby preventing you from starting up, begin in the preceding section.

SEE: • "When Your Macintosh Won't Start Up," earlier in this chapter

Causes:

The most common cause is damage to critical invisible files needed for the Macintosh to interact with the disk—the Directory and the device driver (see Chapter 8 for background on the Directory and related invisible files). Otherwise, if it is a new drive, the disk may not yet be formatted, or the drive may be incorrectly connected.

Hardware problems are also possible. This is especially likely if the hard drive appears to make less noise than usual, or if its indicator lights do not go on or flash as expected. Also suspect hardware damage if symptoms appear shortly after you've jostled a hard drive while it was in use.

What to do:

If an error message appears, skip ahead to the section relevant to that message. Otherwise, try the following steps.

Check Power and Connections

For external drives, make sure the drive is actually on and plugged in. Make sure all cables are firmly connected (remember to turn the Macintosh off before reconnecting loose cables).

Restart or Try to Mount the Drive Manually

If you are starting up from an internal drive and a secondary external drive did not mount automatically as expected, the problem may simply be that you did not turn the hard drive on in time for the Macintosh to recognize its presence. Similarly, external hard drives that are turned on after startup is over do not automatically mount. These problems are usually easy to solve—just select Restart, and everything should now mount as expected. In the future, remember to turn on the external drive a few seconds before turning on the Macintosh.

SEE: • **"Take Note: Where Is My External Drive?," earlier in this chapter, for more on this problem**

Otherwise, try to mount the drive manually. The easiest way to do this is to use a special control panel, such as SCSIProbe. Alternatively, you can usually use the formatting utility that came with your hard drive (except for Apple's formatting utility, Apple HD SC Setup, which has no mount function).

To use SCSIProbe, open its control panel window. Ideally, you should see the name of your hard disk present in its list, even if the disk was not mounted. From this window, click the Mount button. If this mounts the drive, your problems are probably over, and the drive should mount as expected next time.

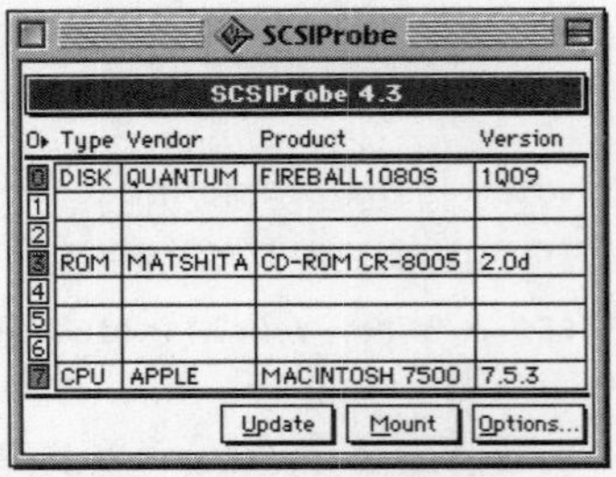

Figure 5-13 *SCSIProbe. Click the Mount button to mount a hard disk without having to restart the Macintosh.*

If SCSIProbe does not even indicate that your drive is present, you can try SCSIProbe's Update button to see if that gets the program to recognize the presence of your drive. If it does, click Mount to see if you can get the disk to mount. Again, if this works, your problems are over.

SEE: • **Fix-It #16 for more details on using SCSIProbe**

Check for SCSI-Related Problems

If you have external SCSI devices—and particularly if you have more than one—check for SCSI-related problems such as device ID conflicts and improper termination. The best way to start this search is by shutting down, detaching the SCSI cable from the back of the Macintosh, and restarting. If things now go well with all SCSI devices detached, suspect a SCSI problem.

Be especially suspicious of SCSI-related causes if you have made recent changes to your SCSI connections. In many cases, these problems cause a system crash at startup, typically just after the "Welcome to Macintosh" message appears.

Also, if you have more than one hard drive, Apple's official recommendation is that they all use the same device driver. This may require shifting to a new driver on one or more of your drives, or even reformatting disks. At the same time, though, I have never seen a problem result from ignoring this advice.

SEE: • **Fix-It #12 for more details on disk device drivers**
• **Fix-It #16 for details on these SCSI-related problems**

Special Case: Problems Mounting Removable Media Cartridges

A removable cartridge (like those used with SyQuest, Zip, or Jaz drives) should mount automatically when you insert it. My experience, however, is that this does not always occur. Success seems to depend on a variety of factors, including whether you started up with extensions on or off, whether certain options are selected from a SCSI mounting control panel (such as SCSIProbe or Drive7's Mount Cache), whether the drive was turned on prior to startup, and whether the cartridge was inserted at startup.

For example, one version of the APS PowerTools control panel (included with APS drives) had "AutoMount" and "Support This Device" checkboxes. Selecting these options should increase the odds that your cartridge mounts when inserted; check your utility's documentation for details. Remember, though, that no icon appears on your desktop until a cartridge is inserted in the drive. I have also found that when I select Restart, the cartridge may or may not automatically eject. If it does eject, be sure to reinsert it, or it will not reappear on your desktop when the restart is complete.

Occasional problems with an inserted cartridge that does not automatically mount can almost always be solved by mounting the cartridge manually. To do this, use a SCSI mounting control panel and click its Mount button. If you are trying to use a cartridge as the startup disk, make sure that the drive is on and the cartridge is inserted before you turn on your Mac. (Cartridges inserted prior to startup can sometimes be the cause of problems, however, including a sad Mac. So if you are unsuccessful in mounting a cartridge in this way, give up using it as a startup disk and insert it after startup is over.)

Problems mounting a removable cartridge can especially occur when you eject a cartridge and insert a different one. Problems are most likely to happen if the new cartridge uses a different disk driver than the previous cartridge (which can happen if they were formatted by different utilities). Control panels—again, such as SCSIProbe and Drive7's Mount Cache—are designed to solve these conflicts, either by getting the Mac to switch to the new disk's driver or by using a universal driver that works with virtually all formats. In the latter case (of which Mount Mache is an example), it is recommended that you do not have any cartridge inserted in a drive until after startup (otherwise, the driver contained on the disk is installed in memory instead of the control panel's universal driver; these may not be the same). Obviously, this makes it impossible to use the cartridge as a startup disk.

Definitely use one of these utilities if you are having problems mounting removable-media drives. As an immediate solution, simply restart.

By the way, Iomega's Zip and Jaz drives come with special software that enable you to attach these drives and mount cartridges in them, even on a Macintosh that has not had the Zip/Jaz Tools software installed. This is convenient for when you take your drive traveling for use on other Macs.

Finally, if you insert a cartridge and get a message that says it is "not a Macintosh disk," the disk may simply be a new unformatted disk. If so, do not click the Initialize button. This will format it improperly. Instead, use your disk formatting utility to format the disk.

If the disk is already formatted, you may have a damaged disk (see next section). SyQuest cartridges, in particular, are susceptible to damage from dust, which is why you should always eject them from the drive and store them in their case when not in use. *Never* open the cartridge's metal shutter.

SEE: • **Fix-It #12 for more details on disk device drivers**
• **Fix-It #15 on formatting disks**
• **Fix-It #16 for more on these SCSI-related problems (especially "Take Note: Mounting Removable-Media Cartridges with Different Drivers")**

BY THE WAY ▶

THE IOMEGA DRIVER EXTENSION COULD NOT LOAD ...

If you restart your computer with a Zip or Jaz cartridge already in the drive (for example, after a system crash), you may get a message such as "The Iomega Driver Extension (version 4.3) could not load because an older version (4.2) is already loaded." Yet your System Folder reveals that only version 4.3 is present. What's going on?

The answer is that there is a "hidden" copy of the driver on the Zip/Jaz cartridge. When (and only when) you start up with the cartridge inserted, its driver is loaded before the one in your internal drive's System Folder is checked. When the Macintosh reaches the one in your System Folder, you get the error message. As long as you don't require the new driver, no problems result from this happening; if you do, however, restart with the cartridge removed.

A long-term solution is to update the driver on your cartridge to the newer version. Fortunately, the latest versions of Zip Tools includes a utility called Iomega Disk Updater that allows you to do this without having to reformat—and thus erase—the cartridge. Version 4.3.2 and later also includes a utility (called Copy Machine) that allows you to copy the contents of one Zip or Jaz drive to another.

SEE: • **Fix-It #12 for more on updating a disk driver in general**

Check for Damaged Files and Disks (Disk Is "Unreadable" or "Not a Macintosh Disk")

If none of the previous solutions work, you probably have damaged files on the disk, most likely the Directory files. Damage is especially likely when you get the message that says that the disk is "unreadable" or "not a Macintosh disk." Check for possible damage with repair utilities, such as Disk First Aid or MacTools. You may also have the Disk Check bug (as described previously in this chapter, in the section on getting a blinking question mark on startup). If so, after the disk is repaired, defragment the disk.

SEE: • **Fix-It #10 and #13 on repair utilities**
• **Fix-It #8 on defragmenting a disk**

If these fail to work, round up the usual suspects (as listed below). Especially try zapping the PRAM.

SEE: • **Fix-It #7 on viruses**
• **Fix-It #9 on rebuilding the desktop**
• **Fix-It #11 on zapping the Parameter RAM**
• **Fix-It #12 on updating the hard disk device driver**

After you try each Fix-It, restart your Macintosh to check whether it has remedied the problem. Unfortunately, if the Finder cannot mount your disk, it probably means that most of these techniques will not recognize the drive either—but it's worth a shot.

Reformat

If all else has failed, reformat the entire drive and start over (but if you are desperate to try to recover unbacked-up files from your disk, check the next section before you reformat). After reformatting, assuming you have backup files, restore them to your disk.

With these sort of problems, it often pays to reformat even if previous attempted solutions seem to have fixed the problem. If you don't reformat, your problems may soon return.

SEE: • Fix-It #15 on formatting disks

Hardware Problems: Stiction and Beyond

If reformatting fails, you probably have a hardware problem. If you couldn't even begin to reformat because the disk showed no signs of life, you almost certainly have a hardware problem. In particular, suspect hardware trouble if the drive is making either unusual noises or no noise at all when you first turn it on. Similarly suspect a hardware problem if the hard drive's indicator light is not going on as expected or is not flashing on and off as it typically does.

Usually, a damaged hard disk cannot be repaired; it will need to be replaced. This can—and often does—mean the loss of all data on your disk. Even here, however, there are a few glimmers of hope.

Stiction This term refers to a hardware problem whereby the drive gets physically stuck at startup and is unable to reach its normal spinning speed—as a result, the Macintosh never starts up at all. As low-tech as it might seem, a sharp slap to the side of the drive case can sometimes get it going again. The problem will return the next time you try to start up, though, so immediately back up all your data if you succeed in getting the drive to work.

A stiction problem is most severe when the drive is first turned on. So, if you manage to overcome stiction temporarily, do not turn the drive off. The Mac will probably continue to run fine as long as you leave it on.

As with other hardware damage to a disk, stiction cannot be repaired. Replacing the disk is the only permanent solution. These temporary fixes, however, should at least allow you to recover any needed data from the disk before replacing it.

Power Supply For external hard drives, the problem may be in the power supply, a separate component from the disk itself. Once it is replaced, your hard drive will function normally again, and all data on your disk will still be there unharmed.

Otherwise... For internal drives, there is a slim chance that the problem is with the connection cable from the drive to the logic board. This should be fixable. Finally, if all else fails and you have important unbacked-up data on a damaged disk, try a repair shop that specializes in recovering data from problem drives. Some of these places, such as DriveSavers (1-800-440-1904), advertise nationally. You can mail them your drive, and they may succeed where you could not. Do this, however, *before* you try to reformat the disk.

SEE: • Fix-It #17 on dealing with hardware problems

A Floppy Disk Won't Mount

Symptoms:

Upon inserting a floppy disk into a disk drive, one of the following things happens:

- The disk drive makes no sound, as if it does not recognize that the disk has been inserted. Obviously, the disk does not mount.
- The Macintosh appears to recognize the disk and attempts to mount it, but ultimately a system freeze occurs.
- An error message appears informing you that the disk cannot be mounted. The most common messages say that the disk is damaged, unreadable, or not a Macintosh disk. Usually, you are given the option to initialize the disk.
- An error message appears telling you that the disk needs minor repairs.

Note that if you are trying to use the floppy disk as a startup disk, you should start with the section earlier in this chapter.

SEE: • "When Your Macintosh Won't Start Up" (especially the topic on the "X" disk icon), earlier in this chapter

Causes:

These vary depending on which of the symptoms you have. In general, similar to what was true for hard disks, the problem is usually due to damage to the files used by the Macintosh to recognize and interact with the disk, particularly the Directory. If the disk cannot be easily repaired, you have a *trashed disk.*

The problem can also be caused by physical damage to the disk or the disk drive.

TAKE NOTE ▶

IF YOU CAN'T GET A DISK TO INSERT

A disk that won't insert probably has a stuck or bent shutter (the metal piece at the bottom of the floppy disk). If it doesn't freely slide, it is stuck. If you can't free it, remove the shutter by bending it open, as if you are trying to straighten a paper clip. Then insert the disk and, if it mounts, immediately copy all data on it to another disk. Discard the problem disk.

If you know that your disk has a stuck or bent shutter, do *not* try to insert it into a drive without first removing the shutter. Otherwise, even if you succeed in inserting it, you may have even greater problems getting it to eject again. A disk with a bent shutter can even damage the drive itself.

What to do:

For the "Disk Needs Minor Repairs" Message

If you get an error message saying the disk needs "minor repairs," follow these steps.

Click OK The error message includes an OK button; click on it. This usually repairs the problem.

If Clicking OK Doesn't Succeed You may have a corrupted Desktop file. To check for this, you can completely delete it and create a new desktop (rather than simply rebuilding it), as explained in Fix-It #9. Otherwise, check for a damaged disk by using Disk First Aid and/or other repair utilities. Some viruses also will cause this message to appear, so check for virus infections using your anti-virus utility.

SEE: • **Fix-It #9 for more on rebuilding the desktop**
• **Fix-Its #10 and #13 on disk repairs**
• **Fix-It #7 on viruses**

For the "Disk Is Unreadable" or "Is Not a Macintosh Disk" Messages

You may also get error messages that say the disk is unreadable or is not a Macintosh disk. Typically, the alert box asks if you want to initialize the disk.

For Unformatted Disks The messages that the disk is unreadable or is not a Macintosh disk appear when you insert an unformatted floppy disk. This is perfectly normal. If this happens, simply click Initialize (or Two-Sided) to format the disk.

SEE: • **Fix-It #15 on formatting and Fix-It #5 on installing system software**

Figure 5-14 *The "Disk is unreadable" message from System 7.1 (top) and System 7.5 (bottom). Don't give up; your disk may be fine.*

For Formatted Disks If the disk has been formatted previously, don't reinitialize the disk! There may be nothing wrong with it, and reinitializing the disk loses any chance you have of recovering any data from it.

Click Eject instead, and then make sure you are using the right type of disk for the right type of drive. For example, do not insert an HD disk into an 800K drive; the drive cannot read HD disks, so it will treat all of them as unreadable, even if they are in perfect condition. If this happens, eject the disk and insert it into an HD drive. All will be fine. Copy the data to 800K disks, if desired. This is just one of several similar problems you may have with inserting a floppy disk into the wrong type of disk drive.

SEE: • **Fix-It #15 for the other reasons why a floppy disk may not mount**

Otherwise, proceed to "After You Eject the Disk," later in this section.

For PC (DOS)-Formatted Disks PC (DOS) computers can now use the same disks that Macintoshes use, but the formats are still different. If you insert a disk formatted for a PC machine, you will probably get the "unreadable" disk message. Again, don't initialize the disk, and don't ever try to repair it with any Macintosh disk repair utilities. Most likely, the disk is just fine, and anything you do to it will risk destroying its data. The solution is to use an extension such as Macintosh PC Exchange (now included as part of System 7.5.X). With this extension, a DOS disk will mount on the Finder's desktop just as if it were a Macintosh-formatted disk. Also note that PC Exchange (together with Macintosh Easy Open) will assist you in opening PC-format files that may be on the PC disk (see Chapter 6 for more on this).

By the way, even with Macintosh PC Exchange installed, the Mac will not recognize "improperly formatted" PC disks—in particular, double-sided (720K) disks formatted as HD (1.4MB) disks, or HD disks formatted as double-sided disks. In these cases, you need to go back to the PC machine and copy the needed files onto a properly formatted disk.

Finally, if you suddenly have trouble mounting PC-formatted disks and PC Exchange is installed properly, it may be that the PC Exchange Preferences file is corrupted. Try deleting it.

For "Disk Is Damaged" or "Disk Error" Messages If you get an error message saying the disk is damaged, it probably is. You may have a choice whether you want to eject the disk or initialize it. Alternatively, there may simply be an OK button to eject the disk, with no opportunity to initialize it.

Click Eject instead of reinitializing the disk. You may be able to repair the damage. Reinitializing it loses any chance you have of saving the disk or recovering any data from it.

Figure 5-15 *"Disk is damaged" (left) and "disk error" (right) messages. Don't accept the offer to initialize the disk.*

Proceed to "After You Eject the Disk," later in this section.

If No Error Message Appears

In some cases, you don't get an error message; the disk simply does not mount. The Macintosh acts as if you never inserted the disk.

Eject the Disk Try to eject the disk by pressing Command-Shift-1 (internal or lower drive) or Command-Shift-2 (external or upper drive). If you cannot get the disk to eject with this method, see "A Floppy Disk Won't Eject," later in this chapter.

After You Eject the Disk

Hope It's a One-Time Glitch Lock the disk (to protect against any possible further damage) and reinsert it. See if it mounts now.

Do this a few more times, if needed. Sometimes, a minor misalignment in the disk drive causes problems that disappear on the next insertion.

Floppy disk drives can get pretty finicky about what disks they accept. It might help to briefly shake the disk or rotate the metal circle on the back side of the disk before reinserting it. Since PowerBook floppy drives seem particularly prone to these types of problems, you may have success by inserting the problem disk into another Macintosh, mounting it, ejecting it, and then reinserting it into the PowerBook.

If reinserting succeeds in mounting the disk, your disk may be okay, but it's also possible that you have media damage on the disk. Especially if the problem occurs repeatedly with the same disk (and not with others), copy its files to another disk and then repair or replace the problem disk, as described shortly.

Restart (with Extensions Off) Sometimes restarting alone will get the Macintosh to mount a disk. More rarely, an extension may prevent the reading of a floppy disk. So, to be extra safe, hold the Shift key down when you restart to keep extensions off. Now try to mount the disk.

SEE: • **Fix-It #4 for more on dealing with extensions**

Special Case: AV and Power Macs AV Macs and Power Macs (and possibly other new models by now) use a new floppy drive controller that is more sensitive to inaccuracies; as a result, these Macs may have problems reading 800K disks that were mass-duplicated. To try to solve this, start up with extensions off, zap the PRAM, and/or use another Macintosh to copy the data on the 800K disk to an HD disk.

Replace or Repair If reinserting or restarting fails to get the disk to mount, you probably have damaged files and/or damaged hardware.

- If you have a backup copy of the disk, throw the damaged disk out. Even if you were to succeed in repairing the disk, your best bet would be to discard the disk, because it would probably have trouble again sometime soon. Better safe than sorry—throw it away, and use your backup copy to make a new backup copy.
- If you do not have a backup of the disk, and the files on the disk aren't important, throw the damaged disk out. You could try to reformat the disk, but disks are cheap enough that you shouldn't risk using a defective disk twice. Certainly, if you try to reformat the disk and get the "Initialization failed" message, it's time to discard the disk.

  SEE: • **Fix-It #15 for more on formatting disks**
- If it is important to save the data on the disk that are not backed up, try to repair the disk using repair utilities. When your attempted repairs are completed, try to mount the disk again. If it still doesn't mount successfully, use utilities to try to recover files from it to another disk.

  SEE: • **Fix-It #10 and Fix-It #13 on disk repairs**
  • **Fix-It #14 on file recovery**
- With a bit of luck, you may be able to recover data from an "unreadable" floppy disk without having to resort to repair utilities. Instead of ejecting the disk, open the application for a document on the disk that you want to save. If you can open the document from the application, save it to another disk and then discard the problem disk.
- Finally, you may have a problem with the disk drive itself, even if you do get the disk to mount. To check for this, insert other disks into the disk drive, and test the problem disk in other disk drives. A specific drive that fails to recognize virtually

every disk that you insert—while those same disks work fine when inserted into other drives—is the classic pattern implying a hardware problem with the drive. At best, the drive is just a little dirty; at worst, it is beyond repair.

SEE: • **Fix-It #17 for more on hardware problems**

If the same disk causes problems in other drives, it may mean a physical problem with the disk itself (such as a stuck or bent slide shutter, as described in "Take Note: If You Can't Get a Disk to Insert," earlier in this chapter) rather than the drive.

A Floppy Disk Won't Eject or Unmount

Symptoms:

You attempt to eject a floppy disk from its drive, using the standard methods, but it does not eject. Sometimes you can get the disk to eject, but you can't unmount it (that is, the disk image will not disappear when you drag its icon to the Trash).

Causes:

This is often a software-based problem. For example, there may be insufficient memory available to permit the disk to be ejected (although this is not likely in System 7). If so, you should get an error message that describes this as the problem. Various bugs in the system software may also be to blame.

In other cases, the problem has a physical cause, such as a damaged disk or a defective disk drive. it may be as simple, however, as a disk label that has come partially unglued and is jamming the eject mechanism.

In any case, unless the problem is a recurring one, understanding the cause is not necessarily critical. The more important task is figuring out how to remove the disk. Regardless of the cause, the methods for removal remain the same.

What to do:

For the sake of thoroughness, I will review both the standard and nonstandard ways of ejecting a disk. You may be surprised to discover how many different ways there are.

Standard Methods for Ejecting a Disk

From the Finder First, select the disk by clicking its icon on the Finder's desktop. Then try either of the following:

- Select Eject Disk (from the Special menu of the Finder) or type Command-E (the command-key equivalent of Eject Disk, as listed to the right of the menu command).
- Drag the icon of the disk to the Trash (no, this does *not* erase any data on the disk), select Put Away from the File menu, or type Command-Y (the command key equivalent of Put Away).

There is an important difference between these two groups of procedures. After you use Eject Disk, a dimmed image (called a *shadow*) of the disk icon remains on the screen. This means that, technically, the disk is still mounted and information about the disk remains in memory. Thus you can still refer to the disk for purposes of copying, moving, or otherwise working with its files. The Finder will ask you to reinsert the disk if it is needed (see more about this in the next section).

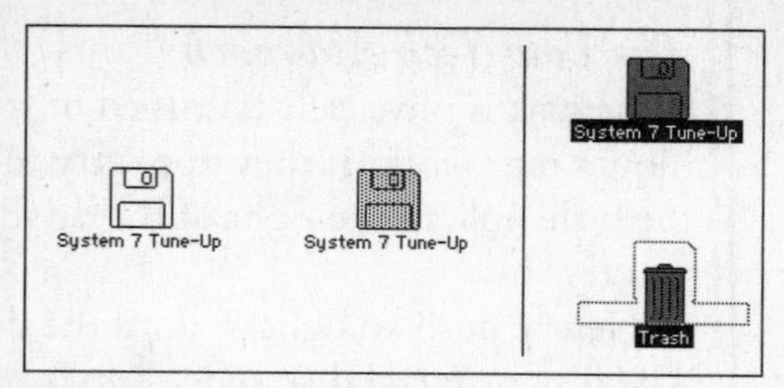

Figure 5-16 *Left: A typical disk icon (left) changes to a shadow disk icon (right) after selecting Eject Disk. Right: Dragging either type of icon to the Trash removes the icon from the desktop altogether (and ejects the disk if it is currently inserted).*

After you select Put Away or drag the disk to the Trash, however, the disk image disappears entirely. The disk is unmounted and is no longer in memory. The Finder acts as if the disk no longer exists.

From Within an Application If you are in an application (such as a word processor), select the Eject button from its Open or Save dialog box. This is the same as selecting Eject Disk from the Finder.

From Any Location Press Command-Shift-1 (for internal or lower internal drive) or Command-Shift-2 (for an external or upper internal drive). This is also similar to selecting Eject Disk from the Finder.

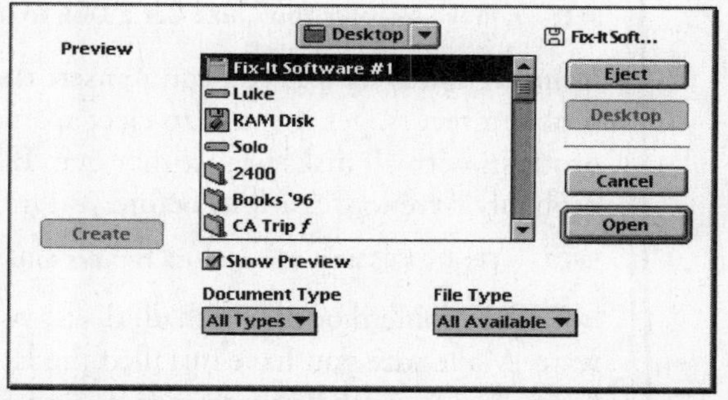

Figure 5-17 *Click the Eject button in this Open dialog box to eject the selected disk.*

Nonstandard Methods for Ejecting a Disk

All of the preceding methods assume that there is no problem with the disk that would prevent it from being ejected normally. If none of those standard techniques work, it is time to get more serious. Try the following techniques:

Restart Your Macintosh This by itself may eject the disk. It should work for any disk that does not have a System Folder on it.

Restart While Holding the Mouse Button Restart the Macintosh, holding down the mouse button until the disk ejects. This should eject a disk even if it has a System Folder on it.

SEE: • **"By the Way: The Sad Mac Makes a Brief Visit," earlier in this chapter, for an example of this method**

Actually, this is a general technique to get the Macintosh to bypass and eject a floppy disk that is present in a disk drive at startup, whether the disk is causing a problem or not. It does not seem to work, however, on at least some PowerBooks (using the track-ball or trackpad button here, since there is no mouse).

The Low-Tech Approach

If the disk is physically damaged or somehow stuck in the drive, none of these techniques may work. If they don't, try to eject it by inserting a straightened paper clip into the little hole to the right of the drive slot. (Ideally, the Macintosh should be off before you try this.)

Gently push straight in until the disk ejects—but if you have to push too hard, stop. The disk or metal disk slide shutter may be damaged or caught in such a way that further force would damage the drive rather than eject the disk. In this case, make a trip to the repair shop.

Reinserting the Disk

Before You Reinsert the Disk Check whether the disk has a torn label that may be getting stuck in the drive; if so, remove the label. Also check if the slide shutter is bent. You may be able to straighten it, or you can remove the shutter altogether.

SEE: • "Take Note: If You Can't Get a Disk to Insert," earlier in this chapter

Reinsert the Disk If you can reinsert the disk successfully, congratulations. If the problem recurs, get the disk to eject again. Insert other disks to determine whether it is a problem with all disks or just that one. If the problem is just with that disk, you will probably have to discard it; before you do, copy files from it to another disk, as needed.

SEE: • Fix-Its #13 and #14 on disk repairs and file recovery for problems recovering files

If the problem occurs with all disks, you may have a problem with the system software. Make sure you have installed the latest System Update for your version of the system software, as these updates may have fixes that solve the problem. Otherwise, reinstall the system software.

SEE: • Fix-It #5 on system software

As a last alternative, you may have a problem with the disk drive itself. Take the drive in for repairs, if necessary.

SEE: • Fix-It #17 on hardware problems

Special Cases

Files on the Disk "Are in Use" You cannot use the Put Away command if any file on the disk is currently open or in use. If you try, an alert message will inform you that the disk "could not be put away, because it contains items that are in use." The simplest solution here is to close all open files from the disk and try again. This includes both application and document files, even if the application that created the document is not on the floppy disk.

Figure 5-18 *A disk cannot be unmounted when applications or documents on the disk are currently open (also see Figure 5-23).*

If you try to unmount a disk that contains the image files currently mounted by ShrinkWrap (or another disk-image mounting utility), the Macintosh will again say that items on the disk are "in use." This may seem a bit mysterious, since ShrinkWrap

BY THE WAY ▶

MORE MEMORY PROBLEMS WITH THE FINDER

Several different Macintosh error messages indicate that you cannot mount, eject, or use a disk because of insufficient memory. Normally, these problems are resolved by reducing the number of open applications and desk accessories. If these problems occur frequently, you should increase the size of the Finder's memory, increase the size of the system heap or add more memory. This is especially likely to be needed in System 7.5.5.

Occasionally, using a disk that is nearly full will result in error messages that appear to be memory related (such as an inability to update the disk's window). These problems can generally be solved by deleting some items from the disk. Also, rebuilding the desktop will generally free up some extra kilobytes.

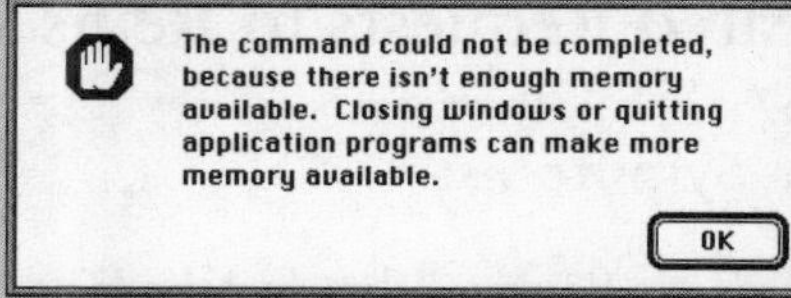

Figure 5-19 *The Finder is having a problem because "there isn't enough memory available."*

"Not enough memory" messages when copying files via file sharing or when a PPP connection is active are due to a bug that is fixed in System 7.5.3, so install System 7.5 Update 2.0 (or later) if you are using an earlier version of System 7.5.

These types of problems are not limited to floppy disks; they can occur with any type of disk or with general Finder operations (such as opening windows).

SEE: • **Fix-It #6 for details on memory management, including how to increase the size of the Finder's memory or of the system heap**

is probably not listed as open in the Application menu at the time, but trashing the image files will allow the disk to eject/unmount.

Otherwise, if nothing else appears to be in use, you may try to run Disk First Aid to see if a Directory problem is the root cause, Disk First Aid may fail as well, though, stopping with a message that says "test was interrupted because another program was using the disk." If this happens, try a Force Quit from the Finder or a Restart (in some cases, you may need to do this with extensions off), which should eliminate the entire problem. The disk will eject; if you then recheck the floppy disk with Disk First Aid, the latter should report it as okay.

SEE • **Fix-It #10 for more on Disk First Aid**

Insufficient Memory to Eject a Disk When you try to put away a disk, it may not eject because, according to the error message that appears, there isn't enough memory available to move the disk to the Trash. The easiest thing to do is to quit an open application, which should free up enough memory to allow the disk to eject. Sometimes increasing the memory size of the Finder or increasing the size of the system heap may help. If the problem still occurs frequently, consider increasing the memory capacity of your machine by adding more SIMM/DIMMs.

SEE: • **Fix-It #6 on memory problems**
• **Fix-It #17 on hardware problems**

PowerBook 500 Problem If you can't get a floppy disk to eject on a PowerBook 500, the drive may not be properly aligned. If you can see the metal frame sticking up more than a couple of centimeters behind the floppy drive door, you'll need to get the drive repaired. Take the PowerBook to a local Apple-authorized service provider or call 800-SOS-APPL.

Repeated Requests to Reinsert a Floppy Disk

Symptoms:

- You eject a floppy disk using the Finder's Eject command, meaning that the disk is still mounted. An alert box message, however, immediately (or soon) asks you to reinsert the same disk.

  You reinsert the disk and once again eject it; the request to reinsert the disk appears. This sequence appears likely to continue indefinitely.

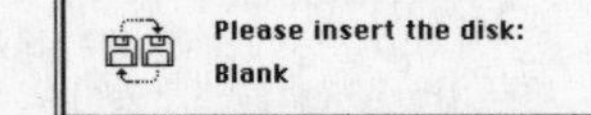

Figure 5-20 *The Macintosh asks you to insert a disk.*

- In a similar situation, the Macintosh may eject a disk and ask that another named disk be inserted. You insert what you believe to be the requested disk. The computer immediately ejects it, however, and asks that the requested disk be reinserted. Again, there seems to be no end to this repetitive cycle.
- The Macintosh may cycle between asking you to insert first one disk and then a second one.

Causes:

If you eject a disk using the Finder's Eject command, the disk remains mounted, as described in the previous section. The shadow(dimmed) icon of the disk remains on the desktop just as it might if an application automatically ejects a disk as part of its normal activity.

So far, you don't have a problem. In fact, it may be necessary that this happen for certain operations, such as when making a disk-to-disk copy with only one floppy drive. In this case, the computer automatically and repeatedly ejects the disks and asks you to insert the other one until the copying is finished. The number of swaps it takes to complete the copying varies depending on how much you are copying, what system software version you have, how much memory you have, and what model of Macintosh you are using. A similar situation can occur when you are using Installer utilities.

Even when you are not copying or installing, however, you may find that the Macintosh unexpectedly asks you to reinsert a disk with a shadow icon. Usually, this is because the computer needs to update information on the disk or otherwise access data from the disk (for example, if you try to launch an application from a disk that is not inserted). Other times, it may seem to be asking you to reinsert the disk for no apparent reason.

In most cases, reinserting the disk settles the matter. If two floppy disks are involved, several swaps back and forth may be required before the system comes to rest, but this is normal. The problem occurs when the swapping back and forth never seems to end—or when the Macintosh repeatedly spits out the disk that you insert, then asks you to reinsert the same disk. The exact cause is often vague, but the problem is usually attributable to bugs in the system software.

What to do:

Make Sure You Are Inserting the Requested Disk

Maybe you're inserting the wrong disk, and that is why it is being rejected. The Macintosh may want Disk 1 of a multi-disk package, for example, and you are inadvertently inserting Disk 2. The obvious solution is to find Disk 2 and insert it.

To Break out of the Cycle, Try Pressing Command-Period

Press Command-Period several times. If necessary, hold down the keys until the request to insert a disk goes away (or until you give up in despair). It may take a minute or more for this to happen.

This solution may lead to another message saying that your command could not be completed (for instance, saying that your folder could not be opened). If you click OK at this point, the insert-disk message may reappear. If so, press Command-Period again, going back and forth like this several more times if necessary. Regardless of what messages you see, at some point you should break out of this cycle. The last message will probably say that the disk "cannot be used, because it is not in any drive."

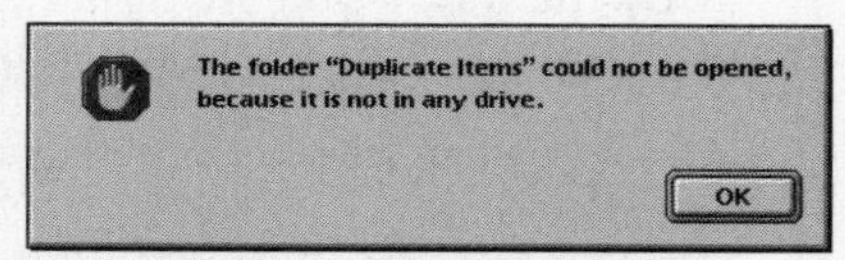

Figure 5-21 *This message appears after you repeatedly press Command-Period to get rid of alert boxes that ask to insert a disk that you do not want to insert.*

Unmount the Disk or Close Windows

If you manage to break out of the cycle, go immediately to the Finder and drag the shadow icon of the problem disk to the Trash (assuming you don't need the disk mounted). This should make the icon disappear and prevent any further recurrence of this looping. Sometimes, the Mac does this for you automatically.

Actually, unmounting is a good preventative measure whenever you have a shadow disk icon that you know you are finished using. Routinely unmounting these floppy disks can prevent problems before they start.

If you want the disk to remain mounted, though, close any open windows from the disk. That way, if you make any changes to the contents of these windows from within applications, the Finder will not need to update the screen display, which would require you to reinsert the disk.

Restart (Possibly with Extensions Off)

If none of the above seems to work, treat this as a system error and restart the Macintosh. Normally, after restarting, the problem does not recur.

Note that a disk-swapping problem of this sort is especially likely to occur when you are using an Installer utility. In this case, the solution is to restart with extensions off. You may have to do a Force Quit to get out of the Installer before you can select to Restart.

SEE: **• Chapter 4 for more on Force Quits**

A CD-ROM Disc Won't Mount

Symptoms:

- You insert a CD-ROM disc into a CD-ROM drive, but the disk icon never appears on the desktop. No error message appears. The CD-ROM tray may even eject the disc.
- When you insert a CD-ROM disc, the Macintosh displays the message, "This is not a Macintosh disk. Do you want to initialize it?"

Causes:

There are a number of possible causes. First, the driver software or related extensions may not have been installed. Second, there may be a problem with SCSI connections. Third, the drive itself may be damaged.

By the way, if you are trying to use the CD-ROM disc as a startup disk, remember that you may have problems doing this on some models of Macintosh.

SEE: **• "Default Rules for Selecting a Startup Disk," earlier in this chapter**

What to do:

Make Sure the Disc Is Inserted Correctly

Insert the disc label side up. While you are at it, make sure that the disc is seated correctly so the tray can close all the way, and that it is clean. Otherwise, the tray may automatically eject the disc instead of mounting it.

Make Sure the Drive Is Turned On Before You Start Up

If you are using the Apple CD-ROM driver and you have an external CD-ROM drive, the drive must be turned on at startup for the driver extension to load (it doesn't matter whether a disc is in the drive or not). If you turn the drive on after startup and then insert a disc, it will not mount, and no icon will appear. The solution is to turn the drive on and restart.

This is not a problem for internal drives, which are turned on whenever you switch on your Macintosh. Similarly, some other CD-ROM drivers, such as DriveCD, avoid this problem. There is also a freeware utility, called LoadADrive, that will mount Apple's CD driver after startup.

Make Sure the CD-ROM Driver Is Installed in the System Folder and Enabled at Startup

Similarly, if the CD-ROM driver extension is not installed, you will typically not be able to use the drive. For Apple drives, the name of the extension is *Apple CD-ROM.*

This driver extension must be loaded at startup for you to use your CD-ROM drive. This means that you can't mount a CD-ROM disc if you started up with extensions off. The utilities mentioned in the previous item should help again here to overcome this obstacle. Power Computing's Mac clones (which use CD-ROM Toolkit) apparently also mount a CD-ROM disc even if you start up with extensions off.

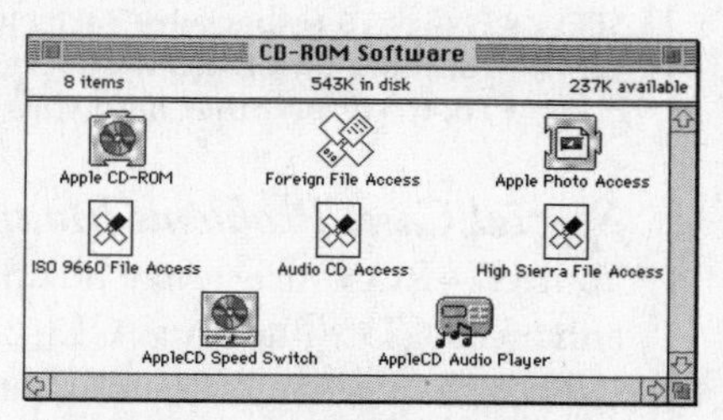

Figure 5-22 *Apple's CD-ROM driver and related files. All except Speed Switch and Audio Player are extensions that may be needed to mount different types of CD-ROM discs.*

Finally, note the issue of extensions (on or off) is not directly relevant if you are using your CD-ROM disc as a startup disk.

SEE: • **"Take Note: CD-ROM Startup Discs," earlier in this chapter**

Make Sure You Have Foreign File Access and Other Related Extensions as Needed

To mount a non-Macintosh formatted CD-ROM disc, such as an audio CD or a photo CD, special extensions such as Foreign File Access and Apple Photo Access (and possibly other relevant access files) must be present and be loaded at startup. Photo CD discs also need QuickTime 1.5 or later. Otherwise, when you insert a "foreign" disc, you will get the message that says that "This is not a Macintosh disk."

You May Have Damaged CD-ROM Files or an Extension Conflict

If you get the "disk is unreadable" message when trying to mount a CD-ROM and the needed CD-ROM extensions are properly installed, the files may be damaged. Reinstall them. Typically, these extensions are included as part of the system software disks, but make sure you are using the latest version (the current version of CD-ROM Setup is available online). If reinstalling the files has no effect, you may have an extension conflict.

Otherwise, Check for Miscellaneous SCSI and Related Hardware-Related Problems

First, make sure that you do not have a SCSI ID number conflict.

If a freeze occurs when you are trying to mount a CD-ROM disc, there may be dirt on the disc. To clean it, wipe the shiny side of the disk gently with a soft cloth or tissue. Look especially for sticky "goop" on the disk. Wipe from the center to the edge of the disk; do not wipe in a circular manner.

If you have a Power Mac 7200 or 7500 and you are having trouble getting CD-ROMs to mount, note the following information from Apple: The Power Macintosh 7200 and 7500 series computers have a "kickstand" or bracket that prevents the internal-component cage from opening. If this bracket is not secure, however, it can cause enough tension on the internal SCSI ribbon cable to pull it from the SCSI connector. If this happens, CD-ROM discs will no longer mount. To resolve this problem, snap the bracket securely into place and then reconnect the internal SCSI ribbon cable.

SEE:
- **Fix-It #16 (especially "Take Note: CD-ROM Drivers and Problems Mounting CD-ROM Discs") for more on CD-ROM drivers, including non-Apple drivers and other SCSI-related problems**
- **Fix-It #17 on other hardware problems**

Special Case: Problems Mounting Multi-Session CD-ROM Discs

Your CD-ROM drive may be unable to mount or work with multi-session CDs or enhanced CDs (known as CD+). A multi-session CD-ROM disc is one that can be written to in separate sessions, such as a Photo-CD disc (which can have additional photo images added until the disc is full). An enhanced CD is one that combines audio CD and CD-ROM data on the same disc. The following are suggested solutions from Apple for problems with these discs.

- The wrong ROM was installed in some Matsushita quad-speed drives installed in PCI Power Macs when they were manufactured. Unfortunately, serial numbers do not necessarily help in identifying these drives, so you may just have to try it to see (although if you have version 2.0d or earlier, as you can find out from utilities such as SCSIProbe, you probably have the problem). If you have trouble with multi-session or enhanced CDs, take your drive to an authorized Apple service provider, and it will be replaced for free. If you are especially lucky, you will get a Sony drive, none of which are known to have problems.
- Install the latest version of CD-ROM Setup (version 5.1.2 or greater) for complete compatibility with multi-session CD-ROM discs.
- CD-ROM discs created with Apple Media Tool version 1.2 and earlier may have a problem known as the "AMK Spinning-Cursor Bug." This can be repaired by a software fix of the same name posted in Apple software updates areas of online services.

A CD-ROM Disc or Removable Cartridge Won't Eject

Symptoms:

When you select Put Away, Eject, or an equivalent command to eject a CD-ROM disc or removable cartridge, it does not eject. Typically, an error message appears that gives you some clue as to why it will not eject.

Causes:

The most common reason that these disks cannot be put away is that a file is "in use." In the same way that you cannot delete a file that is currently open, you cannot eject these disks if they contain a file that is currently open.

Having virtual memory and/or file sharing on can also cause this problem. It is also possible that the disk is somehow physically stuck in the drive.

What to do:

Use the Put Away Command

The Put Away command (Command-Y) or simply dragging the icon of the disk to the Trash are the main ways to eject a CD-ROM or removable disk (the same as for a floppy disk). This unmounts it as well as ejects it.

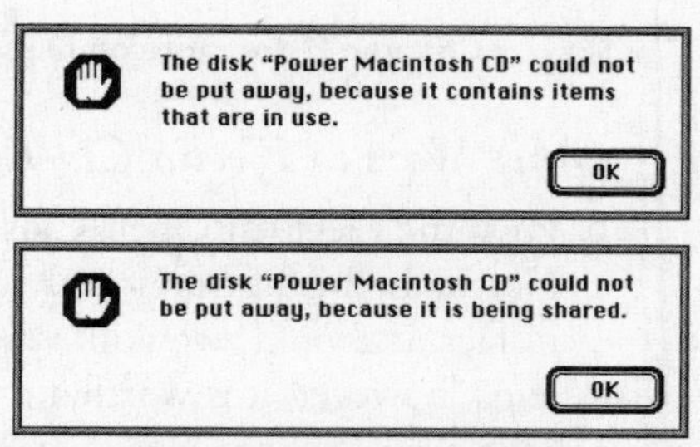

Figure 5-23 *Messages that may appear when you are trying to eject a disk. The top one can occur with any type of removable disk (floppy, CD-ROM, cartridge). The bottom message will not occur with floppy disks.*

Remember, for a removable cartridge (such as a SyQuest cartridge), ejecting a disk may be a two-step process. The disk may spin down and partially eject; after you drag the disk icon to the Trash, you may have to press a stop button as well. In either case, after the drive has spun down, you may have to slide a lever to get the cartridge to eject completely (particularly on SyQuest drives). Do not do this, however, until you are certain that the drive has spun down (often, a light goes off to indicate when it's safe); otherwise, you could damage the disk. Check with your drive's manual for details.

Eject Instead of Put Away

If Put Away does not work, often you can still eject the disk (Command-E), leaving its disk image on the desktop. If ejecting is good enough for what you want to accomplish at the moment, then do it. You can also try ejecting a CD-ROM with the Eject button on the AppleCD Audio Player if you have that installed in your Apple menu.

Be careful, however, if you eject a removable cartridge without unmounting it. When you insert another cartridge, the Mac may think it is the one you just ejected—with the result that it corrupts the Directory files of the second cartridge.

If you still cannot get the disk to eject (or if you must actually put away the disk), proceed to the next steps.

If a File on the Disk Is "In Use," Quit the Relevant Application(s)

If you cannot eject a disk because you get the "in use" error message, quit any and all applications that are currently open on the problem disk or that use documents on that disk. You should now be able to eject the disk.

Turn Off Virtual Memory

Having virtual memory on *may* prevent a CD-ROM disc or removable cartridge from being ejected. If so, you will be able to eject the disk by restarting with virtual memory off (hold down the Command key at startup to do this).

Turn Off File Sharing

Prior to System 7.5.1, a problem ejecting a CD-ROM disc or removable cartridge might also occur if you had file sharing on. In particular, you would get a message that says your disk "could not be put away, because it is being shared." Current systems no longer have this problem. If you do get this message, simply turn file sharing off (from the Sharing Setup control panel of the Control Strip module) and try again to eject the disc.

SEE: • Chapter 11 for more on file sharing in general

Other Ways to Eject a CD-ROM Disc

1. Press the Eject (or Open/Close) button, which should be near the drive tray. Normally this button is only used to open the tray when there is no disc in the tray; in fact, it should *not* work when there is a disc present. When you are having problems, however, it is worth a try.
2. If pressing the drive's Eject button fails to work, turn the drive off and then on again (or, for an internal CD-ROM drive, restart the Mac)—and then immediately press the eject button, repeatedly if necessary. For Macs like the Power Mac 6100 that do not automatically turn off when you select Shut Down, try pressing the eject button when the screen blackens and the "power off" message appears.
3. Otherwise, try holding down the mouse button at startup. The disk may eject.
4. If it doesn't, start up with extensions off. Now try the CD-ROM drive's eject button.
5. If that fails, turn off the drive, take a large straightened paper clip and insert it into the small hole to the right of the eject button. This should cause the disk to pop out.
6. Still out of luck? Follow any instructions that came with your particular drive. If nothing works, you may have a damaged CD-ROM drive. Take it in for repair.

SEE: • "Take Note: CD-ROM Startup Discs," earlier in this chapter, for related information

BY THE WAY ▶

SELECTING RESTART OR EJECT WHEN A REMOVABLE CARTRIDGE IS THE STARTUP DISK

If you are using a removable cartridge as a startup disk:

- If you select the Eject command for the removable cartridge, you are likely to get into an endless loop of the computer asking you to reinsert the cartridge and then spitting it out again. Restarting will be the only way out of this.

  Zip and Jaz drives include a special utility that can be used to make cartridge-to-cartridge copies.
- Selecting the Restart command from the Finder's Special menu may cause the removable cartridge to eject, with the typical result that your Macintosh shifts to its internal drive as your startup disk. To avoid this, select Shut Down rather than Restart. Then reinsert the cartridge and wait for it to spin up before turning your Mac back on. The cartridge will remain as your startup disk. Also note: the formatting utility for your cartridge may include options to prevent ejecting at restart or shutdown.

Other Ways to Eject a Removable Cartridge

For most drives, when standard methods fail,the remaining choices are basically similar to the methods just described for CD-ROM discs—in particular, shut down the Macintosh and press the drive's Stop/Eject button. If that fails, insert an unbent paper clip into the small hole near the drive opening (usually provided as a fail-safe for when nothing else works). Check your drive's manual for details.

A Hard Disk Gets Unmounted

Symptoms:

- A disk icon of a hard disk can become unmounted. Typically, this means that the desktop icon of the hard disk will either vanish or become a dimmed shadow icon.
- In some cases, an undimmed hard disk icon may remain on the desktop, but you are unable to access anything on the disk. Attempts to do so may lead to a variety of problems, including system errors.

SEE: • Chapter 4 for more on system errors

Causes:

Removing a Disk Icon

If you drag the icon of a hard disk to the Trash, the disk is unmounted and its icon disappears from the desktop (unless the disk is the current startup disk, in which case the disk cannot be unmounted). Of course, the Macintosh will not let you do this with the startup disk.

As with the similar unmounting of a floppy disk, the Macintosh no longer has any memory of an unmounted hard disk. This is not a problem by itself. It does mean, however, that you no longer have access to anything on that disk until it is remounted.

Dimmed Hard Disk Icons

Normally, the Eject Disk command is not accessible when a hard disk is selected on the Finder. Thus a dimmed hard disk icon should never occur for a fixed hard disk (though it may occur for a removable-media cartridge, such as SyQuest and Iomega drives).

If the command does occur, its cause is usually unclear. Usually, some sort of software bug has confused the Macintosh so that it is aware of the presence of the hard disk but does not think that the disk is currently accessible. A corrupted System file might be the ultimate cause. Whatever the cause, trouble will likely occur if you try to access anything on the disk.

Turning the Power Off

Turning the power off for an external hard drive *after* you have dragged its icon to the Trash is not necessarily a problem. To be safe, however, I would usually recommend against doing this. For example, if you have several devices attached to a SCSI chain (as discussed in Fix-It #16), turning off one of the devices can prevent the others from working.

If you turn the power off *before* dragging the disk's icon to the Trash, however, you have essentially unmounted the drive without informing the Finder of this fact. This is a definite no-no, and problems are likely to ensue.

What to do:

Drag the Disk Icon to the Trash

If you have turned the power off on an external hard drive without first dragging its icon to the Trash, immediately drag the disk icon to the Trash. Do *not* try to work with any folders, windows, or files from the disk; doing so will probably lead to a system crash. It may also corrupt the hard disk's Directory so that the disk no longer mounts at all.

If you have files that are currently open and in use from that disk, though, you may have problems no matter what you do. Dragging the disk icon to the Trash may not be enough to save you.

Your best bet is to save what open files you can (to another disk, obviously) before a system crash occurs, and then restart. If you don't need to save any files, simply restart.

Drag a Shadow Icon to the Trash

Similarly, if the disk icon appears dimmed, your best bet is to drag the shadow disk icon to the Trash, unmounting the disk before any other problems develop.

Otherwise, some particularly perplexing symptoms may appear. For example, you may get an alert message to reinsert the hard drive (which, of course, cannot be done). You can try to get this message to go away by pressing Command-Period, as you would do for a floppy disk. If this does not work, you have to restart the Macintosh as you would after a system error, either by pressing the Reset button or by turning the computer off and on again.

SEE: • **Chapter 4 for more on system errors**

Even if you do not get the reinsert message, a system crash is likely to occur soon if you ignore this situation. Restart to be safe.

Remount Any Unmounted Disk

Whatever the cause of the unmounting, if you want to use the disk again, you have to remount it. To do this without restarting, you have to do it manually, using a utility like SCSIProbe. Otherwise, simply restart the computer (using the Finder's Restart command), and the disk should remount automatically.

SEE: • **"A Hard Disk Won't Mount," earlier in this chapter**
• **Fix-It #16 for more on using SCSIProbe**

Problems with Restart, Shut Down, or Sleep

Symptoms:

- When you select either Restart or Shut Down from the Finder's Special menu, the shutdown process begins normally but is halted by a system error. You may get an error message, or you may simply get a freeze.
- A similar problem may occur when selecting Sleep on PowerBooks (see Chapter 11, though, for more general problems with the Sleep command).
- When you select Shut Down, the Macintosh spontaneously restarts rather than shutting down.
- A spontaneous restart occurs for no apparent reason at any time during an otherwise normal work session.

Causes:

When you select Restart or Shut Down, the Macintosh attempts to save and close all currently open documents and quit all currently open applications before actually shutting down. It also does a final update of the Directory files of any mounted disks. If for any reason (usually a bug somewhere in the software) the Finder cannot close a given file, the shutdown process halts. The cause could be something as simple as having an unsaved document, or it could be a problem with an application, extension, or control panel. The error could also be due to corrupted system software or directory damage.

In addition, corrupted Parameter RAM may also cause an inability to shut down. Finally, you may have a hardware problem, such as a stuck Power key on your keyboard or a bad power supply.

What to do:

Save Documents, Quit Any Open Applications (and Related Issues)

Save any unsaved documents if you are requested to do so.

Another message you might get is a warning about the contents of your RAM disk being lost when you shut down (assuming you have a RAM disk). This warning will halt the shutdown process until you dismiss the message. Click OK here (unless you wish to save the files).

Sometimes the Macintosh cannot automatically close an open application during a shutdown or restart. If you go to the application and manually select its Quit button, this may let the operation proceed. If not, try the following steps.

Check for Background Application Problems

If you try to shut down and all visible applications have quit, but the Mac sends you a message saying that it "can't shutdown because the 'unknown' application can't quit," it is probably due to a so-called background application (the sort whose name does not appear in the Applications menu, giving you the impression that nothing is left open; sometimes such applications are stored in the Extensions folder as extensions) or some similar process (such as documents left in the PrintMonitor Documents folder).

Otherwise, this message is probably due to a bug in an ordinary extension.

In either case, you will probably have to reset the Mac (as described in Chapter 4) to restart. Restart with extensions off by holding down the Shift key at startup. Then treat it as an extension problem, as described next and in Fix-It #4.

Check for Startup Extension Problems

If the problem recurs, check for startup extension-related problems. For example, I had an anti-virus utility that prevented me from shutting down normally until I rearranged its loading order. Similarly, I had some fax software (FaxSTF 3.0) that prevented me from shutting down normally whenever its Control Panel startup extension was active.

Some versions of Microsoft Office Manager were also known to prevent shutdowns due to a bug in the software (or in Apple's system software, depending upon whom you believe). This problem may have been fixed in System 7.5.3. If you do come across it, a utility that allows you to quit the Finder (such as Terminator Strip) may help to close those pesky applications, allowing you to shut down. Otherwise, you will have to do a reset (as described in Chapter 4).

As mentioned earlier in this chapter, startup extensions are an especially likely cause of a spontaneous restart if it occurs during startup (that is, while startup extensions are loading). Not all of these restarts, however, signal a problem. For example, some startup managers restart the Macintosh if you use them to change the status of any startup extension that loads before the manager itself.

In the worst-case scenario—in which continued spontaneous restarts prevent you from completing a startup—try starting up with extensions off; this is almost guaranteed to work. Then determine the offending startup extension.

SEE: • Fix-It #4 on solving startup extension problems

Restart (by Using the Reset Button If Needed)

If you had a spontaneous restart, and your Mac successfully restarted afterward, your problem may be over already. Check it out by trying Restart once more. If things go smoothly, congratulations. It was probably a one-time glitch.

Otherwise, treat this as a system error, especially for a machine that refuses to shut down or restart. You have to restart your computer by using the Reset button or by turning the computer off and on again. The problem is unlikely to recur after you restart.

SEE: • Chapter 4 for more on system errors

Replace the Finder Preferences File

If the Macintosh fails to restart after you select the Restart command from the Finder's Special menu, you may have a damaged Finder Preferences file. To fix this, restart (using the Reset button if needed) with extensions off (by holding down the Shift key during startup). Go to the Preferences folder in the System Folder and drag the Finder Preferences file to the Trash, then restart again (using Reset again if needed) and empty the Trash.

SEE: • **Fix-It #2 for more on preferences files**

Zap the Parameter RAM

SEE: • **Fix-It #11 for how to zap the Parameter RAM**

Replace the Open Application and/or the System Software

If the problem does recur—and if it always seems to involve the same application—you may have a defective copy of the application; replace it. If this does not work, contact the company to see whether there is a bug in the software that has been fixed by an upgraded version. Otherwise, do a clean reinstall of the system software.

SEE: • **Fix-Its #2 and #3 on replacing application software**
• **Fix-It #5 on system software**

Check for Disk Directory or Hardware Problems

Run the usual repair software (Disk First Aid, Norton Utilities, and/or MacTools) to check for Directory problems. The most likely hardware cause is a stuck Power key. To check for this, restart with the keyboard detached. For this or other suspected hardware problems, take the Mac in for repairs.

SEE: • **Chapter 11 for more on PowerBooks and sleep problems**
• **Fix-Its #10 and #13 on disk repairs**
• **Fix-It #17 for more on possible hardware problems**

BY THE WAY ▶

STOPPING A SHUTDOWN

If you ever select Shut Down or Restart and then suddenly realize that you do not want to shut down or restart after all, you may be able to halt the process by quickly launching an application. Also, if an application that was open when you selected Shut Down or Restart asks whether you want to save a document before quitting, clicking Cancel will halt the shutdown.

Files Missing from the Desktop

Symptoms:

- The most common situation is when many or most files on a particular disk (floppy or hard) seem to have vanished from the desktop, and these files are not listed in any Open or Save dialog boxes. Continued use of the disk may lead to system crashes. You can usually tell that something is wrong right away because the indication of the amount of disk space in use (as shown in the window header of any window from that disk, when using an icon view) indicates that much more disk space is in use than is accounted for by the files that are still visible.
- A special case is when files and/or folders have vanished from the desktop but are still accessible from within applications and seem intact when accessed this way. The disk behaves normally in all other respects. This is an especially likely symptom if you are using System 7.0 or 7.0.1.

Causes:

The problem is almost always due to damage to the invisible Directory or Desktop files that keep track of what is on the disk.

SEE: • **Chapters 2 and 8 for more details on these invisible files**

The special problem that crops up in early versions of System 7 is apparently due to a long-standing yet obscure bug in the Macintosh hardware (ROM) that rarely appeared until System 7.

What to do:

Close and Reopen the Window

Sometimes, especially if the problem is limited to one or a few newly copied files, the file(s) are really there and undamaged. It's just that the Finder may not have been updated properly, and so it does not yet display the files. Usually, simply closing and reopening the window that contains the files will get the files to display.

Use Find

Use the Finder's Find command to search for the name of the missing file, if you can recall it. If it locates the file, this often makes the file visible again, at least temporarily.

SEE: • **"Cursor Alternates Between a Watch and an Arrow (or All Icons in a Window Are Missing)," earlier in this chapter**
• **Chapter 6, "When You Can't Locate a File," for more on locating a single missing file**

Rebuild the Desktop

Rebuilding the desktop can sometimes solve this problem, again at least temporarily. Ideally, you should use TechTool to rebuild the desktop here.

SEE: • **Fix-It #9 for more on TechTool**

Use Disk First Aid

Recent versions of Disk First Aid (shipped with System 7.1 or later) are especially good at solving these problems. They can fix damage that might otherwise cause these problems to occur in the future.

If you have an immediate problem, and if damage is discovered, repair it, or recover data from the disk as appropriate. If the damage cannot be repaired, you need to reformat the disk. Reformatting is probably a good idea even if you think you fixed the problem. If it is a floppy disk, you should probably discard it instead.

SEE: • **Fix-It #10 on using Disk First Aid**
• **Fix-It #13 on disk repairs and Fix-It #15 on reformatting**

Upgrade

Once you succeed in recovering whatever vanished files you could, if you are using System 7.0 or 7.0.1, upgrade to System 7.1 or later. Current system software versions include a fix that prevents this problem. This won't fix an existing problem but will prevent future ones from happening.

The Macintosh's Speed Is Unexpectedly Slow

Symptoms:

- The primary symptom here is that many operations across most or all of your applications are running noticeably slower than usual. This commonly includes delays in opening files, saving documents, menus dropping down, and/or responses to mouse clicks. Other symptoms include increased time to copy or delete files and slow redrawing of the screen.
- Sometimes delays may be restricted to particular applications or situations, usually ones that are processor-intensive, such as running QuickTime movies.

BY THE WAY ▶

WHAT IS THE EXPECTED SPEED OF YOUR MACINTOSH?

If your Macintosh suddenly starts performing at a snail's pace, you will undoubtedly notice. But what if you have a new Macintosh, and you have no idea how fast your machine *should* perform? Is there some way of finding out whether it runs as fast as is typical for its model? Yes, there are a variety of commercial and shareware utilities that do this. MacBench, a freeware program, is one example (described in a bit more detail in Fix-It #17). The current version of Norton Utilities has a similar feature.

Causes:

Having operations run in the background generally slows down the speed of your machine. Using up almost all of your available RAM also tends to cause slowdowns. Operations that require frequent disk access, such as compressing and decompressing files, will also slow down the Macintosh. More unusual causes revolve around problems with system software or even with the drive itself.

The list of solutions is by no means exhaustive, but it covers the most common problems. Some answers require giving up certain features to gain a speed benefit; you'll have to decide if the trade-off is worth it.

What to do:

Try any or all of the following, in the general order listed here, until you get the speed you expect:

- Quit any applications you do not need to keep open.
- Stop any background applications or processes, such as PrintMonitor, or communications software that is downloading a file in the background.
- Turn off file sharing. Do this by selecting the Sharing Setup control panel and clicking the Stop button in the file-sharing section.

  SEE: • "A CD-ROM Disk or Removable Cartridge Won't Eject," earlier in this chapter, for more on how to turn off file sharing

- Turn off any unneeded extensions and restart. Several extensions—particularly those that modify general system function, such as Now Menus (part of Now Utilities) or Apple Menu Options—will noticeably slow down the Macintosh. The cumulative effect of several of these extensions can be substantial.

  Apple Menu Options can cause an especially long slowdown in system operations when an alias to a hard drive is placed in the Apple Menu Items folder. Other similar extensions, such as Now Menus, do not cause the same performance penalty because they accomplish the same goal by a different method. The downside of the Now Menus method, however, is that it will take longer than Apple Menu Options to display its hierarchical menu.

  Of special note, one function of most anti-virus extensions is to check a file for viruses when it is launched. This can significantly extend the time it takes an application to open. Some versions of SAM were particularly prone to this problem and would cause inordinately long launch times.

  Finally, disable Speakable Items in the Speech control panel, if you have it installed and are not using it at the moment. Restarting is not necessary.

- Disable AppleTalk, if not needed.
- Add certain extensions. If you think this contradicts my previous advice, you're right. A few extensions, though, are designed to speed up specific operations, particularly those of the Finder. Included here would be utilities such as CopyDoubler and SpeedyFinder.

But here's an exception to the exception: System 7.5 improved the Finder's speed of copying files and emptying the Trash (as compared to System 7.0/7.1). As a result, speed-enhancing features of utilities such as CopyDoubler and SpeedyFinder may no longer be needed.

Also note that Connectix's Speed Doubler can substantially increase the speed of your Mac, especially a Power Mac. Its Speed Access extension works as a replacement for Apple's Disk Cache. Speed Emulator is an improved faster version of the 680X0 emulator for Power Macs (although the difference is not as great with Apple's most recent software).

- Turn off virtual memory (as set in the Memory control panel) if you are using it, with the possible exception of if you are using a Power Macintosh. Similarly, if you are using a memory-enhancing utility, such as RAM Doubler, turn this off. Typically, this step will require that you restart the Macintosh.

SEE: • Chapter 12 on Power Macintoshes and virtual memory

- The size of the disk cache (as set in the Memory control panel) affects speed. If you start up with extensions off (by holding down the Shift key at startup), the cache will revert to its default size for that session, rather than any potentially larger size that you may have previously set. The custom size will return the next time you restart with extensions on. Up to a point, a larger cache size will generally lead to improved performance.

SEE: • Fix-It #6 for recommended cache size settings

- Increasing the Preferred memory size of an application may increase its speed by allowing more of the program to load into RAM, which in turn will reduce need for frequent "disk swaps" that slow programs down.
- Turn off any automatic compression utility you are using. This is more important for disk-level compression than for file-level compression (see Chapter 2, and specifically the section "Other Ways to Save or Get More Space," for an explanation of this distinction).
- Connecting online with a Geoport Telecom Adapter can slow your Mac's performance. So don't maintain a connection longer than necessary.
- Lower your display depth, using the Monitors control panel. All other things being equal, your Macintosh will perform faster when the display is in black and white, for example, rather than 256 colors. If you don't need the color display, you can speed things up by switching to black and white. (This is not as relevant for today's fastest Macs.)

SEE: • Chapter 10 for more on setting the display depth

- Defragment your disk and rebuild the desktop.

SEE: • Fix-It #8 on defragmenting
• Fix-It #9 on rebuilding the desktop

- Reduce the number of files on your disk, especially if you have folders that contain hundreds of files in them. Keeping track of so many files tends to overwhelm the Mac's operating system and slows things down.

- Turn off Calculate Folder Size in the Views control panel.
- Keeping Key Caps open in the background slows down text processing in the foreground; turn it off.
- If you are using a PowerBook, open the PowerBook control panel. Uncheck the Reduce Processor Speed and Allow Processor Recycling options.

  SEE: • Chapter 11 for more details on finding and using these options

- If you are using a 68040 Macintosh, check the Cache Switch control panel. Make sure it is on.

  SEE: • Fix-It #1 for more on the disk cache

- Update your disk driver. If your Macintosh uses SCSI Manager 4.3, make especially sure you have an upgraded disk driver that is compatible with this new manager.

  SEE: • Fix-Its #12 and #16 for more on SCSI Manager 4.3 and upgrading the disk driver

- Check if your hard drive was formatted with the proper interleave. This is an unlikely issue these days, especially for internal drives that came with your Macintosh, but you can still check it easily enough.

  SEE: • Fix-It #15 on formatting a hard disk and what interleave is all about

- Otherwise, it's time to check whether you have a hardware problem with your hard drive.

  SEE: • Fix-It #17 on hardware problems

- As a long-term issue, hardware additions (such as adding more RAM, a coprocessor, or an accelerator card) can increase the overall speed of your machine. Of course, moving up to a faster Mac (especially a Power Mac) will also help.
- **Special Case: Delays at Startup**
  - **a.** If you are having unusual delays at startup, especially prior to the appearance of the smiling Mac, check your Startup Disk control panel. If no volume is selected, select your desired startup volume. Your startup time should now improve.

    This improvement is especially likely to happen if you had temporarily set a CD-ROM or removable cartridge to be the startup disk and that volume is no longer available. It can also happen after zapping your PRAM.
  - **b.** The initial startup period (prior to the appearance of the "Welcome to Macintosh" message) takes longer when you add physical RAM, as well as when you restart after a system crash. This is normal.
  - **c.** If your Mac suddenly starts taking an unusually long time to start up (with lots of disk activity taking place), it may be that the AppleShare PDS file can become corrupted. To fix this, delete the file and re-create your access privileges as needed. Since AppleShare PDS is an invisible file, you will need to use a utility, such as DiskTop, that lets you view invisible files (as described more in Chapter 8).

  SEE: • Chapter 11 for more on file sharing and the PDS file

Frequent System Crashes and Other Disk-Related Quirks

Symptoms:

The disk apparently mounts successfully, but as soon as you attempt to work with it, you notice serious problems, including the following:

- Multiple copies of the icon for a mounted hard disk appear scattered across your desktop. Continued use of the Mac is likely to result in a system crash. (This unusual symptom is a SCSI-related problem, as described later in this section.)
- Frequent system crashes occur at erratic and unpredictable intervals (but only when the problem disk is the startup disk).
- System crashes occur shortly after you attempt any sort of access to a specific disk, such as trying to open an application or document on the disk.

Other strange symptoms may appear. The critical diagnostic clue in almost all these cases is that the problem is specific to one particular disk but involves almost all general activity related to that disk. These are all one step short of a total disk crash. If the problem is left unattended, you may soon find that the disk does not mount at all.

Causes:

The problem is almost always due to software damage to the Directory or related invisible disk files, or to media damage to the disk itself. Other possibilities include a virus, corrupted system files, SCSI problems, or hardware that needs to be repaired. Again, depending on the nature of the damage, it is often repairable entirely by software techniques.

What to do:

Check for Damage

Check for damage to the disk, and repair it if possible. Start by using Disk First Aid, then try the more industrial-strength repair utilities.

SEE: • Fix-It #10 on Disk First Aid and Fix-It #13 on other repair utilities

Check for Viruses

SEE: • Fix-It #7 on viruses

System Software and Application Problems

Problems such as frequent Type 10 or Type 11 errors are known to be due to bugs, either in some versions of the system software or in specific applications (Netscape Navigator is commonly cited here).

SEE: • Chapter 4 for a more detailed discussion of this issue
SEE • Chapter 14 for more on problems with Netscape and online connections in general

Startup Disk Problems

If the problem occurs only when the disk is the startup disk, you should probably try replacing the system software files. Also consider possible problems with extensions that loaded at startup. You can even try rebuilding the desktop.

SEE:
- **Chapter 4 for more details on system errors**
- **Fix-It #4 on startup extension problems**
- **Fix-It #5 on replacing system software**
- **Fix-It #9 on rebuilding the desktop**

Hard Disk Problems

If the problem is with a hard drive (as opposed to a floppy disk), update the hard disk's device driver. If you have multiple disk drives connected, try to have all disks use the same driver.

Also check for general SCSI-related problems, especially if your symptoms include multiple copies of the hard disk icon appearing across your desktop. This symptom typically indicates a SCSI ID number conflict.

SEE:
- **Fix-It #12 on disk device drivers and Fix-It #16 on SCSI problems**

If All Else Fails

If none of the previous steps has worked, recover essential files from the disk, if possible.

SEE:
- **Fix-It #13 on recovering files from damaged disks**

After file recovery, if it is a floppy disk, discard it; if it is a hard drive, reformat it. Make sure your reformatting utility is a current version.

SEE:
- **Fix-It #15 on reformatting**

If the problem persists after you've reformatted a hard disk (or, for a floppy disk drive, when you use other floppy disks), you may have a hardware problem with the drive itself. If you have not already done so, this would be a good time to seek outside help.

SEE:
- **Fix-It #17 on hardware problems and Fix-It #18 on seeking outside help**

Chapter 6

When You Can't Find, Open, or Otherwise Use a File

It's the Little Things 191

Understanding Opening and Saving 191

Open and Save Dialog Boxes 191

Opening Files from the Finder 192

Using Save versus Save As 192

Solve It! Problems with Files 193

When You Can't Locate a File 193

Can't Find It in the Finder 193

Can't Find It in an Open Dialog Box 193

Avoid Saving Files to Unintended Locations 194

Don't Inadvertently Move a File Instead of Copying It 194

Look for a File from the Finder 194

Modify the Finder's Window Displays 196

Look for a File from an Application's Open Dialog Box 197

If the File Was Inadvertently Deleted 200

If None of the Preceding Steps Succeeds in Locating the File 203

When You Can't Launch an Application or Control Panel 203

Insufficient Memory to Launch an Application 204

Miscellaneous Other Causes 204

Insufficient Memory or Unexpected Quit 204

Incompatible Control Panel Settings 206

You Cannot Open a File from Its Alias 206

You Cannot Open the File Because It Is in a Compressed or Disk Image Format 207

You Cannot Open a File Because You Have the "Wrong" Macintosh 208

Too Many Files Are Currently Open 209

You Cannot Open an Application Because of Duplicate Copies on a Network 209

You Cannot Open Damaged Files 209

Solve It! Problems with Files (continued)

When You Can't Open a Document 213

If a Document's Application Can't Be Found by the Finder 214

An Application Does Not Import a Document File, Even Though the Application Has a Translator Available for the File's Format 220

The File Is in PC/DOS Format and/or on a PC/DOS-Formatted Disk 220

Insufficient Memory to Open the File 222

The File Is Not Intended to Be Opened 222

Opening a Document from the Finder When the Application Is Already Open 223

Opening a Document File from the Finder Launches the Wrong Application 223

The Problem May Be with the Application, Not the Document 224

Damaged Preferences 224

Damaged Documents That Can't Be Opened 224

When You Can't Delete a File or Folder 225

Make Sure the File or Folder Is Really in the Trash 225

If the File or Folder Is on a Floppy Disk, Check if the Floppy Disk Is Locked 226

Check If the File Is Locked 226

Folders Locked via the Sharing Command 227

Check If the File Is Currently Open or in Use 228

Folders That Unexpectedly Remain "In Use" 228

The Folder from Hell Problem 229

Deleting Damaged Files 230

When All of the Preceding Steps Fail to Delete the File or Folder 231

When You Can't Rename a File or Folder or Volume 232

When You Can't Save or Copy a File 233

For Problems with Locked or Full Disks 234

Full Disk Problem with Virtual Memory 234

Files That Are "In Use" and "Illegal Access Permission" 235

For Problems Due to a Disk Error 236

When the Going Gets Weird 238

Scroll, Close, Quit, Restart 238

If the Problem Results in a System Error of Any Sort 238

Check for Hardware Incompatibilities Between Your Hardware and the Application in Use 238

Check for Damage to or Other Problems with the Application's Preferences File 238

Check Whether One of the Application's Accessory Files Is Missing or Mislocated 239

Check Whether the Application or Any of Its Accessory Files Are Damaged 239

Consider Whether the Problem Is Due to a Bug in the Application 239

Check for Startup Extension Conflicts 240

Check for Memory-Related Problems 241

Check for System Software Problems 242

If All Else Fails, Round Up the Usual Suspects 243

Printing Problems? 243

It's the Little Things

Maybe you want to open a file, but you can no longer remember where on your disk it is located. Or maybe when you do finally find it, the Macintosh refuses to open it. Or maybe when you later try to delete the file, the Macintosh says "no dice." (Well, maybe not in those exact words.) These are the sorts of problems that are the subject of this chapter. If the previous chapter focused on problems that affected your use of an entire disk, this chapter narrows the focus to those problems that are limited to your use of a specific file. You will most likely confront these problems in one of two situations:

- When you are using an Open or Save dialog box from within an application to locate, open, or save a file.
- When you are using the Finder to locate, open, copy, or delete files.

As familiar as these procedures are to most Macintosh users, there are some potential misunderstandings about their use. I'll clear these up first, then go on to describe the problems you are likely to confront.

Understanding Opening and Saving

Open and Save Dialog Boxes

The Open or Save dialog box appears after you select the Open, Save, or Save As commands from the File menu of most applications.

To review briefly, using these commands is a two-step process:

1. **Navigate to the desired location.** The folder name (it may also be a volume name, or simply the Desktop) listed above the scroll box is the name of the folder whose contents are currently displayed in the scrolling list. Double-click any folder listed in the scroll box to display the contents of that folder; the folder's name then becomes the one listed above the scroll box. Conversely, select a folder's name from the pop-up menu that appears when you click the name of the currently open folder, and you retreat back to the location you selected. Use these techniques to move to the desired location.
2. **Open or save.** You've arrived at your desired destination. If you are in an Open dialog box, click Open to select the desired file. If you are in a Save dialog box, enter a name for the file (after first clicking in the rectangle where a name is entered, if necessary) and click Save.

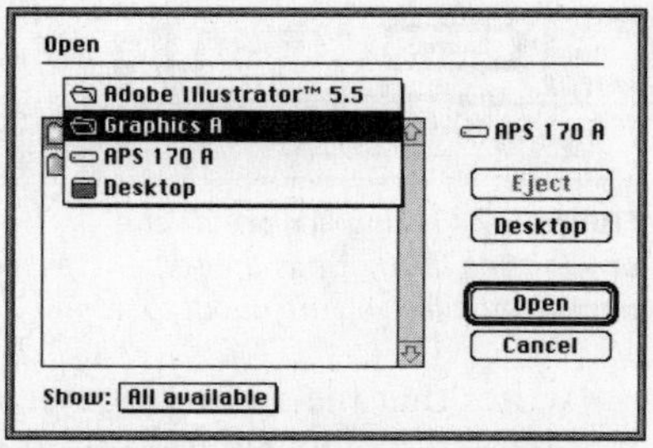

Figure 6-1 *Navigating in an Open dialog box: Choose an item from the pop-up menu to go to the selected location.*

Remember, Open dialog boxes will generally only show those files that can be opened by the application in use. To see a complete list of files on your drive, you need to go to the Finder.

Opening Files from the Finder

You can also open most files (applications or documents) directly from the Finder, either by double-clicking the file's icon or by single-clicking the icon and then selecting Open from the Finder's File menu.

With applications that support *drag and drop* (and most now do), you can drag the icon of a document over to an application icon. If the application can read that type of document file, the application icon will be highlighted. Release the mouse button, and the application needed to open the document launches, followed by the document itself. This is an especially great way to open a document with an application other than the one that created the document (which is what would launch if you just double-clicked the document).

Using Save versus Save As

When you are saving a document for the first time, the Save and Save As commands do the same thing. The difference emerges when you want to preserve changes to a previously saved document.

In this case the Save command simply overwrites the previous version and replaces it with the newly modified version. You will get no dialog box or alert message when this happens, even though the previous version (unless you have a backup copy) is gone forever! It can't even be undeleted (as described in Chapter 2).

The Save As command prompts you to save the document as a separate file with a different name. As a result, you wind up with two documents: the original file, and the modified file. After you do this, if you have not closed the document at the same time, you will be working with the modified document instead of the original one.

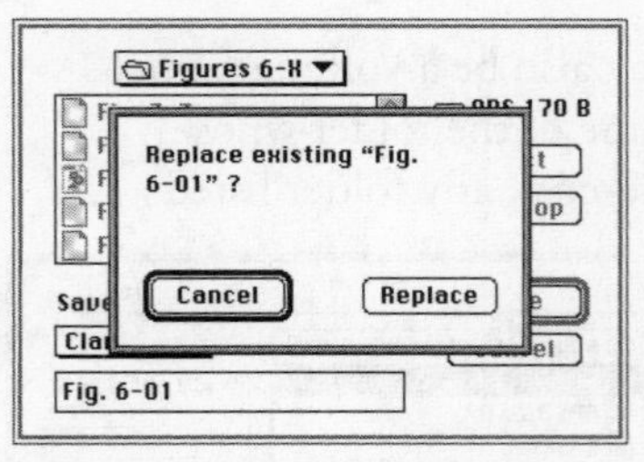

Figure 6-2 *Clicking Replace deletes any existing file that has the same name as the file you are about to save.*

Be careful not to overwrite a file unintentionally with Save As by giving the new document the exact same name as the file you are currently using. If you do this, you will get an alert message asking whether you want to replace the original document. If you click Replace, you essentially wind up with what you would have gotten if you'd simply selected Save instead. If you expected to wind up with two separate documents, you will be sadly surprised.

If you get the Replace alert even though you have changed the name of the file, some other file with the same name already exists at that location. Clicking Replace overwrites that file and replaces it with the current one. Before doing this, make sure you are not deleting a file you still want.

Finally, remember that nothing is saved until you save it! Don't be nervous about making sweeping changes to your document and then not being able to return to the original version. Until you select Save, you can *always* get back to the original version simply by closing the document (click "No" when asked if you want to save it) and then reopening it. A Revert to Saved command, if your program has one, does the same thing. And, of course, if you save your sweeping changes to a new file using Save As rather than Save, the original version remains available. About the only way to save changes unintentionally is if your program autosaves documents without warning at some regular interval. I would advise against having a program set up to do this.

SEE: • "OpenDoc and Live Objects," in Chapter 13, for information on an OpenDoc feature that permits saving of multiple drafts of a document

Solve It! Problems with Files

When You Can't Locate a File

Symptoms:

You are looking for a file that you know is on your disk, but it does not seem to be there. More specifically, one of two situations is likely.

Can't Find It in the Finder

You look for a file from the Finder, navigating through all the folders on the desktop, but you are unable to locate the file. Usually, these missing files are document files. You are less likely to lose track of an application, but it can happen.

Can't Find It in an Open Dialog Box

You are using an Open dialog box from within an application and cannot get the document to appear in the list.

Causes:

Admittedly, in some cases, a file may really be missing from your disk. But before you assume this has happened, calm down. The file is almost always present somewhere on your disk, in perfect condition.

The most common cause of apparently lost files is, to put it bluntly, you. Here are typical examples of what can happen; more details are given in the "What to Do" section that follows:

- You incorrectly recall what you named the file.
- The file was inadvertently saved to an unintended location.
- The file was moved rather than copied.
- You are looking for the file in the Open dialog box of the wrong application.
- The file was inadvertently deleted.

What to do:

Avoid Saving Files to Unintended Locations

When you first use Save or Save As to save a new file, the application you are using may select a default folder in which to place the file. This location, however, may not be where you intend to save the file. If you do not notice this and simply click the Save button, the file winds up buried in a location where you might never think to look. In some cases, you may even save it to a floppy disk when you intended to save it to your hard drive (or vice versa).

When you are using Save for the first time (or whenever you are using Save As), check the pop-up menu above the list of files in the dialog box to see if the currently selected folder (and disk) is the one that you want to use. Change the location if it is incorrect, then save the file.

Don't Inadvertently Move a File Instead of Copying It

Moving a file occurs when you drag the file to a different folder on the same disk. Doing this transfers the file to that new location. There is still only one copy of the file on your disk.

Copying a file occurs when you move a file to a different disk. In this case, you wind up with two copies of the file: one on the original disk, and another on the destination disk.

If you forget this distinction, you may expect to find a moved file still in its original location. Hint: It won't be there.

BY THE WAY ▶

COPYING ON THE SAME DISK

You can make a second copy of the same file in a different folder of the same disk, if you want. Just hold down the Option key as you drag the file. To make a second copy of a file at exactly the same location as the original, use the Duplicate command (Command-D) from the Finder's File menu.

Look for a File from the Finder

Use the Finder's Find File Command If you cannot easily find a particular file, you can at least save yourself the headache of searching manually through every folder on your hard drive by using the Find command (as first described in Chapter 2). Note that there are really two types of Find functions in System 7.5 and beyond. The one that you should see by default is really derived from an application called Find File, stored in your Apple Menu Items Folder, and is only available in System 7.5 or later. The other one, which is built into the system software, exists in older versions of the system software. You will also see it in System 7.5 or later if you start up with extensions off, or if you hold down the Shift key when selecting Find from the File menu. The following instructions apply to both types of Find functions (with exceptions for the System 7.5 Find File added as indicated):

1. Select Find from the Finder's File menu.
2. Restrict the search range, if desired, by selecting a choice from the pop-up menu to the right of "Find items."
3. Type in the name of the file you are looking for (such as "Board Minutes") and click the Find button. If you are not sure of the exact name of the file, type in a portion of the name only. For example, if you don't recall whether you named the file "Board Minutes" or "Meeting Minutes," just type *Minutes* or even *Min*, and the Macintosh will locate every file whose name contains that segment of text.
4. If the Mac finds a file with a similar name that is not the one you are seeking, type Command-G (the keyboard equivalent of the Find Again command), and it will look for the next file that contains the selected text as part of its name. Keep doing this until you find the file or have searched the entire disk.

   System 7.5 Find File: Using Command-G is not necessary with the Find File feature in System 7.5, since it displays a complete list of all found files.

If none of this works, maybe you gave the file a totally different name from what you recall (perhaps you called it "October Notes"). The Find command can still assist you here if you remember some other critical aspect of the file, such as what day you saved it. Let's assume that you know that you saved the file yesterday.

1. To find the file, once again select Find from the Finder's File menu.
2. This time, click the More Choices button (if it isn't already selected).

   System 7.5 Find File: This step is not necessary if you are using the Find File function in System 7.5. Here, the More Choices button is used to set up searches based on multiple criteria, not to access more options for doing a single-criterion search.
3. Select Date Modified from the first pop-up menu (the one that probably says "Name" when you first open the dialog box).
4. The current date should appear. If you click on the day, arrow buttons will let you change the date back to yesterday (or whatever date you want).
5. To find all files created on a single day (or created since that day), select "is" (or "is after") from the middle pop-up menu.
6. Click Find. For the pre-System 7.5 Find function, the first matching file will appear; use Command-G to search for more files if it is not the one you are looking for. For the System 7.5 Find File, just look in the Results window for the file you want. If the correct file appears, you can hopefully recognize it by its name at this point.

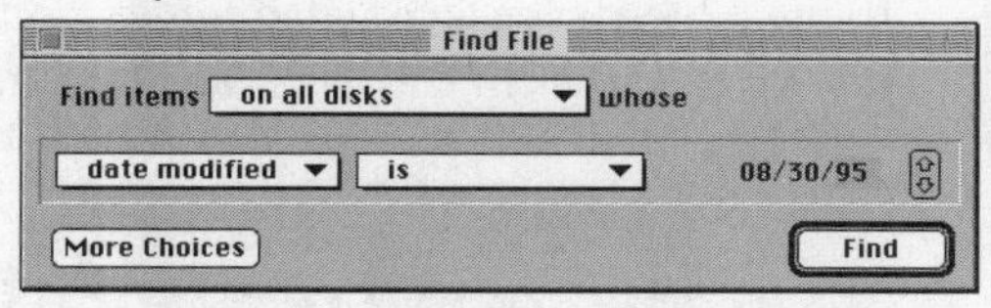

Figure 6-3 *Using the System 7.5 Find File to find all items created on a specific day.*

SEE: • Chapter 2 for more on how Find and Find File works

Modify the Finder's Window Displays

Close and Reopen the Folder Window There is an apparent bug in some versions of system software, such that the Finder does not properly update information about files listed in open windows until after the window is closed. This could cause a file to be listed temporarily with an older, incorrect modification date. In the most extreme cases, the file may appear to be missing altogether. Simply closing and reopening the window usually corrects this problem.

BY THE WAY ▶

WRONG MODIFICATION DATES

If all of your recently saved documents have incorrect modification dates—usually dates that are much older than they should be—you may have a weak or dead battery in your Mac. The correct date is maintained in Parameter RAM via the battery. Check the date in the Date and Time (or General Controls) control panel; if it is wrong, reset it. If the corrected setting is lost again after you reset, try zapping the PRAM. If that doesn't work, you probably need to replace the battery. This problem may also be caused by a corrupted System file, so if the PRAM fix fails, replace the System file.

SEE: • Fix-It #5 on reinstalling system software
SEE: • Fix-It #11 on zapping the Parameter RAM

Select Clean Up by Name Sometimes, if you are using an icon view, a file is located in the extreme corners of a window, far from the other files and almost inaccessible by normal scrolling. To solve this quickly, hold down the Option key and then select the Clean Up command from the Finder's Special menu. What is normally the Clean Up Window command will now most likely read Clean Up by Name (though, depending on your most recent selection from the View menu, it may read Clean Up by Size, Clean Up by Date, and so on). Clean Up by Name moves all icons close together, sorted in alphabetical order.

This sorting process also helps uncover icons that may be hidden from view because they are underneath another icon.

Use View by Date (or Other Non-Icon View) Selecting a non-icon view can help locate a file lost in a crowded folder. For example, if you know that a file you want was just saved earlier in the day, View by Date should bring it to the top of the list.

BY THE WAY ▶

LOOKING FOR A FILE MISSING FROM THE APPLE MENU

The Apple menu lists files only if they are in the Apple Menu Items folder on the startup disk. Check to make sure the missing file is in the folder. Also, make sure you have not started up from a different startup disk than you usually use. If you use a utility such as Suitcase to manage your desk accessories, make sure it is on.

BY THE WAY ▶

SEARCHING WITHIN A TEXT FILE

If you are searching for a text file and you can't remember anything helpful about its name or date, specialized utilities can search for text files based on the actual content within the file. With one of these utilities (Gofer is an example), you could search for any file that contained an expression such as "Academy Award" anywhere in the document itself, not just in the title. Microsoft Word, via its Find function, has this capability built into the program, but it can only search for files that Word can read—in contrast, utilities like Gofer work with all files.

System 7.5's Find File can also search for text within a file via its Contents option. You need to hold down the Option key, when selecting the "name" pop-up menu, to get this choice.

Look for a File from an Application's Open Dialog Box

In general, if you are having difficulty locating a file from an Open dialog box, go to the desktop (Finder) to look for it. Otherwise, when using the Open dialog box, consider the following possibilities.

The Application Is Not Supposed to List the File An application's Open dialog box usually lists only those data files that can be opened by that application. So, for example, don't look for a database document from your word processor's Open dialog box. Make sure you correctly recall what application you used to create your document.

You Are Not Using the Application You Think You Are Using Similarly, when you select Open from a File menu, make sure you have the correct application—that is, make sure your intended application is the active application. There are several ways to do this.

- **Check the Application menu**
  This is the menu at the far right of the menu bar; the active application is the one with its icon displayed in the menu bar itself. Additionally, the menu lists all open applications, with a check mark in front of the active one. If the checked application is not the one you want, select the one you want instead.

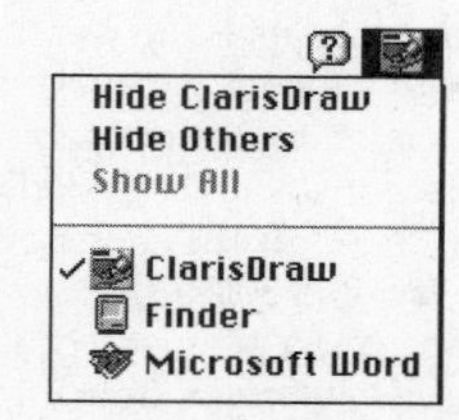

Figure 6-4 *The Application menu, with ClarisDraw as the active application—indicated both by the check mark next to its name in the menu, and its icon in the menu bar (next to the Apple Guide icon)*

- **Check the Apple menu**
  Alternatively, the first line in the Apple menu almost always says "About BusyWorks" (or whatever the name of the active application is). If the name shown is not the one you want, you can use the Application menu to shift to the correct one.
- **Examine the menu bar menus**
  The menu bar contains the menus of the active application. If you are familiar with an application's unique menus, you may recognize if it is currently active just by scanning the names of the menus in the menu bar.
- **Click a window**
  If the application you want to use has any open windows, clicking any one of its windows makes it the active application.

TAKE NOTE ▶

SYSTEM 7.5, NOW UTILITIES, AND MORE: HELPING YOU FIND YOUR WAY

Many novice users get frustrated by what happens when they accidentally click in the desktop background while working within an application. Typically, this causes the active application to shift from whatever they were using to the Finder; its windows may disappear or move to a back layer. Users may have no idea what has happened, may not realize they are no longer in their word processor (or whatever), and may have some difficulty figuring how to return.

All of this is solved in System 7.5 by a new option called Finder Hiding. This makes the Finder inactive while an application is running, so that you remain in that application even if you click outside its windows. To activate this, uncheck "Show Desktop when in background" from System 7.5's new General Controls control panel. This feature complements the Hide Others and Hide <application name> commands in the Application menu.

By the way, other third-party utilities, such as the "Auto-Hide application windows" option in Now Menus, have a similar function.

A related new feature in System 7.5 is WindowShade. With this control panel installed, when you double-click the title bar of any window, the entire window (except the title bar) disappears, like a window shade rolling up. This can reduce screen clutter when you have several applications—each with its own window—open at once.

System 7.5 also includes an option, accessed from the General Controls control panel, to save all documents from all applications to a single folder. This will help prevent documents from being saved to unexpected locations, making finding these documents easier.

The General Controls control panel in System 7.5.3 adds yet another option: "Folder that is set by the application." When you open a document by double-clicking its icon, the default folder for saving documents will be set to the folder containing the document (instead of to the Documents folder, or the folder containing the application that opened that document).

Some problems have been reported with the Documents Folder feature, so disable it if it seems to cause you grief. Actually, you may find it wise to disable the entire General Controls control panel. You can still use many of its features (such as the blinking rate settings) even with the control panel "disabled."

A new control panel in System 7.5, Apple Menu Options, adds Recent Applications, Recent Documents, and Recent Servers hierarchical menus to the Apple menu. The listings in these menus are based on folders (stored in the Apple Menu Items folder) where the Macintosh places aliases of the relevant recently used items. Since selecting a listed item opens the item, you can use these menus to access desired files quickly.

Now Menus from Now Utilities provides a similar, more full-featured version of this idea. Its menu can be totally separate from the Apple menu. Also, if you place an alias of your hard disk's icon in the Apple Menu Items folder, Now Menus will create a hierarchical menu of everything on your disk, nested five levels deep (bear in mind that the more items Now Menus needs to keep track of, however, the more RAM Now Menus uses). It can also create a similar separate menu directly in your menu bar. Now FolderMenus, another Now Utilities option, will pop up a hierarchical menu of folders, subfolders, and files off of any folder listed in an Open or Save dialog box, as well as from any folder icon in the Finder, or from a folder's window header. PopUp Folder is yet another utility that does this. You have to see these utilities in action to truly appreciate them.

SEE:
- **"Take Note: Files Locked by the Performa or by System 7.5's General Control Panel," later in this chapter, for more on this control panel**
- **Chapter 13 for more on System 7.5 and later revisions in general**

Check the Open Dialog Box's Settings Many applications have options to selectively filter which files get displayed in the Open dialog box. If you select a translation filter that does not match your missing file, the file will not be listed. To maximize your chances of success, make sure the most general option for reading files (such as "All Available") is selected.

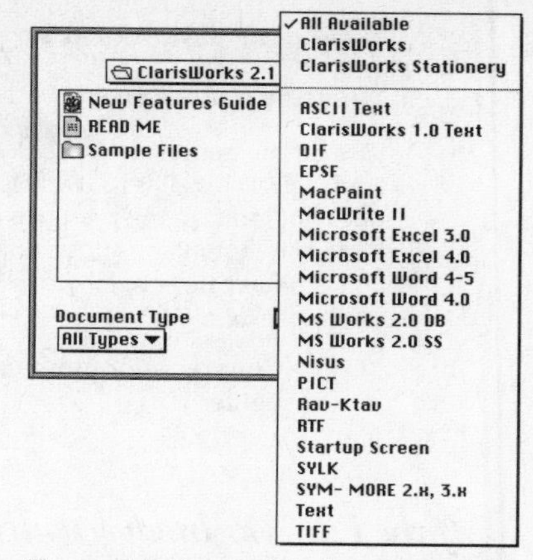

Figure 6-5 *Some of the format translators available with ClarisWorks—select one, and only the files matching that format are displayed in the Open dialog box.*

Check for Unusual File Names For example, if a blank space precedes the name of the file, it will be sorted alphabetically at the top of the list in an Open dialog box. If you look for this file based on where it should be, given the first real letter of its name (which, for a file named "Zoo Animals," would be at the bottom of the list), you will not find it.

The solution is to check the entire file list when a file does not appear in its expected location.

BY THE WAY ▶

FINDING THE ORIGINAL FILE FOR AN ALIAS

If you want to locate the original file linked to an alias, just open the Get Info window for the alias and click the Find Original button. As a shortcut, there are various freeware extensions or control panels that add a "Reveal Original" (Command-R) command to the Finder's File menu (at least in System 7.5.2 or later). These freeware utilities include Finder Extensions Enabler and Secret Finder Features.

If the link between your alias and original file appears to be "broken," check out "Cannot Open a File from Its Alias," later in this chapter.

Check the Desktop "Folder" Normally, all files on a disk are listed as "inside" that disk. Thus, if you click the Desktop button in an Open dialog box, you see the names of all currently mounted disks/volumes. Double-clicking a disk name results in a list of all the folders and files at the top level of the disk. These are the same items you would see from the Finder, in the window that would open if you double-clicked the disk icon.

A file, however, that is located directly on the desktop—that is, not in any window, but directly on the background area where the Trash and disk icons are found—is not listed as being inside the disk. These files are listed at the desktop level alongside the names of the mounted disks. All the items on the desktop appear in this one list, regardless of what disk contains the item.

If you fail to realize this, you may search in vain for a file by looking only at those files and folders inside the disk window. Instead, the file may be relaxing quietly at the desktop level.

TECHNICALLY SPEAKING ▶

THE DESKTOP FOLDER

Files on the desktop in System 7 are actually in a special invisible folder called the Desktop Folder. Each disk has its own Desktop Folder. The Open dialog box of most applications does not indicate the presence of these folders; instead, Desktop Folder files are just listed as if they are not in any folder. If the Open dialog box does show a Desktop Folder, however, you probably have to look there for files that would normally be listed directly at the desktop level.

SEE: • **Chapter 8 for more on invisible files, including the Desktop file and Desktop Folder**

If the File Was Inadvertently Deleted

If you still cannot find your file after trying all of the preceding suggestions, it is time to consider that it is really missing. One way this might happen is if you inadvertently deleted the file. Maybe you discarded a folder that contained the file you want, not realizing that the file was inside it. Whatever the reason, the file is now gone; here's what you can do about it.

Make Sure You Really Deleted the File Remember, the Trash is never emptied until you specifically select the Empty Trash command from the Finder's Special menu. Even if you restart the Macintosh, the items in the Trash remain as shown by the bulging Trash icon. So, if you haven't yet emptied the Trash, just double-click the Trash icon. If the window that opens up shows your items are still there, drag them out of the Trash, and you are back in business.

Unplug Your Mac If you have just accidentally deleted a file, you can probably get it back by *immediately* turning off the power on the Macintosh. Don't select Restart or Shut Down; don't even trust a reset. Pull the plug on the Mac from the wall outlet, then plug it back in and restart. Chances are your file will be back. I don't recommend this as a regular procedure, but it can be useful in an emergency.

Undelete the File If you really have deleted the file, don't despair yet. You may still be able to recover it. This is because when you delete a file, the Macintosh does not erase the data immediately; it simply frees up the space to be overwritten with new data as needed. If you have not added too many new documents since deleting the file, it may still be intact on your disk.

Utilities such as Norton Utilities and MacTools Pro can also recover recently deleted files. As first described in Chapter 2, these utilities work best if you have previously installed special extensions that the utility uses to keep track of what you have deleted (FileSaver and TrashBack, respectively).

SEE: • **Chapter 2 for more on installing and using these control panels**

If you are using Norton Utilities:

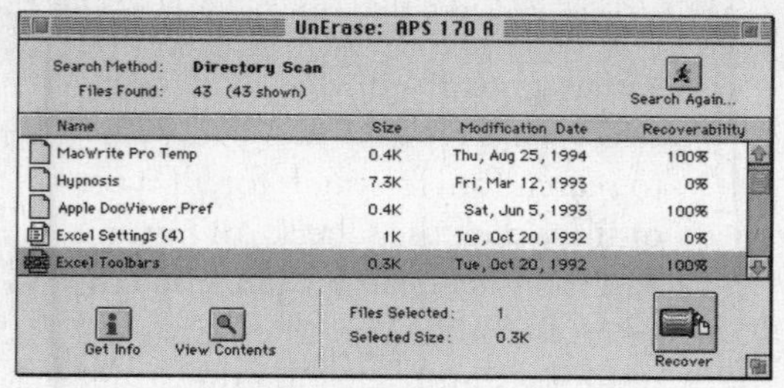

Figure 6-6 *The Norton Utilities UnErase window.*

1. Run Norton Utilities and select the UnErase option (turn File Sharing off if you are asked to do so). You can also directly launch UnErase using the Open UnErase application in the Norton Utilities folder.
2. From the next dialog box that appears, select the disk(s) that you believe may contain the deleted file(s). Then click the Search button. A list of files appears; if you want, you can click the View Contents button to view the contents of a selected file. For text files, this can help you figure out whether the file is truly the one you want to recover.
3. If the FileSaver control panel was installed prior to when you deleted the file(s) you want to recover, the desired file(s) should be listed. Select the files (using Shift-Click to select more than one file) and then click the Recover button. Files will be saved to the location you specify.
4. If FileSaver was not installed in time, click the Search Again button in the UnErase window. From the dialog box that appears, select options as described in "Technically Speaking: Undeleting Files Without First Installing the Special Invisible Files." These will create a list of files in the UnErase window that can then be recovered.

SEE: • **Fix-Its #13 and #14 for more on using UnErase**

If you are using MacTools Pro:

1. If TrashBack is installed and enabled, select the TrashBack command from the Finder's Special menu. This will bring up a window that lists all files currently tracked by TrashBack; if you want, you can click the View button to view the contents of a selected file. For text files, this can help you figure out whether the file is truly the one you want to recover. Otherwise, simply click to the left of the name of each file you want to undelete (this will place a check mark next to each name), then click the Recover button. Files will be saved to the location you specify.
2. If TrashBack was not installed or enabled, launch MacTools Clinic. Select the disk from which you wish to undelete files and click the Undelete button. From the dialog box that appears next, click the File Scan button.

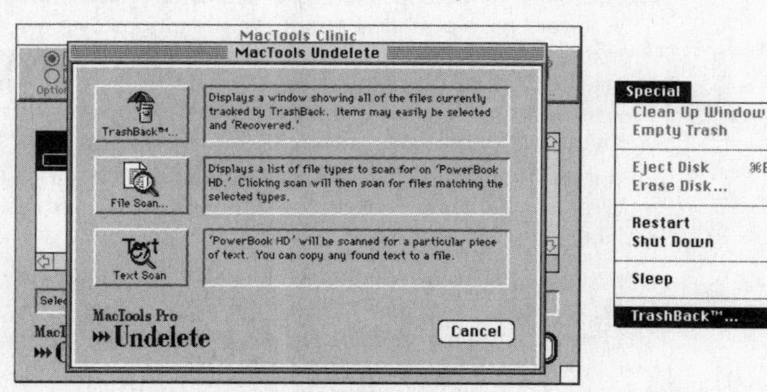

Figure 6-7 *Left: The dialog box that appears after selecting Undelete from MacTools Clinic. Right: MacTools Pro's TrashBack command in the Finder's Special menu.*

You will be then presented with a dialog box from which you can select what types of files you wish to search for. To search for all types of files, click the Check All button, and then the Scan button (though when I tried it, I got the same result by simply clicking the Scan button, leaving all types unchecked).

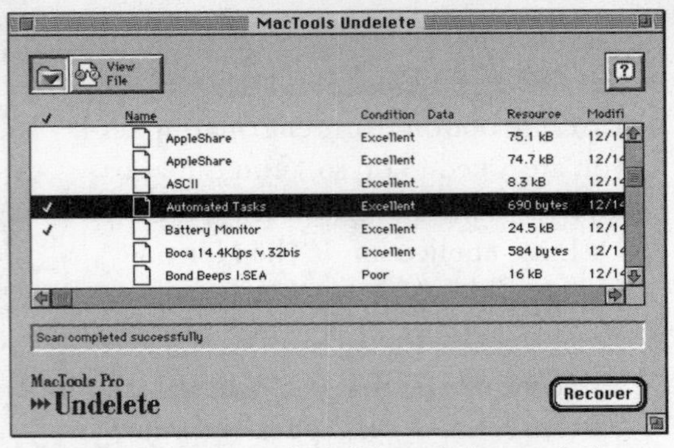

Figure 6-8 *The MacTools Undelete window, used when TrashBack was not enabled.*

You will then see a list of files that you can recover, similar to how TrashBack works. The list may include applications as well as documents. Click the View button to check on the contents of any file. Again, click to the left of the name of each file you want to undelete, placing a check mark next to its name, then click the Recover button. Files are saved to the location you specify.

If even this fails, return to MacTools Clinic, click Undelete again, and then click the Text Scan button.

TECHNICALLY SPEAKING ▶

UNDELETING FILES WITHOUT FIRST INSTALLING THE SPECIAL INVISIBLE FILES

If you have not installed FileSaver or TrashBack before you need to undelete a file, all is still not lost. Packages such as Norton Utilities and MacTools Pro include other options to help recover files.

- The *file scan* or *file pattern scan* method searches for specific types of documents that the utility is designed to recognize (such as Excel documents and MacWrite documents). Both Norton Utilities and MacTools Pro give you options to specifically select which applications' documents you want to search for. With MacTools Pro, if you want to search for a type of document that is not listed, you can add its type (check the MacTools Pro manual for details).
- The text scan method can recover segments of text from a deleted text document (such as a word processing file). Usually you cannot recover more than a few paragraphs of text this way, particularly if the document is fragmented (see Fix-It #8 on defragmenting your disk), but this still may be better than nothing. You enter a string of text that you want to search for, and then initiate a scan of the disk for any document that contains that string. Choose this option only as a last resort.
- UnErase from Norton Utilities also includes a third option, Directory-scan. If you haven't installed a utility like FileSaver or TrashBack, this is your best chance of recovering a file intact.Try this method first.

With MacTools, you access these options by clicking the Undelete button from MacTools Clinic. With Norton Utilities, click the Search Again button in the UnErase window.

In general, these techniques are less reliable than a method that depends on a preinstalled extension. They are only for those times when you are really desperate.

Two important caveats to bear in mind when you are trying to undelete files are discussed below.

- **Some files may be only partially recoverable**
  Eventually, an erased file is written over by a newly created file. The erased file is then gone forever. In some cases, though, only part of an erased file may have been overwritten. These files may still be partially recoverable, although the salvaged parts are mainly useful only for text files. Your undelete utility typically lists the recoverability of each deleted file. If you have problems opening a partially recovered file, refer to "When You Can't Open a Document," later in this chapter.
- **Recovered files may not open properly**
  When you double-click a recovered document file, even if it appears to be fully restored, you may see an error message that says the creating application could not be found. Usually you can still open the document if you select it from within the application using its Open dialog box. If you then save the document to a new name using Save As, the new document should behave normally.

SEE: • "When You Can't Open a Document," later in this chapter, for more details
• Chapter 8 on file types and creators for more technical information

If None of the Preceding Steps Succeeds in Locating the File

The File May Be Missing Because of Problems with the Disk Itself This is the last, and most unhappy, possibility. It often means that your problems go beyond the immediate loss of one file. Sometimes these problems are repairable, usually by a utility such as Norton Utilities or MacTools.

SEE: • Chapter 5, the section entitled "Files Missing from the Desktop"
• Fix-It #13 on fixing damaged disks

Otherwise, It Is Probably Lost for Good It's time to give up. If the file was critical, I hope you had a backup copy.

When You Can't Launch an Application or Control Panel

Symptoms:

You try to open an application or control panel (or desk accessory) from the Finder, usually by double-clicking its icon, but the application does not open. Usually an error message appears with an indication as to why the file did not launch; it also may offer advice on how to solve the problem.

In the worst cases, a system error may occur. In this case, refer to Chapter 4, which covers system errors.

Causes:

Insufficient Memory to Launch an Application

The most common reason an application does not open is because there is less available RAM (memory) than the application requires. Whether you have as little as 1MB of RAM or as much as 80MB, you occupy some of that memory each time you open an application, and you can still reach the limits of your machine. As you keep more and more applications open at the same time, you eventually have too little left over to open one more program.

Actually, some applications require so much RAM that they may not open on your machine even if nothing else is open (other than the Finder, which stays open at all times).

In any of these cases, you probably get an error message informing you that the problem is due to insufficient memory.

Sometimes, an application starts to open but then quits in midstream, accompanied by a message that says that the program "unexpectedly quit" (a problem described in more detail in Chapter 4). This is also usually a memory-related problem.

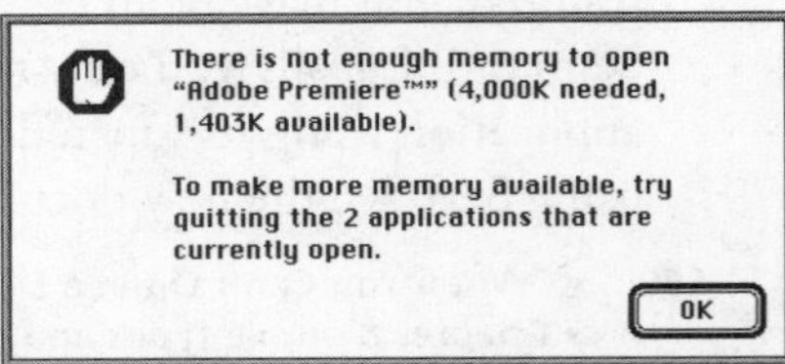

Figure 6-9 *Here's what happened when I tried to open Adobe Premiere with less than the necessary amount of memory available.*

Miscellaneous Other Causes

More explanation of these causes is given in the "What to Do" section. By the way, many of the following causes apply to documents as well as to applications, control panels, and desk accessories.

- A control panel setting is incompatible with the application.
- You cannot open a file from its alias.
- You cannot open a file because it is in a compressed or disk image format.
- You cannot open a file because you have the "wrong" Macintosh.
- Too many files are currently open.
- You cannot open damaged files.

What to do:

Insufficient Memory or Unexpected Quit

Generally, if an error message offers advice on what to do to remedy this problem, follow its advice. Otherwise, try each of the following solutions, as needed:

- Quit currently open applications to free up more memory, then try to launch the application again.

- Restart the Macintosh and try again to launch the application. Sometimes, due to a memory leak (as described in Fix-It #6), restarting will be required to free up enough memory to get the program to launch. Also, sometimes after an unexpected or forced quit (as described in Chapter 4), the application will refuse to launch until after you restart. If you try before restarting, you will get another unexpected quit or a similar error message.

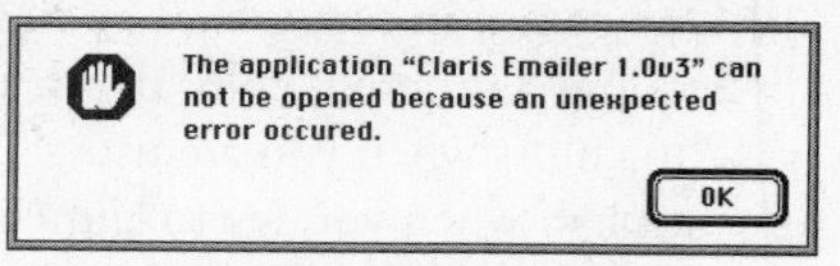

Figure 6-9A *Claris EMailer refused to relaunch after an unexpected quit, showing this error message. After I restarted the Mac, the program worked fine.*

- Restart the Macintosh with all unneeded extensions/control panels (startup extensions) disabled. This reduces the amount of memory allocated to the system software, thereby freeing up more memory for your application. This is a work-around solution (since you will no longer have the benefit of the disabled extensions/control panels), but it at least may allow you to launch the problem application. The simplest approach here is to disable all startup extensions by holding the Shift key down while the Macintosh is starting up. If you need a particular startup extension to remain enabled while using the application in question, you will instead need to disable extensions individually.

  SEE: • Fix-It #4 on disabling extensions

- You may have to open the problem application's Get Info window and decrease the application's Preferred memory size. If none of the previous suggestions work, there are also several other similar memory-related solutions you can try.

  SEE: • Chapter 2 on the Get Info window
  • Fix-It #6 on memory management problems for more potential solutions

TAKE NOTE ▶

MICROSOFT WORD 5.1 MEMORY BUG

Perhaps you are like me and still prefer Word 5.1 to Word 6.x. If so, you probably know that there is a bug in Microsoft Word 5.1 that causes the application to fail to open occasionally, especially on newer Mac models. Instead, an error message informs you that Word would not open because "System memory is too low." It advises you to reduce Word's memory size.

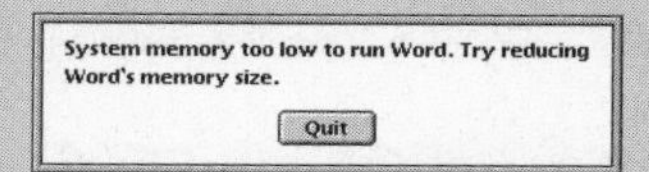

Figure 6-9B *The Microsoft Word 5.1 "memory bug" message.*

Typically you can ignore this advice; this is just a bug and it has little or nothing to do with how much memory you actually have. A few reports, however, suggest that you can eliminate this message simply by making Word's Preferred memory size (in its Get Info window) just a little bit smaller or even a little bit larger than its default setting.

The bug most often appears when Word is the first application you try to launch after startup. If you launch another application and go back to Word, or if you simply try relaunching Word a few times, the problem is usually resolved. This has been my solution.

There is a freeware extension, called FixWordSystemMemory, that supposedly eliminates this problem. When I installed it on my Power Mac 7500, however, it had little or no effect. Some users report that RAM Charger can also solve the Word 5.1 bug. Otherwise, increasing the size of the system heap (such as via Conflict Catcher's Guarantee System Heap command) may resolve this problem (see Fix-It #6 for more details on this).

Incompatible Control Panel Settings

One common example of an incompatible control panel setting is a program that requires a different color depth setting than the one you currently use (for instance, 256 colors when you are using 16 grays). An error message usually explains this problem when you try to launch the application. In other cases, problems may be due to incompatibility with virtual memory or 32-bit addressing options in the Memory control panel.

For color depth problems, assuming that you have the appropriate hardware to adjust the color depth, the obvious solution is to change the setting by using the Monitors control panel. Most game programs these days make this adjustment for you (if you click OK) when you launch the game.

For Memory control panel problems (or similar sorts of problems with any other control panel), you probably have to turn the relevant control panel options off.

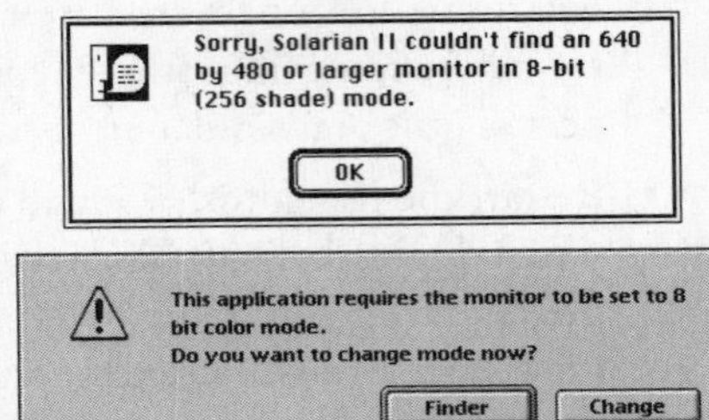

Figure 6-10 *Top: The game Solarian II gives you this error message if your Mac is running in black-and-white. Bottom: Crystal Caliburn gives you this message when you are using more than 256 colors.*

SEE:
- **Chapter 10 on displaying color**
- **Fix-It #1 on hardware incompatibilities**
- **Fix-It #5 on system software problems**
- **Fix-It #6 on memory problems**

BY THE WAY ▶

CAN'T OPEN THE VIEWS CONTROL PANEL?

If you ever have trouble opening Apple's Views control panel, remember that this control panel includes a pop-up menu of all of your fonts. A corrupted font may prevent the control panel from opening, perhaps even resulting in a system freeze. Also, if you have a gargantuan number of fonts in your System Folder, the control panel may take a very long time to open—perhaps fooling you into thinking that it will never open.

You Cannot Open a File from Its Alias

Occasionally, if you double-click an alias file, the original file does not launch. Instead, you get a message that says the original file cannot be located. Usually, this is because the original file has been deleted or renamed.

The easiest solution is to discard the alias file, find the original application, and create a new alias. Several utilities (such as one called Alias Director) are available to facilitate this process.

You also cannot open a file from its alias if the original file is on a disk that is currently not mounted, such as a CD-ROM disc or a shared disk (accessed via file sharing). To access these files, you have to remount the needed disk.

The alias "Interview notes alias" could not be opened, because the original item could not be found.

OK

Figure 6-11 *Here's what you see if you try to open a file from its alias, but the original file is missing or cannot be located.*

Sometimes an alias and its original file are both on the disk, but you still cannot open the file from its alias. This is called a *broken link*. There are various causes for this (including bugs in the system software), with various solutions. Rather than go into details, I will simply say that there are several utilities, such as AliasZoo and Alias Dragon, that can efficiently fix these problems. The latter utility is especially effective at fixing a problem whereby the drag-and-drop ability of an alias is lost.

BY THE WAY ▶

ALIAS (AND PREFERENCES FILE) LINKS LOST AFTER RESTORING OR TRANSFERRING DATA TO A DISK

If and when you reformat your hard drive and restore your files from your backups, or if you transfer the entire contents of your disk to a new disk (as you might do after purchasing a new hard disk), it is possible for most or all of your existing alias links to be broken. In the worst cases, the alias may actually wind up linked to a wrong original. All of this is less likely to occur if you make sure that the new or reformatted disk volume has the same name as the original disk. Similarly, make sure you assign the same name to the volume in the Sharing Setup control panel, and try not to relocate any files that have aliases associated with them until *after* you have used the alias to launch the file.

If you still have problems, there is no easy solution left; you will have to check out and re-create all affected aliases. The two utilities mentioned in the main text (AliasZoo and Alias Dragon) may help.

In some cases, after restoring your disk, you may have a similar problem with an application losing its link to its preferences file. As with aliases, you may have to delete the original preferences file and re-create your preference settings (see Fix-It #2 for more details).

You Cannot Open the File Because It Is in a Compressed or Disk Image Format

This problem is most likely to occur as a result of downloading files from an online service. These files are often stored in a compressed format, and they need to be decompressed before they can be opened. Unless they are stored as self-extracting files, you need special utilities to do this. One popular freeware utility of this sort is StuffIt Expander.

Similarly, sometimes you will download an entire disk, such as an Apple System Update disk. Usually, these are stored in a special disk-image format that requires a special utility, such as Apple's Disk Copy, to convert the files to a usable form.

Finally, if you use SpaceSaver and start up with extensions off, all of your compressed files may display the StuffIt icon. If so, you will have to expand each compressed file separately (using a utility such as Expander) before you can use it. A similar situation exists with AutoDoubler and other background compression utilities.

SEE: • Chapter 14 for more on problems using downloaded files

You Cannot Open a File Because You Have the "Wrong" Macintosh or System Software

This is becoming an increasingly common problem, particularly for control panels and other files from Apple system software. Many of these control panels are designed to work only with certain models of Macintosh (such as PowerBooks or Power Macs) or with other optional hardware. Some only work with certain versions of the system software (such as System 7.5 or later) or with certain other extensions installed (such as the Monitors & Sound control panel, which requires the SystemAV extension in order to work). Also, Apple's Installer may mistakenly install files on a Macintosh even though they do not work with that model. In any of these cases, when you try to open the file, you will get an error message saying that the file cannot be used (sometimes including an explanation as to why).

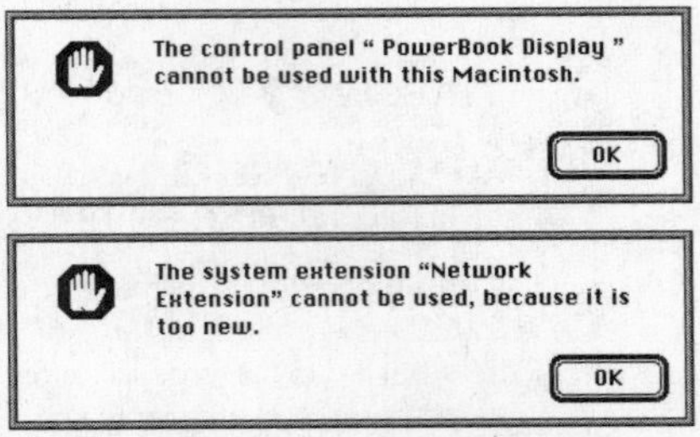

The control panel " PowerBook Display " cannot be used with this Macintosh.

OK

The system extension "Network Extension" cannot be used, because it is too new.

OK

Figure 6-12 *Examples of messages that may appear when you try to open a control panel that does not work with your model of Macintosh and/or your version of the system software.*

Before giving up, however, make sure that the control panel is in the Control Panels folder in the System Folder, restart, and try again. Sometimes this type of message appears when you try to open a control panel that was not loaded at startup (perhaps because you just added it and haven't restarted or shut down since then). After restarting, the problems go away.

You can have the same sorts of problems with applications, since versions of an application that are written specifically for a Power Mac will not run on other types of Macintoshes (see Chapter 12). Similarly, many applications only work with certain versions of the system software (such as 7.0 or later).

SEE: • Chapters 12 and 13 for more examples of these sorts of problems

TECHNICALLY SPEAKING ▶

YOU CANNOT OPEN A CONTROL PANEL BECAUSE NO INITS BIT IS CHECKED

On one strange occasion, upon trying to open a control panel, I got a message that said it would not open because it had not been loaded at startup. This typically means simply that the control panel had been disabled via an extension management utility (as described in Fix-It #4).

In this odd case, however, I knew it had not been disabled. Even odder, when I checked my extension manager's listing, the control panel was not even there anymore! Yet, when I checked in the Finder, the control panel file itself was clearly in the Control Panel folder within the System Folder. What was going on?

What had happened was that a conflict between two other extensions had caused an unusual result: the NO INITS bit on several of my control panels was incorrectly checked. This meant that the Macintosh, and my extension manager, no longer considered these files as ones to be loaded at startup (remember "INIT" is the older, more technical name for startup extensions). After determining and eliminating the conflicting extensions, I used a utility called Snitch to uncheck the bit. After that, things worked fine.

SEE: • Chapter 8 for more on the NO INITS bit and Get More Info

Too Many Files Are Currently Open

The Macintosh has a limit as to how many files can be open at one time. This limit is defined in an invisible area of your disk called the *boot blocks* (described more in Chapters 5 and 8). Typically, the limit is 40 files (though in System 7, it may expand more if needed). Normally, you will not come up against this limit, though some applications keep more files open than may be apparent because of their use of invisible files. If this does become a problem, the easy solution is to close some currently open files and try again. If you frequently have this problem, however, there is a freeware utility called Up Your FCBs that can permanently change the limit. I would use this utility with caution, as raising the limit too high may lead to other problems.

You Cannot Open an Application Because of Duplicate Copies on a Network

Some programs check over a network to see if other copies of the program with the same serial number are running. If there are, the program will not launch. I am not suggesting that you be a software pirate and try to defeat this copy protection. If you have a legitimate reason to do so, however, you can usually avoid the conflict simply by pulling the network plug out of the back of your Macintosh before you try to launch the program.

On a related note, if you use a Force Quit (Command-Option-Escape) to quit one of these programs, the program may not launch again—even if you are not connected to the network—because it mistakenly detects itself as still running. Usually, turning off AppleTalk will serve as a work-around solution; otherwise, you will have to restart as well. In some cases, just turning AppleTalk off will not work, and you will actually have to detach the LocalTalk cable from your Mac.

Panorama 2.0 had this "network" problem when using System 7.5.3, but it was fixed in Panorama 3.0.

You Cannot Open Damaged Files

If a file is damaged, there may be a cryptic error message when you try to open it, or no message at all. It may just fail to open, or a system error may occur. If you suspect a damaged file, here's how to check it out:

- Try again, as always, just in case. The file might open fine the second time.
- Otherwise, there is usually only software damage. In these cases, the best and easiest solution is to replace the application, its preferences file, and (if necessary) any of its accessory files.

  SEE: • Fix-It #2 on preferences files and Fix-It #3 on accessory files

- Sometimes an application may not open because of a damaged font file, rather than a problem with the application itself.

  SEE: • Chapter 9 for more on locating and replacing damaged font files

- For control panels, if you get a message saying that the file cannot be opened or used, perhaps the control panel did not properly load at startup (even if the message offers a different explanation). To check, make sure the control panel is in its correct folder

TECHNICALLY SPEAKING ▶

A FEW WORDS ABOUT SOUND AND SOUND FILES

- **Sound file formats.** In System 7, sounds can exist as independent files on the desktop, much like font files; if you double-click a sound file, the Macintosh will play the sound. If you have sound files that do not work this way, it is probably because these files are not in the standard format. Unfortunately, because Apple failed to provide any standard format prior to System 7, there are a variety of different formats that your sound file could be. The good news is that there are several shareware utilities that can easily convert most sound formats to the System 7 standard format. The one that I use most often is called Sound Extractor.

  These utilities can also be used to change a standard Apple sound file back to other formats (such as AIFF, WAV, or AU) that are commonly needed to use sounds on the World Wide Web. The new SimpleSound utility, which I will describe shortly, may help out here as well.

  SEE: • Chapter 14 for more on the World Wide Web

- **Damaged sound files.** If you still cannot get a sound file to play when you double-click it, the file may be damaged. In this case, a utility such as CanOpener may be able to recover the sound. Also, for those of you familiar with the basics of using Apple's ResEdit, try to open the sound resource using ResEdit. If the file is damaged, ResEdit will identify this and offer to try to fix it for you. If it succeeds, you should then extract the sound resource to a new file.

  SEE: • Fix-It #14 for general information on fixing damaged files

- **Apple's sound-related control panels.** Apple's sound-related software has become more complicated to track in recent months; even something as simple as selecting an alert sound and adjusting its volume can be a daunting task to summarize. Many users still depend on the basic Sound control panel to do this, but PCI-based Macs use the Monitors & Sound control panel (which itself is a replacement for the now defunct Sound & Displays control panel). Monitors & Sound has at least three different sound-related sections: Alerts (for alert sounds), Sound (for overall sound adjustment) and Monitor Sound (for AppleVision monitors that have built-in speakers). If you do not have a compatible PCI-based Mac, AppleVision adjustments will be in yet another control panel, AppleVision Setup. You can also make volume adjustments from the Control Strip's Sound module.

  Of all of these control panels, Sound is the only one that can record new sounds. That's why Apple now has another program, called SimpleSound, that comes with PCI-based Macs (and can be used by other Macs as well) for recording sounds.

- **Accessing alert sounds.** You select an alert sound from the Sound or SimpleSound files. Other applications, such as alarm clock utilities, may similarly access the list of alert sounds. The sounds listed are determined by what sound files have been installed directly into the System file. You can add a sound to the System file simply by dragging a standard System 7 sound file to the System Folder.

  Though System 7.1 and later revisions now use a Fonts folder rather than installing fonts into the System file, there is no equivalent Sounds folder. Several third-party utilities (such as SoundMaster) can bypass this restriction, however, allowing you to access sound files from anywhere on your disk and use them as alert sounds. These utilities also allow you to attach these sounds to almost any sort of event (such as Empty Trash or Eject Disk). In addition, there is a way to access sound files that are not in the System file without requiring any specialized software: change the file's type and creator to match that of a font suitcase. After this, simply place the sound file in the Fonts folder, and the System will correctly list it as a potential alert sound.

  SEE: • Chapter 8, "Add Alert Sounds Without Installing Them in the System File," for details on how to do this

(Continues on next page) ▶

▶ TECHNICALLY SPEAKING ▶

A FEW WORDS ABOUT SOUND AND SOUND FILES *(Continued)*

- **Alert sound volume.** Within the Sound control panel, the volume is regulated by two different volume controls. The main one is the slider visible when Alert Sounds is selected from the Sound control panel's pop-up menu. The other control (assuming you are using the built-in speakers) is the slider for Built-In volume, accessed by selecting Volumes from the pop-up menu. The Built-In volume sets the level for all sounds going to the built-in speaker, not just alert sounds.

  If you are not getting the sound level you expect by adjusting one of these sliders, try adjusting the other instead. For example, try keeping the Alert Sounds volume turned up to its maximum and instead adjust the Built-in volume. In any case, if the Built-in volume is set to zero (or if the Mute box below the volume slider is checked), you will get no alert sounds (or any other sounds from the built-in speaker) no matter what the volume setting of the Alert Sounds slider. If either slider is set to zero, the menu bar will flash when an alert sound would have otherwise occurred.

Figure 6-14 *The Volumes and Alert Sounds sections of the Sound control panel (left) and the alert sound files themselves, as installed in the System file (right).*

  Also, be aware that if you have a cable plugged into the sound-out port (the one with the speaker icon over it), sound will be directed through that port rather than to the built-in speaker (even if you have not made a separate selection from the sound-out section of the Sound control panel). This again can mean that you will be unable to hear alert sounds.

  If none of this seems to explain why you can't hear anything, it is possible that the wire from the logic board to the built-in speaker may have come loose. If you have a Mac whose insides are easily accessible, you can probably check and fix this yourself. If all else fails, you may need a logic board repair.

  If you use Monitors & Sound, the general options are similar, although the details change (especially if you have an AppleVision monitor). Refer to the Apple Guide file if you need additional advice.

  SEE: • **Chapter 12 for more details specific to AppleVision monitors**

- **Application sounds.** If you are having problems with hearing sounds other than alert sounds—such as ones used in games—again, check the setting of the slider(s) in the Volumes section of the Sound control panel (or the Sound portion of the Monitors & Sound control panel). Also, remember again that special rules apply to getting sound from AppleVision's built-in speakers. If virtual memory is on, this can distort sounds, especially in games and QuickTime movies.

- **Problems retaining sound volume setting.** You may have a problem where your Sound volume setting is not saved after a shutdown, reverting to some default value. While there are a number of possible causes and cures for this (zapping the PRAM or reinstalling system software may help, or hardware repair may be needed), the first thing to try is wonderfully simple: delete the Sound Preferences file in your Preferences folder, ideally after restarting with extensions off. Most of the time, this will solve your problem.

(Continues on next page) ▶

▶ TECHNICALLY SPEAKING ▶

A FEW WORDS ABOUT SOUND AND SOUND FILES *(Continued)*

Updating to System 7.5.3 or later also fixes some bugs that could cause this to occur, including a related problem where the mute box setting is not retained after a restart, but reports suggest that this problem still persists. Numerous work-around fixes have been suggested; one that usually works is to install a shareware extension called Unmute-It.

Finally, if you use Energy Saver 2.0 or later, some muting problems can be solved by making sure that the Notification Preferences "Mute sounds while the computer is asleep" option is unchecked.

- **Recording sounds with SimpleSound.** SimpleSound can create two types of sound files. The first, SimpleSound documents, are standard AIFF files that can be used by most sound-editing applications (such as Avid VideoShop or SoundEdit 16) and are also usable on the Web. To create, select New from SimpleSound's File menu.

  The second variety, "system" sounds, are files that play directly when you double-click them from the Finder. To do this, click the Add button from SimpleSound's Alert Sounds window. The newly recorded sound file will be stored in the System file initially (where it can be used as an alert sound), but you can drag it elsewhere for other uses if you wish.

- **CD Audio.** Most older Macintosh models (other than AV and Power Macs) cannot play stereo sound from audio CDs or CD-ROM discs through the Mac itself; instead, you have to attach external speakers or headphones directly to an external CD-ROM drive. For AV and Power Macs (at least those with internal CD-ROM drives), you can play stereo sound through the Mac's internal speakers—though the quality will not be great—if you first make the appropriate settings in the Sound control panel. In particular, select Sound In from the pop-up menu, then click the Options button. From the Options window, select the Internal CD icon and click to mark an "X" in the Playthrough box (remember to uncheck Playthrough when you no longer wish to access CD audio), then select Volumes from the pop-up menu to access and adjust the Built-In volume setting (make sure the Mute button is not checked).

  However, with System 7.5.3 on PCI-based Macs that use Monitors & Sound, life is easier. You should be able to hear stereo sound without any change in settings at all. You do *not* have to select the "Internal CD" option from Monitors & Sound's Sound Input pop-up menu in order to hear an audio CD from internal or external speakers. Similarly, you no longer need to select any "Playthrough" option.

- **PlainTalk Speech.** Macintoshes can now talk to you via MacinTalk 2, MacinTalk 3, or MacinTalk Pro, each of which use Apple's text-to-speech technology, loosely referred to as PlainTalk technology. You will especially need the Speech Manager extension (which has a version of MacinTalk built into it) and assorted other "voice" files (on AV Macs, Speech Manager is in ROM).

  An attempt to explain the differences between the versions of MacinTalk can lead to more confusion than I can possibly disentangle here. If you use an Installer utility to install all this software, however, it will generally turn out okay; check a PlainTalk manual or Apple Guide file for more details. To hear speech output, you will also need an application that supports this feature (Apple included this support in SimpleText; check out its Sound menu).

  Conversely, AV Macs and all Power Macs can obey your commands when they are spoken into a microphone. This capability requires additional components of Apple's PlainTalk software, as well as a PlainTalk-compatible microphone. If you intend to use either of these technologies, make sure you have the needed software and read instructions carefully for proper installation and use. In particular, having Speakable Items turned on from the speech control panel uses additional memory and may conflict with other programs.

(that is, not disabled) and that you did not start with extensions off, then restart normally. If the control panel does not open now, the message's explanation for why you cannot open the file is probably correct.

If you use an extensions manager (see Fix-It #4), make sure it is not set to disable the control panel at startup.

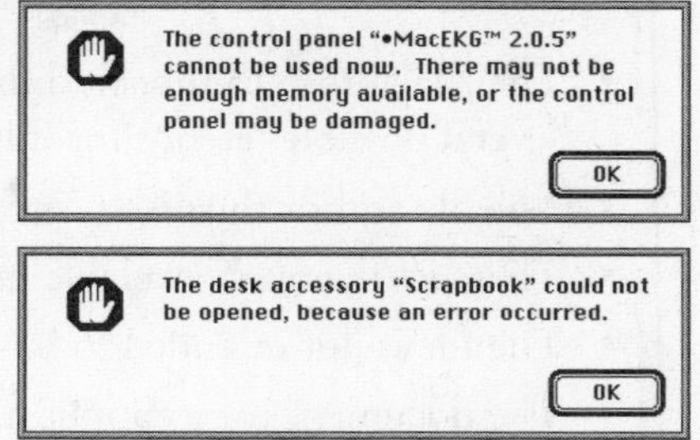

Figure 6-13 *Top: Trouble opening a control panel that may or may not be damaged. Bottom: This message often implies damage to the Scrapbook file (or sometimes the Scrapbook program itself).*

- Trouble opening the Scrapbook is due just as often to a corrupted Scrapbook File (stored in your System Folder) as to a problem with the Scrapbook desk accessory itself. If the file is corrupted, you may or may not be able to recover data from it (using a program such as CanOpener). If you just remove the Scrapbook File from the System Folder, however, you will at least be able to use the Scrapbook again (albeit with an empty Scrapbook File). If you don't need anything inside the damaged Scrapbook File, just delete it. While you are at it, replace the Scrapbook DA as well, just to be safe.

  If you are using System 7.5 and you get a message such as "Sorry, this disk is full or the system is out of memory," you may really have a memory problem. In this case, you can actually increase the Scrapbook's memory allocation via its Get Info window (as discussed more in Chapter 13, "Solve It! System 7.5 Problems").
- An error message that says something like "Unable to read from disk" suggests possible media damage, typically in the area of the file you are trying to open. In this case, before replacing the damaged file from your backups, you should check for and repair any media damage. This usually requires reformatting the disk.
- Otherwise, check for more general damage (such as to system software) that may be causing problems beyond the file in question.

SEE: • **Fix-Its #13 and #14 on fixing damaged files and media damage**
• **Fix-It #15 on reformatting disks**

When You Can't Open a Document

Symptoms:

You attempt to open a data document, either directly from the Finder (usually by double-clicking the file's icon) or from within an application (using the Open dialog box). In either case, though, the file refuses to open. Typically you get an error message indicating the cause of the problem, but in the worst cases, a system error may occur.

Or perhaps the file opens but only part of its contents remain, or the file displays random gibberish rather than the correct data. (More minor display problems, such as incorrect use of fonts or colors, are not covered here. For solutions to these problems, refer to Chapters 9 and 10.)

Causes:

Reasons that you cannot open a document file include the following:

- The Macintosh cannot find the application needed to open the document (there are several possible reasons for this, as detailed in the following "What to Do" section).
- The file and/or the disk it is on is in PC/DOS format.
- There isn't enough available memory to open the file.
- The file is not intended to be directly opened (for example, extensions).
- The document (or its application) is damaged.
- Many of the same reasons that prevent you from launching an application (refer to the previous section for advice on these causes).

What to do:

If a Document's Application Can't Be Found by the Finder

Suppose you double-click a document file from the Finder, but, instead of the file opening, you get an error message. It says that the file could not be opened, because the application program that created it could not be found.

This happens because the Finder "knows" to which application a document belongs (see Chapter 8 for an explanation of how it knows this). For example, it knows that Excel documents belong to the Excel application. So when you try to open an Excel document, the Finder searches the disk until it locates the Excel application. It then launches the application, followed by the document. If the Finder cannot locate the creating application, however, nothing opens—instead, you get the error message just described. What to do about this depends on exactly why the Macintosh could not find the needed application. There are several possibilities.

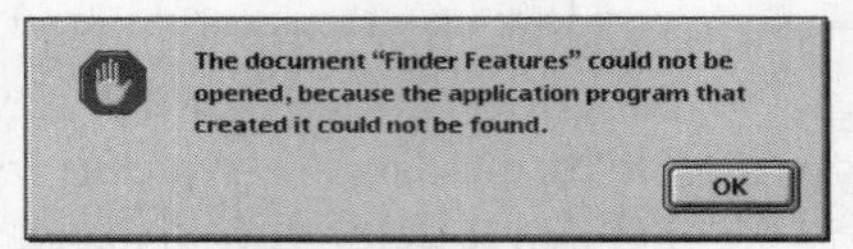

Figure 6-15 *The "application ... could not be found" error message.*

If the Creating Application Has Been Deleted or Is Not Currently Accessible You create a document file using a particular application. For whatever reason, you later delete that application from your startup disk. Or perhaps you have received a document from a colleague that was created by an application that is not on your disk. When you try to launch such documents, you probably get the "application could not be found" error message.

The most obvious solution to this problem is to install the needed application on to your disk. The Kind line in the file's Get Info window (see Chapter 2) may indicate the name of the document's creating application.

You could also try opening the file from within another application you have that is likely to be of the same category (for example, using a word processor for text files of unknown origin). You may get lucky and hit on the right application, or at least find one that can successfully import the file.

If that doesn't work, several utilities can assist in your efforts to open a document.

- **SimpleText**
  If SimpleText (or its older relative, TeachText) is on your disk (it comes with Apple's system software), when you try to open certain text or graphics files (such as plain TEXT or PICT documents) that would normally lead to the "application could not be found" error message, you may instead be given the option to open the file in TeachText/SimpleText. This at least allows you to view the contents of the file.

Figure 6-16 *Similar to the message in Figure 6-15, this message appears if the file cannot be opened by its creating application (usually because it is not on your disk) but can be opened with SimpleText.*

SEE: • Chapter 8 for more on the types of files (TEXT and PICT) that can be opened this way

- **Macintosh Easy Open**
  This Apple utility is included as part of System 7.5 and later revisions. With Easy Open, when you try to open a document whose creating application is missing, you get a window listing all other available applications that can open the document. You can then select which one to use to open the document. On subsequent occasions, the substitution application will be remembered and it will open automatically, without the dialog box. If desired, you can later delete a particular substitution pair from Easy Open's "memory" by using the Easy Open Setup control panel.

  The bare-bones version of Easy Open only recognizes TEXT and PICT documents, making it not much more effective that the basic System 7 alternative just described. With appropriate translators such as those in DataViz MacLink (a set of which come with System 7.5) or Word for Word, however, it will work with a variety of other document types, including documents created by PC applications.

  A related utility, called Easy Open Document Converter (not included with System 7.5), converts a document from one format to another at the Finder level—that is, without even needing to open the document or the application.

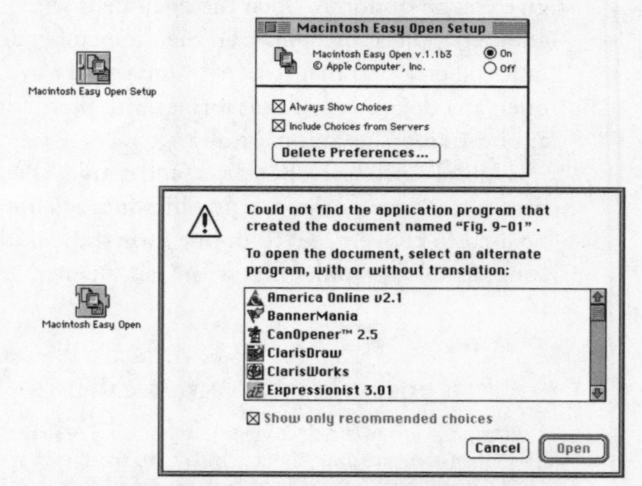

Figure 6-17 *Top: Macintosh Easy Open Setup control panel (used to delete previously created pairing preferences). Bottom: With Macintosh Easy Open extension installed, the dialog box shown here appears (rather than the one in Figure 6-16) if the file cannot be opened with its intended application but can still be opened with SimpleText. With additional translator files installed, this dialog box also appears for other types of files.*

BY THE WAY ▶

MACINTOSH EASY OPEN QUIRKS

Some points worth remembering if you use Macintosh Easy Open:

- Simply installing Macintosh Easy Open can result in frequent rebuilding of your desktop, without you ever requesting it (this oddity is detailed more in Fix-It #9).
- If you select an unintended application to link with a document, you may have trouble figuring out how to undo the link. To do so, go to the Easy Open control panel and click the Delete Preferences button. You should then rebuild the desktop with all extensions (except Easy Open!) turned off.
- For obscure reasons not worth delving into here, Macintosh Easy Open will not list Microsoft Word as a potential application for documents of unknown type, even if Word could open the document.

- **Other utilities**

  Easy Open isn't the only control panel that will let you double-click WordPerfect files in the Finder and have the Mac automatically open Microsoft Word. Other utilities such as the Now Menus control panel from Now Utilities provide similar solutions.

  When you try to open a document for which the Finder does not recognize the creating application, these utilities intercept the normal "application not found" error message and give you an option to open the document with another application. They can then remember any link you create so that the next time you try to open any document of that format, the alternative application opens automatically.

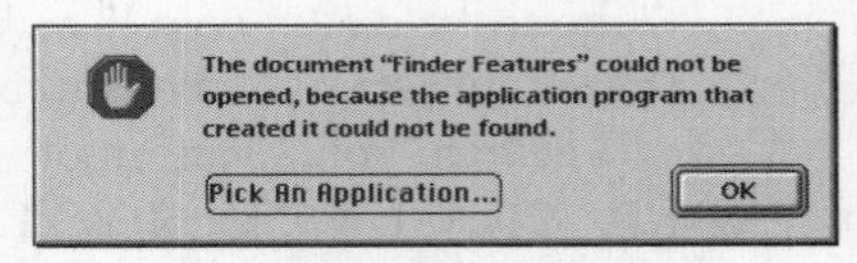

Figure 6-18 *The same alert message as in Figure 6-15, except the Pick An Application button is added because Now Menus is running.*

  Utilities such as DeBabelizer, and similar shareware alternatives, can open graphics files of almost any format. (In addition, they can be used to convert files from one format to another.) You can also try to open "unopenable" graphics files with Can Opener.

BY THE WAY ▶

CREATE DOCUMENTS THAT ANYONE CAN OPEN

If you plan to give a document to other users, you can help them out by saving it in a way that lets anyone open the document, no matter what application you used to create it. You will need special software to create these documents, however, and users will need the free "reader" application to open it. The most popular example of this system is Adobe Acrobat and Acrobat Reader. You can similarly use the portable document (PDD) feature of System 7.5's QuickDraw GX.

Certain programs (such as one called DOCMaker) can create self-opening documents that do not even require a reader.

The Creating Application Has Been Replaced with an Upgraded Version When a new version of an application is released, the format of its document files may be changed. Even if this happens, the new version should retain its ability to read files created by its earlier versions, opening the files and converting them to the new format.

Sometimes, however, this does not work. For example, suppose you are using BusyWorks version 3.0, but you have a file created by BusyWorks 2.0. The file should open in BusyWorks 3.0 without a problem. But in this case, when you try to open the 2.0 document file from the Finder, you get the "application not found" error message.

- **Use the Open command**
  The key here is *not* to try opening the file from the Finder. Open the creating application first, then try to open the document using the application's Open command. If the program is at all capable of reading its older version's files, this should work.
- **Check for special commands and utilities**
  The application may have a special command for opening files of earlier versions, or even be a separate utility for converting these files to the new version's format. Check the manual for any mention of these items. Some programs may include a separate utility for converting files of one version to another.
- **Import to another application**
  You could also try the previously described importing alternative. That is, try to open the file from the Open dialog box of another application that has a translator capability for BusyWorks 2.0.
- **Use the older version**
  If all else fails, you could reinstall the deleted older version of the application (assuming you have retained a copy of it, which you can see now is usually a good idea). Launch the now-reinstalled older version and open the document.

The Document Was Created by a Newer Version of the Application Than the One You Are Using This case, sort of the reverse of the previous situation, usually happens only if you get a file from someone else. For example, perhaps a friend gives you a document created by BusyWorks 3.0, but you are still using version 2.0. When you try to open the document from the Finder, you get the "application not found" error message.

Trying to open the document from within the application itself (BusyWorks 2.0 in this case) may succeed on occasion, but most of the time it won't. Usually, the name of the document won't appear in the Open dialog box's file list. Even if it is listed, you may open the document only to find that it has lost its formatting or contains garbage data (in addition to the actual data). In the worst case, just trying to open the document may result in a system crash!

The crash can occur because the application, in the middle of opening the document, suddenly discovers that it isn't in the expected format. Unable to go forward or back, it decides to crash the system. I have seen this happen when trying to open MacWrite II files with an earlier version of MacWrite.

- **Upgrade your software**
  The easiest (though not necessarily the fastest or cheapest) solution is to upgrade to the new version of the application.
- **Save in a different format**
  Alternatively, you can see if the person who gave you the file can save the file in a format readable by your version. BusyWorks 3.0, for example, may have an option to save the file in version 2.0 format.
- **Import to another application**
  If you have new versions of other applications, you may find that one of them has a translator file for BusyWorks 3.0. You can use this application to open the file.

BY THE WAY ▶

AVOID MULTIPLE VERSIONS OF THE SAME APPLICATION

When you upgrade to a new version of an application, be sure to delete the previous version from your hard drive. Otherwise, when you try to launch a document created by the application, it may incorrectly launch the old version rather than the new one.

In any event, I would be cautious about opening two different versions of the same application at the same time. This could easily cause problems, including a system crash.

The Correct Version of the Creating Application Is Present, Yet the Document File Still Does Not Open from the Finder Since this is not supposed to happen, it indicates that something has gone wrong. Sometimes this happens to a file you have undeleted. Usually, if this does occur, you will also find that the customized icon for the document is lost and that only the generic (that is, blank) document icon is present.

- **Use the Open dialog box**
  Launch the creating application and try to open the file from within its Open dialog box. If this works, create a copy of the document as a new file with a different name. Quit the application and delete the now-unneeded original file. Most of the time, this remedies the situation.

  If the custom icon does not yet appear, select Get Info for the file. This should get the Macintosh's attention and update the icon display. Otherwise, it will probably be displayed correctly after your next restart.
- **Rebuild the desktop**
  If the preceding steps are unsuccessful, try rebuilding the desktop. The Desktop file stores information about the links between documents and applications, and errors in the Desktop file data can prevent the document from opening. Rebuilding the desktop usually fixes these problems.

  SEE: • Fix-It #9 on rebuilding the desktop

BY THE WAY ▶

NOW MENUS CAN LAUNCH THE "WRONG" APPLICATION OR PREVENT QUITTING FROM AN APPLICATION

As mentioned in the main text, Now Menus from Now Utilities (as well as several other competing utilities) can be set up so that when you double-click a WordPerfect file, for example, it launches Microsoft Word rather than WordPerfect. If you create such a link inadvertently, however, (or if you later buy WordPerfect but forget that you made the link), you may be frustrated by your computer's apparently strange insistence that all WordPerfect documents launch into Word. If this happens, check out the substitution list in Now Menus and delete the undesired link.

Now Menus can cause even stranger problems because of its ability to reassign command key equivalents. For example, if you want Command-R rather than Command-H to be the equivalent to the Replace command, you can use Now Menus to do it, but this will override whatever Command-R did previously (if anything). This problem is made worse by how easy it is to make these assignments accidentally with Now Menus. For example, I once mistakenly reassigned Command-Q (normally used to quit the application) to some rarely used function. From that point on, I could not use Command-Q to quit the application; instead, nothing happened. It took me quite a while to figure out what was going on.

If None of the Preceding Steps Work If you are willing to get technical in search of a solution, check for problems with the file's type, creator, and bundle-bit settings.

SEE: • Chapter 8 for explanations of these terms and what to do

TAKE NOTE ▶

WHAT TO DO ABOUT LOST CUSTOM ICONS

One day you start up your Macintosh and notice that some or all of the colorful icons you're used to seeing on your desktop are missing, especially document icons. In their place are plain "generic" icons. This can happen even when there is no problem correctly launching the documents. What can you do?

The simplest solution, if it works, is to select Get Info for the file in question and then close the window again. Other times, a restart of the Macintosh does the trick. Sometimes changing to a different view, as listed in the Finder's View menu, will get the icon to appear. Otherwise, this problem is most often solved by rebuilding the desktop (as long as the creating application for the document is still around).

It is less likely, but still possible, that you have an incorrect Creator code (as explained in Chapter 8, "Type and Creator Code Problems"). Or you may have some Directory file damage—usually a relatively minor problem with what is called the "bundle bit," though sometimes the trouble is more serious. MacTools and Norton Utilities can typically fix bundle-bit as well as other Directory problems (as mentioned in Chapter 8 and Fix-It #13).

Much more detailed coverage of this entire issue can be found in Fix-It #9.

An Application Does Not Import a Document File, Even Though the Application Has a Translator Available for the File's Format

Suppose you try to open a Microsoft Word file from within the Open dialog box of BusyWorks. You select the "All Available" or "Microsoft Word" option from the pop-up menu that lists the types of readable files, but the file you want either does not get displayed in the dialog box or does not open when selected.

The most likely problem is that the importing translation filter you need to open the file (usually stored in the System Folder somewhere) is missing. If you believe the correct filter is present, perhaps it is not an exact match for the file you are trying to import. In particular, the filter may be specific to a different version of the file's creating application (for example, you might be trying to open a Microsoft Word 6.0 file with a Microsoft Word 3.0 translator).

In a related example, Microsoft Word has a Fast Save formatting option that you can select from the Save As dialog box. Doing this is supposed to speed up the process of saving documents. Files saved in the Fast Save format may not be recognized by another application, however, even if the other application does recognize Word files saved in the normal format. Similarly, different types of TIFF document formats exist. A particular translator maybe able to open some formats but not others.

The general solutions to these problems are to resave the document file in a format that matches the filter, get a filter that matches the file (see if the company that makes your application has one available), or use another application that can successfully import the file. If all of these fail or are not feasible, you may have to give up on this approach altogether.

BY THE WAY ▶

IF THE SYSTEM 7 STATIONERY PAD OPTION DOES NOT WORK ...

You check the Stationery Pad option in a document's Get Info window—but when you double-click the document, it still opens as an ordinary document rather than as stationery. The problem may simply be that the application in question does not support this System 7 option. If so, there is nothing you can do about it. Many word processors, however, have their own stationery feature that is separate from the System 7 feature. You could use this instead.

The File Is in PC/DOS Format and/or on a PC/DOS-Formatted Disk

This is really a special case of the previous section on problems with importing files. Many Macintosh applications, such as Microsoft Word and WordPerfect, can read files saved in a PC format (that is, as used on IBM PCs and compatibles), especially those files created using a PC version of the same software. Even then, however, some special preparation may be necessary.

Make Sure the Macintosh Can Read the PC-Formatted Floppy Disk When you first acquire PC files, they will probably be on a PC-formatted disk. Fortunately, if it is set up properly, the Macintosh can mount and read files from these disks just as if they were Macintosh-formatted disks. First, remember that all PC 3.5-inch floppy disks are HD disks, so you will need a SuperDrive to mount them (older 800K drives cannot read HD disks). Second, you will need a special startup extension in your System Folder that is used to recognize PC-formatted disks. Apple includes such a startup extension, the Macintosh PC Exchange control panel with System 7.5. With PC Exchange installed, an inserted PC disk will mount on the desktop as a disk icon in exactly the same manner as a Macintosh disk. Files on the disk will be represented by file icons, and they can be copied back and forth to your hard drive or any other disk.

SEE: • **Fix-It #15 for more on formatting disks**

Make Sure the Application Can Read Files Formatted by the Application That Created It on the PC Some applications have "built-in" translators for reading PC-formatted files—for example, WordPerfect for the Macintosh can open files created by the PC versions of WordPerfect. To access these documents, the most reliable method is to open them from within the application, not by double-clicking the document from the Finder. With PC Exchange installed, however, you may be able to open the document directly from the Finder. Specifically, PC Exchange will match a DOS suffix in a document's name to a particular Macintosh application, as set in the PC Exchange control panel window. (Of course, this only works well if the application in question can read the PC-formatted file.)

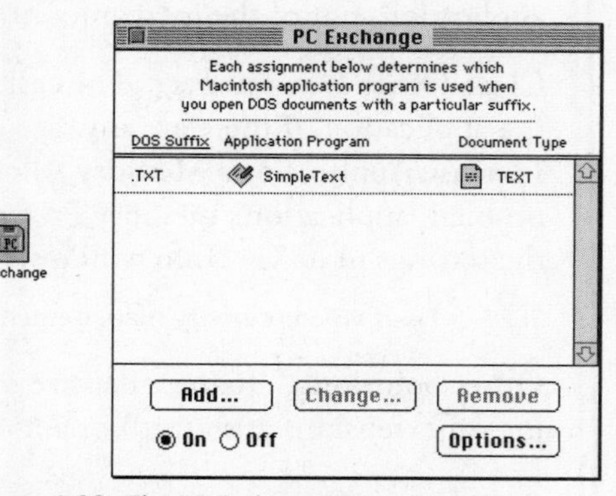

Figure 6-19 *The PC Exchange control panel.*

Opening PC-formatted files directly from the Finder, regardless of their name, is further enhanced if you use Macintosh Easy Open (which, like PC Exchange, is included as part of System 7.5).

Check for the Correct Suffix If you are trying to import DOS-formatted files (such as a PC Works 2.0 file to Microsoft Works 3.0), make sure the document file has the suffix that would be assigned to that file on a DOS machine (for example, "file.*wrk*") Without the suffix, some Macintosh programs will be unable to recognize the file when you try to open it later, even though they include a file translator for that format.

CD-ROM Disc Problem If you are having problems opening PC files from a CD-ROM disk, check that you have the Foreign File Access extension installed. If you don't, install it (either from your System Software disks, or from the CD-ROM Setup discs).

Insufficient Memory to Open the File

Sometimes, even if you can open the application itself, you cannot get it to open a document. This is common if the document is especially large (particularly if it is a large graphics file) or if you are trying to open several documents at once.

This is usually a memory-related problem. Each application is allocated a specific amount of memory, as determined in the application's Get Info window. This amount of memory must contain the application itself plus any documents that you open while using it. If opening a document would require more than this allotted amount of memory, you cannot open it, even though the memory allocation was sufficient to open the application itself. When this occurs, you usually get an error message accurately describing this problem.

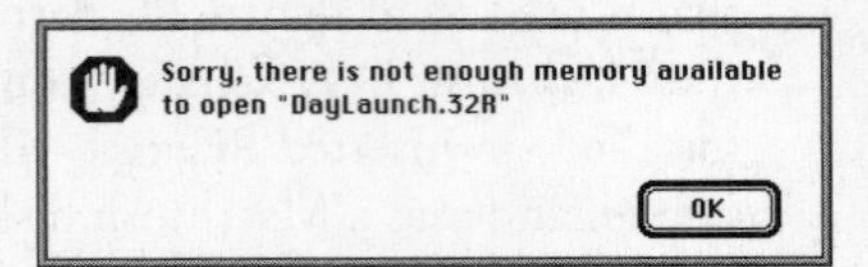

Figure 6-20 *This message may appear when you try to open a document (in this case, a large graphics file).*

The same sort of error may appear if you try to cut or copy a large selection to the Clipboard. These errors can occur no matter how much memory you have installed in your system. They are a function of the amount of memory assigned to an individual application, not of the total amount of available memory.

Close Other Documents The easiest solution is to close other open documents within the application, if there are any. See if the document now opens.

Increase Application's Memory Allocation You can go to the Finder and increase the problem application's memory Preferred size (called Current size in System 7.0) from the settings in its Get Info window.

SEE: • **Fix-It #6 on memory management problems for details**

Other Solutions Reduce the size of your system software memory allocation (by turning off extensions at startup) or add more memory hardware.

The File Is Not Intended to Be Opened

Some files are not intended to be opened from the Finder. For example, After Dark is a screen-saver utility that replaces your normal screen display with some amusing alternative after several minutes of inactivity. It uses numerous plug-in modules to let the user choose what alternative appears on the screen; each module is a separate file. If you double-click one of these files, though, it does not open After Dark—instead, you get the "application could not be found" message. You can only access these modules by first opening the After Dark control panel directly.

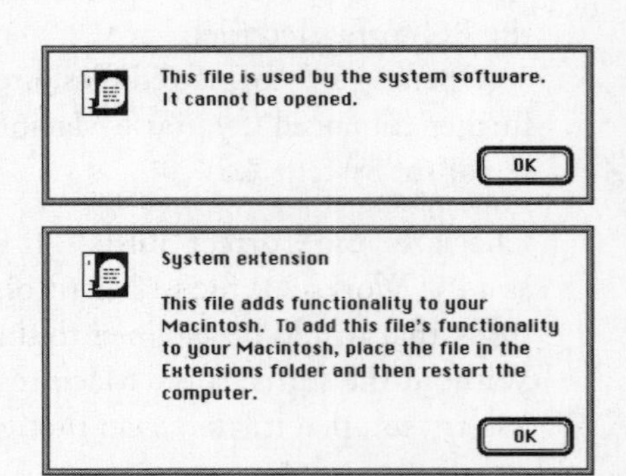

Figure 6-21 *Top: If you try to open the Finder by double-clicking its icon, this message will appear. Bottom: This message appears if you try to open a system extension.*

Similarly, many System Folder files are not intended to be openable (including the Finder itself and most extension files), and if you try to open them, you'll be promptly informed of this fact. There is nothing particular to do in such cases. The files are not supposed to be opened, so don't try.

On a related note, you cannot use an application to open a file that is already open in another application. For example, you cannot simultaneously open a graphics document in ClarisDraw and ClarisWorks. If you try, you will get an error message telling you that it cannot be done.

Opening a Document from the Finder When the Application Is Already Open

You try to open a document file from the Finder for an application that is already open. Unfortunately, you get a message saying that you can't open the document because the application is in use, or just that the document could not be opened.

Technically, this should not happen; you should be able to open the file in this way. Some programs, however, may give you problems with this. The solution here is simple: open the document from within the application, using the application's Open dialog box.

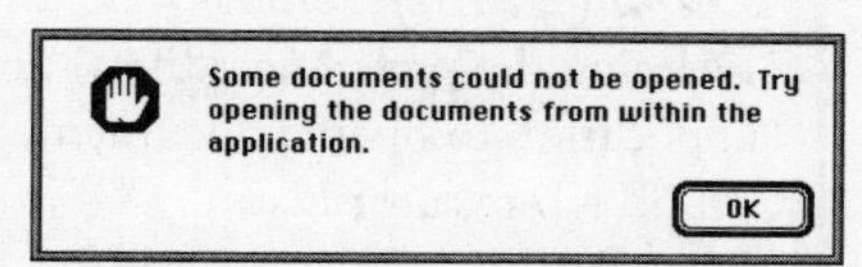

Figure 6-22 *This message may appear when you are trying to open a document from the Finder for an application that is already open.*

Opening a Document File from the Finder Launches the Wrong Application

You create a text file in BusyWorks. The next day, you double-click that file to open it, but for some reason the Macintosh opens the file in TeachText or Microsoft Word. What happened?

Some programs save their documents as plain text files rather than in their own default format (see Chapter 8 for more on this). This practice is common for certain programs that are not really word processors but do produce text reports of some sort. In such cases, if the document is launched later from the Finder, it often opens in a generic text application (such as TeachText). Actually, I just as often have the reverse problem: I save a file in a plain text format, expecting it to launch into SimpleText the next time, but instead it opens into the creating application (which may take a lot longer to open).

A related situation is if you saved the file—inadvertently, perhaps—in a format other than the application's default format, such as saving a BusyWorks file in Microsoft Word format. In this case, trying to open the file from the Finder causes it to launch Word rather than BusyWorks. (If Word is not on your disk, the file may not open at all, and you will get the "application could not be found" message described earlier in this chapter.)

If a text document does open in the "wrong" application, it is also possible that text formatting (such as the font, the size of the text, the line breaks, and the margins) are different from when you saved it.

SEE: • Chapter 9 for more on text-formatting problems

To make sure a file opens with the desired application, open it from within the application (using the application's Open dialog box) rather than from the Finder. If this does not work, you can fiddle with the document's creator code (see Chapter 8 again). Otherwise, there is not much else you can do.

The Problem May Be with the Application, Not the Document

If a particular application refuses to open most or all appropriate documents, the application itself may be damaged, or there may be a software bug involved. To check for either of these flaws, replace the application software. If this fails, you may still be able to open the document(s) in another program that can read files created by the problem application.

Damaged Preferences

Deleting the preferences file(s) associated with an application can sometimes get the application to open a document. For Claris programs, especially look to delete the XTND Translator List.

SEE: • **Fix-It #2 for more on preferences file problems**

Damaged Documents That Can't Be Opened

When none of the preceding solutions opens a document (or, if it does open, much of the data appear garbled or lost), the document itself may be damaged. In most cases, the simplest solution is to revert to a backup copy of the file, assuming you have one. If this works, delete the problem copy, make a new backup, and you are back in business. If you do not have a backup copy, you can try several options that may repair or recover data from the damaged file.

SEE: • **Fix-It #14 on fixing damaged files**

An error message such as "Unable to read from disk" usually means media damage to the area of the disk where the file resides. This damage has to be fixed even if you can recover or replace the file.

SEE: • **Fix-Its #13 and #14 on fixing damaged files, including media damage**
• **Fix-It #15 on reformatting**

If, after trying this and all of the previous suggestions, you still cannot open the file, there is little or no hope of saving it. Just delete the problem file and go on with your life.

When You Can't Delete a File or Folder

Symptoms:

You place a file or a folder in the Trash. You select Empty Trash from the Finder's Special menu, but the item does not get deleted.

Usually, you also get an alert message explaining why the Trash was not emptied (for example, that "items in it are locked," or "because it contains items that are in use").

Causes:

Exact causes vary depending on the error message you get.

- Locked files or files on locked floppy disks cannot be directly deleted. They need to be unlocked.
- Files that are currently open (or in use) cannot be deleted until they are closed. This makes sense; deleting an open file would be like erasing a videotape while you are in the middle of watching it. Similarly, the System and the Finder on the startup disk cannot be deleted, because they are always in use.
- In rarer cases, a problem with the system software, a damaged file, or damaged disk media may prevent a file or folder from being deleted. Most likely it is a Directory problem or a Finder flag problem.

SEE: • **Chapter 8 on the invisible Trash folder and Finder flags**

BY THE WAY ▶

EXCEPTIONAL TRASH BEHAVIOR

As discussed previously, you normally cannot have two files or folders of the same name in the same location. If you try to do this, the Macintosh asks if you want to replace the existing file (or folder) with the new one. The Trash, however, is a partial exception to this rule. If you place an item in the Trash when it already contains an item of the same name, the Macintosh renames one of the items by appending the word *copy* to the end of the name). Both items can then coexist in the Trash while they await your decision to delete them. You will get no message alerting you to the name modification.

What to do:

Make Sure the File or Folder Is Really in the Trash

If you can still see the file/folder on the desktop near the Trash, it is *not* in the Trash. To get it in the Trash, drag it until the cursor arrow covers the Trash and the Trash icon turns black. Then release the mouse; the file/folder icon should disapper. Now select Empty Trash.

If the File or Folder Is on a Floppy Disk, Check if the Floppy Disk Is Locked

A floppy disk is locked if the sliding tab, located in the upper corner on the rear side of the disk, is positioned so that you can see through the hole. Ordinarily you cannot even move an item from a locked floppy disk to the Trash; certainly, nothing can be written to or deleted from the disk.

If a floppy disk is already inserted in the Macintosh, you can check if it is locked without having to eject it. If it is locked, the Finder displays a small icon of a padlock in the upper left corner of any window from the disk.

To unlock the disk, eject the disk and slide the tab down. Reinsert the disk, and you can then delete the file.

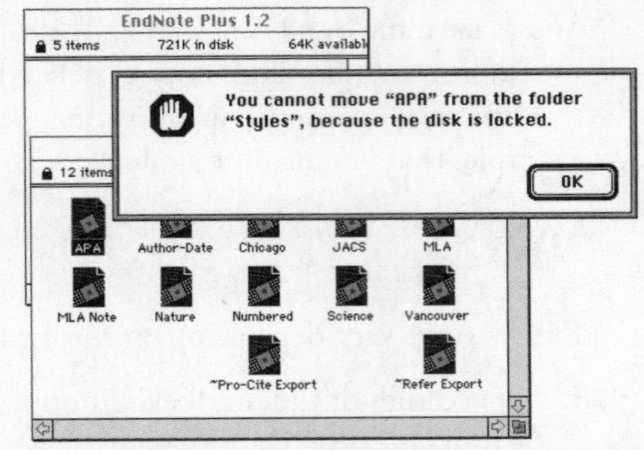

Figure 6-23 *The padlock icon means that the floppy disk is locked. The error message appeared when I tried to move a file on this disk.*

If the Mac wrongly indicates that virtually every floppy disk you insert into a floppy drive is locked, it is probably a problem with the floppy drive itself. In particular, the pin that goes through the hole of a locked disk is likely to be stuck in a way that makes all disks seem locked. You may be able to fix this by opening up the drive and cleaning out the gunk that is making the pin stick, but I'd guess most of you would rather take the drive in for professional servicing.

Check If the File Is Locked

A file is locked if the Locked box in the file's Get Info window is checked (as described more in Chapter 2). If you are viewing files by any view other than an icon view, a locked file will have a padlock symbol at the end of its listing line.

If a file is locked, you can still place it in the Trash. When you try to delete it, however, you will get a message informing you that you cannot do this unless you hold down the Option key while you select Empty Trash. (This allows locked files to be deleted.) Actually, in some cases of files that refuse to delete, it may pay to hold down the Option key even if the file is not locked—or to deliberately lock the file, then try to delete it with the Option key held down.

Figure 6-24 *Top: The padlock symbol appears next to the locked Script Editor file. Bottom: The message that appears if you try to Empty Trash with a locked file in the Trash.*

Alternatively, you can go to a file's Get Info window and uncheck the Locked box. The file is now unlocked and may be deleted normally.

SEE: • **Chapter 2 for more on using the Get Info command**

TAKE NOTE ▶

FILES LOCKED BY SYSTEM 7.5'S GENERAL CONTROL PANEL

The System 7.5 General Controls control panel has two options called Protect System Folder and Protect Applications Folder. If these options are checked, it means that any and all files in these folders cannot be removed from the folder, even if the relevant Locked box in the window Get Info is unchecked (by the way, an Applications folder is automatically created when you first check this protect option). To remove files in these protected folders, you must first uncheck the control panel protection options. Otherwise, if you try to move a file, a message will tell you that you cannot do it because you "do not have enough access privileges."

Overall, my advice is to avoid using these Folder Protection features at all. They cause more problems than they solve, including possible startup crashes and freezes.

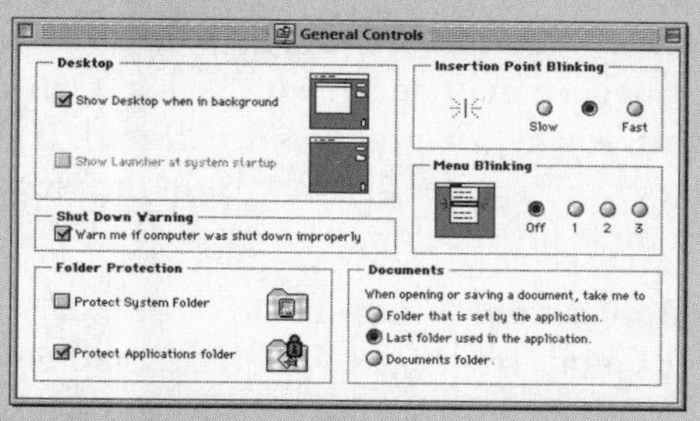

Figure 6-25 *The System 7.5 General Controls control panel, with its Protect Applications Folder option checked.*

In any case, they only prevent removal of files from the main folder; you can still remove files from subfolders within a protected folder.

SEE: • **"Take Note: System 7.5, Now Utilities, and More: Helping You Find Your Way," earlier in this chapter, for more on this control panel**

Folders Locked via the Sharing Command

If you use System 7's file sharing, you probably know that you can restrict users' access to files, preventing them from modifying your files in any way. You do this via the check boxes in the dialog box that appears after selecting Sharing from the Finder's file menu. At the bottom of this dialog box, however, is a lesser-known option that can limit even your own ability to modify a folder on your disk.

To see this in action, turn file sharing on, select any folder, and then select the Sharing command. At the bottom of the dialog box, note the checkbox option called "Can't be moved, renamed, or deleted." If this is checked, the folder cannot be moved, renamed, or deleted by anyone, including yourself, whether it is accessed directly or via file sharing—but only as long as file sharing is on. If you try, you will get a message that the folder can't be moved to the Trash because it is locked.

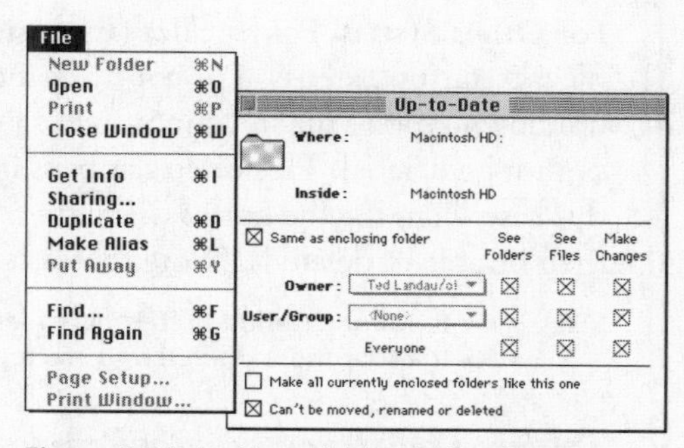

Figure 6-26 *Locking a folder via the Sharing command. This only works when file sharing is on.*

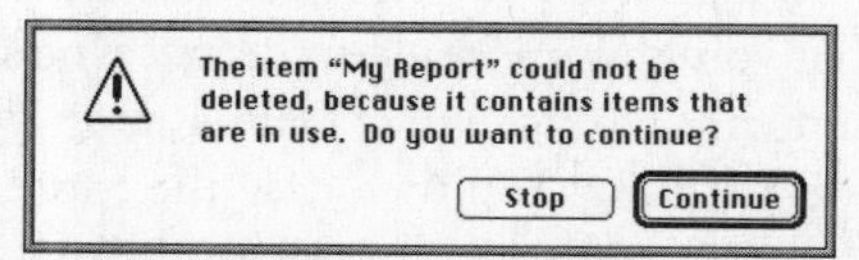

Figure 6-27 *This message appears if you try to delete a file that is currently open.*

The only solution for this is to select the folder, go to the Sharing dialog box, and uncheck this option. If you otherwise have access, however, you can still remove individual files from the folder and delete them separately.

SEE: • **Chapter 11 for more on file sharing**

Check If the File Is Currently Open or in Use

Any application or document file that is currently open cannot be deleted. If you try to do this, you get an error message instead. If you get this message, click Continue to delete any other files that may be in the Trash, then choose the appropriate solution from those listed below.

For Applications If the file to be deleted is an application, quit the application, then select Empty Trash again. The file should now be deleted.

For Documents If the file is a document, all you usually need to do is close the document file, then return to the Finder and select Empty Trash again. If this doesn't work, try quitting the application that created the document, and then try to trash the document.

For Essential System Folder Files If the file is an essential system software file on your current startup disk (such as the System, the Finder, or an Update file), you cannot delete it unless you restart the Macintosh using an alternate startup disk. After doing this, drag the file to the Trash and delete it. Normally, you only want to do this if you are about to replace these files.

SEE: • **Fix-It #5 on replacing system software files**

For Other System Folder Files (Extensions, Control Panels, Fonts, and so on) If the file is a startup extension or control panel on your current startup disk (or any other unknown type of file in your System Folder), you may get an error message saying that it cannot be deleted. This often happens if the file gets loaded into memory at startup. In this case, drag the file out of the System Folder, then restart the Macintosh. You should then be able to delete it. (Note that you don't need to use an alternate startup disk.)

SEE: • **Fix-It #2 for deleting Preferences files**
• **Fix-It #4 for more on deleting startup extensions**

Folders That Unexpectedly Remain "In Use"

Suppose you are working on a file called "Daily Report #6." After printing the file, you decide to delete it—in fact, you have a whole folder of daily reports called "Articles 2" that you now are ready to delete. Knowing that you cannot trash an open file, you remember to close the "Daily Report #6" file, although you do not quit the application you are using. You then drag the entire folder to the Trash.

When you select Empty Trash, you get an alert message saying that the "Articles 2" folder could not be deleted because it contains items that are still in use. When you check the folder, though, it is empty. Every file in the folder was in fact deleted, but the folder itself was not. How can anything in it be still in use? What's going on?

The problem is that the Macintosh considers a folder to be in use until you quit *every* currently open application that has opened *any* of the files that were within that folder, even if the files have since been closed. In this case, if the word processor (for example) that was used to create the Daily Report file is still open, the folder is not deleted, even though you have closed and successfully deleted the Daily Report #6 file. To delete the folder, follow these steps:

1. Click Stop or Continue.
2. Quit the relevant applications.
3. Select Empty Trash again. It should work now.

Trash
1 item
Articles 2
Articles 2
0 items 70.8 MB in disk 4.2 MB available
Trash
The item "Articles 2" could not be deleted, because it contains items that are in use. Do you want to continue?
Stop Continue

Figure 6-28 The folder "Articles 2," now in the Trash, is empty (top). Even though the folder is empty, it does not get deleted when Empty Trash is selected; instead, an error message appears (bottom).

An Invisible File in the Folder? A relatively rare problem is if a folder contains an invisible file that is "in use." In this case, the Macintosh will not delete the folder until you either remove the invisible file or quit whatever application is causing the file to be in use. The best way to check this is with a utility, such as Norton Utilities or DiskTop, that lists invisible files.

Special Case: Deleting Folders from an AppleShare Volume If you are using System 7.1, make sure you have installed System Update 3.0. This fixes a problem with deleting folders that are on an AppleShare volume. Without this update, the Finder may prevent deleting folders by falsely claiming that the folder is "in use."

SEE: • Chapter 11 for more on connecting Macs via AppleShare

The Folder from Hell Problem

Occasionally, you may have a folder that is empty but refuses to be deleted no matter what you try. Everything in the folder can be deleted, but the folder itself does not go away—even after you quit all open applications, even after you restart the Macintosh, even if you hold down the Option key while emptying the Trash. Trying to move or delete the folder may produce various strange symptoms and error messages, such as a –127 error. Often, this problem crops up following a system crash.

This type of folder has been referred to as the *folder from hell.* Its cause probably has to do with the special Directory files that the Macintosh uses to keep track of what is on the disk.

SEE: • Chapter 8 for more on the Directory files

Without getting too technical here, the problem is typically the result of a discrepancy between different areas of the Directory files as to how many files and folders are contained within the problem folder. Because of this confusion, the Macintosh thinks there is a file or folder "in use" inside the problem folder, even though it is empty. This can be an especially difficult problem to solve, but here's how to try.

Rename the Folder Then try to trash it. It's unlikely to work, but it doesn't take much effort to try, either.

Create a New Folder with the Same Name Another easy solution, if it works, is to create a new folder with exactly the same name as the problem folder. Make sure you create it in a different location from the problem folder—for example, within a separate folder—or you will not be able to give the new folder the same name. After you've created it, drag the new folder to the same location as the problem folder. The Macintosh will ask you whether you want to replace the problem folder with the new one. Because replacing that folder is the whole point, click OK. Now try to delete the replacement folder. If it works, the folder from hell is gone!

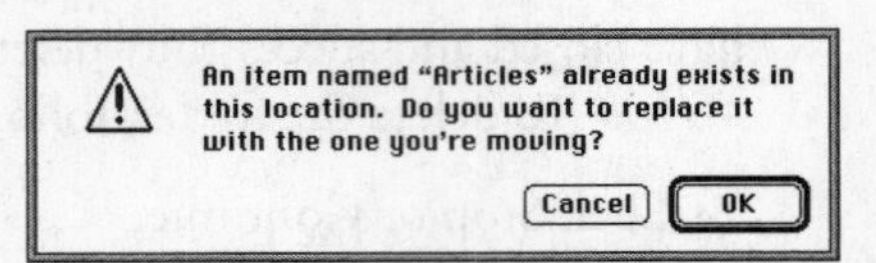

Figure 6-29 *Click OK to try to delete a folder from hell.*

Utilities to the Rescue Disk First Aid or the other repair utilities (such as MacTools or Norton Utilities) can usually fix this problem, and a special shareware utility, called HellFolderFix, is specifically designed to combat this problem. While some reports indicate that HellFolderFix only works in System 6, recent reports have clearly shown that it is still viable in System 7.5. It's certainly worth a try in a pinch.

This folder problem may also be caused by a bug that appears to be limited to System 7.0 (not 7.0.1 or later) when file sharing is in use. The bug also typically prevents renaming of folders—including the hard disk icon itself—in addition to possibly preventing the deleting of a folder. In this case, special utilities such as Apple's Rename Rescue or a shareware utility called UnlockFolder may fix the problem. Again, several reports (including one from Apple itself) suggest that these utilities may still be effective in System 7.5.

SEE: • **Fix-It #10 on Disk First Aid and Fix-It #13 on other repair utilities**

Deleting Damaged Files

Sometimes you will have trouble deleting a damaged file, which will often be accompanied by an ID = –39 error message. Damaged font files and font suitcases seem particularly prone to this sort of problem. If this happens to you, try any or all of the following:

Create a New File with the Same Name Create a new file, of any type, with the same name as the problem file. Drag the dummy file to the location of the problem file. The Macintosh should ask whether you want to replace the problem file. Click OK. If doing so successfully replaces the problem file, try to delete the dummy file. It should work.

Drag the File Out of the System Folder If the file is in your System Folder (such as a font file), try dragging it out of the System Folder, restarting, and then deleting the file. For a problem font file, you may have to drag the entire Fonts folder out of the System Folder.

Restart with Extensions Off Hold down the Shift key at startup, and then try to delete the file. This is also useful for problem font files, especially if you are using an extension such as Suitcase.

SEE: • **Chapter 9 on damaged font files for more specific advice on this problem**

When All of the Preceding Steps Fail to Delete the File or Folder

You may have problems that go beyond an inability to delete a file or folder, so it's time for a more scattershot approach.

Restart the Macintosh If you haven't already done so, restart your Macintosh. This alone may solve the problem.

Rebuild the Desktop Rebuild the desktop, then try to delete the file or folder again.

SEE: • **Fix-It #9 on rebuilding the desktop**

Start Up from Another Disk After restarting, try to delete the file or folder.

Try a Finder Alternative You may be able to delete the file or folder using a utility such as DiskTop instead of the Finder.

Attempt to Repair the Disk If you haven't already done so, run Disk First Aid and, if necessary, any other disk repair utility you have (such as MacTools and Norton Utilities). Repair any problems that you find.

SEE: • **Chapter 5 for more details on disk-related problems**
• **Fix-It #10 on Disk First Aid and Fix-It #13 on other repair utilities**

Reformat the Disk If the problem persists, back up the disk, reformat it, and then restore the contents of the disk from your backups. This almost always solves the problem.

SEE: • **Chapter 2 on Apple HD SC Setup**
• **Fix-It #15 on reformatting disks**

If None of the Preceding Steps Work If even reformatting the disk doesn't work, there is probably some file (most likely in the System Folder) that you are reintroducing to the disk from your backup copy that is causing the problem. If you want, you can continue to search for this problem file by yourself—by testing for startup extension conflicts, for example. If your patience begins to wear thin, though, seek some outside help.

SEE: • **Fix-It #4 on problems with system extensions and control panels**
• **Fix-It #18 on seeking outside help**

When You Can't Rename a File or Folder or Volume

Symptoms:

You try to rename a file in the Finder, but you are unable to get the I-beam cursor to appear, and so the text remains uneditable.

Causes:

Most of the time, there is nothing wrong. You just need to follow correct procedures to get the I-beam to appear. Otherwise, for volume names, the problem may be that file sharing is on or you are experiencing an unusual system software bug.

What to do:

1. To get the I-beam to appear from an icon view in the Finder, click once in the area where the name of the file is (just below the icon itself), then wait for the name to be highlighted and the I-beam to appear. Otherwise, you can click in any part of the icon and press the Return key. You should now be able to edit the name. (Remember that a name cannot be more than 31 characters long, and it cannot contain a colon.)
2. If the previous step fails to work for renaming a file, the file may be locked. Select Get Info and uncheck the Locked box, if it is checked.
3. Some files have locked names even if their Get Info box is not locked, because a special file attribute called "Name Locked" has been checked. This typically would only occur for certain system software files, such as the System and Finder. If for some reason you need to rename these files, you will have to uncheck this attribute and then restart.

   SEE: • Chapter 8, "What Are Finder Flags (Attributes)?," for more details

4. For volume names (such as hard disks) and/or for folders that cannot be renamed, turn file sharing off. (Alternatively, for folders only, select the folder, then select the Sharing command from the Finder's File menu and make sure that the "Can't be moved, renamed, or deleted" option is unchecked.) This will usually solve the problem. Otherwise, you may have a rare bug that can be fixed by special utilities such as Apple's Rename Rescue or a shareware utility called UnlockFolder.
5. If all of these solutions fail, this may be a symptom of a more general problem, such as a damaged file or disk.

   SEE: • Fix-Its #10, #13, and #14 for more on fixing damaged files and disks

When You Can't Save or Copy a File

Symptoms:

- **Saving a File**
  You try to save a file from a Save dialog box, but you are unable to do so. Usually you get an error message, such as "Disk is locked; there is not enough room on the disk" or "Disk is full."

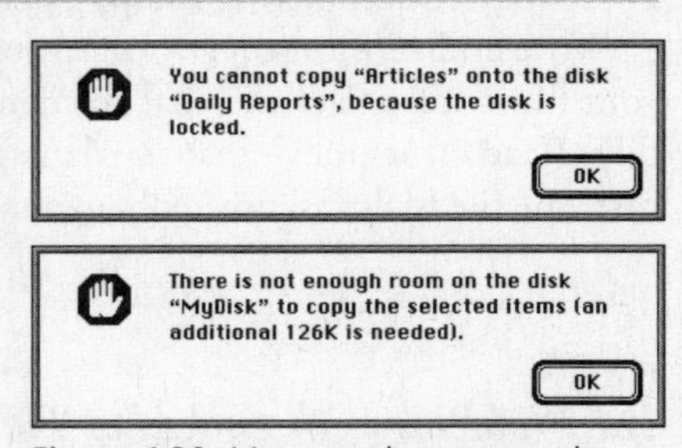

Figure 6-30 *Messages that appear when you try to copy files to a locked disk, or to a disk with less unused space left than is needed for the file(s) to be copied.*

- **Copying or Replacing a File**
  You try to copy a file to another disk, or to another folder on the same disk, but you get an error message. In some cases, it may say that you cannot copy or replace the file because it is "in use" or because you do not have "access permission." In more serious cases, you may be told, "The file couldn't be read and was skipped (unknown error)," or some other similar message.

Causes:

In most cases, the cause is evident from the error message and easy to solve. If you try to save a 100K file to a floppy disk that only has 20K of empty space left, you'll get an error message saying that you cannot do this. Similarly, you cannot copy or save anything to a locked floppy disk. Files that are open also cannot be replaced, and sometimes they cannot be copied.

More rarely, you may be unable to save a file from within an application, even though the disk is unlocked and there seems to be sufficient space available. This probably means there is a bug in the application software.

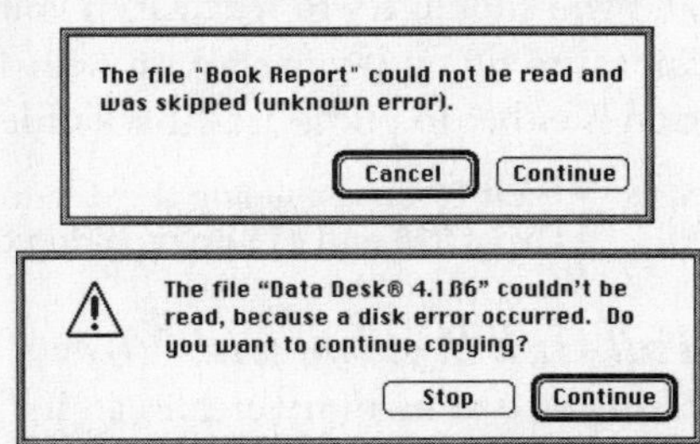

Figure 6-31 *Ominous messages such as these may appear when you try to copy files from the Finder.*

The most troublesome messages inform you that the file you are trying to copy could not be read or could not be written. Usually referred to as *disk errors*, these problems sometimes happen when you are trying to copy too many items at one time. Otherwise, they almost always mean a problem with defective disk media, commonly referred to as *bad blocks.* If the file cannot be read (*read error*), the damage is to the area of the disk where the file now exists. If the file cannot be written (*write error*), the damage is to the area where the Macintosh is trying to create the copy. If you are trying to make a copy from one disk to another, read errors refer to the source disk, and write errors refer to the destination disk.

Sometimes you get a message that says a file could not be *verified.* Functionally similar to a write error, this problem means that the error went undetected when the file was first written, but it was caught when the disk was rechecked (as is normally done by the Finder before completing a copy operation to a floppy disk).

Write and verification errors are definitely the lesser of two evils, since they mean that your file is still intact and that the damage is in a presently unused area of the destination disk. Read errors mean that the damage is to the area presently containing the file. In this case, the file is almost assuredly damaged, perhaps beyond repair.

What to do:

For Problems with Locked or Full Disks

Follow the Advice in the Alert Message These problems are usually remedied simply by paying attention to the alert message that appears. If the message indicates that the disk is locked, for instance, unlock the disk. If the message indicates that the disk is full or that there is not enough room, you either have to go to the Finder and delete some other files from the disk (to free up more space for the file to be saved) or save the file to another disk.

SEE: • "When You Can't Delete a File or Folder," earlier in this chapter, for more on locked disks

For "Disk Is Full" Message When Disk Is Not Full If you know that the disk is not full or think that it should not be full, try restarting and/or rebuilding the desktop. This alone may cure the problem. Also check for temporary files that may have unexpectedly stayed on your disk (if you use PrintMonitor, be sure to look in the PrintMonitor Documents folder in your System Folder). Otherwise, you probably have a damaged disk, and you should try to repair it. If you use TrashBack from MacTools, your disk is likely to appear to fill up if you start up with TrashBack off (as described in Chapter 2). The solution is either to purge TrashBack's files or restart with TrashBack on.

SEE: • Fix-It #9 on rebuilding the desktop
• Fix-Its #10 and #13 on repairing disks

Full Disk Problem with Virtual Memory

Using virtual memory creates an invisible file on your disk that can be quite large. As explained more in Fix-It #6, it is equal in size to the amount of RAM that you have plus the amount of virtual memory that you add (for example, 16MB of RAM plus 16MB of virtual memory will take up 32MB of disk space). If you start up with virtual memory off, this file is not created. Thus, in the example given, you would have 32MB more of disk space when starting up with extensions off (or with just virtual memory off, or when starting up from a floppy disk).

As a result, your mysteriously full disk may just as mysteriously become less full when you start up with a Emergency Toolkit disk in order to try to fix the problem. If this happens, you can be almost certain that your virtual memory file is the cause. By the way, RAM Doubler does not share this problem, which is why it is often a preferred alternative to Apple's virtual memory.

BY THE WAY ▶

DON'T TRY TO SAVE A FILE THAT IS CURRENTLY IN THE TRASH

Don't open the Trash window and select the Save command for a file that is in the Trash. Why anyone would want to do this is unclear to me, but people who have tried quickly learned that it can lead to system crashes and other assorted problems. Using Save As (and saving the file to a new location) is okay, but using Save is not.

BY THE WAY ▶

MOVING FILES ON A LOCKED DISK TO THE DESKTOP

If you try to move a file from a CD-ROM disc or a locked floppy disk to the desktop, you will get a somewhat strange message that says "Items from locked disks cannot be moved to the desktop. Do you want to copy <filename> to the startup disk?" Here the Mac is telling you that, while you cannot move the file to the locked disk's desktop (because the disk is locked), it will copy the file to your startup disk (if you wish) and place it on the startup disk's desktop. If you say OK, you have actually copied the file to the startup disk rather than simply moved the file to the desktop. Often, this is what you are trying to accomplish anyway; if so, click OK. Otherwise, for floppy disks, an alternative is to unlock the disk (CD-ROM discs, of course, can never be unlocked).

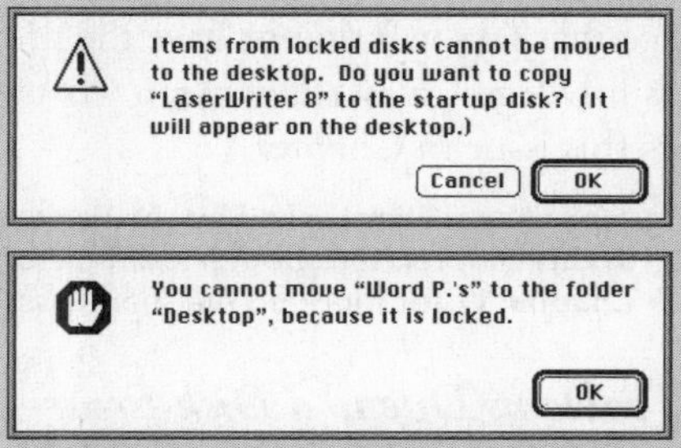

Items from locked disks cannot be moved to the desktop. Do you want to copy "LaserWriter 8" to the startup disk? (It will appear on the desktop.)

Cancel OK

You cannot move "Word P.'s" to the folder "Desktop", because it is locked.

OK

Figure 6-32 *Top: This message appears when moving a file to the desktop of a locked floppy disk. Bottom: This message turned out to be due to Directory damage.*

In one strange case, when I tried to move a folder on my hard drive to the desktop, a message told me that I could not do it because the Desktop folder itself was locked. Since there was no reason to expect this to be the case, I suspected that some software on the disk was damaged. Rebuilding the desktop did not help. Ultimately, the problem turned out to be Directory damage, which I was able to fix using MacTools.

Files That Are "In Use" and "Illegal Access Permission"

If you try to replace a file that is currently open or in use—for instance, by copying a new file with the same name to the same location as the open file—you will get the same sort of "in use" alert message that occurs when you try to delete such a file. This is because replacing the file requires deleting the original version. For application and document files, the obvious solution is to close the open file. For control panels and extensions that are in use, drag the "in use" file out of the System Folder to the Trash, then move the new copy to the intended location. You may have to restart before you can delete the file placed in the Trash.

SEE: • **"Check If the File Is Currently Open or in Use" in "When You Can't Delete a File or Folder," earlier in this chapter, for more details**
• **Chapter 9 for special problems replacing a font file**

In some cases, if you try to copy a file that is currently open, you will get a similar "in use" message. If you are trying to transfer an open file across a network via file sharing, however, you may instead get a message that says you have "illegal access permission," even if you do have proper access permission. For me, this seemed to occur especially if I was using an early version of a copy utility called CopyDoubler. In either of these situations, the simple solution is to close the document (or quit the application) and then make the copy.

When you are using file sharing, however, a message that says you do not have the proper "access privileges" may really mean what it says. I discuss this issue in Chapter 11.

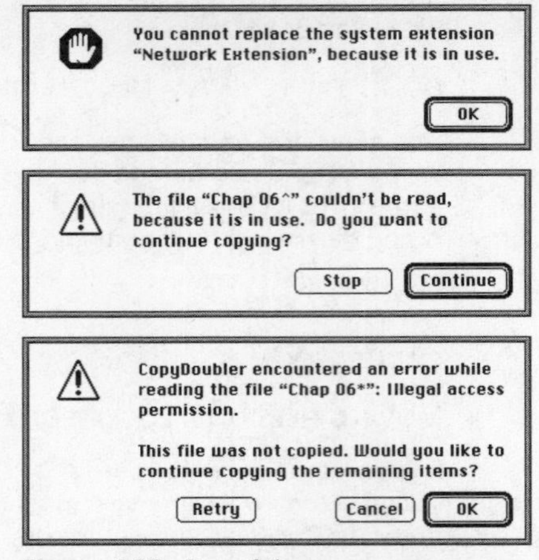

Figure 6-33 *One of these messages may appear if you try to replace or copy a currently open file.*

SEE: • **"Take Note: Files Locked by the Performa or by System 7.5's General Control Panel," earlier in this chapter, for another example of an access permission problem**
• **Chapter 11 for more on file sharing and illegal access permission**

For Problems Due to a Disk Error

Disk errors, as noted earlier, occur while trying to save or copy a file; the error message informs you that the file could not be read or could not be written.

If you were trying to copy more than one file, click the Continue button in the error message in order to copy any remaining files (assuming they are not having problems themselves). Otherwise, click Cancel and try the following solutions.

Try to Copy Files Again, in Smaller Groups If Appropriate Check which file(s) did not copy, and try again to copy any file that was not copied successfully the first time. Then try one or two more times. Sometimes the problem was a short-lived glitch, and one of your next tries will be successful.

This persistence is especially worthwhile if you were trying to copy several files at one time. Copying multiple files can overwhelm the Finder's processing and/or memory capacity, causing disk errors to occur. You may even get a separate error message indicating that there is insufficient memory to copy the files. In these cases, copying one file (or at least a smaller number of files) at a time should solve the problem.

For Floppy Disks, Use a Special Copy Utility If you get an error message from the Finder that the floppy disk could not be read, try instead to make the copy of the entire disk using a special copy utility. Disk Copy is a utility from Apple that can be used for this purpose; Norton Utilities includes a similar program called Floppier, and MacTools has one called FastCopy. These sometimes work when the Finder fails.

Alternatively, you may be able to copy files from a damaged floppy disk using Apple File Exchange software (included on System 7 software disks prior to System 7.5), even though that is not the main purpose of this software.

Also note that if you are using a utility such as Copy Doubler or Speed Copy and you get a "disk error" message when trying to copy files from a floppy disk, the problem may be with the utility instead of the disk. To find out, disable the utility extension and try the copy again.

If These Methods Fail

- **Read errors**

  A read error often means that the file is hopelessly damaged; your best bet is to replace the file with a backup copy. If you do not have a backup copy, you may still be able to repair or recover data from the disk.

  SEE: • **Fix-It #14 on rescuing damaged files**

- **Write (or verify) errors**

  If a write or verification error occurs, try copying the file(s) to a different disk. This should work fine, since a write error indicates that the problem is with the destination disk, not the source disk or the original file you want to copy.

  You should then back up all files on the disk that generated the write error. You may get read errors as you try to do this, indicating that some files on the disk are themselves damaged. Try to recover data from these files, as needed.

  SEE: • **Fix-It #14 on rescuing damaged files**

For both read and write errors, in addition to any attempt to repair files, check for bad blocks. Disk errors of either sort almost always mean there are bad blocks on the disk, usually due to media damage (as first described in Chapter 2); the damage is on the source disk for read errors, and on the destination disk for write errors. If you detect any bad blocks, you probably have to reformat the disk.

If the disk is a floppy disk, you are probably better off discarding it instead of reformatting it. After all, for the price of a floppy disk, why take chances? Even if the read or write error appears to vanish after repeated attempts to copy a file, do not trust the disk—if the media is bad, the error will return! Get rid of the disk, and be happy you were able to copy the file first.

By the way, if after several attempts you are eventually able to copy a file that had triggered a read error, open the file to make sure it is okay. Sometimes, the file is damaged even though the Finder does not report an error.

If the damaged disk is your only copy of an application disk, contact the manufacturer for a replacement. If you are a registered user of the software, you can usually do this for a nominal fee.

SEE: • **Fix-It #14 on damaged files**
• **Fix-It #15 on reformatting**

When the Going Gets Weird . . .

Symptoms:

While you are using an application (or control panel or desk accessory), something unexpected happens—something not covered by or not explained by any of the previous sections of this chapter.

Perhaps a command ceases to function suddenly, or a dialog box doesn't come up when requested. Or anything else occurs that seems to run counter to what the software's documentation (or common sense) says should happen.

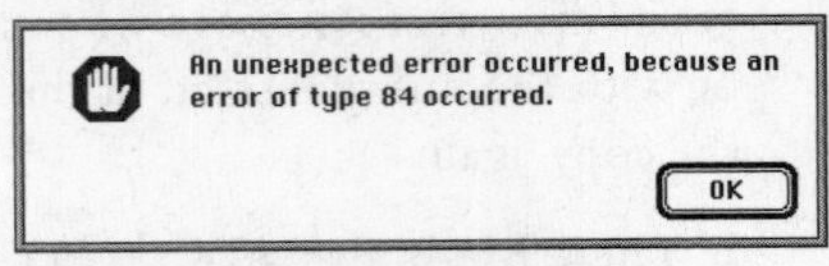

Figure 6-34 *One example of an error message that may appear when you are trying to carry out a command and the "going gets weird." This particular error number may result from problems with purgeable WDEF resources (as explained in Chapter 4).*

This catchall category also summarizes many of the suggestions made earlier in this chapter. Though it is hard to generalize here, the list I'll present tends to run from the most common and easily solved problems toward more complex situations.

Causes:

The most common causes include hardware incompatibilities, software bugs, missing accessory files, corrupted files, startup extension conflicts, and memory problems.

What to do:

Scroll, Close, Quit, Restart

An impressive variety of largely cosmetic problems with an application (such as text that seems to vanish) can be solved by simply scrolling the current display off the screen and then scrolling it back again, closing a window or document and then reopening it, or quitting the application and then relaunching it. The logical extension of these steps, of course, is simply restarting the Macintosh. Give these a try before proceeding further.

If the Problem Results in a System Error of Any Sort

Check Chapter 4 for the information on your particular type of system error. Return to this section only if Chapter 4 fails to provide a solution.

Check for Hardware Incompatibilities Between Your Hardware and the Application in Use

SEE: • **Fix-It #1 on incompatibilities between hardware and software**

Check for Damage to or Other Problems with the Application's Preferences File

SEE: • **Fix-It #2 on problems with preferences files**

TAKE NOTE ▶

FLASHING ICONS IN THE MENU BAR AND UNEXPECTED ALERT NOISES

If you suddenly see a flashing icon in the menu bar or hear an unexpected alert sound, these are usually requests to get your attention.

The most common alert these days is a flashing icon in the Application menu (found on the right side of the menu bar). The icon will always be for an application other than the currently active one. If you pull down the menu, you will notice a diamond symbol in front of the name of the relevant application; select it. Sometimes the flashing icon is something as harmless as an email application telling you that you have just received some mail. Otherwise, it is likely to be an alert or error message of some sort (such as one in the Finder telling you that your printer is out of paper).

The only other likely possibility here is that some extension function is the cause. For example, Apple's old Alarm Clock desk accessory will flash the Apple menu when its alarm goes off; similarly, Retrospect's extension will do this when it is time to run a scheduled backup. In these cases, the extension is not listed in the Application menu. You simply have to know what the cause is by the nature of the icon.

In any case, once you select the relevant application, the flashing (or sound) should stop.

Check Whether One of the Application's Accessory Files Is Missing or Mislocated

SEE: • Fix-It #3 on missing or mislocated accessory files

Check Whether the Application or Any of Its Accessory Files Are Damaged

Start by replacing just the application file from a copy on the original disk (be sure to delete the suspected defective file before making the new copy). If this does not solve the problem, reinstall the application together with all its accessory files. If the program has an Installer utility, use it (if it requires the use of an Installer utility, though, you may not have the prior option to replace only the application).

As always, when dealing with potentially damaged files, check for possible media damage to the disk itself. If the original application disk is damaged, you may still have an undamaged version of the files on your regular backups.

SEE: • "When You Can't Save or Copy a File," earlier in this chapter
• Fix-It #14 on damaged files

Consider Whether the Problem Is Due to a Bug in the Application

There is no way you can repair a bug yourself; this must be done by the manufacturer of the software in the form of a bug-fixed upgrade of the application. If you suspect a bug, you should call the company's technical support personnel to check it out. They may already know about it and be able to tell you what to do.

SEE: • Fix-It #18 on calling technical support and getting upgrades

In general, make sure you are using the latest version of the application, especially if you are using a version of the system software that was released after the version of the application you are using. Newer versions tend to fix bugs and conflicts from earlier versions.

BY THE WAY ▶

PROBLEMS WITH RUNNING IN THE BACKGROUND

A program that continues to work even when it is not the active application is said to run in the *background*. System extensions and many control panels do this, as first described in Chapter 1. Some applications do this as well: for example, the Finder in System 7 can complete a copy operation in the background, and PrintMonitor (see Chapter 7) runs in the background. Background-acting programs make it seem like two things are happening at once. What actually happens, though, is that background activities simply grab time whenever the foreground application is sufficiently idle.

Depending on the nature of the background activity, you may or may not notice an overall slowing down of the foreground activity as the background action proceeds (for example, cursor movements can become jerky, or dialog boxes may take longer to appear). In the most extreme cases, a conflict may occur between a foreground and a background activity, with the result that one or both of the programs cease to function. A system crash may even result.

If you suspect that a problem is due to a background processing conflict, here's what to do:

- **Pause your foreground activity briefly.** Some background activities halt while you type and resume again when you pause. Thus, if you take a brief rest, the background activity is given priority and completes faster. When you resume, you are no longer bothered by a slower response time and jerky cursor movements. Transient problems with PrintMonitor can be avoided this way. Doing this makes practical sense, of course, only if the background activity does not take too long to complete.
- **Turn off the background activity temporarily, if such an option is available.** For example, for control panels, there is usually an on/off button in the control panel window. Turn it back on when you are no longer using a foreground activity that conflicts with the background processing.

Otherwise, you will have to forgo the background processing altogether, either by keeping the potential background activity in the foreground until it is completed or (when all else fails) by not using the background program.

Symptoms due to bugs can be as "simple" as a system crash or so weird and convoluted that you might never expect that a bug is the underlying cause. There are no useful guidelines here.

Check for Startup Extension Conflicts

Startup extension conflicts are a common cause of almost any problem you may have with an application or control panel.

SEE: • Fix-It #4 for detailed procedures on how to identify and resolve startup extension conflicts

Startup extension problems can cause difficulties either with using an application or with using the startup extension itself. Startup extensions that modify either the normal functioning of the Finder or basic system functions (such as Open and Save dialog boxes) are especially likely culprits; the control panels of Now Utilities are a prime example here. Surprisingly, problems with Now Utilities can often be fixed simply by replacing the preferences file associated with the problem control panel (located in the Now Utilities Preferences folder, which is inside the Preferences folder of the System Folder).

RAM Doubler, CEToolbox (used by QuickKeys), ATM, and virtually any fax software are among many other common startup extensions that are prone to causing problems.

Similarly, be wary of any extensions that actively process information in the background, such as Disk Express II, or the prevention-checking features of MacTools and Norton Utilities. Finally, be careful never to use two extensions that do essentially the same thing, such as two screen savers. This is almost a sure way to cause problems.

In most cases, these startup extensions are regularly updated to resolve identified problems, so make sure you have the latest versions.

In general, check the ReadMe files that come with these programs to find out about any already known conflicts. If you have access to them, check online services for problems reported by other users (these are often accompanied by answers from the publisher of the software). If you are still stumped, call the program's technical support line.

Three more specific recommendations are as follows:

- **For RAM Doubler** You can easily start up with just RAM Doubler on, and all other extensions off, by holding down the Shift-Option keys at startup. You can similarly start up with all extensions on, except RAM Doubler, by holding down the Escape or tilde (~) key at startup. Lastly, you can compare the effect of using virtual memory instead of RAM Doubler simply by turning virtual memory on (this automatically disables RAM Doubler). After doing all of this, you should be able to determine if the problem goes away with RAM Doubler off, comes back with RAM Doubler alone on, and is not a general problem with virtual memory. If all three of these conditions exist, then you have almost certainly identified a RAM Doubler conflict, and it's time to contact Connectix (the maker of RAM Doubler).
- **For ATM** With ATM, try turning off (or on) the options in the ATM control panel, particularly the "Substitute for missing fonts" checkbox, to see if that fixes the problem.
- **Extensions and Installer utilities** Installer utilities (used to install a given software product on your hard disk) generally don't get along well with startup extensions. If an Installer utility fails to work correctly for any reason, restart with extensions off (by holding down the Shift key at startup) and try again. You will likely be successful now.

SEE: • **Chapter 9 for more on ATM**
• **Fix-It #2 on preferences files**
• **Fix-It #18 on calling technical support and getting upgrades**

Check for Memory-Related Problems

Insufficient available memory is yet another leading cause of problems. In these cases, you will most likely get an error message that tells you the general nature of the difficulty.

SEE: • **Chapter 4 for resolving memory problems that lead to a system error, such as a freeze or unexpected quit**
• **Fix-It #6 for more general advice on solving memory-related problems**

BY THE WAY ▶

APPLE EVENTS ERRORS

Apple events are an Apple technology that allows an application to send instructions to other programs. It forms the foundation of AppleScript (a feature now included and expanded in System 7.5). Support of Apple events and AppleScript requires that the application be rewritten to understand this feature.

If a program attempts to call another program via an Apple event and does not succeed for any reason, you will likely get an Apple events error message. The cause is usually either not enough memory to open the receiving application or the inability of the receiving application to understand the incoming instruction. For memory problems, you can try to increase your memory availability (as described in Fix-It #6). For the other more specific problems, there is no immediate solution. Contact the application's publisher for possible assistance.

Check for System Software Problems

Some problems with applications can be solved by reinstalling the system software. This is particularly advised if you get an error message that says needed system resources are missing.

Also, install the latest System Update available. For example, if you are using System 7.5.3, get the free update to System 7.5.4 (or later).

TAKE NOTE ▶

A QUICK CHECK FOR PROBLEMS WITH SYSTEM FOLDER FILES

Here's a quick way to determine if anything in your System Folder—other than the System, Finder, or Update files—is the source of your problem:

1. Remove the System file and the Finder (and Update file, if present) from the System Folder.
2. Rename the System Folder with a name like "System Stuff."
3. Using the Finder's New Folder command, create a new folder and name it "System Folder." Place the System and Finder and Update files in it.
4. Restart. The Macintosh should use the new bare-bones System Folder. Under System 7, new System Folder subfolders (such as Extensions and Preferences) are automatically created within the new System Folder during startup.
5. Check if your problem remains or is now gone.

If the symptoms remain, either the problem is with the System, Finder, or Update file or it has nothing to do with System Folder files at all. If the problem goes away, some System Folder file currently stored in the "System Stuff" folder is the cause. (This idea is similar to starting up with extensions off, but it checks for problems that go beyond extension problems.)

In any case, other techniques will now be required in order to determine the precise culprit (whether it be an extension, control panel, preferences file, System file, or whatever) and thereby solve the problem. Such techniques are described throughout this chapter and in relevant Fix-Its (especially Fix-Its #1–#5). This check is only a diagnostic technique designed to help narrow your focus.

By the way, to reverse the above steps, return the System, Finder, and Enabler to their former folder (now called "System Stuff"), delete the newly created System Folder, and rename the "System Stuff" folder as "System Folder." Restart.

If your version of the software is too old to work with the latest update (for example, if you are still using System 7.1 or earlier), strongly consider upgrading unless your Macintosh model is too RAM-deficient to use the newer software.

SEE: • **Chapter 2, "By the way: What Exactly Does a System Update Update?"**
• **Fix-It #5 on system software problems**

If All Else Fails, Round Up the Usual Suspects

The cause may extend beyond the problem application itself. For example, check for a possible virus infection, or for damage to the invisible Directory files. Let your particular symptoms guide you as to which Fix-Its seem most relevant; try those first.

SEE: • **Fix-It #7 to check for viruses**
• **Fix-Its #10 and #13 to check for damage to the Directory files**
• **Fix-It #9 to rebuild the desktop**

Printing Problems?

One major topic not mentioned in this chapter is problems with printing. This is the subject of the next chapter.

Chapter 7

When You Can't Print

The Paperless Office? 247

Your Dialog Boxes May Vary 248
LaserWriter versus LaserWriter 8 248
Desktop Printers 249
QuickDraw versus QuickDraw GX 249
And So 250

When Things Go Right 251
Step 1: Select the Chooser 251
Select Chooser from the Apple Menu 251
Make AppleTalk Active or Inactive 251
Select a Printer by Clicking a Printer Driver Icon 254
Select Printer-Specific Options 255
Step 2: Select Page Setup 259
Working with the Page Setup Dialog Box (LaserWriter 8.4) 259
When Changing Printer Drivers 260
Step 3: Use the Print Command 261
Working with the Print Dialog Box (LaserWriter 8.4) 261
What Happens Next 263
Special Case: Background Printing and PrintMonitor 264
Monitor Your Printing 264
Cancel Printing 265
Error Messages 265
Quitting PrintMonitor 265
PrintMonitor Documents Folder 267
Special Case: Desktop Printers 267
Desktop Printer Software 267
Creating Desktop Printers 268
Selecting a Default Printer 268
Using Desktop Printers 269
Mini-Solve It! Troubleshooting Desktop Printers 270

Solve It! When Things Go Wrong 274

The Macintosh Can't Find the Printer 275

Try Printing Again 276

Make Sure the Printer Is Ready to Print 276

Check the Chooser 277

Investigate Other Possibilities 280

Printing Halts with No Error Message 281

Is the Queue Stopped? 281

If You Are Using Background Printing 282

If You Are Not Using Background Printing 282

Do a Forced Quit or Restart the Macintosh 282

Reinitialize the Printer 282

Try Printing Again 282

For LaserWriters: Is It a Complex Document? 282

For LaserWriters: Check the Status Lights 283

If None of the Preceding Steps Work 283

Printing Halts Due to a System Crash, PostScript Error, or Other Printing-Related Error 284

Bugs in the Relevant Software 285

Corrupted Files 285

Other Causes 285

Try Printing Again 286

Replace Potentially Corrupted Files 286

Serial Port Is Currently In Use? 287

Zap the PRAM 287

Check the Printer Driver 288

Shift to a Different Version of the Printer Software 288

Check the Printer Cable 288

Turn Off Certain Printing-Specific Options 289

Make Sure Enough Free Space Exists on Your Disk 290

Check for Insufficient Memory and Related Problems 290

Problems with Background Printing 292

Widen the Search to More General Causes 294

The Paperless Office?

In the much-prophesied paperless office of the future, there will be no need for printed output. Quite the contrary is true today, however. Printing is one of the most common and critical of all computer activities. For most tasks, the job isn't done until you print it out—which means that if you have a problem printing, you are in serious trouble.

This chapter focuses on just one of the many possible printing-related problems you could have. But it is a big one: the failure of a document to print—either because the printing never gets started or because it stops before it is finished.

Many other types of printing problems are mentioned either only in passing or not at all in this chapter. So, if you are looking for the answer to one of these problems, let me be clear about what is *not* covered in this chapter:

Formatting Problems If the printer spits out your document but the latter's appearance is not what you expected, don't look here for help. These sort of problems are the domain of Chapters 9 and 10.

Problems Specific to Non-Apple Printers Although all printers work similarly on the Macintosh, each has unique options. I stay as general as possible here, addressing issues and problems that are common to all printers. When I do need to be specific, however, I focus on Apple's PostScript LaserWriters. This is because they are the most popular printers currently sold for the Macintosh and because other Macintosh printers tend to have fewer options and therefore fewer specific problems. Information about other Apple printers (especially StyleWriters) is also covered, but to a lesser extent.

If you are looking for advice specific to a Hewlett-Packard or other non-Apple printer, though, you won't find too much help here. I'm sorry, but it may help to note that many non-Apple laser printers use the LaserWriter driver. If this is the case for your non-Apple printer, you will find this chapter to be more directly relevant.

Problems with the Printer Itself This chapter covers some general problems related to printing hardware, such as proper connection of the printing cables. Aside from that, I largely avoid a discussion of hardware-related problems (such as paper jams or replacing the toner). Check your printer's manual for troubleshooting advice concerning your particular printer's hardware.

TAKE NOTE ▶

DIFFERENT TYPES OF PRINTERS

Three major categories of printers are commonly connected to Macintoshes.

- **Laser printers.** Laser printers use a printing method similar to that of a photocopier. The quality of laser printer output is the best of any of the printer types described here. For Macintosh users, Apple's LaserWriters are the most common example of this type of printer.
- **Inkjet printers.** Inkjet printers work by shooting miniature streams of ink from a cartridge onto the page. Apple's StyleWriters and Hewlett-Packard's DeskWriters are two popular examples. Color inkjet printers are the least expensive way to create decent color output.
- **Dot-matrix printers.** A dot-matrix printer uses a series of small pins to hammer against an inked ribbon. Which pins are hammering at a given moment determines what is printed on the paper. These printers are no longer popular, except for printing stencils or forms that have multiple copy layers. The ImageWriter is Apple's dot-matrix printer.

Your Dialog Boxes May Vary

Printer drivers (to be described in more detail shortly) are the files in your Extensions folder with the names of printers. Generally, you want to make sure that you have the driver whose name matches the model of printer you are using.

The information in the Page Setup and Print dialog boxes accessed from most File menus is determined by what printer driver you use. Unfortunately, making sweeping generalizations about these dialog boxes and other printer-related commands is becoming nearly impossible. One obvious reason for this is that with the proliferation of different printers, differences in the appearance of the dialog boxes are similarly multiplying. Even if you stick with the same printer, however, these dialog boxes and commands may vary—sometimes dramatically—because there may be more than one printer driver that you can use with a given printer. The following sections describe a few especially important examples of this.

LaserWriter versus LaserWriter 8

Until 1993, the standard printer driver used for PostScript LaserWriters was called LaserWriter. While minor differences occurred as the system software version changed, it remained remarkably the same for several years. In 1993, though, Apple and Adobe jointly released a major upgrade to the LaserWriter driver called LaserWriter 8. It was designed primarily to take advantage of new features available in Adobe's latest version of the PostScript language, called *PostScript Level 2*; it also increased printing speed with some printers. Using PostScript Level 2 also requires a printer that has the Level 2 instructions built in, which older LaserWriter models do not (check with your printer's manual to find out about your particular printer). Still, most compatibility problems with LaserWriter 8 have now been solved and it is generally recommended that you move up to this software. In fact, several applications now require LaserWriter 8. (But don't get too complacent; PostScript Level 3 is coming soon.)

LaserWriter 8.4 Several versions of LaserWriter 8 have been released since it first arrived on the scene. Each one fixed some bugs and many added one or two minor new features; for example, LaserWriter 8.3 was the first version to support ColorSync 2.0. LaserWriter 8.4 (released in mid-1996) represents a major upgrade, however, with completely redesigned Page Setup and Print dialog boxes (Apple has now done this sort of makeover every time I thought it was safe to write an edition of this book!).

Desktop Printers

Desktop printers (described in more detail later in this chapter) were an innovation first included with QuickDraw GX. The technology was sufficiently well received that Apple created a version of this software for non-GX systems as well. For non-GX systems, it is an optional feature that requires the enabling of a set of desktop printer extensions. Exactly how you set up to print and monitor the printing of a document will vary depending upon whether you have this optional software installed.

QuickDraw versus QuickDraw GX

In order to display or print almost anything, all Macintoshes depend on something called QuickDraw, which is built into the Macintosh ROM and to some extent into the system software. In 1994, Apple released QuickDraw GX, an optional upgrade to QuickDraw that is now included with System 7.5 or later. The user decides whether to install it or instead go with the standard non-GX version of QuickDraw.

Among its other features, QuickDraw GX includes a complete overhaul of the Macintosh printing software. Each printer needs a separate GX version of its printer driver, and so LaserWriter users now have to contend with LaserWriter GX in addition to LaserWriter and LaserWriter 8. The Page Setup and Print dialog boxes for LaserWriter GX are completely redesigned from either of the two previous drivers, with many new options.

In the short run, I expect that many users will choose to ignore QuickDraw GX. This is because it takes up a significant amount of disk space, it increases the minimum RAM you need just to run your system, and many of its features only work if you are using an application that has been rewritten to be "aware" of QuickDraw GX. Because of this, I am putting off a discussion of QuickDraw GX and its associated print-related dialog boxes until the more general discussion of System 7.5 in Chapter 13.

And So …

For the descriptions of LaserWriter printing in this chapter, I will almost exclusively focus on the LaserWriter 8.4 driver. I will also generally assume that you have the desktop printer software installed. For a point of comparison, however, Figure 7-1 shows how the Page Setup dialog boxes differ across the four versions of the LaserWriter driver.

SEE:
- **Chapter 9 on PostScript printers and text printing**
- **Chapter 10 on PostScript printers and graphics printing**
- **Chapter 13 for more on QuickDraw GX**

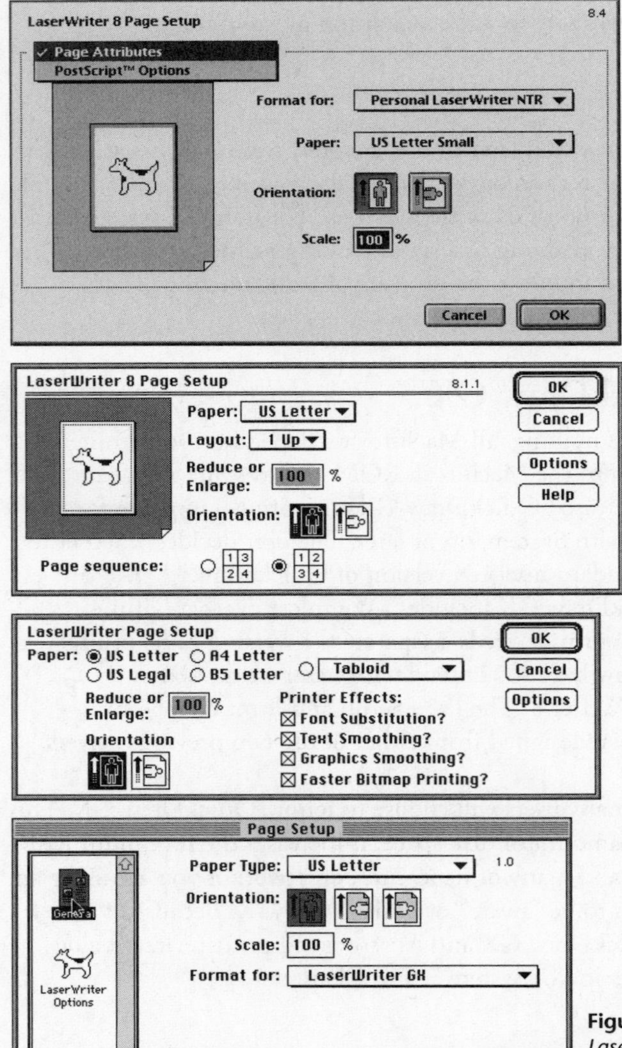

Figure 7-1 *Page Setup dialog boxes of LaserWriter 8.4 (top), earlier versions of LaserWriter 8 (upper middle), LaserWriter (lower middle), and LaserWriter GX (bottom)*

When Things Go Right

Before looking at how things can go wrong when printing a document, let's start by looking at what normally happens when things go as expected (ignoring the use of desktop printers for the moment). The three steps to no-hassle printing are as follows:

1. Select the Chooser.
2. Select Page Setup.
3. Use the Print command.

Remember, for the Page Setup and Print dialog boxes, what you actually see will be different if you are using a version of LaserWriter prior to 8.4 or using another driver altogether (such as the StyleWriter driver). Still, the basic principles remain the same.

Step 1: Select the Chooser

The Chooser is a desk accessory that is an essential part of the Macintosh system software. It's almost certainly on your startup disk already. It should have been installed when your System Folder was initially created; if it wasn't, you should get it onto your startup disk now.

When to use it:

The purpose of the Chooser, as its name implies, is to select which printer to use when printing. Even if you have only one printer connected to your Macintosh, you still need to use the Chooser, at least once, to identify that printer for the Macintosh. After that, the Macintosh remembers your choice; you do not have to use the Chooser again unless you want to change printers.

Note: If you have desktop printing software installed, you can change your printer selection without going to the Chooser, as described in the section on desktop printers later in this chapter.

What to do:

Select Chooser from the Apple Menu

This opens up the Chooser window, from which you make the other selections in this section.

Make AppleTalk Active or Inactive

Certain printers, most notably the majority of Apple's LaserWriter models, require the use of an AppleTalk network in order to work—even if the "network" is just one Macintosh connected to one printer. When the LaserWriters were first released, you see, they were so expensive that no one expected them to be used by just one person. Today, however, individually owned LaserWriters are common.

BY THE WAY ▶

HELP FROM APPLE PRINTER UTILITY

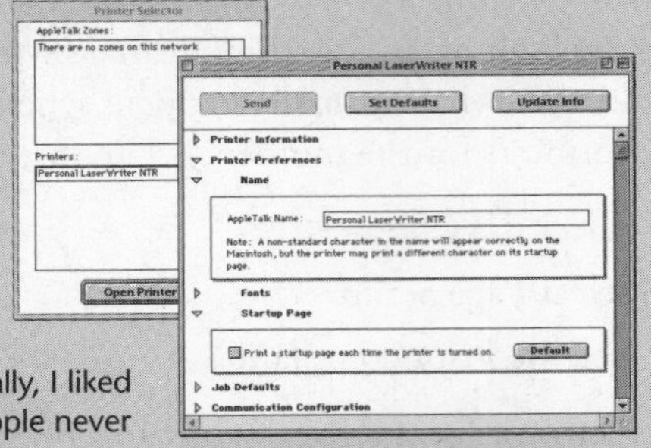

Figure 7-2 *The Apple Printer Utility, with two of its Printer Preferences options displayed.*

Apple Printer Utility is the latest incarnation of a utility that was previously called LaserWriter Utility (and LaserWriter Font Utility before that). Included with your system software and used to interact with laser printers, especially Apple's LaserWriters, it performs a number of useful tasks. Apple Printer Utility only works with PostScript Level 2 printers (all current LaserWriters qualify); for older printers, you need to use the older LaserWriter Utility. Personally, I liked the user interface of LaserWriter Utility better, but Apple never asked my opinion on this matter.

To use Apple Printer Utility, first make sure that the printer is connected to the Macintosh and that AppleTalk is turned on. Then turn on your printer and let it warm up. Launch Apple Printer Utility, click on the name of the printer with which you want to work, and then click the Open Printer button. From the window that appears next, you can select from any number of options. For example:

1. To change the name of a LaserWriter printer as it appears in the Chooser, click on the triangle next to the word Name. Enter the name you want to use, and click the Send button.
2. To stop printing a text page every time you turn on your LaserWriter, click on the triangle next to the phrase Startup Page. Uncheck the option that appears, and click the Send button.
3. To check on what PostScript fonts are built into your LaserWriter (as detailed in Chapter 9, "How to Identify a PostScript Font") or to download fonts to the printer manually (also detailed in Chapter 9, "Technically Speaking: Automatic versus Manual Downloading"), click on the triangle next to the word "Fonts."

With LaserWriter Utility, these same features are selected as menu commands, most often from the Utilities menu.

- **For AppleTalk printers, AppleTalk should be active**

  For AppleTalk printers, you need to turn on AppleTalk before you can print anything. Do this by clicking AppleTalk's Active button, located in the lower right-hand side of the Chooser window.

  By the way, occasionally, the AppleTalk Active button may read "Active after restart," indicating that AppleTalk will not be active until you restart the Macintosh. This indication is especially common after system crashes. Just restart, as it requests, and all will be fine.

  Note: If you have the Control Strip software installed, you can also turn AppleTalk on or off from the AppleTalk Switch module. With Open Transport, you can also use the AppleTalk control panel.

  Finally, make sure the AppleTalk cable is connected to the printer port (if you are using Classic AppleTalk) or the port selected in the AppleTalk control panel (if you are using Open Transport).

- **For non-AppleTalk printers, AppleTalk does not need to be active**

TAKE NOTE ▶

WHAT IS APPLETALK?

AppleTalk refers to a method of networking computers and peripherals together so that, for example, several users could all share the same printer; it is the equivalent of the language that is used to send information over the network. It is a language that all Macintoshes understand. To make an AppleTalk network connection, follow these instructions:

1. Make sure the hardware you want to connect to the network is all AppleTalk-compatible. Every Macintosh computer comes with built-in AppleTalk support, but not all printers do. Some printers, such as the StyleWriter 2500, have an option to add a module that provides AppleTalk network support for the printer. The manual that came with your printer should provide this information; if it doesn't, check with your dealer.
2. Connect the hardware. Usually, this is done via special networking cables. Apple's cabling system is called LocalTalk; other companies make competing cabling systems that connect via the same ports. A popular LocalTalk alternative is PhoneNet, which uses ordinary phone wire to make connections. It is still basically a LocalTalk system.

   On one end, the cable is connected to the Macintosh, typically through the serial port. If your Mac has two serial ports and you use Classic AppleTalk, AppleTalk is available only via the printer port, not the modem port. In this case, AppleTalk printers can never be connected through the modem port (even though non-AppleTalk printers can typically be connected through either port). If you are using Open Transport, you can use the AppleTalk control panel to select which port you want as the AppleTalk port. If your Macintosh has only one serial port, that port supports AppleTalk.

   On the printer end, connect the cable to the serial port. Just remember (especially for PhoneNet-like systems) that the cable connected to the device at each end of the chain may need a special terminating resistor, plugged into the empty slot in the phone plug.

   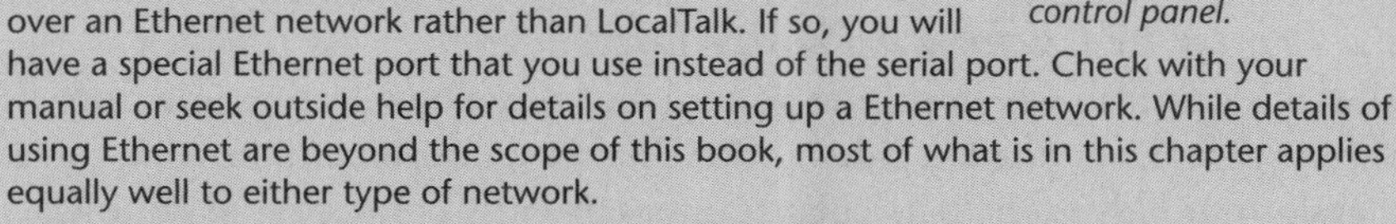

   Figure 7-3 *Selecting the AppleTalk port from Open Transport's AppleTalk control panel.*

   In some cases, you may have the option of connecting over an Ethernet network rather than LocalTalk. If so, you will have a special Ethernet port that you use instead of the serial port. Check with your manual or seek outside help for details on setting up a Ethernet network. While details of using Ethernet are beyond the scope of this book, most of what is in this chapter applies equally well to either type of network.
3. Turn on the AppleTalk option (by selecting Active) from the Chooser (or the AppleTalk control panel or the Control Strip, as appropriate).
4. If you are using Classic AppleTalk, open the Network control panel and select the appropriate icon. Most likely, it will have "LocalTalk Built In" as its default selection. As you are probably using LocalTalk, this is just fine; leave it as it is. If you are using Ethernet or some other type of networking protocol, you will need to select that option.

   If you are using Open Transport, make the appropriate selection from the TCP/IP control panel. If you are using LocalTalk, you can most likely skip this step.

SEE: • **Chapter 14 for more on networking issues, especially regarding Classic AppleTalk and Open Transport**
• **Fix-It #17 for more details on cable connections**

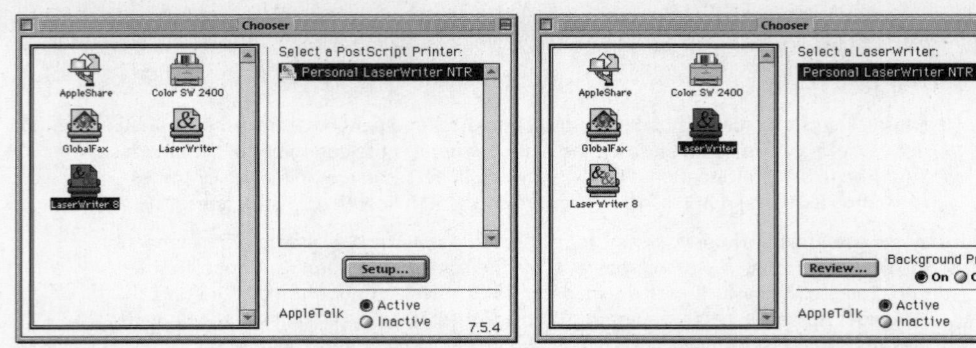

Figure 7-4 *Left: The Chooser display with LaserWriter 8.4 selected (note that no Background Printing options are shown). Right: The Chooser display with LaserWriter selected (Background Printing options are present). Left and Right: AppleTalk can be made active or inactive from the Chooser (as well as from the AppleTalk control panel or from the AppleTalk Control Strip module).*

TECHNICALLY SPEAKING ▶

APPLETALK ON AND OFF?

If you have a non-AppleTalk printer, you may still want your Macintosh connected to an AppleTalk network for other reasons (such as file sharing). In this case, you could connect the printer through the modem port and connect to the network through the printer port. AppleTalk is now turned on for the network, even though AppleTalk is not used by the printer.

Actually, with an option called PrinterShare (or GrayShare or ColorShare) that is available with some non-AppleTalk Apple printers, you can access a non-AppleTalk printer over a network (as long as the computer that the printer is connected to is on and is connected to the network). Details on how to set this up should have come with your printer.

Select a Printer by Clicking a Printer Driver Icon

You tell the Macintosh which printer you intend to use by selecting one from the display of printer icons on the left side of the Chooser dialog box. Normally, you select the icon that corresponds to the particular printer currently connected to your Macintosh.

These icons represent the different printers you can use (as well as possibly some networking options, such as AppleShare, which I will ignore for now). What printers appear in the Chooser window is determined by which printer-related Chooser extensions (also called *printer drivers*) are located in the Extensions folder of your System Folder. If the icon you are looking for is not present, you need to add that printer driver to the Extensions folder before you can proceed. Printer drivers for all Apple printers are included as part of the system software (though you will need the latest version of the system software to have the drivers for the latest printers).

SEE: • **"The Macintosh Can't Find the Printer," later in this chapter, for more details**

Note especially that the LaserWriter/LaserWriter 8 drivers are used only for PostScript LaserWriters. Non-PostScript LaserWriters, such as the Personal LaserWriter 300, have separate drivers.

BY THE WAY ▶

SELECTING A PRINTER DRIVER WHEN THE PRINTER IS OFF

If your AppleTalk printer is off when you select the Chooser, you can still select its printer driver. You will not see the name of the printer appear in the scroll box, but this is not a problem as long as you don't intend to print something yet.You can similarly select the printer driver for non-AppleTalk printers, even when they are off.

In either case, the driver selection forces the document to be formatted as though it will be printed to the selected printer, even though the printer is not currently available. This method can be used (as discussed more in Chapter 9) to format documents for printers that may not be currently attached to your Macintosh but that you intend to use for printing later. When you do print later, you may have to reselect the printer driver, even though you are not really changing drivers.

At the risk of stating the obvious, selecting a particular icon only lets you use that printer if it is physically connected to your Macintosh. The icon has no magical qualities.

Select Printer-Specific Options

- **Non-AppleTalk (serial) printers**

  Printer or modem port If you selected a non-AppleTalk printer, you usually have an option to select an icon representing one of the *serial ports*—either the *printer port* or the *modem port*. Select the icon that matches the port where the cable from your printer is connected; you can check the rear of your Macintosh to find out which port this is. Each port has an icon over it that matches the icon in the Chooser display. Despite their different names, the ports are almost identical. A non-AppleTalk printer can be successfully connected to either port.

  Special case: Only one serial port? Some Macs (especially most new PowerBook models) come with only one serial port; it acts as a combined printer and modem port. Connecting a non-AppleTalk (serial) printer to these models can get a bit complicated, and the task is made harder by the fact that Apple's advice on what to do seems to keep changing as new software and/or hardware is released. So, to be sure I get it right, the following advice comes directly from Apple. If these guidelines do not seem to work, check with Apple for possibly updated advice.

  To use a non-AppleTalk (serial) printer, three conditions must be met: (1) AppleTalk should be set to inactive; (2) if you have an internal modem, you will need to respectively set the PowerBook, PowerBook Setup, or Express Modem control panel to External, to Normal, or by unchecking "Use internal modem instead of modem port" (the location of this setting will depend on what version of the modem and system software you have); and (3) when selecting the serial printer in the Chooser, you must select the modem port or the combined printer/modem port (that is, do not select the printer port).

  If problems persist, you may need to disable the Assistant Toolbox extension (if it is installed). Also, if you have a communications program that does not use Apple Communications Toolbox extensions, this may not work. You may have to use a LocalTalk printer rather than a serial one.

To get back to using a modem again, note the following:

On most PowerBook models that have only one serial port (the 200, 2300, 190, and 5300 models), the serial port is mapped as a modem port. Under normal conditions this isn't a problem; the internal modem can be used at the same time as a serial device such as a printer is being used. The exception to this is if you are using a communications program that does not use the Apple Communications Toolbox (CTB). If this is the case, to use the modem, you will need to respectively set the PowerBook, PowerBook Setup, or Express Modem control panel to Internal, Compatible, or "Use internal modem instead of modem port" (again, the location of this setting will depend on what version of the modem and system software you have). When the PowerBook is set like this, the serial port cannot be used with serial devices; however, it can be used with LocalTalk devices.

- **StyleWriters with LocalTalk Option: Switch Hitters**
  StyleWriter printers are shipped as non-AppleTalk printers. Several models (such as the 2400 and 2500), however, include an optional LocalTalk module that allow the printer to function as an AppleTalk printer. If you have the LocalTalk module installed, the Chooser will still give you the option for a non-AppleTalk connection (via selecting the modem or printer port). There will be a third option, however, to select the name of the printer; in this case, you are using the LocalTalk module.

  With a non-AppleTalk selection, a button at the bottom right of the Chooser will read "Setup." Clicking this button opens up a window from where you can select whether to use the PrinterShare option (see: "Technically Speaking: AppleTalk On and Off?"). With the AppleTalk connection, the name of the button shifts to "Rename," and you are given the option to rename the printer (with LaserWriters, you would use the Apple Printer Utility to do this).

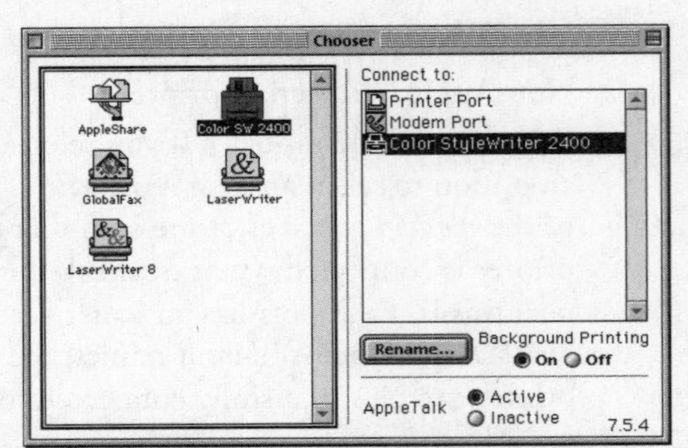

Figure 7-5 *The Chooser with the StyleWriter driver selected. In this case, the StyleWriter has a LocalTalk module installed and so can be selected by name on a AppleTalk network (this is the option currently highlighted). For a non-AppleTalk connection, select either the Printer or Modem port option as desired.*

- **AppleTalk Laser Printers**
  Select a printer name If you selected an AppleTalk laser printer, the name of the printer should appear now in the scrollable box on the right-hand side of the dialog box—but again, only if the printer is currently turned on and properly connected. Click the name of the printer you are using, if it is not already selected. Unless you are on a network with several printers, there should be only one name listed. For example, after you select a LaserWriter printer driver, the name of your printer appears already selected.

LaserWriter 8 driver: Click the Setup button After you click the LaserWriter driver icon, a Setup button will appear in the Chooser window. If this is the first time you are using LaserWriter 8 with this printer, you should select the Setup button before you try any printing. To do this, click the name of the printer (as listed in the right-hand side of the Chooser) and then click the Setup button.

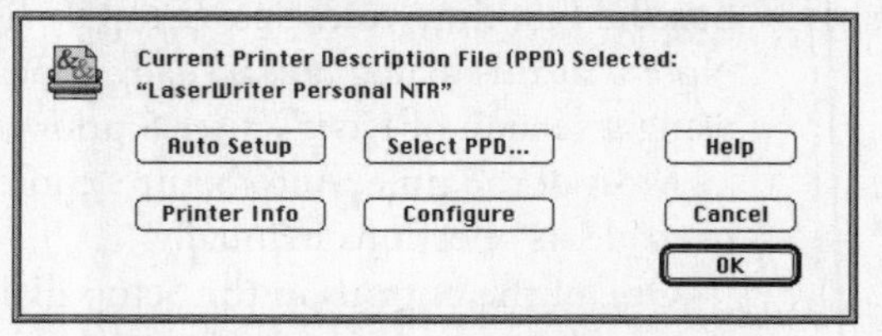

Figure 7-6 *The Setup dialog box in LaserWriter 8.2 or later.*

Note: If you have desktop printing software installed, the button should say Create, rather than Setup, prior to the first time you select it. This is meant to imply that selecting the button will create a desktop printer for you.

(If no printer name is listed in the Chooser, or if you have not yet selected a name, the Setup button will be dimmed and therefore unusable. Since a printer's name only appears here if the printer is connected and turned on, you must connect and turn on a printer before you can select Setup for it. If it is important for you to get around this restriction, try a freeware utility, called LaserWriter Patch, that alters the driver so that the Setup button is never dimmed; just make sure you are using a version of LaserWriter Patch that has been updated to match the version of the driver you are using).

If you are using LaserWriter 8.2 or a later version, after you select Setup (or Create) the first time, the driver will automatically determine the correct setup for your selected printer. A series of messages will briefly appear on the screen; when they are gone, you're done with Setup/Create. You only need to do this once for a given printer, not every time you reselect that printer. If a Setup has already been completed for a given printer, an icon for that printer will appear to the left of its name. If you see this icon, there is no need to bother with Setup unless you wish to make changes to the current settings.

TECHNICALLY SPEAKING ▶

PPD FILES AND WHAT REALLY HAPPENS WHEN YOU SELECT SETUP OR AUTO SETUP FOR LASERWRITER 8

Want to know a bit more about what happens when you select Setup or Auto Setup? Here's the scoop: If you properly installed LaserWriter 8, there will be a folder within your Extensions folder called Printer Descriptions. Within this folder are a collection of PostScript Printer Description (PPD) files that cover every different model of LaserWriter that uses the LaserWriter 8 driver (or at least all those models available at the time your version of LaserWriter 8 was released). Non-Apple laser printers may come with their own PPD file that you can install. When you set up a printer, the Chooser automatically ferrets out the PPD file for your printer and loads it. Additionally, your printer itself is checked for what options it may have available, such as whether an optional paper tray is installed. All of this information is then used to configure your Page Setup and Print dialog boxes to specifically match your printer and its options.

If you never select Setup at all (or if there is no PPD file that matches your printer), the LaserWriter 8 driver will probably default to a PPD named Generic (you can also select Generic from the Select PPD option in the Setup dialog box). If you have a choice, avoid the Generic setup; you will almost certainly be better off by selecting your printer-specific setup.

If you reselect Setup after having already previously set up the printer, you will get a dialog box that lets you select your own Setup options (you can also get this dialog box the first time you select Setup by holding down the Command-Option keys). Note that this dialog box actually appears the first time you select Setup, if you are using a version of LaserWriter 8 prior to 8.2.

Most of the time, Auto Setup's choices work fine. If you need to, however, you can override its selections manually.

One of the buttons in the Setup dialog box is Auto Setup. Clicking this does exactly the same thing as what probably happened automatically the first time you selected Setup. Unless you are having some problem, there would be no reason to select this button.

Another button is the Select PPD button (if you are using LaserWriter 8.1.1 or an earlier version, you will first need to click the More Choices button to access this and other buttons). This will bring up a scroll box listing all the PPD files in your Printer Descriptions folder; just choose the particular PPD for your printer. It is possible to select a PPD file other than the one that matches your particular printer. If you do this, you may find options in the Print dialog box that your printer doesn't support (or supported options may be missing); however, when you simply select Print, the document should print out okay. Still, I wouldn't recommend doing this, and I can't think of any reason you would want to do it.

Next, if desired, click the Configure button to access selection settings for certain printer-specific options. From here, you can select what printer tray options are installed, for example.

The remaining button in the Setup dialog box is "Printer Info." It doesn't allow you to change anything, but it does give you a description of your printer's characteristics (such as its resolution, its installed memory, whether it supports PostScript Level 2, and so on) that you may find informative.

Whatever you do, after you are done, close the Setup dialog box.

(Note: For versions of LaserWriter prior to LaserWriter 8, the PPDs are not used, and the Setup button works differently.)

- **Background printing: On or off**

Background printing will appear as an option only if your printer supports this feature; almost all models of LaserWriter and StyleWriter support it. You turn background printing on or off via buttons in the Chooser dialog box. If you are using LaserWriter 8.4, however, this option is absent. Instead, you select background printing directly from the Print dialog box.

Background printing is a useful feature that allows you to regain control of the Macintosh very soon after you select Print, even before the first page is actually printed. The printing process continues in the background while you return to your other work. Thus, you can continue editing your document or work on a different application without halting the printing process. You can even select additional documents to be printed; they will just be added to the waiting queue.

Without background printing, you would have to wait until your print job was completely finished before you could use your computer for something else. Since this could take many minutes, background printing can often be a big time-saver. Turning background printing off, however, usually speeds up the total time until completion of a given print job—which may be relevant if you are in a big hurry to get the job done. It may also occasionally be necessary to turn it off to prevent certain problems (as described later in this chapter). Still, for most users, background printing is definitely the way to go.

Using background printing requires the presence of the PrintMonitor and/or Desktop PrintMonitor extensions in the Extensions folder (with the exception of QuickDraw GX, which no longer needs PrintMonitor). PrintMonitor is the application that actually carries out the background printing. Normally, you do not need to interact with PrintMonitor in any way; the program handles everything itself automatically as soon as you select Print.

SEE: • **"Special Case: Background Printing and PrintMonitor," "Special Case: Desktop Printers," and "Problems with Background Printing and PrintMonitor," all later in this chapter**

Step 2: Select Page Setup

The Page Setup command brings up a dialog box that is important for formatting a document so that it matches the requirements and limitations of the selected printer. As a result, the options listed in this dialog box differ depending on which printer you are using. Different applications may also add their own custom options to this box.

When to use it:

As with the Chooser, you do not have to select Page Setup prior to every print request. You need only select it after you change printers (from the Chooser) or whenever you wish to change any of its options from their current settings.

What to do:

Working with the Page Setup Dialog Box (LaserWriter 8.4)

1. Select Page Setup from an application's File menu.
2. There should be a pop-up menu with at least two and possibly three choices; Page Attributes and PostScript Options will always be there. In addition, if your application has custom options, there will be an item with the name of the application (for example, Microsoft Word).
   a. **Page Attributes** From this option you can select Paper (for selecting among different sizes of paper), Orientation (portrait or landscape, as indicated by the icons), or Scale (to change the size of the entire printed output). For most common printing tasks, you should not need to change any of the default settings.

If you have more than one laser printer desktop printer created, there is even an option to select which printer you want the document to be formatted for (eliminating the need to go to the Chooser to do this).

Click on the picture of the "dogcow," and you will see the detailed specifications for the paper size you selected.

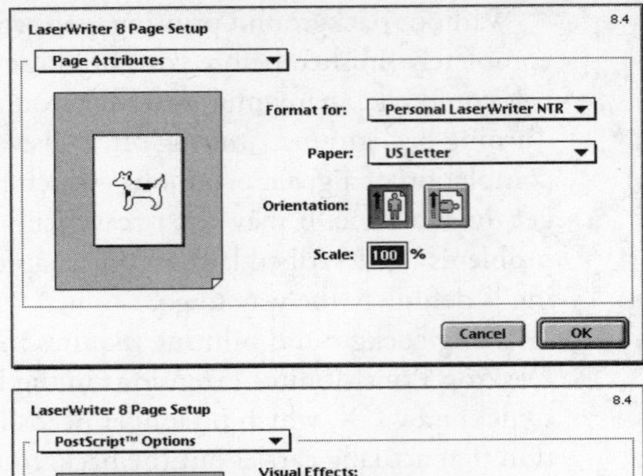

b. **PostScript Options** From here, you choose from among a variety of options, such as Precision Bitmap Alignment and Substitute Fonts; these are covered in more detail in Chapters 9 and 10.

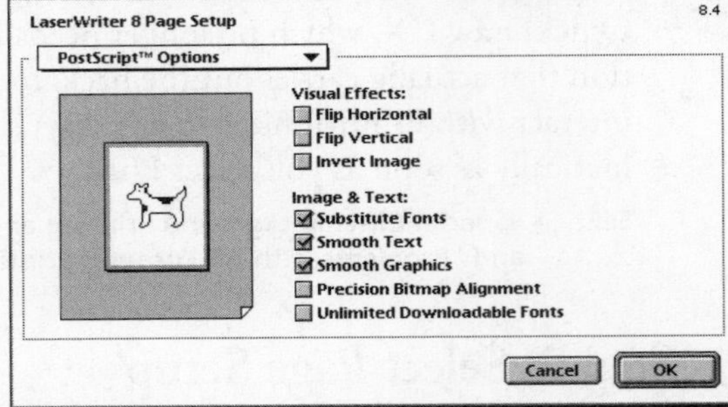

Figure 7-7 *The Page Attributes and PostScript Options displays of the LaserWriter 8.4 Page Setup dialog box.*

c. **Application Name** From here, you get to select special Page Setup options that are specific to the application you are using. Fractional Widths (as described in Chapter 9) would be a common option here.

You can turn on Balloon Help for some additional guidelines.

3. Click OK. This is sufficient to reformat the document to match the requirements of the selected printer. Hold down the Option key when clicking OK to save your changes as new defaults.

SEE: • **Chapter 9 on Page Setup commands and text printing**
• **Chapter 10 on Page Setup commands and graphics printing**

When Changing Printer Drivers

If you change printer drivers, you will automatically receive a message when you quit the Chooser, telling you to select Page Setup. If you get this message while an application is open, simply select Page Setup from within the application and click OK.

If no application (other than the Finder) is open at the time the Chooser message appears, you can usually ignore the message. Applications should adjust to the newly selected printer automatically when they are launched (see Chapter 9, though, for some problems that may occur).

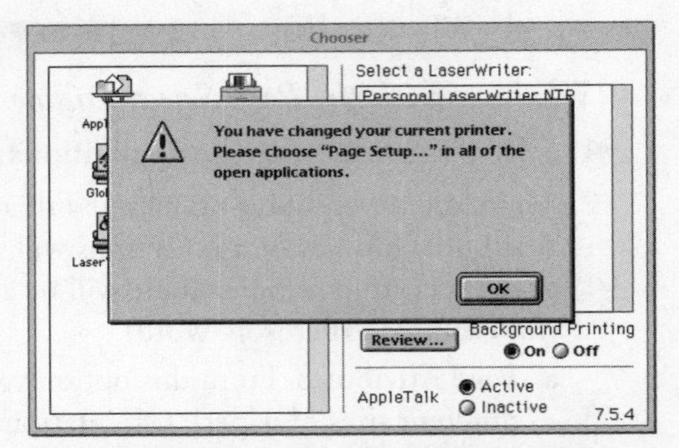

Figure 7-8 *If you change printer drivers, the Chooser (when you go to close it) automatically alerts you to select Page Setup.*

Oddly, if you change default desktop printers (as described in the section on desktop printers, later in this chapter), you do not get any alert message like this.

Finally, if you get a message that says that you cannot use Page Setup because you have never selected a printer, go to the Chooser and select a printer, as the message suggests.

Step 3: Use the Print Command

The Print command brings up a dialog box that is used to select such options as how many copies you want to print and what range of pages you wish to print. As with Page Setup, its options differ somewhat depending on the printer you are using. Different applications may also add their own custom options to this box.

When to use it:

This is the only step that is essential every time you wish to print something.

What to do:

Working with the Print Dialog Box (LaserWriter 8.4)

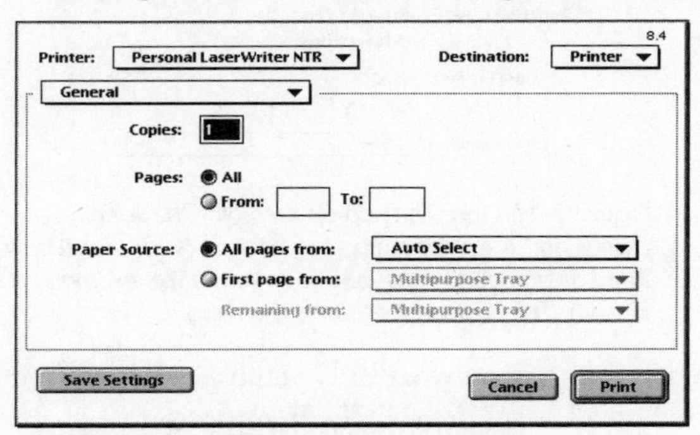

Figure 7-9 *The LaserWriter 8.4 Print dialog box, with General selected.*

1. Select Print from the application's File menu.
2. If you have more than one LaserWriter connected, the Printer pop-up menu lets you select which one you want to use (again eliminating the need to go to the Chooser to make this change). If you want your print job to be saved as a PostScript file (as described in "Technically Speaking: LaserWriter 8.4's Destination Option"), you make that choice from the Destination pop-up menu.
3. There should be a pop-up menu with at least seven choices (possibly more, depending upon your printer and application in use). Several of them involve issues that are beyond what we need to cover here (some, such as Color Matching and Imaging Options, are covered in more detail in Chapter 10). For now, here are the most common options with which you are likely to need:

a. **General** Here is where you select how many copies you want to print, the page range, and the source of the paper.

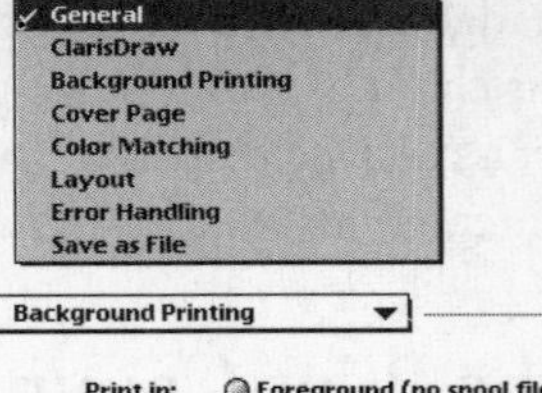

b. **Background Printing** From here, you can select to print in the "Background" or "Foreground (no spool file)." (Background printing is no longer selected from the Chooser in LaserWriter 8.4.)

c. **Layout** Here is where you determine how many pages per sheet you want printed.

d. **Error Handling** Here is where you select if and how you want PostScript errors reported (though these error reports will not be all that informative to most users, I would probably still select either the "Summarize on Screen" or "Print Detailed Report" option if you are retrying a print job that failed the previous time).

For most common printing tasks, you will probably only need to worry about the settings in the General window.

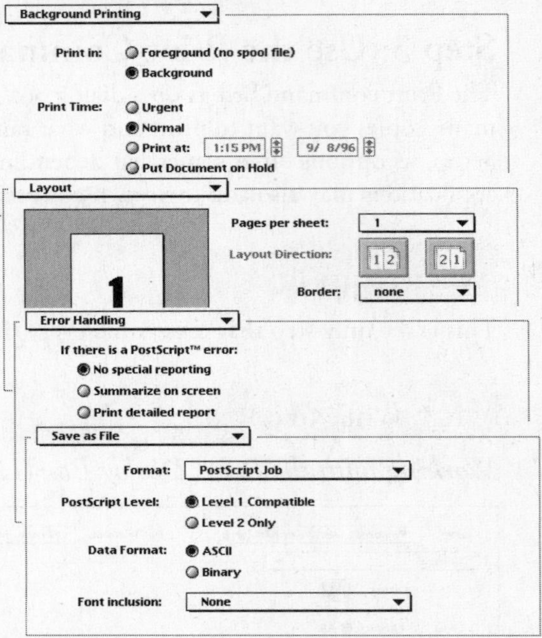

Figure 7-10 *Top: The pop-up menu for the various LaserWriter 8.4 Print dialog box options (with ClarisDraw listed as an application-specific option in this example). Bottom: The displays for four of the options.*

Different options may be available depending upon what PPD you have selected (the dialog boxes in the figures here are based on a LaserWriter NTR). If an option you expect to find is missing (such as PhotoGrade or FinePrint), you may not have installed the appropriate PPD file (see "Step 1: Select the Chooser").

4. Save your settings, if desired. Unlike Page Setup, most selections here are not saved when you close the dialog box; they revert to their default option each time you select Print. Thus, even if you change the number of copies from 1 to 3, it will return to 1 the next time you select Print. If you want to save the settings, however, you can now simply click the Save Settings button. (Of course, if you select some rarely used settings and save them, you may get surprised the next time you print!) Note that settings appear to be saved globally, rather than separately for each document.
5. Click Print. The document now prints.

SEE ALSO:
- **Chapter 9 on Print commands and text printing**
- **Chapter 10 on Print commands and graphics printing**

TECHNICALLY SPEAKING

LASERWRITER 8.4'S "DESTINATION" OPTION

In the upper right corner of the Print dialog box is the option to select Printer or File as the destination of your document. Most likely, you will be selecting Printer. If you select File, though, your document is saved as a PostScript file on your drive rather than being printed. The exact characteristics of the file are further determined by options you select from the Save as File pop-up menu selection. These options include whether to save the file as a PostScript file or an EPS file (see Chapter 10 for more on EPS), whether to include the font information for your document as part of the file (selecting "None" for a text document may mean that the document will print in an incorrect font), and whether you want the file to be PostScript Level 1 compatible.

Why would you ever want to save a document as a file? One reason would be to save the print job as a PostScript file so that you can later print it to any PostScript printer, without needing either the original document or its creating application. Another use would be to import a selection from a program that cannot save in EPS format to a program that does support the EPS format.

By the way, as of this writing, you cannot use the Save Settings button to save File as your destination; the Print dialog box always opens up to Printer as the destination.

What Happens Next

After you select the Print command, printing is handled automatically by the Macintosh. Initially, a message on the screen will tell you that the document is printing, usually adding instructions that you can cancel the print job at any time by holding down the Command-Period keys.

If you are printing to a LaserWriter (and background printing is off), this message is typically followed by the appearance of a second message that informs you of the progress of the print job. The exact messages vary depending on what LaserWriter you are using and what you are attempting to print, but there are generally three or four basic stages:

- *Looking for <name of printer>* or *Waiting for <name of printer>*. This message means that the Macintosh is searching for the printer currently selected from the Chooser. If the printer is on and properly connected, it will be found.
- *Initializing.* This message, if it appears at all, appears only during the first print job after turning on the printer. Essentially, information from the Macintosh, mainly from the printer driver, is sent to the printer to establish how the printer and the Macintosh communicate.
- *Starting job* and *Preparing data.* The Macintosh and printer are working to get the document (referred to as a *print job*) ready to be printed.
- *Processing job.* This is the final stage before your printed output begins to appear. Here is where the PostScript instructions are finally interpreted. For long documents, the printer may alternate between "Preparing data" and "Processing job" messages several times before finally printing.

If your document prints without a problem, you can happily ignore all these messages. If a problem interrupts the printing process, however, it can be diagnostically useful to know exactly where in the printing process the interruption occurred.

Special Case: Background Printing and PrintMonitor

Background printing requires an extension called PrintMonitor (if you are using desktop printers, it also requires a file called Desktop Print Monitor). Assuming that background printing is on, PrintMonitor is automatically launched after you select the Print command. The first thing PrintMonitor typically does is create a special PrintMonitor spool file of the document you're printing (see "PrintMonitor Documents Folder," later in this section, for more on this). On screen, an alert box will appear indicating the page-by-page progression of this spooling, which should average about a few seconds per page for text documents (even with laser printers, this process can be surprisingly time-consuming with large files, although LaserWriter 8.4 appears to be significantly faster than previous LaserWriter 8 versions).

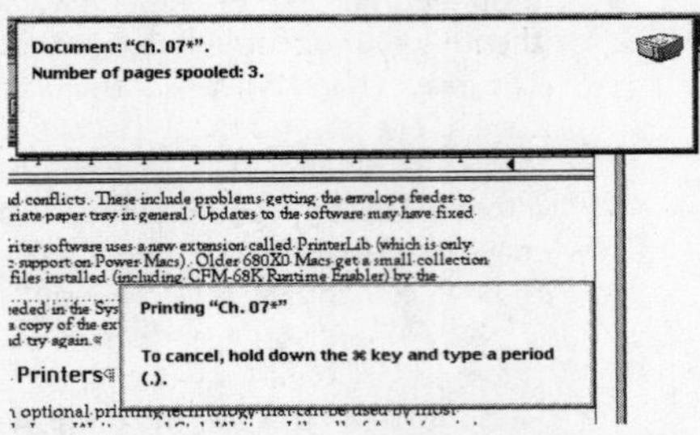

Figure 7-11 *The two message windows that typically appear on your screen shortly after selecting to print, when background printing is on.*

After this initial step, control of the Macintosh is returned to you. Meanwhile, printing begins, and PrintMonitor automatically quits after the print job is through. Normally, that is all there is to it.

While PrintMonitor is active, however, its name will appear in the Application menu (the one in the upper right-hand corner of the menu bar). If spooling has just completed, you may have to wait several more seconds before the PrintMonitor name first appears—in fact, it may briefly seem as if your Macintosh has frozen as it waits for PrintMonitor to gear up. Don't worry; just wait a bit longer, and all will be fine again.

Once its name does appear, you can select PrintMonitor as you would any other application. If you do, it opens the PrintMonitor window.

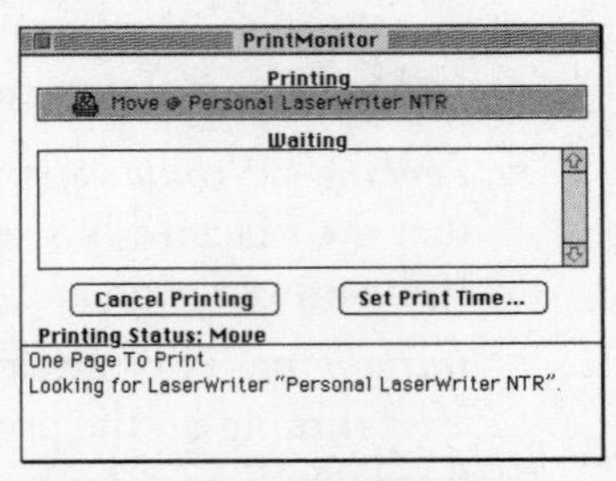

Figure 7-12 *The PrintMonitor window. The information in the box under "Printing" indicates that the LaserWriter is about to print the document named Move; no print jobs are waiting in the queue.*

Note that PrintMonitor usually quits (that is, its name is removed from the Application menu, unless you have its window open) before all your output has been printed. This is a sign that all the information needed to finish the printing job has been sent to the printer's memory, and so the Mac itself is no longer involved.

PrintMonitor works fine whether or not you select it from the Application menu. So why would you ever select it? The following sections explain why.

Monitor Your Printing

Selecting PrintMonitor allows you to follow the progress of the print job. The messages that would normally have appeared on the screen (if you were not using background printing, that is) are instead shifted to the PrintMonitor window. If you have several jobs queued to be printed, you can determine what they are and the order in which they will print by selecting PrintMonitor.

Cancel Printing

You can also cancel any waiting print jobs from the PrintMonitor window. Just highlight the document name you want to cancel from the list in the Waiting box, then click Cancel Printing. This is the only way to cancel a print job at this point; using Command-Period to cancel a print job is *not* an option once PrintMonitor takes over.

If you only want to cancel one job, do not go to PrintMonitor's File menu and select Stop Printing, which will stop *all* scheduled print jobs. To undo this, you will have to return to the File menu and select Resume Printing.

BY THE WAY ▶

NOT QUITE CANCELING PRINTING

If you cancel a print job on the LaserWriter, either by holding down Command-Period or by selecting Cancel Printing from the PrintMonitor window, do not expect printing to stop immediately. As many as a dozen or so more pages may print out before the printer acknowledges your cancel request. The only sure way to prevent these pages from being printed is to turn off the printer itself.

Error Messages

PrintMonitor alerts you when any sort of printing error occurs, even if you haven't selected the PrintMonitor window. Exactly how PrintMonitor alerts you (for example, whether you see a general message appear on the screen or only a flashing icon in the menu bar) is determined by settings that you select via the Preferences command in PrintMonitor's File menu.

If you get one of these alerts, you need to select PrintMonitor to see the specific error message. Most of the likely messages are described in the next sections of this chapter. If you had background printing turned off, the error message would have appeared directly on the screen, without any need to use PrintMonitor. (Note: With LaserWriter 8, you may also want to select to report errors via the Error Handling settings in the Print dialog box.)

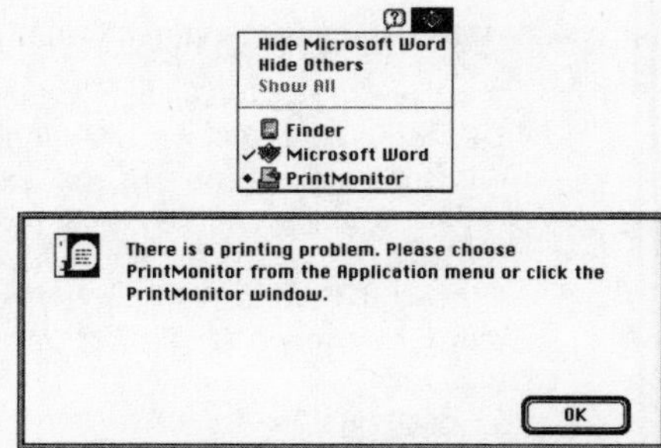

Figure 7-13 *Two ways that PrintMonitor may alert you of a problem: a diamond next to its name in the Application menu (top), or an alert message that appears on your screen (bottom).*

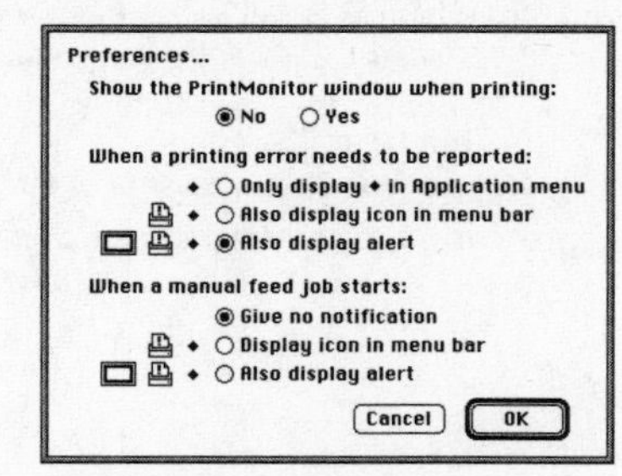

Figure 7-14 *PrintMonitor's Preferences window.*

Quitting PrintMonitor

When you are done working with PrintMonitor, don't close its window (and certainly don't select Stop Printing from its File menu since this brings all printing to a halt). Simply go to another application, either by using the Application menu or by clicking in any window from that application. PrintMonitor looks after itself and quits when it is done.

TAKE NOTE ▶

BACKGROUND VS. FOREGROUND PRINTING WITH LASERWRITER 8.4

Prior to LaserWriter 8.4, the LaserWriter created a spool file for each printed document whether printing in the background or the foreground. As a result, printing required two separate passes through the file: the first pass to analyze the file (spooling), and the second pass to convert the QuickDraw code to PostScript (printing). This incurred a performance penalty for printing large documents and sometimes required significant disk space to store the temporary spooled file. A spool file is really only needed for background printing, however, so creating one for foreground printing unnecessarily interfered with the printing speed.

Happily, this has been fixed with LaserWriter 8.4, which now does what is called "single pass" printing (that is, no spool file is created) when foreground printing is used. This can be especially handy to maximize the speed in which a document is printed. Remember, you make this selection from the Background Printing pop-up menu item in the Print dialog box.

An application may fail when printing in the foreground, however, if the application assumes that the driver will make a spool file. If so, turn background printing back on and try again. Applications known to have some problems of this nature include Persuasion, Photoshop, PowerPoint 4.0, Excel 5.0, Quicken, PageMaker 6.0, ClarisDraw, and Claris Impact.

TAKE NOTE ▶

OTHER LASERWRITER 8.4 QUIRKS, CONFLICTS, AND ODDITIES

The LaserWriter 8.4 software, which includes Desktop Printers 2.0, has been reported to have numerous minor problems and conflicts. These include problems getting the envelope feeder to work, or to select the appropriate paper tray in general. Updates to the software, though, may have fixed those glitches by the time you read this.

Also note that the LaserWriter software uses a new extension called PrinterLib, which is currently only needed for native Power Mac support on Power Macs. Older 680X0 Macs get a small collection of Code Fragment Manager files installed (including CFM-68K Runtime Enabler) by the LaserWriter 8.4 Installer.

The Finder Help file must be in the System Folder for the LaserWriter software to be installed. If you don't have it, a copy of the extension is on the LaserWriter disks themselves; copy it to the Extensions folder and try again.

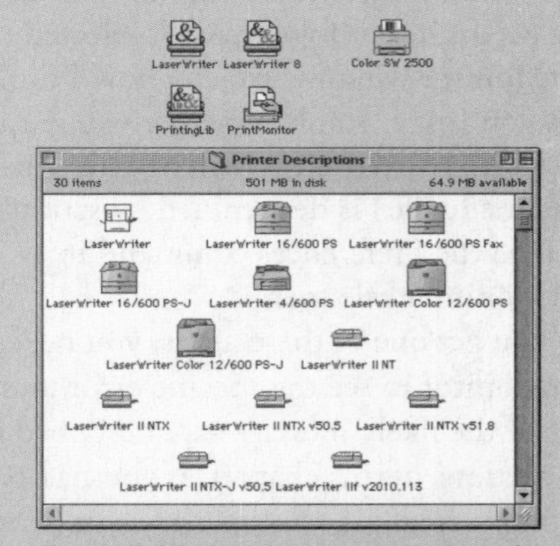

Figure 7-15 *Some common printing-related files in your Extensions folder: the LaserWriter, LaserWriter 8, and Color StyleWriter 2500 printer drivers; the PrintMonitor file needed for standard background printing; the PrinterLib file used by LaserWriter 8.4 on Power Macs; and just a few of the PPD files in the Printer Descriptions folder.*

PrintMonitor Documents Folder

PrintMonitor creates a folder in your System Folder, called PrintMonitor Documents, where it holds temporary "spool" files that it uses to carry out the printing. These files are essentially copies of the documents to be printed, created at the time you selected Print. Any changes you make to the document after selecting Print are not included in the pending printout, even if you make the changes before the document is actually printed. A file in the PrintMonitor Documents folder is automatically deleted when the print job is completed.

If you are using desktop printers, these spooled files are instead held as invisible files inside the desktop printer "folder" itself. Actually, if you are using desktop printers, the PrintMonitor file is not even used; Desktop PrintMonitor is used instead (see the next section for more details).

Special Case: Desktop Printers

Desktop Printers is an optional printing technology that can be used by most printers, including all Apple LaserWriters and StyleWriters. It is included with System 7.5.3 or later, as well as with the printing software for LaserWriters and StyleWriters. It is also available separately with its own Installer.

Like all of Apple's printer software, Desktop Printers seems to be under a constant state of revision. This section assumes you are using version 2.0 or later (the version that first shipped with LaserWriter 8.4).

The essential idea of Desktop Printers is that you create icons for each printer that reside on your desktop. Among other things, if you drag a document to a desktop printer icon, the document will print automatically. Similarly, if background printing is on (which it ideally should be to take full advantage of this technology), double-clicking on the desktop printer icon opens up a window that performs similarly to the PrintMonitor window described in the previous section. Let's look at all of this in a bit more detail.

Desktop Printer Software

The essential Desktop Printers software consists of three extensions: Desktop Printer Extension, Desktop Printer Spooler, and Desktop PrintMonitor. An optional fourth extension is Desktop Printer Menu. Except for the Desktop Printer Menu, all of these extensions should get installed when you do an Easy Install of your system software or printer software. Otherwise, you will need to select them from the Custom Install window of the Installer.

Figure 7-16 *The key files (again, found in your Extensions folder) needed for desktop printing. Among other things, these files, rather than PrintMonitor, handle background printing when enabled.*

Creating Desktop Printers

Creating desktop printers could not be easier; one such icon may have even been created automatically the first time you started up after installing the software. To add or change printers, go to the Chooser and select the printer driver icon (and printer name, for AppleTalk printers) for which you wish to create a desktop printer. If there is a button on the right side of the Chooser window that says "Create" (or possibly "Setup"), click this button, then close the Chooser. A printer icon will now appear on your desktop. You can repeat this for as many printers as you have connected to your Mac (or your network). Actually, you may find that one desktop printer is created automatically, even if you don't specifically create one. Don't worry; this is normal.

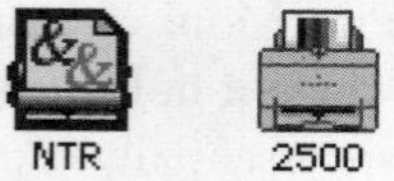

Figure 7-17 *Two desktop printer icons, as they would appear on your desktop; the bold outline around NTR indicates that it is the default printer.*

Selecting a Default Printer

If you have more than one desktop printer, you have to select one to be the default printer—that is, the one the Macintosh will print to the next time you choose to print a document. On the desktop, the default printer's icon is outlined in a heavier bold line than the other printer icons.

There are several ways you can change the default printer:

- Go to the Chooser and select a different printer driver, then close the Chooser.
- Click on a desktop printer icon, then select the Set Default Printer item from the Printing menu that appears.
- If you had the Control Strip installed when the Desktop Printers software was installed, it should have installed a Printer Selector module. With this, you can select the default printer from the Control Strip. Wait a few seconds for the change to take place before selecting the Print or Page Setup commands from an application.
- If you optionally installed the Desktop Printer Menu extension, there should be a printer icon in the menu bar, to the left of the Apple Guide icon. If so, you can select a default printer from here. Wait a few seconds for the change to take place before selecting the Print or Page Setup commands from an application.

Printing
✓ Start Print Queue
Stop Print Queue
Get Printer Info
Change Setup...
Show Manual Feed Alert
✓ Set Default Printer

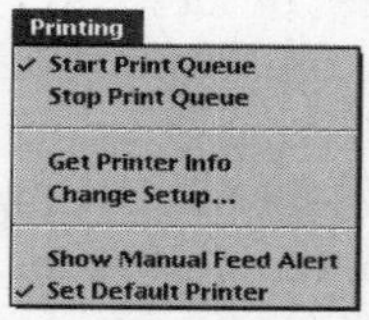

Figure 7-18 *The Printing menu that appears when you click on a desktop printer. Among other things, you can go here to select the given printer as the default printer; you can also select a default printer from the Chooser, the Apple menu, the Control Strip, or a special Printer menu next to the Apple Guide menu (all assuming the relevant software is installed).*

- The printer software should also install a Desktop Printers folder in your System Folder. This should contain aliases of all of your desktop printers. Further, an alias of the folder itself is stored in your Apple Menu Items folder. This lets you select a default printer from the Apple menu.
- With LaserWriter 8.4, you can switch among different desktop printers (for laser printers that use LaserWriter 8.4) from the Print dialog box's Printer pop-up menu.

Using Desktop Printers

Although you can print a document by dragging a document to a desktop printer icon, most often you will probably still use an application's Print command.

You'll prefer the desktop printer drag-and-drop method if you are printing a number of documents from several different applications, especially if you are sending them to different printers (although you should remember that doing this opens all of the separate applications, so be sure you have enough memory first). Simply drag your documents to your selection of printers, and the desktop printing software sorts everything out. You will no longer have to go to the Chooser to switch printers (though Apple says you may occasionally have problems doing this if documents come from different applications).

If you use file sharing, you can even drag a document to a desktop printer on another mounted Macintosh. This works even if the printer is not otherwise directly connected to the network in any way.

No matter how you choose to print (and again, I'm assuming that background printing is on), the major role of Desktop Printers becomes evident after control of the Mac has been returned to you and the background printing process has begun.

- *The desktop printer icon* First, you'll note that the icon for your desktop printer changes. If things are going well, an icon of a piece of paper will appear that will gradually fill up as printing proceeds to completion. If you halt printing, a red "stop" symbol appears. If an error occurs, a yellow alert symbol appears.

Figure 7-19 *The changing face of a desktop printer icon: the paper sheet that appears when printing is in progress; the alert symbol that appears if a problem occurs; the halt symbol that appears if you pause printing yourself; and the standard icon that appears when all is done.*

- *The Printing menu* Second, if you click on the desktop printer icon, a Printing menu will appear. What is in the menu depends upon what type of printer you selected, but at the very least you can select the default printer from here, as well as turn the Print Queue on or off (turning off the Queue brings all printing to a halt). With laser printers, you can also select whether you want to show manual-feed alerts; this is a new option in version 2.0 of the software.

- *The desktop printer window* Third (and most significant), if you double-click the desktop printer icon, it opens to a window that lets you monitor the progress of your printing in more detail. For example:

  To hold or resume printing a document To temporarily pause printing for a particular item (as opposed to the entire queue), select the item and then click on the relevant VCR-like button (in this

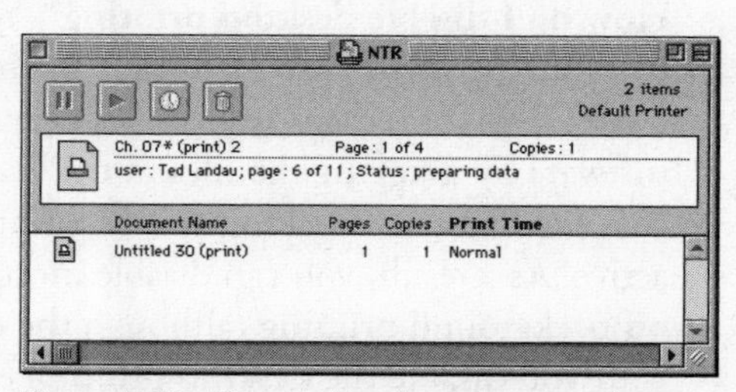

Figure 7-20 *The window that opens up when you double-click a desktop printer icon. Here it shows that the document "Ch. 07*" is currently being printed, while a document called "Untitled 30" is waiting in the queue.*

case, the double-vertical-line button). To resume printing again, click on the button with the triangle on it.

(Note: If you hold down the Option-Shift keys, these two buttons become Stop Print Queue and Start Print Queue buttons.)

To delete a print document To completely remove an item from the desktop printer, click on the item and select the Trash button.

You can also affect the printing process by dragging document items around the window. For example, you can select an item waiting in the queue and drag it so as to make it print sooner or later than its original order. You can even drag an item from the top window (indicating the item currently printing) to the bottom window (the queue), or vice versa.

Note that while you can sort documents in the queue in different orders by clicking on the column headers (for example, clicking on "Name" displays documents in alphabetical order), the actual printing order does not change.

This desktop printer's window is also the area where you can follow numerous messages (error and otherwise) that appear during background printing. Thus, if the error alert symbol appears on a desktop printer, and no error message appears immediately in the Finder, open this window to find out what the error is all about.

In some ways, desktop printers behave like applications. For example, if you select Get Info, you will see that you can adjust the memory size of the desktop printer, just as you can for applications (the relevance of this is discussed next in "Mini-Solve It! Troubleshooting Desktop Printers"). On the other hand, these icons sometimes act as a folder, and they may even appear as a folder in some Open dialog boxes of applications. In fact, it is within this "folder" that documents in the print queue are invisibly stored (again, some of the troubleshooting relevance of this is discussed next).

Mini-Solve It! Troubleshooting Desktop Printers

The main Solve It! section is coming up next, but here are some troubleshooting issues specifically related to using desktop printers.

- **How do I disable desktop printing?** You can temporarily turn off desktop printing by disabling the desktop printing extensions at startup (this is typically done by using a startup management utility). You can permanently remove the desktop printing software by dragging the files to the Trash and restarting.

  Note that most desktop printing features require that background printing be active. As a result, you can disable most aspects of desktop printing simply by turning off background printing (although the desktop printing software itself remains active).

  If you disable the desktop printing extensions, you can still use the older PrintMonitor-based method of background printing, as long as the PrintMonitor extension still resides in your System Folder.

- **Why do my desktop printer icons have an "X" over them?** This usually means that the desktop printing extensions were disabled at startup (either because you selectively disabled them, as just described, or because you started up with all extensions off). You can still print (unless you are using Open Transport and started up with all extensions off), but you don't have access to any of the special features of the desktop printers. Restart with the extensions back on, and everything will return to normal.

  The printer icons will also have an "X" over them if the matching printer driver is missing from the Extensions folder for any reason. In this case, you will not be able to print.

Figure 7-21 *The "X" over each of the icons means that the Desktop Printers software is currently disabled.*

- **Why can't I trash a desktop printer icon?** To get rid of a specific desktop printer, simply drag its icon to the Trash. As long as the software is active, however, you must always have at least one desktop printer. If you throw away the last one, it will be immediately re-created.
- **Why can't I move a desktop printer icon to a folder?** Prior to Desktop Printers 2.0, desktop printer icons could only reside on your desktop, not in any folder. With version 2.0 or later, you can now put the icons anywhere you want. Any version of Desktop Printers will allow you to rename a desktop printer or create an alias of it.
- **Why do I get a message that says the desktop printer cannot be found?** When you try to print, you may get an alert message that your "spool files" have been moved to the Trash because the needed desktop printer could not be found or does not exist. There are two likely causes (and solutions) to this problem.

  First, it is possible that your desktop printer has somehow become damaged. To fix this, drag the desktop printer icon to the Trash and reselect the printer in the Chooser. I once had to solve this problem by reinstalling my entire LaserWriter and desktop printing software.

  Otherwise, if you have third-party printer software, it may be incompatible with desktop printing, particularly Desktop PrintMonitor. In this case, go to the Chooser and turn off Background Printing, then try to print again.

  Finally, if you try to print to a desktop printer that has been disabled because its printer driver is missing, you may get this sort of message. In this case, you need to return the driver to the Extensions folder.

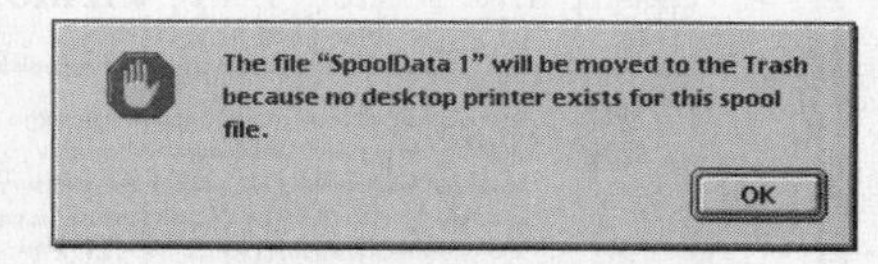

Figure 7-22 *If you get this message even though the needed desktop printer is present, you usually have damaged printing software or are using an incompatible application*

- **Why does nothing happen when I try to print certain documents by dragging them to a desktop printer icon?** If you drag a document to a desktop printer and nothing happens, it is likely that the document's creating application is incompatible with this drag-and-drop feature or with desktop printing entirely. There is nothing you can do about this.

  Also, unlike most ordinary documents, you cannot print "clippings" files via drag-and-drop to a desktop printer icon.

- **Why did I lose my document when I saved it to the desktop printer "folder"?** The Save dialog boxes of applications may list desktop printers as ordinary folders. Saving a document to these folders, however, will not get it to print; in fact, you will lose access to the document altogether. To get it back, you'll have to start up with extensions off and drag the file out of the desktop printer folder.

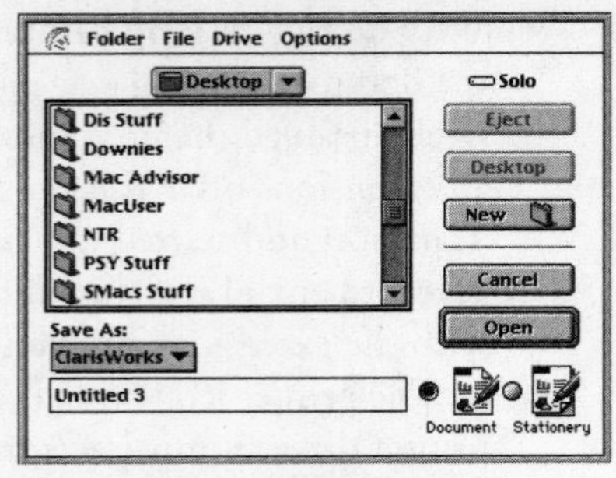

Figure 7-23 *A Save dialog box that "erroneously" shows a desktop printer (NTR) as an ordinary folder.*

- **What if my Macintosh continues to crash when restarting after a printing-related system error?** If a printing problem causes the Mac to crash, forcing you to restart, it may crash again near the end of the startup as it automatically retries to print the problem file. The solution? Start up with extensions off. The desktop printer will have an "X" over it, but double-click it anyway; it will open up like a folder, with the waiting Spool Files inside visible as ordinary-looking documents. Drag the document icons to the Trash and restart as normal, then try printing again. Hopefully, the printing problem will not recur; if it does, check out the sections in the remainder of this chapter for more general advice.

Figure 7-24 *A Spool File as you might find inside a desktop printer icon "folder." To see it, start up with extensions off (while a print job has been left uncompleted) and then double-click the desktop printer icon.*

- **What do I do about an "insufficient memory" message when trying to print?** If you have more than five desktop printers, you may get this message whenever you try to print. To solve this problem, give Desktop PrintMonitor (located in the Extensions folder) more memory by increasing its Preferred memory size as listed in its Get Info window. The default size is typically around 160K to 175K; increase it by 12K for each printer beyond the fifth one.

  Also note that as long as there are any files waiting to be printed, Desktop PrintMonitor remains active in memory, even if background printing is off. If you are not printing in the background, remove all print requests from your desktop printer queue. This will "turn off" PrintMonitor, saving you the 160K or more.

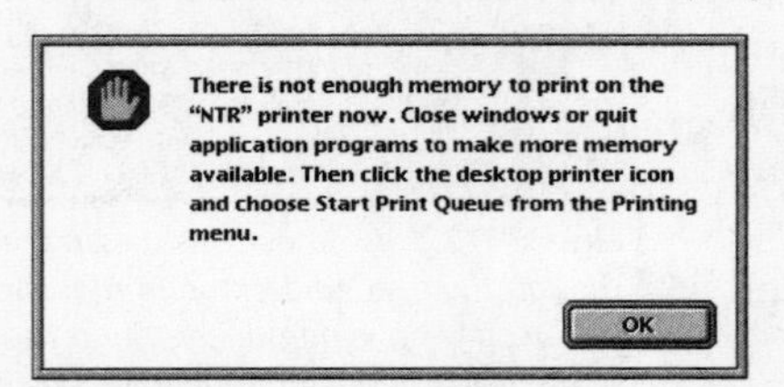

Figure 7-25 *If this message keeps recurring across different print jobs, it often means that it's time to increase the Preferred size of the Desktop PrintMonitor file.*

- **What if I get a message that asks if I want to adjust the memory size of my desktop printer?** If you print large complex documents, a message may appear asking if you want to temporarily adjust the memory size of the desktop printer in use. Click OK, and all should go well. If this adjustment is not sufficient or the problem recurs often, however, you can permanently increase the printer's memory by selecting the Get Info window for the printer icon itself and increasing its Preferred memory size by about an additional 100K to 200K.

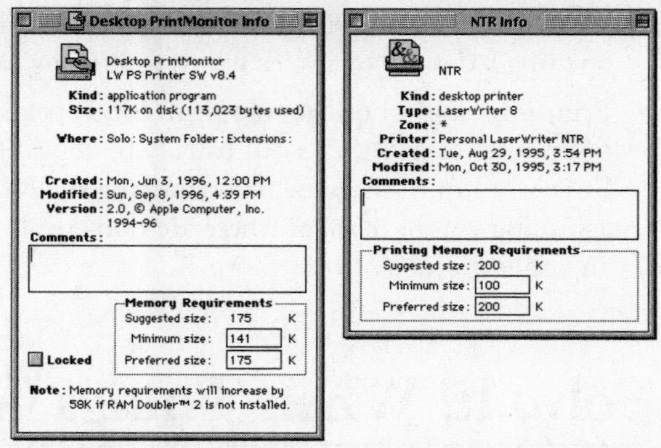

Figure 7-26 *The Get Info windows of the Desktop PrintMonitor extension (left) and a desktop printer (right). Surprisingly, both allow for Memory Requirements adjustments.*

SEE: • **Chapter 2 and Fix-It #6 for more on memory adjustments from the Get Info window**

- **What if I get a message that says I cannot use a desktop printer, or if I have other printing problems, such as freezes and crashes?** If you get a message that says a particular desktop printer cannot be used or if you otherwise cannot get printing to proceed, go to the Preferences folder and delete that printer's Preferences file (for a printer using LaserWriter 8, look for LaserWriter 8 Prefs). Then go back to the Chooser and redo the Setup for the printer, restart the Macintosh, and try again.

  Also, if you are using older versions of the system software and desktop printing software, upgrade to the latest versions.

- **What about –192 or 15 system errors when installing desktop printers?** After first installing desktop printer software and restarting, you may get "–192" or "15" errors when you try opening files or folders in the Finder. This is probably due to corruption of Now Startup Manager's preferences file. The solution is to restart your computer with extensions disabled and delete the preferences file.

- **Type 15 errors and multiple desktop printers on your desktop** Here's a truly weird problem. With desktop printing software enabled, you select to print and get a Type 15 error, maybe a few of them. You dismiss them and your print job finishes successfully. But now crossed-out desktop printers begin to appear on your desktop, with a new one created every second or so. Nothing you can do, short of restarting, can stop them. What's going on? It turns out that this is due to a bug in some versions of Desktop Printing software. The solution is to make sure that the Finder Scripting Extension is enabled. This same symptom may also occur due to conflicts with certain fax software (for example, if GlobalFax GX is present in a non-GX enabled system).

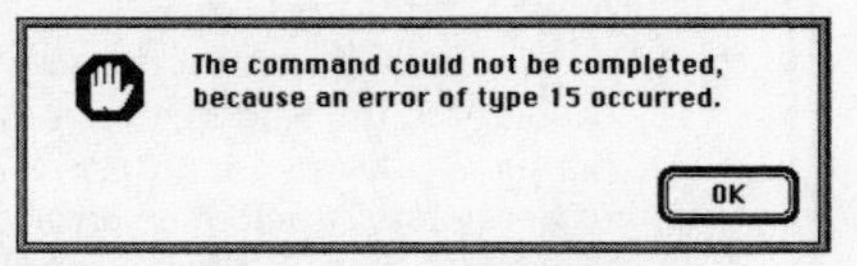

Figure 7-27 *An error message that may appear when trying to print with desktop printers.*

With Finder Scripting Extension disabled, Type 15 errors may also result from opening a desktop printer's window or using any other desktop printer function.

- **Print jobs stall in queue** If a print job appears in your desktop printer window but refuses to print, this can usually be solved by giving more memory to Desktop PrintMonitor. Otherwise, try removing the MathLibMoto or LibMotoSh extensions, assuming you have them (these are non-Apple extensions that are used to speed up an application's math operations).

Solve It! When Things Go Wrong

Most of the time, if you have followed the preceding three steps—select the Chooser, Page Setup, and Print—your printing proceeds without any further problem. Then, however, there are those times when the printer simply refuses to cough up your request. The following sections detail the myriad of reasons that a printing request may fail and what you can do about it.

TAKE NOTE ▶

GENERAL ADVICE FOR ALL PRINTING PROBLEMS: TRY AGAIN

Before you wade through all of the specific advice in the rest of this chapter, simply try printing again. Maybe you had a one-time glitch, and the problem will not repeat itself.

For starters, if you get an error message that includes a Try Again button, give it a try (unless you already suspect what the problem is and know that simply trying again will not work). If the error message offers any explanation or advice, make use of it (such as by adding paper or turning on AppleTalk, as indicated), and then try again. You may have to select Cancel Job or Stop Queue (or whatever) before you can do this.

Otherwise, simply quit the application from which you are trying to print, launch it again, and try to print again. If that fails, turn the printer off; wait about ten seconds or so; then turn the printer back on and try again (this *reinitializes* the printer). If even that fails, shut down the Macintosh and the printer, then turn everything back on and try to print the document one more time. Always make sure the printer is correctly selected in the Chooser.

Obviously, if you had a system crash, you may have little choice but to restart and try again.

If it is practical to do so, before trying to print again, close all open applications and documents not needed for the printing to proceed. This frees up additional RAM, which may solve the problem.

Note that if an error message does not appear on your screen (either while in the application or in the Finder), you may have to select PrintMonitor or open the default desktop printer (if you are using this software) before you can see it. In any case, the Mac may seem to freeze briefly before an error message appears. If so, don't worry; the error message will usually show up in a few moments. If not, you probably did not get any error message.

SEE ESPECIALLY: • **"Mini-Solve It! Troubleshooting Desktop Printers" and "Printing Halts Due to a System Crash, PostScript Error, or Other Printing-Related Error," elsewhere in this chapter**

The Macintosh Can't Find the Printer

Symptoms:

You select Print from the application's File menu, and one of the following events happens:

- The Print dialog box does not appear. You immediately get an error message that says the Macintosh "can't open printer."
- The Print dialog box appears, and you click OK. Then, however, you get the message that the Macintosh "can't open printer."
- You may get a message that says the printer "could not be found" or "is not responding."
- An error message of any other sort appears instead of the Print dialog box.

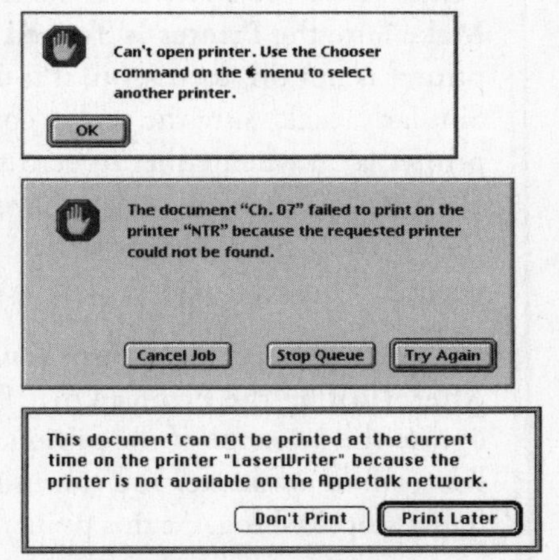

Figure 7-28 *Examples of error messages that may occur after you select Print, if the Macintosh cannot locate or access the selected printer.*

Note that you have to leave your application and go to the Finder to see some of these alert messages. In all these cases, the result is that no printed document ever appears. The good news is that probably nothing is wrong with the printer. Even better, the solutions here tend to be quick and easy.

Causes:

Typical causes are that the Macintosh cannot locate the printer driver, that the wrong printer driver is selected, or that the printer is not properly connected. If your printer requires an AppleTalk connection, it may be that AppleTalk (or PrinterShare, for those printers that can use this option) is not turned on, or that the wrong printer name is selected. In addition, the wrong port (printer as opposed to modem) may be selected, or corrupted Parameter RAM (PRAM) may be causing the problem. Or it may simply be that your printer is turned off.

Often, especially in System 7, you may get an error message that describes the likely cause. For example, it may say, "Use the Chooser to make AppleTalk active" or that the ImageWriter's "Select light is off. Please push the select switch." If you get this sort of helpful advice, follow it.

What to do:

Try Printing Again

SEE: • **"Take Note: General Advice for All Printing Problems: Try Again," earlier in this chapter**

Make Sure the Printer Is Ready to Print

Make Sure the Printer Is Turned On It never pays to overlook the obvious. If the printer is not on, turn it on; if it doesn't turn on, check to see if it's plugged in. Similarly, make sure the power cord is firmly connected to the printer. You'll know the printer is on when either its status lights are on or the printer at least makes some noise.

Several printers these days have an energy-saving feature that turns the printer off (in a sort of "sleep" mode) when it is not in use, automatically awakening it when needed. This saves you the hassle of worrying about whether or not the printer is on.

For LaserWriters: Make Sure You Did Not Select the Print Command Too Soon After Turning the Printer On If you select Print too soon, the Macintosh will not recognize the presence of the printer. Wait for the printer to complete its startup cycle; it takes about a minute. You can usually tell this has happened when the printer status lights stop flashing. At this point, reselect the Print command.

Try Plugging the Printer Cable into the Other Serial Port If you are an individual with a Macintosh and a printer, a cable probably runs from one of the serial ports on the Macintosh (usually the printer port) to the appropriate port on the printer (there is usually only one port that fits the cable you are using).

If your non-AppleTalk printer is currently plugged into the printer port, switch it to the modem port—or vice versa. This may help if one of the ports is damaged (which ultimately requires a hardware repair to fix). You will also have to change the port selection from the Chooser.

For AppleTalk printers using Open Transport, you can also switch your cable to the other serial port. In this case, you also need to make the switch in software via the AppleTalk control panel.

Telecom Software Alert: You cannot connect a printer to the modem port when the GeoPort Telecom software is installed. Telecom assumes all data sent to modem port is for the modem.

Make Sure You Are Using a Correct Cable If you have never used this printer and/or connecting cable before, there is a chance that you are trying to use an incorrect cable. For example, the cable for connecting a modem to the Macintosh may look identical to the one used to connect a non-AppleTalk printer, but they are not necessarily the same. Similarly, the cable used to make an AppleTalk connection is different from the standard serial cable used for non-AppleTalk printers (see "Take Note: What Is AppleTalk?" earlier in this chapter). If you are uncertain whether your cable is correct, take your cable to an Apple dealer (or other knowledgeable source) to check it.

Make Sure the Cable Is Firmly Plugged In and Not Damaged Check if the printer cable is loose; reconnect it if needed. Make sure no pins on the plug are bent or missing. To be certain that a cable is not defective, switch it with a different one that is successfully working with another printer, if such a cable is available. If this solves the problem, then the original cable was damaged.

SEE: • Fix-It #17 for more on cable problems

After Completing the Previous Checks, Try Printing Again Even if you didn't find anything amiss, try again anyway. You may have fixed something without realizing it, and printing may proceed successfully. If the document still fails to print, proceed to the next step.

TAKE NOTE ▶

MISSING OR DAMAGED PREFERENCES (ESPECIALLY WITH LASERWRITER 8)

An error message (either when selecting to print or when opening the Chooser) that says "The LaserWriter 8 Preferences file may be missing or damaged ..." most likely means you have not selected the Setup command for your printer. Go to the Chooser, select the printer driver icon, select the printer name, and then click the Setup button. As a last resort for this or related problems, go to the Preferences folder, locate and delete the LaserWriter 8 Prefs file, then go to the Chooser and select Setup for your printer.

Figure 7-29 *Trash this file if you keep getting messages that it is missing or damaged.*

Check the Chooser

Incorrect settings from the Chooser are a common source of problems at this point in the printing process. Note that if you are using desktop printer software, however, you may be able to bypass the Chooser here and, for example, select or switch default printers by a number of other methods.

SEE: • "Special Case: Desktop Printers," earlier in this chapter

If You Cannot Locate the Chooser in the Apple Menu In System 7, this means that the Chooser is not in the Apple Menu Items folder. If necessary, locate it (either elsewhere on your disk or on a backup disk) and place it in the Apple Menu Items folder in your System Folder. Once you have installed, located, and selected the Chooser, continue with the steps that follow.

Make Sure the Correct Printer Driver Icon Is Selected Thus, if you are using a LaserWriter printer, select the LaserWriter 8 (or LaserWriter) icon. If the correct icon is not present, the driver for your printer is not present in the Extensions folder. To correct this, locate the correct driver from your Macintosh system software disks (or, if you are using a non-Apple printer that has its own driver, locate this driver) and place it in the Extensions folder.

TAKE NOTE ▶

DOES THE CHOOSER SHOW GX DRIVERS INSTEAD OF THE ONES YOU WANT?

If you are looking for a driver (such as LaserWriter 8) and do not find it listed in the Chooser, it may be that you have installed QuickDraw GX. With this installed, only GX-compatible drivers (which all have GX in their name) are displayed, even if the non-GX driver is correctly located in the Extensions folder. If this appears to be your problem (and assuming you don't want to be using GX), the quickest solution is to drag the QuickDraw GX extension out of the Extensions Folder onto the desktop, then restart. For more details on dealing with QuickDraw GX, refer to Chapter 13.

TAKE NOTE ▶

PROBLEMS PRINTING WITH EXTENSIONS OFF: APPLETALK CAN'T BE MADE ACTIVE AND –23 ERRORS

If you start up with extensions off (by holding down the Shift key) and then select Print from an application, you may get an error message that says that AppleTalk is off and that you need to turn it on in the Chooser to get printing to proceed. In some cases, you may instead get a –23 error, which refers to the same problem. In any case, when you go to the Chooser and try to select AppleTalk, you get a message such as one that says "The printer port is in use. AppleTalk cannot be made active now," or simply, "AppleTalk cannot be opened." What's going on? What do you do?

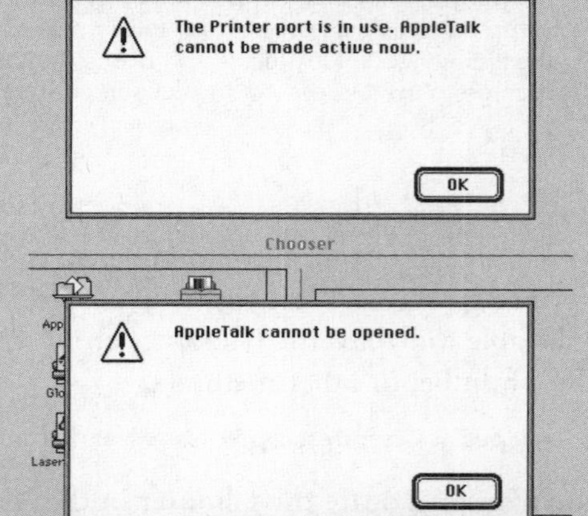

Figure 7-30 *Error messages that you may get, typically when in the Chooser, when you use Open Transport and try to print with extensions off or with Open Transport software otherwise disabled. Doing this prevents you from using AppleTalk, which then prevents you from printing to an AppleTalk-connected printer (such as a LaserWriter).*

The answer here is almost certainly that you are using Open Transport, Apple's new communications software that replaces "Classic AppleTalk" (as described more in Chapter 14). Open Transport requires that its Open Transport extensions be active, which they are not if you started up with extensions off). If these extensions are not active, AppleTalk cannot be turned on, and printing cannot proceed.

The solution is to delay printing until you start up again with extensions on. At the very least, make sure that all the Open Transport Library and "Lib" extensions are enabled. Otherwise, if your computer supports it, you can use Network Software Selector to shift back to Classic AppleTalk; you can then print with extensions off.

If you use desktop printers and start up with extensions off, the desktop printing software is disabled. As long as you don't use Open Transport, you will still be able to print, but without the desktop printing features. Alternatively, if you do use Open Transport and selectively disable desktop printers, but keep Open Transport and other related extensions enabled, you will be able to print, but again without desktop printing features.

If You Are Using AppleTalk, Make Sure It Is Active If it isn't, you will get a message to this effect when you try to print a document.

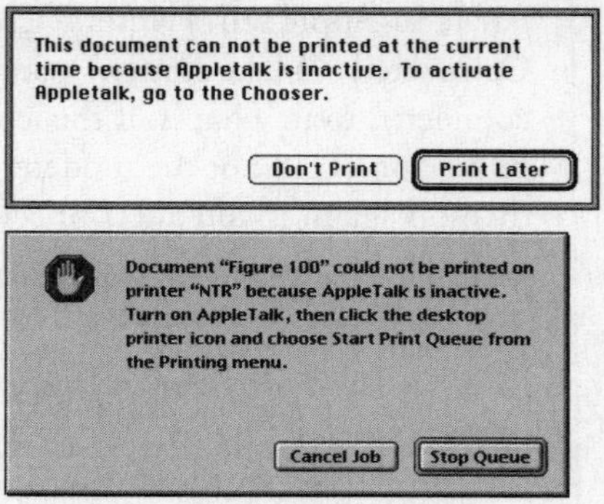

This document can not be printed at the current time because Appletalk is inactive. To activate Appletalk, go to the Chooser.

Don't Print | Print Later

Document "Figure 100" could not be printed on printer "NTR" because AppleTalk is inactive. Turn on AppleTalk, then click the desktop printer icon and choose Start Print Queue from the Printing menu.

Cancel Job | Stop Queue

Figure 7-31 *If you have AppleTalk turned off when trying to use a printer that requires AppleTalk, you may get a message like one of these.*

If You Are Using AppleTalk, Check That the Name of Your Printer Is Listed and Selected The name should appear after you select the printer driver icon, assuming the printer is already on.

SEE: • **"When Things Go Right," earlier in this chapter**

If no name appears, the Macintosh does not recognize the presence of your printer. For laser printers, assuming that you have already checked that the printer is on and connected properly (as described previously), you probably haven't waited long enough for the printer to warm up after turning it on (some printers now have an "instant on" feature and will not require this warm-up period).

To solve this problem, quit the Chooser (even though this step probably isn't necessary). Wait a minute, then select the Chooser again; the name should now appear. Select it if it is not already highlighted.

If this fails to work, and if you are using Open Transport, go to the AppleTalk control panel and reselect the correct port for your printer, even if it is already correctly selected. In one case I saw of a printer connected to an Ethernet port, selecting the Printer port and then reselecting the Ethernet port finally got the printer's name to appear in the Chooser.

Also, if you are on a LocalTalk network that has several Macs and/or printers daisy-chained together, be aware that if someone between you and the printer disconnects from the chain (by pulling their cable out), you will not be able to access the printer. Make sure your fellow office workers keep their cables properly connected.

Finally, note that the top line of the Print dialog box gives the name of the currently selected printer. This may be different from the name of any printer that is now available on your network. For example, if you have a PowerBook and print to one printer at work but another at home, you may have the printer for the wrong location shown as the selected one. To solve this problem, again simply go to the Chooser and select the name of any currently listed printer.

TAKE NOTE ▶

FINDING YOUR PRINTER NAME: WHEN A SHUTDOWN IS BETTER THAN A RESTART

If the Chooser refuses to list your AppleTalk printer's name no matter what you do, sometimes the magic of a restart will do the trick. Try it. I have occasionally found (particularly with PowerBooks) that even if a restart fails to work, a shutdown and subsequent restart will succeed.

For Non-AppleTalk Printers: Check the Port to Which the Printer Cable Is Connected Make sure the selected serial port icon is the one that has the printer cable connected to it. That is, if the icon is for the printer port, make sure the cable is in the printer port and not the modem port. Also, it may help simply to turn the printer off and then on again. If you are connected to the printer port, make sure AppleTalk is turned *off.*

SEE: • "When Things Go Right" (especially the list item "Non-AppleTalk printers"), earlier in this chapter, for more advice, including advice concerning PowerBooks with only one serial port

If you are trying to use PrinterShare (or GrayShare or ColorShare) to print to a computer connected to another Macintosh, remember that in order to access the printer, the computer that the printer is connected to must be turned on, as well as the printer itself. Unlike with AppleTalk, it is not sufficient that just the printer be on. Also, in order for the printer to be shared, the Share This Printer option must be turned on for that printer. This is done through the Chooser; select the printer's icon and then click the Setup button to see this option. Using this feature may also require that the printer be connected to the modem port, not the printer port.

Try Printing Again If you have successfully navigated your way through the Chooser dialog box, close the Chooser, reselect Page Setup if needed, and reselect the Print command. The document should now print.

BY THE WAY ▶

PRINT LATER?

Alert boxes that appear when there is a problem with a print job request may include a Print Later button. In general, I recommend not using this button. Instead, cancel the print job and simply start over once you determine what is wrong. This simplifies the procedure, reducing the risk of other problems down the road.

One exception is with PowerBooks that have Assistant Toolbox installed. In this case, the Print Later option is a useful way to store documents that you are working on when you are on the road and not connected to a printer. When you are back at the office, you can easily print them all in one step. Of course, with background printing on (especially with desktop printers), you can also easily do this by halting the print queue prior to selecting Print.

Investigate Other Possibilities

If none of the preceding suggestions worked, consider any or all of the following, as appropriate.

The Wrong Version of the Printer Driver Generally, you should use either the version of the printer driver that matches the version of your System and Finder or a more recently updated version (see "Take Note: Mixing Versions of Printers, Printer Drivers, and Other System Software," later in this chapter, for more on this).

A Corrupted Printer Driver The printer driver may be damaged. To check for this possibility, replace it with a copy from your backups. For example, if you are trying to print using a LaserWriter, replace the LaserWriter driver extension in the Extensions folder with a backup copy. (For LaserWriter 8, also replace the PPD files.) Reinstall all printing software if in doubt.

Corrupted Parameter RAM (PRAM) The Parameter RAM, a special area of memory, contains information necessary for the serial ports to work. If the PRAM becomes corrupted, information cannot get through the serial ports (printer and modem) to the printer. The PRAM then needs to be reset (*zapped*, is the commonly used term) before printing can proceed.

SEE: • **Fix-It #11 for more about the Parameter RAM and how to zap it**

Hardware Problems If none of the previous suggestions work, a hardware problem is likely. It's time to take your printer (or perhaps the Macintosh itself) in for repairs.

SEE: • **Fix-It #17 on hardware problems**

Printing Halts with No Error Message

Symptoms:

The printing process does not even begin, or it begins but then stops in midstream. In either case, no error message occurs. Everything else seems to be operating as normal. All you know is that a long time has passed and the printer is producing no output.

Causes:

Perhaps everything is fine, and the document just needs a long time to print. Otherwise, an *endless loop* type of system error has probably occurred.

SEE: • **Chapter 4 for more on endless loops and related system errors**

In the latter case, the document never prints out, no matter how long you wait. If this happens with a LaserWriter, you are likely to notice that the print job seems to be stuck forever in the "preparing data" or "processing job" phase.

The ultimate causes of such system errors are the typical ones: software bugs or damaged files (see also the next section for more on these causes). Occasionally, the problem may be due to insufficient RAM in either the Macintosh or the printer itself in the case of laser printers.

What to do:

Is the Queue Stopped?

If all printing seems to have stopped, make sure you have not inadvertently stopped the entire print queue, either by selecting PrintMonitor's Stop Printing command or by selecting desktop printer's Stop Print Queue (in which case a stop symbol will be on the desktop printer icon). If so, select to start/resume printing again.

If You Are Using Background Printing

If you are using background printing, you usually regain control of the computer before the first page prints out. If so, and no error message appears in the Finder, you can check the PrintMonitor window (or desktop printer icon window, if you have this software installed) to make sure no message is waiting there. With desktop printers, you can usually tell that there is a message waiting, because the desktop printer's icon will include a yellow alert symbol. In either case, the Application menu will probably be flashing.

If no message (or at least no message with helpful advice) appears, delete the document from the queue (by selecting Cancel Printing in PrintMonitor, or by trashing the document with desktop printers) and try printing again.

If You Are Not Using Background Printing

If you are not using background printing, you are probably stuck with some sort of "Now printing" message on the screen. Press Command-Period a few times to try to cancel the printing. Wait a minute or so to give it a chance to cancel the process.

Do a Forced Quit or Restart the Macintosh

If none of the previous procedures has any effect, you can treat this as a system freeze and try a forced quit (press Command-Option-Escape) of the application. Otherwise, you have to restart the computer.

SEE: • Chapter 4 on forced quits and restarting

Reinitialize the Printer

In any case, once you regain control of the Macintosh, you should reinitialize the printer. Turn off the printer, wait a few seconds, and turn it back on again.

Try Printing Again

Return to your application and select the Print command a second time. See if it works now.

SEE ALSO: • "Take Note: General Advice for All Printing Problems: Try Again," earlier in this chapter

For LaserWriters: Is It a Complex Document?

If the document still fails to print, don't automatically assume that you have a system error. Consider whether you simply have a document that takes a long time to print.

For laser printers, where an entire page is printed at once, it is not unusual for a considerable amount of time to pass before the printing of the page begins. Particularly if the page contains large or complex graphics, it could take ten to fifteen minutes—or even more—for the laser printer to spit it out.

So if you are printing something out of the ordinary, where you don't have experience with how long it should take, give it a chance before assuming the worst. If everything else seems to be working normally (for example, the green status light on the printer is blinking as expected), go away for a while. By the time you return, it may have been printed.

TECHNICALLY SPEAKING ▶

WHAT ACCOUNTS FOR PRINTING SPEED?

Speed of printing is hard to predict because it depends on so many different factors. Similar to how far an automobile goes on a gallon of gas, your printing "mileage" may vary.

The first factor is the printer itself. Usually, a printer is rated in terms of pages per minute (ppm). This represents the approximate maximum rate that the printer can produce its output; most popular laser printers are in the range of 4 to 10 ppm or even more. The ppm rating is primarily a function of the physical limits of the actual printing machinery. Printers, however, rarely meet this theoretical maximum.

For example, real printing times for laser printers (especially PostScript laser printers) are also influenced by any computer processing hardware built into the printer. Thus, the faster the processor in the printer can get the information to the printing machinery, the more likely the printer is to approach its ppm maximum. Similarly, the greater the amount of RAM in the printer, the faster its printing generally proceeds.

Speed is also influenced by events that take place before the information ever reaches the printer. The specific version of the printer driver can have an effect; newer versions often include improvements designed to enhance printing speed.

Sometimes the printing application itself has an effect as well. Two different word processors, for example, may print similar documents at different rates.

The nature of the document itself has a major effect on speed. Simply formatted text usually prints the fastest. In contrast, heavily formatted text and (especially) complex graphics slow the operation down considerably. Large, multicolored graphics printed to an inkjet printer can take a very long time indeed.

You can speed up printing somewhat by turning background printing off—but then you lose the advantage of more quickly regaining control of the Macintosh. As always, free lunches are hard to find!

For LaserWriters: Check the Status Lights

There is typically one status light that turns on when you are out of paper; another light indicates a paper jam. Attend to these problems as necessary. Check the manual that came with your printer for how to remove jammed paper. If both lights are on at the same time (or are flashing in any way), a hardware repair is almost certainly needed.

SEE: • Fix-It #17 for more general information on hardware problems

If None of the Preceding Steps Work

If none of this works, treat the problem as a more general system error. Continue to the next section.

BY THE WAY ▶

OUTPUT TOO LIGHT, TOO DARK, OR STREAKED?

When LaserWriter output becomes too light or is streaked, you probably need to replace the toner cartridge. Output that is too light or too dark can also be adjusted by changing the print density control, a knob located on the printer (the precise location varies with different models). Sometimes, these symptoms mean that you have to replace a hardware part called the fuser assembly.

Printing Halts Due to a System Crash, PostScript Error, or Other Printing-Related Error

Symptoms:

Printing halts as a result of any of the following mishaps:

- A system crash occurs, usually generating the system-bomb error message.

  SEE: • Chapter 4 for more general information on system errors

- An error occurs that says "the serial port is in use."

  SEE: • Chapter 11, on file sharing and Apple Remote Access, for more on this problem

- A specific printing-related error occurs, usually indicated by a printing-related error message. For example, with PostScript LaserWriters, it is common for the message to read "PostScript error," plus a more specific name such as "Set limitcheck," "VM Storage," "Offending command …," or "Range Check." Usually, additional text follows that sometimes indicates the precise source of the problem (such as too many fonts in use). More commonly, you cannot make any sense out of the often-cryptic content of the message—and it is probably not really worth trying very hard.

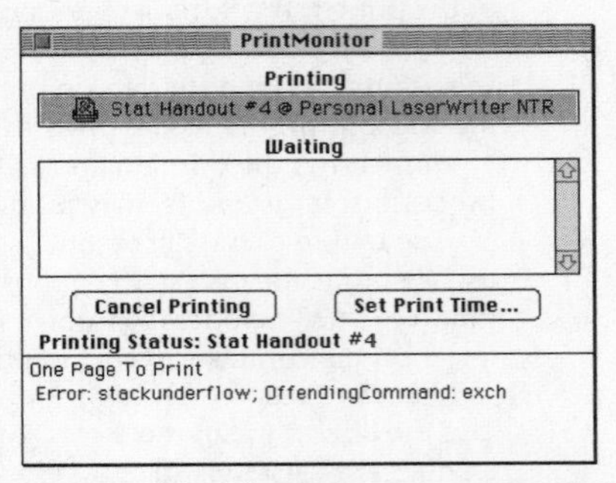

Figure 7-32 *A PostScript error, as reported in PrintMonitor.*

  SEE: • Chapters 9 and 10 for more on PostScript

- An error message suggests a problem with incompatible printer software or system software.
- If you are using PrintMonitor or a desktop printer, a message may suggest that it is the cause of the problem (such as a lack of sufficient memory for PrintMonitor to work).

These events may happen even before the first page is printed, or at some point in the middle of a print job. Particularly for LaserWriters, a print job may succeed at first but then halt at a particular page because of a problem specific to the contents of that page.

Remember that the Macintosh may seem to freeze temporarily prior to the appearance of a printing error message. This is normal; just wait. The Mac will probably "unfreeze" shortly, and the error message will appear.

Many error messages will cite insufficient memory as a cause, but this message cannot be entirely trusted. Often something else is the true cause.

Causes:

There are two likely candidates as the source of these problems: software bugs or corrupted files.

Bugs in the Relevant Software

Technically, any software that is active at the time of printing could be the offending party, including any startup extension or the System file itself. The most likely candidates, however, are the printer driver, the PrintMonitor file or desktop printing software, any other non-Apple background printing software you are using, and the application that issued the Print command.

Sometimes the problem may represent an interaction between one of these files and some particular characteristic of the document to be printed, such as the type of font used or a specific graphic element. The bug may be such that the problem occurs only with a specific model of printer, or it may affect all printers.

As always, there is no way to eliminate the bug yourself. A truly permanent solution must await a future upgrade to the product. Some common work-arounds, however, may allow you to print a document despite the presence of the bug.

Corrupted Files

In this case, the problem is that one of the files involved in the printing process has become corrupted. The most likely guilty parties are the same as for software bugs, especially the printer driver, PrintMonitor, or desktop printers. Additionally, the document itself or the font files that the document uses may be corrupted.

The exact events that caused the damage may never be known, but they don't really matter. The important thing is to recognize the problem and to replace the damaged file with an intact copy from your backup disks.

PostScript errors are typically due to corruption in the output generated when you try to print a file to a PostScript printer. Sometimes, however, these errors may have nothing directly to do with PostScript output. A corrupted font or graphic image may be the actual cause.

SEE: • **Chapter 2, on damage control, for more general information**

Other Causes

Other possible causes include having the wrong printer driver selected, insufficient memory available, insufficient unused space on the startup disk, and corrupted PRAM. Damaged cables may also cause a PostScript error.

What to do:

Try Printing Again

SEE: • **"Take Note: General Advice for All Printing Problems: Try Again," earlier in this chapter**

If simply trying again fails to work, try to determine the exact cause of the problem, as described in the following sections. Unless the specific error message you receive offers guidance as to what to do first, there is no particular recommended order for trying these solutions; all other things being equal, try the ones you find simpler and less disruptive first. The first two suggestions that follow are the most likely to be successful. If those fail, try the subsequent suggestions until one works.

Replace Potentially Corrupted Files

If a printing problem is caused by a damaged file, replacing the file should solve the problem. To check for this, do the following.

Replace Printing-Related Files Use your backup disks as a source of uncorrupted copies of these files. In particular, replace the printer driver, the PrintMonitor file (if you are using background printing), and the application and its accessory files.

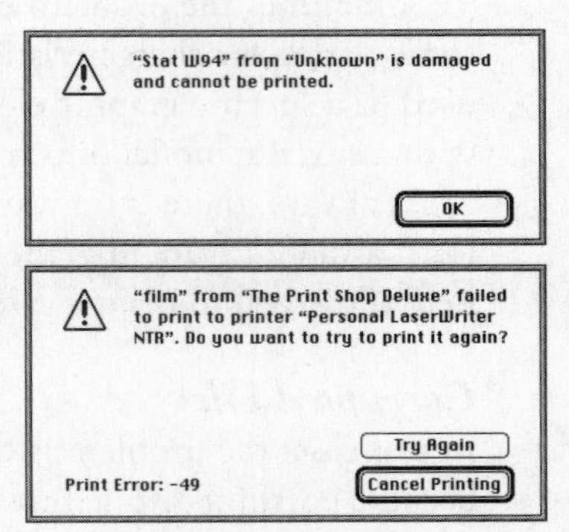

Figure 7-33 *Two examples of messages that could mean that a printing problem is due to a damaged document.*

Replace All or Part of the Document File If a document file is corrupted, you will probably notice this as soon as you open the document. The content of the file will probably be partially missing or garbled in some way; in fact, it may not even open at all. Sometimes you may be "lucky"enough (in terms of finding a cause) to get an error message indicating a damaged document. Even if everything seems normal, however, you may still have damage that somehow prohibits printing of the document. It's worth the effort to replace the document with a (hopefully uncorrupted) backup.

Otherwise, you may find that you only have trouble printing a specific page or paragraph. While this could indicate a corrupted font, it may also mean problems with the document itself. You may be able to fix this by simply deleting the problem text and retyping it.

Delete the "Spool" File If you are trying to print a file with background printing on, and you get a message that the file could not print because it was damaged, the damage may not be to the original document. Instead, it may be with the "spooled" version of the document that is created when background printing is on. If you cannot delete the document from the PrintMonitor window, the solution is to go to the PrintMonitor Documents folder in the System Folder and delete it from there. If you use desktop printers, you instead delete the document directly from the desktop printer icon's window (see "Mini-Solve It! Troubleshooting Desktop Printers," for exactly how to do this). Then try to print again.

Replace a Potentially Corrupted Font File If a font file becomes damaged, documents that contain this font may be displayed correctly on the screen but may be impossible to print (this is particularly likely for TrueType fonts, but it occurs for other font types as well). If a printing problem seems specific to the presence of a particular font, suspect this as the cause. In such cases, you need to replace the corrupted font file (for PostScript fonts replace both the printer font and the screen font).

Shift to a Different Font While replacing a corrupted (or otherwise problematic font) is the recommended course of action, sometimes you may be too rushed to bother, or maybe replacing the font didn't solve the problem. In these situations, an obvious work-around solution is to shift to a different font. For example, I once had a case where printing in Palatino Bold Italic led to a PostScript error, but printing the same text in plain Palatino worked just fine. Shifting fonts does not eliminate the ultimate source of the problem, but it at least gets your document to print.

Even better, sometimes, these errors can be resolved just by changing the troublesome portion of text to another font and then back again to the original "problem" font. Try this before you try more extreme measures.

Retry Printing Retry printing after each replacement to see if the printing problem goes away.

SEE:
- **Fix-Its #2, #3, #5, and #14 for more on replacing damaged files**
- **Chapter 9, "Damaged Font Files," for specifically how to detect and replace a damaged or corrupted font**

Serial Port Is Currently In Use?

If you have a serial printer (non-AppleTalk) connected to the printer port, you mistakenly assign it to the Modem port in the Chooser, and a modem is connected to the modem port—and especially if the modem is in use—you will get a message that the "serial port is currently in use" when you try to print. The solution is to go to the Chooser and select the correct port, then try printing again.

More generally, this "serial port is currently in use" message may mistakenly occur when the serial port settings have become corrupted. To fix this, you have to "reset" the serial port. The simplest way to do this is by restarting your Macintosh; if this fails to work, you may have to zap the PRAM (see next item).

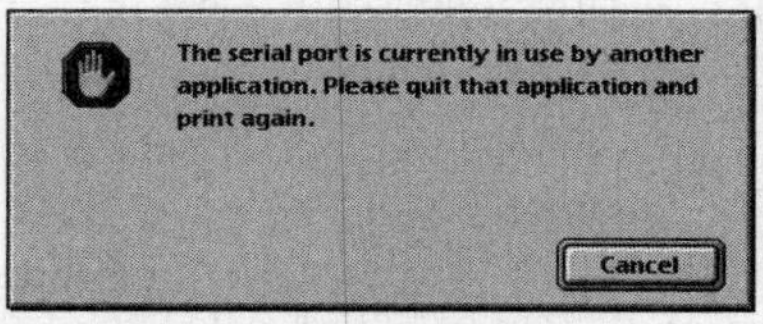

The serial port is currently in use by another application. Please quit that application and print again.

Cancel

Figure 7-34 *This message is often a bit misleading. Selecting the correct port from the Chooser, or otherwise simply restarting the Mac, usually fixes this problem.*

SEE:
- **Chapter 11 for more on this problem**

Zap the PRAM

Consider this especially if you got the message that said printing was unsuccessful because the serial port was in use. If you get system errors while in the Chooser, zapping the PRAM often solves that problem as well.

SEE:
- **Fix-It #11 on zapping the Parameter RAM**

Check the Printer Driver

Make sure the printer driver you selected from the Chooser is the one that matches your printer. The wrong selection can result in a variety of unusual error messages (such as messages that mention a Ready button when printing to a StyleWriter).

Shift to a Different Version of the Printer Software

As a rule, you are safe using the printing software that was included as part of your system software. You may also want to use a more recently updated version, however, as long as that version works with your software. For example, when LaserWriter 8.4 came out, it was compatible with virtually all Macs that were already using some earlier version of LaserWriter 8. (Check the printing software upgrade "Read Me" file for details.)

Whether you are upgrading from LaserWriter to LaserWriter 8 or from one LaserWriter 8 version to another, make sure you use the Installer utility on the system software or printer driver installer disk. Don't just drag a driver to your Extensions folder. For one thing, you need to upgrade PPD files as well as the driver; also, the Installer utility may perform operations that would not be duplicated by simply copying files.

As a rule, don't use printing software from system software that is older than what you are currently using.

If problems persist, try any or all of the following procedures.

Switch from LaserWriter 8 to LaserWriter (or Vice Versa) If you are using one of these drivers and have a problem, try the other. You can keep both in your Extensions folder at the same time, switching back and forth as needed.

Also, try to use the latest version of LaserWriter 8, as it should contain fixes for bugs found in previous versions. A few applications, however, may not work with the latest version; for these cases, you may succeed by using a previous version.

Reinitialize Laser Printers After Changing Drivers With older versions of the system software, if you change drivers while a LaserWriter is on and then try to print a document, an alert message may tell you that the printer has already been "initialized with an incompatible version of the LaserPrep software" and ask whether you wish to reinitialize it. This is perfectly normal; click OK. The printer will be reinitialized, and your document will print.

This message may also appear if you are sharing a printer on a network and some other user initialized the printer with a different version of the driver from the one you are using. Again, click OK, and your document will print. To avoid repeated occurrences of this message, however, make sure everyone on the network is using the same version of the driver.

This message no longer seems to occur with LaserWriter 8 and/or System 7.5.

Check the Printer Cable

Make sure you are using the right cable, and check to see if it is loose. Reconnect it if necessary, making sure that no pins on the plug are bent or missing. To be certain that a cable is not defective, switch it with a different one that is successfully working with another printer, if possible. If this solves the problem, then the original cable was damaged.

Turn Off Certain Printing-Specific Options

Some of the following suggestions apply only to certain types of printers.

Turn Off Fractional Character Widths A Fractional Character Widths checkbox option, if your active application includes this feature, is usually found in the Page Setup dialog box, though in some applications it may be in a separate Preferences dialog box or even directly in a menu (check the manual of your application to determine where it is located). With LaserWriter 8.4, it will be in the application-specific pop-up menu. Making changes to this option affects only the current application; Fractional Widths settings in other applications have to be adjusted separately.

For high-resolution printers, such as LaserWriters and StyleWriters, checking this option should improve the appearance of printed text by adjusting the spacing between letters. It may also cause problems, though, that prevent the document from being printed. For example, I once got a PostScript error while trying to print a particular page of a document with Microsoft Word. Turning off Fractional Widths solved the problem. Thus, if you are having printing problems and Fractional Character Widths is checked, uncheck it and try to print the document again.

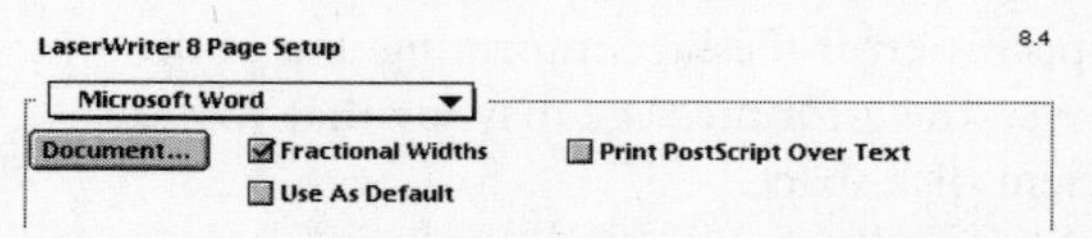

Figure 7-35 *A view of part of the Page Setup dialog box for Microsoft Word (5.1); Fractional Widths is found in the application-specific options.*

SEE: • **Chapter 9 for details on what the Fractional Character Widths option does**

If you are using some versions of Adobe Type Manager (ATM), you may have problems when using Fractional Widths (as described more in Chapter 9). If so, you should turn Fractional Widths off.

Don't Use Flip Options and/or Landscape Orientation in Combination With a few applications, you cannot print if you use the Page Setup options for Flip Horizontal, Flip Vertical, and/or the landscape page orientation in combination. Uncheck these options if you have problems using them.

Turn Off Unlimited Downloadable Fonts This option, also found in the Page Setup box of LaserWriter drivers (it's in the PostScript Options section of LaserWriter 8.4), can sometimes be the cause of a PostScript error. If it is on, try turning it off and see if this solves the problem. As described shortly, however, sometimes turning it *on* rather than off will solve a problem.

SEE: • **Chapter 9, "A Document Prints with a Different Font from the One Displayed," for more on this option**

Turn Off Faster Bitmap Printing This option is found in the Page Setup box of the LaserWriter driver. (It has been eliminated from the LaserWriter 8 driver dialog box.) Some documents refuse to print with this option turned on. In this case, if Faster Bitmap Printing is checked, uncheck it and try to print the document again. Actually, I would avoid ever using this option, since it causes more problems than it solves—if it indeed solves any problems at all. Maybe that's why it was dropped from LaserWriter 8.

Make Sure Enough Free Space Exists on Your Disk

The spool files that get created during background printing may take up a significant amount of disk space (as explained in "PrintMonitor Documents Folder," earlier in this chapter). The computer always looks for this free space on the startup disk, so it doesn't matter if there is a lot of extra room on any other mounted disk.

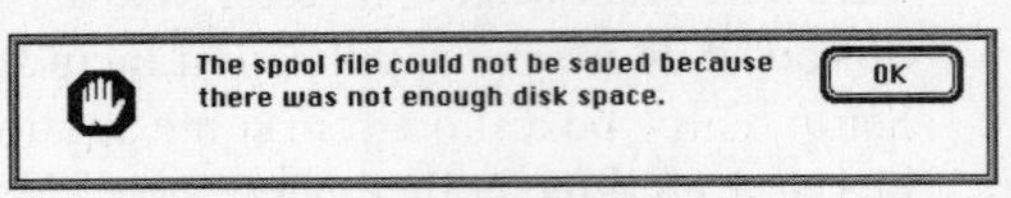

Figure 7-36 *This message may appear when printing a large document with background printing on and too little free space on your disk.*

Unless you are doing a lot of background printing or unless your drive is filled almost to capacity, this is unlikely to pose a problem on a hard drive, as enough free space is almost always available. Trouble is more likely to happen if a floppy disk is your startup disk (itself a rare event these days).

If such problems occur, you usually get a specific error message informing you of the problem. If you are using PrintMonitor, however, the error message may say that you are out of memory when the real cause is insufficient disk space.

In any case, the solution is either to delete files from the disk until you have freed up sufficient space or to use a different startup disk that has additional space already. Then try printing again.

On a related subject, if you are saving a PostScript print job to a disk file rather than sending it to the printer, make sure there is enough disk space available to hold the file.

Check for Insufficient Memory and Related Problems

Does Your PostScript Printer Have Enough Memory? PostScript printers have their own RAM memory; the amount installed varies with different printers. If your document requires more memory than is available in your printer, you will get a PostScript error (insufficient memory in the Macintosh itself usually generates other types of error messages). Be especially wary of this problem if the error is listed as a "limitcheck error," VMStorage," or "VMerror." PostScript error –8993 is another one that typically means you had insufficient memory to print your document. In some cases, additional RAM can be added to your printer; if so, this is the best long-term solution for frequent memory-related PostScript errors. Also, printers that use PostScript Level 2 do a better job of handling memory than was done with the previous PostScript versions. Otherwise, try any of the following suggestions that appear relevant.

BY THE WAY ▶

HOW MUCH RAM IS IN YOUR PRINTER?

You can check how much memory is installed in your printer by using the Apple Printer Utility and checking in the Printer Information section. If you are using LaserWriter 8, RAM information is also available from the Printer Info window, which is accessed by selecting Setup from the Chooser and then clicking the Printer Info button.

Try Printing One Page at a Time A page of text with complex formatting (such as many fonts of different sizes and styles) can cause printing problems, especially if the page is part of a long document. Similarly, graphics imported into a word processor from a drawing program, such as MacDraw or Canvas may not print—especially if the graphic includes many grouped objects.

Too many fonts is an especially likely problem with PostScript LaserWriters if you are using fonts that are not built into the LaserWriter's hardware. Such fonts must be downloaded to the printer's memory before you can print the document. If you have several of these fonts, you can run out of memory to hold them, which then causes problems with printing.

If only those pages with complex formatted text or graphics do not print, try printing that page by itself. Similarly, if you were attempting to print multiple copies of a document, try printing single copies instead.

Turn On Unlimited Downloadable Fonts Turning on this option (accessed from the Page Setup dialog box for LaserWriters) may also help solve problems with too many fonts in a document.

SEE: • Chapter 9, "A Document Prints with a Different Font Than Is Displayed," for more on this option

Simplify the Document If the previous solutions do not work, try to simplify your page layout. In particular, if you are using several fonts on the same page, modify the text to reduce the total number of fonts. For problems with graphics combined in a word processing document, cut out the graphic and try to print it separately from the text. Sometimes, in fact, just reimporting the graphic may solve the problem.

Bugs in the printer driver may cause PostScript errors when certain special effects are in use, no matter how much memory you have in your printer. For example, rotated objects with rounded corners or selection of both Invert Image and Smooth Graphics (selected from the Page Setup dialog box) for the same document, have been reported to lead to PostScript errors. To cite one specific case, PageMaker 5.0 documents containing rotated text do not print correctly with earlier versions of LaserWriter 8.

If the object has a lot of separate elements (for example, a complex object-oriented graphic), see if you can simplify it by reducing the number of elements, then try to print again.

There is nothing you can do about these errors except avoid using the problem effects or upgrade to a newer (and hopefully less buggy) printer driver.

Change the Format of a Graphic If the problem appears to be related to printing a specific graphic object, sometimes saving it in a different format (such as shifting from PICT to TIFF) may eliminate the problem.

SEE: • Chapter 10 for more on graphics formats

Use Split Long Paths in PostScript Graphics Programs Check the Split Long Paths option in Illustrator or FreeHand; long paths can cause a system crash if the PostScript interpreter runs out of storage space. Try to print again.

Turn On 32-Bit Addressing If your Macintosh includes this option in its Memory control panel, turning it on sometimes solves memory-related PostScript errors.

Turn Off RAM-Using Options from the Page Setup Dialog Box In particular, turn off Larger Print Area (no longer available in LaserWriter 8.4). Also turn off Smooth Text and Smooth Graphics.

Make Sure Sufficient Memory Is Allocated to the Application Though insufficient application memory is not a common cause of a printing problem, if nothing else seems to be working, try increasing the Preferred (or Current) memory allocation from the Get Info window of the application you are using. This is likely to help only if you are having a problem printing very long or complex documents.

SEE: • **Chapter 2 on the Get Info command and Fix-It #6 on memory problems for more details**

Make Sure Sufficient Memory Is Allocated to PrintMonitor or to Desktop Printer This is discussed in more detail in the next section and in the earlier section on desktop printers. As an alternative, turn background printing off.

LaserWriter 8.4 and Limitcheck Error When Canceling Printing When canceling a foreground printing job using LaserWriter 8.4, I sometimes get a limitcheck error message prior to the job actually canceling. Everything else seems to work okay, and I have typically just ignored this message.

Problems with Background Printing

This section is relevant only if you are using background printing, particularly as used with LaserWriter drivers. Printing problems related to background printing may or may not be accompanied by an error message. To check if background printing is the cause of your problem, try each of the following suggestions until one works.

Don't Do Anything Else While You Are Trying to Print Don't continue working with your application (actually, it may help to quit the application altogether as soon as the job is sent to the printer). Don't try to copy files, and don't do anything else that may use additional memory until the printing is completed. For example, stop any other nonprinting-related background processing that may be going on at this time (such as a telecommunications program that is working in the background).

All of these efforts minimize the chance that the problem is caused by overloading the processing capacity of the Macintosh. Of course, they also negate the advantage of using background printing, but hopefully you won't be required to do this very often. In general, you should be able to carry out other tasks while background printing is in progress.

Remove Documents from the PrintMonitor Documents Folder If you get a error message that includes a Try Again option, but selecting it simply leads to the return of the same message, click Cancel. Then go to the PrintMonitor Documents folder in your System Folder, and delete any documents you find there. You will now have to reselect Print for whatever documents you were trying to print; they may print successfully now.

With desktop printer software, it is usually sufficient simply to select Trash for the documents from the desktop printer's window, then try again.

Don't Put a PowerBook to Sleep While Printing Putting a PowerBook to Sleep while background printing is in progress will obviously halt the printing. When you wake up the PowerBook, printing may not resume. In this case, you may need to cancel the print job and reselect it.

Turn Background Printing Off Altogether Turn off background printing. Try to print the document again. If you can print the document now, background printing is probably at least a partial cause of the problem. To further isolate the cause, turn background printing on again, and try the following tests.

Check for a Conflict Between Background Printing and the Application (or Document) If the problem appears only when you are using background printing in a particular application, a conflict is a likely possibility. You may not be able to do anything about this immediately, other than keep background printing off when using this application.

The problem may occur with some documents but not others, however, so it may pay to turn background printing back on and print a different document, just to check. If you can successfully print most documents, the easiest solution might be to turn background printing off for those rare documents when it is a problem.

Reinstall or Upgrade Background Printing Software I have already mentioned, in previous sections of this chapter, the possibility of a damaged or incorrect version of the PrintMonitor file. If you haven't already done so, replace the file with a copy from Macintosh system software disks that match the version on your startup disk. Similarly, reinstall the desktop printing software if you use it; make sure you are using the latest versions of these files.

TECHNICALLY SPEAKING ▶

PROBLEMS WITH EMBEDDED FONTS

A special problem can occur with background printing of a document that uses fonts embedded directly in the document or the printing application, rather than somewhere in the System Folder (I discuss this subject in more detail in Chapter 9). The System is aware of an embedded font *only* while the document or application that contains the font is open. If you close these files before the software (PrintMonitor or Desktop PrintMonitor) is finished processing the file being printed (normally an okay thing to do), the software will not be able to find the embedded fonts when it needs them. This has been known to cause serious problems, including system crashes.

As a result, you should avoid using background printing with files that have embedded fonts. But how do you know whether a file has such fonts? Well, you can use Apple's Font/DA Mover to check (again, see Chapter 9 for details). If you find embedded fonts, remove them and transfer them to the System file (or Fonts folder), where they can be accessed correctly for background printing to proceed as normal.

Turning background printing off temporarily, however, also solves this problem. If you are unfamiliar with embedded fonts, you may prefer this simpler, more general solution.

Check for Insufficient Memory for Background Printing You may get an error message that says the document did not print because PrintMonitor or your desktop printer did not have enough memory. With PrintMonitor, the message may say that the Mac will try to print again when more memory is available.

If so, click OK and close any unneeded documents, applications and/or desk accessories. Close any open Finder windows. Printing should now proceed.

Alternatively, the message may offer to allocate more memory to PrintMonitor or your desktop printer. If so, click OK and try printing again by selecting Print.

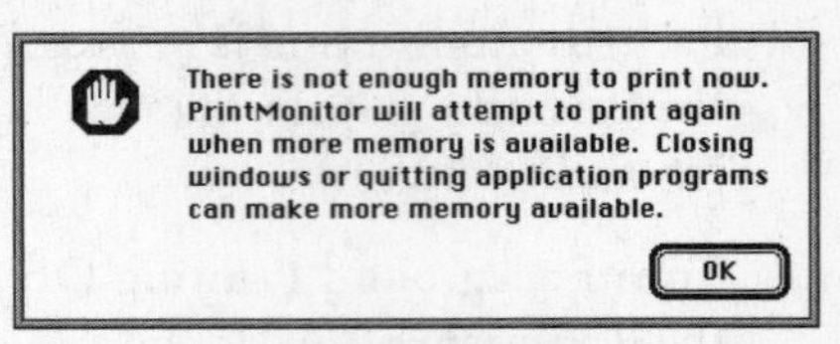

Figure 7-37 *A message indicating that not enough memory is available for PrintMonitor to work.*

Check for Free Space on Your Startup Disk As I have already mentioned (see "Make Sure Enough Free Space Exists on Your Disk," earlier in this chapter), a document may not print in the background if there is too little free disk space to create the needed spool files. Even worse, if this problem occurs, an error message may erroneously claim that the trouble is due to insufficient memory. In either case, if there is very little free space left on your disk, delete some files and try printing again. Alternatively, for multipage documents, try printing the document in smaller segments, waiting until each one is finished before you try the next one. Or simply turn off background printing.

Otherwise (for PrintMonitor) With any other error message that suggests a problem with background printing when using PrintMonitor, manually increase PrintMonitor's memory as follows:

1. Locate PrintMonitor in the Extensions folder, select it, and then select Get Info from the Finder's File menu.
2. Its Preferred (or Current) memory size is probably 80K. Whatever the amount is, increase it by another 50 to 100K, if you have enough memory available to do so.
3. Try printing again. It should work.
4. As a sort of last resort, you can try increasing the Finder's memory allocation; this, too, may help PrintMonitor. In System 7, the easiest way to do this is with a utility called Finder Fixer.

SEE: • **Chapter 2 on Get Info and Fix-It #6 on memory management, as needed**

Otherwise (for Desktop Printers) If you are using desktop printers, there are similar memory adjustments you can make. These and related troubleshooting tips for desktop printers are described earlier in this chapter.

SEE: • **"Mini-Solve It!: Troubleshooting Desktop Printers," earlier in this chapter**

Widen the Search to More General Causes

If all of the preceding options fail to work, you are probably dealing with an inherent software bug or conflict in one or more of the programs involved in printing your document. It's time to begin a more general diagnostic hunt to isolate the cause. Try to print using different documents and applications, to determine exactly how specific the problem is. For example, does the problem occur with some documents but not others?

SEE: • **Chapter 3 for general strategy guidelines**
• **Chapter 4 on general guidelines for system error problems**
• **Chapter 6 for a more general discussion of file-related problems**

Resolve Conflict with the Application The application may turn out to be incompatible with the particular printer you have. Usually, the only immediate work-around solution here is to stop using the problem application, at least until an upgrade comes along.

The application may also have certain incompatibilities with the printing software. In this case, shifting to an older or newer version of the system printing software may help. Check the "Read Me" files that come with Apple's system software or contact the relevant application vendors for more specific advice.

SEE: • **Fix-It #1 on incompatible software and hardware**
• **Fix-Its #2 and #3 on other application-specific problems**
• **Fix-It #18 on calling technical support**

Resolve Conflict with a Startup Extension or System Software Similarly, there may be an startup extension conflict or a more general problem related to the system software. Solutions here may require disabling certain extensions or reinstalling your system software. Again, check with the vendor of third-party software for possible work-arounds and/or upgrades.

SEE: • **Fix-It #4 on problems with system extensions and control panels**
• **Fix-It #5 on system software problems**
• **Fix-It #18 on calling technical support**

Round Up the Usual Suspects If no special problem file can be identified, start rounding up the usual gang of suspects in search of still more general causes. These include rebuilding the desktop and running Disk First Aid. Problems with PRAM, as mentioned earlier in this chapter, are another common source of printer-related problems. See the appropriate Fix-Its for details.

SEE: • **Fix-Its #7 to #13 to check out the usual suspects**

Hardware Problems Finally, if all else has failed, assume that a hardware problem is the cause. Take the printer (and, if need be, the Macintosh itself) in for repairs.

SEE: • **Fix-It #17 on hardware problems**

TAKE NOTE ▶

SLOW PRINTING WITH HEWLETT-PACKARD PRINTERS

If RAM Doubler or Apple's virtual memory is on, and you have a Hewlett-Packard printer, you may find that you get very slow printing performance (or even a complete failure to print) when background printing is also on. Turning off virtual memory and/or background printing will work around the problem. Otherwise, make sure you have the latest version of the Hewlett-Packard printer drivers, which reportedly have fixed this problem.

TAKE NOTE

TROUBLESHOOTING STYLEWRITERS

Most of this chapter focused on printing to a LaserWriter, although information specific to other printers was scattered about. Apple's inkjet StyleWriters are another popular line of printers. For those of you that use them, here is some additional StyleWriter-specific advice.

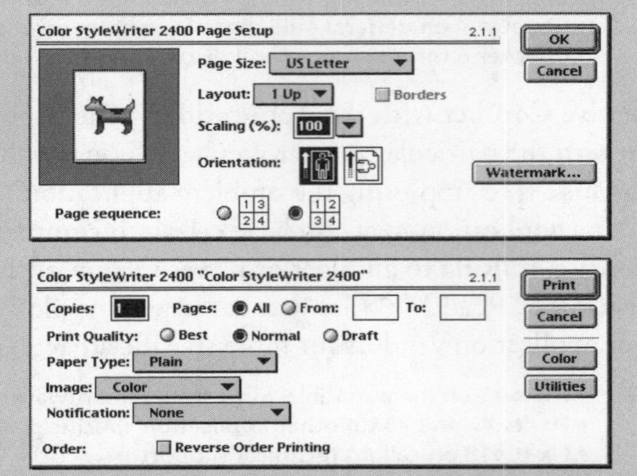

Figure 7-38 *The Page Setup and Print dialog boxes of the Color StyleWriter.*

- **If you have trouble installing StyleWriter software.** For installation problems, here are a couple of tips (beyond the general information found in Fix-It #5). For starters, remove the Fonts folder from your System Folder before doing any install. Otherwise, do a Custom Install to try to install anything that was missing from an Easy Install. If you still have problems, remove the Control Panels, Extensions, and Preferences folder prior to a Custom Install (dragging the items in these removed folders back to the newly created folders after the installation is done). Why do this? Apple says: "The reason you may have to remove these folders is that some installers lock the driver if it is already installed. Also, the printing preferences are sometimes locked, or the General Controls control panel is set to Protect System Folder. Virus software may also remain active even with Extensions off, preventing changes to the System folder. Any of these circumstances can result in the generic 'installation cannot take place on this disk' message."
- **If you get a message that says there is no paper in printer, or the paper is the wrong size (when paper of the right size is actually there), or to check your connections.** You are probably using the wrong type of cable. For example, when connecting a StyleWriter without a LocalTalk module, you must use the standard Macintosh Peripheral-8 cable, not a LocalTalk cable. If you have the right type of cable, make sure it is securely plugged in. If none of this helps, reselect the printer driver and connection port from the Chooser.
- **If a freeze occurs when printing.** Printing to a Color StyleWriter 2400 may result in a freeze if virtual memory is on. The solution is to upgrade to the printer driver used by the newer Color StyleWriter 2500 (version 2.2 or later), which is backward compatible with the 2400. Also, if you are using desktop printing software, make sure you have the latest version. Earlier versions (especially prior to 1.0.3) were known to cause freezes.

  In general, upgrades fix bugs from previous versions. Always check that you have the latest version available.
- **If you have memory problems.** On StyleWriters, system software memory allocation will likely increase by several megabytes when printing. This is normal. If you do not have sufficient free memory, you will get a message that says you are unable to print until more memory is made available; your text may print only in the Geneva font.

(Continues on next page)

▶ TAKE NOTE ▶

TROUBLESHOOTING STYLEWRITERS *(Continued)*

If any of this happens, quit any unneeded open applications and try again. Giving your application more memory, turning off background printing, and/or disabling desktop printers may also help. If you are using desktop printers, check the section earlier in this chapter ("Mini-Solve It! Troubleshooting Desktop Printers") for more advice. Also check the "Read Me" file that comes with the StyleWriter software.

- **If you have very slow printing speed.** StyleWriters are fairly slow printers to begin with, especially when printing complex color graphics. Also remember, though, that StyleWriters use the Macintosh's processor to do all their image processing (unlike PostScript LaserWriters, which have their own processor). This means that if you continue to use the Mac while the StyleWriter tries to print in the background, printing can slow to a mind-numbing crawl. If this happens, just stop using your Mac until the print job is done.
- **If no sign of printing occurs.** For a non-LocalTalk connection, if AppleTalk is active, make sure the printer is not connected to the AppleTalk port (typically the printer port). Otherwise, set AppleTalk to inactive. If your Mac has only one serial port, see the section, "Special Case: Only One Serial Port?" earlier in this chapter for advice.

  Also, much of the advice in the main text is relevant to StyleWriters as well. Check it out.
- **If you can't get PrinterShare to work.** Most StyleWriters can be shared with other Macs through Apple's PrinterShare technology. This is the option selected after clicking the Setup button in the Chooser for the printer.

  Otherwise, to share a Color StyleWriter 2400 or 2500, you can purchase the LocalTalk optional module and put it on a network, just as you can with most LaserWriters. With the newer 2500, there is even an optional Ethernet adapter.

  For more help on setting up PrinterShare, check the documentation that came with your printer.
- **Smeared ink.** Inkjet-printed output can smear more easily than laser-printed output, though newer inks are less susceptible to this problem. Still, be especially careful not to get inkjet output wet. For color inkjet printers, even though they can print on plain paper, using special coated papers usually yield better results.
- **Output too light, thin white lines, distorted image, or colors missing.** Output that is too light typically means that an ink tank is empty or defective and needs to be replaced (you can replace just the tank within the cartridge or the entire cartridge assembly, as suggested by your manual). For color inkjet printers, remember that one color may run out before the others, so if only certain colors are printing incorrectly, you should again replace either a tank or the entire cartridge.

  If you have thin white lines, a wavy image, or colors missing on your printed copy, another possibility is that the ink cartridge for the missing color may be clogged. To try to unclog most StyleWriters using current software, select the Utilities button in the Print dialog box, select the "Clean the printhead before printing" option, and then select Print.

  Finally, make sure that the Paper Type selected in the Print dialog box matches the type of paper you are actually using.

SEE ALSO: • **Chapter 10, "Problems Printing Color/Grayscale to a Color Printer," for more on Color StyleWriter problems**

Chapter 8

Getting Under the Hood: The Invisible Macintosh

Peeking Under the Hood 301

File Type and File Creator 301

How Kind 301

Kind and the Desktop File 302

File Type 302

File Creator 303

Type and Creator Code Problems 303

Application Could Not Be Found 303

Wrong Kind 304

Wrong Icon 304

A File's Type Code or Both Its Type and Creator Codes Are Missing or Corrupted 304

A Document File's Creator Code Is Missing or Corrupted 305

The Creating Application Is Missing 305

Bundle Bit Problems 305

Multiple Versions of the Same Application on Your Disk 305

Try the Simpler Solutions 305

Viewing and Editing Type/Creator Codes 306

Identifying the Correct Creator Code 309

TEXT and PICT Formats: Type and Creator Code Issues 310

Five More Good Reasons to View or Change a File's Type/Creator Code 311

Get Documents to Open in TeachText/SimpleText by Default 311

Make Uneditable TeachText/SimpleText Documents Editable 312

Fit More Utilities on an Emergency Toolkit Floppy Disk 313

Add Alert Sounds Without Installing Them in the System File 314

Search for a File Based on Its Type or Creator Code 314

Finder Flags (Attributes) 315
What Are Finder Flags (Attributes)? 315
The Invisible Bit 315
The Bundle Bit 315
The Inited Bit 316
The Use Custom Icon Bit 316
The No INITs Bit 316
The Name Locked Bit 316
Viewing and Editing Finder Flags 317

Invisible Files and Folders 318
Viewing and Editing Invisible Files and Folders 318
Special Case: Viewing the Contents of the Desktop Folder and Trash Folder 320
Viewing and Editing *Really* Invisible Files and Folders 321
The Directory and Boot Blocks 321
Viewing the Directory and the Boot Blocks 321
Special Case: The Disk Driver and Related Low-Level Data 322

Peeking Under the Hood

This chapter takes you inside the workings of the Macintosh more than any other chapter in this book. Still, you can understand and use the material in this chapter without any special software or any particular skills other than those already described. So, stick around; don't rush through or skip to the next chapter.

If you make an effort to master this material, you will be amply rewarded. For example, what you learn here will help you solve problems locating or opening files, as described in Chapter 6. It will also be immensely helpful in understanding problems with graphics formats, as described in Chapter 10. It covers how applications import and export files of different formats, a subject discussed in several chapters. Finally, it allows you to do some neat tricks that you will discover for the first time in this chapter.

File Type and File Creator

How Kind

Every file on your disk is assigned a particular *kind,* which is a brief description of the general category to which the file belongs. Thus, the kind for all application files is "application," and the kind for a document created by Excel is "Microsoft Excel document." (Note that this description not only lists the general category of the "document" but also the application that created the document.)

As I first noted in Chapter 2, you can easily determine the kind for any file by selecting Get Info for that file and reading its kind description. You can also see the kind for all files in a folder at one time by switching to a non-icon view, such as By Name or (even better) By Kind.

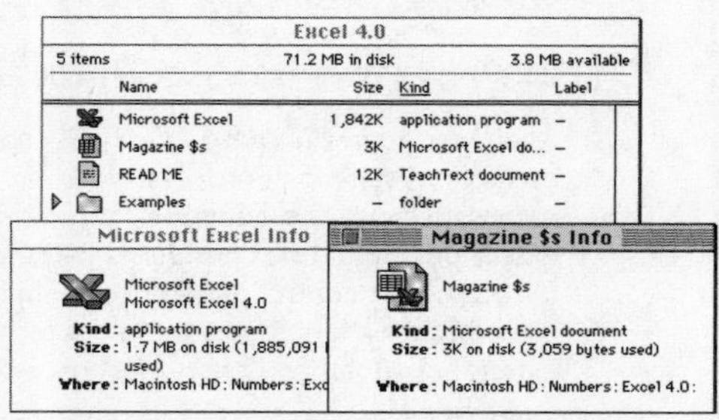

Figure 8-1 *Where to find a file's kind: in a By Kind view of a folder's contents (top), or in the Get Info windows (bottom).*

This information can help you to identify an unfamiliar file; in fact, that's more or less how the Finder uses it. For example, if a file's kind is "application," the Finder knows it can be opened directly and does so when you double-click it. On the other hand, if it is a "system extension," the Finder knows that it cannot be opened at all and belongs in the Extensions folder. If it is a "document," the Finder uses the kind to determine what application is launched along with the document when you double-click it. As a result, a problem with a file's kind can cause difficulty in opening a document. This problem, briefly alluded to in Chapter 6, is described more fully here.

Kind and the Desktop File

How does the Finder identify a file's kind? The general answer is that the needed information is stored in an invisible Desktop file (System 7 actually has two separate Desktop files). Every time you add a new file to your disk, the Desktop file is updated to include the kind information for that file. In fact, the Desktop file is the Finder's storage site for virtually all of the information listed in Get Info windows, including what icon a file should have.

SEE: • Fix-It #9 for more on the Desktop file

So where does the Desktop file get this kind information (and other related data) in the first place? Each file on your disk contains a special area reserved for this purpose. When a file is first copied to a disk, the information from that area is copied to the Desktop file, where it is then accessed by the Finder as needed. Applications are the primary source of this information (for files other than system software), providing the needed icons and document-linking data for all the application's accessory files and documents.

Specifically, a file's kind is determined by two four-letter codes assigned to and initially stored with each file. These are referred to as the file's *type* and *creator* codes.

File Type

A file's type determines whether a file is listed as an application, a document, a system file, or whatever. For example, all applications have a type code of "APPL." System files have several possible codes: the type for desk accessories is "dfil"; for control panels, it is "cdev" (an abbreviation for *c*ontrol panel *dev*ice); and for common system extensions, it is "INIT."

TECHNICALLY SPEAKING ▶

INIT VS. EXTENSION VS. CONTROL PANEL

As alluded to in Chapter 1, the type code INIT describes programs that must load into memory at startup in order to work—in particular, most system extensions and many control panels. Because the file type of common extensions is "INIT," it would seem that only system extensions should be considered INITs. But control panels that load into memory at startup (which not all control panels do) contain the equivalent of an INIT within their program. This is the basis for sometimes using the term INIT to group these control panels and system extensions together. Otherwise, I generally refer to these files as "startup extensions."

SEE: • "Finder Flags (Attributes)," later in this chapter, and Fix-It #4 for more details

For documents, a virtually infinite number of possible type codes are available. Each application uses a unique type code determined by the developers of the software that it assigns to documents saved in its unique format. Thus, for example, all MacWrite Pro data documents created in MacWrite Pro are given a "MWPd" type code (related documents will probably have a different type; for example, MacWrite Pro stationery has the type code "sWPd"). As another example, the type code for Microsoft Word 4.*x*/5.*x* documents is "WDBN" (it's "W6BN" for Word 6.*x* documents).

The type information determines what files get displayed in an application's Open dialog box. Thus, MacWrite Pro recognizes files of the MWPd type as being MacWrite Pro documents. Similarly, MacWrite Pro's file translation feature, if installed, would determine that files of the WDBN type should be interpreted as Word files.

File Creator

The creator code is used to *bundle* (or link) an application and all the documents that it creates. So, for example, the creator code for both the MacWrite Pro application and a MacWrite Pro document is MWPR; for Microsoft Word, it is MSWD. Creator codes, like the type codes, are selected by the software developer.

The creator code is used primarily at the Finder level. For example, it tells the Finder that a MacWrite Pro document was created by the MacWrite Pro application, which is why the Finder launches MacWrite Pro when you double-click on the document. It also partly determines what icon the Finder assigns to a newly created MacWrite Pro document.

For documents, the kind description in the Get Info window is determined primarily by the file's creator, not its type.

Programs can often save files in several different formats. When MacWrite Pro saves a file in Microsoft Word format, for example, it assigns Word's document type and creator codes to the file. As a result, there is no way to tell that the file was originally created in MacWrite Pro and not in Word. The changed creator code means that when you next double-click this file from the Finder, it will launch Word instead of MacWrite Pro (assuming Word is on your disk somewhere). Had only the file's type been changed, double-clicking the Word file from the Finder would launch MacWrite Pro (per the creator code), which would then correctly interpret the file as a Word file (per the changed type code) and translate it.

To solve problems involving type and creator codes, you need to know what a file's codes are and, if necessary, how to change them. The next section describes how to do this.

Type and Creator Code Problems

Symptoms:

One or more of the following symptoms occurs.

Application Could Not Be Found

You are unable to open a document from the Finder; an error message says the application program that created the document could not be found. This message, of course, could appear for many reasons that do not directly relate to type or creator code problems (as I discuss more in Chapter 6). The best tipoff that you have a type/creator code problem is if you get this error message even though the creating application is presently on a mounted disk.

Wrong Kind

The kind for a data document, as listed in the Get Info window, is listed only as "document" when it should be something more specific (such as "MacWrite Pro document"). Although "document" by itself is the correct kind listing for some files, this is usually not the case for data documents such as word processing files.

Wrong Icon

A file, most often a data document, does not display its correct icon in the Finder. Typically, it displays a generic (blank-page) icon instead. You will often find this to be the case with documents whose kind is listed only as "document," as just described. If this is the only symptom you have, you can often ignore it (unless the aesthetic loss bothers you). If it is linked to a problem opening the file, though, you will probably want to fix it.

> **TAKE NOTE ▶**
>
> **ASSIGNING ICONS**
>
> Most file icons in the Finder are not generic; instead, they are *custom icons* (sometimes called *bundled icons*, to distinguish them from the truly custom icons that you make yourself). Generally, an application and all its accessory and document icons have a similar appearance that helps identify them as belonging together.
>
> If no custom icon is present, the Finder instead assigns it one from its standard set of generic icons. The generic document icon, for example, is simply a blank rectangle with a corner turned down. Thus these generic icons can be perfectly normal, even if they are rarely seen these days.
>
> Occasionally, however, a file that has previously displayed a custom icon may unexpectedly appear with a generic icon. This is usually a sign of at least minor trouble.

Causes:

As is true for software in general, the area of a file that contains the type and creator codes can become corrupted. These codes can also be mistakenly altered by other programs. Finally, for various reasons, the Finder may have difficulty correctly interpreting a file's type and creator code information. More specifically, the following situations can occur.

A File's Type Code or Both Its Type and Creator Codes Are Missing or Corrupted

This situation is relatively rare, but it can happen. Files without type or creator codes can often be quite difficult to open, especially from the Finder. They may not even open from within the creating application. Happily, restoring the proper codes is a quick way to restore the document to working condition.

A Document File's Creator Code Is Missing or Corrupted

Be especially suspicious that a document is missing its creator code if you get the message that "the application program that created it could not be found," even though you know the application is on a currently mounted disk. Restoring a document's proper creator code reestablishes the link between the document and its creating application, allowing the Finder to identify the file and open it.

The Creating Application Is Missing

Even if a document has its correct type and creator codes, it cannot be opened from the Finder if the creating application is not currently on a mounted disk. In fact, if the creating application has *never* previously been on the same disk as the document, the document may display a generic icon rather than its correct custom icon.

Bundle Bit Problems

Occasionally, even though a document has its correct type and creator codes and the creating application is on a mounted disk, the Finder still fails to recognize the link between the application and the document. Technically, this is not a type or creator problem. Most often the application's Bundle bit is set incorrectly (as described more in the section on "File Attributes," later in this chapter), or more serious file damage has occurred.

Multiple Versions of the Same Application on Your Disk

If you have two different versions of the same application on your disk, you may find that one of them displays the wrong icon (typically using the icon associated with the other version). Similarly, its documents may display the other application's document icons, or they may display only the generic blank-page icon.

What to do:

For the fastest and easiest route to success, try the following suggestions in the order given.

Try the Simpler Solutions

Copy the Creating Application to a Mounted Disk If the creating application is not on any mounted disk, you can solve most of these problems easily enough by copying it to a mounted disk. (This suggestion assumes, of course, that you know what the creating application is and that you have access to it.) Not only should this solution allow you to open problem documents directly, it usually fixes any icon display and related problems (after you restart).

Open the File from Within the Creating Application If the creating application is on the disk already, you can usually solve the problem by trying to open the file from within the application's Open dialog box rather than from the Finder. If you can open it this way, save a copy of the file with a new name, quit the application, and delete the original file. This usually solves the problem.

Open the File with Another Application If the creating application won't work, try to open the file from within another application (already on your disk) that can import the problem document file.

SEE: • Chapter 6 for more details on these solutions

Rebuild the Desktop This fixes a variety of wrong-icon and related problems. If you have two different versions of the same application on your disk, get rid of one of them before you rebuild.

SEE: • Fix-It #9 for details on rebuilding the desktop and much more on generic icon problems

Use a Repair Utility Run Disk Doctor (in Norton Utilities) or DiskFix or FileFix (in MacTools) to check for incorrect Bundle bit settings and/or minor problems with other file attributes. This is all done automatically as part of the utility's routine disk-checking procedures (as described in Fix-It #13). If a problem is detected, the utility alerts you and asks if you wish to fix it. Say yes.

Viewing and Editing Type/Creator Codes

To view and edit both type and creator codes, you can use Norton Utilities or MacTools; many other utilities also let you do this. Two others, both mentioned later in this chapter, are DiskTop and Snitch. The former is a desk accessory that is an especially good tool for virtually any of the functions described in this chapter. The latter is a shareware extension that is especially convenient when you want to quickly access the codes of a single file.

BY THE WAY ▶

CHANGING A FILE'S TYPE HAS ITS LIMITS

Other than correcting a lost or damaged type code, there is rarely any reason to consider modifying a file's type (though I'll provide a couple of exceptions later in this chapter). Changing a type code does not change the underlying format of a document. For example, changing a document's type code from WDBN to MWPd does *not* magically change a Word document into a MacWrite Pro document; it only leads to confusion. On the other hand, as described here, changing a file's creator can be useful even when the code is not lost or damaged.

Editing type and creator codes is how, for example, you can restore a missing or corrupted code. You can also use these utilities to change a document's creator from a missing application to one that is available. Assuming that the substitute application can import files of the document's type, you would now be able to double-click the document from the Finder and have it launch with its newly assigned application rather than its originally intended one. Other utilities (such as Now Menus and Macintosh Easy Open) accomplish this same goal in a simpler manner (as mentioned in Chapter 6), but sometimes altering the creator code directly is the only thing that works.

Several specific examples of the potential usefulness of editing a file's creator and type codes will be described shortly. But first, let's see how to use utilities to actually make these changes. (A general warning: Before attempting to make any of these changes, make sure the file is closed and that you have a backup of the file.)

With Norton Utilities

1. Open Norton Disk Editor (either from its Finder icon or by selecting it from the Utilities menu of Norton Utilities). This should lead to a dialog box with a pop-up menu of all mounted disks.
2. Select the disk you want and click Open. This opens a window with a directory listing of all files and folders on the disk, including invisible ones. Double-click a folder to reveal the contents of the folder.
3. The type and creator codes for each file are already listed in columns to the right of the file name. To edit any of these codes, select the desired file and then click the Info button at the top of the window. Doing this opens up a new window that lists the type and creator (among other things) of the file. From here, you can modify the code by typing in a different one.

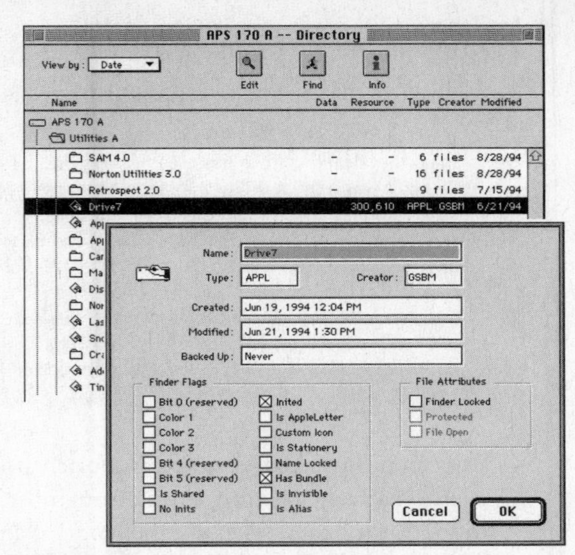

Figure 8-2 *Norton Disk Editor shows the type and creator codes of the Drive7 application.*

With MacTools Pro

1. Open the MacTools Clinic application, then click the FileFix button from the row of buttons at the top of the window. This opens up the FileFix window. Select the File Info button in order to get access to the Type and Creator editing features.
2. From the scrolling list on the right-hand side of the window, locate and select the desired file. To the left of the name of each disk is a triangle that works like the triangles in the Finder's non-icon views. Clicking on a triangle next to a disk name results in a sublist of all files and folders at the root level of the disk; further triangles appear next to each folder. Using this approach, you can eventually locate any file on the disk, including invisible ones.

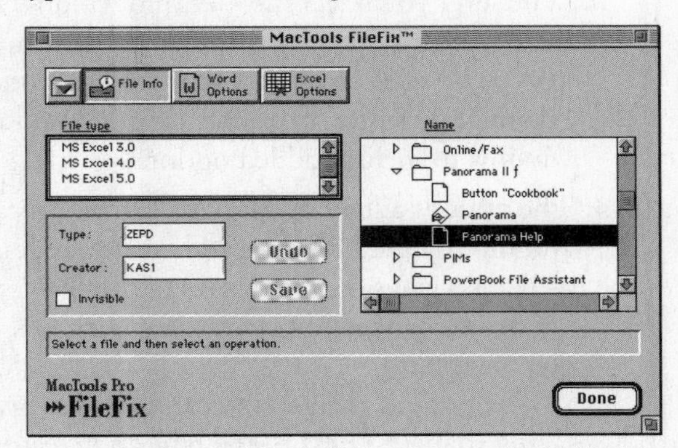

Figure 8-3 *MacTools Pro's FileFix window, with the File Info option selected.*

3. When the desired file is highlighted, its type and creator codes will appear in the appropriate editable boxes on the left side of the window. If the boxes contain question marks or are blank, it means that the codes are unknown. Below these boxes will be a checkbox that will be checked if a file is currently invisible.

BY THE WAY ▶

A GREAT FEATURE OF MACTOOLS DISAPPEARS

If you are familiar with versions of MacTools prior to version 3.0, you will notice that one of the major applications from these earlier versions, DiskEdit, is missing in version 3.0 and thereafter. DiskEdit was a great utility that allowed you to access several of the features that I describe in this chapter, including editing a file's type and creator codes, file attribute bits, boot blocks, hex code for the entire disk, and more. In some ways, it was better for these purposes than anything in Norton Utilities. Although Central Point (before it was taken over by Symantec) decided to drop this application from version 3.0, two important features—editing file type and creator codes, and viewing invisible files—are still available through FileFix. The remainder of DiskFix's features, unfortunately, can no longer be accessed in any manner via MacTools. Of course, now that Symantec has discontinued selling MacTools, this may all soon be moot.

4. You can now modify the type and/or creator codes by typing in different one(s).

    Alternatively, you can scroll through the list of application names above the Type and Creator boxes; selecting the name of any application will result in the current file's type and creator codes shifting to match that of documents belonging to the selected application.

    You can also change the selected file's invisibility status.

5. Click Save to save any changes and click Done when you are finished with all the changes you wish to make.

With Snitch

1. Before using Snitch, install it in the Extensions folder and restart the Macintosh.
2. Whenever you select the Get Info window for a file or folder (either by pressing the Command-I keys or by selecting Get Info from the Finder's File menu), Snitch will automatically modify the window to include added options.
3. The options added by Snitch allow you to view and modify the file's type and creator codes, as well as several other attributes of the file. Type whatever changes you want, then click OK when you are done.

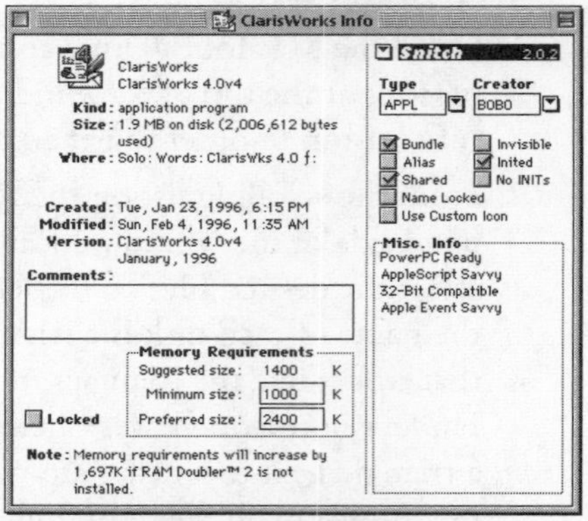

    The pop-up menus (indicated by downward-facing triangles) next to the type and creator fields have a selection of commonly used codes that you can select. For added convenience, you can also add your own codes to these menus.

    Clicking the "Snitch" pop-up menu reveals selections that lead to other options, including the ability to change the creation and modification dates of the file.

Figure 8-4 *The Get Info window for ClarisWorks, with Snitch active; editable type and creator fields are present.*

Most other competing utilities work in a similar manner. For example, DiskTop works very much like Norton Utilities. You simply open DiskTop, navigate to the file you want, and then select Get Info from the DiskTop menu (or type Command-I). This brings up a window where you can edit the type and creator codes.

No matter which utility you use, when you return to the Finder, you may find that the Finder does not yet seem to recognize the changes you've made; for example, the file may still show its old, incorrect icon. If so, select Get Info for the file. Doing this gets the Finder's attention and forces it to update its information. If your changes still don't show up, restart. As a last resort, rebuild the desktop.

Identifying the Correct Creator Code

The ability to alter a file's creator or type, of course, is not of much value if you do not know what creator or type code you need to enter. For example, perhaps you want to restore a missing creator code to a Microsoft Excel document file, but you have no idea what the proper code is. The simplest answer is to find an existing Microsoft Excel document on your disk, use any of the utilities just described to check what its codes are, and then apply them to the problem document. (Note: the use of uppercase and lowercase makes a difference in these codes, so copy codes exactly!)

If you have no document to use as a guide, your best bet is to try MacTools' FileFix, since it provides a built-in list of common file codes. Just select the name of the suspected creating application in the scrolling list, and FileFix will automatically fill in the correct codes for that application. Make sure, however, that the version of the application on your disk matches the version listed in FileFix—sometimes an application's creator and type codes are changed when an upgrade is released.

The commonly used codes in Snitch's pop-up menus will also be of some use here.

TAKE NOTE ▶

A REAL-LIFE EXAMPLE OF CHANGING A FILE'S CREATOR CODE TO OPEN THE FILE

I acquired a graphics file from a colleague that was in a format commonly referred to as GIF (the actual file type is GIFf). Since I had an application that opened GIF files, I did not expect any trouble. When I double-clicked the document from the Finder, however, I got the all-too-familiar message that the creating application could not be found. I launched my GIF utility and tried to open the problem document from within the application, but this did not work either.

At this point, I used MacTools to look at the type and creator of the file. The type was indeed GIFf, but the creator was different from the one used by my application. Since at least a dozen or more programs can save in the GIF format, this was not surprising. Even so, the document should have opened, since my GIF utility is designed to open any GIF file, no matter what its creator. Because the document clearly was not opening, however, I decided to see if modifying the creator code might help.

I used Snitch to change the document's creator to match the creator code of the application on my disk. It worked—the file now opened, both from within the application and from the Finder.

TEXT and PICT Formats: Type and Creator Code Issues

Some file formats (file types) are *generic*—that is, they are not associated with a particular application. These formats are recognized by most applications of a given category.

For example, the *Plain Text* (or just Text) format is recognized by virtually every word processor.

In fact, even spreadsheets and databases can save their data as Text files as well as read Text files created in other applications. Even if these programs have no special translator files, they typically can still read Text format files. There is a cost, however, to this universal acceptance: Text files do not retain any of the special formatting options (such as font styles or pasted-in graphics) available, for example, when you save these files in an application-specific format.

Graphics formats have a whole collection of generic file formats, each with different qualities. Indeed, many graphics applications do not have a unique format for saving documents, instead, depending entirely on the generic formats. These shared formats make it much easier to transfer graphics information from one graphics application to another.

Probably the most common generic graphic file format is called PICT. Almost every graphics application can read and save PICT files; it is the graphic equivalent of the plain Text format.

SEE: • **Chapter 10 for more on PICT and other generic graphics formats**

The file type for plain text documents is TEXT, and the file type for PICT documents is PICT. No single creator code is associated with these file types; each file is assigned the creator code of the application used to save it. Thus, if you create four different PICT files, each with a different application, double-clicking each document from the Finder will launch a different application—even though they are all PICT documents. The same idea applies to TEXT documents.

Figure 8-5 *These icons all represent PICT files, each one created by the application named under the icon.*

As a result of all this, you can't trust icons to identify PICT or TEXT files, as each type of file may have any of several different icons, depending on the application that created them.

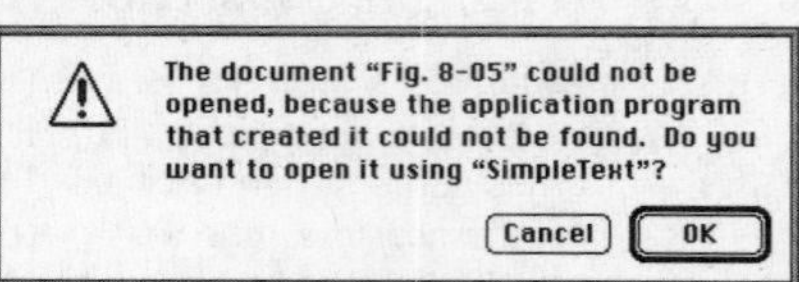

Figure 8-6 *This message appears when you try to open a TEXT or PICT document for which the creating application cannot be found.*

If the creating application is not on your disk, however, the Finder will not launch a TEXT or PICT file when you double-click it. Instead, as discussed for documents in general, an error message typically informs you that the file did not open because the application program that created it "could not be found." (In System 7, however, if you have SimpleText on your disk, the Finder additionally asks whether you want to open the document using SimpleText.)

This problem, though, only affects opening the file from the Finder by double-clicking. All applications that can read TEXT or PICT files can recognize and open these files from within the application itself. In fact, once the document is open, you can usually use Save to save the document, and it should acquire the creator (and type)

> **TAKE NOTE ▶**
>
> **TEACHTEXT VERSUS SIMPLETEXT**
>
> TeachText is a bare-bones word processor that used to come as part of Apple's system software. More recently, Apple replaced TeachText with SimpleText. Because of the widespread availability of these applications, many companies use TeachText/SimpleText documents for their "Read Me" and related files.
>
> SimpleText, while it is still sparse in features (you still can't open files greater than 32K or paste graphics), at least now allows you to vary the font and size of text, and also allows multiple documents to be open at once. Fortunately, the type and creator codes of SimpleText documents remain exactly the same as for TeachText documents. Still, as a precaution, once you shift to SimpleText you should remove any copies of TeachText from your disk.

code of the application you are using. Otherwise, if you wish, you can directly change the creator code of the TEXT or PICT document using the methods described in the previous section.

Alternatively, as described in Chapter 6, utilities such as Now Menus or Apple's Macintosh Easy Open can be used to make substitutions of this sort automatically—so that whenever you double-click a Text file, for example, the Finder will always open ClarisWorks.

SEE: • **Chapter 6 for more on problems with opening files**

Five More Good Reasons to View or Change a File's Type/Creator Code

If you are still not convinced that a working knowledge of how to edit type and creator codes is of value to you, here are a few more practical examples that may change your mind.

SEE: • **"Take Note: Increasing Memory of Files" in Fix-It #6, for yet another reason**

Get Documents to Open in TeachText/SimpleText by Default

Suppose you have saved a text document in a communications program like America Online. The next time you double-click the text document, you would prefer it to open directly in TeachText or SimpleText (which launch rather quickly) instead of the more cumbersome communications software. Unfortunately, it doesn't. What to do?

Simple. Use Snitch (or a similar utility) to access the file's creator and type codes. The type code should be TEXT; if so, leave it alone. Change the Creator codes, however, from whatever it currently is to "ttxt." The file will now open directly in TeachText or SimpleText; its icon should also change to the familiar SimpleText icon.

Similarly, for any PICT file, if you change its creator to "ttxt," it should open in TeachText/SimpleText. You can't edit it from there, but you can view it. By the way, these are the type of PICT files that are created by your Macintosh when you take a picture of your screen by typing Command-Shift-3 (try it!).

Of course, changing a document's creator is not the only way to get a text document to open in SimpleText by default. You could also open the text document from within SimpleText and then use the Save As command to create a new document containing the same text. This new document will now open in SimpleText by default. Changing the creator is simpler and faster, however. Especially with a utility like Snitch.

Make Uneditable TeachText/SimpleText Documents Editable

Have you ever come across those uneditable TeachText documents, the ones with the newspaper icon? If you try just to copy any text from one of these documents (never mind actually altering any of the text!), TeachText/SimpleText won't let you. The commands are all disabled. What to do?

Easy; change the file's type code (not its creator). While the file is closed, change its Type from "ttro" to "TEXT." Presto—you now have an editable TeachText document. Its icon will change accordingly.

Yes Edit No Edit Picture

Figure 8-7 *TeachText/SimpleText icons for editable text files (left), uneditable text files (center), and PICT files (right).*

By the way, with editable TeachText/SimpleText documents, you can copy and paste text and copy graphics, but you cannot paste graphics. To place graphics into a SimpleText document, use a utility like ResEdit.

BY THE WAY ▶

GRAPHICS IN SIMPLETEXT DOCUMENTS

Did you ever wonder how the SimpleText "Read Me" files that come with some software include graphics in them? It seems impossible, because the SimpleText program itself doesn't let you paste graphics.The way it happens is amazingly complicated (especially for a program named SimpleText) and requires ResEdit, but Apple has a Technote file that spells it all out. If you are on the Web, you can find it at http://dev.info.apple.com/technotes/tn1005.html. Alternatively, you can use a shareware program called Text-Edit Plus.

By the way, if you convert a read-only SimpleText file to an editable one, any editing changes you make may result in the document's graphics being lost or not displayed properly.

Finally, note that while you can't edit graphics files (such as screen snapshots) in SimpleText, the application is still great for quickly copying a selected portion of the file's image to the clipboard. In most "draw" programs, you either cannot do this at all or must first paste the graphic into a special "paint" window to do it.

BY THE WAY ▶

TEX-EDIT PLUS

So you want to put graphics in your SimpleText documents but are put off by the ResEdit hassles needed to do so? Don't despair. Get Tex-Edit Plus. This shareware program makes it easy to create SimpleText graphic documents, as well as to create your own read-only SimpleText documents and just about anything else imaginable that can be done with a SimpleText type of document.

Fit More Utilities on an Emergency Toolkit Floppy Disk

In Chapter 2, I described how to make a Finder-less startup floppy disk using a utility called ShortFinder as a substitute for the real Finder. This utility, because of its small size compared to the Finder, frees up about 420K disk space for you to add other utilities (version 1.5 of ShortFinder only takes up 30K, while the Finder takes up more than 450K).

The method I described in Chapter 2 required that all files be at the root level of the startup disk. I promised then that I would later reveal how to create a startup disk with ShortFinder and still keep all relevant files in a true System Folder. Well, that time has come.

First, delete the original Finder from your startup floppy disk. Now copy ShortFinder there instead, placing it in the System Folder—to be really cute, rename ShortFinder to Finder. The key step, though, is to use Snitch (or a similar utility) to change ShortFinder's type and creator codes to match those of the original Finder; in particular, change the type code from "APPL" to "FNDR," and the creator code from "sFdr" to "MACS." When you are done, ShortFinder's icon should change to that of the real Finder. The disk should now function just fine as a startup disk!

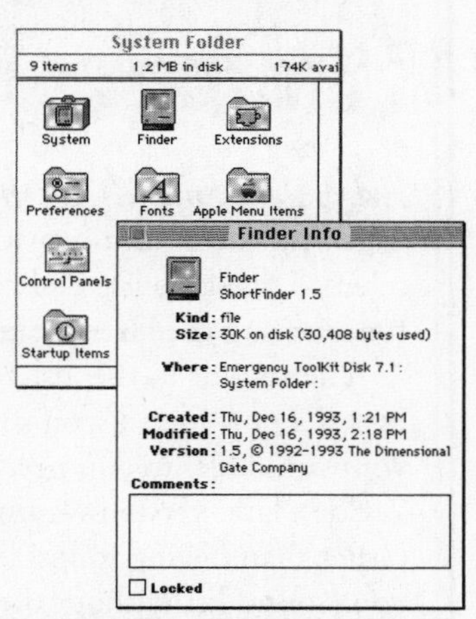

Figure 8-8 *ShortFinder "disguised" as the Finder in the System Folder of a startup floppy disk (take a close look at the top of the Get Info window, and the Size of the file).*

This ShortFinder trick is the only technique I am aware of that will let you launch more than one utility from a Finder-less floppy startup disk. If you need to save even more space (or don't want to use ShortFinder for some reason), and you don't need to run more than one application from the floppy disk, you can use an almost identical method to create a totally Finder-less startup disk. In this case, simply assign the FNDR and MACS codes to whatever single troubleshooting application you wish to access at startup. Combine this application with a System file, and you have a startup disk. These two files needn't even be in a System Folder; just leave them loose at the root level of the floppy disk. Actually, as described in Chapter 2, if you do place the files at the root level of the disk, you may not even have to bother with changing the application's type and creator codes. Simply renaming the application to "Finder" may work (though apparently not in System 7.5).

When you start up with these types of disks, they take you directly to the application that is serving as a Finder substitute. The downside is that you will not be able to shift to any other application (unless you used ShortFinder), you will have no view of the Finder's desktop, and will you have no access to the Apple menu. If you try to quit from the application, the Macintosh will interpret this as a Restart/Shut Down command.

Also, a word of caution is appropriate. With the changes in the new versions of the system software that keep arriving, it is possible that ShortFinder will no longer work with current or future system software.

BY THE WAY ▶

OTHER TYPES OF FINDER-LESS STARTUP DISKS

Some commercial Finder-less startup floppy disks, such as those that come with MacTools Pro, may be created by the same type/creator method described here for ShortFinder, except that they use their own utility (such as DiskFix) rather than ShortFinder. In other cases (such as with recent versions of Apple's Installer disks), these startup floppy disks are not created by changing the application's type/creator codes. Instead, these disks are created by altering the floppy disk's boot blocks (a term explained in more detail later in this chapter) so that the Macintosh is instructed to start up with an application other than the Finder. As a result, the application on these disks does not have to be renamed "Finder," even though it is at the root level of the disk. Beyond this, these disks have no system software except a System file. Like most other Finder-less disks, the Finder-substitute application is the only one that can be opened.

While you can create your own custom disks of this type using Norton Utilities or DiskEdit (from MacTools 2.*x*), I will pass on describing the details here. I recommend using the type/creator code method instead.

In any case, as I described in Chapter 2 ("Take Note: To Make an Exact Copy of an Entire Floppy Disk), if you make a copy of these altered disks from the Finder, the copy may not work as a startup disk, because the Finder does not copy the modified boot blocks. To be safer, use a special copy utility such as Disk Copy.

Add Alert Sounds Without Installing Them in the System File

Open up the Sound control panel, and you'll see a list of all the alert sounds you can select. This same list is also used by a variety of programs for various purposes, such as for selecting the alarm sound in appointment/reminder programs.

The sounds in this list come from the sounds installed directly in the System file; to install a new sound, you simply drag the sound file to the System file icon. But suppose you would like to add new sounds in the same way that you can add new fonts in System 7.1 or a later version—simply by placing the sound in a folder, like the Fonts folder, rather than having to install it directly in the System file? This way you could modify your sound list without the damage risk of having to modify the System file each time.

The trick solution here is to change the file type and creator of the sound file to match that of a font suitcase file. In particular, change its type code from "sfil" to "FFIL," and the creator code from "movr" to "DMOV."

Actually, if you have multiple sounds stored in a sound suitcase file (like the one provided with utilities such as Now Fun!), you can change the entire sound suitcase into a font suitcase. Dragging this lone file to the Fonts folder will add all the sounds in one step.

Search for a File Based on Its Type or Creator Code

In the Finder of System 7.1 or earlier, the Find function cannot search for files based on their type or creator codes. This ability, however, was added to the Find File function of System 7.5. For users of earlier versions of the system software, a host of competing utilities also provide this function, including DiskTop (via its Find command), Fast Find in Norton Utilities, or FindPro (a shareware utility that is the basis of System 7.5's Find File). With this ability, you can search by creator code to locate easily every file on your disk created by a specific application.

True, with most Find utilities, you can probably search by Kind to accomplish the same thing as a search by Creator, but I think searching by Creator is more reliable. Also, System 7.5's Find File limits what you can use as input for Kind, making a search by Type/Creator the only viable alternative in many situations. For example, to find all ClarisWorks documents, you might decide to search for all files whose Kind contains the word *ClarisWorks.* Unfortunately, though, you can't do this with Find File. Instead, you need to search for all files with a Creator equal to "BOBO."

One notable reason to do this type of search, as described in Fix-It #2, is to search for a hard-to-locate preferences file.

Finder Flags (Attributes)

What Are Finder Flags (Attributes)?

Finder flags are a set of "on-off" characteristics that have been separately assigned to each file (and folder) on your disks; these flags are also often referred to as a file's *attributes* or *bits.* They determine important aspects of how the Macintosh (especially the Finder) interacts with a given file—for example, whether it is invisible, and whether it loads at startup. Normally, these flag settings are handled without any user involvement, and so you may not even be aware that these flags exist. As you will soon see, however, you can examine and modify these flags by using the special utilities already described in this chapter. Here are six examples of Finder flags that you might have reason to check on or modify.

The Invisible Bit

If the Invisible bit box is checked for a file or folder, it will not be visible on the Finder's desktop; normal access to these files is thus prohibited. The Desktop file is a common example of a normally invisible file. Unchecking this bit for an invisible file will make the file visible on the Finder's desktop, and you can similarly turn any ordinary visible file into an invisible one by checking this bit.

Of course, if a file is already invisible, you may wonder how to find it so that you can change its flags. I'll explain that shortly.

SEE: • "Invisible Files and Folders," later in this chapter

The Bundle Bit

The Bundle bit is usually turned on for applications. This bit informs the Finder to check the application for information about linked document files, including what icons to assign to documents that the application creates. Programs like Norton Utilities or MacTools, when used to check for disk problems (as described in Fix-It #13), can detect and correct Bundle bit errors (that is, a Bundle bit set to "off" that should be on, or vice versa). This can sometimes help restore the correct icon to a document file. Unless you are sure you know what you are doing, you should depend on these utilities to fix Bundle bit problems rather than altering the Bundle bit yourself.

A utility called Save A BNDL doesn't actually alter the Bundle bit, but it updates the Desktop database for that file, an especially useful function in certain cases where the file would otherwise be ignored by the Desktop database. This can fix a generic icon problem for a specific file without you having to rebuild the entire desktop.

If you really get serious about understanding file icons and what determines when they do and do not appear correctly, you will need to get into using ResEdit and learning about things such as FREF resources. For most people, what is provided here (and in Fix-It #9) will be more than enough.

The Inited Bit

This bit indicates whether or not the Finder has seen the file. If you disable it, you can force the Finder to look at the file again, which can be useful or even necessary to get Finder to recognize changes you have made to other attributes for the file. It may also help to solve a generic icon problem for a particular file. After you uncheck this bit, restart to see if it has any effect. This bit works in conjunction with the Bundle bit to determine the file icons displayed in the Finder.

The Use Custom Icon Bit

This bit indicates that a file's icon has been added by pasting the icon into the icon box of the file's Get Info window. If this icon is not being displayed (and other suggested solutions have failed to work), look to see if this attribute is checked. If not, check it and restart.

The No INITs Bit

The No INITs bit is relevant mainly for certain control panels. If a control panel is designed to act as a startup extension (that is, if it loads into memory at startup along with system extensions), this bit is unchecked. Otherwise, it is checked. You can use this bit to determine for certain which control panels (or extensions) are INITs and which are not.

Normally, you should not alter this bit yourself. In Chapter 6 (see "Technically Speaking: Cannot Open a Control Panel Because No INITs Bit Is Checked"), however, I described one case where certain control panels could not be opened because their No INITs bit had been inadvertently checked. This caused the Mac not to load these control panels at startup, and so they would not work. The solution (after discovering how this had happened in the first place) was to recheck the No INITs bit and restart.

SEE: • **Chapter 1 and Fix-It #4 for more details on startup extensions (INITs)**

The Name Locked Bit

This bit, when checked, prevents the name of the file from being changed from the Finder, regardless of whether the Get Info Locked box is checked or not. This is the reason you cannot change the name of the System, Finder, or Enabler files, for example. If you turn this bit off and then restart, you will be able to change the name of these files.

You might instead, however, simply make a copy of the file, since the copy does not have its locked bit set. You can then change the name of the copy (deleting the original if desired).

Viewing and Editing Finder Flags

One of the conveniences of the Macintosh's design is that you can easily turn these flag settings on or off without any special programming skills—just one click of a mouse can turn an invisible file into a visible one. Still, you don't want to make these changes recklessly. Normally, these flags are set on or off by the developer of the software (or, in some cases, by the Finder), and there is no reason to change them. Nevertheless, a few of these attributes, such as the ones just described, can be relevant to certain problem-solving issues. Even if you don't change them, it pays to know how to check on them.

So, to access the list of flags/attributes for a file, use the same familiar utilities (and similar procedures) that you used to check a file's type and creator: Norton Utilities, MacTools, or Snitch (as well as DiskTop or other competing utilities). Here are the exact procedures (the figures showing these utilities, earlier in this chapter, may be useful to look at again here):

With Norton Utilities

1. Open Norton Disk Editor (either from its Finder icon or by selecting it from the Utilities menu of Norton Utilities). This should lead to a dialog box with a pop-up menu of all mounted disks.
2. Select the disk you want and click Open. Doing this opens a window with a directory listing of all files and folders on the disk, including invisible ones. Double-click a folder to reveal the contents of the folder.
3. Select the desired file and then click the Info button. This opens up a new window that lists the file's attributes (as well as its type and creator codes, as described earlier).
4. Check or uncheck a particular attribute as desired. Older versions of Norton Utilities presented slightly different lists of attributes depending on whether you selected those for System 6 or System 7. This feature has been dropped from version 3.0 and later upgrades.

By the way, you can also get a similar list of information from Norton Disk Doctor. Select "Get Info" (for volumes) or "Get Info for …" (for files and folders) from Disk Doctor's File menu.

With MacTools The latest version of MacTools no longer has the option to list a file's attributes other than the Invisible bit. This bit, as described, is accessed from FileFix using the same procedure used to access the type and creator codes. In earlier versions of MacTools, you could access all attributes via the DiskEdit utility.

With Snitch The basic procedure is the same as for getting a file's type and creator codes. One disadvantage of Snitch is that, since it works from the Finder, you cannot use it to select invisible files.

1. Select the desired file from the Finder's desktop and type Command-I; the list of file attributes will appear. This list is somewhat different from the list in Norton Utilities, but they both list the key attributes described in this chapter.
2. Check or uncheck a particular attribute as desired.

Invisible Files and Folders

Lurking on your disk are invisible files and folders. Among the common invisible items you will find on a typical disk are Desktop DB and Desktop DF (the two Desktop files); AppleShare PDS and Move&Rename (used with file sharing); LoadRAMDblr (an invisible file needed by the RAM Doubler extension/control panel in order to work), the Temporary Items folder, the Trash Folder, and more.

Normally, you access invisible files and folders indirectly. Thus, you can rebuild the invisible Desktop file without ever opening it or viewing it in any way. There are occasions, however, when you may want to view or modify these invisible files and folders directly. The next section describes how to do this.

SEE:
- **Chapter 2 for more on FileSaver**
- **Chapter 4 for more on the Temporary Items Folder**
- **Chapter 11 for more on AppleShare**
- **Fix-It #9 for more details on Desktop files**

BY THE WAY ▶

TWO TYPES OF DESKTOPS

A distinction is usually made between the Finder's desktop (which refers to the display of windows and icons that the Finder creates) and the invisible Desktop file(s). By convention, the word desktop, when used for the Finder desktop, is not capitalized. For the invisible Desktop files, it is capitalized.

Viewing and Editing Invisible Files and Folders

With Norton Utilities or MacTools Pro You can view invisible files and folders with Norton Utilities or MacTools, using the same basic procedures described previously for accessing type/creator codes and attributes. For Norton Utilities, open a disk with the Norton Disk Editor; for MacTools Pro, open the Clinic application and click the FileFix button. From the window that appears, locate the file/folder you want from any currently mounted disk. In either case, a complete list of files and folders—both visible and invisible—is displayed. To see the contents of a given folder, open the folder as indicated for each application.

These utilities list *all* files, but they do not make it immediately obvious which ones are normally invisible. If you are familiar with the file you are looking for, such as the Desktop file, this may not be a problem. Otherwise, the only sure way to determine if a file is normally invisible is to select the file and check if its Invisible bit is turned on, as previously described in the section on "Finder Flags (Attributes)."

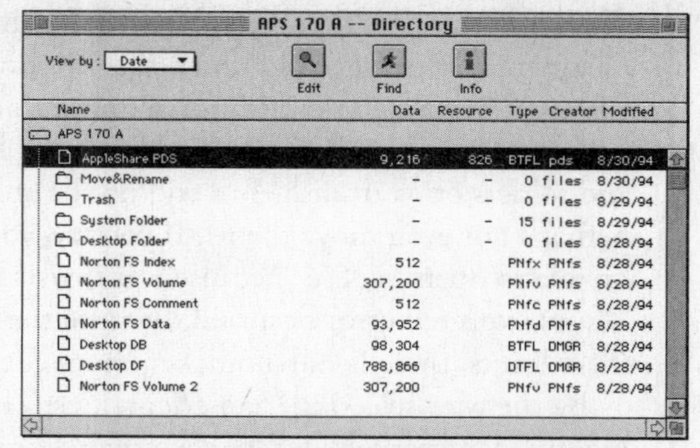

Figure 8-9 *A view form Norton Disk Editor; all of the files and all of the folders (except the System Folder) are invisible on the desktop.*

These utilities typically list only the name and location of these files, so you cannot use them to open a file and examine its contents. Similarly, you cannot directly delete any of these invisible files from these utilities. To do any of these things, you must first make the file visible by unchecking its Invisible file attribute; you can then access the file from the Finder. A shareware utility called InvisiFile works similarly.

With DiskTop DiskTop deserves special mention here because you *can* use it directly to launch any files or delete invisible files from its listing window. This useful utility, as mentioned, also allows you to modify type/creator codes and file attributes, as well as search by type or creator codes.

1. Open DiskTop; a list of the contents of all mounted disks will be displayed. Double-click a volume or folder name to reveal its contents.
2. The listing should include both visible and invisible files. If invisible files are not listed, select Preferences from the DiskTop menu. Check Technical from the Level options, and return to the file listing. Invisible files and folders will now be listed there.
3. To delete an invisible file or folder, simply select it and click the Delete button, located near the top of the window.
4. To launch any file, just double-click it.

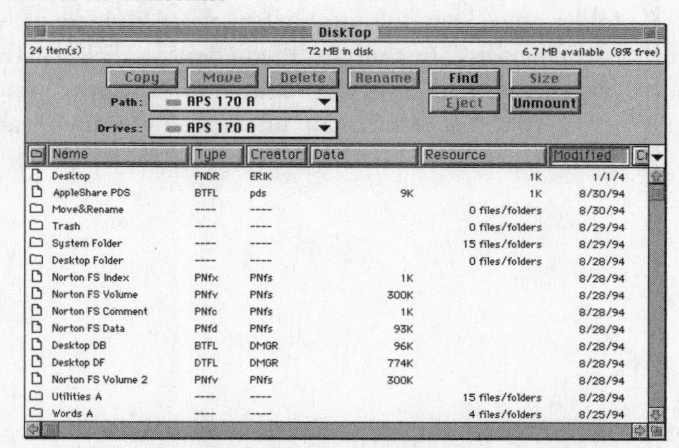

Figure 8-10 *DiskTop is still another utility that lists invisible files and folders—but this one lets you copy, move, delete, or rename them.*

With System 7.5's Find File System 7.5 has a new Find File feature (described in Chapter 2). Open it, hold down the Option key, and select the Name pop-up menu. This will bring up four additional options at the bottom of the menu. Select "visibility" as "invisible," then click the Find button. This will give you a list of all invisible files and folders on your disk. You will not be able to open or edit any of these files (and perhaps not even move them). If you try, you will get a message saying that you are unable to open the file "because it is invisible (or is inside an invisible folder)" or that "An unexpected error occurred, because the original item could not be found." Despite these limits, there is not a quicker, more convenient way to get a list of these files.

By the way, selecting "name/icon lock," another of Find File's special options, conveniently identifies which files have their Name Locked bit turned on.

Special Case: Viewing the Contents of the Desktop Folder and Trash Folder

By definition, an invisible folder is not displayed on the Finder's desktop (though it may appear in Open and Save dialog boxes). Similarly, none of the contents of an invisible folder are visible on the desktop (even though the invisible bits for each item in the folder are not turned on).

The special Desktop Folder and Trash folder, however, are exceptions to this generalization. The contents of the Desktop Folder *are* visible; they are seen as the files and folders on the desktop (those items not in any folder nor in the root-level window of a volume). Similarly, just double-click the Trash icon to open a window that displays all items currently in the Trash folder—you can think of the Trash can as a special folder icon.

Each disk maintains its own set of these invisible Desktop and Trash folders. For example, if you use MacTools Pro's FileFix or Norton Disk Editor to open the Trash folder on a given disk, it only lists those files that are currently in the Trash from that particular disk. In contrast, if you double-click the Trash icon on the desktop, it lists all files placed there from all mounted disks. If you eject a floppy disk, any unemptied items from that disk remain unemptied but disappear from the Trash folder window. They return to the Trash the next time you insert the disk.

Viewing and Editing *Really* Invisible Files and Folders

The Directory and Boot Blocks

Some files are so invisible that they do not even appear in the main listings of utilities like MacTools or DiskTop. In part, this is because these special files are not files in the same sense as typical documents and applications. A disk's *Directory* file and *boot blocks* are two examples of this. Sometimes, however, you can use other special features of these utilities to view—and even alter—the contents of these files.

SEE: • **Chapter 5 for more information on startup disks and boot blocks**
• **Fix-Its #10 and #13 for more information on the Directory**

Viewing the Directory and the Boot Blocks

With Norton Utilities

1. Open Norton Disk Editor (either from its Finder icon or by selecting it from the Utilities menu of Norton Utilities). This should lead to a dialog box with a pop-up menu of all mounted disks.
2. Select the disk you want and click Open. This opens a window with a directory listing of all files and folders on the disk, including invisible ones.
3. Pull down the Objects menu. You will see a list of objects that include the boot blocks and the different components of the Directory (such as Extents B-Tree). Note that near the top of the window is an explanation of the function of the selected component; this explanation shifts accordingly each time you select a different component.

   By the way, the Directory object (the last one in the Objects menu list) is something of a misnomer. It refers to the default listing of the contents of the disk, not to the actual Directory files.

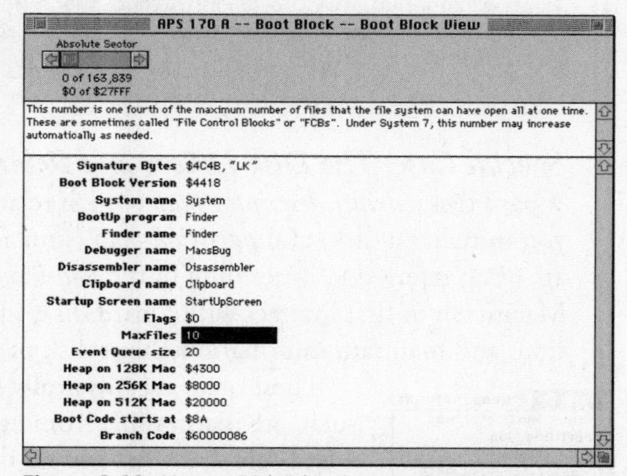

Figure 8-11 *Norton Disk Editor's view of a disk's boot blocks. Since the MaxFiles line is selected, the text near the top of the window gives an explanation of what MaxFiles is.*

It's technically possible to use Norton Utilities to modify any of this boot block and Directory information. To do so, select the View in Hex or View in ASCII commands from the Display menu. You can now directly modify the data.

TECHNICALLY SPEAKING ▶

HEX/ASCII DATA EDITING

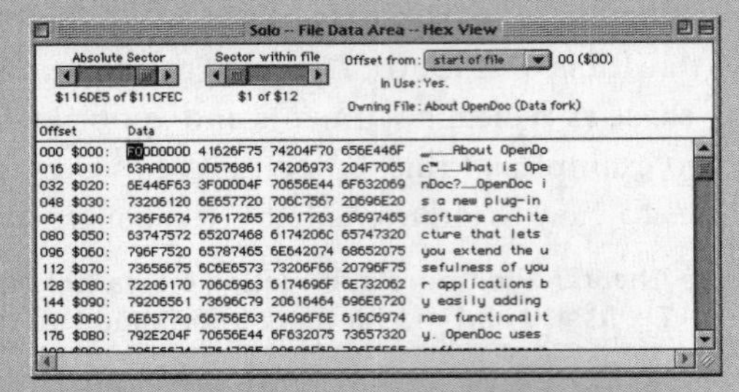

Figure 8-12 *A view of the hex code for the "About OpenDoc" text file, as seen from Norton Disk Editor. Norton Utilities lets you edit this code if you want.*

With Norton Disk Editor, you can get a hex or ASCII listing for any file on your disk just by selecting the file name (when in the Directory view) and clicking the Edit button. There is even a way to access areas of a disk that have not been assigned to any file. Unless you are following detailed instructions or are generally skilled in how to work with hex code, though, I would not mess with any of this. This is the "raw" data level of the computer's contents. Thankfully, you will rarely (if ever) need to edit this information, or even understand more about it than the minimum I have presented here. Refer to the Norton Utilities documentation for more help if you really want or need to try this editing. The MacTools DiskEdit utility, which unfortunately is now extinct, could similarly view and edit this information—and in a way that made making changes easier to do.

When might a person largely unfamiliar with what all of this means have any reason to work at this level? For one example, a vendor helping you to "patch" a program (to fix a minor bug) may provide instructions that require altering the hex code. In this case, you don't need to have any idea what you are actually doing; just follow the vendor's instructions carefully.

Special Case: The Disk Driver and Related Low-Level Data

A hard disk's *driver descriptor map* (which related to the disk driver first installed when you initialize a disk) and *partition map* (similarly determined when you format a disk) are often referred to as residing in the *low-level* areas of the disk. These areas allow the Macintosh to first interact with a hard disk, identify critical components of its operation, and maintain information about disk partitions.

These areas are physically separate from the rest of the disk and, as such, are inaccessible from every function in Norton Utilities or MacTools that I have so far described. In fact, the Norton Utilities manual draws the distinction between the "logical disk" (what we have been working with so far) and the "physical disk" (which includes these additional areas). In essence, this difference is what is implied by saying these areas are at a low level. Normally, you interact with them only indirectly, such as via a disk formatting utility.

If you are really determined, however, you *can* see the driver descriptor map and partition map with Norton Disk Editor. They are listed at the top

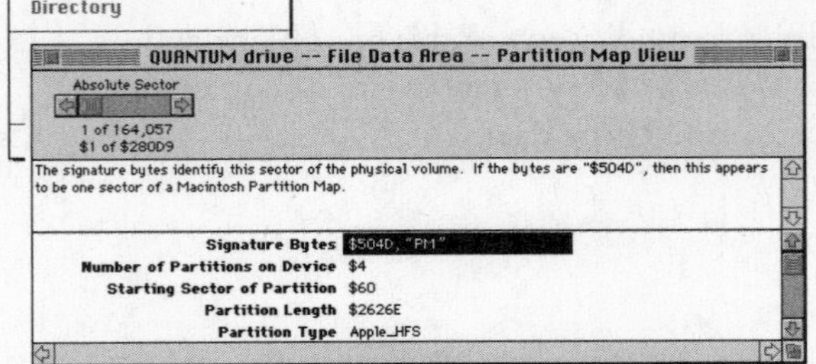

Figure 8-13 *Norton Disk Editor finds friends in low places.*

of the Objects menu. Normally these menu items are grayed out, but you can make them active (leaving the other items grayed out) through a special procedure that involves holding down the Command and Shift keys when selecting a volume from Disk Editor's Open pop-up menu (after first selecting the "Scan SCSI Bus" command). This brings up a list of the additional names of the physical disks (such as "Quantum drive") that you can open; now you will have access to these menu items. Check the Norton Utilities manual for details as needed.

I only mention all of this for the sake of completeness. Typically, you would have no reason to ever work with these areas.

SEE:
- **Fix-It #12 for more details on disk device drivers**
- **Fix-It #15 for more details on partitioning and disk formatting**

TECHNICALLY SPEAKING ▶

USING RESEDIT

Before concluding this chapter, I feel obligated to at least mention the ultimate "under the hood" utility, Apple's ResEdit. It is mainly used to view and edit the variety of *resources* that are stored within a file—such things as fonts, sounds, icons, and more.

Personally, I rarely use ResEdit for troubleshooting. Instead, I use it most often simply to "explore" these resources. By doing so, you can often learn things about the contents of a file that may later prove to be helpful for troubleshooting. For example, you can get a listing of all of the possible error and alert messages that an application might generate or all of the menus generated by an application.

You can also modify all of this stuff with surprising ease: adding custom menus, editing icons, changing the text and default settings of dialog boxes, replacing graphics (including the Mac OS "splash" screen that you see at startup), and much more. You may also be able to turn on or off various options for a file that are otherwise inaccessible (for example, I discovered that you could disable the single-pass-printing foreground of LaserWriter 8.4 in favor of the older double-pass printing, a change that might help eliminate printing conflicts with a few applications).

Finally, you can use ResEdit to do hex editing, as well as modifying the type, creator and Finder flags of any file. It can be a great "Swiss Army knife" utility. If you want to take the time to master it (as easy as it is, it is still more designed for programmers than end users), it can do just about everything that all of the other utilities mentioned in this chapter can do—and then some.

If all of this sounds like it is up your alley, get a copy of ResEdit and try it out. Some sparse documentation may be included with the file; more complete documentation is available from a variety of books (including one called *Zen and the Art of Resource Editing: The BMUG Guide to ResEdit*.

Figure 8-14 *Using ResEdit to get inside Apple's Disk First Aid utility. Double-clicking any of the icons opens the door to further exploration of the resources within.*

Chapter 9

Fonts and Text: Write and Wrong

The Write Stuff 329

Font Basics 330

Font Files versus Font Suitcases 330

Font Files 330

Font Suitcases 330

Where the Fonts Are 330

How Can You Tell What Fonts Are Installed in Your System? 331

Locating, Adding, and Removing Fonts from Your System Folder 331

Fonts in System 7.1 and System 7.5 331

Fonts in System 7.0 and Earlier Versions 333

The Different Types of Fonts 334

Bitmapped Fonts 334

Estimating Font Sizes and Styles: The Jaggies 335

How Do You Know What Sizes of Bitmapped Fonts Are Installed? 335

Outline Fonts: TrueType and PostScript 336

TrueType Fonts 337

How to Identify a TrueType Font versus a Bitmapped Font? 337

PostScript Fonts 338

PostScript Printer Fonts versus Screen Fonts 338

PostScript Fonts and Adobe Type Manager (ATM) 340

PostScript Fonts and QuickDraw GX 344

Locating, Adding, and Removing PostScript Printer Font Files from Your System Folder 344

How to Identify a PostScript Font 345

Combining TrueType, PostScript, and/or Bitmapped Versions of the Same Font ... 345

What Font Format Is Displayed? 346

What Font Format Prints? 346

What It All Means 346

The Different Types of Fonts (continued)

Which Font Format Should You Use? 347

Limit Your Use of Bitmapped Fonts 347

Deciding Between PostScript and TrueType 348

Consider Your Printer 349

Keep It Simple 349

Summing Up 349

***Solve It! Text and Font Problems* 350**

A Document Displays the Wrong Font 350

The Necessary Font Is Not in Your System Folder 350

A Font ID Number Conflict Has Occurred 350

A Font File Is Damaged 351

Check the Font Menu 351

If the Correct Font Is Not Listed in the Font Menu 351

If the Font Is Listed in the Font Menu 353

If You Still Can't Use the Font 354

A Document Prints with a Different Font from the One Displayed 355

A Font File Is Damaged 355

Problems Specific to PostScript LaserWriters 355

Otherwise 355

Replace a Damaged Font 355

StyleWriter: Problems with Low Memory 355

PostScript LaserWriters: Uncheck Substitute Fonts or Change the Font 356

PostScript LaserWriters: Check Unlimited Downloadable 356

PostScript LaserWriters: Uncheck Unlimited Downloadable 357

A Document Displays or Prints with the Wrong Formatting 357

Line Breaks and Margins Change Due to Changing Printers 358

Line Breaks Change Due to Changing Fonts 359

Vertical Alignment and Line Length Problems Due to Font Selection 360

TrueType Incompatibility Problems 360

LaserWriter 8 Incompatibility 361

Changes in Appearance Due to Fractional Character Widths 362

Fractional Widths and ATM 362

Style Selection Does Not Print Correctly Because of Missing Printer Font Files 362

Formatting Problems Due to Out-of-Date or Damaged Font Files 363

The Text Is Clipped at the Margins When Printed 363
Change the Margin Settings of Your Document 363
Select the Larger Print Area Option from Page Setup Dialog Box 363
Turn Off Larger Print Area 364
Select Correct Paper Size and Orientation from Page Setup Dialog Box 364
Change or Upgrade Your LaserWriter Driver 364
PostScript Fonts Do Not Print Using PostScript 364
The Jaggies Appear Unexpectedly 365
With TrueType 365
If You Use ATM 366
With Bitmapped Fonts Printed at Best Quality 367
Extra Help from PostScript Printers 367
A Paragraph Unexpectedly Shifts Its Formatting 367
Make Invisible Characters Visible 368
Be Careful When Copying and Pasting 368
Be Careful When Deleting Text 368
In General: To Correct Unexpected Format Shifts 369
Problems Copying and Pasting Text Across Applications 369
If You Are Unable to Paste Text at All 370
If Format Shifts When Pasting Text Across Applications 371
Use Drag and Drop and Clippings Files 371
Otherwise ... Reformat the Text 373
Text Turns into Bitmapped Graphics 373
Start Over and Repaste the Text 373
OCR 373
Do Not Use Bitmapped Graphics Programs for Text 374
Special Case: Problems with Uneditable Text in Draw Programs 374

Solve It! Font File Problems **375**
Damaged Font Files 375
Locate Any Damaged Font Files 375
Replace the Damaged Font File(s) 377
Problems Removing a Font File from a Fonts Folder 378
Check for Problems with Other Files 378

Solve It! Font File Problems *(continued)*

Damaged Font Suitcase Files 379
- Delete and Replace the Suitcase File 379
- Extract Fonts from the Suitcase File 379
- Watch Out for the Suitcase Utility 379

Solve It! Font Menu Problems **380**

Fonts Unexpectedly Appear or Disappear from Font Menus 380
- Check for Font Differences Among Different Startup Disks 380
- Check for Embedded Fonts in Applications 381
- Check for Fonts Installed by an Installer Utility 381
- Check If Font/DA Management Utilities Are Turned Off 381
- Quit Currently Open Applications 382
- Special Case: Font Names Are Listed in the Fonts Menu But Are Dimmed 383
- In General: If You Are Having Trouble Finding a Specific Font File 383

Font Menu Clutter 383
- Get Rid of the Style Variant Screen Fonts 384
- Use a Utility to Eliminate the Clutter 384
- Do Nothing 385

The Write Stuff

No matter what else you do with your Macintosh, sooner or later you use it to write something. It may just be a note to a colleague or a caption added to an illustration, or it may be a full-length manuscript. Whatever it is, you are using the text capability of the Macintosh to write it—and what a capability it is! The power you have to alter the appearance of text on the Macintosh is one of the computer's most impressive features.

These text features and the applications that use them, most notably word processors, are the focus of this chapter. In most of these applications, changes to text are made by selecting items from the Font, Style, and Size menus. For example, you might start by selecting a basic font appearance from the choices in the Font menu (such as Times or Helvetica), then decide on the style (such as *italics* or **bold**) and size (such as smaller or larger) of the font. A quick trip to the menu bar can change "**this**" to "this." Equally impressive is that when you finally print your text, the output looks virtually identical to what appeared on the screen, sometimes even better! This is the basic "what you see is what you get" (WYSIWYG) appeal of the Macintosh.

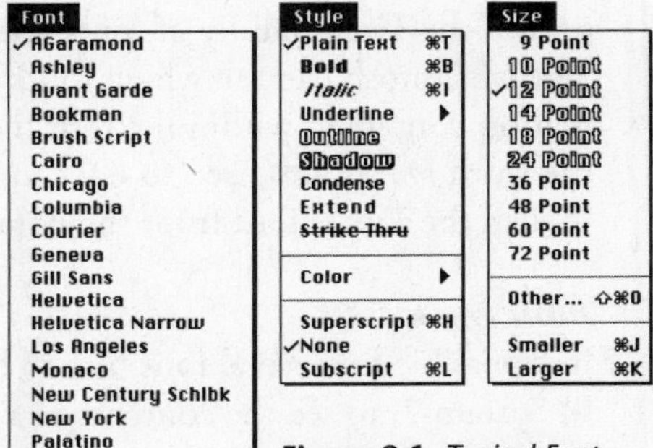

Figure 9-1 *Typical Font, Style, and Size menus.*

What's even better is how easy it is to do all of this. Most people can create and print their text documents without the slightest understanding of how any of these font miracles happen. This is good, because the Macintosh's methods for displaying and printing fonts constitute about the most convoluted topic I'll cover in this book.

Most of the time, the Macintosh succeeds in hiding this complexity from you. Eventually, however, something unexpected happens. Perhaps the line breaks on the printed copy do not match what appeared on your screen, or maybe your document inexplicably displays a different font from the one you expected—or worse. To resolve these problems, you will need to learn at least a little about how all of this works. So take a deep breath, and let's go.

QuickDraw GX Alert: QuickDraw GX is a recent technology that is included with System 7.5 (though it can also be used in System 7.1). It is an optional feature that affects almost everything about the display and printing of text and graphics. I say a lot more about QuickDraw GX in Chapter 13. Since you can use System 7.5 without installing it, however, this current chapter (unless otherwise indicated) assumes you are not using QuickDraw GX.

Font Basics

Font Files versus Font Suitcases

Font Files

Font file is the term used to describe a particular individual font as it appears on the Finder's desktop. It can be moved or copied just like any other type of file.

All characters in a font look related, and this basic design is called the *typeface* of the font. All fonts of the same typeface have the same general name and are said to belong to the same *family.* Thus, Times 10, Times 12, Times (bold), and so on are all part of the Times family of fonts, even though they are a different size and/or style. The Macintosh can tell which fonts belong to the same family because of special information contained within the font files. Sometimes, because it is common practice, the word *font* is also used to refer to the entire family rather than just a single file (as in "Select the Times font from the Font menu").

Font Suitcases

It is possible for several font files to be combined into one superfile called a *font suitcase.* In System 7, to see the contents of a suitcase file, simply double-click the file icon; a new window will open up that lists all of the individual font files stored in the suitcase. In most cases (some exceptions are listed in the following sections), you can modify the contents of a font suitcase simply by dragging a font file out of or into the suitcase.

Figure 9-2 *Font file (left) versus font suitcase (right) icons.*

A font suitcase can contain just one font file, or several (such as all sizes of New York). The fonts in a suitcase do not have to be of the same family; for example, New York and Geneva fonts can be combined into one suitcase.

Where the Fonts Are

Just because a font file is on your disk somewhere doesn't mean it will show up on your Font menus. To be in an application's Font menu, the font file has to be in a special location in your System Folder.

Many new Macintosh users, especially if they work with only one application, are surprised to discover that the available fonts are not part of the application itself. Instead, applications get their font listing from the System Folder. Since all applications' font listings are generated in the same way, the same set of fonts is available to all applications running under that startup disk. Thus, if you were to shift from a word processor to a spreadsheet, you would almost always find the same font listing.

The Macintosh system software includes a basic set of fonts that are automatically installed when you first create a System Folder on your hard disk. These are only a tiny sample, however, of what is available (even though they are probably all that most people ever use). Other fonts are available from Apple as well as from many other companies. All told, you can choose from thousands of possible fonts.

How Can You Tell What Fonts Are Installed in Your System?

One way, of course, is to open your System Folder and check directly (assuming you know where to look, as I will describe shortly). A much simpler solution, however, is to open the Key Caps desk accessory that comes with Macintosh system software disks; its Key Caps menu lists all currently installed fonts. The Font menu of most word processors and related applications would have the same menu.

Locating, Adding, and Removing Fonts from Your System Folder

To add a new font to or remove an unwanted font from your Font menu, you have to install or remove the font at its relevant System Folder location. How to change which fonts are in your System Folder varies depending on what version of the system software you are using. The sections that follow explain what you need to know (except for special issues that pertain only to PostScript fonts, which will be described later in this chapter).

Fonts in System 7.1 and System 7.5

Font files are located in a special folder within the System Folder called Fonts. The Fonts folder can contain both single font files and font suitcases; the Macintosh will deal with both of them appropriately. The Fonts folder must remain in the System Folder, though, in order for applications to access its contents.

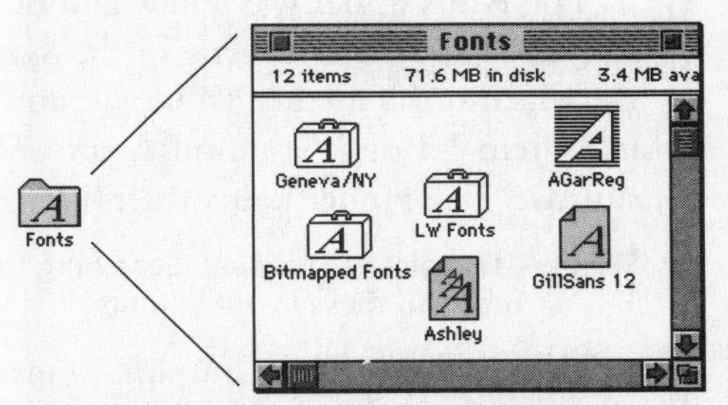

Figure 9-3 *A Fonts folder containing both suitcase files and individual font files.*

Font and suitcase files can be dragged to or from the Fonts folder, similarly to how any other set of files and folders on the desktop would work. You can also add a font or suitcase file to the Fonts folder by dragging the file onto the active System Folder icon. This moves the font directly to the Fonts folder, after first giving you an alert message to confirm that this is what you want to do.

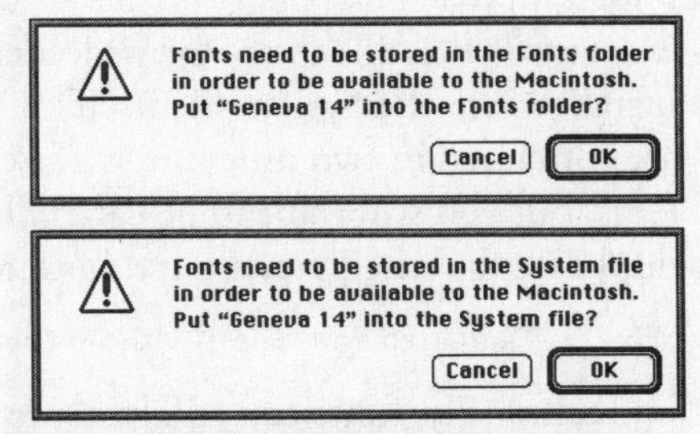

Figure 9-4 *Similar messages that appear when you drag a font file to the System Folder icon in System 7.1/7.5 (top) and System 7.0 (bottom).*

You can add font files or suitcases to the Fonts folder even if other applications are open. If applications other than the Finder are open, however, you will typically get an alert message warning you that the added fonts will not be available to any open applications until after you quit and relaunch them. And you cannot replace a font file with another file of the same name while applications are open, just as you cannot simply remove a file from the Fonts folder while any applications are open. (Sometimes you can remove a font file from a font suitcase within the Fonts folder even though applications are open, but I have found that this doesn't always work.) The solution in each of these cases, of course, is to quit all open applications before you try to make changes that affect existing fonts.

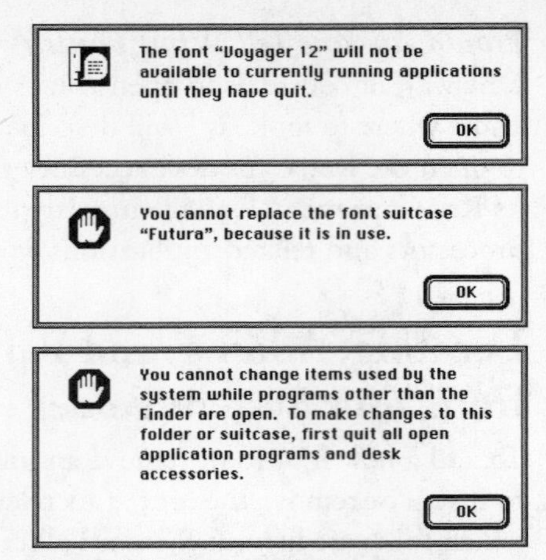

Figure 9-5 *Messages that appear when you try to add (top), replace (middle), or remove (bottom) a font file to or from a Fonts folder while applications are open.*

Helpful hint: The system software doesn't always behave by the rules. Sometimes you get these alert messages when you shouldn't, and sometimes you don't get them when you should. For example, to replace a font, even with all applications closed, you may have to remove the existing font file separately and then add the new one—otherwise, you may get the "font is in use" message. Beyond that, if you are still having these font problems, restarting will usually solve them. If that doesn't work, you may have damaged font files (as described later in this chapter).

The Fonts folder was a new addition in System 7.1; earlier versions of the system software store fonts directly in the System file. Actually, a few critical fonts needed for the Macintosh's menus, windows, and message boxes are still located in the System file in System 7.1 or 7.5, although you will not find them there when you open the System suitcase. The Finder keeps their listing "invisible."

SEE: • **"Technically Speaking: Searching for Reserved Fonts in System 7," later in this chapter, for more on these invisible fonts**

Using a Fonts folder simplifies most font management tasks, and the less frequent need to modify the System file reduces the risk of possible damage to that file. In a few situations, however (such as replacing a font currently in the Fonts folder), the Fonts folder approach can be a bit tricky. For example, it is possible to have two copies of the exact same font file in the Fonts folder at the same time (you could not do this with fonts installed into the System file itself). One way this could happen is if duplicate font files are contained in two different suitcases. Surprisingly, this usually doesn't cause any problems, but you still want to be careful here. For instance, you wouldn't want to add a duplicate file when you are trying to replace an existing file that you suspect is corrupted.

SEE: • **"Damaged Font Files," later in this chapter, for more details**

Technically, fonts can still be stored in the System file rather than the Fonts folder (see "By the Way: Font/DA Mover and Other Font/DA Management Utilities"). Fonts in the System file are recognized and used just as if they were in the Fonts folder. Similarly, any fonts you find in the System file can be removed by opening the System file window and dragging the font files out. The Finder, however, no

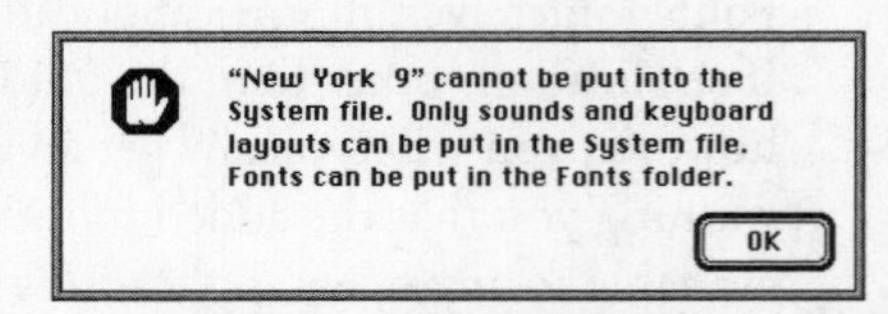

Figure 9-6 *This message appears in System 7.1 or 7.5 if you try to add a font to the System file by dragging the font file directly to the System suitcase icon.*

longer lets you add new fonts to the System file; instead, it insists that you place them in the Fonts folder.

In this regard, if you upgraded from System 6 or 7.0 to System 7.1 or 7.5, check whether there are any fonts still remaining in your System file. If they are duplicated in your Fonts folder, drag the unneeded fonts from the System file to the Trash and delete them. Otherwise, drag the nonduplicate fonts to the Fonts folder.

TAKE NOTE ▶

CREATING NEW FONT SUITCASES

You can create a new empty suitcase simply by duplicating an existing suitcase and dragging all existing fonts out of it. At that point, you are ready to add new files. If there are no suitcases anywhere on your disk, check your system software disks; the fonts included with your system software are typically stored in suitcase format. Otherwise, you can create a new suitcase with a freeware utility called SuitcaseMaker. As a third alternative, you can use Font/DA Mover to create a new suitcase (see "By the Way: Font/DA Mover and Other Font/DA Management Utilities").

Why might you want to create a new suitcase? In System 7.1, there is a combined limit of 128 font files and font suitcases that you can have in the Fonts folder. While this will never present a problem for most users, if you should exceed this limit, you can get back under it (without sacrificing any of your fonts) simply by combining font files into a single font suitcase. You can do this by adding fonts to an existing suitcase or creating a new one.

Fonts in System 7.0 and Earlier Versions

In System 7.0, there is no Fonts folder (this was true for System 6 as well). Instead, font files are stored directly in the System file. Appropriately enough, the System file icon in these versions is a suitcase (and as such is sometimes referred to as the System suitcase), and it works just like a font suitcase. Double-click it, and it opens up a window with a list of installed fonts.

With this edition of *Sad Macs*, I no longer cover these systems in detail. If you have font-related problems with these systems, my advice is to upgrade to a new version of the system software.

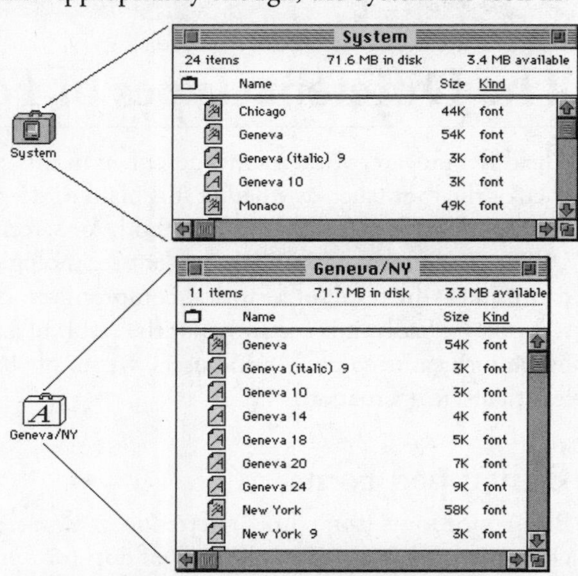

Figure 9-7 *Opening a System suitcase (top) and a suitcase file (bottom) to view the font files within each.*

BY THE WAY ▶

FONT/DA MOVER AND OTHER FONT/DA MANAGEMENT UTILITIES

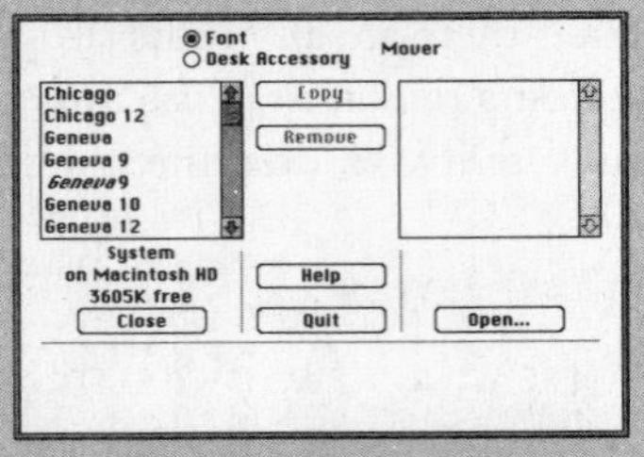

Figure 9-8 *Font/DA Mover.*

In System 6, font files cannot exist as separate files on the Desktop; they need either to be in the System file or in a font suitcase. Moving them from one location to another requires a utility called the Font/DA Mover, which performs a similar function for desk accessories (DAs) and DA suitcases. Font/DA Mover can also create new empty suitcases or modify existing ones.

In System 7, you no longer need Font/DA Mover. (Actually, except for convenience and organizing, you don't really need suitcase files either.) As a result, this utility is no longer included with System 7 software.

Desk accessories in System 7 function almost like independent applications and are typically stored in the Apple Menu Items folder. If you do still have DAs stored in a DA suitcase file, dragging the suitcase to the System Folder icon will automatically empty the suitcase and place the enclosed DAs into the Apple Menu Items Folder. Similarly, fonts are stored in either the System file or the Fonts folder and, in either case, can be moved without Font/DA Mover, as explained in the main text.

As is occasionally mentioned elsewhere in this chapter, Font/DA Mover can still do a few useful tricks even in System 7 (although nothing that cannot also be accomplished by some other method). If you do decide to use it, just make sure you are using Font/DA Mover version 4.1 or later, because earlier versions will not work properly with System 7. The latest version can be obtained from various on-line services and user groups (see Appendix).

Utilities such as Symantec's Suitcase can track fonts anywhere on a disk and allow them to be used as if they were installed in the Fonts folder. You can also use these utilities to open or close specific suitcase files on a temporary or permanent basis without having to move anything into or out of the Fonts folder. If you do use Suitcase, it is recommended that you store your fonts outside of the System Folder entirely.

The Different Types of Fonts

The different categories of fonts described in this section do not refer to the appearance of the font (such as whether it is plain or decorative), but rather to the *technology* the Macintosh uses to create a font, both for screen display and for printing.

The Macintosh's multiplicity of font technologies is evidence of a sorry state of confusion—the result of historical compromises, competing interests, and changing technology. Sadly, it is certainly not the result of a deliberate strategy to make the Macintosh easier to use. As end users, we simply have to make the best of this less-than-great situation.

Bitmapped Fonts

Bitmapped fonts (sometimes referred to as *fixed-size fonts*) are so named because each character is made up of a collection of dots (or *bits*) that create the appearance of the font. Because it is an exact representation of the font, including its size, a separate set of instructions is needed for each different size of a font. Thus a bitmapped font *family* (such as New York) typically would include a collection of separate font files, each representing different font sizes (such as New York 9, New York 10, New York 12, and so on), where each number refers to the *point size* of the font as listed in the Size menu.

Most bitmapped fonts come in a small set of standard sizes, the most common being 9, 10, 12, 14, 18, and 24 points. This is why the Size menus of many applications list only these sizes and do not include odd sizes such as 13 or 17 points. Larger sizes of fonts (greater than 24 points) are similarly rare. This is mainly because, as the font sizes get larger, the amount of disk space needed to store the larger bitmap files increases dramatically.

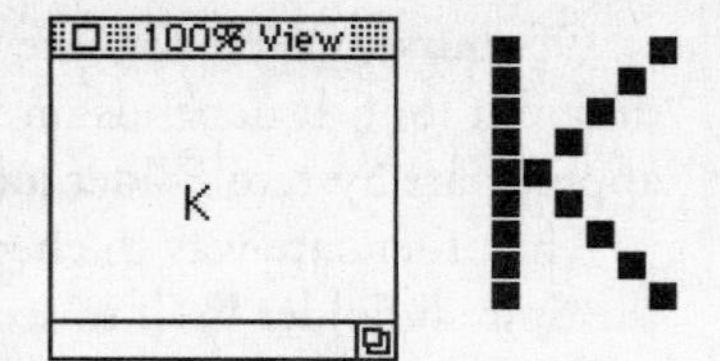

Figure 9-9 *A bitmapped letter K, enlarged to show its underlying bit (dot) structure.*

Estimating Font Sizes and Styles: The Jaggies

For bitmapped fonts, if you select a font size (such as 13 or 17 points), for which you do not have a corresponding font file installed, you get the *jaggies.* What happens is that the Macintosh tries to approximate the appearance of the font by estimating shape information from sizes that are installed. Unfortunately, the Macintosh cannot do a very good job of this estimation, and so the font appears with an unpleasing jagged look.

Technically, the Macintosh uses the same sort of estimation when you select different font styles (such as bold versus italics). The changes necessary to alter a style, however, are generally simpler than what is needed to change a size. This is why you generally don't need separate bitmapped font files for each different style (although separate files do exist and can improve the appearance of the font over using the estimated style).

New York 14 point with jaggies.

Bitmapped New York at 14 point.

TrueType New York at 14 point.

Figure 9-10 *Screen displays of different font types; "jaggies" (top line) occur when bitmapped New York 14 point is displayed without the 14-point size installed.*

At one time in the Mac's history, bitmapped fonts were the only kind there was. Even today, they produce the sharpest screen displays of any type of font, especially at smaller point sizes (12 points or less). Still, because of the jaggies problem as well as their low resolution for printing—bitmapped fonts are designed at 72 dots per inch (dpi), while current laser printers commonly print at 300 to 600 dpi—they have largely been replaced by newer font technologies, as explained in the next sections.

SEE: • **Chapter 10 for details on the meaning of resolution and dpi**

How Do You Know What Sizes of Bitmapped Fonts Are Installed?

A quick way to find out what sizes of bitmapped fonts are installed is to select the Size menu of a text application. Here you may see some numbers in plain type (9) and others in outline style (10). The outlined numbers mean that the current System file contains the bitmapped font file for that particular size of the selected font and can therefore produce a smooth display. Attempts to use the sizes shown in plain type will generally result in jagged fonts on the screen.

Of course, which sizes are and are not installed, may change each time you select a different font. It depends on which sizes for that particular font are installed in the appropriate System Folder location.

The other sure way to check this information, of course, is to inspect the contents of the System Folder itself to see what font files are located there.

By the way, if all the sizes listed in a Size menu are outlined—even odd sizes that are definitely not installed as bitmapped fonts—it is because you are using a TrueType font (described in the next section).

Outline Fonts: TrueType and PostScript

Outline fonts (sometimes referred to as variable-size or scalable fonts) are an alternative to bitmapped fonts. Essentially, with these fonts, the shape of each character is initially derived from a mathematical formula that describes the curves and lines that represent the character rather than by dot-by-dot mapping. For example, an outline font would derive the letter *O* from the basic formula for a circle (the exact formula differs to account for variations in the letter O for each font). This information is then converted to the pattern of dots necessary to display or print the character, a process called *rasterizing.*

BY THE WAY ▶

OUTLINE FONTS VERSUS OUTLINE STYLE

The term *outline,* as applied to outline fonts, has nothing to do with the outline display style of a font. The former refers to a method of generating font characters; the latter refers to the appearance of a particular style of font as selected from a Style menu.

As their name implies, scalable font files are not restricted to a specific size. In fact, with only a single outline font file, you can select any font size you want and never have a problem with the jaggies.

While bitmapped fonts may look better on a typical monitor, outline fonts usually look far superior in printed output. This is because the resolution of outline fonts is *device independent,* taking advantage of whatever resolution is available in the output device. The appearance quality of outline-font text thus improves as the resolution of the printer increases. Laser-printed output, even though it is still a collection of dots constructed similarly to how fonts are displayed on a screen, has a resolution of at least 300 dpi. Since most monitors are limited to about 72 dpi, the appearance of fonts on the monitor display can never match what you can achieve in the printed output from laser printers or any other comparable higher-resolution printer.

SEE: • Chapter 10 for more on resolution

There are two basic types of outline fonts on the Macintosh: TrueType fonts and PostScript fonts.

TrueType Fonts

TrueType fonts are an outline font technology developed by Apple. Several TrueType fonts are shipped with System 7 software disks. TrueType and bitmapped versions of the same font generally look similar (which is what you would expect, of course), but some differences are noticeable.

Only one TrueType font file is needed to display and print all possible sizes. Similarly, you only need the same solitary font file to create the different styles of the font (such as bold or italics), although you may occasionally see TrueType fonts with separate files for different styles (such as Futura Bold and Futura Italic). If you install these additional files, they will be used when you select the Bold or Italic styles from the Style menu.

Otherwise, the Macintosh will estimate the style from the plain-text font file information, as it typically does with bitmapped fonts. This is similar to the situation with PostScript fonts, as described in "Technically Speaking: All in the Family".

How to Identify a TrueType Font versus a Bitmapped Font?

The standard set of bitmapped fonts that ship with the Macintosh include the familiar "city" fonts, such as Geneva, New York, Chicago, and Monaco. Some TrueType fonts, however, use the exact same name and have the same general appearance. In fact, both types of fonts may be contained within a single suitcase file. So how do you know which is which?

Identifying Fonts from the Finder If you go into the System folder and look at the icon of the font file, you can see that a bitmapped font icon has one A, while a TrueType font icon has three overlapping A's. Similarly, if you double-click a font file, it opens up to display a sample of what the font text looks like. Bitmapped fonts show only a sample in their single fixed size; TrueType fonts show samples in three different sizes.

Even their names give them away. Bitmapped fonts are always named with a number representing their size (New York 12), while TrueType fonts are named without any number (New York).

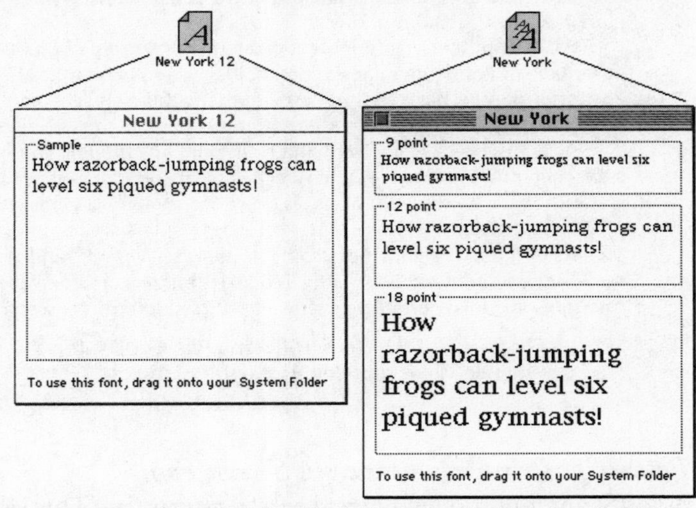

Figure 9-11 *A bitmapped font file (left) versus a TrueType font file (right).*

QuickDraw GX Alert: In QuickDraw GX, PostScript font icons and Get Info windows look just like the ones for TrueType fonts. This can be confusing! Check out Chapter 13 for more information.

Identifying a TrueType Font from Within Applications You can usually distinguish the presence of a TrueType font from directly within a text application. First select the font in question from the Font menu, and then check the Size menu. For TrueType fonts, all sizes in the menu should be in outline style—and if there is an Other size option, the word *Other* is also in outline style. If only bitmapped font files are present, only installed sizes are outlined, and the word *Other* is never outlined.

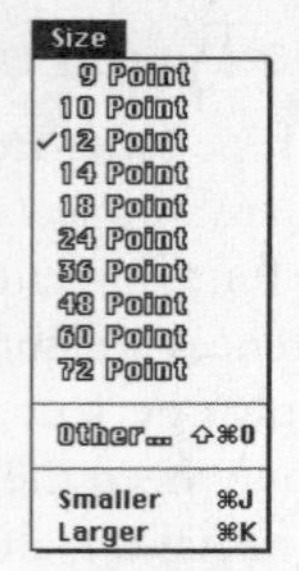

Figure 9-12 *The Size menu for a TrueType font.*

PostScript Fonts

PostScript outline fonts, which predated the arrival of TrueType fonts by several years, were originally developed by a company called Adobe. They instantly became an essential ingredient of high-quality output on a Macintosh. In fact, one of the reasons that Apple developed TrueType fonts was that it did not want Adobe, or any other company, controlling such an important part of the Macintosh technology. TrueType was Apple's answer to PostScript fonts.

TAKE NOTE ▶

WHAT IS POSTSCRIPT?

PostScript is a page description language that describes the location and appearance of text and graphics output, usually to a PostScript printer. When you use a PostScript printer, text and graphics (as displayed on your monitor) are translated into PostScript instructions. These instructions, in turn, are used to create the image of each page. The information needed to interpret these instructions and create the final printed output is built into the hardware of a PostScript printer.

PostScript printers can print text created with any type of font. To take maximum advantage of PostScript's capabilities, however, you need special PostScript fonts. Most PostScript printers have a set of PostScript fonts built into the hardware; other PostScript fonts can be downloaded from the Macintosh. Details are described in the main text.

Similarly, while a PostScript printer can print any graphic you see on the screen, it is at its best when printing graphics that directly utilize PostScript instructions (you need special software to create these graphics, as described more in Chapter 10).

The vast majority of Macintosh PostScript printers are laser printers, but not all laser printers include PostScript. For example, the LaserWriter LS and LaserWriter Select 300 are not PostScript printers. Dot-matrix and inkjet printers are generally non-PostScript devices (though some inkjet printers include a PostScript interpreter or can optionally add one).

SEE: • **Chapter 7, "Take Note: Different Types of Printers," for more on printer types**
• **Chapter 10 for more on PostScript graphics**

PostScript Printer Fonts versus Screen Fonts

A PostScript font is often referred to as a *printer font.* This is because a PostScript font file contains the PostScript instructions needed by a PostScript printer to create text output. Printer fonts, however, are completely unable to create an image of the text on the screen (since only the printer has the PostScript interpreter needed to make use of the

PostScript instructions). This makes them fundamentally different from bitmapped and TrueType fonts, which can generate both printed text and screen images.

Of course, in order to use PostScript fonts, you must be able to see the text on the screen. This problem was initially solved by the use of *screen fonts,* which are essentially ordinary bitmapped font versions of the PostScript fonts' appearance. When you select a PostScript font from a Font menu, you actually select and see the screen font on the screen, but selecting that font also tells the Macintosh to use the corresponding PostScript printer font when you print to a PostScript printer. Both types of font files are necessary to use PostScript fonts on a Macintosh.

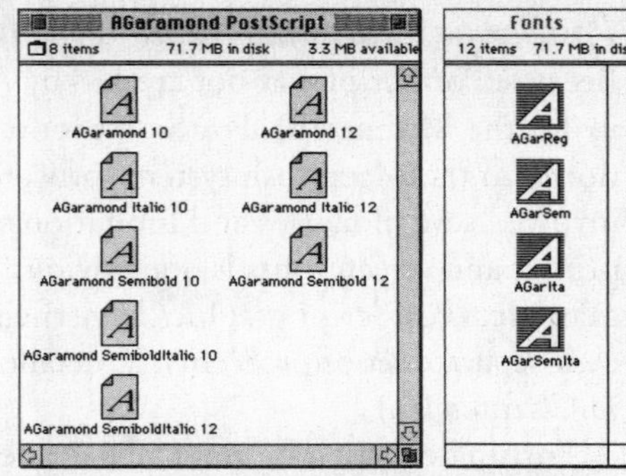

Figure 9-13 *The bitmapped screen fonts for the Adobe Garamond (AGaramond) font (left), and the matching printer font files for AGaramond (right).*

QuickDraw GX Alert: PostScript fonts work differently if you use QuickDraw GX. See "PostScript Fonts and QuickDraw GX," later in this chapter, or Chapter 13, for details.

In general, printer font files are stored in your System Folder (see "Locating, Adding, and Removing PostScript Printer Font Files from your System Folder," later in this chapter, for more details). They are also included directly in the (ROM) hardware of PostScript laser printers; for example, most Apple LaserWriters include Avant Garde, Bookman, Courier, Helvetica, Helvetica Narrow, New Century Schoolbook, Palatino, Symbol, Times, Zapf Chancery, and Zapf Dingbats. Thus, you do not need to place separate printer font files in your System Folder to use these fonts, only the corresponding screen fonts. (If your use of PostScript fonts is restricted to these built-in fonts, you may have never even seen PostScript printer font files.)

No printer font files are included with Macintosh system software, so you have to acquire them on your own. Adobe has a slew of excellent PostScript fonts, although at rather high prices. Other companies make less expensive PostScript fonts.

TECHNICALLY SPEAKING ▶

TYPE 1 VERSUS TYPE 3 POSTSCRIPT FONTS

You may occasionally hear reference to Type 1 versus Type 3 PostScript fonts (for some reason, there is no Type 2). Type 3 fonts are a relic from a time when Adobe tried to keep secret some of its ways of improving the appearance of fonts: Type 1 fonts contained special appearance-enhancing instructions, called hinting, that could not be used in Type 3 fonts. Only Adobe made Type 1 fonts, while Type 3 fonts were for everyone else. Since Adobe gave up on this restriction several years ago, though, you can pretty much assume that all your PostScript fonts are Type 1.

PostScript Fonts and Adobe Type Manager (ATM)

Because PostScript was not created by Apple (in fact, it was not even developed primarily for the Macintosh), PostScript fonts have not had TrueType's almost seamless integration into the Macintosh system software. Using PostScript for text has traditionally involved several hassles and limitations not found with TrueType. The need for separate printer and screen fonts is one obvious example. (PostScript graphics have their own separate set of problems, as detailed in Chapter 10.)

Fortunately, most of these text-related hassles can be overcome by using a control panel utility called Adobe Type Manager (ATM), which is designed to work exclusively with PostScript fonts (although the new version 4.0 also works with TrueType fonts). Adobe keeps releasing new versions of ATM, as it tries to keep up with changes in Apple's software and hardware. To avoid problems, make sure you have a recent (ideally, the latest available) version of ATM.

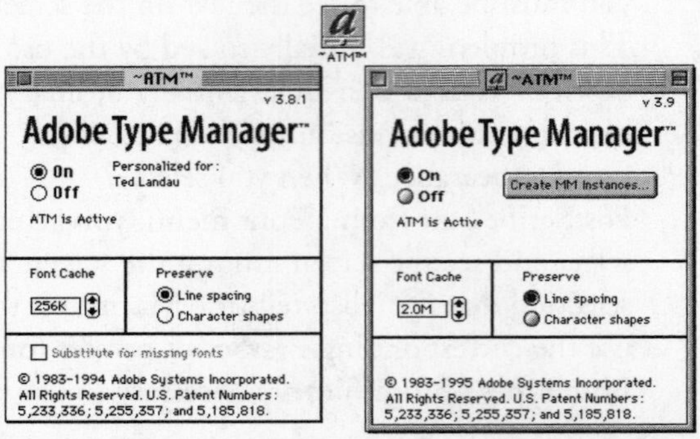

Figure 9-14 *ATM 3.8.1 (with "Substitute for missing fonts" option) and ATM 3.9 (with "Create MM Instances" option); both versions include the "Line spacing" versus "Character shapes" choice. All of these options are described in more detail later in this chapter (see: "Take Note: Substitute Fonts with ATM," "Technically Speaking: A Primer on Multiple-Master Fonts," "Fractional Widths and ATM," and "The Jaggies Appear Unexpectedly").*

ATM has so many benefits that, if you use PostScript fonts at all, ATM is nearly essential. Fortunately, you can purchase it directly from Adobe at a nominal charge (see Appendix); higher-priced versions of ATM typically include additional PostScript fonts on the disk. ATM also comes with almost every other Adobe product (such as Adobe Illustrator), as well as other software packages. Finally, a special version of ATM is included as part of the QuickDraw GX component of System 7.5 (see "PostScript Fonts and QuickDraw GX," later in this section).

Because of the importance of ATM, it is difficult to describe PostScript fonts and how they work without also describing how ATM modifies this process.

- **What about WYSIWYG?**

  Although screen fonts are designed to match what the PostScript printed output looks like, the match is almost never perfect. As a result, the Macintosh's normally close WYSIWYG relationship between the display and the printed output is broken. For example, line breaks might not always appear in the printed copy exactly as they appear on the screen.

  A related problem is the return of the jaggies on the screen. For example, suppose you pick a 17 point font size. Since you probably do not have a 17 point screen font, it will *display* with the jagged look described previously in the section on bitmapped fonts. It will still *print* out smooth as silk to a PostScript printer, however, because the printer font file is used to create the printed copy and the printer font uses PostScript (which, as with TrueType, is an outline font technology that prints smoothly at any point size).

TAKE NOTE ▶

ATM DELUXE:
A MAJOR UPGRADE FOR ADOBE TYPE MANAGER

A major new version of ATM, called Adobe Type Manager Deluxe (version 4.0), was released just around the time this book was going to press. It is a complete and major overhaul of the program, including an entirely new interface. With it, you will be able to create font sets (much as you can with Suitcase), both with TrueType fonts and PostScript fonts. You will even be able to analyze your fonts to check for possible damage. You will also be able to create anti-aliased "smooth font edges" on screen. This creates an even smoother look than the main effect of using ATM.

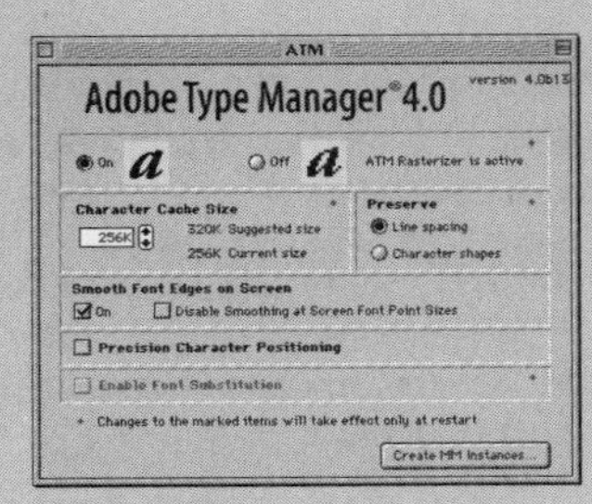

Figure 9-15 *Adobe Type Manager Deluxe, a major upgrade to this essential utility.*

- **ATM to the rescue (part 1)**
ATM solves most of the WYSIWYG problems just described. In particular, it uses printer font instructions to generate an image of the font on the screen that can be smoothly scaled to any selected size! The jaggies vanish, much like what happens with TrueType fonts. The WYSIWYG matching of lines breaks and character spacing, while not necessarily perfect (especially because of likely differences in the resolution of the monitor versus the printer), will also be improved.

A minor problem remains with the look of the Size menus. Unlike TrueType, ATM does not affect what sizes are outlined in Size menus. Thus, if the Palatino 18 screen font is not installed, the 18 in the Size menu will not be outlined. Don't be fooled, though—with ATM installed, the font will still print *and* display without the jaggies.

Bitmapped Palatino 14 point

Bitmapped Palatino 18 point

ATM Palatino 14 point

ATM Palatino 18 point

TrueType Palatino 14 point

TrueType Palatino 18 point

Figure 9-16 *Samples of screen displays of bit-mapped, ATM-generated, and TrueType Palatino text; there are no jaggies, but each type looks somewhat different.*

Given all of this, you may now be asking: If I use ATM, does this mean that I no longer need screen fonts at all? Unfortunately, you still do need screen fonts. More precisely, you need at least one point size of a screen font for every PostScript font you use, because the screen font is necessary just to get the font name to appear in Font menus. Also, since screen fonts at smaller point sizes (12 points or less) generally look better than ATM-generated screen displays, it is common to have 9-point, 10-point, and/or 12-point screen fonts in use, even if you have ATM installed.

Finally, note that if you are using the PostScript fonts that are built into your PostScript printer (such as the previously mentioned Times, Helvetica, and so forth), you still need to install the corresponding printer font files in your System Folder in order for ATM to create smooth screen displays. ATM cannot access the printer font files in your printer.

TECHNICALLY SPEAKING ▶

ALL IN THE FAMILY

If you have ever purchased a PostScript font and tried to install it, you may notice that things are often a bit more complicated than I have implied here (as if they weren't already complicated enough!). In particular, you may find that several printer font files exist for the same font family. For example, the Adobe Garamond font includes four printer font files: AGarReg (for plain text), AGarSem (bold), AGarIta (italics), and AGarSemIta (bold and italics combined). All four printer font files are needed for these common styles to appear correctly in printed copy. For example, if you only installed AGarReg, but not the other AGar printer files, Adobe Garamond text will appear correctly in bold or italics on the screen, but as plain text when printed.

This is also why, for example, you can display the Bold style for the Zapf Chancery font (which is a font built into your LaserWriter) on your screen, but the LaserWriter will not print it as bold. This is because Apple chose to include only the plain-text printer font for Zapf Chancery in the printer.

You may also find that a separate set of bitmapped screen fonts is included to match each of the different style variants of the printer font files. For example, there may be screen fonts of various sizes for AGaramond (plain text), AGaramond Semibold, AGaramond Italic, and AGaramond SemiboldItalic. If installed, these appear as separate fonts in the Font menu (which can considerably clutter up your Font menu). If the font files were created correctly, however, the Macintosh should recognize all these variations as belonging to the same font family.

Unlike for the printer fonts, it is usually not necessary to use these screen font style variants. You could still select different styles from the Style menu without them, because printed appearance is determined primarily by the presence of the printer files, not the screen fonts. For example, when printing with most applications, selecting Italic from the Style menu for the AGaramond font usually duplicates the effect of directly selecting the AGaramond Italic font from the Font menu (assuming all the printer font files are installed). Experiment with this on your equipment—if your printed output is satisfactory with only the plain text screen font installed, you can skip the others.

Actually, there are advantages to using the Style menu method. For example, if you select Italic from the Style menu for AGaramond text but change to a different font later, the text will remain in italics. This would not happen if, instead, you had selected AGaramond Italic from the Font menu.

(Continues on next page) ▶

- **What if the printer font file is missing?**
  As I have already implied, if you select a presumed PostScript font from a Font menu but its PostScript font file is missing, it will not print in PostScript, even if you are using a PostScript printer (unless, of course, it is one of the fonts built into the printer). Instead, the screen font prints directly. A PostScript printer, however, will still probably do a better job of printing the screen font than a non-PostScript printer would. This is because a PostScript printer generates a temporary outline-like font file for the font when it goes to print it. It won't look nearly as good as if a true printer font was present, but you may find it acceptable if you have no other alternative.

  Similarly, even if you are using ATM, you still need PostScript printer fonts. If you just have the screen font, ATM is irrelevant; the printed output and the screen display will be the same as if you were not using PostScript fonts at all!

SEE: • **"Take Note: Substitute Fonts with ATM," later in this chapter, for related information**

TECHNICALLY SPEAKING

ALL IN THE FAMILY *(Continued)*

The main advantage of using the separate style variants of screen fonts is that they typically enhance the WYSIWYG matching of the screen to the printed output. This is because the Macintosh uses the variant file, when available, to create the screen display rather than trying to approximate it from the plain text file (sometimes called a "false style"). The approximation method usually results in a less accurate match than using the style variant. For a few applications, character spacing of printed output may also be improved with the use of the style variants.

By the way, don't be surprised if you do not have these variant screen fonts for your PostScript fonts, because not all PostScript fonts come with separate files for different styles. For example, for the PostScript fonts that come with Apple's LaserWriters, Apple includes only the plain text screen fonts, without the other screen font variants. You would have the style variants only if you obtained the font directly from Adobe.

Also note that screen font variants may come in forms that are not a direct match for the Italics and Bold styles in the Style menu (Demi, Light, and the like refer to different degrees of "boldness"). This is another reason why selecting the screen font variant may lead to different output than selecting the comparable style from the Style menu; this applies to TrueType fonts as well as PostScript fonts. In general, for TrueType fonts, keeping and using style variants will lead to better display and printing quality.

Finally, if you use multiple-master fonts, there are other special factors to consider.

SEE:
- **"Technically Speaking: A Primer on Multiple-Master Fonts," near the end of this chapter**
- **"Technically Speaking: Different Versions of Screen Fonts for the Same PostScript Font," later in this chapter, for related information**
- **"Font Menu Clutter," later in this chapter, for possible problems with using separate screen fonts for different styles of the same font**

- **What if you don't have a PostScript printer?**
  Another traditional problem with using PostScript fonts, again as already implied, is that they require a PostScript printer. If you try to print PostScript text to a non-PostScript printer, the bitmapped screen font once again prints directly (as if it were an ordinary bitmapped font) whether or not the PostScript printer font is present.

- **ATM to the rescue (part 2)**
  Here is the second major benefit of using ATM: You can use it to print PostScript text even to a non-PostScript printer. In essence, the ATM software substitutes for the printer's PostScript interpreter, which would otherwise be needed.

  With ATM, as long as you have the relevant printer font files installed, text output to a non-PostScript printer looks about the same as the output from a PostScript printer *of the same resolution.* ImageWriter output will never look as good as LaserWriter output, even with ATM, because the ImageWriter is a lower-resolution printer. Output from inkjet printers (such as Apple's StyleWriter) and non-PostScript laser printers (such as Apple's LaserWriter Select 300), however, look almost identical to output from 300-dpi PostScript printers.

  By the way, remember that ATM only affects text. If you plan on printing PostScript graphics (see Chapter 10), ATM is of no help; you still need a PostScript printer.

PostScript Fonts and QuickDraw GX

Even though I have postponed the primary discussion of QuickDraw GX until Chapter 13, there is an important change in how PostScript fonts work in QuickDraw GX that I should mention right now: *You no longer need separate printer fonts and screen fonts with QuickDraw GX.* These two components are combined into a single font file that resembles a TrueType font. Though you still need ATM to get everything to work properly, a GX-compatible version of ATM is included with QuickDraw GX. The result is that PostScript fonts in QuickDraw GX work almost indistinguishably from TrueType fonts. Virtually all of the previous "hassles" of using PostScript are gone. Still, because of other overhead associated with QuickDraw GX, users may not rush to adopt this technology (which is why I defer discussing it until Chapter 13).

Locating, Adding, and Removing PostScript Printer Font Files from Your System Folder

In the section on Font Basics, I described the changing location of font files from System 6 to System 7.5. All of that material applied both to bitmapped fonts (including the screen fonts of PostScript fonts) and TrueType fonts. The PostScript printer font files, however, work a bit differently.

First, unless you are using QuickDraw GX (as mentioned in the previous section), printer font files cannot be included in suitcases, nor can they be installed in a System file (no matter what version of the system software you are using).

TECHNICALLY SPEAKING ▶

AUTOMATIC VERSUS MANUAL DOWNLOADING

When you print a document using PostScript fonts that are not built into the printer, the needed information from the relevant printer font files is downloaded to the printer at the time the document is printed, then cleared from the printer's memory when the document is finished printing. This means that the next time you print a document that uses the same fonts, the information has to be downloaded again. This repeated automatic downloading takes time and consequently slows down the printing process.

As an alternative, you can manually download a font to the printer by using Apple's LaserWriter Utility or Apple Printer Utility. Manually downloaded fonts stay in the printer's memory until you shut down (although you can download only as many fonts as can fit into the printer's memory at one time). If you plan to use the same few fonts repeatedly, this can be worthwhile, but in most cases manual downloading does not save much time. Most users prefer the simpler and more transparent automatic downloading.

For fonts that are built into a PostScript printer, no downloading of any sort is needed; they are already there.

(A note for users of Type 1 PostScript fonts converted to QuickDraw GX format: To use the Apple Printer Utility to download the fonts manually to a PostScript printer, you need to select the printer fonts as stored in the •Archived Type 1 Fonts• folder, not the converted GX fonts.)

SEE: • **Chapter 7, "By the Way: Help from Apple Printer Utility," for more on these utilities**
• **Chapter 13 for more on QuickDraw GX**

Second, the correct location within a System Folder to place printer font files varies a bit from what was true for other font files. In particular, in System 6, printer fonts can be located anywhere at the root level of the System Folder. In System 7.0, they should be stored in the Extensions folder. In System 7.1 or 7.5, they should be stored in the Fonts folder (though they will also work if stored in the Extensions folder). Unlike other font types, you can add or remove printer font files to or from any location in a System Folder without getting any alert messages, even if other applications are open.

How to Identify a PostScript Font

There is no clear way to know if you are using a PostScript font just by checking an application's Font menu or Size menu. To find out if a given font is a PostScript font, check the System Folder for the presence of PostScript printer font files. There are several different possible icons for PostScript fonts, but they will all have "PostScript font" as their Kind in their Get Info window.

For fonts that are built directly into your PostScript printer, there may not be a printer font file present for you to check. For a list of these built-in fonts, check the manual that came with your printer (for instant help, the family names of the fonts built into most LaserWriters were listed in a previous section, "PostScript Printer Fonts versus Screen Fonts). Otherwise, you can use LaserWriter Utility or Apple Printer Utility, which will check a PostScript laser printer and create a list of all the fonts built into the printer. To do this, select "Display Available Fonts" from the program's File menu.

SEE: • **Chapter 7, "By the Way: Help from Apple Printer Utility," for more information**

Eventually, you should be able to recall from memory which of your fonts are PostScript and which are not.

If you use Now Utilities, its WYSIWYG Menus control panel has a feature that identifies PostScript, TrueType, and bitmapped fonts from its control panel window.

QuickDraw GX Alert: In QuickDraw GX, PostScript fonts appear exactly like TrueType fonts, even using the same icon. Since the Get Info window provides no clue either way, there is no easy way in this case to tell whether a font is a TrueType font or a PostScript font (although you can see Chapter 13 for more help here.)

Combining TrueType, PostScript, and/or Bitmapped Versions of the Same Font

It is entirely permissible to mix font formats for the same font family within the System Folder. For example, you may have installed the 10-point and 12-point bitmapped versions of Times to use as screen fonts, plus a TrueType version of the Times font. If you are using a PostScript LaserWriter, you also have the PostScript printer font of Times built into the printer.

Are there problems with doing this? Advantages, perhaps? The answer is yes to both questions. To understand why, you first need to understand the rules that determine which font is used for the screen display and for printed output when multiple competing types are present.

What Font Format Is Displayed?

The font format displayed on the screen when more than one format of the same font is installed is determined according to the following priority list. The Macintosh uses the first format on the list, if it is available, skipping to items lower on the list as necessary:

- Bitmapped font, if the selected size is available
- TrueType font
- ATM-generated PostScript font
- Bitmapped font scaled from a different size (which usually results in the jaggies), if selected size is not available

What Font Format Prints?

Which font format is used for printing when more than one format of the same font is installed is governed by a different set of rules from those used for the screen display. Furthermore, the rules vary depending on whether or not you are using a PostScript printer.

PostScript printers use the following, in order of preference:

- PostScript fonts built into the printer's ROM
- PostScript fonts contained in the active System Folder (with or without ATM)
- TrueType fonts
- Bitmapped fonts

Non-PostScript printers use the following, in order of preference:

- TrueType fonts
- ATM-generated PostScript fonts
- Bitmapped fonts

What It All Means

Bitmapped fonts get the highest priority for screen display, but they get the lowest priority for printing! Although this may seem illogical at first, it does make sense.

To understand why, return to the previous example. If you have Times 10 and Times 12 installed, these bitmapped fonts are used for the screen display at those sizes. Such fonts generally offer the best possible screen appearance for these small sizes because, as described in previous sections, even if you use an outline font, the screen display itself remains a bitmap (that is, a collection of dots). The outline font instructions must be converted to a bitmapped approximation in order for it to be displayed. Bitmapped fonts at installed sizes, because they do not depend on any approximation, can best utilize the screen display.

The Times TrueType font kicks in at other sizes. This has the advantage of eliminating the jaggies at these sizes without requiring a separate bitmapped file for each size. (You could have used ATM to obtain this same benefit, but this would have also required installing printer font files. In essence you are using TrueType here, instead of ATM, to avoid the jaggies—the matching TrueType font serves as the screen font for the PostScript font. Many times, however, you will not have a matching TrueType font available, so this option will not apply.)

When you print to a LaserWriter, the printer's built-in PostScript Times font takes over, overriding both the bitmapped and the TrueType instructions in order to provide the highest-quality output possible with your PostScript printer.

Still, many experts recommend not combining TrueType and PostScript versions of the same font. This is primarily because TrueType-based screen display may have a different appearance, in terms of line breaks and character spacing, from PostScript-based printed output. Results can be especially hard to predict if you have different screen fonts and different TrueType fonts for different styles of the same font (such as Times Bold and Times Italic). I have made these sorts of combinations in several cases without any problem, however, so experiment for yourself. In any case, placing TrueType fonts and PostScript fonts from different families in the System Folder is not a problem at all.

Which Font Format Should You Use?

Suppose you have bitmapped, TrueType, and PostScript versions of the same font (such as Times). Assuming you would like to use only one of these formats for creating your text, which should you prefer? Or suppose you are considering purchasing a collection of fonts, and you need to decide whether you want them to be TrueType or PostScript. Which should you get? Here are some guidelines for solving these and other similar dilemmas.

Limit Your Use of Bitmapped Fonts

Use bitmapped fonts mainly for display of text at small sizes. They make a clearer display and will redraw faster than TrueType fonts. If possible, use bitmapped fonts only in conjunction with TrueType or PostScript (with ATM) versions of the same font, so that the bitmapped version is not used for printing. Otherwise, try to avoid bitmapped fonts altogether, especially with a high-resolution (300 dpi or higher) printer.

Occasionally, large point sizes of bitmapped fonts may be useful if you're printing to a low-resolution printer, such as an ImageWriter. They may print better than the ATM or TrueType versions.

If you do print bitmapped text to a PostScript LaserWriter, it probably will look better than you might expect. This is because (as mentioned earlier in this chapter), a PostScript LaserWriter creates a temporary outline-like font file for the font, so that the font prints relatively smoothly at any size. ATM may even create a "substitute font" (see "Take Note: Substitute Fonts with ATM," later in this chapter).

Checking the "Smooth Text" option from the PostScript Options section of the Page Setup box may also help improve appearance of printed bitmapped fonts (the option is irrelevant for other types of fonts). Still, the converted and smoothed bitmapped output remains inferior to the quality you would get from a true PostScript font.

BY THE WAY ▶

PRINTING SCREEN FONTS AS BITMAPPED FONTS

Screen fonts are not usually printed; they serve only to create the screen display for a matching PostScript printer font. If you do not have the matching printer font installed (or if you are using a non-PostScript printer without ATM), however, the screen font prints directly, just like any other bitmapped font. If you try this, you may find that screen fonts do not print as attractively as bitmapped fonts that are specifically designed to be printed. This is because screen fonts are usually designed with an emphasis more on how well their screen display matches the related PostScript printed output than on how they actually print out. (Of course, if you are using TrueType or PostScript fonts for printing, as recommended, all of this is irrelevant.)

Deciding Between PostScript and TrueType

PostScript (especially with ATM) and TrueType are both excellent font technologies. To a large extent, which looks better depends on the design of the particular font, not the technology. If your primary use of text is for minimally formatted documents, such as reports and manuscripts, either type of font is likely to be adequate.

PostScript, however, does have some advantages. As a group, PostScript fonts tend to be superior in appearance to the corresponding TrueType fonts. A wider selection of PostScript fonts than TrueType fonts is available, though this gap is rapidly disappearing. Most notable, PostScript is the standard font format used by typesetters and is likely to cause them fewer problems than TrueType fonts—an important consideration if you plan to have documents printed professionally by a service bureau. Also, if you plan on using PostScript graphics, you will probably prefer to use PostScript fonts as well.

On the other hand, each Macintosh comes with a selection of TrueType fonts at no extra cost. For some people, that alone is reason enough to prefer them. TrueType also has an advantage in its simplicity and better integration with other system software, although using QuickDraw GX sharply reduces this advantage.

With PostScript you can create special effects, such as rotated text and shading of text, that are either not possible or difficult to achieve with standard TrueType. There are also special PostScript fonts (called multiple-master fonts) that let you vary the characteristics of a font, including its weight and width. With QuickDraw GX, however, TrueType can duplicate most if not all of these effects—as long as your software has been rewritten to be QuickDraw GX-savvy (which is still not common).

Finally, if you are really determined to stick to one format, there are software programs that you can use to convert a PostScript font into a TrueType one, or vice versa.

So, should you use PostScript or TrueType? There is no easy answer; I use them both.

SEE: • Chapter 13 for more on QuickDraw GX

Consider Your Printer

- **For PostScript printers**
  Print with PostScript fonts if you can, using ATM to improve screen displays of these fonts. You can also use TrueType fonts. If you have installed TrueType and PostScript versions of the same font, TrueType is not used for printing.
- **For non-PostScript printers**
  Use either TrueType fonts or ATM-generated PostScript fonts.

Keep It Simple

Don't overload your System Folder with fonts you rarely or never use. When you must use bitmapped versions of fonts, keep only those sizes that you use frequently.

Summing Up

Table 9-1 presents a summary of much of the information covered so far in this chapter.

Table 9-1 Font Basics Summary[1]

	BITMAPPED FONT	TRUETYPE FONT	POSTSCRIPT FONT[2]
Icons	or	or	Several possible icons, including: or
Location in System 6 System Folder[3]	System file (via Font/DA Mover)	System file (via Font/DA Mover)[4]	Any location in System Folder
Location in System 7.0 System Folder[3]	System file (can be directly opened)	System file (can be directly opened)	Extensions folder
Location in System 7.1 or later System Folder[3]	Fonts folder	Fonts folder	Fonts folder
Can font be stored in suitcase and/or exist as a separate file?	Font suitcases (in all system versions) or separate files (System 7 only)	Font suitcases (in all system versions) or separate files (System 7 only)	Separate files only (unless using QuickDraw GX)
Is screen display smooth?	Smooth only if selected size is installed	Smooth at any size	Smooth only if bitmapped font for selected size is installed or if using ATM
Is PostScript printer output smooth?	Generally smooth, but looks best if selected size is installed	Smooth at any size	Smooth at any size
Is non-PostScript printer output smooth?	Smooth only if selected size is installed	Smooth at any size	Smooth only if bitmap font for selected size is installed or if using ATM

1 *Changes due to QuickDraw GX are covered more in Chapter 13*

2 *Matching screen font needed to create screen display (except in QuickDraw GX)*

3 *If you use Suitcase or a similar utility, fonts may be stored anywhere on your disk*

4 *Requires System 6.0.7 or later and the TrueType INIT extension*

Solve It! Text and Font Problems

This section gives specific advice about various problems with the display and printing of text and with using fonts in general. The emphasis is on problems that can occur with almost all Macintoshes and most printers. Some advice specific to certain printers (such as LaserWriters and ImageWriters), however, is also included.

SEE: • **Chapter 7 for a more general discussion of printing-related problems**
• **Chapter 10 for display and printing problems specific to graphics documents**

A Document Displays the Wrong Font

Symptoms:

A previously saved text document is opened. The file opens normally, except that the fonts displayed are different from the ones selected when the document was last saved. For example, the document may have been saved using Garamond, but it now opens using Geneva instead.

Causes:

The Necessary Font Is Not in Your System Folder

This could occur, for example, if you open a document that uses a font you have since deleted from your startup disk. Or perhaps you are using a document obtained from a colleague, and the font has never been on your disk.

When this happens, the document typically opens using either a default system font (most likely Geneva or Chicago) or the application's default font (usually Geneva, New York, or Helvetica). You may also get an alert message warning you of what has happened.

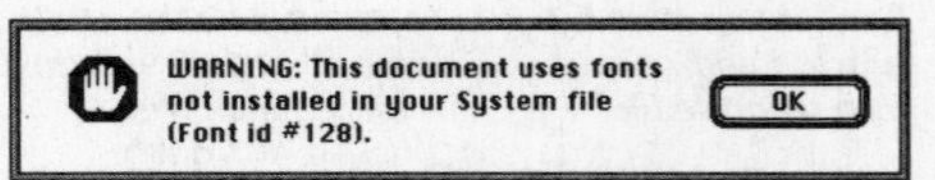

Figure 9-17 *A message that may appear if you open a document that uses a font not currently installed in your System Folder.*

By the way, if you click in an area of text and go to the Font menu, the assigned font name for the text where the I-beam is located should have a checkmark in front of it. If no font name is checked, this probably means that the assigned font is not available and a substitute font has been used instead. (For example, the text might display in Geneva, but the Geneva name will not be checked. If you do not see a checked font in the Font menu when you highlight—rather than just click in—an area of text, however, this could also be because the highlighted area includes text of two or more different fonts.

A Font ID Number Conflict Has Occurred

Though you do not normally need to be aware of this, every font file has its own ID number that is initially assigned by the developer who created the file. The Macintosh uses these numbers to identify the font internally. Within certain limits, what ID number is assigned to a font is arbitrary; as a result, it is possible for two different fonts to wind up with the same ID number.

Two fonts in the same location (the same suitcase file or the same System file) cannot share the same ID number. If you try to install two identically numbered fonts to the same location, the Macintosh automatically assigns a new ID number to one of the fonts to resolve the conflict.

This numbering system is not likely to cause any immediate problems—as long as you stick to your own computer and use only documents you've created. Problems can occur if you send or receive documents to or from other users. For example, suppose you have two fonts, Futura and Frontier, that initially have the same ID number. When you install them both to your System file, Futura is assigned a new ID number to resolve the conflict. Now you create a document using the Futura font. So far, so good—but later, you take this document to be printed elsewhere. Even though the other computer has the Futura font, it probably uses the font's original ID number. As a result, the other Macintosh does not correctly identify the Futura font in your document and probably displays and prints the document in some other font.

The good news is that this problem is becoming increasingly rare, beause new ID numbering formats have reduced the probability of two fonts having the same ID number. Similarly, newer software typically identifies fonts by the font's name rather than its ID number; since names should be unique, conflicts are largely eliminated. For people who regularly take their documents to outside sources to be printed, however, this remains a potential source of trouble.

By the way, a font's ID name is separate from the font's file name in the Finder. This means you could potentially change a font's file name without affecting how the font is listed in a Font menu.

A Font File Is Damaged

If a font file is damaged, text using that font may not be displayed properly.

 **What to do:**

Check the Font Menu

If a document opens in the wrong font (and you know what the correct font should be), check whether the intended font is listed in the Font menu.

If the Correct Font Is Not Listed in the Font Menu

Check Key Caps Some applications don't list all installed fonts in their Font menu. You can always use the Key Caps desk accessory to see a complete Font menu list. If the font shows up in Key Caps, check the problem application's manual for how to access the "missing" font.

If you don't see the font in any Font menu, this probably means that the font is not currently installed. To check and fix this, follow these steps:

1. **Quit Without Saving** Quit the application you are using, but *without* saving the document. This prevents you saving any incorrect font information.
2. **Check Your System Folder** Go to the location in your System Folder where your installed fonts are stored (the System file, Extensions folder, and/or Fonts folder). See if the font is listed there.

   While you're at it, make sure you are using the System Folder. If you are using a startup disk different from the one you normally use, this alone could account for the "missing" fonts.
3. **Get the Font** If the font isn't in your System Folder, the solution is simple. Assuming you have access to the needed font, get it and install it.

   SEE: • **"Font Basics," earlier in this chapter, for more on where fonts are stored and how to install them**
4. **Check for Font Menu Problems** If the font is correctly installed in your System Folder but still does not appear in the Font menu, check for special problems with Font menu listings.

   SEE: • **"Fonts Unexpectedly Appear or Disappear from Font Menus," later in this chapter, for more on locating missing font files and related problems**

TAKE NOTE ▶

SUBSTITUTE FONTS WITH ATM

With ATM, if a text document includes fonts not currently installed in your System Folder, you can still create a nearly identical substitute version of the font that preserves the general appearance and line breaks of the document.

This feature was originally found only in SuperATM (a product that has since been dropped from Adobe's catalog), but it is now included with versions of the basic ATM. In some versions, you may find a checkbox option called "Substitute for missing fonts" in the ATM control panel; if so, you need to check it to turn this feature on. (In even more recent versions, this feature appears to be built in, with no checkbox option included.) You will also need a file called ATM Font Database that is installed at the root level of your System Folder (a mini-version of this file is included with Adobe Acrobat Reader). You also need the Adobe SansMM and Adobe SerifMM fonts. Without these files, the "substitute for missing fonts" checkbox, even if present, will likely be dimmed.

Admittedly this all gets a bit confusing. If you simply install ATM as directed, however, most of the hassle will likely be taken care of for you automatically. On the down side, this feature only works with PostScript fonts, and even then it may be incompatible with some applications.

More generally, programs such as Acrobat—as well as Apple's PPD feature in QuickDraw GX—can create documents that can be viewed and printed in their originally assigned fonts, even if the viewer does not have the needed fonts installed (or even if you are missing the creating application!).

SEE ALSO: • **"Technically Speaking: A Primer on Multiple-Master Fonts," near the end of this chapter, for related information**

BY THE WAY ▶

FONT NOT FOUND

If you select a font from a Font menu and get a message that says "font not found," this may indicate that ATM did not have enough memory to create a substitute font. To solve this problem, increase the size of the ATM Font Cache from the ATM Control Panel.

TAKE NOTE ▶

PROBLEMS WITH QUICKDRAW GX FONTS

PostScript font files are different in QuickDraw GX and in non-GX systems. If you install a GX PostScript font in a non-GX System Folder, its name should appear in the Font menu. If you try to format text with this font, however, the text may display in Geneva rather than the actual font. You may have similar problems if you install the special TrueType fonts used by QuickDraw GX. Conversely, using a non-GX style PostScript font in a GX system will not work, but you can use non-GX TrueType fonts in either system.

Even when you are not running GX, however, QuickDraw GX fonts can *print* okay if you have a LaserWriter with 3MB or more of RAM (unfortunately this requirement excludes most LaserWriters).

SEE: • Chapter 13, on QuickDraw GX, for more details on the new font formats

If the Font Is Listed in the Font Menu

Replace a Damaged Font You may have a damaged font file, so replace it from your backups. This should fix the problem unless your backup copy is also damaged.

SEE: • "Font Basics," earlier in this chapter, for more on deleting and replacing fonts
• "Solve It! Font File Problems," later in this chapter

Check for Font ID Conflict If the trouble persists, you probably have a font ID conflict. The easiest solution for this problem is to select the text with the incorrect font and then select the correct font from the Font menu. The text should now display properly; if it does, you will probably have no further problems. Save the changed document, and it should open properly next time.

Otherwise, go to the System Folder location of your fonts. Delete both the font currently used to display the text and the font that should have been used, then reinstall both of them from your backups. Try opening the document again, and see if the font now displays as expected.

For Documents Sent to Outside Sources If you are regularly plagued by ID conflicts because you send documents to outside sources (such as professional typesetters) and the documents you send print in the wrong font, you may need some special solutions. For example, you could include a copy of your System file and the related Fonts and Extensions folders to be used when printing your document.

Check for Duplicate ID Numbers You may encounter a related ID conflict problem if you use a font management utility, such as Suitcase, or if you use System 7.1 or 7.5. In these cases, fonts can be installed and accessed by the System directly from font suitcase files. If two different fonts in different suitcases have the same ID number, neither ID number is changed, and the conflict remains. The usual result is that you can use only one of the two fonts, even though both may be listed in your Font menu. The solution is to get the Macintosh to renumber the ID of one of the fonts. Typically, this is easily done by combining both fonts into one suitcase, thus forcing a renumbering.

Older versions of Suitcase included a supplemental utility, called Font Harmony, designed to resolve this sort of conflict. The current version does not have this utility anymore, probably in recognition of the decreased probability of this type of problem occurring.

Seek Outside Help ID conflicts can be messy to diagnose and difficult to solve. If the explanations given in this section are not sufficient to resolve your problem, it's time to seek outside help.

SEE: • **Fix-It #18 on seeking outside help**

If You Still Can't Use the Font

If none of this works, or you have no idea what the missing font should be or you do not have access to it, you are out of luck. You will have to reformat the text using a font that is available.

TAKE NOTE ▶

INCORRECT TEXT CHARACTERS AND INTERNATIONAL KEYBOARD LAYOUTS

If pressing a keyboard key results in an incorrect character appearing on the display (such as "y" appearing when you press the "z" key) or if foreign-language characters appear instead of the expected English characters, you probably have shifted inadvertently to an international keyboard layout. Normally you would do this by selecting a layout from the Keyboard control panel, which would be difficult to do by accident. Because a keyboard shortcut (Command-Option-Spacebar) also cycles you through the different available layouts, however, you may have changed layouts without realizing it by pressing this key combination.

If this happens, go to the Keyboard control panel and reselect the "U.S." layout (unless you actually need an international layout). To prevent the problem from happening again, double-click the System file icon to open its window (this is where the keyboard layouts are stored) and delete all layout files (the ones with names like British, Danish, and French). The default U.S. layout is built into the system software and does not require a special layout file.

Otherwise, to prevent this inadvertent switching of keyboard layouts permanently, you can simply disable the Keyboard extension. Even better, System 7.5 Update 1.0 or later adds a checkbox to the Keyboard window that allows you to turn off the keyboard shortcut. (The checkbox is off by default.)

A Document Prints with a Different Font from the One Displayed

Symptoms:

- A document displays on the screen with the selected font, but a different font is used when printing.
- Specifically for PostScript printers: The displayed font is Geneva, New York, or Monaco, and the printed font is Helvetica, Times, or Courier.
- Specifically for PostScript printers: The displayed font is any PostScript font, and the printed font is Courier.

Causes:

A Font File Is Damaged

If a font file is damaged, text using that font may not print in that font, even if it is displayed correctly on the screen.

Problems Specific to PostScript LaserWriters

Some problems are a direct result of checking a specific option in the Page Setup dialog box (for example, fonts changing because the Substitute Fonts option was selected). Others may have a more general cause, such as insufficient memory in the printer.
By the way, the dialog boxes described and pictured here are those of the LaserWriter 8 driver. Users of previous versions of the LaserWriter driver will have similar options, but with a somewhat different layout of the dialog box (as briefly described in Chapter 7). If you use the QuickDraw GX version of the LaserWriter, check out Chapter 13.

Otherwise ...

Problems with low memory are usually the cause.

What to do:

Replace a Damaged Font

You may have a damaged font file. If so, replace the font from your backups. This should fix the problem unless your backup copy is also damaged.

SEE: • **"Font Basics," earlier in this chapter, for more on deleting and replacing fonts**
• **"Solve It! Font File Problems," later in this chapter**

StyleWriter: Problems with Low Memory

If a document's font changes about halfway down a page when printing to a StyleWriter or StyleWriter II with background printing on, you usually are having trouble with low memory. To solve this problem in the short run, turn background printing off (or add more memory to your desktop printer); in the long run, add more memory to your Macintosh. Actually, these same solutions apply to any other printer that exhibits similar problems.

SEE: • **Chapter 7, especially "Take Note: Troubleshooting StyleWriters," for related information**

PostScript LaserWriters: Uncheck Substitute Fonts or Change the Font

LaserWriter 8's Substitute Fonts option, located in the PostScript Options window of the Page Setup dialog box, is usually checked by default. In older LaserWriter driver versions, this option is called Font Substitution and is found in the main Page Setup dialog box.

If this option is checked, any text displayed in the Geneva, New York, or Monaco fonts will be printed in Helvetica, Times, and Courier, respectively. It will do this whether these screen fonts are bitmapped or TrueType, although it will not substitute for any other fonts. This option will not only cause your display and printout to have different fonts but result in differing line and page breaks as well. The purpose of Substitute Fonts, which originated before TrueType fonts existed, was to use the higher-quality PostScript fonts for printing instead of the bitmapped fonts that were displayed.

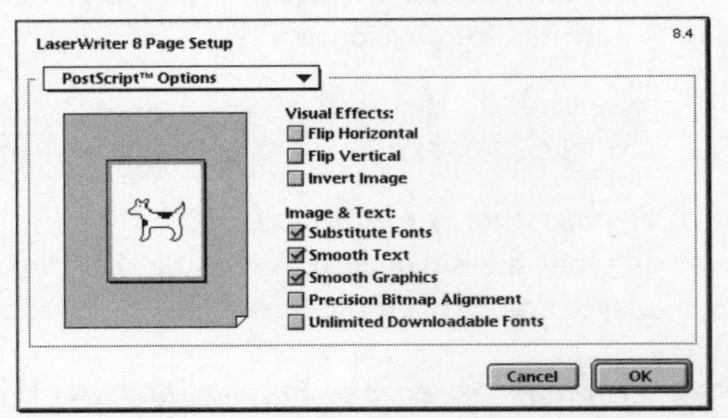

Figure 9-18 *The PostScript Options window from LaserWriter 8.4's Page Setup dialog box, accessed by selecting PostScript Options from the pop-up menu. Here is where the Substitute Fonts and Unlimited Downloadable Fonts options are found.*

To avoid these problems, uncheck the Substitute Fonts option. This forces the document to print using the actual font displayed on the screen. The LaserWriter will use TrueType if it's available for that font; if not, the bitmapped font prints directly.

Alternatively, if you want to print using a PostScript font, then simply select it for screen display as well—for example, select all instances of the Geneva font in your document and change them to Helvetica (or any other PostScript font of your choosing).

PostScript LaserWriters: Check Unlimited Downloadable Fonts in a Document

Sometimes, especially if your document uses many different PostScript fonts, the document will print out entirely in the Courier font rather than the fonts you selected.

The cause here is usually that there isn't enough memory in the printer to hold all the different PostScript information needed to print your document. Usually you should get an alert message informing you of this problem, but sometimes things get mixed up and your document simply is printed in the Courier font instead.

One way to try to solve this problem is to select the Unlimited Downloadable Fonts in a Document option (available from the Page Setup dialog box). This doesn't always work, but it is worth a try. It allows the needed font information to be swapped in and out of the printer's memory as needed, rather than be loaded in all at once (as would otherwise be required). Although this option permits an unlimited number of fonts to be used, it tends to slow down the printing process.

Simplify the Document An alternative solution is to simplify the document by using fewer fonts or by dividing up the document into separately printed segments.

PostScript LaserWriters: Uncheck Unlimited Downloadable Fonts in a Document

I know, I know, this is the opposite of what I just told you. The resolution of this contradiction is that the advice to *un*check this option only applies when you are printing fonts as part of a graphic (such as an EPS or PICT file) and the fonts print incorrectly. In this case, unchecking this option may help. By the way, printing fonts, especially PostScript fonts, are often a source of trouble with PICT documents. Try to avoid this combination if you can.

SEE:
- **"PostScript Fonts Do Not Print Using PostScript" and "The Jaggies Appear Unexpectedly," later in this chapter, for related problems**
- **Chapter 7 for a more general discussion of memory-related printing problems**
- **Chapter 10 for more on graphic file formats**

BY THE WAY ▶

RIGHT FONT, WRONG CHARACTER

Sometimes, particularly with a PostScript font, your text may correctly print out in the same font as displayed on the screen, except that an occasional character is different—usually some special character accessed via an Option key combination. There is probably a difference, in this case, between the character set in the screen font file (used to display the text on the screen) and the printer font file (used to create the printed text). While technically this should not happen, it can occur if the screen font file is from an older version of the font while the printer font is a newer version, or vice versa; these versions may have minor differences in their character set. If this error occurs, there is usually not much you can do about it other than switch to a different font (or font version) that does include the desired character, assuming you can find such a font.

SEE:
- **"Technically Speaking: Different Versions of Screen Fonts for the Same PostScript Font," in the next section, for related information**

A Document Displays or Prints with the Wrong Formatting

Symptoms:

Wrong formatting refers to incorrect margins, line breaks, alignments, or character spacing, often occurring when you change fonts or printers. More specific symptoms are as follows:

- A previously saved text document is opened. The file opens normally, except that margin settings and/or line breaks are different from what they were the last time you opened the document.
- Margin settings and/or line breaks shift when you change fonts.

- Vertically aligned columns, such as those in tables, lose their alignment when you change fonts.
- Text characters are squeezed too closely together, perhaps even overlapping. Or there may be other unusual irregular spacing. Working with this text may ultimately cause a system crash.
- Formatting (such as bold, italics, spacing) appears correctly on the screen but does not print correctly.

Causes:

- A change in the printer selection from the Chooser can result in unexpected changes in margins and line breaks.
- A change in the fonts used in a document can result in margin and line break shifts, changes in the vertical alignment of tables, changes in the length of lines created by using the dash or underline keys, and more.
- TrueType fonts may occasionally cause problems with the appearance of text, especially if the application you are using is not a new enough version to recognize and work with TrueType.
- Squeezed-together text, overlapping characters, or solid lines that print as dashed lines are all usually traceable to an option, found in most word processors, called Fractional (Character) Widths.
- Missing printer font files can cause problems with appearance of printed text, such as bold or italics not printing.
- The wrong font may be used when printing as a result of options selected from the printer's Page Setup dialog box (see previous section for details).

What to do:

Line Breaks and Margins Change Due to Changing Printers

When you shift printer drivers via the Chooser, you get a message informing you to select Page Setup for all your open applications. Recall that all you have to do here is to open the Page Setup dialog box and click OK. The readjustment to the new printer is then accomplished.

SEE: • Chapter 7 for more on Page Setup and using the Chooser

Different printers, however, have different page-margin limits. Unfortunately, this often means that if you select a new printer driver, the document's line breaks, page breaks, and tab alignments may all change.

There is no quick fix for this; you simply have to reformat the document manually. The best long-term strategy is to select the printer driver you intend to use *before* you start working on the document. Remember, when you select a particular printer driver, the printer itself does not have to be on or even connected to your computer (see Chapter 7). In such cases, an alert box may claim that the Macintosh cannot find the current printer. If so, select Continue rather than Cancel. At this point, the driver is still selected and the document will be formatted correctly for that printer.

If the desired printer driver is not in your System Folder, you obviously cannot select it, so copy it from your system software disks.

Line Breaks Change Due to Changing Fonts

Line breaks can change when you change text to a different font, even if you do not also change the size or style. This can happen because the number of characters that fit on a line can be different with different fonts, even those that have the same point size. Point size has more to do with the height of the font than the width.

```
Here are four lines of text using New York 12 point font. Compare the
difference between the line breaks for this paragraph when the text
is formatted for a LaserWriter (the top paragraph) vs. when it is
formatted for an ImageWriter (the bottom paragraph).

Here are four lines of text using New York 12 point font. Compare the
difference between the line breaks for this paragraph when the text is
formatted for a LaserWriter (the top paragraph) vs. when it is formatted for
an ImageWriter (the bottom paragraph).
```

Figure 9-19 *A paragraph formatted for a LaserWriter versus an ImageWriter. Note the difference in where the line breaks occur.*

In particular, shifting from a *monospaced* font (such as Monaco or Courier) to a *proportional* one (such as Geneva or Times), or vice versa, causes dramatic changes to the layout of your text.

There is no quick fix for this problem, other than to select Undo and not to use the alternative font. If you need to switch fonts for some reason, you have to readjust all the text formatting manually as needed.

Line Break and Spacing Problems with Downloaded Files Text files downloaded from online services frequently require a monospaced font (especially Monaco 9 or Courier 9) in order to be displayed correctly. This sort of problem can be particularly severe for text in the form of a table. While shifting to a monospaced font will usually be a quick fix here, a more general solution is to use tabs, rather than spaces, to create table text (see next section).

TAKE NOTE ▶

MONOSPACED VERSUS PROPORTIONAL FONTS

Monospaced fonts allocate the same amount of space per letter, regardless of the width of that letter (for instance, an *i* and a *w* take up the same space on a line). Such fonts simulate how a typical typewriter works and guarantee that each line has the same number of characters on it; however, they also tend to have an unattractive, nonprofessional look. Monaco and Courier are examples of monospaced fonts.

```
Here is a sample of text in Monaco 12 (a monospaced font).

Here is a sample of text in Geneva 12 (a proportional font).
```

Figure 9-20 *A line of text in Monaco (a monospaced font) versus Geneva (a proportional font).*

The alternative is a proportional font, where the space allocated per letter varies appropriately with the width of each letter. Proportional fonts are found in most books, including this one. Most Macintosh fonts are proportional.

Another potential problem with downloaded files is that they may have a line break (an invisible character) at the end of each line. This means that if you reformat a paragraph by using a different font, or even just changing the margins, the text will not rewrap properly, as it would do with most word-processor-created text. Sometimes using a monospaced font will solve the immediate problem. For a more flexible, long-term solution, though, you will want to get rid of the unnecessary line-break characters; you can do this with shareware utilities such as Add/Strip. For a more quick and dirty approach, try an extension called MagicBullets, which lets you copy the text to the clipboard and paste it back with the return characters stripped.

BY THE WAY ▶

SPACING AND THE IMAGEWRITER'S DRAFT MODE

The ImageWriter prints in a monospaced font when using Draft mode. If your original document uses a proportional font, the Draft mode printout will have very irregular, almost unreadable spacing. The only solution to this, assuming you must use Draft mode, is to change your document's text to a monospaced font prior to printing.

Vertical Alignment and Line Length Problems Due to Font Selection

Shifts in the vertical alignment of columns of text (such as those used to create a table) are a related problem that may occur after you change a font. Such problems usually happen if you've used the spacebar to align the columns, rather than the Tab key.

The solution is to use the Tab key or, even better, your word processor's Table commands, if it has them (Microsoft Word, WordPerfect, and MacWrite Pro all are good at this).

Even if you do not change fonts, the spacebar is a poor choice for aligning columns, especially if you are using a proportional font. The variable width of proportional font characters makes vertical alignment across lines nearly impossible. If you must use the spacebar for such alignments, switch to a monospaced font, such as Monaco or Courier.

Similarly, to create a dotted line of a specific length, do not simply type a series of dots or dashes. Instead, use your word processor's Tab Fill option (if it has one). This causes a series of dots or dashes (usually you have some choice here) to fill in the space between tabs, rather than just having blank space. This method preserves the length of the line even if you change fonts; consult your word processor's manual for details.

TrueType Incompatibility Problems

A problem can occur whenever TrueType and bitmapped versions of the same font are in use. What happens is that the bitmapped version, when used for the screen display, may show different line breaks on screen than will be printed out. Eliminating *all* bitmapped font files for that font will eliminate this problem; it will probably also improve the way italics and bold form on the screen (since they will be based on TrueType technology rather than an estimate from the bitmap). The plain-text style of

TECHNICALLY SPEAKING ▶

DIFFERENT VERSIONS OF SCREEN FONTS FOR THE SAME POSTSCRIPT FONT

When you buy a PostScript LaserWriter, Apple includes a set of screen fonts that match those built into the LaserWriter (Times, Courier, Helvetica, and so on). These are also now included on System 7 software disks. These screen fonts were designed by Apple, but Adobe makes its own screen fonts for these same PostScript fonts. You may also own these Adobe screen fonts, especially if you have purchased any Adobe software (such as ATM, Illustrator, or Photoshop) or font disks.

Does it matter which ones you use? Usually, not much. Even when using just the plain-text style variant (as described earlier in this chapter), however, the two sets of screen fonts are somewhat different. Some people claim that Adobe's screen fonts are a more accurate match to the printed output than Apple's version. In any case, a document created with one version may become formatted differently if you later substitute the other version in your System Folder. A well-known example of this involves the use of the Palatino font in some versions of HyperCard's tutorial stacks. Palatino text displays correctly in HyperCard's text boxes if you use Apple's screen fonts, but the character spacing is too wide if you use Adobe's screen fonts. You can choose to ignore this, as it is just an aesthetic problem and should not otherwise affect the functioning or printing of the document. Otherwise, you can switch back to Apple's screen fonts.

If this problem appears after you have upgraded to System 7.1 or a later version, you are probably using an older incompatible version of the screen fonts. This is especially likely if you are having spacing problems using the Helvetica or New Century Schoolbook fonts. The solution is to replace the screen fonts with newer versions, from Adobe or Apple.

the font, however, will probably appear slightly worse (which is the main reason for retaining the bitmapped fonts in the first place).

I am also aware of a more general problem that may occur when a selection of text in a TrueType font is included in a paragraph that otherwise uses a PostScript font. While the screen display is fine, there may be an unusually large space before and after the TrueType font text when the paragraph is printed to a PostScript printer. The solution here is to not use the TrueType font.

Finally, old versions of some applications may not be compatible with TrueType. While such applications are rare these days, the resulting problems may include overlapping characters in display and/or printing; system crashes may even occur. The solution here is either to upgrade or discard the problem application or to stop using TrueType fonts when using the program.

SEE: • Chapter 7 for more on printing problems with TrueType

LaserWriter 8 Incompatibility

Some applications may not work correctly with any given version of LaserWriter 8; even the latest version of LaserWriter 8.4 includes a list of incompatibilities in its "Read Me" file. Problems are especially likely with programs, such as PageMaker, that depend heavily on PostScript. If you are using LaserWriter 8, try switching to LaserWriter or to another version of LaserWriter 8 to see if that fixes the problem.

Changes in Appearance Due to Fractional Character Widths

As I first mentioned in Chapter 7, the Fractional (Character) Widths option is found in most text-oriented applications, usually in the Preferences or Page Setup dialog box (it would be in the application-specific pop-up menu in LaserWriter 8.4). Changing its setting from off to on (or vice versa) may change the line breaks and/or character spacing of any text you are currently editing.

With Fractional Character Widths off, the result may be that line breaks are different in the printed output than they are in the display. Here is how the screen display looks with Fractional Character Widths turned OFF.

With Fractional Character Widths off, the result may be that line breaks are different in the printed output than they are in the display. Here is how the screen display looks with Fractional Character Widths turned ON.

Figure 9-21 *A sample of text with Fractional Widths turned off (top) and on (bottom).*

This option is designed to be used primarily when printing to higher-resolution printers, such as LaserWriters. Because of their higher resolution (300 dpi or more), these printers can print thinner (fractional) lines than can be displayed on the screen (which is usually at 72 dpi) and so text can be effectively squeezed closer together in the printed copy.

With Fractional Widths off, the result may be that line breaks are different in the printed output from the way they are in the display.

With Fractional Widths on, line breaks on the screen and the printed output should match correctly, but individual characters in the display may be squeezed together too closely for the monitor to display them properly. Because the option adjusts the spacing on the screen to match the higher-resolution capability of the printer, an irregular, less legible, sometimes even overlapping character display frequently is the result.

Also, if you are using a solid underline and it prints out as a dashed line, turning on Fractional Widths should solve the problem.

Turning on Fractional Widths is generally preferred when printing to LaserWriters. If the screen appearance is less than desirable, don't worry; it should all still print okay.

Fractional Widths and ATM

If you are using ATM, the ATM control panel has two checkboxes that also influence character and line spacing: Preserve Line Spacing and Preserve Character Shapes. These address the same sort of problems as does Fractional (Character) Widths. In fact, ATM has been known to conflict with Fractional Widths, leading to improper spacing of text when both are active. You may need to experiment to see which options produce the most attractive output.

Style Selection Does Not Print Correctly Because of Missing Printer Font Files

For PostScript fonts, you may find that a style selection (such as bold or italics) looks correct on the screen but does not appear in printed output. This is probably because the needed printer font file for that style is not present; it needs to be installed.

SEE: • **"Technically Speaking: All in the Family," earlier in this chapter, for more details**

Formatting Problems Due to Out-of-Date or Damaged Font Files

If you are having any other font-related formatting problem, or if your problem was not amenable to any of the previously suggested solutions, you may have an out-of-date or damaged font file.

Various versions of the fonts included with LaserWriters have been shipped over the years, and earlier versions may not work correctly with current software and hardware. If this seems to be a possibility in your case, seek the versions from Apple's current software. Otherwise, simply replace damaged fonts with your undamaged backups.

SEE: • **"Solve It! Font File Problems," later in this chapter**

The Text Is Clipped at the Margins When Printed

 **Symptoms:**

Text appears fine when displayed on the screen but is clipped (that is, cut off at the margins) when printed. Often, you will get an alert message warning that this may occur, such as one that says "Some margins are smaller than the minimum allowed by the printer. Your document may be clipped."

 **Causes:**

This is usually because the top, bottom, left, and/or right margin settings for your document (or for a particular paragraph within a document) go beyond the minimum limit that can be accommodated by your printer. Changes to the default settings are usually made via Document or Paragraph menu commands within your application. Sometimes, margin settings will be in the Page Setup dialog box.

 **What to do:**

Change the Margin Settings of Your Document

Locate where margins are set for the application in use. Increase their size as needed.

Select the Larger Print Area Option from Page Setup Dialog Box

If your printer supports the Larger Print Area option, select it. For PostScript LaserWriters prior to LaserWriter 8.4, it is found in the Options window of the Page Setup dialog box. This allows for narrower margins than the default printer settings. This option uses additional memory from the printer, however, and therefore it reduces the number of downloadable fonts the printer memory can hold. Checking this option therefore increases the likelihood that you may also want to check the Unlimited Downloadable Fonts option, located in the same dialog box. This option helps prevent memory problems associated with printing documents that use many fonts.

Turn Off Larger Print Area

Some programs do not properly support the Larger Print Area option. In this case, the edges of a document may become clipped only after Larger Print Area is turned *on.* If so, simply turn the option off.

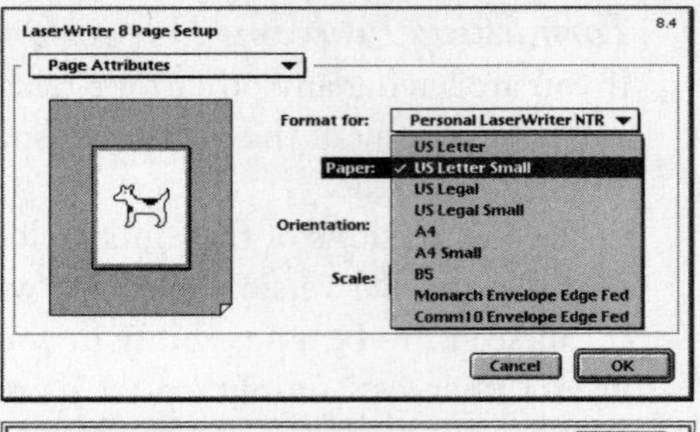

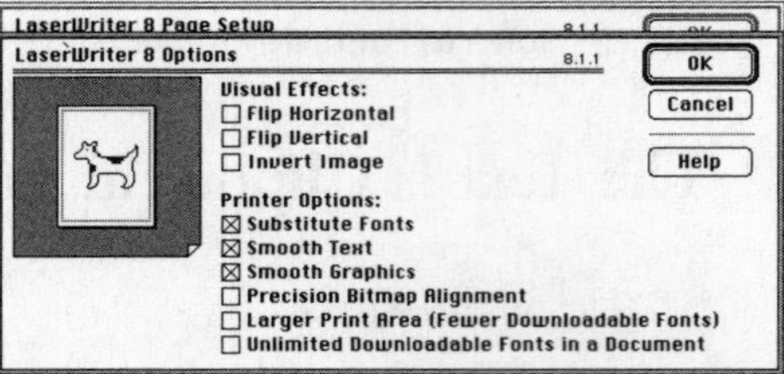

Figure 9-22 *Top: LaserWriter 8.4's page size option, with US Letter Small selected. Bottom: The Options window from previous versions of LaserWriter 8 (accessed by clicking the Options button in the main Page Setup dialog box); here is where the Larger Print Area option is found.*

Select Correct Paper Size and Orientation from Page Setup Dialog Box

Starting with LaserWriter 8.4, the Larger Print Area option has been eliminated. If your printer supports it, however, you will have Paper Size options of US Letter and US Letter Small (with the same choice for Legal and A4 sizes). According to Apple, "To prevent text from clipping or wrapping to the next line on different printers, use US Letter Small. To get the widest possible margins from your printer model, use US Letter." Experiment to see what works best on your printer.

Also, remember that whether you select the Portrait or Landscape orientation can affect whether your text fits on the page.

Change or Upgrade Your LaserWriter Driver

The LaserWriter 8 driver allows some printers to print using a larger print area on the page, regardless of Page Setup settings. If your printer does so, you may find that text in some documents reflows or is clipped to fit the new larger area. An upgraded version of the LaserWriter 8 driver may exist that corrects this problem. Otherwise, you need to either change the margins of your document or return to using the LaserWriter (*not* LaserWriter 8) driver.

SEE: • **Chapter 7 for more on LaserWriter 8 and printer drivers in general**

PostScript Fonts Do Not Print Using PostScript

Symptoms:

You select a PostScript screen font. It displays correctly, but when you print it, it does not print using PostScript. Typically, the bitmapped screen font version of the PostScript font prints instead.

Causes:

The typical cause is that the needed PostScript hardware and/or software is not present.

What to do:

- Make sure you are using a PostScript printer and/or ATM software.
- Make sure that the printer font files for the font are either built into the printer (as described in "PostScript Fonts," earlier in this chapter) or are in the correct location in the System Folder. For example, for System 7.1 or 7.5, these files should be in the Fonts folder.
- If you are manually downloading a printer font file to the printer (as explained in "Technically Speaking: Automatic versus Manual Downloading," earlier in this chapter), make sure you downloaded it prior to printing the document.

The Jaggies Appear Unexpectedly

Symptoms:

Happily, with the popularity of TrueType fonts and ATM, jaggies are largely a thing of the past. Nevertheless, they still crop up from time to time. If text characters display and/or print with ragged, irregular shapes, this is commonly referred to as the *jaggies.* The "expected" reasons for this have been described previously.

SEE: • **"Bitmapped Fonts" and "PostScript Fonts and Adobe Type Manager (ATM)," earlier in this chapter**

The jaggies, however, may also appear unexpectedly in a text document that previously displayed and/or printed without them.

Causes:

- A TrueType font was inadvertently deleted.
- ATM was inadvertently turned off or is not working as expected.
- Bitmapped fonts will print with a jagged appearance, even though the correct size is installed, if you use the Best quality option (as selected from the Print dialog box of certain printers, such as the ImageWriter) and you do not have the bitmapped font file installed that is double—or even triple—the size selected in the Size menu.

What to do:

With TrueType

You may have inadvertently deleted the TrueType file for a font (when updating your system software, for example), leaving behind only a scattered selection of bitmapped files for that same font. If you did, any text in sizes not represented by bitmapped files will now have the jaggies.

To check for this, look in the Fonts folder and/or your System file in the System Folder to see if you have somehow deleted any TrueType fonts that you expected to still be there. If so, reinstall the TrueType fonts as needed.

If You Use ATM

Some of the specifics of what follows may need to be modified if you are using the new ATM Deluxe.

- Make sure that ATM loaded into memory at startup. (You didn't hold down the Shift key at startup, did you? If you did, this prevents the loading of all startup extensions and control panels, including ATM.)
- The ATM control panel is named deliberately (with a tilde in front of its name) so that it loads near the end of the list of startup extensions. This is to avoid certain potential startup extension conflicts that may prevent ATM from working, so do not rename the control panel.

  SEE: • Fix-It #4 for more on startup extension conflicts

- Check the ATM control panel to make sure ATM is actually turned on. If it isn't, turn it on and restart the computer.
- Make sure that all the needed printer font files are present and in their correct location (typically the Extensions or Fonts folder). ATM will not work for a particular font without the printer font files in your System Folder, even if the fonts are built into your PostScript printer. Remember, printer font files should be stored in the Extensions folder in System 7.0. For System 7.1 or 7.5, they can be either in the Extensions or the Fonts folder.
- Make sure you are using a version of ATM that is compatible with the system software. For example, System 7.1 needs at least version 3.0 of ATM (this is especially important if you are storing printer font files in the Fonts folder).
- If your problem is limited to a specific application and you are using System 7.1 or a later version, make sure you are using an application that is new enough to know that it should check for printer font files in the Fonts folder. Contact the manufacturer of the application to get this information, if needed.
- If ATM seems to work slowly or improperly when displaying fonts (or if you get a message that says ATM cannot render text because of a low cache size), increase the Font Cache setting in the control panel to as much as 512K or beyond, if you can afford the extra memory. The font cache is used to determine how much memory is assigned to ATM at startup. Especially if you are working with a relatively large number of fonts or are using Adobe's multiple-master fonts, proper functioning of ATM may require that the cache size be increased from its default setting.
- Replace the ATM file(s), just in case they have gotten corrupted. Restart the Macintosh and try printing again.
- If you are still having problems getting ATM to work, check the ATM manual or Apple Guide files (in ATM Deluxe) for further information.

Helpful Hint: Checking on ATM hardware compatibility Starting with ATM 3.8, if you use the ATM Installer, the Easy Install option automatically builds in the correct "driver" for your hardware (for example, PowerPC or 680X0). If you click on the version number in the upper right corner of the ATM 3.8 or 3.9 control panel (this feature appears to have been dropped in ATM 4.0), you will see one or more letter codes. These indicate the type of support for your version of ATM. For example, "p" means Power Macintosh support, "g" means QuickDraw GX support, and "2" or "k" means 68020/030/040 support.

With Bitmapped Fonts Printed at Best Quality

When you print bitmapped fonts using Best quality (as opposed to Faster or Draft), as selected from an ImageWriter's Print dialog box, the Macintosh accesses a font size double the size you selected, then prints this double-sized font at a 50% reduction. The result is that the font prints at the selected size but at a visibly higher resolution. If the double-sized font is not present, the Mac estimates the size, which can result in the jaggies. For example, to print New York 12 correctly at Best quality, you need the New York 24 font file, not the New York 12 file.

You can avoid this problem by having the double-sized font installed, by using a TrueType version of the font, or by using ATM with a PostScript version of the font. A similar situation exists for StyleWriters, where you may need the triple-sized font (New York 36 in the example above) to print bitmapped fonts at Best quality.

Extra Help from PostScript Printers

Some LaserWriters include an option called FinePrint (accessed from the Print dialog box) that helps smooth out jagged edges, especially of text, even beyond what PostScript normally does. This can be useful even if nothing is really wrong with the text.

SEE ALSO: • "By the Way: Anti-Aliasing and the Jaggies," later in this chapter

A Paragraph Unexpectedly Shifts Its Formatting

 **Symptoms:**

In a word processor, a paragraph is typically assigned a specific set of margins, justification, indents, tabs, and line spacing. In some word processors, a paragraph may even have a particular default font, size, and style setting. Taken together, these characteristics define a paragraph's formatting. Problems can occur in either of the following cases:

- When you are editing text, a paragraph's formatting suddenly shifts to the format settings of an adjacent paragraph.
- When you are pasting text from one location to another, the formatting of the pasted text is not retained. Instead, the selection adopts the formatting of the surrounding text or uses the application's default format settings.

Causes:

The most likely cause of these problems is the selection (or lack of selection) of special invisible text characters. For example, in a typical word processor, every time you press Return, a special character is created, typically called the *return character* or the *paragraph marker*. This character indicates where a paragraph has ended. It also acts as a marker for all the formatting instructions unique to that paragraph. Other invisible characters are used to identify tabs, page breaks, and paragraph indents.

As implied by their name, these characters are not normally visible on the display or in printouts, but they can still be deleted, copied, and replaced. Unintended modifications of invisible characters is usually the cause of the unexpected problems described above. If you delete a paragraph marker, any customized formatting for that paragraph is lost. Also, the paragraph merges with the adjacent paragraph to form one larger new paragraph.

What to do:

The key to avoiding these problems is to understand the consequences of selecting versus not selecting an invisible character when you make modifications to its related text. Once you understand the consequences, making the appropriate choice is usually easy.

Make Invisible Characters Visible

Showing invisible characters is a key first step whenever you suspect that a problem is caused by invisible characters. Word processors typically include a command, with a name like Show Invisibles or Show ¶, that makes these characters visible. Select this command.

Here's a sample of text with normally invisible characters made visible. A tab is inserted here:→ A return character is inserted here:¶

This starts a new paragraph. Note how the selection of text at the end of this paragraph has been extended to include the return character.¶

Figure 9-23 *A sample of text from Microsoft Word, with its invisible characters made visible.*

Be Careful When Copying and Pasting

If you copy the return character along with a paragraph, the text should paste with the same format as it had when you copied it. Depending on exactly how and where you are pasting, it may even cause surrounding text to shift to the format of the newly pasted text. If a pasted selection does not contain a return character, it adopts the format of whatever paragraph now contains the selection.

Be Careful When Deleting Text

If you press the Delete key while the cursor is at the start of a paragraph, you backspace to the end of the previous paragraph. This causes the two paragraphs to merge, with both paragraphs now sharing the formatting of the second paragraph (a similar result occurs if a return character is cut or replaced by any other means).

If, instead, you want the merged paragraphs to share the formatting of the first paragraph, cut the text of the second paragraph (without cutting its paragraph marker), and then paste this text at the end of the previous paragraph. Finally, delete the "empty" line containing the paragraph marker of the second paragraph.

In General: To Correct Unexpected Format Shifts

If pasting or deleting text results in a format change that you did not want:

1. Select Undo immediately. This will reverse the undesired change.
2. If you have not already done so, turn on Show Invisibles or an equivalent command, if your program has such a command.
3. With the formerly invisible characters now visible, begin the procedure again. This time, be careful to select or not select the relevant invisible character(s), as desired. Experiment if necessary; if you make a mistake, select Undo. Continue trying different variations until you get the result you want. For example, to paste text and minimize problems due to merging of formats across paragraphs, press Return immediately prior to selecting Paste. This usually achieves the desired effect.
4. Optional: Select Hide Invisibles (or the equivalent command) when you are done. This command should have replaced the Show Invisibles (or equivalent) command at the same menu location. The so-called invisible characters are now once again invisible.

Problems Copying and Pasting Text Across Applications

Symptoms:

You select a passage of text and cut or copy it to the clipboard. When you attempt to paste the selection into a document of another application, however, one of the following problems occurs:

- The Paste command is dimmed and cannot be used.
- Nothing at all appears when you select Paste.
- Something other than what you most recently copied is pasted.
- The text is pasted successfully, but its formatting is incorrect (for instance, the font and/or style is wrong).

Causes:

Unless you are working with an application that simply does not accept pasted text, the most likely cause has to do with the operation of the clipboard. Although this may not be immediately apparent to most users, the Macintosh maintains one clipboard for use within an application (called the *application clipboard)* and another for use between applications (called the *system clipboard)*). If you copy and paste within the same application, only the application clipboard is used. This generally preserves all formatting, and the copy-and-paste transfer works just fine.

When you transfer to another application, however, the copied information is sent to the system clipboard, which does *not* typically retain application-specific text-formatting instructions. System 7.5 in general, however, and QuickDraw GX in particular have new features (such as drag-and-drop clippings) that help minimize this problem.

More to the point, simply switching among two or more open applications is usually sufficient for information in the application clipboard to pass to the system clipboard and then to the application clipboard for the receiving application. That is why you likely never notice the presence of these separate clipboards. The system clipboard, however, may not always be properly updated. If that happens, whatever is currently present in the system clipboard (which may be totally different from what you just copied) appears when you select Paste in a second application. If nothing is currently in the system clipboard, nothing pastes.

Even if the text is pasted successfully, it may be incorrectly formatted. This may occur (even if the needed invisible characters are included) either because the pasting application cannot interpret the formatting instructions of the original application or because differences between the application and system clipboards cause the instructions to be removed during the transfer. In either case, expect pasted text to conform to the format in effect in whatever document is receiving the text.

This section is limited to problems with the transfer of text. Transfer problems with graphics are covered in Chapter 10 (see "You Are Unable to Paste a Graphic Across Applications").

What to do:

If You Are Unable to Paste Text at All

You copy text in one application and select Paste in another, but nothing happens. No text appears. Here's what to try:

- **Select Show Clipboard**
  Select the Show Clipboard command in the Finder's Edit menu, and look in the Clipboard window to see its contents. If the desired selection is not there, you need to update the system clipboard. To try to do this, go to the next step.
- **Quit the application or go to the Finder**
  Quit the application you were using when you copied the text (if you get a message such as one that says "Save large clipboard?" select Yes), then return to the receiving application and try pasting again. Alternatively, go to the Finder and then back to the receiving application, then try pasting again. Both of these operations are likely to force an updating of the system clipboard. If neither of them works, copy the selection a second time and try again; it may work now.
- **Transfer the selection in segments**
  If you are trying to paste a large selection, you may get a message saying that there is not enough memory to copy the selection to the clipboard. If so, the easiest thing to do here is to transfer the selection in separate segments rather than all at once.

Alternatively, you might try *importing* the selection instead (see the next section), assuming your application supports this option.

- **Make sure the pasting application accepts text**
  If the previous methods all fail, make sure that the pasting application currently accepts text in your selected location. For example, a database does not accept text into numeric or graphic fields.

If Format Shifts When Pasting Text Across Applications

You copy text in one application and select Paste in another. The text appears, but in the incorrect font or style. Here's what to try:

- **Make sure the needed invisible formatting characters were copied**
  It may simply be a case of the pasted text adopting the style of the surrounding text.

  SEE: • "A Paragraph Unexpectedly Shifts Its Formatting," in the previous section

- **Import the text rather than paste it**
  In many applications you can directly import text from another document, bypassing the clipboard altogether, either via the Open command or via special Import or Insert commands. Doing this successfully depends on the receiving application having a translator capability for the format you want to import (usually listed in a pop-up menu found in the needed dialog box).

  This method is not guaranteed to work, but is worth a try if the clipboard fails. Try importing even if this means having to transfer more text than you need—you can always delete the unwanted text later.

  SEE: • Chapter 6, "When You Can't Open a Document," for more on importing files
  • Chapter 10, "Take Note: Foreign Imports"

Use Drag and Drop and Clippings Files

Drag and Drop is a System 7.5 feature (also partially available in System 7.1) that allows you to drag a highlighted selection directly from one document to another, even across applications, without needing the intervening copy-and-paste steps traditionally used by the clipboard.

You can even drag a selection to the Finder's desktop and create a special *clippings* file that can later be dragged to another document, largely bypassing the need for the Scrapbook. You can have multiple clippings files on your desk; double-clicking one of these files opens up a window showing its contents.

Among standard Apple programs, you can drag clippings or selected text directly to or from the Scrapbook, SimpleText, or the Notepad. Third-party software will work only if it has been designed to use these features.

If these feature does not work with any software, make sure you have the needed extensions installed and enabled (such as the Clippings extension). They should be installed automatically when you select an Easy Install of the system software.

These methods may have no more chance of success than using the clipboard, but they're worth a try.

SEE: • Chapter 13 for more general information on System 7.5

BY THE WAY ▶

COSMETIC BUG WITH CLIPPINGS FILES

Clippings files are great for those applications that support this feature. Any time I want to save a text selection in a word processing document, I can simply highlight it and drag it to the Finder's desktop. Later on, I can move the file to whatever folder I want or drag it to another open document to paste the text there.

There is at least one common "bug," however, that you will likely find if you use these clippings files often enough. If you open a clippings file, place another window over its open window, and then move the window away, the text in the clippings file may have vanished. In some cases, the text may even mysteriously reappear in other windows and locations on your desktop. This bug is known to Apple, and they intend to fix it eventually. In the meantime, they contend it is only a cosmetic bug that will not lead to any system freezes or crashes. If you simply reclose the clippings window and re-open it again, the missing data will return.

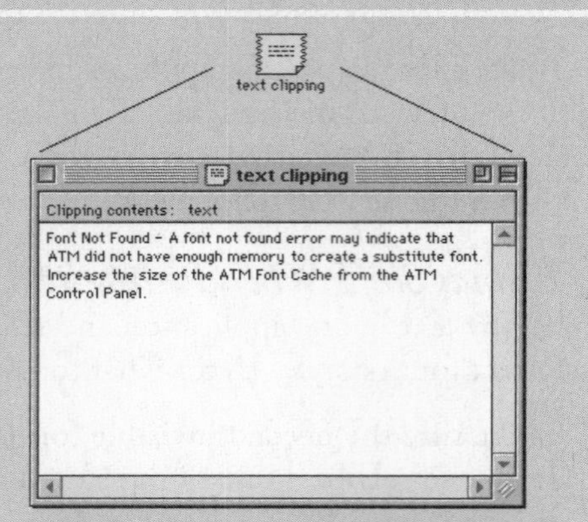

Figure 9-24 *A text clippings file with its window open. To paste the contents into a document, you can select Copy when the window is active and then select Paste from within the desired application, or simply drag the file icon to an open document window (if the application supports this feature).*

BY THE WAY ▶

MORE WAYS TO BYPASS THE CLIPBOARD

Drag and Drop is just the latest in a series of ways that you can transfer data across applications without using copy and paste. They all offer different advantages and/or limitations, and they all require that software be written specifically to support the feature.

System 7's Publish and Subscribe lets you place a copy of your selection into a document while retaining a link to the original. Whenever you update the original, the linked copy can be automatically updated as well, eliminating the need to repaste the modified data. Unfortunately, this feature has never become very popular, and many applications do not support it.

Another alternative, less well-known and even less often used, is EGO (Embedded Graphic Objects). An equation editor, Expressionist, uses this method for transferring an equation to other documents, such as a word processing document. The advantage of an EGO-placed equation is that if you double-click it from the word processor, it automatically opens Expressionist to allow editing of the equation and then automatically places the modified equation back in the original document. The only trick to doing this is that the object must first be selected with "handles" showing, rather than highlighted; if it is highlighted, you are just selecting it to be cut or copied.

Another related and very rarely implemented technology, called Word Services, is specific to text applications. For example, it can allow a stand-alone spelling checker to work within another application, adding its commands to the menu bar as if it were actually part of the other application. If you are interested, WordPerfect can make use of this feature.

Finally, with OpenDoc, separate OpenDoc files (called parts or Live Objects) can be combined into one "super-document," open files, eliminating the need to transfer data at all.

SEE: • **Chapter 13 for more on OpenDoc**

Otherwise ... Reformat the Text

The only remaining solution if the above techniques fail is to give up. Paste or drag the text as best you can, then reformat it as needed.

Text Turns into Bitmapped Graphics

Symptoms:

The text is no longer editable in any way; you can't select it or change it. In addition, the printed output looks distinctly inferior in quality to what you have come to expect from the font and/or printer you have been using. This problem is limited largely to typing text in certain graphics applications.

Causes:

If you are using a *paint* (not a *draw*) graphics program, any text gets converted to a bitmapped graphic once you finish typing the text and move on to use another tool.

SEE: • **Chapter 10 for more on paint versus draw programs**

The most immediate consequence is that the text can no longer be edited in any way. In particular, you can no longer delete or add characters or change fonts, styles, or sizes. Instead, the text is treated as another part of the overall bitmap that makes up the picture, as if it were a graphic element drawn by the paint program. For example, it can now be erased using the paint program's Erase tool.

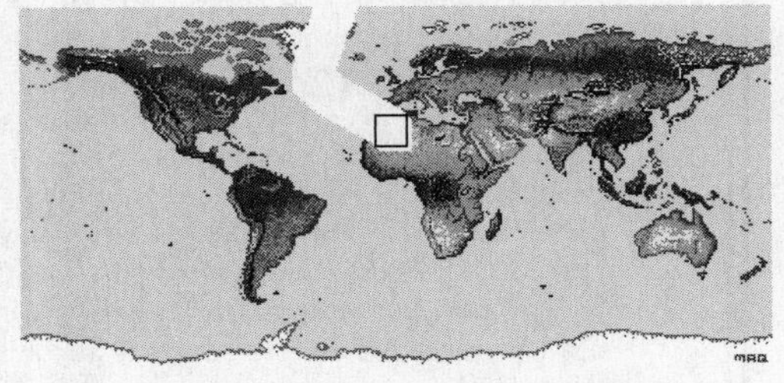

Figure 9-25 *If you can erase the text as shown here, the Macintosh no longer recognizes it as text.*

Similarly, any TrueType scaling or PostScript instructions that would have been used when printing are now ignored. The text simply prints as a duplicate of the screen display, with any jaggies retained.

What to do:

Start Over and Repaste the Text

If it is necessary to make changes to the text in a paint program, about the only thing you can do is erase the text using the paint program's tools (such as the Eraser), then start over and repaste the text. Make the needed changes before selecting another tool.

OCR

If you are desperate to recover a large amount of text that has been lost in this fashion, you may be able to convert it back to text with an optical character recognition *(OCR)* program, such as OmniPage.

Do Not Use Bitmapped Graphics Programs for Text

Text remains editable in draw programs, similarly to how it would be in a word processor. If it is important that your text remain editable and print in its highest quality, do *not* use a paint program (or a paint module in a combination paint/draw program) to create the text; use a draw program or module instead. To see the difference, compare the paint versus draw modules in a program like ClarisWorks. (Also, avoid image-processing programs such as Photoshop.)

Finally, note that if text has already been converted into a bitmapped graphic, copying and pasting the text into a draw program or word processor does not restore it as editable text.

Special Case: Problems with Uneditable Text in Draw Programs

Editable text in a PICT file created by a draw program typically remains editable the next time you open the file. It may become uneditable, however, especially if it is transferred to an application other than the one that created the graphic. For example, I had this happen when opening a ClarisWorks-created PICT file with ClarisDraw (and even when I reopened the PICT document in ClarisWorks itself).

BY THE WAY ▶

ANTI-ALIASING AND THE JAGGIES

For bitmapped graphics, objects in your image may have unattractive jagged edges. This can be a problem both for text and picture parts of your image, whether in on-screen displays or printed output.

When you first create the text part of the graphic, using TrueType fonts or Adobe Type Manager (for PostScript fonts) can help minimize this problem. Still, these font technologies will not completely eliminate the jaggies, and they have no effect at all on jaggies in the non-text parts of your graphic.

This problem is especially apparent with on-screen displays, because monitors have less resolution than the typical printer and thus do not benefit as much from a smoothing effect. Thus, this residual jaggies problem can be a particular concern for Web authors who include graphics on their pages.

Here is where a technique with the strange name of *anti-aliasing* can come to your rescue. Basically, it is a method of blurring the edges of images so as to make their edges appear more smooth. The effect, which can be quite dramatic, is especially noticeable with color documents.

To take advantage of this, you need software that has an anti-aliasing function. Photoshop has one, and there is a shareware program called Smoothie that does a quick and easy job of anti-aliasing PICT documents. Adobe Type Manager 4.0 also includes an anti-aliasing feature (called "Smooth Font Edges on Screen"), but it only works with PostScript fonts.

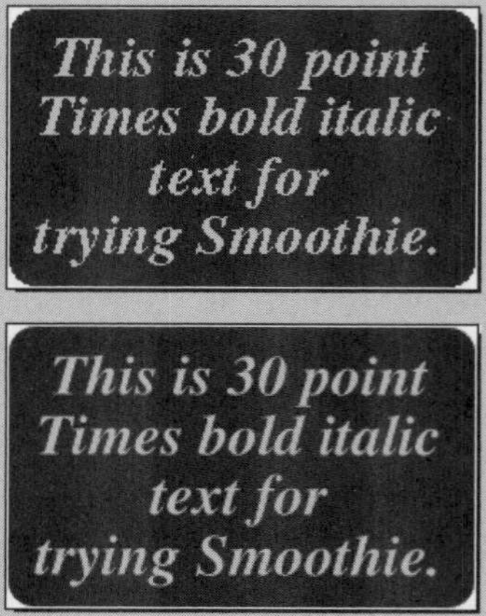

Figure 9-26 *Smoothie uses anti-aliasing to eliminate the jaggies (bottom), both for text and graphics, in bitmapped images. The difference is more pronounced when viewed on a monitor.*

Solve It! Font File Problems

Damaged Font Files

Symptoms:

A damaged font file should be suspected whenever you have any of the following symptoms (especially if other solutions, as described in previous sections of this chapter, have failed to work):

- Text is displayed in the wrong font or with otherwise unexpected formatting.
- Any document containing a specific font will not print correctly or will not print at all (see Chapter 7 for more on printing errors).
- Whenever you try to open a certain application, a system freeze occurs. This can happen even if you are not using a document that contains the damaged font (see Chapter 4 for more on system freezes).
- Every time you open or modify any document that contains a certain font, a system error occurs. Sometimes simply selecting the font from a Font menu will result in a crash.
- Trying to open a font file from the Finder results in either a message that says the file is damaged or that your system has crashed.
- An inability to remove a font file from a font suitcase, a Fonts folder, or the System Folder (even if no applications are open). If you try to do this, an error message appears.
- Trying to delete a font file in the Trash results in an error message that says the file could not be deleted.
- The icon for your hard disk looks like a generic text document icon.

Causes:

A font file can get damaged just like any other file. Damaged font files are a potential cause of incorrect font displays and the other symptoms I have just listed. These problems can occur not only in text-oriented programs, such as word processors, but in virtually any application.

What to do:

Locate Any Damaged Font Files

Your first job is to determine if you do indeed have a damaged font file and, if so, which one it is. This can be difficult because the symptoms of a damaged font file are so varied and often have other possible causes.

Thus, your first step should be to rule out other likely causes, such as a damaged document or a damaged application. Use the general guidelines detailed in Chapter 3. For example, try different documents and different applications to see how narrow or widespread the problem is. Replace possibly damaged documents and applications with backup copies. Try changing the font of a problem document to see if that eliminates the problem. If the printing problem is specific to a certain page of your document, replace fonts that appear only on that page.

Sometimes you may find that symptoms are indeed linked to the use of a certain font. While this suggests (but does not prove) that you have a font problem, the damaged font may not be the one that you think it is. For example, I once had a problem with a calculator desk accessory that displayed its numbers in an incorrect font, making it difficult to read the numbers. The cause did turn out to be a damaged font file, but neither the correct font nor the one that was being displayed incorrectly was damaged. Replacing a totally unrelated font remedied the problem.

Use a Spare System File to Check for Damaged Fonts A clever way to check for damaged bitmapped fonts is to build a small streamlined System file and drag all of your fonts to it. The system checks the integrity of the font before "accepting" it and gives it a unique ID number. If a corrupted font is present, it will be flagged. This ID renumbering can also help resolve ID conflicts among these fonts (as described in "A Document Displays the Wrong Font," earlier in this chapter).

Use Utilities to Check for Damaged Fonts There are now several utilities specifically designed to check for damaged fonts as well as a host of other potential font problems (such as duplicate fonts). One is Font Box, which is shareware, and another is the FONDler, a commercial product. ATM Deluxe will also include this function.

If you are using WYSIWYG Menus from Now Utilities and a system error occurs as a result of a damaged font, you may get some help with your diagnosis: after you restart, the utility should tell you the name of the font that caused the error. An antivirus utility, Disinfectant, will also identify font files that appear to be damaged as part of its normal check for virus infections.

Some of these utilities may even be able to repair a damaged font.

Remove Fonts from the System Folder Otherwise, your main hope to isolate the damaged font is to remove fonts from the Fonts folder (or other System Folder locations), one by one, until the problem disappears. Obviously, start with the fonts that appear most likely to be the cause of the problem.

SEE: • **"Font Basics," earlier in this chapter, for more on how to remove fonts from a System Folder**

To isolate a problem font, you can use the same techniques used to identify problem startup extensions. (For example, you can first remove half the fonts and see if the problem goes away; divide that half into two smaller halves and return one of the halves to the Fonts folder, then see if the problem reappears; and so on.) A utility such as Fonts Manager can assist in doing this; it works like an extensions manager, except it is specific to fonts. The latest versions of Conflict Catcher and Now Startup Manager can also do this.

SEE: • **Fix-It #4 for more details on this procedure and startup management utilities**

Replace the Damaged Font File(s)

If you don't have a utility that can repair a damaged font, your only alternative is to replace the suspected damaged font file with an undamaged copy from your backups (you *do* have backups, don't you?). Hopefully, the problem is now gone.

Usually, you have to replace only the exact font file that was causing the problem. You shouldn't need to replace all of the files for other sizes and/or styles that are part of the same font family.

In most cases, replacing a damaged font file should be no different from replacing an undamaged font; use the procedures as described earlier in this chapter (see "Font Basics"). For the sake of clarity, however, here is a specific example of how to replace a suspected damaged font file (in System 7.1 or later). Let's assume that the suspected font in this case is a TrueType font called Ashley.

1. First quit all open applications. You cannot remove *any* font files, damaged or undamaged, from your active System Folder (or Fonts folder within your active System Folder) if any applications besides the Finder, are in use.
2. Open the Fonts folder inside your System Folder and locate the Ashley font. In this case, it is a separate font file (that is, not in any suitcase). If it had been in a suitcase file, you would need to open the suitcase (by double-clicking on its icon) to locate the Ashley font file.
3. Drag the Ashley font from its location in the Fonts folder to the Trash. Select Empty Trash. (If the Finder says the font file is "in use" and refuses to delete it, restart and try again. It should delete now.)
4. Locate your undamaged backup copy of Ashley, and drag the backup copy of the Ashley font to the Fonts folder. You are done.

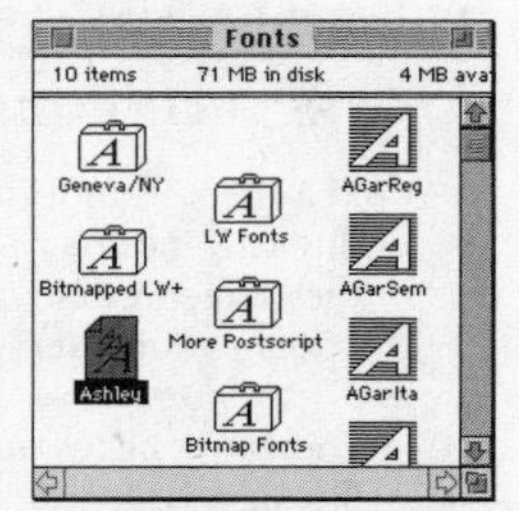

Figure 9-27 *The inside of a Fonts folder, with the Ashley font file highlighted.*

Note that I removed the Ashley font from the Fonts folder before adding the new font; I recommend replacing font files this way. The alternative is to drag the replacement font to the Fonts folder before you remove the damaged font, letting the Macintosh do the replacement in one step (after confirming that you want to replace the font). While the one-step method should work—and may sometimes be necessary if the two-step procedure fails—I don't trust it to be as reliable.

This advice is especially important if your suspected damaged font is stored in a suitcase. In this case, if you drag the replacement font to the System Folder icon or to the Fonts folder before removing the damaged font, the damaged font will *not* be replaced. Instead, you will wind up with two versions of the same font stored in your Fonts folder: the problem one in the suitcase, and its replacement loose in the Fonts folder. Alternatively, if your replacement font has the same name as its suitcase, dragging the font to the Fonts folder could cause the entire suitcase to be deleted, not just the single font. To replace a font stored in a suitcase, you should remove the font first and directly drag the replacement font to the suitcase. If it makes things simpler, you could remove and replace the entire suitcase, rather than just one font in it.

Problems Removing a Font File from a Fonts Folder

Occasionally, even when all applications are closed, you may be unable to remove or replace a particular font file (or font suitcase) from your Fonts folder. No matter what you try, you probably get an error message, perhaps saying that you cannot use the font because it is "in use." Usually, this is because the font is damaged. If this happens, try the following:

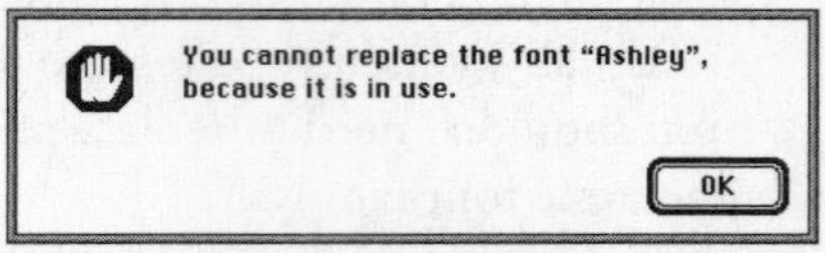

You cannot replace the font "Ashley", because it is in use.

OK

Figure 9-28 *This message may appear when you try to remove a damaged font from a Fonts folder, even if all applications are closed.*

1. Drag the entire Fonts folder from the System Folder to the desktop.
2. Restart the Macintosh, ideally with extensions off.
3. Drag the problem font file(s) to the Trash. It should now delete successfully.
4. Return the Fonts folder to the System Folder.

SEE: • **Chapter 6, "When You Can't Delete a File or Folder," for more on this problem**

TECHNICALLY SPEAKING ▶

THE 31-CHARACTER FONT NAME LIMIT

In System 7, font names cannot have more than 31 characters. If, by some oddity (usually due to a font name assigned in System 6), a font name has more than 31 characters, you may have trouble deleting the font. You may even have problems if and when you try to update your system software.

The font name refers to an internally stored ID, used by applications to identify the font. This is not necessarily the same as its file name in the Finder, which means that changing its file name will not help you here. Actually, most fonts have their file "name locked" attribute turned on, so that you could not readily change the name anyway (see Chapter 8, "Finder Flags," for how to get around this if you are curious). If you have this problem, your best bet is to open Font/DA Mover 4.1 (or a later version), locate and select the problem font, and click Remove. This should work.

Check for Problems with Other Files

If all else fails to solve your problem, you should suspect more generalized trouble, such as damaged system files, startup extension conflicts, or a bug in the application itself. In the worst-case scenarios, you may have to repair the Directory or reformat the entire drive.

SEE: • **Chapter 6 for more general advice on problems with files**
• **Fix-It #2 and #3 on application problems**
• **Fix-It #4 on startup extension conflicts**
• **Fix-It #5 on system software problems**
• **Fix-It #10 and #13 on Directory problems**
• **Fix-It #14 for more information on damaged files**
• **Fix-It #15 on reformatting the drive**

Damaged Font Suitcase Files

Symptoms:

You double-click a font suitcase to view its contents, but the suitcase will not open. Instead, you get an error message that says the font suitcase cannot open because it is damaged.

Causes:

A variety of causes is possible, most of them rather unlikely these days, and most of them not really a case of a damaged file. Some examples follow.

- You have two fonts in a suitcase with names greater than 31 characters (a length possible in System 6), but the first 31 characters of each name are identical. In System 7, the Finder only checks the first 31 characters and so it believes that the two fonts are identically named. The Finder will typically react to this by thinking that the font suitcase is damaged.
- The Suitcase utility was used to compress font files. This may also fool the Macintosh into thinking a font suitcase is damaged.
- A suitcase file in the Fonts folder is also in use by Suitcase (or a similar utility).

  Of course, it is also possible that the suitcase file or one of the specific fonts within the suitcase file really is damaged.

What to do:

Delete and Replace the Suitcase File

If you have undamaged backup copies of the fonts, the best thing to do is simply to delete the font suitcase and reinstall fresh copies of the font.

If the Macintosh refuses to let you delete the suitcase file, refer to the previous section, "Damaged Font Files." Follow its advice on how to delete problem font files.

Extract Fonts from the Suitcase File

If you do not have usable backup copies of your fonts, you can try to extract the fonts (assuming they are really not damaged) from the supposedly damaged suitcase. You can do this with a copy of Font/DA Mover (at least version 4.1 if you are using System 7). Otherwise, if you don't care about saving the fonts, just delete the suitcase.

Watch Out for the Suitcase Utility

If the problems seem related to your use of Suitcase, refer to the Suitcase manual for specific advice in order to avoid a repeat of the problem. Alternatively, stop using Suitcase altogether. The same rule applies to any similar utility.

Solve It! Font Menu Problems

Fonts Unexpectedly Appear or Disappear from Font Menus

Symptoms:

You check the Font menu of your word processor (or other text application) and find that one of the following glitches occurs:

- One or more new fonts are listed that were never there before, and you do not recall installing them.
- One or more fonts that have always been listed are unexpectedly absent, and you do not recall removing them from their System Folder location.
- One or more font names are listed in the Font menu but are dimmed.

Causes:

There are a variety of probable causes for these Font menu disappearing and reappearing acts, none of them very serious, and all usually easy to correct. These include font differences across startup disks, fonts embedded in an application, fonts installed automatically by Installer utilities, and font management utilities inadvertently turned off. In general, remember that a font will not appear in a Font menu unless it is installed in its proper location (usually the System Folder), as detailed in the beginning of this chapter.

What to do:

Check for Font Differences Among Different Startup Disks

You may be using a startup disk that is not the one you normally use. If this new startup disk has different fonts in its System Folder than your normal startup disk, these differences are reflected in the Font menu. The same thing is true, of course, when you are working with someone else's computer; their fonts are probably different from yours.

Fonts are usually installed in the System file or Fonts folder. As stated earlier in this chapter (in "Font Basics"), fonts are usually not part of the application itself. The fonts listed in an application's Font menu vary depending on what fonts are installed in the startup disk's System Folder.

If a change in startup disks is the apparent cause of unexpected changes in your Font menu, simply return to your original startup disk, and all will return to normal. If this is not possible for any reason, you have to either give up on using the missing fonts or install them into the current startup disk's System Folder.

Check for Embedded Fonts in Applications

You *can* install any font directly into an application (similarly to how you install fonts into the System file; such fonts are called *embedded fonts.* It is rare to use embedded fonts these days. If they are used, however, they are listed only in the Font menu of the application that contains them. Thus, when you shift to another application, the embedded font will seem to have disappeared.

SEE: • **Chapter 7, "Technically Speaking: Problems with Embedded Fonts," for a problem with printing documents that use embedded fonts**

TECHNICALLY SPEAKING ▶

LOCATING AND UNEMBEDDING EMBEDDED FONTS

You can use Font/DA Mover to access embedded fonts by holding down the Option key and clicking Font/DA Mover's Open button. The Open dialog box that appears will list all files on your disk (without using the Option key, it lists only suitcases and System files). Select the application that contains the embedded fonts; the names of these fonts (if there are any) should now be listed in the Font/DA Mover window. Assuming you are familiar with the use of Font/DA Mover, you can now easily copy these fonts to a suitcase file or even a System file. This procedure lets you essentially unembed the font, making it available to all applications. You can similarly use Font/DA Mover to delete the embedded font from the application.

You can also check an application for embedded fonts without Font/DA Mover. Simply make a copy of the application and change the copy into a suitcase, using a utility that can change a file's type and creator codes (such as Snitch). Change the type code to "FFIL" and the creator to "DMOV." Then double-click the suitcase to open it, and any embedded fonts will be revealed.

Check for Fonts Installed by an Installer Utility

If you recently upgraded your system software or installed a new application that uses an Installer utility, you may have automatically installed new fonts without realizing it. Usually the manual tells you about this, though not all do. Apple's system software Installer, in particular, reinstalls any of Apple's standard fonts that you may have deleted since the previous installation.

If you wish to delete new fonts that have been added by the Installer, it is usually safe to do so.

Some applications, however, use these fonts for special purposes that may not be immediately apparent, so be careful. Save a copy of the font before you delete it, and be prepared to reinstall it if problems appear when you use the relevant application.

SEE: • **"Locating, Adding, and Removing Fonts from Your System Folder," earlier in this chapter**

Check If Font/DA Management Utilities Are Turned Off

Font/DA management utilities, such as Suitcase, are system extensions. This means that if you use one of these utilities and you start up with extensions off (for example, by holding down the Shift key at startup), any fonts that are accessed through these utilities will not appear in Font menus. Anything else that you do to turn off these utilities has the same result.

SEE: • **"By the Way: Font/DA Mover and Other Font/DA Management Utilities," earlier in this chapter, for more on these utilities**

Quit Currently Open Applications

If you just made a change to the fonts in your System Folder, don't expect to see it reflected in any currently open applications. To see the change, you have first to quit the application and relaunch it—ideally, you should close all open applications prior to making any changes. In some cases, you may need to restart the Macintosh.

TECHNICALLY SPEAKING ▶

SEARCHING FOR RESERVED FONTS IN SYSTEM 7

The Macintosh needs certain fonts for displaying system information such as menus and dialog boxes. These fonts (Chicago 12, Geneva 9, Geneva 12, and Monaco 9) are called *reserved fonts*. Because of their importance, you should never delete these fonts from your System Folder. Usually this is not an option anyway, as the Macintosh does not easily let you delete them. In all versions of System 7, in fact, you won't find these font files listed anywhere, even if you were to open a suitcase file that contained these fonts. In System 7.1 or 7.5, these fonts are "invisibly" installed in your System file, even though remaining fonts are in your (quite visible) Fonts folder. Despite their absence from these Finder-level listings, these fonts still work correctly and appear in Font menus.

Chicago 12 is even more reserved than the other reserved fonts; it is included directly in the Macintosh's ROM hardware. It can therefore never be truly deleted, even if you manage to remove all traces of it from your disk.

You can use Font/DA Mover to view and copy reserved fonts, though you cannot remove them from an active System file.

BY THE WAY ▶

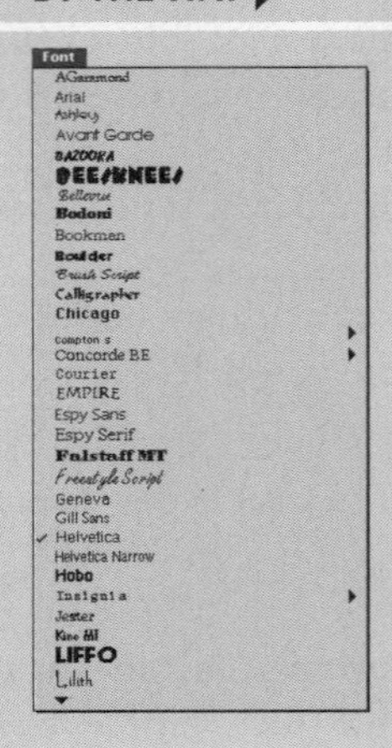

FONT MENUS: GOING IN STYLE

If you pull down a Font menu and each font name is displayed in the "look" of the font itself, you either have installed an extension that provides this feature (such as Now Utilities WYSIWYG Menus) or are using an application that can do this (such as ClarisWorks). It's a nice feature that can make choosing a font easier.

Figure 9-29 *A Font Menu as it looks with Now Utilities WYSIWYG Menus (or other similarly acting feature) modifying the appearance of the font names.*

Special Case: Font Names Are Listed in the Fonts Menu But Are Dimmed

If font names are dimmed, it usually means that a program is keeping track of the fonts that were used when a particular document was created and saved (this habit is often characteristic of PostScript drawing programs). If you later open that document on any system where one or more of those fonts is not installed, the fonts will appear in the menu as dimmed. The solution, of course, is either to obtain the missing fonts and install them or to go back to your original system.

In General: If You Are Having Trouble Finding a Specific Font File

To check if a font file has been inadvertently moved from its proper location, or to locate a font file on your startup disk for any reason, follow these guidelines:

- Check all the relevant System Folder locations—the System file, the Extensions folder, and (if present) the Fonts folder. Even in System 7.5, some fonts may be in the System file. Conversely, in System 7.0, some fonts may be in the Extensions folder.
- Otherwise, use the Find command from the Finder (or another similar Find utility). Type the likely name or partial name of the font file you wish to locate, then click the Find button.
- You can check for possible embedded fonts using Font/DA Mover.

  SEE: • **"Technically Speaking: Locating and Unembedding Embedded Fonts," earlier in this section**
- Font/DA management utilities such as Suitcase can access fonts from anywhere on your disk, not just the System Folder. In these cases, your missing font may be hiding anywhere on the disk. The utilities themselves usually have a function for locating the files that they are accessing; use it.

Font Menu Clutter

Symptoms:

The only symptom here is a Font menu that seems to contain several separate listings for the same basic font—for the Palatino font, you might see B Palatino Bold, BI Palatino BoldItalic, and I Palatino Italic, as well as Palatino itself.

If you are lucky, all of these fonts may appear together in the Font menu. In the worst cases, the variants of a font are listed in different locations because they do not all start with the same letter. Multiply this by a half dozen or more similarly structured fonts, and you can quickly see the potential scale of this problem.

Causes:

There is nothing actually wrong here. This chaotic listing is what is "supposed" to happen, given the nature of these fonts. The names shown are all style variants of screen fonts, designed to match separate PostScript printer font files for each style. Recall that four (or even more) separate printer font files may exist for the same font (either in your

System Folder or built into the PostScript printer); in these cases, you may also have a matching set of four screen fonts.

SEE: • **"Technically Speaking: All in the Family," earlier in this chapter, for details on these style variant font files**

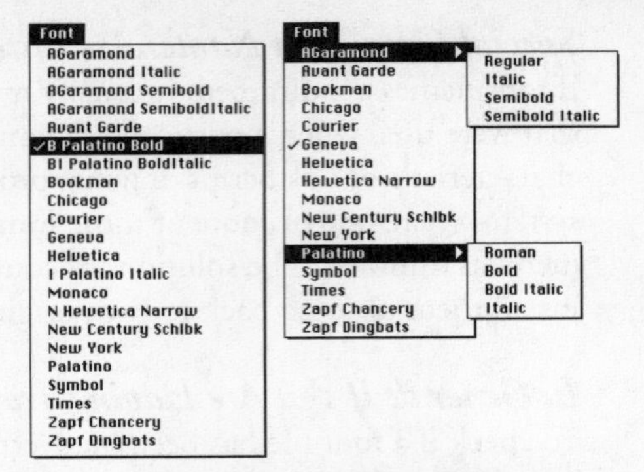

Figure 9-30 *Font menu clutter (left), cleaned up with Now Utilities WYSIWYG Menus (right).*

If this part of the Macintosh interface were perfectly designed, all the different screen fonts would be considered part of the same family and would not result in separate listings in the Font menu. For example, your Font menu does not list Times 10 and Times 12 separately as different fonts, even though a separate bitmapped font file may be present for each size. Similarly, this problem does not occur when you install different TrueType fonts of the same family, such as Palatino and Palatino (bold).

As it turns out, however, these style variant screen fonts are often considered to be separate families and thus get listed separately. This is the cause of the menu clutter problem.

What to do:

Get Rid of the Style Variant Screen Fonts

If you are not using ATM or a PostScript printer, these style variants are irrelevant, so get rid of them. (How did they get there in the first place?)

If you are using ATM and/or a PostScript printer, but the menu clutter still bothers you, just remove all the screen fonts for the style variants. Keep only the plain-text screen font (such as Palatino and AGaramond). You can even use a TrueType font as a screen font if you have one from the same family (Apple provides a TrueType version of Palatino, for example, as part of System 7). In most cases, this should eliminate the menu clutter without unduly affecting the monitor display or printed output.

SEE: • **"Technically Speaking: All in the Family," earlier in this chapter, for more details on pros and cons of eliminating these screen fonts**

Use a Utility to Eliminate the Clutter

If you really want to keep the style variant screen fonts, you can use special utilities such as WYSIWYG Menus (part of Now Utilities) or Adobe Type Reunion. These are designed to clean up menu clutter, typically by creating a hierarchical menu off each main font that lists all the variants. Occasional anomalies occur; for example, two common LaserWriter fonts, Helvetica and N Helvetica Narrow, are considered to be from separate families even when you use these utilities.

Adobe Type Reunion has had a reputation for causing more compatibility problems than the others. The new Adobe Type Reunion Deluxe (not yet out as I am writing this), however, should be improved in this regard.

Do Nothing

If you don't like either of these choices, you can just live with the menu clutter. It will do you no harm.

TECHNICALLY SPEAKING

A PRIMER ON MULTIPLE-MASTER FONTS

Adobe's multiple-master fonts are fonts in which you can vary the style characteristics of the font itself, such as weight (how thick the characters are) and width (how spread apart they are). The details of how all this works are too involved to get into here. If you have at all ventured into the world of multiple-master fonts, however, you are probably a bit mystified by the meaning of all those strange-looking names that appear in your Font menus (yet another contributor to Font menu clutter, these can again be fixed by using a utility such as WYSIWYG Menus). In any case, here are a few tips that may help you sort things out:

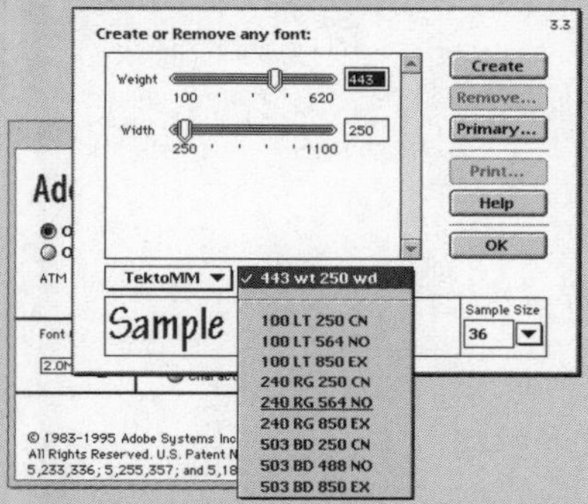

Figure 9-31 *The Make MM Instances window of ATM 3.9.*

- Adobe Manager 3.9 includes a button called "Make MM Instances." With this feature, you can easily create a new multiple-master screen font of any weight and width you select. ATM Deluxe has a similar capability.
- Most of the naming information that follows refers to screen fonts that are stored in a multiple-master font suitcase (such as in the Tekton MM suitcase for the TektoMM printer font). Typically, you should not discard these screen fonts, or you will lose the multiple-master variations of the font.
- "MM" after a name means it is a multiple-master font (you might have guessed this).
- Optional designations immediately after "MM" describe the style of the font (such as "Obl" for oblique or "Ita" for italics). Other letters may indicate the company that made the font.
- Letters and numbers that follow the underscore in the name describe the particular attributes of the font (typically, its weight and width). For example, "MyriaMM_347wt423wd" indicates a weight of 347 and a width of 423. Other fonts with the same numbers should be comparable in these attributes.
- Alternatively, after the underscore, you may see something like "540 BD" and/or "200 CN." The letters are abbreviations reserved by Adobe to describe the font; in this case, "BD" means bold and "CN" means condensed. The numbers again describe how bold or condensed the font is. If the abbreviations are in caps, the specific font was supplied by the company that created the font. If the abbreviations are in lowercase, you created the specific font yourself (typically via Font Creator or perhaps a recent version of ATM).
- If the font name begins with "%M," it is the master font that all other variations are based on. Such fonts typically do not appear in Font menus, but they are critical. If you remove a master font from the System Folder, none of the other related fonts will work.
- Adobe SansMM and Adobe SerifMM are two key multiple-master fonts—also not shown in your Fonts menu—that are needed for the "substitute fonts" feature of some versions of ATM. They work in conjunction with a file called ATM Font Database, which is installed at the root level of your System Folder (a miniature version of this file is included with Adobe Acrobat Reader).

SEE ALSO: • Chapter 13 for information about similar abilities of QuickDraw GX fonts

Chapter 10

Graphics: What's Wrong with This Picture?

Picture This 390

Resolution and Display Depth 390

Understanding Resolution 390

Monitor Basics 390

Multiscan Monitors 392

Printers 392

Understanding Display Depth: Color and Grayscale 393

What Is the Display Depth? 393

Display Depth and Dithering 394

Display Depth and Printing 394

Setting the Depth and Resolution of the Display 395

Monitors Control Panel 395

Monitors & Sound Control Panel 397

Control Strip 397

Types of Graphics, Programs, and Files 399

Bitmapped versus Object-Oriented Graphics 399

Bitmapped Graphics 399

Object-Oriented Graphics 399

Editing Bitmapped versus Object-Oriented Graphics 401

Paint versus Draw versus PostScript Programs 402

Paint Programs 402

Draw Programs 403

PostScript Programs 403

Graphics File Formats 404

Generic Graphics File Formats 404

Application-Specific File Formats 406

How to Determine the File Type of a Graphics Document 407

Movies, Video, and More 408
QuickTime and Beyond 408
Basic QuickTime Files 408
Playing and Editing Movies 409
Video Formats 409
Recording Video and Playing TV 410
QuickTime VR and QuickDraw 3D 410
Mini-Solve It! Problems with Movies and Video 411
Problems Installing and Starting Up with QuickTime 411
Problems Playing QuickTime Movies 411
Recording Movies 412
Problems with Apple Video Player 412

Solve It! Problems Transferring Graphics Across Applications 414
You Are Unable to Paste a Graphic Across Applications 414
Check Show Clipboard 415
Update the System Clipboard If Necessary 415
Check If the Application Supports Graphics Placement 415
Use Drag and Drop, Clippings Files, and Scrapbook 416
Import the Graphic 416
Otherwise 417
File Format Shifts When Transferring Graphics Across Applications 418
Copy and Paste, Publish and Subscribe, Drag and Drop 418
Importing 418
Use the Option Key to Copy PostScript Code to the Clipboard 418
Import Rather than Copy or Publish 419
For LaserWriter Users: Save the Selection as an EPS File 419
Try a Different Application 419
Use QuickDraw GX 419
Ignore the Problem 419
Related Problems 420

Solve It! Problems Displaying Color/Grayscale 420
Color Shift Problems 420
Color Palettes 421
Quit and Relaunch the Application 421
Use Another Application, If Possible 422
Select the Desired Document to Be the Active Window 422
Change to a Higher Color Depth 422
Problems Displaying at Different Color Depths 423
Make Sure You Have the Necessary Hardware and System Software 423
Select the Desired Setting from the Monitors/Monitors & Sound Control Panel 424
Allocate Enough Memory to Run in 24-Bit (or 16-Bit) Mode 424
Make Sure Your Application Can Run in the Desired Display Depth 425
Make Sure the Document Can Be Displayed at the Desired Display Depth 425
Give Up 425

Solve It! Problems Printing Graphics 426
Problems Printing Color/Grayscale to a Black-and-White Printer 426
Select Enhancement Options from the Print Dialog Box 426
Use Halftone Options Built into Specific Applications 427
Dither the Image Prior to Printing 428
Problems Printing Color/Grayscale to a Color Printer 429
Select Color Options from the Print Dialog Box 430
Use Apple's ColorSync 430
Special Case: Color StyleWriter Output is in the Wrong Colors or Otherwise Distorted 431
Problems Printing PostScript Graphics 432
Make Sure You Are Using a PostScript Printer 432
Make Sure the Application Supports PostScript 433
Make Sure the File for an Imported EPS Graphic Is Still Available 433
Avoid PICT Files If Possible 433
Problems Printing Bitmapped Graphics 433
Change the Graphic to an Object-Oriented Image 434
Check If Your Application Supports Higher-Resolution Bitmaps 434
Use Preferred Formats 434
Select Enhancements from the Page Setup Dialog Box 434
Use Anti-Aliasing 435
Special Case: Problems with ImageWriter Printers 436

Picture This

If you think the graphics features on the Macintosh are just for artists and designers, you are wrong. From the Finder's icons to a spreadsheet's charts to a word processor's paragraph borders, the Macintosh lives and breathes graphics that you use and create. Even if you can't draw a straight line, your computer can draw one for you. If you have a scanner, you can use it to convert almost any printed copy into a digitized computer image. You can buy prepackaged images, called clip art, or even have your photographs developed onto a compact disc that can be read by CD-ROM drives.

This chapter deals with graphics-related issues and problems that are likely to confront even the most casual of users; for better or for worse, it is not designed to meet the specialized needs of graphics professionals. As in the previous chapter on text problems, I begin this chapter with some basics about how graphics are created, stored, displayed, and printed. I then shift to specific solutions for a selection of common problems.

Resolution and Display Depth

To solve graphics problems, you first need to understand two issues that are fundamental to the operation of the Macintosh: resolution and display depth. While these issues affect all aspects of Macintosh display and printing, they are particularly relevant to graphics.

Understanding Resolution

How does the quality of the image you see, either on the screen or in a printed copy, relate to the resolution of the display or printing device? In answering this important question, I'll try to avoid technical jargon as much as possible.

Monitor Basics

All monitor screens are made up of a series of square dots (usually called *pixels*). The combination of dots that are on or off at a particular moment makes up what you see as the screen display. The number of dots that fit across an inch of space is referred to as the *dots per inch (dpi)* or *pixels per inch (ppi)* measurement of the monitor. The higher the dpi, the more dots you can fit in an inch of space.

The *resolution* of the screen refers to how clearly you can see images on the screen and how finely detailed those images can be. The dpi measurement is the most important (but not the only) factor that determines a screen's resolution.

To see how this works, assume you are comparing two different monitors of exactly the same size; the only difference is in the size of the individual dots or pixels. Let's assume Monitor A has 72 dpi, while Monitor B has 144 dpi. Since the screen sizes are the same, this must mean that each dot in Monitor A is twice the size of each dot in Monitor B.

Now, assume further that, despite this difference in dpi, a displayed image takes up the same amount of screen space on both monitors. Thus, if you displayed the same document on both machines, they would both fit the same amount of the document onto the screen. This means that an object in the document that is 2 inches long on either monitor will be 144 dots long on Monitor A, but 288 dots long on Monitor B.

As a result, the object will be seen in higher resolution on Monitor B than Monitor A. For example, if the object displayed is an irregularly curved line, the subtle nuances of the curves can be better captured when you have 288 dots to do so than when you only have 144 dots. To understand this more clearly, imagine how hard it would be to display an intricately curved 2-inch line with a resolution of only 4 dpi. Simply put, you could not do it.

Higher resolution is generally considered desirable, because it offers the potential for smoother, finer, more detailed, and more realistic-looking displays. Similarly, since you cannot create a line thinner than the width of a single dot, the higher the resolution of your monitor, the thinner the lines you can display.

But dpi is not everything when it comes to screen image quality; you must also consider the size of the screen. For example, suppose that the 72-dpi Monitor A we have been considering is a 14-inch monitor, with a typical screen dimension of 640 pixels across by 480 pixels down. Monitor C, with a screen size half as large as Monitor A, also has dimensions of 640 x 480 pixels. Therefore, each pixel in Monitor C must be half the size of those in Monitor A, which means that Monitor C is measured at 144 dpi. Monitor C will thus appear to have higher resolution, but everything on Monitor C will also be shrunk 50 percent compared to Monitor A. For example, a 2-inch curved line in Monitor A will now only be 1 inch long in Monitor C, using 144 dots in both cases. This, of course, makes everything in Monitor C harder to see, even if the images are sharper.

If Monitor C's resolution is 72 dpi, any image will appear just as large as it would on Monitor A (for example, a 2-inch line would display at 2 inches in both cases). Because the Monitor C screen is half the size, however, it could only show half of what Monitor A could show at any one time.

This sort of dilemma has been faced by some users of PowerBooks, whose screens are smaller than the 14-inch or larger monitors common on desktop Macs. Some older PowerBook models maintained 72 dpi resolutions, and by doing so they were unable to show as much on the screen. In particular, these PowerBooks cut off the bottom 80 rows of what would be seen on a desktop screen, using a dimension of 640 x 400, rather than 640 x 480. All recent models of PowerBooks duplicate the 640 x 480 dimensions of desktop monitors by making the pixel size smaller. The actual dpi may be as high as 92, which gives images a crisper look. These PowerBooks display identical images to those on the desktop Macs, but everything on the PowerBook is significantly smaller.

Here's one more complication: The original Macintosh monitor had 72 dpi and all applications were written based on this assumption. Thus, a graphics program wanting to draw a 1-inch line would draw a line that was 72 pixels long. Today, though, many monitors vary from this 72-dpi standard; for example, your monitor may have only 69 dpi. Still, most applications still draw a 72-pixel line for a 1-inch line. With a 69-dpi monitor, this means that a 1-inch line will actually appear as slightly longer than 1 inch.

When monitors get much larger than 14 inches (sizes of 16 to 21 inches are common these days), they typically still hover close to the 72-dpi standard. This means they have many more pixels on the screen and can thus show much more of an image at one time. As a result, you will not need to scroll through a document as often with a larger screen.

To summarize: As pixel size gets smaller, the number of pixels per inch (dpi) increases. All other things equal, this means a higher resolution. By increasing its dpi, a smaller screen may show exactly the same image (though reduced in size) as a larger screen with a lower dpi. Thus the size of the screen and its pixel dimensions both play a role in resolution. Finally, the depth of the display (described in the next section) has an effect on your perceived resolution.

Multiscan Monitors

What Are They? *Multiscan monitors,* the most popular monitors today, allow you to choose from among different pixel sizes (or resolution) of the display. Changing resolution will change how much of an image you can see on the screen at one time. You might choose to use a higher resolution (such as 1152 x 870) when you want to see a lot on the screen at one time (albeit with everything, especially text, smaller and harder to view), but shift to a lower resolution (such as 640 x 480) when you are more interested in a larger image. On a 17-inch monitor, the resolution that most closely matches the image size from the old 640 x 480 13-inch monitor standard is 832 x 624.

In some cases, you may have options to select the same resolutions at different Hz (such as 67Hz and 75Hz). Never mind exactly what Hz means here. Generally speaking, use only the highest Hz indicated. If some Hz resolution options are listed in italics, avoid them. These options are generally for when the monitor is hooked up to a PC rather than a Macintosh, and selecting them may lead to distorted displays.

Overall, the resolution of Apple monitors varies from 64 to 80 pixels per inch (ppi). A multiscan monitor's ppi will change when you shift resolutions, typically ranging from 64 to 79 ppi.

AppleVision Monitors AppleVision monitors (such as the 1710 and 1710AV) are Apple's latest version of multiscan monitors. They are distinguished by new software that gives you more flexible and easier control over many monitor settings, including such options as recalibrating color levels. The 1710AV is also a multimedia monitor, which means that it comes with built-in stereo speakers.

SEE: • **Chapter 12 for more on AppleVision monitors**
• **Fix-It #17 for more on troubleshooting monitor problems**

Printers

Printed images, like their screen display counterparts, are made up of a series of dots. Printer resolution is thus also measured in dots per inch (dpi). Actually, the situation is a lot less complicated with printers than with monitors, because you don't have to deal with an interaction comparable to that of pixel size versus monitor size. With printers, dpi *is* the total indication of resolution.

At the low end, Apple's dot-matrix ImageWriter printers have a resolution of 72 dpi. This is the same as that of a typical monitor, which (while not very high) is great for having the printed output perfectly duplicate the screen display.

Laser printers typically have a resolution of at least 300 dpi, although 600 dpi is now common on newer models. With some printers, you can select what resolution you want to use (for example, via a Printer Specific Options or Imaging Options pop-up menu choice in the LaserWriter 8.4 Print dialog box). Commercial quality printers have even higher resolutions. Inkjet printers, such as StyleWriters, have resolutions in a similar 300- to 720-dpi range. In other words, most printers in use today have resolutions far higher than that of the monitor display; this is why printed output typically looks much better than what you see on the screen. But the discrepancy in resolution between screen and printer also opens the door to potential problems, as you will soon see.

Understanding Display Depth: Color and Grayscale

What Is the Display Depth?

Each pixel of a typical color monitor can be any one of up to millions of different colors. Because of other hardware restrictions in the Macintosh, however, a pixel may be able to show only a subset of these millions of colors in a given situation. More precisely, there is usually a limit to the total number of different colors that can appear on the screen at any one time; this is referred to as the *depth* of the display. Noncolor monitors, by definition, have even greater restrictions on their display depth.

In the simplest case, each pixel—or each bit of the bitmap, to phrase it differently—can be in either one of two states: on (white) or off (black). This simplest case produces a black-and-white display and is called a *1-bit depth.* A basic black-and-white monitor (as in a Macintosh SE, for example) is only capable of a 1-bit depth display.

With most displays today, though, each pixel can assume more than just two values. For example, several PowerBook models, such as the PowerBook 180, can have up to 16 different states. This is called a *4-bit depth.* Each different state of a pixel corresponds to a different shade of gray that the pixel can assume, from very light to almost black. Thus, a graphic image with gray shadings will appear more accurately on a 4-bit display than on a 1-bit display, although these PowerBooks cannot display color. Any monitor that can only display different shades of gray is referred to as a *grayscale* (or *monochrome*) *display.*

Most current monitors attached to desktop Macintoshes are *color displays,* and most new PowerBooks have color displays as well. In these cases, what determines the maximum number of colors you can display at one time is not the display itself but the hardware on the Macintosh's logic board, the size of your monitor, and the software on your disk.

SEE: • **"Problems Displaying at Different Color Depths," later in this chapter, for more on hardware/software requirements for different color depths**

The default setting for most older color Macintoshes is to display 256 different colors (also called an *8-bit depth*). With current Macs (which come with at least 16MB of RAM), the default is typically *thousands of colors* (16 bits). If you have the right equipment, you may be able to show millions of colors at one time (over 17 million, to be more precise), a capability referred to as *24-bit color.*

Display Depth and Dithering

If you have ever looked at a grayscale graphic on a black-and-white monitor, you may think you are actually seeing different shades of gray, but you are not. This illusion is achieved by a careful mixing of dots, called *dithering*. For example, alternating black and white pixels, when viewed at a slight distance, simulate the appearance of a medium gray. By altering the proportion of black to white dots in a given area of the screen, as well as by varying the pattern in which the dots are mixed, a range of shades of gray can be simulated.

Figure 10-1 *At left, a 256-bit grayscale display of a cat; at right, a dithered display (resulting from shifting to a 1-bit display depth) of the same image.*

The Macintosh uses dithering with reasonable success when you change display depths, which you may need to do because the depth level of a document (determined when the file is created) is greater than the current display depth. Thus, if you display an 8-bit grayscale image at a 1-bit display depth, what you see is a dithered equivalent of the grayscale image. Similarly, if you display a 24-bit color graphic at an 8-bit color depth, you get a dithered approximation of the colors that are outside the 256-color range.

Display Depth and Printing

With resolutions of 300 to 600 dpi, most popular printers (such as Apple's LaserWriters) are great for printing text. They can produce finely detailed fonts in almost any variety, as well as thinner lines, smoother curves, and sharper, more finely detailed graphics than can be seen on the screen. Most of them, however, are black-and-white printing devices; that is, they have a 1-bit depth. This makes them distinctly limited as devices for reproducing grayscale and color graphics. Any shades of gray that seem to be in an image are accomplished by dithering or by a conceptually similar technique called *halftoning*.

Of course, color printers do exist, but they vary widely in terms of the color range and quality they can print. At the low end, you have inkjet printers such as the Apple Color StyleWriters or Hewlett-Packard's DeskWriters. They are inexpensive and can produce a rich color printout, even of a 24-bit color image, but their color quality is far from professional. Even the best printers (which use different printing methods and cost thousands of dollars more than inkjets) still have difficulty exactly matching their colors to those on the screen display.

SEE: • **"Problems Printing Color/Grayscale to a Black-and-White Printer," later in this chapter, for more on dithering, halftoning, and color-matching problems**

Setting the Depth and Resolution of the Display

You have some control over what color depth and, if you have a multiscan monitor, what resolution is actually displayed on your monitor. On many Macs, you make this selection by using the Monitors control panel; on most PCI-based Macs, the control panel is called Monitors & Sound. In either case, you can also use the Apple Control Strip utility.

BY THE WAY ▶

CHANGING RESOLUTIONS "ON THE FLY"

When Apple first came out with multiscan monitors, to change resolutions you had to restart the Macintosh. Happily, you can now select a new resolution and see the change instantly. This process was initially managed by a special extension called Display Enabler. Starting in System 7.5.3, this software was built into the system software, and (at least in most cases) the separate extension is no longer needed.

Monitors Control Panel

Display Depth You select a bit depth from the options listed in the scroll box at the top of the control panel: for example, Black & White is a 1-bit display, 256 is an 8-bit display, and Millions is a 24-bit display. To reiterate, these numbers refer to the maximum number of different colors the screen can display at any one time. This means that, with an 8-bit display, you can still vary which 256 colors get displayed. In essence, this is what you do when you shift from 256 grays to 256 colors, for example.

Actually, switching between the Grays and Colors options will only make a difference for 4-bit, 16-bit, or 256-bit displays. Black & White is always black and white. Thousands and Millions are always capable of showing color; only those images that do not contain any color will display in all grays at these settings. If your hardware/software is not adequate to display a certain depth (such as Millions), that option will not appear in the scroll box.

A setting of 256 grays is sufficient to display a black-and-white photograph with smooth gradient transitions and subtle shadings. Overall,

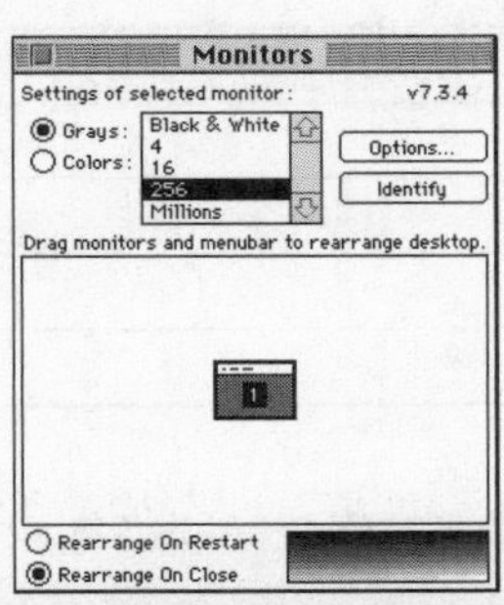

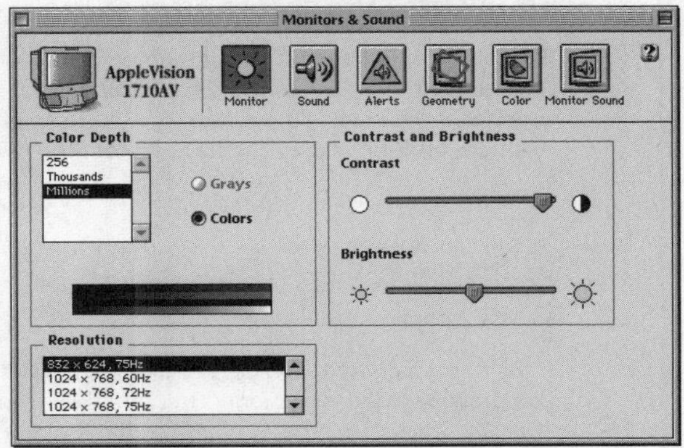

Figure 10-2 *The Monitors (top) and Monitors & Sound (bottom) control panels.*

the image quality is almost equal to that of a photograph. Note that the term *black-and-white*, when used to describe a photograph, is not accurate; these photographs actually contain a multitude of shades of gray. To achieve the same level of image quality for a color photograph, you need 24-bit color.

Table 10-1 summarizes the relationship between the Monitors control panel settings and display depth (as measured in bits).

Resolution (and Gamma) To change resolutions, click the Options button. From the window that opens, you can "Select a monitor setting." If you hold down the Option key when selecting Options, you may get additional resolutions listed. This window (with or without holding down the Option key) may yield additional video options such as "gamma corrections" (which modify the overall color balance of the display).

SEE: • **"Technically Speaking: Why 24-Bit Color?"**
• **"Problems Displaying at Different Color Depths," later in this chapter, for more on color depth issues and problems**

Table 10-1 Display Depth and the Monitors Control Panel

Depth (in number of bits)	Depth (as listed in Monitors control panel)	Does shifting from Colors to Grays change the display?
1	Black-and-White	No
2	4	Yes
4	16	Yes
8	256	Yes
16	Thousands	No
24 (or 32)	Millions	No

TECHNICALLY SPEAKING ▸

BIT NUMBERS AND COLORS

The relationship between the bit number (such as 8 bits) and the number of colors (such as 256) is determined as follows: Each bit of information can have 2 possible values. The total number of different values is thus 2 raised to an exponent equal to the number of bits. For example, an 8-bit display can have 2^8 (or 256) different values.

BY THE WAY ▸

BLACK APPLES

If the Apple icon for the Apple menu is black, even though the rest of your screen is in color, you probably have your monitor set to display Thousands or Millions of colors but have selected Grays rather than Color from the Monitors menu. The solution is to switch to Color. Note that this problem will not crop up on most newer Macs, as they no longer allow the Grays option to be selected at higher than 256 colors.

Monitors & Sound Control Panel

If you have a PCI-based Macintosh, you no longer use the Monitors control panel. Instead you use one called Monitors & Sound (which itself is a redesigned version of a short-lived clunker called Sound & Displays that was shipped with the original PCI-based Macs as part of System 7.5.2). From the panel window (labeled Monitors) that first appears when you open the control panel, you can select a display depth and (if you have a multiscan monitor) a resolution. You may also be able to adjust brightness and contrast. With these Macs, you can no longer select fewer than 256 colors/grays. Otherwise, the basic logic of what depth to select is the same as just described for the Monitors control panel.

(Note: To open the Monitors & Sound control panel, the System AV extension must also be installed.)

Control Strip

A third way of selecting different display depths or resolutions is via Apple's Control Strip modules (the Control Strip, once available only for PowerBooks, is now available for all Macs, starting with System 7.5.3). These changes are temporary in that the former setting will return the next time you restart; you typically have to open the Monitors (or Monitors & Sound) control panel to make a permanent change.

By the way, other third-party utilities have a capability similar to the Control Strip. For example, with Now Utilities' Now Menus, you can make changes from a hierarchical menu off of the Apple menu.

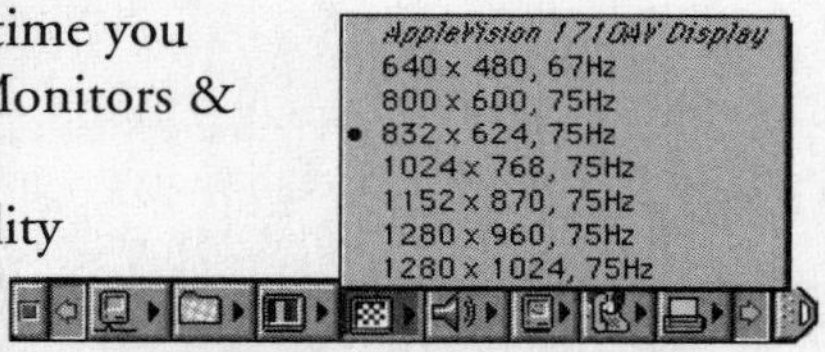

Figure 10-3 *Selecting resolutions (for an AppleVision monitor) from the Control Strip.*

TAKE NOTE ▶

MISSING RESOLUTIONS

Occasionally, when you click to see a list of possible resolutions, you will only see one choice (typically 640 x 480). There are several possible reasons for this.

For starters, Apple notes the following: "Many older Macintosh computers did not support resolution switching using software and require a cable adapter to produce different resolutions. Other computers do not provide the proper sync signals to work with the monitor and require an adapter to get any picture."

There are other causes that will not require additional hardware to fix. Some of these, as especially relevant to AppleVision monitors, are covered in Chapter 12.

BY THE WAY ▶

WHAT ELSE ARE THESE CONTROL PANELS GOOD FOR?

Selecting display depth and resolution are the main functions of the Monitors (and Monitors & Sound) control panels. One other important function is coordinating displays with multiple monitors attached; this is described more in Chapter 11.

Exactly what other options you have with Monitors & Sound will depend upon your setup. If you have an AppleVision 1710 monitor, for example, there will be options to set the sound of the monitor's speakers, to recalibrate the color of the monitor, and to modify such "geometry" as position and pincushioning. Some adjustments can be made from buttons on the monitor itself. Apple Guide files specific to your monitor should be available to give more detailed advice.

If you have an AppleVision monitor connected to a non-PCI-based Mac (which therefore uses the Monitors control panel), many of these special options are instead available via a separate control panel called AppleVision Setup.

SEE: • Chapter 12 for more on AppleVision monitors

TECHNICALLY SPEAKING ▶

WHY 24-BIT COLOR?

The Millions setting on the Monitors control panel is also referred to as 24-bit color. Assuming you have the necessary hardware to select this setting, why would you want to use it? After all, if you were going to draw a picture with crayons, would you feel a need for 17 million different crayons? Probably not, but the Macintosh is a bit different.

- **The pros of 24-bit color.** Higher depths are especially useful for viewing photographic images, such as those digitized from a scanner or used in QuickTime movies. The subtlety and naturalness of 24-bit color far exceeds what is possible with a 256-color limit. Similarly, the color gradient fill commands found in many graphics applications produce a much smoother transition of colors with 24-bit color than with 8-bit color. To see this difference, look at the color bar at the bottom of the Monitors control panel when you shift from 256 to Millions of colors. The difference is dramatic. At 256 colors, distinct bands are visible; with Millions selected, the color transitions are so smooth as to be imperceptible. Twenty-four-bit color also eliminates color shift problems (as described in the "Solve It!" section of this chapter).
- **The cons of 24-bit color.** The speed with which the screen image is updated slows down as the depth level increases. Working with a 24-bit color document can mean, for example, that every time you scroll your image, your computer slows to a crawl (unless you have a lot of RAM, a fast CPU, and/or a graphics accelerator card). Actually, this slowdown occurs even in nongraphic, noncolor documents. As a result, scrolling through a black-and-white text document is faster in 8-bit mode (and faster still in 1-bit mode) than with 24-bit color. Also, since 24-bit documents contain a lot more information than 8-bit (or other lower-depth) documents, they require much more disk space and need more memory to open than comparable 8-bit documents. By the way, creating 24-bit documents requires more than just a 24-bit display; you also need 24-bit-capable software (as explained more in the "Solve It!" section of this chapter).

Types of Graphics, Programs, and Files

Bitmapped versus Object-Oriented Graphics

The Macintosh uses two basic methods to create graphic images: bitmapped graphics, and object-oriented graphics. The differences between these two categories are analogous to the distinction between bitmapped and outline fonts (as described in Chapter 9).

Bitmapped Graphics

A bitmapped graphic is created as a series of individual dots (also called *bits*). A bit-mapped graphics file contains the instructions that detail the status of every single bit that makes up the image (which bits are off, which ones are on, and with what color). These instructions are called the *bitmap*.

Technically, the bits in a bitmapped image can be of any size (or *resolution*), but the most common size is 72 dpi. This is approximately the same as the minimum dot (or pixel) size of most Macintosh monitors.

This similarity is not a coincidence; it ensures that a bitmapped graphic file stores the exact information needed to re-create a screen image. When you consider that the Macintosh's first printer, the ImageWriter, also had a 72-dpi resolution, you can clearly see the origins of the WYSIWYG aspect of the Macintosh.

Some applications create bitmapped graphics at higher resolutions, such as 300 dpi (which conveniently matches the resolution of most LaserWriters). These images have a greatly improved printed appearance. If the monitor's resolution is limited to 72 dpi, however, this higher-resolution detail cannot be translated to the monitor display image; at best, it can be approximated. In such cases, the WYSIWYG relationship between the display and the printed output is partially broken.

On the other hand, a bitmapped graphic created at 72 dpi looks no better in the printed output than it does on the screen. Even if the printer has a higher resolution, bitmapped graphics print only at the resolution with which they were created—for instance, 72-dpi bitmapped graphics print out at 72 dpi even on a 300 or 600-dpi LaserWriter. In some cases, smoothing options are available from the Page Setup dialog box to reduce the jagged look of these images, but this does not alter the basic resolution.

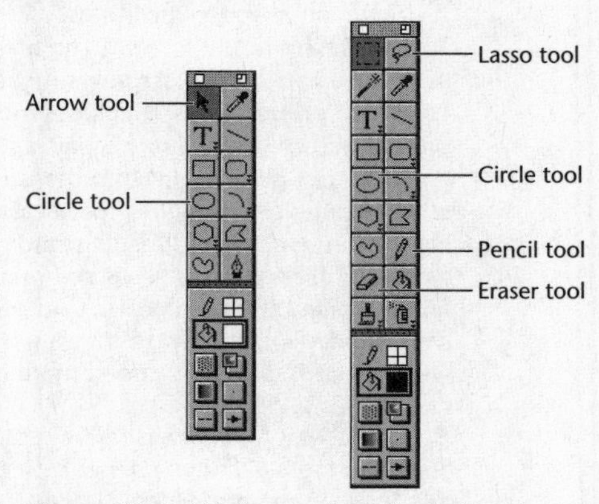

Figure 10-4 *At left, a tool palette designed primarily to work with object-oriented graphics (taken from a program's draw module). At right, a tool palette designed to work with bitmapped graphics (taken from a program's paint module).*

Object-Oriented Graphics

Object-oriented graphics are defined and stored as individual objects (lines, circles, squares, and so on). A document of this type is typically made up of a collection of these separate objects. Analogous to outline fonts (as described in Chapter 9), this method frees the graphic from dependence on a specific level of resolution.

Object-oriented graphics display or print at whatever resolution is used by the output device. So an object-oriented graphic will print at a typical LaserWriter's resolution of 300 dpi, even though the screen display is still translated into a 72-dpi image, because that is the monitor's resolution. This means that the appearance of printed output is likely to be superior to what you see on the screen.

To further clarify the distinction between bitmapped and object-oriented graphics, consider the differences between a bitmapped versus an object-oriented circle. You create both circles in exactly the same way: select the relevant application's Circle tool from its tool palette, hold down the mouse button, and drag the mouse. Similarly, if both monitors use a 72-dpi resolution, the display images of both types of circles usually are indistinguishable from each other. The increased resolution capability of the object-oriented circle becomes apparent mainly when you print the circles with a higher-resolution printer.

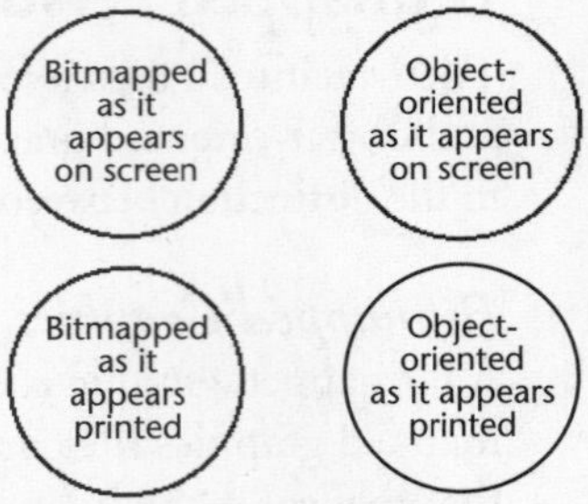

Figure 10-5 *At top, a 72-dpi bitmapped circle (left) versus an object-oriented circle (right) as they appear on the screen (note the similarity). At bottom, the same bitmapped circle (left) versus an object-oriented circle (right) as printed by a LaserWriter (note the difference).*

Bear in mind that all Macintosh displays and printed output are necessarily bitmapped. The difference between object-oriented versus bitmapped graphics is that bitmapped graphics begin with bitmapped instructions, while object-oriented graphics are converted to a bitmap from the object-oriented instructions.

TECHNICALLY SPEAKING ▶

QUICKDRAW VERSUS POSTSCRIPT GRAPHICS

In most cases, the basic set of instructions used to create both bitmapped and object-oriented graphics is obtained from the Macintosh's ROM; these built-in instructions are referred to as QuickDraw routines. QuickDraw is used for both screen display and printing.

The alternative to QuickDraw is PostScript, a page-description language used to create and print high-resolution text and graphics. The PostScript language interpreter, which is needed to convert PostScript instructions into printed copy, is built into the ROM of PostScript printers (which includes most Apple LaserWriters). PostScript can affect only printed output; the screen display is still based on QuickDraw.

PostScript graphics fall into the category of object-oriented graphics. Creating PostScript graphics, however, requires special applications that generate the necessary PostScript instructions (such as Adobe Illustrator and FreeHand). The advantage of these applications, when combined with a PostScript printer, is that you can create and print graphics with finely detailed smooth lines and other special effects that surpass what you can do with the more limited QuickDraw routines. (However, QuickDraw GX, an optional feature included with System 7.5 and described more in Chapter 13, comes close to matching PostScript's capabilities.)

By the way, all of this is relevant to text as well as graphics. Both bitmapped and TrueType fonts ultimately depend on QuickDraw for printing; you can probably guess what PostScript fonts depend on.

SEE: • Chapter 9 for related background on PostScript and PostScript fonts

Editing Bitmapped versus Object-Oriented Graphics

A major difference between bitmapped and object-oriented graphics, as explained in the previous section, is that the resolution of objected-oriented graphics is device independent. Other notable differences become apparent when you edit these graphics.

Selecting and Moving Bits versus Objects

If you draw a circle directly on top of an object-oriented square, the shape and location of the square (now hidden from view) is still remembered. The circle can be later selected, typically by clicking the mouse while the Arrow tool cursor is over the object, and dragging to a new location; the square, now no longer hidden from view, will reappear. It is as if the circle had been stacked on top of the square, which is, metaphorically speaking, exactly the case.

A.

B.

Figure 10-6 *At top, an object-oriented circle is selected (indicated by the four "handles" at the corners) and moved (indicated by the dotted-line circle). At bottom, when the move is completed, the square previously hidden underneath the circle becomes partially visible.*

In contrast, when you edit bitmapped graphics, placing a circle on top of a square changes the map of the pixels in that area. There is no separate recognition of a square and a circle; only one layer of dots exists, and nothing can be hidden underneath it. You can still select and move the circle, for instance with a Lasso tool, but you would no longer find a square underneath. There would be only white space.

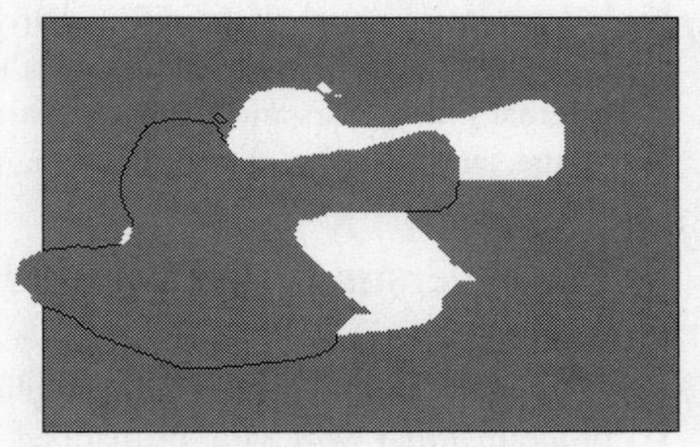

Figure 10-7 *Moving this irregularly shaped bitmapped object (selected with a Lasso tool) leaves behind a blank white space; whatever may have been underneath the selection is no longer there.*

Pixel-by-Pixel versus Object-by-Object Editing

Bitmapped graphics can be edited on a pixel-by-pixel basis, while object-oriented graphics can be edited only on an object-by-object basis. For example, with bitmapped graphics, you can use a Pencil tool to add or delete a single pixel from the circumference of a circle; you can similarly use an Eraser tool to remove part of a bitmapped graphic. This precise editing ability is the main reason that bitmapped graphics are the preferred type for creative artwork and image retouching.

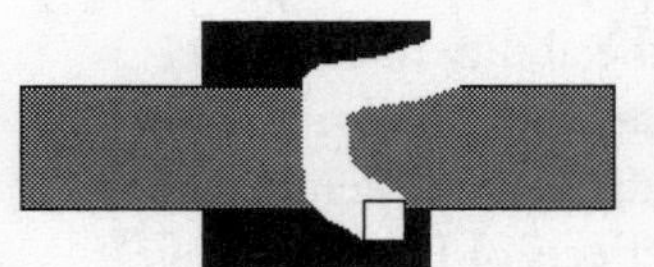

Figure 10-8 *Using an Eraser tool to partially erase objects, as shown here, can be done only with bitmapped graphics.*

With object-oriented graphics, on the other hand, you can make modifications only to an entire object. Thus you cannot remove one pixel from an object-oriented circle; you must instead erase the entire circle (typically by selecting it and pressing the Delete key). Still, this approach has its advantages. For example, you can change fill patterns and line thicknesses of object-oriented graphics at any time with a single command, while comparable changes are far less convenient with bitmapped graphics.

Reducing, Enlarging, and Rotating Bits versus Objects For object-oriented graphics, reducing, enlarging, or rotating an object does not alter the quality of the image. For bitmapped graphics, such operations usually reduce the quality of the selected image.

To change the size of an object-oriented circle, for example, the Macintosh uses an appropriate numeric substitution in the formula used to define the circle. The quality and accuracy of the image are maintained as before. In some cases, the screen display may suffer because of its 72-dpi bitmapped restriction, but higher-resolution printed output still looks fine.

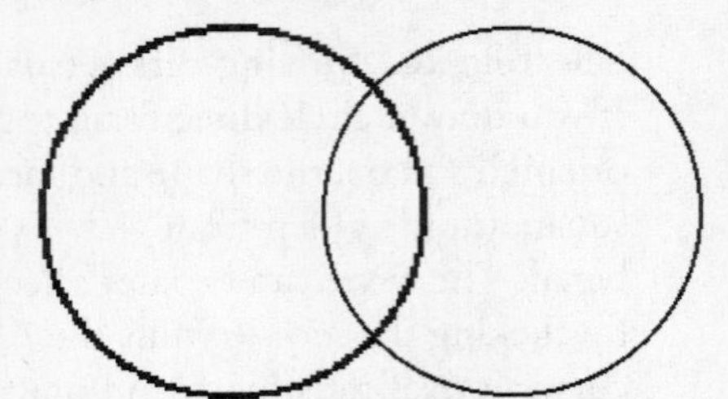

Figure 10-9 *At left, the bitmapped circle from Figure 10-5, after enlarging it on the Macintosh; at right, the object-oriented circle from Figure 10-5, similarly enlarged.*

For bitmapped graphics, however, these same operations are likely to produce distortions that affect both the screen display and the printed output. Enlarged images tend to have increased jaggies, reduced images lose fine detail, and rotated images look messier. Reductions are a particular problem for bitmapped graphics, since shrinking the image results in a smaller number of bits in the bitmap. For example, if you reduce an irregularly curved line that was 200 dots long to a length of 100 dots, you have only half as many dots to create the same appearance. Some of the details of the original line's twists and turns almost certainly will have to be omitted in this smaller image, since the size of the dots remains the same.

Paint versus Draw versus PostScript Programs

How do you know whether you are working with bitmapped or object-oriented graphics? Generally, it depends on the application you are using. Programs (or modules of programs) that work with bitmapped images are called *paint* programs, while those that work with object-oriented images are called *draw* programs. Many applications can work with both types of images. Detailed information should be somewhere in the application's manual.

Paint Programs

Paint programs or modules work exclusively with bitmapped graphics. The term *paint* is meant to suggest their preferred use for artistic purposes, where the ability to edit pixel by pixel allows for freehand drawing and subtle texture effects that would be impossible with object-oriented graphics. Programs in this broad category range from the minimalist black-and-white approach of MacPaint to the color and texture effects of Painter. Image-processing applications, such as Photoshop, are designed to work primarily with digitized artwork (that is, images typically created by using a scanner). Since digitized artwork uses bitmapped images, these applications are functionally similar to paint programs. Most integrated packages, such as ClarisWorks, include both a paint and a draw module.

TAKE NOTE ▶

DIFFERENT TOOLS IN PAINT VERSUS DRAW PROGRAMS

Just as the previous chapter made frequent reference to word-processing programs, this chapter makes reference to graphics applications. In particular, it assumes at least a passing familiarity with the basic array of "tools" used by these programs, such as Lasso, Eraser, and Polygon.

If you don't know whether a program is a paint or a draw program (or whether you are in the paint or draw mode of a program that can do both), you can often figure this out simply by examining the collection of tools currently in its toolbar. For example, paint programs/modules will show an Eraser tool, but draw programs/modules will not. This is because erasing requires editing of individual pixels—something that is possible only with bitmapped graphics in paint programs/modules.

Some primarily draw programs, such as ClarisDraw, also have an ability to shift to a paint mode so that you can edit bitmapped graphics with them.

Any object-oriented graphics that are pasted into a paint program/module become part of the bitmap and lose their object identity. As a result, they can now be edited on a pixel-by-pixel basis.

Draw Programs

Applications that use primarily object-oriented graphics are often called *draw* programs. These applications are preferred for architectural and engineering drawings, or any other use where precision and layout are more important than creative touches. (However, you can still create some fine artwork with draw programs.) Typical programs in this category include ClarisDraw and Canvas.

Draw programs are *not* limited to object-oriented graphics; they can contain bitmapped graphics as well. In "pure" draw programs, the bitmapped graphic simply becomes another separate object. In some draw programs, though, you can actually shift into a paint mode to edit it on a pixel-by-pixel basis. Again, integrated packages such as ClarisWorks and Microsoft Works include separate draw and paint modules.

PostScript Programs

PostScript programs such as Adobe Illustrator and FreeHand form a special class that doesn't quite fit into either category. In most ways they are similar to draw programs, because PostScript is basically an object-oriented language—in fact, some draw programs (such as Canvas) incorporate PostScript features. With PostScript, however, what you see on the screen is often only a rough approximation of the printed output, because the PostScript graphic instructions only go to the printer and do not determine the screen display. More details about this distinction are covered in the next section on graphics file formats.

BY THE WAY ▶

POSTSCRIPT GRAPHICS WITHOUT A POSTSCRIPT PRINTER

Only PostScript printers can print PostScript-based graphics. If you try to print a graphics document that contains PostScript code to a non-PostScript printer, the document will print incorrectly, in poorer quality, or not at all. A utility called Freedom of Press, however, can interpret PostScript graphic instructions so they can be used with non-PostScript printers. Another utility, StyleScript, offers a similar capability specifically for Apple Color StyleWriters. Hewlett-Packard offers a competing software package for its non-PostScript printers. While printing with any of these utilities typically takes much longer than printing to a PostScript printer (as the Macintosh needs to do all the processing that would normally be handled by the printer), it can be a cost-effective alternative for people who only occasionally need to print PostScript graphics.

Graphics File Formats

When you save a graphics document, you save it in a particular *file format.* This is really no different from what I have previously described for documents in general, such as with text documents (as described in Chapters 6 and 8). For example, Microsoft Word saves documents in its own Word file format, and generic text is also available in almost all text-oriented applications. To open a text file in a format other than the one specific to the application in use generally requires that the application have a translator file for that format. These same general rules apply in the world of graphics.

Generic Graphics File Formats

There is only one generic text format, but there are several different generic graphics formats. Graphics applications do not depend on application-specific formats to nearly the extent that most other categories of applications do. In fact, many graphics applications do not even have an application-specific format, instead relying entirely on generic formats. When things are working well, this considerably simplifies the process of transferring information across applications by reducing the number of translator files needed.

Each of the different generic formats has different limitations and advantages. For example, some are better for bitmapped graphics, while others are better for object-oriented graphics.

The most common generic graphics formats are PNTG, PICT, TIFF, and EPSF.

TECHNICALLY SPEAKING ▶

WHERE DO THESE NAMES COME FROM?

Typically, generic file formats are referred to by the four-letter code used to name the file type (not file creator) of the document. Each different generic or application-specific format has a unique file type.

SEE: • Chapter 8 for more on file types and file creators

PNTG or Paint The PNTG format (often referred to as Paint) was originally considered an application-specific format for the Macintosh's first graphics program, MacPaint. The format is so commonly available today, however, that it is now considered generic.

It is a limited format, though, and so it is rarely used anymore. It can store only black-and-white bitmapped information at 72-dpi resolution. This worked well for accurately transferring the screen image from early 72-dpi black-and-white Macintoshes to the original 72-dpi black-and-white ImageWriters, but it hardly keeps pace with today's color monitors and high-resolution printers.

A common misconception is that all paint programs use the Paint file format. This is not true. What makes a program a paint program is how it works with bitmapped images, not what file format it uses. Paint programs can use any of several formats, especially the PICT format that is described next.

PICT The PICT format was originally derived from MacDraw, the first object-oriented graphics program for the Macintosh. As with PNTG, however, it is now widely used by many other applications and is considered a generic format.

In fact, PICT is the most versatile and common of all the generic graphics formats. For example, it is the graphics file type used by Apple's TeachText/SimpleText utilities. In this sense, it is the complementary format to the TEXT file type used for text. Also, when you take a picture of your screen (using Command-Shift-3), the Mac saves the picture as a PICT document.

PICT images can be used by both draw and paint programs and can contain either bitmapped or object-oriented graphics. PICT images are notorious for causing problems for PostScript printers, however, especially those used by professional printers. If you plan to send your documents to a printing service, you will be better off using the TIFF or EPS formats described next.

TECHNICALLY SPEAKING ▶

PICT VERSUS PICT2

The basic PICT format is limited to using only eight colors. A newer PICT2 format breaks this color restriction and can potentially use any number of colors, but its file type remains PICT.

TIFF TIFF stands for Tagged Image File Format. Like PNTG, it is a bitmapped-only file format. Actually, several different versions of the TIFF format are available. The resolution and color limitations of the format depend on the exact version of TIFF in use (as well as the specific application in use).

TIFF is the preferred format for working with digitized images, particularly scanned photographs. This format is similarly ideal for use in imaging programs, such as Photoshop, that permit brightness and contrast adjustments to a document.

TIFF can save files at very high resolutions, permitting high-quality printouts, but at the cost of requiring enormously large files. As a result, it is common to see special compressed TIFF formats.

EPSF or EPS EPSF (often called EPS) stands for Encapsulated PostScript File. This file format can be used with either bitmapped or object-oriented graphics. The primary reason for using EPS, however, is that it stores the graphic information as PostScript instructions, which are then used to create the graphic on a PostScript printer.

Using EPS files requires an application that supports the use of PostScript instructions; Adobe Illustrator and FreeHand are the two best-known examples of graphics applications that have this capability.

EPS files generally include a separate PICT image of the file in addition to the PostScript information. The PICT image—an approximate visual representation of the PostScript commands—is displayed on the monitor, while the PostScript information is used only when printing. Thus, as is generally true when using PostScript, the screen display of an EPS file is not identical to the printed output.

You may be able to open an EPSF file with an application that does not support PostScript. If so, the display and printing are both generated from the PICT information; the PostScript information is ignored entirely.

By the way, if you are using LaserWriter 8, you can save any file as an EPS file via the print-to-disk option in the Print dialog box (as described in Chapter 7, "Technically Speaking: LaserWriter 8.4's 'Destination' Option").

SEE: • **"File Format Shifts When Transferring Graphics Across Applications" and "Problems Printing PostScript Graphics," both later in this chapter**

Application-Specific File Formats

In addition to the generic file formats, some graphics applications have a unique application-specific format that is comparable to the specific formats created by most word processors. These unique file formats may allow the creating application to save certain special formatting effects that are not possible with the generic formats.

Graphics programs with application-specific file formats also have options to save files in generic formats. In fact, you may have to save in a generic format if you wish to transfer the image to another program, such as a word processor or a page-layout program. Word processors and the like rarely have file-translation filters for application-specific graphics formats; they tend to support only generic formats.

BY THE WAY ▶

WHAT ABOUT GIF AND JPEG?

GIF and JPEG are two more graphics file formats that you may have heard about. Actually, they are special ways of encoding/compressing graphics that have become useful for transmitting graphics on the Internet, especially graphics displayed on Web pages. I will have a bit more to say about these formats in Chapter 14.

How to Determine the File Type of a Graphics Document

A graphic document's file type can be the key to solving a problem with displaying or printing the file. So how can you determine the file type of a specific document?

The Kind description in the file's Get Info window, though useful in identifying file types of most nongraphic documents, is generally not helpful here. It tells you only the name of the application that *created* the document, not necessarily what format it was saved in. For example, a ClarisDraw file saved in ClarisDraw's application-specific format and a ClarisDraw file saved in the PICT2 format are both listed in the Kind description as simply "ClarisDraw document."

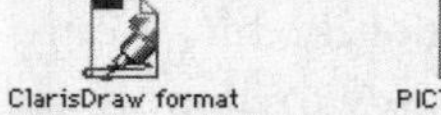

Figure 10-10 *Different icons for a ClarisDraw document saved in its application-specific format (left), a PICT2 format (center), and an EPSF format (right).*

You will have better luck by checking the icons for each document. Many programs use different Finder icons to indicate the different file formats; for example, ClarisDraw uses different icons for files saved in its custom format, PICT files, and EPSF files. If checking icons doesn't help, determine an assigned format from the Open dialog box, assign a format using the Save As command, or use a disk-editing utility. Details of these options are given in the following paragraphs.

Determine an Assigned Format from the Open Dialog Box Open a graphics application—ideally, the application that created the document. Select the Open command, and navigate to the folder where the unidentified file is located. Most graphics applications offer a variety of file format-translation options, typically from a pop-up menu in the Open and/or Save dialog boxes. Select the different format options listed there one by one. Each time, check whether the file you are interested in is listed in the scroll box. Because only those files that match the selected file format appear in the list, the currently selected format when your file appears is the one used by that file. Alternatively, if your document has an All Files option, you might try using it to open your file. If this works, an alert message may inform you of the file format as the file is being read (such as "Converting TIFF document").

By the way, an application may not be able to export all the file types it can import. Therefore, the file types listed in its Save (or Export) dialog box may be different from those listed in its Open (or Import) dialog box.

Assign a Format Using the Save As Command Whenever you first save a graphic (or use the Save As command), you assign a format to the file. Usually, the default format is the application-specific format, if there is one.

If you want to make sure that a file is in a particular format (such as PICT) regardless of what its present format may be, you can assign the file a specific format with the Save As command. Just select Save As, choose the desired format from the options listed there, and click Save. Whatever file format you selected is now assigned to your document; give the file a new name if you do not want it to replace the original file.

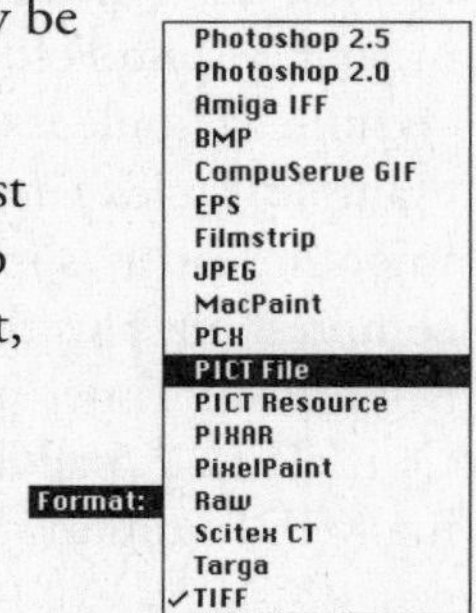

Figure 10-11 *Graphics file formats listed in the Format pop-up menu in Photoshop's Open As and Save As dialog boxes.*

If no selections are given, it usually means that all files in the application are saved in some generic file format (often PICT), with no other options available.

Use a Utility If the preceding methods do not apply, you can directly read a document's file format by using a utility that identifies a document's file type, such as Get More Info. The four-letter name (such as PICT or TIFF) of each generic format is the code you see listed as the file type for these documents. By definition, this tells you the file's format, since application-specific formats have their own unique codes.

Generally, do not use this method to change a file's type code. Doing so does not change the format of the file; it only causes problems for subsequent use of the file. Use this method primarily to identify the file's type.

There are also a host of commercial and shareware/freeware utilities that are designed to open files of a variety of formats and convert them into other formats. DeBabelizer is probably the best-known commercial product, while GraphicConverter is a well-known shareware utility. Photoshop, among its many other virtues, also serves well here.

SEE: • **Chapter 8 for more details on file type codes and related utilities**

Movies, Video, and More

These days, graphics on the Macintosh mean more than just the two-dimensional pictures emphasized in this chapter; they mean 3D graphics, animated graphics, QuickTime movies, and more. What follows is a general overview of these features, together with specific troubleshooting issues.

QuickTime and Beyond

Apple's QuickTime, the technology that changed the nature of Macintosh graphics, is the major application for viewing "movies" on your Mac. For you to view QuickTime movies, the QuickTime software must be installed in your System Folder. Make sure you have the latest version, as Apple is constantly improving it. For example, QuickTime 2.1 included support for smoother video, sprite animation, and 16-bit audio compression, plus the capabilities of the Apple Multimedia Tuner (formerly a separate extension). QuickTime 2.5 added several more features, including MIDI support.

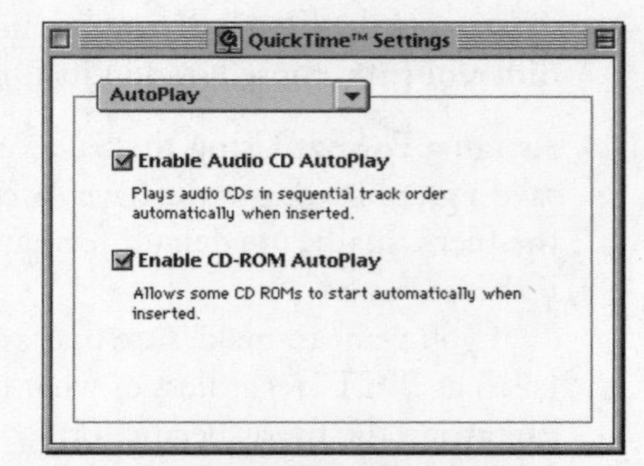

Figure 10-12 *QuickTime 2.5's QuickTime Settings control panel.*

Basic QuickTime Files

The essential file for using QuickTime is the QuickTime extension. Additionally, on Power Macs, you need to have an extension called QuickTime PowerPlug (it comes as part of the QuickTime package).

For improved sound, QuickTime Musical Instruments is an optional add-on.

Finally, QuickTime 2.5 adds a QuickTime Settings control panel. From here, you can select whether you want audio CDs and/or certain CD-ROMs to play automatically when inserted. You can also select for different music-related options, such as a MIDI connection port.

Playing and Editing Movies

Movie Player, included as part of Apple's QuickTime package, is sort of the SimpleText of movie software. With it, you can view movies and do some simple editing. A wide variety of other shareware, freeware, and commercial programs go beyond the capabilities of Movie Player, including such products as Avid Cinema and Adobe Premiere. At the lowest end, even SimpleText itself can play movies!

For the World Wide Web, Apple makes a QuickTime plug-in (included with Netscape Navigator 3.0 or later) that allows QuickTime movies to be played as "embedded" within a Web page rather than requiring a separate window.

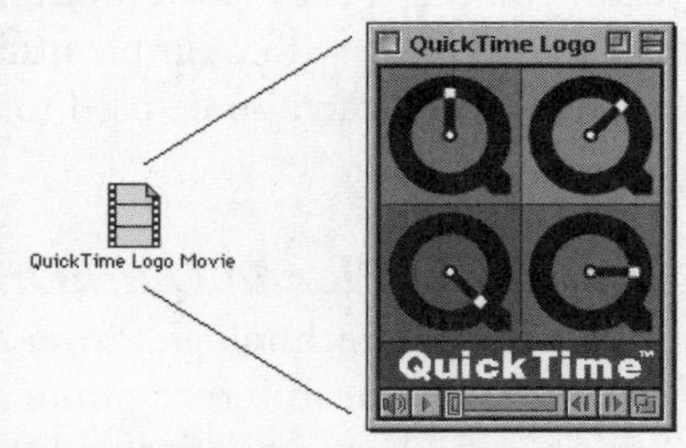

Figure 10-13 *A movie of the QuickTime logo, as seen from Apple's Movie Player.*

TECHNICALLY SPEAKING ▶

PUTTING QUICKTIME MOVIES ON THE WEB

To place QuickTime movies on a World Wide Web page, you first need to "flatten" the movie (that is, remove the resource fork from the file, leaving just the data fork). There are freeware utilities that can do that for you, including one called FlattenMoov. You might also try the "Playable on non-Apple computers option" in the Save dialog box of Apple's Movie Player application.

SEE: • Chapter 14 for more on the World Wide Web in general

Video Formats

Movies can come in different formats, just as graphics files come in formats such as PICT or TIFF. The following are two examples:

MooV (or Mov) This is the basic QuickTime movie format. You'll need the QuickTime extension to view these files, plus some movie player application (such as Movie Player).

MPEG This compressed format was developed for professional video transmissions, but it is commonly used on the Internet as well. There are several different versions of the MPEG format, with newer versions having improved quality. If you want to convert your QuickTime movies to the MPEG format, use a utility such as Sparkle. In combination with an additional MPEG extension, QuickTime 2.5 can work directly with MPEG files, but earlier versions of QuickTime cannot directly play back MPEG files unless you have additional hardware.

You may see a few other movie formats, especially on the Internet—for example, Microsoft's AVI format—but these are by far the most common in the Macintosh world. By the way, QuickTime does not support AVI files, though you can play them through Microsoft's Internet Explorer software.

Recording Video and Playing TV

If your Macintosh comes with AV input jacks (like those found on the PCI-based Power Mac 7500, 7600, and 8500), or if you add such capability yourself via a NuBus or PCI card, you can record video input from a TV, VCR, or camcorder. Macs that include this capability come with a simple utility called Apple Video Player for this purpose.

This utility can also be used to view TV on your Macintosh screen if your Mac has a TV Tuner card.

QuickTime VR and QuickDraw 3D

Two emerging technologies from Apple, QuickTime VR, and QuickDraw 3D, will likely be popular in future games and multimedia applications. Sometimes, though, it is a bit hard to keep straight the differences between them. Accessing these technologies requires that the relevant extensions be installed in your System Folder and/or that you use applications that were written to take advantage of these features (such as QTVR Player for QuickTime VR).

QuickTime VR QuickTime VR lets you create graphics that a user can navigate around in a 360-degree space. For example, you could view a picture of a room and rotate around to see all four walls, look up to the ceiling or down to the floor, even move through a door. The VR software includes a simple VR player application that can be used to view VR documents. If it did not come with your Mac, it is available online.

QuickDraw 3D QuickDraw 3D is a technology that makes 3D rendering easier to do than was previously possible on a Mac, creating a standard that most developers are likely to adopt. With an optional QuickDraw 3D accelerator card added, it also becomes the Mac's fastest method of 3D-processing. While this is more of a graphic technology rather than a video one, I placed it here because it is likely to be used in conjunction with movies. For example, QuickTime 2.5 includes QuickDraw 3D support. If it did not come already pre-installed on your Mac, the QuickDraw 3D software is included on Apple's system software CD-ROM disc. Otherwise, as always, the latest version is available online.

Apple also has announced a QuickDraw 3D RAVE technology, that allows game developers to "transparently access 3D graphics accelerators for maximum speed and throughput, while also providing exceptional 3D rendering speed in software" even if they are not using QuickDraw 3D.

All of this will be especially prevalent in game programs and on multimedia pages of the World Wide Web.

Mini-Solve It! Problems with Movies and Video

Problems Installing and Starting Up with QuickTime

Startup Problem Due to Two Copies of QuickTime If you install a new version of QuickTime, the older version should be removed or deleted. Sometimes the Installer utility does not do this, however, especially if the old version's name—as listed in the Finder—is slightly different than the new version's name (for example, QuickTime 2.1 versus QuickTime 2.5 or QuickTime). In this case, both versions may remain in the Extensions folder after an upgrade. If so, when you try to start up, you will get a message that says QuickTime cannot be installed because another version is already installed. If this happens, simply delete the older version and restart the Mac. In the meantime, despite what the message says, one of the versions of QuickTime did load.

This exception aside, as a general rule, it is wise not to rename system software files. Otherwise, more problems such as this one are likely to occur.

QuickTime PowerPlug and "Can't find QuickTimeLib" If you get system crashes when trying to use QuickTime on your Power Mac, you probably don't have the QuickTime PowerPlug extension installed. Failure to have this extension installed may also result in a message that says, "Can't find QuickTimeLib." If you do have PowerPlug installed but you still get this message, there is most likely a bug in the application you are trying to use. Contact the vendor about possible upgrades.

QuickTime 2.5 and Sound Manager 3.2.1 QuickTime 2.5 came with Sound Manager 3.2.1. Even if you use System 7.5.3, which has Sound Manager 3.2 built-in to the system software, you should leave this extension installed; it is a bug-fixed update. With System 7.6, the separate extension may no longer be needed.

Problems Playing QuickTime Movies

To get QuickTime movies to play smoothly, with good image resolution and proper speed, consider the following tips:

Lower Display Depth Playing a movie back at 16-bit or even 8-bit depth, rather than at 24-bit depth, can improve the performance of the movie. The image, however, will appear grainier (for 8-bit depth, there is a way for the creator of the movie to add a "custom color table" that will improve the quality; details of how to do this are beyond the scope of this book).

Reduce Screen Size Reducing the screen size of a QuickTime movie will improve the smoothness of the display.

Turn Virtual Memory Off, Etc. Turning virtual memory off, quitting other open applications, and starting up with only essential extensions can all lead to improved performance when recording or playing back movies.

Get More VRAM and a Faster Mac Faster and more powerful Macs, particularly those with the extra video RAM (usually around 4MB these days), can play and record video with the best performance capability. If you really need this ability, you'll need to spend the bucks on better hardware.

Recording Movies

If you are recording your own QuickTime movies, the speed and smoothness of the movie (as well as the size of the file) are affected by options that you can set, especially the compression method and frames-per-second setting. While details here are beyond the scope of this book, I will touch on a few key points.

Decrease Frames Per Second and Reduce Compression In some applications, when recording movies, you can record them at different frame rates (such as 15 or 30 frames per second). Thirty frames per second is considered ideal for producing realistic video, but most Macs don't have the muscle to record or even play back at that rate and still have the movie appear smooth. In most cases, unless you have a high-end Macintosh with lots of video RAM, you'll get better results by recording at a slower rate.

While leading to bigger movie file sizes, recording with Normal or No compression (rather than Most) selected in Apple Video Player's Preferences dialog box will lead to improved playback performance.

One common recommendation for preparing QuickTime files for the Internet is to use Cinepak compression. (For those of you who know about these matters, set Cinepak to 50 percent, 8 to 10 frames per second with a key frame every 30 frames.)

Record to a RAM Disk or a Fast AV Hard Disk Recording movies to a RAM disk, rather than a hard disk, can also help the movie to play back more smoothly. Using the fastest hard disk available is advisable if you are recording to a hard disk. Special so-called AV hard disks will also lead to improved performance.

Problems with Apple Video Player

Who Can Use It? Apple Video Player only works with Macs that have a video input or TV Tuner capability. This group includes the PCI-based Power Mac 7500, 7600, and 8500, for example, or Macs that have a video card added. On other Macs, if you try to run it, you will get a message that says the Video Startup extension was not installed properly. Ignore the message; Apple Video Player won't run no matter what you do.

Video Startup On the other hand, for those Macs that *can* use Apple Video Player, it is true that it won't work unless the Video Startup extension is installed.

Insufficient memory If you get a message that says "An error occurred while trying to copy (via Command-C) the video display to the Clipboard" when you try to capture a large (640 x 480) image in the Apple Video Player, or if you get a message that says "An error occurred while trying to freeze the video display" when you click the Freeze button, the Apple Video Player is running out of memory. Quit the program, increase its memory allocation (via its Get Info window), and try again.

Can't Launch Apple Video Player (or Can't Use a Speech Program with Apple Video Player Open) You may find that you are unable to launch Apple Video Player even though your Mac model should work with it. Instead, you may get a message that says "Apple Video Player could not find the necessary video hardware. Make sure that your computer has video input capabilities and that you are not running any other video applications," or "Apple Video Player could not find the necessary audio hardware. Make sure you are not running any other audio applications."

The most likely reason for these messages is that you have PlainTalk installed and have Speakable Items turned on. Because both PlainTalk and Video Player need to access the Mac's digitizing hardware, you cannot use Apple Video Player and Speech Recognition simultaneously on PCI-based Power Macs. Apple says it will fix this conflict eventually. Until then, to get the Video Player to launch, turn off Speakable Items from the Speech control panel.

Conversely, if you have Apple Video Player running and you try to turn on Speakable Items from the Speech control panel, you will also get an error message (for example, "Speakable Items could not run because another application is using sound input. Quit that application to use speech recognition."). In this case, the solution is to quit Apple Video Player.

Apple Video Player appears to have a similar problem with launching while SoftWindows 95 is open. Conversely, opening SoftWindows 95 while Video Player is open may result in a Type 11 error.

Launching Apple Video Player will result in an error message if you are using a version of QuickTime earlier than 2.0.9.

Problems with Avid Cinema Apple Video Player and Avid Cinema don't mix well. For example, you may get an error if you launch Cinema while Apple Video Player is open. Conversely, Apple Video Player won't record while the Avid Cinema Extension is installed. Of related interest, the Avid Cinema Extension may display an X through its icon at startup if virtual memory is on or if Cinema loads before QuickTime 2.5.

TV Tuner Won't Work If you have a Performa with a TV Tuner card installed, you may find that Apple Video Player won't work after you upgrade to System 7.5.3 via System 7.5 Update 2.0. The reason is almost always that the Installer did not correctly install the upgraded versions of Apple Video Player and/or Video Startup. The solution is to go back to the System 7.5 Update 2.0 disc and do a Custom Install to get the updated files.

TV Remote Control Does Not Work The remote control from the Apple TV/Video System may not work after you upgrade to System 7.5.3 (which uses version 1.4 of the Video Player software). The problem has been confirmed by Apple for all machines in the 630, 5200, 5300, 6200, and 630 families. This problem is fixed by upgrading to System 7.5.5.

Menu and Control Strip Disappear When you are displaying video on television from a Power Macintosh 8500, the menu and control strip may disappear when you select a new resolution. To get them back, reset the PRAM and delete Display Preferences while extensions are off.

SEE: • Fix-It #11 for how to reset (zap) the PRAM

Apple Video Player and MPEG problems If the Apple Video Player window is blank during a playback with an MPEG card, there are a number of possible reasons. The two most likely causes are corrupted Apple Video Player Prefs (the solution is to delete them) or an old version of QuickTime (the solution is to upgrade to version 2.1 or later).

By the way, if you use an MPEG card, note the following warning from Apple: "MPEG movies designed for software decompression by applications such as Sparkle may not be compatible with the hardware decompression methods employed by the MPEG card and the applications that support it. There is no work-around for this. You cannot play software decompression movies with applications that support the MPEG card."

Solve It! Problems Transferring Graphics Across Applications

You Are Unable to Paste a Graphic Across Applications

Symptoms:

You copy a selected graphic to the clipboard and shift to another application (a word processor, graphics application, or whatever) to paste the graphic into a document. Unfortunately, one of the following events happens:

- The Paste command is dimmed and cannot be used.
- Nothing at all appears when you select Paste.
- Something other than what you most recently copied is pasted.

These symptoms are not limited to graphics and may occur whenever you use the clipboard.

SEE: • Chapter 9, "Problems Copying and Pasting Text Across Applications"

Causes:

- **The graphic never copied to the system clipboard**
  Obviously, a graphic image will not paste successfully if it was never copied successfully. This can happen for the same general reason first discussed for text transfers in Chapter 9, which involves the distinction between the application versus system clipboards.

To review briefly, there are really two clipboards, an application clipboard (used in the creating application) and a system clipboard (used when going between applications). Information is supposed to be converted from the application clipboard to the system clipboard when you switch programs, but it does not always work properly if you have multiple applications open.

- **The application does not support graphics placement**

If either of these problems occurs, the Paste command will either be dimmed, will paste nothing, or will paste whatever was previously in the system Clipboard.

What to do:

Check Show Clipboard

To check if the graphic was transferred to the system clipboard, select the Show Clipboard command in the Finder's Edit menu. Look in the Clipboard window to see its contents.

Figure 10-14 *The Finder's Show Clipboard command, and the Clipboard window that opens when you select this command.*

Update the System Clipboard If Necessary

If the image is not in the clipboard, you will need to update the system Clipboard. To do this, try any or all of the following steps.

1. Quit the application you were using when you copied the graphic. (If you get a message such as one that says "Save large clipboard?" select Yes.) Return to the receiving application and try pasting again.
2. Go to the Finder and then back to the receiving application. Try pasting again.
3. Recopy the graphic and paste it to the Scrapbook. Then shift to the application where you wish to paste the graphic, go to the Scrapbook, and copy the desired graphic. Now return to the application and select Paste.
4. Go to the System Folder and locate the file called Clipboard. Drag it to the Trash; a new file will be created automatically. Now try to recopy and paste your graphic. This may work, especially if the Clipboard file was damaged.
5. If none of the above succeeds, try copying and pasting a few more times. Sometimes, for unknown reasons, it may eventually work.

Check If the Application Supports Graphics Placement

If the image is in the clipboard but you cannot get it to paste, the application probably doesn't accept graphics (for example, a spreadsheet may not accept graphics in its cells). In such cases, when a graphic is on the clipboard, the Paste command is usually dimmed so that you cannot select it. Even if it is not dimmed, nothing will appear when you select Paste. Check the application's manual for more details as to what can be pasted into it.

Use Drag and Drop, Clippings Files, and Scrapbook

Drag and Drop is a System 7.5 feature (also partially available in System 7.1) that allows you to drag a highlighted selection directly from one document to another, even across applications, without needing the intervening copy-and-paste steps traditionally used by the clipboard.

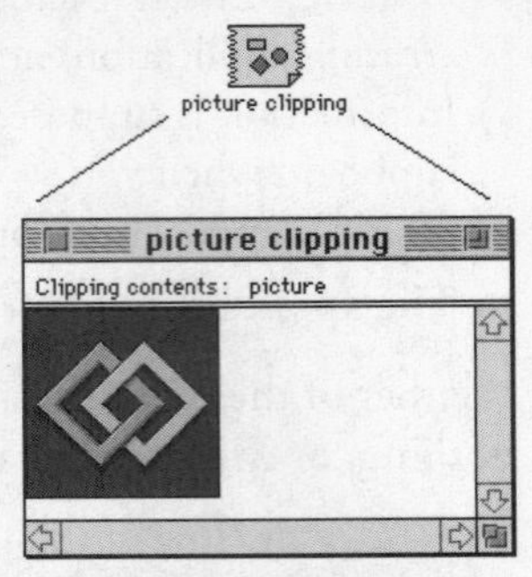

Figure 10-15 *A picture clippings file with its window open.*

You can even drag a selection to the Finder's desktop and create a special *clippings* file, that can later be dragged to another document, largely bypassing the need for the Scrapbook. You can have multiple clippings files on your desk; double-clicking one of these files opens up a window showing its contents.

Among standard Apple programs, you can drag clippings or selected items directly to or from the Scrapbook, SimpleText, or the Notepad. (The Scrapbook in System 7.5 also gives information about the format of what is stored there.) Third-party software will work only if it has been designed to use these features.

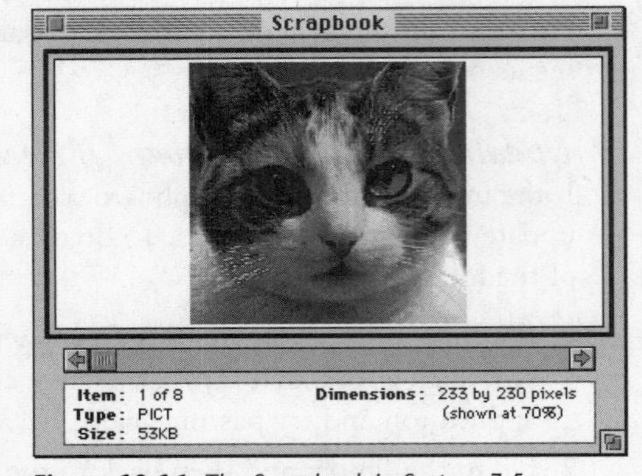

Figure 10-16 *The Scrapbook in System 7.5.*

If these features do not work with any software, make sure you have the needed extensions installed and enabled (such as the Clippings extension). They should be installed automatically when you select an Easy Install of the system software.

These methods may have no more chance of success than using the clipboard, but they're worth a try.

SEE:
- **"By the Way: Cosmetic Bug with Clippings Files," and "By the Way: More Ways to Bypass the Clipboard," in Chapter 9, for related information**
- **Chapter 13 for more on the Scrapbook, as well as more general information on System 7.5**

Import the Graphic

If none of the preceding suggestions solves the problem, try importing the graphic. This often succeeds even when the clipboard fails.

Successful importing depends on the receiving application having the relevant file-translation filter for the format of data to be imported. Even if you have the correct filter, however, the import may still fail. (If so, you typically get an error message.) This is a particularly common problem with the TIFF format, because there are several variations of the format. You can't do much about a failure at this point, other than return to the original application and see if you can save the file in a different format

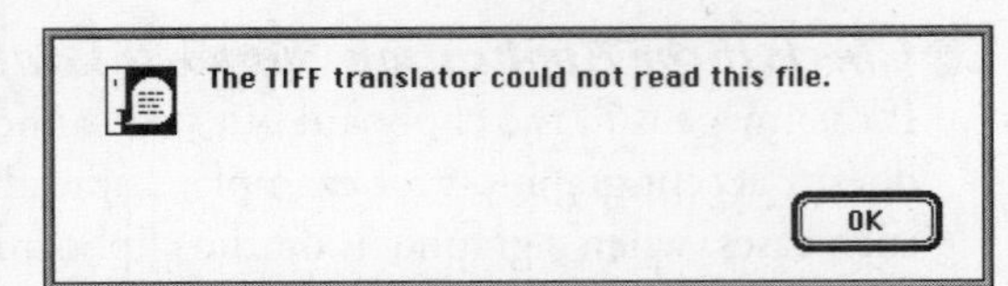

Figure 10-17 *This message appeared when a program was unable to import a TIFF file, even though the application had a TIFF translator.*

that will be accepted by the importing application. In general, avoid application-specific formats, as these are the least likely to be importable; use generic formats instead.

By the way, beware of using Mac OS Easy Open when importing graphics (for example, EPS or TIFF files into PageMaker). If you are having problems, turn Easy Open off.

SEE: • **Chapter 6 for more on importing problems**

TAKE NOTE ▶

FOREIGN IMPORTS

I use the term *importing* to refer to the process where an entire file created by one application is opened in another application. This process bypasses the clipboard. When you import a file, you usually open the entire file via the Open dialog box as a separate document in its own window, exactly as if it were being opened by the application that created it.

In other cases, you may be able to import a file to a specified location of an already open document, rather than opening it as a separate document. Applications that can do this usually have special commands for this feature (with names such as Import, Place, or Insert).

In either case, the import procedure still requires the relevant file translation filter.

Otherwise ...

If none of the previous suggestions succeed, you are probably stuck and will not be able to transfer the graphic to the application in question. If you do finally get the graphic to transfer, however, you may find that your problems are still not over. In particular, you may find that the graphic is no longer in its original file format. If this happens, check out the next section ("File Format Shifts When Transferring Graphics Across Applications").

BY THE WAY ▶

SPECIAL PROBLEMS WITH THE PLACEMENT OF A GRAPHIC IN A TEXT DOCUMENT

When you are trying to paste a graphic image into a word processor or similar type of application, you may find that the graphic itself pastes just fine—it's just that you can't get it in the desired location within the document. For example, you may want the graphic to appear to the left of a paragraph of text, or you may want the adjoining text to wrap around the shape of the graphic. Instead, what you may get is the graphic appearing by itself on a separate line below the paragraph, or directly overlaying the paragraph and obscuring your view of the text.

Neither the graphic itself nor a problem related to the clipboard or importing method is responsible for this sort of incorrect placement. Rather, it is inherent in how the application treats pasted or imported graphics. Because different word processors use different methods, you should consult your application's manual for the details of its approach; look especially for features related to "text wrapping."

Many word processors and integrated packages (like ClarisWorks) are now quite flexible in how they handle graphics placement. Still, if you are not satisfied with the limitations of your application, the only solution is to use a different one. If this is a frequent problem, you might consider investing in a page-layout program (such as PageMaker or QuarkXPress). These programs provide the greatest flexibility in how graphics and text can be combined.

File Format Shifts When Transferring Graphics Across Applications

Symptoms:

A graphic image is successfully transferred from one application to another (typically by copying and pasting), but one of these errors occurs:

- The display quality of the transferred image is poorer than when it is displayed in the original application.
- When you print the transferred graphic, its quality is distinctly inferior to that obtained when printing it from the original application.

These problems are most common with documents originally formatted in TIFF or EPSF.

Causes:

The primary cause is that when graphics are transferred across applications, they are typically converted to a PICT format, regardless of the format of the document from which they originated. This is especially a problem with TIFF and EPS files, since these formats contain special printing-related information (such as an EPS file's PostScript instructions) that are lost in the conversion to a PICT format.

Copy and Paste, Publish and Subscribe, Drag and Drop

This PICT conversion most commonly occurs when you use standard system software methods—such as the clipboard (copying and pasting), publish and subscribe, or drag and drop—to transfer a graphic image. For example, if you paste an image from a TIFF file to the Scrapbook, it will be converted to a PICT file. You can confirm this by checking the format of the pasted file in the Scrapbook window; in the lower left corner of the window, you might see a graphic's "Type" indicated as PICT. Fortunately, this conversion problem does not occur when transfers are made within the same application.

Importing

This conversion problem may also occur when you import graphics documents. Don't assume that because an application has a translator for the TIFF format, for example, the imported file is retained in TIFF format. The outcome depends on the features of the importing application.

What to do:

Use the Option Key to Copy PostScript Code to the Clipboard

If you are trying to transfer EPS images via the Clipboard, note that graphics applications supporting this format (such as Adobe Illustrator) can usually copy both the PICT image and the embedded PostScript code. To do this, hold down the Option key when you select Copy. If you then paste this copied image into any other program that can accept the PostScript code, both the image and the PostScript code will paste. Check with the manual of your program to see if it accepts PostScript code.

Import Rather than Copy or Publish

In general, if you were unsuccessful in preserving the format of an image when using either the clipboard or a publish-and-subscribe approach, try importing instead (if this option is available). Importing is often more successful in preserving a graphic's format.

SEE: • **"Take Note: Foreign Imports," in the previous section, for more details**

For LaserWriter Users: Save the Selection as an EPS File

If you want to transfer a graphic to another application with its EPS format preserved and standard importing methods did not or could not work, try selecting Print and saving the selection or file in EPS format (by selecting File, rather than Printer, as the Destination). Then try to open the file in the receiving application.

SEE: • **Chapter 7, "Technically Speaking: LaserWriter 8.4's 'Destination' Option"**

Try a Different Application

If transferring to your first-choice application does not succeed in preserving the format, try transferring to a different application (assuming that you have another one suitable for your needs). Perhaps the alternate application will preserve formats correctly.

For example, page-layout programs such as PageMaker tend to preserve most formats they import. Word processors, in contrast, often convert all graphics to a PICT format, though some can preserve the EPS format. Graphics programs vary in this regard.

Photoshop is particularly good at being able to open and/or import a variety of graphics formats.

SEE: • **Chapter 6 for more general problems in opening files**

Use QuickDraw GX

Apple has claimed that the QuickDraw GX clipboard can retain graphics format information (such as TIFF and EPS) when transferring graphics across applications. This eliminates the problem of all formats being converted to the PICT format when they are transferred, but it only works with software upgraded to support this new feature. Given the overall lack of popularity of QuickDraw GX, I am not sure how much value this option has at this time.

SEE: • **Chapter 13 for more on QuickDraw GX**

Ignore the Problem

Otherwise, these format shifts cannot be avoided if they occur; they are inherent to the operation of the system and/or application software. You may, however, choose to ignore this problem. Even in its changed file format, the image may be satisfactory for your needs. In this case, you need do nothing at all. To maintain the original application's format, however, you are limited to editing or printing the file from its original application.

Related Problems

Two other issues related to this general problem are discussed in detail elsewhere.

Problems with the Importing Application When you transfer a graphics selection to another graphics application, its appearance and the methods available to edit the graphic depend more on the features of the importing application than on the document itself. For example, a paint program converts all transferred graphics to bitmapped images, regardless of their original format. For PostScript graphics, such as EPS files, other special problems may occur.

SEE: • **"Paint Versus Draw Programs," earlier in this chapter**
• **"Problems Printing PostScript Graphics," later in this chapter**

Color Problems The displayed colors of a transferred graphic may be different from the way they were in the original application.

SEE: • **"Color Shift Problems," in the following section**

Solve It! Problems Displaying Color/Grayscale

With the increased amount of RAM and video RAM common on today's Macintoshes, and the increased speed of the Macs themselves, problems here have lessened considerably (since most of them can be solved simply by using a faster Mac with more RAM). Still, for those still facing these challenges, here's what you need to know.

Color Shift Problems

Symptoms:

- When you are transferring graphics (such as via the clipboard, by using publish and subscribe, or by importing), the colors of the image shift. As a result, the transferred graphic now displays in colors different than it did in the creating application.
- If two or more documents are open within a single application, changing to another document as the active document may cause the displayed colors of the previously active document to shift temporarily.
- When you are using a color graphics program, the colors displayed in other open applications (including the Finder) may temporarily shift to the wrong colors.

Causes:

This is more of a minor irritation than a real problem. No damage or permanent change has been done to your document; your graphic remains fully capable of displaying correctly. Often, in fact, just closing a window will solve the problem.

Understanding why this happens, however, does provide some useful information about how the Macintosh works. The primary cause in all of these cases is a limitation of working in less than 16- or 24-bit color.

Color Palettes

Even at an 8-bit color depth, you have access to all of the millions of colors that a color monitor can display. The problem is that only 256 can be displayed at one time. So the question becomes, what 256 colors get displayed?

The default system-level choice (at 8-bit color depth) is a set of 256 colors called the *system colors* (there is a similar default choice for other depths). Depending on the application in use, your available colors may differ from the system colors. In some cases, you may be able to select from separate sets of 256 colors that are called *color palettes.* In such cases the system-color palette becomes just one of many possible palette choices. (For example, there may also be palettes for earth tones and pastels.) A palette need not fill all 256 available colors, but no more than one palette can be in use at the same time.

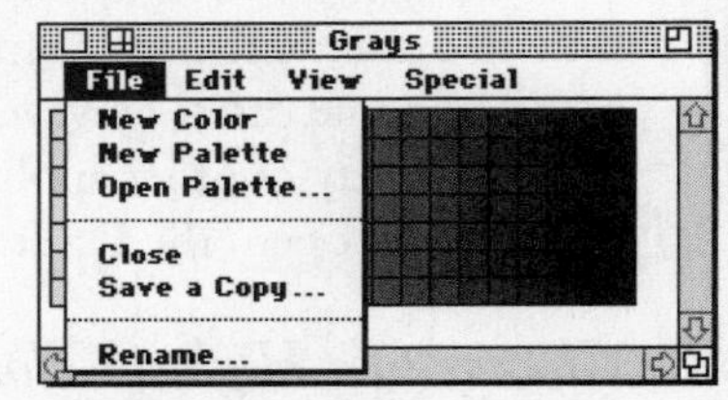

Figure 10-18 *A graphic application's color palette window, displaying a palette of different shades of gray.*

This restriction can lead to what I call *color shift* problems. For example, if you open a document that was created using the system-color palette while an earth-tone palette is active, the document may be displayed in the wrong colors (that is, in the earth tones rather than the system colors). Similarly, if two graphics are open at the same time and they use different palettes, the system may correctly display the active window while the back window shifts accordingly to the wrong colors. Finally, in some cases, if a graphic uses a palette other than the system palette, it may be displayed in the wrong colors whenever it is opened in an application other than its creating application, no matter what depth setting is in use.

What to do:

Quit and Relaunch the Application

Just quitting and relaunching the current application could solve the problem. This is especially likely to work if your colors shifted immediately after you changed resolutions with a multiscan monitor.

BY THE WAY ▶

DISPLAY ODDITIES WITH MULTISCAN MONITORS

With Apple's multiscan monitors, changing a resolution while an application is open may result in the colors displaying incorrectly, or windows that have moved halfway off the screen or are missing altogether. These problems can usually be fixed by quitting and reopening the problem application. Otherwise, you may have to return to your original resolution.

SEE: • **"Multiscan Monitors" and "Setting the Depth and Resolution of the Display," earlier in this chapter**

Use Another Application, If Possible

Assuming you have more than one application that can display the graphic, try another application; it may work better. For example, I have found differences between two word processors in their ability to import color TIFF documents. Both word processors opened the TIFF file, but only one displayed the colors correctly.

Select the Desired Document to Be the Active Window

At 8-bit (or less) color depths, the display of the entire monitor—that is, all windows from all open applications—typically reflects the color palette of the currently active document. If other open documents use different palettes, they may display incorrectly when they are not the active document (using the colors of the document that is active).

This is an aesthetic problem, and you can ignore it if you wish. The monitor should shift to display the correct colors for each document when it is made the active document. In some cases, however, you may have to quit the relevant graphics application to get the display of other applications to return to normal. For example, with certain applications open, the Finder's desktop is always displayed in incorrect colors.

Change to a Higher Color Depth

Shifting to 24-bit (or even 16-bit) color from the Monitors control panel, if this option is available, generally solves all these problems, since this removes the 8-bit restriction of 256 colors. Besides allowing a greater range of colors, these higher depths use a different method to determine what colors to display. This method tends to ensure more accurate matching of colors for graphics transferred across applications. The main potential problem here is if you are using an application that does not run at higher than an 8-bit depth, as explained more in the next section.

BY THE WAY ▶

APPLE'S COLOR PICKER

In many programs, there are instances where you have the option to select your own choice of color from all the colors that are available. For this task, they often depend upon Apple's Color Picker, a system extension. One way to access it is to select the Color control panel and then select "Other ..." from the choices for highlight color.

Note that in recent versions of this software, if you select More Choices, you get two options: HSL (for Hue, Saturation, and Lightness) and RGB (for Red, Green, and Blue). In the first option, you get the familiar color wheel, which you click on to make a choice. In the latter option, three sliders can be adjusted to your desired RGB values.

Problems Displaying at Different Color Depths

Symptoms:

- You want to display a document at a high color depth, typically Thousands (16-bit) or Millions (24-bit), but these options are not listed in the Monitors control panel.
- You select Thousands or Millions from the Monitors control panel, but the document still does not display in these depths.
- An application will not open in certain color depths.
- A document does not display in the selected color depth.

SEE ALSO: • **"Setting the Depth and Resolution of the Display," earlier in this chapter**

Causes:

Hardware and/or system software that is inadequate to the task is the main cause of this problem. Perhaps you have never attempted to use 24-bit color before. In this case, part of the problem is to determine if your machine can even display in this mode, and if not, why not.

Other causes have to do with software, such as incorrect settings from the Monitors (or Monitors & Sound) control panel or problems with the application and/or document itself.

What to do:

Make Sure You Have the Necessary Hardware and System Software

This is not the place for a complete course in what you need to display at higher color depths. Here, however, are the main things to consider:

- You need a color monitor.
- You need a Macintosh model with the necessary color-display instructions built into its ROM. Virtually all recent models fit this bill.
- You need sufficient video RAM (called VRAM) to display at higher color depths. Some amount of VRAM is included on the logic board of most Macintoshes; if it is not sufficient, you may be able to add more. For example, Apple's current PCI-based Macs have four slots for holding VRAM cards. They typically only come with two of these slots filled.

  Otherwise, you will need to add a special *video card* to increase the available VRAM. These hardware additions will require opening up your Macintosh.

- You need sufficient ordinary RAM as well. These days, figure on having at least 8MB of RAM if you regularly use 24-bit color on a 14-inch monitor. If you don't have enough RAM, you usually will get an alert message of some sort when you try to open a 24-bit color document. Some Macs make use of a portion of ordinary RAM as a substitute for VRAM; in these cases, your RAM needs will be even higher than on other Macs (though you may be able to bypass this use of RAM by installing a separate VRAM video card).
- The larger the size of your monitor, the more RAM and/or VRAM you will need to achieve a particular color depth. In other words, for a given RAM/VRAM, you may be able to display 24-bit color with a 14-inch monitor, but only up to a maximum of 8-bit color with a 21-inch monitor.

SEE: **• Fix-It #1 for more on hardware incompatibilities**

Select the Desired Setting from the Monitors/Monitors & Sound Control Panel

Assuming you now have the appropriate hardware, the higher depth options in the Monitors (or Monitors & Sound) control panel should be listed. Still, they don't work unless you select them. If you are not seeing 24-bit color, the solution may be as simple as going to the Monitors control panel and selecting the Millions options.

Allocate Enough Memory to Run in 24-Bit (or 16-Bit) Mode

If you can't open a document in 24-bit color because of insufficient memory, you may not necessarily need to buy more RAM or VRAM. First, try the following steps:

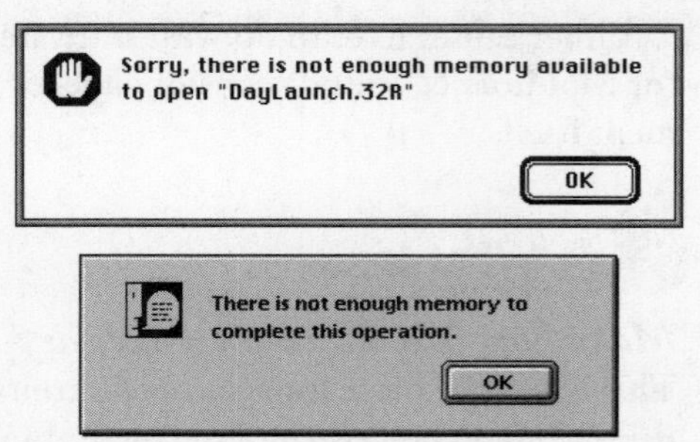

Figure 10-19 *Top: An error message that appeared because of insufficient memory to open a 24-bit color document. Bottom: A message that appeared in ClarisDraw when working with bitmapped graphics.*

1. Increase the memory allocation of the application, typically via its Get Info setting. Some applications do not set their default allocation at a high enough level to open 24-bit documents. In some cases, the application may provide its own options for temporarily increasing its allocation.
2. If you don't have enough free RAM available to increase the application's memory allocation, make more memory available by quitting other open applications, restarting with extensions off, or using virtual memory (or RAM Doubler).

SEE: **• Fix-It #6 for more on these memory-enhancing techniques**

BY THE WAY ▶

BITMAPPED "BOXES" AND MEMORY

In programs such as ClarisWorks and ClarisDraw, you can open up a bitmapped graphic "box" within a draw document. These take up much more memory than other objects in the document. As a result, you are more likely to get "out of memory" messages, especially if you make the box too large and then try to copy and paste anything to or from it. One solution is to close other open documents in that application; another is to try to use a smaller bitmapped box. Otherwise, you will have to quit the application, increase its memory allocation, and try again.

Make Sure Your Application Can Run in the Desired Display Depth

Some programs will only run at one color depth (such as 256 colors); using either a lower or a higher depth will not work. Others require a certain minimum depth. Usually, if there is a problem, you will get an alert message informing you of the situation when you try to launch the application. Use the Monitors control panel to change the depth as needed.

In some cases, the application will successfully launch at a 24-bit depth setting even though it is actually incapable of displaying documents in 24-bit color. Check your application's manual for details on this glitch.

These are increasingly rare problems today, as most current software is 24-bit compatible. If you want to run at 24-bit depth and the application is incompatible with that setting, however, there is nothing you can do about it aside from using a different application that is compatible.

Make Sure the Document Can Be Displayed at the Desired Display Depth

Remember, even if you are at a 24-bit depth setting and using a 24-bit compatible application, a particular graphic document may not be able to take advantage of that depth level. For example, a document originally created and saved at an 8-bit color depth will not change its appearance if displayed in 24-bit depth. Similarly, a black-and-white image still displays in black and white even if you are using 8-bit color.

Conversely, an image's display cannot exceed the current depth-level setting. Thus, if you open a 24-bit color document while in 8-bit mode, you will not see all the colors that may have been in the original document, because no more than 256 can be displayed at one time. Typically, what you will see is an 8-bit dithered approximation of the 24-bit image. Similarly, all documents opened in 1-bit mode will be displayed in black and white.

Bear in mind that changing the color depth (via the Monitors control panels) affects only the display, not the contents of the graphics document itself. The color information is remembered even if it isn't seen. When you shift back from the 1-bit to the 8-bit depth, for example, an 8-bit color graphic will once more be displayed using its proper colors.

Give Up

If all has gone well, your color image should now be on display in all its spectacular glory. Otherwise, it's time to give up.

Solve It! Problems Printing Graphics

The printer is the final arbiter of what the printed output looks like. No matter what other hardware and software you have, the quality of the printed copy can never exceed the capabilities of the printer.

SEE:
- **Chapter 7, "Take Note: Different Types of Printers," for an introduction to different types of printers**
- **Chapter 7 for an introduction to the Page Setup and Print dialog boxes, printer drivers, and problems getting any printout to appear**
- **Chapter 9 for printing problems specific to formatting of text documents**
- **"Types of Graphics, Programs, and Files" and "File Format Shifts When Transferring Graphics Across Applications," earlier in this chapter, for printing problems related to different graphic formats**

Problems Printing Color/Grayscale to a Black-and-White Printer

Symptoms:

When you print a grayscale or color image to a black-and-white printer such as a LaserWriter, the image quality appears distinctly different from the way it appears on the screen (usually worse).

Causes:

Printing a color or grayscale image to a black-and-white printer requires the printer to approximate the look of the image with its limited one-color (black) capability.

Sadly, this approximation is often less than wonderful. The resolution may be great (because it is at 600 dpi instead of the screen's 72 dpi), but the overall image may still be reduced to a disconcerting set of large black-and-white blotches that render the image almost indiscernible. The quality of the approximation depends on a number of factors, including the particular application in use, the features of the printer, and the printer driver.

What to do:

Short of using a color printer, there is no perfect solution to this problem. Here, however, are some partial solutions.

Select Enhancement Options from the Print Dialog Box

The success of these solutions depends partly on whether a particular application is written to be aware of them. As a result, your success may vary across different applications.

- **Color/Grayscale**
  For PostScript LaserWriters, select the Color/Grayscale option rather than the Black & White option (accessed by selecting Color Matching in LaserWriter 8.4). Doing this causes the printer drivers to generate an improved dithered (or halftone) output; it does not alter the file or the screen display in any way.

  This is probably the most important thing you can do to improve print quality. If you leave the setting at Black & White, you will likely get an extremely poor output.

Figure 10-20 *The Color/Grayscale option, as listed in the Color Matching window of the LaserWriter 8.4 Print dialog box.*

  With LaserWriter drivers, the rationale for a choice between Black & White versus Color/Grayscale is that Black & White is faster. With LaserWriter 8, though, the print speed is apparently the same with either option, so you should always use Color/Grayscale.

- **PhotoGrade, FinePrint, and GrayShare/ColorShare**
  Some Apple LaserWriters may include other Print options, such as PhotoGrade, that further enhance printing of grayscale images. These printers typically have a companion option (useful whether or not you are printing grayscale/color), called FinePrint, that helps make edges appear extra smooth. Some non-AppleTalk Apple printers have a feature similar to PhotoGrade that is called GrayShare or ColorShare. (Yes, this is the same GrayShare/ColorShare mentioned in Chapter 7 as a networking utility; hence its two-part name.) Other printers may have their own unique halftone/dither options. These are all printer-dependent processes that have no direct relationship to the screen display.

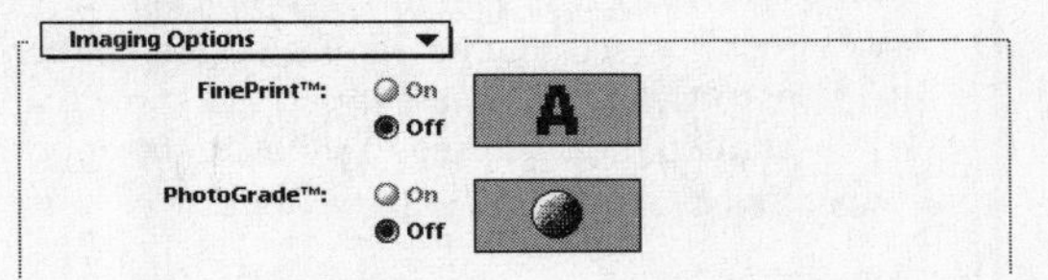

Figure 10-21 *Depending on your selected printer, the Print dialog box may have special options such as PhotoGrade and FinePrint, as seen in this Imaging Options window of the LaserWriter 8.4 Print dialog box for a LaserWriter Pro 630.*

Use Halftone Options Built into Specific Applications

Some applications, particularly page-layout programs and image-processing software (including Photoshop), have options to override a PostScript LaserWriter's default halftoning routines. With these applications, you could select a halftone dot pattern different from the LaserWriter's default choice. Depending on the particular graphic, a different pattern can significantly improve the graphic's printed appearance. Experiment with these choices if they are available in your application (see the relevant manuals for more information on how and why to do this).

Using these halftone options typically requires that your image be saved in the TIFF format. Color/Grayscale should also be selected from the Print dialog box.

TECHNICALLY SPEAKING ▶

HALFTONES

Halftoning is the name for a printing process used to simulate the appearance of grays by printing black-and-white dots. It has the same function as dithering. Technically, halftoning is based on a special photographic process where the image is broken up into a series of differently sized dots (small black dots for lighter areas, larger black dots for darker areas). On the printers commonly used with a Macintosh, however, halftoning is not handled the same way, since these printers can only print dots in a single size (such as 300 dpi). Instead they use digital halftoning, which involves setting up equal-sized cells of a given number of dots. The more dots in a cell are filled in (that is, black instead of white), the darker the shade of gray represented by that cell.

There is a trade-off here. Larger cells allow for more shades of gray (because there are more dots per cell), but they result in lower resolution of the image (because the number of cells per inch decreases as cell size gets larger). The result of this trade-off is that, at typical LaserWriter resolutions, halftoning cannot simulate anything close to the full 256 shades of gray seen on an 8-bit display. Under the best circumstances (using Apple's best LaserWriters with PhotoGrade enhancement), you can get only about 90 shades of gray; with other LaserWriters, you may get as few as 36 shades of gray. Still, this may result in satisfactory printouts, at least for nonprofessional uses.

If you need more shades of gray than you can currently get, the best solution is to shift to a printer that has a higher overall resolution. For example, a 600-dpi LaserWriter can simulate more shades of gray than an equally full-featured 300-dpi LaserWriter. Printers with a resolution higher than 600 dpi can do even better.

This topic is a lot more complex than I have presented here; for example, I could get into such subjects as lines per inch, screen patterns, and screen frequency and angle. For present purposes, though, it is enough to know that halftoning is a first cousin to dithering—a printing method used to simulate the appearance of shades of gray using only black ink.

Dither the Image Prior to Printing

Some graphics applications have an option to create a dithered image from a grayscale or color image. In some cases, the application may automatically do this prior to printing; in others, you must manually request for this to be done. For example, in Photoshop, look for the Bitmap command in the Mode menu. If you want to save the new dithered image, however, be sure to save it as a separate document and not to discard the original document, because the dithering process strips away all the color/grayscale information from the original image. If you later want to display the dithered image in color, you will not be able to do so.

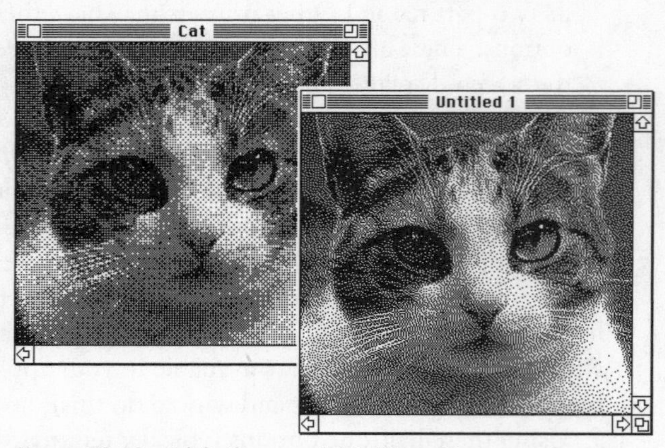

Figure 10-22 *At left, the same 1-bit dithered image as shown in Figure 10-1; at right, an application-generated dithered image of the same graphic. Notice the improvement in the image on the right.*

The printout resulting from a dithered screen image is often better than if you print directly from the grayscale or color image, depending on the printer's dithering process. If you have a PostScript LaserWriter, however, you will usually be better off using the printer's enhancements, as described in the previous sections.

By the way, do not use the 1-bit (Black & White) setting from the Monitors control panel as a substitute for an application's 1-bit dithering options. These options are by no means equivalent. The printout resulting from shifting to the Monitors 1-bit setting, while perhaps improved from the original printout, is still distinctly less attractive than an application-generated dithered pattern.

TECHNICALLY SPEAKING ▶

A WORD ABOUT SCANNERS

This book doesn't delve much into the use of scanners, but here is one useful tidbit worth knowing: When scanning something to be printed, you are typically better off selecting a dpi resolution that is *less* than that of your black-and-white printer (at least half the resolution is often good). This is because halftoning typically requires at least two dots on a printer to print a dot of scanned image. Actually, a preferred alternative is to scan at a high resolution and then use a program, such as Photoshop, to *downsample* the image to the lower resolution.

In general, it doesn't pay to save your finished image at a higher resolution than that of the device (printer or display) you intend to use as the output for your image.

Problems Printing Color/Grayscale to a Color Printer

Symptoms:

A color document displays fine on the screen but prints incorrectly. In particular, either the document is printed in the wrong colors or the entire image quality is poor.

Causes:

Color printers have difficulty getting their printed output to match what appears on the screen. This can be due to any of the following:

- Limitations of the printer technology
- Problems resulting from the fact that screen colors (which are from a light source) are produced differently from printed color (which is from a pigment source)
- Especially for inkjet printers, one or more colored inks may have emptied for the ink cartridge

SEE: • **"Technically Speaking: Professional Color Matching"**

By the way, if your problem is not specific to the use of color, then the same causes and solutions described in the previous section ("Problems Printing Color/Grayscale to a Black-and-White Printer") apply here as well. If this is the case, refer first to that section for advice.

What to do:

Select Color Options from the Print Dialog Box

- **For color LaserWriters: Color/Grayscale and more**
  With LaserWriter 8.4, make sure you have at least selected Color/Grayscale from the Print Color pop-up menu in the Color Matching window. You will be better off selecting PostScript Color Matching, however, and then also selecting the printer-specific name from the Printer Profile pop-up menu. These settings are critical; if you leave the setting at Black & White, you will get extremely poor output.

  You may alternatively choose to select ColorSync Color Matching (which then invokes ColorSync, as described more in the next section), although my understanding is that PostScript Color Matching remains the preferred choice here.

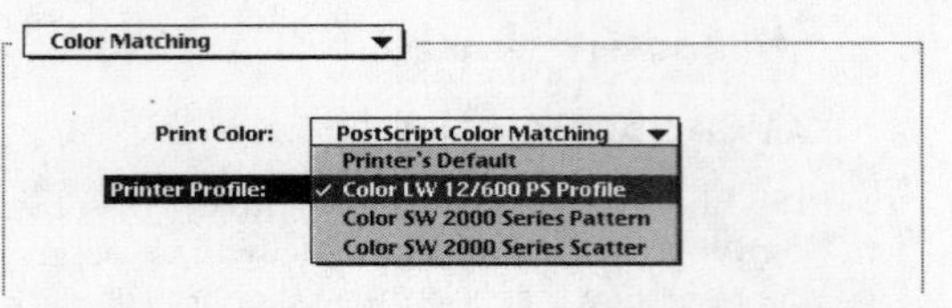

Figure 10-23 *The Color Matching window of the LaserWriter 8.4 Print dialog box. PostScript Color Matching has been selected as the Print Color, and the Printer Profile for the Color LaserWriter is highlighted in the pop-up menu.*

- **For color StyleWriters (and other inkjet printers)**
  Check what printer-specific options may be available for enhancing color output.

  For example, for Color StyleWriters, select Color from the Image pop-up menu in the Print dialog box. Then click the Color button and, from the window that appears, select whether you want Pattern or Scatter as a Halftoning Option (Scatter is generally better for photograph-type images).

  Optionally, you may also select to use ColorSync, as described next. This choice apparently does not remain selected by default, so you may have to reselect this and other options each time you print.

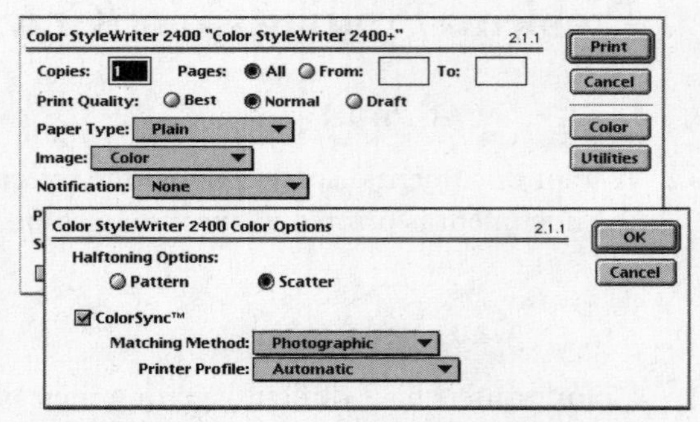

Figure 10-24 *The Color options for Apple's Color StyleWriters.*

  Hewlett-Packard's printer drivers may include proprietary color matching software, called ColorSmart.

Use Apple's ColorSync

ColorSync's sole function is to give the user easy automated control over color matching by having one simple set of options that will work with all your different hardware.

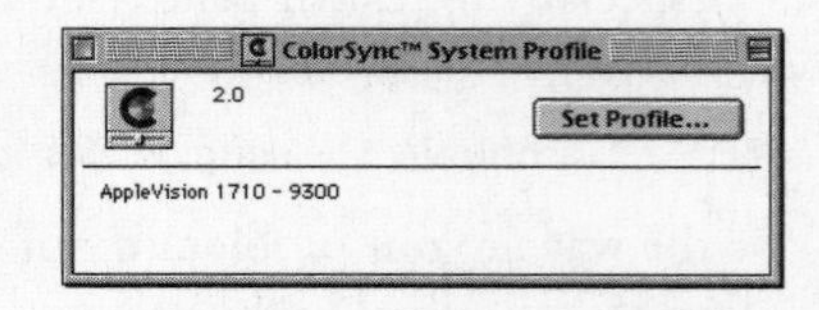

Figure 10-25 *The ColorSync System Profile control panel, with the AppleVision 1710AV monitor selected.*

Assuming that the needed ColorSync software is installed (it is included as part of System 7.5 and comes with all Apple color printers), your first step

TECHNICALLY SPEAKING ▶

PROFESSIONAL COLOR MATCHING

If you are really serious about color printing, you need to get into color matching techniques that go well beyond the solutions covered in this section. Here are some key issues:

- The colors on a monitor are produced by a combination of red, green, and blue lights (RGB), whereas most printers use a combination of cyan, yellow, magenta, and black inks (CYMK). Because translating an RGB display into a CYMK printed output is not an exact science, the two images are rarely an exact match. Many high-end graphics and page-layout programs have (often complex) features that attempt to compensate for this difference. Apple's ColorSync extension is basically an attempt to make this process more accessible to nonexperts.
- Many specialized graphics and page-layout programs can perform a process called *color separation*. This is where the document is separated into four (or more) colored layers that are each saved separately and then combined by a professional printing process to produce the final multicolor output. This process is essential to professional-level full-color printing as seen in glossy magazines.

As usual in this area, things are even more complicated than this summary may suggest. If you went further, you would soon find yourself talking about matters such as process versus spot colors, Pantone color selection, and more. But take heart! Nonprofessionals often find that the less-than-perfect output they get, without any special knowledge or effort, is still satisfactory for their needs.

is to select the ColorSync's control panel and select the name of the monitor that is connected to your Mac. All Apple monitors should be listed; whether non-Apple monitors are listed will depend upon whether a profile file (as stored in the ColorSync Profiles folder in the Preferences folder) was included with the software that came with your monitor.

For printing, the remaining ColorSync options are selected from the Print dialog box (the exact location is described in the previous section). ColorSync can potentially work with any printer, scanner, or other imaging device, whether it is from Apple or not. You just need to have the appropriate profile file for the device.

In general, make sure that both the ColorSync extension and control panel are enabled. Otherwise, ColorSync will not work.

For more detailed advice on using ColorSync, check your Mac's Users Guide or Apple Guide file.

Special Case: Color StyleWriter Output is in the Wrong Colors or Otherwise Distorted

If the colors of your document look wrong, the image is distorted, or certain colors are missing—and you are sure that all software options (such as ColorSync, if you use it) are set correctly—then it is time to consider the printer itself as the cause. Typical causes are as follows:

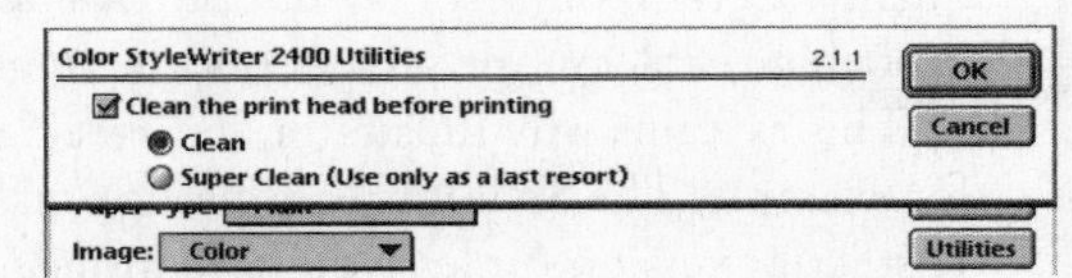

Figure 10-26 *The Utilities window for the Color StyleWriter.*

- A clogged nozzle is blocking the ink. To fix this, clean the print head by clicking the Utilities button in the Print dialog box, then select "Clean the print head before printing."
- One or more of the colors in the ink tanks is empty; you need to replace the ink tank or the entire ink cartridge. The four-color cartridge in a Color StyleWriter holds two separate ink tanks: one for cyan, magenta, and yellow and the other for black. Each tank can be replaced separately. (If you run out of yellow ink, for example, you will have to replace the tank that holds all three colors.) After several tank refills, you will want to replace the entire ink cartridge that houses the tanks.
- The Paper Type selected in the Print dialog box does not match the paper type that you are using. Alternatively, you may be using an inappropriate type of paper (such as erasable typing paper).

Otherwise, check the manual that came with your printer for more detailed advice.

SEE ALSO • **"Take Note: Troubleshooting StyleWriters," in Chapter 7**

Problems Printing PostScript Graphics

Symptoms:

- You print a document that contains PostScript instructions, such as an EPS file, but it does not print out with the overall image quality you expect.
- Certain graphics objects, such as hairlines, do not print at all.

Causes:

Either you are not using a PostScript printer or you are not using an application that supports PostScript printing. In these cases, what will happen is that you will typically print a less detailed PICT-based image approximation of the PostScript instructions.

What to do:

Make Sure You Are Using a PostScript Printer

Obviously, with a non-PostScript printer, the printed graphic image will be of inferior quality. Certain objects may not print at all. For example, hairline graphics, though probably visible on the screen, may be totally missing from printed output.

This explains why Illustrator and FreeHand files will print incorrectly to a StyleWriter, for example. The StyleWriter at best prints the PICT version of the file, not the PostScript version (unless you have installed a software PostScript interpreter, such as Freedom of Press or StyleScript, as mentioned earlier in this chapter in "By the Way: PostScript Graphics Without a PostScript Printer").

Make Sure the Application Supports PostScript

Many graphics applications do not support PostScript printing. If you transfer a PostScript graphic to one of these programs, the PostScript information will not print—even if you have a PostScript printer.

Sometimes, this can be a problem for data transferred from programs whose use of PostScript instructions may be unfamiliar to you. For example, Microsoft Word uses PostScript to produce some special effects, such as background watermarks. These effects may not be printed if you import a Microsoft Word file to another non-PostScript supporting application.

Make Sure the File for an Imported EPS Graphic Is Still Available

Some programs, particularly page-layout programs such as PageMaker, import EPS graphics in a special way: instead of importing the full EPS information from the graphic, they create a link to the original EPS file. The screen display appears fine in such cases, displaying the PICT version of the graphic. When you print the file, however, PageMaker searches for the original linked graphic. To find it, the graphic file must still be present and bear the same name as when it was linked. If the graphic file cannot be found, the graphic will not print correctly.

Avoid PICT Files If Possible

Object-oriented PICT files, though they will normally print fine to your LaserWriter, sometimes cause problems when printing to PostScript printers, especially those used by professional printing services. The graphic may take unusually long to print, or print with inferior quality. Even fonts may print incorrectly when they are part of a PICT file.

Problems Printing Bitmapped Graphics

Symptoms:

Bitmapped graphics look distinctly inferior to the quality of printed text and/or object-oriented graphics.

Causes:

This is an inevitable consequence of the fact that most bitmapped graphics are at 72 dpi while the resolution of most printers is at 300 dpi or higher. Unlike object-oriented graphics, bitmapped images do not change their resolution to match that of the printer.

What to do:

Change the Graphic to an Object-Oriented Image

Redraw the graphic using an object-oriented graphics application. If the graphic is something simple, like a plain circle, this should not be hard to do. Otherwise, this may be impractical. For something like scanned photographic images, this is obviously not relevant advice.

Check If Your Application Supports Higher-Resolution Bitmaps

Some applications can create bitmapped images at higher resolutions, such as 300 dpi.

Use Preferred Formats

For example, the TIFF format will generally lead to better results for scanned photographs than the PICT format, especially when used in combination with image-processing software such as Photoshop.

Select Enhancements from the Page Setup Dialog Box

Some of these enhancements are available only with PostScript LaserWriters. With LaserWriter 8.4, they are found in the PostScript Options window of the Page Setup dialog box.

- **Select Smooth Graphics**
  Checking the Smooth Graphics option alters the appearance of bitmapped graphics by smoothing out curved lines and reducing jagged edges. This is supposed to improve the appearance of the graphic, but finely textured artwork may not look any better with this option on. It may even look worse. Similarly, if you selected Color/Grayscale, also selecting Smooth Graphics will probably make things worse. Try it both ways if you are in doubt.

  By the way, most LaserWriters also offer a Smooth Text option (for smoothing bitmapped text).

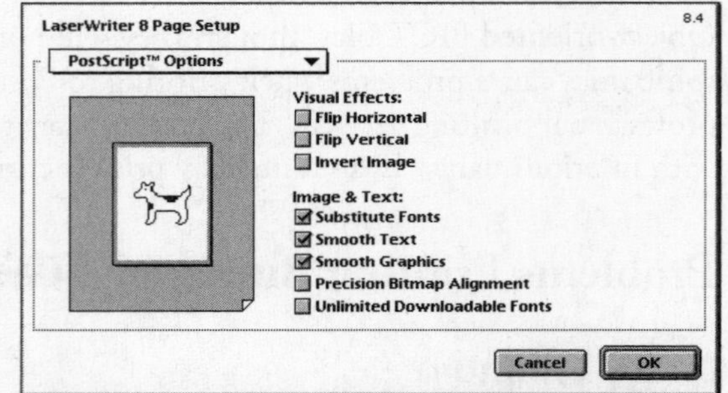

Figure 10-27 *The PostScript Options of the LaserWriter 8.4 Page Setup dialog box (seen after selecting PostScript Options from the pop-up menu near the top of the box).*

- **Select Precision Bitmap Alignment or Exact Bit Images**
  For PostScript LaserWriters, select Precision Bitmap Alignment. Other printers may have an essentially identical option called Exact Bit Images (Shrink 4%). These options reduce the size of the entire document by 4 percent, which generally improves the printed appearance of bitmapped graphics.

TECHNICALLY SPEAKING ▶

WHY A 4 PERCENT REDUCTION?

Precision Bitmap Alignment appears to be a strange option. Why reduce a document 4 percent, rather than 5 percent or whatever?

The reason has to do with the typical 72-dpi resolution of bitmapped graphics. A LaserWriter has a different resolution (typically 300 or 600 dpi). The LaserWriter must adjust the bitmapped image to match its own resolution. Because the printer cannot print a fraction of a dot, it does the best job of this conversion if the ratio between the resolution of the bitmapped image and the printer's resolution is a whole number. This cannot be done with an image resolution of 72 dpi and a common printer resolution of 300 dpi. If you reduce the image by 4 percent, however, the resolution is effectively raised to 75 dpi. Now the conversion process to 300 dpi can work with only whole dots, putting four dots in the printed image for every one dot in the bitmapped image (since 4 x 75 = 300). Thus, the 4 percent reduction eliminates distortions that might otherwise occur. Other reduction percentages that have a whole-number ratio are 72, 48, and 24 percent.

By the way, StyleWriter printers have no reduction option. Why not? Because its basic resolution is 360 dpi, which is exactly equal to 5 x 72. As a result, it prints at a whole-number ratio to the screen display without any adjustment needed.

Reducing everything by 4 percent (not just bitmapped graphics), though, can be a problem if your document is a mixture of text, object-oriented graphics, and/or bitmapped graphics. In these cases, I would avoid this option unless the appearance of your bitmapped graphics is critical.

- **Don't select Faster Bitmap Printing**
  This option is of little value and often causes more problems than it solves. In fact, it may prevent your document from being printed at all, even if your document contains no bitmapped graphics. If you are having any general printing problems with this option on, uncheck this option and try again. This option is no longer included in the LaserWriter 8 driver.

Use Anti-Aliasing

Anti-aliasing is a technique that can reduce the jagged edges of objects in bitmapped graphics, both text and non-text. It can help both for on-screen displays as well as in printed output. Anti-aliasing requires special software (such as Photoshop or a shareware program called Smoothie).

SEE" • "By the Way: Anti-Aliasing and The Jaggies," in Chapter 9, for more on anti-aliasing

Special Case: Problems with ImageWriter Printers

Symptoms:

An ImageWriter-printed graphic is either distorted or printed in an unacceptably poor resolution.

Causes:

I almost decided to drop this section from this edition of *Sad Macs*, as I expect that very few readers still use an ImageWriter. But for those of you who still do, I will explore this problem one last time.

The resolution of the ImageWriter is 72 dpi, which is rather paltry compared to the 300-dpi or greater capabilities of most current printers. No matter what software you use or what Macintosh model you own, you cannot alter this basic fact. This rather low resolution makes the ImageWriter of only limited value for graphics-oriented tasks.

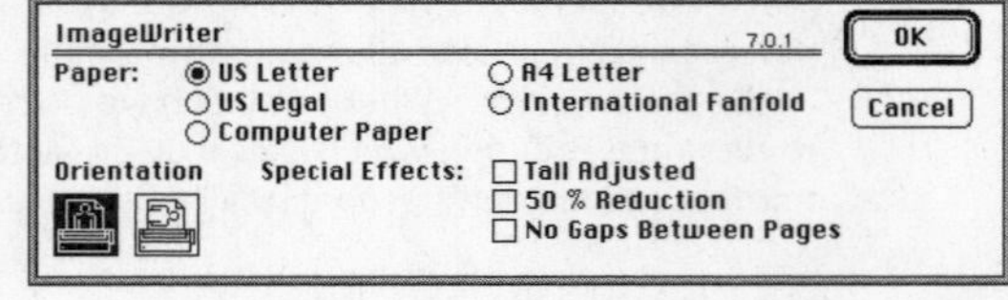

Figure 10-28 *The ImageWriter's Page Setup dialog box.*

What to do:

There are two options from the ImageWriter's Page Setup dialog box that can help improve the quality of ImageWriter output.

- **Select 50% reduction**
  This option, in effect, simulates raising the resolution to 144 dpi, because you are trying to squeeze 144 dots of information into the space normally occupied by 72 dots.

  The problem with this solution, however, is that everything is now 50 percent smaller. Aside from the fact that you may not want everything smaller, this technique cannot actually make the size of each dot any smaller. Too often, therefore, the result is a packed group of dots that resembles little more than an ugly blob of black ink.

  In order for this option to be of much value, you must first double the size of the image, typically by using whatever scaling commands you have available in your graphics application. The reduced image then prints at the original intended size.

  This is similar to the logic behind the improved appearance of text obtained by using the Best quality option from the Print dialog box, as described in Chapter 9. Shifting from the Faster to the Best option, however, does not affect the appearance of printed graphics. (With Draft, of course, the graphic does not print at all.)

- **Select Tall Adjusted**
  Macintosh monitors display an equal number of dpi horizontally and vertically, with each dot forming a square (usually at a resolution of about 72 dpi). The ImageWriter's overall resolution is also listed at 72 dpi, but it has a slightly different number of dots per inch in the vertical direction than in the horizontal direction.

BY THE WAY ▶

PRINTING COLOR ON AN IMAGEWRITER

ImageWriter IIs and LQs can print in color if you replace their standard black ribbon with the optional color ribbon (which has three colors plus black). There is no trick to using this ribbon; you install it exactly as you would a black ribbon. ImageWriter color, however, has two big limitations:

- Under standard conditions, ImageWriters can print only eight different colors (including black and white as two). Software packages such as MacPalette II and CheapColor (if you can still find them) can extend this range via dithering techniques.
- In order for ImageWriters to print in color, the application in use must be written to be aware of the color-printing option; otherwise, the printer always prints in black-and-white. Given how rare these printers are today, I don't know if developers even worry about this anymore.

Even with everything working well, the output is not nearly as good as you can get from a StyleWriter or other color inkjet printer. Given how inexpensive these inkjets are, if color printing is important to you, give up on your ImageWriter and get a new printer!

The result is that printed output has a rectangular appearance—a bit more tall than wide—compared to the screen display. To most people, this effect gives text a more pleasing appearance, and so it is generally ignored rather than considered a problem. At the same time, however, it causes graphics to print in a manner that is slightly distorted from what you see on the screen. For example, a square on the screen prints as a slight rectangle, and circles appear as ovals.

If you want graphics printed with correct proportions, select Tall Adjusted. This option compensates for the discrepancy between the screen and the printer; correct proportions are maintained, and a square prints as a square. Unfortunately, any bitmapped text will probably now look worse.

Chapter 11

Trouble To Go: Not Just PowerBooks

You Can *Take It with You* 442

Basics for PowerBooks and Beyond 443

PowerBook Models 443

The All-in-One PowerBooks 443

The Duo PowerBooks 443

Some Other Distinctions of Note 444

PowerBook Control Panels (and Control Strip) 444

PowerBook 444

PowerBook Setup 444

PowerBook Display 445

Control Strip 445

PowerBook Battery Conservation 446

Use Features That Conserve Battery Power 446

Don't Use Features That Drain Battery Power 450

Running out of Battery Power 451

Using RAM Disks 452

Create and Use a RAM Disk 452

Why RAM Disks? 452

Making a RAM Startup Disk 452

Saving the Contents of Your RAM Disk 454

Using an External Monitor 456

Connecting an External Monitor 456

Activate the External Monitor 456

Other Monitors Control Panel Options 457

Video Mirroring 457

Disconnecting an External Monitor 458

Solve It! Basic PowerBook Problems 458
Restarting a PowerBook After a System Error 458
Try the Finder's Restart or Shut Down Menu Commands 458
Press the Reset Button or Reset Keyboard Combination 459
Do a Hard Shutdown 459
Reset the Power Manager 460
If the System Error Recurs After a Successful Restart 462
Problems Running on Battery Power 463
Use Battery Conservation Features 464
Check for Power Adapter Problems 464
Check for a Dead or Incorrectly Installed Battery 466
With NiCad Batteries, Check for the "Memory Effect" 466
Recondition Batteries 467
Intelligent (500 Series) Batteries: Recondition 467
Intelligent Batteries: Special Recharging Problem 467
Reset the Power Manager 467
Zap the PRAM 468
A Blown Fuse? 468
PowerBook Appears Dead 468
Check the Battery and Power Adapter 468
Reset the Power Manager 468
Try More General Solutions 469
Sleep Problems 469
Automatic Sleep Disabled 470
Automatic Sleep Works, But Not at the Expected Interval 471
Manual Sleep: AppleTalk Warning 471
System Freeze Immediately After Waking Up from Sleep 472
PowerBook Quick Fixes 472
Do You Qualify for the PowerBook Repair Extension Program? 472
Defective Pixels on Active Matrix Screens 472
Ghosting and Submarining on Passive Matrix Screens 474
Sound Problems 474
Backing Up Your System Software and Your Hard Drive 474
Forgot Your Password? 475
Can't Insert a Duo into or Can't Eject a Duo from a Duo Dock 475

Trouble Ejecting PCMCIA Cards 475
PowerBook 1400 Glitches 476
TrackBall and TrackPad Problems 476

Transfer Files to and from a PowerBook 476
Transfer Files Via the SCSI Port 477
To Connect an External Hard Drive to Your PowerBook's SCSI Port 477
To Connect Your PowerBook as an External Drive to a Desktop Mac 477
Transfer Files Via File Sharing 479
File Sharing: Initial Setup 479
File Sharing: Disconnecting 484
Accessing File Sharing After the Initial Setup 485
Transfer Files Via a Modem (Apple Remote Access) 486

Solve It! File Transfer Problems 488
Can't Get File Sharing to Work 488
If You Get a Message That Says "File Sharing Could Not Be Enabled" 488
For Other Problems with Enabling File Sharing 489
If You Get a Message That Says the Shared Disk Could Not Be Opened Because It "Could Not Be Found on the Network" 491
If You Get the Message That Says the Shared Disk "Could Not Be Opened, Because You Do Not Have Enough Access Privileges" 492
Problems with Turning File Sharing or AppleTalk Off 493
Other Problems with Using File Sharing 494
If Any File-Sharing Problems Lead to a System Freeze or Crash 495
You Can't Get a PowerBook Modem to Work 496
External Modems 496
Internal Modems 496
Communications Software 497
Serial Port "In Use" 497
Problems Using Apple Remote Access 498
Switch Options from the Network or AppleTalk Control Panels 498
Check the Serial Port Arbitrator Extension and Remote Access Setup 500
Miscellaneous Other Problems 501

You *Can* Take It with You

Apple's PowerBook line of notebook computers has been an enormous success. Many Macintosh users now own two Macs—a PowerBook in addition to the traditional desktop machine. Other users, finding that a PowerBook has all the computing power they need, make it their only computer.

Fortunately (or unfortunately, depending on your point of view), most of the problems that plague desktop Macintoshes are no different from the ones that travel with you when you use your PowerBook. As a result, most of this book applies equally well to either type of Macintosh. Where important differences do exist, they have probably already been covered (such as in Chapter 4, where I explained the unique variations on how to shut down or restart a PowerBook).

But this still leaves several topics that are only relevant to PowerBook users; running on battery power is one obvious example. These PowerBook-specific issues are the main focus of this chapter.

In this edition, however, that focus has blurred a bit. The differences between PowerBooks and desktop Macs continue to shrink as new models and new software are released. For example, there was a time when the Control Strip was available only to PowerBook users, but no more. Thus, while the coverage of the Control Strip in this chapter still focuses on its use with PowerBooks, much of the information will be relevant to all Mac users. The same thing goes for coverage of RAM disks and especially for file sharing. So even if you don't own a PowerBook, check out this chapter. You are still likely to find it helpful.

BY THE WAY ▶

CURRENT POWERBOOKS: GOOD NEWS AND BAD NEWS

Between hardware problems, production delays, and marketing mishaps, 1996 was a terrible year for PowerBooks. Things got so bad that during the fall, Apple had *no* PowerBook models in its catalog at all! Happily, new models have now arrived, and they look great. The PowerBook 1400s feature an optional internal CD-ROM drive and the largest PowerBook display ever. The even newer PowerBook 3400s are Apple's fastest PowerBooks ever.

Basics for PowerBooks and Beyond

PowerBook Models

You already know that PowerBooks are different from desktop Macintoshes. What you may not know as clearly is that different PowerBook models are often quite different from one another. In particular, there are two main lines of PowerBooks, as presented in the following paragraphs.

The All-in-One PowerBooks

These PowerBooks, typified by models such as the older 180 (which uses a trackball) and the newer 5300 (which uses a trackpad), all include a floppy drive in addition to their internal hard drive. They also have a full set of connection ports on the back of the machine to hook up with SCSI devices, an external modem, a printer, possibly an external monitor, and more.

The Duo PowerBooks

These PowerBooks, typified by models such as the 2300, do not include the floppy drive or external ports found on the all-in-one PowerBooks. (The more general name for this type of computer is *subnotebook.)* To access these absent features, you need to connect the Duo to either a Duo Dock or MiniDock. You can also attach a floppy disk drive directly, without a dock, via a special adapter cable.

In particular, if you insert a Duo into a Duo Dock that has an external monitor and a keyboard attached to it, the unit performs like a desktop Mac, bypassing the Duo's built-in screen and keyboard. This is a main attraction of the Duo. On the one hand, you get the lightest possible portable device; on the other hand, you get a single Mac that can adequately serve as both a portable and a desktop computer. Using a MiniDock is more like turning your Duo into an all-in-one PowerBook rather than a desktop Mac, except that the MiniDock does not include a floppy drive.

The main disadvantage of Duos is that, if you need access to a floppy drive and/or connection ports when you travel, you will need to take additional hardware along (eliminating the lightweight advantage of the Duo).

For better or worse, the Duos are reportedly on the way out. Apple appears to have no plans to release new Duo models.

BY THE WAY ▶

INSERTING A DUO INTO A MINIDOCK OR DUO DOCK

When inserting a Duo into a MiniDock, remember to put it to sleep first. Before inserting a Duo into a Duo Dock, you should shut it down altogether.

Some Other Distinctions of Note

Here are a few other commonly noted variations among PowerBook models:

- Although early PowerBook models were limited to black-and-white or grayscale displays, most recent PowerBooks include color (8-bit depth or greater).
- Early PowerBooks also had a non-standard display size that could not duplicate the image size of a typical desktop Mac monitor (basically, PowerBooks would omit the bottom fifth of the screen image). More recent PowerBook models have a display that does duplicate the image size of a standard desktop Mac display.
- The PowerBook 5300 and 2300 models were the first to use a PowerPC processor, thus qualifying as "Power Macs" in addition to being PowerBooks (that's a lot of "power"). They use a 603e processor, a low-energy processor that is actually slower than the PowerPC 601 used in the first generation of desktop Power Macs. The next generation of PowerBook models promise to be a lot faster.
- Most newer models can accept expansion cards (called PCMCIA cards).
- Overall, the PowerBooks continue to evolve into true feature-for-feature portable versions of desktop Macs. For example, the newest PowerBook models include CD-ROM drives.

PowerBook Control Panels (and Control Strip)

All PowerBooks come with several control panels and other utilities that you use to access and modify features unique to PowerBooks. The layout of these control panels has undergone significant revisions over the years; the descriptions in this chapter assume that you are using the latest versions, as shipped with System 7.5 or later. If you are using earlier versions, you may find that a particular option has a somewhat different name or a different location (or possibly is even in a different control panel). The functions, however, generally remain the same.

Figure 11-1 *The Control Strip is not just for PowerBooks anymore; this strip was taken from a desktop Mac. Its modules include (from left to right) AppleTalk, File Sharing, Monitor Bit Depth, Monitor Resolution, Sound Volume, Terminator Strip (a third-party module that lets you "quit" the Finder), FreePPP's module, and Printer Selector.*

PowerBook

This control panel's primary purpose is to set battery conservation options (as described in more detail in "PowerBook Battery Conservation," later in this chapter).

PowerBook Setup

This is used to select whether you are using an internal or external modem, as well as to select a SCSI ID number for your PowerBook (which you will need if you are going to use your PowerBook as an external hard drive connected to another Macintosh, as described later in this chapter).

TAKE NOTE ▶

CONTROL STRIP BASICS

What Is the Control Strip? The Control Strip control panel (now a standard component of System 7.5 and its revisions) creates a strip of buttons that stay on the screen at all times. To use a button, click it and hold down the mouse button; a pop-up menu of choices will appear.

What buttons appear on your Control Strip depends upon what modules are stored in the Control Strip Modules folder inside your System Folder. When you first install the Control Strip, it comes with Apple's basic set of modules.

Since the first versions of the Control Strip were only compatible with PowerBook models, the original modules focused on features relevant to PowerBook users (such as a battery monitor). These features will be the focus of this chapter.

Starting with System 7.5.3, however, the Control Strip works with virtually all Mac models, and so additional modules are now included. For example, as covered in Chapter 10 ("By the Way: Control Strip: Bypassing the Monitors Control Panel"), there are buttons for displaying color depth and monitor resolution. As mentioned in Chapter 7, there is also a module for changing your default desktop printer. Some of the original PowerBook modules (such as for file sharing, AppleTalk, and Sound Volume) work with desktop Macs as well. In addition, a variety of third-party modules do things such as connect online, list your control panels, or allow you to restart/shut down.

Moving and Resizing the Control Strip If the Control Strip is in your way but you still want to have it readily available, you can collapse it to just a little tab by clicking its close box (on the strip's left side) or its tab (on the right side). Clicking the tab reopens the strip again. You can resize the strip by click-dragging the tab to the left or right, or move the entire strip to another screen location by click-dragging the tab while holding down the Option key. If the strip has more buttons than it can display at once, click the scroll arrows to see the other buttons.

The Control Strip control panel The Control Strip control panel (which is separate from the strip itself) offers only a few options, mainly whether or not to display the Control Strip at all.

PowerBook Display

This is used primarily to turn video mirroring on and off. This feature, which is not available in all PowerBooks, is only relevant if you are using an external monitor (as described later in this chapter).

Control Strip

The PowerBook-related Control Strip modules include a battery module that displays a multi-bar indicator of the current battery charge level. The fewer filled bars there are, the less battery power you have left.

This indicator, however, is notoriously inaccurate (especially with nickel-cadmium battery PowerBooks), commonly showing more power left than you really have (other non-Apple utilities with battery indicators have similar problems). The battery icon adjacent to the indicator bars changes depending on whether the PowerBook is running on battery (just the battery icon appears) is fully charged and running on AC power (a plug appears over the battery icon), or is charging

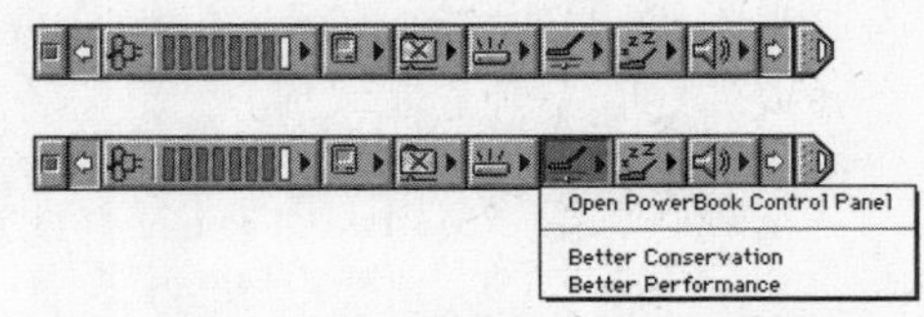

Figure 11-2 *The Control Strip from a PowerBook 180, before (top) and after (bottom) clicking the module that accesses the PowerBook control panel.*

(a lightning bolt appears over the battery icon). Different PowerBook models have different variations on this battery display.

Other modules are used to access the PowerBook control panel, check or change the status of file sharing, or otherwise access features that affect battery conservation (as described in more detail in the next section).

PowerBook Battery Conservation

Other than their small size, the single most distinguishing feature about PowerBooks is that they can run on batteries. Batteries, though, have a big problem: they can run out of power. If you expect to be away from a convenient power source for any length of time (on an airplane, for instance), conserving battery power becomes a primary concern. Fortunately, there are a wide assortment of battery conservation options. The more of these features you use, the better your battery savings will be.

Use Features That Conserve Battery Power

- **Sleep: Put the PowerBook to sleep whenever you aren't using it**

  To put a PowerBook to sleep, select Sleep from the Finder's Special menu. Alternatively, you can use the Sleep selection in the Control Strip.

  To wake up a sleeping PowerBook, press any key except Caps Lock (on some models, you must press the Power key). The PowerBook will reawaken almost instantly, returning you to where you left off without needing to go through the startup sequence. This is because the RAM contents of a PowerBook are maintained while it is asleep. This is a very convenient way to save battery power without the hassle of shutting down and restarting.

Figure 11-3 *Two ways to select Sleep—from the Finder's Special menu (left), and from the Control Strip (right).*

TAKE NOTE ▶

WHY SHUT DOWN WHEN YOU CAN SLEEP INSTEAD?

When you don't plan on using your PowerBook for a while, an obvious alternative to Sleep is to shut down (via the Shut Down command in the Finder's Special menu). But why bother with it? Shutting down means that all open applications quit, all contents of RAM (including RAM disk contents) may be lost, and you will have to go through a potentially long startup sequence the next time you want to use your computer.

You can travel with your PowerBook just as well while it is in sleep mode as when it is shut down. You can even safely connect and disconnect cables (such as modem and printer cables) while in Sleep mode, though you need to shut down to connect a Duo to a Duo Dock.

In fact, the only clear advantage of shutting down a PowerBook rather than using Sleep is that a shut down PowerBook drains less battery power than one that is asleep. Shutting down thus makes some sense if you don't expect to use your PowerBook for at least several days and do not have it plugged into a wall outlet.

- **Use an AC outlet, instead of battery power, whenever possible**
When you connect the PowerBook to the Power Adapter and plug the adapter into a wall outlet, the PowerBook will run on AC power rather than battery power.

  Since a PowerBook's battery is slowly losing power even when it is asleep or shut down, it pays to keep your PowerBook plugged in whenever possible. While the computer is plugged in, the battery will charge until fully charged and then stay that way (though it will take longer to reach full charge if the PowerBook is in use instead of sleeping or being shut down). Because you cannot "overcharge" a battery, you can keep the PowerBook plugged in even if it is fully charged.

- **Spin down the hard drive**
An active hard drive is one of the two major drains on battery power (the light for the screen is the other). So, to save battery power, temporarily "turn off" the hard drive by selecting the Spin Down button from the Control Strip. This shuts off the motor that otherwise spins the drive constantly.

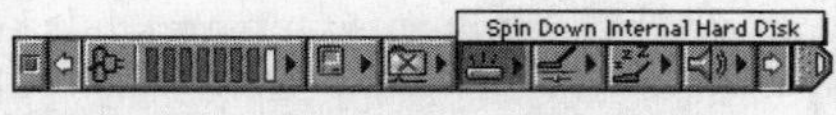

Figure 11-4 *The Control Strip's Spin Down button.*

  Spinning down does not prevent you from using your PowerBook. As soon as the PowerBook needs to access any information on the drive, it will automatically turn the drive back on. You will hear the drive spin up, and there will be a slight delay until the PowerBook responds to your command. This delay is normal; do not be concerned.

  This option is of little value, of course, if your application keeps turning the hard drive back on every time you turn it off. But if your task mainly involves accessing information that is already in RAM, you can keep working while the hard drive is off for an extended time. This can be an especially effective battery-saving strategy when used in combination with a RAM disk (as described in "Using RAM Disks," later in this chapter).

  Also note that the features of some extensions will force the drive to spin up, including the hourly chime of a clock extension. To avoid these minor demands on the drive, turn such features off or disable the extension altogether.

  On a related note, higher disk cache settings, as set from the Memory control panel (see Fix-It #6), will help minimize how often a hard drive will need to spin up again after you have selected Spin Down.

- **Screen dimming**
Screen dimming turns off the light to your PowerBook's screen. Unless you are in a dimly lit area, you should still be able to see the screen images (though dimmed color displays may be hard to see in any light). In fact, it may be possible to continue working while the screen is dimmed, just using external light. Doing this will save considerable battery power.

  You can also dim the screen by turning the Brightness control down to its minimum setting (see the next item in this list). Alternatively, several utility programs (I use QuicKeys) include features that let you dim the screen either by pressing a keyboard combination or by clicking on-screen buttons.

BY THE WAY ▶

ASSISTANT TOOLBOX

Current system software includes an extension called Assistant Toolbox (it was originally sold separately as part of a product called PowerBook File Assistant, which also included File Assistant and AutoRemounter). Assistant Toolbox adds a useful collection of features to your PowerBook, and I highly recommend it.

At the top of the list, pressing Command-Shift-Zero is a shortcut that puts the PowerBook to sleep. Similarly, pressing Command-Shift-Control-Zero spins down the hard disk. Assistant Toolbox also adds the option for a "persistent RAM disk" (as described later in "Saving the Contents of Your RAM Disk"). Other features include a "later laser" option that lets you save print jobs indefinitely, in case you are not connected to a printer at the time (although desktop printer software works just as well for this function); a special cursor for minimizing the "submarining effect" (as mentioned later in "PowerBook QuickFixes"); and a feature that makes sure you can activate AppleTalk without having to restart your PowerBook.

- **Turn down brightness**
  All PowerBook models have some sort of brightness control, typically a slider of some sort on the front of the computer. On the 100 series, this control is near where the top and bottom halves of the PowerBook join, while on the 500 series, the slider is to the right of the screen. Turning down brightness conserves battery power; if you turn it down enough, it is the equivalent of dimming the screen.
- **Use PowerBook control panel options**
  A friendly reminder: The exact locations of the options I'm about to describe can be quite different in older versions of the system software (and, knowing Apple, they may change again in future versions!).

  Easy View: Better Conservation versus Better Performance Most battery conservation features worsen performance, either by inconveniencing you (for example, by dimming the screen sooner than you would want) or by decreasing the PowerBook's overall performance speed. If you open the PowerBook control panel in Easy view, all you will see is a slider control for choosing along a scale of Better Conservation versus Better Performance. You select how much performance you're willing to sacrifice in favor of battery conservation for the time being.

  Custom View: Automatic Sleep, Screen Dims, and Hard Disk Spins Down If you want to know exactly what the Easy view's slider is controlling, or if you want more authority over the various settings, switch to the Custom view. Here you will see separate controls that determine how many minutes will pass before the PowerBook automatically goes to sleep, dims the screen, or spins down the hard disk (if you want any of these options to kick in before their automatic time, you can usually do this manually, from the Control Strip, as previously described). For the Sleep and Screen Dims settings, the numbers on the sliders refer to minutes of idle activity (that is, an interval when you are not pressing any keys, clicking any buttons, or otherwise actively using the PowerBook) that must pass before the automatic kick-in occurs (at the most extreme, you can select "Never"). For Hard Disk Spins Down, the setting refers to minutes without any hard disk access, even if you are otherwise using the PowerBook.

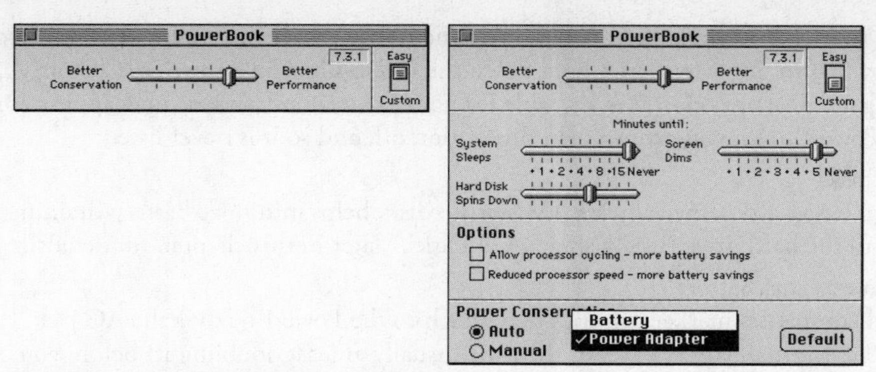

Figure 11-5 *The PowerBook control panel shown in Easy view (left) and Custom view (right).*

If you move the Easy view slider (which remains visible here) along, you will see how the other three sliders change accordingly. From the Custom view, however, you can change each separate slider independently.

Custom View: Power Conservation As an added bonus, the Power Conservation feature at the bottom of the window lets you assign one set of options for when you are running on battery power (select Battery from the pop-up menu) and another for when you are using AC power (select Power Adapter). The idea here is that although you will probably opt for better performance when the PowerBook is running from the adapter, you'll want better conservation when it is running on batteries. If you have the Auto button selected, this means that the settings will shift automatically whenever you plug in or unplug the Power Adapter. (By the way, in older versions of the PowerBook control panel, the only option like this was a "Don't sleep when plugged in" checkbox. To mimic this with the new control panel, simply select "Never sleep" as a setting for Power Adapter but not for Battery.)

Custom View: Reduced Processor Speed and Allow Processor Cycling For most PowerBook models, the PowerBook control panel includes two more options: Reduced Processor Speed and Allow Processor Cycling. When turned on, these two options save battery power and help reduce the already small risk of the PowerBook overheating. The first option does exactly what its name implies by reducing the processor's speed, which of course slows down the Mac's operations in general. The second option allows your processor to "rest" while the PowerBook is idle (though, if you really want to save battery power, you shouldn't leave an idle computer on for very long!). It, too, will slightly slow down your PowerBook's operations.

Some people leave these options on by default, but I don't. I prefer to use the higher performance options, if possible. I use the slower options only in situations when I know that saving every drop of battery juice is important, or if I want to check if persistent system crashes may be due to an overheating problem (see "Defective SIMMs and PowerBook Warmth," later in this chapter).

The Reduced Processor Speed option is not available on 68040 (the 500 series) or PowerPC PowerBooks.

On some PowerBooks, you may not see the Allow Processor Cycling option listed. If so, switch to Easy view, then hold down the Option button and select Custom view again. The option, if it is available for your PowerBook, should now appear. On some PowerBooks, you cannot turn this option off, and so it is never listed.

- **RAM disks**
  Using a RAM disk, especially a RAM startup disk, helps minimize battery-draining access to the hard drive (see "Using RAM Disks," later in this chapter, for details).
- **Add an external battery**
  Several companies market batteries that attach to the PowerBook via the AC jack. Using an external battery extends the time (usually at least doubling it) before you run out of battery power.

Don't Use Features That Drain Battery Power

- **Turn AppleTalk off**
  You can do this from the Chooser or from the Control Strip. Just remember not to do it while a shared volume is mounted; unmount the volume first (see "File Sharing: Disconnecting," later in this chapter).

  Unless you have Assistant Toolbox installed, you may have to restart in order to turn AppleTalk on or off.
- **Turn off file sharing**
  Turning off file sharing also saves battery power. Do this from the Sharing Setup control panel by clicking the Stop button in the File Sharing middle section. If the button says Start, file sharing is already off.

  By the way, if you set up the file-sharing software the way I describe later in this chapter (see "File Sharing"), you can share files with a desktop Mac without ever turning file sharing on.
- **Don't use virtual memory**
  Turn it off from the Memory control panel (see Fix-It #6). Never use virtual memory when running on battery power; if you even try to use it, the PowerBook will give you a warning message. Using virtual memory increases access to the hard disk, one of the bigger eaters of battery power.

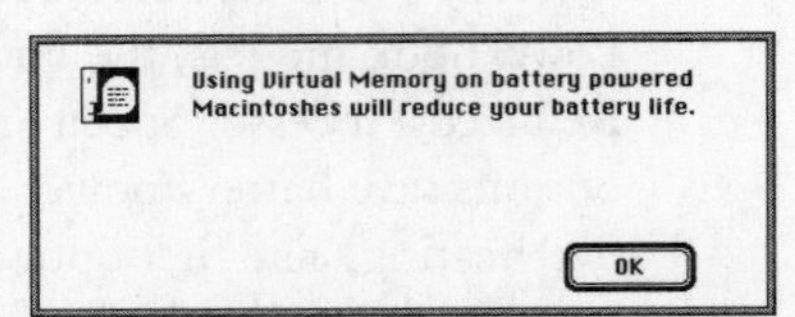

Figure 11-6 *Don't use virtual memory when running on battery power.*

  Using RAM Doubler may present similar battery-draining problems, but if you have at least 8MB of physical RAM, it should not be nearly as big a drain as virtual memory. Many users keep RAM Doubler on while working with battery power.
- **Turn the modem off, and quit all communications software**
  Quit all telecommunications software that you are not using. The modem is on and draining power as long as a telecommunications program is open, even if you are not connected online. Apple does not include a module with the Control Strip that tells you if your modem is on or not, but some other competing utilities, such as PowerStrip, include this feature.

- **Don't use the floppy drive**
  If your PowerBook has a built-in floppy drive, using it will drain battery power.
- **Turn down sound volume**
  Playing sound uses battery power. Keep the volume as low as is feasible, and turn it off altogether if you don't need it. You can do all this from the Sound control panel or the Control Strip.
- **Don't plug anything into the PowerBook's ports**
  Almost anything that you plug into a port, such as an external monitor or an external hard drive, will cause the PowerBook's battery to drain faster. In fact, in some PowerBooks, you can't even use an external monitor unless you are running on AC power.
- **Use a "white" desktop pattern**
  On PowerBooks, a screen pixel is "on" if it is dark, and "on" pixels require more energy than "off" ones. Since your Finder's desktop pattern is frequently on the screen, you can probably save a little power by using a pattern of mostly "off" pixels. You choose the pattern via the Desktop Patterns control panel in System 7.5, or via the General Controls control panel in earlier system software versions.

Running out of Battery Power

As you start running low on battery power, a series of three different messages will appear on the screen (such as "You are now running on reserve power and your screen has dimmed," or "Very little of the battery's reserve power remains"). Each succeeding message means you have less time left until the PowerBook will automatically go to sleep.

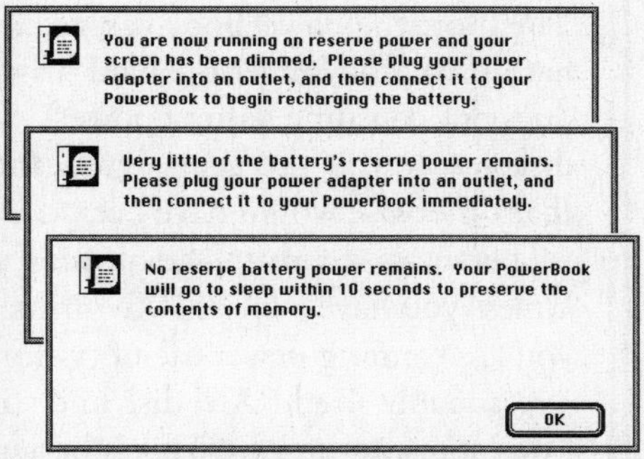

You are now running on reserve power and your screen has been dimmed. Please plug your power adapter into an outlet, and then connect it to your PowerBook to begin recharging the battery.

Very little of the battery's reserve power remains. Please plug your power adapter into an outlet, and then connect it to your PowerBook immediately.

No reserve battery power remains. Your PowerBook will go to sleep within 10 seconds to preserve the contents of memory.

OK

Figure 11-7 *The three messages that appear as you run progressively low on battery power.*

When the first message appears, a battery icon will begin flashing over the Apple icon in the menu bar. If you can, plug in the power adapter immediately; this puts a stop to the messages and starts recharging the battery. Otherwise, if you continue to work on battery power, save your work frequently. Don't wait until the third message to take action, since you may not even have time to save your work at that point.

Figure 11-8 *The battery icon that appears in the menu bar, over the Apple icon, when battery power is low.*

If you ignore all these warnings and wait until the Macintosh finally is forced to sleep, you have about one or two days to get AC power to the PowerBook and recharge the battery before it is totally out of juice. If you wait until this happens, the Mac will need to be restarted from scratch after you recharge the battery; any unsaved data will be lost. If you recharge sooner, the PowerBook will wake up normally where it left off before going to sleep.

Using RAM Disks

Create and Use a RAM Disk

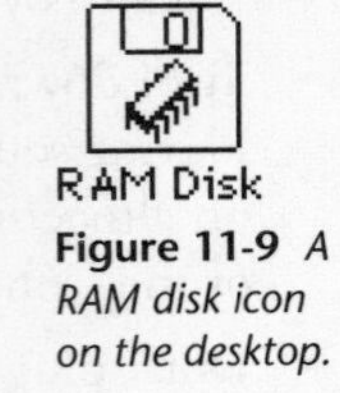

Figure 11-9 *A RAM disk icon on the desktop.*

With the right software, your PowerBook can be "fooled" into thinking that a portion of its RAM is actually a physical disk. This RAM disk appears on the desktop with its own icon, just like any other disk. You can then, for example, copy applications to the RAM disk and launch them just as if they were on your hard drive.

You already own the software you need to create a RAM disk: it's the Memory control panel. To use it, just click the On button in the RAM Disk section of the control panel and use the slider to adjust how large you want the RAM disk to be. Then restart, and presto—your RAM disk will appear.

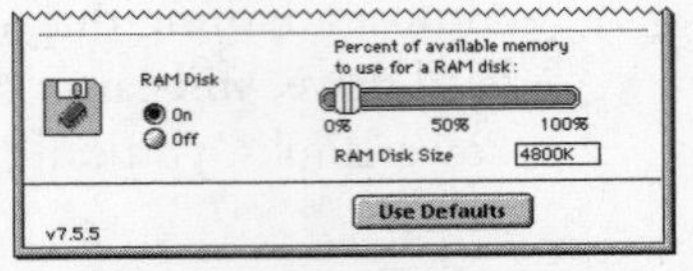

Figure 11-10 *The RAM Disk settings from the Memory control panel.*

With current system software (System 7.5.3 or later), you need at least 6MB of installed RAM simply to activate the RAM Disk option in the Memory control panel. The minimum size of a RAM disk is 416K.

SEE: • **Fix-It #6 for more details on creating and removing RAM disks**

Why RAM Disks?

The main advantage of a RAM disk for PowerBook users is that it saves battery power. The more the PowerBook can access information from the RAM disk rather than the hard drive, the longer the hard drive can remain "spinned down" (a state in which it does not consume battery power). Since RAM disk access is many times faster than hard disk access, you also get a significant speed boost by doing anything from the RAM disk that otherwise would have been done from your hard drive.

The main disadvantage of using a RAM disk, of course, is that it takes up RAM. Unless you have a lot of RAM installed (at least 16MB and ideally more, especially if you are running newer memory-hungry software), you may find that you cannot create a reasonably sized RAM disk and still have enough RAM left over to open the applications you want to run. This is because an application copied to a RAM disk still requires the same amount of additional RAM to run as it would ordinarily need.

When you are running an application from a RAM disk, however, you *can* often lower its memory allocation from its Preferred size to closer to its Minimum size and still not see any speed decrement. While lower memory allocations typically mean more frequent access to the disk, the greater speed of access to the RAM disk over the slower hard drive makes up for the lost time. You can change an application's memory allocation from its Get Info window.

SEE: • **Chapter 2 and Fix-It #6 for more on the Get Info window**

Making a RAM Startup Disk

Suppose you set up a RAM disk and copy your Microsoft Word folder to it (or at least the essential files in the folder; a full installation of Word 6.0 has no chance of fitting on even the largest of PowerBook RAM disks). You now launch Word, but you find that hard disk access is still annoyingly frequent. This is because most applications, including Word, make frequent calls to System Folder files—and, in any case, the Finder is still accessed from the hard disk's System Folder. Thus, to make really effective use of a RAM disk, you need to create a System Folder for it and use it as a startup disk. (In fact, you will probably access a hard disk less often if there is a System Folder on the RAM disk and nothing else than if there are applications and no System Folder.)

Unfortunately, most users' System Folders are so huge that fitting it on a RAM disk would mean creating a RAM disk so large that there wouldn't be enough RAM left over for other uses. The solution here is to create a minimum System Folder. Here are the steps for doing this:

1. Create a RAM disk (as described in the previous section, "Create and Use a RAM Disk"), and set it to at least 4MB (make it even larger if you can afford to set aside that much RAM). Try to estimate the size properly the first time, because if you want to change the RAM disk's size after you create it, you will have to start over, deleting everything currently on the RAM disk.
2. Install the minimum version of the system software for your PowerBook, using the system software Installer (as explained in Fix-It #5). Alternatively, you can install the minimal floppy disk software from a compatible Disk Tools disk onto a RAM disk (see the section in Chapter 2 on creating an Emergency Toolkit disk).

   Using these options, however, may prevent you from having access to certain features available in the standard system software installation. Other than making an enormous RAM disk (assuming you have enough RAM to do so), there is not much you can do about this. Using virtual memory to give you the extra memory you need to make a RAM disk is not a solution here either since virtual memory requires disk access.
3. **a.** Delete any unneeded control panels, extensions, or other nonessential files you may find on the RAM disk, then copy from your hard disk's System Folder any control panels, extensions, and fonts you still need. You'll probably want at least the Chooser, a printer driver, and a few key fonts. Since control panels that are not INITs (see Chapter 1 and Fix-It #4), such as Startup Disk, work just as well whether or not they are in the startup disk's System Folder, you don't need to copy these control panels to the RAM disk.

   b. Alternatively, you can save space by creating aliases of your hard disk's control panels and extensions and placing them in the relevant folders within your RAM disk's System Folder. Ideally, the Macintosh should still load these extensions into RAM at startup as if the originals were on the RAM disk. If not, you will need a utility such as Conflict Catcher II, which has an option called "Recognize Aliases" in its Preferences window. With this option checked, you should have no problems at all using aliases on your RAM disk. The 5.0 version of Startup Manager (in Now Utilities) has a similar feature, called "Resolve Aliases."
4. If space permits, copy one or two of your most frequently used applications. Similarly, if your applications access special folders in the System Folder (such as the Claris folder used by Claris applications), copy relevant files from that folder as well.

5. Open the Startup Disk control panel and select the RAM disk as the startup disk, then restart. The RAM disk will now boot as your startup disk, with all the files you placed there still intact.

   You may get a message at startup saying something to the effect that this system software should only be used on floppy disks. Ignore it; click OK, and everything should boot exactly as if the RAM disk were an actual floppy disk. If problems persist, you may have to give up on using the minimal software for your RAM disk (as indicated in step 2). Instead, copy the System and Finder (and Enabler, if needed) directly from your hard disk's System Folder.

Saving the Contents of Your RAM Disk

At this point you may be saying "But wait! Doesn't a restart wipe out all RAM? Won't the contents of the RAM disk be lost when I restart?" Fortunately, for most Mac models (including all PowerBooks), a RAM disk is an important exception to this generally true axiom. *Everything on a RAM disk is preserved when you restart, even if you do so using the Reset button after a system crash* (as described in Chapter 4).

Even so, your RAM disk's contents are still more vulnerable to being lost than if they were on a hard disk. Here are some tips to help make sure you never lose any of the valuable data on your RAM disk:

- Never keep documents on your RAM disk that are not backed up elsewhere. This is a good idea for any hard disk, but it is even more important for RAM disks.
- Be careful not to shut down the PowerBook. When you select Shut Down, rather than Restart, the RAM disk's contents *are* lost. You will normally get a message warning you of this problem.

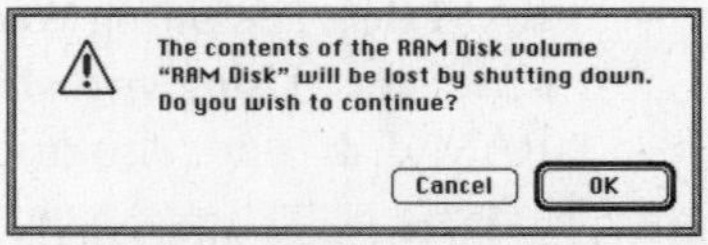

  The contents of the RAM Disk volume "RAM Disk" will be lost by shutting down. Do you wish to continue?
  Cancel OK

  Figure 11-11 *Your RAM disk's contents may be lost if you click OK here.*

  PowerBook users who routinely use the Power button (rather than the Reset button) to restart after a system crash should be especially careful here. While using Reset preserves the RAM disk's contents, using the Power button is the equivalent of shutting down and will not save the RAM disk's contents.

  SEE: • **"Restarting a PowerBook After a System Error," later in this chapter, for more details**

- Happily, you can overcome the previous problem and preserve a RAM disk's contents—even after a shutdown! To do this, install Apple's Assistant Toolbox extension. Assistant Toolbox writes a copy of the RAM disk's contents to a special file stored in the Preferences folder of the System Folder (called Persistent RAM Disk); when you restart after a shutdown, it copies these contents back to the RAM disk.

  If you shut down immediately after a system crash, Assistant Toolbox will be unable to update the Persistent RAM Disk file. Even in this case, however, all is not lost. The next time you start up, Assistant Toolbox restores your RAM disk to its state at the time of your last normal shutdown (not the last time you put the PowerBook to sleep!). Depending on how often you shut down your PowerBook and how often you modify your RAM disk, this could mean that you lost very little (if any) of the contents of the RAM disk.

SEE: • "Restarting a PowerBook After a System Error," later in this chapter, for more details
• Chapter 4 for more general information on restarting after a system error

- Zapping the Parameter RAM (see Fix-It #11) will erase the contents of a RAM disk.
- If you select Restart (from the Finder's Special menu) and then start up with extensions off (by holding down the Shift key at startup), don't worry. The RAM disk will still appear with its files intact (even though the Memory control panel, used initially to create the RAM disk, is not active).

TECHNICALLY SPEAKING ▶

AN "UNREADABLE" RAM DISK

Even with an extension like Assistant Toolbox installed, you will get a message warning you that the contents of your RAM disk will be lost if you shut down during a session where you started up with extensions off. Don't worry; just click OK. The next time you restart with extensions on, the RAM disk's contents will appear as normal.

Figure 11-12 *An "unreadable" RAM disk. This message usually does not mean that anything is wrong; it often happens when you start up with extensions off.*

Here, however, is a strange situation to watch out for: You shut down (rather than just restarting), then start up later with extensions off. As startup is completed, you get a message saying that the RAM disk is "unreadable" and asking if you want to initialize it. If you click Initialize, a new RAM disk is created, but all the contents of the previous RAM disk are erased (as expected after a shutdown in any case). If you click Cancel, the RAM disk will not appear at all for that session, but its contents are still gone forever—unless you have previously installed Assistant Toolbox. (If you have Assistant Toolbox installed, go ahead and click Cancel. The RAM disk will still not appear in this session, but the next time you restart normally with extensions on, it will reappear with its files intact.

Otherwise, the "unreadable" message probably means that you need to decrease the size of the RAM disk. (For example, if you have only 8MB of RAM, you supposedly get this message if you allocate more than 544K to a RAM disk.) Experiment until you find a size that works.

- To be extra safe, you should store a copy of at least the RAM disk's System Folder on your hard disk. This will help you re-create it if it should ever be lost. To avoid any possible problems with two System Folders on your hard disk, as well as to save hard disk space, store this copy as a compressed file (using a utility such as StuffIt or Compact Pro, as described in Chapter 2).

BY THE WAY ▶

THE SHRINKWRAP ALTERNATIVE

The popular shareware program ShrinkWrap is used to mount disk image files on your desktop without having to copy them first to a floppy disk (see Fix-It #5: "Take Note: Why Can't I Open The System Software I Just Downloaded?"). You can also use it, however, to create a "blank" mounted image that acts pretty much like a RAM disk. Just select its Preferences to "Mount images unlocked by default" and "Keep mounted images in RAM," then create a new image file and mount it. Copy whatever you want to the mounted file, and place the image file (or its alias) in the Startup Items folder. You will now have a RAM disk mimic whose contents are always saved to disk whether you select to restart or shut down (an advantage similar to using Assistant Toolbox).

Using an External Monitor

With all but the earliest PowerBook models, you can connect an external monitor to your PowerBook. I will focus here on those setups where both the external monitor and the PowerBook's own screen are active at the same time (with Duos, you do this with the MiniDock). This sort of hookup is common when you want a larger screen for making a presentation on the road.

Problems with connecting external monitors are typically solved by understanding how to use the relevant control panels, especially the Monitors control panel. You also have to make sure the hardware is connected correctly.

Note: If you have a PCI-based Macintosh and use Monitors & Sound (rather than Monitors), the procedures in the control panel will be different. In this case, when both monitors are connected, the Macintosh Guide file (accessed from the Apple Guide menu when you are in the Finder) will provide the details about what to do.

Connecting an External Monitor

1. Use AC power to run the PowerBook. Some PowerBooks will not even start up on battery power with an external monitor attached.
2. Put the PowerBook to sleep or shut it down, then connect the monitor to your PowerBook. If you are using a Duo's MiniDock, simply plug the monitor's cable into the video port. For most all-in-one PowerBooks, you will need the separate video adapter cable that came with the PowerBook. Plug one end of the adapter into the video port of the PowerBook, and the other end into the external monitor's video cable.
3. Plug the monitor's power cord directly into an AC outlet; do not use a monitor with its power cord plugged into a desktop Macintosh. You may have to purchase a separate cord to do this, as the power cord that connects to a Macintosh typically has a hood on it that will prevent you from connecting it to a wall outlet.
4. Turn the monitor on, followed by the PowerBook.

Activate the External Monitor

Even if you have correctly followed the previous steps, your external monitor will still not show anything other than a blank screen. To get the monitor to actually show something, you need to "activate" it through the Monitors control panel. On some PowerBooks you only have to do this the first time you attach an external monitor; on others, you have to do it every time you connect one.

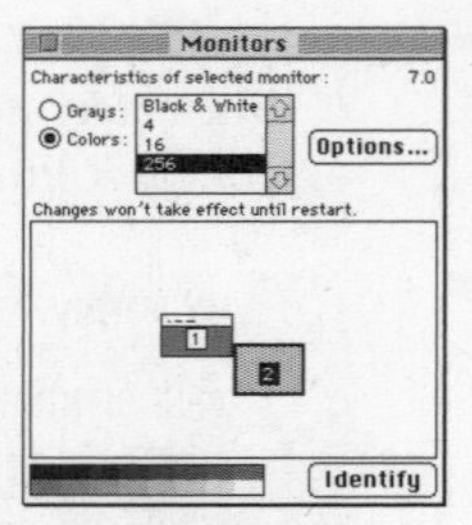

Figure 11-13 *The Monitors control panel. The two adjacent rectangles represent the PowerBook screen and an external monitor.*

1. Open the Monitors control panel. You will see two rectangles that represent your two monitors. If there is any doubt which one is which, click the Identify button, and the number "1" will appear on the monitor screen that corresponds to rectangle 1 in the panel. If you do not see a number appear over each rectangle, you may have a hardware or cable problem; see if using another video cable works. Otherwise, if your cables appear to be connected correctly, take the monitor in for a possible repair.

2. Click on the rectangle that represents your external monitor; it is now activated. At this point you can select its color depth (via the Monitors control panel, of course), which can be set differently from that of the PowerBook screen.

SEE: • Chapter 10 for selecting color depth

3. Close the Monitors control panel. The external screen is probably still empty, but you can now drag items to it from the PowerBook screen as if the two monitors were adjacently connected. As you move the cursor, you can see it disappear off one end of the PowerBook screen and reappear on the other end of the external monitor. Unless you have video mirroring turned on (as described shortly), this is how an external monitor works.
4. By the way, in order to prevent overheating, you should also turn on processor cycling when using an external monitor.. (See "PowerBook Battery Conservation: Use PowerBook Control Panel Options" for how to turn this feature on.) If you are using a 16-inch or larger monitor, the PowerBook will automatically turn this feature on.

Other Monitors Control Panel Options

Open the Monitors control panel to access these options.

- To move the menu bar from one monitor to another, drag its image from one monitor's rectangle to the other.
- To change the spatial relationship between the two monitors, move the two rectangles that represent the screens. Its placement in the control panel determines whether the external monitor acts as if it is to the right, left, above, or below the PowerBook screen.

  The cursor will only be able to move from one monitor to the other in locations where the two rectangles touch. To minimize the passing of the cursor from one monitor to another, adjust the rectangles so that they only touch in one small area.

Depending on your system software, you may have to restart to see these changes, especially if the Monitors control panel does not include buttons for the "Rearrange on Restart" versus "Rearrange on Close" options.

Video Mirroring

Video mirroring occurs when both the PowerBook screen and the external monitor display the exact same image. This option might be useful, for example, when you are giving a presentation to a large audience and you want the PowerBook display in front of you to show exactly what is on a larger screen behind you.

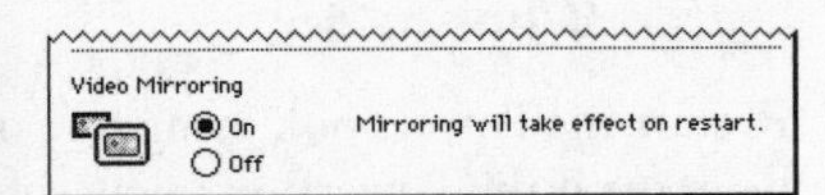

Figure 11-14 *The video mirroring option in the PowerBook Display control panel.*

Not all PowerBooks have a video mirroring option. If your model does, you will find it in the PowerBook Display control panel (at least you will if you are using the latest version of this control panel). To get it to work, simply turn it on and restart. Also, some applications are not compatible with video mirroring, and using them may result in incorrect display of information.

Disconnecting an External Monitor

When you are ready to disconnect the monitor, shut down the PowerBook. (You cannot put a PowerBook to sleep with an external monitor attached.) Once you have shut down, simply disconnect the cable(s) and restart.

Solve It! Basic PowerBook Problems

Restarting a PowerBook After a System Error

Symptoms:

A system crash, system freeze, or other system error has occurred that requires that you restart your PowerBook. You are having trouble, however, figuring out how to do this.

Causes:

Most causes of system errors are the same for PowerBooks as for any other Macintosh. This section focuses specifically on those techniques and problems that are unique to PowerBooks, especially solving the basic problem of just restarting the PowerBook. Most of these techniques were briefly mentioned in Chapter 4, but they are covered in more detail here.

By the way, Apple particularly cites extension conflicts (as described in Fix-It #4) as a possible cause of a variety of ills. Here's a quote: "With PowerBooks, symptoms that are typical of being caused by an extension conflict are: freezing, Type XX errors (where XX is a number), 'floating point coprocessor not installed' errors, not coming out of sleep properly, not auto-dimming the display, not auto-sleeping, not spinning down the hard drive, not reading floppy disks correctly, displaying anomalous information or 'garbage' on the screen, getting errors when printing, not accessing external devices, modem not connecting properly or dropping the line, not connecting to a network properly, and many others."

What to do:

Restart the PowerBook using one of the methods that follow. After each step described here, see if the PowerBook now successfully restarts; if not, go on to the next step. The last step considers what to do if the system error recurs after a successful restart.

Try the Finder's Restart or Shut Down Menu Commands

These methods are called a *soft restart* or *soft shutdown,* respectively. After most types of system errors, these probably will not work (you probably can't even get the menu to drop down), but give them a try.

TAKE NOTE ▶

WAIT BEFORE YOU (RE)START

If you are having a system freeze, wait a few seconds before you assume that the freeze is for real. Recent PowerBook models have a problem where they temporarily freeze for about 20 to 30 seconds when you try to move an icon in the Finder. This glitch was supposedly fixed, however, in System 7.5.3.

Also, if you are having any trouble getting your PowerBook to start up after you shut down or when trying to restart after a system error or sad Mac, wait at least 10 seconds before restarting.

Press the Reset Button or Reset Keyboard Combination

- On the PowerBook 100, the Reset button is on the left side of the machine.
- On all other 100 series PowerBooks, the Reset button is on the rear of the machine, recessed into a small hole. It can only be accessed with something like an unbent paper clip. If you don't have a paper clip handy, you may have to pass on this technique.
- On all other PowerBooks, life is simpler—just press the Command-Control-Power keys at the same time (though this may not work after some particularly nasty system crashes). PowerBook 190 and 5300s also have an easily accessible Power/Reset button in the back panel.

Do a Hard Shutdown

This technique almost never fails, but it may result in the loss of a RAM disk's contents that might otherwise have been saved (as mentioned in the previous section on RAM disks).

- On a PowerBook 100, press the Reset and Interrupt buttons at the same time.
- On a PowerBook 140, 145, or 170, press the Power button on the rear of the machine.
- On other 100 series PowerBooks or any 200 and 2300 series Duo, press the Power button on the rear of the machine and hold it down for at least five seconds. This initiates a *hard shutdown.* If you hold it for less time, it will attempt the equivalent of a *soft shutdown* (similar to what would happen if you selected Shut Down from the Finder's Special menu). Unfortunately, a soft shutdown does not work after a system crash, so a quick press of the Power button in this case will do absolutely nothing.

  In addition, Duo users should not forget that there is also a power button on the rear of a Duo Dock.
- On 500 series PowerBooks, press the Command-Control-Option-Power keys all at the same time. (This is necessary because the 500 series PowerBooks have no Power button.) If this combination fails to work, your only other solution is to remove the batteries and disconnect AC power temporarily.
- On 190 and 5300 PowerBooks, pressing the Power/Reset button in the back of the machine should turn off power instantly. (There appears to be no distinction between hard and soft shutdowns.) Pressing the button again will turn the Mac

back on; holding it in for a few seconds before letting go has been known to cure some startup problems.

Also note that these Macintoshes have a Power key on the keyboard that works just as the similar key does on desktop Macs (for example, if you are using System 7.5.1 or later, pressing the key should bring up a dialog box asking if you want to shut down).

Will this also work on the new PowerBooks released in late 1996 and 1997? I am not sure. Consult the documentation that came with your PowerBook for more help here, if needed.

BY THE WAY ▶

FIXING POWERBOOK PROBLEMS WITH SHUT DOWN INSTEAD OF RESET

In this book, I often recommend restarting the Macintosh as a potential cure for almost any immediate problem you may have, from minor malfunctions to system errors. Usually, no distinction is drawn between simply restarting and shutting down before restarting. With PowerBooks, however, a shutdown may cure a problem that a restart (even via a Reset button) will not. So, if a reset or restart fails to work as you had hoped, try shutting down and then restarting.

Reset the Power Manager

This is a last resort that should only rarely be necessary to solve a system crash problem (it is more commonly used for battery-related problems, as described in the next section). Still, here are the basic instructions (which, unfortunately, can and do vary for nearly every different PowerBook line):

1. Shutdown the PowerBook (that is, do not just put it to sleep).
2. Disconnect the power adapter, remove the battery, and let the PowerBook sit for at least 5 minutes. On some PowerBooks, removing the battery is not required to reset the Power Manager, but remove it if you have any doubt. (Actually, this step alone should reset the Power Manager on some PowerBooks.)
3. Reset the Power Manager, using the appropriate instructions for your PowerBook.
   a. On a PowerBook 100, 140, 145, or 170: Press and hold the Reset and Interrupt buttons for at least 30 seconds (on all but the 100, you'll need two unbent paper clips to follow this rather awkward procedure).
   b. On the PowerBook 150: Push the Reset button in the back of the unit with a paper clip and hold it in for 5 to 30 seconds (estimates of the proper time length have varied here), then plug the power adapter back in. Next, push the reset button in the back again, but just briefly. You should hear a small pop from the speaker; do not be concerned. If the PowerBook did not already turn on, push the main power button in the back of the unit (large exposed button). The unit should now power up. Finally, reinsert the battery and let it charge for at least 8 hours.
   c. On any other 100 series PowerBook (except the 190) and 200 and 2300 series Duos: Press the Power button on the rear of the machine and hold it down for at least 30 seconds. On Duos, some people have claimed that you should

simultaneously press both the Power button on the rear of the machine and the Power key on the keyboard. Try it.

d. On a 500 series PowerBook: Press the Command-Control-Option-Power keyboard buttons all at the same time (this will appear to do nothing, but don't worry). This is the same combination used to initiate a hard shutdown after a system error, as just previously described. In either case, the Power Manager is reset. You can also try this key combination on other PowerBooks, just to cover all possible bases.

e. On the PowerBook 190 and 5300 series: Shut down the PowerBook (do *not* restart it), then turn it back on and zap the PRAM (as described in Fix-It #11). In some cases, you will get the expected two startup chimes. When you let go of the keys, the computer may continue to start up, or it may shut down. If it shuts down, press the Reset button (on the rear of the machine) to turn it back on.

In other cases, there will be one chime, but then the screen will go dark and the green sleep light will stay on. In this case, press the Reset button (on the rear of the machine), and the PowerBook should start up after a brief pause. If it does not, then turn it on by pressing the Power key in the upper right corner of the keyboard.

These procedures should reset both the PRAM and the Power Manager.

SEE ALSO: • **"Take Note: Special Method for Reviving 'Dead' PowerBook 5300 or 190," later in this chapter, for yet another method of resetting the Power Manager**

f. Though it's not certain at this writing, the PowerBook 1400 and 3400 series should be similar to the 5300 in terms of resetting the Power Manager.

4. If you haven't already done so, reinsert the battery, plug in the power adapter (if desired), and turn the PowerBook on. Hope that your problem is gone.

5. If you still cannot get the PowerBook to start up successfully, remove the battery again and wait at least 15 minutes before you try the above procedures. Some people claim that you should leave the battery out overnight to be certain that the procedure has succeeded. Go for the overnight approach—if you are having this much difficulty, why take chances with shortcuts?

   In addition, for some PowerBooks, you may need to remove the internal backup battery (see "Take Note: What Is the Power Manager?") and let it sit for at least a minute. This is guaranteed to reset the Power Manager. Accessing the backup battery may require opening up the PowerBook case, however, and you may not want to do

BY THE WAY ▶

A POSSIBLE SHORTCUT FOR RESETTING THE POWER MANAGER

There is a freeware utility called ResetPwrMgr that, when launched, resets the Power Manager. It saves you the trouble of having to figure out and remember the correct procedure for your particular model of PowerBook (and with all of the different methods, no one finds it easy to keep them all straight!). The only downside is that it restarts the Mac without the proper checking that is done when you select the Finder's Restart or Shut Down commands, but this is no worse than what happens when you restart after a system crash.

I am not certain if this program works for the latest PowerBook models. Also, of course, it is only useful if your problem does not prevent you from starting up your PowerBook.

TAKE NOTE ▶

WHAT IS THE POWER MANAGER? (AND ONE REASON IT MAY GET CORRUPTED)

The Power Manager is hardware—sort of like a little microprocessor, located on the PowerBook's logic board. It is used to control most battery- and power-related operations. The Power Manager also maintains some information in memory (such as the time settings used by the PowerBook control panel for automatic sleep and screen dimming). This information is preserved, even when there is no AC or main battery power, via the PowerBook's internal backup battery.

This small battery is also used to maintain the contents of the PRAM, just as a similar battery is used in all Macintosh models (see Fix-It #11).

Like the PRAM, the Power Manager data can get corrupted. The most common result of this corruption is an inability to start up your PowerBook; oddly, this may happen even if you are running on AC power. Corrupted Power Manager data may also cause a variety of other symptoms, such as a battery that takes an unusually long time to recharge.

Apple notes the following: "While there are several reasons a PowerBook may need its power manager circuitry reset, most of which involve some kind of power interruption to the unit, there is one very common cause—improper use of the AC Adapter. The PowerBook Power Manager circuitry is most often 'corrupted' by the AC Adapter not being plugged into the PowerBook in the proper order. The AC Adapter should *always* be plugged into the AC (wall) outlet before it is plugged into the PowerBook itself. If you are using a power surge protector bar, make sure the power bar is powered on (usually it has some kind of indicator light) before you plug the PowerBook AC Adapter into it. Also, never turn off the power to the PowerBook by turning off the power bar's switch."

The solution to all of these problems is to reset the Power Manager data, as described in the main text. For PowerBooks, resetting the Power Manager is one of those generic fix-it procedures, much like zapping the PRAM; it may fix many problems beyond the ones specifically mentioned here.

In the worst case, hardware damage to the Power Manager may cause symptoms similar to those caused by corrupted data. Fixing this will require a trip to the repair shop.

this yourself. For specifics, consult your PowerBook's manual or simply take your PowerBook to an authorized service provider.

6. Check your PowerBook control panel. You will have to redo any customized changes you may have made there, because resetting the Power Manager reverts those settings to their default values.

SEE:
- **"Problems Running on Battery Power," later in this chapter, for another situation where you need to reset the Power Manager**
- **Chapter 4 for more on Reset buttons, Power buttons, and what to do to solve system error problems**

If the System Error Recurs After a Successful Restart

Consider the following possible causes:

- **Defective memory and PowerBook warmth**

  All PowerBooks get warm as you use them, some more so than others—color PowerBooks, in particular, get almost hot. In most cases, this is normal and not a cause for concern.

If you install a memory module card that is at or near the maximum possible amount for your PowerBook (typically 10MB or more), however, this also adds to the heat level of the PowerBook. If you didn't get the best-quality memory chips (even though they are not technically defective), the RAM may overheat, causing any number of weird symptoms, including freezes and system crashes. Defective memory chips, no matter what quantity you have installed, may cause similar symptoms.

Turning on Processor Cycling (from the PowerBook control panel) helps to keep temperatures down. Otherwise, your only cure is to replace the defective memory.

Another point about keeping your PowerBook cool: Keep the unit's legs up when it is in use, and don't shut its cover.

SEE: • **Fix-It #17 for more on memory problems**

- **Screen dimming may not work with certain programs**
  The result can be a system freeze as soon as screen dimming turns on. If you suspect this, turn off screen dimming from the PowerBook control panel prior to using the problem application.
- **PowerBook freezes when hard drive spins up after a spindown**
  This is probably the result of having rebuilt the desktop with extensions turned on. The solution is to disable all extensions, restart, and rebuild the desktop again.

SEE: • **Fix-It #4 on extensions**
• **Fix-It #9 on rebuilding the desktop**

- **System error may be related to using file sharing**

SEE: • **"Solve It! File Sharing and Modem Problems," later in this chapter, for examples of system errors related to these issues**

- **Consider more general causes and solutions (especially extensions conflicts)**

SEE: • **Chapter 4 for more general information on system errors**
• **Fix-It #4 on extension conflicts**

Problems Running on Battery Power

Symptoms:

- After following procedures to recharge a battery, the battery remains uncharged.
- The battery indicator in the Control Strip (or another similar utility) indicates that the battery is nearly out of power, even though you just recharged it.
- The battery successfully charges, but it then drains its charge much more rapidly than expected.
- The PowerBook will not start up at all with battery power but works normally when using AC power.

Causes:

- The power adapter may be defective, not plugged in correctly, or is the wrong power adapter for your PowerBook.
- The battery may be dead, or nearly so; if so, it needs to be replaced. This is especially likely if the battery either never successfully recharges or loses its charge very rapidly.
- With some types of PowerBook batteries, you may have something called the "memory effect," which causes batteries to discharge rapidly (as explained later in this section).
- The charger may be stuck in "trickle" mode. This can make it take an unusually long time to recharge the battery.

TAKE NOTE ▶

WHAT IS TRICKLE MODE?

The process of recharging a battery (particularly a nickel-cadmium battery) is typically divided into two stages. In the first stage, called fast mode, the charge proceeds at its fastest pace. In the second stage, which typically begins after the battery is more than 80 percent charged, the remaining charge occurs at a much slower pace, called trickle mode. This helps prevent overcharging of the battery. Apple's Control Strip does not have separate icons to indicate which mode you are in, though some competing utilities do.

Sometimes the charging process may get stuck in trickle mode, never shifting to fast mode when appropriate. This will mean that charging the battery will take an unusually long time. Corrupted Power Manager data can cause this.

- The Power Manager's data may have become corrupted.
- A corrupted PRAM may also cause these symptoms.
- Finally, you may be using your PowerBook in a way that excessively drains battery power.

What to do:

Use Battery Conservation Features

If your battery is simply losing power faster than it typically has in the past, but all battery and charger operations otherwise seem normal, you may be using your PowerBook in a way that drains battery power excessively (for example, by using virtual memory or a modem). The solution is, where possible, to select battery conservation options.

SEE: • **"PowerBook Battery Conservation," earlier in this chapter, for details**

Check for Power Adapter Problems

The typical way to recharge a battery is to use the power adapter. Just connect it to your PowerBook and you are automatically recharging, even as you continue to use the PowerBook (though using it will lengthen the time needed to recharge). If the

TECHNICALLY SPEAKING ▶

DIFFERENT POWERBOOKS, DIFFERENT BATTERIES, DIFFERENT ADAPTERS

Different models of PowerBooks use different types of batteries. When you replace the battery that came with your PowerBook, make sure you replace it with the right one.

All-in-one PowerBooks of the 100 series (such as the 160 and 180) use nickel-cadmium (NiCad) batteries. These are the type susceptible to the "memory effect" problem described in the main text. The 500 series PowerBooks use a nickel-metal-hydride (NiMH) battery called the PowerBook Intelligent Battery; it includes a built-in microprocessor that actually sends information to the PowerBook which is used to help conserve battery power.

Duos and the 190, 5300, and 1400 series PowerBooks use different NiMH batteries that are classified as Type I, Type II, or Type III; the Type III battery is the newest and lasts the longest. Using these newer battery types may require that additional enabler files be installed in your System Folder, depending upon what version of the system software you are using and what PowerBook model you have (older Duo models are most likely to need some sort of enabler file, such as one called Type III Battery).

By the way, the PowerBook 100 and the original Macintosh Portable used still another type of battery, of the lead-acid variety.

Different models of PowerBooks also use different power adapters. In particular, NiCad all-in-one PowerBooks have an entirely different adapter from Duos, and the new Intelligent Battery PowerBooks use still another type of adapter. Also, Apple periodically makes minor improvements in their power adapters (and even to the batteries themselves), typically to give them increased power load capacity. For example, Apple has upgraded the adapters used with NiCad PowerBooks several times; while they may look identical, they have different part numbers. Older NiCad PowerBooks will benefit from using the newer adapters, but otherwise you cannot mix and match different styles of adapters with different PowerBooks.

PowerBook is asleep or shut down, recharging should only take about 2 to 3 hours. If the power adapter doesn't seem to be doing its job, explore the following possibilities:

- Check that the power adapter plugs are correctly and fully inserted at both the PowerBook end and the wall outlet end.
- Check that the power outlet is working. For example, a wall outlet connected to a wall switch will not work if the wall switch is in the off position.

  Don't trust the on-screen icons as a reliable indicator of a charging battery. For example, the lightning-bolt icon (indicating a charging battery) in the Control Strip appears as soon as you plug the adapter into the PowerBook, even if the power outlet end is not plugged into anything! (Eventually, if this condition persists, the PowerBook will figure out it has almost no power left and will inform you of this.)
- Remove the power adapter from its power source, wait briefly, and then plug it back in. This may correct a problem with the charger being stuck in trickle mode.
- Be sure you are using the power adapter that came with your PowerBook or another compatible one obtained from Apple. Using any other adapter may not work and may even damage your PowerBook.
- If possible, check whether the power adapter itself may be broken by trying to charge the battery with another adapter. If you succeed, this means that the original adapter is broken.

By the way, Apple sells an optional external charger that allows you to recharge a battery while it is not in the PowerBook (this is convenient if you like to keep a spare battery charged at all times). If the charger can recharge the battery but the adapter cannot, this situation also would suggest a defective adapter.

BY THE WAY ▶

WHAT ABOUT LITHIUM ION BATTERIES?

PowerBook 5300 models originally used a new type of battery called a lithium ion battery (LiIon). These PowerBooks were recalled, however, and later versions were shipped with NiMH batteries. The problem was that Apple, as the company put it, "experienced two isolated instances within the company where a lithium ion battery pack failed, damaged the unit and could have posed a safety risk." In plain English, the PowerBooks caught fire.

Reportedly, the 3400 series of PowerBooks will give LiIon batteries another chance.

Check for a Dead or Incorrectly Installed Battery

If your battery will not hold a charge, it may be dead or nearly so. A battery should last for about 500 charges; under normal use, this may be expected to take about two years. The solution for a dead battery is to replace it.

While you are at it, check that the battery is installed correctly, following the instructions in your PowerBook User's Guide. Sometimes, an improperly installed battery may be the total cause of your problem.

Also make sure you have the right type of battery and software enabler for your PowerBook (see "Technically Speaking: Different PowerBooks, Different Batteries, Different Enablers, Different Adapters").

With NiCad Batteries, Check for the "Memory Effect"

If your PowerBook has a NiCad battery (see "Technically speaking: Different PowerBooks, Different Batteries, Different Adapters") that seems to lose its charge very quickly after recharging, you may have the mysterious *memory effect* problem. Essentially, the theory of this effect is that if you do not fully discharge a battery before recharging it, it will eventually begin to act as if its total charge is limited to the pre-recharging level. Similarly, if you typically recharge a NiCad battery to less than its full capacity, it may start to "think" of this lesser level as its full capacity and no longer allow itself to be fully charged. Even in worst-case scenarios, you will probably have to recharge the battery 50 or more times before you start to notice this effect.

The solution to this is to periodically (maybe after every 20 recharges) let the battery discharge completely, then recharge it. To be safe, a regular PowerBook user might do this every month or two, no matter how often the PowerBook is recharged. To let the battery discharge completely, simply keep the PowerBook active until it goes past all of its low-battery warning messages and finally shuts off; then recharge it.

To speed up the time to discharge the battery fully (and bypass the warning messages), use a shareware control strip module called BatteryAmnesia.

Newer versions of these NiCad batteries are less subject to this problem, and some experts claim that the memory effect is a myth altogether. You be the judge.

Recondition Batteries

PowerBook 270c, 280, 280c, 2300, 190, and 5300 models can use a program called Battery Recondition (currently up to at least version 2.0) to recondition the battery automatically. Use this program whenever these NiMH batteries fail to hold a charge for as long as expected; its approach is similar to that for eliminating the memory effect in NiCad batteries. Check with your PowerBook's manual for details. Also, note that the PowerBook 200 and 2300 series computers use a different version of Battery Recondition than do the PowerBook 5300 and 190 series computers.

BY THE WAY ▶

PRESERVING RAM WHEN REPLACING BATTERIES

Suppose you are on an airplane and you run out of battery power for your PowerBook. Fortunately, you have a fully charged spare battery ready to swap with the now discharged one. That's great, unless swapping the batteries results in losing what is currently in RAM. With most PowerBooks, this can be avoided.

With a Duo, first put the PowerBook to sleep, then swap the batteries. The Duo's backup battery (the small internal one that maintains the contents of PRAM, and so on) will maintain the contents of RAM long enough for you to make the swap. When you wake up the PowerBook, you will be right where you left off.

You can do the same thing with the newest PowerBook models. In fact, the 500 series has an option to hold two batteries at once. In this case, you can swap one battery at any time; you don't even have to put the PowerBook to sleep.

With the 100 series of all-in-one PowerBooks, though, the backup battery does not maintain the contents of RAM while you swap batteries. Therefore you must shut down the PowerBook first, rather than just putting it to sleep. Your only alternatives are to purchase an attachment that provides temporary backup battery power to the PowerBook (sold at most stores that sell Macintoshes) or find a way to get AC power to the PowerBook while making the swap. In these cases, it is not necessary to shut down.

Finally, you may consider purchasing special higher-capacity batteries that attach to the PowerBook case. These can double the time before you need to recharge.

Intelligent (500 Series) Batteries: Recondition

Under certain conditions, the information stored in the "intelligent" batteries used by the 500 series PowerBooks can become corrupted and cause the system software to incorrectly report the battery status. The software updates this information in the battery and restores normal operation.

Intelligent Batteries: Special Recharging Problem

An intelligent battery may have a problem where its charge level is so low that the PowerBook does not recognize its presence and so does not begin to recharge it. You may be able to fix this by removing and reinserting the battery (preferably in the right-hand compartment, with the left compartment empty). Try this several times before giving up; if it doesn't work, you will have to get the battery replaced. Your best bet is to call Apple for assistance (1-800-SOS-APPL).

Reset the Power Manager

See the previous section, "Restarting a PowerBook After a System Error," for details on how to do this.

Zap the PRAM

To zap the PRAM, hold down the Command-Option-P-R keys at startup. Obviously, if you can't get the PowerBook to start up from battery power, you will need to do this while running on AC power.

If the computer shuts itself off after a PRAM zap, press the Reset key on the back of your computer to turn it back on.

SEE: • **Fix-It #11 for more on zapping the Parameter RAM**

A Blown Fuse?

Using a damaged power adapter can cause hardware damage to the logic board itself. In particular, it may blow a fuse so that the PowerBook can run on AC power but not on battery power. This is particularly known to happen with the 140, 160, 170, and 180 PowerBook models. If this happens, replacement of the power adapter is obviously required. Replacement of the main logic board may also be required. Call 800-SOS-APPL for advice here. You should be able to get it repaired at no cost.

PowerBook Appears Dead

Symptoms:

Whether operating on battery power or with the power adapter, the PowerBook shows no sign of life. You cannot even get it to turn on and begin a startup sequence.

Causes:

- The battery and/or power adapter may be damaged and need to be replaced.
- The Power Manager data may be corrupted.
- Otherwise, the cause is probably a general one not specific to PowerBooks.

What to do:

Check the Battery and Power Adapter

Try another battery and/or a different power adapter, if either is available. If you fix the problem this way, your old battery may be dead or damaged, or your power adapter may be damaged. Replace them if necessary.

Reset the Power Manager

Though the Power Manager is primarily associated with problems specific to running on battery power, trouble with it may prevent you from running on AC power as well.

SEE: • **"Restarting a PowerBook After a System Error," for details on this topic**

TAKE NOTE ▶

SPECIAL METHOD FOR REVIVING A "DEAD" POWERBOOK 5300 OR 190

If your PowerBook 5300 or 190 (and possibly a newer model) appears dead, there is a special method for resetting the Power Manager than may revive it. Here's what to do:

1. Shut down and then disconnect the power adapter and remove the battery.
2. Press and hold the Reset button on the back of the PowerBook (under the external video port) for about 30 to 45 seconds.
3. Reconnect the power adapter, making sure it is connected to an AC outlet first. Don't replace the battery yet.
4. Press the Reset button again, just briefly. After a slight pause, the PowerBook should start up; if it doesn't, push the main Power button on the keyboard.
5. If startup is successful, you can now replace the battery.

Try More General Solutions

Check Chapter 5 ("The Macintosh Is Dead") for more general possibilities. As a last resort, take the PowerBook in for repair; you may have a damaged Power Manager or some other serious problem. If the PowerBook is still under warranty, call 800-SOS-APPL for advice on possible free repairs (see Fix-It #18).

Sleep Problems

Symptoms:

- The PowerBook does not go to sleep automatically.
- The PowerBook automatically goes to sleep sooner (or later) than expected.
- A message warns you about some potential problem if your Macintosh goes to sleep.
- A PowerBook freezes or has a system error immediately after waking up from sleep.

Causes:

Most of these problems are due to variations in the settings in the PowerBook control panel. Messages warning against putting a PowerBook to sleep are usually due to selecting Sleep while AppleTalk is on.

Note that the most common way to put a PowerBook to sleep is to select Sleep (or use a keyboard shortcut) from the Finder's Special menu. On some PowerBooks, such as the 190 and 5300, just closing the lid puts the PowerBook to sleep.

Also note that the Sleep command "works" on desktop Macs as well. Exactly what it does depends upon your Mac, your monitor, and what software (such as Energy Saver) you have installed. On some setups (such as PCI-based Macs with Energy Saver monitors), it will completely turn off your monitor and spin down your hard drive; on others, it will simply activate a screen saver, if you have one installed.

What to do:

Automatic Sleep Disabled

Automatic sleep refers to when the PowerBook goes to sleep without your specifically requesting it. When this happens is determined by the interval set in the PowerBook control panel.

Obviously, if the System Sleeps setting is set to "Never," there is no automatic sleep. (If you have an older version of this control panel and your PowerBook is operating on AC power, you get the same result by clicking the Options button and checking "Never Sleep When Plugged In.")

Similarly, be wary if you use the Manual setting for Power Conservation. In particular, make sure you have not selected Power Adapter mode when you are running from battery power, as the power adapter settings generally set a longer time until automatic sleep occurs (or prevent it completely).

SEE: • **"PowerBook Battery Conservation," earlier in this chapter, for details on the PowerBook control panel**

If your PowerBook control panel settings suggest that you should be getting automatic sleep, but it doesn't happen, check for any of the following possible causes. They all prevent automatic sleep from kicking in.

- AppleTalk is on and the power adapter is plugged in, whether you are actually connected to a network or not.
- You are connected to another volume on a network.
- The modem is in use (or auto-answer is on for an internal modem), a document is printing, or a serial port is in use for any other reason.
- Any background activity is occurring.
- An external monitor is in use.
- A Duo is plugged into a Duo Dock, or MiniDock with an external monitor attached.
- An Apple Guide window is open (Apple Guide is a System 7.5 feature described in Chapter 1).
- A 500 series PowerBook is connected to an Ethernet network.
- For Power 5300 and 190 models, make sure you have Password Security 1.0.3 control panel (it comes with System 7.5.3 or later). It fixes a bug whereby the PowerBook would not go to sleep if it was set to ask for the password on waking.
- Some startup extensions may cause the PowerBook to think that the system is busy, thereby preventing sleep (for example, FocalPoint II INIT has been shown to do this).
- Similarly, some application processes may cause the PowerBook to think that the system is busy, thereby preventing sleep (for example, Microsoft Word's automatic repagination option will keep the system awake).

- Finally, here's a direct quote from Apple: "An extension called Insomnia came on the Install Me First disk with some versions of the system software. If this extension is mistakenly put into the Extensions folder in the active System folder on the hard drive, the PowerBook will not sleep. It should be removed from the hard drive. Insomnia is an extension that keeps the PowerBook from going to sleep during the installation process when starting from the Install Me First disk."

  By the way, don't confuse Apple's Insomnia with third-party files of similar names, such as Sleep Deprivation (a cute extension that makes interesting screen patterns when you put your PowerBook to sleep) or Insomniac (a Control Strip module that lets you program automatic wake-ups).

Automatic Sleep Works, But Not at the Expected Interval

In some cases, automatic sleep works, but it kicks in sooner (or later) than you expected. A similar problem can occur with automatic screen dimming. If any of this happens, the most likely cause is that the PowerBook control panel settings are not what you think they are. For example, they may somehow have been set to too short a time (or you may be using the Battery setting, even though the power adapter is attached).

Manual Sleep: AppleTalk Warning

If you select Sleep manually (such as via the Finder's Sleep command) and AppleTalk is on, you will get a warning message informing you that by putting the PowerBook to sleep, you may lose connection to all currently shared volumes on your network. You will get this message even if you aren't connected to any volumes at the time. If you don't care if currently shared volumes get disconnected (or if you have no currently shared volumes) just ignore the message and click Sleep.

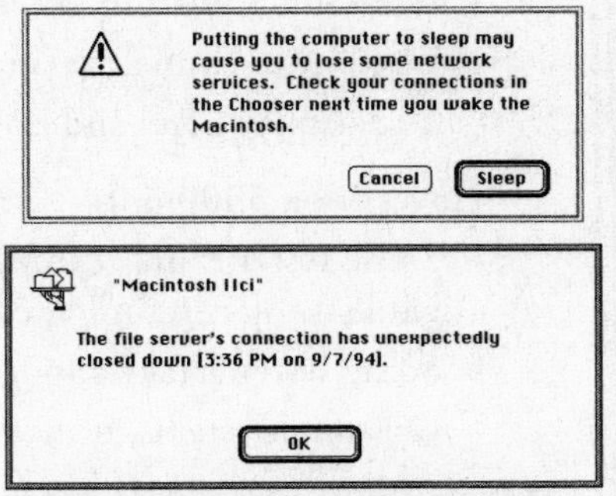

Figure 11-15 *Top: A warning message about selecting Sleep while AppleTalk is active. Bottom: A message that may appear when you reawaken.*

Otherwise, it is generally advised to unmount networked volumes before selecting Sleep. As another alternative, Apple provides a control panel called AutoRemounter (originally part of the PowerBook File Assistant package, but now available as part of System 7.5), which you can use to remount any shared disks automatically after awakening from sleep. Unless this feature is important to you, however, I would not use this extension, since it has been reported to lead to an increase in system crashes. It also doesn't work on some older PowerBook models.

By the way, if you find this AppleTalk warning message annoying and wish to stop it from appearing, you can simply turn AppleTalk off whenever you don't need it to be active. Even better, there are utilities (such as PBTools or Jeremy's Control Strip Modules) that allow you to bypass this message even when AppleTalk is on.

Finally, if shared volumes do get disconnected because of sleep, you will get another message to that effect when you reawaken the PowerBook.

SEE: • **"Transfer Files via File Sharing," later in this chapter, for more on shared volumes**

System Freeze Immediately After Waking Up from Sleep

If your PowerBook freezes or has a system crash (such as a Type 8 error) immediately after waking up from Sleep, there are a whole host of possible causes. Most are fixed by upgrading to the latest software. For instance, a Type 8 error I know of was fixed by upgrading to the latest versions of RAM Doubler and/or installing at least Revision 2 of System 7.5.3. Another freeze problem can be solved by upgrading to at least version 1.0.3 of Drive Setup, assuming your PowerBook can use Drive Setup (as covered in Fix-It #15).

PowerBook Quick Fixes

Here are a few miscellaneous, largely unrelated symptoms and solutions that are too minor to deserve their own sections.

 **Symptoms, Causes, and What to do:**

Do You Qualify for the PowerBook Repair Extension Program?

You do if you have any of the following symptoms (as quoted from Apple):

- **PowerBook 5300 and PowerBook 190:**
  - The power connector on some systems can become loose or inoperative.
  - The display bezel and housing on some systems can crack at the hinge.
- **PowerBook 5300 only**
  - Some systems may exhibit problems when accessing a device in the media bay while using certain PC cards that draw higher levels of power.
  - Some systems take a long time to boot when plugged into AC power.
  - On some systems, devices intermittently drop off LocalTalk networks.

In any of these cases, you qualify for a free repair courtesy of Apple. (Note: if your PowerBook has an "AA" in the lower right-hand corner of the serial number label, you do not need the repair). Call 1-800-801-6024 for more details.

SEE: • **"Take Note: Apple's Repair Extension Program," in Fix-It #17, for more general information**

Defective Pixels on Active Matrix Screens

Check for Void or Stuck Pixels PowerBooks with active matrix screens may have defective pixels (this problem is not relevant to passive matrix screens). To see if you have this problem, turn your PowerBook on and check for either of the following:

- **"Void" pixels**

  This means that the pixel is always off (that is, white). For example, if you look at a screen that should have all dark pixels and one or more pixels are white—staring at you like stars in the night sky—you have void pixels.

- **"Stuck" pixels**
  This means that the pixel is always on (that is, dark). For example, if you look at a screen that should have all white pixels and one or more pixels are dark—looking like periods on a sheet of white paper—you have stuck pixels.

  If you have any doubt as to whether you have defective pixels, a simple test is to use a graphics program to create a large black (or white) rectangle. Now move the window around the rectangle until you have tested all of the screen with it, looking for defective pixels as you go (though you may not be able to test the area of the menu bar this way). Programs that can create slide show presentations can do the same thing. This advice applies best to non-color Macintoshes, though the basic logic is the same in all cases.

Rebuild the Desktop Rebuilding the desktop (see Fix-It #9) may sometimes fix defective pixels, but don't count on it.

Replace the Screen Apple's official position is that if you have six or more void pixels, or even one stuck pixel, you should replace the screen. A stuck pixel is considered more serious because, since it is always in an "on" position, it is constantly draining power. Fortunately, stuck pixels are less common than void ones.

If your PowerBook is still under warranty and has a grayscale (not color) active matrix display, Apple will replace the screen for free under the following conditions: "If it has six or more voids or if any two voids are within one inch of each other, or if a display has even one stuck pixel." Color active matrix screens are not similarly protected.

TECHNICALLY SPEAKING ▶

PASSIVE MATRIX VERSUS ACTIVE MATRIX SCREENS

While PowerBook screens now come in an array of sizes and color capabilities, there are two main types of technologies behind all of these screens: passive matrix and active matrix.

You needn't be concerned about the technical basis for this difference. Suffice it to say that for active matrix screens, each pixel is turned on or off individually; in contrast, passive matrix screens work by activating rows and columns of pixels all at once (a pixel is turned on when an activated row and column intersect).

The main thing to understand about all this is that active matrix screens offer much more rapid and precise control over each pixel than do passive matrix ones. As a result, active matrix screens have much clearer and sharper images than passive matrix screens, and they respond to movement more quickly. An active matrix screen also does not appear to dim or distort as your angle of view moves to one side (as do passive matrix screens), and they are brighter overall. In addition, active matrix screens do not have the ghosting/submarining problem described in the main text. Overall, color passive matrix screens show these problems to a lesser degree than grayscale ones.

The only real disadvantage of active matrix screens is that they are more expensive. If you can afford one, you will be happier with an active matrix screen.

Ghosting and Submarining on Passive Matrix Screens

A disadvantage of passive matrix screens is that when you move the cursor rapidly, the cursor may disappear temporarily. This is a symptom of a more general display problem with passive matrix screens, particularly grayscale ones, called *ghosting* or *submarining*.

Of course, moving the cursor more slowly helps resolve this problem. A better solution is at hand, however, if you have a recent version of Apple's Mouse control panel and Assistant Toolbox installed. At the bottom of the control panel should be an option called Mouse Tracks (not Mouse Tracking, which is at the top of the panel). Selecting longer mouse tracks helps keep the arrow cursor in view by leaving a trail behind it; checking the Thick I-beam option similarly helps make the I-beam more visible. Other PowerBook utilities, such as CPU Tools, have similar options.

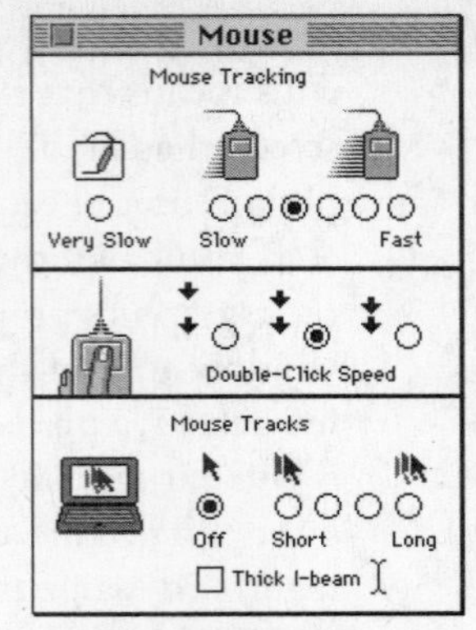

Figure 11-16 *The Mouse Tracks options at the bottom of the Mouse control panel (you'll find it if you have Assistant Toolbox installed).*

Sound Problems

No Sound If your can't get any sound at all from your PowerBook, try zapping the PRAM (see Fix-It #11).

Too Much Sound Persistent white-noise sound "blips" are due to a bug in the hardware of some PowerBook models; there is no real solution to this as yet. I have found, however, that some extensions seem to particularly aggravate this problem. For example, turning off my fax software made this problem go away in my PowerBook 180.

SEE: • **Chapter 6, "Technically Speaking: A Few Words About Sound and Sound Files," for more on problems with using sound**

Backing Up Your System Software and Your Hard Drive

On the PowerBook 5300 series and the 190, rather than including a full set of system software disks, Apple included the disk images of all the disks on the PowerBook itself (although they do come with a Disk Tools floppy disk for startup emergencies). A special utility called Floppy Disk Maker is included so that you can easily make a set of floppy disks from these images. Alternatively, you can try another included utility called Disk Image Mounter, which mounts the system software images and attempts to reinstall the system software from them (apparently, these disk images are different from the standard image format used by Disk Copy).

If you deleted the 5300/190 disk images before making the floppy disks, or to order a backup set of the system software for you PowerBook 145B and 150, call 1-800-SOS-APPL and Apple will send you a set.

The PowerBook 145B and 150 models came with special and somewhat limited utilities to back up and restore the information on your disk, similar to those shipped with Performas. Check the manual that came with your PowerBook for details.

The next generation of PowerBooks is slated to include CD-ROM drives. For these models, users will probably get the system software on a CD-ROM disc, just as desktop Mac users do.

Forgot Your Password?

Newer PowerBook models have a password protection feature. If you forget your password, there is no way to bypass it and start up your PowerBook, because the password is written to your drive at the driver level; even starting from a floppy disk won't work. The only option, according to Apple, is to "take your PowerBook with your proof of purchase (receipt) to an authorized Apple service center where a technician has the means to bypass the security on the system."

So what happens if you don't have your proof of purchase anymore? Is your only hope to reformat the disk? Hmmm …

Can't Insert a Duo into or Can't Eject a Duo from a Duo Dock

Insert Problems If you are having problems inserting a Duo into a Duo Dock, check the following items:

- Make sure the Duo is off (not just asleep) before trying to insert it into a dock.
- Make sure you are not using a Duo with a cover that is too big for that model of Duo Dock. In particular, some newer Duo models did not fit into older versions of the Duo Dock (check with Apple for details).
- Make sure the Duo Dock is unlocked (the key should be in the vertical position).

Eject Problems If pressing the Eject button fails to get a Duo to eject from a Duo Dock, check the following possible solutions:

- Make sure the Duo Dock is unlocked (the key should be in the vertical position).
- Otherwise, you can manually eject the dock by inserting a small screwdriver into the hole on the left side of the Duo Dock. Press it in gently.

Trouble Ejecting PCMCIA Cards

PCMCIA stands for Personal Computer Memory Card International Association, and PCMCIA cards (often just called PC Cards) are memory cards that conform to this association's standard. For Macs, these can be used only on certain PowerBooks, specifically the PowerBook 500 series (which uses a PCMCIA Expansion Module) and the built-in PCMCIA bay for the PowerBook 190 and 5300 series. PCMCIA cards supplement the features of the PowerBook (for example, by adding a modem or Ethernet support), with the exact features depending upon the contents of the card.

Also note that unless newer software incorporates the fix, a file from Apple called PCMCIA Update may be needed to solve compatibility and performance problems with PowerBook 500s.

When a PCMCIA card is installed, one of the more frequent problems users report is difficulty in ejecting it again. Normally, you do this either by dragging the icon of the card to the Trash or selecting Put Away from the Finder's Special menu (just as you do for disks). If this doesn't work, however, here are some other suggestions:

- If you get a message that says that the card cannot be ejected because it is "in use," and you have quit all open applications, the PCMCIA modem may be in auto-answer mode. To eject the card, you'll have to launch your communications software and turn this option off.

  Otherwise, make sure file sharing is turned off. In either case, try again to eject the card.
- For other eject problems, a paper clip can be inserted into the small hole next to the PCMCIA slot to eject the card manually. Try to avoid pulling the card out of the computer.
- If even this fails, Apple offers the following advice: "You can pull the card out yourself with a pair of needle nose pliers or sometimes with your fingers, if you have strong fingernails. Once the card is pulled out, try inserting the paper clip again to release the spring mechanism. If you hear the springs release, you can try inserting the card (or a different card) again. Of course, the problem may recur." If so, the card may be damaged. If the problem occurs with several cards, the Expansion Module (or bay) may be damaged and need to be repaired.

PowerBook 1400 Glitches

- The PowerBook 1400 does not work with System 7.5.5. It does work with System 7.6 or later, however.
- Unlike other Power Macs, holding down the "c" key at startup will not get the PowerBook 1400 to start up from a CD-ROM. Instead, you have to resort to holding down the Command-Option-Shift-Delete keys (as explained more in Chapter 5).
- If you use Disk First Aid and get a message that says "This is not an HFS disk," use the PowerBook 1400 Updater fix utility from Apple.

TrackBall and TrackPad Problems

A few quick fixes for these hardware devices are covered in Fix-It #17.

Transfer Files to and from a PowerBook

If you are fortunate enough to own both a PowerBook and a desktop Macintosh, you will inevitably find yourself wanting to transfer data from one computer to the other. Of course, you can do this by using a floppy disk as an intermediate step. Except for infrequent transfers of small files, though, this is a slow, tedious, and inefficient process. Fortunately, there are better alternatives. This section outlines these alternatives and the problems to avoid when using them.

Transfer Files Via the SCSI Port

To Connect an External Hard Drive to Your PowerBook's SCSI Port

You can connect an external drive to your PowerBook in the same way that you would with any desktop Macintosh. This is an easy way to transfer files. For example, if you have an external hard drive normally connected to a desktop Mac, you can temporarily hook it up to a PowerBook to transfer files to the drive, then reconnect it to your desktop Mac. You will need to take the usual precautions here, such as making sure that there are no ID conflicts and that all devices are turned off before you connect or disconnect any cables.

SEE: • **Chapter 5 and Fix-It #16 for more on SCSI mounting, connections, cables, IDs, and termination**

In addition, there are a few special considerations when connecting an external drive to a PowerBook:

The PowerBook SCSI Port Is Different from the One on Desktop Macs The PowerBook's SCSI port is an almost square 30-pin port, while a desktop Mac's SCSI port is a larger rectangular 25-pin port. To connect an external drive to the PowerBook port, you will need a special cable called the HDI-30 System Cable.

As an alternative, you can get a device such as APS's SCSI Boy adapter, which plugs into a PowerBook's SCSI port on one end and leaves an open 25-pin port on the other end. You can now connect an ordinary 25-pin SCSI cable to the PowerBook.

Extra Termination May Be Needed You may need to insert a terminator at the end of the system cable that gets connected to the external drive, even if the external drive is already terminated. Do this if you are having any problems getting the hard disk to mount.

To Connect Your PowerBook as an External Drive to a Desktop Mac

There is a special feature of PowerBooks called SCSI Disk Mode or HD Target Mode. It is available on all PowerBooks except the 140, 145, 145B, 150, and 170, as well as on Duos through use of the MiniDock. In disk mode, the PowerBook acts as if it is just a normal external drive. With this method, you connect the PowerBook itself to another Macintosh. When the PowerBook's drive is mounted on the other Mac's desktop, you can transfer files between the two Macintoshes. If you have a lot of data to transfer, this is probably the quickest way to do it. Here's how to set it all up:

1. **Before making any connections, open the PowerBook Setup control panel**

   Select a SCSI ID number from the SCSI Disk Mode section of the control panel, then close the panel. Which ID number you select is not important, as long as you make sure it is different from that of any other device already on the desktop Mac's SCSI chain.

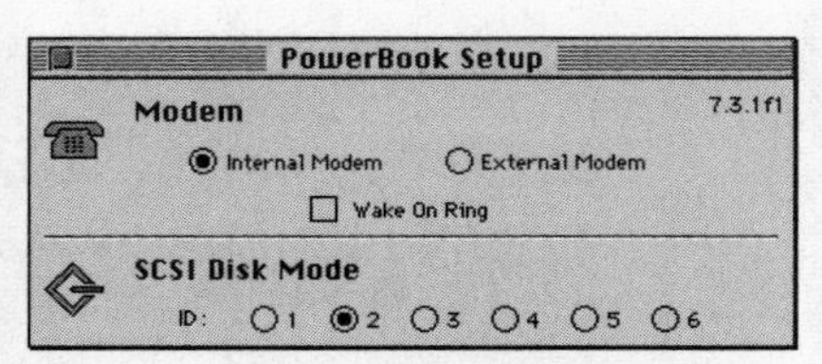

Figure 11-17 *SCSI ID number 2 is selected from the PowerBook Setup control panel.*

2. **Turn off all devices**
   It is especially important to shut down the PowerBook at this point; just putting it to sleep is not sufficient.
3. **Make the cable connections**
   For disk mode, you need a special cable called the HDI-30 Disk Adapter (*not* the HDI-30 System Cable described in the previous section). It is dark gray in color, as opposed to the lighter gray of the HDI-30 System Cable. One end of the HD-30 Disk Adapter plugs into the PowerBook's SCSI port; the other end plugs into the 50-pin end of an ordinary SCSI cable. The other end of this second cable then connects either to a desktop Mac or to the *last* device in a desktop Mac's SCSI chain (depending on which you do, the cable will have either a 25-pin or a 50-pin plug on the end not connected to the adapter). You will probably also need a terminator connected to the SCSI Adapter cable. Consult your PowerBook User's Guide for more details, if needed.

   SEE: • Chapter 5 and Fix-It #16 for more on SCSI mounting, connections, cables, IDs, and termination
4. **Turn on the PowerBook**
   You should now see a large SCSI icon (with an ID number inside it). If so, you are in SCSI Disk Mode.

   If this doesn't happen, immediately disconnect the PowerBook from the desktop Mac and try again, repeating all steps. If you mistakenly connected the cable while the PowerBook was asleep rather than shut down, you should get a warning message when you try to wake it up, telling you *not* to use the PowerBook until you shut down first. Do what it says.

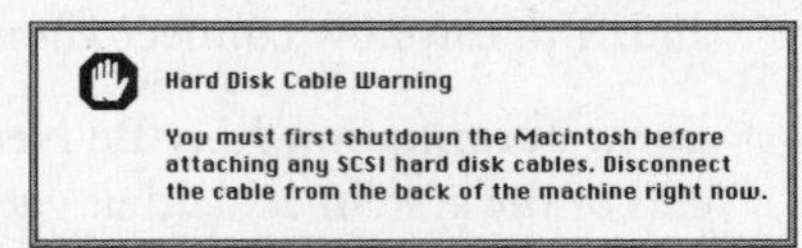

Figure 11-18 *This warning message appears when you awaken a PowerBook after having attached a SCSI cable to it.*

5. **Turn on the desktop Mac**
   When the desktop Mac finishes starting up, you should see the icon for the PowerBook's drive mounted on the desktop Mac's desktop. You can now transfer files.

   (Note: Some Macintoshes won't recognize a SCSI-mode PowerBook if the PowerBook is turned on before the desktop Mac. In this case, turn the desktop Mac on first, then the PowerBook. Experiment to see what works.)

When you are done, turn everything off and disconnect/reconnect cables as needed to return things to how they were when you started.

TAKE NOTE ▶

SCSI DISK MODE VERSUS HD TARGET MODE

Apple now refers to SCSI Disk Mode as HD Target Mode. This change was made because several PowerBook lines (such as the 190 and 5300 series) use IDE internal drives instead of SCSI drives (making the term *SCSI Disk Mode* technically incorrect for those models). Functionally, the two terms mean the same thing.

Three special considerations apply to this process:

Password Protection If your PowerBook has a Password Protection option, you must turn this protection off (from the Password Security control panel) before connecting your PowerBook in SCSI Disk Mode.

PowerBook 500 and 5300 freeze If you have a PowerBook 500 or 5300 connected to a desktop Mac in HD Target Mode, and if you shut down the desktop Mac with the PowerBook still mounted, the PowerBook may freeze. To avoid this, Apple recommends unmounting the PowerBook first (via the Put Away command) and then shutting it off by pressing and holding down the Power key (in the upper right-hand corner of the keyboard) for approximately three seconds. You can then turn off your desktop Mac.

If your system does freeze, you'll probably have to restart the PowerBook with its Reset button (which, Apple warns, may corrupt the Power Manager when done in these circumstances).

Norton Utilities problem Do not use Norton Utilities Speed Disk or Disk Doctor from a desktop computer to check your PowerBook while it is in SCSI Disk Mode. This can cause the desktop computer to crash or freeze. To check your PowerBook with these utilities, do not connect it in SCSI Disk Mode; instead use an Emergency Toolkit startup floppy disk to start up your PowerBook (as described more in Chapter 2).

Of course, updated versions of these utilities may remedy this problem.

Transfer Files Via File Sharing

With System 7, Apple introduced personal file sharing, a method by which up to ten Macintoshes can share information over a network. PowerBook users can use it to transfer information between their PowerBook and their desktop Mac. Though the transfer rate is slower than via the SCSI connection methods, I prefer the file-sharing approach for most transfers (such as copying a few documents from one Mac to the other) because the connection procedure is so quick and simple. You don't have to shut down your Macs to make the connection, and you needn't be concerned about SCSI ID conflicts or termination problems. The lone potential drawback is the required one-time-only installation and setup of the file-sharing software.

File Sharing: Initial Setup

Using file sharing requires several special extensions and control panels that are a standard part of the system software. The key thing to realize here is that 90 percent of the features in these control panels are designed solely for security—to prevent unauthorized users on a network from gaining access to information on your computer. If all you are going to do is connect your own PowerBook to your own desktop Macintosh, security is not an issue.

What follows, then, is a bare-bones, foolproof method of getting file sharing going when security is not a concern. This method eliminates almost all of the hassles you would otherwise have. If you ever use file-sharing software to connect your Mac to a

TAKE NOTE ▶

WHAT IS APPLETALK?

This note is similar to one that appears in Chapter 7. Because of its direct relevance here, however, the information seems worth restating.

AppleTalk refers to a method of networking computers and peripherals together; it is the equivalent of the language that is used to send information over the network. All Macintosh computers have built-in AppleTalk support, which makes it easy to connect them together for file sharing.

Making a connection typically requires special networking cables. Apple's cabling system is called LocalTalk, but other companies make competing cabling systems that connect via the same ports. A popular LocalTalk alternative is PhoneNet, which uses ordinary phone wire to make LocalTalk connections. With PhoneNet, the cable connected to the end device at each end of the chain needs a special terminating resistor, which is plugged into the empty slot in the phone plug.

Once the cables are in place, using a connection also requires turning on AppleTalk and selecting the appropriate driver from the Chooser (as explained in the main text). Finally, if you are using Ethernet or other non-LocalTalk networking system, and you are not using Open Transport, you will additionally have to open the Network control panel and make the appropriate selection. With Open Transport, you may need to make an appropriate selection from the AppleTalk control panel (see "Problems Using Apple Remote Access," for one example).

TAKE NOTE ▶

BEYOND FILE SHARING: TIMBUKTU PRO AND INTRANETS

If you don't want to bother with all of these file-sharing setup procedures, there are at least two other ways you can accomplish the same goal.

- **Timbuktu Pro** One way is to use a product such as Farallon's Timbuktu Pro. With it, you can send files from one Macintosh to another via a LocalTalk connection (or even via a modem connection). It has only minimal setup hassles, primarily a one-time installation of the Timbuktu software. Once installed, using it is even easier than using file sharing. It has the added feature of being able to take "control" of a remote Macintosh: you get to see the other Mac's screen and manipulate via your mouse and keyboard, just as if it were sitting in front of you.
- **Intranet** Another option is to set up an Intranet, with your Macintosh (or at least some Mac) as a mini-server. Rather than having the server connect to the outside world of the Internet, however, you use it only for your local network (which can be as small as two Macs). For infrequent connections, such as for making file transfers to and from a PowerBook, it can be practical to do this via a LocalTalk connection (you'll need to make adjustments to your MacTCP or TCP/IP settings to get it to work). From an Intranet, you can send or receive files to others on your network using FTP software, just as you would on the Internet. You can even have a local-only Web site set up this way, using a program such as WebSTAR or the even simpler personal Web server programs (such as Web For One). While you may balk at the work involved in setting this all up, it keeps getting easier as the software evolves. Still, this is admittedly the most difficult of all of the connection methods described in this chapter. While the setup details are beyond the scope of this book, I wanted you at least to be aware of this increasingly popular option—which obviously has uses beyond connecting a PowerBook to a desktop Mac.

SEE: • Chapter 14 for coverage of more general Internet topics

multi-user network, however, don't use the method described here! (For information on more secure setups, consult System 7 software manuals.)

This method assumes that you will be accessing your desktop Mac from your PowerBook. It also assumes you will use the built-in LocalTalk network (as opposed to EtherTalk, or whatever) and that you have the necessary LocalTalk or PhoneNet cables correctly installed.

BY THE WAY ▶

INFRARED CONNECTIONS

Some PowerBooks, such as the 5300 and 1400 series, include the ability to communicate with another PowerBook via a wireless infrared connection. This requires the Apple IR File Exchange software included with your PowerBook and with System 7.5.3 or later—and it eliminates the need to use physical cables for file sharing.

Needless to say, numerous problems can occur as you try to get this relatively new technology to work. For example, Apple states: "When you select IRTalk in the Network control panel, your computer chooses a random network address. Occasionally, you may come within range of another computer using the same network address and experience difficulty communicating with it. When this occurs, you'll see a dialog box telling you that a duplicate AppleTalk address has been detected. Click OK in the dialog box, then open the Network control panel and select IRTalk again. This will give your computer a new network address and will correct the problem. (Alternately, you can activate and inactivate AppleTalk from the Control Strip or the Chooser.)"

If you want to use this feature to "connect" your PowerBook to a desktop Mac that does not have infrared capability (none do as of this writing), you need to get Farallon's Air Dock and attach it to your desktop Mac.

1. **Make sure you have the needed file-sharing software installed**

You probably already do. This software should have come preinstalled on your hard disk (assuming you have System 7); it also gets installed automatically if you select Easy Install when installing system software yourself. If you have this software installed, you will see files such as Sharing Setup, Users & Groups, File Sharing Extension, and Network in your Control Panels and Extensions folders.

If these files do not appear, you need to install them. To do this, launch the Installer utility on your system software disks. Select Customize, open the Networking Software section and click the File Sharing box, and then click Install. After all this is done, restart your Macintosh.

Install this software on both your PowerBook and your desktop Mac. This process will actually install more files than you really need, especially on your PowerBook; for example, you will need Sharing Setup on your desktop Mac, but not on your PowerBook. As you get familiar with the

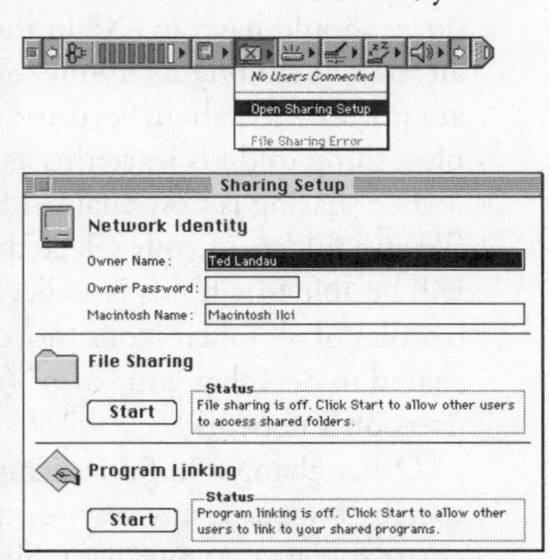

Figure 11-19 *Select Open Sharing Setup from the Control Strip (top) and get the Sharing Setup control panel (bottom).*

procedure, you can delete the files you know you don't need. In the meantime, it will be easier to just leave everything where it is.

SEE: • Fix-It #5 for more details on using the Installer

2. **From your desktop Mac, turn on AppleTalk**
You can do this from the Chooser. Make sure AppleTalk is active; if it isn't, click the Active button. If you are using the Control Strip, you can make AppleTalk active from there. If you are using Open Transport, you can also turn it on from the AppleTalk control panel.

3. **From your desktop Mac, select Sharing Setup**
Open the Sharing Setup control panel directly or from the Control Strip.

In the Network Identity section, you must type in your name (however you want it to appear) and a name for your computer. You can change these names later if you want, but the Mac will not let you leave these spaces blank. You don't have to type a password, but the Mac will send you a warning message, if you do not.

From the File Sharing section, click Start. Wait a minute or so until this process finishes.

Leave Program Linking off. This is a rarely used feature that does not affect what you are trying to do here.

Close the control panel.

4. **From your desktop Mac, highlight the icon of the hard disk you want to share**
To do this, just click the icon once.

5. **From your desktop Mac, select "Sharing…" from the Finder's File menu**
After you select the Sharing command, a dialog box appears. From here, click the check box that says "Share this item and its contents." At this point, all the See Files, See Folders, and Make Changes boxes should have an "X" in them—for all rows, including Everyone. Since you are not worried about security, the simplest thing to do is leave this as it is.

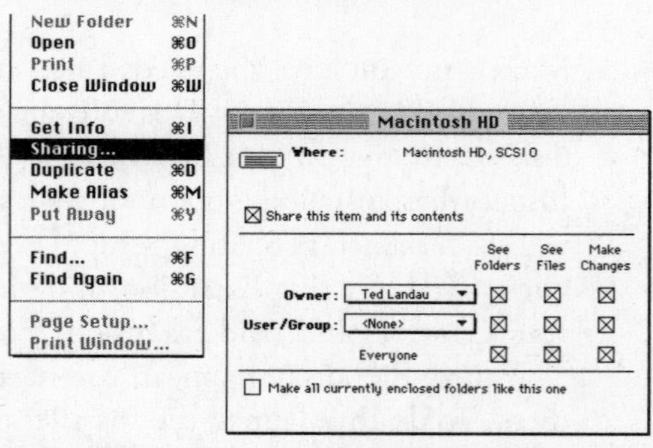

Figure 11-20 *The Sharing… dialog box. Check "Share item and its contents" to share the disk.*

File sharing is now enabled for every file and folder on your selected disk. You will be able to tell this is so because the handles of all folder icons on your disk will become double thick. This happens to all shared folders that you "own" (that is, that were placed there by you, not by other users on a network).

Other changes in folder icons occur if you restrict access to specific folders in any way (or if you let other users on a network create folders on your disk). Since you won't be doing any of that here, however, I won't bother you with the details.

Figure 11-21 *A folder that you own when file sharing is off (left) versus when it is on (right).*

Finally, you can repeat Steps 4 and 5 for any additional mounted disks you want to share.

6. **From your desktop Mac, select the Users & Groups control panel**
   You should see two "face" icons here, one with your name on it (this icon will have a bold outline around it) and the other called Guest. Double-click the Guest icon. From the window that opens, click the "Allow guests to connect" option.

   Again, be warned that this means that any user on a network to which you connect will have access to your entire hard drive. As a safer alternative, you can bypass this step and plan to connect using your own name, as listed on the other icon. Using your name rather than Guest, however, may require additional steps to make a file-sharing connection.

   Close the icon's window and the control panel. You are now done with the desktop Mac's side of the setup.

   (Note: You can create new icons for specific users here, but I am skipping over this option.)

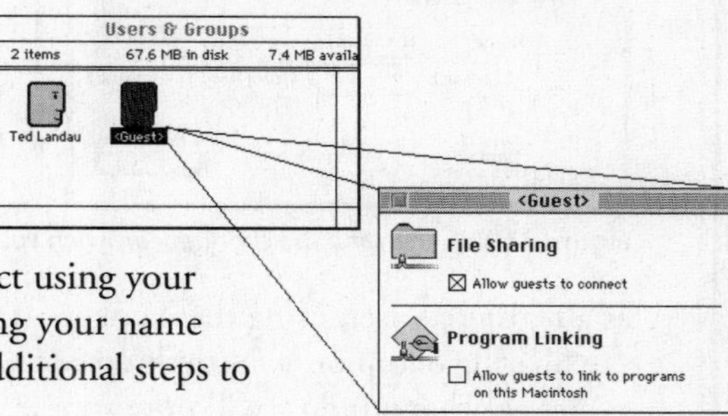

Figure 11-22 *The Users and Groups control panel. Check "Allow guests to connect" to set up a convenient zero-security connection.*

7. **Connect your PowerBook to your desktop Mac**
   To do this, you need a LocalTalk or PhoneNet type cable (see "Take Note: What Is AppleTalk?"). If you are using Classic AppleTalk, connect each end of the cable to the printer ports (not the modem ports) of each computer. For Open Transport, connect the cable to the port selected in the AppleTalk control panel. If your PowerBook has only one serial port, it supports AppleTalk and is obviously the one to use. You can make these connections even while both computers are on.

   If you already have a PostScript LaserWriter connected to your Macintosh, you already have the right kind of cable in a serial port (probably the printer port). In this case, you can simply unplug it from the back of your printer and plug it into the appropriate serial port of your PowerBook (remembering to return the cable to the printer when you are done with file sharing).

SEE: • **Chapter 14 for more on Open Transport and Classic AppleTalk**
• **Fix-It #17 for more on cables and cable connections**

8. **From your PowerBook, select the Chooser**
   Make AppleTalk active, if it isn't already, then select the AppleShare icon. At this point, the name of your desktop Mac should appear in the window on the right. Double-click the name (or single-click the name and click OK).

   From the window that appears next, click the Guest button, then click OK. Alternatively, if you left Guest access turned off in the Users and Groups control panel (in Step 6), you will need to connect

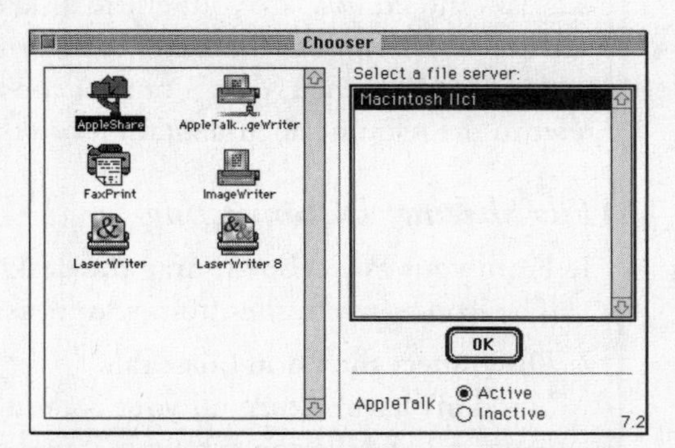

Figure 11-23 *The Chooser, with my desktop Mac's name highlighted.*

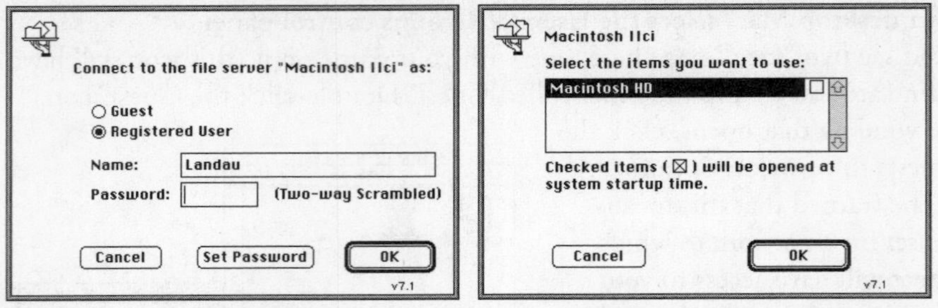

Figure 11-24 *The windows that appear when you mount the desktop Mac from the Chooser.*

as a registered user, using the name (and password, if you entered one) you entered in the Sharing Setup on your desktop Mac.

Yet another window will now appear. The name of the volume(s) you set up for sharing should now appear, already highlighted. (If they are not highlighted, click on them to select them.) Click OK, ignoring the checkbox about having the item open automatically at startup.

Now close the Chooser. The icon of your desktop Mac's hard disk should appear on your PowerBook's desktop. You are now ready to share files—but don't get to work quite yet.

9. **From your PowerBook, select the desktop Mac's disk icon**
   After selecting the icon, make an alias of it by using the Make Alias command from the Finder's File menu. Place the alias in any convenient location on your desktop. The advantage of this alias will become clear the next time you want to use file sharing, as I will describe shortly.

10. **The initial setup is now complete; you can share files**
   Any time you access the desktop Mac from the PowerBook, you will see a pair of opposite facing arrows flashing on and off in the upper left-hand corner of the menu bar, to the left of the Apple icon. This is normal.

Helpful hint: Remember, these instructions assume that you intend to share files between a PowerBook and a desktop Mac, that you are the only user doing the sharing, that you intend to share your entire disk, and that you care nothing about security. If you are on a network with other users or if access has been separately set for individual folders for any reason, things can get considerably more complicated. If this is the case, refer to the relevant documentation or other outside help, as needed.

File Sharing: Disconnecting

1. **From your PowerBook, drag the desktop Mac's icon(s) to the Trash**
   The icon now vanishes from your desktop. The Macs are no longer connected.

2. **Disconnect the LocalTalk cable**
   You don't have to turn off your computers to do this. This is also an optional step; you can leave the cable in place if you plan to leave your PowerBook where it is and have no other need for the cable.

3. **If you want, you can now turn file sharing and AppleTalk off**
   To do this, select the Sharing Setup control panel on your desktop Mac and click the Stop button. Turning file sharing off has the benefit of reducing the amount of RAM used by the system software. You can also turn AppleTalk off if you no longer need it for any other operation. Doing this on your PowerBook helps conserve battery power, but don't forget that you need AppleTalk to be active in order to use most PostScript printers. In any case, you will need to make sure these features are on again the next time you want to share files.

SEE: • **"Problems with Turning File Sharing or AppleTalk Off," later in this chapter, for more information**

Accessing File Sharing After the Initial Setup

Once you have completed the initial setup, as just described, accessing file sharing on future occasions is much easier. Here's all you have to do:

1. **Connect your PowerBook to your desktop Mac**
   Follow the directions in Step 7 of the Initial Setup section.
2. **From your PowerBook, double-click the alias of the desktop Mac's icon**
   This is the alias you made in Step 8 of the Initial Setup section.

That's it! Assuming that file sharing and AppleTalk are both still on, and all needed extensions and control panels are present and active, the desktop Mac's disk should mount on your PowerBook. You are ready to share files without any other steps needed. (If you are mounting as a registered user rather than a guest, you may still get a dialog box where you need to enter your name and password.)

TAKE NOTE ▶

FILE SYNCHRONIZATION

Once you have file sharing set up, one of the best uses you can make of it is to update files that you keep on both disks, so that both computers always have the same version of these files. For example, suppose you are working on a report on your desktop Mac. When you leave for a trip, you copy the report to your PowerBook so you can work on it while you are on the road; when you get back home, you replace the now-outdated version on your desktop Mac with the newer copy from your PowerBook.

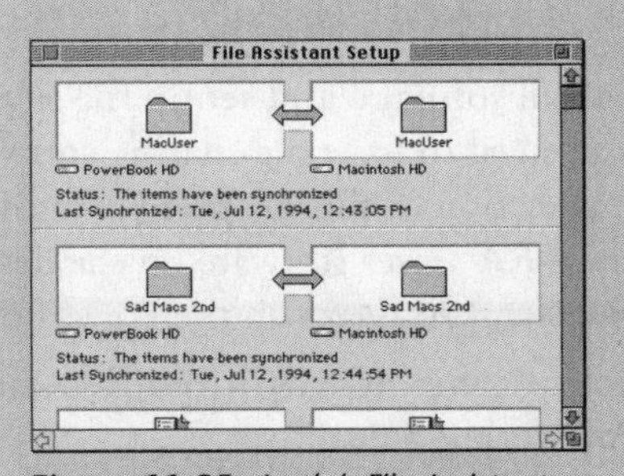

Figure 11-25 *Apple's File Assistant.*

If you only do this occasionally, it is easy enough to do by simply dragging the file from one computer to another via file sharing. If you do this frequently and with a variety of files, however, you will benefit from a method that automates this procedure and makes sure that everything is updated correctly. Doing this is called *file synchronization*.

There are several utilities for this purpose. Apple includes a decent one, called File Assistant, as part of System 7.5 and its revisions.

By the way, the only extensions/control panels you absolutely need at this point are the File Sharing and Network extensions on your desktop Mac and the AppleShare Chooser extension on your PowerBook. To use file sharing in the way I have described here, you don't need any other extensions or control panels active. Still, I would keep control panels such as Sharing Setup around, since you may need them to make changes later.

Transfer Files Via a Modem (Apple Remote Access)

If your desktop Macintosh is at home and you are on the road somewhere with your PowerBook, you can still connect the two machines and directly transfer files between them without using email, or a similar online feature, as an intermediary. You'll need a modem connection and some special software, however, to do this.

The Apple software for this purpose is called Apple Remote Access (ARA). It allows you to connect directly to another Mac via a modem and then access files through Apple's file sharing. Starting with version 3.0, you will be able to use ARA over a PPP connection; for now, you have to make a direct dial-up modem connection.

SEE: • **Chapter 14 for more on Open Transport and PPP**

Farallon's Timbuktu Pro is a potential alternative to ARA that actually has two options. The Dial Direct option is useful for connecting two machines together; it does not require any server or other networking software. In contrast, the second option requires using ARA to link your remote Mac to a server; your remote Mac becomes a node on the network.

Make sure you have a fast modem (at least 14,400 bps) to get a reasonable rate of data transfer with Timbuktu Pro. Even so, your speed will be slower than you would get from the direct LocalTalk network connection described in the previous section.

For the details on how to set up and use ARA and/or Timbuktu Pro, consult the documentation that comes with the software. To give you a basic idea of how all of this works, however, here is a brief overview of the setup procedures required for ARA:

1. **Install software and set up file sharing**
   You need to have file-sharing software installed and set up as described in the previous section of this chapter ("Transfer Files via File Sharing"). You also need to install the ARA server software on the desktop Mac and the client software on the PowerBook machine.

2. **Select "Answer calls" from Remote Access Answering Setup**
   From the desktop machine, which will presumably be receiving the incoming calls, open the Remote Access Setup control panel. Check the "Answer calls" checkbox in the Remote Access Answering Setup portion of the dialog box.

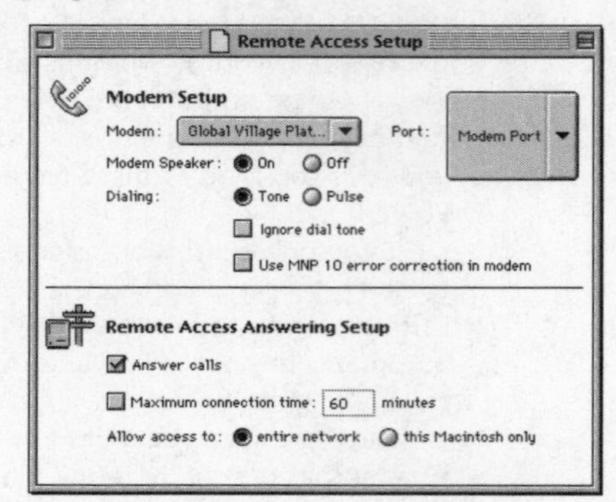

Figure 11-26 *Remote Access Setup. To receive incoming calls, check "Answer calls."*

You will also need to make the appropriate selections, of course, in the Modem Setup portion of the dialog box for both the desktop and PowerBook machines.

3. **Select "Allow to dial in" from Users & Groups**
From the desktop machine, go to the Users & Groups control panel (you can get there from Remote Access Setup by selecting the Users & Groups command from the Setup menu). Double-click the Guest icon. The window that appears will include a new section called "Remote Access." Check the "Allow guests to dial in" option within this section. Again, this allows *anyone* to access your system; for greater security (which is especially relevant here, since anyone could dial in over a modem), use the icon with your own name rather than the Guest icon. From this window, check the "Allow user to dial in" option. Doing so allows you registered-user access to the ARA server on your desktop Mac.

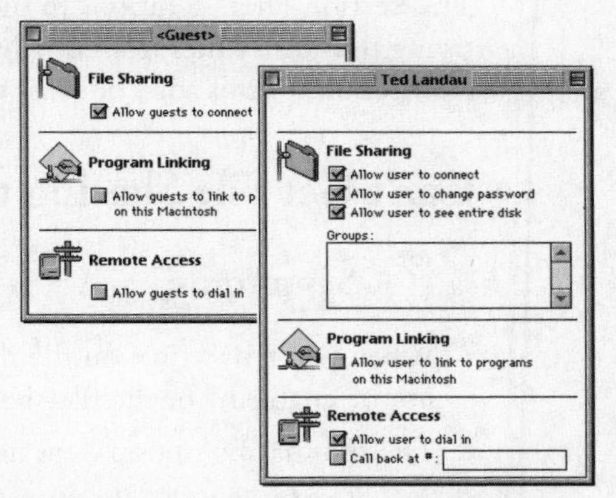

Figure 11-27 *Users & Groups windows for Guest and for Ted Landau; in both cases, ARA's Remote Access sections are seen.*

4. **Connect from Remote Access Personal**
From the PowerBook (the sending machine), open the Remote Access Personal program and select whether you are a Registered User or a Guest. If you are a Registered User, enter your name and password. In either case, enter the phone number needed to connect to your desktop Mac, then click Connect. If all goes well, your desktop Mac should mount on your PowerBook desktop just as it would via a local network using file sharing.

   If you have problems connecting, you may want to try ARA's DialAssist option. To activate it, click the checkbox in the Remote Access Personal window. It accesses a control panel that can help you figure out the correct phone number settings.

   If you still are unsuccessful in getting a connection, go to "Problems Using Apple Remote Access," later in this chapter. It covers such matters as when and how to select the Remote Only option.

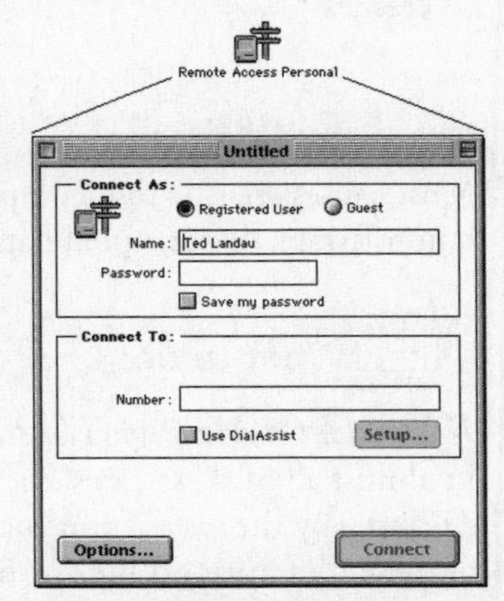

Figure 11-28 *An new Remote Access Personal document.*

SEE ALSO: • **Chapter 14 for more general information on setting up and using a modem and communications software.**

5. **Disconnect**
When you later want to disconnect, select the Remote Access Disconnect item that should be present in the Apple Menu. Alternatively, you can disconnect from the Remote Access Personal program.

Solve It! File Transfer Problems

This section offers solutions to the more common problems you may encounter when trying to transfer files from one Mac to another. Most of the advice here applies to all connections of this sort, not just those involving PowerBooks.

Can't Get File Sharing to Work

Symptoms:

- When you try to turn on file sharing, you get a message that says "File sharing could not be enabled," or the file-sharing startup simply never finishes.
- The file-sharing option does not appear in the Sharing Setup window.
- When trying to connect to another Macintosh, you get a message that says the shared disk could not be opened because it "could not be found on the network."
- When trying to connect to another Macintosh, you get a message that says it can't be opened because "you do not have enough access privileges."
- You cannot enable file sharing or connect to a shared disk for any other reason.
- While sharing information across disks, problems occur, such as system freezes or crashes.

Causes:

Most causes are due to incompatible software, incorrect software settings, bugs in certain software, or corrupted data.

What to do:

If You Get a Message That Says "File Sharing Could Not Be Enabled"

In almost all of these cases, the problem is due to a corrupted file that needs to be deleted. (By the way, if you succeed in enabling file sharing but still want to delete any of these files, turn off file sharing first.)

- **Corrupted Users and Groups data file**
  The Users & Groups data file is located in the Preferences folder. Locate it and delete it, then restart the Macintosh; a new default version of the file will be created. You will then need to re-create any custom settings you made in the Users & Groups control panel. After doing so, see if you can now turn file sharing on.
  By the way, some versions of AppleShare subtly modify this file so that System 7 file sharing will no longer work if the AppleShare extension is replaced with another version. This, too, is fixed by deleting the Users & Groups data file and restarting.

BY THE WAY ▶

APPLESHARE PDS AND CD-ROM PDF FILES—AND KILLER RABBITS, TOO

If you have a CD-ROM drive and use file sharing, go to the Preferences folder and look for a folder called File Sharing. Inside, you will see a collection of files with PDF (*not* PDS) at the end of their names. The reason these files are created is that, since CD-ROM discs are read-only, the Macintosh cannot create the more typical invisible AppleShare PDS file it would otherwise place on the CD-ROM disc. Instead, it creates these PDF files and stores them in your startup disk's System Folder. You can delete them if you wish; the Mac will re-create them if it needs them again.

By the way, speaking of invisible stuff related to file sharing, you may find an invisible folder on your hard disk called Move & Rename. It, too, is created and used by AppleShare. Should you delete it by mistake, don't worry; the Mac will again create a new one when it needs one.

Also note that in some older versions of the system software, the AppleShare PDS file and the PDF files may have a weird "killer rabbit" icon. Don't worry about it. It's just a sign of Apple engineers having some fun.

- **Corrupted files in File Sharing folder**
  The File Sharing folder is located in the Preferences folder. To check for corrupted files, drag the File Sharing folder from the Preferences folder to the desktop, restart and try file sharing again. If it now succeeds, delete the removed folder; a new one will be created automatically and its contents restored as needed. Otherwise, you can return the folder to its original location.
- **Corrupted AppleShare PDS file**
  AppleShare PDS is an invisible file used by AppleShare that is located at the root level of the hard disk. To check whether the file is corrupted, you need to delete it—but since it is an invisible file, you will first need to use a utility (such as DiskTop) that lists and allows you to delete invisible files.

  Some utilities, such as MacTools, may allow you to make an invisible file visible but not to delete the file. If you are using this type of utility, make the file visible, go to the Finder to locate and delete the file, and restart; the Mac will automatically create a new PDS file. Check if you can now enable file sharing.

  By the way, a corrupted PDS file has also been known to be a cause of unusually long startup times. Deleting the file corrects this problem.

For Other Problems with Enabling File Sharing

You may have problems enabling file sharing that do not result in the "file sharing could not be enabled" message. Here are some common situations and their solutions:

- **AppleTalk is not active**
  If AppleTalk is not active, you should get a message telling you this when you try to turn file sharing on. If so, go to the Chooser (or use the Control Strip) and make it active. While you are at it, make sure *all* needed file-sharing software is installed (as described in "File Sharing: Initial Setup," earlier in this chapter).

- **The Sharing Setup control panel cannot be opened**
  The Sharing Setup control panel will probably not open unless the Network Extension (which is different from the Network control panel) is installed in Extensions folder. If you try to open Sharing Setup without the Network Extension active, you will get a message telling you to install the extension and restart your Mac. Do what the message says.
- **The File Sharing section is missing from the Sharing Setup control panel**
  If this happens, the File Sharing Extension (which is not the same thing as the Sharing Setup control panel) is not present or was disabled at startup. Replace or re-enable it, restart the Mac, and check the Sharing Setup control panel again.
- **Corrupted PRAM**
  Zap the PRAM (see Fix-It #11). You will probably have to turn AppleTalk on again after this.
- **Disk limitations**
  You should ideally have at least 1MB of free disk space to use file sharing. Also, some removable cartridge drives do not work with file sharing, and some non-Apple formatting utilities are not compatible with file sharing. Finally, you can't share a PC-formatted volume.
- **Memory limitations**
  You need at least 340K of free memory to use file sharing. If you are having problems, restart with some or all unrelated extensions off.
- **Problems with the "Sharing" command and dialog box**
  If you select the "Sharing …" command for a particular volume from the Finder's File menu and get a message that says "One or more items could not be shared, because not all items are available for file sharing," you are probably trying to share a removable cartridge (such as in a SyQuest drive) that was mounted after file sharing was turned on. Try turning file sharing off and then back on again. Otherwise, restart, making sure the cartridge is present at startup, and then try the Sharing command again. It should now work.

  Once you get the Sharing dialog box to appear and you check the "Share this item and its contents" item for your disk, you may get a message that says the disk "could not be shared because there is a shared folder inside it." This unlikely event means that sharing has already been turned on for some folder on your disk (see "Technically Speaking: The Sharing Dialog Box for Folders" for information on how this could happen). In this case, select File Sharing Monitor to get a list of currently shared folders. (By the way, this control panel only works if file sharing is first turned on from Sharing Setup.) Then go to the Sharing dialog box for each shared folder and unselect "Share this item and its contents;" you will now be able to select this option for the disk you want to share.

If You Get a Message That Says the Shared Disk Could Not Be Opened Because It "Could Not Be Found on the Network"

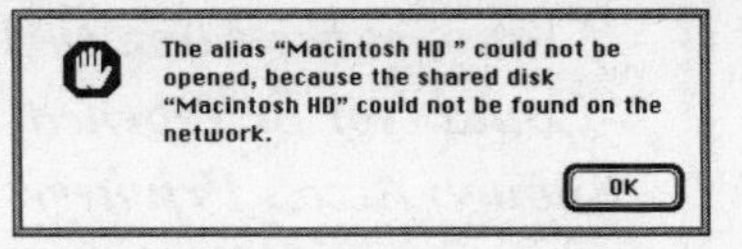

Figure 11-29 *A message that indicates a problem accessing a shared disk.*

There are several possible reasons you may get a message that says that a shared disk "could not be found." These include the following:

- **Cables not connected**
  Make sure that the cable connecting the two computers is present and plugged into the AppleTalk active ports (probably the printer ports) of each Mac.
- **Needed file-sharing software not installed or not active**
  In general, make sure that all software related to file sharing is in place. In particular, look for AppleShare on the guest machine and for Sharing Setup, File Sharing, and Network (control panel and extension) on the host machine. Make sure AppleTalk is turned on for both machines. Similarly, make sure that File Sharing is turned on for the host machine.

  The Network control panel is not present if you are using Open Transport. In this case, however, you will need all the Open Transport software active (as described more in Chapter 14).

  SEE ALSO: • **"Transfer Files Via File Sharing," earlier in this chapter**
- **Shared disk not finished with its startup sequence**
  Even after the startup sequence appears to be over and the desktop icons appear, it may take a minute or so before file sharing is actually enabled. So before trying to mount a shared disk, wait until it completely finishes its startup. You can usually tell this has happened when the noise associated with hard disk access at startup stops, and the double-thick handles appear on folder icons.
- **Alias no longer works**
  If you are trying to open a shared volume by opening a previously created alias of the volume, the problem may be that something on the shared volume has been modified so that the alias no longer works. The solution is to start over and create a new alias (as described previously in "File Sharing: Initial Setup").
- **CD-ROM disc not mounted at startup**
  If you are trying to use a CD-ROM disc as a shared volume, it may not work if the disc was not present when the Mac started up. If this happens, just restart with the disc inserted.

  This problem is not likely to occur with System 7.5.3 or later.
- **Otherwise ...**
  Check in the next sections for other possible solutions.

If You Get the Message That Says the Shared Disk "Could Not Be Opened, Because You Do Not Have Enough Access Privileges"

The alias "Macintosh HD " could not be opened, because you do not have enough access privileges.

OK

You cannot move "Message" from the folder "Desktop Folder", because you do not have the privilege to make changes.

OK

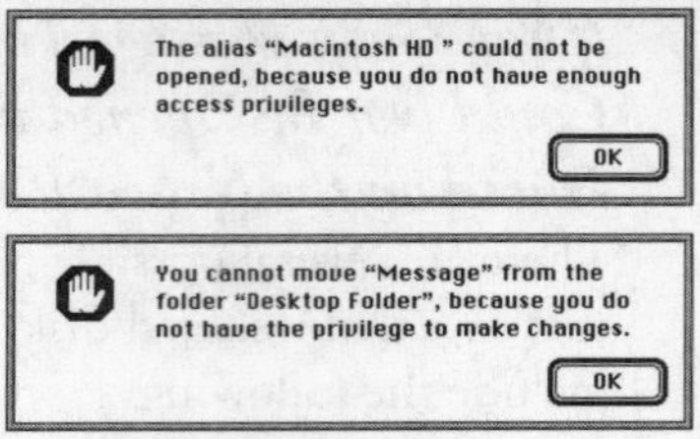

Figure 11-30 *Messages indicating insufficient access privileges.*

While trying to connect to a shared disk, you may get a message that says "you do not have enough access privileges." Sometimes, this is simply because file sharing is not turned on or active on the host machine. The obvious solution here is to make sure file sharing is on, using the procedures outlined earlier in this section.

SEE: • **"Transfer Files Via File Sharing," earlier in this chapter**

Otherwise, you may have inadvertently limited access privileges via the Finder's Sharing command. To fix this, go to the host machine, not the machine where the error message appeared. Select the icon of the problem disk and then select Sharing from the Finder's File menu; this opens up the Sharing dialog box. Then check for the following items:

- **Sharing dialog box: "Share this item and its contents" is unselected**
  If the "Share this item and its contents" option is unchecked, it is usually functionally equivalent to having turned off file sharing for the entire disk. The solution is to turn this option on and try file sharing again.
- **Sharing dialog box: "See Folder, See Files, Make Changes" options modified**
  Even if the "Share this item and its contents" option is checked, you can still separately limit access to Owner, User/Group, or Everyone categories. You do this by unchecking the boxes in the rows following these categories. Normally, for the low-security setups described in this chapter, you would never have reason to do this, but you may find that it has happened anyway.

  In the extreme case, unchecking these boxes can totally block a user's access to the disk. For example, if all three boxes ("See Folders, See Files, Make Changes") are unchecked in the Everyone row, a Guest user will get the "do not have enough access privileges" message when he or she tries to mount the disk—even if access to Guests has been granted in the Users & Groups control panel. As another example, if only the Make Changes box is unchecked, the same Guest will be able to mount and view the disk, but unable to make any modifications to it. Should he or she attempt any modifications, such as discarding a file, an alert message will appear warning that he or she does not have the privileges to make changes In any cases of this sort, the solution is to reselect these options and start over again.
- **Sharing dialog box: If you have shared folders**
  If you try to turn on file sharing for your entire hard drive (via the Sharing Setup control panel) but the hard drive already includes shared folders, you will get the following error message: "Cannot share selected drive because there is a shared folder contained within it." The solution is first to turn off file sharing for all shared folders

TECHNICALLY SPEAKING ▶

THE SHARING DIALOG BOX FOR FOLDERS

In the main text, I only described selecting the Sharing command for an entire disk; however, you can select any folder on the disk and similarly select Sharing. If you do so (and assuming you have turned on "Share this item and its contents" for the whole disk), a variation on the Sharing dialog box will appear. From here, if you uncheck the "Same as enclosing folder" option, you can separately modify the other access options for the folder, overriding the options that were selected for the disk as a whole. On the other hand, if "Share this item and its contents" is off for the disk, you can still turn this option on separately for individual folders on the disk. (Watch for the folder's icon to change as you make these modifications.)

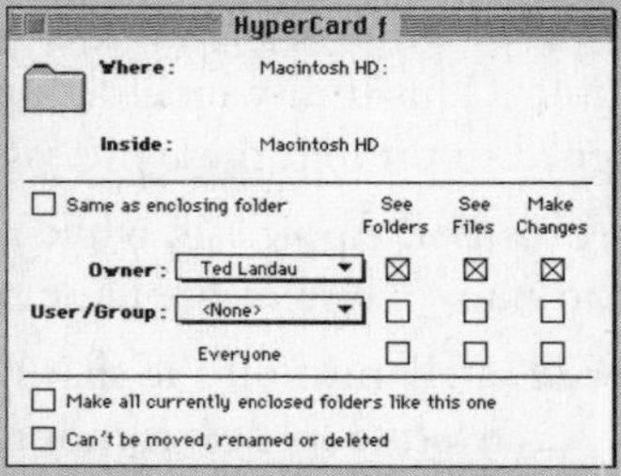

Figure 11-31 *The Sharing dialog box for a folder, with the "Same as enclosing folder" option seen (compare to Figure 11-20).*

There's obviously more to know about how all this works than I have just presented. If you are not concerned about limiting file-sharing access to other users (which has been a working assumption throughout this chapter), however, you should never have any need to alter these settings—don't bother them, and they won't bother you. If you really do need more details on this topic, check out the relevant documentation that came with your system software or seek other outside help.

By the way, the "Can't be moved, renamed or deleted" option is briefly mentioned in Chapter 6 as it relates to an inability to delete a file or folder.

(via the Sharing command in the Finder's File menu), and then to turn on file sharing for the entire drive.

SEE:
- **"Technically Speaking: The Sharing Dialog Box for Folders," for related information**
- **Chapter 6, "When You Can't Save or Copy a File," for related information, especially regarding a message that says "Illegal Access Permission"**

Problems with Turning File Sharing or AppleTalk Off

If you want to turn file sharing or AppleTalk off, take note of the following:

- When you try to turn AppleTalk on, you get a message reminding you to connect to an AppleTalk network. When you turn AppleTalk off (which you may regularly do on a PowerBook in order to conserve battery power), you are likely to get an alert message reminding you to make sure you are disconnected from a network. Usually you needn't do anything to respond to these messages; you can turn AppleTalk on or off whether or not you are connected to a network (as long as no shared volumes are mounted). Just click OK and continue.

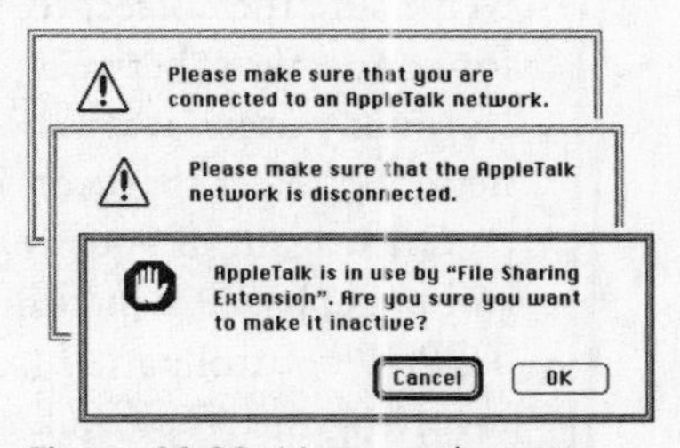

Figure 11-32 *Messages that may appear when you turn AppleTalk on (top) or off (bottom two).*

If you try to turn AppleTalk off when the File Sharing Extension is active, you will get an additional warning that AppleTalk is in use by that extension. You can still turn AppleTalk safely off, you just can't use file sharing until you turn it on again.

By the way, if you get fed up with these messages, try Jeremy's Control Strip Modules. This utility includes a module called Jeremy's AppleTalk CSM that is designed to prevent these messages from appearing.

- Don't turn off AppleTalk while a shared disk is actually mounted. This is almost certain to cause a system freeze or crash.
- You *can* safely turn off file sharing from your desktop Mac, even while its disk is mounted on your PowerBook. If you try to do so, you will first get a message asking you to enter how many minutes should pass before file sharing is disabled. This is provided as a way of giving other users on the network some advance warning, should they be connected to your computer. Since only your desktop Mac and PowerBook are involved, there are no other users to worry about, so you can safely select zero minutes for immediate disabling. If you do disconnect this way, without first unmounting the shared disk, the PowerBook will eventually display an error message informing you that the connection has "unexpectedly closed."

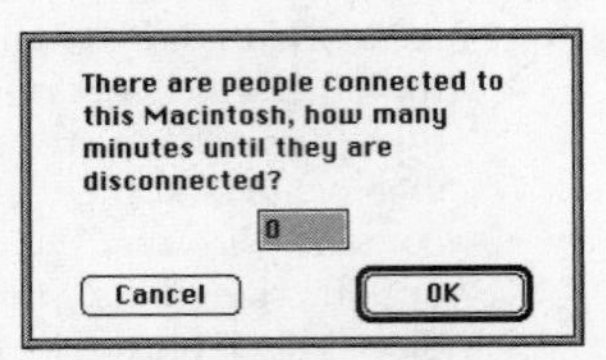

Figure 11-33 *This dialog box appears when you try to turn off file sharing from a host Macintosh.*

Special case: Unexpected disconnection Actually, an "unexpectedly closed" message may occur anytime a file-sharing connection is suddenly broken, such as after a system crash on the host machine. If this happens and you still see the shared volume's icon on your desktop, drag the icon to the Trash before trying to reconnect to the volume.

Other Problems with Using File Sharing

The following are miscellaneous problems and solutions related to file sharing. Several of these problems involve system freezes and crashes; read the list over to see if your problem is contained here.

- Make sure the correct icon is selected from the Network control panel. In most cases, for connections between a PowerBook and another Mac, you should select LocalTalk (for many users, it will be their only option). If you have connected via an Ethernet network, select that icon instead.

  Once again, if you are using Open Transport, you no longer use the Network control panel because its functionality has been incorporated into the AppleTalk and TCP/IP control panels (see: "Problems Using Apple Remote Access" for an example involving the AppleTalk control panel). In most cases, file sharing will work regardless of the settings in the TCP/IP control panel. If you are having problems, however, try selecting "AppleTalk (MacIP)."

  SEE: • Chapter 14 for more on Open Transport

- Make sure connected computers use the same version of networking and file-sharing software. This minimizes the risk of problems, including system freezes. The best policy here is to upgrade to the latest available versions of this software.
- When files are being transferred over the network, other operations are likely to slow down. For example, you will notice that tasks like moving icons on the desktop, opening and closing windows, launching applications, and copying files will all take longer. This is normal.
- Try not to have other background activities going while a disk is currently being shared—especially while transferring files over the network, and most especially when the PowerBook is first trying to access and mount the desktop Mac's disk. In particular, don't have other file copying or printing in progress (especially on the host machine), and don't use your modem. Any of thse actions may lead to a system freeze.
- Be careful about putting a PowerBook to sleep while a shared disk is mounted. If you do, the connection will be lost. If files are currently being transferred, the transfer will halt, and a system crash is possible.
- If you try to eject a CD-ROM disc or unmount a hard disk while file sharing is on, you may get a message that says you cannot do it because the disc is being shared or is in use. In this case, turn off file sharing to unmount the disk; this problem should no longer occur in System 7.5.1 or later.

SEE: • **Chapter 5 for more on problems ejecting CD-ROM discs**

If Any File-Sharing Problems Lead to a System Freeze or Crash

If a system freeze occurs while a shared disk is mounted, and especially during a transfer of files, you will likely find that both the host and the guest Macintoshes have frozen. You will usually have no recourse here other than to restart both machines; a forced quit (as described in Chapter 4) will typically have no effect.

If you are transferring files when a freeze occurs, the first symptom that you will probably notice is that the double arrows next to the Apple menu stop their periodic flashing, and the watch cursor appears and stays on indefinitely.

If freezes occur often when you use file sharing, the most likely culprit is an extension conflict. Try restarting with extensions off; if the problem goes away, you almost certainly have an extension conflict.

SEE: • **Chapter 4 for more on system freezes and crashes**
• **Fix-It #4 on solving extension conflicts**

You Can't Get a PowerBook Modem to Work

Symptoms:

- You have installed an internal modem in or connected an external modem to your PowerBook, but you can't get it to work at all.
- You may get a message that says the serial port can't be used because it is "in use." Freezes or crashes may occur.

Note: *Check out Chapter 14!* The section you are now reading covers just a few modem-related issues that are specifically relevant to transferring data with PowerBooks and/or Apple Remote Access. There are numerous other modem-related symptoms and solutions that apply to all Macs, PowerBooks included. These revolve around incorrect settings in communications software, corrupted data, problems with using a particular serial port, and more. All of this is covered in Chapter 14.

Causes:

Control panel connections are incorrect, needed extensions are missing, and/or cables are not connected properly.

What to do:

External Modems

If you use an external modem, select External Modem from the PowerBook Setup control panel. Make sure the modem cable is correctly connected and the modem is on. If your PowerBook has only one serial port, you must turn AppleTalk off to use an external modem; select the Chooser or Control Strip to do this.

Internal Modems

If you have an internal modem, select Internal Modem from the PowerBook Setup control panel. For Duos with an internal modem, however, you may have to switch back to External Modem to use a printer.

If your PowerBook has only one serial port, it acts as a combined printer and modem port; if you have an internal modem, you will probably only use this port to connect a printer. Still, you may have problems getting your internal modem to work.

Here's what you need to know: On most PowerBook models that have only one serial port (such as the 200, 2300, 190, and 5300 models), the serial port is mapped as a modem port. Under normal conditions this isn't a problem, since the internal modem can be used at the same time as a serial device (such as a printer) is being used. The exception is if you are using a communications program that does not use the Apple Communications Toolbox (CTB). If this is the case, to use the modem, you will need to set the PowerBook, PowerBook Setup, or Express Modem control panel to Compatible, Internal, or "Use internal modem instead of modem port," respectively (which of these settings you will find will depend on what version of the modem and system software you have). When a PowerBook is set like this, the serial port cannot be used with serial devices, but it can be used with LocalTalk devices. (If this all sounds confusing, that's because it is. What is even worse is that Apple keeps changing the rules as it comes out with new software.)

Note, if you have zapped the PRAM, this may reset the Internal Modem selection back to External Modem (or make comparable other changes). If so, you will need to change this back again to get the modem to work.

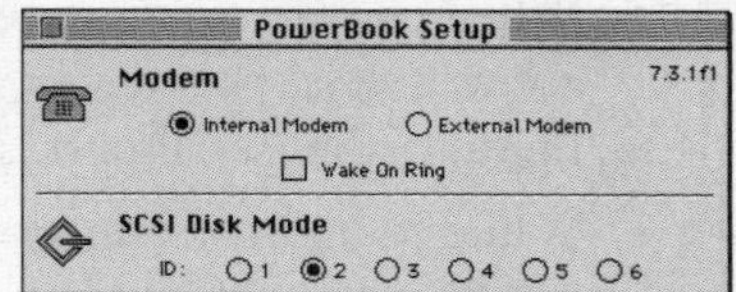

Figure 11-34 *The PowerBook Setup control panel; select Internal Modem to use an internal modem.*

Finally, when using an internal modem, make sure the phone cable is connected directly to the PowerBook's phone outlet.

By the way, much of this advice also applies to those Performas that come with internal modems.

SEE: • **Chapter 7 for more advice on printing problems, especially "Special Case: Only One Serial Port?" for details on printing from PowerBooks with only one serial port**

Communications Software

Many communications programs work with special files called *modem drivers*; each different modem model has its own driver. Another similar set of special files, called CCLs, are used by programs such as Apple Remote Access (as described in more detail shortly). If you don't have the correct modem driver or CCL file for your modem, the software will not work.

You may also have to make a selection such as "Apple Modem Tool" or "Express Modem Tool" from the Method pop-up menu in the Connections or Communications dialog box of your communications software. Check the documentation that came with your modem and/or your communications software for more details.

Serial Port "In Use"

If you get an alert box message that says you can't use a modem because the "serial port is in use"—or if the serial port doesn't seem to be working for any other reason—check if you have a file in your Extensions folder called Serial Port Arbitrator (it would normally be installed there by Apple Remote Access software). If so, delete it and restart. This file is especially likely to be the source of your problem if you use the Express Modem.

This message may appear for other reasons as well. More generally, if the alert box includes an option to reset the port, click OK; if not, try restarting. If restarting fails, resetting the Power Manager and/or zapping the PRAM should fix the problem. If the trouble persists, a hardware problem is likely.

SEE:
- **"Restarting a PowerBook After a System Error," earlier in this chapter, for how to reset the Power Manager**
- **"Problems Using Apple Remote Access," later in this chapter, for more on the Serial Port Arbitrator and serial port problems**
- **Chapter 4 for what to do after a system freeze or crash**
- **Chapter 14 for more on modem, networking, and online problems**
- **Fix-It #11 on zapping the Parameter RAM**
- **Fix-It #17 for more on general modem and related hardware problems**

Problems Using Apple Remote Access

Symptoms:

- When you are trying to set up a connection via Apple Remote Access (ARA), or to access a serial port device (such as a printer) with ARA installed, a message appears that says the "serial port is in use."
- While trying to set up a connection via Apple Remote Access (ARA), you get a message that says the modem could not be detected.
- A system freeze or crash occurs when you are either trying to access ARA or you are accessing any serial port device while ARA is active.
- You cannot successfully make a connection with ARA for any other reason.

Causes:

Most problems specific to using ARA center around the unusual way this utility works. Though you are using ARA to make a network-like connection between two computers, you are not actually using the Mac's networking software; rather, you are using a modem connection. In fact, in certain cases when you use ARA, you actually disable the Mac's LocalTalk network connection.

In other instances, problems can develop because information from an ARA/modem connection and data for another serial port device (such as a printer) are simultaneously trying to be transmitted through the same port. This can happen, for example, if you connected a modem to the printer port, or if you only have one serial port on your PowerBook.

At still other times, you may be connected to a local network while simultaneously accessing a remote network over ARA.

In all of these cases, there is a potential for the Macintosh to get confused and for signals to get crossed. ARA software does its best to anticipate and deal with these problems, but is not always successful.

What to do:

Switch Options from the Network or AppleTalk Control Panels

With System 7.5.3 or a later revision, you may choose between using Classic AppleTalk (the software used prior to System 7.5.3) or Open Transport (the new software first introduced in System 7.5.2). Open Transport is what Apple expects everyone to adopt eventually.

SEE: • **Chapter 14 for more details on Classic AppleTalk versus Open Transport**

If You Are Using Classic AppleTalk With ARA installed, the Network control panel will have at least two icons that you can select: LocalTalk and Remote Only. Which icon should you select? Here's how to decide.

- **Network control panel: Select the LocalTalk icon** Selecting the LocalTalk icon obviously permits LocalTalk connections, but it also permits remote access. If you aren't having any problems, this is therefore the preferred option. In addition, if you are having trouble accessing a local network but not a remote network, select LocalTalk.
- **Network control panel: Select the Remote Only icon** Selecting Remote Only (an option installed by ARA) turns off LocalTalk at the serial ports; you will not be able to use any local network features with this selected (even including a connection to an AppleTalk printer). Still, this is the preferred option if you are having trouble accessing the remote network with the LocalTalk icon selected. Also select Remote Only if you are having trouble printing to a non-networked local printer, especially while connected to a remote network. When you are done using ARA, you can reselect the LocalTalk icon again, if needed.

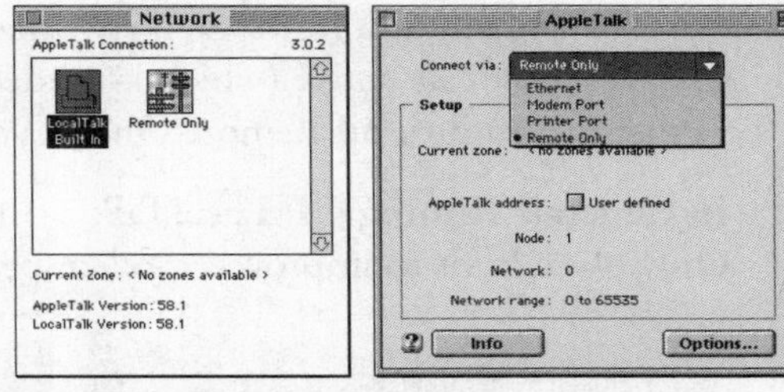

Figure 11-35 *Left: The Remote Only and LocalTalk options in Classic AppleTalk's Network control panel. Right: The Remote Only option selected in Open Transport's AppleTalk control panel.*

- **Don't switch icons while connected to a remote network** If you change the icon selection while you are connected to a remote network, you will probably get disconnected from the network no matter what icon you select. You should get a message warning you about this when you attempt to make the switch.

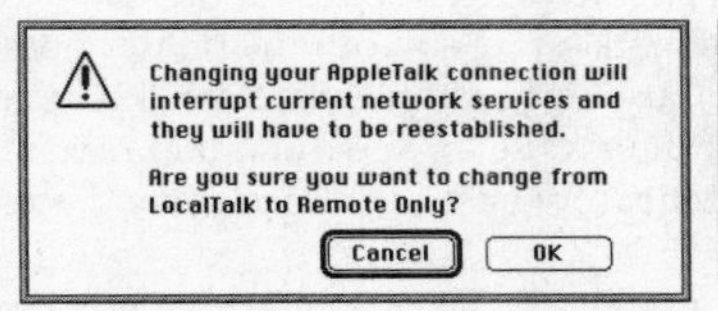

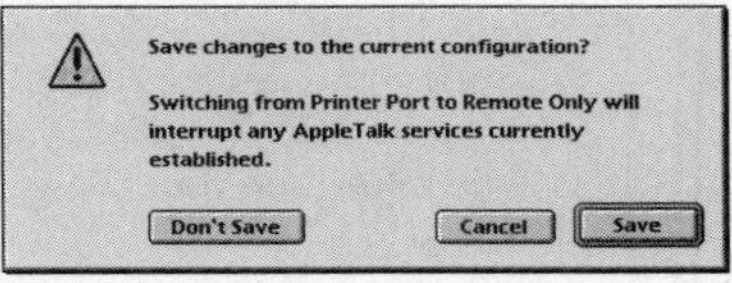

Figure 11-36 *Left: A message that may appear when you try to switch from one Network control panel setting to another while connected to a network. Right: A message that may appear when trying to switch settings from the AppleTalk control panel while connected to a network.*

If You Are Using Open Transport Similar principles apply as just described for Classic AppleTalk; the main difference is that you need to make selections from the AppleTalk and TCP/IP control panels instead of from the Network control panel. There is no Network control panel with Open Transport.

- **AppleTalk control panel** The default AppleTalk control panel selections (printer or modem port) are equivalent to having selected LocalTalk. To select Remote Only, if desired, make that selection from the control panel's "Connect via:" pop-up menu.
- **TCP/IP control panel** Set up your host machine as usual (see Chapter 14 for more details on using this control panel). In particular, you should find a "Connect via:" option listed as AppleTalk Remote Access Protocol (ARAP). If so, select it; otherwise, select AppleTalk (MacIP).

PPP support is available only in ARA 3.0 or later. In general, use ARA 3.0 or later to minimize possible compatibility problems with Open Transport.

SEE: • **"Technically Speaking: Upgrade Network and Communications Software," later in this chapter**

Special Case: Single Serial Port, External Modem, and "Modem Could Not Be Detected" If you try to use Apple Remote Access (ARA) on a single-serial-port PowerBook (200/2300/500/5300/190 series) with an external modem, you may get an error message saying that the modem could not be detected. The reason is that ARA's default AppleTalk designation is for the single port to be for LocalTalk, not for the external modem. What should you do? Once again, you need to select the Remote Only option from the Network or AppleTalk control panels. This allows you to have AppleTalk active (which is needed for ARA) and still use an external modem. Remember to turn off Remote Only if you ever need the LocalTalk connection back.

In General: Turning Off LocalTalk Turning off LocalTalk and switching to Remote Only often leads to improved modem performance with ARA.

BY THE WAY ▶

MORE USES FOR "REMOTE ONLY"

Remote Only has relevance whether your Mac has two serial ports or just one. In addition to being included with ARA, Remote Only (currently version 2.1) is included with the latest versions of Open Transport. According to Apple, Remote Only "is an extension that allows you to turn on AppleTalk networking when both the printer port and the modem port on your computer are already in use (for example, for a serial printer and a modem). Without this extension installed, you cannot use an applicatin that requires AppleTalk to be active at the same time your computer is connected to a modem and a serial printer."

Check the Serial Port Arbitrator Extension and Remote Access Setup

Serial Port "In Use" When Remote Connection Is Active As soon as a remote connection is established, Remote Access prevents other applications from using whatever serial port (printer or modem) you selected in the Remote Access Setup control panel. If a program tries to access that port, you will typically get a message that says the port is "in use."

Serial Port Is "In Use" When "Answer Calls" Is Selected If you checked "Answer calls" in the Remote Access Setup control panel, Remote Access would ordinarily block other programs from using the serial port, even when ARA is not actually using it. This block should not occur, however, if you have also installed a system extension called the Serial Port Arbitrator. This extension normally is installed automatically in your Extensions folder when you install Apple Remote Access (and it only works if ARA is installed). With this extension in place, other programs are still allowed to use the serial port, even though "Answer calls" is selected—in effect, the latter option is temporarily disabled when another program is using the serial port. When the program is finished,

Remote Access re-enables the Macintosh to answer calls. If you have Serial Port Arbitrator installed and aren't experiencing any serial port problems, leave it installed!

SEE: • "Transfer Files Via a Modem (Apple Remote Access)," earlier in this chapter, for more on setting up Remote Access Setup and ARA in general

Conflicts with Serial Port Arbitrator Unfortunately, some programs are not compatible with this extension. In this case, when they try to access a serial port (for example, when printing), you will either get the message that says the serial port is "in use" (despite the presence of the Serial Port Arbitrator extension) or the Macintosh may freeze altogether.

The Serial Port Arbitrator also may conflict with SerialDMA (formerly an extension, but now built into System 7.5.3 software) on PCI-based Macs. The conflict will also cause a crash at startup, although it may have been resolved in System 7.5.3. Upgrading to ARA 2.1 or later also reportedly fixes most, if not all, of these problems. Otherwise, one of the following options should resolve the trouble:

- Remove the Serial Port Arbitrator file from the Extensions folder and restart.
- Turn off the "Answer calls" option from the Remote Access Setup control panel, if you don't need that option for the moment.
- Disable the Remote Access Setup control panel altogether, until you plan to use ARA again. Typically you should use a startup management utility (such as Extensions Manager) to do this (see Fix-It #4), then restart your Mac.

Miscellaneous Other Problems

System 7.5.3 Upgrade If you upgrade to System 7.5.3, install (or reinstall) ARA 2.1 or a later revision *after* installing System 7.5.3. This is good advice for later system upgrades as well.

Can't Locate a Communication Command Language (CCL) Script To use ARA over a modem, you must select the name of your modem from the Modem Setup area of the Remote Access Setup control panel. What modems are listed here are determined by special files, called CCLs, that are located in your Extensions folder. ARA comes with a selection of CCLs and automatically installs them in your Extensions folder when you first install ARA. With ARA 2.1 or later, they are stored in a folder called Modem Scripts. (These modem scripts are also used by Open Transport/PPP, as described in Chapter 14.)

The selection list, however, may not include your particular modem. If this is the case, check the software that came with your modem; it may include a CCL file that you can use. If not, call the modem company for advice. By the way, unless you plan to connect to a variety of different modems on different occasions, you can delete all CCLs other than the one for your modem.

SEE: • "Transfer Files Via a Modem (Apple Remote Access)" and "Can't Get a PowerBook Modem to Work," earlier in this chapter, for more on CCLs and ARA in general

Can't Connect to a Remote Mac Because It Is Turned Off To use ARA to call your desktop Macintosh from your PowerBook, the desktop Mac must be turned on. But what if you forgot to leave it on when you left your office, or just don't want to leave it on all the time? Fortunately, there is a device, (called PowerKey Remote, from Sophisticated Circuits) that will automatically turn on a Macintosh when a phone call comes in and turn it off again when the caller hangs up.

AppleTalk Active? Apple Remote Access (ARA) needs AppleTalk to be active in order to work. Otherwise you may get –5555 errors or other strange problems.

Remote Mac Cannot See You? While you can "see" the remote Mac from your PowerBook while you are connected via ARA, the remote Mac cannot "see" you. This is normal.

Check for More General File-Sharing or Modem Problems Your problem may not be specific to ARA.

SEE: • **"Can't Get File Sharing to Work," earlier in this chapter**
• **"Can't Get a Modem to Work," earlier in this chapter**

Problems Caused by Incompatible Software Upgrade the relevant software.

SEE: • **"Technically Speaking: Upgrade Network and Communications Software"**

TAKE NOTE ▶

OPENTPT SERIAL ARBITRATOR AND UNIMPLEMENTED TRAP ERRORS

Open Transport PPP (OT/PPP 1.0 or later) installs a file called OpenTpt Serial Arbitrator. It functions similarly to the Serial Port Arbitrator file mentioned in the main text. In particular, it allows the Open Transport Serial extension to open the serial port even if the port is in "standby" use, such as when fax software is set to answer calls. Thus, the Arbitrator file would keep the serial port open for other software to use.

Unfortunately, this file appears to conflict with several other extensions, possibly leading to an unimplemented trap system crash at startup. It may also cause "serial port in use" errors. Once again, if you find you do not need this file, get rid of it to avoid these problems.

TECHNICALLY SPEAKING

UPGRADE NETWORK AND COMMUNICATIONS SOFTWARE

- **File sharing and Apple Remote Access problems** AppleTalk is built into all system software. There is no AppleTalk file in your System Folder; it is actually contained within the System file itself. Periodically, however, Apple releases upgrade software (such as a utility called Network Software Installer, available from various online services) that may contain a later version of AppleTalk than the one that came with your system software. If you are having any problems with file sharing or ARA, make sure you have the latest available version of AppleTalk. Of course, the ARA Installer itself installs a compatible version of AppleTalk, but this may not be the latest version, or you may inadvertently install an earlier version via some other communications-related software's Installer. In general, if you make a point of staying current with the latest system software, you should be okay.

  To find out what version of the AppleTalk driver you have installed, check the listing in the Network control panel. If you are using Open Transport, open its AppleTalk control panel and click the Info button; for ARA compatibility, you need AppleTalk version 7.0.1 or later.

  By the way, should a problem with ARA lead you to decide to remove it from your disk entirely, use the ARA Installer disk to do so. (If it still uses the old-style Installer, you need to select Customize, then hold down the Option key; the Install button should change to a Remove button. For the newer Installer, simply select Custom Remove from the pop-up menu.) This is the safest way to make sure you are removing all relevant software.

- **Modem problems (and more ARA problems)** For any modem problems (including those involving ARA), if your software uses Communications Toolbox extensions, make sure you have the latest versions of them. This Apple-made software provides a standard set of tools for interacting with a modem. You can recognize Toolbox extensions because they typically have icons in the shape of a jigsaw-puzzle piece and their names end in the word Tool (such as Serial Tool).

  Many communication programs use the Toolbox and include the software as part of their package; even versions of System 7.5 come with a few basic Toolbox extensions. You may have several applications that use this software, however, each shipping with a different version of Toolbox extensions. If so, you may have deleted a newer version and installed an older one. To correct this, find the disk with the newer version and reinstall it. Otherwise, you can get Toolbox upgrades directly from Apple.

  Note that with Open Transport, Communications Toolbox extensions seem to be on the way out. You may not need them at all in the not-too-distant future.

  Finally, to avoid problems specific to Apple's Express Modem, make sure you are using the latest version of the Express Modem software (at least version 1.1). For example, with an older version of the Express Modem software, the PowerBook may freeze if it goes to sleep while you are accessing a remote network via ARA.

- **Open Transport and ARA** While using Open Transport software sidesteps some of these previous concerns, it may add its own general compatibility problems.To minimize them, again at least make sure that you have the latest version of this software.

  Also, ARA 3.0 should be out by the time you read this. It will include numerous new features, including better support for Apple's Open Transport and support for using ARA via a PPP connection. If you are having any problems using ARA with Open Transport, this new version should solve them. ARA 2.1, the last version before 3.0, added better high-speed modem support and revised CCLs.

SEE: • **Chapter 14 for more on modems, Open Transport, and online problems in general**

Chapter 12

Powerful Problems: Power Macs, PCI-Based Macs & AppleVision Monitors

New Technology, New Problems 507

Power Macintosh Basics 507

What Makes a Power Mac Different from Other Macs? 507

Running in Emulation Mode versus Native Mode 510

Power Macintosh Native Software 511

Upgrading to Native Software 511

Buying and Installing Native Software 511

Is It Native or Not? 512

Virtual Memory and Native Software 512

PCI-Based Power Macintoshes 514

Solve It! Power Macintosh Problems 515

Compatibility and Memory Problems 515

Emulation Mode Problems 516

Insufficient Memory Problems 518

Shared Library Problems 518

System Error and Related Problems 520

Type 11 (Hardware Exception) System Errors 520

QuickTime PowerPlug 520

Power Mac Crashes When You Press the Command Key 520

Power Macintosh Crashes on Startup or When Printing 521

Freezes and PowerPC Interrupt Extension 521

Persistent System Freezes (Apple's Repair Extension Program) 521

Sound Problems 522

Solve It! Power Macintosh Problems (continued)

Monitor Problems . . . 522

The Ghost Monitor Problem . . . 522

Sync-on-Green Problem . . . 523

Monitor Cable Adapter Needed . . . 523

Vertical Lines That Follow the Cursor? . . . 523

Sudden Changes in Monitor's Hue (Apple's Repair Extension Program) . . . 523

PCI-Based Macintosh Quick Fixes . . . 523

Screen Blinking at Startup . . . 523

Sleep and Energy Saver Problems . . . 524

Screen Stays Black? Hard Drive Won't Spin Up? Try the Cuda Button . . . 526

SCSI ID 5 Problems? . . . 526

Erased Disk and Disk Spot Check . . . 526

Floppy Disk Won't Initialize or Erase . . . 526

Why a Graphics Accelerator? . . . 526

Pointer Mode Control Panel . . . 527

Monitors & Sound Control Panel Problems . . . 528

Video Problems . . . 528

Memory Matters . . . 528

Networking and Communications Matters . . . 529

Zapping the PRAM . . . 529

AppleVision Monitors . . . 529

AppleVision Software . . . 530

AppleVision Extension . . . 530

Monitors & Sound versus AppleVision Setup . . . 530

Display Enabler . . . 531

Solve It!: AppleVision Problems . . . 531

Installation Problems . . . 532

Monitor Display and Sleep Problems . . . 534

Sound Problems . . . 536

Miscellany . . . 537

New Technology, New Problems

Pundits may claim that Apple needs to revamp its operating system by yesterday in order to keep pace with the competition. Critics may carp that Apple is no longer on the cutting edge of computer innovation. My guess, though, is that most end users have a somewhat different view. To them, keeping up with all of Apple's latest developments (assuming they even bother to try) gets more difficult with each year.

It's not only that changes are appearing at an ever-increasing rate. It's the exponentially growing number of directions where the changes are going. If you don't believe me, try these terms out for size: GeoPort, IDE, PCI, built-in Ethernet, PlainTalk, PowerTalk, QuickTimeVR, OpenDoc, Open Transport, CHRP (or is it PPRP?), and more. If you're still uncertain about what some (or all!) of these terms mean or how they will affect your use of your Macintosh, you're not alone.

The bright side is that you can still buy a Macintosh, set it up easily, and start using it productively, without bothering to learn about most of this stuff. Still, as you start to expand your use of the Macintosh in almost any way—by adding peripherals, hooking up to a network, or getting into multimedia applications—understanding these new technologies will become increasingly important.

What's new (or at least relatively new) in the Macintosh world is the focus of the next two chapters of this book. In this chapter, I focus on hardware: especially Power Macs, including the more recent PCI-based Power Macs. The next chapter focuses on software: mainly all of the different iterations of System 7.5 (plus System 7.6 and beyond).

Of course, these are not the only chapters where you will find answers to questions about Power Macs and System 7.5. By now, these "new" items have been around long enough that information about them is integrated throughout the rest of this book. The purpose of these chapters is to concentrate just on those issues that are unique to or especially relevant to these recent technologies.

Power Macintosh Basics

What Makes a Power Mac Different from Other Macs?

The main thing that is different in a Power Macintosh is its processor. Instead of using the line of Motorola 680X0 processors that had been the heart of every Macintosh before them, Power Macs are based on a new line (also developed by Motorola) called *PowerPC processors.* Over time, you will see different variations and generations of the PowerPC processor, just as there were for the 680X0 line. Each variation will have its own unique name: PowerPC 603 versus PowerPC 604, for example.

While I am throwing around new terminology, you might as well know that all PowerPC processors are referred to as RISC processors (which stands for Reduced Instruction Set Computing). In contrast, the 680X0 processors were CISC (Complex

TECHNICALLY SPEAKING ▶

SPEED OF YOUR POWER MAC: BEYOND PROCESSOR MEGAHERTZ

When comparing different Power Mac models, people are inevitably interested in which one is faster. The first statistic that people turn to for the answer is the megahertz (MHz) of the processor, also known as the *clock speed*. This is the statistic typically indicated in the model name: a Power Mac 7600/132, for instance, has a 132 MHz processor. But figuring out how this translates into the relative speed of different Macs can get tricky. A 150 MHz machine should certainly be faster than a 75 MHz—but is it twice as fast? Not necessarily, because other statistics also play an important role. Some of these are outlined below.

- **Processor type.** A 604 PPC processor is inherently faster than a 601, even at the same clock speed. That is why a Power Mac 7600/132 (which comes with a 604 processor) may seem even faster than a Power Mac 7500/100 (which comes with a 601) than the difference in MHz would suggest. Similarly, a 603e processor is slower than a 601 (which is an important reason why, for example, 100 MHz 603e PowerBook 5300s ran much slower than 90 MHz 601 desktop Macs). And the makers of the PPC chips claim that "Everything in the system being equal, the 604e is about 50 percent faster than the 603e at the same speed. The reason? The PowerPC 604e can initiate four instructions in the processor for every clock cycle, while the 603e initiates two instructions each cycle."
- **Bus speed and multipliers.** The *bus speed* of the logic board itself—how fast information can shuttle in and out of the processor—also plays a limiting role in the processor's speed. Unfortunately, the logic board bus speed is not "advertised" as much as processor speed, so you may have to dig a little to find out what it is for your model. Still, it can have a significant effect on the performance of your Mac. To cite one interesting case, the 7500/100 Power Mac came with a 50MHz bus speed, while the 7600/120 Power Mac had only a 40 MHz bus speed—one reason why the 7600 did not perform much faster than the 7500, despite the faster processor.

  Things get even more complicated when you consider yet another factor: the *multiplier*. Essentially, your processor must work at a speed that is an exact multiple of the bus speed; this ratio is an inherent part of the processor's design. For example, a 150MHz processor with a 3:1 multiplier will attain its maximum speed when hooked up to a bus that goes at 50MHz (50 x 3 = 150). If the bus speed is 40MHz, though, the processor will only be able to achieve a speed of 120MHz (40 x 3 = 120). A processor may have more than one multiplier built-in, allowing it to choose the optimal one. Also, devices called clock-chip accelerators may help circumvent some factory-set limitations and push the processor beyond its stated specifications.

(Continued) ▶

Instruction Set Computing) processors. You might think that CISC is somehow a superior approach (aren't more advanced computers also more complex?), but this is not the case here. The current thought is that RISC processors can accomplish more in less time than CISC ones. That is why Apple made the switch.

More specifically, compared to 680X0 processors, PowerPC processors tend to be easier and cheaper to manufacture, which is great for Apple (and may ultimately translate into lower computer prices for you). More important, though, they are faster—much faster. Do you recall me saying in Chapter 1 that MHz is the measure of a computer's speed? Well, the fastest Quadra topped out at about 40 MHz; the *slowest* Power Mac starts at 60 MHz. Actually, the full name of the model gives you its speed: the Power Mac 7500/100 runs at 100 MHz, a 7600/132 runs at 132 MHz, and you can probably guess what a Power Mac 9500/150 runs at. To put it simply, this is a

▶ TECHNICALLY SPEAKING ▶

SPEED OF YOUR POWER MAC: BEYOND PROCESSOR MEGAHERTZ *(Continued)*

There are still other complications—aren't there always?—including the fact that the processor can actually set the bus speed itself. But for now, the bottom line is that all of these factors combine to determine the "true" speed of your processor.

- **L2 RAM cache and other factors.** A Level 1 (L1) RAM cache is built on to the processor itself. L2 RAM caches are separate, optional add-on cards of varying sizes. Both cache types are designed to help speed up the processor's ability to get work done (as explained more in Fix-It #17). How much L2 RAM cache is installed will have at least some effect on the speed efficiency of the processor, especially with faster processors (it doesn't seem to have much of an effect with a 601 or slower processor, but can speed things up by as much as 15 percent with a 604 processor).

  RAM cache has its own speed limits, and when paired with today's fastest processors, it may create a bottleneck. The main way to test for this is to remove your RAM cache and see if your computer's performance increases.

  Of special note: To take full advantage of the speed benefits of the PowerPC 604/604e processors (and faster ones still to come), software may need to be rewritten to be "optimized" for them. Otherwise, a given program may actually run faster on a comparable 601-based machine. Eventually, in fact, vendors may ship separate 601 and 604 versions of their Power Mac software.

  Finally, there are a host of more general items that affect the overall speed of your Mac: the amount of RAM, the speed of the disk drive, and so on (as covered in Chapter 1).

Ready for a test? Here's what Apple had to say about the differences between the 604 and 604e processor. See how much of this now makes sense to you: "The 604e is a second version of the 604 with double the internal L1 cache sizes that total 64K (32K for the instruction cache and 32K for the data cache). The 604 has a total of 32K L1 caches (16K instruction and 16K data). Additionally, the 604e shrinks the 5.6 million transistors to 148 sq mm (from 196 sq mm). The smaller die also provides a lower power requirement and can use up to a 5:1 bus multiplier (604 has 3:1). With the 5:1 multipliers, these cards can support 250 MHz."

In the end, at least two things are clear: (1) a 200MHz 604e processor is unbelievably fast; (2) a year from now, it will seem slow.

SEE: • **Chapter 5, "The Macintosh's Speed Is Unexpectedly Slow, " for more on speed-related issues**

quantum leap forward. Even a relatively slow Power Mac can be more than thirty times faster than a Mac Classic performing the same task, and at least twice as fast as the speediest Quadra. With today's Power Macs already breaking the 200 MHz barrier, the word *fast* keeps getting redefined.

Now, some of you may say, "So what? What good is a faster Mac for my word processing? My current Mac already works faster than I can type." That's true. But imagine being able to spell-check a long document in one-tenth the time it takes now, or applying a filter in Photoshop in seconds rather than minutes. Most of all, imagine being able to do things on your Mac that were previously impossible because of speed limitations. In the original version of QuickTime, for example, only small movie images could be processed quickly enough to achieve smooth movement. With Power Macs, smooth full-screen video—in 3D, no less—will be common.

Running in Emulation Mode versus Native Mode

To me, the single most amazing thing about Power Macintoshes is that when you first sit down to use one, they do not seem any different from 680X0 Macintoshes. The Finder and the desktop are still there and work the same way they always have, and almost all the software that runs on older Macs still runs on Power Macs. A Power Macintosh is still a Macintosh; the fact that you are using a completely different processor seems almost irrelevant.

To fully appreciate the significance of this accomplishment, consider this: Software is written to match a particular processor. This means that software written for a 680X0 processor should not be able to run on a machine using a PowerPC processor—and a person upgrading to a Power Macintosh should have to throw out all of his or her existing software. But you don't, because Apple included a *68040 emulator* in the ROM of all Power Macintoshes.

How does this emulator work? When you launch an application, the Power Macintosh automatically determines whether the program is written for a 680X0 Macintosh or a Power Macintosh. If it is a 680X0 application, the Power Mac shifts into *emulation mode.* If it is a Power Mac application (also referred to as a *native code* application), the computer shifts into *native mode*—using the PowerPC processor directly, without any intermediary emulation. The Power Mac can even accommodate software in which part of the software's code is native while other parts are not, again switching modes automatically and transparently as needed. (Unfortunately, this compatibility across machines is a one-way street: There is no way to run Power Mac software on a 680X0 Mac.)

The main problem with emulation mode is that you lose the PowerPC processor's speed advantage—which was the primary rationale for developing the Power Mac in the first place. Emulation mode, almost by definition, can be no faster than the speed of the 680X0 Macs that it is emulating.

Actually, running software in emulation mode on a Power Mac can result in *slower* speeds than running the same software on a true 68040 Macintosh. This was particularly true of the first generation of Power Macintoshes, released in 1994. Things have gotten better, however, with the improved version of the emulator included in PCI-based Power Macs (specifically called the *Dynamic Recompilation Emulator,* or DRE). Also, the Speed Emulator component of Speed Doubler (from Connectix) offers an alternative that generally outperforms Apple's emulator. Combined with their ever-faster processors, today's Power Macs equal or outperform all 680X0 Macs, even in emulation mode.

Still, emulation mode can never equal the performance you can get when running in native mode. When the Power Mac was first released, though, there was virtually no native software available. It took until 1995 before the floodgates finally opened; now, almost all popular Mac software has a native version.

Even if you are running a native application, you still may not get the maximum speed benefit you might expect, because sometimes the program will shift you into emulation mode anyway.

Even in the latest versions of System 7.5 or 7.6, much of the system software is not written in native code. This is important because system software kicks in regularly while using almost any application. For example, commands to open and save documents are typically handled by system software, not by the application itself. And there is a double penalty here: not only is the Mac slowed down as a result of being in emulation mode, however briefly, but just the act of switching from one mode to another causes a tiny delay. Thus, the more often you switch back and forth, the more of a penalty you pay.

Also, the Finder is still not written in native code, so you will go into emulation mode whenever you go to the desktop (which is almost always lurking behind your application windows).

Similarly, many third-party extensions and control panels still run in emulation mode. If the extension is active while a native application is in use, this too will result in temporary switches into emulation mode, with resulting delays.

Power Macintosh Native Software

Upgrading to Native Software

If you own a 680X0 Macintosh and replace it with a Power Mac, you will likely transfer your current software to your new machine—thus, you will be mostly running the Power Mac in emulation mode. Even if you find that a given application runs satisfactorily in emulation mode, though, you should probably still upgrade to the native version when possible. Otherwise, you are not taking full advantage of what your hardware can do.

By now, virtually every major Macintosh application exists in a Power Mac version. If you don't already own it, you can usually get the Power Mac version of a product for free or a minimal charge (unless it is part of a major upgrade that included lots of other new features, in which case you will have to pay the usual upgrade fee).

As always, you may decide that some rarely used programs are not worth paying to upgrade, and some programs may never get rewritten for the Power Mac. Aside from those exceptions, however, use the native code version of software whenever possible.

Buying and Installing Native Software

Some software exists only in Power Mac native form; you can't get a version that runs on 680X0 machines. Most software today, however, still comes in both Power Mac and 680X0 versions.

While some companies may still market these different versions as separate products—forcing you to make two separate purchases to get both versions (as you might need to do, for example, if you own a desktop Power Mac and a 680X0 PowerBook)—most companies include both versions in a single purchase. They may come on two separate sets of disks, or they may come on a single set with an Installer utility that lets you choose which version to install. In the latter case, if you select Easy Install (or an equivalent command), it will automatically install the correct version for your hardware.

In most instances, the Installer also gives you the option to install a special version of the application that combines both the 680X0 and Power Mac code in the same file. This option, called a *fat binary* application, has the advantage of allowing the same copy of the program to run on either type of machine. These fat versions, however, earn their names by taking up more disk space.

In a few cases, a fat binary version is the only option, so you get stuck with non-native code in your software even if you don't want it. While a few programs exist that can strip out the unwanted code, I would be cautious about using them, since doing this may lead to problems down the road (for example, if you strip non-native code from Apple system software, you may have trouble updating the software later).

Is It Native or Not?

Most native code software will identify itself as "Accelerated for Power Macintosh" right on its package and/or manual. But if you have an application already installed on your Macintosh and aren't sure whether or not it is native code, you can quickly find out by opening its Get Info window. If you see a message at the bottom of the window saying how turning virtual memory (or RAM Doubler) on or off will affect the program's memory requirements, the application is native.

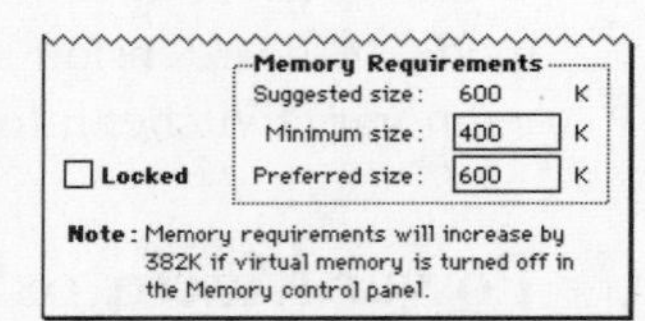

Figure 12-1 *A message like the one at the bottom of this Get Info window indicates that you are running in native mode.*

BY THE WAY ▶

POWERPC FINDER UPDATE EXTENSION: WHERE IS IT?

Prior to System 7.5.3, the appearance of messages about virtual memory at the bottom of applications' Get Info windows depended on the presence of the PowerPC Finder Update extension in the Extensions folder of your System Folder. If this extension was not present, or if you disabled it (such as by holding down the Shift key at startup), these messages would not appear.

Similarly, without the PowerPC Finder Update extension, the numbers listed in the memory requirements boxes in the Get Info windows would remain the same whether or not virtual memory was on. In particular, these numbers were incorrect when virtual memory was off; the application actually needed more memory than indicated.

Starting with System 7.5.3, however, this extension has been rolled into the Finder and is no longer needed.

Virtual Memory and Native Software

Programs running in native mode require significantly *less* RAM (by as much as several megabytes) with virtual memory turned on than they would with it off. This is the implication of the Get Info messages just described in the previous section. You don't need to allocate much virtual memory to achieve this application-memory benefit (just 1 or 2MB should be enough; much less than the Memory control panel's default selection). When you turn virtual memory on or off, the numbers in the memory requirements boxes will shift accordingly after you restart.

BY THE WAY ▶

UTILITIES TELL YOU WHEN YOU ARE RUNNING NATIVE

As described in the main text, your Mac can slip back and forth between emulation mode and native mode even when it is running a native application. If you want to find out precisely when your Mac is or is not in native mode, check out a freeware extension called PowerPeek. It puts a little "light" in your menu bar that flashes green when the Mac is in native mode, and red when it's in emulation mode. Not only does this give you an indication of when mode switching occurs, it can confirm whether a supposed native mode application is really running in native mode.

Another shareware utility, PowerPCheck, can check any selected application and report whether or not it contains native PowerPC code.

In general, although using virtual memory is often of dubious benefit on older Macs (because of disk space requirements and possible slowdowns), it is recommended on Power Macs. In fact, running a native application on a Power Mac with virtual memory off may require significantly more memory than running the non-native version of the same application on the same machine! Apple recommends having at least 1 MB of virtual memory on, which is enough to get the benefit described here. (You can use more if you want, but Apple recommends no more than 50 percent of your physical memory.)

By the way, RAM Doubler has the same benefit as virtual memory on application memory requirements. Even better, because RAM Doubler tries to store information in RAM that System 7's virtual memory stores on disk, you should find RAM Doubler to be faster than using System 7's virtual memory. Just be sure you are using a Power Mac–compatible version of RAM Doubler (version 1.5 or later), and turn off the Mac's virtual memory. Better yet, with RAM Doubler 2, you can choose to turn on this RAM-savings effect (it is called *file mapping*) without adding any additional RAM. This can be nice for those who want this benefit but do not want to use RAM Doubler otherwise because of possible performance deficits.

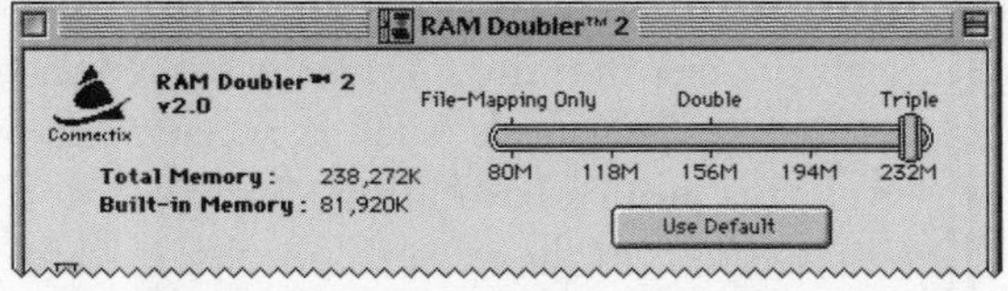

Figure 12-2 *The File-Mapping Only option (on the left end of the slider) of the RAM Doubler 2 control panel.*

Some Power Mac native applications may load faster with virtual memory or RAM Doubler on than off. Aside from that, though, these programs still slow down your machine (exactly how much of a delay you get depends on how much physical RAM you have, how many applications are open, and so on). That's why some experts still recommend keeping virtual memory or RAM Doubler off as long as you have enough physical RAM installed that running out of memory is not a problem (*at least* 32MB these days, and probably more like 64MB). Virtual memory, although not RAM Doubler, can also use up a lot of hard disk space (the more physical memory you have, the more disk space it will need). On the plus side, Apple improved virtual memory in System 7.5.5 so that it should run faster on Power Macs.

SEE: • **Fix-It #6 for more on the Memory control panel, virtual memory, and RAM Doubler**

TECHNICALLY SPEAKING ▶

WHY DO NATIVE APPLICATIONS NEED LESS RAM WHEN VIRTUAL MEMORY IS ON? (FILE MAPPING AND CODE FRAGMENT MANAGER)

Native code applications are written in a new way that allows the Mac to perform a neat trick when virtual memory is on. With 680X0 applications, a certain amount of data must be loaded into memory (physical and/or virtual) before the application can even open. There is a similar requirement for native software when launched with virtual memory off. With virtual memory on, however, a significantly smaller portion of this information is loaded into memory (actually, it goes exclusively to physical RAM). Additionally, a "file map" of the remaining data that would normally be loaded is created on the area of the disk used by virtual memory. This map points to the locations within the application file (as stored on the main part of the disk) that the Mac needs to go to find the data. Since it takes up a lot less space than if the actual data had been loaded, this map is the source of the memory savings. This file mapping is handled by something called the Code Fragment Manager (instructions built into the Macintosh ROM and/or system software). 680X0 Macs relied instead on something called a Segment Loader (although Apple now has Code Fragment Manager software extensions that 680X0 Macs can use).

A side effect of this is that application developers must now ensure that their applications are not self-modifying in any way. Otherwise, if the file on the disk is altered while the application is open, the map in memory may no longer be accurate. System crashes would likely result.

By the way, the Total Memory size, as listed in the About This Macintosh window, may be larger than expected when virtual memory is on. This is not a cause for concern; everything will still work fine, although you really don't have the extra memory. The mislisting is a consequence of the presence of the 68040 emulator causing the Power Mac to make an incorrect calculation.

PCI-Based Power Macintoshes

In 1995, Apple released its second generation of Power Macs: the PCI-based Power Macs (with models such as the 7500, 7600, 8500, and 9500). The "PCI" name comes from the fact that these were the first Macs to use PCI slots rather than NuBus slots for adding optional cards (such as accelerators or video cards) to the Mac. At its simplest level, this means that NuBus cards that worked on older Macs will not work on these Macs; you need the newer PCI type of card.

The differences in the design of these Macs versus the first generation of Power Macs, however, went far beyond optional card slots. Whereas the first generation of Power Macs (6100, 7100, and 8100) were basically Quadras with a PowerPC processor added, the PCI-based Macs were redesigned from the ground up. For starters, they were much faster than their elder siblings, more so than even the differences in clock speed would suggest. They were the first Macs to use DIMMs for memory rather than SIMMs; they had dual SCSI buses; and their fully integrated AV features (especially in the 7500, 7600, and 8500 models) surpassed the sort of patched-together AV features of the first generation Power Macs.

Another innovation included on all PCI-based Macs (except the 7200) was that the processor was on a separate "daughterboard" card that could be removed and replaced as easily as replacing memory. This, for the first time, allowed for easy upgrading of your Mac to a speedier processor.

Yet another innovation added in some PCI-based Macs in late 1996 were multiple processors (see: "By the Way: Multiple Processor Macs").

The Performa 6400 series were the first of the Performa line to be PCI-based Macs. PCI-based PowerBooks are expected in 1997. Eventually, the entire Mac product line will be PCI-based.

SEE: • **Fix-It #16 for more on dual SCSI buses**
• **Fix-It #17 for more on PCI versus NuBus and DIMMs versus SIMMs**

Of relevance to troubleshooting, PCI-based Power Macs came with their own special set of problems, not found in any other Macs, even other Power Macs. These are covered later in this chapter ("PCI-Based Macintosh Quick Fixes") as well as in other sections of this book, as relevant.

BY THE WAY ▶

MULTIPLE-PROCESSOR MACS

There are now PCI-based Macs that ship with two separate processors in them (the Power Mac 9500MP is an example). This allows for the possibility of dividing up tasks between them, thereby providing true multi-tasking. Future Macs may include even more than two processors. If you decide to get a multi-processor Mac, however, don't necessarily expect them to have much effect on the speed of your applications. For starters, to take full advantage of multiple processors, an application needs to be written specifically to be aware of the processors and divide its sub-tasks among them.

Solve It! Power Macintosh Problems

For general problems with running in emulation mode or managing memory, check out the previous section on Power Macintosh Basics. What follows is an assorted collection of more specific problems and solutions.

Compatibility and Memory Problems

Symptoms:

- A program will not run on any Power Mac, although it appears to run fine on other Macintosh models.
- A program runs slower on a Power Mac than on other types of Macintoshes (or has other quirks that are unique to the Power Mac version).

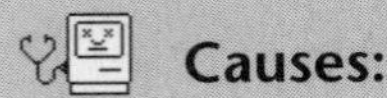

Causes:

The software in question is most likely a non-native code version that is forcing the Macintosh to run in emulator mode. Even though the Power Mac's 68040 emulator should permit most non-native software to run correctly, some compatibility problems will inevitably occur.

Other related causes include problems with memory management or with special extensions.

Running in emulator mode also means that you will not get the full speed advantage of using a Power Mac. In many cases, the emulator speed may be slower than running the same software on a 68040 Mac.

SEE: • **"Running in Emulation Mode versus Native Mode," earlier in this chapter**

What to do:

Emulation Mode Problems

Extensions/Control Panels That Are Not Native Control panels and extensions running in emulator mode can cause unexpected delays. For example, versions of ATM (Adobe Type Manager) prior to 3.8 run in emulator mode. ATM is active any time a program, such as a word processor, needs it for the display or printing of text. The resulting need for the Mac to shift into emulator mode for ATM, even if the application itself is in native code, can cause a slowdown of as much as 15 percent or more. The solution is to use native versions of all startup extensions, whenever possible (version 3.8 or later in the case of ATM).

Programs That Can't Run with the Modern Memory Manager Power Macs handle memory management differently than previous Mac models. They use something called the Modern Memory Manager (selected on or off from the Memory control panel), which is basically a PowerPC native code rewrite of the original Memory Manager (present in all Macs). Keeping Modern Memory Manager on should speed up your Power Mac's performance and reduce memory-related system errors. Since turning it off means you are running the older—and slower—Memory Manager in emulation mode, Apple advises leaving it on at all times.

Some (especially non-native) applications, however, are still incompatible with the Modern Memory Manager (and may trigger Type 11 errors, for example). If this appears to be a possibility for you, turn off Modern Memory Manager and see if the problem disappears.

SEE: • **Fix-It #6 for more on the Memory control panel**

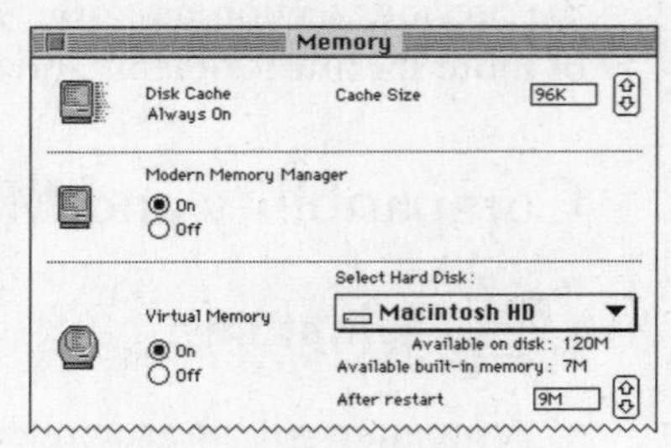

Figure 12-3 *Turning off the Memory control panel's Modern Memory Manager may eliminate a compatibility problem.*

By the way, the Memory control panel for a Power Mac no longer has an option for turning off 32-bit addressing (which traditionally has been another source of memory-related incompatibilities). With a Power Mac, 32-bit addressing must always be on. Actually, starting with System 7.6, Modern Memory Manager cannot be turned off.

Programs That Need a Math Coprocessor (FPU) The Power Mac's 68040 emulator is technically a 68LC040 emulator. Since this particular flavor of 68040 processor does not include an FPU (floating point unit, also called a math coprocessor). This means that non-native versions of programs that use the FPU, including many statistics and scientific applications, will run much slower on a Power Mac than on a 68040 Mac with an FPU. In the worst cases, the program may not run at all, giving you a "No FPU Installed" or "No Coprocessor Present" error message instead.

You may be able to partially solve this problem by using an FPU emulator called Software FPU, but don't count on it. The best solution is to get the native code upgrade to your problem application (if there is such an upgrade!).

By the way, your Power Mac *does* have an FPU; it is built into all PowerPC processors. This can only be accessed, however, by programs running in native mode.

SEE: • **Fix-It #1 for more on Software FPU, and FPU problems in general**

A "No FPU Installed" False Alarm A program may fail to open or may unexpectedly quit, followed by a message that identifies the problem as "no FPU installed." Sometimes (as just described) this relates to the absence of an FPU in the 68LC040 emulator.

With surprising frequency, however, this can happen even if the program does not try to access an FPU. Turning off the Modern Memory Manager (as also just described) may help here. Even more often, though, the real problem may have nothing to do with a coprocessor or emulation mode or Modern Memory Manager. You still have a system error; it's just that the Mac, unable to determine what the appropriate error message should be, may be fibbing about the cause. The actual causes are many, varied, and often mysterious, involving native as well as non-native code programs.

SEE
- **Chapter 4, "Special Case: Type 11 and 'No FPU Installed' errors," for more general help on what to do**
- **"Type 11 System Errors," in the next section of this chapter**

Totally Incompatible Software Some software (even programs that don't access an FPU) will just not run in emulator mode under any circumstances. If all of the preceding tips fail to resolve the problem, you will probably have to give up on the software. If there is a native code upgrade available or coming soon, get it!

The "Read Me" files that come with your Power Mac or system software upgrade typically include a variety of specific incompatibility and related troubleshooting information. Check them out for further advice.

Insufficient Memory Problems

System software tends to require more memory on a Power Macintosh than it would on a 680X0 Macintosh. As a result, you might find that there is not enough unused memory left to open an application on a Power Mac, even though the same application could open on a 680X0 Mac running the same system software. The standard techniques to make more free memory available (as described in Fix-It #6) may help here, but ultimately this difference across machines will remain.

Also recall that keeping virtual memory off will increase a native application's memory requirements, possibly preventing a given application from opening. So keep virtual memory (or RAM Doubler) on unless you have more than enough physical RAM. In any case, native software tends to require more memory than the 680X0 version of the same program. Nothing can be done about this; ultimately, you will have to face the basic fact that Power Macs need more memory than 680X0 Macs.

PCI-based Macs and the latest system software make an especially RAM-hungry combination, often demanding 32MB or more of physical RAM in order to run comfortably. Fortunately, since RAM prices are much cheaper than they were a few years ago, keeping up with these needs is less likely to empty your bank account.

SEE: • **"Virtual Memory and Native Software," earlier in this chapter, for more details**

Shared Library Problems

Power Macintosh native applications increasingly use *shared libraries,* a technology designed to minimize the need to have the same code in RAM more than once at the same time. Thus, if two programs use essentially the same code, it can be stored in a special shared library file that both programs can access (called *dynamic linking*).

While this method should help to reduce the total amount of RAM needed to keep multiple applications open, the memory requirements listed in an application's Get Info don't include any extra memory that may be needed to access a shared library. Thus, you may need more memory to open an application than the Get Info window would suggest—and this may mean that you do not have enough available memory to open the application.

SEE: • **Fix-It #6 on how to solve problems due to insufficient available memory**

A missing shared library file on your hard drive can also prevent an application from opening. If this happens, try reinstalling the application software, making sure to use the application's Installer utility (if it includes one) and carefully following the directions given. This should get the needed library file onto your disk.

Shared Library Manager and Documents The key files that you need to use shared libraries are the Shared Library Manager and Shared Library Manager PPC extensions (the latter is needed to run native code libraries). They are installed as part of System 7.5.3 and later revisions. Examples of shared library "document" files that are shipped with the system software are the AppleScriptLib and ObjectSupportLib files. Used especially with

AppleScript, these files are also needed by several other third-party programs, so do not discard them. In addition, if you use Open Transport, you will see shared library files with names such as "Open Transport Library" and "OpenTransportLib." The files that end in "Lib" are used for running native code applications, while those that end in "Library" are needed to run 680X0 applications in emulation mode. Neither file type loads into RAM at startup; they are loaded only when needed.

Shared library technology is not limited to Power Macs. For example, if you are running Open Transport on a 680X0 Mac, you will likely have the Shared Library Manager, ObjectSupportLib, and a set of three Open Transport files that end in "68K Library" (such as Open Transport 68K Library). These latter three files are special shared library documents needed for 680X0 machines. (By the way, if you find these "68K" files on a Power Mac, they can be deleted.)

Because of differences in design, however, Power Macs take better advantage of shared libraries. In fact, when they were first released, shared libraries only ran on Power Macs.

SEE: • **Chapter 14 for more on Open Transport**

Note: There is a similarly named (and similarly functioning) extension called Shared Code Manager. This is not part of Apple's system software, but a Microsoft extension that is used in conjunction with some Microsoft applications.

Code Fragment Manager The Code Fragment Manager (CFM) is essentially a replacement technology for the Shared Library Manager—by Mac OS 8 (if not sooner) all code (including applications) will be code fragments. The Shared Library Manager will be history, since a shared library document is just one type of code fragment.

Even in System 7, use of the Shared Library Manager is diminishing as applications are being updated to depend instead on the Code Fragment Manager (which is already part of System 7.5 and later revisions). As a result, you may find that these library files work fine even if the Shared Library Manager is not installed.

There is no CFM extension, at least not on Power Macs; it is built directly into the system software. On 680X0 Macs, you may find a file called CFM-68K Runtime Enabler. This allows Code Fragment Manager-dependent software to run on these Macs.

SEE ALSO: • **"Technically Speaking: Why Do Native Applications Need Less RAM When Virtual Memory Is On? (File Mapping and Code Fragment Manager)," earlier in this chapter**

BY THE WAY ▶

ICONS DISAPPEAR FROM THE FINDER'S DESKTOP

For some reason, Finder icons on a Power Mac's desktop can be moved beyond the edges of the screen, so that you can no longer see them. If you suspect this may have happened, click on any visible icon on the desktop and then select Clean Up Desktop from the Finder's Special menu. This should get the icons to return; if it doesn't, try again with the Option key held down.

System Error and Related Problems

Symptoms:

- A system crash or other unusual event occurs at startup.
- A system crash occurs at any other time.

Causes:

Power Macs, of course, are subject to the same system crash and startup problems that plague all Macintoshes. As a result, the cause and solution for your problem will most likely be found in the earlier parts of this book that are devoted to these subjects: Chapters 4 and 5.

A few startup and system crash problems, however, are unique to Power Macs. The exact causes vary, but several common examples are summarized in the paragraphs that follow.

What to do:

Type 11 (Hardware Exception) System Errors

Type 11 system errors are *much* more common on a Power Macintosh than on other Mac models. One source for these errors is corruption of the Power Mac's 68040 emulator as it loads into RAM. Sometimes simply restarting can cure this problem. If the emulator has been corrupted by incompatible software, though, the problem will recur each time you use the software.

The complete story on the causes and cures for Type 11 errors on a Power Mac, however, is much more involved than this.

SEE: • **Chapter 4, "Special Case: Type 11 and 'No FPU Installed' errors," for all the messy details**
• **"Emulation Mode Problems," earlier in this chapter**

QuickTime PowerPlug

In order to play QuickTime movies on a Power Mac, you need not only the QuickTime extension itself, but an extension called QuickTime PowerPlug. If it is not installed and enabled, system errors are almost guaranteed.

Power Mac Crashes When You Press the Command Key

A Power Mac may crash when you press the Command key, particularly if it can be turned on via the Power keyboard key (as is the case for the 7100 and 8100 and all the PCI-based Power Mac models). Why? If you hold down the Power key too long at startup, a bug causes the Mac to "see" the Power key as pressed down all the time. When you later press the Command key, the Mac thinks that you have simultaneously pressed the Command-Power key combination, which acts as a substitute for pressing the Interrupt button.

The result is not really a system crash; you actually wind up getting the debugger window. If this happens, you can probably exit the debugger simply by pressing the "G" key and then Return; otherwise, you will have to restart. In general, to avoid this problem, do not keep your finger down on the Power key at startup—press it once lightly, then let go.

This problem may also occur on certain 680X0 Mac models. Happily, though, it was fixed in System 7.5.3, so upgrade if you're looking for a permanent solution.

SEE: • **Chapter 4 for more on the Interrupt function**

Power Macintosh Crashes on Startup or When Printing

Make sure you are using a compatible version of the system software. Power Macs that are not PCI-based require System 7.1.2 or a later version; PCI-based Power Macs need version 7.5.2 or later. Earlier Power Macs cannot use this version, and some variations of System 7.5.3 only run on PCI-based Macs as well.

Problems were also reported with serial port devices (modems and printers), such as freezes when printing to an inkjet printer. Initially, this was solved by upgrading to the latest version of an extension called SerialDMA (described more in Chapter 14). This extension was rolled into System 7.5.3, however, and thus it is not needed with this system software version.

Happily, all Power Macs can use version 7.5.3 or later. In general, for Power Macs, always use the latest available version of the system software.

SEE: • **Chapter 13, on System 7.5, for coverage of both Power Mac and 680X0 problems specific to the latest system software**

Freezes and PowerPC Interrupt Extension

With any Power Mac running System 7.5.5, freezes can occur while using certain applications—especially game software—that did not occur with prior system software. This is due to a bug that can be squashed by installing an Apple extension called PowerPC Interrupt Extension. As of this writing, it only works with System 7.5.5. The fix is scheduled to be built into the basic software of System 7.6. Meanwhile, if installing this extension seems to have the reverse effect—increasing the number of freezes you have—move the extension to the end of the loading order (typically by using an extensions management utility, as described in Fix-It #4).

Persistent System Freezes (Apple's Repair Extension Program)

Do you have a Power Mac or Performa in the 5200, 5300, 6200, or 6300 series? Are you also plagued by persistent system freezes? If so, these freezes may be caused by "specific, known component issues that have been identified by Apple," in which case you will qualify for a free repair under Apple's Repair Extension Program. To check this out, get a free utility from Apple called 5XXX/6XXX Tester, or call 800-SOS-APPL for assistance.

SEE: • **Fix-It #17 for more details on the Repair Extension Program and related issues**

Sound Problems

Some of the Performas in the above series have a defect in the logic board that causes a crackling or static noise to occur when playing sound files. Before you decide you need your logic board replaced, however, or if you are having a similar problem with 16-bit sounds on any other Power Mac models, get Apple's free Audio Volume extension. It will likely solve the problem.

BY THE WAY ▶

NEW STARTUP SOUNDS ON POWER MACINTOSHES

Power Macs have a sound to indicate a successful startup. On a less friendly note, they also have a new startup crash sound, the one usually associated with a sad Mac appearing on your screen. It sounds like a car crash.

SEE: • Chapter 5 for more on sad Macs and unusual startup sounds

BY THE WAY ▶

POWER MACINTOSHES AND CD-ROM STARTUP DISCS

All Power Macs are shipped with a CD-ROM disc that includes a System Folder and can be used as a startup disk if you have an Apple CD-ROM drive. This alternate startup disk is especially useful for those times when your hard disk crashes at startup. Your Mac will boot from the Power Macintosh CD-ROM if you insert it at startup and hold down the "C" key.

SEE: • Chapter 5 for more on using a CD-ROM disc as an alternate startup disk

Monitor Problems

Symptoms:

Your monitor either does not connect to or does not work with a Power Macintosh. No such problem occurs when you use the monitor with a 680X0 Macintosh.

Causes and What to do:

The Ghost Monitor Problem

If you have a non-PCI-based Power Macintosh with an AV card installed, and your monitor is attached to the Power Mac's built-in video jack, the Mac may mistakenly think you also have a monitor attached through the AV card input jack. This will be apparent when you open the Monitors control panel and see two monitors indicated. The "Read Me" file that accompanies these Power Macintoshes describes what to do to avoid this so-called ghost monitor.

SEE: • Chapter 10 for more on the Monitors control panel

Sync-on-Green Problem

Some non-Apple monitors are incompatible with Power Macintoshes (as well as AV 680x0 Macintoshes) because of something called the "sync-on-green" problem. Ask your dealer about this before purchasing a monitor; don't buy one that may have this problem.

If you do connect a monitor that has this problem, you will likely have a green or purple tinge to your entire monitor display. On some Power Computing clones, this can be fixed by turning off "sync-on-green" from the Twin Turbo control panel.

SEE: • **Fix-It #17 for more details on the sync-on-green and other monitor-related problems**

Monitor Cable Adapter Needed

Some monitors need a special cable adapter in order to attach to the new monitor port on the back of the Power Macintosh. This adapter should come with your Power Macintosh.

Vertical Lines That Follow the Cursor?

On some PCI-based Power Macs (especially the 7500 or 8500), two vertical lines may appear to follow the cursor; this is due to improper installation of VRAM. If you have 2MB of VRAM, you must install the VRAM DIMMs into the slots labeled "1" (which is the way these models are shipped if the VRAM is already installed). If you should get a logic board replacement be especially careful that the VRAM modules are installed in the same slots that they occupied on the original board.

Sudden Changes in Monitor's Hue (Apple's Repair Extension Program)

Do you have what Apple describes as "sudden or intermittent changes in the monitor's color hue on Power Macintosh and Performa 5200 and 5300 series computers, due to a particular cable"? If so, you qualify for a free repair under Apple's Repair Extension Program. To check this out, get a free utility from Apple called 5XXX/6XXX Tester; otherwise, call 800-SOS-APPL for assistance.

SEE: • **Fix-It #17 for more details on the Repair Extension Program and related issues**

PCI-Based Macintosh Quick Fixes

Here are several miscellaneous, largely unrelated symptoms and solutions, all related to PCI-based Macintoshes. Some of these issues are covered separately (and often in more detail) in other sections of the book, as indicated by the cross-references listed.

Symptoms, Causes, and What to do:

Screen Blinking at Startup

Does your Mac's screen "blink" a second time at startup, just after the MacOS screen appears? Don't worry, nothing is wrong; the Mac is just loading an updated version of the video driver software. If you really want to avoid the flash, hold down the Command-Shift-N-D keys at startup, but this also means you'll be using the older (and presumably buggier) driver. Aside from being a bit irritating, the only problem the "blink" causes is that it wipes out any custom startup-screen display.

Starting with System 7.5.3, this blinking has been reported to occur with other desktop Macs. On the other hand, it appears to have been corrected with an updated ROM on some machines. For example, I have a Power Mac 7500 that blinks like this, but some friends whose 7500 apparently has a different logic board (based on the serial number) have never encountered this "problem."

Sleep and Energy Saver Problems

For most desktop Macs, selecting Sleep from the Finder's Special menu merely invokes a screen saver. For PCI-based Macs, however, selecting Sleep can result in the hard drive spinning down and the monitor (if it is capable of doing so) completely shutting off, somewhat similar to what this command does in PowerBooks. Further, the version of Energy Saver designed to be used with PCI-based Macs can be set to do these tasks automatically (for example, after several minutes of inactivity). Energy Saver also has some unusual "problems," however, as detailed below. Fortunately, many of these problems can be solved by correctly adjusting Energy Saver's Preferences file.

More Than One Energy Saver Before I go any further, you should know that there are two different Apple programs named Energy Saver. The older version worked merely to dim monitor screens. The newer Energy Saver (version 2.0 or higher), which only works on PCI-based Macs, is the one that can actually turn off the monitor and spin down the hard drive. This section focuses on the version for PCI-based Macs (if you have a PCI-based Mac, you can install both by renaming one of them).

There are also numerous other energy-saving control panels that Apple has released over the years—such as CPU Energy Saver and Auto Power On/Off—but that's another (equally confusing) story.

Mac Goes to Sleep Automatically Even with Energy Saver Disabled Energy Saver works by combining of a control panel (Energy Saver, which is really an ordinary application) with an extension (Energy Saver Extension).

Some users have noted that if they try to disable Energy Saver by setting the control panel's sliders to "Never" and then disabling the extension, their Mac still goes to sleep after about an hour; the hard drive may also spin down at some point. I have had success preventing this by leaving Energy Saver installed—with settings still at "Never"—rather than disabled. (If you want an alternate program that can similarly invoke automatic sleep, try the shareware program called Sleeper.)

Also note the following statement from Apple: "The Energy Saver sleep settings are not stored in PRAM, they are stored in the Energy Saver Preferences file, located in the Preferences folder within the System Folder. Moving or throwing the Energy Saver Preferences file away, and restarting your Macintosh resets the Energy Saver control panel back to the default sleep time of 30 minutes." It will also cause the splash screen that appears the first time you start up with Energy Saver installed to reappear.

Sleep from Energy Saver or Finder's Special Menu If you do set your Macintosh to go to sleep automatically via Energy Saver, it may be a different sleep than you get by selecting the Sleep command from the Finder. If you use the Finder's Sleep command, the monitor shuts off completely (as shown by the indicator light on the monitor, which goes off). If you wait for the Energy Saver to put the Mac to sleep automatically, and the monitor is set to sleep before the system is set to sleep, it only darkens the screen (the indicator light stays on, and pressing a keyboard key brings the screen back instantly).

You Can't Get the Hard Drive to Spin Down If your hard disk refuses to spin down at the time interval selected in the Energy Saver's main window, go to Server Settings Preferences and make sure that "Never put the hard disk to sleep" is unchecked. If it is checked, spinning down is prevented, despite any other settings to the contrary.

The Macintosh Restarts Instead of Shutting Down If your Mac keeps restarting every time you select Shut Down, go again to Server Settings Preferences and make sure that "Restart after a power failure" is unchecked. If it is checked, it will likely cause the Mac to restart after *any* sort of shutdown.

The Macintosh Goes to Sleep Instead of Shutting Down If your Mac goes to sleep rather than turning off after you select Shut Down, go to Energy Saver's Document Auto-Save Preferences and make sure that "Put the system to sleep instead of shutting down" is unchecked. Otherwise, if you have unsaved documents when you select to Shut Down, the system also will go to sleep instead of shutting off.

Audio CD Problem On PCI-based desktop computers, Energy Saver is known to interrupt the play of Audio CDs if "Put the system to sleep instead of shutting down" is selected from the Document Auto-Save Preferences. To avoid this problem, uncheck this option.

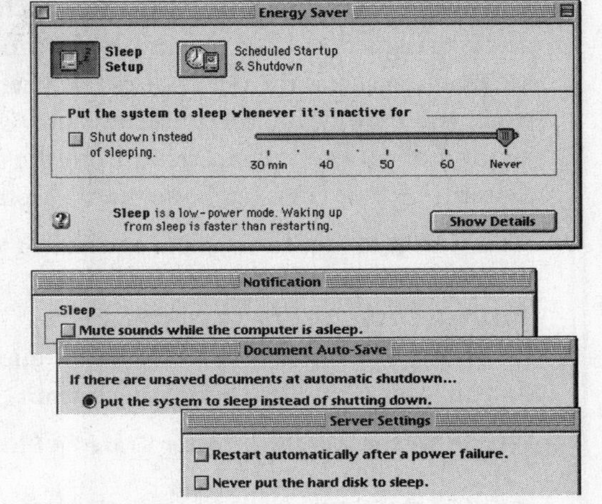

Figure 12-4 *The Energy Saver control panel for PCI-based Macs, with portions of its Preferences settings windows shown.*

Persistent Mute If your Mac's sound suddenly goes "mute" (for instance, when waking up from sleep or after a restart), the Energy Saver control panel may be at fault. To possibly solve the problem, select its Notification Preferences and uncheck "Mute sounds while the computer is asleep."

SEE: • **"Solve It!: AppleVision Monitors," later in this chapter, for still more problems with Sleep**
• **"Technically Speaking: A Few Words About Sound And Sound Files," in Chapter 6**

Screen Stays Black? Hard Drive Won't Spin Up? Try the Cuda Button

The Power Mac 7500, 7600, and 8500 models (and possibly other PCI-based Macs) have a small button near the processor daughter board (called the "Cuda" button) that, when pressed, resets the Mac's default settings even more thoroughly than a reset (or "zap") of the PRAM. You should only use this button as an absolute last resort for PRAM-related problems.

One known problem this button may help resolve, is if your monitor screen goes black and stays that way, even though its power light is on and everything else seems to be working normally. If restarting and zapping the PRAM has no effect (or only works sporadically), try the Cuda button. If you have an AppleVision Monitor with this problem, another option is to try the AppleVision Recovery software (described more in the next section of this chapter, "AppleVision Monitors").

The Cuda button may also help if your hard drive seems to be unwilling to even start spinning at startup. Since defective RAM may also cause these symptoms, it may also help to remove and reseat all RAM.

SEE: **• Fix-It #11 for more on the Cuda button and zapping the PRAM**
• AppleVision Monitors, later in this chapter, for still more problems with screens staying black

SCSI ID 5 Problems?

PCI-based Macs appear to have a bug such that SCSI devices (especially array or tape drives) assigned to ID 5 may not work properly. The computer may freeze when attempts are made to access the device, especially when another SCSI device is in use at the same time; you may even have problems starting up your Macintosh. Even so, no loss or corruption of data appears to result from the bug. This problem was reportedly fixed with System 7.5.3 or later, but some users dispute this.

SEE: **• Fix-It #16 for more on this and related SCSI issues**

Erased Disk and Disk Spot Check

If you run Norton Disk Doctor and it appears to erase your entire disk (yikes!), don't despair. You need Disk Spot Check from Symantec.

SEE: **• "By the Way: Disk Doctor 'Erases' A Disk," in Fix-It #13, for more details**

Floppy Disk Won't Initialize or Erase

If your PCI-based Mac has a 180 MHz or faster processor, you may have trouble initializing or erasing floppy disks. To fix this you need Apple's Power Mac Format Patch extension (which may have come with your Mac). If you have a Power Computing clone, you may instead need an extension called Floppy Tuner. If you are using System 7.5.5 or later, though, this problem supposedly has been fixed.

Why a Graphics Accelerator?

The Power Mac 7200 has a graphics accelerator chip on the motherboard. To take advantage of this chip, though, you need the 7200 Graphics Acceleration extension. Without this file, the graphics are run solely by the CPU, which will result in slower graphics,

TAKE NOTE ▶

PERFORMA PROBLEMS

By 1996, both Performas and PowerBooks had joined the Power Mac family. While this book has a whole chapter on PowerBooks, Performas may seem to be overlooked. This is mainly because, in most cases, Performas share the same problems that affect the rest of the Macintosh line. There is a growing list, however, of problems specific to (or mainly affecting) Performas. I mention several of these in the relevant sections of this book (such as problems with TV tuners and remote controls, as described in "Problems with Apple Video Player" in Chapter 10). Here's a brief look at a few more:

- **PlainTalk** PlainTalk 1.4.1 or earlier did not work with Performa 6200 and 6300 series. Upgrading to PlainTalk 1.5 fixes this. There are reports, though, that when Speakable Items is turned on you will have problems making a PPP connection with a Global Village modem.
- **Serial port slowdowns and/or system errors** Serial ports on Performas in the 5200, 5300, 6200, and 6300 series are somehow different from the serial ports on standard desktop Macs. I'll skip the details, but the net result is that serial port connections (such as a modem) may be unexpectedly slow. Various work-arounds have been suggested, including disabling RAM Doubler and removing Global Village extensions. Nothing, however, is guaranteed to work.

  Actually, I have seen some reports that RAM Doubler 2 and these Global Village extensions may conflict with each other, leading to Type 1 errors. Expect software upgrades to resolve all of this.
- **Volume control button crashes** Freezes or crashes can occur when you press the hardware volume control buttons on Performas such as the 5215CD, 6200CD, 6214CD, and 6300. It turns out that installing the Video Startup extensions (normally needed only if you use Apple Video Player) will fix the problem. The problem may ultimately be related to Apple's disk driver, and has supposedly been fixed in System 7.5.5.
- **Running out of memory after a fax** After sending a fax by choosing Fax Window from the Finder's File menu with a 5200, 6200, 5300, or 6300 Mac, you may start getting out-of-memory messages. This (again) appears to be due to a problem with Global Village extensions. Faxing from within an application will work around the problem, and restarting will get the error messages to go away. Future software upgrades should fix the problem.

Also, Apple's Repair Extension program, as described in Fix-It #17, addresses some problems with Performas.

SEE ALSO: • **Chapter 13 for more on general problems with System 7.5 and beyond**

particularly so with QuickTime. Some Power Computing Macs also use this extension; with it installed, certain QuickDraw operations are taken over by the accelerator chip.

By the way, a similarly named extension, Graphics Accelerator, is needed for video acceleration in PCI-based Macs that use a video card (primarily the Power Mac 9500).

Pointer Mode Control Panel

System 7.5.3 may install a Pointer Mode control panel (it may be in the Apple Extras folder if it is not installed in the System Folder). Primarily intended for the Power Mac 7200, it allows the cursor to remain in screen snapshots taken via the Command-Shift-3 method. More generally, it also may reduce cursor flickering when the cursor is over a graphic.

TAKE NOTE ▶

MAC CLONE PROBLEMS

When discussing problems in this book, I do not mention Macintosh models by name very often. This is because most of the problems covered here are true for all or nearly all Mac models (at least all recently released models). When specific models are mentioned, however—as in the previous section on PCI-based Macs—I almost always refer to Apple-brand models. There is little mention of Mac clones, such as the popular series from Power Computing. The main reason for this, once again, is that Mac clones are so similar to comparable Apple Macs that whatever I say here usually applies to clones as well.

Of course, some specific differences do exist. Perhaps the most notable example is that these clones are shipped with a version of the system software that has an "L" (for "license") at the end of its name, such as System 7.5.3L. While these versions are just about identical to the "non-L" versions, small differences can be detected. For example, Power Computing substitutes their own CD-ROM driver in this software, rather than using Apple's. This means that if you do a clean reinstall of system software from an Apple version of the software, the CD-ROM drive on your Power Computing clone will not work unless you go back and install the Power Computing driver. A few other problems unique to clones are covered throughout this book, as relevant to the topic in question.

One other quick note: Some persistent freeze and crash problems with early versions of Power Computing's Power 120 models were due to a hardware problem. Power Computing will fix this for free, so contact them if you have one of these machines.

SEE: • Fix-It #16 for more on drivers in general

Monitors & Sound Control Panel Problems

The Monitors & Sound control panel needs another extension called System AV in order to work. The older Sound & Displays control panel (used only in System 7.5.2) also needed AppleScript and another extension called AV Setup; happily, these are no longer required for Monitors & Sound to work.

Neither of these control panels can record sounds. To do that, use the SimpleSound utility.

Video Problems

Display problems that occur when you try to run a video program, such as Avid Cinema, on an early unit of a Power Mac 7500 or 8500, are probably due to a flaw in the DAV (digital audio-video) chip on the logic board. Call 1-800-SOS-APPL, and Apple will determine if you qualify for a free replacement.

Memory Matters

PCI-based Macs have a number of special issues related to memory: (1) They use DIMMs rather than the SIMMs commonly used on older Mac models. (2) Most can benefit from memory "interleaving," which is a boost in performance that occurs if memory modules are installed in matched pairs. (3) 16MB or larger DIMMs may not work when installed in some slots, but will work when installed in others. (4) Some (especially third-party) Level 2 (L2) RAM cache may not work at all, especially in the Power Mac 7500.

Much more detail about these and related issues are described in Fix-It #17 ("Memory I: Adding or Replacing Memory" and "Memory II: Getting the Correct Modules for Your Machine").

Networking and Communications Matters

A variety of problems specific to PCI-based Macs with setting up Ethernet networks, making PPP connections, and more are discussed as part of the more general coverage of these issues in Chapter 14.

Zapping the PRAM

There is a special procedure for zapping the PRAM (and non-volatile video RAM) of PCI-based Macs. It is covered in Fix-It #11.

TAKE NOTE ▶

POWER MAC POWERBOOK PROBLEMS

In late 1995, Apple released the 5300 series of PowerBooks, the first line that had a PowerPC processor. They were not especially well-received: they ran more slowly than expected, and they were plagued with glitches that required several software updates and eventually a hardware recall, called the Repair Extension Program (as described in Chapter 11 and Fix-It #17). Then there was the incident of a few of the lithium-ion batteries used in early units of these machines catching on fire.

All in all, these were snakebit machines, but they were Power Macs nonetheless, and most of the general issues described in this chapter apply to them as well as other Power Macs.

Apple's replacement line of PowerBooks (starting with the PowerBook 1400) are also PowerPC machines. These machines appear to be much more reliable.

AppleVision Monitors

When AppleVision monitors work, they are superb. When they don't … well, read on.

The name AudioVision was first given to monitors that combined built-in stereo speakers with a multiscan monitor, giving the user an all-in-one audio-video setup. More recently, the name AppleVision has been applied to a similar line of monitors that do not necessarily have built-in speakers, but do include new AppleVision technology for adjusting the monitor's settings (such as convergence and color calibration). With this technology, you can control many of these settings either from software or from easily accessible buttons on the front of the monitor.

The first generation of AppleVision monitors were Apple's 17-inch multiscan AppleVision 1710AV (the one with the speakers) and 1710 (without the speakers). These monitors (especially the 1710AV, particularly when it is hooked up to a PCI-based Mac) have numerous special features that require some unique troubleshooting. They have also been plagued with an unusual number of hardware glitches that have required many owners to send their monitors back for repair (or replacement!) several times. This section gives you the scoop on all of these issues. Several of these issues will also apply to Apple's "non-AppleVision" multiscan monitors.

AppleVision Software

AppleVision software can be installed via the AppleVision Software disk(s) that come with the monitor. System 7.5.3 or later revisions also include this software, but it may be a *newer* version than what comes with the monitor. In this case, do not install from the disk included with the monitor. For example, if your AppleVision software disks are version 1.0.2 or earlier, you should not use them. Use the files from System 7.5.3 (or later) instead.

Other updates, such as Display Software disks, may be available online with updated versions of some of the needed software.

AppleVision Extension

This extension is critical for use in any setup—make sure you have it installed, and make sure you have the latest available version. As of this writing, however, there was a problem insofar as PCI-based Macs were supposed to use version 1.0.4 of this file, while all other Macs needed 1.0.2. Hopefully, this need for separate versions will be eliminated in the next iteration of the software.

Note: When I moved up to AppleVision 1.0.4, the icon that had previously been shown at startup stopped appearing. The extension, however, still seems to install and work okay.

Monitors & Sound versus AppleVision Setup

The software controls for adjusting the monitors settings are found in one of two places.

Monitors & Sound If you have a PCI-based Mac, use the Monitors & Sound control panel. Note that this is one control panel, not the two separate older ones (Monitors *and* Sound). This control panel combines most of the functions of the separate control panels and adds new features.

This control panel works regardless of what type of monitor you have. If you have an AppleVision monitor and install the AppleVision software, however, special AppleVision-specific options are added. These include the options to set the calibration of the monitor, the "geometry" settings, and (with the 1710AV) the monitor's sound.

If you are still using System 7.5.2 (which I would not recommend), it uses a different control panel, called Sound & Displays (except on the Power Mac 7200, which did not use this control panel). Most users found Sound & Displays difficult to figure out, and happily, it is now defunct.

AppleVision Setup For all non-PCI Macs, since they do not use Monitors & Sound, the AppleVision software installs a separate control panel called AppleVision Setup. Unlike the AppleVision extension, this file appears not to be included on system software disks. In this case, the only way to get it is from special display software disks (such as the AppleVision Software disks).

By the way, make sure you do not have both AppleVision Setup *and* Monitors & Sound installed. If you do, this will cause problems. The solution is to disable the one that is inappropriate for your Mac (running the AppleVision Fix utility, described later in this section, may also fix this).

SimpleSound Those Macs that use Monitors & Sound no longer use the Sound control panel. For recording sound, there is another new file called SimpleSound that should be installed (as further described in "Technically Speaking: A Few Words About Sound and Sound Files," in Chapter 6).

Display Enabler

Apple has claimed that this file (which lets you change resolutions without restarting) is needed for all Macs with multiscan monitors—except PCI-based Macs, which do not need any additional extension.

The situation, however, is actually a bit more complicated. First, a version of Display Enabler was rolled into the system software of System 7.5.3, eliminating the need for this extension for *all* Macs. Later, Apple released a supposed "newer" version of this extension that they again recommended (at least for non-PCI-based Macs); it was included as part of Display Software 2.0.2. Although there is still some confusion on this point, it still appears as if the version built into System 7.5.3 (or later) supersedes this version. My guess is that Display Enabler will no longer be needed with any current system software.

By the way, Apple has reported a conflict between Display Enabler and Now Utilities 6.

Solve It!: AppleVision Problems

Symptoms:

- The AppleVision monitor shows incorrect resolution or color in its display.
- Diagonal lines appear in the display, or other unusual display symptoms occur.
- AppleVision software is not installed or does not work properly (for example, resolution options do not appear as expected).
- Strange sounds are emitted from the monitor speakers, even when the monitor is asleep or off.
- There is no sound from the AppleVision speakers.
- The screen goes black and will not reappear.
- A variety of other minor symptoms occur, as described below.

Causes:

Most problems are caused either by improper installation of the AppleVision software or by a hardware problem with the monitor itself. Other problems are not really problems at all, but are resolved either by setting the AppleVision software options correctly and/or by simply understanding certain limitations of the software and hardware, as described below.

What to do:

Installation Problems

Getting the right AppleVision software for your particular setup installed correctly has occasionally generated into something of a nightmare. For example, System 7.5 Update 2.0, the first update used to upgrade Macs to System 7.5.3, commonly made all sorts of mistakes during installation. The AppleVision extension would be incorrect or missing altogether; for PCI-based Macs, the Update would not install the updated AppleVision 1.0.4 extension except via an Easy Install—and then only if an older version of AppleVision was already present. Other problems cropped up especially with the Power Mac 7200, such as the Monitors & Sound control panel not getting installed by the Update. In addition, the SimpleSound program often did not get installed, and sometimes both Monitors & Sound and AppleVision Setup were erroneously installed in the same System Folder.

The result of all of these mix-ups were a host of symptoms, including brightness/contrast buttons on the monitor that would not work (you would instead get an error message that said "No AppleVision display is connected"), an inability to change the monitor's resolution (only a single default resolution was available), or missing monitor-related software. To remedy all of this, you need to adopt one of the following methods.

Clean reinstall method (pre-System 7.5.3) You could avoid most of these problems by doing a clean reinstall of System 7.5 or 7.5.2, installing the AppleVision software, and then updating to 7.5.3 via an Easy Install of System 7.5 Update 2.0. If files are still incorrect or missing, a subsequent Custom Install may be required.

System 7.5.3 Unity method Alternatively, at least on PCI-based Macs, simply installing the "Unity" version of System 7.5.3 may be sufficient to get the needed AppleVision software. Since new Macs come with System 7.5.3 or later already installed, you may need to take no further action here.

SEE • **Chapter 13 for more details on the different variations of System 7.5.3 and related matters**

AppleVision Fix utility method Finally, because all of this *is* as much of an incredible hassle as it sounds, Apple released a disk called AppleVision Fix. If you run this after installing any version of System 7.5 (especially System 7.5.3 via System 7.5 Update 2.0), it should sort things out and make sure that the correct files are where they should be. For example, on a Power Mac 7200, it should make sure that the Monitors & Sound control panel gets installed, rather than the separate Monitors and Sound control panels.

On the down side, there is a chance that AppleVision Fix will not install at all if you are running the Unity version of System 7.5.3 (or any later system software version). Instead, it may claim that you already have the "fix"—sometimes correctly (that is, you do in fact already have all needed files), but sometimes not.

Even if you run AppleVision Fix and it appears to install successfully, your problems may not be over. For example, for PCI-based Macs, you may find copies of AppleVision Setup and Display Enabler in your System Folder. If so, trash them. Otherwise, the new software won't work, and you may get a message that says "No AppleVision display is connected." On non-PCI-based Macs, if you previously installed Monitors & Sound by mistake, AppleVision Fix will not de-install it; you still need to do this yourself.

BY THE WAY ▶

EXACTLY WHAT IS FIXED BY APPLEVISION FIX?

If things go well, here's what you can expect AppleVision Fix 1.1 to do on your Macintosh.

- **PCI-based Macs** The Fix makes sure you have a host of needed files that you may be missing, including Monitors & Sound, AppleVision 1.0.4, and even the SimpleSound utility.
- **68040 Macs and non-PCI Power Macs** It makes sure you have Display Enabler 2.0.2 and AppleVision 1.0.2 installed.
- **All other Macs** No other Mac models need the AppleVision Fix.

If AppleVision software fails to load at all, check the ADB cables If the software fails to load on restart after you've installed it, make sure the keyboard is plugged into the 1710 monitor's ADB port, not the computer itself. Otherwise, the AppleVision software will not recognize that there is an AV-capable display attached, and the software will not load. (Of course, you also have to make sure that the monitor's ADB plug is plugged into the computer.)

If problems persist If you have installation-related problems even after an apparently correct installation, try zapping the PRAM and/or deleting the Display Preferences, Monitors & Sound (or Sound & Displays) Preferences, and Sound Preferences files. If you still have problems, contact Apple (1-800-SOS-APPL) or seek other outside help for the latest advice.

SEE: • Fix-It #11 on zapping the PRAM

Monitor Display and Sleep Problems

Monitor stays black and will not turn on when waking up from sleep or after recalibrating This problem may persist even after you've restarted the Macintosh. If so, here's what to do:

1. Try restarting a few times. Also, press the Power button on the front of the monitor to turn the monitor off and back on.
2. Unplug the monitor from the wall outlet and replug it after a few minutes. If it doesn't work the first time, try again. This may bring your monitor back to life.
3. Call 1-800-SOS-APPL and request the AppleVision Recovery disks. Follow the instructions that come with the disks. (Basically, you simply use one of the disks as a startup disk.) These disks are specifically designed to fix this problem; however, they are not guaranteed to fix it.
4. Zapping the PRAM or resetting the Cuda button (if you Mac has one) may help (as described in Fix-It #11).
5. You may have defective RAM; this is especially likely if the monitor's power indicator light comes on but the monitor stays dark. Try to check for this (as described in Fix-It #17).
6. If all of these steps fail, you probably have a hardware problem with the monitor itself. The monitor will need to be repaired or replaced.

Color recalibration request In the Color section of the AppleVision Setup or Monitors & Sound control panel, there is an option to recalibrate the color. Doing this may correct a variety of color-related problems. Run it a few times in a row, if needed.

From the Preferences section of this display, you can select whether or not you want to automatically recalibrate every two weeks. If you have it set to "ask before recalibrating," you will get an alert box when the two-week interval is up. This is normal.

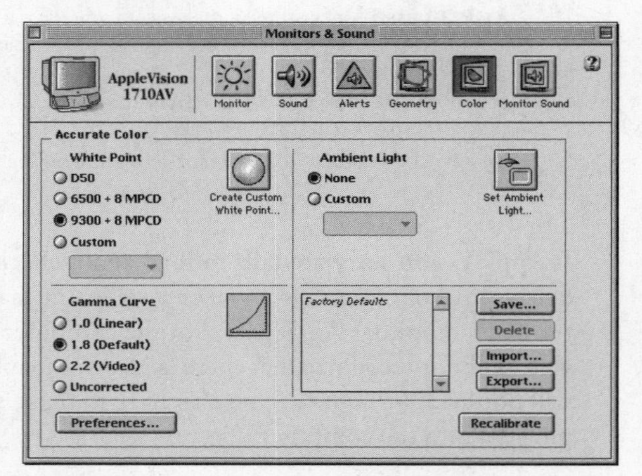

Figure 12-5 *The Color section of the Monitors & Sound control panel for a Mac with an AppleVision 1710AV attached.*

Note: Most non-professionals will be happy to leave the other Color settings (Accurate Color, Gamma Curve, and Ambient Light) at their default settings.

Screen "blinks" at startup The AppleVision Display Enabler in particular can cause the same sort of screen blinking at startup as previously described for PCI-based Macs in general (as mentioned in "Special Section: Troubleshooting PCI-based Macs"). This is normal; don't worry about it.

Only a 640 x 480 resolution is available Most often, your currently selected resolution will be something other than 640 x 480. Holding down the Shift key at startup, even though it disables most extensions, still preserves AppleVision 1710's current resolution setting. Using a startup manager to start up with "all" extensions off (which disables the key AppleVision extension—and Display Enabler, if present), however, results in a 640 x 480 resolution regardless of the current setting.

Similarly, if you start up with a CD-ROM startup disc, the 1710AV reverts to 640 x 480 resolution (unless you also hold down the Shift key at startup to turn extensions off). Oddly, though, if you use a startup floppy disk, the correct currently selected resolution is retained whether or not you start up with extensions off. A 640 x 480 resolution will also occur if you start up with the monitor off and turn it on only after the AppleVision extension has loaded.

Also, make sure you connected the ADB cable (as well as the standard monitor cable) from the 1710 to the Mac—it is not optional. Otherwise, you will probably get (again) only a 640 x 480 resolution; you will also be unable to recalibrate the monitor and will likely have other problems as well.

Finally, the AppleVision software will occasionally fail to load at startup for no discernible reason, resulting again in only a 640 x 480 resolution option. In this case, simply restarting gets everything back to normal until the next time it happens; no permanent cure is known at this time.

SEE: • "Installation Problems," previously in this section, for related information

Color depth options are missing There is an interaction between the monitor resolution and the color depth you select. Unless you have sufficient video RAM, the higher color depth options (Millions and sometimes even Thousands of colors) are no longer available at higher resolution. For example, with a 7500 and 2MB of VRAM, you are limited to 256 colors at the highest resolution.

This is normal, and it is true even for non-AppleVision monitors (as described in Chapter 10). Adding more VRAM is the main solution.

Lack of convergence Some users have reported problems with an excessive lack of convergence (blurriness) along the borders of the display. Adjusting the convergence controls in Monitors & Sound (or AppleVision Setup) cannot remedy the problem. This is a sign of hardware trouble, and you'll need to get the monitor replaced.

Diagonal lines in the display Many users have complained about barely noticeable diagonal lines that traverse across their AppleVision 1710 display (these are most visible when the screen is dark). According to Apple, this is not a defect in the monitor; they are caused by certain hardware inside the monitor resetting itself. You can usually get rid of these lines by turning down your brightness to about 50 percent and leaving contrast at 100 percent—Apple, in fact, recommends these settings as a general rule for all AppleVision monitors. If this doesn't work, recalibrating the monitor will probably do the trick, although you may have to recalibrate a few times before the lines go away. If the trouble persists, you may indeed have a hardware problem, especially if your screen has other irregular discolorations.

Energy Saver and Sleep There are a variety of problems related to the Energy Saver program, especially the version of it that comes with PCI-based Macs and particularly in regard to sleep (such as the Mac not going to sleep when it should, or going to sleep when it should not). While these problems can affect a variety of monitors, AppleVision monitors are at the top of the list.

If you have any problems with Energy Saver, my first advice is to set the slider for putting the Mac to sleep to "Never," then restart. You can then disable the Energy Saver Extension (although there are reports that leaving it enabled results in fewer problems).

SEE: • "Sleep and Energy Saver Problems," in the "PCI-Based Macintosh Quick Fixes" section earlier in this chapter, for more information on Energy Saver and sleep

Sound Problems

Chronic "blipping" sound from AppleVision speakers when monitor is asleep If you ever hear a blipping sound from the monitor's speakers after the monitor goes to sleep, here's what to do:

1. Set the "Put the system to sleep ..." setting in the Energy Saver control panel to "Never," then do not put the monitor to sleep again by *any* method. Otherwise, you may find that, after going to sleep, your monitor never wakes up again. Apple has admitted that the sound (which is caused by the monitor repeatedly turning on and off very rapidly) can signal imminent permanent damage to the monitor. Apparently, this is a hardware problem with early units of the monitor that Apple has since corrected.
2. Contact Apple at 1-800-SOS-APPL. You should be eligible for a replacement monitor.

Chronic "blipping" sound from AppleVision speakers when monitor is off or at any other time Unplugging the monitor from the wall outlet for a minute or two usually clears this up. It again probably indicates a hardware problem, so you should call 1-800-SOS-APPL for help.

Startup chimes are not heard You probably won't ever hear the Mac's startup chimes with a 1710AV monitor attached to your Mac. This is because the computer's internal speakers are automatically muted when the 1710AV is attached, and the monitor doesn't turn on—or doesn't turn back on after a warm restart—until after the chime has occurred (so you don't hear it through the monitor's speakers either).

This is all related to a special energy-saving feature that causes these monitors to shut down completely whenever the signal from the computer to the monitor is absent (even for the second or so after you select Restart).

Microphone problems With Power Macs, if you have problems using a PlainTalk microphone connected to the AppleVision's microphone port, connect the microphone to the port on the computer instead.

Other sound problems Many sound problems (such as no sound from speakers) are not really problems at all. Instead, they suggest improper adjustments of the admittedly confusing array of sound volume options available in the Monitors & Sound (and/or related) control panels. Some general discussion of this can be found in Chapter 6 ("Technically Speaking: A Few Words About Sound and Sound Files"). Otherwise, check the Apple Guide help for the control panel in question.

Miscellany

Desktop icons are rearranged At startup, icons on the desktop may get rearranged in alphabetical order on the right side of the screen (as if you had selected "Clean up all" from the Special menu). Otherwise, if you have left a Finder window open, icons in that window may get rearranged. This is due to a bug in some versions of the AppleVision software. If this happens to you, leave an empty Finder window open so that it (rather than the desktop) is the affected "window" at startup.

Buttons on the monitor do not work If the buttons on the monitor (especially the ones that adjust sound, brightness, and contrast) do not work, make sure the software was correctly installed (as described in "Installation Problems," earlier in this section). If it was, simply restarting the Macintosh often fixes this problem. Also note that you can disable the contrast and brightness buttons from the Monitors & Sound control panel (select the Preferences button of the Color dialog box to see this "lock out" option).

Otherwise The AppleVision 1710/1710AV has been plagued with more hardware-related problems than any other Apple monitor in history. If you have any sort of problem not covered here, call 1-800-SOS-APPL for help and advice; you may qualify for a free monitor repair or replacement. Whether future AppleVision monitors (such as the newer 20-inch AppleVision monitor) improve on this record remains to be seen.

Chapter 13

Mac OS System 7.5/7.6 and Beyond

System 7.5/7.6 Basics 542

Why This Chapter? 542

Apple's Mac OS Release Strategy 542

Getting Help from Apple 543

"Read Me" Files 543

Apple Guide and Balloon Help 543

Online Help 544

Solve It! System 7.5/7.6 Problems 544

Installation Problems 545

System Software on CD-ROM Disc 545

Installing with a Non-Apple CD-ROM Drive 546

Step-by-Step, Hassle-Free Installation 548

Custom Install System Software Options. 552

Compatibility and Memory Problems 554

What About Enabler and Update Files? 554

Are Extensions and Control Panels Installed (or Deinstalled) as Needed? 555

Delete Preferences Files 558

Are Your Applications "Capable," "Savvy," or Not? 558

Audio and Video Problems 558

Memory Problems 559

System 7.5.5-Specific Memory Problems 560

Apple Guide Does Not Work 562

Apple Guide Not Installed or Not Enabled 562

Incorrect Location of Apple Guide Documents 562

Third-Party Conflicts and Macintosh Guide. 563

Problem with Apple Guide Additions Is Fixed 563

OpenDoc and Live Objects 564
What Is OpenDoc? 564
Is It a Container? 564
Editors, Viewers, and Stationery 565
OpenDoc Software: What Goes Where? 566
Installing and Using OpenDoc 567
The Documents and Edit Menus 568
Combining Parts 570
Missing Editors and Orphaned Parts 570
Wrapping It Up 571

QuickDraw GX 572
Installing and Using QuickDraw GX 572
QuickDraw GX and Printing 573
QuickDraw GX-Specific Printer Drivers 573
QuickDraw GX and the Chooser 573
Select to Print a Document 575
Respond to Error Messages, If Any Appear 577
QuickDraw GX Page Setup and Print Dialog Boxes 577
The Printing Menu 579
The Print Queue Window 580
Special Case: Portable Digital Documents (PDDs) 581
QuickDraw GX and Fonts 583
Bitmapped Fonts 583
TrueType Fonts 583
PostScript Fonts 584
QuickDraw GX and Graphics 588

Solve It! QuickDraw GX Problems 589
Memory Problems 589
Problems Running with Only 8MB of Memory 589
Memory Problems Caused By Inactive Desktop Printers 590
Printing and Printing-Related Problems 590
QuickDraw GX Features Are Missing 590
Printing Fails 591
"SimpleText Cannot Display This Document" Message 594
Desktop Printer-Related System Crashes Due to a Locked System File 594
You Cannot Delete or Move a Desktop Printer File 594
Font Problems 595
Make Sure Any PostScript Fonts You Use in QuickDraw GX Have Been Enabled 595
Text Displays in Incorrect Font or Style, Displays with Jaggies, or a System Crash Occurs When Using a Specific Font 595

On the Horizon 596
Software 596
Mac OS 7 597
Rhapsody 597
BeOS 597
Hardware 597

System 7.5/7.6 Basics

Why This Chapter?

When the second edition of *Sad Macs* was published, System 7.5 was still relatively new. The point of this chapter then was to introduce you to the new features (and new problems) specific to this system. By now, I expect that most readers of this book are using some version of System 7.5, and information about this system software has been integrated throughout the rest of the remaining chapters. It may seem, therefore, that a separate chapter on System 7.5 is no longer needed.

Since the publication of the last edition of this book, however, System 7.5 has become an entire family of system software versions: System 7.5.1, System 7.5.2, System 7.5.3, System 7.5.3 Revision 2, and System 7.5.5. And now Mac OS 7.6 is upon us.

The purpose of this chapter, then, is to help you understand these different variations, what version(s) you can use, and how to get everything to work properly.

This chapter also introduces coverage of OpenDoc, a new technology from Apple that (if it is successful) represents a major change in how applications and documents work together. OpenDoc is not covered elsewhere in this book.

This chapter also retains and updates the coverage of QuickDraw GX, as first included in the second edition. If you haven't tried QuickDraw GX yet, you may want to give it a spin. Current statements from Apple claim that it will eventually be a required part of the Mac operating system.

Speaking of the future, the last part of this chapter offers a preview of some of the features that you can expect to see in the Mac OS of the not-too-distant future.

Apple's Mac OS Release Strategy

At one point, it all seemed very clear and simple: Apple would release a substantial upgrade of its system software (such as System 7.5) from time to time. These upgrades would be called *reference releases* because they combined and included all new and existing current system software. It might then release one or two updates (such as System 7.5 Update 1.0), largely for the purpose of fixing bugs. These *update releases* could only be installed on top of the most recent reference release; you could not create a functional System Folder just from an update release. The whole cycle would then start over with the next reference release.

The next (and eagerly anticipated) reference release was supposed to be Mac OS 8 (also known as Copland), but it got derailed somewhere along the way. Instead, we now have Apple's new system software release strategy: a new reference release every six months (with a change in version number, usually in the digit after the first decimal) and an update release (with a change in the digit after the second decimal) at the three-month interval between reference releases. In other words, you can expect to see some significant system software upgrade four times per year.

Added to this, Apple is concurrently developing updates to System 7 as well as working on an entirely new OS (code named "Rhapsody" and based on its recently acquired NeXT OS.

Apple can always change its mind about all of this—and there is certainly a precedent for it doing so. For now, though, we are faced with a near-constant arrival of incremental changes in the system software.

Whatever benefits this approach may have (for example, getting new features as soon as they are ready rather than waiting for some future mega-release), it makes troubleshooting more difficult. For starters, with more and more variations of the system software around, there is a rapidly decreasing chance that most users have the same basic system software configuration. And with change occurring at such a frequent rate, keeping one's troubleshooting knowledge current is more difficult than ever. For a book like this, it also means that whatever I write will probably become obsolete even sooner! Alas, there is nothing I can do about this—except to do the best I can.

Getting Help from Apple

No matter what version of System 7.5 (or later) you are using, there are two important sources of information that you should check out for troubleshooting assistance:

"Read Me" Files

"Read Me" files have always been included with system software disks, but they are especially relevant here. System 7.5.3 and Mac OS 7.6, for example, come with an entire collection of "Read Me" files, that explain what all of the control panels and extensions in your System Folder do, what files have been dropped from or added to this new version, what bugs have been fixed, what known problems remain, and tips on how to install the software. Taking some time to at least browse through this material can save you a lot of grief.

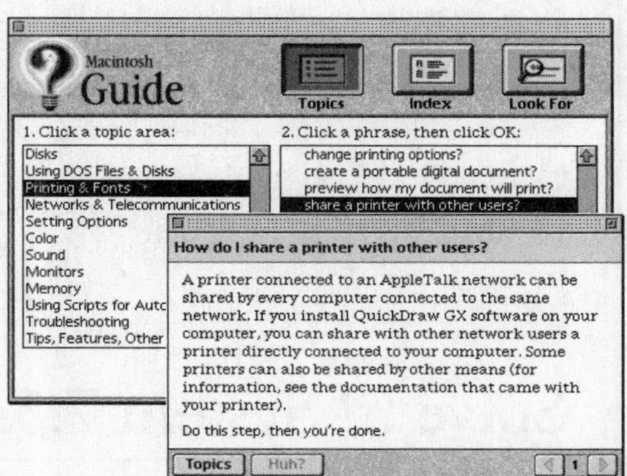

Figure 13-1 *Apple Guide*

Apple Guide and Balloon Help

These days, the written documentation that comes with your system software tends to be woefully incomplete. This is apparently part of a deliberate strategy on Apple's part to shift the burden of documenting its software to its computer-based help, notably Balloon Help and (especially) Apple Guide. You should be able to get answers to most of your questions from these sources. To access the main Apple Guide listing, go to the Finder and select Macintosh Guide from the Guide menu (formerly called the Balloon Help menu). For some programs, there are separate application-specific Apple Guide files. These files are accessible from the Guide menu only when the relevant application is active.

By the way, Apple Guide 2.0 or later works with all versions of System 7 (that is, from 7.0 to the present version).

Newer versions of Apple Guide, as yet unreleased, promise to be even better. Not only will they show you what to do, they will actually do it for you!

The easy accessibility and interactive nature of Apple Guide can make it preferable to printed documentation in many situations. Still, there are times that I would prefer printed material, primarily because many of Apple Guide's explanations require that you actually carry out an operation in order to find out how to do it. If you just want to learn about something without actually doing it, Apple Guide can be frustrating. It is also quite slow.

Perhaps, though, I shouldn't complain too much. It is just this sort of thing that encourages people to seek out books like this one!

SEE: • **Chapter 1 for background on Apple Guide and Balloon Help**

Online Help

More and more of Apple's software support is being moved to the World Wide Web. Apple has numerous sites that include technical documentation, Q & A files, and more. I describe these in more detail in Fix-It #18.

BY THE WAY ▶

"SECRET" SYSTEM 7 FEATURES

Apple has completely hidden some helpful features of the Finder in System 7.5 and its revisions. The code for these additions is included in the Finder file (starting at least in System 7.5.3), but Apple has the code "turned off" so you can't use them, for reasons that remain a bit mysterious. What are these hidden gems?

- A Reveal Original (Command-R) command, in the Finder's File menu, takes you directly to the original file of a selected alias (bypassing the need to access the Find Original button in Get Info windows).
- If you drag a file icon out of its folder while holding down the Control key, you automatically create an alias of the file.
- Selecting a file and then pressing Command-Delete automatically moves the file to the Trash.

Fortunately, there is an easy way to enable these hidden features by installing one of several freeware utilities. Two popular ones are Hidden Finder Features and Finder Extensions Enabler.

Solve It! System 7.5/7.6 Problems

This section covers problems specific to System 7.5 and beyond. For example, while Fix-It #5 covers general issues about installing system software, this section covers a variety of issues specific to installing the different variations of System 7.5.

If you don't find what you are looking for here, check out the appropriate sections of the rest of this book (such as Chapter 7 for a printing problem).

Installation Problems

Symptoms:

The primary symptom is that you are unable to install System 7.5 or one of its revisions successfully. Related problems that immediately result from a System 7.5 installation are also considered. Mac OS 7.6 issues are also noted.

Causes:

Most of the causes are related to the increased complexity and variety of the software and hardware. As a result, it's almost impossible for a single Installer to easily install the correct software on every Mac.

Other problems appear to be due to corrupted software, software conflicts, and some mysterious causes that are as yet undetermined.

SEE: • Fix-It #5 for more on the basics of a clean install of the system software and related problems

BY THE WAY ▶

REVISION 2 ODDITY

The System 7.5.3 Revision 2 update was mainly needed for PCI-based Macs and a few PowerBook models running System 7.5.3. Oddly, it also contained some minor updates for all PowerBook models, even if they were running earlier versions of System 7.5. Among other things, it fixed a problem with Type 8 errors that occurred when a PowerBook woke up from sleep with RAM Doubler installed.

If you have the Unity version of System 7.5.3, don't worry about this Revision 2, since it is already built into the software. In contrast, upgrading to System 7.5.5 is advised for *all* Macs running System 7.5.3.

What to do:

System Software on CD-ROM Disc

Since most Macs now have CD-ROM drives, the primary way that Apple distributes its system software is on a CD-ROM disc. You can directly install the software from these discs.

The CD-ROM disc also contains disk images of floppy disks containing the system software. You can use these to create a backup set of floppy disks, if desired, by Disk Copy (see Fix-It #5, "Take Note: Why Can't I Open the Software I Just Downloaded?").

In some cases, you may want to start up from the CD-ROM disc. Depending upon the CD-ROM disc and the Mac you have, you may be able to do this (usually you need to hold down the "C" key at startup with the CD-ROM disc already inserted to do this). Otherwise, you can always start up with the Disk Tools floppy disk; if one was not included with the system software, you can make one from the disk image on the CD-ROM disc.

SEE: • Chapter 5 for more details on using a CD-ROM disc as a startup disk

TAKE NOTE ▶

SYSTEM 7.5/7.6 CONFUSION: UPDATES, REVISIONS, AND UNITY

Apple, which is now up to System 7.6 and beyond, has promised that the naming of updates will be simplified and the variations within each version eliminated. Let's hope so, because the confusion started by System 7.5.3 has left many users disgruntled. I'll provide a brief overview here.

First came System 7.5, followed by System 7.5.1 (which you got by updating via the System 7.5 Update 1.0 software) and System 7.5.2 (which could only be used by PCI-based Macs, such as the 7500 and 8500). Then came System 7.5.3 (for all Macs), and the fun really began.

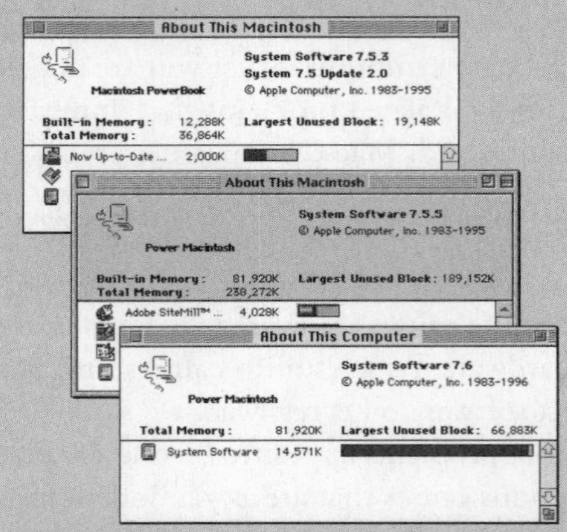

Figure 13-2 *Top: About This Macintosh, System 7.5.3 (System 7.5 Update 2.0 variation). Middle: About This Macintosh, System 7.5.5 (with the Mac OS 8 look via the Aaron extension). Bottom: About This Computer, System 7.6.*

The first way to get to System 7.5.3 was with System 7.5 Update 2.0 (a naming convention that is already confusing), which was available on one CD-ROM disc or on a set of 14 floppy disks. This update could not be used to do a clean install of System 7.5.3; it could only update existing systems (which turned out to be a hassle when various installation problems occurred). Further, it resulted in two slightly different System 7.5.3 versions (using different Update files), depending upon whether you had a PCI-based Mac (updating from System 7.5.2) or any other Mac (updating from System 7.5.1 or System 7.5).

Next Apple started shipping an installed version of System 7.5.3 (with a CD that *could* do a clean install of the system software) on its newly released PCI-based Macs. This was called "System 7.5.3 (PCI-only)."

Then Apple released a small update, primarily to fix bugs, that bumped the software up to System 7.5.3 Revision 2 (and again, exactly what Update file it installed varied based on whether you had a PCI-based Mac). There was some confusion as to whether users of System 7.5.3 (PCI-only) should also install this Revision 2 update. The consensus was that they should, but apparently some fixes included in System 7.5 Update 2.0 were missing from System 7.5.3 (PCI-only) even after users added Revision 2 (for instance, the latest versions of Apple Menu Options and Apple Video Player). This led some people to first install System 7.5 Update 2.0 over the preinstalled System 7.5.3, then add Revision 2 ... are you still following all of this?

(Continued) ▶

Installing with a Non-Apple CD-ROM Drive

If you are installing system software from a CD-ROM disc onto an Apple-brand Macintosh and you do not have an Apple CD-ROM drive, be careful. Normally you would use your hard disk as a startup disk prior to installation. If the installation fails for any reason, however, and you can't boot from the CD-ROM disc itself, you may have to resort to the Disk Tools disk to start up again. If you have an Apple CD-ROM drive, there is no problem, since the CD-ROM driver extension (which is needed to get the Mac to recognize the CD-ROM drive) is included on the Disk Tools disk. If you have a non-Apple drive, however, you may now find that you can no longer access the CD-ROM disc. This would happen if the drive requires its own CD-ROM

▶ TAKE NOTE ▶

SYSTEM 7.5/7.6 CONFUSION: UPDATES, REVISIONS, AND UNITY *(Continued)*

Next, Apple started shipping some Macs with System 7.5.3 Revision 2 already installed.

At last, Apple shipped a single version of System 7.5.3 that worked with all Macs and included all of the updates (including Revision 2). Usually referred to as the Unity version of System 7.5.3, it was available as a commercial product and could be used to do a clean install of the software. It also included two Disk Tools disks, one for people that needed Apple HD SC Setup and another for people that needed Drive Setup (as explained more in Fix-It #15).

Using this Unity version assured that you had all of the updates included in the previous versions. The bad news, however, was that newer versions of some included files, such as Drive Setup 1.0.5 and QuickTime 2.5, were already available separately online even before Unity was released. In contrast, Unity (unlike System 7.5 Update 2.0) was not free, and it was not available online.

System 7.5.3 Unity was only out for a few months when System 7.5.5 arrived, followed three months later by Mac OS 7.6. And so it goes.

Also note that version numbers with an "L" at the end (such as System 7.5.3L) are ones that ship with Mac clones.

Just in case you don't know, you can find the name of the system software you're using listed in the About This Macintosh window. Here's what the names mean:

- **System 7.5.3; System 7.5 Update 2.0:** You are running a Macintosh that was updated to System 7.5.3 by System 7.5 Update 2.0.
- **System 7.5.3:** You are running a Mac that came pre-installed with a special PCI-only version of System 7.5.3 (such as a Power Mac 7600).
- **System 7.5.3; Updated to Revision 2:** You are running any of the above configurations, after having additionally installed System 7.5.3 Revision 2.
- **System 7.5.3; Revision 2:** You have a Mac (such as a 5400) that came with Revision 2 pre-installed, or you have the Unity version of the software.
- **System 7.5.3; Revision 2.1:** You have a version that came pre-installed on Performa 6400s and perhaps some other models released about that time (summer 1996).
- **System 7.5.3; Revision 2.2:** You have a version that came pre-installed on the Power Mac 9500/200 and the Performa 6360.
- **System 7.5.5:** You have moved beyond System 7.5.3 (congratulations!). System 7.5.5 can be installed over any version of System 7.5.3 and includes all of the fixes in the Revision 2 update.
- **Mac OS 7.6:** Actually, you know you have at least Mac OS 7.6 even before you open the window, because "About this Macintosh" has been changed to "About This Computer"! Note: Apple now refers to its system software as "Mac OS 7.6," rather than "System 7.6." For convenience, I still use both terms in this book.

driver, which of course is not found on the Disk Tools disk. Since you can't access the CD-ROM disc anymore, you can't try again to install system software.

This is one situation where a backup set of floppy disks would be useful. Otherwise, you'll need to create a startup floppy disk that includes the needed CD-ROM driver extension. One way to do this is to delete the Apple CD-ROM extension from the Disk Tools disk and replace it with the driver for your non-Apple CD-ROM.

Mac clones, such as those from Power Computing, come with their own custom CD-ROM system software discs, thereby bypassing this problem.

SEE: • Chapter 5 and Fix-It #16 for more on CD-ROM drivers

Step-by-Step, Hassle-Free Installation

Starting with System 7.5.3, just getting new system software to install successfully became more and more of a hassle. The following guidelines should help you avoid most problems. Note that starting in Mac OS 7.6, there is a new Install Mac OS utility that helps you walk through some of this. This, and more general information about installing system software, is covered more in Fix-It #5.

1. Before you even get started, make sure you have enough memory to support the software (especially if you are upgrading from a pre-System 7.5 version). You need at least 8MB (and, on a Power Mac, more like 16MB) to adequately run this software. Without sufficient RAM, the Installer will not even permit the installation to take place, giving you an alert message that informs you of the memory problem.

   Also, make sure you have enough free disk space to hold the software. If you plan to install such extras as QuickDraw GX, you will need even more memory and disk space.

2. In case you run into trouble later on, it pays to back up your System Folder (for example, to a removable cartridge) before updating. That way, if problems occur, you can always easily return to your original System Folder. At the very least, have backups of your System, Finder, and Update files.

   Remember, not all Installers have a Custom Remove option. And even if they do, they only remove new files; they don't typically restore the previous files.

   Actually, if it's practical, you should back up your entire hard drive just before an installation. You won't likely need to restore every file, but better safe than sorry.

3. It is recommended, but not required, that you zap the PRAM before installing the new system software. Try it again after installing the software if problems persist. (Note that with PCI-based Macs, there are new procedures for doing this.)

   SEE: • **Fix-It #11 on zapping the PRAM**

4. If you use Apple HD SC Setup or Drive Setup, update your driver with any newer version that may have been included with the system software. Be sure to use the right utility for your Mac model.

   SEE: • **Fix-Its #12 and #15 for more on these utilities**

5. Run Disk First Aid to check for possible Directory damage.

   SEE: • **Fix-It #10 for more on Disk First Aid**

6. Turn off any security protection before installing an upgrade. For example, if you use At Ease, turn it off. Similarly, turn off any virus protection software (see next item for more general advice on turning off extensions).

   Also, make sure that you do not have the System or Finder (or any other critical) files locked, either via the Lock box in the Get Info window or by selecting Protect System Folder in the General Controls control panel. If you do, when you try to install the new software you will get an error message saying that you are prohibited from modifying the System file.

7. If you are planning on doing an Easy Install, Apple recommends that you do it with Apple Extensions on (you can do this most easily by using Apple's Extensions Manager to enable only System 7.5 extensions). I have not found this to be necessary, but it is good advice—if you choose not to follow it, start up with all extensions off as an alternative.

   Make sure that optional software that you expect to be updated is present before you run the Installer; a good example of this is AppleVision software (if you have an AppleVision monitor). This is especially important for system software updates such as System 7.5.5, which generally do not install optional software unless they find an older version already in your System Folder.

   Also, make sure you have not changed the name of any Apple extensions. The Installer may not recognize the extension under a different name, and therefore it may not update the file.

   Note: Current versions of the Installer correctly check for and update extensions and control panels whether or not they have been disabled. For example, if an extension to be updated is in the "Extensions (Disabled)" folder, the updated version will be there after the installation is over. This was not true in previous versions of the system software, so it should matter less now whether your extensions are enabled or disabled.

8. Launch the Installer; select Easy Install in most cases. If you are lucky, all will go well at this point.

9. If an Easy Install does not work, or you just want to be cautious right from the start, try a clean reinstall. For an update release, this means going back and reinstalling the previous reference release, followed by an installation of the update. If you try to do a clean install from an update, an error message will inform you that you cannot do it.

   When you are doing a clean reinstall, it is obviously preferred (and sometimes required) to start up from an alternate startup disk. You may then try a quasi-clean install by simply deleting the System, Finder, and any Enabler/Update files from your existing System Folder and selecting Easy Install. Otherwise, you may do a true clean Install by holding down Command-Shift-K after the Installer has launched and selecting the clean install option. The latter option only works if you already have a System Folder on your disk. (Of course, if you do not have one, then an Easy Install accomplishes the same goal.)

   Ideally, you should have the Installer software on a separate disk/volume than the one that is the destination for the system software.

   By the way, with a clean reinstall, you may lose various customized settings such as your current TCP settings (if you do the update without a clean install, these are preserved). Taking a screen snapshot (Command-Shift-3) of your customized control panel settings before updating will help you out if you need to re-enter these values.

   Also note that after doing a clean install, you will want to return various third-party software to your active System Folder. Be cautious, since some older software may not be compatible with the update. Also, do not accidentally replace updated Apple software with older versions that you drag back.

SEE: • Fix-It #5 for more on doing a clean reinstall and/or a Custom Install

BY THE WAY ▶

DO NOT INSTALL SYSTEM SOFTWARE ON A POWERBOOK IN SCSI MODE

If you connect your PowerBook to another Mac via its SCSI mode option (as described in Chapter 11), do not try an Easy Install or "for this Macintosh" install of system software to the PowerBook. If you do, it will install the software needed for the Mac that the PowerBook is connected to, not the PowerBook itself.

10. Various files may get installed that you had previously deleted; if you still don't want them, remember to delete them again. For example, I do not like Macintosh Easy Open (or Mac OS Easy Open, as it is now called), so I always delete it when I see it reappear. I also delete Apple Menu Options and Extensions Manager, using Now Menus and Conflict Catcher instead.
11. Remember, these Installers are not perfect. Even if you have done everything correctly, they may omit files that should have been installed. Especially if you are doing an Easy Install, the Installer may fail to update files already on your disk to a newer version or it may fail to install files for which you do not currently have an older version already installed. If you discover this to be the case (usually carefully reading the "Read Me" files or checking online sources of information will clue you in to these problems), you can usually solve the problem by going back and doing a Custom Install of the missing features.

    Sometimes, even this is not enough. One prominent example is with AppleVision software, where the situation got so messy that Apple released a separate utility, called AppleVision Fix, to try to sort things out. (This is covered more in the section on AppleVision monitors in Chapter 12.) There was also a case where the Installer mistakenly warned you that you were about to install an older version of Apple Video Player, when actually it was a newer version.

    A final note: Some non-system software may have to be separately reinstalled after you install the system software, especially if the software had modified your System file. Such modifications may get wiped out during a system software installation, requiring the reinstallation of the separate software to get the modifications back. There is no sure way to know which programs do this. Typically, you discover the problem when the software no longer works.
12. You may find new and strange extensions in your Extensions folder. For instance, you are installing Open Transport networking and communications software for the first time, it will certainly install a new collection of extensions with names like OpenTransportLib. Actually, the move to Open Transport is handled differently in various Macintosh models; these matters are complex enough that I cover them separately in Chapter 14.

    In general, don't assume that unfamiliar extensions can be deleted, since many of these are essential to the use of your system software. Delete nothing unless you are sure it is safe to do so; otherwise, you may later find that some feature of your software no longer works.

If you are installing other optional system software that requires a separate Installer, such as QuickDraw GX, do so now. In Mac OS 7.6, the new Install Mac OS utility helps automate this process.

TAKE NOTE ▶

PROBLEMS GETTING STARTED WITH SYSTEM 7.5.5 AND BEYOND

System 7.5.5 introduced no new interface features; it simply fixed bugs and added several performance enhancements, especially involving virtual memory. It also deleted a few files from System 7.5.3 that were no longer needed (most notably the System 7.5.*x* Update file). Your System file will be a bit larger after updating, though, because the Installer decompresses some of the System file's previously compressed resources (in order to help speed things up).

The biggest problem with System 7.5.5 has turned out to be getting it to install successfully. First off, because it is an update instead of a reference release, you can only install it over an existing System 7.5.3 System Folder. Doing a clean install requires starting over with System 7.5.3. Also note that a few models (notably the PowerBook 1400 and Motorola's Mac clones) cannot run System 7.5.5 at all.

If you follow the general guidelines in the main text of this section, you will usually be okay. If things do not go as planned, however, check out this section for additional advice. Although you may have moved on to System 7.6 or later by now, I'd still advise looking all of this over, since many of these problems are likely to be relevant to future upgrades.

- **Energy Saver 1.*x* glitch** There are two different versions of the Energy Saver control panel: version 2.*x* is used for PCI-based Macs, while version 1.*x* is used for most other Macs. If you have version 1.*x*, remove it from your System Folder before running System 7.5.5. The Installer only updates version 2.*x* and will incorrectly try to update version 1.*x* if it finds it there.
- **"Cannot copy the file 'System' Please delete this file and try again."** If you get this message when trying to install System 7.5.5, start over with a clean reinstall of System 7.5.3. Otherwise, deleting third-party sounds from your System file may help. Having the Installer on a separate disk from your startup disk also seems to help, especially if the separate disk has a lot of unused space.
- **"Installation has been canceled, leaving your disk untouched."** If you get this message when trying to install System 7.5.5, try the same solutions as described in the previous item. Some reports, however, have said that this could be due to corrupted Installer software. Assuming you downloaded the software, try to download it again.
- **"Need System 7.5.3"** If you get a message that says you cannot install unless you have System 7.5.3, even though you are running System 7.5.3, make sure the System 7.5 Update file has not been renamed. If the name is okay, and you still have this problem, you probably need to do a clean reinstall.
- **54xx/64xx Update** If you find a file with this name in your System Folder, and you are not using a 54xx/64xx model of Macintosh, delete the file. It is only needed on those Macs.
- **Freezes on startup** If a system freeze occurs at startup after you update to System 7.5.5, start up from an Emergency Toolkit disk and delete the Finder Preferences file. This should eliminate the freeze.
- **Just weird: AppleTalk and Virtual Memory "gone"** There have been occasional reports of an inability to get AppleTalk to be active, and of the Virtual Memory section of the Memory control panel disappearing, following an installation of System 7.5.5. Once again, a clean install is the most popular solution; for the AppleTalk problem, simply reinstalling the latest version of Open Transport may work. Otherwise, see outside help for these problems.

Custom Install System Software Options

If you select Custom Install and then click the triangle next to "System Software," you will typically see several additional sub-options (at least you will if you are working with a reference release). Exactly what sub-options you see varies among the different system software Installers, but they should resemble the following list.

System Software for This Macintosh This option installs essentially the same main system software as an Easy Install—in other words, only those resources needed for your particular Mac model.

Minimal System Software for This Macintosh Originally designed to install a set of system software small enough to fit on a floppy disk, in most recent Installers even this minimal installation is too big for a floppy (the Minimal option on the System 7.5.3 Unity Installer is a notable exception). If a floppy install is what you want, the main alternative—as explained in Chapter 2—is to copy the System Folder from the Disk Tools disk.

This option is gone in Mac OS 7.6.

Minimal System Software for Any Macintosh This install option will not fit on a floppy disk; I am not sure why it is even needed. If you are using something like a Zip cartridge, you might as well install the full Universal System, which is described next.

Universal System for Any Macintosh This option installs a set of software that should work on any Macintosh model. This system software would be useful on a removable cartridge, for example, that you could use for troubleshooting in an environment with many different Mac models.

BY THE WAY ▶

PROBLEMS DOING A UNIVERSAL INSTALL

Doing a universal install from System 7.5 Update 2.0 presents a problem. Since this basic problem also occurs in other situations, I will explain it in detail here.

To create a Universal System Folder with Update 2.0, you must start with System 7.5, not System 7.5.1 or 7.5.2. This in turn requires you to do a clean reinstall of System 7.5 using the universal "for any Macintosh" option, and then install the Universal System Folder option in the Update 2.0 Installer.

This presents a real "catch-22" for PCI-based Mac users, however, since the System 7.5 Installer won't launch on these machines. Instead, you get an error message to the effect that the Installer script does not recognize your hardware—which makes sense, since the PCI-based Macs came out after System 7.5 and require at least System 7.5.2.

Happily, you can get around this by holding down the Option key when you launch the Installer. This takes you directly to the Custom Install view and lets you select the desired "For Any Macintosh" option. The only other solution is to perform the installation on an older Mac model that does let you install 7.5.

The "Installing This Update" file that comes with the Update gives more detailed step-by-step instructions for a universal installation.

Using the Unity version of System 7.5.3 eliminates all of these hassles.

Note that if you choose this option, you will get items installed that are not needed for your particular Mac model, even though you have not specifically selected them from the other Custom Install listings. That is why I recommend not installing a universal system on your startup drive.

Note that in the Mac OS 7.6 listing of these options, "Macintosh" has been replaced by "computer" or "supported computer."

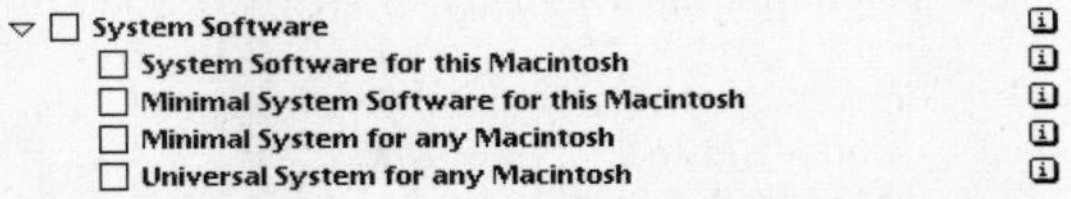

▽ ☐ System Software
- ☐ System Software for this Macintosh
- ☐ Minimal System Software for this Macintosh
- ☐ Minimal System for any Macintosh
- ☐ Universal System for any Macintosh

Figure 13-3 *Custom Install System Software options for System 7.5.3.*

BY THE WAY ▶

IF YOU CAN'T ACCESS SYSTEM 7.5 UPDATE 2.0 CD AFTER INSTALLING SYSTEM 7.5.5

If you launch the Installer from the System 7.5 Update 2.0 CD after installing System 7.5.5, you will not be able to access anything. Even the trick of holding down the Option key when you launch the Installer (described in "By The Way: Problems Doing a Universal Install") will not work. The reason here is that the Installer is designed not to work unless it sees certain versions of the system software present, and System 7.5.5 is not one of those versions.

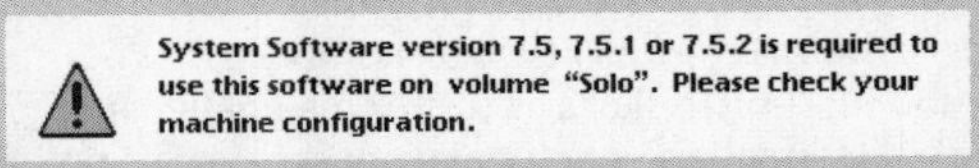

System Software version 7.5, 7.5.1 or 7.5.2 is required to use this software on volume "Solo". Please check your machine configuration.

Figure 13-4 *The message you will get from the Installer when trying to run System 7.5.3 Update 2.0 after System 7.5.5 or later is installed.*

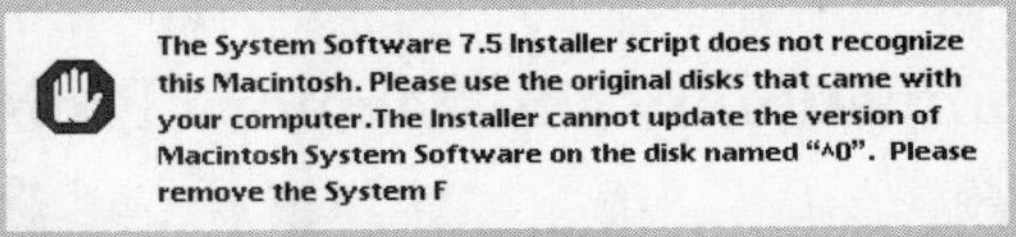

The System Software 7.5 Installer script does not recognize this Macintosh. Please use the original disks that came with your computer.The Installer cannot update the version of Macintosh System Software on the disk named "^0". Please remove the System F

Figure 13-5 *One of several other error messages you may get from the Installer when it doesn't like what you are trying to do; various solutions are covered in the text.*

This can be a problem if you want to access the Custom Install list to install an item. One solution is to get the "Unity" CD for System 7.5.3, which should work okay. Otherwise, if you are ready, willing, and able to use Apple's ResEdit utility, try the following:

1. Make a duplicate of your System file and drag it out of the System Folder to the desktop.
2. Open up the System file in ResEdit and go to the "vers" resource.
3. Open up each of the two resources there. The top line of each should say "Version Number," followed by three boxes that together contain the numbers for 7.5.5. Change the last digit to a zero for both resource IDs; you can ignore the rest of the information. Close and save your changes.
4. Drag your 7.5.5 System file out of the System Folder and put it in any other folder. Now drag your newly created "7.5.0" System file into your System Folder.
5. Launch the Installer on your System 7.5 Update 2.0 CD; you should be able to access everything now. I doubt that you could safely use this to go back to System 7.5.3, but you can use it to get to the various control panels, extensions, and utilities listed in the Custom Install.
6. When you are done, simply swap the System files back.

If you are reluctant to use ResEdit, you can always install System 7.5.2 or earlier on any disk anywhere, then delete everything but the System file itself. You can now use this System file in exactly the same way as just described.

BY THE WAY ▶

WHERE DID THE NAME OF MY MACINTOSH GO?

After installing a version of System 7.5, you may find that the exact name of your Macintosh model (such as "Macintosh IIci," "PowerBook 5300," or "Power Macintosh 7600") is no longer listed in your About This Macintosh window (instead, it now simply says "Macintosh," "Macintosh PowerBook," or "Power Macintosh"). Apple says this is a normal consequence of doing a clean install of System 7.5 (using Command-Shift-K, as explained in Fix-It #5), but it is not supposed to happen after a typical update installation. Still, many users report that it happens in all cases.

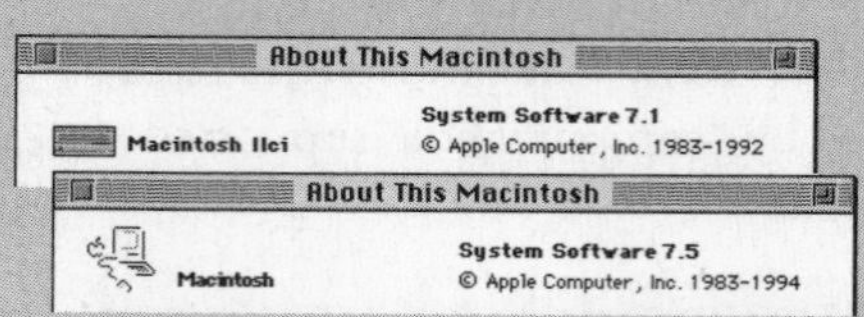

Figure 13-6 *The About This Macintosh window before and after upgrading to System 7.5; note that the name of the Macintosh model is missing from the window in System 7.5.*

This may seem like a trivial problem, and most often that's all it is. Some utilities and networking applications, however, look for this information to determine model-specific options related to the running of the program; with this information gone, more serious problems can occur. Currently, the best way I know to get the model name back is to use a shareware utility called MacIdentifier.

Compatibility and Memory Problems

Symptoms:

- You install System 7.5.*x* but are unable to access certain of its new features. Either the feature simply does not appear, or you get an error message when you try to use it (such as an "out of memory" message).
- You have more general trouble using some version of System 7.5 or Mac OS 7.6 (or later), possibly including an inability to start up, even though you had no such problem with your previous version of the system software.

Causes:

In most cases, the problem is the result of insufficient RAM, needed extensions/control panels that are not installed, applications that are not able to use new System 7.5.*x* features, or conflicts with certain non-Apple extensions and control panels.

What to do:

What About Enabler and Update Files?

Enabler and Update files are stored in the System Folder. They are used to supplement the basic System file with added code that is especially relevant to the new system software or new hardware.

SEE: • **"Take Note: System Enablers, Updates, And Universal System Folders," in Fix-It #5, for more details**

Sometimes it can be hard to tell exactly what Update file you should or should not have. Once again, System 7.5.3 is a perfect example of this problem. When installing System 7.5 Update 2.0, a file called System 7.5.2 Update would be installed (in the root level of your System Folder) if you had a PCI-based Mac; a similar file called System 7.5 Update would instead be installed on any other Mac. To make matters more complicated, the PCI-only version of System 7.5.3 needed no Update file at all, but if you further updated this to System 7.5.3 Revision 2, a file called System 7.5.3 Enabler would be installed. And no matter what version you had, when you updated to System 7.5.5, all of the Update and Enabler files were removed!

Basically, if you find these files (or other similarly named ones) after an installation, leave them there. Conversely, do not simply drag Update files to a System Folder if they are not installed by the Installer; otherwise, problems are likely to occur. Usually, the Installer does the right thing.

Finally, do not try to rename any of these files. While they may work fine after being renamed, you may have problems later when you try to update the software. For example, if you try to use an Installer and get a message that says "This system cannot be updated," it is probably because you have changed the name of a needed Update or Enabler file and the Installer cannot locate it. A similar message may appear if you try to install an Update in a system that already has the Update installed.

SEE: • **"Take Note: Problems Getting Started with System 7.5.5," earlier in this chapter, for related information**

Are Extensions and Control Panels Installed (or Deinstalled) as Needed?

Many System 7.5 features, even nearly essential ones, depend on extensions and control panels. Often it is difficult to determine what a particular file does and what would happen if you removed it. Sometimes Balloon Help or Apple Guide may give you a hint; otherwise (as mentioned in "Getting Help from Apple," earlier in this chapter), the "Read Me" files that come with the Update are especially helpful. For example, if a file in your System Folder disappears after updating, check the section of the "Read Me" files that says "Files No Longer Needed." It may be that this file has been incorporated into the System, Finder, or System Update files and thus no longer exists as a separate file. With System 7.5.3, examples of these files that should no longer be in your System Folder are Finder Update, SCSI Manager (including SCSI Manager 4.3), SerialDMA (and 7.5.2 Printing Fix), and ThreadsLib. System 7.5.5 eliminated the System 7.5.*x* Update file, Startup Tuner, and Power Mac Format Patch.

If you are prone to surfing the Internet, there are also a couple of Web sites devoted to helping you figure all of this out. My favorite is the Mac Pruning Pages (*http://www.AmbrosiaSW.com/DEF/*). It also provides a separate file you can download, called InformInit, that includes all of the information on the Web site.

Finally, here is a sampling of some of the more common extension and control panel problems you may encounter:

Make Sure You Have Find File Extension and Finder Scripting Extension System 7.5 includes a new Find File feature, available both from the Apple menu and from the Finder's File menu. To access Find File from the Finder's File menu, however, you need to have the Find File Extension installed in your Extensions folder.

A slick feature of Find File is that you can drag an item from the Results window list to any location on the desktop. This causes the item to be moved to the new location. For this feature to work, however, you need the Finder Scripting Extension installed in the Extensions folder.

SEE: • Chapter 2 for more on using Find File

Make Sure You Have the Clipping Extension This is needed to create clippings files via System 7.5's new Drag and Drop feature (as explained in Chapter 10).

ObjectSupportLib and AppleScriptLib Technically, these files are only needed if you use AppleScript, but several other applications make use of their AppleScript features. These applications will give you trouble if you don't have the extensions installed, so don't delete them. Also, be sure to get the latest version; problems were reported with a confusing variety of versions floating around for most of 1996. In particular, ObjectSupportLib 1.1.2 or later should remedy problems with earlier versions.

Video Startup and SystemAV Video Startup is needed for Apple Video Player, and SystemAV is needed for the Monitors & Sound control panel. Speaking of Monitors and Sound, you may occasionally need to delete its Preferences file to get it to work.

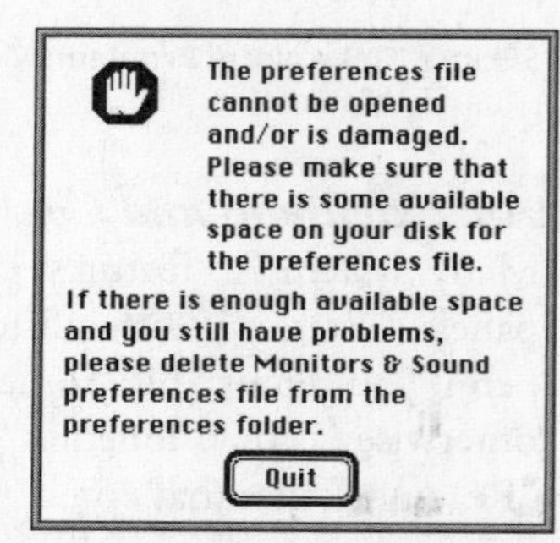

Figure 13-7 *An error message that may appear when you try to open the Monitors & Sound control panel if its Preferences file is damaged.*

Monitors Extensions Are Not Required System 7.5 installs an extension specific to your particular model of Macintosh (with a name such as IIci/IIsi Monitors Extension or PowerBook Monitors Extension). These extensions are not essential in order to use a monitor; your Mac will still work fine without them. They potentially affect what choices are available when you select the Options button from the Monitors control panel.

Be Careful of Apple Menu Options The Apple Menu Options control panel adds hierarchical menus off the Apple menu (as described in Chapter 6, "Take Note: System 7.5, Now Utilities, and More: Helping You Find Your Way"). It is known to conflict with a variety of other non-Apple software, however, as well as to slow down hard disk performance significantly. Many experts suggest using some comparable alternative program (such as Now Menus) instead. Certainly don't use both Apple Menu Options and a program such as Now Menus at the same time.

Also, if you find that Apple Menu Options does not work in any way (for instance, your hierarchical menus disappear), delete Apple Menu Prefs. This fixes most of these problems. It may even fix a problem that causes an "insufficient memory" message to appear at startup.

Where is MacTCP? If you use MacTCP and find it gone after updating, it is because Open Transport software has replaced it. This, of course, means you should be careful not to delete the Open Transport software.

SEE: • Chapter 14 for more details on Open Transport and MacTCP

Shutdown Items Folder Note that the items in this folder are only accessed at shutdown if the Finder Scripting Extension is installed and enabled. Thus, it will not work if you start up with extensions off.

WorldScript Power Adapter Most people think of this extension as only needed if you have a foreign-language Macintosh that uses the Mac's WorldScript software. It includes PowerPC native code that improves text processing speed even for English-language text, however, so use it if you have a Power Mac.

Multiprocessing Software If you are using Apple's multiprocessing software (with a Mac that has multiple processors, of course), turn off virtual memory or RAM Doubler, as well as the Energy Saver control panel. Multiprocessing may not work otherwise.

Disable Features That Are Common Causes of Problems Several features of recent versions of Macintosh system software have been implicated as frequently conflicting with other software. If problems persist, try disabling these features to see if doing so cures the problem. These features include virtual memory, file sharing, PlainTalk speech recognition, and ColorSync software.

Two Different Versions of Energy Saver As noted earlier, there are currently two different versions of Apple's Energy Saver control panel—version 2.*x* is just for PCI-based Macs, while version 1.*x* is for most other Mac models. Be sure you have the right one.

Also note that resetting the PRAM does not affect the settings of the Energy Saver 2.*x* control panel; its settings are stored in an Energy Saver Prefs file. The current settings remain active even if you start up with extensions off. Thus, the only way to prevent Energy Saver from putting your Mac to sleep is to change its control panel setting to "Never."

SEE: • "PCI-Based Macintosh Quick Fixes," in Chapter 12, for much more on Energy Saver 2.*x* troubleshooting

Third-Party Startup Extension Problems Third-party extensions are always a potential source of conflict for new system software, at least until they themselves are updated to work with the new software. If problems develop, suspects to consider first (because past history has shown them to be frequent sources of trouble) include After Dark, Adobe Type Manager, RAM Doubler, Speed Doubler, SAM, and Now Utilities. Disable them to see if your problem goes away. If it does, check that you have the latest version; if not, upgrading may fix the problem. A more general search for possible extension conflicts (using a utility such as Conflict Catcher) is also recommended.

Special Case: Now Utilities Many problems with Now Utilities 6.0 or later, and particularly with Now Menus, are solved by disabling the Menu Blinking option in Apple's General Control control panel. As always, deleting the Now Utilities Preferences files is another good bet to try (as described next).

Another unusual problem with Now Utilities 6.0 or later is that, when you are trying to launch other unrelated applications, you may get a message that says the program won't open because you need "System 7.1 or later"—even though you are running System 7.5 or later. The culprit here seems to be the Now Mail server plug-ins of Now Utilities, which are background-only applications (also known as *appes*, as explained more in Fix-It #4). Apparently, a bug in the system software causes this error when more than one appe is running at the same time; System 7.5.5 is supposed to have fixed this bug.

Delete Preferences Files

Many of the new control panels in System 7.5 and its revisions have preferences files associated with them. Trouble with a specific control panel may be due to a flaw in its preferences file (for example, if it is damaged) rather than an actual compatibility problem with the control panel itself. Usually this is remedied by deleting the preferences file, ideally after restarting with the control panel disabled (Macintosh PC Exchange is one well-known example, as is Apple Menu Options). This remedy also applies to several third-party control panels.

SEE: • **Fix-It #2 for more on preferences files**

Are Your Applications "Capable," "Savvy," or Not?

Some of the features of System 7.5 and its successors (such as Drag and Drop, AppleScript, and QuickDraw GX) can only be used with software that has been specifically written to support these features. A further complication is that there are usually different levels of support possible for each feature. For example, a program may be able to receive data from via the Drag and Drop method, even though it cannot send it; this is called being "Macintosh Drag and Drop aware." If a program can fully use all of the new Drag and Drop features, the program is said to be "Macintosh Drag and Drop capable." A similar distinction is used to differentiate programs that are only "QuickDraw GX-aware" versus "QuickDraw GX-savvy" (a distinction I explore more in the QuickDraw GX section of this chapter).

If you are unable to access a particular System 7.5*x* feature from within a specific application, the application probably does not yet support this feature.

Audio and Video Problems

Sound Manager 3.2 is built into the System 7.5 Update file, eliminating the need for a separate extension; this new version includes asynchronous sound playback and better Power Mac performance. QuickTime 2.5, however, came with a bug-fixed Sound Manager 3.2.1, so you will find that the extension has returned to your System Folder after installing this version of QuickTime. Leave it there.

This sort of flip-flopping between when a given extension should or should not be in your System Folder is likely to continue as new software gets released.

A variety of other audio-video problems are covered elsewhere in this book.

SEE;
- **"Movies, Video and More," in Chapter 10, for problems related to Apple Video Player and movies/video in general**
- **"PCI-Based Macintosh Quick Fixes," in Chapter 12, for problems related to the Monitors & Sound control panel**
- **"AppleVision Monitors," in Chapter 12, for installation problems**

Memory Problems

Most memory problems that you will have will not be specific to System 7.5. Since System 7.5 and its revisions generally need more memory than previous systems, however, you are more likely to have memory problems. Here are three examples of the few System 7.5-specific memory pitfalls lurking out there:

"Out of Memory" Messages (and Other Problems) in the Scrapbook The System 7.5 Scrapbook is a genuine application rather than a desk accessory (which it had previously been). As a result, you can now change its memory allocation from its Get Info window.

This shift is important because "out of memory" messages may appear when you try to cut from or paste to the Scrapbook, especially if you have a large number of items in the Scrapbook file. Sometimes these commands will simply refuse to work, with no error message appearing. If any of this happens, try each of the following as needed:

- Restart the Mac and try again. Sometimes, this is all you need to do.
- Quit the Scrapbook, go to its Get Info window, and increase its Preferred memory size by 100 to 200K (or more, if you can afford it).
- Cut unneeded items out of your Scrapbook. A utility called Scrapbook Burster can automate this process for you.
- Drag the file called "Scrapbook file" from the root level of your System Folder (*not* the Scrapbook program in the Apple Menu Items folder!) to the desktop. The next time you open the Scrapbook, a new, empty Scrapbook file will be created and used. You can still access the original Scrapbook file by double-clicking its icon.

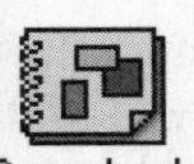

Figure 13-8 *The Scrapbook application (left) versus the Scrapbook file (right).*

- In a few cases, the problem may be a damaged Scrapbook file. In this case, you can try to recover images from the file, using a utility such as CanOpener. After that, delete the Scrapbook file.
- Use a utility (such as MacUser's ScrapBoard) that substitutes for the Scrapbook but has multi-file capability.

"Out of Memory" Messages with Desktop Patterns Desktop Patterns is an application, even though it is designed to look like a control panel (this appears to be a growing trend). Increase its memory allocation from its Get Info window to eliminate "out of memory" messages that occur while using it.

You can paste your own patterns into the Desktop Patterns control panel window. If and when you try to do this, you may get a message that says "Sorry, there is not enough memory to complete this operation." If what you are trying to paste is not very large, the problem may have nothing to do with memory; instead, you are probably trying to paste something that is in an unacceptable format. For example, I got this message when I tried to paste a text selection. When I instead tried to paste a graphic object, everything worked fine.

SEE: • **Fix-It #6 for more on the Get Info window and memory problems in general**

Shared Library Problems You may find that your system software takes up more and more memory as the day goes on. This is because of System 7.5.3's increased use of shared libraries. When you run an application that uses a shared library, the library loads into system software memory but doesn't necessarily get released again when you quit the application (especially so if virtual memory is off). Thus, as you continue using shared library files, your available memory starts to shrink. This sort of trouble is especially likely on a Power Mac.

SEE: • **Chapter 12, "Shared Library Problems," for more on this subject**
• **Fix-It #6, "Check for Memory Leaks (A Step Beyond Memory Fragmentation)," for still more details**

System Heap Size Increases After Installing RAM If you install additional physical RAM in your Mac, you may notice that the size of your System Software memory (as indicated in the About This Macintosh window) is significantly larger after you restart than it was before, especially if you also reinstalled your system software. At least in some cases, this may be because the size of the disk cache has increased automatically to equal 32K times the number of MB of RAM installed. You can manually lower this amount from the Memory control panel if you wish.

System 7.5.5-Specific Memory Problems

System 7.5.5 included new math library routines (which are built into the System file) that require slightly more memory than the old routines. As a result, some programs that ran fine in System 7.5.3 may need additional memory to run in System 7.5.5. Apple stated that if you get an "out of memory" message when launching or otherwise using a particular program, go to its Get Info window and increase its Preferred memory size by 23K.

This worked fine for applications—and even worked for some applications in disguise, such as Desktop PrintMonitor—but it turned out that some extensions and control panels also needed this boost. These programs do not have a Memory Requirements box in their Get Info windows, so how do you change their Preferred size? It turns out that you can do this in a variety of different ways, either via utilities such as Snitch or via ResEdit.

The Finder itself was also more subject to out-of-memory problems after updating to System 7.5.5. It, too, could benefit from a memory boost (to at least 256K)—but again, you can't do this from its Get Info window. So what do you do? You can use a special freeware utility, designed just for this purpose, called Finder Heap Fix.

The details on all of these memory-boosting procedures can be found in Fix-It #6. Note that Mac OS 7.6 reportedly solves these problems by assigning the Finder a boosted memory allocation and by eliminating the System grabbing the extra 23K of memory from applications.

SEE: • **"Increase the Finder's Memory Size" and "Take Note: System 7.5.5 Memory Problem and Increasing Memory Size of Extensions," in Fix-It #6**

TAKE NOTE ▶

MAC OS 7.6: A CLOSER LOOK

Because Mac OS 7.6 was released just as this book was going to press, it is too new for me to offer detailed troubleshooting advice here. Here, however, are some key highlights:

- It includes a new version of the Extensions Manager (see Fix-It #4 for a look).
- It includes a new Installer utility called Install Mac OS. Details on how to use it are in Fix-It #5.
- To install Mac OS 7.6 over a network, you will first need to install the updated version of AppleShare included with the new OS.
- The revised Disk Tools disks include special Enabler files in their System Folders.
- It includes an improved version of something called Mount Check, which has been around in the Macintosh's ROM for a long time. It is basically a partial implementation of Disk First Aid code, designed to check for and repair Directory problems that may have occurred after a system crash; the need to run Mount Check is why, after a crash, the happy-Mac icon stays visible for such an unusually long time. A new and improved Mac OS 7.6 version is supposed to speed up this process substantially.
- Mac OS 7.6 will no longer work with Macs that are not "32-bit clean." This means that all Macs prior to the Mac IIci (and even a few that were released later than that) are no longer supported.
- Modern Memory Manager is not an option on Power Macs; it is always enabled.
- It includes a host of related software, such as OpenDoc, QuickDraw GX, QuickDraw 3D, Cyberdog, ARA Client, Open Transport, OT/PPP, and even America Online. Expect a full install of everything to take up about 120MB of disk space.
- Open Transport is required with Mac OS 7.6.
- It installs Open Transport 1.1.1. If you already use a later version, you will need to reinstall it after installing Mac OS 7.6. Certain other optional software (such as QuickDraw 3D) included with Mac OS 7.6 is also not the latest version.
- The "Welcome to Macintosh" message no longer appears at startup. The Mac OS splash screen appears directly.
- "About This Macintosh" is now "About This Computer"; "Macintosh Easy Open" is now "Mac OS Easy Open." These and other similar changes are in deference to Mac clones—they use the Mac OS, but only Apple makes Macintoshes.

Apple Guide Does Not Work

Symptoms:

You try to access an Apple Guide file from the Guide menu, but the relevant Guide file is not listed.

Causes:

The needed Guide file (or the Apple Guide extension itself) probably is either not installed or not in the correct location.

What to do:

Apple Guide Not Installed or Not Enabled

With the Finder as the active application, select the Guide menu. The top line should read "About Apple Guide." If it reads "About Balloon Help" instead, perhaps the Apple Guide extension was not installed or has been disabled. Check for this; if this is the case, no Apple Guide files will be accessible, even if they are correctly located.

If Apple Guide was never installed and thus is nowhere on your disk, you need to run the System 7.5 Installer to install it (use Custom Install and select Apple Guide from the Utility Software submenu). If it is disabled, re-enable it (for example, by using a startup management utility) to get it back in the Extensions folder.

A basic reminder: Apple Guide is disabled if you start with extensions off (by holding down the Shift key at startup), although Balloon Help will still work. Still, to get Balloon Help in the Finder, you will need the Finder Help file in your Extensions folder.

SEE: • **Fix-It #4 on enabling and disabling extensions**
• **Fix-It #5 on using the Installer**

Incorrect Location of Apple Guide Documents

In addition to needing the Apple Guide extension, accessing specific Apple Guide documents from the Guide menu (such as the Finder's Macintosh Guide) requires that the relevant document file be correctly located on your disk. For example, the Macintosh Guide file must be in the Extensions folder.

Guide documents are only accessible when the appropriate application is active. For example, Macintosh Guide is only available when you are in the Finder; you will not see it listed when another application is active. Similarly, individual applications may have their own Apple Guide documents, which in turn are only available when you are using that application.

You cannot directly open a Guide file by double-clicking its icon in the Finder. Doing so will lead to an error message that says something like "It can only be run from within the application it is associated with."

Complicating matters a bit more, different Apple Guide documents may need to be stored in different locations in order to be accessible. For example, most of Apple's Guide documents are stored in the Extensions folder, but most application-specific Guide documents will be found in the same folder as the application itself (thus, you will find File Assistant Guide in the same folder as the File Assistant program). Other Guide documents may need to be at the root level of the System Folder. Generally, if a program uses an Installer utility, it will install its Guide documents in the correct location. If so, do not move them to another location, or they will not work.

Figure 13-9 *The Apple Guide extension, with Macintosh Guide and just a few of the other Guide documents you are likely to find in your Extensions folder.*

Third-Party Conflicts and Macintosh Guide

A third-party Guide file may prevent your access to Macintosh Guide. In this case, you will have to either give up on Macintosh Guide or delete the third-party file.

Problem with Apple Guide Additions Is Fixed

An Apple Guide Additions file (sometimes referred to as a "Mixin") acts to add additional topics to a main Apple Guide file. You can't separately select an Additions file from the Apple Guide menu; instead, its topics are seamlessly integrated within the overall topic list of a main file (such as Macintosh Guide). Typically, Additions files get installed automatically only when the software that they describe is also installed. For example, the Speech Guide Additions file is installed when you install PlainTalk software, and its topics are then integrated into the listing of the Macintosh Guide file.

Prior to System 7.5.3, all Apple Guide files would become totally inaccessible from the Apple Guide menu if you happened to install an Additions file for software that was not available with your Mac model (which might happen via a Custom Install, for instance). Examples of this would be if the PowerBook Additions file was installed on a desktop Macintosh, or if the Video and Speech Additions files were installed on any non-AV Power Mac. The loss of the Apple Guide function may similarly occur if you delete the software referred to in an installed Additions file, but do not remove the Additions file itself (such as if you delete the PlainTalk software, but let the Speech Guide Additions file remain).

Happily, this problem appears to have been remedied in System 7.5.3.

OpenDoc and Live Objects

What Is OpenDoc?

OpenDoc software is included with System 7.5.3 or later revisions as an optional installation.

Simply put, OpenDoc is a radical new approach to how software works. In the past, you opened an application and created documents with it. Except in some limited ways, though, applications could not interact with each other—so if you wanted to have additional features available to use with a document, the primary way to do it was to add those features in the next update of the the application itself. This approach eventually gave us behemoths like Microsoft Word 6.0, where you wind up paying for dozens of features that you don't want simply because someone else may want them.

In the OpenDoc world, though, the center of the universe is the document, not the application. In fact, there need not be any applications at all; instead, you have OpenDoc parts (now called Live Objects).

With OpenDoc, you combine different Live Objects together in a sort of super-document. So, for example, what appears to be a word processing document may also contain a spreadsheet part and a Web browser part within it. It's a bit like how ClarisWorks now works, except that you can mix and match on your own (depending upon what parts you have) rather than having to depend upon what ClarisWorks gives you.

The motive behind this technology is to encourage smaller, more compartmentalized, and more specialized software that you can combine into your own customized applications. The idea of OpenDoc is clearly great, but how well it succeeds in the marketplace remains to be seen.

(Note: Microsoft's OLE is a competing technology to OpenDoc. Apple is betting on OpenDoc winning the day.)

Is It a Container?

Understanding how all of the different components of OpenDoc fit and work together is admittedly a bit confusing—there are several different components, and different ways to categorize them.

The first distinction to know is whether or not an OpenDoc file is a *container*. A container can hold other Live Objects (also called OpenDoc parts) inside its document window. Actually there are two types of containers, which are defined as follows:

- **Container applications**
  These are ordinary applications that can contain other OpenDoc parts; the first OpenDoc-based version of ClarisWorks, for example, is a container application. They are like a hybrid between OpenDoc parts and traditional applications.
- **Container parts**
  These are true OpenDoc parts. When you open them, however, they may look just like container applications, since they can also contain other OpenDoc parts. The main thing that makes them different from a container application is that

BY THE WAY ▶

OPENDOC ESSENTIALS

Mac OS 7.6 comes with a basic set of container parts grouped together under the name OpenDoc Essentials (formerly called KickStart). It features a basic drawing container part called Apple Draw. It also includes assorted other parts, such as Apple QuickTime Viewer and Apple Button. With luck, these may have the same stimulating effect on OpenDoc software development that the original MacWrite and MacPaint had years ago for the Macintosh itself.

they themselves may be contained in another container part (whereas container applications cannot do this).

- **Noncontainer parts**
  These parts can be within a container, but they cannot contain things themselves. A clickable button (to which you can assign a link or command) might be an example here. A button-making part could allow you to insert the button within any OpenDoc container, but the button cannot contain anything itself.

Editors, Viewers, and Stationery

This is a second basic distinction in OpenDoc. These elements can be broken down as follows:

- **Editors**
  The grunt work of OpenDoc is done by editors. With editors, you can open, modify, and save the contents of an OpenDoc document. Most OpenDoc Essentials parts are thus examples of OpenDoc editors. They are like mini-applications.
- **Viewers**
  Viewers are similar to editors in that they let you open and view an OpenDoc document. Unlike editors, however, they cannot modify a document—they can only view it. Viewers are likely to be a critical component of OpenDoc, since they will often be free and will allow users who have not purchased a given editor to view the documents created with it. In this sense, viewers resemble runtime-only applications or readers, such as Adobe's Acrobat Reader (which can view Acrobat files but cannot create them).
- **Stationery**
  Editors and Viewers are very close relatives; as you will see in a moment, they are stored in the same special location on your disk. Stationery is something else again. Stationery files are the documents that editors create. They are what you actually open to access OpenDoc and do some work. For example, to access Apple Draw, do not double click on the Apple Draw editor itself. Instead, launch the Apple Draw stationery file.

  There are really two different types of OpenDoc stationery: one is actually called *stationery* and the other is called *documents.* The distinction is similar to the distinction between these terms for traditional applications. *Stationery* opens up a copy that, when you save it, leaves the original file untouched. In contrast, when *documents* are saved, the original file itself is modified.

Further, when you go to save either a document or stationery, you may have an option to "Save as Run-only." As this name implies, this version cannot be modified at all when it is reopened.

Understanding the distinction between editors/viewers versus stationery requires a new way of thinking that will take some time to get used to. For example, editors, viewers, and stationery are all OpenDoc parts. If you select Get Info for any of these files, their Kind may be "OpenDoc document" (in some cases, it may say "OpenDoc stationery" or just plain "document"). Despite this apparent similarity, they are all slightly different, as just explained.

Figure 13-10 *Left: Apple Draw editor (from the Editors folder). Right: Apple Draw stationery (from the Stationery folder).*

Adding a bit more confusion, an OpenDoc document usually gives little or no indication—other than possibly via its icon—as to what editor (or editors) will open when you open the document. For example, the Kind for a document created via Apple Draw will not say "Apple Draw document" in its Get Info window; it will simply be identified as an OpenDoc file.

OpenDoc Software: What Goes Where?

When you install OpenDoc, it places a lot of different software in different locations on your disk. The rules of exactly what goes where may change as the software evolves, but here are the basics as they now stand:

- **OpenDoc Libraries Folder**
  This is found in the Extensions folder of the System Folder. It is where the basic OpenDoc "application" is found, as well as several other critical extensions, such as Memory Manager and OpenDocLib. Without these extensions enabled, you cannot use the rest of the OpenDoc software.

Figure 13-11 *The OpenDoc Libraries Folder.*

- **Editors Folder**
  This is found at the root level of your System Folder. It is the folder where all editors and viewers must reside; if an editor is not here, OpenDoc cannot access it. The Editors folder must, in turn, be in the System Folder.

  Unlike ordinary applications, you do not double-click an editor to launch it—if you try, you will get an error message. The only way to access an editor or viewer is by opening a stationery or document that needs it. This is why editors can be safely tucked out of the way in the Editors folder, and it is also why stationery is so important. Discarding all stationery that refers back to an editor means you cannot access the editor at all; it is almost the equivalent of trashing a traditional application.

  Note: A file called ODFLibrary is located in the Editors folder. If any OpenDoc software comes with a newer version of this file than you currently have installed, make sure the newer version gets installed or you may be unable to use your new software.

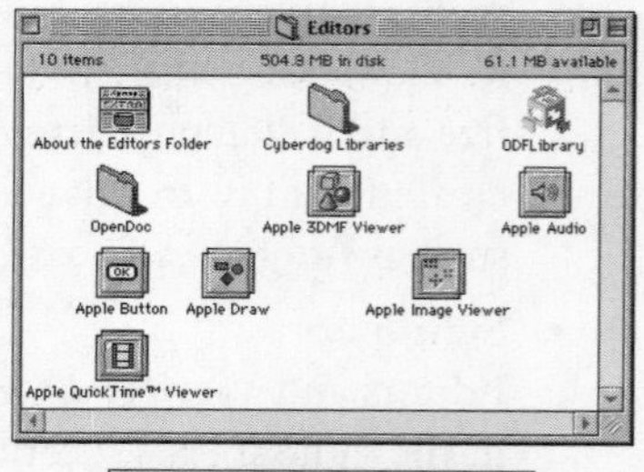

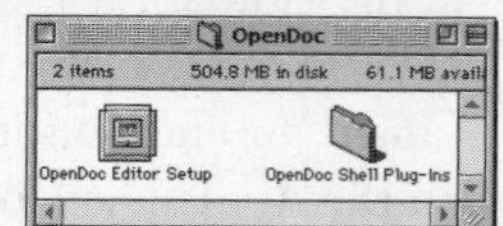

Figure 13-12 *An OpenDoc Editors Folder (top) and its OpenDoc folder (bottom).*

Inside the Editors folder, there may be any number of other subfolders, including one called OpenDoc. The OpenDoc folder contains a file called OpenDoc Editor Setup (which is needed to assign alternative editors for orphaned parts, as described in a moment) plus a folder called OpenDoc Shell Plug-Ins (whose files, called plug-ins, allow an editor to add features to OpenDoc that are not part of the basic feature set).

Note: If you drag an Editor to the System Folder icon, you may get a message asking whether you want the Editor to go into the Extensions folder. Say no; it should go in the Editors folder.

Figure 13-13 *An error message that appears if you try to launch an OpenDoc editor directly, rather than opening one of its stationery or document files.*

- **Stationery Folder**
  A *Stationery* folder starts out at the root level of your hard drive (although you can move it, or any files within it, to any other location). It contains the OpenDoc stationery and documents that the editors work with. To open a document and "launch" its editor(s), just double-click it. You may also have a separate folder called *Documents* for holding OpenDoc document files that are not stationery (as explained in the previous section).

  If you check the Application menu or select the "About this Computer" command in the Finder, it will list the names of the stationery files that you have open (not the editors themselves). If you select the "About" box when a given OpenDoc file is active, however, it will describe the base editor of the active document. Actually, in some cases, two or more base editors may be listed.

Things can get complicated fast. For example, Apple's Cyberdog is a collection of OpenDoc parts—including an OpenDoc container application called Cyberdog, a main OpenDoc document called Cyberdog Starting Point, and a collection of other documents—all located in the Cyberdog folder. Plus, there are associated Cyberdog documents in the Cyberdog Libraries folder in the Editors folder. There is even a separate Cyberdog extension.

Installing and Using OpenDoc

To install OpenDoc, simply run the OpenDoc Installer and restart your Macintosh. One such Installer is included with some versions of System 7.5.3, and a newer version is part of Mac OS 7.6. The software should also be available as a separate component that can be downloaded from Apple's software libraries.

When you purchase any OpenDoc-based software, if there is no Installer to assist you, it will be important to follow instructions carefully and make sure you put the appropriate parts of the software in the appropriate locations. Apple's Installer should help put everything in its place. (Aladdin also has an OpenDoc-based version of its InstallerMaker.)

Once everything is installed, simply clicking on an OpenDoc stationery or document will launch that document, activating whatever editors are needed to work with it. At this point, you will need to make some further adjustments to your traditional view of Macintosh software. Several familiar sights are gone, and new ways of doing things are required.

The Documents and Edit Menus

When you first open an OpenDoc document, you will know right away that something is different. The familiar File menu is replaced by a menu called Document.

Figure 13-14 *Two examples of Documents menus, one from Apple Draw (with no Quit command) and another from Cyberdog (with a Quit command).*

- **Documents Menu: Quit or Close**
  The Documents menu may not contain a Quit command. This is because there may be no applications to quit, just OpenDoc parts. You can still close each document part, even if you cannot "Quit" anything; OpenDoc itself then quits when all its parts are closed. As the software now works, this can be a hassle if you have a lot of parts open—without a global Quit command, you'll have to separately select each part to close it.

  With an OpenDoc container application such as Cyberdog, however, there will be a Quit command.

- **Documents Menu: Open/New versus Insert**
  With an OpenDoc document open, if you choose New or Open, you will open a new document in a separate window. If you instead select Insert, you will insert your selection into the presently open window. This is how, for example, you would insert a button (using Apple Button) into an Apple Draw document.

  Each separate window has its own separate listing in the Mac's Application menu.

- **Documents Menu: Delete**
  Every time you open a document from a stationery pad file, a new file is created. After a while, your desktop can get cluttered with files that you really don't want to save. That's probably why the Document window contains a Delete command (not found in the traditional File menu).

- **Documents Menu: Drafts**
  The Drafts command lets you save multiple versions of your document, allowing you to go back to a previous version if you wish (sort of like an enhanced Revert to Saved command).

- **Documents Menu: Document Info (and memory allocation via Size)**
  What is assuredly the most important new command in the Documents menu (at least for troubleshooting) is the Document Info command. From the Document Info window, you can learn about and manipulate several important aspects of your document.

  Document Info window For starters, the Editor line will tell you the current base editor of the document. The Kind line tells you what type of document it is (which may often be the same as the name of the editor); however, Kind is also a pop-up menu that may allow you to change the Kind of the document to that of a different editor.

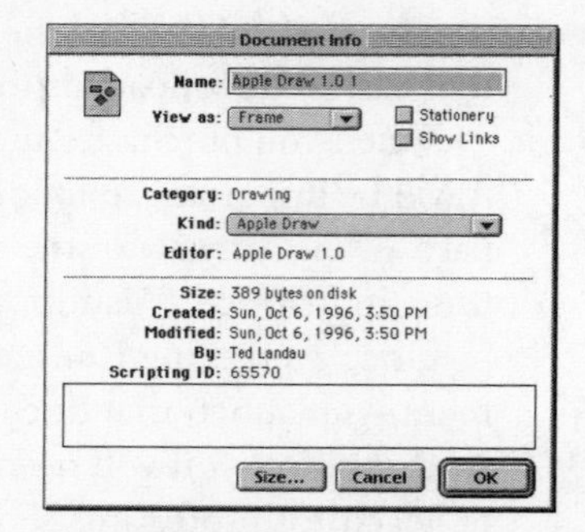

Figure 13-15 *A Document Info window for Apple Draw.*

From this main window you can also change the name of the document, among other options.

Size window If you click the Size button in the Document Info window, you move to another important window; this one allows you to select the memory allocation for the document. Remember, as OpenDoc does not depend upon traditional applications, there is no Get Info window application memory allocation. Editors do not have their own memory allocations, so you select memory allocation for the document instead.

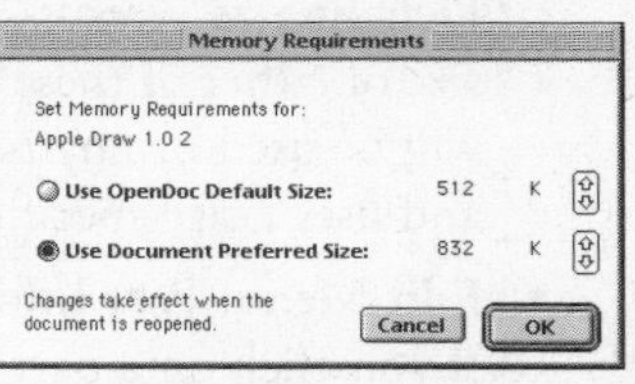

Figure 13-16 *Document Info's Size dialog box (again for Apple Draw).*

BY THE WAY ▶

MORE ON MEMORY MANAGEMENT IN OPENDOC

The OpenDoc extensions (in the OpenDoc Libraries folder) require some memory beyond what is allocated from this Size window of each document (although they only use this memory when at least one OpenDoc part is open). They require a minimum of 1.8MB of memory; without this available, you cannot even use OpenDoc. The size of the increase is greater if you are not using virtual memory or RAM Doubler (it can be 5MB or more).

To see more about how this memory allocation works, check out the About This Macintosh (or About This Computer, in Mac OS 7.6 or later) window. It reveals that when you open an OpenDoc file, the name of the stationery or document (not the editor) gets added to the listing, together with its memory allocation. If more than one document from the same stationery is open, the stationery name will be listed separately for each additional document.

If you are using an OpenDoc container application (such as Cyberdog or ClarisWorks), things are a bit different again. Here, as with traditional applications, all the OpenDoc parts are included in a single entry (such as the name Cyberdog).

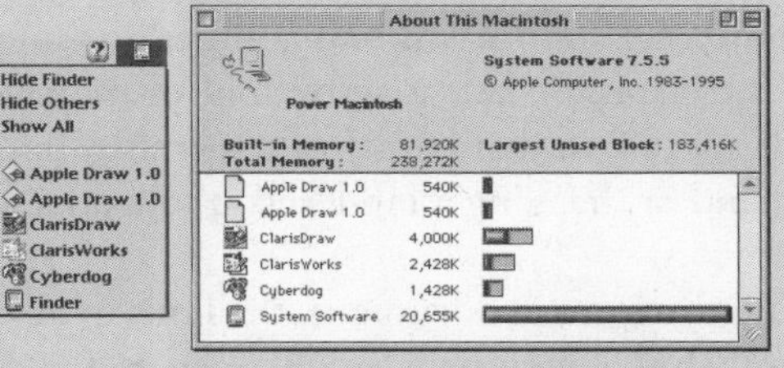

Figure 13-17 *The Application menu (left) and About This Macintosh window (right), with Cyberdog and two Apple Draw documents open.*

In either case, as you open more parts, the size of the System Software line is likely to increase as well; in some cases, it may hold onto that memory increase even if you later close the relevant parts. I found this to be true for Cyberdog parts: the Cyberdog memory allocation stayed the same as I opened more Cyberdog parts, but the System Software allocation kept increasing. The system software memory was only reduced after I completely quit all Cyberdog parts. Clearly, OpenDoc can quickly eat up a lot of memory. If your memory supply is getting low, you may occasionally need to quit an OpenDoc program and relaunch it to reduce the system software memory allocation.

Note: The OpenDoc file itself (in the OpenDoc Libraries folder) does have a Memory Requirements box in the Get Info window, because it is actually an application. Even here, however, you can't really open OpenDoc by double-clicking this file; trying will only get you an error message telling you to open stationery instead. Also, you won't see this file listed in the Application menu or the About This Macintosh window, even when OpenDoc files are open.

If you are getting "out of memory" messages when you use OpenDoc, the Size window is the place to go. For starters, you can select between "Use OpenDoc Default Size" versus "Use Document Preferred Size." You can also adjust the memory size of either of these options. The former selection sets and uses a default size that will be used by any new OpenDoc document that is opened; the latter option sets and uses a size specific to that document.

- **Edit Menu: Part Info**
  If you click on a part embedded in a document, so that the corner handles of the part appear, you will then be able to select Part Info from the Edit menu. This opens a dialog box that is similar to the Document Info dialog, except that it is specific to the selected part and has no Size button.

Combining Parts

Once you have an OpenDoc document window open, you can go to the Finder and drag and drop any other OpenDoc stationery or document icon to the document's window. This will result in an embedded object for that part appearing in the window (just as if you had used the Insert command). For example, if you drag a part for a spreadsheet into a word processing document, a spreadsheet part will appear in the document. When you click on the spreadsheet part to make it active, it is "live," and you will be able to work with it just as if you had opened it as a separate document (again, the analogy to ClarisWorks is appropriate here). Using Cyberdog (as described a bit more in "Take Note: What About Cyberdog," in Chapter 14), you can even embed a live Internet connection into another document, such as a page layout.

When a specific part is active, one or more additional menus will appear for commands specific to that part. Just remember, inserting a new part requires using the Insert command or dragging a Finder icon to a document *window* (not to another document Finder icon).

When you save a document, the links to all editors in use are saved. The next time you launch the document, it will open and re-access all needed editors.

Missing Editors and Orphaned Parts

Given that several different editors might contribute to the creation of an OpenDoc document, a real concern is what happens when you want to give such a document to someone else. In the world of traditional applications, if you wanted to give someone a ClarisWorks document, all you needed to know was whether they owned a copy of ClarisWorks (or at least another application that could read ClarisWorks documents). With an OpenDoc document, you need to know that they have all the different editors that you used (which, in turn, may have been created by several different vendors). It is less likely that such a perfect match will be found.

So what happens when you try to open a document for which you are missing at least one or more needed editors? For starters, you are likely to get an error

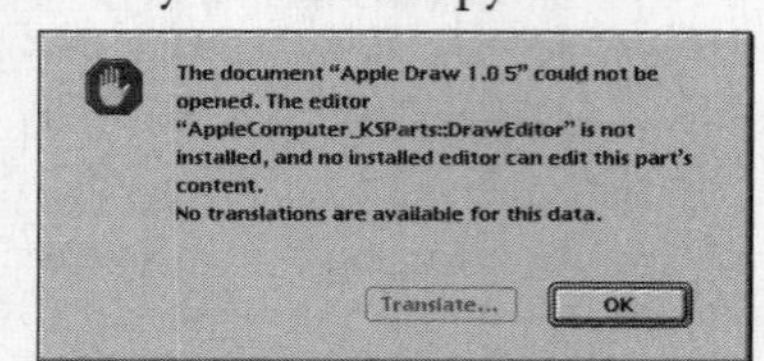

Figure 13-18 *An error message that may appear when you try to open an OpenDoc document whose editor is missing or not properly installed in the Editors folder.*

message informing you of this fact. This leads to the next big question: What can you do to solve this problem? Some answers are listed below.

- If a particular editor is not available, there may be a (possibly free) matching viewer that can be used instead. This obviously prohibits the other person from editing that part, but at least they can see it.
- The other person may have another part that can act as an alternative editor (for example, just as with traditional applications, one drawing part may be able to substitute adequately for another). In this regard, OpenDoc is shipped with an OpenDoc part called OpenDoc Editor Setup that is accessed from the Editor Setup control panel (which is really an OpenDoc document). Working a bit like Mac OS Easy Open, you can use Editor Setup to tell OpenDoc what editor part to use when a particular needed one is missing.

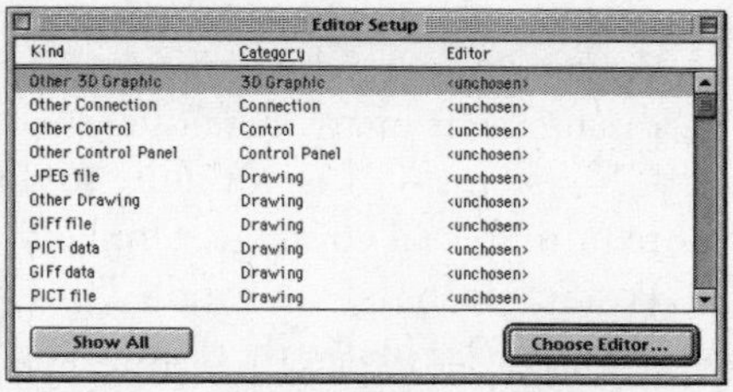

Figure 13-19 *The Editor Setup control panel, used to reassign orphaned parts.*

- You can do nothing and hope for the best. A given part whose editor is missing (called an *orphaned part*) may show up just as it normally would if another pre-assigned substitute editor automatically kicks in; it may show up in some more limited way (for example, a scrollable picture may show up as a static picture instead); or you may just get a generic icon—or nothing at all—occupying the space where the orphaned part of the document should be (sometimes accompanied by an error message). In the case of complex base container documents (such as those created by Wav, an OpenDoc word processor), however, you may be unable to open the document at all unless you have the appropriate editor or viewer.
- If you have a document that has orphaned parts and you have no idea what editors are needed, a product called PartFinder (from Kantara Development) may be able to help. It can automatically find Live Object components at its Internet site.

Wrapping It Up

OpenDoc is still an emerging technology; as of this writing, in fact, third-party OpenDoc software barely exists. Still, this section covers the basics of how to use OpenDoc and explores possible problems you may encounter along the way. Just be aware that some of this information may change as the software matures.

It's obviously a lot easier to see how OpenDoc works by installing the software and trying it out than by reading the description here. In any case, if you haven't done so already, you ought to take a good look at OpenDoc very soon, since it promises to loom larger and larger in importance in future versions of the Mac OS. Some day, not too far away, it will likely be an essential component of your Mac.

QuickDraw GX

QuickDraw GX, as its name implies, is an enhancement to QuickDraw, the set of routines built into your Macintosh's ROM that ultimately determines how almost everything on your Macintosh is displayed and printed (as first described in Chapter 10).

The most immediately obvious change resulting from installing QuickDraw GX is the new way in which printing is handled; it is so completely different that I omitted discussing it in any detail in Chapter 7. With desktop printers now in use even for non-GX systems, GX is not quite so different anymore, but it is still different enough to require special coverage. Similarly, there are major changes in how fonts (particularly PostScript fonts) are handled in QuickDraw GX; I only briefly described these in Chapter 9. Finally, there are some new graphics-related features associated with QuickDraw GX that were only slightly mentioned in Chapter 10.

As with OpenDoc, QuickDraw GX remains an optional and separately installed part of your system software—at least for now. You can easily use System 7.5 or later without using QuickDraw GX. If you do install QuickDraw GX, however, it will have wide-ranging effects on how your Macintosh works.

Here, I will finally go into the details of these matters. In the following sections, I assume that you are at least minimally familiar with non-GX aspects of these topics, as presented in these previous chapters.

Installing and Using QuickDraw GX

To install QuickDraw GX, use the separate QuickDraw GX Installer. In most cases you will be best off selecting Easy Install; a couple of instances where you might prefer to use a Custom Install are described later in this chapter. If you ever decide to remove QuickDraw GX software permanently, launch the GX Installer and select Custom Remove.

The key component of the QuickDraw GX software is the QuickDraw GX extension. If this extension is disabled or deleted, you lose access to all QuickDraw GX features, even if all the other GX software remains on your disk.

Simply installing QuickDraw GX, though, does not mean that you can now use all of its features. Some features, such as desktop printers and portable documents, are indeed immediately usable with almost all current applications (except a few that are totally incompatible with QuickDraw GX), but others (such as the redesigned Page Setup and Print dialog boxes and the improved clipboard) are available only in programs that are at least "GX-aware" (that is, the programs have been rewritten to permit use of these GX options). Finally, a few remaining features of QuickDraw GX (such as its new font-related features) are only available to programs that have been completely upgraded to be "GX-savvy." As a result, your ability to use the new features of QuickDraw GX will very much depend on the current status of the applications you use. Specific examples of this are cited in the sections that follow.

QuickDraw GX and Printing

This section covers what is different about printing with QuickDraw GX. If you already use the desktop printing software employed in non-GX systems, you will find much of this familiar, since all desktop printers were based on this GX technology. Otherwise, as you first read this material, it may seem like there is a lot of new things to master. Once you get things set up and rolling, however, printing with GX is no more difficult than before—in fact, you may find it even easier. In most cases, you can still simply select Print from within an application and make the standard choices in the Print dialog box. Your document will then print without any further hassle.

QuickDraw GX-Specific Printer Drivers

To print with QuickDraw GX, you need a GX-specific printer driver file for your particular printer. When you install QuickDraw GX, GX-specific drivers for all of Apple's printers are installed in the Extensions folder of your System Folder (non-GX versions of the printer drivers also remain installed).

If you have a non-Apple printer, you will need to get a GX-compatible driver from the company that made the printer. If you do not have a GX-specific driver for your printer, I would recommend against installing QuickDraw GX at all.

If you use fax software, the fax driver must also be GX-compatible. Apple's Telecom (2.0 or later) and Global Village's GlobalFax (2.5 or later) are examples of compatible drivers.

QuickDraw GX and the Chooser

The first step in setting up to print with QuickDraw GX is to select the Chooser, which has been redesigned in QuickDraw GX. First, the GX Chooser does not even list non-GX printer drivers in its window. Thus you will not find LaserWriter 8 listed, even though the driver may be present in your Extensions folder; to use a PostScript LaserWriter, you must select LaserWriter GX. Don't be in a hurry to remove the non-GX version of your printer drivers from your System Folder, however, as they may still be needed. For example, if you ever start up with the QuickDraw GX extension disabled, the Chooser will revert to its former non-GX format, and only non-GX printer drivers will be listed. This way you can still print without GX being active.

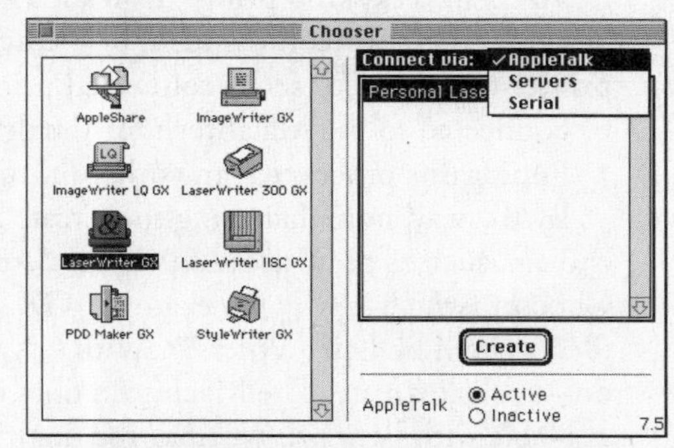

Figure 13-20 *The QuickDraw GX Chooser, with a selection of GX-specific drivers listed.*

To use the Chooser in QuickDraw GX, follow these steps:

1. **Select a printer driver**
   Click on the icon for the printer driver you want to use (I will use LaserWriter GX in most examples here).

2. **Select a connection type (and select AppleTalk active or not)**
   From the "Connect via:" pop-up menu, select the desired connection type. Typically, the options you can choose among are AppleTalk (used for AppleTalk printers), Serial (used primarily for non-AppleTalk printers), or Server (relevant only if you are on a network that uses a server).

   Thus, there is no longer a need for separate printer drivers for AppleTalk and non-AppleTalk versions of the same printer (as was the case for the ImageWriter, for example). The option to switch between AppleTalk and Serial for LaserWriters reflects the fact that some printers using this driver (notably the LaserWriter Select 310) employ a serial connection rather than the much more typical AppleTalk connection.

   Regardless of your choice here, you still need to select separately whether you want AppleTalk active (via the radio buttons at the bottom right of the Chooser).

3. **Create a desktop printer icon for your printer(s)**
   To create a desktop printer icon for an AppleTalk-connected printer, first make sure the printer is on and actually connected to the Macintosh. If so, when you selected the appropriate printer driver, the name of your printer should appear in the right-hand side of the Chooser window (just as it does in the non-GX Chooser). At this point, click the Create button. After a few moments, an icon with the name of your printer will appear on your desktop.

   Personal LaserWriter NTR PDD Maker GX

   Figure 13-21 *LaserWriter GX and PDD Maker GX desktop printer icons.*

   To create a desktop printer icon for a serial-connected printer, simply select the desired serial port icon (Modem or Printer), then click Create. There is no named printer to select. For serial-connected printers, the printer does not have to actually be connected to the Macintosh for the desktop printer icon to be created.

   Repeat this process for any other printers connected to your Macintosh.

   By the way, note that using the Create button does not provide for any optional choices, such as those accessed via the Setup button found in non-GX versions of the Chooser (which is why, for example, GX software does not include printer description files, as used by LaserWriter 8). With GX, all you have to do—indeed, all you *can* do—is click Create. The Macintosh does not actually check what setup options are available with your printer until the first time you print a document. Thus, some printer options may not be immediately accessible for a newly created desktop printer.

   Desktop printer icons must remain on the desktop; if you try to move them into any folder, you will get a message saying you cannot do this. You can delete them, however, by moving them to the Trash.

4. **Create a PDD Maker GX desktop icon**
   Select the PDD Maker GX driver icon and click Create again. This will create a special desktop icon whose function I will describe more in an upcoming section. This step is optional (and you can always come back to the Chooser and do it later), but I recommend taking care of it right away.
5. **Quit the Chooser**
   Unlike with non-GX systems, after you quit it, you may never have to select the Chooser again. The only reason to do so would be to create a new desktop printer icon.

> **BY THE WAY ▶**
>
> **WHAT ABOUT BACKGROUND PRINTING?**
>
> There are no longer any on/off buttons for background printing in QuickDraw GX, because background printing is always on automatically. Also, background printing with QuickDraw GX does not use PrintMonitor. Instead, it uses a new method, directly built into QuickDraw GX, that should be faster and more reliable. The PrintMonitor file remains in your System Folder only for those occasions when you choose not to use QuickDraw GX.

Select to Print a Document

You have a choice of two ways to print a document with QuickDraw GX. Each is outlined below.

- **Print from the desktop printer icon**
  To do this, drag the document icon to be printed to the desired desktop printer icon. This will force the selected document to open from within its creating application. If the application is GX-aware, printing will immediately begin at the current print settings, and the application will quit when done. If the application is not GX-aware, the process will instead halt at the Print dialog box. In this case, select options as desired and click Print.

  You can add more documents to the printer's queue via this method without having to wait for the completion of the current print job. You can even simultaneously assign documents to icons for different printers.
- **Print from within an application**
  To do this, select Print from an application's File menu. Select options as desired from the dialog box, then click Print. Just as with non-GX printing, you may first wish to select Page Setup to access other print-related options.

  The exact nature of the Page Setup and Print dialog boxes that appear will vary depending on whether the particular application supports QuickDraw GX or not. If it does not support QuickDraw GX, you will see dialog boxes similar to those that appear in non-GX systems (for example, with

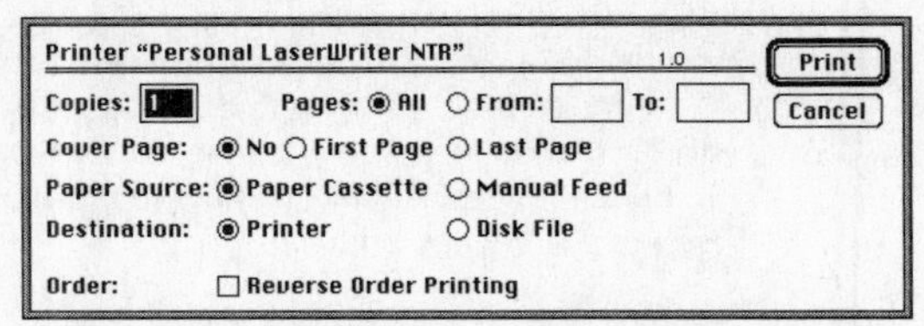

Figure 13-22 *The LaserWriter GX Print dialog box, as it appears with QuickDraw GX running, for an application that is not "GX-aware."*

TAKE NOTE ▶

FOR APPLICATIONS INCOMPATIBLE WITH QUICKDRAW GX, USE QUICKDRAW GX HELPER

Figure 13-23 *The QuickDraw GX Helper and PrinterShare GX extensions.*

Some applications are incompatible with QuickDraw GX and will not print while QuickDraw GX is active. This does not necessarily mean, however, that you have to restart with GX disabled in order to get the document to print—instead, you can temporarily turn off QuickDraw GX just for that application. To do this, you must first have installed an extension called QuickDraw GX Helper. This is not installed as part of an Easy Install of QuickDraw GX; you have to select Custom Install and then choose to install QuickDraw GX Utilities.

With Helper installed, you will see a new command called "Turn Desktop Printing Off" when you select the Apple menu. Select this when the incompatible application is active; you will then get a dialog box telling you what non-GX driver will be used instead. Clicking OK turns off the GX driver for that application (but not for any other application) and substitutes the non-GX driver.

File Edit View Layout
About ClarisDraw...
Help
Turn Desktop printing Off
AppleCD Audio Player
Automated Tasks
Calculator
Chooser

Figure 13-24 *The "Turn Desktop Printing Off" command that appears in the Apple menu when QuickDraw GX Helper is installed.*

For this to work, you must have the alternative compatible non-GX driver present in your Extensions folder. For example, if you are turning off LaserWriter GX, either the LaserWriter or LaserWriter 8 driver must be in the Extensions folder (if both are present, LaserWriter will be selected). Without the needed non-GX driver(s), QuickDraw GX Helper will be of no help.

By the way, since Helper enables a non-GX printer driver, you will not have access to GX PostScript fonts. If this is a problem, you will need to install the appropriate non-GX PostScript printer font files into the Fonts folder (see "QuickDraw GX and Fonts," later in this chapter, for more details).

If you wish, you can later turn GX printing back on for that application by returning to the Apple menu while the relevant application is active and selecting the command that now reads "Turn Desktop Printing On."

If even this technique fails to get your document to print, you will need to restart with the QuickDraw GX extension turned off (use Extensions Manager or a similar utility to do this). You can then select the non-GX driver and print as if you had never installed QuickDraw GX.

(Note: QuickDraw GX Helper may not work with non-Apple printer drivers.)

BY THE WAY ▶

PRINTER SHARING

With the PrinterShare GX extension installed and file sharing turned on, you can let other users share your desktop printer icons in the same way that you can share any other files (as described more generally in Chapter 11). To get the dialog box needed to set access options for the printer icon, select the printer icon and then select Sharing from the File menu.

A printer does not have to be an AppleTalk printer to be shared in this way; in fact, a similar sharing feature is available for non-GX systems via the optional PrinterShare extension. To print with QuickDraw GX, however, the PrinterShare GX extension is required, even if you are not sharing any printers.

LaserWriter GX, you will get dialog boxes that are like those used with LaserWriter 7). If the application does support QuickDraw GX (as SimpleText does, for instance), you will get the new GX-specific dialog boxes, as described in the next section.

If your application supports QuickDraw GX printing, after completing either method of print selection you will briefly see a Printing Status dialog box appear on the screen as a background-printing spool file is created. Shortly afterward, your printing should begin. If you selected manual feed from the Print dialog box, a dialog box, however, will appear in the Finder asking you to confirm that you have inserted paper into the manual feed tray. To print with manual feed, make sure that paper is present, then click Continue.

Respond to Error Messages, If Any Appear

If something goes wrong after you select Print, an error alert should appear. Although the exact wording of a message may be different from those in non-GX systems, most error messages are similar across both systems. For help in determining the meaning of these general messages, refer to Chapter 7. (A selection of GX-specific error messages is covered in the section on "QuickDraw GX Problems," later in this chapter.

Generally, error messages appear in the Finder. If you are not in the Finder at the time the message appears, an alert sound occurs—this is the Mac's way of telling you to go to the Finder to view the message.

Some error messages result in the printing of your document being placed on hold. Assuming you fix the cause of the error, you must then choose to resume printing either by clicking the Resume button in the Print Queue window or by selecting the Resume command in the Printing menu (details on how to do this are described in following sections).

If your application is not QuickDraw GX-aware, printing will proceed similarly to how it would in a non-GX system (including using PrintMonitor, if available).

QuickDraw GX Page Setup and Print Dialog Boxes

Both the Page Setup and Print dialog boxes have a button to toggle between Fewer Choices and More Choices. Though the Fewer Choices displays should be adequate for most basic printing tasks, the descriptions that follow explain the additional options available via More Choices.

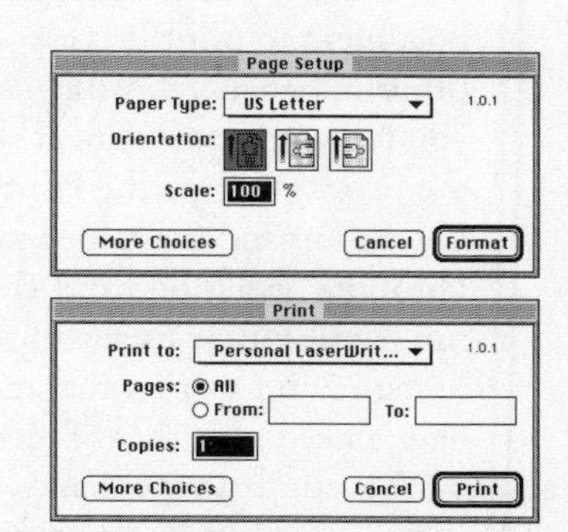

Figure 13-25 *The Fewer Choices Page Setup and Print dialog boxes for LaserWriter GX.*

Page Setup Dialog Box With More Choices selected, icons appear along the left-hand border of the dialog box; with LaserWriter GX, for example, you should see General and LaserWriter Options icons. General is the one selected by default when you open the Page Setup dialog box. From here, you can select the type of paper and printer for which your document is formatted—via the "Paper Type" and "Format for" pop-up menus—even if you do not have the selected paper loaded or selected printer currently attached to your Macintosh. If you click on the LaserWriter Options icon, the dialog box display shifts to a listing of image manipulation choices similar to (though actually fewer than) what is available with the non-GX LaserWriter driver, such as Flip Horizontal and Invert Image. In any case, when you are done making your choices, click the Format button.

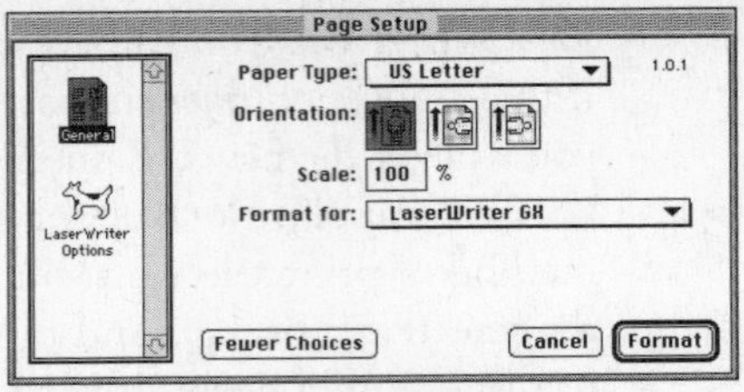

Figure 13-26 *The LaserWriter GX Page Setup dialog box, with the General icon selected.*

Print Dialog Box and Printer Extensions With More Choices selected, a column of icons appears along the left-hand border of the Print dialog box; again using LaserWriter GX as an example, the default selection is General. From here, you use the "Print to" pop-up menu to select what desktop printer you wish to use. Ideally, it should match the type of printer that you selected in Page Setup (otherwise, your document may print with incorrect margins). You can also select from other options, such as whether you want the paper feed to be automatic or manual (if you select Manual, you will get a "Manual Feed Alert" message when printing actually begins, requesting that you insert paper as needed) or whether you want the document's destination to be the printer or a PostScript file (a distinction explained in more detail in Chapter 7). Of course, you also have the standard options to set the number of copies and page range to be printed (also available with Fewer Choices selected). Most of these options are essentially the same ones available with non-GX drivers.

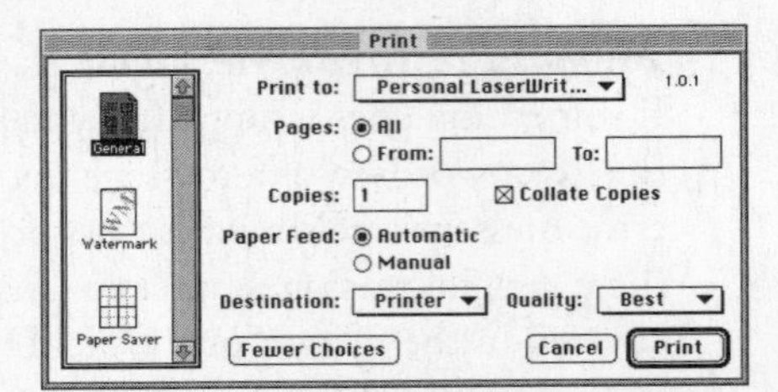

Figure 13-27 *The LaserWriter GX Print dialog box, with the General icon selected.*

Besides General, you will find at least two other icons: Print Time and Paper Match. Print Time allows you to schedule when you want a document to print (in case you don't want it to print immediately), while Paper Match allows you to override the default setting for the size of the paper as set via the Printing menu's Input Tray command (described in the next section). For more details on using these extensions, consult Apple Guide or any of several books on System 7.5; I suspect that most users will never have a need for either of these two extensions.

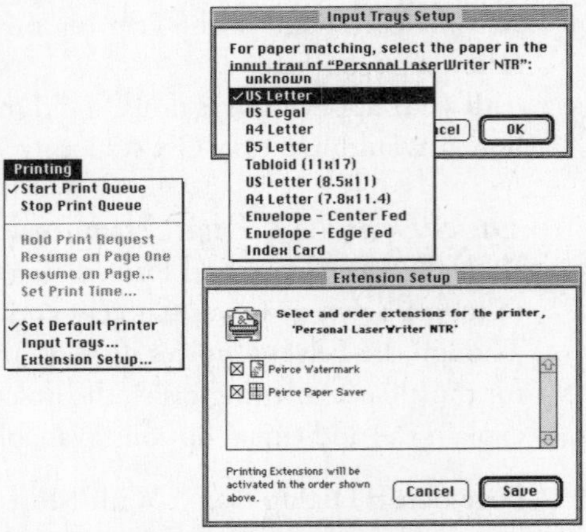

Figure 13-28 *Left: The Printing menu as it appears after selecting a LaserWriter GX desktop printer icon. Right: the dialog boxes that appear after selecting the Input Trays and Extension Setup commands from the Printing Menu.*

You can further enhance the functions of the Print dialog box by adding optional printer extensions. For example, Apple includes an N-Up Printing Options extension (for printing up to 16 pages on a sheet of paper) and an EPS Extension (relevant if you intend to create PostScript files via the Print dialog box, which may be useful for importing graphics into applications that do not support QuickDraw GX). Otherwise, these extensions come from companies other than Apple (as examples, Apple includes Peirce's Watermark & Paper Saver extensions on its System Software CD-ROM).

You install extensions by dragging the extension files to the System Folder icon or directly to the Extensions folder; you do not have to restart to begin using them. You can separately select which extensions will be available for a particular printer via the desktop printer icon's Printing menu (described in the next section).

When you are done making your selections, click the Print button.

The Printing Menu

When you single-click on a desktop printer icon, a Printing menu is added to the menu bar. These commands only apply to the selected printer; you need to select these options separately for each desktop printer icon.

By using the two commands at the top of the menu (Stop Print Queue and Start Print Queue), you can choose to stop or start printing of all items currently in the queue of the selected printer. The middle items are only available when a specific file is selected from the Print Queue window (described in the next section). Finally, there are three special commands at the bottom of the Printing menu:

- **Set Default Printer**
  If you have more than one desktop printer icon, you need to select one as the default printer. This is the one to which all print requests will be directed, unless you specifically select otherwise from the Print dialog box. Actually, for applications that do not yet support the GX Print dialog box, the default printer will be the only printer you can use; to use another printer in this case, you will have to change the default selection.

  To change the default printer for any reason, simply select the Set Default Printer command from the Printing menu of the desired desktop printer icon. The Set Default Printer command of the default printer will have a check mark in front of it; also, the desktop icon for the default printer will have a bold outline.
- **Input Trays ...**
  Select the Input Trays command, and choose the default size of paper for each tray listed. Typically, you would select the size(s) you most commonly use in your printer's input tray(s).
- **Disable Manual Feed Alerts**
  This turns off the alerts for manual feed printing on PostScript printers.
- **Extension Setup ...**
  When you select the Extension Setup command, you will see a list of all optional extensions available for your printer (such as the Watermark and Paper Saver extensions mentioned previously). To turn off a particular extension (so that it will not be available in the Print dialog box of the selected printer), click the checkbox next to it so as to remove the "*x*." To change the processing order of the extensions, drag an extension up or down the list. This feature is provided because the operation of some extensions may vary depending on which extension is processed first.

> **TECHNICALLY SPEAKING ▶**
>
> **SOLVING PAPER SIZE SELECTION CONFUSION**
>
> You can select a paper size format from the Page Setup dialog box. You can select the default size of the paper in the input tray from the Input Tray command in the Printing menu. You can then override that selection from the Paper Match extension in the Print dialog box.
>
> All of this can admittedly get a bit confusing. How do you decide what paper size to select, and from where do you select it? Here are some simple guidelines: From the Input Trays command for your printer, select the size you most commonly use (US Letter, typically). If you ever print at some odd size, such as an envelope, select that size from the Page Setup dialog box.
>
> Use the separate manual feed tray, if available, to load the odd-sized paper, rather than your standard input tray. In this case, also remember to select Manual Feed from the Print menu. I would avoid bothering with the Paper Match extension altogether. In some cases, though, you may get the Tray Mismatch Alert message when you try to print. If so, assuming you have the correct paper in place, simply click the Print button; the document should still print normally.
>
> **SEE:** • **"Printing and Printing-Related Problems," later in this chapter, for more on the Tray Mismatch Alert**

The Print Queue Window

If you double-click on a desktop printer icon, it opens up the printer's Print Queue window. The item listed in the top half of the window, if any, is the item currently printing; items in the bottom half of the window are waiting to be printed.

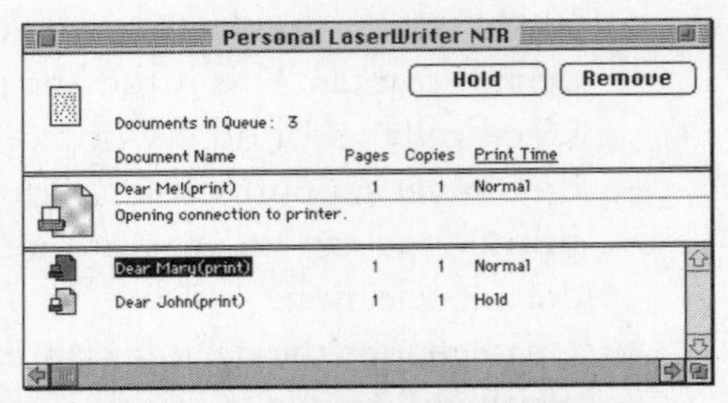

Figure 13-29 *A desktop printer's Print Queue window, seen just as the document "Dear Me" is about to print.*

When a print job is in progress, messages concerning the print job will appear in this window, much as they appeared in the PrintMonitor window of non-GX printers.

Meanwhile, back on the desktop, the desktop printer icon actually changes to reflect changes in current printing status. For example, if there are any documents waiting in the print queue, a mini-picture of a document is added to the icon. If there is currently a printing problem, a triangular yellow alert symbol is added to the icon.

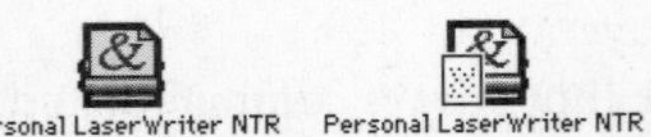

Figure 13-30 *The changing face of a desktop printer icon—normal (left), when a document is in the queue (center), and when an alert has occurred (right).*

Print Time Each item has its own Print Time category. Most often, the setting will be Normal, meaning that the item is scheduled to be printed as soon as the print jobs ahead of it in the queue are completed.

Location in the queue is initially determined by the order in which the print requests were made. By default, document names are sorted in the queue based on their Print Time order; you can tell this is so because "Print Time" is underlined. To sort the list based on another column (and have that column name be underlined), simply click that column's name (though this will not change the print order of the currently listed documents).

If you select an item in the queue and click the Hold button (or select Hold Print Request from the Printing menu), the document's print time will be listed as Hold. These documents are not printed until you again select the document name in the queue and either click the Resume button in the Print Queue window (the Hold button toggles to a Resume button when you select a held document) or select one of the Resume commands from the Printing menu.

Other Print Time options are available by selecting "Set Print Time ..." from the Printing menu. From here, you can schedule an item as Urgent (so that it jumps to the head of the queue), or set it for delayed printing at some future scheduled time. The functions of the Print Time printer extension (described previously) largely overlap with the Print Time option in the Printing menu; choose whichever one is more convenient for you.

You can also drag a document from the (lower) queue list area to the (upper) print area of the Print Queue window, or vice versa. This has the similar effect of changing a document's status from either Hold to Normal or Normal to Hold.

You can completely delete an item from the print queue by selecting it and then clicking the Remove button.

Print Preview If you double-click an item in the queue, it will open up a print-preview version of the document in SimpleText. This preview information is taken from a special print version of the file stored in the PrintMonitor Documents folder (similar to how spooled printing files are stored in the PrintMonitor Documents folder when using background printing in non-GX systems).

Actually, you can even drag a document directly out of the Print Queue window altogether. This creates a print file version of the document on the desktop (identical to the same type of file in the PrintMonitor Documents folder). You can drag this print file back into a queue when you want to print it. If you double-click the print file while it is out of the queue, it will still open up in SimpleText.

Special Case: Portable Digital Documents (PDDs)

QuickDraw GX offers a special bonus—the ability to create documents, called Portable Digital Documents (PDDs), that can be viewed and printed on any Macintosh. Even if the original document's creating application is missing, and even if the fonts that were used to create the document are not available, the display and printed copy of the PDD will be an exact match of the original document. The main limitation is that you cannot edit this document in any way (there had to be some drawback to this!). Still, this means that someone could open or print a PDD file that you created from a PageMaker document, for example, and have it appear exactly as you created it, without needing to have their own copy of PageMaker. All they need is QuickDraw GX and SimpleText. (Before you run out and install GX just so you can create PDDs, though, bear in mind that this is still more limited than what you can already do with programs such as Adobe Acrobat.)

Figure 13-31 *A print file document (left) and a PDD document (right); both function similarly in QuickDraw GX.*

To create a PDD, use the PDD Maker GX desktop icon (created via the GX Chooser, as described earlier in this chapter). Either drag a document directly to the PDD Maker icon or select PDD Maker GX as the "Print to" location in the Print dialog box of a GX-savvy application. When you do this, a PDD is created.

PDDs only work with QuickDraw GX installed. For example, if you double-click on a PDD icon when GX is not running, you will get an alert message that says "SimpleText cannot display this type of document." If you try to open the document from within SimpleText, it will not appear in the Open dialog box. Conversely, unlike with ordinary text documents, you should use only SimpleText to open a PDD. If you try to open a PDD in another word processor (whether or not GX is installed), it will appear as gibberish.

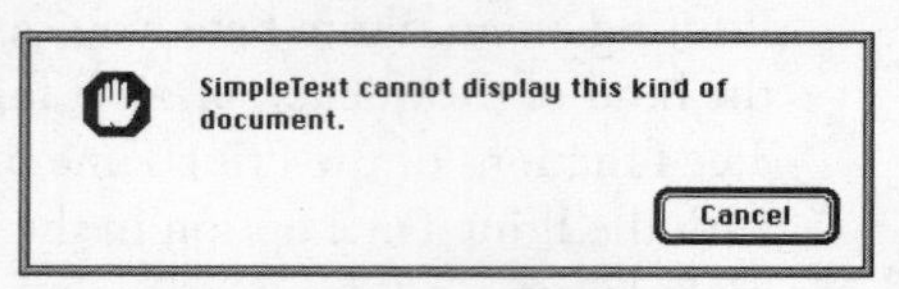

Figure 13-32 *The message that appears if you try to open a PDD document when QuickDraw GX is disabled.*

Finally, you may be thinking that PDDs sound suspiciously similar to the print file documents you can create with any desktop printer (as described in "Print Preview" in the previous section). If so, you are right. Both the PDD files and print files described here, though, are separate from the PostScript print files that you can create by selecting PostScript as the Destination in the LaserWriter GX Print dialog box.

PDD Maker GX and the Printing Menu The Printing menu for the PDD Maker GX icon is a bit different from that for other desktop printer icons. In particular, it has a special command called "PDD Maker Setup" that you can use to designate a default folder for saving PDDs.

TECHNICALLY SPEAKING ▶

THE FILE TYPES OF SIMPLETEXT DOCUMENTS

In Chapter 8, I explained the difference between read-only and read-write SimpleText (and TeachText) text documents. I explained how each had a different file type (" TEXT" for read-write versus "ttro" for read-only). I also explained how you could change a document from read-only to read-write or vice versa, simply by changing the file's type code (via a utility such as Snitch).

PDDs are still listed as SimpleText documents in the Get Info window, but they have a different file type from either of the previous two text document types. The file type code for a PDD is "sjob." Print file documents (the ones stored in the PrintMonitor Documents folder, or created by dragging a file from the Print Queue window to the desktop) have a slightly different file type, "tjob." Aside from the fact that these two document types have separate icons, though, they function almost identically. In fact, you can successfully change a document from a PDD ("sjob") to a print file ("tjob") document just by changing its file type (again via a utility such as Snitch). You cannot change either of these into a TEXT or ttro document (or vice versa), however, by changing the document's type code—the icon will change, but the document will not open successfully.

PDDs and SimpleText What PDD Maker actually does is create a special type of SimpleText document (see "Technically Speaking: The File Types of SimpleText Documents," for more details). Ordinary SimpleText documents are simply plain text documents that can be opened by virtually any word processor. When you use the scroll bars for these type of documents, you scroll through the pages of the document.

In contrast, the scroll bars of PDDs only take you up and down a single page. To move to another page of a PDD, you have to use SimpleText's page navigation commands, which are located in the Edit menu (Next Page, Previous Page, and Go to Page). These commands are dimmed and unavailable when you view a plain text document.

Figure 13-33
SimpleText's page navigation commands become active when viewing a PDD file.

QuickDraw GX and Fonts

It's hard to ignore QuickDraw GX's new printing features; if you don't master them to some extent, you won't be able to print anything. At the same time, though, it's almost too easy to ignore GX's new methods for handling fonts. You can install and use QuickDraw GX for quite a while without necessarily noticing the significant font-related changes that have taken place. If you don't understand these changes, however, you will eventually have problems.

This section focuses on the new types of fonts specific to QuickDraw GX: how to recognize them, and how they are different from the previous type of fonts. I also explain how you can still use your older styles of fonts in GX. Finally, I explain how to fix things when they go wrong.

Bitmapped Fonts

First, the good news: You can still use all your existing bitmapped fonts. They will work exactly the same in QuickDraw GX as they do in non-GX versions of the system software.

TrueType Fonts

With QuickDraw GX, there are now two types of TrueType fonts. Simple (non-GX) TrueType fonts, the standard types prior to the release of System 7.5, can be used equally well in GX or non-GX systems. In contrast, complex (GX) TrueType fonts are designed to take advantage of the new capabilities of QuickDraw GX. Using these fonts without GX installed may cause the text to be displayed and/or print incorrectly.

Installing QuickDraw GX does not convert non-GX TrueType fonts to GX TrueType fonts.

SEE: • **"Technically Speaking: A Primer on Using QuickDraw GX Fonts" and "Take Note: Identifying GX Versus non-GX Fonts" for more details**

PostScript Fonts

There is no compatibility between the GX and non-GX versions of PostScript fonts. As a result, you should not use non-GX PostScript fonts with QuickDraw GX running, nor should you use GX PostScript fonts without QuickDraw GX running. Similarly, avoid using GX PostScript fonts in a document if you plan on opening that document later when GX is not running. If you ignore all these warnings, text is likely to be displayed and/or print incorrectly at the very least; at worst, you may get a system crash.

TECHNICALLY SPEAKING ▶

A PRIMER ON USING QUICKDRAW GX FONTS

New font capabilities with QuickDraw GX You may wonder why Apple bothered to create this new GX-specific font technology. The answer is that QuickDraw GX greatly expands your ability to manipulate the appearance of a font. For example, with non-GX fonts, about the only way you can vary the thickness of a character is by shifting from plain style to bold. Sometimes you might find a "light" style that appears thinner than plain style of the same font, but that's about it. With QuickDraw GX, though, you are able to vary the thickness (technically referred to as the *weight*) of a character in a virtually limitless series of gradations, as well as the width of the character set and the spacing between characters. After you set these characteristics for an entire font, with the help of special typographic software, the manipulated font can then be used by any GX-savvy application. These abilities were previously available for PostScript, but only if you had Adobe's multiple-master PostScript fonts. With QuickDraw GX, however, they are available for virtually all GX TrueType and PostScript fonts.

A technical discussion of the details of these new options is beyond the scope of this book. Suffice it to say that when you start to explore these new capabilities, you will add a whole new collection of terms to your vocabulary (can you say *glyphs* and *ligatures*?). There are, however, a couple of basic points that you should be aware of right away:

- Using these new font capabilities requires QuickDraw GX-savvy applications as well as QuickDraw GX fonts. It may also require special typographic software capable of creating the desired modifications to the font. Since Apple presently is not shipping any software of either sort with System 7.5 (not even SimpleText qualifies), you may not be able to take advantage of any of these new features at first. The CD-ROM version of System 7.5, however, came with a presentation file (called GX Type Expo) that at least demonstrated all of GX's new font tricks.

  Without GX-savvy applications, GX fonts behave just like non-GX fonts, even though QuickDraw GX is active. The good news is that GX fonts will work at some level with almost any application, even if the application is not GX-savvy.
- A primary difference between GX and non-GX fonts is that non-GX font characters are all based on a single keyboard keystroke (or modifier-character keystroke combination). QuickDraw GX fonts no longer have this restriction; separate characters can be combined into a single character. Examples of this would include a lowercase *i* with an asterisk for its dot, or combining the "1," "/," and "2" characters into a new "1/2" character. This is why QuickDraw GX fonts are referred to as complex fonts, while non-GX fonts are referred to as simple fonts.
- When you install QuickDraw GX via Easy Install, it installs the following GX fonts: Apple Chancery, Hoefler Text, Skia, and Tekton Plus. The first three fonts are TrueType fonts; Tekton Plus is a PostScript font (with *Plus* added to indicate that it is a GX font).

TAKE NOTE ▶

IDENTIFYING GX VERSUS NON-GX FONTS

Unfortunately, there is no easy way to identify whether a font is a GX PostScript font, a GX TrueType font, or a non-GX TrueType font. Neither looking at the font file's Get Info window, or double-clicking the font file to open its display window, or seeing how the font is listed in a Font menu yields any useful clues.

The only sure way to know if a font is a GX font or not requires using Apple's ResEdit utility. For those who are willing to try it, here it is: First, open up the font file (or suitcase) in ResEdit, and then open up its "sfnt" resource window (this is where the PostScript information that used to be in the printer font file is now stored). Finally, open one of the resources listed in the window, and look in the right-hand column. If the first four letters are "typ1," the font is PostScript. If the first four letters are "true," it is is a GX TrueType font. If the first four letters are anything else, it is probably a non-GX TrueType font. If you can't find an "sfnt" resource, it is probably a bitmapped font.

A simpler way to distinguish TrueType from PostScript fonts in QuickDraw GX (if they are still in their original suitcase file) is to open up the suitcase file containing the font. If the files in the suitcase have size numbers in their name (such as "Times 12"), the font is PostScript; if not, it is TrueType. This method should work as long as you haven't modified the contents of the suitcase or changed the names of the font.

The fact that GX PostScript fonts and TrueType fonts now behave almost identically will probably be the most confusing part of shifting to QuickDraw GX. The good news, however, is that this distinction will be less important in QuickDraw GX than it was before. Hopefully, some shareware author will write a utility that simplifies the identification process.

Also bear in mind that there are really two kinds of GX PostScript fonts. Those converted from non-GX fonts will be unable to take advantage of the new typographic features possible with GX fonts. In contrast, fonts specifically designed to be GX fonts can naturally use all of GX's new font features. The ResEdit identification procedure described here does not distinguish between these two types.

(Note: QuickDraw GX fonts *can* print okay, even when not running GX, if you have a LaserWriter with 3MB or more of RAM. Unfortunately this requirement leaves out most LaserWriters).

The main reason for this lack of compatibility is that QuickDraw GX PostScript fonts no longer use separate screen font and printer font files (see Chapter 9 for details on this subject). The printer font file information is now included in the basic font file, just as it always has been for TrueType fonts. In fact, a PostScript font file now looks and behaves on the desktop exactly like a TrueType font.

In this regard, with QuickDraw GX, I would recommend against having a TrueType and a PostScript version of the same font in your Fonts folder. This is more likely to cause problems than it would in non-GX systems.

Ultimately, eliminating the need for printer font files will be a great advantage, as it eliminates many of the hassles and complexities associated with their use. For example, you no longer have to worry that if you select a font because its screen font is in your Font menu, it might not print correctly because the matching printer font file is missing.

In the short run, however, you are faced with the problem of making sure that your PostScript fonts are in the right format to be used with your version of the system software. In particular, if you are using QuickDraw GX, you must *enable* your non-GX PostScript fonts before you can use them.

Two ways to enable a PostScript font are detailed below.

- **When You Install QuickDraw GX**
  If there are any non-GX PostScript fonts in your Fonts folder when you install QuickDraw GX, they are automatically converted to the GX format. In addition, all of the now-unneeded screen fonts and printer font files are placed in a special folder inside your System Folder called "•Archived Type 1 Fonts•" (recall from Chapter 9 that Type 1 fonts are a type of PostScript font; virtually all commonly used PostScript fonts are Type 1). The derived GX version of the font is then placed in the Fonts folder.

  For this method to work, you must have enough free disk space when installing QuickDraw GX to hold both the existing and converted forms of any PostScript fonts that are currently in your System Folder.

  The non-GX version of the fonts is saved so that you can return to them if you later wish to abandon using QuickDraw GX. (This return becomes necessary because, as I stated, you should not use the converted-to-GX form of the PostScript fonts when QuickDraw GX is not running.) To re-enable the non-GX versions of your fonts, remove the GX version of the fonts from the Fonts folder and drag the files from the •Archived Type 1 Fonts• folder back to the Fonts folder.

  Even better, if you reinstall just the non-GX printer font files (and do not remove the matching GX font files), the Mac will be able to access either the GX or non-GX versions of these PostScript fonts as appropriate. (This method also applies to fonts enabled with Type 1 Enabler, described next.) Fonts remaining in the •Archived Type 1 Fonts• folder may not be used, although LaserWriter 8.3 (or later) checks in the •Archived Type 1 Fonts• folder for PostScript fonts.

- **Using the Type 1 Enabler utility**
  Type 1 Enabler, a utility included with QuickDraw GX, lets you convert any non-GX PostScript font that was not present in your System Folder when you first installed the software to a GX PostScript font. Before you do this, Apple recommends that you make sure each screen font suitcase contains only one font family. Thus, for example, if Garamond and Hobo font files are in the same suitcase, you should separate them into two suitcases (see Chapter 9 for more on how to do this if needed). When I have ignored this recommendation, however, the conversion has still appeared to be successful.

  Figure 13-34 *The Type I Enabler utility is used to convert non-GX PostScript fonts to the GX format (it is not needed for fonts that were in your System Folder when you first installed QuickDraw GX).*

  After completing any suitcase modifications, launch Type 1 Enabler. Select the Enable command if necessary, and locate each font (suitcase) you wish to enable. The utility will ask you for a destination folder for the enabled font; typically, you will choose the Fonts folder of your GX System Folder. After determining this, the enabled font is created (don't forget, you will still need the matching printer font file present, ideally in the same location as the screen font, for this conversion to succeed).

The enabled suitcase will contain copies of the previous screen fonts, plus the newly created PostScript font file (actually, it should contain one PostScript font file for every style variant printer font file of the font that was present). The original font files remain unmodified in their original location (or moved to a special folder called Saved Suitcases if you are saving the enabled font to the same location as the original font).

SEE:
- **"Technically Speaking: A Primer on Using QuickDraw GX Fonts"**
- **"Take Note: Identifying GX Versus Non-GX Fonts"**
- **"Take Note: QuickDraw GX and ATM"**
- **"By the Way: QuickDraw GX Utilities"**

TAKE NOTE ▶

QUICKDRAW GX AND ATM

Adobe Type Manager (ATM) is still required with QuickDraw GX for proper display and printing of PostScript fonts (this is one key difference between TrueType and PostScript fonts in QuickDraw GX). A special GX version of Adobe Type Manager was included with QuickDraw GX when the latter was first released. Current versions, however, are shipped with a standard version of ATM (3.8.2 or later) that works well with both GX and non-GX fonts. This is a native PowerPC code version of ATM. Also note the following:

- Even with ATM 3.8.2 or later, you cannot use GX fonts unless GX is running. Otherwise, at the very least, the fonts' screen displays will be subject to the same jaggies that would occur if you were not using ATM at all. Similarly, unless their printer font file information is built into the printer's ROM, the fonts will not print correctly.
- It might seem that the screen font files in an enabled GX font suitcase are not required anymore (much as they are not required when using TrueType fonts). At least one screen font file (typically at 10- or 12-point size) however, is still needed for ATM to work with the GX font (this is similar to the ATM requirement for non-GX fonts, as explained more in Chapter 9).
- With GX running and ATM installed, PostScript fonts appear as Geneva when displaying a character at a point size less than one half the size of the smallest bitmap available. For example, a font with a single 24-point bitmap would display as Geneva at 11 points and lower.
- If you separately install ATM with QuickDraw GX already installed, it installs GX versions of its "substitution fonts" (Adobe Sans MM and Adobe Serif MM). If you later disable GX, ATM will not work, giving you a message that you need to reinstall the non-GX substitution fonts. To do this, you need to reinstall ATM with QuickDraw GX off—apparently, the ATM installer will not install both. This can get to be a hassle if you switch back and forth between GX and non-GX. One solution is to add an asterisk at the end of the substitution fonts you want to be disabled, move them to the disabled Fonts folder, and then reinstall ATM to get the other version of the fonts. Now, with a utility such as Suitcase or Now Startup Manager, you can shuttle the appropriate fonts back and forth depending on whether GX is on or off.

BY THE WAY ▶

GX FONTS AND REMOVING QUICKDRAW GX

If you decide to remove QuickDraw GX, note that in the original version of QuickDraw GX, the Installer's Custom Remove feature did not remove QuickDraw GX fonts. You had to remove these yourself and, if appropriate, replace them with matching non-GX fonts, as stored in the •Archived Type 1 Fonts• folder. Current versions of QuickDraw GX apparently do all of this housework for you as part of the Installer's Custom Remove process. Even in this case, however, QuickDraw GX fonts that do not have a match in the •Archived Type 1 Fonts• folder are not removed.

QuickDraw GX and Graphics

QuickDraw GX has features that assist in better graphic color matching (by making use of the ColorSync extension). In addition, built-in routines make it easy for almost any application to include enhanced graphics manipulation features, that previously were only possible with high-end graphics applications and/or PostScript. Finally, as mentioned in Chapter 10, QuickDraw GX improves transfers of graphic images via the clipboard. In particular, an image's format (such as EPS and TIFF) is more likely to be preserved (rather than converted to a PICT format) when it is copied and pasted. As is true for most other GX features, however, making use of the enhanced clipboard requires software that is QuickDraw GX-savvy. Apple's Scrapbook is one example of a GX-savvy program.

BY THE WAY ▶

QUICKDRAW GX UTILITIES

There are four utilities included with QuickDraw GX. To install them on your hard disk, select Custom Install and then select "QuickDraw GX Utilities." Two of these utilities, QuickDraw GX Helper (used to disable desktop printing) and Type 1 Enabler (used to enable non-GX PostScript fonts), are described in the relevant sections of the main text of this chapter. The other two are Paper Type Editor (used to create extensions that add custom paper sizes to the Paper Type menus in various dialog boxes) and LaserWriter Utility (which has actually now been superseded by Apple Printer Utility, as described more in Chapters 7 and 9).

Solve It! QuickDraw GX Problems

Much GX-related troubleshooting advice has already been described in the immediately preceding sections, as part of the general overview of QuickDraw GX. What follows is a more focused look at troubleshooting issues, emphasizing the error messages you may receive.

Remember, most of the error messages described in this section appear in the Finder. If you are not in the Finder at the time, you will have to leave your application and return to the Finder to see the message.

Memory Problems

Symptoms:

- Low-memory message alerts appear when running QuickDraw GX.
- More rarely, a memory-related problem may prevent the Macintosh from starting up when GX is active.

Causes:

Almost by definition, the main cause here is insufficient memory to run QuickDraw GX adequately. Recall that running System 7.5 with QuickDraw GX requires at least twice as much memory as you need to run it without QuickDraw GX. This means that the absolute minimum required memory to run GX is 8MB.

What to do:

Problems Running with Only 8MB of Memory

If you only have the minimally required 8MB of memory installed (it would have to be 16MB on a Power Mac), you can still expect to have memory problems when you use QuickDraw GX. For example, Apple claims that in this case you can enable no more than seven printing extensions and seven desktop printers at one time without getting a low memory alert (admittedly, this is not a major concern for most of us). If you want to have more than seven desktop printers, removing a printing extension may help alleviate memory difficulties, and vice versa.

Personally, I have had problems using QuickDraw GX with only 8MB of RAM even with just one or two extensions and desktop printers. In one case I was unable to open any windows in the Finder, even though I had several megabytes of unused RAM.

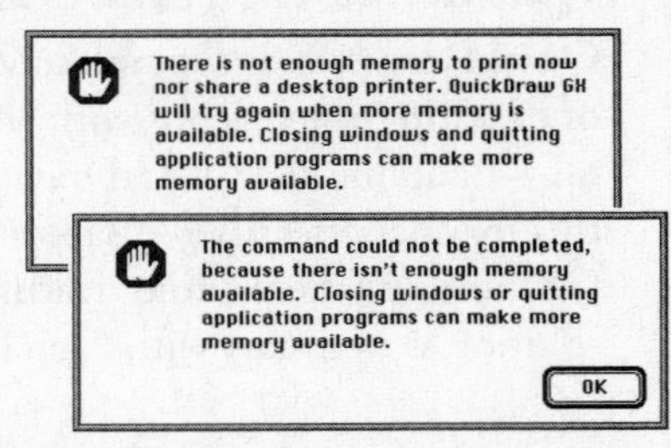

Figure 13-35 *Examples of low memory alerts that may appear when running QuickDraw GX.*

If a low memory alert does appear, try deactivating printing extensions or deleting desktop printers. Also, try closing any open windows in the Finder, close any unneeded documents in any open applications, and (even better) quit any applications that do not need to be open. Using RAM Doubler to double your RAM will also help. As always, adding more physical RAM is the best long-term solution.

Memory Problems Caused By Inactive Desktop Printers

The presence of several inactive desktop printers (as described in the next section) on the desktop or on disks other than the startup disk can cause low-memory alerts to appear. In some cases, they may prevent your computer from starting up. The solution here is to start up with extensions off (by holding down the Shift key at startup), drag the inactive desktop printers to the Trash, and then restart normally.

Printing and Printing-Related Problems

Symptoms:

- Some or all aspects of QuickDraw GX printing features are not usable. In the worst case, all of QuickDraw GX appears disabled. Desktop printer icons may appear with an "X" over them.
- Page Setup and Print dialog boxes in specific applications are not the expected GX dialog boxes.

Causes:

GX-specific causes include needed extensions not loading at startup, desktop printing turned off by QuickDraw GX Helper, a printer driver not selected from the Chooser, no desktop printer created, an incompatible application, a mismatch between the selected paper-size format and the paper size in the printer, or damaged files.

What to do:

QuickDraw GX Features Are Missing

QuickDraw GX Is Completely Disabled The most likely reason for the appearance of desktop printer icons with an "X" over them is that you started up with extensions off—disabling the QuickDraw GX extension in this manner effectively disables all of QuickDraw GX, not just the printing features. The obvious solution is to restart with QuickDraw GX active.

Figure 13-36 *Desktop printer icons with an "X" over them, indicating that you cannot use them for desktop printing.*

It may also happen if you start up with ColorSync disabled, as this extension (which should load before QuickDraw GX) is needed for QuickDraw GX to load. If ColorSync is missing, you should get a message indicating this at the end of the startup sequence.

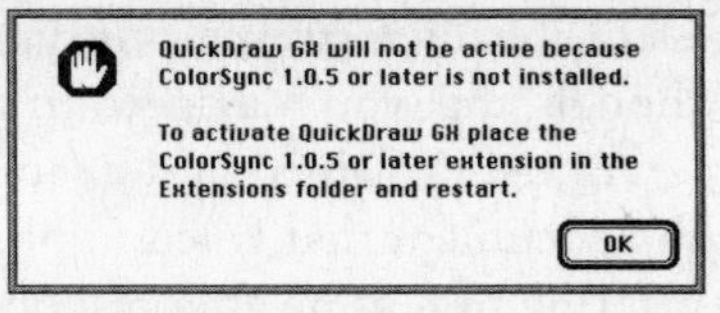

Figure 13-37 *This message appears if you try to load QuickDraw GX when ColorSync is missing or disabled.*

In any case, if you try to open one of the desktop printer icons marked with an "X," you will get the message that says it could not be opened because the creating application could not be found.

Figure 13-38 *This message appears if you try to open the queue window for a desktop printer that has an "X" over it.*

By the way, if you copy a desktop printer icon to another disk, the copied icon will probably have an "X" over it even if the original did not. This is normal and does not affect your use of the original unmarked desktop printer.

QuickDraw GX Is Enabled at Startup But Does Not Work In this situation, as in the previous one, desktop printer icons will have an "X" over them. QuickDraw GX nevertheless seems enabled because when you select the Chooser, you see the GX printer drivers rather than the non-GX ones. If you try to select a GX printer driver, however, you cannot do so.

If this happens, you probably have a damaged GX-related file. For example, when this happened to me, I ran Norton Disk Doctor, and it reported a file length problem with LaserWriter GX. Since this was not a problem that Disk Doctor could fix, the solution was to delete the driver and reinstall a new one (I used the GX Installer to do this). After that I restarted, and everything worked fine.

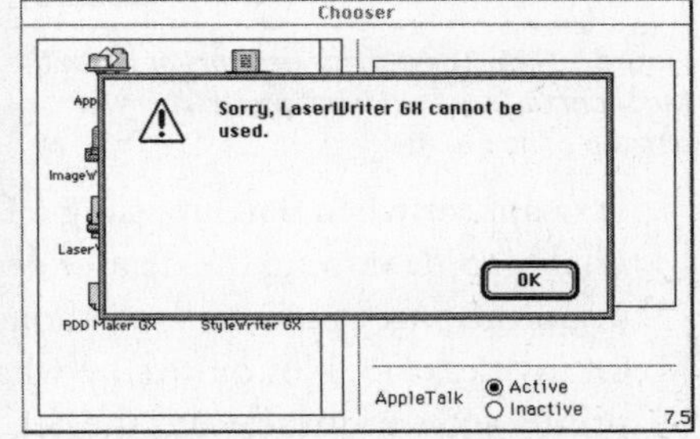

Figure 13-39 *This message may appear in the Chooser if you have damaged GX-related software.*

By the way, if you select Print from within an application before you fix this problem, you will get an error message.

QuickDraw GX Page Setup and Print Dialog Boxes Are Missing This happens when you are using an application that is not GX-aware. There is nothing you can do to fix this.

It can also happen if you have installed QuickDraw GX Helper and turned off desktop printing for a particular application. To reverse this, go to the Apple menu and select the Turn Desktop Printing On command.

Printing Fails

Sometimes QuickDraw GX appears to be enabled and running correctly (desktop printer icons are not crossed), yet printing still fails. Typically an alert message appears, either as soon as you select Print from an application's File menu or after you click the Print button in a Print dialog box (or after dragging a file to a desktop printer).

Occasionally, however, printing fails without any message appearing (remember, though, that you may need to go to the Finder to see a particular error message).

As first explained in the section on"The Print Queue Window" earlier in this chapter, the document that failed to print is likely to be placed on Hold. In this case, to get printing to resume after responding to an error message, go to the Print Queue window, select the document name, and click the Resume button. Alternatively, you can terminate the print process altogether by clicking the Remove button.

The Mac Cannot Find a Valid Printer In this situation, the Macintosh is unable to determine which desktop printer you intend to use (or it may be unable to find any desktop printers at all). The exact message varies with the particular situation. For example, if you have never created any desktop printer icons, you should get a message such as "Your request could not be completed because there are no desktop printers."

Figure 13-40 *These messages appear when the Mac cannot figure out what printer driver or desktop printer to use.*

If, instead, you get a message that says "not a valid printer chosen," you are probably trying to print without GX being enabled, after having used GX to print in a previous session. As a result, the Mac may not know which non-GX printer driver to use. The simple solution here is to go to the Chooser and select a driver.

A message that a particular application is "unable to print" or "unable to set up the page" may appear when you are using a GX-aware application (such as SimpleText) and it is unable to determine the default desktop printer. For example, I once got the "unable to setup the page" message even though it seemed that a valid default desktop printer was on my desktop. Not quite sure what else to do, I simply clicked on the default desktop printer icon and reselected the Set Default Printer command from the Printing menu. When I tried to print again, it succeeded.

These messages (or other related ones) may also appear if any of your printing-related software is damaged or if you have QuickDraw GX disabled (so that each of your desktop printer icons has an "X" over it).

Print Failure Alert Appears Most reasons for this are similar to causes described in Chapter 7. For example, an alert message saying that "the requested printer could not be found," most likely means that your printer is not turned on, is not yet warmed up, or its cables are not properly connected. A message that refers to an "unknown error" more likely indicates a PostScript error or similar document-specific error.

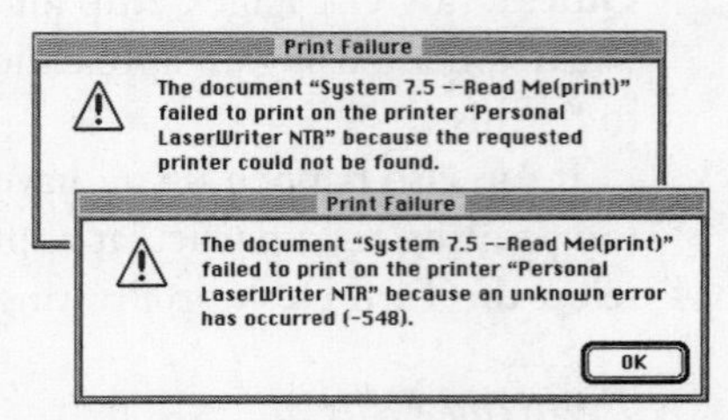

Figure 13-41 *Two examples of Print Failure alert messages.*

Documents May Get Stuck in the Queue Occasionally, jobs waiting in a desktop printer's queue may not be printed, even though no error message appears. If this happens, check the status of the document in the desktop printer's Print Queue window to ensure that it is not on Hold. If it is, select the document name and click the Resume button to change its status. If the current status of the document is Normal but it is still not printing, a system software bug may have caused the document to get "stuck." In this case, restart the Macintosh; the document should now print.

PrinterShare GX Is Missing The PrinterShare GX extension is not optional when printing with QuickDraw GX, even if you aren't sharing any printers. If you try to print without PrinterShare GX in your Extensions folder, you will get an error message informing you about this. The solution is to re-enable PrinterShare GX (by getting it to the Extensions folder) if it has been disabled, or to reinstall it (using the GX Installer disks) if the extension cannot be found anywhere on your startup disk. As always, after making these changes, restart the Macintosh before trying to print again.

Figure 13-42 *This message may appear if you try to print a document without PrinterShare GX in your Extensions folder.*

Tray Mismatch Alert Appears When a Tray Mismatch Alert appears, the paper format you have selected for your document (via the Page Setup dialog box) does not match the paper size that the Macintosh believes is in the selected input tray of the printer (as determined via the Input Trays command from the printer's Printing menu, or via the setting in the Paper Match extension as selected from the Print dialog box). If you want the printer's paper type selection to change to match the format as selected in Page Setup (presumably because that is the type of paper you are now actually using), click "Manually changed to ..." (if you have also checked the Save checkbox, the changed selection will become the new default size for the input tray). Otherwise, you can click the "Continue printing" option if it is undimmed (additionally indicating whether you prefer the document to be cropped or scaled, if needed).

A pop-up menu lets you switch to different input trays (which presumably have different sizes of paper), if your printer has this option.

In any case, when you are done, click Print (to continue printing) or Cancel (if you have given up in despair).

The options in the Tray Mismatch Alert box are not the easiest to understand. When in doubt, you can always experiment with different selections until you get the desired result.

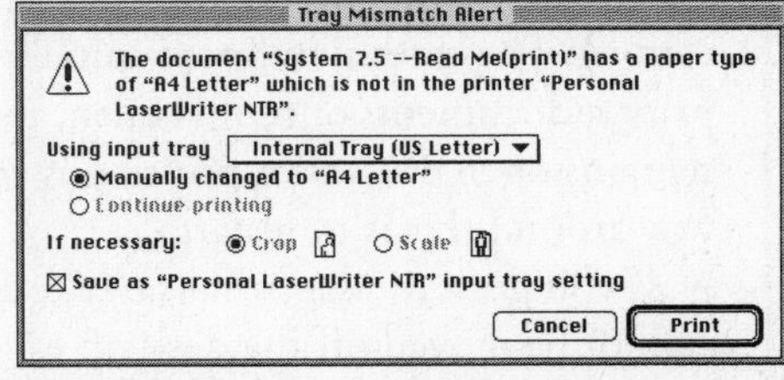

Figure 13-43 *A Tray Mismatch Alert message may appear just before a document begins to print.*

SEE: • **"Technically Speaking: Solving Paper Size Selection Confusion," earlier in this chapter, for more on this topic**

Other Problems The application you are using may be incompatible with QuickDraw GX. If so, you may get messages such as "No PostScript fonts are present, You will be unable to print since no outline fonts are present," or "Font Mismatch" (followed by the name of a font). To determine if any of this means that your application is incompatible, select Turn Desktop Printing Off from the Apple menu (available only if QuickDraw GX Helper is installed) or start up with the QuickDraw GX extension disabled. Now see if your document will print. If it does, and you still want to use QuickDraw GX, your only hope lies with an application upgrade; check with the application's vendor for information.

SEE: • **"Take Note: For Applications Incompatible with QuickDraw GX, Use QuickDraw GX Helper," earlier in this chapter, for more details on QuickDraw GX Helper**

"SimpleText Cannot Display This Document" Message

The most common cause of this message is that you are trying to open a PDD document when GX is not active, as explained in "Special Case: Portable Digital Documents (PDDs)," earlier in this chapter.

Desktop Printer-Related System Crashes Due to a Locked System File

QuickDraw GX stores the name of the default desktop printer (and the name of its Chooser extension) in the System file. If the System file is locked (which means it cannot be modified), a crash may occur when the Macintosh tries to change any of its contents which is exactly what happens when, for example, you change or delete the default desktop printer. To prevent a crash, make sure the System file is not locked: select the System file's icon, choose Get Info from the File menu, and click the Locked checkbox to remove the "X" (if one is there). Similarly, avoid turning on System Folder Protection in the General Controls control panel.

You Cannot Delete or Move a Desktop Printer File

If you try to delete a desktop printer file and get a message that says "the desktop … is busy," restart the Macintosh; you should now be able to delete the desktop printer. What's usually going on here is that you cannot delete the desktop printer file because the PrinterShare GX extension is open (you can see that it is open by going to the Extensions folder and looking at its icon; it has the grayed appearance of an open application). The extension opens initially whenever you print a document; once it is open, though, it apparently remains open even after printing is completed. The only way around this is to restart.

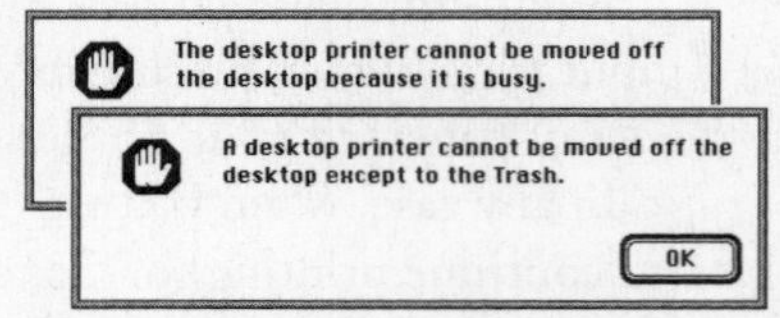

Figure 13-44 *Messages that may appear if you try to move a desktop printer icon off the desktop.*

If you get a message that says "A desktop printer cannot be moved off the desktop except to the Trash," however, there is nothing you can do. Currently, QuickDraw GX does not allow you to move a desktop printer icon anywhere except to the desktop, the Trash, or to another volume altogether. You cannot move it to within any folder on the volume from which it was created. Current versions of non-GX desktop printing software, though, do allow desktop printers to be moved into folders. I expect that an eventual upgrade to QuickDraw GX will add this feature.

Font Problems

Symptoms:

- The display and/or printed font is not the font originally selected for the text.
- A given font displays in some generic font, such as Geneva or Helvetica, rather than in its own font.
- Text unexpectedly displays the jaggies.
- A system crash occurs shortly after selecting a specific font from a Font menu.

Causes:

If the trouble is GX-specific, the cause is almost assuredly some mismatching of the system software and the problem font (for example, using GX fonts when not running GX). General guidelines were given in the "QuickDraw GX and Fonts" section, earlier in this chapter.

SEE: • Chapter 9 for non-GX-related causes of these symptoms

What to do:

Make Sure Any PostScript Fonts You Use in QuickDraw GX Have Been Enabled

You cannot use non-GX PostScript fonts in QuickDraw GX unless they have been enabled, either when you first installed QuickDraw GX or via the Type I Enabler utility. Even after they have been enabled, they will not acquire the characteristics needed to create special GX font effects; the fonts will only be usable in the same way they were in non-GX systems. To use GX font effects, you need specially designed GX fonts.

SEE: • "QuickDraw GX and Fonts," earlier in this chapter, for more details

Text Displays in Incorrect Font or Style, Displays with Jaggies, or a System Crash Occurs When Using a Specific Font

Avoid Switching Back and Forth Between GX and Non-GX In general, try to avoid switching between running with GX on and with it off. Switching back and forth—especially when opening and saving the same document in both situations is likely to result in problems, including loss of correct font information.

In one case, for example, I created a document when a non-GX System Folder was the startup folder. The document contained PostScript fonts that were not present in a separate GX System Folder that I sometimes used; when I later opened the document while that folder was the startup folder, not surprisingly it was displayed in the incorrect font. I made a few minor spelling changes (but no font changes) and saved the document. When I later opened the document under the original non-GX System

Folder, though, it was displayed in the same wrong font that had appeared when GX was active!

If you do expect to enable and disable QuickDraw GX periodically, make sure both GX and non-GX versions of your fonts are in the Fonts folder of your System Folder.

Make Sure You Have a Screen Font For PostScript fonts, make sure you have at least one size of its matching screen font remaining in the Fonts folder. These screen fonts are needed for ATM to work.

Make Sure You Do Not Have Missing Printer Fonts With PostScript GX fonts, since the printer fonts are "hidden" inside the GX font file, there is no clear way to tell if or which "styles" (such as bold or italics) of printer fonts may be missing (especially a potential problem with GX fonts originally converted from non-GX fonts). Missing styles could result in fonts unexpectedly printing with the jaggies. If this happens, you'll have to reconvert the non-GX version of the font to GX format—this time with all its needed printer fonts included—using Type 1 Enabler.

On The Horizon

Finally, here's a peek at some of the new software and hardware improvements that are coming in the months ahead.

Software

The future of the Mac OS is very much in flux (see also "Apple's Mac OS Release Strategy," at the start of this chapter). Not too long ago, Apple was promising a major upgrade: Mac OS 8 (originally code-named Copland). It was to be the biggest rewrite of the Macintosh operating system in its history. Major new features expected to be in Mac OS 8 included:

- Current extensions and desk accessories would no longer work; all of this software would need to be rewritten.
- The Finder interface would be completely redesigned and much easier for the user to customize.
- Protected Memory should minimize system crashes by preventing a fatal error in one program from leading to a systemwide problem that necessitates restarting your Mac.
- All code will be on disk, eliminating the need for the Mac ROM altogether. This will make it easier to put the Mac OS on clones.

However, Apple has now officially abandoned development of Copland. In its stead will be two separate development lines that will eventually be merged.

Mac OS 7

Apple will continue to develop upgraded versions of Mac OS 7.x for at least another couple of years. These will include at least some of the technologies originally developed for Mac OS 8.

Tempo The summer of 1997 will see the arrival of a major update, currently code-named Tempo and likely to be called Mac OS 7.7. It should include many of the user-interface features of Mac OS 8.

New and upgraded technology Progress continues on Apple's other supplementary software; you should expect major upgrades to Open Transport, OpenDoc, QuickDraw 3D, and more in the year ahead. Apple is also hard at work on several Internet-related technologies, especially those that can be used for navigating the World Wide Web and searching Web site contents.

Rhapsody

In December 1996, Apple acquired NeXT Software, Inc. The major reason for doing so was to acquire the NeXT operating system software. This software will now form the basis for an entirely new Mac OS, currently code-named Rhapsody, that is intended to contain all of the key advantages of Copland and then some! Eventually, this software will be merged with the Mac OS 7, and there will finally be one unified Mac OS! It won't be until 1998 before we get to see how all of this ultimately shakes out.

BeOS

BeOS was once rumored to be the OS that Apple would purchase, rather than the NeXT OS. While Apple has passed on it for now, development of the software continues by Be, Inc. There is now a version of the BeOS that runs on Power Macs. There is also software, called VirtualMac, that lets you run the Mac OS from within the BeOS environment. The BeOS is an extremely fast OS that already has the key advantages originally planned for Copland. While not an Apple product, BeOS may yet play an important role in the future of the Macintosh platform.

Hardware

Faster and Multiple Processors Ever faster high-end Power Macs are on the way. Expect processor speeds to vault to new heights, with a new line of processors that can push speeds past the 500MHz barrier. Macs with two or more processors will also become increasingly common.

Low end Macintoshes Apple is not forgetting the entry level. A whole new line of less expensive PCI-based Macs is due out in 1997.

New PowerBooks Look for a complete revamping of Apple's PowerBook line. The 1400 series, with its internal CD-ROM drive, started it off. The first PCI-based PowerBooks, the PowerBook 3400 series, have now also arrived.

PPRP Macs Still waiting in the wings is the Apple and IBM collaborative computer, formerly called Common Hardware Reference Platform (CHRP) and now called Power PC Reference Platform (PPRP). Designed to run a variety of operating systems, besides just the Mac OS, the future of these machines appears a bit uncertain at the moment (especially in light of the recent changes in MacOS development).

And more Look for significant changes in the exterior design of Apple's desktop Macintosh computers. FireWire, Apple's SCSI replacement technology, may be standard on all Macs by 1998.

Chapter 14

Road Service for the Infobahn: The Internet, the Web, and the Online World

No Mac is an Island ... Anymore 602

Understanding Modems 603

Modem Speed 603

Bits Per Second (bps) 603

Line Noise 604

Connection Location 604

Other Potential Roadblocks 604

Modem Data Compression and Error Correction 605

Carrier (DCE) versus Connect (DTE) Speeds 605

Selecting the Right Port Speed: Getting Maximum Throughput 606

Bottom Line? 607

Flow Control 607

Xon/Xoff versus Hardware Handshake (And Using the Correct Cable for Your Modem) 607

Selecting the Right Flow Control: CTS and RTS (DTR), CTS Only, or RTS (DTR) Only 608

Modem Initialization Strings 608

AT Commands and Init Strings 608

Selecting Your Init String 608

Understanding Open Transport, TCP, & PPP 609

Why Open Transport, Anyway? 609

What Files Are Needed For Open Transport (vs. Classic AppleTalk)? 610

Open Transport 610

Classic AppleTalk 610

Choosing Between Open Transport and Classic AppleTalk 610

What Mac Models Can or Cannot Use Open Transport? 610

Network Software Selector 611

Understanding Open Transport, TCP, & PPP (continued)
Memory Requirements 612
Making a TCP (and PPP) Connection 612
A Bit of Background on TCP/IP and PPP 612
TCP/IP and AppleTalk Control Panels 615
FreePPP and Open Transport PPP/Modem Control Panels 617

Solve-It! Open Transport Problems 622
Compatibility Problems 622
Modem and PPP Connection Problems 623
When You Can't Get Connected: General Advice 624
When You Can't Get Connected: Specific Advice 624
Dropped Connections 627

The Internet (especially the World Wide Web) 629
Understanding Internet Addresses 629
Domain Names 629
Email Addresses 630
World Wide Web Addresses 630
URLs: Using Your Browser for More Than Just the Web 632
Working with Downloaded and Uploaded Files 632
Downloaded Files 634
Uploaded Files 636

Solve-It! Web Browser Problems 637
Web Pages Won't Load or Load Slowly 637
No Pages Load 637
Unable to Connect to Host 638
No DNS Entry, 404 Not Found, and Related Messages 638
Network Connection Refused, No Response from Server, or No Message at All 639
Pages Load Slowly 639
A Long Delay Before a Page Starts to Load 641
Downloads Transfer Slowly or Not At All 642

System Freezes, Crashes, and Directory Damage 642
Try Netscape Defrost 642
Not Enough Memory 643
Trash Browser Preferences File 644
Incompatible Files 644
Browser Caches and Corrupted Directory Files 645
Avoid Public Betas 646
Getting out of a Freeze or Crash 646
Pages Display Incorrectly or Have Features Missing 648
Netscape Extensions 648
Plug-Ins 648
Preference Settings 649
Helper Problems 650
Setting Up a Helper 650
Get a Missing Helper 651
When Your Browser Can't Find a Correctly Listed Helper 651
Binhex Files Appear as Text in a Browser Window 652
Web Pages Do Not Get Updated as Expected 653

Ethernet Quick Fixes 655
Ethernet Extensions Solve Problems 655
Cables and Hardware for Ethernet Mini-Networks 656

No Mac is an Island … Anymore

When I wrote the first edition of this book, I deliberately omitted almost all coverage of online and/or networking problems. There were several reasons for this. First, far fewer people were connected online than is the case today, so it did not seem as critical to include it. Second, I wanted to target the book to individual users trying to solve problems on their own, and most networking/online problems seemed too technical and too difficult for that audience. It was better to leave those problems to another book, I recall thinking.

Things are different today; the Internet is *everything.* Using a browser to cruise the World Wide Web is fast becoming the single most popular use for personal computers. The popularity of the Web (and online services in general) is now so great that it demands coverage in this edition.

Fortunately, getting up and running online is significantly easier than it was years ago (I will not soon forget the unbelievable hassles I had trying to make my first PPP connection!). Even so, the technically complex world of modem connections and networks is still among the least user-friendly of troubleshooting topics. And to make matters worse, those people who seem to understand this stuff the best seem the least capable of explaining it to others. (If you want proof, try reading the manual that came with your modem.) While I don't consider myself an expert in this particular field, I hope that I can compensate for this by being at least a bit better at explaining what I do know. I'll try to focus here on practical answers rather than just technical ones.

This chapter covers a lot of ground, from setting up a PPP connection to troubleshooting your Web browser. Since thorough coverage of even a fraction of the topics described here could fill up a book by itself, I am forced to be selective in what I cover. For example, my focus is on Open Transport rather than MacTCP, and LocalTalk connections are emphasized over Ethernet ones, since I believe these topics face the greatest number of users. I am sorry if I omitted a particular topic that you wanted covered.

Cheer up, though; plenty of problems *are* covered. Chances are good that you'll find what you are looking for.

Understanding Modems

You don't necessarily need a modem to get connected online. Particularly in work settings, you may have a direct connection through a LocalTalk or Ethernet network. Still, since the vast majority of users—especially home users—get online via a modem, I will focus on modem issues here.

A modem is a hardware device that connects your Macintosh on one end to your telephone line on the other end. With the right software, you can use these devices to connect to other computers or to computerized information services anywhere in the world.

Setting one up is usually a fairly simple affair. For an external modem, you simply connect it to a wall outlet for power, to your phone line (for obvious reasons!), and to your Mac via its serial port, then turn it on. Aside from any software you need, that's all there is to it. Of course, as you will soon learn, things can go wrong even here, but most users quickly succeed in getting past this point.

It's actually making an online connection via the modem that presents more problems. But before we explore the specific troubleshooting issues, it will help to delve more into what different modem settings mean and how they affect the way your modem and Mac work together.

This section covers the three most common modem settings that you need to know about when troubleshooting online connection problems: modem speed, flow control, and initialization strings.

Modem Speed

Modems can run at different speeds. Faster speeds have the obvious benefit that everything you do, from downloading files to loading Web pages, can be done more quickly. As is true in every other part of the computer world, faster is better.

You would think a modem's speed would be relatively easy to determine and comprehend—if someone says that a car is going 60 mph, after all, you don't need a manual to figure out what that means. Sadly, modem speeds are not at all like automobile speeds. Here is what you need to know to get up to speed on modem speed.

Bits Per Second (bps)

Most modems are described as having a basic speed listed in *bits per second* (bps). This speed is the maximum rate at which the modem is capable of sending and receiving data.

These days, the most common bps for modems is 28,800 (also referred to as 28.8K or simply 28.8—or, more mysteriously, as a V.34 modem; never mind why). The slowest modem you can probably buy is 14.4K (anything slower is useless for the World Wide Web and can be interminably slow for downloading software). Actually, through some minor tinkering, you can get a 28.8K modem to run at 33.6K (if you have a flash-ROM upgradable 28.8K modem—I'll explain this jargon later—you can do this entirely via software, if the vendor provides it). Even faster modems capable of 56K in certain circumstances, are on the way.

Some telecommunications software may display this bps speed when you first connect (or perhaps another measure of speed, as described shortly). Other software may make speed measures difficult to find; check with the documentation for your software for guidance here.

By the way, while bps is sometimes interpreted as the same thing as baud rate, they are different. The term *baud rate* is no longer technically correct and is not used much anymore.

Line Noise

The bps rating is the maximum speed you can hope to get, and you won't hit that maximum very often. In fact, the faster the modem, the less likely you are to reach its top speed. The actual speed is partially determined when you first make a connection and is affected by such factors as telephone line noise. The result is that most connections from 28.8K or 33.6K modems are lucky to reach 26.4K. Even lower speeds are not uncommon.

To some extent, it's like driving a Ferrari in rush hour traffic. It doesn't matter if your speedometer can go up to 200 mph; the needle won't be going anywhere near there for the moment.

Connection Location

For a modem even to approach its maximum speed potential, both connected sites must operate at that speed (or faster). If you connect to a service that sends information at 2,400 bps, your 28,800 bps modem has to slow down to match the slower rate of the service. Fortunately, all modems can downshift to lower speeds if necessary, so you don't need a separate modem for each speed.

In years past, an online service such as America Online would have separate phone numbers for different connect speeds (such as a 2,400 bps line and a 14,400 bps line). Much more common today is a single high-speed line that can accommodate the full range of modem speeds. Similarly, services used to charge extra for connecting at higher speeds, but this is usually no longer the case. Now there is a one-price policy regardless of the connection speed.

Other Potential Roadblocks

Especially on the Web, your data transfer rate may vary even further from your modem's bps speed because of a host of factors that are largely beyond your control, such as the speed of the server you are addressing, how many other users are trying to access the page at the same time, and the nature of what you are trying to view (graphics take an especially long time to transfer). If things slow to a crawl, it might pay to come back later when the traffic is less heavy.

Modem Data Compression and Error Correction

While your modem may have a limit of 28.8K, it can increase its apparent transmission speed through compression of the data. This hardware-based data compression is similar to how a software utility like StuffIt works. By analogy, suppose you wanted to send a telegram as fast as you could, but the fastest it could go was 10 letters per second; your 500 letter telegram would take 50 seconds to send. Now suppose you found a way to eliminate 20 percent of the letters and still retain all the meaning of the telegram; your message would now take only 400 letters and thus 40 seconds. Since the recipient essentially "decompresses" the telegram by reading it, in some sense he or she has received all 500 letters in less time.

The designation for the most popular data compression process in use today on 28.8K and 33.6K modems is V.42bis. Its advantage over other methods (such as one called MNP) is that it can detect if a file has already been compressed. For example, if you are trying to send a StuffIt file over the modem, it cannot really be compressed any further. V.42bis will detect this, although a compressed file will not transmit any faster with V.42bis in place than it would without the modem compression. Actually, in some cases, compressed files will transmit more slowly with V.42bis turned on, although the difference is rarely enough to worry about. In brief: sometimes data compression will appear to speed things up, but sometimes it won't.

These same high-speed modems also include error-correction protocols to ensure that the data gets transmitted correctly at these high speeds. You can turn these compression and error correction protocols on and off; how you do this depends again on your modem software. For example, Global Village modems let you do this from the TelePort control panel. Other modems may require that you modify the modem initialization string (described later in this section).

In any case, the maximum data compression that most 28.8K modems can handle is 4X (that is, compression to ¼ size). This means that once a 28.8K modem decompresses incoming data, it is as if it received the data at a rate of 115,200 bps (4 x 28.8K). A few modems can do an 8X compression and thus receive data at an apparent rate of 230,400 bps. Of course, this raises the question of whether your Mac itself is able to receive data at this high rate. The answer depends upon what Macintosh you have and the type of serial port it uses to connect to your modem.

Carrier (DCE) versus Connect (DTE) Speeds

The speeds referred to thus far are only half the story—the speed with which information travels from its external remote source to your modem, and vice versa. This is technically referred to as the *carrier* (or DCE) speed.

Once the data hits your modem (and gets decompressed), it has to travel to your computer through the serial port connection. This is called the *connect* (or DTE) speed; it is also referred to as the *port* speed. The fastest connect speed is referred to as the *maximum throughput.* The connect speed can be (and usually should be) set to higher level than the carrier speed, for reasons I will explain shortly.

Selecting the Right Port Speed: Getting Maximum Throughput

The connect (DTE) speed represents a potential bottleneck for a high-speed modem, since your Macintosh may not be able to receive data at anything close to the modem's ability to send it. In particular, the maximum port speed on Macs slower than a IIfx (virtually all 68030 and slower Macs) is limited to 9,600 bps; on 68040 Macs, it is 19,200 bps. On Quadra AVs and Power Macs, the port speed can be as high as 230K, due to an improved serial port technology present in the GeoPort serial port of these Macs (called DMA). Thus a 28.8K modem will seem to work slower on a Mac IIci than on a Power Mac 7600, no matter how otherwise identical the setups are.

Additionally, to get these maximum throughputs, you need software that allows you to select these speeds. For example, FreePPP's Port Speed selections do go as high as 230K, but other software may not support this high a rate.

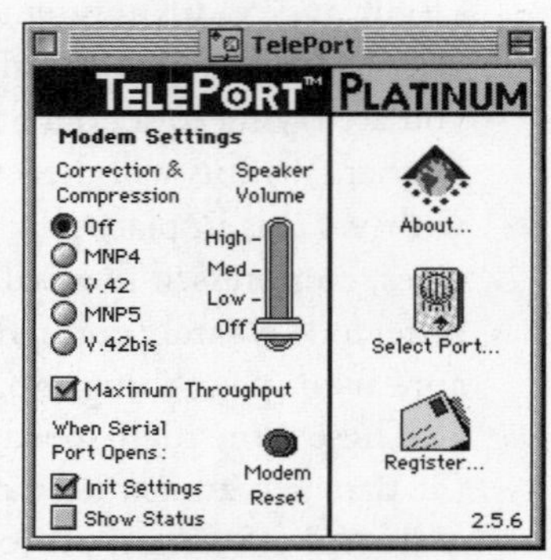

Figure 14-1 *Global Village's TelePort control panel, with options to set Correction and Compression protocols as well as Maximum Throughput.*

On the other hand, the TelePort control panel of Global Village Platinum modems includes a "Maximum Throughput" option that boosts transmission to 115K even if your software does not include this speed option (there is no 230K support because this modem does not have 8X compression). You will only see this option, however, if you have a Mac that includes the DMA serial port architecture (AV and Power Macs). In this case, you may see 115K throughput even with a 14.4K connection.

Typically, you should set your port speed optimistically at a somewhat higher rate than the modem's maximum compressed speed. In general, if you are connecting with a 14.4K modem, set your software's port speed to 19,200 bps (this relatively small increase is because these modems do not typically have the much better compression methods found in 28.8K modems). If you are connecting with a 28.8K modem, you should set the port speed to at least 38,400 bps or even 57,600 bps. If you have an AV or Power Mac, the latest SerialDMA software (as built into System 7.5.3 or later), and telecommunications software that supports these higher speeds, you can set your port speed as high as 115,200 bps (or even 230,400, if your modem has 8X compression). For a variety of reasons, your actual speed will almost certainly turn out to be less—but at least you tried.

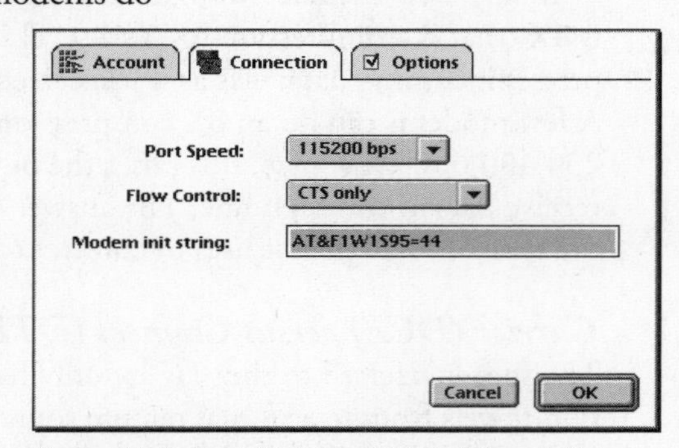

Figure 14-2 *FreePPP Setup 2.5's Port Speed, Flow Control, and Modem Init String settings.*

If your system can't support that selected speed, it will usually just automatically adjust downward to a speed it can handle. If problems such as freezes and crashes occur, however—and they become more likely at 115K and 230K—you may have to select a slower speed yourself.

Bottom Line?

Your modem data transfer speed at any moment is a combination of the bps and compression technology of the modem, the throughput of the Mac's serial port, the settings of your software, the type of information being transmitted, the noise in the phone line, and the location to which you are connected. Clearly, as they say in the car ads, your mileage may vary.

TAKE NOTE ▶

THE "MODEMS" OF THE FUTURE

When even the fastest modem speed is not fast enough for you (and all it takes is a day of Web surfing for you to decide that this is the case), you'll have to start looking at the telecommunications technologies of the future, such as ISDN (which stands for Integrated Services Digital Network). These technologies require special digital phone lines that may or may not yet be available in your neighborhood, but they are coming. Connecting via your TV cable lines is another promising superfast connection of the near future. Otherwise, there are T1 and T3 connections (which you can afford to install in your home only if you happen to be in the same financial league as Bill Gates).

Flow Control

Okay, I am going to throw around some more jargon here. It's not critical that you know what it all means, just that you know how to make practical use of it.

Xon/Xoff versus Hardware Handshake (And Using the Correct Cable for Your Modem)

The speed with which your modem sends data to your Macintosh, in turn, must be matched with the capability of your Mac to receive at that speed. If the modem sends data too fast, some will get lost. This matching is handled by something called *flow control* or *handshaking*. On lower-speed modems, flow control is accomplished by a software method (usually set via options in your communications software) called *Xon/Xoff*, while higher speed modems (9,600 bps and above) use what is called *hardware handshaking*. Because this method is hardware-dependent (that is, the protocols are built into the modem and handled by dedicated wires) rather than a function of your communications software, it is faster and more reliable.

So, first off, if you have a fast modem (and you should), make sure your software has not enabled an Xon/Xoff option, assuming such an option is given. Second, make sure you have a cable connecting your modem and Macintosh that is hardware-handshaking capable. Such a cable should come with every Mac high-speed modem. If you use an incompatible cable from some slower modem (which is easy enough to do, since the cables look identical; I've done it once), or you may find that you can't connect at high speeds.

Selecting the Right Flow Control: CTS and RTS (DTR), CTS Only, or RTS (DTR) Only

Often, communications software will give you a choice of the exact type of hardware handshaking you want. For example, the Connections window in FreePPP does this in its Flow Control pop-up menu. There are three options (the fourth option, None, means you don't want hardware handshaking at all): CTS and RTS (DTR), CTS Only, and RTS (DTR) Only. Most times, you will be best off selecting the "CTS and RTS (DTR)" option. If that appears to cause trouble, try CTS Only. (Don't you just love telecommunications abbreviations [TCAs]?)

Modem Initialization Strings

AT Commands and Init Strings

Back in the online Dark Ages, when everyone communicated via text-only command line processors, your modem needed a way to know whether the text you were typing was a command to the modem or data to be transmitted. The primary method to do this was to type AT (short for "ATtention") at the start of a line intended as a modem command. This was followed by a series of numbers and characters that all had special meaning for your modem. Today you can still operate this way via a terminal session window, an option that is available in most current communications software. Happily, though, software generally does most of the necessary work for you.

Still, the one place you typically still need to enter this sort of information is called the initialization (or *init) string.* These commands tell the modem how to set up any and all of its parameters, including whether data compression should be on or off, whether hardware handshaking should be used, whether the modem's speaker should be on or off, and so forth. When you first try to make a connection, your software initializes the modem based on the init string that you have given it (for example, in FreePPP's init-string box of its Communications window).

Some settings are clearly optional, and you can do whatever you prefer (such as turning the speakers off if they annoy you, or turning them back on if you want to do some troubleshooting). Some of these options must be set a certain way, however, in order for you to make a successful online connection.

Selecting Your Init String

The exact init string you should use varies depending on the brand of modem you are using, the communications software you are using, and sometimes even the remote location to which you are trying to connect. It is impossible for me to give general advice here, other than to say that "AT&F1" (a command to use the modem's default settings) is a good starting point if you have no other guidance. Otherwise, your modem's manual, your communications software's manual, or your online service may all have suggestions as to what init string is best for minimizing trouble; you should follow their advice.

In some cases, init string decisions can be made for you automatically. As described in the next section (see: "FreePPP and Open Transport PPP/Modem Control Panels"), FreePPP has an AutoDetect option that will select a string for you. Apple's TO/PPP (like America Online and most other online services) has a collection of *modem script* files, offering an option for you to select the script for your modem. The script includes an init string plus lots of other goodies that should smooth the road ahead of you. If not, you may have to edit the string (again, based on advice from other sources).

Understanding Open Transport, TCP, & PPP

The original system software Apple used for making online and network connections did not have a specific name; it was just there. Starting with System 7.5.3, though, Apple made a completely different set of communication software available. The new software was called Open Transport, and the old software was belatedly named Classic AppleTalk. Open Transport actually first appeared for PCI-based Macs only in System 7.5.2.

Users typically become most aware of the difference between Classic AppleTalk and Open Transport when they make a direct connection to the Internet. With Classic AppleTalk, you needed to set up a control panel called MacTCP (as well as possibly another one called Network); with Open Transport, you instead use a control panel called TCP/IP (as well as one called AppleTalk).

Open Transport is clearly the wave of the future, so this section will focus almost exclusively on it.

Why Open Transport, Anyway?

Why was Open Transport even needed? What can you do with it that you could not do with Classic AppleTalk? While there are many differences, here are the three that are most likely to be immediately relevant to you:

- TCP/IP is usually easier to configure than MacTCP, since many of its fields are automatically filled in by your server when you make a connection.
- With Open Transport, you can switch from one networking configuration to another (such as from PPP to Ethernet) simply by selecting a different previously saved configuration setting. You don't have to reconfigure the control panel and restart the Mac each time, both of which were problems with MacTCP.
- There is a potential for increased performance speed with Open Transport as compared to Classic AppleTalk. How much of a speed increase you actually see, though, will depend upon whether your application software has been rewritten to take advantage of Open Transport. To get a speed boost, a program must be not only compatible with Open Transport, but "Open Transport Ready." This means it will run native on Power Macs and has modified code needed to support the performance-enhancing features of Open Transport.

What Files Are Needed For Open Transport (vs. Classic AppleTalk)?

Open Transport

I already mentioned that the TCP/IP and AppleTalk control panels are part of the Open Transport software. In addition, on Power Macs, the following shared library files will be in the Extensions folder: Open Transport Library, Open Tpt AppleTalk Library, Open Tpt Internet Library, OpenTransportLib, OpenTptAppleTalkLib, and OpenTptInternetLib. The first three files are for running 680X0 applications in emulation, while the latter three are for Power Mac native applications.

On 680X0 Macintoshes, only three shared library files are installed: Open Transport 68K Library, Open Tpt ATalk 68K Library, and Open Tpt Inet 68K Library. (If these three files appear on Power Macs, they may be deleted; in fact, online performance may actually improve if you do this.)

Open Transport will likely also install Ethernet (Built-In) and Serial (Built-In) and Open Transport Guide Additions. It makes use of the Network Extension, and other supplementary files may be present as well.

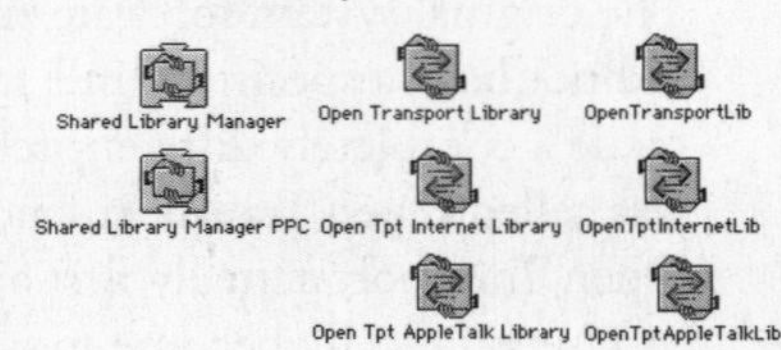

Figure 14-3 *Some of the shared library extensions/files (as found in the Extensions folder) needed for running Open Transport on a PowerPC.*

SEE: • **Chapter 12 and 13 for more on shared libraries**

Classic AppleTalk

Classic AppleTalk requires MacTCP, the Network control panel, and the Network Extension. It does not use any shared library files.

Choosing Between Open Transport and Classic AppleTalk

What Mac Models Can or Cannot Use Open Transport?

Some models can use only Open Transport or only Classic AppleTalk; some can use both. Here's the breakdown:

- Open Transport is required for all PCI-based Macs (such as the Power Mac 7600 and 8500). Although there are tricks you can use to get around this, I don't recommend them. Stick with Open Transport on these machines.
- Open Transport does not work on 68000 and 68020 Macs (such as a Mac SE). Users of these machines must stick with Classic AppleTalk.
- Both Open Transport and Classic AppleTalk work on 68030 and 68040 Macs, but you can only use one at a time. If both are installed (as is done in System 7.5.3 or later), Classic AppleTalk is probably selected as the default on these machines. You can change this selection via the Network Software Selector, which is described in the next section; the only reason to prefer Classic AppleTalk here is if you are having problems with Open Transport.

  Also note that you need at least version 1.1.1 of Open Transport to work with 5200/5300/6200/6300 Performas and Power Macs.

Installing System 7.5.3 (or later) should install the correct software for your machine. If not, do a Custom Install as needed. Mac OS 7.6 only works with Open Transport.

Network Software Selector

At least on those Macs (using System 7.5.3 or later) that can switch between Open Transport and Classic AppleTalk, you should find a file—probably in the Apple Extras folder—called Network Software Selector. If you launch it, you will get a window that lets you choose which system you want active on your next restart. Simply make your selection, quit, and restart your Macintosh.

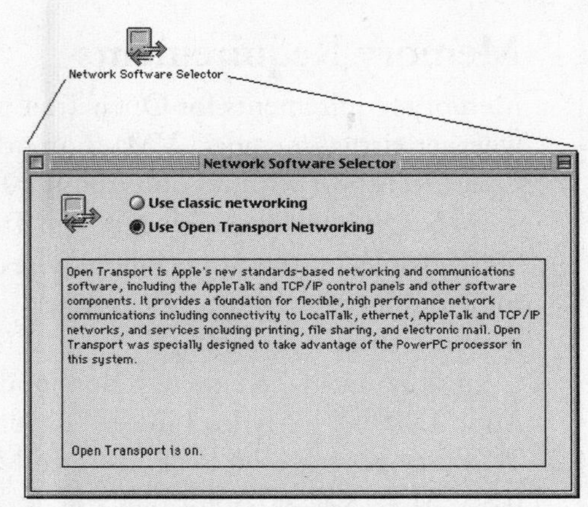

Figure 14-4 *The Network Software Selector.*

Note that the NSS selection is simply an indication of a user preference, however, not a directive. That is, NSS may allow you to select a networking option that does not work on your Mac (such as Classic AppleTalk on a PCI-based Mac). In this case, the Mac will override your selection when you restart, instead loading the software that works with your Mac.

Any changes you make to your TCP settings while using one system, will probably not be converted to the other system after your switch. Also, if you are using Ethernet or any other type of networking besides LocalTalk, switching from Open Transport to

TECHNICALLY SPEAKING ▶

NETWORK SOFTWARE SELECTOR'S MAGIC

Network Software Selector (NSS) makes the switch between Open Transport and Classic AppleTalk in a very unusual way—rather than simply disabling the unneeded control panels, it makes them invisible!

In particular, MacTCP and Network are invisible when Open Transport is active; TCP/IP and AppleTalk are invisible when Classic AppleTalk is active. They are still in the Control Panels folder, but you just can't see them. To further make sure they are not used, their file type (described in Chapter 8) is different when they are invisible.

Other Open Transport files (such as the shared library files) remain present in either case, but they are only used when Open Transport is active.

If files that were supposed to be made invisible are still visible after a restart, it is probably because you have renamed the file. It must have its original name to become invisible.

If you try to copy a temporarily invisible file (such as MacTCP) to the Control Panels folder, you will get a message that would seem mysterious if I hadn't just told you what is going on): "You cannot move 'MacTCP' to the folder 'Control Panels,' because an invisible item with the same name already exists in this location."

Note: The preference for which network system to use is stored as a part of the AppleTalk Prefs file. If you delete this file and then launch the NSS utility, you will re-establish the default preference for your Mac. If the NSS appears to be making a mistake (such as saying you cannot switch to Open Transport on your Mac model, when you know that you can), deleting the Preferences file may cure the problem.

Classic AppleTalk (or vice versa) may cause the network connection to revert to LocalTalk. To get back your original networking selection, use the Network control panel (in Classic AppleTalk) or the AppleTalk control panel (Open Transport).

Memory Requirements

Memory requirements for Open Transport can vary a great deal depending upon whether virtual memory (VM) is on or off. In particular, on a Power Mac with VM on, Open Transport requires only about 200K to load; with VM off, it can require up to 1.2MB. On non-Power Macs, Open Transport should not require more than about 500K, while Classic AppleTalk requires about 350 to 450K in any situation. (All of these numbers are subject to change as Apple revises the software; relative differences, however, should remain.)

In situations where there is not enough memory to load Open Transport, Classic AppleTalk will likely load instead (assuming both networking systems are installed). This may be true even for PCI-based Macs! According to Apple, though, on these PCI-based Macs, Classic AppleTalk will be "limited to support only for AppleTalk on LocalTalk; no TCP/IP services will be available."

Making a TCP (and PPP) Connection

Once again, I emphasize that this is a troubleshooting book, not a how-to guide for using software. I cannot teach you everything you might need to know about setting up a TCP connection here. Still, because of all the things that can go wrong, I will go into more of the basics than usual. While setting up a successful TCP/IP and PPP connection can be one of the most daunting tasks you will likely do with your Mac, don't despair. Once you do get things working, you can usually forget about all of this stuff and just connect in one easy step.

A Bit of Background on TCP/IP and PPP

To access the Internet via a modem (or *dial-up*) connection, you do not necessarily have to bother with the TCP/IP control panel at all. Using a program such as ZTerm, you could make a shell account connection, where your Mac acts like a "dumb terminal." Similarly, online services such as America Online and CompuServe have also provided access to the Internet (including the World Wide Web) through their own connections without requiring the use of TCP/IP (or MacTCP).

For the most flexible and best access to the Internet, however, you should have your computer directly linked to the Internet network. This allows you to use any of the rich variety of Internet-specific software available, many of which feature Mac-enhanced graphical interfaces that are not otherwise available; such programs include Anarchie, Fetch, NewsWatcher, Netscape Navigator, Microsoft Explorer, Claris Emailer, and Eudora. For this type of setup, you *do* need TCP/IP.

SEE • **"Technically Speaking: TCP/IP and MacTCP Control Panels—What Exactly Do They Do?" for why you need TCP**

TECHNICALLY SPEAKING ▶

OPEN TRANSPORT, MEMORY LEAKS, AND "LOAD ONLY WHEN NEEDED"

The "About This Macintosh..." box, as selected from the Apple menu when in the Finder, reports on the Largest Unused Block of memory. Theoretically, this should be the same number that you would get if you subtracted the sum of all of the memory allocated to open applications from the Total Memory. Often, however, the Largest Unused Block is significantly less than this subtraction.

Where did the missing memory go? It disappears due to what are called "memory fragmentation" and "memory leaks," as explained more in Fix-It #6. One significant problem of this sort associated with Open Transport appears to result in at least some of the memory allocated to TCP/IP applications, such as Netscape Navigator, not being released when you quit the application. What follows are some technical details about how and why all of this happens (although some mystery still remains):

A memory leak can occur if you launch and quit multiple applications that use networking services, and especially if you have set Open Transport TCP/IP options to "Load only when needed." The apparent cause of this "leak" is that the TCP/IP Stack, which loads into memory when you launch a TCP/IP application (such as Netscape Navigator), does not unload as it should when you quit the application. Normally, Apple claims that it may take about two minutes after you quit an application before TCP/IP Stack unloads. However, especially with PPP connections, it may never unload. Quitting all open applications may alleviate some of this problem but not completely eliminate it.

One potential solution to this is to uncheck "Load only when needed" in the TCP/IP control panel. To do this, first make sure that you have chosen Advanced as your User Mode (as selected from the Edit menu). If you click the Options button in the control panel window, you will see the "Load only when needed" option. Uncheck it, but leave TCP/IP "active."

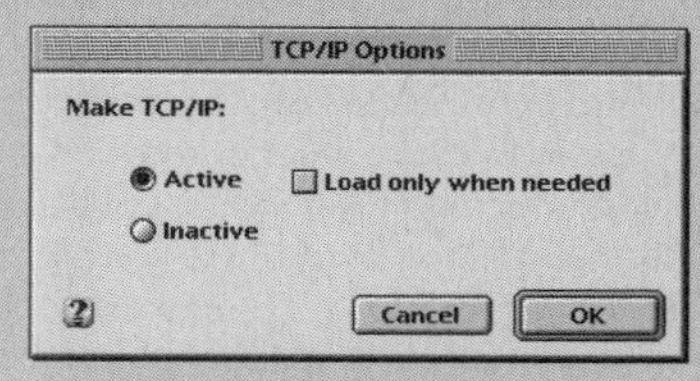

Figure 14-5 *The "Load only when needed" option (unchecked) in the TCP/IP control panel Options window.*

After restarting, TCP/IP Stack should now load at startup and remain loaded "permanently." This eats up additional memory (which is the downside of this solution) but can help prevent memory leaks and associated memory fragmentation.

Also, according to Apple: "When TCP/IP is set to 'Load only when needed,' the first TCP/IP application launched normally will cause Open Transport to load into memory. Some older applications don't cause Open Transport to load, and then report errors similar to those encountered when MacTCP is not installed. If this is a problem, again turn off the 'Load only when needed' option and restart your computer."

In general, experimenting with the "Load only when needed" option (checking or unchecking it) is a good thing to try for almost any TCP/IP-related problem.

If you still have a memory leak after trying this solution (especially one where *all* of Netscape's memory allocation is mysteriously retained after quitting it), you have a problem that appears to occur only with the first Open Transport-related program that is launched each session. One suggested work-around answer, therefore, is to launch an OT-related program that uses very little RAM, quit it, and then launch your more RAM-hungry applications (such as Netscape). Otherwise, restarting the Macintosh will always reclaim the missing memory.

Future versions of Open Transport may fix these problems, although they still appear to be present in version 1.1.1 and 1.1.2.

SEE: • Fix-It #6 for more on memory leaks and related issues

There are two basic ways to make the desired TCP/IP connection: through a hard-wired network connection, or over a modem. But with a modem (which is what I am focusing on here), you need a further translator after TCP/IP has done its translating work in order to prepare the data for modem transmission. Two solutions to this problem appeared, called SLIP (Serial Line Internet Protocol) and PPP (Point-to-Point Protocol). Of the two, PPP is far more popular today; it will be the only method described here.

TECHNICALLY SPEAKING ▶

TCP/IP AND MACTCP CONTROL PANELS: WHAT EXACTLY DO THEY DO?

The short answer is that the Internet communicates via a special "Internet protocol" (or IP, for short). Since your Mac does not "speak" this language, these control panels serve as an intermediary, doing the necessary conversions and translations. You don't need these control panels if you are accessing the Internet via some commercial online service (such as America Online) or via a text-only "shell account" connection; in these cases, the conversion problem is handled by your service provider. The control panels are required for direct access to the Internet, however, which is typically the case if you use programs such as Netscape, NewsWatcher, or Eudora for access via an Internet service provider (ISP).

To understand the logic of configuring MacTCP or TCP/IP, you need to understand the concept of the *domain name*. To get to any destination in the Internet, you need to know its address. Internet addresses are numeric; domain names are assigned to these numeric addresses to make it easier for humans to remember them. These domain names and/or their corresponding numeric equivalents should be entered in the Domain Name Server Information area of the MacTCP control panel, or the Name Server Addr and Search Domains fields of the TCP/IP control panel.

When you try to make a connection (and especially if there is any problem locating a numeric address or if you didn't provide a numeric address), an attempt is made by the control panel to "resolve" the non-numeric name. That is, it will figure out the actual numeric address that most closely matches the non-numeric domain name you gave; it then uses that address to connect you to the Internet. If it fails altogether, you will get an error message saying something to the effect that it was unable to resolve the domain name. In most cases, your ISP uses special software (called a *domain name server*) to try to resolve your domain names when it receives your request.

More rarely, your ISP may provide you with a *host file*, which you should store at the root level of your System Folder. This file contains a table of domain names and IP addresses, which is used by the TCP control panels for domain name resolution. TCP/IP has a button to select a specific host file.

To get the needed domain names and numeric addresses (and, indeed, for any further location-specific advice on how to get set up), contact your ISP. Even if you don't understand them all, just follow their instructions *exactly*. Some more general guidelines are given in the main text.

By the way, TCP/IP stands for "Transmission Control Protocol/Internet Protocol."

SEE: • "Troubleshooting Internet Addresses," later in this chapter, for more on domain names

TCP/IP and AppleTalk Control Panels

1. TCP/IP control panel: Change your User Mode?

Select User Mode from the control panel's Edit menu. If you have never done this before, you are probably in Basic mode, which is fine for most users. Additional options, however, become available if you select Advanced or Administrator mode. The most relevant of these additional options is the Options button that appears in the main window, which in turn gives you access to the "Load only when needed" checkbox (as discussed in "Take Note: Open Transport, Memory Fragmentation, and 'Load Only When Needed,' earlier in this chapter).

Use Apple Guide for more information on these different modes.

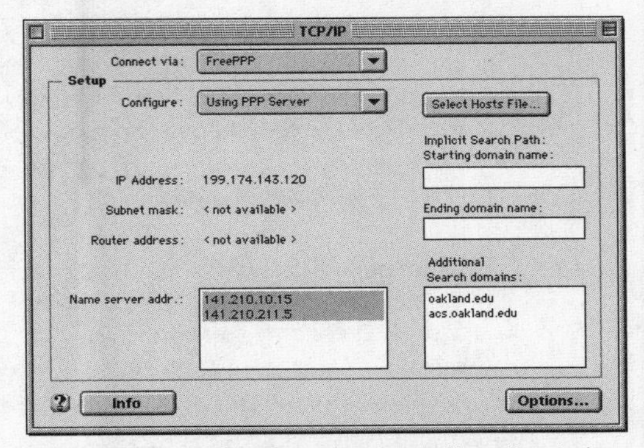

Figure 14-6 *The TCP/IP control panel's main window in Advanced mode.*

2. Setting up TCP/IP control panel for a PPP connection

a. From the "Connect via:" pop-up menu: Assuming you want to make a PPP connection using either FreePPP or Apple's OT/PPP (which is the assumption in this section), select FreePPP or PPP (for Apple's OT/PPP) as appropriate.

b. From the "Configure:" pop-up menu, select 'Using PPP Server.'

c. Enter IP (numeric) addresses into the Name Server Addr field and (optionally) domain names in the Search Domains field, as advised by your ISP. Conversely, if you enter a Search Domain name, entering an IP in the Name Server Addr field may be optional.

That's it; you are done. The other options should be "supplied by server," which means that you can ignore them.

SEE ALSO: • **"Technically Speaking: TCP/IP and MacTCP Control Panels: What Exactly Do They Do?"**
"Technically Speaking: TCP/IP Control Panel: Connections Other Than PPP"

3. Do you need to have multiple settings?

After you complete Step 2, you are basically done with the TCP/IP control panel. If needed, however, you can create other configuration settings. This might be useful, for example, if you connect via PPP sometimes but via an Ethernet network at other times.

To do this, select Configurations from the control panel's File menu. Then, from the window that appears, select Duplicate and give the duplicate settings a new name. Now select the new settings and click Make Active. This will take you back to the main window; you can now change the settings as you wish.

After this, any time you want to switch back or forth, go to the Configurations window and select which settings to Make Active.

By the way, there is a similar multiple-settings option in the AppleTalk control panel, which is described next.

TECHNICALLY SPEAKING ▶

TCP/IP CONTROL PANEL: CONNECTIONS OTHER THAN PPP

For connections other than PPP, here are some hints as to what to do for a first-time setup:

- For a LocalTalk network connection, typically select "Connect via: AppleTalk (MacIP)" and "Configure: Using MacIP Server." This can also be used for a LocalTalk network that is connected via a router to a larger network. You may also have to select your AppleTalk zone from the Select Zone window.
- For an Ethernet connection, select "Connect via: Ethernet," then select "BootP", "DHCP," or "RARP," as directed by your network administrator or Internet service provider.
- "Configure: Manually" should only be needed if you have a static IP address. If you are like most Mac users, you have a dynamic address (which means you get a different IP address every time you connect).
- Fill in the remaining blanks (such as IP Address or Subnet Mask) as directed by your network administrator or Internet service provider.

Technical details aside, the protocols such as BootP and DHCP are designed to reduce the need for you to enter information manually, so as to reduce the chance of a user error. They also help administrators deal with large networks that include a variety of different computer platforms.

Want to know your current IP address while you are online? Programs such as FreePPP will give it to you. For example, with FreePPP, simply click on the "i" (information) button in the FreePPP Setup window.

SEE: • Chapter 11, "Problems Using Apple Remote Access," for help on setting up connections for Apple Remote Access

4. **Set up the AppleTalk control panel, if needed**
   Modem users can largely ignore the AppleTalk control panel. Just make sure that if AppleTalk is active, the AppleTalk port (Printer or Modem), is not the same port to which your modem is connected.

   But if you are connecting via Ethernet, for example, you will need to go here and select Ethernet from the "Connect via:" pop-up menu. For LocalTalk network connections, make sure the port that carries your network (Printer or Modem) is selected. Also, click the Options button and make sure AppleTalk is active.

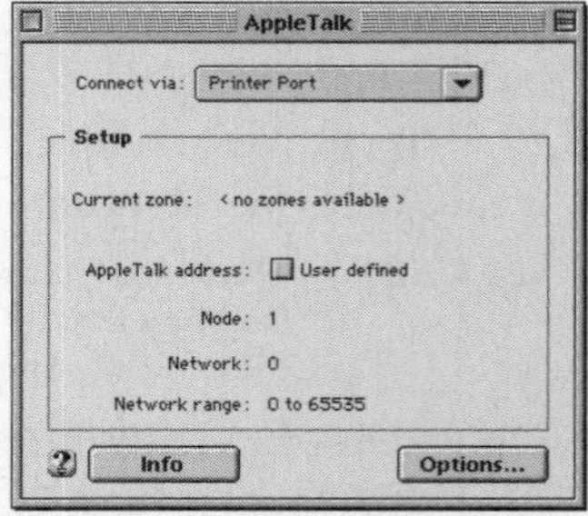

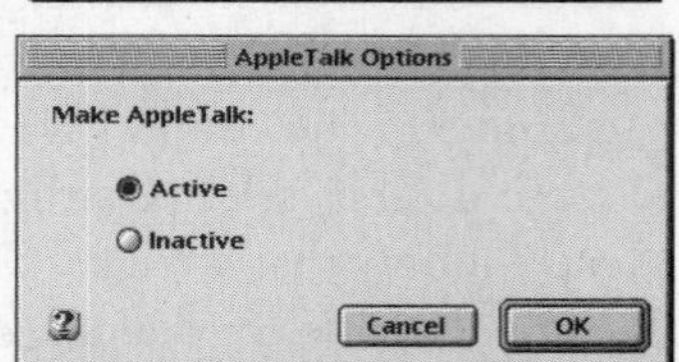

Figure 14-7 *The AppleTalk control panel and its Options window.*

5. **For more help**
   The CD-ROM disc versions of System 7.5 Update 2.0, System 7.5.3, and presumably newer major updates come with an exceptionally good collection of documents on Open Transport, including an Acrobat-format manual. Also, check with Apple Guide for quick help; otherwise, consult with your ISP or network administrator.

BY THE WAY ▶

MACTCP DNR

If you see a MacTCP DNR file at the root level of your System Folder, leave it there—even though you are using Open Transport. While technically not required for Open Transport, it is left there for older TCP applications that expect it to be there and won't run without it.

If you are having problems getting online, however, you might try deleting the DNR file (especially if it is a pre-Open Transport copy). The system software should create a new one—hopefully one that is less problem-prone—when it is needed.

FreePPP and Open Transport PPP/Modem Control Panels

Implementing PPP on a Mac requires special software. Initially most people used a program called *MacPPP*, a version of which may still be included with Apple's Internet Connection Kit (AICK). More generally, however, it has been superseded by a superior product called *FreePPP* (which costs you exactly what its name implies). Since FreePPP is not an Apple product, though, Apple has recently released its own PPP software, called *Open Transport PPP (OT/PPP* or just *PPP)*. Apple's PPP runs in native code on a Power Mac (FreePPP does not), giving it a potential speed advantage. Also, as it is directly supported by Apple and will be included in future system software releases (as well as in other products such as AICK and Apple Remote Access), its popularity is sure to grow.

Unfortunately, PPP is not yet as convenient to use as FreePPP; in fact, from a design point of view, FreePPP is vastly better. The basics of both FreePPP and PPP are covered here—I'll let you decide which one to use.

Setting up FreePPP The main task is to set up an account, which is mainly what I will describe here. For help with FreePPP's many other setup options, check the documentation and/or Apple Guide file that comes with the program. For help with matters such as setting up a connection script, if needed, you will probably also need to get help from your Internet service provider.

Before getting started, make sure "FreePPP" is selected from the "Connect via:" pop-up menu of the TCP/IP control panel, as described previously.

1. **Open FreePPP Setup and click the Accounts tab**
   After installing the FreePPP software, launch FreePPP Setup. Then click the Accounts tab, and click to Edit or create a New account.

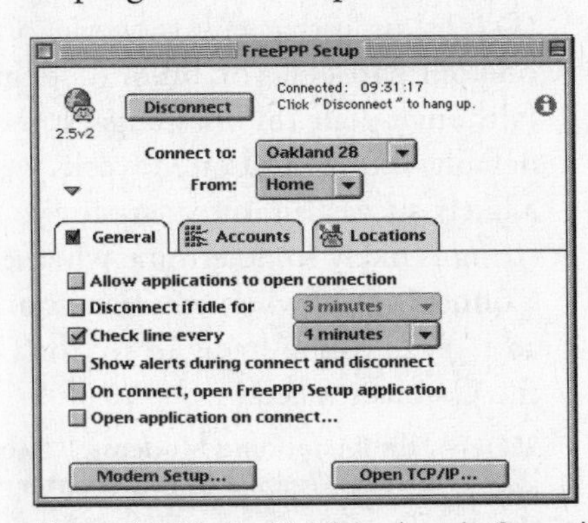

Figure 14-8A *FreePPP Setup's main General window.*

2. **From the window for a given account: The Account tab (and Location tab)**
   From the Account tab, type in a Server Name (anything you like can go here) and enter the phone number of your Internet service provider. Assuming you don't need to use a Connection Script, select "Directly" from the Connect pop-up window. Then enter your user login name and password in the spaces indicated.

   The Location tab allows you to set up certain options specific to a given location. By creating more than one location, you can have settings ready to go whether you are at home, at the office, or on the road. Users with just a single location can largely ignore this.

   You can create more than one account and location, if desired, and select the ones you want to use for a given connection from the "Connect to:" and "From:" settings, as described in Step 5.

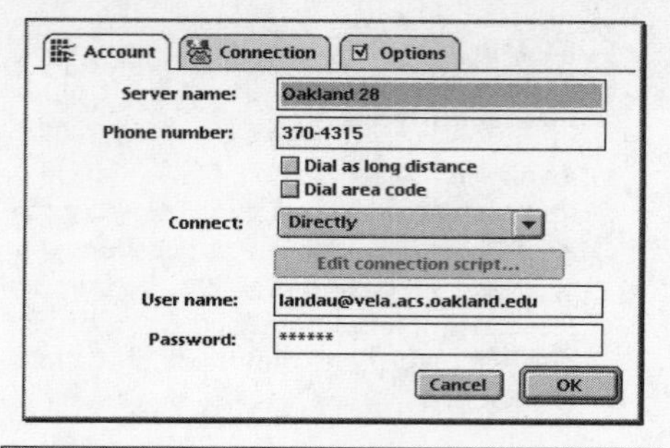

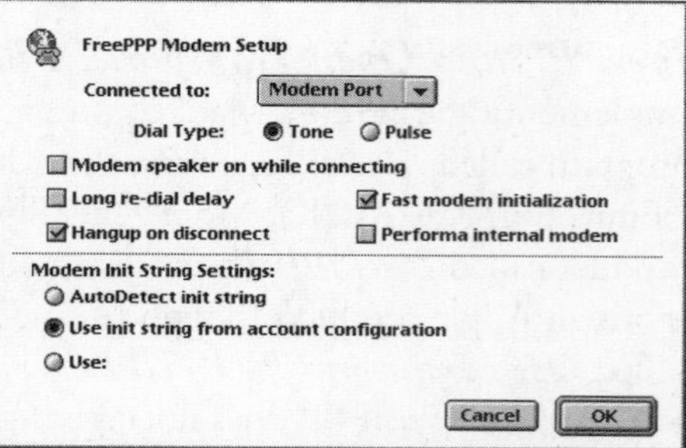

Figure 14-8B *FreePPP Setup's Modem Setup window (top) and an Accounts window (bottom).*

3. **From the window for a given account: The Connection tab**
   From the Connection tab, select a Port Speed and Flow Control setting, then enter a Modem Init String. These are the three most critical variables in determining the success or failure of your connection.

   For example, for a 28.8K modem connected to a Power Mac, you will probably select a port speed of "115200 bps." Flow control will probably be "CTS & RTS (DTR)" or, if that fails to work, "CTS Only." The modem init string depends on your particular brand of modem, and so is typically obtained from its manual (although your ISP may suggest modifications). "AT&F1" typically selects a modem's default settings and often works well. Alternatively, FreePPP has the ability to pick a likely successful init string for you (as described in Step 4). Note that your init string is likely to determine whether FreePPP lists your Carrier speed or your Connect speed when you first connect. For example, with Global Village modems, add "W2" to the string to see the Carrier speed. Otherwise, you will most likely see the Connect speed.

   SEE: • **"Understanding Modems," "Modem Speed," "Flow Control," and "Initialization Strings," earlier in this chapter, for more details**

4. **Modem Setup**
   Close the Account window and select the General tab, then click the Modem Setup button. Make sure the options here, such as the port to which your modem is connected (modem, printer, or internal), are correct. Most importantly, if you did not enter a modem init string previously, click "AutoDetect Init String" rather than the

option to use the string from the account configuration. After you're done, close the Modem Setup window.

If the AutoDetect option fails to work (which might result in a message that says "Link established but was not reliable and was disconnected"), turn it off and enter an init string yourself.

5. **Make the connection**
   Select the account name from the "Connect to:" pop-up menu. (If you have more than one Location, pick the desired one from the "From:" pop-up menu.) Assuming all other options have been set up as needed, you can now simply click the "Connect" button, and a connection should be made.

6. **Disconnect**
   To disconnect, simply click the Disconnect button. Alternatively, you can disconnect via FreePPP's Control Strip or menu bar options.

7. **Connect again**
   For subsequent connections, just open the FreePPP Setup control panel and click the Connect button. Alternatively, you can connect from the Control Strip or menu bar options.

Other options in the General window of FreePPP Setup are fairly self-explanatory (and the Guide file explains them more if needed). Uncheck "Allow applications to open connection" if you have connection problems (it is used to connect via FreePPP automatically when you open an Internet application). Also, checking "Check line every X minutes" may help prevent unwanted disconnects.

SEE ALSO: • **"Dropped Connections," later in this chapter**
• **"Take Note: Troubleshooting FreePPP," later in this chapter**

Setting up Open Transport PPP (OT/PPP) Setting up and using Apple's Open Transport PPP requires the use of a pair of new control panels: Modem and PPP.

Before getting started, make sure "PPP" is selected from the "Connect via:" pop-up menu of the TCP/IP control panel (as described previously).

1. **Open the Modem control panel**
   You should only need to access this control panel when you first set it up, or if you change to a new modem.

2. **Set Modem's "Connect via:" and "Modem" options**
   From the "Connect via:" pop-up menu, select the serial port to which your modem is connected.

   From the "Modem" pop-up menu, select the modem name that matches the name of your modem. Assuming you find a match, this selects a script from a folder called Modem Scripts that is stored in the Extensions folder of your System Folder.

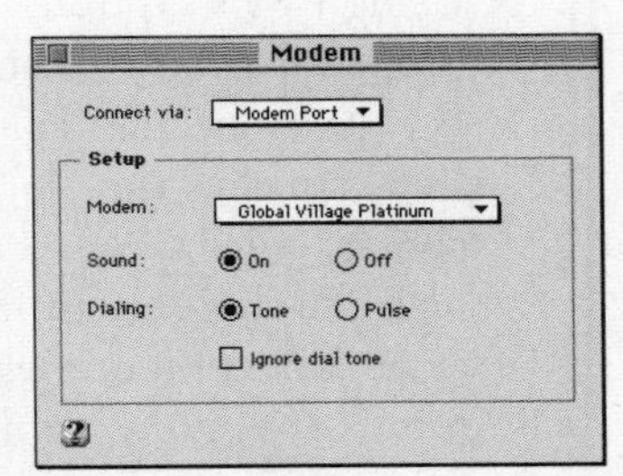

Figure 14-9 *Apple's Modem control panel.*

If things work well, you don't have much left to worry about. If problems occur, however, you may have to modify the modem script (which is basically a text file), or even create a new one. This is likely to be considerably more difficult than making similar modifications to FreePPP. This is one of the main disadvantages of PPP. To help out, Apple does include a program called Modem Script Generator. Be sure to check out its Help files for more guidance, but the process is still far from pleasant.

By the way, modem scripts are essentially the same as Apple Remote Access CCL files (as described in Chapter 11), except that CCL scripts did not permit data compression or error correction to be turned on.

3. **Open the PPP control panel and enter basic settings**
The first time you use PPP, open the PPP control panel and enter the login name and password that you need to access your ISP account. If you want your password to be retained for future use (a possible security risk), check the Save Password checkbox, then enter the telephone number of your ISP.

If you want to have more than one PPP configuration, you can set up and select from different configurations via the Configuration command in PPP's File menu. It works the same way as the similar command in TCP/IP, described previously in "TCP/IP and AppleTalk Control Panels."

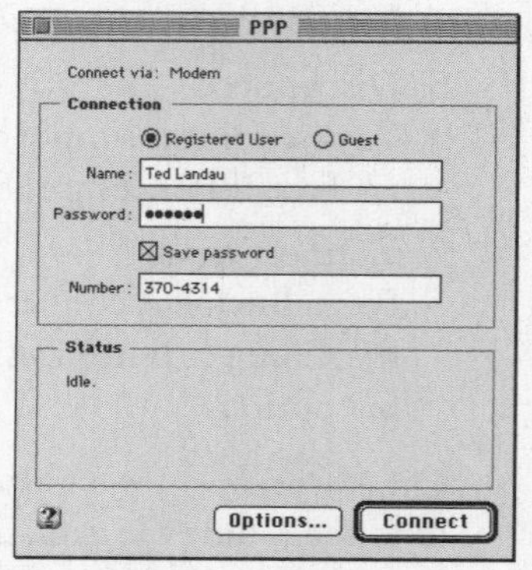

Figure 14-10 *Apple's PPP control panel.*

4. **Make the connection**
At this point, the Connect button should be enabled. Simply click it and, if all goes well, you should get connected.

Note: "Connect Automatically when starting TCP/IP applications" functions similarly to FreePPP's "Allow applications to open connection," allowing automatic connection when you open an Internet application. Again, uncheck this option if you are experiencing problems.

5. **Using PPP's Options (hopefully, you will not need them)**
If your connection fails, your probable next step is to click the Options button in the PPP control panel. From the Protocol tab, you will have the choice to turn data compression and error correction off (which can help solve some connection problems). Most importantly, if you select "Connect to a Command Line Host" and then check "Use terminal window," you will be able to log on from a terminal window session, record and save the session, then select "Use Connect Script" and

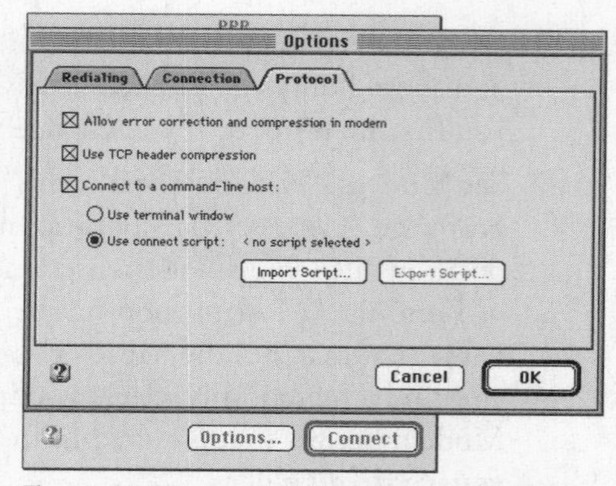

Figure 14-11 *Apple's PPP control panel options; the option to "Use Connect Script" is selected here.*

import the script you just saved. (FreePPP has similar options, by the way, accessed from its Account tab window).

If you ever modify an existing Connect Script (which, since it is just a text file, can be modified in any word processor), you will need to re-import it to get PPP to recognize the changes.

If even this fails to work, then consider changing to the modem script used by the Modem control panel. Consult PPP documentation for more help and for descriptions of other options, if needed.

6. **Disconnect (and Connect Again)**
   To disconnect, simply click the Disconnect button. For subsequent connections, all you need to do is open the PPP control panel and click the Connect button.

TECHNICALLY SPEAKING ▶

MULTI-HOMING

Many of Apple's more recent PCI-based Macs (such as the 7600, but not the 7500) include a new feature called multi-homing. It is only relevant to those users who want to connect online via two different methods at the same time (such as via a modem *and* via Ethernet). As I am far from an expert in this area, I will give you the following quote from Apple to help explain exactly what is going on here: "The enhanced models of the PCI-based Power Macintosh computers have a new version of the Curio IC, CurioPrime, that supports multi-homing. Multi-homing, also called multi-porting, makes it possible for AppleTalk to be active on more than one network port on the computer at the same time. Multi-homing is most important for Macintosh computers with PC Compatible cards installed so users can have simultaneous TCP/IP and Netware sessions."

BY THE WAY ▶

AMERICA ONLINE AND COMPUSERVE VIA PPP

I have focused here on connecting online to the Internet via a PPP connection. As mentioned in the main text, you do not need to use a PPP connection to access services such as America Online or CompuServe, although you can use a PPP connection with them.

For example, with America Online, you can select "TCP Connection" as the Locality in its Welcome screen (assuming you have installed AOL's TCP software for this option). This will likely be faster than your normal modem connection (and perhaps cheaper, if your PPP connection is not a toll call and your standard connection is). With AOL 3.0, you have a new option called AOL Link. This allows you to connect to AOL in a way that mimics a true TCP connection. To avoid problems, do not install AOL Link if you already use a separate ISP to make TCP connections.

Similarly, with CompuServe, you can use your CompuServe phone number to make a PPP connection just as if CompuServe was an Internet service provider (you'll need to set up a connection script to do it; CompuServe has files online that give the details). After making this CompuServe connection, you can use any Internet software.

Basically, the lines between these services and the Internet are blurring. A common expectation is that within a few years, these services will be gone altogether, at least in their present form. If they are around at all, they will be based on the World Wide Web.

Solve-It! Open Transport Problems

Compatibility Problems

Symptoms:

- Programs do not work properly after installing Open Transport.

Causes:

Typically, this is caused by older versions of software that are incompatible with Open Transport in some way.

What to do:

Update to current versions of the problem software. Here are a few specific examples:

- Some incompatibilities are addressed by updates to Open Transport itself. For example, you need at least version 1.1 of Open Transport to use Netscape Navigator. You need at least version 1.1.1 of Open Transport to work with 5200/5300/6200/6300 Performas and Power Macs.
- You need version 1.3 or later of Apple's Assistant Toolbox extension (it's already included with System 7.5.3).
- Panorama 2.*x* doesn't like Open Transport. When you launch it, you will get a message that says another version of Panorama is already in use, and the application will quit automatically. Upgrading to version 3.0 fixes this problem; otherwise, turning off AppleTalk or reverting to Classic AppleTalk (if your Mac model supports this) are work-around solutions.
- Virtual memory (or RAM Doubler) are periodically reported to have conflicts with Open Transport, although this is less likely with current versions. You may need to disable these features if problems persist.
- Make sure you are using the latest versions of FreePPP or Apple's Open Transport PPP (described more in the prior section of this chapter).

TAKE NOTE ▶

WHEN STARTING UP WITH EXTENSIONS OFF: SERIAL PORT FUNCTIONS DON'T FUNCTION WITHOUT OPEN TRANSPORT

With Classic AppleTalk, if you started up with extensions off, you could still print to an AppleTalk printer (such as a LaserWriter) and usually connect to a modem. Not so with Open Transport. With Open Transport disabled (and assuming that Classic AppleTalk is not active either), you will be unable to do just about anything that requires going through the serial ports! Although AppleTalk will not function, you can still print to non-LocalTalk printers. (This is also covered in Chapter 7 in regard to printing.)

TECHNICALLY SPEAKING ▶

A MYSTERIOUS CURE FROM SOME TYPE 1/TYPE 11 ERRORS WHEN USING TCP SOFTWARE

When you install Open Transport PPP 1.0 (OT/PPP, it adds two files to your Extensions folder: OpenTptModem and OpenTptRemoteAccess. It turns out that these two files may have some benefit even if you don't want to use OT/PPP. In particular, many users have reported that installing just these two files (actually OpenTptRemoteAccess seems to be the key file), and no other part of OT/PPP, completely eliminates Type 1 and/or Type 11 errors occurring when using Netscape Navigator, Claris Emailer, or almost any other TCP application. For the most part, these users were using FreePPP, rather than OT/PPP, to make their modem connection (they were also using Open Transport rather than Classic AppleTalk). Of course, actually installing and using all of OT/PPP has the same beneficial effect. To get just these two extensions, and not use OT/PPP, the simplest procedure is to select Custom Install from the OT/PPP Installer and check to install either "OpenTransport/PPP files (68K only)" or "OpenTransport/PPP files (PowerPC only)," depending on the type of Mac you have.

Why does this cure work? No one I have contacted had a good explanation. But it is clear that it does work.

Modem and PPP Connection Problems

Symptoms:

- When you try to make a connection with your modem, especially a PPP connection, the connection consistently fails.
- After making a successful connection, you still cannot get any response from your relevant applications (for example, pages do not load in your Web browser).

SEE: • **"Troubleshooting Web Browsers," later in this chapter, for related problem solving help**

- Online response time (such as for data transfers) is unexpectedly and unusually slow.
- A successful connection unexpectedly gets lost ("dropped"), although your PPP software indicates that it is still connected.
- A system freeze occurs while you are online and using a network services application (such as a Web browser)
- You have problems with faxing over a fax modem.

Causes:

These problems are typically caused by a bad connection, problems with your modem, problems with your online service (or Internet service provider), incorrect settings in your Open Transport and/or PPP software, or software incompatibilities.

Generally, if you cannot even get the phone number you are dialing to answer and attempt to establish a connection, the problem is usually with your modem, modem cables, or the serial port, unless there is trouble at the receiving end (a busy signal, the server is down, etc.).

If you get stuck at the point of trying to establish a connection, though, or if a connection appears to be established successfully but you get no response when you try to access the host via your communications software, the problem is more likely due to incorrect settings in your communications software or other software-related issues.

What to do:

I am assuming here that you have followed the advice in the previous section of this chapter on setting up a TCP and PPP connection.

When You Can't Get Connected: General Advice

- Make sure that you are getting a dial tone, that the modem is really attempting to dial, and that the receiving end is answering. This is best accomplished if you can listen to the sounds emitted by your modem's speakers. So turn this option on, either from FreePPP's Modem Setup options or by changing your modem init string (where M0 turns sound off, and M1 turns it back on) if it is currently set to off.
- Turn the modem off and back on again. This is good general advice, but try it especially if you can't get a dial tone from your phone line after a failed attempt at connecting.
- Disconnect the phone cable from the modem and reconnect it. Use this as a last resort if turning the modem off did not work, or if you have an internal modem that thus cannot be turned off.
- Restart your Macintosh.

After each of these steps, try to connect again to see if it works.

When You Can't Get Connected: Specific Advice

- If you have call waiting, make sure it is disabled by dialing *70 prior to the phone number. Getting a separate phone line for your modem eliminates the need to worry about this!
- Your ISP may be having troubles at its end that are preventing you from connecting. In some cases, trouble may allow email to work, but not your Web access (or vice versa).

  In any case, give the ISP a call to see what's up.
- Check your speed, flow control, and modem init string settings. Consider trying a lower speed, especially if this is a phone number that you have not tried before.

  Error messages may be misleading here. For example, I once got an error message that told me to check the Domain Name Server addresses in the TCP/IP control panel as the likely source of the problem. It turned out, however, that FreePPP's AutoDetect modem init string option was selecting a less-than-ideal string. When I entered my own custom string (based on advice given in the modem manual), everything worked.

SEE: • **"Modem Speed," "Flow Control," and "Initialization Strings," earlier in this chapter, for more details**

- Check your TCP/IP control panel settings, just in case.
- If you get a "serial port in use" message that includes an option to reset the port, click OK. Otherwise, use a freeware utility called CommCloser to close the serial port. If that option fails or is not available, you'll have to restart your Macintosh.
- If you get "waiting for port" or "PPP" time-out message errors, make sure you have entered your name and password correctly.
- If AppleTalk is on, turn it off. This can resolve some serial port problems. Since turning off AppleTalk is also known to improve speed and reduce transmission errors, try it if you have persistent problems.

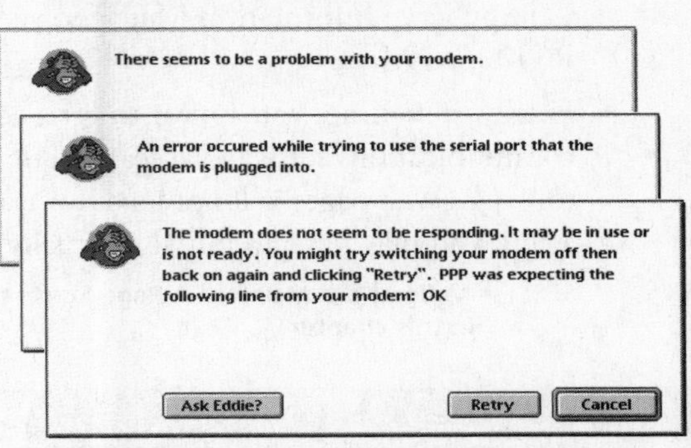

Figure 14-12 *Some error messages you may get from FreePPP when it fails to connect. Top: You may have a problem at the receiving end (such as a dead line) or a problem with the modem (try turning it off and back on again). Middle: Do you mistakenly have AppleTalk turned on for your modem's serial port? Bottom: Did you forget to turn on the modem?*

- At least on PCI-based Macs, the GeoPort Telecom Adapter (which needed to use modem features via the GeoPort), does not work, if you also have an active LocalTalk connection—which includes something as simple as a laser printer connected to your Mac. This conflict may be fixed in the most current release of the Telecom software; check the "Read Me" file that comes with the Telecom software for details. If it is not fixed, you'll have to unplug your LocalTalk cable before you can use the GeoPort. Simply turning off AppleTalk is not sufficient to prevent this problem.

  Current versions definitely fix a bug that caused older versions of the Telecom fax software to cause a crash at startup if Apple Guide was also present.
- If you use Apple's GeoPort Telecom Adapter as a modem, select Express Modem (rather than External Modem) from the Express Modem control panel.
- Consider whether you have a dead modem. See if another modem works.
- If you have fax software installed, turn it off (or at least any "fax receive" options) unless you are actually trying to receive a fax. Disabling this software has been reported as necessary for both Global Village and Supra modems, although upgrades may have fixed this problem.

  On a related note, Global Village extensions (such as Global Village Toolbox) reportedly conflicted with the initial release of RAM Doubler 2, leading to Type 1 errors. The solution is to disable the Toolbox and related fax extensions, at least temporarily. They are only needed for faxing, not for connecting to the Internet.
- If you updated the firmware of your modem—and especially if you had any problems or interruptions when doing so—your modem's firmware may now be damaged. Contact the vendor for help.

SEE ALSO: • **"By The Way: Firmware Updates"**

- In general, make sure you have the latest version of the modem and fax software, especially important with PCI-based Macs. If problems start as soon as you upgrade, consider going back to the prior version.
- Similarly, you may have incompatible communications software. For example, CompuServe Information Manager, versions 2.x work sporadically at best on PCI-based Macs.
- Finally, sometimes you appear to get a connection—according to your modem and/or communications software, at least—but you can't get any communications applications to work (Web pages will not load, for example). Wait awhile before you give up and try again; you may have an initial unusually slow response that will clear up on its own.

SEE: • **"A Long Delay Before A Page Starts to Load," in "Solve-It! Web Browser Problems," later in this chapter**

BY THE WAY ▶

FIRMWARE UPDATES

Some modems, such as the popular Global Village Platinum modem and top-of-the-line Supra modems, can actually have their ROMs (firmware) upgraded by the user. This is because the modems use a "flash ROM" that can be "permanently" recoded by running special updater software.

If your modem has a flash ROM, check with the vendor to make sure you have the latest ROM update. Updates fix bugs or provide improvements such as faster throughput.

If you have a Global Village modem, and want to check what version of firmware you are using, here is how: Open the Global Village Fax Center software, hold down the Option button, and click anywhere on the word "GlobalFax" at the top of the window. The window that appears will include the firmware number. If it says you are using an older version than you think you have installed, go to the TelePort control panel and click the Modem Reset button, then try again.

BY THE WAY ▶

PROBLEMS FAXING WITH A FAX MODEM

Over the years, fax software (of all brands!) has been notorious for causing conflicts and generally not working well. Many users simply give up and buy a dedicated fax machine. Happily, the software seems to be improving of late (and Global Village's software remains the most reliable, in my opinion). Bear in mind that you can still use your modem to make online connections, even with all fax software disabled. If you are having problems using your fax software, here are a few tips to check out:

- If you use PPP software and you are having problems with your faxes, make sure you have closed any PPP connection before trying to send or receive faxes.
- With MS Office applications and FAXcilitate, select Fax Setup (and then click the Print button) rather than directly selecting the Fax command. Otherwise, you may get Type 1 errors.
- With Global Village, changing the loading order of its Toolbox extension (earlier or later in the sequence, depending upon your specific setup) may help resolve problems.
- Try a clean reinstall of system software.

Dropped Connections

Sometimes you appear to be connected just fine when, unexpectedly, your connection gets lost in the middle of a session. This is called a "dropped connection," and here's what you should know about it:

Short-Term Causes and Solutions

- A problem with your ISP, such as its server going down, could cause this. In this case, you will not be able to reconnect (with any reliability anyway) until the ISP fixes the problem.
- Your ISP may have a time limit on how long you can stay connected. There is not much you can do about this, other than reconnect when it happens.
- Your ISP may have a feature to disconnect you after a certain period of inactivity. Aside from simply keeping busy, turning on an option such as FreePPP's "Check Line Every X Minutes" may keep things going.
- You may have an option set in your software (such as FreePPP's "Disconnect If Idle for X Minutes" option) that disconnects you automatically after a certain period of inactivity. If so, uncheck this option.
- Line noise may cause a disconnection.

In many of these cases, the disconnect will occur at the modem even though your PPP software (such as FreePPP) still says you are connected. In this case, you first have to "disconnect" via your PPP software before you can try to reconnect again.

In general, the solution to almost all of these problems is to try to connect again. In some cases, you may need to restart the Macintosh first.

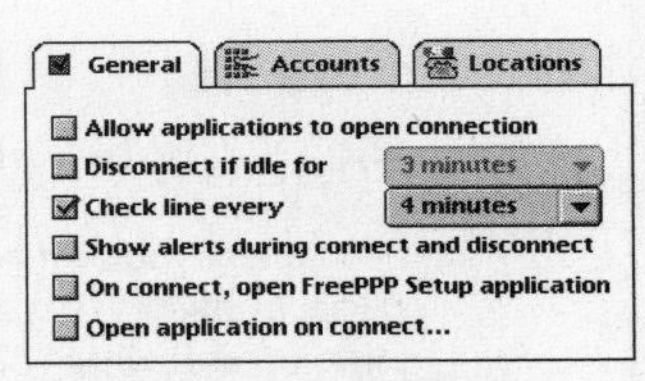

Figure 14-13 *Another look at FreePPP's General options.*

Long-Term Causes and Solutions These most often have to do with init string settings.

- If you have a Global Village modem, disable its extensions (especially the Global Village Toolbox extension). They are only really needed if you are sending or receiving faxes. Sometimes, just rearranging the loading order of the extensions may help.
- Turn off the error correction and/or data compression options of your modem. Depending on your software, you may be able to do this directly from the software itself; otherwise, you do it by modifying the modem's init string. This might make the modem operate a little slower, but the connection will be more stable.
- Switching flow control from "CTS & RTS (DTR)" to "CTS Only" may help.
- Make other changes to the modem init string, as specified by your online service or ISP. Assuming "AT&F1" did not work, another somewhat generic suggestion to try is "AT&F%C0\NO."

SEE: • **"Modem Speed," "Flow Control," and "Initialization Strings," earlier in this chapter, for more details**

TAKE NOTE ▶

TROUBLESHOOTING FREEPPP

Though Apple's OT/PPP has now arrived, FreePPP remains a popular alternative. Here is some troubleshooting advice specific to this software that is especially relevant if you are having problems getting or keeping a PPP connection:

- Make sure you have no older copies of FreePPP Setup (or other FreePPP components) or older versions of MacPPP still on your drive, no matter where on the drive they may be.
- Be careful of using third-party PPP add-ons, such as Control PPP or PPPFloater. They often conflict with FreePPP 2.5 or later.
- If you are experiencing very slow data transfer rates, disable RAM Doubler, especially if you have a Macintosh that uses as 603 or 603e processor. There have been reports that RAM Doubler and PPP software somehow conflict on these Macs, resulting in the slowdown.
- If "Allow applications to open connections" is checked and you have any weird symptoms—including the modem dialing at startup or shutdown—disable this option, especially if TCP/IP's "Load only when needed" is unchecked. In fact, to play it safe, always connect with FreePPP prior to opening your Internet applications. Among other things, this tactic reportedly reduces the probability of memory leak problems.

SEE: • "Technically Speaking: Open Transport, Memory Leaks, and 'Load Only When Needed,'" earlier in this chapter

TAKE NOTE ▶

PROBLEMS GETTING CONNECTED ON THE ROAD

If you take a modem and a Macintosh with you when you travel, you may discover some special problems that crop up when trying to get online from your hotel/motel. Here's what's going on and what you can do about it:

- Beware if the hotel/motel uses a digital phone system. Not only won't your modem work with it, but it may actually damage your modem if you try. Some better hotels that use a digital system also have a special "data port socket" for use with modems; ask the front desk about this. Otherwise, you may be able to purchase a digital-to-analog converter to use with your modem. Global Village makes one for its modems called GlobalSwitch; a similar product by Radish Communications Systems is called InsideLine.
- If your hotel uses a special digit (usually an 8 or a 9) to access an "outside" line, this may prevent your modem from working if it doesn't pause long enough to wait for the outside line to appear. You can probably solve this by adding a couple of commas between the special digit and the rest of the phone number.
- You can use the "W" character to tell the modem to wait for a dial tone. Otherwise, the "@" character will cause the modem to wait for five seconds of silence. One of these, inserted after the initial special digit, may work (depending upon how the system is set up).
- Finally, some problems may be due to the modem not recognizing the odd sound that some hotel phone lines use as a dial tone. If none of the previous solutions work, check if your modem supports an AT command for bypassing the need to hear a dial tone. If so, use that command. Otherwise, your software may provide such an option; for example, Apple's Modem control panel (used with its Open Transport PPP software) has an option to "Ignore Dial Tone."

SEE: • Chapter 11 for more details on problems using a modem with a PowerBook

The Internet (especially the World Wide Web)

If you have made it this far in the chapter, I will assume that you have successfully connected and made it onto the Internet. Congratulations! It is probably also safe to assume that surfing the World Wide Web is one of the more common things that you do. You may also be familiar with some of the other basics of Internet surfing, such as getting email or downloading files. This section will explore some of the common questions and problems that people confront when engaged in these activities.

If you need more basic help on telecommunications and/or the Internet, there are approximately a zillion books out there offering to help you. For starters, the latest edition of *The Macintosh Bible* (Peachpit) has an excellent set of chapters on these topics.

Understanding Internet Addresses

When the World Wide Web first exploded on our cultural landscape, surely among the things that most puzzled Web neophytes were the weird names that made up a Web site's address. How, for example, was anyone supposed to make sense of something like *http://www.amherst.edu/~mkbhatia/otppp.html* (which happens to be a site that covers Open Transport and PPP questions, in case you still have any)? Well, it turns out that these names are just one more variation of a basic naming structure that pervades the entire Internet. Here is basically how it works.

Domain Names

Each location along the Internet has its own IP address sending or retrieving information, much like the post office mail address for your home. These addresses, however, are made up of a string of seemingly meaningless numbers (such as 141.210.10.15). Fortunately, to make things easier for you, a domain name can be assigned to a numeric address. Examples of these are typically found in the Search Domains file of the TCP/IP control panel. For example, instead of 141.210.10.15 (the IP of Oakland University, where I work), I can use its assigned domain name address: *oakland.edu.*

Each period (or "dot") in a domain name separates different hierarchical levels of the name (much as a comma separates a city and state in a post office mail address). In the simple example of *oakland.edu, oakland* represents the name of the university while *edu* identifies it as an educational institution. The final part of all domain names (such as *edu* in the previous example) is typically one of a limited set of identifiers, including *com* (for commercial), *gov* (for government), and *org* (for non-profit organizations).

SEE: • **"Technically Speaking: TCP/IP and MacTCP Control Panels: What Exactly Do They Do?" earlier in this chapter, for related information**

Email Addresses

Internet email addresses are based on the domain name scheme just described. They are divided into two parts—the user's name and the user's location—separated by the "@" symbol. For example, my email address, *landau@oakland.edu.*, essentially identifies me (*landau)* as being located at Oakland University (*@oakland.edu*).

Here's one more example. My America Online name is "Ted Landau." If you want to send email to that account over the Internet, however, you will have to send it to *TedLandau@aol.com*. Note that the space between my first and last name is eliminated on the Internet-based address (Internet addresses do not permit spaces, although AOL does for its own screen names). The location name tells you that it is an America Online location (*aol)* and that America Online is a commercial institution (*com)*. Capitalization also matters when typing these names.

BY THE WAY ▶

IF YOUR SENT EMAIL BOUNCES BACK TO YOU

If you send an email message and it gets returned to you unsent (sometimes called a *bounce-back*), make sure you entered the address correctly. If you did, the problem is at the receiving end (perhaps the mail server is down). All you can do is wait—minutes, hours, or days—and try again later. The error message that accompanies the bounce-back may give you some insight as to what is going on, but don't count on it.

World Wide Web Addresses

To get your browser to go to a specific location on the Web, you must enter its Web address (do this in the "Location:" box of Netscape Navigator, for example). Web addresses all begin with the expression *http://,* whose letters stand for "HyperText Transfer Protocol." This is the protocol that allows you to click on a word or a picture on a Web page and have the browser jump (or *link*) to another site. Just be careful to enter the address exactly how it is written; even the most trivial variation will result in the address being rejected (that's why users depend upon ways of saving these addresses, as described in "By the Way: Saving and Using URLs"). Also, note that whenever you jump to a location by clicking on some hyperlinked text or graphic on a Web page, it is using these same Web addresses "behind the scenes."

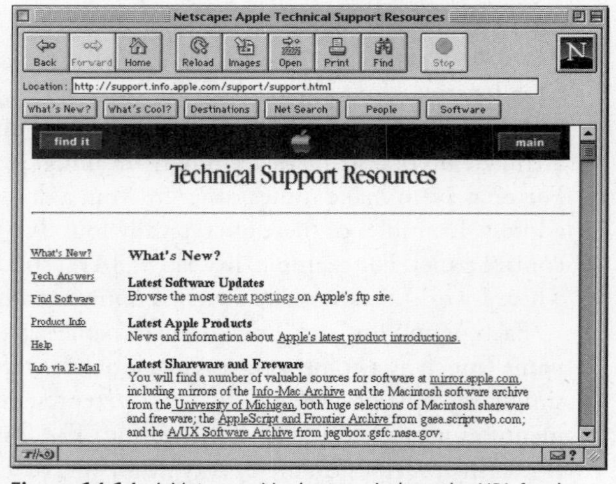

Figure 14-14 *A Netscape Navigator window; the URL for the page displayed is in the "Location:" text box.*

A typical address is *http://www.macintouch.com/* (one of my favorite sites). Everything after the colon identifies the specific location. If the last character is a slash, the address refers to a directory of files; selecting it will open the default (or index) file associated with that directory. Otherwise, the address refers to a specific file within a directory and takes you directly to it. If you are having trouble getting an address to work, you might try adding a slash on the end (if one is not there), or vice versa. Web addresses never end in a period.

The slash divisions represent another hierarchical level of organization (similar to how the dots within each slashed area work). For example, the address for a list of Apple utilities on my own MacFixIt Web site is *http://www.macfixit.com/library/applelinks.html.* The first expression (*www.macfixit.com)* identifies that you are going to the MacFixIt site on the World Wide Web. The subsequent expressions further hone you in on the exact page with the utilities listing. If you simply delete any rightmost slashed segment of an address (such as *applelinks.html)*, you will typically be taken either to a directory index or to the next higher level in the directory hierarchy—try it out and see.

You can often guess an unknown Web location in a similar manner. Do you want the home page for Widgets, Inc.? Try *http://www.widgets.com/*—more often than not, this will work. Actually, since Netscape Navigator knows the same trick, if you just typed "widgets" into the "Location:" box, the browser will automatically try out *http://www.widgets.com/* for you!

Finally, remember that since every Web address also has a numeric address hidden beneath it, you can use these numeric addresses instead of names to go to Web sites. In fact, sometimes you will see these numeric addresses appear when you are connecting to a Web site.

BY THE WAY ▶

SAVING AND USING URLS

No one wants to remember and retype URLs in their browser. Fortunately, you rarely have to. Here are some popular alternatives:

- In Netscape Navigator, as you already know if you have ever used it, you can save a URL as a "Bookmark," then open it next time from the Bookmarks menu. You can later edit, rearrange, or delete bookmarks by selecting Bookmarks from the Window menu. Microsoft's Internet Explorer browser works similarly via its Favorites menu.
- In Navigator, you can drag a URL to the desktop. This will create a document that will go directly to that page when you double-click it.
- If you save a Web page to the desktop using Navigator's Save a Copy command, it will include the URL for that page in the file's Get Info Comments window.
- For URLs from other sources, such as word processing documents, you can always copy and paste. Several programs such as Aladdin's CyberFinder, however, have options that let you select a URL in text and (via a special keyboard and/or mouse-click combination) directly launch that page or save the URL as a "file."

Also note that browsers have a Go menu that tracks recently visited pages. You can select a URL from there as well as from the Bookmark menu.

URLs: Using Your Browser for More Than Just the Web

The Internet is not only a loosely connected worldwide network, it is also a loosely held collection of different services. You can use the Internet for email, for downloading files (called *file transfer protocol* or FTP), for checking out newsgroups, and for browsing the Web—and those are just the main options).

With a TCP connection on a Macintosh, you can use different software specialized for each function (such as Eudora for email, NewsWatcher for newsgroups, Anarchie or Fetch for FTP, and Netscape or Explorer for Web browsing).

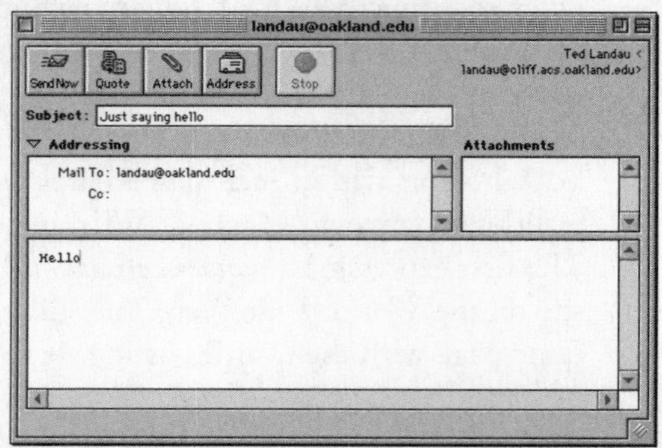

Figure 14-15 *Using Netscape Navigator to send email.*

One of the beauties of Web browsers such as Netscape Navigator or Microsoft's Internet Explorer, however, is that you can access all of the services listed here from the browser itself, which becomes sort of a Swiss Army knife for the Internet. The other applications are not obsolete by any means. They retain certain specialized advantages, offering more features than the Web browser could include, but the browser is a great place to start.

The main reason this can work is that all of these different services can be referenced via a common naming system, called a URL (or Uniform Resource Locator). URLs are based on the same domain name system already described. A *http://* address is just one type of URL. Your Web browser can also access FTP sites (where files that you can download are stored) via URLs that begin with an *ftp://* prefix (such as *ftp://ftp.info.apple.com/Apple.Support.Area/Apple.Software.Updates/US/Macintosh/).* Today's browsers can similarly access newsgroups (via a *news://* prefix) and send email (via a *mailto:* prefix). These latter two features take you to special windows that are separate from the main Web browser windows. For example, to send me email from a browser, you should enter *mailto:landau@oakland.edu*.

SEE: • **Fix-It #18 for more on these Internet services**

Working with Downloaded and Uploaded Files

Downloading a file means getting a copy of it from some remote online location and transferring it to your Macintosh; *uploading* is the reverse process. Most times these tasks, especially downloading, are as simple as clicking a button and letting your software do the rest of the work. Common problems that confront users, however, include downloaded files that do not open and uploaded files that are not received in an openable form. This section explains why these problems occur and what to do about them.

If you are having problems even getting a file to download successfully, especially with a Web browser, check out "Solve-It!: Web Browser Problems," later in this chapter.

SEE ALSO: • **Fix-It #5, "Take Note: Why Can't I Open The System Software I Just Downloaded?" for another look at this subject**

BY THE WAY

A WORD ABOUT WEB PAGE AUTHORING AND HTML

Just how do you go about creating a home page for the World Wide Web (a popular activity these days)? First, you create a text document written in a special language called HTML (HyperText Markup Language). The document is then loaded to a *Web server* and assigned a specific address (actually, with very little effort, your own Macintosh can become a Web server). Here it can be viewed by anyone with access to the Web.

The basics of using HTML are quite simple—in particular, much simpler than learning a programming language. It depends on special tags (contained inside brackets) that indicate instructions on how the page should appear; your Web browser then interprets these instructions to construct the page. For example, "<TITLE>Ted Landau's Home Page</TITLE>" tells the browser that "Ted Landau's Home Page" is the title of the page. Note that the actual text needs to be correctly enclosed by an opening tag and a closing tag (which has the slash); this is a general principle of almost all HTML "commands."

Still, since designing fancy pages can get complicated quick enough, there are a host of Web page editors on the market to help you out. The most recent trend is for these editors to completely hide the HTML code from you, allowing you to lay out a page almost as easily as if you were using a word processor or page layout program. Currently, the most popular of these so-called WYSIWYG (for "What You See Is What You Get") editors are Adobe's PageMill and Claris Home Page.

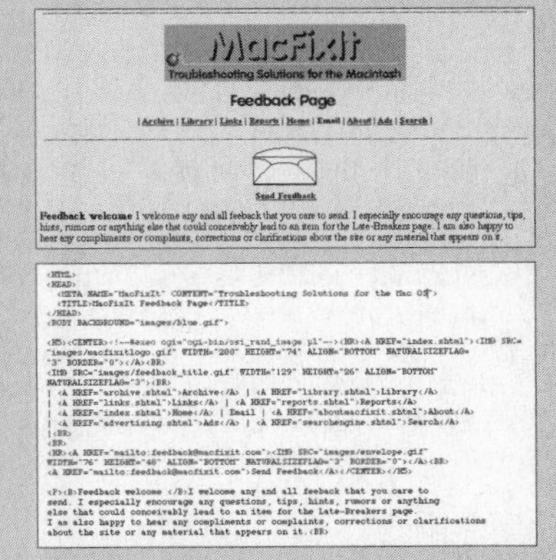

Figure 14-16 *Top: A Web page as viewed in a browser. Bottom: the source code behind the Web page (from Navigator, select Document Source for the View window to see the source code).*

There are, of course, a host of troubleshooting issues that might confront a Web author trying to get a page to look and work exactly the way he or she wants. Although this is best left as a subject for another book (of which there are already many), here are a few key reminders:

- If you are entering your own HTML code, make sure that every opening tag has a matching closing tag.
- You have limited control over the appearance of ordinary text. You can control its relative size (compared to other text) but its absolute size and specific font are handled by the user's Web browser. Similarly, paragraph indents, special characters (such as an em dash) and other common text features do not show up on a Web page. So be sure to actually check out how your page looks in a browser before going public; you can do this by simply opening your finished page in your browser while you are offline. (Text control will improve with new font features coming soon.)
- GIF and JPEG graphics are the only graphic formats directly supported on Web pages. Other graphic formats will require special plug-ins to be viewed. (Plug-ins are discussed later in this chapter.)

  GIF graphics are especially flexible. There is a special GIF-89 format used to create *transparent* GIF graphics, which let the page's background show through. You can also create *interlaced* GIF graphics that load progressively, thereby speeding up the initial view of the graphic. There are even *animated* GIFs that provide a simple way to have movement on your page without any plug-ins or fancy tricks required.
- Creating forms, using counters, and some types of imagemaps generally require special software on your server (called CGI scripts) that do most of the work. Simply setting up a form on your Web page will not, by itself, get the form to work.

BY THE WAY ▶

A WORD ABOUT USING YOUR MAC AS A WEB SERVER

If you do create a Web page, you will most likely upload it to a remote server (often the same ISP you use to access the Web). You may be surprised, however, to learn that your Macintosh can be set up as a Web server with amazing ease. You can do it with relatively high-powered software (such as WebSTAR) or more personal-oriented software (such as Microsoft's Personal Web Server or Personal WebSTAR). In either case, even a neophyte can get it up and running in minutes.

While this is truly easy to do and has numerous advantages over other methods (you have much more control over how the site works, for instance, and can customize it more easily), it has one big disadvantage for most individual users—it is expensive, primarily because of the connection costs. Since a 28.8K modem simply will not be fast enough to support any sort of decent-sized Web traffic, an ISDN line is the minimum you will need. If you get fancy, you will also need routers and possibly other expensive networking devices. Also, you will need to get a dedicated line (that is, one that connects your Mac to the Web 24 hours a day), which again is more expensive than your typical dial-up line.

Along with this, you will need a *static address*—that is one that stays the same every time you connect. Users who just browse the Web can get by with a *dynamic address*, which means that they are assigned a new IP address each time they connect. Again, static addresses are more expensive to get. So, unless you are rich or expect to make a profit with your Web site, the costs are too high to make this a viable option (other than as a temporary setup on your existing system, just to see how it works).

Even if you get past the cost, you will find that a Macintosh server cannot work fast enough to support the high volume of access requests you might get if your site gets very popular.

Downloaded Files

Sleeper.sit.hqx Sleeper.sit Sleeper

Figure 14-17 *A downloaded file in binhex format (left); after decoding the binhex file into a StuffIt format (center); and after unstuffing the file into a folder containing the usable files (right).*

You've just downloaded a file. If you did this in a program such as Netscape Navigator, it probably used "helpers" (such as StuffIt Expander) to "decode" and "decompress" the file. As a result, you may find as many as three different versions of the file on your drive. If so, you can delete the two files that have suffixes such as ".sit" or ".hqx" and just save the finished usable file/folder. Otherwise, if you have a downloaded file that refuses to open or gives you other similar problems, the following tips should help you sort things out.

Encoded Files: Binhex (.hqx) If your downloaded file ends in the suffix ".hqx," this means it has been encoded as a *binhex* file. This encoding is used because most Internet servers (especially for email) do not support direct transfers of Macintosh binary data (although commercial services, such as CompuServe and America Online, typically do without requiring any separate encoding or decoding on your part). Files to be downloaded from the Web also commonly use the binhex format, though some sites additionally have unencoded binary (".bin") files that you can try as an alternative.

Before you can use a binhex file on your Mac, you will first have to decode it. Conversely, to send a Macintosh file other than an ordinary text file over the Internet (such as a file attached to email), your best bet is to encode it first into binhex format.

A binhex file is essentially a ordinary text file, but the content of the file is in "code." The code, in turn, can be decoded with the right software, in order to re-create the original Mac document or program. The first line of a binhex file will typically read "(This file must be converted with Binhex 4.0)," while the remaining text will be appear to be meaningless nonsense—this, of course, is the coded information. If needed because of file size restrictions, a program can be converted into several smaller binhex file segments, with each segment rejoined when it is decoded, so as to re-create the original single file. Unencoded bin files can also similarly be split into segments.


```
(This file must be converted with BinHex 4.0)¶
:'P0PBh*PG#"'D@jNCA)J4Q9KG(9bCA-ZFfPd!&0*9%46593K!*!%#-%!N!35jP0¶
*9#%!!3!!#-&b6'&e![m!N!-@IrmJ)"c6C@0bCA3J4QPZC'9b)%CPBA4eFQ9c!*!¶
*9T8!!!(P!&m#`J&d!*!$!J#3$iB!!!%Jrj!%!3#Y6$8RVDTEJ`#3"J11!*!'#$X¶
!N!Th`Jd0(8&LEfpeG#"6C@0bCA3J4QPZC'9b)%CPBA4eFQ9c!!!4T3#3%4B!!!D¶
8!*!$&J#3!pY849K88LTMD!%!V8`eE+e-0@`!!!@Z!!!(43!!!CN!!!3&hdQ,"3#¶
3"[[h)d31)LT1%EP35@[`ccfRpEleYj0hPCfd5qITeb@kGF)T,feG121h%hpq`Pr¶
0'LHGdYbVD9Q64AK-jbCVPG8ieeNVPmbXcJdR,2caIIZH$ej!90S#epXq+ff[2IM¶
0edlrR[rZZXqHXVcpG(j5ddhM[M01[R,a0rlkrQp1krQ!ji-66rQHDm+fPUQIr-Q¶
D1rXHH2d"Sqj$1mjkBGN(V[YN@9)jrHkpEDH-DqKC9(R#09m[rXcFcjHkVVVdXfq¶
X6Rrlh)S,2rc4crh&PKmmmpA8,&I[V62DRPVhaS)2aVlqYr+j*lCXQUPIqaZeG8B¶
h!V'3!,Y68k@B4Ypjr5Z1!r)MMJ16,h)F'(SFXm'JMi''NP`8TSR1[h81&[T[Gba¶
81"baLR2%6qkH(8[4m(mr"Ti+(P0L41RQhh")`22$diJae,4aTCqEFN`UkIbh@BC¶
!&p$8K"cRULP,5TQ11GpSf35`N!!C9&c'VST-aLSH'1*`hPR-JI1DTZ&q)#G6+cN¶
k`a&aLIMkrC%SqU#LRq9bPLCH)A8@PZ8iX$Rc2J!!#U)!J#!$Q"`MakP(MZ+[bli¶
```


Figure 14-18 *What binhex coding looks like if you load an ".hqx" file into a word processor.*

Some communications software automatically decodes downloaded binhex files for you. Otherwise, use a freeware utility (available online itself) from Aladdin called StuffIt Expander. The enhanced shareware version of it includes additional translation options as well as another utility, called DropStuff, that you can use to encode files that you want to send. To use either of these utilities, just drag the file to be converted to the program's icon and let go ("drop" it); the utility will launch and automatically convert the file.

These Aladdin utilities can also decode/encode files using other formats, including the much less common UUencode format, which is occasionally found on Mac sites on the Internet.

Compressed Files Even after decoding (or if decoding was not necessary), the file may still not be usable. This is because it may be in a compressed format (a StuffIt archive will typically have the suffix ".sit," while other types of compressed files may have suffixes such as ".cpt" and ".zip"). Sometimes these files are "self-extracting," (often with a suffix such as ".sea"); if so, they can be decompressed simply by double-clicking the file. Again, some online services automatically decompress downloaded software for you. Otherwise, StuffIt Expander can decompress all of these formats.

If you are in doubt, open the Expander program and select its Preferences command. Here you will have the chance to see what types of files it can decode and decompress, and to select exactly what you want it to do.

Segmented Files Segmented files will usually all have the same name except for a number indicating its place in the sequence of files (such as "BusyWorks.1.sit.hqx" versus "BusyWorks.2.sit.hqx"). When you are downloading these files, download them in the reverse order, so that the segment numbered 1 downloads last. Note that the freeware version of Expander cannot join segmented files; you need the shareware version (DropStuff with Expander) to do this, or the commercial StuffIt Deluxe. When it works correctly, Expander will join all the segments together into a single functional file.

Graphics, Sound, and Movie Formats After Expander has finished decoding and decompressing the file, it still may not open. Most often, this is because you do not have the needed application for the file. For example, many graphics on the Internet will have a ".GIF" or ".jpeg" suffix. These suffixes indicate that the file is in a special graphics compression format that many standard Mac applications cannot open. If you are having trouble, you will need a shareware utility (such as JPEGViewer) to open these.

Similarly, sound files of the ".wav" or "AIFF" format may need special applications to open them. Again, there are shareware utilities that can open almost any type of sound file (a popular one is Sound Machine).

Most movies are in QuickTime format (MooV), and will work if you have QuickTime installed (you probably do). Some movies use Microsoft's "avi" format, however, and you will likely need a special viewer to see them (although they are viewable with Microsoft's Internet Explorer). MPEG is yet another movie format that shows up on the Web.

SEE: • **"Movies, Video, and More," in Chapter 10, for more on these file formats**

Acrobat Files Some files will not open unless you have the right "viewer." The most common example these days are Adobe Acrobat (or pdf) files. Viewing Acrobat files requires the Acrobat Reader program (or the Acrobat plug-in for your Web browser). These, too, are available online as freeware.

Disk Images Especially in the case of many of the update files from Apple, the file may be in a disk image format (often with a ".image" or ".img" suffix). In this case, you will need a program called Disk Copy (it comes on the CD-ROM disc that is included with most Mac models these days; otherwise, it is available online). With this program, select its "Load Image File" command and open your ".image" file. You can now "Make A Copy" of it to a floppy disk, just as if you were copying a real disk; the floppy disk will now finally contain the files you can open.

An alternative to this that I prefer uses a shareware program called ShrinkWrap. Simply drag and drop the disk image file to ShrinkWrap, and ShrinkWrap will mount an image of the file on your hard drive exactly as if it were a floppy disk. This saves you the hassle of actually having to copy the stuff to a real floppy disk. Of course, this pseudo-floppy disk is just temporary, but it doesn't matter. In most cases, what will be on this disk is not the file you ultimately want, but an Installer utility. After you run the Installer utility to install the files on your hard drive in a usable form, you can trash the ShrinkWrap-mounted disk image (but save the original image file as a backup in case you ever need to reinstall the files).

Uploaded Files

When uploading files, you will need to specify what type of file is being transmitted. Text files and binhex (".hqx") files will transmit as "Text." Other files will most commonly transmit as "Binary" (or "raw data") with a ".bin" suffix. If you are sending a Macintosh program to another Mac user, however, you should choose "MacBinary." The difference between Binary and MacBinary is that MacBinary files include a "resource fork" that is only interpretable by Macintoshes.

When sending an attached file in an email, you will typically want to compress and binhex the file. Programs such as Claris Emailer can do this automatically for you. If you send a file without binhexing it, there is a good chance that the recipient will be unable to open it regardless of what software (as described in the previous section) he or she has available.

Similarly, if you are uploading a file (for example, to your Web site) using a program such as Fetch, you can set it to binhex a file automatically prior to uploading it. Of course, make sure these programs do not duplicate your effort by compressing or encoding files that you have already compressed or encoded yourself.

Solve-It! Web Browser Problems

Because Web browsers are both a relatively new category of software and one of the most frequently used applications today, it seems almost mandatory for me to spend some time on Web browser troubleshooting. The focus of this section is clearly on the Web browsing part of these programs (as opposed to a browser's newsgroup or email features). Still, many of the points covered will have a general applicability that applies to other parts of the browser, as well as to all online software.

Web Pages Won't Load or Load Slowly

Symptoms:

- Pages won't load at all. There is no error message; the browser simply "hangs" at the point of trying to make a connection.
- One or more pages won't load. Any of a variety of error messages do appear.
- Pages load, but at a very slow rate, or with a long delay before starting to load.

Causes and What to do:

No Pages Load

If your browser steadfastly refuses to load any pages at all, you are probably not really connected, or you have a bad connection. Even if you modem seems to have connected successfully, there may still be problems. Specific messages in this category include "Netscape was unable to create a network socket connection" or "Attempt to load" [name of page] failed."

Most likely, these messages appear from the first moment you launch your browser. Due to a dropped connection, however, these problems can also appear at any point in your use of a browser. Often, if you are using a modem, your PPP software may indicate that you are connected even though you are not.

- In general, the best approach is to quit your browser, click the Disconnect button from your PPP software (if you are using a modem), and start all over by reconnecting and then relaunching your browser.
- Sometimes, I have found it also necessary to restart the Macintosh to sort matters out (probably because of a problem at the serial port).

- If none of this works, there may be a problem with your ISP; perhaps their hardware is down. Try to check by giving them a phone call.
- Otherwise, you probably have a problem with your communications hardware or software. If so, it's time for more run-of-the-mill troubleshooting, as detailed in other parts of this book.
- Also be aware that if you have your software set to make a PPP connection automatically when your browser launches, you should make sure that this actually happened. In fact, if a problem occurs, it is even better to turn this option off (typically from your PPP software) and make a separate manual connection. Sometimes this solves the problem.

SEE: • "Modem and PPP Connection Problems," earlier in this chapter, for details on dropped connections

BY THE WAY ▶

PAGES LOAD EVEN WHEN YOU ARE DISCONNECTED. HOW?

Sometimes even after you have been dropped from your connection, you may find that some pages still appear to load. Inevitably, these are pages that you have recently visited and are still stored in your browser's cache; the browser is drawing the page from the cache file rather than from over the online connection. If you want to see if your browser has really lost its connection, try to go to a new page or update the current page by selecting the browser's Reload button.

SEE: • "Browser Caches and Corrupted Directory Files" and "Web Pages Don't Update As Expected," later in this chapter, for more on cache files

Unable to Connect to Host

If you ever select an address and get a message that says something like "Unable to connect to host" or "invalid host," this doesn't necessarily mean that there is anything wrong with your address. For example, the computer you are trying to connect to may simply be turned off for the moment! Try again later.

No DNS Entry, 404 Not Found, and Related Messages

You may get a message that says the server does not exist or the address cannot be found (or something similar). More specifically, in Navigator the message might say "The server does not have a DNS entry" or "404 Not Found;" In Explorer, it might say "The server could not find ..." or "The name is illegal."

The most common causes of these errors are that (1) you entered the URL incorrectly, such as by misspelling a word, or (2) the page you are looking for no longer exists (this happens quite often if you browse through the backwaters of the Web!). Sometimes, though, it again may mean that the server is temporarily down or is overloaded (that is, too many people are trying to access the same page all at once). If so, simply trying again later should succeed.

Additionally, Netscape claims that some "404 Not Found" errors can be prevented by making sure the buffer size (found at Options: Network Preferences: Connections) is bigger than 4K. After making this change, quit Navigator, relaunch it, and try again.

The message "File Contains No Data" may be telling you the truth, but often it lies. It once happened on my Web site because my home page had gotten inadvertently deleted. In fact, there was no file. In other cases, however, the data may still be present. In this case, problems due to this message may sometimes be fixed by adding ":80" to the URL's domain name segment (such as *http://www.oakland.edu:80/~landau/sadmacs/).*

A "403 Forbidden" or "Access Denied" error message means that the site is password protected and you don't have the password.

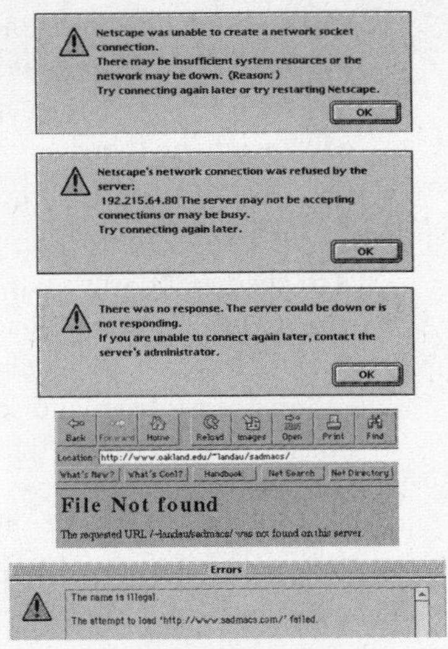

Figure 14-19 *Some messages that may appear in your Web browser when it can't load a requested page.*

Network Connection Refused, No Response from Server, or No Message at All

If you get messages such as "Network connection refused by server" or "There was no response. Server could be down" (or if you receive no error message at all but the page never begins to load), the two most likely causes are (1) the page is being overloaded with more requests that it can handle (so your connection request was refused), or (2) the server you are trying to connect to is truly down (for instance, it may have just had a system crash).

Even if you do finally connect, an overloaded server can also lead to agonizingly slow data transfer times no matter how fast your modem or network connection is. Since the source of the problem is not at your end, there is not much you can do about any of this. Trying again later (hopefully at a less busy time) is the time-honored solution.

The same rules apply if you receive no error message at all but your page still refuses to load.

Pages Load Slowly

If your requested page actually begins to display on your screen, don't applaud yet. Your problems may not be over. The page may be loading so slowly that you begin to wonder whether someone pressed the pause button. Most often, this happens when the page contains large graphics (especially imagemaps); text transmits a lot faster. The main culprit for the slowdown can be at your end (where even a 28.8K modem is not all that fast for some graphics-rich pages) and/or at the server's end (where they, too, may be using equipment that's not fast enough or does not have enough bandwidth to support many simultaneous requests for access).

Other than wait patiently and take a coffee break, curse your computer (which rarely has any effect), or install an ISDN or T1 line to replace your modem (if money is no object), what can you do to speed up these slowdowns? Not all that much, unfortunately. But you can try the following:

- For starters, you can click any link button as soon as it is visible; there's no need to wait for the entire page to load.

- You could click your browser's Stop button. While this stops the loading of the remainder of the page, it also forces whatever has already loaded (even though it may not yet be displayed) to appear on your screen. If you are lucky, whatever you need will already be there. If not, you can always click the Reload button and try again.
- If you don't really need to see all the graphics on the page, a more long-term solution is to change the way graphics and text load, so as to get the text to load faster. To do this in Netscape, go to Options: General Preferences: Images and select "Display Images After Loading" instead of "…While Loading." In Explorer, go to Edit: Options: Display and make sure "Refresh document after each image is loaded" is checked. Otherwise, although I know this sounds like voodoo, try checking the opposite of whatever item is currently checked and see if it helps.

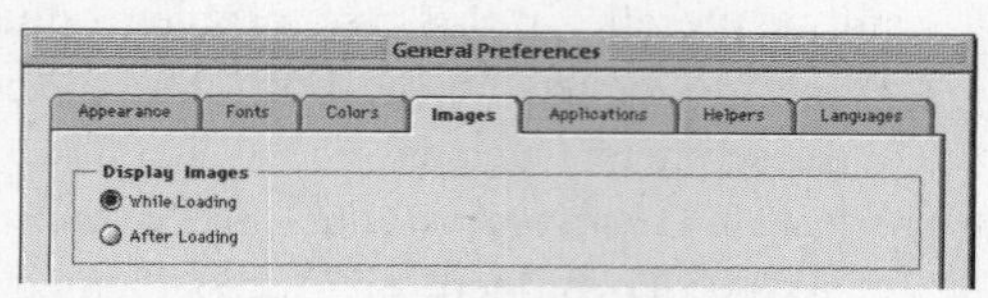

Figure 14-20 *Netscape Navigator's options to display images "While Loading" versus "After Loading;" try them both to see which results in pages loading faster for your Macintosh.*

- Next, you can tell your browser not to load any graphic images at all. To do this in Navigator, uncheck Autoload Images from the Options menu. In Explorer, go to Edit: Options: Page & Link and then uncheck "Show Pictures." Be careful here, though: some sites require the display of images to access all of their features, so this may not always work out well. In any case, both Navigator and Explorer include toolbar buttons to load a page's graphics "manually" at any time. You can even click on an individual graphic's placeholder icon to get that particular image to load.

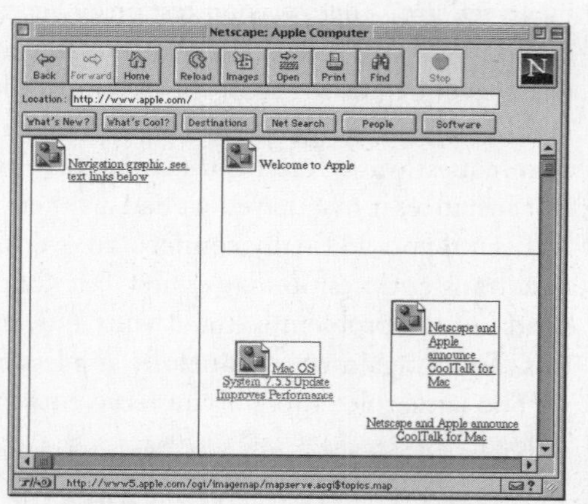

Figure 14-21 *Apple's home page with graphics images not loaded.*

- Some sites may include an optional "low graphics" or "text-only" version of their site for the benefit of those with slow connections. Use these to speed things up.
- Insufficient memory can cause slow loading of all your pages. I have seen this happen in Netscape, for example, when it is run on a Mac with 8MB of RAM. In addition to everything loading slowly, there was incessant access of the hard disk, probably related to its frequent access of cache files. RAM Doubler or virtual memory is not a solution here; you need more physical RAM.

A related point: As described in more detail elsewhere, proper use of your browser's cache and buffer can help speed page loading.

SEE:
- **"Browser Caches and Corrupted Directory Files" and "Web Pages Don't Update As Expected," later in this chapter, for more on cache files**
- **"System Freezes, Crashes, and Directory Damage," later in this chapter, for more on dealing with memory problems**

TECHNICALLY SPEAKING ▶

IMAGE LOADING SPEED: WEB AUTHORS CAN HELP YOU

In some cases, no text will begin to appear on your page until after all graphic images have started to appear, no matter what Web browser options you choose. There is nothing you can do about this; the problem is in the design of the Web page itself. It is possible for the page author to include instructions about the size of graphic images on the page. If he or she does, then the text will start appearing almost immediately. Otherwise, the text does not appear until after all the graphic size information has been calculated, which can only happen after the images have started to appear. Not all authors include this helpful size information.

You will also notice that some graphics appear first in a very blurry form, or in a partial form that looks a bit like a series of slats in a window blind; gradually, the parts fill in until you have a finished image. Called an interlaced image, this is another technique used to help speed things up by allowing you to see an approximation of the image before it is completely loaded. Again, there is nothing you can do to turn this feature on or off, since it is determined by the Web page author.

- Deleting Netscape Navigator's Global History file (located in the Netscape *f* folder inside the Preferences folder) can increase the subsequent speed of loading pages. Do this with Navigator closed.

  With Internet Explorer, you can accomplish the same thing by clicking the "Empty" button in the Options:Advanced:History box.
- Sometimes, slow loading of pages may indicate a problem with you modem connection, in which case disconnecting and reconnecting again may help.
- One last caution: if you click on a link that goes to another location on the same page, and that part of the page has not yet loaded, loading of the page instantly halts. To solve this problem, you will need to reload the page and wait for the part of the page with the link destination to appear.

A Long Delay Before a Page Starts to Load

I have occasionally had a problem where, when I click to go to a page, nothing at all happens for 30 seconds or so. It appears as if I have a dropped connection or even a system freeze. Suddenly everything kicks into gear, however, and all is normal (that is, the page starts to load at a normal speed). The same thing may happen when you are trying to check email. This problem is usually sporadic (perhaps linked to a previous system crash or some exotic extensions conflict). If it persists beyond going to one or two pages, try disconnecting and reconnecting again.

One time, the problem persisted for several days; the only way I got it to go away was by reinstalling my system software. Otherwise, suspect the cause to be the software or firmware that works with your modem. Check if there are upgraded versions.

Downloads Transfer Slowly or Not At All

If a Web site is busy, a page may take a few more seconds to load than it ordinarily would. Downloading a file from a busy Web site, though, can mean having a transfer slow to such a crawl that download times increase dramatically. Sometimes, you will have better luck if you cancel the download in progress and simply try again immediately. Otherwise, give up and try again at a later time.

There is a bug in some versions of Netscape that will prevent FTP downloads from successfully downloading a file. The work-around solution is to download the file from an FTP program such as Anarchie.

SEE: • **"Working with Downloaded and Uploaded Files," earlier in this chapter, for tips on getting downloaded files to work**

System Freezes, Crashes, and Directory Damage

Symptoms:

- A system freeze or crash occurs while you are trying to load or use your Web browser.
- Utilities such as Disk First Aid report frequent disk repair problems, especially B-tree Directory errors

Causes:

Type 10 and Type 11 errors are particularly common. Aside from the generic causes of system errors (as described primarily in Chapter 4), there are a variety of causes unique to the Internet and Web browsers, which I will discuss below.

The Directory damage issue is primarily related to the browser's frequent writing to the disk to create and update its cache files.

What to do:

Try Netscape Defrost

For system freezes and unexpected quits in your Web browser, install a freeware extension called Netscape Defrost and/or upgrade to Netscape version 2.0.1 or later.

Does the Netscape Defrost utility still help to prevent freezes in the current versions of Netscape Navigator? Maybe not. According to Netscape, the freezes that Defrost prevented will no longer occur with Navigator 2.0.1 or later. According to Scott Sykes (the creator of Netscape Defrost), however, the bug that caused the problem is really in the system software, not in Navigator, and it is still present in System 7.5.3. Since the Defrost utility is a general patch for the buggy code, not specific to Navigator, it may still help to prevent freezes in any Internet software—including the latest versions of Netscape—if the software "calls the ReadXPRam trap to read the MachineLocation." I have seen several reports that indicate that this utility still helps; give it a try.

Not Enough Memory

Web browsers, especially Navigator, are memory-hungry animals that happily devour whatever extra memory you give them. Navigator 3.0 won't be real happy unless it has at least 9 or 10MB of RAM, preferably more. Without enough memory to satisfy its hunger, your browser will pay you back with slowdowns, frequent disconnects, freezes, or system crashes. These problems become even more likely if you are loading pages that use plug-ins or frames, or if you simply have several browser windows open at one time.

There are a few common solutions to these sort of problems, assuming you have enough physical RAM (and/or virtual RAM) to use them.

- The simplest solution is to increase your browser's Preferred memory size from its Get Info window. Make it several megabytes higher than whatever it is currently set at.

  As an alternative, you can try to reduce how much memory your Web browser needs. For example, with Navigator 3.0 or later, you can do this by removing all the plug-in files and by turning off Java and JavaScript (from the Language tab of the Navigator's Network Preferences). You lose access to the now-disabled features, but you may find that Navigator performs better overall. You may now even be able to reduce Navigator's Preferred memory size (in its Finder Get Info window) without causing any negative side effects.

- Otherwise, increase your browser's cache size to 10MB or higher. Using less may work, but try this if problems occur. To do this in Navigator, go to Options: Network Preferences: Cache; in Internet Explorer, go to Edit: Options: Advanced.

  Make sure, however, that you have enough empty disk space to accommodate this increase. In fact, if your hard drive is nearly full, *reducing* the size of Netscape's cache may prevent some system crashes from occurring!

- Next, increase the size of your disk cache setting in your Memory control panel (which is completely separate from your browser's cache) to at least 32K per MB of physical RAM.

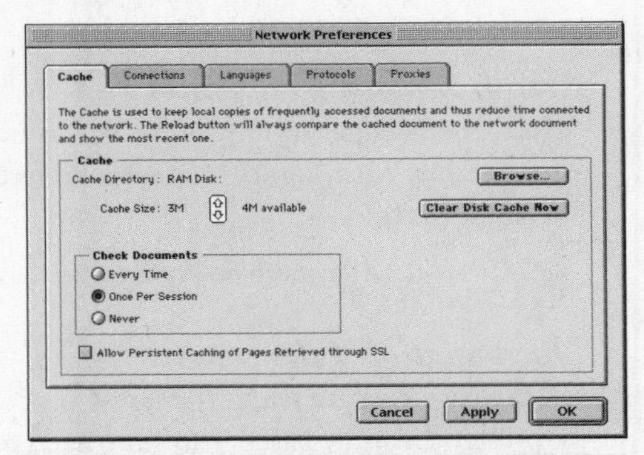

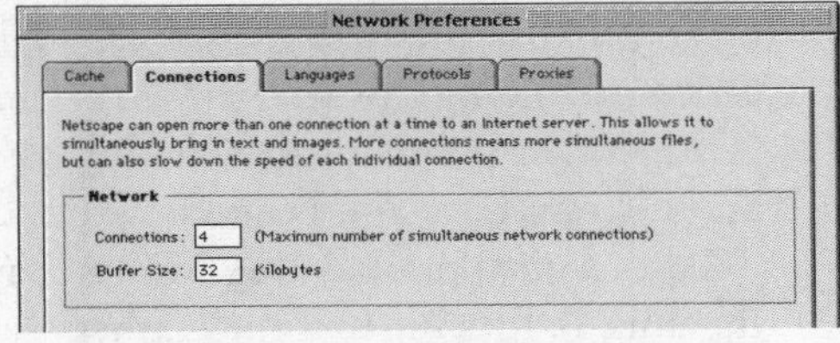

Figure 14-22A *Netscape Navigator's option to change its Cache setting (top) and its Connections settings (bottom); changing these settings (as described in the main text) can help prevent system freezes, prevent corruption of data on your disk, and speed up Navigator's performance.*

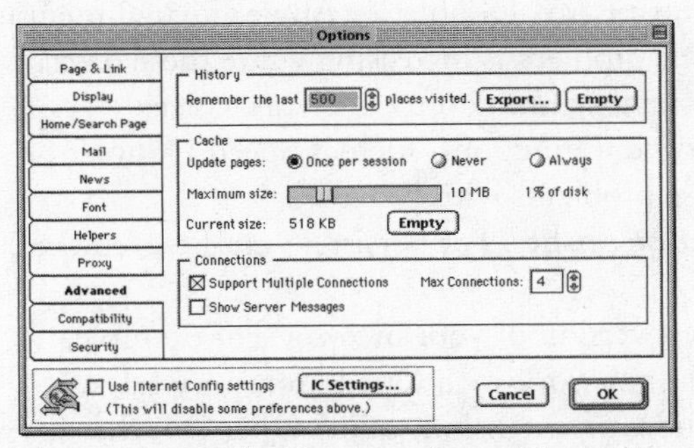

Figure 14-22B *The History, Cache, and Connections settings of Microsoft Internet Explorer.*

- In Navigator, go to the Connections tab of the Network Preferences window. Increasing the number of connections and/or decreasing the buffer size has been reported to solve certain memory-related problems.

  Note: Increasing the number of connections allows more elements of a page (such as graphics images and text) to load "simultaneously." Increasing it too much, however, may slow down the overall speed of the loading. Too large a buffer may also overwhelm the capacity of your computer to handle the incoming information.
- Otherwise, the only practical solution is to get more RAM.

TAKE NOTE ▶

OPEN TRANSPORT, BROWSERS, AND MEMORY LEAKS

Browsers can give you memory grief even after you quit the application—namely, the memory occupied by the browser may not be freed up after you quit (this is typically referred to as a *memory leak*). Restarting the Macintosh is guaranteed to reclaim the memory; otherwise, there are several utilities (such as Mac OS Purge) that may reclaim the memory without forcing you to restart.

This is especially known to be a problem with Netscape and Open Transport. Open Transport 1.1.1 is supposed to largely fix this leak; if it doesn't, look for later versions of Open Transport to do so.

SEE: • **"Memory Requirements" in "Understanding Open Transport, TCP, and PPP," earlier in this chapter (especially: "Technically Speaking: Open Transport, Memory Leaks, and 'Load Only When Needed'")**
• **"Check for Memory Leaks," in Fix-It #6 for more discussion of this**

Trash Browser Preferences File

Netscape Navigator, in particular, has been reported to have crashes at launch that can be cured by trashing its Netscape Preferences file (found in the Netscape *f* folder in the Preferences folder).

SEE: • **Fix-It #2 for more on Preferences files**

Incompatible Files

Make sure you are using the latest versions of software, such as FreePPP and RAM Doubler. In some cases, you may need to turn RAM Doubler or Apple's virtual memory off to get your browser to work (though this problem is increasingly rare these days). Of course, doing this will only make any memory limitation problems worse!

Any other programs that modify basic system functions, such as Speed Doubler or Speed Copy, have also been known to cause problems with browsers.

Also, some optional plug-in files may cause crashes. For persistent crashes, remove the plug-in files to see if the crashes cease.

Finally, make sure you are using the latest version of your browser. For example, Netscape Navigator versions prior to 2.0 do not work with Open Transport 1.1.x.

Also note that America Online 3.0 includes an extension, called OpenOT, that fixes certain crashes that may result from using Open Transport. A future version of Open Transport is expected to fix this bug.

Browser Caches and Corrupted Directory Files

Getting Out of Trouble When your browser reads a Web page, it typically creates a "snapshot" of that page that it stores in a *cache file,* either temporarily in RAM memory on your disk (typically in the Cache *f* folder of the Netscape *f* folder in the Preferences folder). In a typical setup, you may have dozens or even hundreds of these cache files stored on your disk. Their value is that if you revisit a page, the browser can use the cache to load the page rather than grabbing the data from the Internet each time. This results in much faster loading times.

Because of the frequency with which these cache files are added and updated, however, your browser writes to your disk especially often. This increases the chance that your disk's directory will get corrupted. Especially if you have a crash while using a browser, there is a higher than usual probability of the Mac's Directory files getting corrupted as a result.

Figure 14-23 *Netscape Navigator's cache files.*

To check for this, periodically run Disk First Aid (or some other repair utility) at the first sign of trouble, or even before there is any trouble at all. Make repairs as needed. If your repair utility reports recurring B-tree errors, your browser is probably the culprit.

SEE: • **Fix-It #10 and #13 on making disk repairs**

Preventing Trouble Even if your disk checks out okay, you should still try to minimize the risk of data corruption down the road. To do this, you need to change the way your browser creates and stores these files.

- One short-term option is to clear (or empty) the cache completely, although this will slow your browser's performance significantly. To do this in Navigator, go to Options: Network Preferences: Cache, then click the "Clear Disk Cache Now" button. In Internet Explorer, go to Edit: Options: Advanced and click the "Empty" button in the Cache section.

  Do not try to clear the cache by trashing the cache folder in the Finder while your browser is running. This could lead to a system crash.
- Although it may slow the performance of your browser, you can keep the cache "permanently" cleared by setting its size to zero.
- A longer-term solution that should not result in slower performance is to create a RAM disk (from the Memory control panel) and set it as the location for the cache files. To do this in Navigator, click the Browse button in the Cache dialog box and select the RAM disk as the cache location (Explorer 2.1 or later has a comparable option).

  SEE: • **Chapter 11 for more on creating RAM disks**

- Alternatively, instead of a RAM disk, you could use ShrinkWrap to create a disk image file. To do this with Netscape Navigator, follow these steps:
  1. Open ShrinkWrap (version 2.0.1 or later) and select its Preferences menu command from its Edit menu.

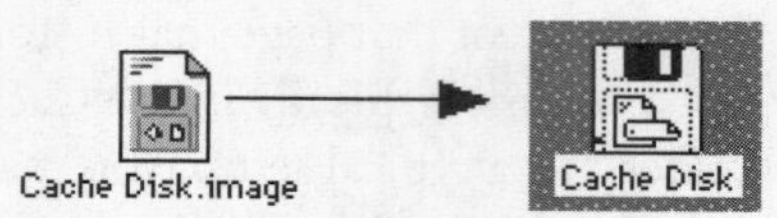

Figure 14-24 *Using ShrinkWrap to create a RAM-like disk at startup.*

  2. From the collection of choices that appear, make sure you have checked "Keep mounted images in RAM" (this is what gets the image to behave like a RAM disk) and "Mount images unlocked by default" (this allows you to write to the image). The latter option may not be available in older versions of ShrinkWrap.
  3. Select New Image from the Image menu. Name the image and assign a desired size (the larger you make it, the more RAM it eats); click the Create button. This will create a ShrinkWrap image file document as well as an actual mounted disk image.
  4. Drag the ShrinkWrap document to the Startup Items folder of your System Folder (this will get ShrinkWrap to automatically mount the image at each startup).
  5. Finally, go to the Cache preferences of Netscape Navigator's Network Preferences. Click the Browse button, select your mounted disk image as the destination for the cache files, and close the window.

  Using ShrinkWrap has the added bonus that, unlike with a RAM disk, the cache contents will be preserved after a shutdown (although you could similarly save the caches on a RAM disk by using the persistent-RAM-disk feature of Apple's Assistant Toolbox, designed primarily for PowerBooks but included with System 7.5.3 or later).
- In contrast to the previous advice to set your cache size to zero, increasing your browser's cache size (to 10MB or higher) may also reduce the risk of system crashes while using your browser. This can also help minimize Directory damage caused by crashes. Experiment with different cache sizes to see what works best for you.

Avoid Public Betas

On another front, Netscape and Microsoft both encourage free downloading of beta versions of the next release of their browsers. This is getting to be such a widespread practice there is even a term for it, *public betas.* Be cautious about using these unless you like to see your Macintosh crash. Your best bet is to stick with the latest officially released versions, although even these continue to be plagued by too many Type 10 and Type 11 errors.

Getting out of a Freeze or Crash

If you get a freeze, try a forced quit (Command-Option-Escape) to get out of it. If that fails and you have MacsBug installed, you may still be able to recover from the freeze, or even a system crash, without having to restart your Macintosh (as described in Chapter 4).

TAKE NOTE ▶

TED'S TOP TWO RULES ON USING BETA SOFTWARE

With the explosion of availability of "public" beta software on the Web and the increasing number of problems reported from using these programs, you should be aware of these two rules about using beta software:

1. Don't install beta system software in your default startup System Folder. This especially applies to beta software for such things as Open Transport, OpenDoc, or any other software that may modify the contents of your System Folder.

   Beta software is beta for a reason. That reason is usually that there are significant bugs in the program that make it not yet ready for prime time. Sometimes these bugs can bring your entire system down, forcing a clean reinstall or worse. That's why you should keep them out of your main System Folder.

   If you still want to use the beta software, install it on a separate System Folder stored on a removable cartridge (or similar alternative) and test it from there. Even if it appears to work well, unless the beta version's improvements are critical to your needs, avoid regular use of it; wait for the release version to come out. If you follow this rule, you will have a happier and less stressful life.
2. Read Rule #1 a few more times.

If you want to try to reconnect online after recovering from a system error, but without restarting your Mac, remember first to turn your modem off and then back on; you may also need to disconnect from your PPP software. Still, to be safe, restarting is always advised.

SEE: • **"System Freezes" and "By the Way: Recover From a System Crash Without Restarting (Maybe)," in Chapter 4, for more details**
• **"Modem and PPP Connection Problems," earlier in this chapter**

TAKE NOTE ▶

MAGIC COOKIES

Netscape Navigator creates a "MagicCookie" file which it stores in your System Folder. When you log onto a Web site that is set up to access the file, it can save a cookie to your MagicCookie file. This means that it stores a line of text in the file. The next time you log on to the Web site, it can check for the cookie that it left. The cookie can identify who you are and what you have visited. This means that each visitor to a site can see something different on the same site as determined by what they did on their previous visit. Advertisers can also use cookies to track how many people visit a site.

The idea that a Web site can modify the contents of your hard drive, even in this minimal way, makes many people nervous. There are concerns about invasion of privacy and breach of security. Indeed, in some very early versions of Navigator, this was a potential risk. With current versions, however, a Web site can only read a cookie it created—it cannot read all your cookies or anything else on your drive. Still, if this idea disturbs you, you have a variety of alternatives. My favorite is to use a freeware utility called Cookie Cutter. It allows you to selectively remove and/or block the cookies from individual Web sites. You can also set Navigator to give you a message each time a Web site attempts to set a cookie, with the option to allow it or not. I have found that disallowing a cookie can result in Netscape crashing.

Mostly, you can just ignore cookies. Most people feel they represent no threat and can actually be useful for sites that you visit often.

Pages Display Incorrectly or Have Features Missing

Symptoms:

- You go to a Web page that claims to include animation (or some other special feature), but all you see are static images that don't move anywhere (or don't otherwise display the special feature). In Netscape Navigator, an empty box with the Navigator symbol may be displayed, indicating that something is amiss.
- Text or graphics overlaps are missing or are in incorrect locations.
- Colors on a page are wrong.

Causes:

Netscape Extensions

You just went to a site and it looks like it was designed by Picasso during his blue period. Why does it look so messy? The most likely reason is that the page uses some aspect of HTML (the language used to create Web pages) that is not supported by your browser. In particular, Netscape has built-in support for a number of features of its own design that may not appear if you use other browsers, including such things as background colors and patterns. Although these are called "Netscape extensions," they are not separate extensions files stored in your System Folder but features actually built into the Netscape application itself (or sometimes stored in Netscape's Preferences folder).

Fortunately for Microsoft Internet Explorer users, version 3.0 of that browser supports most Netscape extensions. (Explorer 2.0 did not support frames, for example.)

Also, there are continual additions to the HTML standard. For example, older versions of browsers may not support newer features that have been added to HTML 3.0—although the latest versions of both Navigator and Explorer tend to be very current here (often anticipating changes that are not yet official).

SEE: • **"By the Way: A Word About Web Page Authoring and HTML," earlier in this chapter, for more about HTML**

Plug-Ins

Another likely cause of these problems is that a needed plug-in file is missing. Plug-in files (stored in the Plug-Ins folder in your browser's folder, not in the Preferences folder) extend your browser's capabilities. For example, to load pages that feature animated images created by Macromedia's Shockwave technology, you'll need to drop the Shockwave plug-in into your browser's Plug-Ins folder. Plug-ins are optional, and most are typically not included as part of your browser's basic installation (although the latest version of Navigator does include a QuickTime plug-in, among a couple of others).

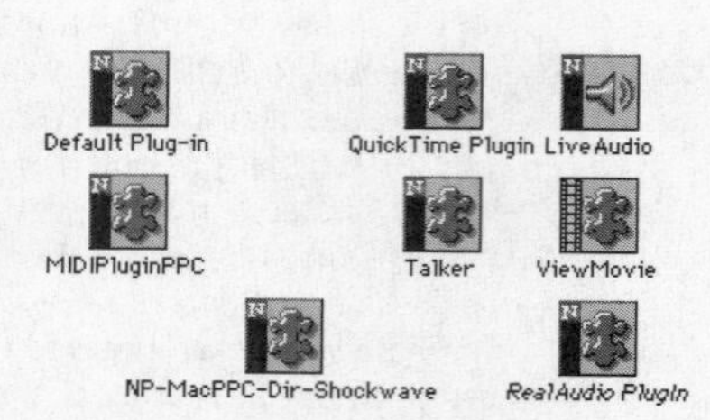

Figure 14-25 *Some Netscape Navigator plug-ins, as found in the Plug-Ins folder located in the same location as the Navigator application.*

A related problem is whether your browser has the support needed to display pages that use Java applets (Java is another technology that can add enhanced features to Web pages). The latest versions of Netscape and Explorer do support Java.

Preference Settings

A last possibility is that a preference setting of your browser is incorrect. Preference settings are found by selecting Options from Explorer's Edit menu or by selecting one of the Preferences items in Navigator's Options menu.

What to do:

Try a Different Browser If Internet Explorer doesn't do what you want, try Netscape Navigator. The Web browser included with America Online (prior to version 3.0) is a notoriously bad one, so avoid it if you can. In either case, make sure you have the latest version of the browser you use (with the caution, mentioned previously, of avoiding beta versions).

Check For Special Accommodations To best view pages that use frames in Internet Explorer 2.*x*, Microsoft recommends going to Edit: Options: Compatibility and selecting "HTML 2.0 and Internet Explorer Features." Newer versions of Explorer will support frames directly. Check your browser's documentation for accommodations it may make for other missing features.

Get The Plug-In Viewing a page correctly may require optional plug-in files that do not come packaged with your browser.

Netscape, which first developed the plug-in technology, maintains a library of third-party plug-ins that work with Navigator (be careful here, since some of these only work with the Windows version of Navigator). *MacWEEK* also maintains a list (at *http://www.zdnet.com/macweek/plugins.html)* of dozens of the most popular Macintosh plug-ins. Get what you need and simply drop them in your browser's Plug-Ins folder. Though plug-ins were first designed by Netscape, Microsoft Explorer supports them also.

Remember that additional plug-ins may increase the memory requirements for your browser.

Check for Alternate View Options Some Web sites have options to get an alternate view of a site (for example, a view that does not use frames). This is useful if you do not have a browser capable of using these special features, or even if you just don't like the feature. Many sites do not give you this choice, of course, so don't count on it.

Font Problems The fonts displayed by your browser, in terms of both the font type and (in Navigator) the base size of the font, can be selected from the Fonts preferences of your browser. If text is too small, too large, or otherwise unreadable, check this out.

Color Problems Browsers typically can only display 256 different colors. If a Web page includes colors that are not among these 256, Navigator will dither the display to attempt to approximate the color. Success here may vary; colors may thus appear different than the page designer intended.

BY THE WAY ▶

TWO TIPS ABOUT FRAMES

- One complaint about frames has been that they prevent a browser's Back and Forward commands from working as desired. In particular, when you select to go back to a previous frame of a page, you instead are taken back to the page you were viewing before the frame-based page loaded. Latest versions of browsers, notably Navigator 3.0 and its revisions, fix this problem.
- If you want to open up a frame so that it is a separate frameless page, you can do so. In Navigator, simply click and hold the mouse down anywhere in the frame; a pop-up menu will appear with an option to open a "New window with this frame."

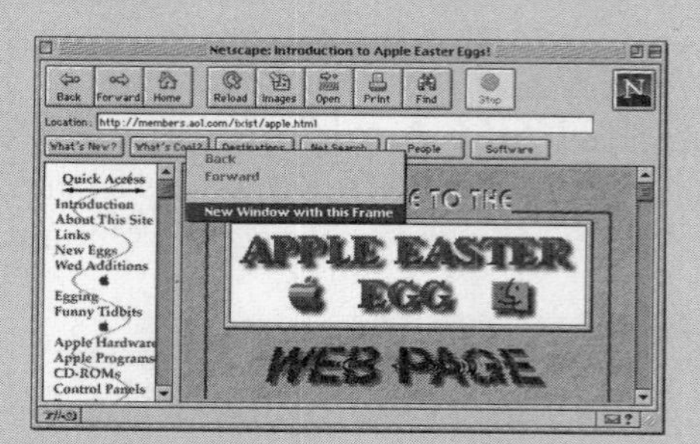

Figure 14-26 *A Web page that uses frames, with the pop-up option to open a "New window with this frame" selected.*

Helper Problems

Symptoms:

- Your browser does not call a helper application or plug-in as expected.

  In one common example of this problem, binhex files appear as text in a browser window rather than downloading as expected.

Causes and What to do:

Setting Up a Helper

When called upon to do something that is not in its built-in repertoire, a browser calls for outside help—typically in the form of other separate applications stored on your hard disk. For example, if you click a button for a QuickTime movie, your browser will probably open a movie player application on your disk, which will then show the movie in a separate window.

Probably the most common of these "helpers" is StuffIt Expander, used to decode and expand downloaded binhex (.hqx) files. It comes included with Navigator 3.0 or later.

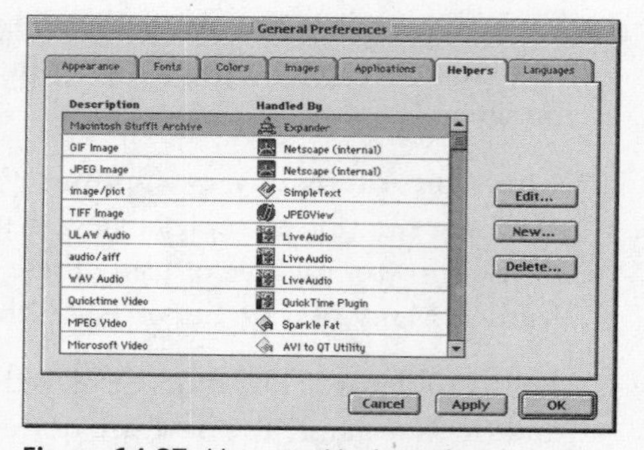

Figure 14-27 *Netscape Navigator's Helpers list, as selected from its General Preferences Options.*

So how does your browser know which helper application to open? It maintains a table that links specific file types to specific applications. After identifying the file type, the browser launches the appropriate helper as listed in the Helpers table, which is located at Options: General Preferences: Helpers (in Navigator) or Edit: Options: Helpers (in Explorer).

The browser comes with many helpers preassigned. If you want to assign a file type to a different helper than the table's current selection, or if you are trying to open a type of file that your browser does not recognize, you need to edit the table information.

Current versions of Navigator simplify this process by providing a helper dialog box that appears automatically whenever Navigator is uncertain what to do, giving you the chance to create a helper link automatically. In Navigator 3.0, you can also assign plug-ins to act as helpers.

Finally, note that plug-in files may also be assigned as a helper. Doing this may, for example, allow a certain type of file to be viewed directly within a Web page, rather than opening up in a separate window. The QuickTime plug-in does this for QuickTime movies. PDFViewer works similarly for Acrobat files.

SEE: • **"Technically Speaking: Understanding MIMEs," for more technical advice on working with helpers**

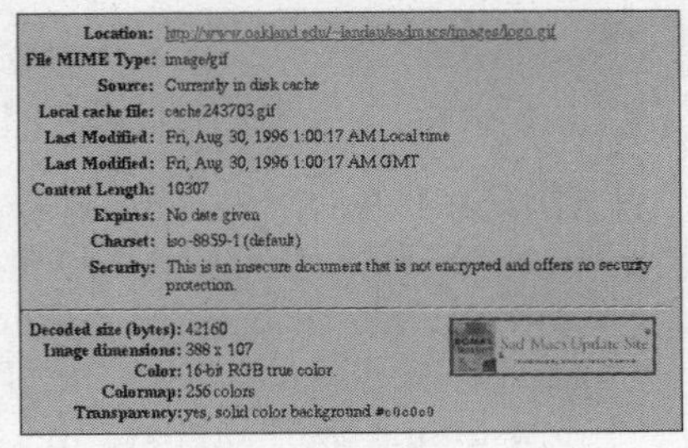

Figure 14-28 *Select Document Info from Navigator's View menu and get a window that includes the MIME for your current "page"; in this case, the document is an "image/gif" MIME.*

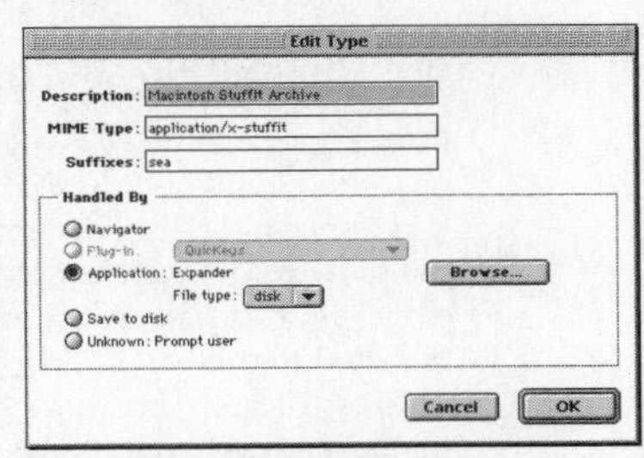

Figure 14-29 *The Edit window for a helper from Netscape Navigator's Helpers listing.*

Get a Missing Helper

What if you don't have the default application needed to open a particular type of file? One solution is simply to get it; they are usually shareware or freeware programs. The other solution is to change your browser's Helpers table to list a helper that you do have (for example, you may want to open up QuickTime movies with QuickTime VCR rather than Movie Player). To do this in Navigator 3.0 or later, for example, click on the listed file type in the Helpers table (such as "QuickTime Video"), then click the Edit button. From here, click the Application radio button, then click the Browse button; an Open/Save dialog box will appear. Locate and select the application you now wish to use as a helper. Close all windows, by clicking Apply and OK as appropriate.

When Your Browser Can't Find a Correctly Listed Helper

Occasionally, you may find that a helper does not get called when expected, even though it appears to be correctly listed in the Helpers table. This has been most noted with StuffIt Expander and Navigator (especially when the user is upgrading to a new version of Expander), sometimes leading to a –43 error. If this happens, try one of the following:

- Make sure you have not changed the name of the program, as listed in the Finder.
- If there is a new version of the helper application recently added to your disk, go to the browser's Helpers table and specifically select the new version as a replacement for the existing listing. Ideally, move the new version to the same location as the prior version, deleting the prior version.

- Rebuild the desktop.
- Delete the Finder Preferences file (after first restarting from another disk).

Binhex Files Appear as Text in a Browser Window

When downloading a binhex file via a Web browser, if the download URL is an HTTP address rather than an FTP address, it may appear as text in a Web browser window rather than download as a file. This is obviously not what you want.

Assuming that you have an appropriate helper (such as StuffIt Expander) on your disk and it is correctly assigned in the Helpers table (as described in the immediately preceding sections), you may have a problem with the setup of the server you are trying

TECHNICALLY SPEAKING ▶

UNDERSTANDING MIMES

Most pages that you view with your Web browser are HTML documents. These are the typical pages that contain the links and graphics for which the Web has become famous. Reading and displaying HTML documents is what your browser was mainly designed to do. It can do the same with only a few other file types (such as GIF and JPEG graphics); for any other type of file, your browser requires helper applications or plug-ins. The files on the Web are then matched to their appropriate helper based on the information in the browser's Helpers table. Most of the time this works just fine without you even being aware of what's going on. Since things may go wrong, however, it pays to understand in more detail how all of this works.

When a file is sent to a browser, the browser first checks for the MIME type of the file. MIME (which stands for Multipurpose Internet Mail Extensions) was developed to permit sending documents over the Internet beyond the plain text files typically required by email. Each different category of file has its own MIME name (usually divided into a main type and a subtype). For example, the MIME for a binhex file is "application/mac-binhex40" (where "application" is the main type, and "mac-binhex40" is the subtype). Similarly, for QuickTime movies, the MIME is "video/quicktime." When one of these files is placed on a Web site's server, it is assigned its appropriate MIME type (usually also identified by the suffix of the file's name, such as "file.hqx" for binhex files). When your browser receives the file, it also receives its MIME name, then compares this MIME with those listed in its Helpers table. When it locates the correct MIME, it determines what Helper is linked to it (such as StuffIt Expander for binhex files or Movie Player for QuickTime movies) and takes the appropriate action.

Occasionally the server may fail to send the MIME, or it may send a MIME that your browser does not recognize. In this case, your browser checks the suffix of the file name and again compares it to the list of suffixes in the Helpers table (such as ".hqx" for binhex files or ".mov" for QuickTime movies) to determine the appropriate action.

If your browser is still unable to sort things out after all of this, it will treat the file according to the browser's default MIME, which is typically "text/html." When this happens, the file—whatever its contents—will appear as text characters on a Web page (which is usually not what you want). To fix this, you may need to add a new Helper listing or edit an existing one. In some cases, however, even this won't help. When this happens, it usually means that the problem is at the server end; for example, the server may incorrectly list a file's MIME. To solve this, you'll have to contact the Webmaster of the server for assistance.

Particular MIME names are decided by a central registry called the Internet Assigned Numbers Authority (IANA). Developers of new file types submit requests here to register new MIME names. Getting permission to add a new subtype is fairly easy; to add a new main type, though, you'll have to convince the registry that it is really necessary.

to download from. This will need to be fixed by the Webmaster of the server; contact that person to alert him or her of the problem.

Similar problems may occur with other types of encoded files.

SEE: • **"Technically Speaking: Understanding MIMEs," for a more technical view of this issue**

BY THE WAY ▶

DOWNLOADING BINARY FILES WITH NETSCAPE NAVIGATOR

Most downloadable files on the Web will be in binhex format, as described in the main text. You may still find binary files to download, however, and these have the advantage of being smaller in size. Unfortunately, they often do not transfer successfully over the Internet. If you want to increase your chances of success when downloading a binary file with Netscape Navigator, hold down the Option key when you click on the file's link.

Web Pages Do Not Get Updated as Expected

Symptoms:

- You go back to a page that you had previously viewed during a session, with the expectation that the page has been updated in the meantime (for example, a counter should have been increased). Instead, you find that the page remains unchanged.

Causes:

Assuming that the page really has been changed since your last look, why does this happen? The answer is that the browser is getting the page from its cache on your drive rather than from the remote source.

For the same reason, a page may load from its cache even if you are no longer connected to the Internet, fooling you into thinking that you are still online.

SEE: • **"Browser Caches and Corrupted Directory Files," earlier in this chapter, for more on what these caches are**

What to do:

If you want to get your browser to load a page from the remote server rather than your cache, try the following:

Use Reload The primary solution is to click your browser's Reload button from its toolbar. Click it a couple of times if necessary.

Note: At least with Navigator 3.0, Reload does not work if there is still some part of the page that has not yet loaded. In this case, first click Stop, then click Reload.

Use Option-Reload Netscape Navigator continues to have bugs in its cache algorithm that can prevent a reload from working correctly. The result is that your browser may be pulling the image from your local cache instead of reloading, even after you click the Reload button.

In these cases, holding down the Option key when you Reload almost always works.

Quit and Relaunch If you are still having problems, quit your browser and relaunch it. This should always work as long as you have not set your cache updating option to "Never."

SEE: • **"By The Way: How Often Does Your Browser Update Its Cache Files?"**

Clear the Cache If even this fails to work, you can clear (or empty) the cache, although this will slow your browser's current performance significantly. To do this in Navigator, go to Options: Network Preferences: Cache and click the "Clear Disk Cache Now" button. In Internet Explorer, go to Edit: Options: Advanced and click the Empty button in the Cache section.

Do not try to clear the cache by trashing the cache folder in the Finder while your browser is running. This could lead to a system crash.

BY THE WAY ▶

HOW OFTEN DOES YOUR BROWSER UPDATE ITS CACHE FILES?

How does your browser decide whether to load a page from its cache or from the remote source? It depends upon a preference setting that you can adjust (for Navigator, it's found at Options: Network Preferences: Cache; for Explorer, it's at Edit: Options: Advanced). The default setting for both Navigator and Explorer is to check the network only "Once Per Session." This means that it updates the cache only the first time you go to a page after launching your browser. Thus, if a page has changed since you last looked at it, your browser will not normally update the page to reflect these changes until after you quit and relaunch the browser.

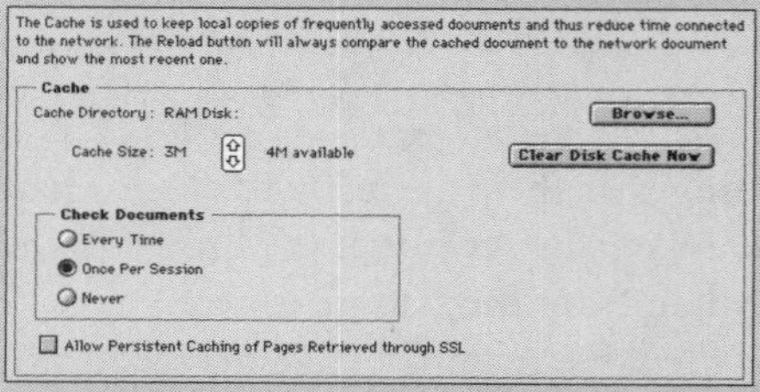

Figure 14-30 *Netscape's Cache settings again. Note the options to "Check Documents;" changing this affects how often your Web page is reloaded from the remote location vs. your cache file. Also note the option to "Clear Disk Cache Now;" this can force a reloading of a Web page when all else has failed to do so.*

You can change this to update "Every Time," but this will result in slower loading of previously viewed pages.

Alternatively, you can choose to have the cache "Never" update. This means it will pull the item from the cache even after relaunching. You should typically not check this, except on a temporary basis to view pages after you have disconnected. To do this, you may also want to make the cache size very large.

In any case, you can always force your browser to check for updates at any time simply by clicking your browser's Reload button, as described in the main text.

Finally, even if your browser is set to update your pages once per session, it may update them more frequently, depending upon what method you use to return to a page. For example, using the Back button on the browser's toolbar is less likely to update a page than using a Back button found on a page itself. You may have to experiment a bit to see what works best.

TAKE NOTE ▶

WHAT ABOUT CYBERDOG?

Figure 14-31 *Cyberdog's Starting Point window.*

Apple has its own Web browser, called Cyberdog. Actually, it's more than just a Web browser; it's is a collection of OpenDoc parts (or Live Objects) that provide a full suite of Internet features (including email, FTP, and a newsgroup reader). Not only can these parts be used from within the basic Cyberdog Starting Point document, they can be integrated into other OpenDoc objects. So, for example, you can embed a Web page into a word processing document; if you computer is connected to the Internet when you open the word processing document, you will automatically have a live connection to that Web page.

Even more exciting news is down the road. Netscape and Apple have announced that Netscape will provide an OpenDoc-based version of Navigator that will function with Cyberdog (to be called Netscape Navigator for Cyberdog). This will eventually be integrated into the MacOS and be shipped with all Macintosh computers.

SEE: • **Chapter 13 for more on OpenDoc**

Ethernet Quick Fixes

Coverage of networks in this book has focused on LocalTalk, Apple's built-in networking that has been around almost as long as the Mac itself. Ethernet is a networking alternative to LocalTalk. With many recent Macintosh models, especially PCI-based desktop Macs, Ethernet is now much easier to use (but still not as easy as LocalTalk) because of the Mac's built-in ports and hardware support for making Ethernet connections.

The main advantage of Ethernet over LocalTalk is increased speed. With Open Transport, if you have an Ethernet connection, your first step will be to make sure you select "Ethernet" from the "Connect via:" pop-up menu in the TCP/IP control panel. Beyond this, space constraints—as well as my own lack of expertise in this area—prevent me from going into details about how to set up and manage Ethernet networks.

Still, for those who plan to use or are using Ethernet, two sets of troubleshooting tips are provided below.

Ethernet Extensions Solve Problems

Apple Built-in Ethernet and Ethernet (Built-in) Extensions Apple's built-in Ethernet hardware (the "MACE" controller) in Quadras and some Power Macs can cause freezes and/or corruption of data. The "Apple Built-in Ethernet" extension (for non-PCI based Macs) and "Ethernet (Built-in)" extension (for PCI-based Macs) are needed to fix these problems.

ENET Compatibility Extension If you have a PCI-based Mac connected to a Novell Netware network, you need the ENET Compatibility extension. If it does not get installed by an Easy Install of your system software, use a Custom Install (look for an Ethernet Driver Update section) to get it. This note from Apple explains why you need it: "The extension fixes a problem in the system shutdown code. A side effect of this fix is a two-minute delay in shutting down the computer. It may appear that the machine has hung, however after two minutes, the machine will resume the shutdown process. This delay can be avoided by logging out of the Netware tree before shutting down or restarting. Without the Ethernet Compatibility extension, when a PCI-based machine running System 7.5.*x* selects Shut Down or Restart, the machine would crash."

Figure 14-32 *Useful extensions for Ethernet users.*

System 7.5.5 Updating to System 7.5.5 (or later) fixes problems that might occur transferring large files over an Ethernet network when virtual memory is on.

Cables and Hardware for Ethernet Mini-Networks

To get the speed advantage of Ethernet, some users have decided to use it rather than LocalTalk for functions as simple as connecting a LaserWriter to a Mac or connecting two local Macs together. This can be done, but the following are a couple of caveats to bear in mind.

- PCI-based Macs come with a built-in 10Base-T Ethernet port. This can allow you to connect two Macs together (or a Mac and a printer together) via an Ethernet connection with just a simple cable connection (other Macs with Ethernet ports need a AAUI transceiver). You can't, however, use the standard Ethernet RJ45 cable. Instead, get a special cable called a cross-over cable, then select "Ethernet" from the Open Transport AppleTalk control panel.

  Connecting three or more devices can get more complicated and will probably involve getting an Ethernet "hub."

- Some reports indicate that connecting two Macs together poses a special problem that is not relevant when connecting a Mac and a printer together. In particular, the Mac does not start up with Ethernet active if it does not "see" a device connected on the Ethernet network; it defaults to LocalTalk instead. Whichever Mac starts up first will therefore default to LocalTalk, preventing the connection from working. The solution once again is more hardware (including something similar to Farallon's Etherwave transceiver to act as a hub), plus switching back to the standard cable. (Other reports indicate that this will be unnecessary, since the cross-over cable trick should work.)

Part III:

Disaster Relief: The Fix-Its

Meet the Fix-Its—a collection of eighteen topics that cover the entire range of problem-solving techniques. Think of them as a set of descriptive troubleshooting tools, the metaphorical equivalent of such traditional tools as a screwdriver or a hammer. Whereas previous chapters were organized according to symptoms, the Fix-Its are organized according to the tools themselves.

There are two ways to use this Fix-It section. First, and most often, you will be sent here via a cross-reference from an earlier chapter of this book. In this case, these Fix-Its are an extension of the step-by-step procedures listed in the previous chapters. Assuming you are still hunting for a solution to your problem, here is where you continue the hunt. These Fix-Its detail frequently cited techniques, helping me avoid the need to repeat this information every time it is relevant.

Second, I have tried to make each Fix-It stand as a self-contained tutorial on its subject. For instance, if you want to learn about viruses—what they are, how they originate, and how to protect yourself against them—turn to Fix-It #7. This self-teaching can be useful regardless of whether you are referred to this section from a previous chapter. To make these Fix-Its independent, some material presented earlier in the book is repeated here, but I have tried to keep this to a minimum.

Each Fix-It is divided into five parts:

1. **Quick Summary.** This briefly describes the key procedure(s) of the Fix-It.
2. **When to Do It.** This section summarizes the common situations and symptoms that suggest the use of the Fix-It. Scanning these "When to Do It" sections is especially useful if you are browsing through the Fix-Its without having been directed here from a previous chapter.

   Be aware that many of the symptoms described in this section appear in more than one Fix-It. For example, a system crash may point to many different causes, including an extension conflict, a damaged preferences file, or a virus. Therefore, when you see your symptom listed for a particular Fix-It, do not immediately assume you have found the cause of your problem. Actually, to diagnose a particular problem, you are better off starting your search in Part II of this book, which also gives suggested sequences for trying the Fix-Its, with the precise order varying according to the particular problem at hand.
3. **Why to Do It.** This section briefly summarizes the rationale behind each procedure and what you can expect it to accomplish. Here, more than in the other sections, you can gain insight as to why a given solution works.
4. **What to Do.** This is the main section of each Fix-It—the actual procedures and step-by-step instructions. Some of these sections are relatively brief; others are lengthy. In general, they follow the "What to Do" format of the previous chapters.
5. **For Related Information.** This last section is a list of cross-references that tell you where to go to further investigate selected topics mentioned in the Fix-It.

This "disaster relief" section makes more than occasional reference to utilities needed to assist in repairs, particularly disk repair and recovery utilities such as MacTools and Norton Utilities. I go into considerable detail on how to use these utilities—more detail than you are likely to find in other troubleshooting books. Even so, the instructions are not a substitute for the documentation that comes with each utility. If anything here seems unclear, please check your software manuals before proceeding.

Disaster Relief: The Fix-Its

Fix-It #1: Check for Incompatibilities Between Hardware and Software 665
Application Software Is Too New or Too Powerful for the Hardware 666
Hardware Is Too New for the Application Software 666
Hardware Is Too New for the System Software 666
General Strategies 666
A Few Common Hardware Incompatibilities 668
Monitor Incompatibilities 668
Card Incompatibilities 669
Peripheral Hardware Incompatibilities 669
No Math Coprocessor 669
Insufficient RAM 670

Fix-It #2: Check for Problems with Preferences Files 671
Loss of Customized Settings 672
Corrupted and Upgraded Preferences Files 672

Fix-It #3: Check for Mislocated or Missing Accessory Files 678

Fix-It #4: Check for Problems with Extensions and Control Panels (Startup Extensions) 682
Startup Extension Conflicts 683
Startup Extensions That Do Not Load or Run 684
Disable Startup Extensions to Determine If You Have a Startup Extension Conflict 685
Method #1: Disable Startup Extensions by Holding Down the Shift Key at Startup 686
Method #2: Disable Startup Extensions by Using a Startup Management Utility 686
Method #3: Disable Startup Extensions by Removing Startup Extensions from Your System Folder 692
Identify the Problem Startup Extension 693
Check Recently Added Startup Extensions 693
Check Suspicious Startup Extensions 693
Check for Known Incompatibilities and Bugs 693
Disable and Re-Enable Individual Startup Extensions 694
Special Case: Conflict Between Two Startup Extensions 696
Special Case: Conflict Occurs Only When Using a Startup Extension 697
Special Case: If a Startup Extension Causes a System Crash at Startup 697

Resolve the Conflict 699
Rearrange the Loading Order of Startup Extensions 699
Upgrade the Problem Startup Extension or Other Software 702
Replace Potentially Damaged Files 702
Check for Memory-Related Problems 703
Delete the Problem Startup Extension. 703
If the Startup Extension Does Not Load or Run 704
Is It a Codependent Startup Extension Problem (or Other Startup Extension Conflict)? 704
Did You Restart After Installing the Startup Extension? 704
Is the Startup Extension in the System Folder? 704
Is the Startup Extension in Its Proper Location in the System Folder? 705
Was the Startup Extension Disabled by Your Startup Manager? 705
Is the Startup Extension Turned On? 706
Special Case: Startup Icons Appear with an "X" Over Them or Disappear 706

Fix-It #5: Check for Problems with System Software 708
Complete Install/Reinstall of System Software 710
Doing a Clean Reinstall of System Software 710
Using the System Software Installer 716
Selective Install/Reinstall/Deletion of System Software. 724
Basis for a Selective Install/Reinstall 724
Install/Reinstall Selected System Software Files 725
Special Case: Delete Multiple System Folders 727

Fix-It #6: Check for Problems with Memory Management 729
Memory Problems When Trying to Open an Application 732
Check the Advice, If Any, in the Alert Message 732
Quit One or More Other Open Applications 732
Reduce the Size of a Large Clipboard 732
Check for Fragmented Memory Space 733
Check for Memory Leaks (A Step Beyond Memory Fragmentation!) 734
Reduce the Minimum/Current Memory Size. 736
Remove Plug-In Modules and Other Accessory Files 737
If None of the Preceding Steps Work 738
Memory Problems When Using an Open Application 738
Close Any Open Documents That Do Not Need to Be Open 739
Reduce the Size of the Clipboard 739
Do Not Try to Open the Document from the Finder 739
Quit the Application and Relaunch It, Restarting If Needed. 739
Increase the Preferred/Current Memory Size. 740
Special Case: Finder-Related Memory Problems. 741
Quit Applications and Close Windows 741
Increase the Finder's Memory Size 742

How to Increase Overall Memory Availability. 742
Reduce Applications' Preferred/Current Memory Size 742
Reduce the Memory Size Needed by System Software 746
Increase the Size of the System Heap 749
Increase the Total Available Memory. 750

Fix-It #7: Check for Viruses. 756
Use an Anti-Virus Utility 760
Install an Anti-Virus Utility. 760
Keep Your Anti-Virus Utility Updated. 761
Customize Your Anti-Virus Utility 762
Prevent a Virus Attack from Infecting Your Disk 763
A Virus Is Detected 763
A Suspicious Activity Is Detected. 763
Suspicious-Activity False Alarms 764
Eradicate an Existing Virus. 764
Scan for and Delete Infected Files 765
Repair an Infected File?. 767
If the Anti-Virus Utility Didn't Solve Your Problem 767
Determine the Source of Your Virus Infection 767

Fix-It #8: Defragment/Optimize the Disk 768
Optimizing/Defragmenting Basics. 769
Before You Optimize. 770
Optimize the Disk. 770
Beyond the Basics 771
Check for Fragmentation of Individual Files 771
Make Sure Files Are Free to Defragment (Startup Disk Problems and More) 772
Create Free Space. 772
Don't Optimize Floppy Disks 772
A Disk Is Optimized When You Reformat and Restore It 773
The Downside of Optimizing and Defragmenting 773
Defragmenting Takes Time. 773
Defragmenting Can Erase Files That Otherwise Could Have Been Undeleted 773
Defragmenting Can Cause Disk Damage 774

Fix-It #9: Rebuild the Desktop 775
The Desktop File Can Become Bloated 776
The Desktop File Can Become Corrupted or Incorrectly Updated 776
Generic Icon Problems 776
Rebuilding Basics 777

Beyond the Basics 778
Fixing Generic Icon Problems 778
Losing (and Saving) Get Info Comments After Rebuilding the Desktop 782
Minor Repairs Alert Message 782
Don't Bother to Rebuild the Desktop After Initializing a Disk 783
Desktop Files and Reusing Floppy Disks 783
The Desktop Rebuilds Every Time You Start Up 783
Keep Extensions Off When You Rebuild? 784
Really Rebuild the Desktop 785

Fix-It #10: Run Disk First Aid 787
Using Disk First Aid 788
Getting Started 788
Verify or Repair a Disk 789
Further Damage Checks 792

Fix-It #11: Zap the Parameter RAM 793
Zapping Basics 795
For All Macs Running System 7 (except PCI-based Macs) 795
For PCI-Based Macs (PRAM and NVRAM) 795
Optional: Remove the Battery 796
After Zapping the PRAM 796
Really Zap the PRAM: Use TechTool 798

Fix-It #12: Update the Disk Device Driver 801
Update to Accommodate New System Software 802
Update to Accommodate New Hardware 802
Update to Repair Damage to the Driver 803
Get the Latest Version of the Formatting Utility 804
Update the Driver 807

Fix-It #13: Check for Damaged Disks: Repair, Restore, or Recover 810
Repair 811
Restore 811
Recover 812
Repair a Damaged Disk 812
Before Using Your Repair Utility 812
Make Repairs 815
Restore a Damaged or Accidentally Erased Disk 821
Before Attempting to Restore a Disk 821
Restore the Disk 822
Recover Selected Files from a Damaged Disk 823

Fix-It #14: Check for Damaged Files: Replace or Recover 827
Damaged Files Due to Miscopied Information 828
Damaged Files Due to Bad Blocks 828
Caveats 828
Replace the Damaged File 829
For Applications 829
For Documents 830
Recover the Damaged File 830
Make a Copy of the Damaged File 830
Try to Open the Damaged Document 831
File Recovery Via CanOpener 831
File Recovery with MacTools or Norton Utilities 832
Resolve Problems with Bad Blocks 833
Recover Damaged Files and Repair Bad Blocks 833
Repairing Bad Blocks: Recovery Utilities versus Reformatting 835
Special Case: Recovering Files from Floppy Disks with Bad Blocks 836

Fix-It #15: Format, Initialize, and Verify Disks 838
Floppy Disks 839
Formatting an Unformatted Disk 840
Reformatting an Already Formatted Disk 841
Reformatting versus Deleting 842
Unreadable or Damaged Disks That Really Aren't 842
Macintosh PC Exchange and PC-Formatted Disks 843
Damaged Disks 843
Hard Disks 844
Formatting and Reformatting in General 844
Apple HD Setup versus Drive Setup: Which One Do You Use? 845
Reformatting Using Apple HD SC Setup 847
Reformatting Using Drive Setup 848
Reformatting Using Other Formatting Utilities 850
Reformatting versus Erasing versus Deleting 851
Partition the Disk 852
Verifying Disks and Media Damage 855
For Floppy Disks 855
For Hard Disks 856

Fix-It #16: Check for Problems with SCSI Devices and Connections 858
What's a SCSI Chain? 859
What's the Problem? 859
Using a SCSI Utility 862
Mounting SCSI Devices with SCSIProbe 862
If SCSIProbe Lists a Device, But Doesn't Mount It 864
If SCSIProbe Doesn't List or Mount the Device 867
Special Case: Disk Drives That Don't Automatically Mount at Startup 868

SCSI-Related Problems 869
- Make Sure the SCSI Port Is Functioning 871
- Check If All SCSI Devices in the Chain Are Turned On 871
- Be Careful When Turning Off a Non-Startup Drive 871
- Disconnect All SCSI Devices 872
- Make Sure No Two SCSI Devices Have the Same ID Number 872
- Make Sure All SCSI Devices Are Properly Terminated 873
- Reconnect and Rearrange the Connection Order of SCSI Devices 873
- Confront Cable Connection Confusion 875
- Running with Devices Disconnected 876
- Check for Damage 876

Fix-It #17: Check If Hardware Repairs or Replacements Are Needed 877

Diagnose Hardware Problems 879
- Preliminary Checks 879
- Use Hardware Diagnostic Utilities 879

Repair Selected Hardware Problems 881
- Hard Drives and Other SCSI Devices 882
- Floppy Drives 882
- Keyboard and Mouse/Trackball/TrackPad 884
- Monitor I: No Display or Dimmed Display 886
- Monitor II: Quality of Display Problems 889
- Serial Port Devices: Printers, Modems, and Networks 891
- The Macintosh 893
- Memory I: Adding or Replacing Memory 894
- Memory II: Getting the Correct Modules for Your Machine 898

Fix-It #18: Seek Technical Support or Other Outside Help 903

Product Technical Support 904
- When to Call Technical Support 904
- When to Seek Other Types of Technical Support 905
- Be Prepared Before You Call 905
- Using Utilities to Help Get Prepared 906
- Make the Call 907

Seeking Other Outside Help 909
- Online Information Services 909
- The Internet (especially the World Wide Web) 910
- User Groups 913
- Magazines 913
- Books 913
- Other Options 914

Fix-It #1: Check for Incompatibilities Between Hardware and Software

QUICK SUMMARY ▶

Read the manuals (as well as any on-disk "Read Me" files) that come with your software and hardware in order to determine what known incompatibility problems may exist. Check to see if changes to control panel settings can resolve a problem. Otherwise, check if a software upgrade is available that eliminates any incompatibility.

When to do it:

- Before installing or using any new program—or, even better, before you purchase a program, looking for incompatibility information before the fact may save you from buying software you cannot use.
- If an application fails to launch successfully the first time you use it (especially if it causes a system error).
- Similarly, if an application fails to launch successfully the first time you try it after having made a change in your hardware configuration.

Why to do it:

In the early days of the Macintosh, there was only one model (or few very similar models) available, and the only printer that worked with it was the ImageWriter. Similarly, the original system software was quite modest and fit entirely on one or two floppy disks. What you lost in versatility, you gained in simplicity. And, unlike other computers at the time, including Apple's own Apple II, Macintoshes were designed to prevent you from accessing the inside of the machine.

All of this was intentional. The Macintosh vision was to keep things simple and consistent, so that each software application could be assured that it was interacting with the same hardware, no matter who was using it. This in turn, would make it easy to ensure that all software ran without any problems on every Macintosh.

Obviously, this is true no more. There are now dozens of Macintosh models, past and present, with different CPUs, different ROMs, different amounts of RAM preinstalled, and a number of other critical differences. With modular Macintoshes, you can add any variety of monitors. The number of possible printers is staggering, from inkjet to laser and beyond. Storage devices are increasingly diverse, from CD-ROMs to Zip drives. PowerBooks will include software not found on desktop Macs, PCI-based Macs will include software not found on other Macs, and so on.

The amazing thing, considering all of this diversity, is that most software still runs admirably well almost all the time in almost all of the various possible configurations. But "almost" doesn't mean "always." Thus, when things go wrong, one of the first possibilities to consider is that your software is incompatible with your hardware. The most common sources of such problems are as follows.

Application Software Is Too New or Too Powerful for the Hardware

For example, a particular application may require more memory, a faster processor, or a particular color display capability that your particular Macintosh does not or cannot have. Often this is because the newer Macintoshes have updated ROMs containing new options not available in the older models.

Hardware Is Too New for the Application Software

Software released prior to the arrival of certain models of Macintosh may have problems due to added features in the new hardware. This is often the case when the new hardware includes some significant departure from previous Macintoshes.

One obvious example is that when Power Macintoshes first came out, several programs would not run on these machines, even in emulation mode. Typically, these are temporary problems that are corrected (within a few months or so) by upgrades in the software.

Hardware Is Too New for the System Software

Typically, you can expect problems—possibly including startup crashes—if you try to use a version of the system software older than the version that was current when your Macintosh model was first released. For example, PCI-based Macs only run System 7.5.2 or later. You also need to make sure you have any needed Enabler or Update file installed.

SEE: • **Fix-It #5, for more on System Enablers and Updates**

What to do:

General Strategies

1. **Check manuals, "Read Me" files, and Apple Guide Help**
   If you suspect incompatibility between a particular application and your hardware configuration, the first thing to check is the documentation that came with the application; the critical information is usually in the opening pages. Manuals typically inform you of potential incompatibilities as well as minimal hardware requirements. For example, if an application needs a math coprocessor, the manual should tell you that, as well as what models of Macintosh come standard with a math coprocessor.

TECHNICALLY SPEAKING ▶

LEARNING THE LOWDOWN ON YOUR HARDWARE

The more you understand the characteristics of your Macintosh model, the easier it will be to discover hardware incompatibilities. Throughout this book, I have referred to the different characteristics of the various models of Macintosh, but often only in a general way. To get a good summary of the current hardware details for every Mac ever made, check out Apple Spec, a FileMaker document that Apple updates every time new models come out. It's available at many online locations, including Apple's software updates sites (such as *http://www.support.apple.com/pub/apple_sw_updates/US/Macintosh/Utilities/*).

Of course, a poorly written manual may omit this information. Similarly, even a good manual cannot anticipate conflicts with hardware that was not released until after it was published. Thus, problems may occur that are not cited in the manuals. Sometimes, "Read Me" files included on the software disks will contain important information about conflicts discovered too recently to have made it into the manual.

If this information cannot be found in the software manual or "Read Me" files, check the manual(s) that came with your hardware. Also check the documentation included with any peripheral cards you may have added. If you did not set up your Macintosh yourself, and you are not sure what peripheral cards or other add-ons you have, find someone who does know this.

Since vendors are increasingly depending on the use of Apple Guide rather than printed material for their critical documentation, you should check there as well. Another trend is shipping software on CD-ROM discs, with all of the documentation on the disc (often in Acrobat format); you then have to read the documentation on your monitor or print it out.

If you cannot find the relevant manuals, or they don't contain the information you are seeking, call the manufacturer of the program directly.

2. **Adjust control panel settings**

   Some hardware-related incompatibilities can be partially solved by a work-around approach with your current software. In particular, certain control panels have options that inactivate or modify problem-causing hardware features, enabling you to use otherwise incompatible applications. There is an obvious trade-off here, since you lose the advantage of whatever feature you turn off in order to obtain the needed compatibility.

   Many of these control panel options are described elsewhere. Here are a few examples:

   a. **Memory control panel.** A program may be incompatible with 32-bit addressing. To solve this, simply turn off 32-bit addressing from the Memory control panel and restart. On newer Macintoshes, this may not be an option, as they only run in 32-bit mode. On Power Macintoshes, turning off an option called Modern Memory Manager solves some incompatibility problems (but leave it on otherwise). Starting in System 7.6, this can no longer be turned off.

b. **Monitors control panel.** A program may require a particular color depth to run (some games, for example, only run in 256 colors). Assuming that your hardware is capable of displaying 256 colors, you simply need to make the proper selection from the Monitors control panel (as described more in Chapter 10).

c. **Fax software.** Some programs do not work if fax software is set to receive faxes. Putting your fax software into "suspend" mode can solve this problem. Depending on your software, this may be done via an option in a control panel or an item in the Apple Menu.

3. **Upgrade software or hardware, as needed**

With luck, a new version of the application software that eliminates the incompatibilities either already exists or will be released shortly. In any case, as a preventative measure, you should keep your software current.

If you have a current version of the application, it may be your system software that is not current—for instance, an application may require System 7.5 or later, and you may be still using System 7.1. If so, upgrade it (as described in Fix-It #5), and make sure your disk driver is current as well (as described in Fix-It #12).

Otherwise, if it is critical to use the application, you may need to purchase new hardware that eliminates the incompatibilities. This hardware can include anything from more memory to getting a logic board upgrade that essentially transforms your machine into a newer model; you may even have to purchase a new Macintosh. If you don't wish to invest in new hardware, your main remaining choice is simply not to use the problem software.

4. **Don't be a pioneer**

In general, you can keep compatibility problems to a minimum by not being the first on your block to purchase a newly released model of Macintosh or upgrade to a major revision in the operating system. I try to wait at least six months after a machine comes out before I consider buying it. By then, most of the software companies have had a chance to upgrade their software to meet the demands of the new machine, and Apple has had a chance to correct any minor glitches in the product. For system software upgrades, I confess to upgrading immediately—but I often pay for this with several months of frustrating problems until the kinks get worked out.

A Few Common Hardware Incompatibilities

Monitor Incompatibilities

The standard pixel dimensions of a Macintosh 13- or 14-inch monitor are 640 x 480. Many applications are written assuming that the monitor has at least these dimensions. In some cases, if the screen has smaller dimensions, the program can adapt by resizing windows accordingly. Some programs, however, cannot—in particular, games may be unplayable on screens that use lesser dimensions. Certain PowerBooks and Apple's now-defunct 12-inch monitor are examples of Macintoshes that have this problem.

There is no good solution here other than to avoid those applications that do not work with your monitor size. Some utilities fool the Mac into creating a larger screen display (as if it were displaying to a larger monitor), but you then need to scroll around to view the parts of the display that are cut off from your monitor. I generally do not find this to be a practical solution.

Just remember, it is not the screen size that matters here but the pixel size. For example, a very small screen with equally small pixels may still be 640 x 480 in its dimensions. In this case, it will display correctly, but everything will be at a reduced size (see Chapter 10 for more on monitor resolutions).

At the other end of the spectrum, larger monitor screens (16 inches and greater) require more memory than smaller ones to display at the same color depth. Thus you may find that your Macintosh can display in 24-bit color on a 13-inch monitor but not with a 20-inch monitor. This problem can typically be solved by adding RAM, video RAM, and/or special graphics cards to your Macintosh. If you are unfamiliar with the requirements of your particular hardware, seek outside advice.

Card Incompatibilities

Most desktop Macintosh models have special slots located on the main logic board of the computer for you to insert *cards* that look like smaller versions of the set of integrated circuits found on the main logic board. These cards either add new functions to or enhance existing functions of your machine. For example, they may enhance the number of colors that can be displayed, accelerate the speed of the Macintosh, or add video input capabilities. Occasionally, a program may be incompatible with a particular card; if so, you will have to give up on either the application or the hardware.

Peripheral Hardware Incompatibilities

Every time you connect a peripheral device (such as an external hard drive, scanner, or modem) to your Macintosh, some software may be incompatible with it. For example, you may have some imaging or optical character recognition (OCR) software designed to work in conjunction with a scanner, but it may not work with your particular scanner. This may be because the OCR application requires special software drivers customized for each type of scanner. If the application did not come with a driver for your scanner or cannot recognize the drivers that may have been included with the scanner, it will not work with that scanner.

No Math Coprocessor

Most Macintosh models include a *math coprocessor* (also called a *floating point unit,* or FPU); a few models (mostly older ones) do not. On 680X0 Macs the FPU is a separate component from the processor, but on Power Macs it is actually integrated into the processor itself (see "By The Way: Software FPU, Power Macs, and 68LC040 Processors," for more details on this). If you are using a Macintosh that does not have a math coprocessor, some math-oriented programs, such as some statistics programs, may not run. If you try, you may get an error message—possibly as part of a system crash—that says "floating point processor not installed." Be wary of this message, however, since it

can also mistakenly result from causes having nothing to do with an FPU (such as a bug in the software, an extension conflict, or a call to a memory location that does not exist). In these cases, refer to Chapter 4 for more general advice on system errors. For Power Macintoshes, turning off the Modern Memory Manager from the Memory control panel may eliminate this problem.

If you do not know whether an FPU is in your Mac or not, there are various utilities that can tell you, including the previously mentioned Apple Spec (see "Technically Speaking: Learning the Lowdown on Your Hardware").

BY THE WAY ▶

SOFTWARE FPU, POWER MACS, AND 68LC040 PROCESSORS

There is a shareware utility called Software FPU that adds math-coprocessor capability to Macintoshes that lack it. Using it, however, does not produce the same speed as using a hardware-based FPU. Non-FPU Macintoshes that can benefit from this utility include 68000 Macs (such as the Mac Plus and SE) and 68LC040 Macs (such as the Quadra 605 and 610, and LC 475).

Also note that the 680X0 emulation mode on Power Macs actually emulates a 68LC040. As a result, PowerPC Macs will not work with non-PPC native code applications that require an FPU. If you try to run such software on a Power Mac, you will get a "No FPU installed" or similar error message. Software FPU (or its related commercial version, is written in native code) will help here as well. The best solution, however, is to get a native code version of the application itself if one exists.

SEE: • **Chapter 12 for more on Power Macintoshes**

Insufficient RAM

A program may require a minimum of 12MB of RAM, but you may only have 8MB of RAM installed. Problems of this sort are so important and so common that I cover them in a separate Fix-It (#6) on memory problems.

For related information

SEE:
- **Fix-It #5 on system software problems**
- **Fix-It #6 on memory-related problems**
- **Fix-It #12 on disk drivers**
- **Fix-It #17 on diagnosing hardware problems**
- **Fix-It #18 on calling technical support and seeking outside help**
- **Chapter 10 on monitor-related problems**
- **Chapter 11 on PowerBooks**
- **Chapter 12 on Power Macs**
- **Chapter 13 on new system software**

Fix-It #2: Check for Problems with Preferences Files

QUICK SUMMARY ▶

Replace an application's preferences file and/or system software preferences files (such as Finder Preferences), usually found in the Preferences Folder of the startup disk's System Folder.

When to do it:

- When any changes you have made to preferences settings are unexpectedly lost. For example, customized settings in a word processor, such as fonts and margin settings, may be different from the defaults.
- Whenever you have a problem using a specific feature of an application or control panel, such as a command that does not work or a dialog box that does not appear as expected. Be especially suspicious if that feature had worked properly on previous occasions.
- Whenever an extension does not load or work—in particular, you should suspect system software preferences files such as Finder Preferences. Examples of system software known to have problems related to preferences files include the Finder, the Network extension, and PC Exchange.

Why to do it:

Preferences files are used mainly to store customized settings. For example, a word processor may include a checkbox to turn smart quotes on or off. Whichever selection you make, the program remembers it even after you have quit the application; it usually does this by storing your choice in the application's preferences file. This way, you do not have to reselect the desired settings each time you relaunch the application or open a new document.

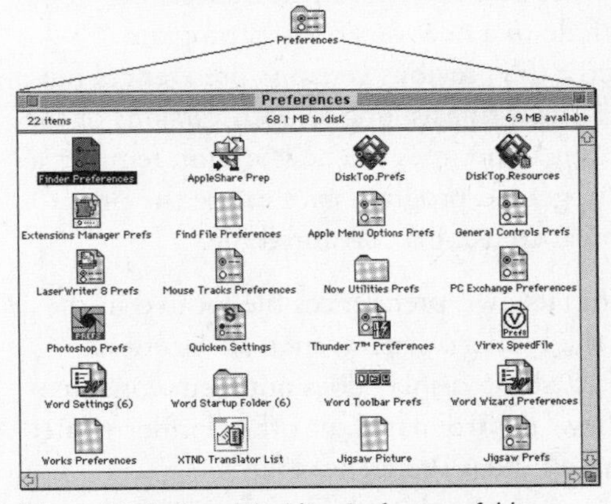

Figure F2-1 *A peek inside a Preferences folder.*

Preferences files typically have names like Word Settings or Works Preferences and they are usually located in the System Folder (most often in a special folder called Preferences). In some cases, preferences files can be stored in the same folder as the application. Usually the program can correctly locate its preferences file whether it is stored with the application or in the System Folder.

Not all programs have preference files. For programs that have them, though, preferences files are a common source of trouble. Problems with these files fall into two categories: customized settings are lost when preferences files are moved or deleted, or various problems occur because of a damaged or upgraded preferences file.

Loss of Customized Settings

Most applications automatically create a preferences file the first time the application is launched. If the preferences file is moved or deleted, the program simply creates a new one the next time you use it. Thus, even if a preferences file was missing or in the wrong place, it is unlikely that you would be alerted to any problem. The real threat here is that since a newly created preferences file contains the program's default settings, any customized settings are lost when the previous file is trashed.

A few programs, however, halt during launch if they cannot locate their preferences files. In most of these cases, an alert message should then appear, requesting that you either locate an existing copy or reinstall a new copy of the preferences file.

Changes in preferences files settings due to unexpectedly "lost" preferences files can occur for numerous reasons. For example, you could shift to a different startup disk, thereby accessing the preferences file (perhaps a default file you just created) in the alternate disk's System Folder. Or you might completely replace your System Folder, deleting all preferences files that were in it—normally this is not a recommended procedure—and thereby forcing a new preferences file to be created when you next use the application. Similarly, if you use the same application in two different settings, such as at home and at work, each site may have a different customized preferences file.

Corrupted and Upgraded Preferences Files

Preferences files seem particularly susceptible to becoming damaged, often for no discernible cause. When you launch an application that uses a corrupted preferences file, it may refuse to launch. More often, it opens successfully but exhibits unusual problems, from menu commands that do not work to system crashes. For example, I once had the Save command of a program stop working because of a corrupted preferences file.

A related problem can occur when you upgrade to a new version of a program. Often, even if you follow the instructions exactly, the previous version's preferences file is not replaced during the upgrade procedure. This is fine as long as both versions of the application can read the same preferences file, but sometimes the new version requires a new format. If the latter is the case, when the upgraded program tries to use the previous version's preferences file, results will be similar to using a corrupted file.

Finder Preferences In System 7, the Finder has its own preferences file located in the Preferences folder. It stores settings that affect the Finder's display, such as selections made in the Views control panel. If the Finder's desktop display does not seem consistent with the settings you have selected from the Views control panel, or other Finder-related problems develop, you probably have a corrupted Finder Preferences file.

A corrupted file of this sort may sometimes cause problems seemingly unrelated to the Finder. For example, a corrupted Finder Preferences file has been known to prevent the use of the Network extension on Power Macintoshes.

System 7.5 Software Preferences Files The Finder Preferences file is far from the only preferences file associated with Apple's system software. Especially if you have are using System 7.5 or later, you are likely to find a whole cornucopia of system software preferences files. These include AppleScript Preferences, Find File Preferences, Desktop Pattern Prefs, Apple Menu Options Prefs, Launcher Preferences, and even Jigsaw Preferences. If these get corrupted, they can also be a source of problems.

What to do:

1. **Quit the problem application (or close the problem control panel)**
   If a problem is specific to a particular application that is currently open, quit the application before taking any further steps. Relaunch the application only after you have completed these changes.

2. **Before replacing/deleting preferences files for control panels, restart with extensions off**
   When deleting preferences files of control panels, first restart the Macintosh with extensions off. Otherwise, even though you delete the preferences file, the new preferences file may be created from the corrupted information still present in RAM.

   By the way, Now Utilities is notorious for having problems that can be remedied by deleting the Preferences files of its various components.

3. **Find or replace missing customized preferences files**
   If you lose an application's customized preferences settings when you switch startup disks, it is because you are now using a different preferences file. The ideal solution is to locate the original customized file, presumably in the System Folder of your original startup disk, and use it to replace the preferences file currently in use. Thus, if your customized settings are on startup disk A but you are using startup disk B, copy the preferences file from disk A to disk B. When the Macintosh asks if you want to replace the existing file, click OK. Make sure you copy the preferences file to its required location; for example, if you place it in the Preferences folder and it seems to have no effect, check whether it needs to be placed in the same folder as the application instead.

   On the other hand, if the problem is that your original customized preferences file has been deleted, the easiest course of action is simply to re-create your customized settings with the new preferences file. In some cases, however, this can be a time-consuming process. For example, Microsoft Word allows you to customize all of its menus; if you make extensive alterations, having to re-create all the changes can be a real annoyance, especially if you can't remember them all. In such cases, if you have installed an undelete utility (described in Chapter 2), use it to try to recover a recently deleted preferences file. Alternatively, see if you have a copy on your backup disks; it might be a good idea to maintain a separate backup copy for just these occasions.

4. **Find and delete (or replace) preferences files that you believe are corrupted or incompatible**
If you suspect a corrupted or incompatible preferences file, delete it. Remember, since many control panels now use preferences files, you should check for those as well.

If you are having trouble locating a specific preferences file, remember to check for it in both the System Folder (especially in the Preferences folder) and in the folder that contains the application. Also note that in some cases, preferences files may be contained in a special folder (created by the application) located within the System Folder; a well-known example of this are the preferences files in the Claris folder (a folder created and used by virtually all Claris applications).

For example, suppose you want to check if there is a preferences file for BusyWorks. First you look, naturally enough, in the Preferences folder. If you are using an icon view, it might help to switch to the By Name view here (from the Finder's View menu). The By Name view lists all files in alphabetical order, making it easier to locate a file that begins with "BusyWorks" (which is probably the start of the name of the preferences file). Alternatively, you could view files By Kind, looking for files of the kind "BusyWorks document" in this case.

What if you come up empty here but you still suspect that your sought-after preferences file exists on the disk somewhere? Use the Find command! Simply select Find (or Command-F) and type in any portion of the suspected file name (such as "BusyW"), then select Find (or simply press Return). For System 7.0 or 7.1, the Macintosh locates the first instance of any file that contains that section of text in its name. If the first identified file is not the one you are seeking, you can use Command-G (Find Again) repeatedly to search for more matching files. With System 7.5's Find File, you get a complete list of all files that match the criteria.

If even this method fails to locate a specific preferences file (perhaps because the file has an unusual name that you do not recognize as belonging to the application), do the following:

a. **Get a utility, such as Snitch, that can list a file's Creator code.** Use it to learn the code for your problem application ("BOBO" is the creator for ClarisWorks, for example). See Chapter 8 for more details on doing this.

b. **Next, get another utility that can search for files based on Creator codes.** In System 7.5, you can do this with the same Find File feature you've already been using (as described in Chapter 2).

   In earlier versions of the system software, the Find function does not include this option. Instead, the best you can do is to search by Kind (such as "ClarisWorks document"), which is a close substitute for a search by Creator but not quite as reliable. Alternatively, you can get any number of other shareware or commercial utilities that can search by Creator (such as DiskTop).

c. **Using whatever utility you select, search for all files that have the same Creator code as the problem application.** Among the found files will almost certainly be the sought-after preferences file. Delete it.

 If you find two preferences files with similar names, both apparently for the same application (such as "BusyWorks Pref-3" and "BusyWorks Pref-4"), you have probably upgraded your application, thereby creating separate preferences files for both the older and newer versions. Check the creation date of both files (using the Get Info command from the Finder), and delete the older of the two files. If this doesn't solve the problem, delete both files.

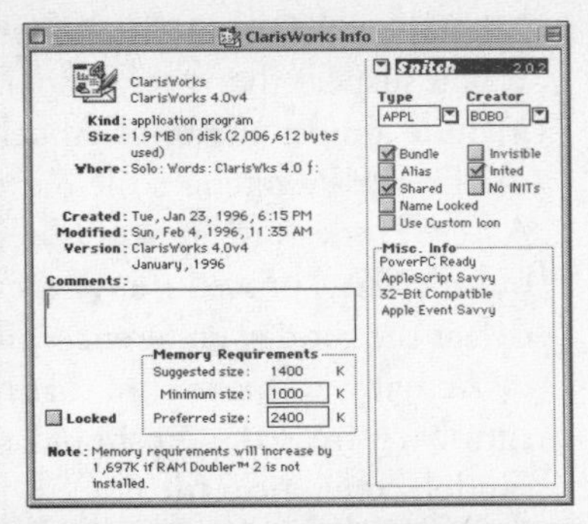

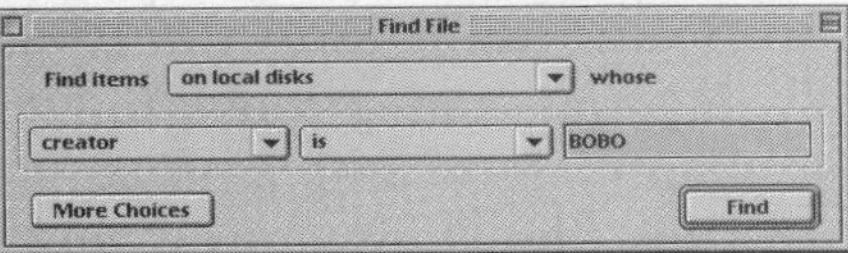

Figure F2-2 *After determining the creator for ClarisWorks is "BOBO" (top), do a search for all files with that creator (bottom). This search should locate any ClarisWorks-specific preferences files (although, in this case, you may miss some more general preferences that apply to all Claris applications, such as XTND Translator List).*

Normally, this is the end of your problem—a new, uncorrupted, and compatible preferences file will be created the next time you launch the application. If this does not happen, check the application's original disks for a preferences file; if you find one, copy it from there. In either case, any customized settings you have entered are lost and need to be re-created.

TECHNICALLY SPEAKING ▶

MORE PROBLEMS DECIDING WHAT PREFERENCES FILE TO DELETE

Deciding what preferences files to delete can get more complicated than just a difficulty in locating a specific file. For example:

- Some preferences files are used by several applications (examples include XTND Translator List, which is a quasi-preferences file shared by most Claris applications and stored in the Preferences folder, and Claris Fonts, located in the Claris folder within the System Folder). Conversely, some programs may have more than one preferences file. Try deleting these additional preferences files if you are having any problems associated with an application that uses them.

 Deleting XTND Translator List is definitely known to fix a variety of ills with Claris programs. Recently, it solved a problem I had with an inability to open PICT files.
- Sometimes a symptom may give no suggestion that a particular program's Preferences file is the cause. This is particularly true for control panel preferences; for example, a corrupted Apple Menu Preferences file can result in a message that says "not enough memory to load all of your extensions" appearing at startup. In these cases, figuring out what to do may require getting advice from others who have had the same problem.

5. **Special case: Delete the Finder Preferences file**
   If you suspect that your Finder Preferences file is corrupted (for reasons that may include almost any unusual behavior in the Finder itself), delete it. To do this, drag the Finder Preferences file out of the System Folder, and then restart the Macintosh. A new Finder Preferences file is created automatically, and you can then delete the old file. This procedure is necessary because the Macintosh does not allow you to delete the Finder Preferences file of the current startup disk.

   Actually, to make sure that the old (and possibly corrupted) preferences data is not simply re-created, you should restart from an alternate startup disk, then delete the Finder Preferences file.

6. **Special case: Delete other system software preferences files**
   If you are having trouble with other system software files (such as control panels), check if there is a preferences file associated with the problem software; these preferences files are especially common in System 7.5. If so, delete the relevant preferences file(s). To do this, you may have to drag the files(s) out of the System Folder and restart (as was done with the Finder Preferences file).

   Two examples of this sort of trouble are as follows:

   a. Some cases of an inability to use PC Exchange (or otherwise mount PC-formatted disks) can be fixed by deleting its preferences file.
   b. Deleting the preferences file for Apple Menu Options fixes a problem where the hierarchical menus generated by the control panel do not appear. It also fixes the "memory" problem mentioned in "Technically Speaking: More Problems Deciding What Preferences File to Delete."

TAKE NOTE ▶

DELETE YOUR ENTIRE PREFERENCES FOLDER? (NO!)

Because of all of the problems that corrupted preferences files may cause, you may sometimes see advice that suggests deleting your entire Preferences folder from time to time, as a sort of maintenance procedure. Generally, I would not follow this advice.

The primary reason is that files in the Preferences folder have assumed more critical functions in recent years. In particular, you are more likely to find larger files, a greater number of files, and more essential files in this folder than ever before. QuicKeys, for example, has long kept many of its key files in the Preferences folder. The Netscape cache files (and Netscape's 3.0's Java library file) also are stored there, as is the Users & Groups Data file (which is important for file sharing). Files that contain registration number data needed even to launch an application, may be stored there, along with your selection of Desktop Patterns. You probably don't want to delete most of these files.

So instead of simply deleting your entire Preferences folder, your best bet is still to try to determine what, if any, preferences file is causing a problem and then delete it individually.

If you are still uncertain about what can or cannot be deleted, check your software manual(s) or ask for outside help.

TAKE NOTE ▶

CLEANING UP UNNEEDED PREFERENCES FILES (AND MORE)

Yank One of the more common complaints among Mac users is that "uninstalling" an application is often not as easy as installing it (particularly when the application's Installer forgot to include a Custom Remove option). You may delete the application but often leave behind a bunch of related files—including preferences files—that should also be deleted. Coming to the rescue here is a shareware utility called Yank, which will search your disk for all files that have the same creator as a selected application and then delete them (if you want, it will ask before moving any item to the Trash). It won't pick up certain files, such as extensions and fonts, that may have been installed as part of an application package but that have a different creator. Otherwise, though, it works just as advertised.

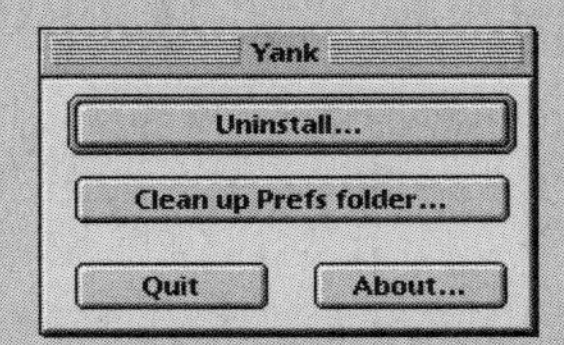

Figure F2-3 *Yank can help you clean up your unwanted preferences files.*

Spring Cleaning Aladdin's Spring Cleaning is a relatively new utility that goes beyond even what Yank can do. It can do the following:

- Delete unneeded preferences files
- Uninstall applications completely
- Identify and reassign "orphan" files (documents for which the application is missing) with Orphan Adopter.
- Trim unnecessary code from fat binary applications
- Repair and update invalid alias files
- Work with entire font families, including PostScript font files

Other Utilities If you simply have a whole bushel of out-of-date and otherwise unneeded Preferences files, you can get rid of them with a shareware utility such as PrefsCleaner or Clean Sweep.

7. Try related solutions

If the previous steps do not solve the problem, the trouble is not with the preferences file. The application itself or its accessory files may be damaged and need to be replaced; damaged control panels or system software damage are also possible.

For related information

SEE:
- **Fix-It #3 on replacing accessory files**
- **Fix-It #5 on replacing system software**
- **Fix-It #14 on damaged files in general**
- **Chapter 2 for more on using Find and Find File**

Fix-It #3: Check for Mislocated or Missing Accessory Files

QUICK SUMMARY ▶

Locate and/or move incorrectly located accessory files as needed. If they cannot be located, reinstall them from your backups.

When to do it:

- If an application specifically requests that you locate a missing accessory file, either via an Open dialog box or via an alert message.
- If selected features (such as menu commands or dialog box options) of an application are dimmed, missing, or do not work. On rare occasions, the program may not even launch.

Why to do it:

Most productivity applications use accessory files (such as dictionary files and translator files) as part of their normal operation. Most of these accessory files are optional, and the program launches just fine without them. A missing accessory file, however, means that you cannot use the feature or option that requires the file. Thus, for example, a program's spell-checking utility does not work without its dictionary file.

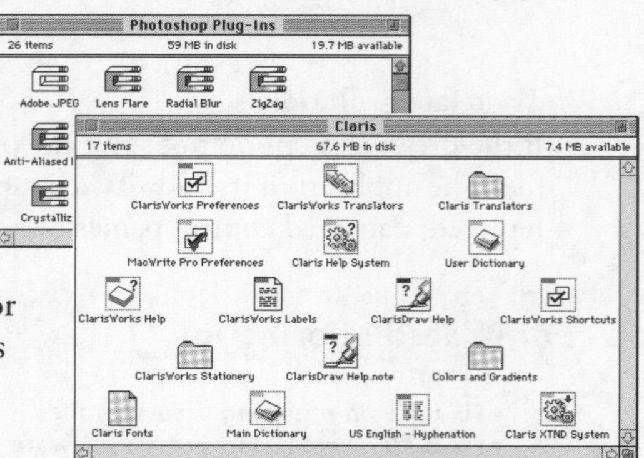

Figure F3-1 *Two examples of accessory file folders: at top, Photoshop's Plug-Ins folder, which is normally located with the Photoshop application; at bottom, the Claris folder, normally located in the System Folder.*

These accessory files often have to reside in specific locations in order to be recognized by the application. Typically, they have to be either in the same folder as the application or in the System Folder. If they are in the System Folder, they are often in a folder of their own, usually named after the parent application or software company (such as Claris). In some cases, these files and/or subfolders are located in the Preferences folder.

Normally, if you use the Installer utility that comes with an application, all of these accessory files are installed in their proper location, including any needed subfolders. The Installer may give you the option to decide which accessory files to install, however, and you may choose to leave out some noncritical files in order to save disk space and/or reduce memory requirements. Similarly, if there is no Installer utility, you get to choose which accessory files to install. Finally, you may (inadvertently?) move or delete previously installed accessory files. In any of these cases, the application's functions that depend on these accessory files will not work.

Technically, preferences files (described in Fix-It #2) are also accessory files. Trouble with preferences files, however, is sufficiently different from other accessory file problems that I discuss it in a separate Fix-It.

What to do:

1. **Determine if you have missing or mislocated accessory files**
   a. **When an Open dialog box appears.** If an application cannot find a needed accessory file needed for a feature you are trying to use, it may present you with an Open dialog box and ask you to locate the file. This could happen, for example, if you select an application's Help command and it cannot locate the needed Help file.
   b. **When an alert message appears.** If you get an alert message that says an accessory file is missing but you do not get an Open dialog box, this also means the application could not locate the needed file.
   c. **When no dialog box or message appears.** Missing or mislocated accessory files can cause problems even though no dialog box or alert message appears; for example, a given menu command or a dialog box option may be dimmed or missing. Similarly, if an application does not list as many file translation formats as the manual says it should, the needed translator files probably are not properly located or were never installed.
2. **Locate missing or mislocated accessory files**
   Try the following suggestions, in the order given, to locate the needed file(s).
   a. **Use the Open dialog box.** If you get an Open dialog box and the mislocated file is on your disk, use the dialog box to find the file, select it, and then click Open or Select. If this solves the problem (and it usually does), the Open dialog box should not reappear the next time you use the feature. If the Open dialog box does reappear, you may have to move the accessory file to a particular location where the program expects to find it (see Step 3).
   b. **Go to the expected location.** Otherwise, to find a missing or mislocated accessory file, go to the file's expected location (typically the System Folder or the application folder) as described in the "Why to Do It" section of this Fix-It.
   c. **Check other mounted disks with System Folders, if any.** If you have two or more mounted hard disks that both contain System Folders, be careful when installing an application onto your non-startup disk. This is because some Installers automatically

place accessory files in the System Folder of the same disk that contains the application, while others place accessory files in the startup disk's System Folder, regardless of where the application is placed. If accessory files wind up in the System Folder of the non-startup disk, they are not accessed by the application when you launch it (since it looks only in the startup disk's System Folder). If you think this has happened, reinstall the application to your startup disk, or locate the needed accessory files in the secondary disk's System Folder and move them to your startup disk's System Folder.

d. **Use the Finder's Find command.** Follow the same basic procedures as outlined in Fix-It #2 for locating preferences files. If you do not know the accessory file's name, take a guess by using the application's name as a search criterion. This procedure should find most (if not all) accessory files that belong to that application. Even if it doesn't, it should at least bring you to the folder where remaining files are located.

e. **Install it from your backups.** If you still cannot find the file you are seeking, it may not be anywhere on your disk(s). You will need to install it from your backups.

TECHNICALLY SPEAKING ▶

BEYOND TYPICAL ACCESSORY FILES

Some programs require special fonts, sounds, or other special system-related files to work correctly. If the application includes an Installer, it usually installs these files properly for you (often placing them in the Extensions folder). Otherwise, you may be instructed to install them yourself. Check the application's manual for details. Remember that omitting these files or deleting them (which you may be tempted to do, if you don't even know how they got on your disk) may present problems when you later use the application.

3. **Relocate or replace accessory files, as needed**

a. **Relocate mislocated accessory files.** If you find mislocated files, move them to their correct location. The manual should tell you where the correct location is, but sometimes this information is not clearly stated. If you have found the apparently missing accessory files and they seem to be in the correct location, but they still do not work, you may need to experiment. For example, if an accessory file does not work when it is in the System Folder, make sure that it is in the correct subfolder within the System Folder. Otherwise, try moving it to the same folder that contains the application.

b. **Install missing or replace damaged accessory files.** If the accessory file is missing altogether, install it from your original disks. If the file is present and in its correct location, but the problem is still not resolved, you may have a damaged accessory file. Once again, the solution is to replace it with a fresh copy from your original disks.

BY THE WAY ▶

LOCATION, LOCATION, LOCATION

I had one unusual variation on this problem of accessory file location—one that also involved a preferences file. An application would not list its plug-in modules in the appropriate menu, even though the modules were properly located (according to the manual). It turned out that the application's preferences file needed to be placed in the same folder as the modules in order for the application to use the modules. When I moved the preferences file to the plug-in modules folder, the problem was solved.

c. **Reinstall the application and all of its accessory files.** If all else fails, the main application file itself may be damaged. At this point, your best bet is to completely replace the application and *all* of its accessory files. Use the Installer utility if one is provided.

Similarly, if you can't find missing accessory files anywhere—even on your backup disks—then you need to reinstall the application.

For related information

SEE:
- **Fix-It #2 on preferences files, especially "Take Note: Cleaning Up Unneeded Preferences Files (and More)"**
- **Fix-It #5 on Installer utilities**
- **Fix-It #14 on damaged files**

Fix-It #4: Check for Problems with Extensions and Control Panels (Startup Extensions)

QUICK SUMMARY

Temporarily disable all startup extensions (system extensions and certain control panels that load into memory at startup). In System 7, you can do this by holding down the Shift key at startup. If the symptoms disappear as a result, you have a startup extension problem. To solve it, first identify the offending startup extension(s), then either rearrange the loading order of the problem startup extension(s), remove the startup extension(s), or replace the startup extension(s).

When to do it:

- When a system crash occurs at startup, particularly while the "Welcome to Macintosh" or Mac OS screen (or your customized startup screen) is visible. Typically, the crash occurs at exactly the same point each time you start up (for example, just after a certain icon appears along the bottom of the screen).
- When a startup extension does not load, even if the startup sequence otherwise proceeds normally.
- When a system error or other disruption occurs while you are using a specific system extension or control panel.
- When a specific command or function in a given application does not work, possibly resulting in a system error. This problem can have numerous causes, a startup extension conflict being one of them—even if the problem appears unrelated to the functioning of the startup extension.
- When a problem occurs in similar situations across several or all applications, such as when you are trying to save a document. Again, this type of symptom has many possible causes besides problems with startup extensions.
- Whenever a message at startup (from system software or other startup utilities) indicates that a likely startup extension conflict occurred during your previous startup.
- Just about any other time something isn't working as expected. Startup extension conflicts are one of the most common sources of Macintosh problems.

 **Why to do it:**

Some (but not all) of the extensions and control panels in your System Folder load into memory during the startup sequence. These files perform any number of functions, usually in the background—placing a clock in your menu bar, for example, or monitoring for virus infections, or enabling file sharing. Apple includes many such extensions and control panels as part of its system software. Some are almost essential to use; others (including many from third parties) are desirable because they greatly enhance the capabilities of a bare-bones system.

On the helpful side, icons for these so-called startup extensions typically appear along the bottom of the Mac OS screen as each one loads into memory. By identifying the icons, you can get a sense of which extensions and control panels load at startup and which do not (though, unfortunately, not all startup extensions display these icons).

Startup extensions, like any software, are subject to the general problems associated with bugs or corrupted files. The two most specific problems associated with these extensions, however, are conflicts among them at startup and extensions that do not load or run.

TECHNICALLY SPEAKING ▶

TERMINOLOGY: STARTUP EXTENSIONS VS. INITS

Even though some startup extensions are control panels, and not all extensions load into memory at startup, Apple generally refers to these programs simply as "extensions." Is this confusing? You bet it is. To try to disentangle this, as described in Chapter 1 (see "Take Note: What's a Startup Extension?"), I typically refer to all of these special programs as "startup extensions." In previous editions of *Sad Macs,* I referred to these files by their more technically correct name, INITs (where "INIT" is the file type of typical system extensions). Except in a few cases (such as in the discussion of the "No INITs" bit in Chapter 8), however, I have dropped that name in this edition.

Startup Extension Conflicts

Most startup extensions remain in memory, working in the background from the moment you start up until you shut down. This presents a unique challenge for these programs: they must function smoothly no matter what other startup extensions or applications you are using at the same time, without preventing the normal functioning of these other programs. Failure to meet these goals is referred to as a *startup extension conflict.*

Sometimes these conflicts are easy to diagnose. At other times, though, they can be *very* subtle. For example, an application may have some quirk that appears only when you are using a new AutoSaver startup extension, with virtual memory turned on, and with the QuicKeys startup extension also installed.

Regardless of the symptoms, the cause of these conflicts is typically a software bug, either in the startup extension or in the software with which it conflicts. Three basic types of startup extension conflicts occur, as described in the following paragraphs.

1. **Conflict with another startup extension**
   Conflicts with another startup extension are often the hardest to diagnose because even when you think you have found the problem extension, another one may be at least partially responsible. This type of conflict is the one most likely to lead to system crashes during the startup sequence.
2. **Conflict with another application**
   The symptoms of a conflict with another application may show up as a malfunction of the startup extension or as a problem with the application (often one that is seemingly unrelated to the startup extension, such as a menu command that does not work).
3. **Conflicts with system software**
   The worst-case scenario is when the startup extension is incompatible with the version of the system software you are using. In this case, problems are likely to occur in a variety of contexts across applications. The startup extension may not work at all, and startup problems are also possible.

Although a startup extension conflict is not the only possible cause of many of these symptoms, it is usually an easy one to either confirm or eliminate. That's why it should be one of the first things you check.

TECHNICALLY SPEAKING ▶

WHERE IN MEMORY ARE THE STARTUP EXTENSIONS?

Applications and documents occupy an area of memory (RAM) referred to as the *application heap*. Startup extensions, in contrast, load into the special area of RAM reserved for the system file and related software, called the *system heap*. To check how the size of the system heap is affected by the presence of startup extensions, select About This Macintosh from the Apple menu when you are in the Finder. A bar representing the amount of memory occupied by the system software will appear in the window shown (as explained more in Chapter 2); as you add to or subtract from the number of extensions that load at startup, the bar becomes larger or smaller accordingly on subsequent restarts.

This has some practical implications. For example, if you do not have enough RAM available to launch a particular application, you can free more memory by disabling a few rarely needed startup extensions and restarting. Similarly, the less RAM in your machine, the fewer extensions you can load at startup before you run out of memory. Startup management utilities (as described in this Fix-It) are especially useful for temporarily disabling selected startup extensions.

SEE: • **Fix-It #6 for more on application and system heaps**
• **Chapter 5 for more on memory and startup problems**

Startup Extensions That Do Not Load or Run

A startup extension may simply not work at all—even without any sign of conflict with other software. Often, this is because the startup extension is never loaded into memory at startup (which it must do in order to work!). A startup extension conflict may still be the underlying cause here, but other causes are possible. For example, remember that you cannot use a newly installed startup extension without first placing it in the System Folder (typically in either the Control Panels or the Extensions folder) and then restarting.

What to do:

Described here are the three main steps to solving startup extension conflicts: (1) Disable startup extensions to determine if you have a startup extension conflict; (2) identify the problem startup extension; and (3) resolve the conflict. The final section of this Fix-It deals with what to do for a startup extension that appears not to load or run at all.

Disable Startup Extensions to Determine If You Have a Startup Extension Conflict

The logic is simple: If the problem goes away when you temporarily disable *all* of your startup extensions, then you know you have a startup extension conflict. There are three different ways to disable your startup extensions: hold down the Shift key during startup, use a startup management utility, or remove all startup extensions from your System Folder.

The quickest way to disable all of your startup extensions is the Shift key method. It is both simple and guaranteed to disable virtually all system extensions and startup extension-type control panels in your System Folder.

Using a startup management utility is more likely to leave some startup extensions enabled (including the utility itself, of course). This method is still fine to use, however, if those remaining startup extensions are not the source of your problem.

TAKE NOTE ▶

A STARTUP EXTENSION IS DISABLED BUT ITS SETTINGS REMAIN

The settings of some control panels (especially those that come with Apple's system software) remain in effect even if you start up with extensions off—for example, this is true for the battery conservation settings of the PowerBook control panel. The reason for this is that although you need the control panel to change the settings, the current settings are stored in the Mac's Parameter RAM (see Fix-It #11) or Power Manager (see Chapter 11), which remain active even when startup extensions are off.

Similarly, the settings for the Energy Saver "control panel" used with PCI-based Macs are retained even if you later disable the extension. If you want to turn these settings off, you should set the settings to "Never" in the control panel, restart, and then disable the separate Energy Saver Extension (or simply leave it enabled with the settings at "Never").

Dragging startup extensions out of the System Folder is recommended only for extreme cases where you have some reason to believe that the Shift key technique or a startup manager did not disable a suspect startup extension (as described in "Technically Speaking: Startup Extension Oddities," later in this Fix-It).

The details of each method are provided below.

Method #1: Disable Startup Extensions by Holding Down the Shift Key at Startup

To disable all of your startup extensions at startup, do the following:

1. **Restart the Macintosh**
2. ***Immediately* after the Mac restarts, press and hold down the Shift key**
   If you do not press it soon enough, it will not work. If it fails to work, restart and try again. The first sign that it worked is that the words "Extensions off" (or "Extensions disabled") appear directly below the words "Welcome to Macintosh" (or "Mac OS") on the startup screen. You can now release the Shift key; your startup extensions have been disabled for this startup. No startup extension icons will appear along the bottom of the startup screen. Everything will return to its previous condition, though, the next time you start up.

   By the way, if you are using a customized startup screen that replaces the "Welcome to Macintosh" screen, the "Extensions off" message will not appear. To be safe here, hold down the Shift key until the startup screen disappears.

The Shift key technique also bypasses any programs found in your Startup Items folder (which is totally separate from your startup extensions!). In fact, if you wait to hold down the Shift key until just after your extensions have loaded, you can bypass Startup Items files without similarly disabling the extensions.

Method #2: Disable Startup Extensions by Using a Startup Management Utility

Startup management utilities are themselves startup extension-type control panels. Startup Manager (from Now Utilities), Conflict Catcher (from Casady & Greene), and Extensions Manager (from Apple) are the three best examples. They all give you a list of the extensions and control panels in your System Folder that are startup extensions. Some may even list other extensions (such as printer drivers, or fonts stored in your Fonts folder).

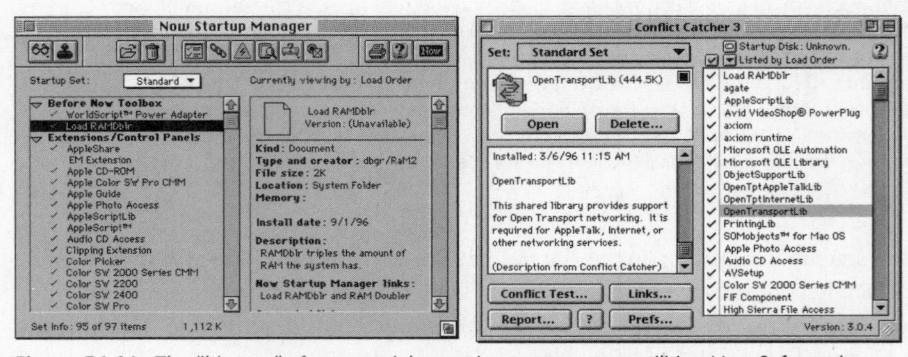

Figure F4-1A *The "big two" of commercial extension management utilities: Now Software's Startup Manager, and Casady & Greene's Conflict Catcher.*

> **BY THE WAY ▶**
>
> **STARTUP MANAGEMENT UTILITIES: CONTROL PANELS AND EXTENSIONS**
>
> Today's startup management utilities work as a combination of an extension and control panel. The main file that you deal with is the control panel—yet Conflict Catcher also uses an extension called Conflict Extension, Extensions Manager uses EM Extension, and Now Startup Manager uses the Now Toolbox. When you enable or disable these startup management utilities, make sure you enable or disable the accompanying extensions as well, or unexpected effects are likely to occur (for instance, control panel options may not work, even though the control panel is installed). The one exception here is that since Now Toolbox is used by other parts of Now Utilities, it can remain even when Now Startup Manager is disabled.

FIX-IT #4

Apple first included a version of Extensions Manager as part of System 7.5. This version has a few less features than a previous freeware generic version (for example, it cannot customize what types of files it lists, and it does not list Apple Menu Items or Fonts), but it does let you start up with all extensions off except those that come with System 7.5 (just select "System 7.5 Only" from the pop-up menu—for System 7.5.5 users, this choice should read "System 7.5.5 Only," and so on). This unique feature can help diagnose conflicts specific to non-Apple extensions. Unlike the commercial startup management utilities, though, Extensions Manager cannot rearrange the loading order of extensions. Although Extensions Manager has been completely redesigned and expanded in System 7.6, it still does not include this "loading order" feature.

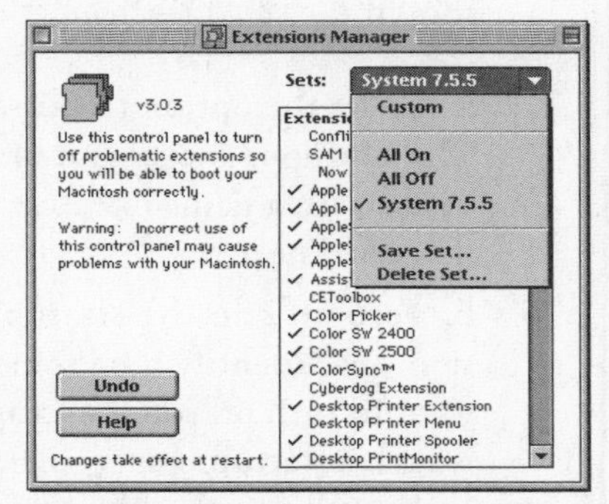

Figure F4-1B *Apple's System 7.5x version of Extensions Manager.*

Conflict Catcher has the most features of any of these utilities. Among its special features is the ability to display actual startup extension names, rather than icons, during startup. Version 3.0.4 or later also has a feature that can scan for damaged startup files (click its Prefs button, go to the Testing window, and click "Scan for Damaged Resources"). Now Software has now released Startup Manager 7.*x*, however, a completely rewritten version (available as a stand-alone product, as well as part of Now Utilities) that is more competitive with Conflict Catcher. It even includes a database of more than a thousand extensions, complete with information the utility can use to help diagnose potential conflicts.

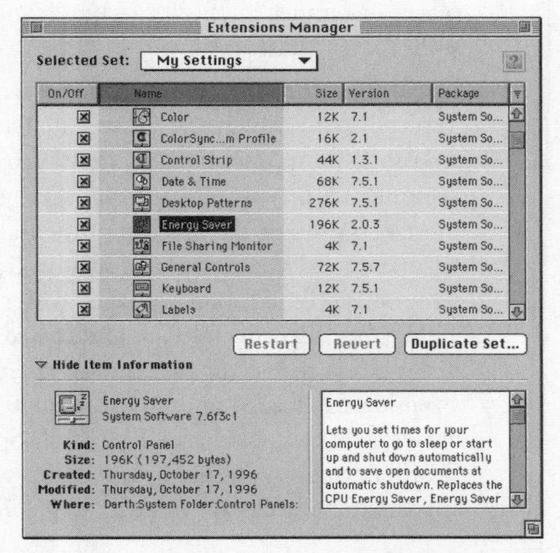

Figure F4-1C *Apple's redesigned Extensions Manager for System 7.6.*

All of these startup management utilities work similarly. Use whichever one you like best, but don't use more than one at the same time. Another word of caution: when shifting from one utility to another, the set of extensions you currently have enabled (and disabled) may change.

Here's how to use them to disable startup extensions:

FIX-IT #4

1. **Hold down a specified "hot key" at startup**
   Each program has a self-defined hot key—usually the space bar. When the management utility loads at startup, it detects the held-down hot key. It then halts the startup sequence and opens the utility's dialog box.

   (Alternatively, some startup utilities have an additional hot key that, if held down at startup, immediately instructs the utility to skip all startup extensions, bypassing the need to access the dialog box.)

2. a. **Select the option to skip loading all startup extensions**
   The startup management utility's dialog box should have a button or menu command with a name like *Skip All* or *All Off*. Select it, or turn off selected extensions as described next.

   b. **Turn off selective startup extensions.** To help identify a problem startup extension (see "Identify the Problem Startup Extension," later in this Fix-It), you will want to turn off some startup extensions but not others. The easiest way to do this is with a startup management utility—in fact, this is the biggest advantage of using such a utility rather than the Shift key method. For example, with Now Startup Manager, double-clicking a name in the list of startup extensions in its dialog box places or removes a check mark in front of the name; only checked startup extensions load at startup.

3. **Decide whether the change is to be temporary or permanent**
   Typically, you can choose between having your changes affect only the current startup (a temporary change) or all subsequent startups (a permanent change). For example, with Now Startup Manager, you do this by clicking either the *Temporary* or the *OK* button at the bottom of the dialog box; the OK button makes the change permanent. When doing this sort of diagnosis, I would preferably make the changes temporary. (Extensions Manager, unfortunately, has no temporary option.)

   In either case, after selecting the desired button, the startup process now resumes normally, except that all disabled startup extensions do not load. If you chose to disable a startup extension that loaded prior to your extension management utility, the Macintosh will probably restart at this point (see "Technically Speaking: Startup Extension Oddities," later in this Fix-It). Actually, with the System 7.5.*x* version of Extensions Manager, restarting appears to be necessary in order to get any changes to take effect immediately.

You are not limited to using these utilities only at startup; you can access them to make similar changes at any other time, as you would any control panel. Changes do not take effect, however, until the next time you start up. Also, the temporary option is not available except at startup (at other times, the Temporary button will not even appear).

Finally, as an alternative to the temporary option, you can create separate "sets" of extensions to choose among at startup, as desired. Check your management utility's documentation for details.

SEE: • **"Take Note: How Startup Management Utilities Do (and Do Not) Disable Startup Extensions" and "Technically Speaking: Startup Extension Oddities," for more on disabling startup extensions**

TAKE NOTE ▶

HOW STARTUP MANAGEMENT UTILITIES DO (AND DO NOT) DISABLE STARTUP EXTENSIONS

What exactly does a startup management utility do to prevent a startup extension from loading? In the past, various utilities accomplished this task by different methods, but now all use the same method: moving the disabled extension to a special folder.

The management utility does this by creating folders with names like "Extensions (disabled)" and "Control Panels (disabled)" and placing these folders in your System Folder. Any startup extensions that you choose to disable are then placed in these folders by the management utility. Removed from their normal location, these extensions and control panels do not load at the next startup.

A minor disadvantage of this approach is that when you select Control Panels from the Apple menu, disabled control panels do not appear (since they are now in a different folder). At first, you may think they have vanished, but they will return to the Control Panels folder automatically after you use the management utility to turn them back on. You can also re-enable these startup extensions manually, by simply dragging them back to their previous folder location (except that some startup management utilities may move them back to the disabled folder the next time you restart, continuing to do so until you re-enable them in the startup management utility listing).

Also note that there are differences between what may get disabled by using your startup management utility to skip all extensions versus holding down the Shift key at startup. For example, Apple's Extensions Manager's "All Off" setting switches off Chooser extensions, while holding the Shift key down at startup does not. Similarly, extension files of the type "thng" (such as for System AV) get disabled if you hold down the Shift key at startup, but may not be disabled by startup management utilities.

There are also differences among startup management utilities in terms of which files get listed and which ones do not. These differences can become important if a given file is the source of a conflict that you are trying to identify by disabling extensions. For example, I once had a case where a file (the now-defunct Multimedia Tuner) that was not listed by (the then-current version of) Now Startup Manager was the source of a conflict. This obviously made it impossible for me to use the Now Utilities program to help identify the conflict.

Finally, both Conflict Catcher and Now Startup Manager have an option to *link* extensions so that, for example, if one extension is turned on, the other is automatically turned on also (see "By the Way: Create Links with Startup Management Utilities," later in this Fix-It). This feature is designed to prevent conflicts and related problems that would otherwise occur. If you disable a linked extension but do not disable the link itself, however, it may get re-enabled automatically the next time you restart (and vice versa). Since these programs come with a built-in set of links, check for this possible cause if you are having a problem getting a change in settings to "take."

TECHNICALLY SPEAKING

STARTUP EXTENSION ODDITIES

Startup Extensions That Refuse to Be Disabled ... and Other Oddities There are a couple of occasions when the Shift key technique and/or startup management utilities will be unable to disable an extension at startup. The reason usually has to do with a growing list of odd types of files lurking in your System Folder.

A general note: Many of these odd-type extensions do not load into memory at startup. They only load when actually needed. Still, startup management utilities often include them (typically in a list that precedes and/or follows the main list of system extensions and control panels).

- **Extensions that load prior to the startup management utility** Some startup managers cannot turn off any startup extensions that may load prior to the manager itself (for example, an anti-virus utility) especially if you are accessing the manager during startup. Some startup managers may not even show such startup extensions in their list. To get around this problem, you may have to rename the early-loading startup extension so that it loads later in the sequence, though this is not always advised (see "Take Note: The Loading Order of Startup Extensions, or What's in a Name?" later in this Fix-It). Current versions of Conflict Catcher and Startup Manager, however, not only list startup extensions that load before them, but allow you to turn these extensions off, even during the startup sequence (by setting the extension to be disabled and then issuing a restart command). Extensions Manager has a similar feature that is accessed by holding down the Command key when you close its window during a startup access.

  A few special files load prior to all other extensions and control panels, no matter what they are named, including the System Enablers/Updates (such as System 7.5 Update). These files (often with a file type "gbly") are typically stored at the root level of your System Folder and are not disabled by any startup management technique (including holding down the Shift key). This is just as well, since (if they are present) they are often essential for a successful startup and should never be disabled.
- **Background-only applications ("appe" files)** There is a category of extensions that has a file type of "appe." These are sometimes referred to as background-only applications. They are sort of a hybrid of extensions and ordinary applications. One example of this is a shareware utility called Folder Watcher; there are many others. Email programs (such as Claris Emailer) often include an appe component. These special extensions do not really launch until the end of the startup sequence, regardless of where their icon may appear during the startup process. In some cases, they only launch when a related other application is in use. Again, some startup managers may not even list these extensions and thus you would not be able to disable them selectively. Holding down the Shift key, however, should disable them.

  By the way, how do you know if one of these background applications is running or not at any given moment? It's hard to tell because their memory allocation is often lumped in with the System Software memory line in the About This Macintosh window (see Fix-It #6). Still, if you have RAM Doubler 2 installed, go to its control panel and click the triangle to see the breakdown of the System Software allocation. You will see background applications listed.

  Also note: If multiple background-only applications are running at the same time, odd symptoms may appear (such as messages saying that you cannot open a certain application because you are not running System 7, even though you are). This error was supposedly fixed in System 7.5.5.
- **Network Extension and "fext" files** Network Extension (the startup extension, not the control panel) is not listed in the menu of some startup management utilities (though Conflict Catcher does include it in the special grouping at the bottom of its list), and for a very good reason: It is not really a startup extension, even though it looks for

Continues on next page

STARTUP EXTENSION ODDITIES *(Continued from previous page)*

all the world like it is. Its file type is "fext" (not "INIT"), and its "No INITs" Finder flag is checked (which means it does not load at startup and thus is not listed in most startup management utilities' lists).

The extension is actually needed for the File Sharing Monitor, Sharing Setup, and Users and Groups control panels to work correctly; if you get Balloon Help for that extension, you will be informed of this fact. Similarly, if you try to open one of those control panels when the Network Extension is not available, you will get a message that you need this extension. It appears to act as a sort of accessory extension that is only active when the primary extension (one of the previously mentioned control panels) is loaded at startup.

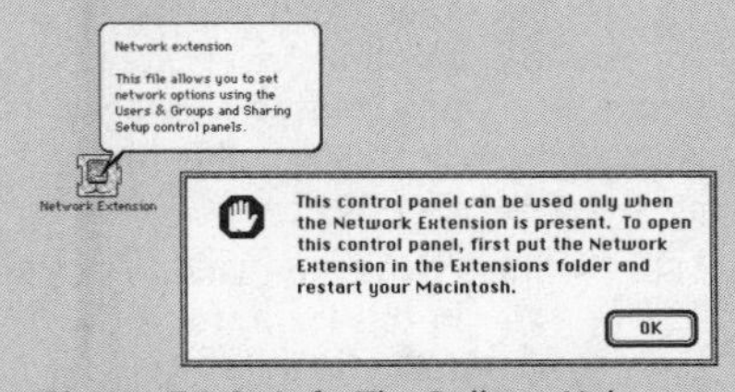

Figure F4-2 *Left: The Balloon Help message for the Network extension. Right: The message that appears if you open File Sharing Monitor without the Network Extension in the Extensions folder.*

- **Shared Library files** Apple's Shared Library Manager extension defies logic by having a file type of "INIT," but still having its "No INITs" flag checked.

  Meanwhile, most shared library files (such as the Open Transport Library files) have a file type of "shlb" or "libr." Although they are stored in the Extensions folder, they are not typical extensions. Conflict Catcher, for example, if it lists them at all, lists them in the group of files that load before the typical startup extensions. Actually, these files typically do not load into memory at startup; they only load when needed by an application that uses the shared library.

  Still, the presence of these files can be critical for other files to work. For example, without the Open Transport shared library files present, you will be unable to use the TCP/IP or AppleTalk control panels.
- **Wild things ("thng" files)** A similar bunch of files of the type "thng" (such as System AV or QuickTime Musical Instruments) are also in this general early-loading category. These files generally work in conjunction with other extensions (such as QuickTime in the case of the Instruments file).
- **Applications in the System Folder** There are some files (such as Print Monitor or Energy Saver 2.*x*) that are stored in the Extensions and Control Panels folders but that are really applications (of the type "APPL").
- **Chooser extensions** As described in Chapter 1, chooser extensions usually do not have a startup extension code and do not load at startup. But some, such as AppleShare (with a file type of "rdev"), break this rule and act as a typical startup extension.
- **RAM Doubler** RAM Doubler actually consists of two extensions. The first one to load, called Load RAMDblr, is invisible and located at the root level of the System Folder. The other extension, RAM Doubler, is visible and located in the Extensions folder. The Load RAMDblr extension (which is what causes the "RAM Doubler is installed" message in the "Welcome to Macintosh" box) loads prior to virtually all other extensions, including RAM Doubler itself. Apparently, it is the critical file needed to actually install RAM Doubler. For example, if you use a utility like Extensions Manager to disable the visible RAM Doubler extension at startup, RAM Doubler will still be active for that startup because the Load RAMDblr file has already loaded (thus overriding your disabling attempt). You will have to restart again to really disable RAM Doubler.

Despite all these exceptions, problems with these unusual-loading extensions are rare. Be an optimist here, and you will usually be rewarded.

Continues on next page ▶

TECHNICALLY SPEAKING

STARTUP EXTENSION ODDITIES *(Continued from previous page)*

One final note: Don't depend on Balloon Help for guidance as to what these files do. For example, it's semi-clueless about shared libraries—mistakenly telling you, among other things, that Open Transport Library is a document designed to be opened by the Shared Library Manager application (which is actually an extension and cannot open itself or anything else from the Finder).

SEE:
- **"Take Note: The Loading Order of Startup Extensions, or What's in a Name?" later in this Fix-It, for more on dealing with startup extensions that load before a startup manager**
- **Chapter 8 for more on file types and finder flags**

Method #3: Disable Startup Extensions by Removing Startup Extensions from Your System Folder

Removing startup extensions from your System Folder is the least convenient way to disable your startup extensions, but it is the only method guaranteed to work under all situations. Here's what to do:

1. **Create a new folder on your desktop (anywhere but in the System Folder)**
   Name it "Extensions Folder," or whatever else you like.
2. **Drag all of the startup extensions from your System Folder and place them in this newly created folder**
   Of course, you may not know which of the files in your System Folder are startup extensions. To determine this, go to the Extensions folder and Control Panels folder, select List view, and check for files whose kind is "control panel" or "system extension." Also remember to check at the main level of the System Folder for these files.

   A few startup extensions list their kind simply as "document," and so they cannot be identified by the technique just described. If you are in doubt, then, you should also remove unfamiliar files in your System Folder that are identified only as "document" if they are in the Control Panels or Extensions folder or at the root level of the System Folder.

   This will inevitably catch files that are not startup extensions, but there is little you can do about that with this method.
3. **Restart your Macintosh**
   The Macintosh will now boot without any startup extensions loading. If your symptoms disappear, you have a startup extension conflict.

BY THE WAY ▶

DON'T DEPEND ON A CONTROL PANEL'S ON/OFF BUTTONS

Some control panels have on and off buttons. In some cases, selecting the off button instructs a startup extension-type control panel not to load at the next startup, but not always. Often, selecting a control panel's off button simply stops the immediate background functioning of the control panel—it still remains in memory, available to be turned back on (without having to restart) if desired. It also may continue to load into memory (although in the off position) at subsequent startups. Even though it is "off," since it loads into memory, it can still be the cause of a startup extension conflict.

Identify the Problem Startup Extension

If your problem disappears as a result of turning off all your startup extensions, you have a startup extension conflict. The next step is to determine *which* startup extension (or combination of startup extensions) is the source of the problem. To do this you will have to selectively enable and disable various startup extensions. Of the three methods for disabling startup extensions described in the previous section, a startup management utility is clearly the best here, since it offers the most convenience and flexibility. Dragging startup extensions in and out of your System Folder from the Finder also works, but it is much more time-consuming. The Shift key technique is useless here; you cannot selectively disable startup extensions with it.

Bearing this in mind, try the following suggestions, in the order indicated, as appropriate.

Check Recently Added Startup Extensions

If you added a startup extension to your startup disk just prior to the appearance of a problem, this extension should be a prime suspect. To check it out, disable just that startup extension. To do this with a startup management utility, access the list of startup extensions from the manager's control panel window, and enable all the ones that you normally use. Now disable the suspect extension and restart. If the problem disappears, you have identified the likely culprit (though the problem may actually involve a conflict with another startup extension).

Check Suspicious Startup Extensions

If the symptoms suggest a particular startup extension or group of startup extensions as the cause of the conflict, disable these startup extensions and restart. For example, if a problem appears across a variety of applications whenever you try to save documents, and you use an autosave control panel, this control panel is a likely source of the problem. Start by disabling it, and see if the problem goes away.

Check for Known Incompatibilities and Bugs

Because you are probably not the first person to experience your particular startup extension conflict, remember that others may be able to identify and solve the problem for you. Check the documentation of all of your startup extensions for any advice.

If you discover a possible culprit, disable it to see if the problem goes away; check with the software vendor for specific help if needed.

Similarly, if you are having a problem only with a particular application and you suspect it may be caused by a startup extension conflict, contact the technical support staff for that application. They may be able to identify the problem and offer a solution. When there is a conflict between a startup extension and an application, however, it can be hard to determine which one is the cause, and so occasionally you may get a run-around. For example, if startup extension A conflicts with Application X, the developer of A may blame the developer of X for the glitch, and vice versa. Unfortunately, while each one waits for the other to correct the problem, you are left without a solution.

Disable and Re-Enable Individual Startup Extensions

If none of the preceding methods succeed, you should systematically disable and re-enable all your startup extensions. This is a time-honored method for identifying problem startup extensions, but it is also a potentially long and tedious one, and it requires your active involvement throughout the process. You can't just walk away for an hour and come back after the procedure is over; you must constantly be present to watch what happens and make changes accordingly. If you use dozens of startup extensions, as I do, this procedure can take hours.

Unless you only have a few extensions (six or less) or are a masochist, don't try to isolate an extension conflict without some sort of startup management utility. They make the testing process much easier and somewhat faster than dragging files in and out of the System Folder and then restarting. Even with just a few extensions, these managers help because they typically identify which extensions and control panels really load at startup and which do not, saving you the effort of worrying about files that cannot possibly be the cause of your problem.

1. **Disable all startup extensions**

   Essentially, start by repeating what you did in the previous section ("Disable Startup Extensions to Determine If You Have a Startup Extension Conflict"). Do this either by restarting after dragging all startup extensions out of your System Folder or by using a startup management utility; do *not* use the Shift key technique here (there is no way for selective re-enabling with this method). As you have presumably already determined that you have a startup extension conflict, your problem should now no longer appear.

   If you are using a startup management utility, you may need to disable any extensions that normally load before the utility itself (see "Technically Speaking: Startup Extension Oddities" for details). This will be necessary only if it turns out that one of them is the actual culprit. If you cannot get the startup manager to disable them, drag those particular startup extensions out of the System Folder and test them separately.

   By the way, you could do this whole process in reverse: Start with all startup extensions enabled and then disable them one by one. If your symptom is a system crash that keeps recurring until you finally remove the guilty startup extension, however, this can be a more frustrating alternative.

2a. Re-enable startup extensions individually, restarting each time

If you are using a startup management utility. Access its control panel, either prior to restarting or during the startup process (as described in "Disable Startup Extensions to Determine If You Have a Startup Extension Conflict"), and use it to turn one startup extension back on; start with any extension you want. See if your problem has returned.

If you are not using a startup management utility. Start by returning one startup extension to the System Folder—in System 7, you can do this by dragging the startup extension to the System Folder icon; the Macintosh will relocate it to the Extensions or Control Panels folder for you—and then restart the Macintosh. See if your problem has returned.

In either case, continue to re-enable startup extensions one at a time, restarting each time, until the problem reappears. Hopefully, you had no other plans for the day. The order in which you re-enable startup extensions doesn't matter—when the problem does reappear, you know that the most recently returned startup extension is the source of the conflict.

2b. An alternative shortcut if you have a large number of startup extensions

Note: Adjust this procedure according to the specifics of whether you use a startup management utility, as outlined in 2a.

Divide all of your startup extensions into two groups, and then re-enable the first half. If the problem reappears, you know that the problem startup extension is in this first group. If it does not, the problem is presumably in the second group. Re-enable the second half to confirm this. Once you have isolated the half that contains the problem startup extension, divide that group into two smaller groups, then re-enable only the first of those two. Continue this technique until you have isolated the problem startup extension by the process of elimination.

3. Is it the startup management utility itself?

If you reach the end of the line and no problem startup extension has been identified, you may have a conflict with your startup management utility itself—after all, these utilities are themselves startup extensions. Especially suspect this if the problem goes away if you disable all startup extensions with the Shift key technique, but not with your startup management utility.

Otherwise, if the manager has a startup hot key that can be used to disable itself, you could conveniently use this to check for a conflict caused by the management utility.

4. Confirm that you have identified the problem startup extension

Once you have identified the suspected problem startup extension, re-enable all startup extensions except the problem one, then restart. If the problem no longer occurs, the lone disabled startup extension is confirmed as the source of the trouble.

As an extra check, disable all startup extensions except the problem startup extension. If the trouble reappears, this is added confirmation that the lone enabled startup extension is to blame.

If these tests do not confirm the identity of the problem startup extension, you probably have one of the special cases described in the following sections.

TAKE NOTE ▶

CONFLICT IDENTIFICATION MADE SIMPLE

If you don't want to do all the work involved in checking for extension conflicts, there's good news: you may not have to. Conflict Catcher (as its name implies) and Now Startup Manager both provide special help for identifying conflicts, essentially automating the procedure for disabling and re-enabling startup extensions. You simply click a button to start the process, and the utility takes over, telling you what to do and what it all means. They can even diagnose conflicts involving two or more startup extensions. These automated methods, however, may have problems properly testing codependent startup extensions; see "Is It a Codependent Startup Extension Problem (or Other Startup Extension Conflict)?" later in this Fix-It.

These utilities also have a separate feature for identifying a startup extension that causes a crash at startup. With Startup Manager, it is called "Disable crashing extensions," and it is available from the Preferences dialog box. If this option is active and a startup extension causes a system crash at startup, that extension is automatically disabled on the next restart. Even more helpful, Startup Manager displays an alert box identifying the name of the disabled startup extension. From this alert box you can also click an Isolate button that takes you directly into Startup Manager's conflict isolation feature (which lets you check if the disabled startup extension was truly to blame for the crash).

Conflict Catcher's similar preferences option is called "Report Startup Crashes."

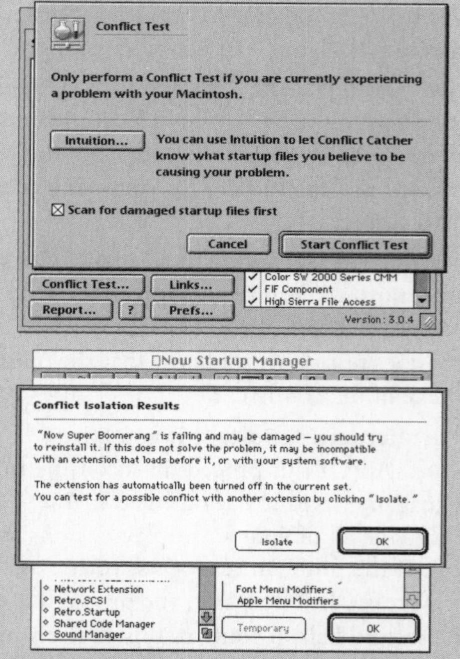

Figure F4-3 *Top: requesting a conflict test from Conflict Catcher. Bottom: the results of a conflict test with Startup Manager.*

Preferences — Advanced
☒ Display startup icons
☒ Show invisible extensions
☒ Prevent screen erasures
☒ Wrap icons
☒ Disable crashing extensions

Figure F4-4 *Now Startup Manager's "Disable crashing extension" option (seen at the bottom of the partial view here).*

Special Case: Conflict Between Two Startup Extensions

The technique of disabling and re-enabling individual startup extensions may not succeed if a problem appears only when two startup extensions are active at the same time. This can be especially problematic if you are using the shortcut grouping method and you have placed two conflicting startup extensions in separate groups. In this case, you can still hope to identify one of the likely problem startup extensions. If so, you can then repeat the basic technique, except leaving the identified startup extension always

enabled while you begin re-enabling others. When the problem reappears, you have identified the second half of the pair causing the conflict.

Helpful hint: Make sure you don't install two startup extensions that do essentially the same thing. For example, don't use two different screen savers, or two different startup extensions that create hierarchical menus off the Apple menu. Doing so will inevitably lead to conflicts. (And, of course, do not try to use two different startup management utilities at the same time!)

FIX-IT #4

SEE ALSO: • "Take Note: Conflict Identification Made Simple," for using your startup management utility to check automatically for this problem

Special Case: Conflict Occurs Only When Using a Startup Extension

Sometimes a conflict may be apparent only when you actually access a startup extension's features (for example, by selecting a pop-up menu that it creates). If so, disabling the startup extension will prevent you from knowing if the problem has gone away. In this case, restart the Macintosh with *only* the identified problem startup extension(s) enabled; ideally, you should do this by using a startup management utility. If the problem does not now occur, it typically is being caused by an interaction between that startup extension and another one. Start re-enabling startup extensions, as just described, until the problem reappears. At this point, you have identified the additional conflicting startup extension.

On the other hand, if the problem does recur with only the one startup extension enabled, treat this situation as a startup extension that will not load or run. Refer to the section on this topic, later in this Fix-It.

Special Case: If a Startup Extension Causes a System Crash at Startup

The procedures just described apply generally to all startup extension conflict situations, including where a startup extension causes a system crash at startup. Special problems can occur in this case, however. because the startup conflict prevents the Macintosh from successfully reaching the desktop. For example, without access to the desktop, you cannot drag items into or out of the System Folder.

There is one bit of good news in all this: startup extensions that cause problems at startup are often the easiest ones to isolate. Because the crash usually occurs precisely when the problem startup extension is loading into memory, the timing of the crash indicates which extension is to blame. Here's what to do:

1. **Bypass the system crash at startup**

   a. **If you are using a startup management utility.** When the system crash occurs, restart the Macintosh. Then invoke the startup management utility at startup (as described in previous sections of this Fix-It), using it to disable all startup extensions. Presumably, you can do this before the system crash has a chance to recur.

   Conflict Catcher has a special feature that can help determine if the utility itself is the source of a problem at startup. To do this, click its Prefs button, then click Disable Startup Features and restart. If Conflict Catcher was the cause of a problem at startup time, the trouble should now go away.

b. **If you are not using a startup management utility.** Either hold down the Shift key to bypass all startup extensions at startup, or start up from an alternate disk that has only a minimal set of extensions and is thus not likely to contain the problem startup extension.

2. **Identify the problem startup extension**

   a. **Locate and disable the startup extension *after* the last one whose icon appeared during startup.** The last icon to appear before the system crash typically indicates the last startup extension to have loaded successfully (if you don't recall what icon that was, you will have to restart again with extensions enabled so as to get the system crash to recur). You can usually identify the name of this startup extension because the icon is similar to or identical to the icon of the system extension or control panel file as it appears on the desktop. If you do not recognize the icon, go to the System Folder and examine the icons of all startup extensions until you find the one that matches the icon that last appeared on the startup screen.

   Of course, this is *not* the likely problem startup extension—the next startup extension scheduled to load is. If you use a startup management utility, you can find out the name of this extension or control panel by checking the list of names in the utility's dialog box. Since startup extensions are listed there in the order that they load, the problem startup extension is the one listed immediately below the name you just identified.

   If you don't use a startup manager, remember that startup extensions load in alphabetical order (first extensions, then control panels). Examine the names of your startup extensions to determine which one was scheduled to load when the system crash occurred.

   SEE: • **"Take Note: The Loading Order of Startup Extensions, or What's in a Name?" later in this Fix-It, for additional details**

   b. **When the startup icon method does not apply.** A potential pitfall with using startup icons to identify the source of a crash is that not all startup extensions display an icon while loading. Some have no startup icon to display, and for others, the icon's display may have been turned off (usually from an optional setting in the startup extension's control panel window). In these cases, referring to startup icons may turn out to be of limited value. If so, you will have to determine the likely cause of trouble either from the Finder's alphabetical listing of extensions and control panels (view By Name) or, if appropriate, from the loading order as listed in your startup management utility. Again, disable the likely culprit, typically by dragging it out of the System Folder.

   c. **Use special features of startup management utilities, if available.** Some startup management utilities have special options for dealing with extensions that cause system crashes at startup. For example, Now Startup Manager has an option called "Disable/Isolate crashing extensions" that disables and identifies the name of the startup extension that was loading at the time of the crash (see "By the Way: Conflict Identification Made Simple," earlier in this Fix-It, for more details).

BY THE WAY ▶

THE MACINTOSH HELPS OUT

If a system error occurs while startup extensions are loading during startup, the Macintosh may display an error message with the following advice: "To temporarily turn off extensions, restart and hold down the Shift key." This is the Mac's way of telling you that you have a startup extension conflict.

3. **Confirm that you have identified the problem startup extension**
   Once you have identified and disabled the suspected problem startup extension, re-enable all startup extensions except the problem one, then restart. If the crash no longer occurs, the lone disabled startup extension is confirmed as the culprit.

   The problem, however, may actually involve a conflict between this startup extension and another one that loaded before it. To test for this, disable all startup extensions that load before the known culprit, then re-enable it and restart. If all goes well now, it means that the crash involves at least two startup extensions. Begin re-enabling the early-loading startup extensions one by one, restarting each time until the crash happens again. The startup extension that triggers the return of the crash is your second culprit.
4. **Expand the search to other startup extensions, if needed**
   If the suspected problem startup extension turned out not to be the true culprit, successively disable and re-enable other startup extensions that loaded anywhere near when the crash occurred, especially the last startup extension that seemed to load successfully. If that still fails to isolate the cause of the crash, follow the general guidelines given previously to disable all startup extensions ("Disable and Re-Enable Individual Startup Extensions") and successively re-enable them until the problem recurs.

Resolve the Conflict

Once you identify the problem startup extension, the simplest solution is to stop using it. Alternatively, if the startup extension causes problems only with one application, you might find it preferable to stop using that application. The ideal solution, though, is to find a way to continue to use all of your startup extensions and applications, but minus the problems. This may be possible; here's how to give it your best shot.

Rearrange the Loading Order of Startup Extensions

Sometimes a startup extension causes a problem only if it loads before (or after) a certain other startup extension. Rearranging the order in which the startup extensions load can thus eliminate the problem. Typically, to test this out, move a problem startup extension toward the beginning or end of the loading order, then restart to see if the problem goes away.

FIX-IT #4

TAKE NOTE ▶

THE LOADING ORDER OF STARTUP EXTENSIONS, OR, WHAT'S IN A NAME?

Startup extensions load in alphabetical order according to name—a startup extension named AutoSaver, for example, loads before one named VirusKiller. All startup extensions in the Extensions folder load first, though, followed by startup extensions in the Control Panels folder, and finally any startup extensions in the top level of the System Folder. Thus a system extension named VirusKiller, located in the Extensions folder, loads before a control panel called AutoSaver, located in the Control Panels folder.

Remember, loading order is determined by folder location, not by the type of startup extension. Thus a system extension placed in the Control Panels folder loads alphabetically with the other control panels, not with the other system extensions in the Extensions folder.

For some startup extensions, it is critical (from a functional point of view) that they load early in the loading process. For example, you want an anti-virus startup extension to load first so that it can detect possible viruses in other startup extensions. Similarly, you want a startup management utility to load first (or just after an anti-virus startup extension) so that it can manage all the remaining startup extensions. To accomplish this, creators of these startup extensions give them special names designed to move them to the top of the loading order. A typical trick is to place a blank space in front of the name of the startup extension (since the Macintosh considers a blank space to be alphabetically before the letter "A").

Adding a blank space to the start of a startup extension's name can be tricky, though, since the Finder does not ordinarily let you type a blank space as a first character. To circumvent this prohibition, select the startup extension's name, type any letter as the first character, follow it with a blank space, and then delete the initial letter.

A few startup extensions (such as startup management and anti-virus utilities) always seem to load near the start of the list, even though they may not appear to have a special character in front of their name. Most often, they do have a special character—typically, a control character. For example, at least some versions of SAM use Control-A, which loads even before a blank space.

To place a control character in front of any startup extension's name, go to the Key Caps desk accessory and type Control-A (or Control-B, or whatever). Copy the character symbol that appears. Now go to the startup extension file in the Finder, select its name, and place the text cursor in front of the first character. Finally, select Paste. To cut a control character from a name, you must also select a character adjacent to the control character.

Other startup extensions (Adobe Type Manager is one well-known example) work best when they are loaded last (or late) in the loading process. To ensure that this happens, Adobe adds a tilde (~) to the name of its extension, which the Macintosh arranges after the letter "Z."

In general, unless you use a startup management utility to maintain the loading order, you should not change the name of startup extensions that begin with these special characters, because you do not want to alter their intended loading order. Finally, note that some special startup extensions load at the start of the startup sequence, regardless of their name. Typically, you cannot use a startup management utility to rearrange the loading order of these special extensions, even if the utility lists their name.

SEE: • "Technically Speaking: Startup Extension Oddities," earlier in this Fix-It

The manual that comes with a startup extension may offer advice about where it should load and what other common startup extensions should precede it or come after it (be careful not to reverse the order of codependent startup extensions, as described in "If the Startup Extension Does Not Load or Run," later in this Fix-It). Otherwise, you have to experiment. Of course, there is no guarantee that any amount of reordering will help, so give up if a few reshuffles don't seem to do anything.

To rearrange the loading order of startup extensions, try one or more of the following suggestions, as appropriate:

- **Use a startup management utility**
  Using a startup management utility is the preferred method of rearranging startup extensions. From the utility's dialog box that lists all of these extensions and control panels, you can usually reorder the names by dragging them to a new location in the list. The startup extensions will then load in this new order, regardless of the names and whether they are in the Extensions or Control Panels folder.

  Apple's Extension Manager does not include this option; this omission is a major drawback for it as compared to other competing utilities.

- **Rename the startup extension**
  If you don't use a startup manager, you must rename a startup extension to change its position in the alphabetical hierarchy. For example, if you want a startup extension to load late, go to the Finder, select the startup extension's icon, and add a tilde in front of its name. To get it to load early, add a blank space or a control character. Of course, simply putting an extra "A" or "Z" in front of the name often works just as well, though it is less aesthetically pleasing.

  SEE: • **"Take Note: The Loading Order of Startup Extensions, or, What's in a Name?" earlier in this Fix-It, for details on how to add a blank space or control character to a name**

  One word of caution: Some startup extensions work only with their original name. Such extensions or control panels often have their name "locked" so that you cannot change it; ideally, their manuals should alert you to this as well. Clearly, you should leave these names alone. If you are determined to change them, however, you can unlock these names (as explained in the section on Finder Flags in Chapter 8).

- **Use an alias**
  Using an alias is especially useful if you want a startup extension located in the Control Panels folder to load before one in the Extensions folder. Simply renaming the startup extension, no matter what name you choose, would not change the rule that all items in the Extensions folder load before any items in the Control Panels folder. Of course, you could get the control panel to load earlier by moving it to the Extensions folder, but then it would no longer appear in the Control Panels window.

  To solve this dilemma, create an alias for the control panel. Place the control panel itself in the Extensions folder, and the alias in the Control Panels folder. Now it loads from the Extensions folder, but the alias shows up in the Control Panels display.

  Of course, a startup management utility that permits reordering of the loading order is more convenient than this alias technique. Still, the alias technique may be useful for establishing the loading order of the startup management utility itself, or for a control panel that you want to load prior to the startup management utility (such as an anti-virus utility). In these cases, this alias technique is useful even if you don't have a startup extension conflict that you are trying to resolve.

BY THE WAY ▶

CREATE LINKS WITH STARTUP MANAGEMENT UTILITIES

Now Startup Manager and Conflict Catcher both have a feature that can create special links among any group of startup extensions. These links can prevent certain startup extension conflicts involving two or more startup extensions. For example, you can create a link to guarantee that one startup extension will always load later than another one, that both startup extensions get turned on or off in unison, or that certain incompatible pairs of startup extensions cannot both be on at the same time. Once you identify one of these problems as the cause of your symptoms, these links provide a permanent solution.

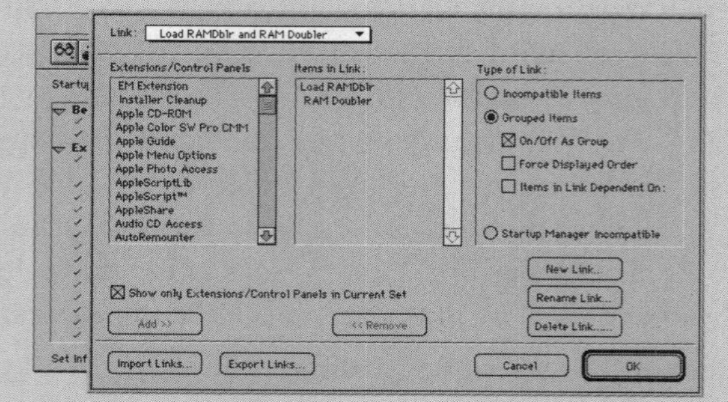

Figure F4-5 *The Links list in Now Startup Manager (Conflict Catcher has a similar feature).*

In most cases, startup management utilities are designed to solve the problem automatically as part of their installation process. For example, the Extensions Manager control panel uses a companion EM Extension to load from the Extensions folder.

SEE: • **"Take Note: The Loading Order of Startup Extensions, or, What's in a Name?" earlier in this Fix-It, for more details**

Upgrade the Problem Startup Extension or Other Software

Many of these startup extension problems are due to bugs in either the extension itself or the application with which it conflicts. If none of the steps offered so far has succeeded, check if there is a newer, nonconflicting version of the startup extension available. If this is the case, get the upgrade and see if it resolves your problem. If a newer version of the application is available, upgrading to it may offer another route to a solution.

If the startup extension conflict appears to be with the system software, upgrading to a newer version of the system software (or downgrading back to the previous version, if the problem began as a result of an upgrade) can also eliminate the conflict.

SEE: • **Fix-It #5 for checking on system software incompatibilities and upgrading system software**

Replace Potentially Damaged Files

Conflicts due to damaged files can obviously be resolved by replacing the files with undamaged copies, as described below.

- **Replace a control panel's preferences file**
  Some control panels have their own preferences files, located in the Preferences Folder. These files may get corrupted and need replacement. If you think this may be your problem, restart with the suspected control panel temporarily disabled, then

delete the potentially corrupted preferences file. The control panel will make a new file automatically, as needed.

- **Replace the startup extension or application or system software**
  Delete the problem startup extension (as described in the next section) and replace it with a fresh copy from your backups. Alternatively, if the problem only occurs when using a specific application, replace the application software to see if that helps. Some startup extension conflicts may be traced to corrupted System and/or Finder files; consider replacing them if all else has failed.

Conflict Catcher has a feature that scans your startup files (including the System File itself!) to test for damaged resources that may cause these startup problems. To access it, select Testing Preferences after opening the utility and click the "Scan for Damaged Resources" button.

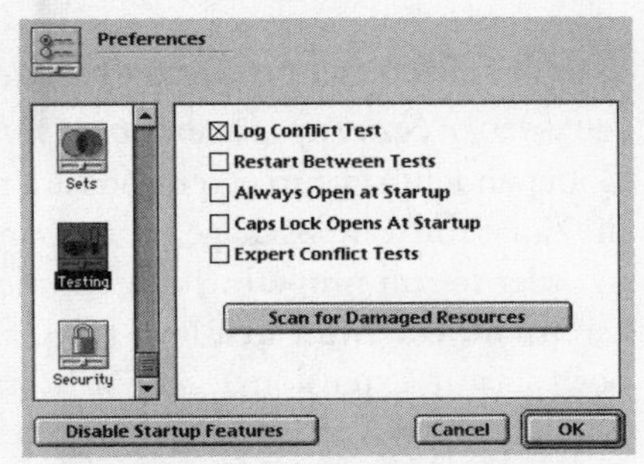

Figure F4-6 *Conflict Catcher's option to "Scan for Damaged Resources." If corruption of a startup extension is causing a startup problem, this may locate the problem file.*

FIX-IT #4

Check for Memory-Related Problems

Some problems involving startup extensions are not directly caused by the extension. For example, if you are using many startup extensions, insufficient memory may be the cause. You might test for this by turning off virtual memory (accessed via the Memory control panel) and file sharing (accessed via the Sharing Setup control panel) if they are on. Also try turning off 32-bit addressing, if you have that option, and see if that cures your problem. If not, refer to Fix-It #6, where memory problems are covered in more detail.

There may also be occasions when you need to increase the memory allocation of certain extensions. This, too, is covered in Fix-It #6.

Delete the Problem Startup Extension

If nothing you've tried so far has helped, you probably will have to stop using the startup extension altogether. As previously discussed, if your problem is caused by a conflict between two different startup extensions, removing one of the startup extensions is likely to resolve the problem. If not, remove them both.

Most often, if you decide to permanently stop using a startup extension, you'll want to place it in the Trash and delete it from your disk. If the startup extension is currently in use (that is, if it was loaded into memory at startup), however, this may be tricky. If you try to empty the Trash when an active startup extension is in it, an alert message may say that the startup extension cannot be deleted because it is in use.

Even if you can trash the startup extension, be careful, since it is probably still present in memory and functioning. If the extension subsequently tries to access data from the now deleted file, it will find it missing. This can cause problems, including system crashes.

The safest way to delete an active startup extension is as follows: (1) Drag the startup extension from the System Folder to the desktop, (2) restart the Macintosh, (3) drag the startup extension to the Trash and discard it.

If the Startup Extension Does Not Load or Run

A startup extension may not load sometimes, even though the startup otherwise proceeds normally. Alternatively, if it does appear to load properly, it still may not function; for control panels, you may even be unable to open its dialog box. If any of these or similar problems happen, ask yourself the following questions.

Is It a Codependent Startup Extension Problem (or Other Startup Extension Conflict)?

Codependent startup extensions are two or more startup extensions—typically from the same software package, or the same company—that must load in a specific sequence in order to run properly. For example, in order to use CE Software's QuicKeys startup extension, you must first load the CEToolbox startup extension (QuicKeys ships with both startup extensions). Similarly, many Now Utilities files will not function unless you first load Now Toolbox. Without these toolbox extensions installed, in fact, the second startup extension of the pair will not load at all.

The solution to this type of problem is either to install the missing codependent startup extension (if only the second startup extension is present) or to rearrange the loading order of the pair (so that the one that needs to load first does).

In the end, this is just a special case of the general problem where any startup extension can cause a conflict if it loads before (or after) a certain other startup extension. The quickest way to check this is to disable all startup extensions except for the one that did not load (see "Special Case: Conflict Between Two Startup Extensions," earlier in this Fix-It), then restart the Macintosh. If the startup extension now loads and runs properly, there is a conflict between it and another startup extension on your startup disk, probably one that normally loads prior to the extension you just checked. Rearranging the loading order will often solve the problem; if it doesn't, you may have to disable one of the incompatible startup extensions.

SEE: • "Resolve the Conflict," earlier in this Fix-It, for more general advice

Did You Restart After Installing the Startup Extension?

Remember, since startup extensions load into memory at startup, they do not immediately work when they are first installed on your startup disk (after all, the startup process has to be finished before you can install anything). To get them to work, restart the Macintosh after installing the startup extension.

Is the Startup Extension in the System Folder?

Startup extensions do not disappear from your System Folder by themselves. Don't forget that if you switch to a different startup disk, however, the new startup disk may contain different startup extensions. In this case, some of those you normally expect to see will not be present.

Is the Startup Extension in Its Proper Location in the System Folder?

Remember, startup extensions load only if they are in the Extensions folder, the Control Panels folder, or the root level of the System Folder (that is, not in any subfolder). Some startup extensions work properly only if they are in a particular one of these locations.

Normally, to add a new startup extension to the System Folder, either use the startup extension's Installer utility or drag the startup extension file to the System Folder icon (*not* the System file icon or the System Folder window). In the latter case, the Finder determines the startup extension's correct folder (Extensions or Control Panels) and asks you if you want it to be placed there. If you add startup extensions by any other method, you may inadvertently place them in a wrong location; in such cases, they may either not work properly or not load at all. I must admit, however, that the automatic method sometimes makes mistakes as well (for example, ordinary applications designed to look like control panels and go in the Controls Panel folder; will be placed in the root level of the System Folder instead). The solution is to determine the startup extension's correct location (check its documentation if needed), move it there, and then restart the Macintosh.

Figure F4-7 *Drag a control panel to the System Folder icon, and you will get this message (unless the "control panel" is really an ordinary application).*

Helpful hint: If a control panel is located outside the System Folder, you may still be able to open it successfully. If it is a startup-type control panel, however, any changes you make to its settings will likely have no effect until you correctly locate the panel and then restart.

BY THE WAY ▶

SOME STARTUP EXTENSIONS DO NOT WORK IF THEY ARE IN A SUBFOLDER

Some startup extensions—usually older ones—may not work properly (or at all) in System 7 if they are placed in the Extensions folder or the Control Panels folder. Often, these startup extensions still work fine if they are relocated to the main level of the System Folder. If this does not completely resolve the problem, create an alias of the startup extension and place the alias in either the Extensions folder or the Control Panels folder, as appropriate. Leave the startup extension at the main level of the System Folder, and restart the Macintosh.

For example, I had a system extension that would not load unless it was placed at the main level of the System Folder. Even after it loaded, however, I could not access its preferences settings dialog box. When I placed an alias of the startup extension in the Extensions folder, with the original at the root level everything worked perfectly after I restarted.

Was the Startup Extension Disabled by Your Startup Manager?

Most startup managers have a user-definable hot key that, when held down at startup, prevents all startup extensions from loading. (This is faster than having to access the manager's control panel at startup.) After defining such a key, of course, you will need to be careful not to press this key inadvertently at startup. Be especially careful if you define Caps Lock as the hot key, since this can be left locked and will thus prevent your startup extensions from loading even if you aren't touching the keyboard!

Also recall that you can set your startup manager always to disable a particular startup extension or automatically skip all startup extensions (by selecting its Skip All or equivalent command). Make sure you do not do this unintentionally.

Similarly, startup managers can save different startup sets (groups of startup extensions that are on or off), from which you can then select extension sets (making it convenient to turn on some startup extensions only when you know you will need them). If you do this, of course, make sure you are using the right set.

Finally, be aware that some of these startup managers have an optional preferences setting that automatically disables any newly added startup extensions. In such cases, you must manually enable the new extension from the startup manager's control panel window before it will load. Then, of course, you still need to restart the Macintosh.

Also, any extension links that have been established (see "By The Way: Create Links with Startup Management Utilities") may result in one extension being turned off automatically as a result of the presence or absence of another extension.

In general, check the startup management utility's control panel to make sure that the startup extension is not currently disabled.

Is the Startup Extension Turned On?

Many control panels have on/off buttons in their dialog box. These buttons must be in the on position for the control panel to work, even if the control panel file is in its proper location at startup. If you discover a startup extension in the off position, turn it back on. If this has no immediate effect, restart the Macintosh; this should get it to work again.

Figure F4-8 *The Spell Catcher control panel, with On and Off buttons in the upper left corner.*

Special Case: Startup Icons Appear with an "X" Over Them or Disappear

Many extensions have an assigned key or key combination that can be used to disable it selectively at startup; no other startup extension is affected unless it uses the same hot key(s). (By the way, although these hot keys can selectively disable startup extensions, I would avoid using them as a means of diagnosing startup extension conflicts. Instead, stick with the other methods described earlier in this Fix-It.)

If you disable a startup extension with this hot-key method, the startup icon (in the "Welcome to Macintosh" screen) for the relevant startup extension may appear with an "X" through it, indicating that the startup extension did not load; alternatively, the startup icon may disappear altogether. This is all perfectly normal. Of course, inadvertently holding down these keys at startup may lead to icons unexpectedly having an X over them. By the way, sometimes turning off a startup extension from its control panel (as described in the previous section) will also cause an icon to appear with an "X" over it.

If these possibilities do not account for a crossed-out icon, consider the following:

- As described more in Fix-It #6, this problem can happen the first time you turn RAM Doubler back on after having previously disabled it via the Shift key or a startup manager. Skipping over the details, this is due to the fact that RAM Doubler actually loads two separate startup extensions, one of which has no icon and loads first. If this first extension does not load at startup (which it may not do after RAM Doubler has been previously disabled and turned back on again), the icon for the second startup extension, if present, will appear with an "X" over it. When startup is complete, you will get a message that says that RAM Doubler did not load but will load correctly the next time you start. To solve this problem, just restart as it suggests.
- You may be trying to use a startup extension that does not work on your Macintosh model (for instance, a PowerBook-only extension installed on a desktop Mac).
- The startup extension's preferences file may be damaged. If you believe this might be the case, locate the file and delete it (see "Replace Potentially Damaged Files," earlier in this Fix-It.).
- If the problem persists, the startup extension itself may be damaged, or it may have a bug that has been fixed in an upgraded version. Replace the startup extension; if that fails, contact the startup extension's vendor for help.

For related information

SEE:
- **Fix-It #2 on problems with preferences files**
- **Fix-It #5 on system software problems**
- **Fix-It #6 on memory problems**
- **Fix-It #13 on damaged disks**
- **Fix-It #14 on damaged files**
- **Fix-It #18 on seeking outside help**
- **Chapter 1 on System Folder subfolders**
- **Chapter 4 on system errors in general**
- **Chapter 5 on system crashes at startup**
- **Chapter 11 on file sharing**
- **Chapter 13 on startup extensions in System 7.5 and later revisions**

Fix-It #5: Check for Problems with System Software

QUICK SUMMARY ▶

If a system software problem is suspected, update or replace the system software files as needed. Generally do a "clean reinstall" of the system software, using the Installer utility that came with your Macintosh system software disks.

When to do it:

- Whenever you have made a change to your system software shortly before the onset of the problem.
- Whenever you have a specific problem using system software (such as a problem with the functioning of the Finder).
- Whenever you have trouble with recently added software that does not appear to be due to the causes described in previous Fix-Its, or any other identifiable cause—even if you have made no changes to the system software.
- Whenever a symptom, such as a system crash, occurs in a variety of different contexts or across a variety of applications.
- Whenever you need to upgrade to a newer version of the system software.

For some of these symptoms, other possible causes exist, but system software remains a prime candidate.

Why to do it:

System software, particularly the System and the Finder, forms the essential background against which all other programs must work. It is in use from startup to shutdown. Thus, since the system software is never dormant, you should suspect it as the potential cause of almost any problem—especially one that is not easy to diagnose.

Besides the System file and the Finder, Macintosh system software includes other files normally found in the System Folder, such as various control panels, extensions, and Apple menu items. The definitions and explanations of all categories of system software files are described in Chapter 1; if the distinctions described here are unfamiliar, check that chapter before proceeding.

Most system software problems fall into two familiar categories.

Incompatibility Problems A new upgrade of your favorite application may only work with the latest version of the system software; if you are still using an older version, you have trouble. In particular, many applications now only work with System 7. The severity of the symptoms of any incompatibility can vary from a refusal of a program to launch to minor display problems to system crashes. The primary solution here is to upgrade your system software.

Because the symptoms range so widely, it can be difficult to know for sure whether a particular problem is due to incompatible system software. Fortunately, there are several ways to get some help (see "Take Note: Identifying System Software Compatibility Problems and Bugs").

Corrupted File Problems Any system software file may become corrupted. The more likely candidates, however, include the System file, the Finder, Enabler files, PrintMonitor, printer drivers, and font files. The System file is particularly prone to damage, mainly because it is modified more often than other files. (It gets modified almost every time you use your Macintosh, even though you are not directly made aware of this.) Unfortunately, damage to the System file is also likely to cause more serious symptoms than damage to

TAKE NOTE ▶

IDENTIFYING SYSTEM SOFTWARE COMPATIBILITY PROBLEMS AND BUGS

You have a problem that may be due to a system software incompatibility, but you are not certain that this is the cause. Before you rush to unnecessarily do a complete system software reinstall, here's something to consider.

When Apple first releases a major upgrade to its operating system, it sometimes includes a utility to help identify third-party programs that will not work with the new system software. For example, with System 7.0, there was a utility called Compatibility Checker; with System 7.5, there was one called Safe Install. I would not bother much, if at all, with these utilities. First, since they were not updated after their initial release, they have little relevance to the current crop of third-party software. Second, they were not all that accurate to begin with. Their warnings tend to be overzealous, citing programs as problematic when they are really fine. If a program is listed as incompatible but you don't experience any problem with it, feel free to continue to use it. If an upgrade is available for the program, however, it probably pays to get it.

Other third-party applications (such as Help!) perform similar functions, identifying conflicts and incompatibilities not only with system software, but with all software and hardware. These programs, however, are only as good as the database of information that the program uses as the basis for its decisions. For these databases to remain current, you have to purchase updates regularly.

Don't forget to check any printed documentation and Apple Guide files that came with your software for possible advice. Outside help, in the form of technical support lines, magazines, users groups, and online services, may also provide an answer (see Fix-It #18 for details).

On a related note, sometimes a problem may be caused by a bug in the system software itself. No version of the system software is free of bugs. Apple tries to eradicate bugs via its System Updates (as described more elsewhere in this Fix-It), but it never entirely succeeds. In fact, new system software may introduce new bugs as much as fixing old ones.

Reinstalling system software, as advised in this Fix-It, will not fix bug-related problems. Fixing these problems will require waiting for the appropriate bug-fixed upgrade. In the meantime, try to stay informed about such bugs so that you can understand the cause of whatever symptoms they produce.

other system software files. The main solution in all cases is to replace the corrupted file. If you cannot determine which system software file is the actual culprit, you may have to replace all system software files. (Note: This is not a type of "damage" that can be fixed by Norton Utilities.)

TAKE NOTE ▶

REFERENCE RELEASES VS. UPDATES

Apple's current policy is to periodically release two types of system software upgrades. The first type, a *reference release*, contains all the necessary software to do a clean reinstall. It also contains all (or almost all) of the updated files from previous releases. After a reference release upgrade, you should never need to go back to earlier system software releases.

The other type of upgrade is called an *Update*. It primarily contains bug fixes, with perhaps some minor new features added. Typically, it can only be used to update existing system software; you could not do a complete clean reinstall from an Update. In addition, it may not contain key software found on the reference release because there are no updated changes to those components. To do a clean reinstall here, you need to start with the previous reference release and then install the Update (as explained more in the main text).

Also note that an Update's Installer typically does not add updated software unless the older files are already in your System Folder. For example, even if an Update includes a new version of Energy Saver, it will not install the file unless it finds the older version of Energy Saver already in your System Folder.

What to do:

This section is divided into two parts. The simplest and most direct approach to most system software problems is to completely reinstall the system software; how best to do this is explained in the first part. Sometimes less drastic solutions are possible, though, such as just replacing a single file that is known to be damaged. These solutions are described in the second part.

Complete Install/Reinstall of System Software

Doing a Clean Reinstall of System Software

When you use the Installer utility on your system software disks to replace existing system software, the Installer may update an existing file by modifying it rather than by completely replacing it. Similarly, the Installer may fail to modify or replace a file if the new version is not any different from what is already on your drive (if both files are from version 7.5, for example). This is actually preferable in many situations. For example, if you have customized a System file with your own set of sound files, a normal reinstall will update the System file, but leave the customized sounds intact. The problem with this approach is that if the System file is damaged, the damage may be left intact. To solve this problem, you need to do what is called a *clean reinstall*—that is, a complete replacement of all existing system software files.

BY THE WAY ▶

REINSTALLING SYSTEM SOFTWARE ON PERFORMAS

Although Performas now use the same system software as the rest of the Macintosh line, the exact software you get with your purchase of a Performa has not been identical to what comes with other Macs (this situation seems to change so often, though, that what I am about to say may be out of date by the time you read this). Currently, Performas are shipped with a CD-ROM that does include a complete set of system software; however, it apparently still does not include the standard set of installation software (that is, the disk images and/or folders that you need to run the standard Installer utility). In fact, there is no standard Installer at all—instead, you are supposed to use a program called Restore System Software (or Restore All Software). Unfortunately, since this software only works with Apple-formatted drives and has numerous other minor quirks, it makes doing a "clean reinstall" much more awkward.

Performa owners should still try to get the standard system software Installer disk(s). If Apple won't send you a copy for free, consider buying it. Having the "real" installer software is especially important if you are doing something like updating via System 7.5 Update 2.0. Otherwise, if this sort of Update should fail, you may find that you have no ready tools to reinstall a working System Folder.

While a clean reinstall is intended primarily to deal with suspected damaged files, it will do no harm (other than the possible loss of some customized settings) even when no damage is suspected. Actually, I recommend doing a clean reinstall almost anytime you upgrade to a new reference release, especially if any problems develop when you try to upgrade via an Easy Install. Sometimes a clean reinstall is specifically recommended in order to avoid problems that are reported to occur after an ordinary upgrade/install. Such was the case, for example, in upgrading to System 7.5.3 via System 7.5 Update 2.0.

Finally, many experts recommend a clean reinstall of your system software every few months as a preventative measure to forestall any problems caused by unrecognized damage. Personally, I have never done this sort of maintenance reinstall.

If you want to do a clean reinstall, continue with this section. If instead you simply want to do an ordinary reinstall (or to install system software on a disk for the first time), skip ahead to the next section, "Using the System Software Installer."

The logic of a clean reinstall is to delete those files that would not have been replaced by an ordinary reinstall, then do the ordinary installation. This forces a completely new copy of the software to be installed. It might appear that the simplest way to do this is to delete the entire old System Folder (after restarting with an alternate startup disk). If you do this, however, you will lose the dozens of files that are in the System Folder but are not included on the Macintosh system software disks, including any fonts, Apple menu items, preferences files, extensions, or control panels that did not come from Apple. As mentioned, you will also lose any customized changes to Apple system software files. So what is needed, then, is an efficient way to delete Apple system software files while preserving all the added items you want to save. The method described here is designed to do precisely this.

TAKE NOTE ▶

AN "INSTANT" CLEAN REINSTALL OF SYSTEM 7.5

After launching the Installer, when you get to the window with the Install button, press and hold Command-Shift-K. A new window will open with two additional options: Update Existing System Folder, and Install New System Folder. Update Existing Folder is the default option; if you select the Install New System Folder option, though, the "Install" button will change to read "Clean Install." You must have an existing System Folder on your disk to use this option (otherwise, you can simply do an Easy Install, which will amount to the same thing).

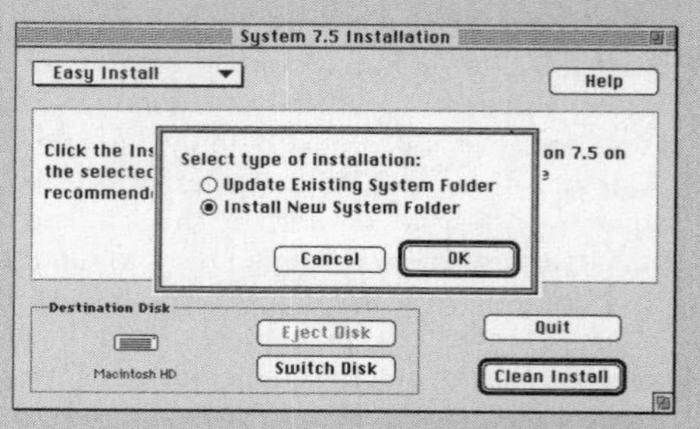

Figure F5-1 *Press Command-Shift-K to get the Installer's "secret" Clean Install option.*

A clean reinstall includes an entirely new System and Finder, leaving your old System Folder still intact and renamed as Previous System Folder. After you quit the Installer, you can drag items from the old folder to the new one as needed, discarding the remainder of the old folder. In order to take advantage of this shortcut, however, you must have enough disk space to hold both System Folders at the same time.

If you use this shortcut, you can skip most of the "Doing a Clean Reinstall of System Software" section of this book. Just browse through it for any relevant advice (such as returning third-party software to the System Folder), and then proceed to the "Using the System Software Installer" section for more detailed instructions, if needed.

One warning: If you cancel this Clean Install in progress, your original System Folder may be left with the name Previous System Folder (with an empty folder named System Folder now on your disk), and it may even be unblessed (that is, the System icon will not be on the folder). This can cause problems for your use of System Folder files and may even prevent you from restarting successfully. The solution is to delete the empty folder, rename your original System Folder correctly, and then open and close the folder (to rebless it if needed).

The procedure for selecting a clean install is a bit different in System 7.6 or later. See "Take Note: Installing System Software with Mac OS 7.6" for details.

You may read about other methods for doing a clean reinstall that are somewhat different from what is given here. Apple even includes instructions for a clean reinstall in the documentation that comes with some Macintoshes. Don't fret about the differences in instructions; they all accomplish the same goal.

1. **Rename the System Folder**
   Locate the System Folder to be replaced. Rename it "X System Folder" (or any other name of your choosing).
2. **Remove the System file contents**
   Create a new folder and name it "System File Stuff." Double-click the System file in the X System Folder to view the files within it. Remove any and all files (such as sound and possibly font files) from within the System file by dragging them out of the window and placing them in the System File Stuff folder.

BY THE WAY ▶

SYSTEM SOFTWARE THAT IS "LOST" AFTER UPDATING

Removing and saving the resources inside your System file (as accessible by double-clicking the file) may not save all of the customized changes to this file. In particular, some Installer utilities for other software modify the System file, often without telling you they are doing this. No later examination of the System file will directly tell you that this modification has been made. In such cases, when you reinstall the basic system software (even assuming that it is the same version you used previously), you will lose these customized changes. If this happens, you may notice that certain features have disappeared.

Similarly, you may wind up with an older version of some system software component, such as AppleTalk, than you had been using. The only solution here is to relaunch the Installers for the other software that is more recent than what you just installed (assuming you remember what they are!) when you are done with the system software reinstall.

3. **Remove the Finder from the System Folder**

   One way to do this is to create a new folder called "Old Finder." Move the Finder to that folder. Now close the X System Folder window; this folder should no longer be blessed (that is, you should no longer see the Macintosh icon on the folder icon). This means that the Mac no longer considers this to be a valid System Folder. When you run the Installer, it should therefore create a new System Folder rather than update the X System Folder.

   I have found, however, that this method does not always work—sometimes the Mac still installs the new software in the X System Folder. In this case, it may be helpful to bury the System file within a folder (such as the Extensions folder) inside the X System Folder, in addition to moving the Finder. It might also help to create a new empty folder at the root level of your disk and name it System Folder.

   The surest procedure is to start up with an alternate startup disk and delete the Finder and the System file (and any Enabler/Update file, if present) from your disk altogether. Because you're going to delete these files in the end anyway, this is my personal recommendation. Of course, you have to start up from an alternate startup disk to do this, but you will be doing this in the next steps in any event. If you are really the cautious type, you may want to first be certain that these files have been backed up before you delete them. If something goes wrong with the reinstall, you then may return to using these files.

4. **Restart the Macintosh**

   Restart with no floppy disk inserted or other alternate startup disk mounted, and wait. You should get the blinking-question-mark icon. This establishes that there are truly no active System Folders on your hard drive.

   If a startup does occur at this point, you had more than one System Folder on your disk. If so, you should locate (using the Find command, if needed) and delete all System Folders except the one you intend to update. If you need to delete the System Folder that is now active, you will first need to restart from an alternate startup disk.

TAKE NOTE

INSTALLING SYSTEM SOFTWARE WITH MAC OS 7.6

Mac OS 7.6 (originally code-named Harmony) introduces some major changes in the user interface for installing system software. Here's an overview of how it all works:

- **Before you install** As always, it is best to install system software with all or at least all non-Apple extensions off. If you use At Ease, you must turn it off before installing Mac OS 7.6. Preferably, use the Mac OS 7.6 disc as the startup disc.
- **Launch Install Mac OS** This is a new utility designed to simplify the installation process and ensure that you do not omit any important steps. When you first launch it, a screen appears with four numbered options. By clicking the appropriate buttons, you will be guided through: (1) checking the system 7.6 Read Me file, (2) updating the disk driver, (3) selecting a volume for installing the system software, and (4) installing the software.
- **Install the software: Start** When you click the "Install the software" button, it brings up a list of all the available software components beyond the Mac OS 7.6 "base system." For example, it will list OpenDoc, QuickDraw GX, QuickDraw 3D, and more. A default set of options is automatically selected for installation. Via the check boxes provided, you can select or deselect which options you want to install. If you then click the Start button, the equivalent of an Easy Install of all of the options selected begins. If no problems occur, all the software should be installed without any further action required on your part.
- **Install the software: Customize** If you click the Customize button prior to selecting Start, you are presented with a similar set of check boxes (now including one for Mac OS 7.6 itself). If you now click Start, you will be taken to the separate installer for each selected software component. From here, you can select Custom Install just as you would in previous versions of the system software.
- **Install the software: Options** If you select the Options button prior to selecting Start, you will be given the option to do a "Clean Install." If you have selected Customize, you will also be given the option to turn off "Verify Destination Disk," which otherwise runs a Disk First Aid-like check prior to the installation.

Note: The pre-System 7.6 style Installers are still present in Mac OS 7.6 (in a folder called "Software Installers"). There is a separate installer for each software component. Each can be launched individually, rather than going through the Install Mac OS utility. Indeed, Install Mac OS

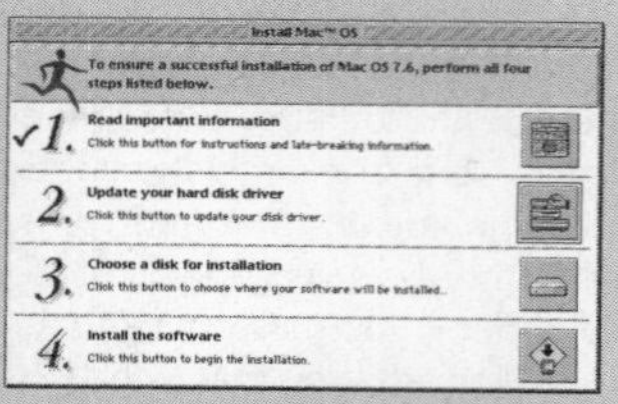

Figure F5-2A *The main window of the Mac OS 7.6 Install Mac OS utility.*

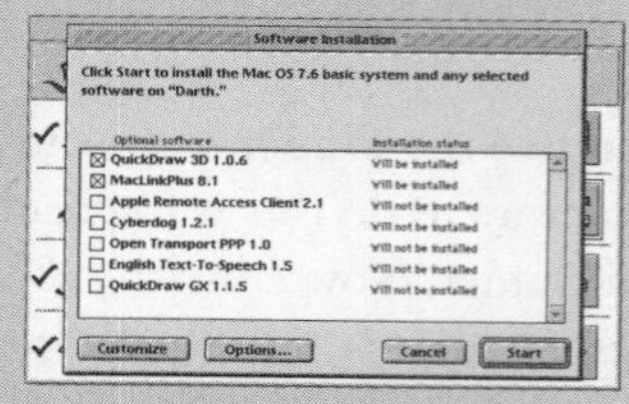

Figure F5-2B *This window appears after you click the "Install the software" button in the Install Mac OS window.*

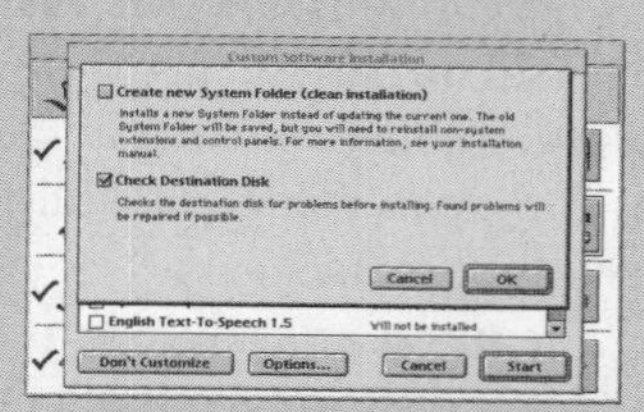

Figure F5-2C *This window appears if you select to Customize and then click the Options button of Install Mac OS.*

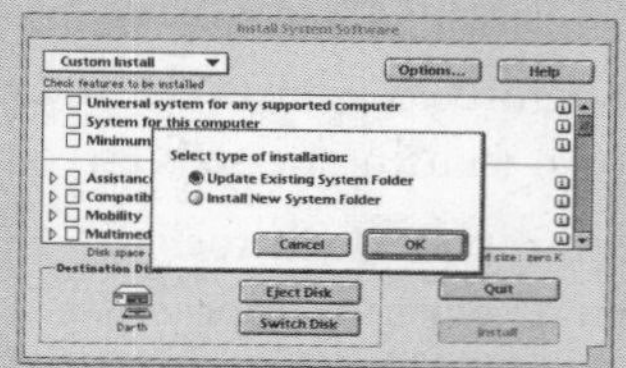

Figure F5-2D *The basic Mac OS 7.6 Installer now includes an Options button; click on it to access a check box for a clean install (you no longer need to use the Mac OS 7.5 Command-Shift-K technique).*

Continues on next page

TAKE NOTE

INSTALLING SYSTEM SOFTWARE WITH MAC OS 7.6 *(Continued)*

ultimately launches these separate Installers anyway. Install Mac OS is really just an overlay that attempts to simplify the installation process for the end user. Thus, the majority of the advice in the main text of this Fix-It still applies even in Mac OS 7.6.

One exception: The Installer for Mac OS 7.6 system software includes a button called "Options." Similar to the Options button in Install Mac OS, clicking it brings up a check box to select to do a Clean Install. Thus, you no longer need to know the "secret" Command-Shift-K shortcut to access this feature (as described in "Take Note: An 'Instant' Clean Reinstall of System 7.5").

SEE • **Chapter 13 for more on System 7.5 and Mac OS 7.6**

5. Insert the relevant system software disk and install a new System Folder

Follow the directions as detailed in the next section ("Using the System Software Installer").

Briefly, if you are using floppy disks, insert the Install 1 (or similarly named) disk (or Install Me First disk, if needed). Wait for the Installer to launch; select Easy Install (or make selections from Custom Install, if desired) and click the Install button.

If you are using an Apple System Software CD-ROM disc, you typically hold down the "C" key at startup to use it as a startup disk. After the disk has mounted, launch the Installer utility, which is typically located in a folder called "System Software Install." Select Easy Install.

6. Restart the Macintosh again

You will probably be forced to restart by the Installer when you quit it; if not, restart anyway. You should now start up from the newly installed System Folder. At this point, check to see if your problem has disappeared. If damaged system software (or one of the files now in the X System Folder) was the cause, your problem should now be gone. If it wasn't, something else is to blame.

7. Return files from the X System Folder

Open the X System Folder. Open each subfolder (Preferences, Control Panels, and so on) within that folder, and drag all the items in each to the identically named folder in the new System Folder. (Note: Do not simply drag the entire subfolder back to the new System Folder, or you will simply delete the entire contents of the new folder and replace it with the old one!)

If you get any messages asking whether you want to replace a specific file, say no (click the Cancel button)—otherwise, you will undo the effect of reinstalling new copies of those files. If you know which files in X System Folder come from Apple, just delete them rather than dragging them back to the new System Folder. This will keep you from repeatedly getting the query about replacing files.

Now drag all other files and folders (except the System and System Enabler/Update files, if still present) from the root level of the X System Folder to the new System Folder.

By the way, if possible, it would be better to install non-Apple files from their original disks rather than from the X System Folder (just in case the version on your hard disk is damaged), but this is not necessary if your primary purpose is to just do a clean reinstall of the Macintosh system software.

Helpful hint: Alternatively, you could drag all of the files from the new System Folder to the X System Folder, then *allow* everything to be replaced when asked (make sure you first saved resources from the inside the old System file before you do this, as explained in Step 8). This will delete all the old Apple files, leaving new ones in their place; at the same time, all other files are untouched. This path is a bit riskier in my view, as it seems more likely that you may make some changes that you had not intended, but it is more convenient overall. When you are done, rename your X System Folder back to "System Folder" (deleting the "new" System Folder), and skip Step 9.

FIX-IT #5

8. **Return files from the System File Stuff folder**
   Open the System File Stuff folder, and drag these files to the System Folder icon (not the System file icon) of the new System Folder. The Macintosh will offer to correctly place these files, installing them to the System file. Accept its offer; again, if you are asked to replace any files, say no.
   As in the previous step, since there is a possibility that one of these files may be the source of the suspected damage, you might prefer to replace any non-Apple files from their original disks rather than from these copies.
9. **Delete the X System Folder, System File Stuff, and Old Finder folders**
   Delete the X System Folder with all of its remaining contents, including the System file and Enabler. Also delete the System File Stuff folder with all of its remaining contents, and the Old Finder folder, which still contains the old Finder.
   If you have already deleted the System Finder and any Enabler files (optionally suggested in Step 3), you obviously won't need to delete them here.
10. **Restart again**
    Restart the Macintosh one more time. You will again start up from the same newly installed System Folder, but now with all your control panels, extensions, and other files returned.

With any luck, your problem will not return. If it does, perhaps non-Apple files in your System Folder that were not replaced are the source of the problem. For such problems, refer to other relevant Fix-Its as needed.

Using the System Software Installer

Helpful hint: Disk Formatters and Disk First Aid An Installer does not update the disk driver, nor does it check for disk damage. For Apple-formatted drives, you should update the disk driver with any potentially new version of the disk formatting software included with the new System software (either before or after installing the system software); you should also check for disk damage (prior to the installation) with the latest version of Disk First Aid. This process is "automated" with Mac OS 7.6's Install Mac OS utility.

SEE: • **Fix-It #10 on using Disk First Aid**
• **Fix-It #12 on updating the disk device driver**

The following is the main procedure for installing or reinstalling system software on a disk.

1. **Restart from a system software Install floppy disk or CD-ROM disc**
   For system software on floppy disks, restart your Macintosh from the system software's Install 1 disk (or Install Me First disk, if needed) as the startup disk. For system software on a CD-ROM disc (as typically comes with Macs that have an internal CD-ROM drive), start up from that disc by holding down the "C" key at startup. Using this CD-ROM disc instead of floppy disks simplifies the installation, as you no longer need to deal with swapping multiple floppy disks. Alternatively, you can place a "net install" version of the software onto a second hard disk and start up from that disk.

   By the way, you do not absolutely need to have these disks act as startup disks in order to do an installation. You can use disks while still running from your hard drive as the startup disk (even if you have moved the location of the Finder on your hard disk, as suggested for a clean reinstall). You just have to quit all applications other than the Finder first (the Installer will volunteer to do this for you if you have forgotten). If you are doing a clean reinstall or are having any problems with your hard disk, however, it is safer to start up from these system software disks. Certainly, if you intend to delete the System and Finder prior to doing a clean reinstall (as optionally suggested in

FIX-IT #5

TAKE NOTE ▶

MUST YOU USE THE INSTALLER?

The Installer utility is the key to installing your system software. Actually, almost all companies now use some sort of installer utility to install their software. Many use the Apple Installer described here.

You may be wondering, "Must I use an Installer, or could I copy the files directly using the Finder?" These days, you must use the Installer. The files are stored in a special compressed format, typically called "tomes," and only the Installer can install the uncompressed usable versions of the needed files. The Installer also helps by installing the files in their correct location (usually!), saving you the hassle of figuring out where that is.

I have a number of gripes, however, with the way the Installer works. Foremost among them is that the Custom Install window doesn't always give you enough options to install just the component you want. This can sometimes force you to do a complete reinstall when you are only looking to replace one file. Similarly, the Custom Remove option is not always enabled, making it difficult to remove the software if you discover that it causes more problems than it solves. Although this is a minor complaint, I also don't like that the Installer forces you to restart when you are done. Sometimes I want to do some other work before restarting with the new software, and I would like the option to exit the Installer without restarting. Happily, this option is now available in some recent Installers that I have used. Otherwise, another alternative, although riskier, is to Force Quit (Command-Option-Escape) from the Installer to avoid having to restart.

Finally, especially with Installers for software other than Apple software, I would like it if you had the option *not* to have extensions automatically installed in the System Folder when you install an application package. There are times when I want to install some software—just to "look" at it, perhaps—without worrying that the required installation may modify my System Folder in unexpected ways.

At the very least, the Installer should give you a report of everything it installed and where it installed it, so you know what happened and how to undo it if necessary.

the previous section), you are required to restart from another disk, presumably the Install disk (see "Take Note: System Enablers, Updates, and Universal System Folders," "Take Note: System Software Upgrade Variations," and "Take Note: Why Can't I Open the System Software I Just Downloaded?" later in this Fix-It, for related information).

TAKE NOTE ▶

SYSTEM ENABLERS, UPDATES, AND UNIVERSAL SYSTEM FOLDERS

Starting with System 7.1, when Apple shipped a new model of Macintosh, it did not automatically release a new version of the system software, as it had done in the past. Instead, it included a special System Enabler file for that model. This file provides the special information needed for the system software to work with the new model.

The benefit of this is that the same basic version of the system software can remain the current version for all users, despite the release of new hardware. Given the frequency with which Apple releases new machines, this is no trivial benefit. These Enablers, however, do have their downside. The most notable problem is that a given disk cannot be used as a startup disk unless it contains the Enabler that matches the machine to which it is attached.

Exactly how Apple deals with this problem continues to evolve. Originally, with your purchase of a Mac, Apple included an Install Me First disk that contained the needed Enabler for your model. You ran this disk first, as its name implied, instead of the Install 1 disk that came with the standard system software.

These days, there appears to be less use of these Enablers. Instead, the needed Enabler information is now rolled into a more general Update file that contains the machine-specific information for all recent Mac models. This is how it worked, for example, when updating from System 7.5.*x* to System 7.5.3 via the System 7.5 Update 2.0 software. A System 7.5 Update file is installed instead of an Enabler, and there is no Install Me First disk to worry about.

Whenever a new major (reference) version of the system software is released, however, it rolls the information for all previous Enabler/Updates into the System file itself, typically eliminating the need for any of these Enabler or Update files (at least until new software and/or hardware is released).

In any case, if you try to start up using a disk that does not contain the correct Enabler or Update file, the startup sequence is likely to halt with a message that says something like "System 7.5 does not work on this model."

One problem that results from all of this is that you can no longer make a floppy disk that will work on all Macintosh models, because there is no way that you can get all of the different varieties of Enabler/Update files on one disk. With the increasing popularity of removable cartridge systems (such as Zip drives), however, it is becoming common to create a "universal" System Folder on a cartridge. To do this, you will need to do a Custom Install rather than an Easy Install. From the Custom Install window, look for the "Universal System Folder" or "System for Any Macintosh" (or similarly named) options under the System Software heading.

One caution: If you select the "universal" System Folder option when your first install system software, you may have a problem if you later try to update using this option to install software only for a specific Mac model—in particular, it will still install the "universal" set of software. This is because, during the initial installation, the Installer places information in the System file about the type of installation selected. This information is used for updates, rather than the information you select from the Installer. To get around this problem, either do a clean reinstall or simply remove the System file from the System Folder prior to your update installation.

SEE:
- **Chapter 2 for details on how commercial recovery software, such as Norton Utilities, create separate startup floppy disks for different Mac models**
- **Chapter 13 for more details relevant to System 7.5 and its revisions**

2. **Launch the Installer utility**
   If it doesn't automatically launch at startup, launch the Installer application. After the "Welcome to Macintosh" screen, you will arrive at the main window.
3. **Select the desired destination disk**
   Click the Switch Disk button until the name of the desired disk is listed.
4. **Decide whether to use the Easy Install or Custom Install method**
   Select the desired option from the Installer's pop-up menu. Which one should you use? There is no automatic answer here. Most people are content with the Easy Install option, which automatically installs the correct versions of all system software needed for your hardware.

   One disadvantage of this method, though, is that it usually installs a variety of files that you do not want or need (for example, printer drivers for printers that you do not have). You can sometimes avoid this by making more specific selections via the Custom Install option. Usually, however, you can just as easily delete the undesired files from your hard drive after the installation is complete. If you are a novice user, uncertain of what you want to keep or delete, just select Easy Install and don't worry about it for now. Unless you need the extra disk space that the files occupy, there is no reason to be in a hurry to delete them.

   Another potential disadvantage of Easy Install is that it will not install files that are designed for features found on other Macintoshes but not available on your model. Normally, this is what you would want; it avoids adding unneeded files to your disk and unnecessarily increasing the size of your System file. If you ever plan on using this System Folder with another Macintosh model, though, Easy Install can present problems. In some cases, it may prevent you from starting up at all from another model. If you see this as a possibility, select Custom Install and create a Universal System Folder (as described in "Take Note: System Enablers, Updates, and Universal System Folders").

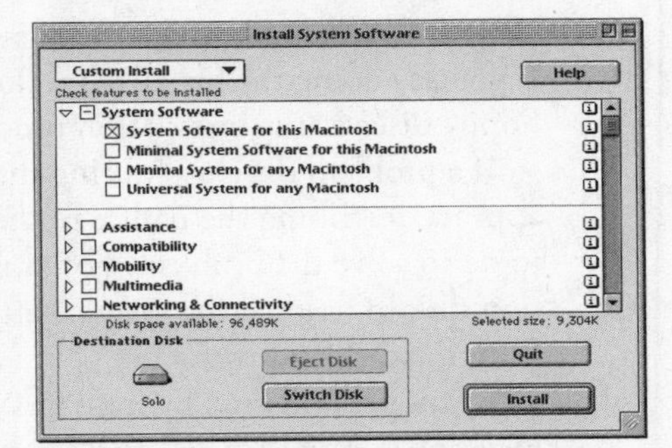

Figure F5-3 *The Custom Install view of Apple's System Software Installer.*

   By the way, another Custom Install option you may find is "Minimal System" (there should be one for "this Macintosh" and another for "any Macintosh"). Note: in Mac OS 7.6, there is just a "Minimum System for any supported computer" option. These used be the options to select for installing system software on a floppy disk. For some versions of the system software, however, this "Minimal" installation is still too big to fit on a floppy disk! In this case, to create a System Folder on a floppy disk, just copy the System Folder from the Disk Tools disk.

   Custom Install is also useful when you are not doing a complete reinstall, but instead want just to add or replace a few selected files (as described in "Selective Install/Reinstall/Deletion of System Software," later in this Fix-It). For example, you can install just printer drivers or just networking-related software without the hassle of a complete reinstallation. Actually, there are some specialized components of the system software that can *only* be installed by a Custom Install; Easy Install does not install them. Check for this if you appear to be missing some expected software after an Easy Install.

5. **Install the software**

   a. **Easy Install.** Click the Install button. The Installer takes care of the rest, prompting you to insert other disks as required. When it is finished, your installation is complete.

   b. **Custom Install.** If you select this option, a scrollable list of software categories (such as System Software, Printing, and Networking Software) will appear in the center of the window. To the left of each name will be a checkbox, and to the left of some checkboxes will be a triangle. Clicking the triangle will reveal a sublist of the files that comprise the larger category (similar to how folders can be manipulated in non-icon views of the System 7 Finder).

      Click the checkbox of an item to select it. Each file in the sublist can be selected separately; selecting the larger category automatically selects all files in the sublist. If you are going to bother to do a Custom Install, I would advise viewing all the sublists and selecting precisely what you want. If you need help deciding what to install, select the "I" button to the right of each name to learn more about what it is. Select the Help button to get more details about what Easy Install does or does not install.

      When you are finished with your selections, click the Install button.

6. **Wait and watch while the installation proceeds**

   If you are doing the install from floppy disks, you will be asked to insert the needed floppy disks as the installation proceeds.

   If a problem develops during the installation procedure, an error message typically appears describing the nature of the problem. Usually, it also offers advice about what to do to solve the problem. For example, if there is insufficient room on the destination disk to hold all the system software, you will be advised to remove some items from the disk and try again.

   If you get bothered by messages from your anti-virus utility while installing, you may find it easier (or even necessary) to halt the installation, temporarily turn off your anti-virus utility, and try again. Doing this is officially recommended anyway.

   SEE: • "Take Note: If the Installation Fails"

7. **Quit the Installer and restart using the destination disk as the new startup disk**

   The Installer will probably force you to restart when you quit it. If it doesn't, restart anyway.

FIX-IT #5

TAKE NOTE ▶

IF THE INSTALLATION FAILS

Apple now recommends that you use its Extensions Manager utility, and select the set that installs only Apple startup extensions, prior to installing a system software update. In some cases, it may be preferable to have *all* extensions off. To be safe, certainly do one or the other prior to installation (or start up from the Installer floppy disk or CD, as they contain essentially no extensions). Otherwise, a variety of problems may develop, from the annoyance of repeated requests to reinsert floppy disks (if you are installing from floppy disks) to messages such as "There is a problem with the disk you are trying to install onto" or "An error occurred while installing onto the active startup disk ..." to freezes or crashes during the installation.

Corrupted fonts are also a possible source of these problems. A corrupt font, however, will likely only cause problems if the Installer attempts to install a font (as is common in printing software installations) that has the same name as a corrupt font currently in your System Folder. To work around this, remove the Fonts folder from the System Folder before installing. Then discard all the fonts with names identical to the new ones that were installed, returning the others to the new Fonts folder.

If you downloaded the software from an online source and you get a message that says "An error occurred while trying to complete the installation. Installation was canceled leaving your disk untouched" while trying to install the system software, you probably got a corrupted copy of the software when you downloaded it. Try to download the software again, perhaps from another source.

When you are running an Installer, make sure that all system software files in your current System Folder have not been renamed from their original name. Wrong names can confuse the Installer and cause problems.

Be aware that if you try to run an Installer for a version of the system software that is too old for your hardware (such as System 7.5.0 on a PCI Mac), the Installer will refuse to let you do it. The solution is to get the correct version of the system software.

The Installer cannot update the version of Macintosh System Software on the disk named "Solo". Please remove the System Folder on "Solo" and try the installation again.

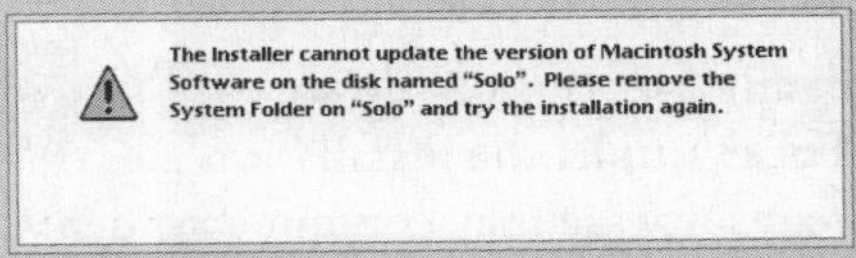

Figure F5-4 *This error message may appear in the Installer window if you are trying to install a version of the system software that is older than the version that you already have. This is just one of several error messages that may occur when using the Installer.*

If problems persist, try zapping the PRAM (see Fix-It #11).

If you are using a CD-ROM as a startup disk, dirt on the disc may cause an installation failure. To check for this, wipe the shiny side of the disk gently with a soft cloth or tissue, looking especially for sticky "goop" on the disk. Wipe from the center to the edge of the disk; do not wipe in circles.

Special note: System 7.5.5 While System 7.5.5 works reasonably well once you get it installed, there are an unusual number of installation problems that can occur. Most of these are remedied by starting over with a clean reinstall of System 7.5.3, while others are addressed by following the advice just given here. Some problems, however, require more specific fixes; these are covered in Chapter 13.

SEE: • **Chapter 13 for more advice on installation failure problems specific to System 7.5 and later**

8. Install/reinstall Updates or other additional system software

If you plan to install or reinstall QuickDraw GX or OpenDoc, for example, do it now. If you are installing a reference release of software and there is a subsequent Update (such as System 7.5.5), install the Update now.

The "Read Me" file included with the installation software may contain instructions about other special procedures for replacing/updating/removing certain software. Follow that advice.

An important note: If you had previously installed newer versions of files that are also contained on the software you are now installing, you will likely need to reinstall these newer versions. If you get messages during the initial system software installation asking you to click OK to replace a newer version of a file with an older version, do so.

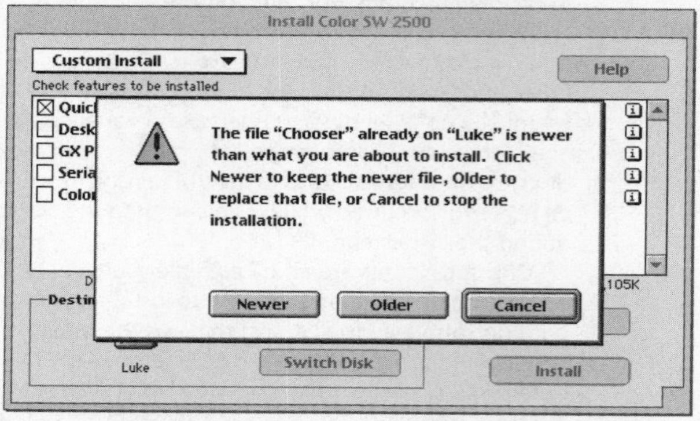

Figure F5-5 *The Installer asks what to do about a file in your System Folder that is "newer" than the one the Installer is about to install. In this case, it gives you a choice (sometimes you are forced to either delete the "newer" file or cancel the installation entirely). What to do here depends on the file; sometimes an "older" file will be considered new if you have modified it in some way. Generally, these files should be discarded in favor of the truly new version you are about to install. Other times, the file already in your System Folder is a truly new version that you have separately installed; if so, you should keep the file if possible (otherwise, you will have to reinstall it again later).*

For example, the installation system software may contain an older version of QuickTime than the current version you are using. As a result, it may replace the newer version with the older one. If so, you will need to reinstall the newer QuickTime separately to get it back.

TAKE NOTE ▶

SYSTEM SOFTWARE UPGRADE VARIATIONS

Because of the increasing complexity and variety of Apple's system software, the odds that any two people are using an identical system software setup, even if they are using the same hardware, is fairly low.

Making the task of sorting all of this out even more difficult has been Apple's frequently changing and often confusing policy on naming upgrades. For example, when PCI-based Macs first came out, they needed System 7.5.2; all other Macs users were relegated to System 7.5.1. Apple then came out with System 7.5 Update 2.0, however, which upgraded all System 7.5.*x* users to System 7.5.3. Later PCI-based Macs received a special version of System 7.5.3 that was different than the one you got by running System 7.5 Update 2.0 (and that only ran on PCI-based Macs). Around the same time, Apple came out with System 7.5.3 Revision 2, which further upgraded selected Macintosh models. This chaos was finally simplified by the release of a reference version of System 7.5.3 that brought everyone up to the same level, for a brief time anyway. (This subject is covered in even more detail in Chapter 13.)

Apple now appears to be striving for more consistency and simplicity in their upgrades. I hope so.

If you are doing a clean reinstall, you will not get these messages, because all the relevant files are in the X System Folder.

SEE: • **"Take Note: System Software Upgrade Variations"**
• **Chapter 13 for more on QuickDraw GX and PowerTalk**

9. Do some final cleanup
If desired, you can do some final cleanup at this point, discarding any files that you do not need. For example, the Installer may have installed some printer drivers, control panels, or Apple menu items that you do not want; if so, delete them. Also check for and delete duplicate copies of fonts that may have been inadvertently installed (as described in Chapter 9).

FIX-IT #5

If you are doing a clean reinstall, return now to the previous section for instructions on completing the procedure. Otherwise, you are done.

TAKE NOTE ▶

"WHY CAN'T I OPEN THE SYSTEM SOFTWARE I JUST DOWNLOADED?"

Many users acquire supplementary system software, such as Update disks, from online services or the Internet. In almost all cases, these files are compressed and/or encoded in some way; how to deal with this issue is described in more detail in Chapter 14. Once you get the decompressed file, however, you may still not be done. If you double-click the file and it still does not open, you probably have what is called a *disk image file*. (It may have a special suffix, such as ".img".) If you don't know what's going on, you may begin to worry that an error occurred while downloading and that you have a damaged file. Don't worry, all is fine—and here's what you need to do.

Disk Tools.image

Figure F5-6 *If you see an icon like this, you need a utility like Disk Copy or ShrinkWrap to use the file.*

First, you need a utility called Disk Copy (or another similar copy utility). It is from Apple and should be available from the same online service where you downloaded your Update file. It is also included on some system software installer CD-ROM discs.

When you get Disk Copy, launch it and click the "Load Image File" button. From the Open dialog box, select the file you downloaded. Now click the "Make a Copy" button, and follow the instructions to insert a floppy disk. Because some disk images are for 800K disks, while others are for 1.44MB disks (by the way, you may need to increase the memory of Disk Copy to at least 1500K when working with 1.44MB disk images), be sure to insert the appropriately sized disk. Disk Copy will now create a floppy disk from the disk image that is an exact duplicate of what you would have gotten if you had obtained the disk directly from Apple—down to the precise location of every icon. Quit Disk Copy; all of the needed files should now be on the floppy disk, in a usable form.

If you get a –620 or a –74 error message when using Disk Copy, you probably have a conflict with virtual memory. Turn virtual memory off and try again.

Alternatively, rather than using the floppy disk directly, you can copy the entire floppy disk to your hard drive (by dragging the floppy disk icon to the hard drive) and perform the Update installation from there. Another alternative is to use a great utility called ShrinkWrap. This program allows you to "mount" a disk image file directly, as if it were a real floppy disk, bypassing the need to use Disk Copy or any floppy disks at all. With ShrinkWrap, you can mount multiple images and do a complete install from them without the hassle of having to insert and eject a series of floppy disks.

SEE: • **Chapter 14 for more on opening and using downloaded files**

Selective Install/Reinstall/Deletion of System Software

Basis for a Selective Install/Reinstall

The main purpose of a clean reinstall of your system software is to solve a problem that may be due to damaged or incompatible system software files. In some cases, however, you may be able to solve such problems by replacing only one or a few selected system software files, saving yourself the time and hassle of a complete reinstall. Examples of this process follow.

Selective Damage Suspected You may suspect, because of the nature of your symptoms, that damage is to a particular file (for instance, if your problem is just with the Scrapbook, you obviously would suspect the Scrapbook file). If so, you can choose simply to replace that file; it typically pays to delete any associated preferences files as well.

Otherwise, for any system software problem, the main suspects are the System, Finder, and Enabler/Update files. Here are a few checks to consider:

- To check for potential damage to the System file, try to open the System suitcase (by double-clicking its icon). If it refuses to open, it is almost certainly damaged and should be replaced. Unfortunately, even if it does open, it may still be damaged.
- If a Mac cannot maintain the correct date or time, and you know the battery is not dead or defective, you may have a corrupted System file.
- The freeware utility TechTool (v. 1.07 and later) includes an option to check if your System file is corrupt and needs replacement. Make sure, however, that you have a current version of TechTool for the system software you are using; otherwise, the utility will either refuse to do this check or may even falsely claim that you have a corrupted file. TechTool Pro can check for the integrity of the System, Finder, and Update files. Conflict Catcher can also do a minimal check of the integrity of these files: go to its Testing Preferences and select "Scan for Damaged Resources."

  You can also check for damage using Norton Utilities or MacTools. Do not assume, however, that these system files are okay just because Norton Disk Doctor or MacTools gave them a clean bill of health. TechTool checks for the sort of damage that is more common to these files.

Figure F5-7 *TechTool's Analyze feature can check for a corrupted System file; the commercial TechTool Pro can additionally check for damage to the Finder and Update files.*

To replace the System (or Finder) file on your normal startup disk, you may need to use an alternative startup disk to access and/or delete the problem file(s).

Files or Resources Missing Some system software problems are due to software that is missing rather than damaged software. This situation is especially likely if you initially did a Custom Install. For example, you may not have installed the files needed for file sharing or EtherTalk because, at the time, you did not intend to use these features; if you later try to access these features, you will probably get a message that needed resources are missing. Similarly, if your System file was customized for your particular

BY THE WAY ▶

SYSTEM SOFTWARE VERSION MATCHING

To see the version of your system software (such as "System Software 7.5.5"), open the About This Macintosh window. Don't rely on checking the Get Info window of the System file to give you the correct information—it may be inaccurate, especially if you have installed an Update to a reference release. Other utilities (such as TechTool) may also provide system version information.

Also note that the version numbers of your System file and your Finder may not be the same. This is probably not a serious concern as long as the difference is only in the digit after the second decimal place (such as System 7.5.2 versus Finder 7.5.5). Otherwise, you probably have a Finder/System mismatch, and one or both of the files should be replaced. With other system software files, it is impossible to make any reliable generalizations about whether or not version numbers should match each other.

If you do decide to check the Get Info windows for system software version information, check both the line below the name of the file and the version number. For example, in System 7.5.5, the Get Info file for Finder still says "System 7.5.3" below the file name (often indicating the original system software source of the file), but the version number indicates System 7.5.5.

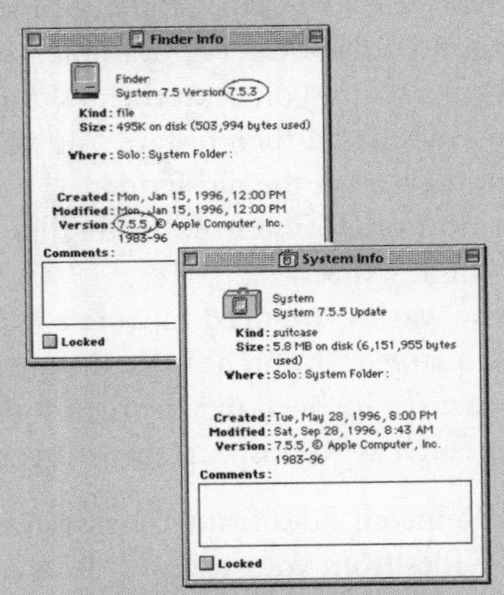

Figure F5-8 *The Finder's Get Info window in System 7.5.5, with different version numbers indicated in two different locations (as circled). The System file's Get Info window indicates the same version (System 7.5.5) in both locations.*

model of Macintosh, it may not work properly if you later copy the same System file for use on another type of Macintosh. In this same situation, you may not have the Enabler needed for that Macintosh.

In still another common example, if you switch to a different printer, you may find that your System Folder does not contain the printer driver for that printer. If you are having a problem getting background printing to work, PrintMonitor may be missing or not in its proper location in the Extensions folder. Finally, certain applications expect specific fonts, available from the Macintosh system software disks, to be installed on your startup disk. If these are not installed, you get a message saying that the font is missing. Subsequent screen displays and printed output may not be correct.

Install/Reinstall Selected System Software Files

To resolve any of the problems just described in the previous section, you can try installing or reinstalling selected files to your System Folder rather than doing a complete reinstall. There are three basic ways to do this; choose the one that is most appropriate for your situation.

Reinstall Files from Your Backups You can do this if you suspect that (or simply want to check if) a particular file is damaged, as long as you believe that your backup copy is still okay. For System, Finder, and Enabler/Update files, you could maintain a special set of backups—separate from your system software disks and your hard disk backups—just for this purpose.

To replace the System, Finder, or Enabler/Update files, you do not need to start up from another disk first. For example, to replace the Finder, you could drag the Finder from your System Folder to the desktop, then copy the replacement Finder to your System Folder, and then restart. You will restart using the new Finder; if all goes well, you can then trash the old Finder.

For most other system software files, simply replace the file from your backups as you would for any file.

FIX-IT #5

By the way, if you need to store a backup of your System file on floppy disks but the file is too large to fit on a single disk (even when compressed), you can back it up to multiple disks by breaking the file up into segments. This can be done by most backup utilities (such as Retrospect) or with compression utilities (such as StuffIt Deluxe).

Install/Reinstall Files from Your System Software Disks To replace specific system software files from your original disks, you typically use the Custom Install option. To add or replace selected categories of software, such as file sharing software, the Installer typically has a separate Custom Install option you can select. If the particular item you want is not listed in the Custom Install listing (which does happen), however, you may have to do a Custom Install of a broader set of software or even a complete Easy Install to get it.

In general, I prefer this Custom Install method over the previous method of using your backup files. This is because the files on the system software disks (especially CD-ROM discs) are less likely to be damaged (remember, you may have backed up a file after it was already damaged!). The main advantages of using backups is that it avoids possibly having to install additional unwanted files. Also, the backups can contain any customized changes you may have made to the file.

SEE ALSO: • "Take Note: Must You Use The Installer?" earlier in this Fix-It

Whatever you do, restart the Macintosh using the now-modified disk as the startup disk when you are done. If your problem is gone, congratulations.

If none of this worked, you probably need to do a complete reinstall of the system software after all (as described in "Complete Install/Reinstall of System Software"). Also, consider checking for media damage (with Norton Utilities or equivalent), especially if you receive any sort of error message that says the Macintosh was unable to successfully replace a suspected damaged file.

Otherwise, if the problem is due to an incompatibility with a particular application, you may be able to solve it by upgrading to a newer version of the application rather than by dealing with the system software. If the problem is specific to an optional feature of the system software—possibly because of a bug—you may work around the problem by not using that feature (such as turning off a control panel).

SEE: • "Take Note: Identifying System Software Compatibility Problems and Bugs," earlier in this Fix-It

Special Case: Delete Multiple System Folders

Multiple System Folders on your startup disk are a potential source of problems (see "Take Note: The Multiple System Folder Controversy, or Why Worry About More than One System Folder on Your Disk?"). To eliminate them, follow these steps:

1. **Check for any multiple System Folders on your startup disk**
   The simplest way to locate multiple System Folders is to use the Find command from the Finder to search for all files that contain "System." Alternatively, the Apple System Profiler Utility (used by most recent Macintosh models) can also check for this; simply select the System Folder Information menu item.
   By the way, there is no problem with having another disk with a System Folder on it mounted at the same time as the startup disk. The potential problem is restricted to multiple System Folders on the same startup volume.
2. **Delete any extra System Folders that you find**
   If you find more than one System Folder on your disk (no matter how many layers of folders they are buried under), delete all except the one that you intend to be the startup System Folder. Restart immediately after deleting these folders.

FIX-IT #5

TAKE NOTE ▶

THE MULTIPLE SYSTEM FOLDER CONTROVERSY, OR WHY WORRY ABOUT MORE THAN ONE SYSTEM FOLDER ON YOUR DISK?

It is best to have only one valid System Folder on your startup disk—or, to put it more precisely, only one System file and Finder should be on your startup disk.

With more than one System Folder present, you may develop problems with applications that store accessory files and preferences files in the System Folder. If these files are stored in one System Folder and another folder on the same disk is used for startup, applications will not access their accessory and preferences files and thus may not function as expected. In general, confusion may develop as to which of the multiple System Folders should be the blessed (or startup) System Folder.

More serious problems, including system crashes, may result when the Macintosh tries to access conflicting information from both System Folders, although some experts claim that the likelihood of this occurring is highly exaggerated. Everyone, at least, seems agreed that problems are especially unlikely if you are using System 6.0.7 or later (including any version of System 7). In these cases, one folder is blessed as the startup System Folder and any other ones are essentially ignored, so all should otherwise proceed as normal. Even Apple now admits that you can (and I quote) "safely store multiple System Folders on your drive."

Nonetheless, to play it safe, avoid having extra System Folders on your startup disk unless you have some deliberate need for them (for example, if you want the option to switch between two different versions of the system software).

If you are determined to have multiple System Folders on the same disk, a freeware utility called System Picker enables you to easily select or switch which System Folder you intend to use as the startup System Folder.

Sometimes you may be surprised to find an extra System Folder on your disk in the first place, since you may not recall placing it there. This commonly happens when you copy an entire floppy disk to your hard drive without realizing that there is a System Folder on that disk (in addition to whatever you intended to copy). You should certainly get rid of these extraneous System Folders.

If the System Folder you want to delete is currently the blessed System Folder, you may need to unbless it before you can delete it. To do this, drag either the Finder or the System file out of the folder, then open and close the System Folder that you want to preserve. This latter folder should now have a Macintosh icon on it. Restart; the correct folder should act as the startup System Folder, and you can now delete the unwanted System Folder. Alternatively, you could restart with an alternate startup disk and then discard any System Folders from the original startup disk.

For related information

SEE:

- **Fix-It #1 on incompatibilities between hardware and software**
- **Fix-It #2 for more on replacing preferences files**
- **Fix-It #12 on updating the disk device driver**
- **Fix-Its #10, #13, #14, and #15 on damaged files, disks, and media**
- **Fix-Its #17 and #18 on diagnostic software**
- **Chapter 1 for details on the locations of system software files**
- **Chapter 5 on startup problems and blessed System Folders**
- **Chapter 9 for more on replacing damaged font files**
- **Chapter 13 for more on problems specific to System 7.5 and its revisions**

Fix-It #6: Check for Problems with Memory Management

QUICK SUMMARY ▶

Increase free memory by closing unneeded documents and applications, adjust an application's memory allocation from its Get Info window, or make more global adjustments to memory allocation (such as by modifying options in the Memory control panel).

FIX-IT #6

When to do it:

- When you cannot perform a task because of insufficient free memory. This generally occurs when you are trying to open an application or a document; usually, you get an alert message such as "There is not enough memory to open [name of application]."
- Whenever you get an alert message stating that memory is running low.
- When software is running unusually slow, especially if it seems to be accessing the disk more frequently.
- Whenever an application quits suddenly and unexpectedly. Insufficient memory is not the only reason for an unexpected quit, but it is a common one.
- Whenever you get a system freeze, a system crash, or any less serious malfunction while using an application, particularly if you were engaging in a memory-intensive operation at the time (such as making a change to a large area of a complex graphics file). No error message need appear; the only system acknowledgment of the error may be a system beep.
- Whenever applications and/or system software have less (or more) memory assigned to them than you expected.

Why to do it:

No matter how much RAM you have, it is not enough. It may seem adequate now, but someday soon it will not be. As memory becomes cheaper, computers include more RAM in their standard configurations. But as soon as software developers expect users to have more RAM in their machines, they develop applications that require the additional memory. The original Apple II computers came standard with as little as 4K of RAM. Today, in contrast, most Macintoshes come standard with at least 12 to 16MB of RAM, which many users then upgrade to 32MB and beyond. Programs are already on the market that require this extra RAM just to launch. This Fix-It can help you deal with the inevitable memory-related problems you will face.

Almost all of your Macintosh's memory is divided into two components. The *system heap* contains the memory needed for the System file, as well as for most extensions and control panels. Meanwhile, the *application heap* contains the memory needed by applications and their documents.

TECHNICALLY SPEAKING ▶

SYSTEM HEAP VERSUS SYSTEM SOFTWARE

In the About This Macintosh window (as selected from the Apple menu), there is always a bar representing the size of the memory occupied by the system software. This is not, however, exactly the same as the size of the system heap. In particular, the Finder, as it is technically an application, is located in the application heap, but its memory size is combined with the system heap size to calculate the system software size in the About This Macintosh window. That's why you don't see the Finder listed as a separate bar. Desk accessories, on the other hand, are listed separately in the application heap.

The size of the system heap can vary depending on such things as how many extensions are in use; whatever is left over is assigned to the application heap. For example, if you have 16MB of RAM in your machine and the system heap occupies 9MB, that leaves 7MB of RAM for all applications. Every application needs a minimum amount of RAM to open and run properly (the amount is listed in the Memory area of the file's Get Info window)—if insufficient RAM is available, the application does not open. Thus, in this example, you could never open an application that required more than 7MB of RAM.

In System 7, multiple applications can be open at the same time. All open applications share the available RAM in the application heap. Each application has a maximum amount of RAM that it occupies; it does not exceed this value even if more memory is available. Again, this limit is determined by the Memory settings in the file's Get Info window. Documents opened within an application use the memory space assigned to the application. So even if an application successfully opens, it may run out of memory as you open a series of documents within the application.

If you work at the limits of your total available RAM, you are likely to get frequent memory-related alert messages. Occasionally, you may even get a system error, such as an unexpected quit, a freeze, or a system crash. These errors generally happen when, as a result of the low memory availability, the program gets "confused" and tries to address an area of memory that does not exist or has already been assigned to another use. Ideally, a program should avoid these errors and simply warn you about low memory via an alert message, but this ideal is often not attained.

SEE: • "Take Note: About 'About This Macintosh' and 'Get Info'" for more on these features

TAKE NOTE ▶

ABOUT "ABOUT THIS MACINTOSH" AND "GET INFO"

If you have any problems with memory management, it's a good idea to assess the allocation of your Macintosh's memory. Details of how and why to do this were first described in Chapter 2. Here's a summary of the essential steps:

1. Select the About This Macintosh option from the Finder's Apple menu, and check the size of the Largest Unused Block in the window that appears. The Largest Unused Block is a measure of how much memory is still free to be assigned to applications or other uses; it can never be larger than the Total Memory size minus whatever is used by the system software. Any application that needs more memory than this cannot be opened without first increasing the size of the Largest Unused Block (as described in the main text). Reminder: "About This Macintosh" becomes "About This Computer" in System 7.6.
2. Select Get Info (from the File menu of the Finder) for the application you wish to open. In the Get Info window, the Minimum size (in System 7.1 or greater) or Current size (in System 7.0) is the minimally required amount of RAM needed to open the application. In System 7.1 and beyond, the application will use more than its Minimum allotted size, if memory is available, up until it reaches the Preferred size. (The Preferred size is the maximum that the program will use.) The more closely a program opens toward its Minimum rather than its Preferred size, the more likely it is to have memory-related problems such as an inability to open large documents.

   By the way, desk accessories, though they are mostly treated like ordinary applications in System 7, do not have these memory allocation options in their Get Info windows.
3. Compare the information in the application's Get Info window and in About This Macintosh. If the program's Minimum size in the former window is larger than the Largest Unused Block in the latter, you cannot open the program. Solutions to this problem, which is probably the most common reason for the appearance of memory-related alert messages, are described in the main text of this Fix-It ("Memory Problems When Trying to Open an Application").

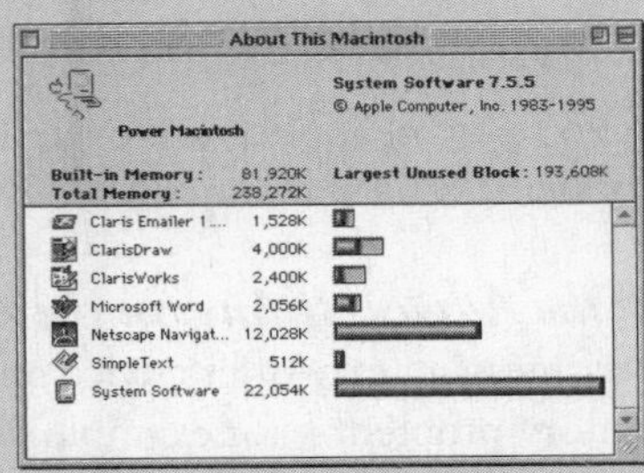

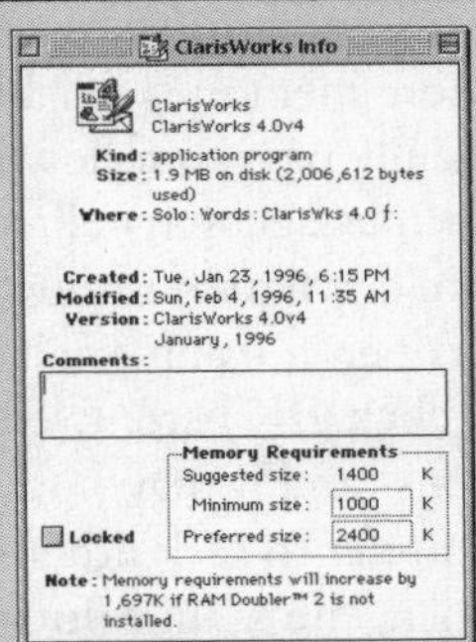

Figure F6-1 *Check these windows for helpful information about memory allocation: the About This Macintosh window (top), and an application's (ClarisWorks, in this case) Get Info window (bottom).*

Finally, note that some programs use special memory allocation schemes that differ from the standard procedures outlined here. For example, Adobe's Photoshop has its own virtual memory allocation method that may not be reflected in the About This Macintosh display.

SEE: • **"Take Note: More About 'About This Macintosh': Bar Shading" and "Take Note: Still More About 'About This Macintosh': Built-In Versus Total Memory," later in this Fix-It, for more on this feature**

What to do:

This section is divided into four parts, based on the type of memory problems you may be trying to solve.

Memory Problems When Trying to Open an Application

You try to open an application or desk accessory, but an alert message says "There is not enough memory available to open." What should you do?

Check the Advice, If Any, in the Alert Message

The alert message may offer advice on how to solve the memory problem—for example, it may say "Closing windows or quitting application programs can make more memory available." If you get such advice, it usually pays to follow it. Occasionally, however, an alert message may tell you that less memory is available than a program ideally needs, yet asks, "Do you want to open it using available memory?" Usually, I would *not* click OK here. Even if the application successfully opens (and it may not), it is likely to give you problems. I prefer to seek other solutions instead.

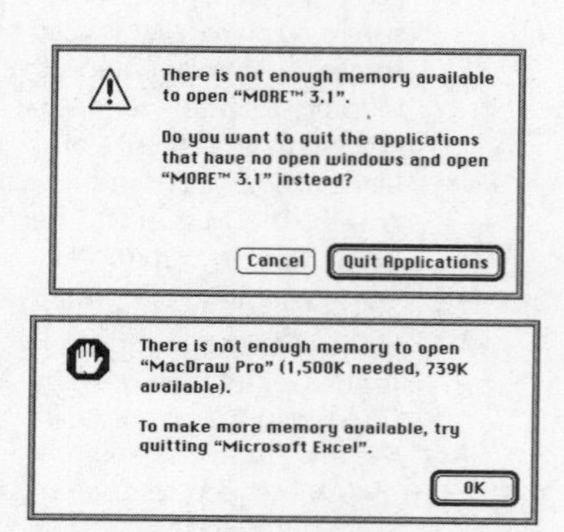

Figure F6-2 *Two examples of alert messages indicating insufficient memory to open an application.*

In particular, the main solution to any of these problems is either to make more free memory available or to reduce the amount of free memory needed by the application. To do this, try one or more of the following methods, as appropriate.

Quit One or More Other Open Applications

In System 7, you can have more than one application open at a time. Quitting open applications frees the memory occupied by those applications. Assuming you have enough total memory available to launch the problem application, quit as many programs as necessary to free enough memory. If you can relaunch the problem application successfully at this point, you may also be able to reload the other applications that you have just closed (see "Check for Fragmented Memory Space," below, for details).

Reduce the Size of a Large Clipboard

Select Show Clipboard from the Finder's Edit menu. If it indicates that a large segment of data is there (such as all of a 50-page document), get rid of the selection. Storing a large selection in the clipboard can take up extra system heap memory; reducing its size may increase the Largest Unused Block enough to allow the application to open.

To try this, go to the Finder, select something small (such as one letter of text in a file's name), and copy that selection to the clipboard. This replaces the large selection, hopefully reducing the clipboard's memory allocation.

TAKE NOTE ▶

QUICK FIXES TO "ABOUT THIS MACINTOSH" ODDITIES

Occasionally, the information displayed in the About This Macintosh/Computer window may suggest that something is wrong. Here are two common examples and their quick solutions. More details are given in the relevant sections of this Fix-It:

- If the sum of the memory used by all software together with the Largest Unused Block size is substantially less than the Total Memory size, you have memory fragmentation or a memory leak. Quit all open applications. If this does not work, the surest (although not necessarily the most convenient) solution is to restart your Mac.
- Sometimes you have more than 8MB (for example) of RAM installed, but everything over 8MB is allocated to the System Software line. If there is a 32-bit addressing option in your Memory control panel, make sure it is turned on; then restart. If 32-bit addressing is already on (or you do not have this option), restart anyway; this will fix a similar but unrelated problem that may exist.

Check for Fragmented Memory Space

What Is Fragmented Memory? You may find that an application does not open, even though enough unused memory is available to meet the requirements of the application. To understand what is probably happening, picture the total memory space as a long loaf of bread that gets divided into smaller slices, where each slice represents an

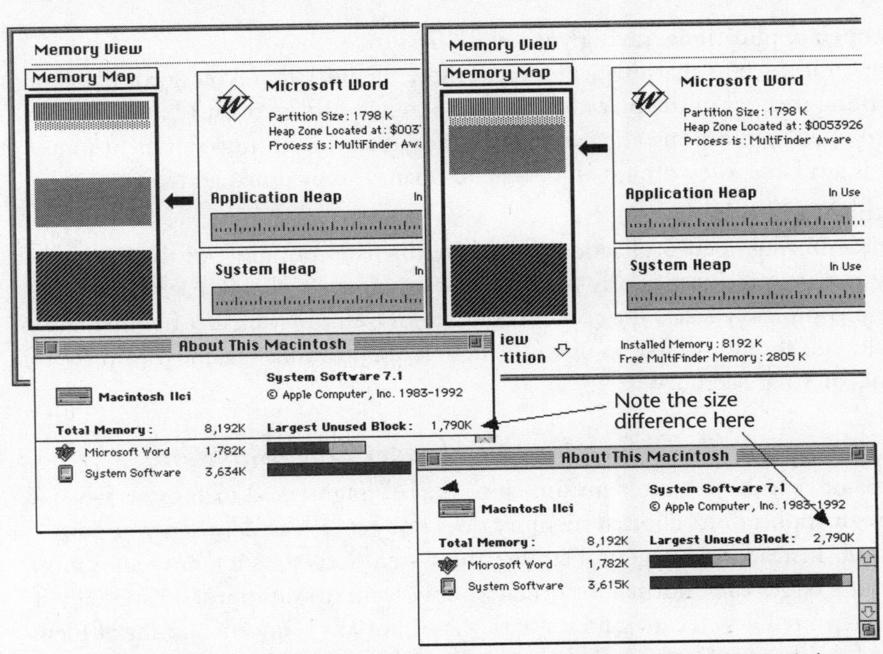

Figure F6-3 *Top: Memory maps (taken from the Memory View feature of Now Menus) that correspond to the change in the size of the Largest Unused Block shown in the bottom part of the figure. The memory map on the left shows unused memory (white space) divided into two separate fragments surrounding Microsoft Word (gray bar). On the right, after defragmenting, Word's location has shifted so that all unused memory is now contiguous. Bottom: After memory is defragmented (by quitting and relaunching Word), the Largest Unused Block increases from 1790K to 2790K.*

open application. Ideally, the slices should be adjacent to each other, so that the remaining unsliced bread forms one big block. If, for some reason, you removed slices from random locations in the loaf, however, the unused portion of the bread would be broken into smaller, noncontiguous segments.

This can happen with memory as well. Normally, applications open into contiguous (that is, adjacent) memory space. If you open, close, and reopen several applications over the course of a session, though, noncontiguous or fragmented memory blocks may exist. (Note that this is not the same as disk file fragmentation, the subject of Fix-It #8.)

The Largest Unused Block size in the About This Macintosh window indicates the largest contiguous block. If memory is fragmented, though, this amount is less than the amount of unused memory. This would mean that the sum of all the memory used by open applications plus the Largest Unused Block size would be less than the Total Memory.

In some cases, memory fragmentation can contribute to an insufficient amount of space for the system heap to expand as needed. This, in turn, can result in system crashes.

How Can You Eliminate Fragmented Memory? Unlike disk storage, where a file can be stored in fragments, an application must load into RAM as a single contiguous block. Thus, any application you want to open must fit within the Largest Unused Block. If an application needs 800K of RAM and only two separate 500K blocks are currently unused, the application does not open, even though 1MB of memory is in fact available. The solution here is as follows:

1. **Quit *all* open applications, saving your work first**
   Do this even if it seems that this will free far more memory than you need. (This is like returning the loaf in the preceding example to its unsliced form.) Now, when you try to open applications, they will load contiguously; assuming sufficient total memory is available, they should all be able to open. If they don't, go to step 2.
2. **Restart the Macintosh**
   Sometimes quitting open applications fails to restore the contiguity of the memory space; System 7 seems particularly prone to this problem. In this case, restarting the Macintosh completely resets the contents of memory, eliminating any fragmentation. As a result, you should be able to open the desired applications (again, within the constraints of Total Memory size).

Check for Memory Leaks (A Step Beyond Memory Fragmentation!)

What is a memory leak? A problem similar to that of fragmented memory is when all or part of an application's allotted memory does not get "released" when you quit the application. Instead, it may get rolled into the system software's memory allocation, making it much larger than normal, or it may simply seem to "disappear." Especially if this happens repeatedly, you can wind up with a substantially reduced amount of memory available for other applications. This is called a *memory leak*.

The difference between memory leaks and memory fragmentation is sufficiently subtle that one problem may be frequently mistaken for the other. For example, what appears to be a leak (because it occurs even when all applications are closed) may really be fragmentation due to a background application that you are not aware is still running. Basically, anytime you have a suspected memory loss of this type, try the relevant solutions for both fragmentation and leaks.

What causes a memory leak? The most common cause is a bug in Apple's system software. "Read Me" files for system software updates frequently cite that they have fixed some of these leaks, but others always seem to remain. Sometimes bugs in the application itself may cause a memory leak.

Also, programs that use shared library files may result in a particular type of memory leak. Because these files load into the system heap memory when needed, the memory they use may remain in the system heap even after you have quit the application that needed it.

SEE: • Chapters 12 and 13 for more on shared libraries

What can you do about a memory leak? The ultimate solution to memory leak problems is for developers to fix the software that causes the leak. What you can do in the meantime depends on whether you are trying to get rid of a leak you have now or are simply hoping to prevent one in the future.

Because the most common memory leak problems revolve around the use of TCP-related software (such as FreePPP and Netscape Navigator), especially with Open Transport, several of the solutions point to these programs.

SEE: • Chapter 14 for more on Open Transport and PPP

How Do I Get Rid of a Memory Leak That I Have Now?

- First, quit all open applications and see if your memory loss is still present. This ensures that your "leak" is not merely memory fragmentation.
- Use the freeware utility Mac OS Purge, which often can eliminate a memory leak. Another utility called FixHeap may sometimes help, though it is not as likely to succeed.
- Quit the Finder, preferably using a utility such as Terminator Strip (a Control Strip module that can send a Quit command to the Finder without requiring that you restart). This is more graceful and less likely to have undesirable side effects than a traditional Force Quit command from the Finder (via Command-Option-Escape), as described in Chapter 4. Any forced quit may succeed here in a pinch, though, so try the latter if necessary.
- Memory leaks related to Open Transport can be minimized—immediately after starting up and getting online—by opening up a Open Transport-dependent application that requires only a minimum of RAM and then quitting it. You will have a leak here, but it will be a small one, and subsequently opened applications that use much more RAM (such as Netscape) should then not leak. To prevent leaks, however, you will have to redo this procedure each time you restart your Macintosh.
- The only other short-term solution is to restart your Mac. As with memory fragmentation, this is guaranteed to work.

How Do I Prevent Memory Leaks From Recurring in the Future?

- If you use Open Transport, go to the TCP/IP control panel. If you are in Advanced or Administration User Mode, there is a button called Options; click it. From the window that appears, make sure that the "Load only when needed" checkbox is unchecked (although in the voodoo of how this works, some users report that *checking* this can help avoid the memory leak problem, so you may want to experiment here). This should prevent most—though not all—memory leaks that are specific to using Open Transport and applications (such as Web browsers) that use Open Transport.

  If you still seem to have a memory leak when quitting Netscape, it is probably due to a bug in Open Transport. Upgrades to Open Transport may fix it.

  SEE: • **"Technically Speaking: Open Transport, Memory Leaks, and 'Load Only When Needed,'" in Chapter 14, for more on this**

FIX-IT #6

- If you use FreePPP, do *not* check its "allow applications to open connections" option (or any other similarly named option that may be in your PPP software). This is used to have FreePPP connect automatically when an application is launched. For some reason, though, it may also contribute to memory leak problems.
- Turn on virtual memory (even at a 1MB size) or install RAM Doubler. This appears to reduce memory leak problems, at least on Power Macs, and especially so for leaks that would otherwise occur due to use of shared library files.
- Upgrading to the latest system software will help. For example, System 7.5.3 fixes a few memory leak problems, including one that occurred every time an Apple Guide file was opened. Some memory leak problems with Netscape and Open Transport have also been reportedly fixed by updating to System 7.5.3 or later versions.
- Install more RAM. Even if this doesn't prevent memory leaks, it makes them less noticeable, as you are less likely to run out of RAM when you have a lot more installed.

Reduce the Minimum/Current Memory Size

In System 7.1 and 7.5, what can you do if you want to open an application that has a Minimum size of 750K, but you cannot afford to free more than 680K of memory? You could reduce the application's Minimum size to 680K and see if it now opens. Technically, if 750K is truly the minimum needed to open the application, this should not work. In fact, when you try to close the Get Info window, you will get a message warning you about the potential dire consequences of what you are about to do. Often the posted Minimum is not really the rock-bottom minimum, however, so the application may successfully open.

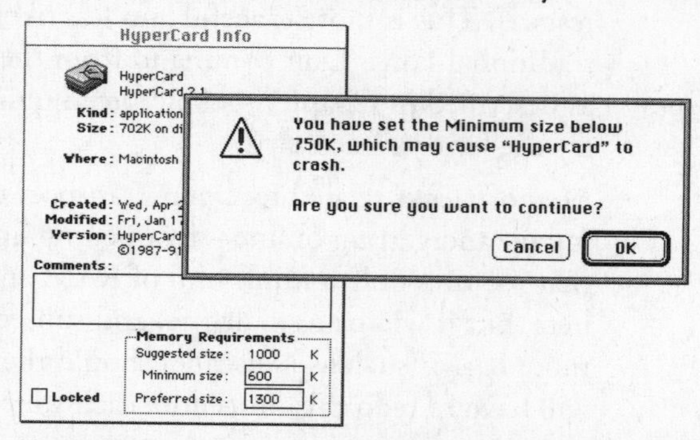

Figure F6-4 *The Macintosh warns you not to set the Minimum memory setting below its preset default value.*

I would only consider doing this if you do not intend to go very far below the Minimum size (and if the default Minimum size is not too far below the Suggested size); otherwise, you are asking for trouble in the form of an eventual system error.

In System 7.0 you have a better chance for success with this method, because the Memory settings in the Get Info window are set up differently. Here, no separate Minimum and Preferred sizes are listed; instead, there is only a Current memory size, which is often preset to a size larger than the Suggested size. If so, reducing the Current size to match the Suggested size will often get the application to open. Again, you may be able to open the application at a memory size below the Suggested memory size, if necessary.

In any version of system software, if the application is opened at reduced memory settings, you may find that not all of its features work. Still, if you only need to do this on rare occasions, it can be preferable to not being able to open the application at all.

By the way, if you do change an application's Minimum (or Preferred or Current) Memory setting, there is no button you can click to get the settings to return to their default values. If you forget the default values, you may need to check with a backup copy to find out what they were (though the message you get when trying to go below the Minimum value at least tells you the default Minimum value).

Power Macintosh Alert: If you have a Power Macintosh, turning on virtual memory may reduce the Minimum size needed to open an application (see "Increase the Total Available Memory," later in this Fix-It, for more details).

Remove Plug-in Modules and Other Accessory Files

If reducing the memory size did not succeed in getting the application to open, and if your application uses plug-in modules (such as Web browsers) or other accessory files, delete any modules you do not need. Since each of these modules typically uses a portion of the application's allocated memory, removing them lessens the amount of memory needed to run the program. If so, the application may now open in your reduced memory size setting.

TAKE NOTE ▶

UNEXPECTED QUITS AND OTHER SYSTEM ERRORS

If an application quits unexpectedly, either while you are trying to launch it or anytime after it has opened, this is a form of system error. The cause is usually a memory-related software bug in the application. It is more likely to occur when your demands on memory are high, such as when you have several applications and documents open at once. Sometimes, after an unexpected quit, you can simply relaunch the application without a problem, but just as often, doing so will result in a recurrence of the unexpected quit. Memory problems may also lead to other types of system errors (including system freezes, system crashes, or a spontaneous restart of the Macintosh). Most often, simply restarting the Macintosh—if it hasn't already done so itself—and relaunching the application clear up these problems. Sometimes, increasing the Preferred memory size of the application, as described in this Fix-It, may help. Otherwise, refer to Chapters 4 and 6 for more specific advice.

By the way, if an application already opens successfully at a given memory size, you may still wish to remove unneeded modules. Doing this leaves a greater portion of the application's allocated memory available for documents to be opened within the application (a problem discussed more generally later in this Fix-It).

If None of the Preceding Steps Work

If you are using a new, more memory-hungry version of an application, you can return to the previous version, assuming it is compatible with your other software. Alternatively, try methods to increase the amount of unused memory available; for example, eliminate unneeded extensions or turn on virtual memory.

SEE: • **"How to Increase Overall Memory Availability," later in this Fix-It**

Memory Problems When Using an Open Application (Including an Inability to Open a Document)

There is something of a paradox here. As just described, when you can't open an application, the solution typically requires freeing up more memory. When you can't open a document within an open application, however, freeing up even an infinite amount of memory is not likely to help. This is because, if the application has already opened in its Preferred memory size, freeing up more memory will not affect how much memory the application can use (barring some rare exceptions). For example, a program that has a Preferred memory size of 1MB won't use any more even if 32MB of free memory is available. Thus, these problems require a different set of solutions than those just described.

Common memory problems within an application include an inability to open a document or the application's failure to carry out a selected command (such as Copy or Paste). Typically, these symptoms are signaled by an alert message. For example, you may get a message that "there is not enough memory" to open a document, or it may say "out of memory" or "memory low." Finally, you may simply get a system error (such as an unexpected quit or a system crash).

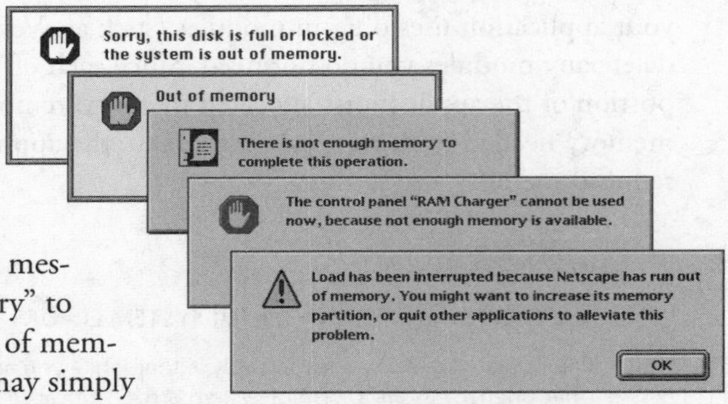

Figure F6-5 *Five examples of "out of memory" alert messages.*

For system errors, see "Take Note: Unexpected Quits and Other System Errors." Otherwise, try one or more of the following solutions, then retry opening the document (or carrying out whatever other operation was not working).

TAKE NOTE ▶

MORE ABOUT "ABOUT THIS MACINTOSH": BAR SHADING

Here's another way that the About This Macintosh/Computer window can help diagnose potential memory problems. The light-shaded portion of each application's bar indicates how much of its allocated memory is still unused; if this area is very small for a given application, memory problems may be imminent. Remember, turning on Balloon Help and placing the cursor over a bar will give you the exact amounts represented by the shaded areas.

The sum of a bar's dark- and light-shaded portions is the application's total memory allocation (and is equal to the number to the right of the application's name).

For the System Software bar, don't worry about how little white space there is, because the system software is designed so that there will always be very little white showing. If the Macintosh needs more memory for the system software, it can dynamically increase its allocation (up to some limit, of course).

FIX-IT #6

Close Any Open Documents That Do Not Need to Be Open

This increases the amount of unused memory available to the application and may permit your requested operation to proceed successfully.

Reduce the Size of the Clipboard

In some cases, the clipboard uses the application's memory allocation. Reducing the size of the clipboard is thus another way to increase the unused portion of the application's memory. To do this, select something small (such as one word from an open text document) and copy it to the clipboard.

Do Not Try to Open the Document from the Finder

When an application's unused memory is low, you may be able to open a document from within the application that would not open if you double-clicked it from the Finder.

Quit the Application and Relaunch It, Restarting If Needed

Select Save, quit the application, and then relaunch it—often, this alone will solve the problem. In fact, if you have received an "out of memory" warning message, do this before trying either of the previous two suggestions. Such messages are typically a warning to bail out immediately; if you ignore this warning, unexpected quits, system freezes, or crashes are likely to occur very soon.

If you had several document windows open previously, work with fewer open documents after relaunching. This will help avoid the return of these memory-related problems.

If relaunching alone does not work, restart the Macintosh and then relaunch again. If this still fails to work, you probably don't have enough memory allocated to the application. To correct this, continue to the next step.

Increase the Preferred/Current Memory Size

Assuming you have free memory available, increase the Preferred (or Current) memory size of the application, as listed in its Get Info window. (Note: This is somewhat the reverse of what you try to do when the application cannot open at all.)

1. **Quit the application**
   You cannot modify the memory size of an application while it is open.
2. **Check the About This Macintosh window**
   Check the About This Macintosh window to see the size of the Largest Unused Block of memory. This will be the maximum size that you can set as the Preferred size (in System 7.1) or Current size (in System 7.0) of the application.
3. a. **Increase Preferred/Current Memory size**
   Assuming free memory is available, increase the Preferred/Current memory size in the application's Get Info window. To be conservative, unless the program gave you an alert message specifically informing you how much of an increase was needed, I would increase the size by no more than 500K at first (often, 100 to 200K is enough).

   If you have enough free RAM, however, increasing this size is a good general preventative measure to reduce possible memory-related problems for almost all of your applications. Netscape Navigator, in particular, is a program that will benefit from doing this.

   b. **If the application's allocation is less than its Preferred size**
   For System 7.1 or later, the method in Step 3a assumes that the application is currently open at its Preferred memory size. If it isn't, there may be a simpler solution.

   Particularly if other applications are open, select About This Macintosh before you quit the application in order to check its actual memory allocation (see "Take Note: More About 'About This Macintosh': Bar Shading"). If the allocation is less than the application's Preferred size, there probably was not enough free memory available when you launched the program for it to open at this size. To remedy this, quit all open applications and launch just the problematic application. It should now open in its Preferred size, and you can probably now open the problem document(s). If not, quit the application again and increase the Preferred size, as described in Step 3a.
4. **Repeat the process, if needed**
   Relaunch the application and try opening the document that would not open previously (or try whatever other memory-related problem you were having). If it still does not work, increase the memory size further until you either succeed or run out of memory.

   If you do not have enough free memory available to increase the application's memory allocation sufficiently, try to increase free memory availability by using methods described later in this Fix-It.

SEE: • **"How to Increase Overall Memory Availability," later in this Fix-It**

5. **Divide the document into smaller files**
   If you succeed in getting the application and document to open by increasing the Preferred or Current memory size, consider dividing the document into separate files for future use—for example, if it is a large word processing document, divide it into two smaller segments and save each one as a separate document. You may now be able to reduce the memory size to its previous level and still avoid a recurrence of this problem. (Obviously, this technique does not work as well for graphics files or other documents that do not lend themselves to being subdivided.)
6. **Reduce memory demand of graphics files**
   Bitmapped graphics, such as TIFF files, can require a large amount of memory to open. The lower the depth and resolution of these documents when they are created, the less memory they will require to open (I am talking here about how they are saved, not how they are displayed). For instance, using 256 grays rather than millions of colors, using 72 dpi rather than 300 dpi, and so on will help reduce memory demands. If you need the higher depth and resolution, so be it, but don't use more than you need. If you succeed in getting a troublesome document to open, consider resaving it with a reduced depth or resolution to reduce its memory demands in the future.

SEE: • **Chapter 10 for more on depth and resolution**

Special Case: Finder-Related Memory Problems

Like every other application, the Finder has a memory size assigned to it. Normally, this size is adequate and does not need readjustment. At times, however, the Finder may have insufficient memory to carry out a request, most often when you are trying to copy files, eject disks, show the clipboard, or open folder windows. Usually, you will get an appropriate alert message informing you of this problem; here's what to do.

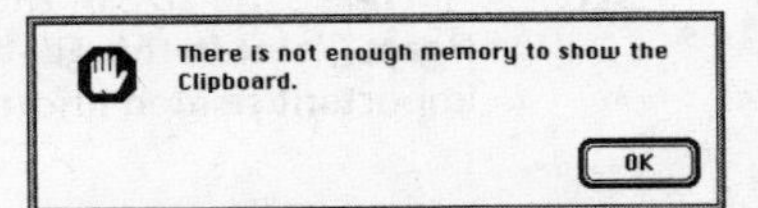

Figure F6-6 *This message may appear after the Show Clipboard command is selected from the Finder's Edit menu. If the object on the Clipboard is not unusually large, the Finder is probably running low on memory.*

Quit Applications and Close Windows

Quit any applications that do not need to be open, and close all open Finder windows that you do not currently need. Try your request again. If this fails to work, restart the Macintosh and try the desired operation once more, still maintaining a minimum of open applications and/or Finder windows.

If you get a memory error only when you are trying to copy several files at once, you should also try copying the files in smaller groups. This reduces the memory demand for each copy request.

Increase the Finder's Memory Size

If Finder-related memory problems occur often, you may be able to resolve the problem permanently by increasing the memory allocation of the Finder. Remember that this reduces the amount of memory remaining for other applications to use, so don't be in a hurry to do it.

As a rule, you should not have to bother with this solution. Apple has assigned what it believes to be an adequate amount of memory to the Finder, and usually it is right (especially if you have 12MB or more of memory). Still, if you start getting "out of memory" messages when you try to open windows or move files (or whatever) in the Finder, you could have a problem with the Finder memory allocation, or possibly even the system heap. In this case, increasing the Finder's memory is worth a try.

The simplest way to increase the Finder's memory size is via a utility; two that I know about for this purpose are called FinderFixer and Finder Heap Fix. Just launch the utility, type in your desired memory allocation for the Finder, quit the utility, and restart.

SEE: • **"Increase the Size of the System Heap," later in this Fix-It, for important related information**

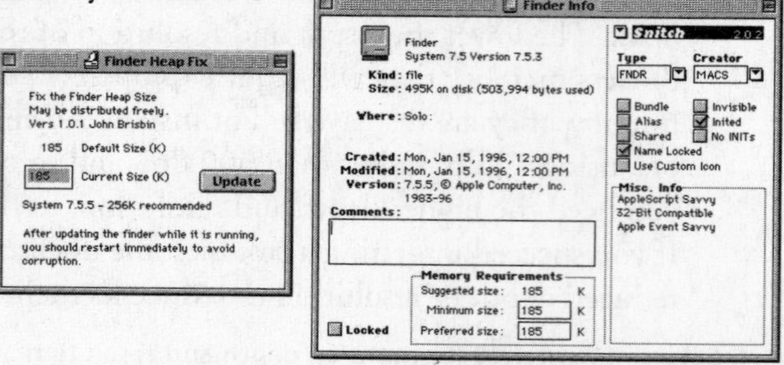

Figure F6-7 *Left: Finder Heap Fix can increase the Finder's memory allocation. Right: Using Snitch to get the Finder to show a Memory Requirements box. This method can be similarly used to increase the Finder's memory size; you can also use it with a variety of other files that would not normally show this box (details are in "Take Note: System 7.5.5 Memory Problem...").*

How to Increase Overall Memory Availability

The previous sections of this Fix-It focus on techniques that affect a single application (such as adjusting Memory settings in the application's Get Info window). If memory problems persist despite these techniques, or if they occur across numerous applications, you need to try more general solutions.

After you try any of the following techniques, relaunch the problem application and/or documents (as well as the other previously opened programs, if enough memory is available). See if all goes well.

Reduce Applications' Preferred/Current Memory Size

Many applications have a Preferred (or Current) size that is larger than the amount of memory the program typically needs in order to run. If you reduce this setting for these applications, they will be assigned less memory when opened, leaving more free memory available for other applications to use. I do not recommend doing this as a general rule, but it can be useful occasionally if you find yourself without enough memory to do what you want.

TAKE NOTE ▶

A SYSTEM 7.5.5 MEMORY PROBLEM, AND INCREASING THE MEMORY SIZE OF EXTENSIONS

The 23K problem When System 7.5.5 came out, Apple reported that users may have new problems with programs reporting insufficient memory (especially when they are first launched), because System 7.5.5 Update requires these programs use an additional 23K of memory. To fix the problem, increase the Preferred Memory size of the application by 23K.

This increased memory requirement is due to a new math library routine, added in System 7.5.5, that takes up an additional 23K. Only programs that use the library should need the increase; as it turns out, though, programs that seem to benefit from it include Desktop PrintMonitor and the Finder itself. To increase the memory size of the Finder, use the Finder Heap Fix utility mentioned in the main text.

Note: The System 7.6 Finder comes with its memory already boosted. The system software has also been fixed so that it does not grab this extra 23K. Thus, the fixes described here may no longer be needed in System 7.6 or later. Still, in case such problems crop up again, these are useful techniques to know.

Increasing memory size of extensions A few other files that seemed to need this memory boost were extensions, especially background-only applications (also known as "appe" files, as described in Fix-It #4). The problem here is that, as with the Finder, these files do not have a Memory Requirements box in their Get Info window—so how can you change their memory size? If you are familiar with ResEdit, you can do it by opening each file and directly editing its Size resource.

Alternatively, you can actually get the file's Get Info window to display a Memory Requirements box. There are several ways to do this; I will describe one that uses a utility called Snitch (described more in Chapter 8). You can do the same thing with utilities such as File Buddy, OtherMenu, or ResEdit (again). Pick the method you like best, but always work with a backup copy when you try any of this.

How to increase memory size of extensions with Snitch:

a. Go to the Get Info window of the file you want to fix, and change its Type to "APPL."

b. Close the Get Info window.

c. Make a copy of the file with the Finder's Duplicate (Command-D) command. (This is needed to get the Memory Requirements box to appear with Snitch; other similar utilities may not require this step.)

d. Open the Get Info window for the duplicate file; a Memory Requirements box will now be there.

e. Make the increase in memory as desired, then change the Type back to "appe" (or whatever it was).

f. Close the Get Info window. You can now delete the original modified file and rename the copy to match the original. The Memory Requirements box will remain visible in the Get Info window, even though it is an "appe" file again. It will disappear after a restart.

By the way, this method can also be used to adjust the memory size of the Finder, as well as desk accessories.

SEE: • **Chapter 8 for more on changing file types**

This technique is similar to what was described previously in this Fix-It as a way to get a specific application to open when free memory is low. Here the emphasis is on changing the Preferred size (rather than the Minimum size) in order to allow more applications to stay open at the same time.

TAKE NOTE

THE MEMORY CONTROL PANEL

Many of the solutions described in this section make reference to the Memory control panel. This note serves as a brief and general explanation of how and why to use it. (Always remember, you typically must restart the Macintosh before any changes you make to Memory settings take effect.)

The options listed in the Memory control panel window may differ depending on which model of Macintosh you are using. It only displays those options that are applicable to the model in use. The most common ones include the following:

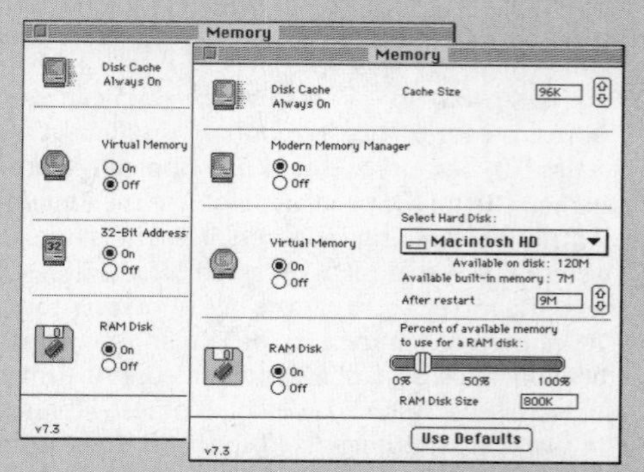

Figure F6-8 *The Memory control panel as viewed from a PowerBook 180 (left) and from a Power Macintosh 6100 (right).*

- **Disk cache.** The disk cache is a specified amount of RAM set aside to hold information that has recently been accessed from your disk. When you access new information from your disk, the new information replaces what is currently in the cache. By itself, this offers no benefit. If you request information that is already waiting in the cache, however, it is accessed directly from the cache rather than from the disk. Since RAM access is much faster than disk access, as discussed in Chapter 1, the disk cache speeds up the performance of operations that would otherwise require repeated reading of the same disk-based data.

  You can adjust the size of the disk cache, but you cannot set it to below 32K. How much benefit you get will depend on your setting size and the extent to which your use of the computer takes advantage of the cache. Apple recommends setting the size of the disk cache to 32K times the number of MB of physical RAM you have installed. Recent versions of the Memory control panel use this value as the cache's default setting. When you start up with extensions off, the Mac may not use the disk cache at all.

  Note: The Speed Access (Faster Disk Performance) component of Speed Doubler (by Connectix) is a substitute for this feature, designed to make your Mac run even faster than with Apple's disk cache.

- **RAM disk.** A RAM disk is a specified amount of RAM that has been set aside to act as if it were a physical disk mounted on the desktop. A RAM disk's icon, which looks similar to a floppy disk icon, appears on the desktop just like for any other disk. For reasons similar to the rationale for a disk cache, the speed of operations involving files copied to the RAM disk should be greatly increased. Indeed, the effect can be spectacular, since items on a RAM disk are always accessed from RAM—not just if they are repeatedly accessed.

(Continued on next page)

To see if this technique is viable for a particular application, check its Get Info window. If its Preferred memory size is set higher than its Suggested size, reduce it to as low as its Suggested size. If this causes no problems with your use of the application, leave it that way. You can get a hint if this is likely to work by initially selecting About This Macintosh when the application and a typical number of its documents are open. If the light shaded area of the bar representing the application's memory allocation is quite large, you are not using much of the memory assigned to the program; if so, reduce it.

▶ TAKE NOTE ▶

THE MEMORY CONTROL PANEL *(Continued)*

Because the disk is only in memory, though, you cannot permanently save files to a RAM disk as you can to a physical disk. Any information on a RAM disk is lost whenever the RAM is cleared; typically, this will happen every time you shut down or restart. As described in Chapters 4 and 11, you can sometimes preserve the contents of a RAM disk after a restart (even after a system crash), but you should still be cautious about saving data to a RAM disk.

The RAM disk option is available on all current Macintoshes. To create a RAM disk, select the disk's size by adjusting the slider in the RAM Disk area of the control panel, then select the On button and restart. To change the size of an existing RAM disk (or to turn it off altogether), you must first delete all files currently on it. At a practical level, the size of a RAM disk is limited by your total available memory. Because many users will need all the memory they have to run their software adequately, a RAM disk is a dispensable luxury.

- **Virtual memory and 32-bit addressing.** While the disk cache and RAM disk options use up available RAM, virtual memory (together with 32-bit addressing) is a way to increase your apparent available RAM. Virtual memory is like the mirror image of a RAM disk—instead of allocating a portion of RAM to act like a disk, it allocates a portion of a disk to act as if it were RAM. With virtual memory, you can open applications that require more memory than you physically have in memory chips. Using 32-bit addressing similarly lets you use more RAM and/or virtual memory than you otherwise could. To use either of these options, just click their On button; for virtual memory, you will also need to select a size. For more details, see "Increase the Total Available Memory," later in this Fix-It.

  On Power Macintoshes, 32-bit addressing must always be on.

  In a few rare cases (such as if a disk driver does not support virtual memory), the virtual memory box may be missing from the Memory control panel.

  Starting in System 7.5.5, Apple significantly improved the performance speed of its virtual memory.

  Connectix RAM Doubler is an alternative to virtual memory.

- **Modern Memory Manager.** This option appears only on Power Macintoshes (starting in System 7.6, it is no longer an option; it is always on). The Modern Memory Manager is essentially a new native code version of the "old" Memory Manager; its practical function is to speed up performance and reduce memory-related problems. Turning it off, however, may eliminate compatibility problems with particular applications. On System 7.5.2 or later, certain common routines of the Modern Memory Manager are also present in 680X0 emulated versions; this helps prevent compatibility problems. Finally, the makers of RAM Charger claim that their product includes fixes that prevent system crashes Modern Memory Manager would otherwise cause.

SEE: **• Chapter 11 for more on RAM disks and PowerBooks**
• Chapter 12 for more on special features of Power Macintoshes

FIX-IT #6

If necessary, you can reduce the Preferred size all the way down to the Minimum size, though this is more likely to cause other memory-related problems. You shouldn't set the Preferred value below the Minimum listed—the Macintosh will give you an alert message if you even try.

SEE: **• "Take Note: More About 'About This Macintosh': Bar Shading," earlier in this Fix-It**

Helpful hint: Using RAM Charger Syncronys Software's RAM Charger is a memory enhancement utility that essentially makes the same sort of allocation adjustments as described in this section. It does a better job of this, however, than you can do. First, it works automatically, without you having to worry about anything. Second, it can add or decrease to an application's memory allocation *while the application is open* (you cannot do this from the Get Info window). It can also borrow unneeded memory from one application and give it to another that has a greater need. The result is an effective memory management system capable of recovering many megabytes of RAM that would otherwise be wasted. RAM Charger's custom settings for each application can make the utility a bit complicated to use, but it works.

Reduce the Memory Size Needed by System Software

The system software on your startup disk occupies a portion of memory at all times. Its size varies, depending on the particular activity you are engaged in at the moment, but it generally stays within a relatively narrow range during any one session. Substantial reductions in the memory size of the system software require that you make changes that affect its initial startup size. Doing this should make more memory available for use by applications, which should hopefully solve your problem. In particular, you can turn off or remove nonessential startup extensions, turn off file sharing, remove unnecessary fonts and sounds, and reduce the size of (or turn off) the disk cache and RAM disks.

Turn Off or Remove Nonessential Startup Extensions (INITs) Because startup extensions take up memory, you should turn off any that you do not absolutely need. Remember, though, that simply turning off a control panel by selecting its Off button (assuming it has one) may not free any RAM. To recover any memory, you must disable it at startup (typically via a startup management utility, or by dragging it out of the System Folder before you restart). In extreme cases of scarce memory, you may need to disable all startup extensions by holding down the Shift key at startup.

Some startup management utilities have a feature that tells you how much memory each startup extension occupies. You can use this feature to help determine which startup extensions require especially large amounts of RAM. Occasionally, a bug in a startup extension can cause "out of memory" messages to appear even though enough memory is available; identifying and turning off these buggy startup extensions solves the memory problem.

SEE: • Fix-It #4 for more on solving startup extension problems

Turn Off File Sharing File sharing involves several related extensions. When it is in use, it takes up about 200 to 300K of system software memory; turning it off recovers this memory for other uses. To turn file sharing off, you do not have to disable the extensions at startup—instead, open the Sharing Setup control panel. If file sharing is on, the button in the File Sharing field of the control panel will read "Stop," and the Status description will say that "File sharing is on." To turn it off, click the Stop button. Of course, you should only do this if you do not plan to use this option for the time being; you typically would use file sharing to connect to other Macintoshes over an AppleTalk network.

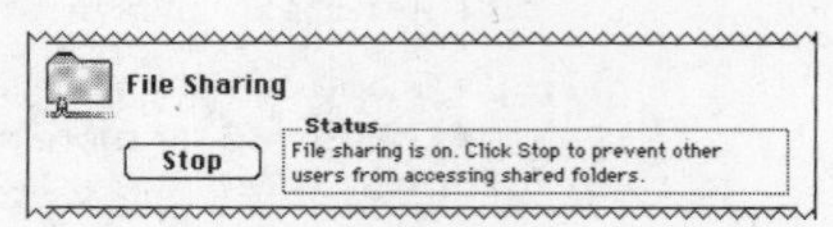

Figure F6-9 *The File Sharing section of the Sharing Setup control panel, as it appears if file sharing is currently on.*

SEE: • Chapter 11 for more on File Sharing, especially as it relates to PowerBooks

Use Classic AppleTalk instead of Open Transport I hesitate to recommend this, as Apple is steadily moving toward making Open Transport the required software for networking and online connections. If your Mac can still use Classic AppleTalk (as discussed more in Chapter 14), however, doing so will generally require less RAM. If memory is a problem, it is therefore something to consider.

Remove Unnecessary Fonts and Sounds Fonts and sounds require memory. Actually, in System 7.1 or later versions, fonts take up very little system software memory (just enough to keep track of their names), but they may increase the amount of memory needed by any application that includes a Font menu. Sounds, on the other hand, are assigned to system software memory (typically, they are stored in the System file itself)—so the more sounds you have, the more memory you use. In any case, it is best to delete fonts and sounds that you rarely or never use. Detailed instructions for removing fonts are described in Chapter 9; the procedures for removing sounds are similar.

By the way, there is a bug in System 7.1 that may cause all of your fonts to be loaded into system software at startup, a mistake that can cause significant swelling of your system software memory allocation. Upgrading to System 7.5 eliminates this bug.

FIX-IT #6

Reduce the Size of (or Turn Off) the Disk Cache and/or RAM Disks The memory required by these options is included in the system software allocation. Turning them off, while obviously eliminating whatever speed enhancement benefit they had, allows you to recover the memory they would otherwise use. You access these features from the Memory control panel (as described in "Take Note: The Memory Control Panel").

- **Disk cache**
  The disk cache cannot be turned off, but you can adjust its size via the arrow keys on the right side of the control panel window (next to the current cache size listing). Starting with System 7.5.3, the default size for the disk cache is 32K for each megabyte of physical RAM installed, up to a maximum of just over 4MB. The larger the size setting, the more RAM the cache uses, and the more performance benefit you can get—at least up to a point. You'll have to decide how you want to balance this trade-off.

  Note that the RAM cache is less effective with applications that handle mostly nonrepeating data (such as Photoshop's loading and editing of different graphics). If this is your primary use of the Mac, you can set the RAM cache to a near minimum with little or no speed loss.

- **RAM disks**
  You can reduce the size of a RAM disk or turn it off altogether. Just remember that you must delete *all* files from the RAM disk before you can change its size or turn it off. To do this, drag all files on the RAM disk to the Trash, or simply select Erase Disk from the Finder's Special menu (don't worry if you get a message that says "Initialization failed"). Although any modifications to the RAM disk settings should result in the disappearance of the RAM disk icon, you must still restart the Macintosh to see any change in memory allocation.

Also note that, starting with System 7.5.3, the minimum size for a RAM disk is 416K. If you do not have that much free RAM, the RAM Disk option will be dimmed. You also need at least 6MB of physical RAM installed to create a RAM disk.

BY THE WAY ▶

DRIVER-LEVEL VERSUS SYSTEM-LEVEL DISK CACHES

Disk formatting utilities often have options to create a disk cache separate from the one created by the Memory control panel. If you own a third-party hard drive, cartridge drive, or CD-ROM drive, such a utility may have come with your drive. Drive7 and DriveCD are two such utilities that you can purchase independent of any hardware product. The disk cache created by these utilities should show a much better performance benefit than Apple's disk cache, because they operate at a machine-specific device driver level rather than a more generic system software level. Additionally, to avoid duplication of effort, these utilities come with an option to "Disable System Cache" (which essentially prevents data used by the cache from also being sent to Apple's disk cache).

If you are using one of these utilities, be sure to check it—rather than the Memory control panel—to reduce the size of the disk cache. Also, if you select Disable System Cache (which I recommend), you can lower the size of Apple's disk cache to conserve RAM (though Apple's cache will still be used by any devices not using the third-party driver).

The Speed Access (Faster Disk Performance) component of Speed Doubler, by Connectix, is a system-level alternative to Apple's disk cache.

BY THE WAY ▶

RUNNING APPLICATIONS FROM RAM DISKS VERSUS HARD DISKS

Any application, whether it is on a hard disk or a RAM disk, loads into RAM when it opens. Thus you might think that running an application from a RAM disk offers no speed advantage over running it from a hard disk, but this is not the case. In fact, running applications from a hard disk is typically slowed down by the frequent need to access the hard disk, because only a portion of the application is in RAM at any one time. Some applications do have an option to load entirely into RAM, but this is not common. Instead, different parts get swapped in and out as needed, with the Macintosh accessing the drive each time a swap is made.

Actually, even if you run an application from a RAM disk, it will still access the hard disk whenever it requires information from the System Folder. Avoiding even this access is the rationale behind creating a startup RAM disk.

By the way, when you are running an application from a RAM disk, you can often lower its memory allocation from its Preferred size toward its Minimum size and still not see any speed decrement. Although lower memory allocations typically mean more frequent access to the disk, the disk in this case is RAM rather than the slower hard disk, so the loss of speed is not as noticeable.

For PowerBooks, a RAM disk has the additional benefit of saving battery power (because RAM access uses less power than disk access).

SEE: • **Chapter 11 for much more on RAM disks and PowerBooks**

Increase the Size of the System Heap

If you are experiencing periodic system crashes—or other strange and serious symptoms—across a variety of applications, you may have a system heap size problem. If you cannot load all of your extensions at startup due to insufficient memory, increasing the size of the system heap may help (although simply getting more memory would be even better).

A system heap problem may also underlie "out of memory" messages in the Finder, such as when you are opening a lot of windows (or, strangely, even with all applications quit and all windows closed). Thus, although they affect different areas of memory—remember, the Finder is really in the application heap—increasing the size of the system heap may fix some of the same problems solved by increasing the Finder's memory size (a technique explained in "Increase the Finder's Memory Size," earlier in this Fix-It).

Under System 6, the amount of space occupied by the system heap was largely fixed. This meant that, as you used up more of it, you had less and less left over. Eventually, you could run out of heap space altogether, which would inevitably lead to problems.

In System 7, however, the size of the system heap is dynamically regulated. This means that the Macintosh automatically adjusts the system heap's size as needed to accommodate additional files, theoretically eliminating the need to readjust the heap size yourself. Sometimes this dynamic size readjustment is insufficient, however, because the Mac finds itself needing more system heap space than it can create. This can happen, for example, when several RAM-hungry applications and startup extensions are all active simultaneously, thereby using up all available RAM and giving the system heap no room in which to grow.

When this blockade of system heap growth happens, you might think that quitting an application or two would help eliminate the problem. Unfortunately, it may not work for reasons similar to the memory fragmentation problem described earlier in this Fix-It. In particular, the system heap and the application heap ultimately share the same total memory space; the system heap starts at the "bottom" of the memory space and grows upwards, while the application heap starts at the "top: and grows downward. In the middle, there is a common area where the space can be assigned to either heap as needed. To give the system heap as much room to grow as possible, the Mac assigns applications to this middle "border" space only as a last resort. But once assigned to that space, the application stays there until you quit the application, even if space is freed above it. Because the system heap must be one contiguous block of memory, any application currently occupying the space near the border may block system heap growth.

When system heap growth is blocked for any reason, you will start getting system heap related "out of memory" messages. Quitting *all* open applications should definitely alleviate this problem (unless some "invisible" background file that does not close when you quit applications is causing the block). In some cases, you may be able to clear the system heap of unneeded data without having to quit applications. Otherwise, you can minimize the chance of a system heap block by guaranteeing more initial space for the system heap, although this leaves less memory space for applications. Here's how to do all of this:

- Use either Now Startup Manager or Conflict Catcher. With Startup Manager, open it and select its Preferences dialog box; you will find an option there called "Reserve System Heap Space." If you check this, you will have the further option to specify how much of an increase you want (generally, 20 percent is a good choice). Read the Now Utilities manual for more details.

  With Conflict Catcher, click its Prefs button. In the "General" display check the option to "Guarantee System Heap." Again, you can adjust the size; typically, 20 percent is a good size to choose.

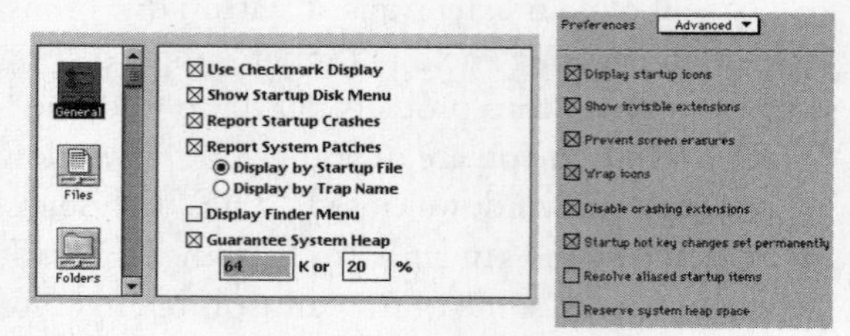

Figure F6-10 *Left: Conflict Catcher's Preferences, showing "Guarantee System Heap." Right: Now Startup Manager's Preferences, showing "Reserve System Heap Space."*

- RAM Charger includes an option called "Auto-Stretch System/Finder" that works similarly to the options for Startup Manager and Conflict Catcher.
- When you find yourself faced with the symptoms described above, it may be too late to adjust the system heap size without restarting. In this case, you might instead try to clear the system heap of unneeded data (for example, memory assigned to extensions that are not currently in use). The freeware utility Mac OS Purge can do this; it may save you from needing to restart.

If you use a lot of extensions and don't have a lot of physical RAM, you will eventually reach a limit beyond which the system heap size cannot reasonably increase no matter what you try. If this becomes a problem, your best immediate alternative is to reduce the system software memory size by following the advice in the previous section ("Reduce the Memory Size Needed by System Software"). Otherwise, just get more memory, as described next.

Increase the Total Available Memory

To increase the total available memory, you can add virtual memory, use RAM Doubler, or add more physical RAM.

Use Virtual Memory Virtual memory, accessed from the Memory control panel, fools the Macintosh into treating part of your hard disk space as equivalent to RAM. After you turn it on, select the desired size of total memory (physical plus virtual) by clicking the arrows on the right side of the control panel. The option does not let you select a higher value than your Macintosh and disk can accommodate.

Virtual memory is quick and easy to use, and it is a lot less expensive than buying more physical RAM. There are some limitations, however, to using this feature. First, some software may be incompatible with virtual memory, though this is relatively rare now. Second, if you do not have enough unused disk space to accommodate what virtual memory needs (and it usually needs a lot), you cannot use it. Third, your Macintosh will run somewhat slower when it uses virtual memory. Still, as long as no

TAKE NOTE ▶

WHY 32-BIT ADDRESSING?

Every location in memory is given an "address" by the computer, but there is a maximum number of possible addresses. The original Macs used 24-bit addressing (the bit number refers to how many digits make up an address); starting with the Mac IIci, Apple shifted to 32-bit addressing. Because this increase meant that many more addresses were now available, Macs could use more memory.

If you use virtual memory, another advantage of having 32-bit addressing on is that virtual memory and physical memory are then viewed as one contiguous space. As applications typically must load in contiguous memory, this can allow you to open memory-hungry applications that you could not open with 32-bit addressing off.

This difference in addressing schemes is determined by information built into the computer's ROM. A computer that has the necessary ROM is called "32-bit clean," a description that applies to all current Macintosh models. From a troubleshooting point of view this has several important consequences:

- Not all Macintoshes show a 32-bit addressing option in the Memory control panel; older Macintosh models (those prior to the Mac IIci) do not support this option and thus do not list it in the control panel. Power Macintoshes similarly do not list this option, because 32-bit addressing is required for these models and cannot be turned off.

  Note: An extension called MODE 32 (available free from Apple) can simulate 32-bit addressing on older Macintosh II series computers (such as the IIcx) that otherwise do not support 32-bit addressing.
- The only reason to turn 32-bit addressing off (on those models that allow you to do this) is to avoid compatibility problems with software that is not itself 32-bit clean. By now, however, almost all recent software is compatible, so it should not be much of an issue anymore.
- If 32-bit addressing does get turned off for any reason, the maximum amount of RAM that the Mac can then address is 8MB (or up to a possible maximum of 14MB of physical and virtual memory combined). If you install more than 8MB of physical RAM in your machine with 32-bit addressing off, the About This Macintosh window will show the additional RAM as included in the System Software bar, which will be now larger than it has ever been before. You will thus get no benefit from this extra RAM—until you turn 32-bit addressing back on and restart.

  Note: System 7.5.5 is the last version of the system software that will run on a Mac that does not support 32-bit addressing.

single open application requires more memory than is available with physical (built-in) memory, the slowdown should not be significant. This is because the Macintosh shifts the active application into the faster built-in memory whenever possible.

Helpful hint: Once virtual memory has been set from the Memory control panel, you can temporarily turn it off by holding down the Command key at startup. This will not disable any other Apple startup extensions. (It is possible that some non-Apple startup extension uses the Command key to similarly disable it at startup, however, so check for this first.) Virtual memory will return automatically the next time you start up. Thus, this technique allows you to toggle virtual memory on and off without having to go to the Memory control panel each time.

TAKE NOTE ▶

STILL MORE ABOUT "ABOUT THIS MACINTOSH": BUILT-IN VERSUS TOTAL MEMORY

You can, of course, use the Memory control panel to see if you have virtual memory turned on (and, if so, how much virtual memory you have). You can also check this, however, from the About This Macintosh/Computer window. If virtual memory is in use, a new listing called Built-in Memory appears above the Total Memory listing; the difference between these two numbers is how much virtual memory you have. Using RAM Doubler similarly results in the appearance of the Built-in Memory versus Total Memory distinction.

Also, on Power Macs, the Total Memory may be larger than expected when virtual memory is on. This is not a cause for concern, although you really don't have the extra memory. Without going into details here, the mislisting is a consequence of how the Power Mac deals with the presence of its 68040 emulator (which is needed to run non-native applications on a Power Mac).

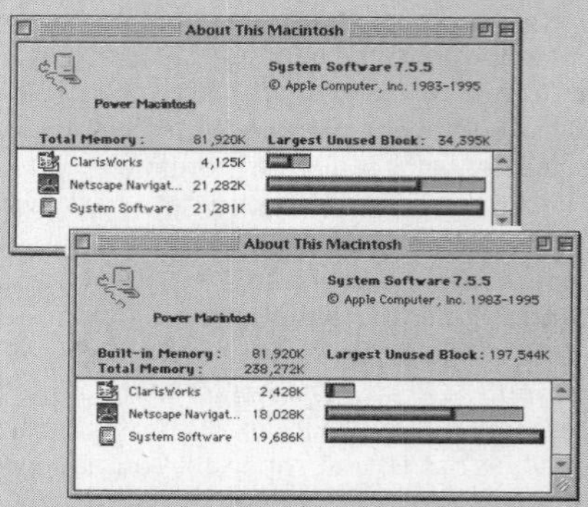

Figure F6-11 *The About This Macintosh window with RAM Doubler off (top) or on (bottom). Note the added Built-In Memory line when RAM Doubler is on; using Apple's virtual memory has a similar effect. Also note how the Power Mac native applications (ClarisWorks and Netscape) take up more memory when RAM Doubler (or virtual memory) is off.*

Power Macintosh alert: If you have a Power Macintosh, you may notice that the Get Info windows for PowerPC native code applications have a message about virtual memory at the bottom of the window. These messages basically tell you that the amount of memory needed to open the application will be less when virtual memory is on; this is due to file mapping, which is described more in Chapter 12. Indeed, if you turn virtual memory on (even using as little as 1MB), the Suggested, Minimum, and Preferred values will all change to lower numbers. Thus, for Power Macintoshes, turning on virtual memory has a double benefit: it makes more memory generally available to all applications, and it allows native code applications to open with less memory.

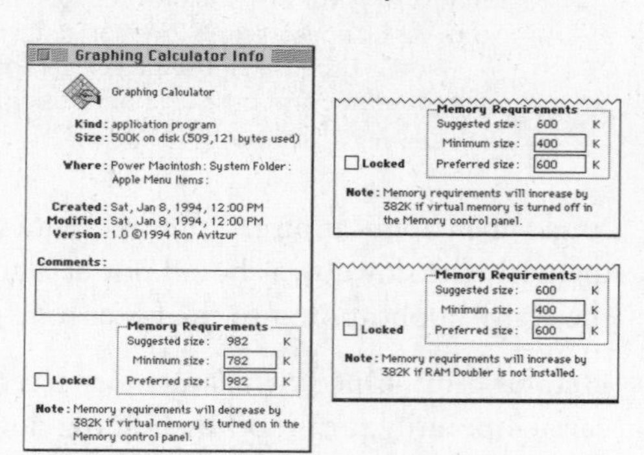

Figure F6-12 *The memory savings effect of using virtual memory or RAM Doubler, as seen from the Get Info window. Left: The Get Info window for a native code application on a Power Macintosh, with virtual memory off. Right: The bottom of the Get Info windows of the same application when virtual memory is on or RAM Doubler is on.*

Running native applications on a Power Mac with virtual memory off often requires significantly more memory than running a non-native version of the same application on a 680X0 Mac! Even with virtual memory on, native versions can be memory hogs.

If you should change any Preferred or Minimum values with virtual memory on, the values that appear when you turn virtual memory off will be altered by the same absolute amount (and vice versa).

RAM Doubler works similarly to System 7's virtual memory and leads to similar messages in Get Info windows.

SEE: • **Chapter 12 for more information on Power Macs and memory**

TECHNICALLY SPEAKING ▶

MORE ON LIMITATIONS OF SYSTEM 7'S VIRTUAL MEMORY

If you have problems using virtual memory, this information may help you figure out what's going on:

- Using virtual memory requires that your Macintosh have a Paged Memory Management Unit (PMMU). This is a small piece of hardware that is built into the 68030, 68040, and PowerPC processors. Models using the 68000 and 68020 processor (found in older models, such as the Macintosh Plus and SE) do not include a PMMU.
- For a given amount of virtual memory, you need disk space equal to the amount of virtual memory you want, plus the amount of physical RAM you have installed. Thus, adding 1MB of virtual memory to a machine that currently has 8MB of RAM requires at least 9MB of available disk space. If your disk space is getting tight, you may not want to give up this much space for use as virtual memory.

  This requirement can be especially problematic for those of you who have installed lots of extra physical RAM. For example, if you have 80MB of physical RAM, you will need 81MB of hard disk space just to add 1MB of virtual memory (of course, with hard disks now commonly larger than 1 gigabyte in size, this may not be too much of a problem).

  If disk space does become a problem, one solution—other than keeping virtual memory off—is to use RAM Doubler, which doesn't require the disk space that Apple's virtual memory does.
- Virtual memory also requires that your disk driver be compatible with this feature. If you haven't updated your driver since moving to System 7, you may need to update it to use virtual memory (see Fix-It #12 on drivers). A driver problem is especially likely if your Memory control panel does not even show a virtual memory area.

Use RAM Doubler In many ways, RAM Doubler behaves just like System 7's virtual memory; it even results in the same Built-in Memory versus Total Memory listing appearing in the About This Macintosh window. In fact, Connectix (the makers of RAM Doubler) refer to both of these techniques as examples of *extended memory*. However, because RAM Doubler accesses the hard disk much less frequently than does System 7's virtual memory, it is usually faster.

RAM Doubler effectively doubles or even triples your apparent RAM, getting your Macintosh to act almost exactly as it would if you actually added an equivalent amount of physical RAM. Speed decrements may occur at times (especially as you approach the limits of available memory), but they are usually minor. Also note that RAM Doubler works best when you use it to open more programs at once, rather than to assign increasing amounts of memory to a single program.

Because of its pervasive effect on your system, compatibility problems with RAM Doubler are more common than with most other programs. To keep these to a minimum, always check with Connectix to make sure you are using the latest version of RAM Doubler.

SEE ALSO: • **"Reduce Applications' Preferred/Current Memory Size," earlier in this Fix-It, for information on RAM Charger, another memory enhancement utility**

Helpful hint: You can turn off RAM Doubler at startup, leaving all other extensions on, by holding down the tilde (~) or Escape keys at startup. Conversely, you can start up with all extensions off except for RAM Doubler by holding down Shift-Option at startup.

TAKE NOTE ▶

NEW FEATURES OF RAM DOUBLER 2

RAM Doubler 2, the successor to RAM Doubler, offers three major new features:

- It can *triple* your RAM and still work just as fast, if not faster, than the original RAM Doubler.
- It includes a control panel that provides information similar to that in the About This Macintosh window, but you can also see how the System Software memory is split among such things as the System file, the Finder, the disk cache, and any RAM disk. It will even show any background applications that may be hidden in the system software allocation. In addition, control panel settings allow you to adjust how much of a memory boost you want RAM Doubler 2 to give.

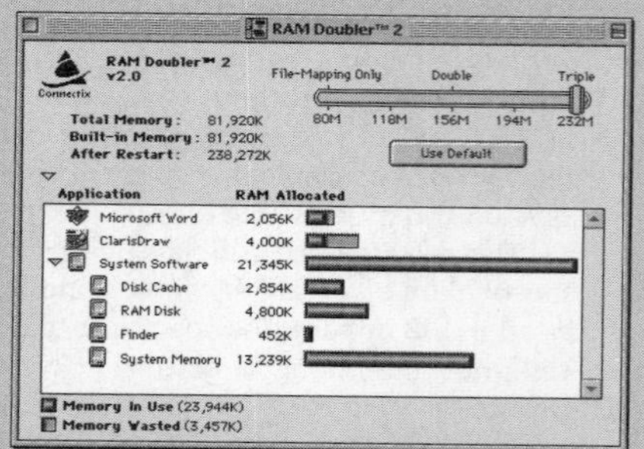

Figure F6-13 *The RAM Doubler 2 control panel, where you can adjust how much of a memory boost you want. Also note the listing of the separate components of the system software RAM allocation.*

- For Power Macs: If you don't really need RAM Doubler 2 to give you any additional memory (and you want to minimize any slowdowns in performance that using RAM Doubler 2 might cause) but you do want to take advantage of the reduced memory requirements of Power Mac native programs that using RAM Doubler 2 permits—as described in the "Power Macintosh Alert" in the main text—simply adjust the slider in the control panel to the left end, where it says "File-Mapping Only."

Add More Physical RAM As a last resort, if memory problems persist, you can solve them by adding more dynamic RAM (or DRAM) memory chips (SIMMs/DIMMs) to your Macintosh. If you frequently find yourself short of needed RAM, though, adding memory should *not* be a last resort, because there is no better solution to memory problems. It has no disadvantage other than price (and, as of this writing, prices are incredibly low). These days, you should have at least 16MB of RAM on a Power Mac—more, if you can afford it.

Adding new SIMMs/DIMMs (or replacing existing ones) is a hardware modification that, depending on your particular model of Macintosh and your willingness to try, can be easy to do yourself or may require that you take your Mac to a dealer. Essentially, you insert the memory into special slots located on the computer's main logic board. (One important caveat: Whenever you add or replace memory, there is a chance that the memory may be of the incorrect type, defective, or incorrectly installed. This can lead to *very* serious problems, including an inability to start up the Macintosh.)

The details of which types of SIMMs/DIMMs to buy, how to install them, how much you can increase your RAM, and in what increments vary significantly among the different Macintosh models. Additional details on these matters are covered in Fix-It #17. If you need still more information, contact an authorized Apple dealer or seek other outside help.

For related information

SEE:
- **Fix-It #4 on extensions and control panels**
- **Fix-It #17 on hardware repairs and upgrades, including adding SIMMs**
- **Fix-It #18 on seeking outside help**
- **Chapter 1 on hardware terminology (SIMMs, processor, and so on)**
- **Chapter 2 on the Get Info command and the About This Macintosh window**
- **Chapter 4 on unexpected quits and other system errors**
- **Chapter 5 on startup problems**
- **Chapter 6 on applications and files that will not open**
- **Chapter 9 on installing and removing fonts**
- **Chapter 11 on RAM disks and file sharing**
- **Chapter 12 for special memory issues regarding Power Macintoshes**
- **Chapter 13 for more on memory problems specific to System 7.5**
- **Chapter 14 for memory issues related to Open Transport and using Web browsers**

Fix-It #7: Check for Viruses

QUICK SUMMARY ▶

Use an updated anti-virus utility to scan your disk for viruses. Replace any infected files with clean copies from your backups. If no backup is available, use the anti-virus utility to eradicate the virus and repair the infected file.

When to do it:

FIX-IT #7

- Whenever you get a warning message from your anti-virus utility that a virus attack has occurred.
- If you have frequent and unpredictable system crashes.
- When you replace an apparently corrupted file and it soon becomes damaged again.
- If the Macintosh system beep, or any other sound, occurs at unusual times and for no discernible reason.
- If files have been inexplicably erased from your disk.
- If a strange or nonsensical alert message unexpectedly appears on your screen.
- If you have just installed an anti-virus utility for the first time or are using a new disk that has not been previously checked for viruses.
- When any of an assortment of system-level problems occur: for example, applications take unusually long to open, all (or almost all) applications have trouble printing documents, cursor movement is erratic, or windows refuse to open or close. These symptoms have several possible causes, as covered in other Fix-Its. The probability that a virus is the cause increases if you have recently engaged in high-risk activity for virus infections (see "Take Note: How to Catch a Virus," later in this Fix-It).

These are just some of the more general symptoms associated with various viruses. For more specifics, see "Technically Speaking: A Few Known Viruses and Their Symptoms."

Why to do it:

A virus is a special type of software program with two main purposes in life. Its first (and most critical) purpose is to duplicate itself—in particular, to spread copies of itself to other disks and other computer systems. Its second function is to carry out some activity on each disk where it resides. This activity can be as benign as sending a message that says "Peace," or as vicious as erasing your hard disk.

TECHNICALLY SPEAKING ▶

A FEW KNOWN VIRUSES AND THEIR SYMPTOMS

You don't have to know anything about the specific names or even the symptoms of known viruses in order to use an anti-virus utility, because the utility does all the necessary checking for you. Still, should you be interested, your anti-virus software probably includes a description of all viruses known at the time it was released (or updated). Here is a selected sampler of the specific symptoms of four well-known viruses, taken from Disinfectant's documentation:

- **nVIR.** It infects the System file but does not create any invisible files. It exhibits no symptoms other than a periodic message ("Don't Panic") or system beeps at startup.
- **INIT29.** This will infect almost any application or system file. It does not do deliberate damage, but every time you insert a floppy disk, you will get a message that the disk is damaged and needs "minor repairs."
- **T4 virus.** Computers with this virus will be unable to load startup extensions at startup. It infects applications and system files.
- **INIT-M virus.** Designed to act on Friday the 13th, this virus attacks system files, applications, and documents. The damage it does includes changing folder names and the creator and type codes of files.

In general, be wary of extensions and invisible files with strange names that seem to have appeared out of nowhere. Also beware of familiar system files that suddenly appear with strange icons. These are all possible symptoms of a virus.

TAKE NOTE ▶

SCRIPTABLE VIRUSES: A NEW VARIATION ON VIRUSES

A new form of virus is among us: *scriptable viruses*. One type, in the form of HyperCard scripts (using the HyperTalk language), only infects HyperCard stacks. An example of this is the "Merryxmas" virus that was inadvertently present in some copies of (a now out-of-date version of) Apple's SIMM Stack. It does no active harm to your Mac. "HC 9507," a more recently reported HyperCard virus, types the word "pickle" and makes the system behave strangely.

Another form of scriptable virus, Word Macro viruses, can infect Microsoft Word 6.0 documents and templates (examples include viruses named "Word Macro 9508" or "WordMacro.Concept"). Written in the Microsoft Word macro language, Word Basic, they have an effect only when using Word 6; infected documents appear with the template icon, rather than the usual document icon. The simplest solution here is to delete infected files, although a file available online from Microsoft, called "mw1222.hqx" at Internet locations, can supposedly eradicate the virus.

Although older anti-virus utilities (including Disinfectant) ignore these HyperCard and Word Macro scriptable viruses, the latest versions of SAM and Virex do check for them.

Viruses duplicate themselves in a variety of ways. The most common method is for a newly arriving virus to locate a specific system software file on your disk and infect it (that is, place a copy of itself within the file's code/resources. It then uses that file as a base of operations for further infections. The system and Finder files, control panels, and extensions are frequent initial sites of infection (it varies according to the particular virus).

TAKE NOTE ▶

HOW TO CATCH A VIRUS

The only way your files can be infected by a computer virus is if they come in contact with a file that is already infected. The probability that this will happen depends on the nature of your computer activity. Activities that place you at higher risk include the following:

- Using a modem to connect to an electronic bulletin board or information service. In particular, you can become infected if you attempt to use a downloaded file that contains a virus. The major services check files for viruses before listing them for downloading, but sometimes a bad file sneaks through. For example, just within the last few months, I downloaded a HyperCard stack from the Info-Mac archive on the Internet and found it was infected with the "Merryxmas" virus. Happily, I had SAM installed and set to scan files at launch, and it picked up the virus before it spread.
- Using a disk given to you by someone else. It doesn't matter whether the person giving you the disk is a close friend or a total stranger; a friend could give you an infected disk without realizing it contains a virus.
- Inserting an unlocked floppy disk into a computer other than your own and then later inserting it in your computer.

Conversely, the odds of coming in contact with a virus are relatively low if you stick to using only shrink-wrapped copies of commercial software, downloaded files from information services that are known to check for viruses, and disks from friends or reputable user groups whom you know to take adequate precautions against viruses. Also, keep your floppy disks locked as much of the time as possible, especially when taking them from one machine to another.

By following this advice, I have had only one (attempted) virus infection in the last several years, even though I work at a university and frequently access a campuswide network.

Once the virus has successfully infected a file on your disk, the virus code typically acts as a startup extension (see Fix-It #4), loading into memory at startup. From there it executes its code, with instructions on how and when to duplicate itself as well as whatever else it may have been programmed to do. For example, every time an application on the disk is launched, the virus code is alerted and typically will infect that application. Occasionally, a virus might attach itself to a driver (such as a printer driver) and execute its code when you access the driver (such as when you attempt to print something).

Transfer of the virus to a different disk usually involves some inadvertent help from the user. For example, a virus on a hard disk can transfer to a floppy disk either when you copy an infected file to the disk or if you run an application from it while the infected hard disk is mounted. When the newly infected floppy disk is mounted on another computer, the process begins anew, with the virus transferring itself to the startup disk of the other machine.

A few viruses work by attaching themselves to a disk's invisible Desktop file (see Fix-It #9 for more on this file). These viruses spread to other disks as soon as an uninfected disk is inserted and mounted; no copying of files across disks or launching of applications is necessary.

Though a few exceptions exist, most viruses cannot infect an application until it is launched, and they cannot affect document files at all.

Viruses are created by unscrupulous programmers. Other than the misplaced sense of pride they may give their creators, viruses have no purpose other than to cause trouble for unsuspecting users. Fortunately, most viruses are relatively benign—that is, they do not deliberately alter or damage your software other than to do what is necessary to duplicate the virus. Because legitimate software is not designed to accommodate viruses, though, even a so-called benign virus can cause problems. Frequent system crashes or damaged files can easily result. Ironically, viruses occasionally have bugs that result in their causing even more harm than their creator intended.

A few viruses are deliberately destructive. Most threatening in this regard is a variation on viruses called a *Trojan horse*—a phony program, often disguised as a game. The real purpose of the program is to do damage to your disk, often erasing all the files on it (an insidious task it begins as soon as you launch the program). The only good news is that, unlike a true virus, a Trojan horse cannot replicate itself; to be transferred to another disk, it must be deliberately copied by the user.

Benign or malicious, viruses and Trojan horses are things that you do not want to have around.

FIX-IT #7

TAKE NOTE ▶

VIRUS HOAXES (AND GETTING VIRUSES FROM EMAIL)

As if dealing with real viruses wasn't enough of a pain, now you also have to worry that the latest virus threat you read about is really a hoax. The most well-known example of this is the fictional "Good Times" virus, which you may get warned about via an unsolicited email. According to the "warning," you should beware of any email message with the subject "Good Times," because even reading such a file could erase your hard drive or destroy your processor. Do not believe this message; it is a hoax.

More generally, at least on a Macintosh, you can *never* get a virus from an email message itself (although you could get one from a file that you receive via email, if you launch the file).

Similarly—although I worry about exceptions to this rule—you cannot get infected from any file that you download until you attempt to open the file.

TAKE NOTE ▶

AUTOMATIC PROTECTION FROM A POSSIBLE VIRUS IN A DOWNLOADED FILE

Starting with version 4.5, SAM includes a new feature called SafeZone. When installed, an area of your drive is designated as a SAM SafeZone; This is where you should initially receive any files that you download from online sources. SAM then automatically scans each file as you download it, thereby preventing any chance that it can infect your drive. Latest versions of Virex include a similar feature.

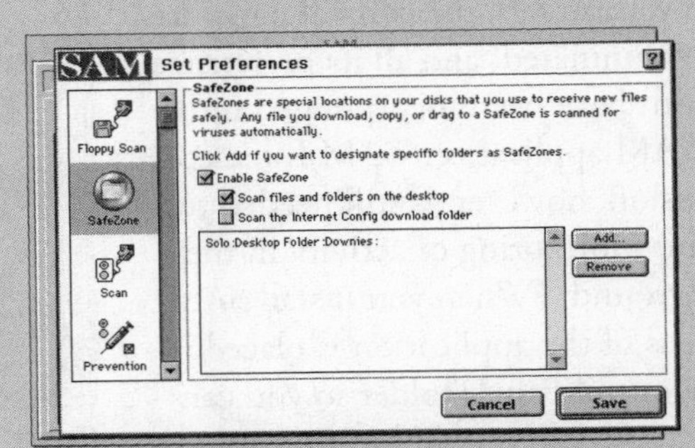

Figure F7-1 *SAM's SafeZone Preferences settings.*

What to do:

Your best defense against viruses is to prevent them from infecting your disks in the first place (see "Take Note: How to Catch a Virus"). Failing that, check for ones that may already be present and get rid of any that you find.

Use an Anti-Virus Utility

Install an Anti-Virus Utility

A current version of a good anti-virus utility is your main line of defense against viruses, so be sure to install one on your startup drive. As mentioned in Chapter 2, the most popular anti-virus utilities these days are Symantec Antivirus for Macintosh (SAM) and Virex. Disinfectant has not been updated in over a year. However, a new anti-virus utility, McAfee VirusScan, is a commercial product based on Disinfectant. It seems promising.

FIX-IT #7

I will use SAM as the primary basis for examples in this Fix-It. Although other anti-virus utilities work differently, enough similarity exists that these guidelines should be helpful no matter which one you use.

Most anti-virus utility packages include an application plus a system extension and/or control panel. The application can scan a disk (or just selected folders/files within a disk) and eradicate all copies of any virus it detects, either by deleting or by repairing infected files. SAM's application is simply called SAM (it was called SAM Virus Clinic in older versions).

The extension/control panel is designed primarily to detect a virus before it infects your disk. For example, once installed, a typical anti-virus control panel continually monitors for potential attempted infections, working in the background while you do other tasks. It can also be set to trigger a complete scan of a disk, checking for viruses that may somehow already be present. In particular, you can configure it to scan floppy disks immediately after a disk is inserted (that is, before it is actually mounted). You can also set it to scan your startup disk every time you start up or shut down your computer.

Versions of SAM prior to 4.0 included a SAM Intercept control panel that you opened to select the various background checking options. Starting with version 4.0, the control panel has been eliminated, and all its preference options have been incorporated into the SAM application. SAM Intercept extension, however, is still needed to permit monitoring of activity in the background. (When you install SAM, an alias of the application is placed in the Control Panels folder so you can access SAM from that location.)

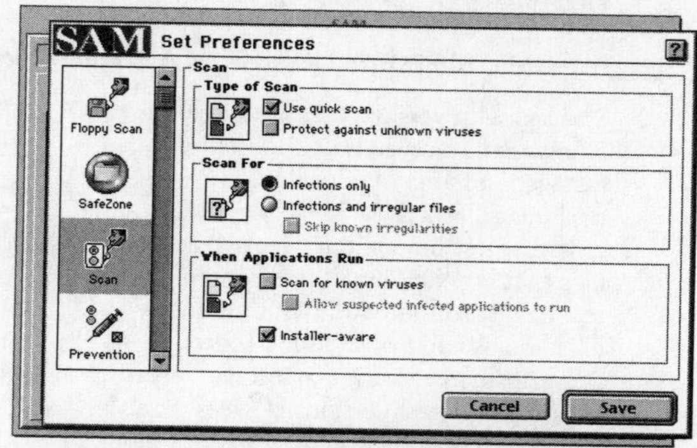

Figure F7-2 *SAM's Scan Preferences with Quick Scan turned on.*

The latest versions of SAM and Virex also include a feature designed to speed up the scanning of your disk for viruses (QuickScan for SAM, or SpeedScan for Virex). They similarly reduce the time needed to check an application for viruses each time it is launched, if you use this option. Older versions of SAM were particularly slow in doing this launch checking of applications; the new QuickScan option is a definite improvement.

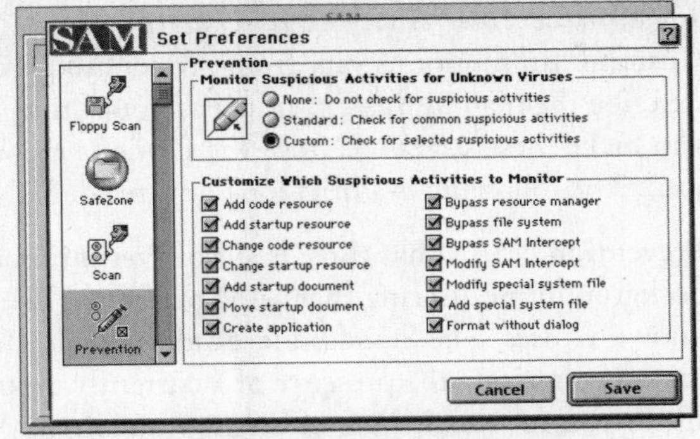

Figure F7-3 *SAM's Prevention Preferences with Custom Prevention selected.*

Keep Your Anti-Virus Utility Updated

When you install SAM, a file called SAM Virus Definitions is placed in your System Folder. This file contains the information needed by SAM to identify and repair specific viruses; new versions are released every time a new virus is discovered. Thus, if you want to detect new viruses reliably, you need to replace your Virus Definitions file periodically with updated versions. Symantec also occasionally releases updates for the program itself as well as the Virus Definitions file.

Depending upon what anti-virus utility you have, what level of service you may have paid for, and the vagaries of your vendor's changing policies, you *may* receive a notification via a postcard or email when a new virus is discovered. Of course, you must at least be a registered user to get this benefit. Otherwise, check online (at the locations listed in your utility's documentation) for updates as needed; your anti-virus utility may have a built-in feature to assist you in doing this. In fact, SAM 4.5 or later has an Auto Update option that automatically downloads SAM's latest virus definition file at scheduled intervals.

TECHNICALLY SPEAKING ▶

USER DEFINITIONS

Some anti-virus utilities, including SAM, allow the user to enter a virus definition directly (or "manually"). With this information, as would be obtained from Symantec, you can add new virus definitions to a file in your System Folder called SAM User Definitions. This is an unneeded hassle these days, however, and updating this way may mean that you can only use SAM to detect the added virus, not to repair it. Preferably, you should instead use your modem to download the latest SAM update (or an equivalent update for other utilities).

Customize Your Anti-Virus Utility

Customization options vary from product to product, and there are too many for me to describe them all in this Fix-It; check your utility's documentation for help. With SAM, you make these selections from the Options menu (or by clicking the Preferences button). The following is a brief look at three of SAM's Preferences options.

Prevention SAM has three levels of Prevention checking, which determine the sort of background monitoring that SAM performs. The lowest level (None) checks only for known viruses. The Standard level additionally checks for certain suspicious activities that may indicate the presence of a currently unknown virus. The third level (Custom) allows you to select which of these suspicious activities you want checked. The None level is probably sufficient for most situations, as long as you keep your Virus Definitions file up-to-date. Unless you are in a very high-risk environment (see "Take Note: How to Catch a Virus"), you are unlikely to come in contact with a virus not covered by the latest Virus Definitions file.

Scan From the Scan Preferences window, you select what SAM does when it scans your disk; for example, here is where you select whether or not to use QuickScan. You can also select whether SAM should "Protect against unknown viruses" and scan for "Infections and irregular files" (you can additionally request that it overlook irregularities that are commonly considered "legitimate"). Since irregular files are a signal of a potentially unknown virus, these two options are simply different methods of achieving the same goal—one method may catch something that the other method does not. Similarly, checking for irregular files during a scan checks for the same sort of oddities as does the "suspicious activities" background monitoring just described. While this overlap of features makes it a bit confusing to figure out which setting does what, don't worry too much: as I have already noted, attacks from unknown viruses are rare, and most users can safely leave all of these options off.

Next, you can decide here if you want SAM to scan applications for viruses each time an application is launched. This is a good idea, but do *not* select the suboption to allow infected files to run (otherwise, you run the risk of spreading the infection). Finally, you have a special option here called "Installer-aware," which disables SAM when it detects that Apple's Installer is in use. Unless this is checked, using the Installer is likely to trigger false alarm virus alerts (as described more in "Suspicious Activity False Alarms," later in this Fix-It).

Compression Some anti-virus utilities cannot scan for and detect viruses contained within compressed files on your disk, such as those created by DiskDoubler or StuffIt; you would have to decompress the files to check them. Both SAM and Virex, however, can check compressed files. To do this with SAM, go to its Compression options window and select what types of compressed files you want it to check. The downside of selecting this option is that scanning compressed files takes more time than checking normal files.

Prevent a Virus Attack from Infecting Your Disk

A Virus Is Detected

If SAM Intercept detects an attempted infection by a known virus (either while Intercept is scanning an infected disk or when you are launching an infected application), an alert message will appear, telling you the name of the virus and which file is infected. The alert box will also give you the choice to Proceed (thereby ignoring the warning), Stop (aborting the launch of an infected application), or Run SAM (if it is currently installed on your disk).

In most cases, you should select stop. Definitely do not click the Proceed button, which essentially bypasses SAM's anti-virus protection, thereby risking further infection. With some other anti-virus utilities, the equivalent command supposedly launches the application (if possible) in a manner that prevents the spread of the virus. Even so, I would avoid using this command—it is far better to eradicate the virus before proceeding.

Though it is probably safe to do so, I would also avoid going directly to SAM. Instead, when SAM detects a virus and identifies a specific file on your startup disk as the source, immediately go to the desktop, locate the infected file, and delete it. If SAM detects a virus while scanning a floppy disk, immediately eject the disk. In either case, now restart with a locked startup floppy disk that includes SAM; use this disk to check for and eradicate any remaining virus infections.

By the way, if you have SAM set to protect against unknown viruses, you may get a similar virus alert message that does not include the name of a virus. This does not necessarily mean that you have a virus infection—it could be a damaged file or a false alarm. Similarly, Disinfectant may mistakenly report that a damaged font file is infected with a virus.

SEE: • **"Eradicate an Existing Virus," later in this Fix-It, for what to do next**

A Suspicious Activity Is Detected

SAM can detect a variety of suspicious activities that may or may not indicate an infection attempt by a new or unknown virus. These notifications do not depend on information in the Virus Definitions file; rather, they are determined by SAM's Prevention settings (as described in "Customize Your Anti-Virus Utility," earlier in this Fix-It).

When SAM detects a suspicious activity, an alert box appears with buttons to either Allow or Deny the continuation of the activity. If you want to allow the activity, and suspect that this same situation will recur, you can select Remember rather than Allow (the Remember button only appears if you have previously checked the option for it in the Alert preferences window). If you select Remember, it tells SAM not to give you this alert for any future repetition of this suspicious activity. It is up to you to decide what button to press; make this decision based on whether you believe the alert indicates a real virus threat or a false alarm.

Suspicious-Activity False Alarms

A suspicious-activity alert does not mean a virus attack is under way, because these alerts often occur during normal activities. For example, you can set SAM to alert you every time a new extension or control panel is copied to your disk. The rationale for this is that viruses are often transmitted as extension code.

If a suspicious-activity alert message appears when you are intentionally copying a new extension to your disk, there is nothing to worry about. Click the Allow button. If this message appears when you are not copying anything, however, you should probably click the Deny button to halt the activity immediately. Be aware, though, that because clicking Deny short-circuits whatever was going on at the time, it can damage the affected file even if no virus attack was occurring.

Running any Installer utility (as described in Fix-It #5) is another activity that commonly triggers these alert messages. Again, nothing is amiss, so click the Allow button. Suspicious-activity alert messages may appear repeatedly while an installation is in progress. In some cases, it can prevent the installation from successfully completing. To avoid this, temporarily turn off your anti-virus utility prior to using the Installer. Even better, if you select its "Installer-aware" option, SAM should temporarily disable itself whenever you run Apple's Installer (in older versions of SAM, you may get an alert message when you launch the Installer asking if you want SAM Intercept turned off until you are finished).

BY THE WAY ▶

KEEP YOUR FLOPPY DISKS LOCKED

Viruses cannot infect a locked floppy disk. So if you suspect your hard disk is infected, make sure that all floppy disks inserted into the machine are locked; after you eradicate the virus, you can use unlocked disks again. Similarly, when you are using a floppy disk on someone else's machine, keep the disk locked if possible. If you need to unlock it (because you want to copy something to the disk), be sure to scan the disk for infection before you use it again on your machine.

Eradicate an Existing Virus

If SAM (or whatever other anti-virus utility you use) does detect an infected file, your next step should be to get rid of it. Even if you subsequently delete the identified infected file from the Finder, however, there may still be other infected files on your disk. Because any further activity risks spreading the virus, you should immediately use the SAM application to do a complete scan of all disks that were mounted at the time the alert message appeared. Delete (or repair) any files that are reported to be infected.

Even if you have not gotten a virus alert message, you may still choose to run your anti-virus utility periodically on a preventative basis. Similarly, if you have just installed your anti-virus utility or are using a new hard disk, you should run the utility before proceeding.

By the way, Virex can repair files directly via its control panel, so you don't have to open the separate Virex application.

Scan for and Delete Infected Files

To use the SAM application to scan for and eradicate viruses, do the following:

1. **Restart your Macintosh with a locked copy of a startup floppy disk that contains the SAM application**

   Recall that you may have to customize your startup disk to include any needed Enabler files (as described in Chapter 2 and Fix-It #5). Most anti-virus utilities either include their own startup disk or have procedures to facilitate the creation of such a disk. With SAM, if the included startup disk does not work with your Mac, you can create a workable startup disk via its Startup Disk Builder option.

   If you are just doing a preventative scan, with no virus suspected, you can skip this step and run SAM from your hard disk (assuming you have installed a copy of it there). But be prepared to restart from a floppy disk if any virus is reported.

TECHNICALLY SPEAKING ▶

TAKING EXTRA PRECAUTIONS WITH FLOPPY DISKS

If the disks you need to scan include a floppy disk, scan the floppy disk(s) before scanning any hard disks. Ideally, in fact, you should not have any hard disks mounted when working with infected floppy disks. This eliminates the chance of infecting your hard disk while you try to disinfect a floppy disk.

To do this with an external hard disk, simply turn it off before you restart with your anti-virus startup floppy disk. For an internal hard disk, insert the startup floppy disk, then restart while holding down the Command-Option-Shift-Delete keys. Wait until the "Welcome to Macintosh" message appears, and then release the keys; typically, the internal hard disk will not mount. After you have eliminated problems with the floppy disks (by using the methods described in the main text), restart again with any hard disk(s) mounted. Now check the hard disk(s) for virus infection.

FIX-IT #7

2. **Launch SAM and select what disk(s) or folders or files you want to check**

   You do this from the directory listing in the window, much as you would select items from the Finder's similar listing of volumes, folders, and files. Most of the time you will select an entire disk.

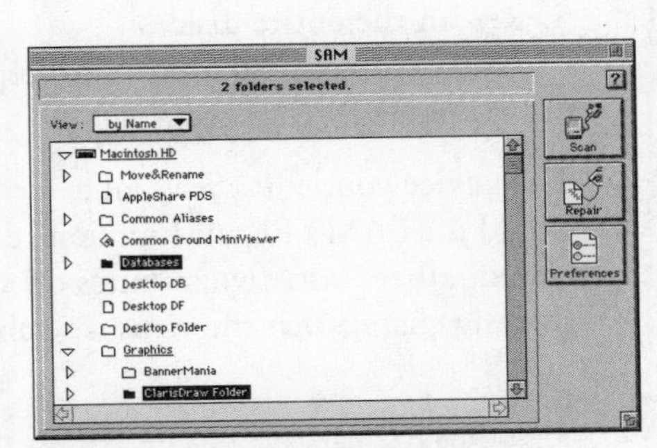

Figure F7-4 *Select what items you want SAM to scan.*

3. **Click either the Scan or Repair button to initiate the scan**

   If you select Scan, SAM will simply report any infected files it finds. If you select Repair, SAM will repair any infected files that it detects (assuming it can do so successfully), although it will also warn you that you should delete rather than repair infected files. I agree with this advice (for reasons I explain in the next section, "Repair an Infected File?"). Still, if you persist, SAM will allow you to select Repair.

Assuming you selected Scan, when the scan is complete, SAM creates a list of all infected, suspicious, or otherwise problematic files. For example, SAM may list a file as a problem because "this file is probably not a valid resource"; the status will be "Error" rather than "Infected." This message typically means the file is damaged and that SAM was therefore unable to check it. The error probably has nothing to do with any virus. Still, because the file may be damaged, you should probably delete and replace it anyway.

4. **Delete and replace any reported problem files (or repair infected files)**
   To delete one or more files, simply select their names from the list and click the Delete button. To attempt to repair them, click the Repair button instead. In either case, you will get a message asking you to confirm what you have selected before SAM takes any action. Alternatively, you can delete files from the Finder.

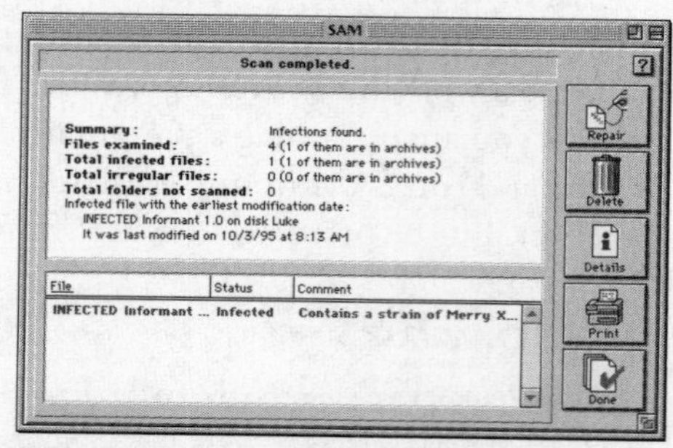

Figure F7-5 *A virus is detected during a scan. Select whether to Delete or Repair the file (If SAM Intercept was on, this virus would also have been detected when you first tried to open the file).*

FIX-IT #7

   You will next want to replace any deleted files from your uninfected backup copies (ideally from a locked floppy or CD-ROM original disk). If there is any doubt about whether the backup is infected, scan the backup disk before making any replacements.

   Replace the deleted files from presumably uninfected backups. Scan the replacement files after you have reinstalled them. If SAM reports a virus is still present, it probably means the backup file(s) are infected and should also be deleted. Other alerts probably mean the problem is not virus related (it could be a damaged file).

5. **Rescan the entire disk**
   After completing the previous steps, scan the disk(s) a second time to be certain that no reinfection has occurred.

The advice you've just read takes a conservative approach. For example, some users would use SAM's Repair function (described next) more freely than I recommend. I would rather waste five minutes on a probably unnecessary precaution, however, than risk any chance that the virus is retained on my disk.

TAKE NOTE ▶

INFECTED DESKTOPS

As mentioned in the "Why to Do It" section, some viruses attach to the invisible Desktop file on your disk. Anti-virus utilities typically report when this has happened and may automatically disinfect the file. Still, the surest way to eradicate these viruses is to completely rebuild the Desktop file. This creates a new uninfected file.

SEE: • Fix-It #9 on rebuilding the Desktop file

Repair an Infected File?

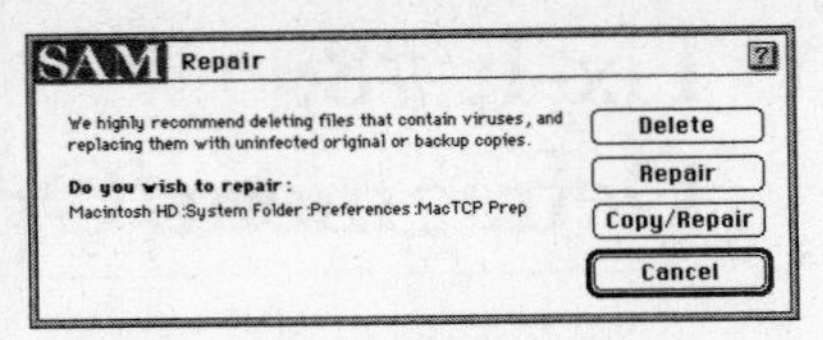

Figure F7-6 *The message that appears if you select to Repair, rather than delete, a file.*

At times, you may not have a backup available for an infected file. For such occasions, most anti-virus utilities, including SAM, give you the option to repair these files. This means that the utility removes the virus program from the infected file and attempts to restore the file to its preinfected state.

SAM (or any other anti-virus utility), however, cannot always repair files successfully. Even if the virus is successfully removed from the file, the file may still not function normally. That's why replacing the file with a backup is the preferred method for eradicating a virus.

Trojan horse programs can never be repaired; they must be deleted.

Anti-virus utilities can only, at best, repair damage due to known viruses. To repair any non-virus-related damage, you need to try other types of repair utilities, as described in Fix-It #14.

If the Anti-Virus Utility Didn't Solve Your Problem

If you use your anti-virus utility and update it as needed, you should be safe from almost any type of virus infection. If your problem persists despite these efforts, it's probably time to look elsewhere for the cause. You might, however, first call the technical support line for your anti-virus utility and ask if your symptoms indicate an unknown or newly discovered virus.

If you remain concerned that you have an unidentified virus, you could reformat the entire disk and restore it from your (hopefully) uninfected backups. This step should eliminate any virus infections, even if they were not detected by your anti-virus utility. Normally, though, this should not be necessary.

By the way, if a virus or Trojan horse did succeed in infecting your disk and appears to have erased files, don't despair yet—even if the files aren't backed up. It may only be the disk's Directory that has been damaged or erased; if so, you may be able to repair or restore the disk, as described in Fix-Its #10 and #13.

Determine the Source of Your Virus Infection

Whenever you find a virus on any of your disks, try to determine where the original infected file came from, and use this knowledge to prevent future infections. For example, did symptoms start shortly after you used a particular floppy disk borrowed from a friend? If so, alert your friend to the problem, and be more careful the next time you borrow a disk from him or her!

For related information

SEE:
- **Fix-It #4 on extensions and control panel problems**
- **Fix-Its #10, #13, and #14 on repairing damaged files and disks**
- **Chapter 2 on preventative maintenance**
- **Chapter 4 on system crashes**

Fix-It #8: Defragment/Optimize the Disk

QUICK SUMMARY ▶

Use a disk optimizing utility (such as Speed Disk from Norton Utilities) to defragment/optimize the files on your hard disk.

When to do it:

FIX-IT #8

- Whenever the overall speed of operations on your disk slows down significantly.
- Whenever symptoms appear that get worse as less and less free space is available on your disk; especially problems opening or correctly displaying a document.
- Whenever your undelete utility is unable to restore or is only able to partially restore even the most recently deleted files.
- Whenever you use a defragmenting utility to analyze a disk and it suggests that defragmenting is desirable.

Why to do it:

This is the first of a trio of Fix-Its that refer to topics first mentioned in Chapter 2, under the heading "Give Your Macintosh a Tune-Up." At that time, I briefly considered them as preventative maintenance procedures. Now let's look at them, in more detail, as specific problem-solving techniques. For this Fix-It, the problem is file fragmentation.

Suppose that a 50K file is stored on your disk, tucked between two 900K files. If the 50K file is deleted, it leaves a small 50K gap between the two larger files. The larger files cannot automatically slide over to fill in the gap, because files can be moved to different physical locations on a disk only when they are copied or modified. (Remember, *location* refers to the physical area of the disk that the file occupies. This is different from its location on the desktop, which refers to the folder where it resides. It is also different from the area of memory occupied by a file after it is launched.) After you've spent months adding, deleting, and modifying files on your disk, the unused space on your disk may consist mostly of these small gaps.

Now suppose that you want to copy a new 1.2MB file to your disk but no longer have a single block that large anywhere on the disk. A total of 5MB of unused space may be on the disk, but it is all in blocks smaller than 1.2MB. By itself, this is not a problem, because the Macintosh can divide the physical storage of a file into separate fragments. These fragments, which don't have to be stored near one another on the disk, then fit into the smaller empty blocks. This is called *disk fragmentation* or, more accurately, *file fragmentation.* Similarly, existing files on your disk can become more fragmented each time they are modified (for example, when you save changes to a document file).

The information needed to link together the data from all of a file's fragments is stored in the invisible files that make up the Directory area of the disk (as described more in Chapter 8). By accessing this information, the Macintosh can combine a file's fragmented data as needed (for example, it would do this when opening a file and loading its data into memory). This does not actually eliminate the fragments; it just allows the Mac to work around them. Thus, most of the time, you could not tell the difference between using a file that is stored as a single block versus using the same file stored in fragments.

If the amount of fragmentation gets too great, however, problems (usually minor ones), can result. Because of the added time needed to skip around the hard drive to find the fragments of a file, the operational speed of the Macintosh may slow down noticeably. Also, especially if an individual file is severely fragmented, you may have trouble using the file—a fragmented word processing file, for example, may unexpectedly display incorrect formatting. Also, disk repair utilities and some undelete utilities work less effectively with highly fragmented disks. Finally, if your free space is fragmented, you may have trouble using certain virtual memory utilities that require contiguous free space in order to work (Apple's virtual memory does not have this restriction). If you are experiencing any of these problems, and you haven't defragmented your disk recently, it's time to check it.

What to do:

Optimizing/Defragmenting Basics

Defragmenting and optimizing refer to different but similar operations. *Defragmenting* means to restore fragmented files into single undivided files. *Optimizing* means to rearrange the location of files on your disk so as to minimize future fragmenting. Optimizing works on the principle that files can only get fragmented as they get used, and especially as they get modified. As a result, you can minimize fragmenting by locating all rarely modified files (such as most applications) in one location and frequently accessed files (such as most documents) in another. A related optimizing technique is to combine all unused space into one block. In general, optimizing a disk implies that you have also defragmented it; this is how I will use the term here.

Special utilities are used to optimize a disk. Examples of these utilities are Speed Disk (from Norton Utilities), Optimizer (from MacTools Pro), and Disk Express (from AlSoft).

Disk Express is noteworthy because it can optimize your disk in the background, working whenever your Macintosh is idle for a few minutes. When you resume work, it halts; at your next break, it returns to where it left off.

Since Symantec recently halted production of MacTools Pro, Optimizer will not remain a viable option in the years ahead.

As Norton Utilities is by far the most popular product, specific instructions in this Fix-It focus on using its Speed Disk utility. The more general principles covered here apply to all of these utilities.

Before You Optimize

Check for Damage Optimizing an already damaged disk can further damage files, resulting in irretrievable loss of data that could have otherwise been saved. To check for possible damage before you optimize a disk, run Disk First Aid as well as the relevant utility from your repair package (such as Disk Doctor from Norton Utilities). Be especially sure to use these utilities to check for media damage. Some optimizers, particularly Speed Disk and Disk Express, can directly check for such damage; repair whatever damage you find before you attempt any defragmentation.

Other Precautions For reasons explained more in later sections of this Fix-It, you should make sure you have a current backup of the disk to be optimized, that all files on the disk to be optimized are closed, and that you have deleted all unneeded files from the disk. Ideally, start up from a disk other than the disk you want to optimize.

Optimize the Disk

FIX-IT #8

1. **Launch your optimizing utility and select the disk you want to optimize**
   With Norton Utilities, click Speed Disk from its Main Menu. From the window that appears, select the disk you want to optimize.
2. **Select the command to display the current status of the disk**
   For Speed Disk, click the Check Disk button in the Speed Disk window. This creates a graphic map showing the distribution of files across the entire disk. Different types of files are assigned different colors (or shades of gray, if you don't have a color display), based on the key shown in each window. The status display also lists the percentage of total files that are fragmented (if you have Fewer Choices selected for Speed Disk, it will describe the fragmentation as "moderate," "severe," and so forth, rather than as a percentage). Finally, it may suggest whether defragmentation is recommended. As a general guideline, if fragmentation is greater than five percent, I would defragment the disk—if you are in doubt, defragment the disk just to be safe.

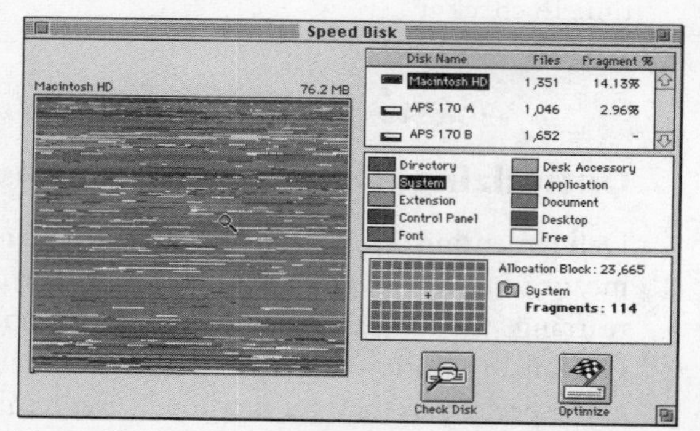

Figure F8-1 *Norton Utilities' Speed Disk display; it shows an impressive 114 fragments for my System file (one of these fragments is located under the magnifying glass cursor).*

3. **Prior to defragmenting/optimizing, select desired options**
   With Speed Disk, you have the option to Prioritize Files. This rearranges the location of files during optimization according to a priority system based on how often the file is likely to be modified (and therefore potentially refragment), as explained in "Why to Do It." When you first select Optimize, Speed Disk also gives you the option to Defragment the disk rather than Optimize it. If you choose Defragment, the locations of files are not rearranged, which means that unused space is not consolidated into one large block.

Selecting the options that do more work typically increases the time it takes to complete the process. Because they help minimize the rate of future refragmentation, however, I recommend using them.

4. **Optimize**
   Click the Optimize button to begin optimization/defragmentation of the disk. This can take quite awhile; be sure to wait until it is finished.

BY THE WAY ▶

DEFRAGMENTING WITH MACTOOLS PRO'S OPTIMIZER

The main text especially covers defragmenting with Norton Utilities' Speed Disk. If you are using MacTools Pro's Optimizer instead, here are some brief instructions:

1. From MacTools Pro's Clinic, click the Optimizer button. (If you are using the startup floppy disk with Optimizer on it, you are taken directly to its special Optimizer window at startup.)
2. Click the Analyze button in the window that first appears. This will open up the Map window.
3. Click the Options button in the Optimizer Map window. Select "Arrange files by kind then date" for maximum prioritizing, or select "Defragment files without arranging" to bypass all prioritization. From here, you can also select to "Remove TrashBack files," a step that helps free up extra space on the disk.
4. Click the Optimize button.

As with Speed Disk, Optimizer has the option to list fragmentation of individual files. To do this, select Optimizer's Fragmented Files button (the last button in the row of buttons at the top of Optimizer's Map window). A list of fragmented files will appear to the left of the map. Unlike with Speed Disk, however, you cannot select individual files for defragmentation.

When you click on a name in the list, its fragments are displayed in white on the map. Conversely, clicking on a block in the map highlights the file to which that fragment belongs.

FIX-IT #8

Beyond the Basics

Check for Fragmentation of Individual Files

Prior to defragmenting a disk, defragmenting utilities can report the number of fragments of any specified file. Even if the overall fragmentation percentage for a disk is at an acceptably low level, a particular file on the disk may still be excessively fragmented. If you are having problems with a file, you can check its fragmentation as follows:

1. **Display the current status of the disk**
   Follow the instructions in Step 2 of "Optimize the Disk."
2. **Select the option to display fragmentation of individual files**
   With Speed Disk, select "More Choices" from the Options menu and then select "Show Fragmented Files" from the Explore menu. You will see a separate window listing each fragmented file and the number of its fragments. If a file cannot be defragmented because it is currently open or because there is not enough free space ("disk is too full"), this will be indicated as well. From this list, you can select individual files and defragment only those files.

Alternatively, if you move your cursor over the graphic map of your disk's file fragmentation, the program will identify the name of the file under the cursor's location and the file's number of fragments.

3. **Decide whether to defragment/optimize**
   As a general guideline, if a file you've been having trouble with is divided into more than five or six fragments, strongly consider optimizing the entire disk (or, with Speed Disk, optimize at least just the problematic files).

Make Sure Files Are Free to Defragment (Startup Disk Problems and More)

Currently open files typically cannot be defragmented. Similarly, the System and the Finder files on the startup disk cannot be defragmented, as they are considered to be open files. If you optimize the disk that contains the optimizing utility, the utility itself cannot be defragmented, because it is an open file.

Defragmenting a disk with files that cannot be defragmented reduces the effectiveness of the procedure. Therefore you should close all files on the disk to be defragmented, and you should not defragment the startup disk or the disk that contains the optimizing utility.

FIX-IT #8

To defragment your normal startup disk, you may need to create a special startup floppy disk that contains the optimizing utility. Norton Utilities and MacTools Pro both give instructions on how to do this. With MacTools Pro, you can also use its new RAMBoot feature (described more in Fix-It #13) to create a startup RAM disk with Optimizer on it.

Disk Express is an exception to these guidelines. It can effectively defragment the disk that contains it, even if the disk is the startup disk.

Create Free Space

Successful defragmentation requires a minimum amount of free space on your disk. If your hard drive is almost full, you may not be able to defragment your disk completely. In particular, you may not be able to defragment larger files.

The solution is to remove files from your hard disk until there is enough free space for the optimizing utility to work—ideally, at least 10 percent of your hard drive should remain unused. Delete any and all unneeded files from your disk.

If you are using MacTools' TrashBack to protect deleted files, Optimizer has an option to delete these files as it optimizes; you can select it from the Options list. Conversely, MacTools TrashBack (described more in Chapter 2) has an option to prevent fragmentation by preserving unprotected space.

Maximizing the amount of free space available on your disk also helps minimize future fragmentation. The Macintosh prefers to store files in a single large block. As the total amount of free space on your disk declines, however, large blocks become increasingly rare, and file fragmentation becomes increasingly common.

Don't Optimize Floppy Disks

In general, don't bother optimizing floppy disks. They are not large enough for fragmentation to be a significant problem.

A Disk Is Optimized When You Reformat and Restore It

Reformatting a hard drive and restoring its files from backups also completely defragments the disk. I would not usually reformat and restore a disk simply to defragment it, but if you are going to do this for some other reason, it's nice to know that you are also optimizing the disk.

TECHNICALLY SPEAKING ▶

THE DISK CHECK BUG AND DEFRAGMENTATION

A bug in the Macintosh ROM may, under certain conditions, cause the Macintosh to treat a perfectly okay disk as if it is corrupted, with the result that the disk does not mount. If it is a startup disk, you will not get past the blinking-question-mark disk icon. The only way to mount the disk in this case is with a disk recovery utility such as MacTools or Norton Utilities (as described in Fix-It #13).

Thankfully, this bug (called the "disk check bug") is a rare cause for these symptoms. It requires a specific combination of events before it can occur; for starters, it can happen only after a system crash or other improper shutdown. Because it also can occur only if the disk is excessively fragmented, it is yet another reason to defragment your disk regularly.

A free utility called Disk Bug Checker will tell you if you are susceptible to this bug. The utility is available from my MacFixIt Web site; it was also included as part of MacTools 3.*x* but is no longer included with MacTools Pro. If Disk Bug Checker says you are susceptible, and you are experiencing any unusual symptoms, you should optimize your disk immediately. A fix for this problem is built into System Update 3.0 and System 7.5 or later. So if you use any of these you can probably ignore this whole issue.

SEE: • **Chapter 5 for more general information on startup and disk mounting problems**

FIX-IT #8

The Downside of Optimizing and Defragmenting

If you follow the preceding steps, defragmenting/optimizing should proceed smoothly. A few cautions to note, however, are described in the following paragraphs.

Defragmenting Takes Time

Defragmentation can take a *long* time; you can easily enjoy a leisurely lunch while an 80MB or larger hard drive is optimized. You might have to take the entire day off waiting for a 1GB drive to be optimized.

Defragmenting Can Erase Files That Otherwise Could Have Been Undeleted

Defragmenting your disk can eliminate the capability of some utilities to undelete previously deleted files, because the optimizing process usually overwrites files that have been deleted but otherwise would have still been recoverable. MacTools Pro's TrashBack feature avoids this problem, no matter what optimizing utility you use, but it apparently still exists for Norton Utilities.

With any optimization utility, of course, defragmentation does not prevent the recoverability of files deleted after the defragmentation process is completed.

Defragmenting Can Cause Disk Damage

The optimizing process rearranges and rewrites so much data that if there is a bug in the optimizing utility, the process could easily damage files on your disk (although the publisher of the utility will almost certainly release upgrades that fix these bugs as soon as it becomes aware of them). Even without a bug, there is a small risk that damage may occur if there is an unexpected interruption in an optimization, such as from a system crash or a power failure.

To save yourself from potential disaster here, be sure you have current backups for your disks before you optimize them.

In particular, Speed Disk 3.0 and (in certain rare cases) Speed Disk 3.1 were known to cause disk damage. Make sure you have upgraded to newer versions.

For related information

SEE: • Fix-Its #10, #13, and #14 for how to check for and repair damaged files and disks
SEE: • Chapters 2 and 6 on using undelete utilities

Fix-It #9:
Rebuild the Desktop

QUICK SUMMARY ▶

To rebuild the Desktop, hold down the Command-Option keys at startup until a dialog box appears asking whether you want to rebuild the desktop. Click OK.

When to do it:

- If a file's desktop icon displays as a blank generic icon rather than its correct customized icon.
- If a file's desktop icon displays an icon for an older version of the creating application rather than the icon for its current version.
- When you drag a document icon to its application, the drag-and-drop highlighting does not occur and the application does not launch, even though it worked previously.
- When you double-click on a document to open it, a message incorrectly claims that the creating application is missing (or other unusual error messages appear).
- If the overall response speed of the Macintosh slows down significantly.
- If the size of available space on a disk, especially a floppy disk, is considerably less than what you would expect based on the files visibly located on your disk.
- If files are inexplicably missing from the Finder's desktop.
- When you get a message that "the disk needs minor repairs," but clicking OK does not remedy the problem.

Why to do it:

The Desktop file is an invisible file created on each disk when the disk is initialized. It stores information about the contents of the disk that is particularly important to the Finder. For example, it keeps track of what custom icons are assigned to files, the links between documents and their creating applications, and the links between aliases and their original files. The text in the Comments boxes of Get Info windows is also stored here. Every time a file is added, deleted, or modified, the Desktop file is updated accordingly.

Without the Desktop file, the Finder could not create its desktop display. When you rebuild the desktop, it means that the Desktop file is largely re-created from scratch by scanning the current contents of the disk to get the required information. The following are reasons why you would need to do this.

The Desktop File Can Become Bloated

Even after a file is deleted, the Desktop file retains the information about that file. Particularly because it retains this now-unneeded information, the Desktop file can become quite large over several months of adding and deleting files. By purging this unneeded information, rebuilding the desktop reduces the size of the Desktop file, freeing up some disk space (an especially relevant advantage for floppy disks) and helping to speed up Finder operations. You can see exactly how much disk space you recover (it can be as much as several hundred kilobytes) by comparing available disk space immediately before and after rebuilding the desktop.

The Desktop File Can Become Corrupted or Incorrectly Updated

These days, virtually every program and document on your hard drive has its own unique customized icon. These icons give the Finder's desktop a wonderfully varied and colorful appearance, an aesthetic experience that you may miss if you select the "By Name" or other non-icon view from the Finder's View menu (although even these views can show custom icons if you select the relevant option from the Views control panel).

FIX-IT #9

Generic Icon Problems

Unfortunately, if the Desktop file is not correctly updated, a file's custom icon may not be displayed. Instead, documents may sport the generic "blank" document icon, or (more rarely) applications may display the generic application icon. This is considered a problem of the Desktop file, rather than the Finder, because the Desktop file is where all of the icon information used by the Finder is stored.

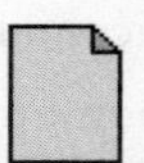

Figure F9-1 *The generic document icon (left) and the generic application icon (right).*

For example, custom icons often get "lost" if you upgrade to a new version of an application that uses a different icon from the older version. The Macintosh may get confused about which icons to use, with the result that the new version's files continue to display either the old version's icon or a generic icon.

Happily, rebuilding the desktop updates the Desktop file and usually fixes these icon problems (though some incorrect icon displays can be caused by a problem with a file's Bundle bit, as described in Chapter 8).

Like all software, the Desktop file(s) can get corrupted. If this happens, the link between a document and its creating application can get lost, and the "application could not be found" error message might appear when you double-click a document file to open it from the Finder. Occasionally, a damaged Desktop file may even cause system crashes. Rebuilding the Desktop is a likely solution to all of these problems.

What to do:

Rebuilding Basics

The basic procedure for rebuilding the desktop was described in Chapter 2 (in the section called "Give Your Macintosh a Tune-Up"). I'll explain it in more detail here.

1. **Hold Down the Command and Option Keys at Startup**

To rebuild the Desktop file on the startup disk (or any other disk mounted at startup), hold down the Command and Option keys during the startup sequence until you see an alert box asking "Are you sure you want to rebuild the desktop file on the disk [name of disk]?"

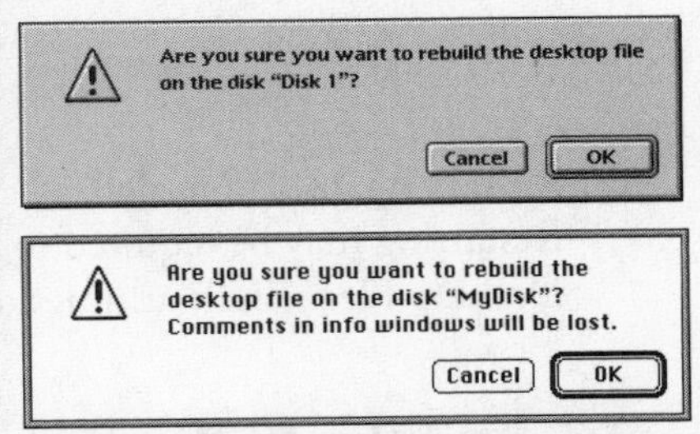

Figure F9-2 *This alert box appears when you hold down the Command-Option keys to rebuild the desktop. The bottom box is from a pre-System 7.5.3 System Folder. Note that in this case, it warns you that "Comments in info windows will be lost." Comments are saved in System 7.5.3 or later.*

To rebuild the Desktop file on any other disk, at any time, hold down the Command and Option keys before mounting the disk. For example, for a floppy disk, do it just prior to inserting the disk. If you want to rebuild the Desktop file on a floppy disk that is already mounted, eject the disk using the Put Away command from the Finder's File menu, then reinsert it while holding down the Command and Option keys. In all cases, wait for the alert box message to appear before you release the keys.

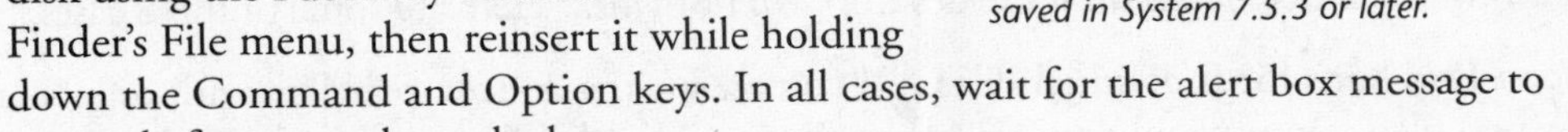

FIX-IT #9

Note that when you are rebuilding the desktop at startup, the message asking you whether you want to rebuild will not appear until after all startup extensions have loaded. If you have a lot of extensions, this can take a while; be patient. Actually, you don't even have to hold down the Command-Option keys until the end of the extension loading sequence approaches.

At Ease Alert: This method may not work if At Ease is running. If it doesn't, you must turn At Ease off and then restart before you can rebuild the desktop.

2. **Click OK to the Alert Box Message**

Click the alert box's OK button and wait. A progress bar should appear, monitoring the rebuilding process. Within a minute or two, the Desktop file is rebuilt, and the progress bar will disappear. You are done.

If you have more than one disk that gets mounted at startup (for example, an internal and external hard disk) you will get a separate message request for each disk, as well as for each partition on a hard disk. Click OK just for the volumes you wish to rebuild. You do not have to rebuild all of them, but I have occasionally fixed an icon display problem on my internal hard drive by rebuilding the desktop of my external hard drive. (This might happen, for example, if a document on the internal drive was created by an application on the external drive.) It usually pays to rebuild all regularly mounted volumes if you are having problems.

BY THE WAY ▶

REBUILDING THE DESKTOP ON POTENTIALLY DAMAGED DISKS

If you plan to rebuild the desktop because of symptoms that suggest file damage on the disk, it is a good idea to first run Disk First Aid or a similar utility to check for and repair possible Directory file damage (see Fix-It #10). Otherwise, there is a slim chance that rebuilding the desktop can make things worse.

In this regard, note that the Desktop file is not the primary method by which the Macintosh keeps track of the contents of disks; the Directory file is far more critical for this task. The Desktop file is needed only by the Finder.

3. **Restart Again, If Needed**
   Restarting may be required to get correct icons to appear. This is especially likely for Desktop files rebuilt at times other than during startup.

Beyond the Basics

Fixing Generic Icon Problems

As described in the "Why to Do It" section, rebuilding the desktop can fix problems with incorrect (generic) icon displays. There are cases where simpler solutions are preferred, however, or where rebuilding the desktop will not work. Here are some of these cases.

FIX-IT #9

Icon Problems for Individual Files If you are having an icon problem with only one or two files, you probably can avoid the time and hassle of rebuilding the desktop and instead selectively update the information for the problem files. With Norton Utilities for Macintosh, you do this via the Add File to Desktop command in Norton Disk Doctor's Tools menu; a freeware utility called Fix Icons does the same thing. In either case, you may need to restart before the change takes effect.

Otherwise, open the Get Info window of the file, click on its icon box, then select Copy, Paste, and Cut (this is not guaranteed to work, but may be worth a try).

Generic Icon Problems with Unmounted Disks If you save a document to your startup hard disk from an application stored on a floppy disk or removable cartridge, the document should still display the appropriate icon. The next time you restart without the application disk/cartridge mounted, though, the document may have a generic icon (especially if the creating application has never been copied to the hard disk). This is because the icon information on the unmounted disk may never have been copied to the Desktop file on your hard drive.

Getting the correct icon to appear typically requires that the needed disk/cartridge be present at startup. If you mount it later, the correct icon will still not be displayed.

You can usually solve these problems by copying the creating application to your startup disk. If you then launch the application, open the document, and save it using Save As, the correct icon should be restored. If not, you need to rebuild the desktop after all, ideally with all relevant disks mounted. This should almost always work.

After this, you can delete the application from your startup disk, if desired. If you do so, however, the generic icon may return if you later rebuild your desktop (as explained in "When Rebuilding the Desktop Causes Generic Icon Problems," later in this section).

Generic Icon Problems with Disk Partitions, External Drives, and Removable Media This situation is similar to the one just described. In this case, though, the problem can occur even if all relevant files are on your startup disk. It can also occur with external drives and removable media, even if they are mounted at startup.

The problem is typically specific to document icons or aliases that are stored on the startup disk's desktop area (that is, not in any folder). In this case, these files may display generic icons if the creating application is on a different volume (partition or disk), even if the other volume mounts at startup. The reason is that the Finder checks for the icons of files on the desktop before the secondary volumes mount. If the icon data is not present in the startup disk's Desktop files, the generic icon is displayed. A similar situation can arise if the file is in a folder on the startup drive whose window is set to open at startup.

The problem is avoided if the Finder does not actually have to display the icon until after the secondary volume(s) are mounted. The easiest solution, then, is to keep these icons off your desktop and out of any windows that are automatically opened at startup.

If you must keep these icons on your desktop, you can use a program such as SCSIProbe or SCSIManager (as explained more in Fix-It #16) that allows for mounting of volumes during the time that extensions load (which is earlier than the volumes would normally load). This will mean that the volume(s) are mounted prior to the Finder loading—with the result that the icons appear correctly.

If the file is an alias, another solution is to create the alias on the non-startup volume and then drag it to the desktop. This keeps the alias file on the non-startup volume. If you create the alias directly on the desktop, it is stored on the startup volume and will likely display a generic icon when you restart.

Lastly, a quick fix is to use a Force Quit command (Command-Option-Escape) or a utility that quits the Finder (such as Terminator Strip); when the desktop reappears, the custom icons will be restored. Similarly, rebuilding the desktop will bring the icons back. With these fixes, however, the problem is likely to return next time you restart.

When Rebuilding the Desktop Causes Generic Icon Problems Occasionally, a file may display its correct custom icon and then lose it because you rebuilt the desktop. Most often, this happens to a document file whose creating application has been deleted from the startup volume prior to rebuilding. Rebuilding the Desktop file purges all information about the deleted application, including what is needed to display the document's custom icon. There is no solution to this other than to return the deleted application to your drive (rebuilding the desktop again if needed).

When the System, Finder, and/or Enabler/Update Files Become Generic If your System and Finder (and possibly Enabler/Update) icons become generic (sometimes *after* rebuilding the desktop), this typically means that the System file's Bundle bit information has gotten corrupted in the Desktop files, or (more likely) that the file's Bundle bit attribute has somehow gotten unchecked.

In the first case, rebuilding the desktop should get the icon back. You can again save yourself the hassle of a complete rebuild, though, by simply updating the desktop for the System file alone (via a utility such as Save a BNDL or by using Norton Utilities' "Add File to Desktop" command). Otherwise, using a utility such as Snitch (as described in Chapter 8), look to see if the System file's Bundle bit is unchecked; if so, turn it back on. While you are at it, *uncheck* the Inited bit, then restart. This should get your icons back. If nothing else works, doing a clean reinstall should get the job done.

By the way, some versions of Apple's Telecom software are known to cause this problem.

In any case, this is only a cosmetic problem that should not signal any other problems with your software.

TAKE NOTE ▶

CUSTOM ICONS VS. REALLY CUSTOM ICONS

The expression *custom icon* often has two different meanings. One refers to the normal, application-specific icons used by almost all applications and their documents. These icons are established by resources stored in application files, placed there by the creator of the application. This is the main meaning of the term *custom icons*, as used in most of the discussions in this Fix-It; sometimes, though, these may also be called *bundled icons*.

The other meaning of the term is when you create a personal custom icon by pasting an image into the icon box of a file's or folder's Get Info window. With this method, you can change the icon for any file, folder, or volume. More specifically, here's one way to do it:

1. Select a file that has an icon you like. Open its Get Info window and click on its icon picture; the icon should now be surrounded by a box. Select Copy. (You can also get icons from other sources, including by making one yourself in a graphics program.)
2. Now go to the Get Info window of the file whose icon you want to change. Click on its icon and select Paste. The copied icon now replaces the existing icon, overriding any bundled icon that an application or document would normally have. The bundled icon information, however, is not lost; if you subsequently cut your personal custom icon, the bundled icon will return.

By the way, if you want to create a folder icon that looks like a generic folder icon but with a smaller custom icon "inside" it (similar to the System Folder icon), you can do it easily with various shareware utilities, such as one called Folder Icon Maker.

Problems with Custom Icons for Folders and Volumes The information about custom icons for a particular program (and its document files) is stored in the resource area of the program as well as in the volume's Desktop file. This is true for both bundled icons and true custom icons.

Custom icons for folders and volumes work a bit differently. Since there is really no file that corresponds to folders or volumes, their icon information is stored in special invisible files, named "icon," located within each folder that has a custom icon. Thus, if volumes or folders with custom icons unexpectedly revert to displaying generic icons, rebuilding the desktop is not likely to have any effect.

Here are some suggested solutions that should work:

- In general, use a utility such as Snitch to make sure that the folder/volume's "Use Custom Icon" bit is checked.
- If the missing custom icon is for a volume (such as a hard disk), check the disk's formatting utility to see if icons can be selected from there. If so, use it to reselect the one you want.
- For folders and volumes, an unexpected generic icon can mean that the custom icon file is damaged. If so, you may be able to fix or create a new icon via the Get Info window method (as explained in "Take Note: Custom Icons Vs. Really Custom Icons").

Figure F9-3 *A Get Info window for a folder, with Snitch enabled. For missing custom folder or volume icons (and sometimes even for missing custom file icons), make sure that "Use Custom Icon" is checked. For problems with your System file having a generic icon, make sure that the Bundle bit is set and that the Inited bit is not set. In all cases, restart your Mac when you are done; with any luck, the missing icon(s) will return.*

- For folders, if the file damage is such that the Get Info method does not work, remove all files from the folder. Then trash the folder (the invisible icon file goes with it), create a new folder to replace it, and make a new custom icon.
- For volumes, the invisible icon file may be missing or "lost" even though the volume's "Use Custom Icon" bit is still set (which means that the Finder thinks the icon is still around). In this case, if you try to use the Get Info method to paste a new custom icon over the generic icon, you will probably get a message such as "The icon could not be deleted because the file can not be found." To get around this, try using a freeware utility called Disk Rejuvenator.

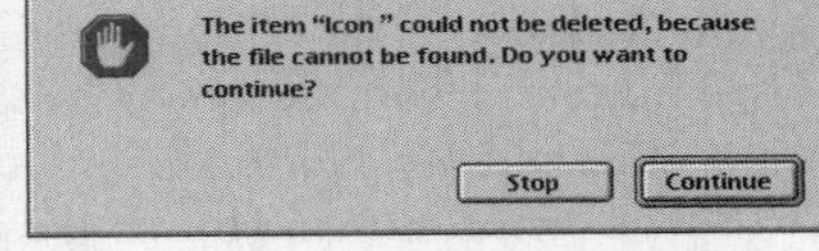

Figure F9-4 *If you get this message when trying to paste a custom icon into the Get Info icon box of a folder, try using Disk Rejuvenator.*

- If all of this fails, open any utility that can delete invisible files. Use it to delete the invisible icon file, then add a new custom icon.
- As a last resort, reformat the entire disk.

Bundle Bit Damage and More Unusual Problems If the preceding fixes do not help, use Norton Disk Doctor or DiskFix (from MacTools) to check for Bundle bit problems or possible damaged files. Otherwise, try a "complete" rebuild of the desktop with TechTool (see later in this Fix-It).

You may be able to fix some nasty icon problems by using ResEdit to modify a file's icon resources directly, but this gets beyond the scope of this book.

Finally, be aware that not all generic icon problems need fixing. For example, I found that if I restart QuickDraw GX disabled after installing QuickDraw GX, many of the custom icons associated with GX switch to generic icons. When I return to GX, everything reverts back to custom icons.

SEE: • **Chapter 8 for more on invisible files, Bundle bits, other file attributes, and related information**

BY THE WAY ▶

WEIRD SIMPLETEXT ICONS

If your SimpleText document icons are missing their left border, don't fret. It is merely a cosmetic problem and is usually remedied by rebuilding the desktop.

The actual cause appears to be out-of-date or damaged copies of TeachText/SimpleText that are on your disk. The solution is to get rid of all copies of this application except the most recent version.

Losing (and Saving) Get Info Comments After Rebuilding the Desktop

Prior to System 7.5.3, rebuilding the Desktop file normally resulted in the loss of any data in the Comments boxes of all Get Info windows. Starting with System 7.5.3, these comments are (at last!) retained when you do a basic rebuild of the desktop.

Even if you are still using an older version of the system software, losing comments is usually of trivial concern, since most users do not store any important information there. If you want to save these comments when rebuilding, however, some utilities can help. One especially slick utility is a system extension called, appropriately enough, CommentKeeper (its upgraded incarnation is called SuperComment). Just drop it into your Extensions folder and restart; it will work automatically the next time you rebuild the desktop via the Command-Option method. When you get the dialog box, it will indicate that comments will be saved.

Alternatively, Norton Disk Doctor (in its Tools menu) has its own command to rebuild the desktop. If you select it, you will get a dialog box with an option to save comments. Also, if you have FileSaver installed and its Comments option checked (see Chapter 2), you can restore the lost comments via the "Restore Finder Comments" command in the Options menu of Norton Utilities.

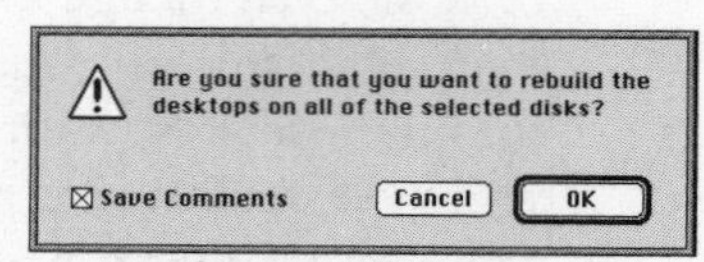

Figure F9-5 *Norton Disk Doctor gives you a chance to save Comments when rebuilding the desktop.*

Comments and TechTool If you use a utility such as TechTool to rebuild the desktop (as described later in this Fix-It), comments still get wiped out, even in System 7.5.3 or later. This is because TechTool completely deletes the Desktop files rather than just updating them. Starting with TechTool 1.1.1, though, you can now save the Desktop files (including comments) before rebuilding. This could be useful, for example, if a rebuild of the desktop has no effect on whatever problem you were trying to solve and perhaps even makes the situation worse. If so, you can replace the original Desktop files and get the comments back.

If saving Comments is really critical to you, and you still want to do a TechTool-like rebuild of the Desktop, use the Norton Disk Doctor method just described.

Minor Repairs Alert Message

Occasionally, at startup or whenever you are trying to mount a disk (most often a floppy disk), you may get a message that the disk "needs minor repairs" (see Chapter 5, "Problems While Launching the Finder and the Desktop"). If you click OK, the problem is typically fixed, and that's the end of it.

This message apparently appears either as the result of damage to the Directory or to the desktop. Clearly, however, it does not rebuild the desktop (it works too fast to have done that). So if the problem persists even after clicking OK, rebuild the desktop and see if that helps. In my experience, this message occurs only rarely, if at all, in System 7.

Don't Bother to Rebuild the Desktop After Initializing a Disk

Any time you reinitialize a disk, it creates a new Desktop file. You do not have to rebuild the desktop separately.

Desktop Files and Reusing Floppy Disks

Many users reuse floppy disks without reinitializing them—that is, they drag all the files on the disk to the Trash and then begin to fill the disk with new files. I don't recommend this. Instead, when you start over with a disk, reinitialize the disk first. Not only does this reconfirm that the disk is not damaged (otherwise, initialization would fail), but it also forces a rebuild of the desktop. This, in turn, purges unneeded information from the Desktop file and may thus reclaim a significant amount of disk space (more than 100K in some cases).

If you don't wish to reinitialize the disk, at least rebuild its desktop after deleting all items from the disk. In System 7, however, at least one file or folder must be on a floppy disk in order to rebuild its Desktop file. If the disk currently has zero items on it (which it presumably has at this point), create an empty folder on the disk and then rebuild. The rebuild will be successful, and you can then delete the empty folder. By the way, this problem is the result of a bug that may get fixed in newer versions of System 7.

FIX-IT #9

The Desktop Rebuilds Every Time You Start Up

A Desktop Folder on Your Desktop If you are using a version of System 7 earlier than System 7.5.3 and your desktop rebuilds every time you start up, check to see if you have created a folder called Desktop. If so, this is the source of your problem; rename the folder.

What is happening is that the Macintosh is confused into thinking that your folder is actually a System 6 Desktop file (see "Technically Speaking: More Than One Desktop File: DB and DF"). This causes the Macintosh to try repeatedly to rebuild the desktop, among other potential problems.

Starting in System 7.5.3, the Finder no longer rebuilds the desktop if it finds a *folder* named Desktop in the root level of your Mac. It will still rebuild, though, if it finds a *file* called Desktop.

Macintosh Easy Open Problems Macintosh Easy Open (called Mac OS Easy Open, starting in Mac OS 7.6) directly modifies the Desktop file. Normally this is not a problem, but conflicts with other programs may lead to an assortment of strange desktop-related symptoms. If you use Easy Open and are experiencing any desktop-related problems, turn it off; your problems will probably go away.

Also, every time you start up with Macintosh Easy Open off (such as by holding down the Shift key at startup to turn all extensions off), the desktop will rebuild the next time you restart with it turned back on—often taking an atypically long time to do so.

This appears to be a necessary feature of Easy Open, as it needs to check what might have changed in the Desktop file since it was last in use.

With some versions of Macintosh Easy Open, users complained that the desktop got rebuilt at every restart, as long as Easy Open was on. This does not seem to happen with the latest version of the extension.

The permanent solution to any and all of these problems is to disable Easy Open (for example, by dragging it out of your System Folder) and restart. The desktop will rebuild once more, and then not again as long as you leave Easy Open off. Of course, this means you lose the features of Easy Open.

TECHNICALLY SPEAKING ▶

MORE THAN ONE DESKTOP FILE: DB AND DF

System 6 had only one Desktop file, called Desktop. In contrast, System 7 has two such files, Desktop DB and Desktop DF, both of which are needed. The DB file stores icon information, while the DF file stores the information about where on the desktop files are located.

You may occasionally find a System 6 Desktop file on disks running System 7. In such cases, System 7 software still uses only the Desktop DB and Desktop DF files; the Desktop file, if present, is used only when the disk is run under System 6. (If desired, you can view all of these files by using a utility that lists invisible files, as discussed in Chapter 8.)

Even if they were formatted under System 7, floppy disks don't have Desktop DB and DF files. This is because these files are created only on volumes greater than 2MB in size. Because floppy disks have a maximum size of only 1.44MB, all floppy disks use the System 6-style single Desktop file.

Keep Extensions Off When You Rebuild?

Some extensions may cause problems when you rebuild the desktop, even going so far as to prevent the rebuild from successfully completing.

For example, with certain anti-virus programs running, rebuilding the desktop may not correct all icon problems.

Rebuilding with extensions on can occasionally result in the loss of all Finder links between documents and applications. If this happens, you may get unusual error messages (with negative error codes) when you double-click on a document from the Finder. Rebuilding the desktop again, this time with extensions off, will solve this problem.

To avoid these and most other extension problems, the general solution is to turn all extensions off prior to rebuilding. To do this, hold down the Shift key at startup until the "Extensions Off" message appears; then let go of the Shift key and immediately hold down the Command-Option keys to get the desktop to rebuild.

Unfortunately, there are a few exceptions even to this generalization.

Macintosh Easy Open Problems … Again Because Easy Open forces a rebuild of the desktop when you turn it off and then back on again, Apple recommends that you leave Easy Open on when you rebuild.

Compression Utility Problems If you use AutoDoubler or StuffIt SpaceSaver and rebuild the desktop without these extensions turned on, all files that had been compressed may adopt the compression utility's icon instead of the file's own icon. If this happens, rebuild again with the compression utility on.

By the way, the ideal way to leave just one or two extensions on without permanently changing your normal selection of enabled/disabled extensions is to use the Temporary feature of a startup management utility (as described in Fix-It #4). With Apple's Extensions Manager, which has no such feature, you will need to create a "Set" to store your normal selection.

If none of this works, and you still have problems (such as a system error) when trying to rebuild the desktop, you probably have a more serious Directory-level problem. You will need to try to repair the disk.

SEE: • **Fix-Its #10 and #13 on repairing disks**

Really Rebuild the Desktop

The information that follows is sufficiently important that I've carved out a separate section for it. When you rebuild the Desktop file(s) using the Command-Option key method, it does not *completely* rebuild the desktop. The effect is more like a thorough updating of the existing file(s) as opposed to deleting them and replacing them with new ones. This can be a problem if you are rebuilding the desktop because you suspect a corrupted Desktop file. In this case, rebuilding may not repair the damage, and the symptoms may persist. In such cases, it pays to delete the Desktop file and thereby force a completely new one to be created (the Macintosh will create the new one automatically when it finds the old one missing). This may solve a problem that a normal rebuild would not.

Completely deleting the Desktop files may also enable you to rebuild the desktop on those occasions when the standard Command-Option technique does not work.

Of course, reinitializing a disk accomplishes a complete rebuild. There are less drastic ways to do this, though, as described below.

Use TechTool My favorite way of completely rebuilding the desktop is to use a freeware utility called TechTool. To use it, just launch the utility and click the "Rebuild Desktop" button. TechTool will ask permission to quit any open applications; let it do so. You will then have the option to select which disks to rebuild, if more than one is mounted. After you have made your selection, TechTool deletes the Desktop file(s) and initiates a rebuild without restarting the Macintosh. When the rebuild is finished, you are returned to the Finder.

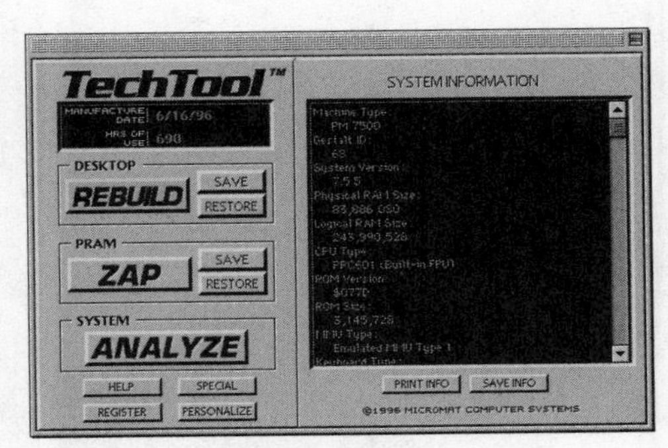

Figure F9-6 *The TechTool dialog box.*

Starting with TechTool 1.1.1, you can also save the Desktop files prior to a rebuild. You can use this to restore your original data later in cases where the desktop files were actually undamaged and rebuilding the desktop had no beneficial effect on your problem.

Use Desktop Reset Another solution is to use a freeware system extension called Desktop Reset. When it is installed, you still request a rebuild the normal way—by holding down the Command-Option keys at startup. When you do this, however, the extension intercepts the normal procedure, gives you a slightly different alert message, and (after you click Reset) deletes the Desktop files, initiating the complete rebuild.

Use Norton Disk Doctor This utility's Rebuild Desktop command also does a complete rebuild.

Use Norton Utilities or DiskTop Some utilities, such as Norton Utilities or DiskTop (as described in Chapter 8), let you view and modify invisible files. In System 7, you can use these utilities to move the invisible Desktop DB and DF files from their location at the root level of the disk to inside a folder on the disk (also making them visible when you do this). This should force a complete rebuild, creating new Desktop file(s) when you restart. After restarting, delete the now-obsolete Desktop file(s) from the folder where you moved them. I see no reason to bother with this method, however, since all of the previous methods work just as well and are easier to do.

For related information

SEE:
- **Fix-It #4 on turning extensions on and off**
- **Fix-It #13 on damaged disks**
- **Chapter 2 on preventative maintenance**
- **Chapter 6 on files that do not open**
- **Chapter 8 on invisible files and on icon problems**

Fix-It #10: Run Disk First Aid

QUICK SUMMARY ▶

Run Disk First Aid to check for and repair corruption of the Directory area of a disk.

When to do it:

- Whenever you are unable to get a disk to mount.
- Whenever you have problems related to using files, including an inability to open, copy, or delete files, as well as files that mysteriously disappear.
- Any time you have a problem that is not easily diagnosed or solved. Running Disk First Aid is such a simple and effective procedure that it is almost always worth trying.

Why to do it:

FIX-IT #10

Disk First Aid is part of Apple's system software; it comes on the Disk Tools disk (and/or the system software CD) that accompanies virtually every Macintosh purchase or major system software upgrade. It can detect and repair a variety of common problems. It is far from the most sophisticated tool of its kind, but Disk First Aid has three distinct advantages over its more industrial-strength competitors: (1) It is free, (2) it is extremely easy to use, and (3) because it is made by Apple and frequently updated, it can sometimes diagnose or fix problems that the more sophisticated tools cannot. That's why I recommend starting with Disk First Aid as a first line of defense before moving on to more powerful utilities and techniques.

What Disk First Aid primarily does is to check for possible damage to a disk's Directory. It can repair many, although not all, of the problems that it finds.

The Directory area of a disk, as detailed in Chapter 8, is a collection of invisible "files" that contain the essential information that the Macintosh needs to access the disk and the files on it. Each area of the Directory has its own (often esoteric) name, such as "extent BTree" or "catalog hierarchy."

The Directory maintains a continually updated catalog of exactly what is on a disk, where everything is, and how it is organized. One very important specific function of the Directory is to keep track of the number of fragments of each file (see Fix-It #8) and where each fragment is located. Without this information, fragmented files on the disk are unusable.

Because the Directory is continually modified as you change the contents of your disk, and because most disk damage occurs when a file is modified, it is common for the Directory to become corrupted. Minor problems may cause symptoms so subtle that you do not notice them, at least not at first. This is why, in Chapter 2, I recommended using Disk First Aid as a preventative measure even if nothing seems wrong. You should eliminate even the most minor Directory problems as soon as you discover them, because minor problems tend to get more serious if left unfixed. Serious Directory problems can render the files on a disk inaccessible—in fact, you may not even be able to mount the disk.

What to do:

Start by making sure you have the latest version of Disk First Aid. If you have upgraded your system software since purchasing your Macintosh, don't rely on the version on your original Disk Tools disk. If a new version was included as part of the system software upgrade, use it!

For preventative maintenance, run Disk First Aid about once a month. If you suspect that you may have Directory problems, run it immediately.

Using Disk First Aid

Getting Started

FIX-IT #10

1. **Before you launch Disk First Aid**

Although Disk First Aid can always verify a disk (that is, check for problems without making any repairs), certain preconditions must be met before you repair one. In particular, Disk First Aid cannot repair the current startup disk, the disk from which Disk First Aid is running, a write-protected disk (including CD-ROM disks), a disk with any open files on it, or any disk at all while file sharing is active. Thus, to save time, do the following before you even launch Disk First Aid:

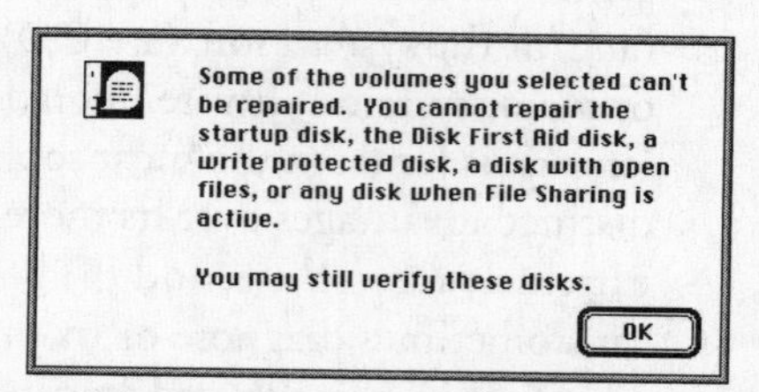

Figure F10-1 *Disk First Aid warns you about its limitations.*

a. Restart your Macintosh from a floppy disk or alternate hard disk that contains a copy of Disk First Aid (for example, the Disk Tools disk that comes with Apple's system software).
b. Make sure file sharing is off (via the Sharing Setup control panel).
c. Make sure any floppy disks or removable cartridges that you want to repair are not locked.
d. Make sure no files are open on the disks you want to repair.

You can choose to bypass these steps for now and just verify a disk. If a problem is found, however, you will have to make these adjustments and start over.

2. Launch Disk First Aid

If you ignored Step 1, you may get warning messages concerning the matters just described. Regardless, you will eventually get to Disk First Aid's window. A brief set of instructions is displayed; if you have not read them yet, do so now.

BY THE WAY ▶

THE NEW DISK FIRST AID

Starting with version 7.2, Disk First Aid underwent a major revision in its interface. The new design makes Disk First Aid significantly easier for novices to understand and use—and, of course, it is capable of fixing problems that previous versions could not. So while you should always use the latest version of Disk First Aid, be sure you are at least using version 7.2.

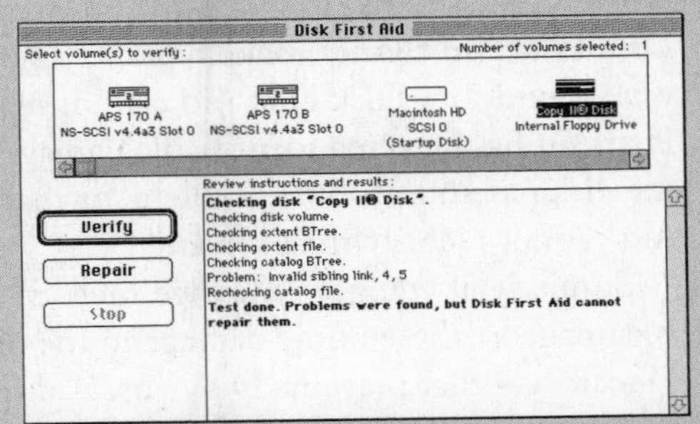

Figure F10-2 *The Disk First Aid (version 7.2 or later) window, indicating that the utility has found a problem it could not repair.*

Verify or Repair a Disk

FIX-IT #10

1. Click the disk icon of the disk you want to check

From the Disk First Aid window, click the icon of each disk you want to check; use Shift-click to select more than one volume at a time. By the way, if a disk is so damaged that it cannot be mounted from the Finder, Disk First Aid may still list it as openable, so give it a try. (Insert floppy disks that cannot be mounted into a drive only after Disk First Aid is open and currently selected as the active application.) If Disk First Aid cannot access the damaged disk, try other repair utilities, as suggested in the end of this Fix-It.

2. a. Click the Repair button to begin verification and repairs.

If the repair button is dimmed, you cannot select it; you can only verify the disk. The reasons this might happen were described in "Getting Started."

b. Click the Verify button to just verify the disk. Most users will do this only if the Repair button is dimmed. Even if Repair is enabled, however, you might consider verifying first. This way, if problems are detected, you can back up critical files on the disk before repairing (just in case the repair attempt makes things worse).

3. Wait while Disk First Aid goes to work

After you select Verify or Repair, the instructions will be replaced by a growing list of items that indicate what Disk First Aid is checking. Don't worry about what any of it means; just wait for it to finish.

4. **If no problems are found**

   Whether you selected Verify or Repair, a message will say "The volume [volume name] appears to be OK" for each volume checked. If this happens, you should still run Disk First Aid a second time, just to confirm the diagnosis. If nothing pops up this time, skip to Step 6.

5. a. **If a problem is found after having selected Repair**

   If you clicked Repair and Disk First Aid spots problems, one of two outcomes will generally occur:

   - **Disk First Aid cannot make repairs.** A message will say "Test done. Problems were found, but Disk First Aid cannot repair them." This means either that Disk First Aid has detected identifiable damage but does not know how to fix it, that the disk has an unfixable problem, or that the disk is so damaged that Disk First Aid cannot identify the problem.

     Similarly, if you get a message such as "Unable to read from disk" or "The disk is damaged," these imply damage to the disk—probably media damage to the Directory—that prevents Disk First Aid from successfully completing its tests. In these cases, testing is aborted or never begun.

     Most likely, Disk First Aid cannot repair such disks no matter what you do. Still, before giving up, try running Disk First Aid a few more times. Sometimes layers of problems exist, and repairs are made incrementally. Disk First Aid may fix one problem but still report that the disk could not be repaired because of other remaining problems. It may take Disk First Aid several runs before it detects and repairs all problems. With luck, you may eventually get the "OK" message.

   - **Disk First Aid successfully repairs the disk.** If this happens, you will get a message saying something like "Repair done. The disk is OK." As a precaution, run Disk First Aid a few more times even if you get this sort of message. It may still detect and repair other problems on subsequent runs.

   b. **If a problem is found after having selected Verify** If you clicked Verify and Disk First Aid spots problems, one of the same basic two outcomes described in Step 5a will occur. The only difference is that Disk First Aid will not attempt to repair any damage even if it can fix what is wrong. If Disk First Aid detects a fixable problem, you will get a message such as "The volume [name of volume] needs to be repaired" (other messages may appear if Disk First Aid does not know how to make the repair). To make repairs, you will have to click the Repair button. If it is not enabled, you will have to do whatever is necessary to enable it (as described in the "Getting Started" section). In either case, make sure critical files on your disk are backed up before proceeding with repairs.

   c. **If you get an unusual message such as "Test interrupted because another program is using the disk"** Quit Disk First Aid, and quit all other open applications as well. Launch and try Disk First Aid again. If this fails, try a forced quit from the Finder or restart the Macintosh (in some cases, you may need to do this with extensions off).

Then run Disk First Aid again. If the message still appears, treat it like a repair problem that Disk First Aid could not fix. Proceed to the next step.

6. **If Disk First Aid could not make repairs or if symptoms persist, try other repair procedures**

No matter what the outcome of the test—even if Disk First Aid initially or eventually reported no problems—you may still have trouble with the disk, because there are many problems that Disk First Aid does not detect. If symptoms persist despite your use of Disk First Aid, you need to use other procedures to try to fix them (see "Further Damage Checks," later in this Fix-It, for suggestions).

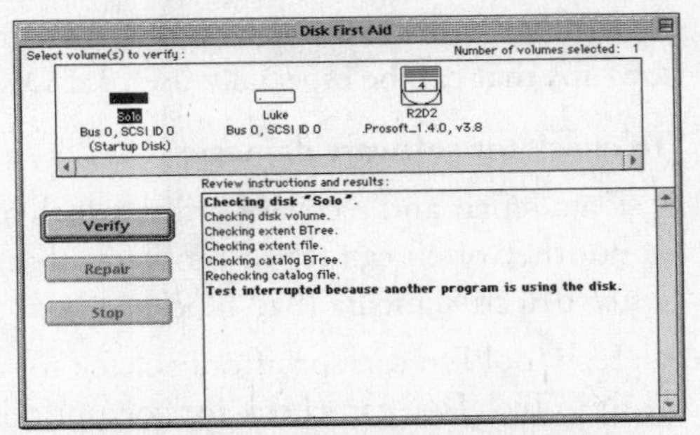

Figure F10-3 *The Disk First Aid window, indicating that a test was interrupted. If this happens, restart your Macintosh and try again.*

TECHNICALLY SPEAKING ▶

WHAT DO THOSE SYMPTOM MESSAGES MEAN?

If it finds a problem, Disk First Aid will often (but not always) include a line describing what the trouble is. For example, it might say "Invalid sibling link, 4, 5" or "Invalid PEOF." Most of the time, these will provide very little insight as to how to solve the problem, should Disk First Aid be unable to do so.

I don't know for sure what an "invalid sibling link" is, although I suspect it has to do with links between fragments of the same file. I do know, however, that an "invalid PEOF" refers to an "invalid Physical End of File." This typically means there is a file on the disk that is bigger or smaller than the Directory file thinks it is. More precisely, the Mac makes a distinction between the PEOF and the Logical End of File (LEOF). It is okay for the LEOF to be smaller than the PEOF (since this means the end of the file falls within the physical limit set by the PEOF), but not vice versa. If the PEOF is too small, you will get the "invalid PEOF" error message. If you get this message and Disk First Aid cannot fix the problem (and it typically can't), try Norton Utilities and/or MacTools; even if repairs are successful, you may still need to replace the affected files. Also, rebuild the desktop. If the problem persists, the System or Finder files are probably corrupted and should be replaced. If all else fails, you will have to reformat the drive.

BY THE WAY ▶

DISK FIRST AID'S ERASE DISK OPTION

Disk First Aid's Option menu includes a command called "Erase Disk." Only use this for floppy disks that you wish to reformat (typically because they are reported to have problems that cannot be repaired). Even here, you may want to try other repair utilities, such as Norton Utilities, before erasing the disk. Do not use this option to erase a hard drive of any sort!

See: • **Fix-It #15 for more details on erasing/reformatting disks**

Further Damage Checks

Disk First Aid is a good starting point, but it is certainly not the end of what can be done to solve possible software and/or hardware damage. Below are some suggested follow-ups that can be especially useful if Disk First Aid fails to correct your problem.

To check for software damage:

- Data repair and recovery utilities such as Norton Utilities check for similar damage, but they often can repair problems that Disk First Aid cannot. They can also check for defective media (bad blocks).
- TechTool Pro can specifically check for corruption of the System, Finder, and Update files. TechTool can check for corruption of the System file.
- TechTool and TechTool Pro can also repair damage to the Desktop file and the Parameter RAM (as can the standard procedures for rebuilding the desktop and zapping the PRAM).
- Adobe Type Manager 4.*x*, Font Box, and other competing utilities can check for damage to fonts.
- Conflict Catcher can check for damage to startup extensions.
- Updating the disk driver (with Apple HD SC Setup or Drive Setup, for example) may repair problems due to a damaged driver. Formatting utilities can also check for defective media (bad blocks).
- Checking for viruses sometimes detects damaged files, even if they are not infected.

To check for hardware damage:

- Use utilities such TechTool Pro or Peace of Mind. These are commercial products that test for problems with an extended selection of hardware components, including SIMMs/DIMMs, floppy disks, hard disks, and monitors.

For related information

SEE:
- **Fix-It #1 on hardware/software incompatibilities**
- **Fix-It #4 on solving extension conflicts**
- **Fix-It #5 on system software problems**
- **Fix-It #7 on checking for viruses**
- **Fix-It #9 on rebuilding the desktop**
- **Fix-It #11 on zapping the Parameter RAM**
- **Fix-It #12 on updating the disk device driver**
- **Fix-It #13 on disk repair utilities such as MacTools and Norton Utilities**
- **Fix-It #14 on repairing files**
- **Fix-It #15 on damaged media and reformatting disks**
- **Fix-It #17 on hardware diagnostic utilities and hardware repairs in general**
- **Chapter 2 on preventative maintenance**
- **Chapter 5 on startup and disk problems**

Fix-It #11: Zap the Parameter RAM

QUICK SUMMARY ▶

Hold down the Command-Option-P-R keys at startup until the Macintosh restarts itself a second time. Release the keys and let startup proceed normally.

When to do it:

- Whenever control panel settings, such as the current date/time and volume level, are inexplicably incorrect (especially if you reset these values, but the settings are wrong the next time you turn on your Macintosh).
- If your Mac starts up in a Black-and-White or Gray display mode, even though you have selected Colors from a Monitors control panel.
- Whenever you are unable to start up from a hard drive, especially an external hard drive. Symptoms as serious as a "sad Mac" may occur.
- If you cannot mount or otherwise access any externally connected SCSI device.
- Whenever you cannot access a modem, or other serial port device, because its port is claimed to be in use.
- When you cannot get documents to print at all or if garbage characters print instead of the correct output, especially if an error message appears indicating a problem with the serial port.
- If, in certain PowerBook models, you have a loss of sound from your speakers.
- If a monitor's screen will not come on at startup.
- If, after you select Shut Down from the Finder's Special menu, the Macintosh restarts instead of shutting down.
- If you get persistent and frequent system errors, especially Type 11 errors, at random times.

A PRAM problem is not the only cause of many of these symptoms, but it is a very common one.

Why to do it:

Parameter RAM, usually referred to as PRAM, is a small amount of RAM maintained by special hardware on the main logic board of the Macintosh. It is separate from both the main memory (see Fix-It #6) and the video memory (see Chapter 10) referred to elsewhere in this book.

So, what exactly does PRAM do? Primarily, it stores the settings of several control panels included with the Macintosh system software. Most notably, the PRAM stores the current date and time, your choice of startup disk (set by the Startup Disk control panel), and whether AppleTalk is active (set by the Chooser desk accessory), as well as settings from the General Controls, Memory, Mouse, Sound, Keyboard, and Color control panels. The PRAM also stores information regarding the status of the serial and SCSI ports of your Macintosh. Some items not technically stored in PRAM are also reset to default values when you zap the PRAM; these include the settings for the desktop pattern and the color depth of the monitor.

The rationale for storing this information in PRAM is that, unlike other forms of memory, PRAM information is retained after the Macintosh is turned off (or even after you unplug it). That is why, for example, you do not have to reset the time each time you turn your Macintosh on.

If (as I said in Chapter 1) RAM gets wiped out when you turn the Macintosh off, how is the information in PRAM retained? It is saved because a battery inside the Macintosh keeps the PRAM powered at all times (similar to how some bedside alarm clocks use a backup battery to keep going in the event of a power failure).

The problem is that the information stored in PRAM can get corrupted. A good sign that this has happened is if the time and date are suddenly wrong and, even if you reset them, the corrected settings are not retained. Another similarly common symptom is when control panel settings, such as the Monitors control panel, are not retained when you restart. If this happens, all other PRAM settings are likely to have the same problem.

A corrupted PRAM can also prevent the Macintosh from transmitting information to or receiving information from the SCSI port and/or serial ports (modem and printer), causing problems with all devices connected to those ports.

BY THE WAY ▶

PRAM VERSUS THE FINDER PREFERENCES FILE

The Finder Preferences file also stores some user-selected settings. In particular, it stores the settings of the Views control panel and the on or off status of the "Warn Before Emptying" checkbox (located in the Trash's Get Info window). These settings are separate from PRAM settings and are not reset when you zap the PRAM. Problems with these settings are usually solved by replacing the Finder Preferences file, as described in Fix-It #2.

There are a variety of other system preferences files you may have, especially if you use System 7.5. These include AppleScript preferences, Find File preferences, and more. Again, none of these settings are reset when you zap the PRAM.

These PRAM problems do not occur often—but when they do, the solution is to "zap the PRAM." This is a cute way of describing the method for erasing the presumably corrupted current PRAM data and returning all PRAM settings to their default values. If zapping the PRAM does not eliminate these symptoms, it may mean you have a dead battery or system software damage.

Finally, note that some third-party extensions may use parts of the PRAM for their own purposes, contrary to Apple's guidelines. This usage may conflict with Apple's own changing uses of PRAM, leading to freezes, crashes, and the like. The only solution here, short of an upgrade to the extension, is not to use the problem third-party software. Contact the vendor for information if you suspect a conflict like this.

What to do:

Zapping Basics

If corrupted PRAM is preventing your startup hard disk from mounting—and especially if it causes a sad Mac to appear—you may need to start up with a floppy disk (such as your Emergency Toolkit disk) before you can zap the PRAM.

TAKE NOTE ▶

WARNING FOR USERS OF RAM DISKS

Zapping the PRAM will erase all data on a RAM disk created via Apple's Memory control panel. Be sure to back up any critical data on your RAM disk before you zap!

For All Macs Running System 7 (except PCI-based Macs)

1. Simultaneously hold down the Command-Option-P-R keys at startup. Wait until the Macintosh startup tone chimes again and the Mac restarts itself a second time.

   Actually, if you continue to hold down these keys, the Mac will continue to chime and restart indefinitely. Some reports suggest holding down these keys until three or more starts have occurred, but Apple's official position is that two starts are enough.

2. Release the keys and let startup proceed as normal.

For PCI-based Macs (PRAM and NVRAM)

Most Macs store display settings in PRAM. PCI-based Macs, however, store this data in yet another special area called non-volatile video RAM (NVRAM). You can clear this NVRAM area at the same time as you zap the PRAM, but you'll have to be a bit more precise about what you do. In particular, do the following:

1. Shut down the Mac (do not use Restart).
2. After shutting down, restart and *immediately* hold down the Command-Option-P-R keys. Wait for the Mac to chime twice. (If you don't hold these keys down immediately, you will only reset the PRAM.)

3. Release the keys and let startup proceed as normal.
4. After the startup has been completed, go to the Preferences folder and trash the Display Preferences file (ideally, this should be done on a startup where extensions were disabled by holding down the Shift key; you can still do this after zapping the PRAM).

By the way, current versions of TechTool and TechTool Pro (as described later in this Fix-It) do *not* zap the NVRAM. According to MicroMat (makers of TechTool), this ability is planned for a future version.

Optional: Remove the battery

If you want to be absolutely certain that you zapped the PRAM, you can remove the Mac's internal battery (the one that is used to maintain the PRAM information after you turn the computer off). Note for PowerBooks: This internal battery is separate from the main battery used to power the computer.

In the Macintosh Plus, the battery is stored in a special compartment on the back of the computer and can easily be accessed. Although the battery looks similar to a common AA battery, it is a special 4.5V battery; make sure you get the right one.

On all current Mac models, the battery is located on the logic board; this means you will have to open up the computer case to remove the battery. It also means that you will have to learn where the battery is located and any specific information about how to remove it on your particular model (details may have come with your Macintosh). This may, of course, be more than you care to learn. Note that in some cases, the battery is soldered to the board; if so, you almost certainly will want to take the Macintosh in for servicing to get it replaced.

If you decide to remove it and replace it yourself, first shut off your Mac, then open it up and remove the battery. Wait at least a half hour to let the capacitor that maintains the PRAM information "drain." Now reinsert the battery, close up your Mac, and turn it back on.

More details on how to replace these batteries can be found on the World Wide Web at *http://www.academ.com/info/macintosh/*.

After Zapping the PRAM

1. **Reset customized settings**
   Zapping the PRAM wipes out any customized changes you may have made to certain Apple control panel settings, returning values to their default state. As a result, you will now need to reset any changes you had previously made. For example, if you use 32-bit addressing, be sure to turn it back on from the memory control panel (if you have a model that allows it to be turned off); otherwise, you will be unable to access more than 8MB of RAM (as described more in Fix-It #6). Also, you probably need to reselect "Internal Modem" from the PowerBook Setup control panel if you use an internal modem. If you keep AppleTalk off, you will need to turn it off again. You may also have to reset the color depth of your monitor's display. (See the "Why to Do It" section for a more complete listing of affected settings.)

If the time and date were correct before you zapped, however, you should not have to reset them. These two settings are temporarily stored elsewhere while the PRAM is reset and then written back to the PRAM afterward.

Finally, due to a bug in the system software, certain monitors (particularly budget Apple color monitors), when used in combination with Quadra or Centris Macintoshes, may display an overly green tint after zapping the PRAM. To fix this, install Apple's Basic Color Monitor extension (available online).

2. **Replace a dead battery**

If your newly reentered settings are lost again after you turn the Macintosh off, you probably have a weak or dead battery, so replace it.

Don't worry too much about this, though, because a battery should last at least five to seven years. Many users will replace their Macintosh before the battery wears out!

A dead battery can cause some surprising and disturbing symptoms, however, that go well beyond lost control panel settings. These range from a monitor display that will not turn on to a Mac that appears completely dead.

TECHNICALLY SPEAKING ▶

THE CUDA BUTTON (AND MONITORS THAT DO NOT WORK)

The Power Mac 7500, 7600, and 8500 (and possibly other PCI-based Mac models) have a small button near the processor daughter board (called the "Cuda" button) that, when pressed, resets the Mac's "permanent" settings even more thoroughly than a reset of the PRAM. You should only need to use this button as an absolute last resort for PRAM-related problems.

One known problem where doing this may help, is if your monitor screen goes black and stays that way, even though its power light is on and everything else seems to be working normally. If restarting and zapping the PRAM has no effect, or only works sporadically, try the Cuda button.

The Cuda button may also help if your hard drive seems to be unwilling even to start spinning at startup. Removing and reseating all RAM may also help, because defective RAM can cause these symptoms.

By the way, the Cuda button resets the data stored in the Cuda Microcontroller Chip. This chip is not present in all older Mac models, but it is present on all Power Macs (whether there is a Cuda button or not). According to Apple, the main functions of the Cuda Microcontroller Chip are as follows:

- Turn system power on and off
- Manage system resets from various commands
- Maintain parameter RAM
- Manage the Apple Desktop Bus (ADB)
- Manage the real-time clock
- Let an external signal from either Apple GeoPort serial port control system power

SEE ALSO: • **"AppleVision Monitors," in Chapter 12, for more on monitors that go black**
Fix-It #17 for more on hardware-related problems

3. **Replace a corrupted System file**
   If you still have a problem with an incorrect date and/or time, you may have a corrupted System file, so replace it as well. By the way, the freeware utility TechTool (described in the next section) can both zap your PRAM and check for a corrupted System file.

   Also, check the Date & Time control panel to make sure you have actually entered the correct date and time there and have set the formatting for how you want them displayed.

SEE ALSO: • **Fix-It #5 on replacing system software**

BY THE WAY ▶

RESETTING THE POWER MANAGER ON POWERBOOKS

PowerBooks have another special type of RAM, similar to the PRAM, that is mainly used to maintain information regarding operating a PowerBook on battery power. It is called the Power Manager. As with the PRAM, the Power Manager data may get corrupted and need to be reset. The details of exactly why and how to do this are described in Chapter 11.

Really Zap the PRAM: Use TechTool

Unfortunately, the standard method (Command-Option-P-R) to zap the PRAM does not reliably zap *all* of the PRAM data. If the remaining unzapped portion of the PRAM is corrupted, the previous zapping of the PRAM will not fix the problem. This seems to happen particularly with the PRAM data that affects the SCSI and serial ports. For example, you may find that even after zapping the PRAM, you cannot access external SCSI devices—or it may be that when you try to use your modem, you get an error message that says the serial port is "in use." In these cases, you need to *completely* zap your PRAM.

Fortunately, there are several freeware utilities that do this complete zap for you: my favorite is TechTool. (Yes, this is the same utility used to completely rebuild the desktop, as described in Fix-It #9.) As an added bonus, TechTool will save your PRAM settings before you zap, allowing you to restore them when you are done. Here's what to do:

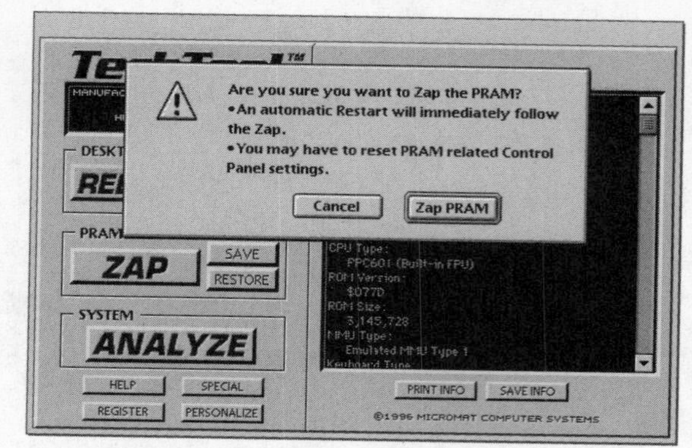

Figure F11-1 *TechTool getting ready to zap the PRAM. Note also the System Analyze button, which can be used to check if your System file is damaged.*

1. **Click the PRAM "Save" button**
   Doing this saves a copy of your current PRAM data for later use by TechTool. Obviously, the ideal time to save is before you suspect that your PRAM is corrupted; otherwise, you may be saving corrupted data. If you have not previously saved the PRAM before you

BY THE WAY ▶

RESTORE MANDATE FEATURE OF TECHTOOL PRO

Figure F11-2 *TechTool Pro features an ability to "Restore Mandate" prior to zapping the PRAM. This will preserve your date of manufacture and hours of use data.*

TechTool is freeware. TechTool Pro is a commercial product that includes all of the features of TechTool and much more (as described more in Fix-It #17). For zapping the PRAM, TechTool Pro includes one additional feature called Restore Mandate. If you have saved the PRAM data previously, this feature allows you to restore the data on the date of manufacture of your Mac and its hours of use, without having to restore any other PRAM data. This is useful if you want to retain this information after zapping your PRAM. Otherwise, every time you zap your PRAM, this information gets reset back to its default values (which would include resetting hours of use to zero).

Current versions of TechTool also preserve this mandate information. In particular, before TechTool clears the PRAM, it stores the mandate into the TechTool Preference file. When you reboot, TechTool will automatically launch itself and restore the mandate information.

If you ever remove the Mac's internal battery, there is no way to restore the mandate.

zap, though, you might as well do it in any case. If the symptoms still remain afterwards, then the PRAM was not the cause, and you can safely restore your saved PRAM data.

2. **Click the PRAM "Zap" button**
Active applications must be closed before you can zap the PRAM. If you have any open applications, TechTool will offer to close them for you before you zap. The Macintosh will restart as part of the zap process.

   Note: After selecting the Zap button, a dialog box will ask: "Do you want to save the current PRAM data to disk before zapping it?" If you have already saved a copy of the PRAM that you know is current and clean, say "no" here. Otherwise, you will be saving PRAM data that may be corrupted.

3. **Optional: Click the PRAM "Restore" button if zapping the PRAM has no effect**
If you have previously saved your PRAM (and the saved data appear to be uncorrupted), return to TechTool and click the Restore button (again, active applications must be closed before this can be carried out).

   The PRAM data are now restored to what they were when you last saved them, eliminating the need to re-create manually all of the customized control panel settings that were lost as a result of the zap.

   One caution: Never restore data saved from one machine onto another machine. Doing so could prevent your Mac from starting up; you will have to remove the battery to fix the problem.

4. **Optional: Click the System "Analyze" button to check for a corrupted System file**
Replace the System file if TechTool identifies it as corrupted. Remember, you must use a version of TechTool that is at least as recent as the version of the system software you are using, or Analyze may not work (see Fix-It #5 for more details).

5. **For PCI-based Macs: Zap the NVRAM**
   If you have a PCI-based Mac, you may also want to zap the PRAM again—via the standard method—in order to zap the NVRAM (as described in "Zapping Basics," earlier in this Fix-It).

Note that removing the Mac's battery or using the Cuda button, as described previously in this Fix-It, will also do this complete zapping (and then some). Using TechTool, however, is a lot easier.

For related information

SEE:
- **Fix-It #12 on disk device drivers**
- **Fix-It #16 on problems with SCSI devices and connections**
- **Fix-It #17 on hardware problems**
- **Chapter 2 on preventative maintenance**
- **Chapter 5 on startup and disk mounting problems**
- **Chapter 11 on resetting the Power Manager and on file sharing and modem problems**
- **Chapter 12 on AppleVision monitor problems**

Fix-It #12: Update the Disk Device Driver

QUICK SUMMARY ▶

Use a disk formatting utility to update the device driver on hard disks and removable media cartridges. For Apple hard disks, you can use Apple HD SC Setup or Drive Setup. Click the Update button or select the Update Driver menu command, as appropriate to the application in use. Though not always required, it is best to start up from a separate disk that contains the formatting utility before updating a driver.

When to do it:

- Whenever a new version of the driver is released, especially if you have upgraded your hardware or software and the new driver is needed to use selected new features of the upgrade. In this regard, be particularly concerned when upgrading to a Macintosh that requires (or at least recommends) a shift from Apple HD SC Setup to Drive Setup.
- If you are experiencing frequent system crashes or other serious problems, especially if the problems do not occur when you are using a floppy disk as a startup disk.
- If you cannot get your Macintosh to start up. Obviously, a driver problem is only one of many possible causes of this symptom.
- To make sure your drive is compatible with SCSI Manager 4.3 (if your Macintosh uses this feature) particularly if your machine is running slower than expected.
- If you are using System 7 and cannot get virtual memory to work properly.
- If a PowerBook crashes while spinning up after a power down (for example, after it has been asleep for awhile).

Why to do it:

A hard disk's *device driver* is software. It is located in a special section of the disk that is created when the disk is first formatted. Thus, any hard disk you own that came preformatted came with a driver already on it. It is normally completely invisible and inaccessible to the user. Even disk repair utilities such as MacTools or Norton Utilities do not directly access it when making disk repairs.

The driver contains critical *low-level* instructions that tell the Macintosh how to communicate initially with the drive. A copy of a disk's driver is loaded into memory whenever the disk is mounted; without the driver in memory, in fact, the disk cannot be mounted.

Updating a disk driver requires using the same formatting utility that you would use to reformat the disk (see Fix-It #15). Apple now has two main formatting utilities: Apple HD SC Setup and Drive Setup. Different brands of drives typically come with their own formatting utilities that, in turn, install their own disk drivers. The whole updating process takes only a few seconds, and it leaves the rest of your drive untouched. You do not have to reformat the drive in order to update it—which is convenient, because reformatting would erase all the data on the drive (requiring you to restore the files from your backups) and would take much more time.

If you "update" your disk driver with the same version of the utility that originally installed it, it will simply replace the existing driver with a duplicate. Like system software, however, disk formatting utilities are periodically upgraded. Updating the driver from a newer version of the formatting utility will replace the older version with the newer one.

In terms of problem solving, there are three basic reasons to update a driver: to accommodate new system software, to accommodate new hardware, or to repair damage to the driver.

Update to Accommodate New System Software

When Apple releases a new version of its system software, newly added features may require changes to disk drivers. For example, when you are updating from System 6 to System 7, make sure you also update to a System 7-compatible driver, because System 7's virtual memory feature usually does not work with pre-System 7 disk drivers. Similarly, when System 7.5.3 came out, it included new versions of Apple's disk drivers that were necessary in order for System 7.5.3 to work properly.

Note that when you use the Installer utility to upgrade the system software, this does *not* upgrade the driver, even if you have an Apple hard drive. You need to update the driver separately (see the "What to Do" section for details).

Update to Accommodate New Hardware

Occasionally, you may need to update to a new version of a driver in order to accommodate features added to newer Macintosh models.

For example, using a hard disk with Apple's PowerBooks requires special modifications to the disk driver that are not necessary with desktop Macintoshes. If you are using an Apple drive that was shipped with your notebook machine, you don't have to worry about this; the preinstalled driver works fine. If you bought a third-party drive, though, it may have been shipped with a driver incompatible with the notebook models (though this is less likely now that the PowerBooks have been around for several years). In this case, you have to either get a newer version of the formatting utility that updates the driver appropriately (call the drive manufacturer for information) or switch to a different driver that is already compatible with the PowerBooks.

Similarly, AV and Power Macintoshes (and any other Macintoshes that use Apple's new SCSI Manager 4.3) require an updated driver in order to take full advantage of the features used by these new machines. The most noticeable symptom of having the wrong driver is slower performance speed. At one time in late 1993, the only driver compatible with SCSI Manager 4.3 was the driver installed by the latest version of Apple's own formatting utility, Apple HD SC Setup. By now, however, most other major formatting utilities have been updated as well.

Most recently, Apple drives in PCI-based Macs need the latest version of Drive Setup's driver in order to work properly.

Update to Repair Damage to the Driver

Despite its relative inaccessibility, the driver (like any software) can get damaged. For example, sudden power failures, particularly during startup, can cause it to be damaged. A damaged driver usually causes serious problems, including an inability to mount the disk on the desktop. Updating the driver can repair the damage and eliminate the problem.

A special problem with the write cache of some disk drivers (solved by updating to a newer driver that addresses the problem) is covered more in Fix-It #16 (see "Take Note: The Write Cache Problem and Data Corruption"). Also note that some driver-related problems can be fixed by a more general update of Apple's system software (updating to System 7.5.3, for example, fixed some known bugs).

TAKE NOTE ▶

BEWARE: UPDATING THE DRIVE MAY *CAUSE* PROBLEMS (NOT FIX THEM)!

The disk driver lives on your hard drive in an area referred to as the *driver partition*. When a disk is first formatted, a certain amount of space is set aside for this partition. When you go to update a driver, it may be that the new driver takes up more space than the space allotted to the driver partition. When this happens, your formatting utility should warn you and prevent the update. The solution is to reformat your drive with the new formatting utility (or not to do the update at all).

In some unfortunate cases, the formatting utility may incorrectly try to fit a too-large driver into a too-small space. The result is a corrupted driver—and when you next try to start up your Macintosh, it won't work. Symptoms range from startup system crashes to the disk icon with the blinking question mark to a Sad Mac. You may be able to reinstall your previous driver at this point, but it is more likely that you will have to reformat your disk. As a result, you should make sure you have things backed up before updating a driver.

For example, problems such as these were reported when updating from version 3.*x* to version 4.*x* of APS PowerTools. In one case, the drive and the Mac itself simply shut down near the end of the startup process. APS said that with this major upgrade, they recommended reformatting prior to updating the driver; this would have avoided the problem. If you already have the problem, reformatting will still work. You might also be able to fix it, however, simply by mounting the drive using APS PowerTools and selecting the correct partition options for each partition on the drive ("Startup Drive" for the startup partition and "Mount at Startup" for the others).

What to do:

Get the Latest Version of the Formatting Utility

You should almost always use the latest version of your formatting utility, even if you are not experiencing any of the problems described in the "Why to Do It" section. At the very least, the new version probably contains fixes to bugs found in the previous versions.

For Apple drives, you typically update the driver via Apple HD SC Setup or Drive Setup (included on the system software disks). If you get your Macintosh from Apple, one of these utilities was almost certainly used to format the drive installed in your computer.

Note that Apple HD SC Setup and Drive Setup only work with Apple fixed drives (see "By the Way: Switching to a Different Formatting Utility").

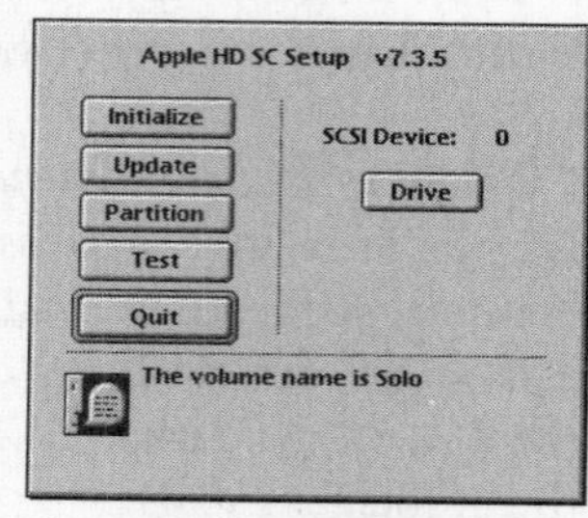

Figure F12-1 *Apple HD SC Setup; click the Update button to update the driver.*

Apple HD SC Setup Do not use a version of HD SC Setup older than the version that came with the system software and/or system Update you are currently using. If you upgrade to a later version of the system software, check to see if it includes an upgraded version of Apple HD SC Setup; if so, use it to update your disk driver. You can also check with online services or other similar sources (see Fix-It #18) to make sure you have the latest version.

Drive Setup Drive Setup can be used by almost all Power Macs, even those that have drives that were originally formatted with Apple HD SC Setup. If your disk can use Drive Setup, switch to it—at the very least, it will probably give you faster performance. Beyond that, the same advice about using the latest version, offered above for Apple HD SC Setup, applies here.

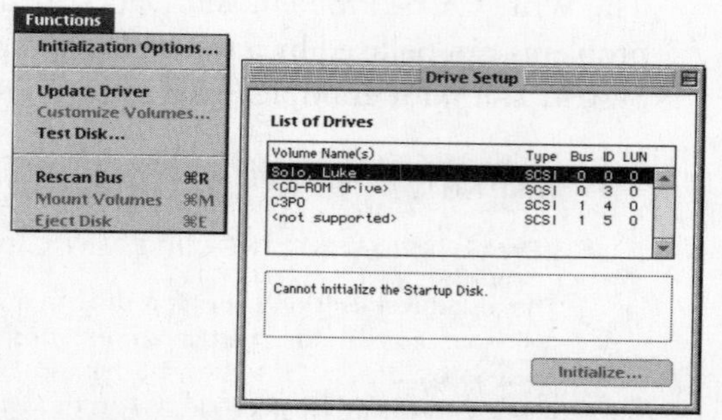

Figure F12-2 *Apple's Drive Setup; note the Update Driver command in the Functions menu.*

TAKE NOTE ▶

APPLE HD SC SETUP VS. DRIVE SETUP: WHICH ONE DO YOU USE?

Apple now has two major formatting utilities: Drive Setup and Apple HD SC Setup. Drive Setup is used mainly with Power Macintoshes and those Macintoshes that have IDE drives, especially if they are using System 7.5.2 or later. Apple HD SC Setup is used with all other Macs. Unfortunately, there are exceptions to these generalizations; check out Fix-It #15 for the complete details.

Be especially sure *not* to use Apple HD SC Setup on PCI-based Macs, or problems will occur. For example, if you launch Norton Disk Doctor, it may list a mysterious and otherwise invisible hard drive volume called "unknown." Other problems may be reported if you try to analyze this or other drives. If this happens, update the driver using the latest version of Drive Setup.

Custom Formatting Utilities If your drive is not an Apple drive, it came with its own formatting utility and associated driver. Often, this is a custom utility developed by the maker or reseller of the drive (for example, APS drives come with a utility called APS PowerTools). If so, contact the company that sold the drive to get information about upgrades to its formatting utility (or check the manual that came with the drive for possible advice). In some cases, these utilities should only be used with drives sold by the same company that makes them.

Universal Formatting Utilities Finally, you may choose to use a universal formatting utility. These are separately sold software products not associated with Apple system software or any particular drive. As their name implies, they may be used with virtually any drive you own, including Apple drives (but see "By the Way: Switching to a Different Formatting Utility" for a warning regarding Apple drives). Drive7 and Hard Disk ToolKit are two popular examples. In this case, contact the publisher of the utility for upgrade information.

Why would you ever want to use a universal utility? Some users may want advanced features available in the formatting utility that are not present in utilities such as Apple HD SC Setup (which is actually minimal in terms of features). Also, if you have multiple drives connected to your Mac, it is advised that all drives have the same driver; using a universal formatting utility can simplify doing this. A mix of different drivers on different drives can lead to problems, including system errors, but the risk of this problem is probably overstated. I have routinely used mixed drivers connected to the same Mac and have never experienced a problem.

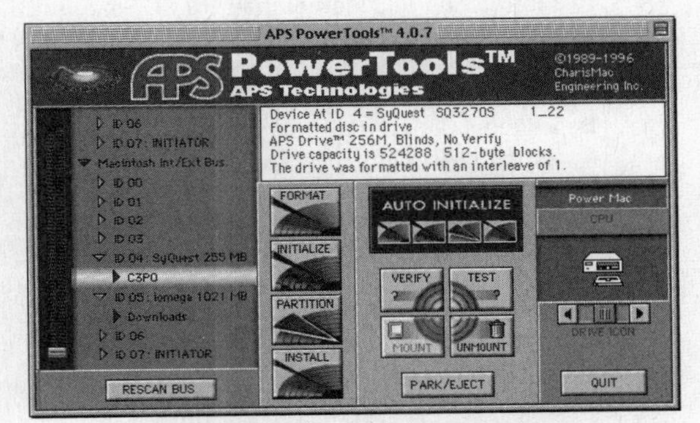

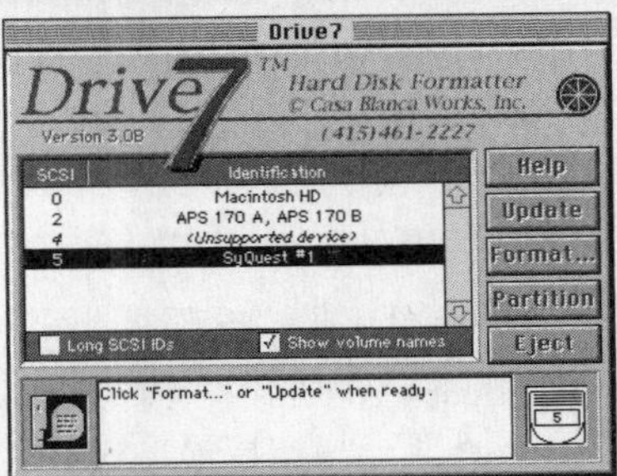

Figure F12-3 *Top: APS PowerTools, a custom formatting utility. Bottom: Drive7, a universal formatting utility.*

Special Case: Updating Drivers on Removable Media Each removable media cartridge/disk (such as SyQuest and Iomega cartridges or optical disks) contains its own disk driver. When updating to a new version of a driver, ideally you should update all of your cartridges that use that driver. Certainly try to avoid using different brands of drivers for different cartridges that use the same drive; try to standardize on one utility. Otherwise, problems may occur, especially when you are switching from one cartridge to another during a session (see Fix-It #16, "Take Note: Problems Mounting Removable Media Cartridges with Different Drivers," for more details).

BY THE WAY ▶

SWITCHING TO A DIFFERENT FORMATTING UTILITY

You can update a driver using a different formatting utility from that used to format your disk (such as using Drive7 to update a disk formatted by Apple HD SC Setup). This can usually be done without reformatting the disk. Still, as I discuss more in Fix-It #15, I prefer to reformat when switching to a different driver.

There is, however, a special problem to watch out for here: Apple HD SC Setup and Drive Setup both only work with Apple fixed drives—Apple HD SC Setup, especially, will not even indicate the presence of non-Apple drives. As a result, you cannot use or switch to these utilities for any drive that did not come from Apple (except that Drive Setup can work with removable cartridge drives, even if they have not been formatted by any Apple utility).

You can go in the reverse direction—that is, if you have an Apple drive, you can switch to a formatting utility other than HD SC Setup or Drive Setup—but there is a problem here as well. After you switch, you can never switch back to using the Apple utilities, because the switch deletes the special coding information on the drive that these utilities use to recognize that it is an Apple drive. (Although I have not tried it, there are some reports that you may be able to switch back if you are using Drive Setup.)

By the way, the name "Apple" on a drive doesn't mean that Apple really made the drive. The actual drive mechanism is made by a company that specializes in drive manufacture (such as Quantum); these vendors sell their drives to various other companies who package them and sell them to end users. Thus, both Apple and APS, for example, may use exactly the same Quantum manufactured drive (see Fix-It #16 for more on this). Nevertheless, the Apple formatting utilities will recognize only an Apple drive because of the special coding information that Apple places on the drive before it is shipped.

SEE ALSO:
- **"Take Note: Beware: Updating the Drive May *Cause* Problems (Not Fix Them)," earlier in this Fix-It**

BY THE WAY ▶

CHECKING THE VERSION NUMBER OF THE DRIVER

If you want to know the version number of your formatting utility, it is usually present somewhere in the window that appears when you launch the utility. Otherwise, just open the Get Info window and check the line labeled "Version." But what if you can't find this utility anymore? Or what if you want to confirm whether your currently installed driver is the one actually installed by this utility? A potential solution is to check the version number of the driver itself, which you can usually do by selecting the Get Info window for the disk in question. In the line labeled "Where," you should see a version number (oddly, drives formatted by Apple HD SC Setup do not show a version number here). In many cases, the version number here should match the version number of the formatting utility itself; however, it is not uncommon for it to be an entirely different number. In this case, contact the technical support staff of the company that made the utility and give them this number. They should be able to tell you if you are using the latest version of the driver (or at least a version compatible with the rest of your software and hardware).

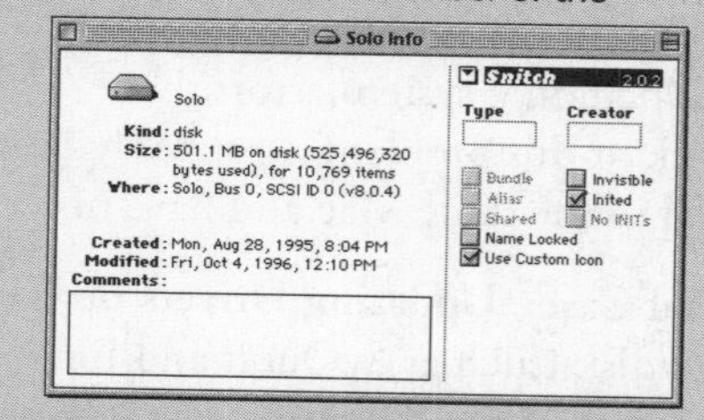

Figure F12-5 *The Get Info window for a drive formatted by Apple's Drive Setup 1.0.5; the version number of the driver (as seen in the "Where" line) is listed as 8.0.4.*

FIX-IT #12

BY THE WAY ▶

REMOVABLE CARTRIDGE DRIVES: DRIVERS AND EXTENSIONS

With removable cartridge drives such as those from SyQuest or Iomega, there is an extension in your System Folder that serves as a driver, in addition to a more typical "invisible" driver found on each cartridge. The extension allows the driver to load even when there is no cartridge inserted at startup (as long as the drive is turned on at the time). As a result, the drive is ready to mount a cartridge as soon as you insert it.

If a cartridge is present at startup, however, the driver from the cartridge typically loads before the one in your Extensions folder is checked. If the two drivers are different versions, you may get an error message such as "The Iomega Driver Extension (version 4.3) could not load because an older version (4.2) is already present." This is normally nothing to worry about, although you probably should update to get everything using the same driver.

A similar situation can occur with any format utility that uses an extension to mount drivers at startup (such as Hard Disk ToolKit or APS PowerTools). These may try to mount a driver for an Iomega drive if no cartridge is present at startup; if so, when the Iomega extension later tries to load, it will be unable to do so. Again, you will get some error message saying that the driver could not load because another driver is already present. The solution here is to change the loading order of the extensions so that the Iomega extension loads first. Alternatively, you could give up on one of the drivers altogether (deleting the extension from your disk) and just use the other driver—because the Iomega driver only works with Iomega drives, this is often the one you would give up. In these cases, make sure you also update your cartridges with the alternate driver.

Finally, if you start up with a removable cartridge drive turned off, you may get a message saying that the extension could not find the drive and thus did not load.

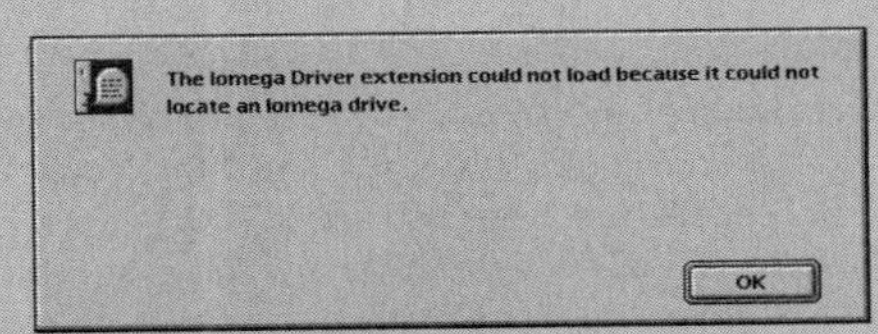

Figure F12-4 *With some versions of Zip Tools, this message appears if you start up your Macintosh with the Iomega Driver Extension installed, but with the Iomega Zip or Jaz drive off.*

Update the Driver

1. Make sure your data are backed up and your disk is not damaged

As with most of these types of procedures, there is the slim chance that updating will do more harm than good. So, before attempting any updating, make sure all your data are backed up. It is also a good idea to check for possible disk damage (see Fix-Its #10 and #13) before updating or switching drivers.

SEE ALSO: • **"Take Note: Beware: Updating the Drive May *Cause* Problems (Not Fix Them)!," earlier in this Fix-It**

2. Restart from a startup disk other than the one you want to update

With some formatting utilities, you cannot update the current startup disk or the disk from which you launch the formatting utility. The simplest solution for this problem is to start up with an Emergency Toolkit disk (see Chapter 2) or any other startup floppy disk or CD-ROM disc that contains the formatting utility. If you have more than one startup hard drive, use the alternate drive.

With Apple HD SC Setup or Drive Setup, you *can* update the driver on the current startup disk, but you will still have to restart before the new driver is actually used.

(If you are unable to start up because the problem disk causes a crash at startup, even when using an alternate startup disk, check Chapter 5, "Starting with an Alternate Startup Disk," for advice.)

3. **Launch the formatting utility and select Update**
With Apple HD SC Setup, click the Update button. With Drive Setup, select Update Driver from Drive Setup's Function menu. In either case, wait a few seconds, and you are done.
Just remember that HD SC Setup and Drive Setup do not work on non-Apple drives or Apple drives that have been updated and/or reformatted by another utility (although Drive Setup does work with removable cartridges).
For most other formatting utilities, such as Drive7, the procedure is essentially the same—just click the Update (or equivalent) button.

BY THE WAY ▶

WARNING FOR PASSWORD SECURITY USERS

Some software, such as At Ease for Workgroups, includes a security feature that "locks" access to a password-protected disk so that you cannot access the hard drive even if you start up from a floppy disk. It does this by modifying the disk's driver. If you lose the password, you may still be able to regain access to the drive by updating the disk driver, but some security programs will even block this. In this case, you will need to reformat the drive.

Users of the PowerBook password security software face a similar problem. If you forget your password, contact Apple for what to do.

Also note: If you remove At Ease on a protected disk by any method other than its Installer utility, it may similarly prevent you from starting up from the disk.

4. **If the Update selection is dimmed and cannot be selected (or if the update process fails for any reason)**

If you are using Apple HD SC Setup or Drive Setup, the drive probably has been formatted using a different utility. In this case, the Apple utility will not recognize the drive; the solution is to use a utility other than an Apple utility.
Sometimes, for a variety of reasons (a few of which are cited here), these Apple utilities may let you reformat a disk but not update the driver. In these cases, you will need to reformat the disk before you can use the utility with it.
In general, for any formatting utility—including Apple utilities—a dimmed Update button may mean that you are using a version of the format utility older than the one used to create the driver now on your disk. (For Apple HD SC Setup, for instance, this will be the case if the first or second digit of Setup's version number is lower than that of the version that installed the driver currently in use.) Conversely, it can mean that the version of your driver is so old that the newer utility cannot update it. Finally, it may mean that your driver (or the partition map, a related low-level area of the drive) is damaged.
To solve these problems, start by making sure you are using the latest version of whatever formatting utility created the driver currently on your disk. If this fails to work, you could try updating with another utility. In the end, however, you will

probably need to reformat the disk (especially if the driver or partition map is damaged). Prior to reformatting, use a data recovery package to recover files from the disk, as needed. MacTools, in particular, has special options to mount a disk with a damaged driver (as described in Fix-It #13).

Special case: Drive Setup problem Drive Setup cannot update the driver on some IDE drives. In these cases, the "Update driver," "Customize volume," and "Test disk" options will be dimmed; to get everything working again, you will need to re-initialize the drive. This problem mainly occurs with the first IDE drives used in Macintosh computers (prior to the release of Drive Setup and therefore never formatted with it), which were initialized without partitioning information on them. Drives that show "Where: Macintosh HD, AT_0" in the volume's Get Info window are such drives.

SEE ALSO: • **Fix-It #15 for more special problems using Drive Setup**

Special case: Compression utilities After installing certain programs that modify the driver (such as disk-level compression utilities), you may be unable to update the driver. If this happens, your only recourse may be to reformat the drive.

5. **Whatever you do, do *not* click the Format or Initialize buttons/commands!**
   Clicking a format utility's Format button sets you up to reformat the entire drive. With Apple HD SC Setup and Drive Setup, Initialize is the name of this button (with other utilities, "initialize" and "format" commands do different things, as explained in Fix-It #15). Reformatting your disk will irretrievably erase all data on the disk, which is probably not what you want to happen when you are just trying to update a driver.

   Actually, the situation with Drive Setup is a bit more complex. While it does not have separate Initialize and Format buttons, it does include separate options to "zero all data" or to do a "low level format." Again, this is described more in Fix-It #15.

   True, the driver gets updated when you reformat a disk, but reformatting a disk just for this reason is like using a machine gun to swat a fly. As noted, however, (see "By the Way: Switching to a Different Formatting Utility"), I would consider selecting Format/Initialize rather than Update if I were switching to a different driver entirely—after first backing up my data, of course.

6. **Quit the utility and restart the Macintosh**
   After updating is complete, quit the format utility. If you started up from a disk other than the one you are updating, the updated hard drive may be unmounted as a result of the update (that is, its icon will have vanished from the desktop). Don't worry. Restart the Macintosh, and the hard disk should now mount using the new driver.

For related information

SEE: • **Fix-It #15 on reformatting disks, partitioning disks, and formatting utilities in general, as well as more detailed coverage of Drive Setup versus Apple HD SC Setup.**
• **Fix-It #16 on SCSI problems**
• **Chapter 5 on problems mounting disks**

Fix-It #13: Check for Damaged Disks: Repair, Restore, or Recover

QUICK SUMMARY ▶

Use a data recovery utility package (primarily Norton Utilities for Macintosh) to repair or restore a damaged disk. If the disk cannot be fixed, recover files from the disk, as needed.

When to do it:

- Whenever you cannot start up your Macintosh with a known startup disk.
- Whenever you are unable to get a properly formatted disk to mount to the Finder's desktop. Especially with floppy disks, you may get a message that says the disk is "unreadable," "not a Macintosh disk," or "damaged" and asks if you want to initialize it.
- Whenever you have systemwide problems with a particular disk, especially problems related to keeping track of files. These commonly include an inability to open, copy, or delete files/folders on the disk, as well as files/folders that mysteriously disappear.
- If you accidentally erase a hard disk with the Finder's Erase Disk command.
- If you used Disk First Aid and it identified a problem that it could not repair.

FIX-IT #13

Why to do it:

Although utility packages such as Norton Utilities include dozens of features, their ability to resurrect a damaged disk is undoubtedly the single most important one. These programs accomplish this task in a manner similar to how Disk First Aid works (see Fix-It #10). Compared to Disk First Aid, however, these programs do more extensive checks, fix more problems, give you more options, and provide more feedback about what they are doing. If you have a disk that will not mount or otherwise seems in serious trouble, and if Disk First Aid could not remedy the problem, these are the utilities to use. If they fail to save the disk, usually your only remaining options are to reformat the disk or (for a floppy disk) to discard it.

Similar to Disk First Aid, these utilities check mainly for damage to the invisible Directory files. The Directory area of the disk (as detailed in Chapter 8) contains a continually updated catalog of what is on a disk, where everything is, and how it is organized. This is the essential information that the Macintosh needs to recognize, locate, and access all the files on a disk. For example, if a file is stored on a disk in fragments, the Directory contains the information needed to link all the fragments together when you launch the file. The Directory (together with related "hidden" areas of the disk) also contains the critical information necessary for the Macintosh to recognize whether the disk is a Macintosh-formatted disk as well as whether it is a startup disk. Thus, even a small amount of damage to the Directory can render an entire disk virtually inaccessible.

Fortunately, if Directory damage occurs, there is still a very good chance that your disk—or at least most of the data on it—can be saved, because the remaining areas of the disk (where the documents and applications actually reside) may still be unharmed. The files contained on the disk are often all usable, if only they can be accessed. Working with a disk with a damaged Directory is a bit like trying to use a library without a catalog: the books are all fine, but there may be little hope of finding the ones you want.

The working assumption in this Fix-It is that Directory damage is the cause of a problem mounting a disk (commonly referred to as a *crashed* or *trashed* disk). Related problems are covered in other parts of this book, especially the remaining Fix-Its. This Fix-It covers details of how to use both MacTools and Norton Utilities to fix these problems. Although the guidelines given here are not intended as a complete substitute for the documentation that accompanies these programs, in many cases, they will be sufficient to convey what you need to know. Additionally, this Fix-It should make clear—in a way often obscured in the manuals—exactly what these recovery utilities can and cannot do.

Disk recovery utilities such as Norton Utilities provide up to three methods of rescuing these Directory-damaged disks: repair, restore, and recover.

Repair

To *repair* a disk means to return the damaged files to their predamaged state. If the damage to the Directory is simply a garbling of the data stored there, these utilities can often scan the remaining undamaged areas of the disk and determine what the ungarbled data should be, and then re-create it. If this works, it is the ideal solution. It is almost like magic: an apparently dead disk is restored to full working order in a matter of minutes, with no loss of data.

Restore

Sometimes, though, Directory damage is so extensive that it cannot be repaired, usually resulting in a crashed disk. Similarly, if you accidentally erase a hard disk (via the Finder's Erase Disk command), the original Directory information is hopelessly lost, causing the Finder to list the disk as empty. In both cases, however, the rest of the files on your disk may still be perfectly intact (in the case of the "erased" hard disk, this is because the Erase Disk command does not actually erase or reformat a hard disk; it only alters the Directory, as described more in Fix-It #15).

In these cases, you may still be able to resurrect (or *restore)* the hard disk by using a utility to completely replace the current presumably damaged or erased Directory with an undamaged backup copy.

Recover

Sometimes a disk cannot be repaired or restored. Among other reasons, this can happen when media damage occurs to the area of the disk where the Directory resides. In these cases, you usually can still use these utilities to *recover* individual files from the disk (a helpful feature if files are not backed up elsewhere), because these utilities can identify the files from non-Directory information and then copy them to a separate disk. Assuming that the files are not themselves damaged, this procedure saves the files from an otherwise unsavable disk. Since recovery does not repair or replace any damage, you will typically have to reformat (or discard) the disk after recovery is completed.

SEE: • **Chapter 2 and Fix-Its #14 and #15 for more on the subject of media damage**

What to do:

This Fix-It, as already noted, describes three main options: repairing a damaged disk, restoring a damaged or accidentally erased disk, and recovering selected files from a damaged disk. This Fix-It further assumes that you are using either (a) MacTools Pro or (b) Norton Utilities 3.*x*, as indicated in the steps that follow. If you are using an earlier version of these programs, be aware that the specific instructions given here may not apply to you.

MacTools Pro is no longer being marketed, and there will be no more updates to this product. As a result, I considered dropping coverage of MacTools from this edition. The word, however, is that a forthcoming update to Norton Utilities will include some of the unique features of MacTools. When that happens, some of the points covered here about MacTools will likely prove useful—and in the meantime, there are still many MacTools users out there. For both of these reasons, MacTools makes one last appearance here in *Sad Macs.*

More generally, for Norton Utilities (and even for MacTools), it pays to contact Symantec and make sure you have the latest versions of these programs. There have been several minor updates to keep pace with the latest changes in Apple's system software.

Repair a Damaged Disk

Before Using Your Repair Utility

1. **Mount the disk from the Finder, if possible, and copy unbacked-up files to another disk**

   If the problem disk mounts on the desktop from the Finder without any problem, you are lucky. Immediately copy any essential files you haven't already backed up to another disk, just in case your repair attempts make things worse.

   If you cannot mount the problem disk, and it is your normal startup disk, you will have to restart with an alternate startup disk (such as your Emergency Toolkit disk, as described in Chapters 2 and 5) before you can proceed. The problem disk may now mount normally as a secondary disk; if so, now copy any essential files that lack backups to another disk.

TAKE NOTE ▶

USING MACTOOLS OR NORTON UTILITIES TO CREATE STARTUP DISKS

Current versions of Norton Utilities and MacTools Pro include an emergency startup disk that is ready for use. They also have special options, however, for creating customized emergency startup floppy disks that are designed to ensure that this disk works with your particular hardware (by including needed Enabler files, if any). You will have at least two options: one to create a startup repair disk (as described here) and another to create a startup disk for defragmenting (as described in Fix-It #8). Ideally, you should use these options *before* you run into trouble.

- **MacTools Pro.** With MacTools Pro, you are given the option to build an emergency startup disk during the installation of MacTools on your hard drive. Otherwise, you can select the "Build DiskFix Disk" option from the Clinic menu at any time.

  If you have a Macintosh that can create a RAM disk via System 7's Memory control panel, MacTools Pro can automatically create a RAM disk, copy the needed files to it, and then restart and boot from this RAM disk (assuming that the problem is not so serious as to prevent the RAM disk from setting up). You do this by clicking the "RAMBoot" button in the MacTools Clinic main window. Follow the instructions carefully, as I have had numerous problems getting this RAMBoot option to work; be especially aware that you will not be able to use RAMBoot unless you have a healthy amount of RAM available (for example, you appear to need more than 8MB of RAM to use this feature on a Power Mac running System 7.5). Still, when it works, this can be a wonderful convenience, freeing you from the need to have a bootable emergency disk handy when a problem appears. I have found it especially helpful for when I travel with my PowerBook.
- **Norton Utilities.** With Norton Utilities, you are similarly given the option to create an emergency startup disk when you first install Norton Utilities. Otherwise, select "Startup Disk Builder" from the Utilities menu and then select to build a "Norton Disk Doctor/UnErase" disk.

  By the way, when you first install Norton Utilities, you are also given the option to create something called a VIF (Volume Information File) for each currently mounted disk. You can also create VIF files at any later time via the "Create VIF Files" command in the Norton Utilities Options menu. These VIF files can help Norton Disk Doctor to identify and recover from certain types of damage to the disk. In most cases, you can use Disk Doctor quite successfully without these files; still, it does no harm to create them.

SEE: • **Chapter 2 for more general advice on creating emergency startup disks**

Even if the damaged disk does not mount as a secondary disk, you can still try to recover important files (if any) via the recover capability of the utilities before attempting repairs (see "Recover Selected Files from a Damaged Disk," later in this Fix-It).

2. **Preferably, start up from an undamaged disk that contains the repair utility** Norton Utilities will let you make repairs to the current startup disk and/or the disk that contains the Norton Utilities application. MacTools Pro (unlike earlier versions of MacTools) similarly lets you make many, though not all, of its repairs to the startup disk or the disk that contains MacTools. Still, I recommend against doing this, because it increases the chance that repairs will be unsuccessful; in the worst case, you may actually precipitate more damage. To be safe, use an alternate startup disk to repair problems to the startup disk.

If you have two hard drives, an acceptable strategy is to start up and run the utility from one hard drive to check the other one for damage. You can also start up from an Emergency Toolkit disk you have created (you may have already started up in this way in Step 1), or you can use the special emergency startup disks included with repair utility packages. These special disks contain and automatically launch the relevant repair utility upon startup (see "Take Note: Using MacTools or Norton Utilities to Create Startup Disks" and "Take Note: If You Can't Start Up with Your Emergency Disk").

One advantage of using the special emergency disks that come with the repair utilities is that there is typically no Finder on them. Normally you would not consider this an advantage, but it may be one in this case. This is because the Finder attempts to mount disks in the background, even if the data recovery utility is the active application. As the Finder is usually less effective in dealing with problem disks than data recovery utilities, the Finder's attempt to mount a problem disk may interfere with the ability of repair utilities to work, sometimes even causing a crash to occur. By not including a Finder, the emergency disks bypass this problem.

In this regard, if you insert a damaged floppy disk when your repair utility is not active and a dialog box asks if you want to initialize the disk, eject the disk instead. Then launch the repair utility and insert the floppy disk.

TAKE NOTE ▶

IF YOU CAN'T START UP WITH YOUR EMERGENCY DISK

First of all, before disaster strikes, check whether your emergency startup floppy disk will actually work as a startup disk—a hard disk crash is *not* the ideal time to discover that your startup floppy disk does not start up. If you do have a problem getting the floppy disk to work, make sure the disk was set up properly (see "Take Note: Using MacTools or Norton Utilities to Create Startup Disks"). Otherwise, problems starting up with an emergency disk are usually indirectly caused by problems mounting the damaged disk you want to repair. To bypass these problems, try the following (more detailed procedures are described in the manual for each utility):

- For damaged floppy disks, do not insert the floppy disk at startup. Insert it after the data recovery utility launches from the emergency disk.
- For a damaged external hard disk, turn off the disk at startup. Turn it on after the data recovery utility launches.
- For a damaged internal hard disk, hold down the Command-Option-Shift-Delete keys at startup until the "Welcome to Macintosh" message appears; the Macintosh should bypass the internal drive so that it does not mount. Launch the data recovery utility from the emergency disk. If this does not work, you may also have to zap the PRAM (see Chapter 5, "By the Way: The Internal Drive May Still Mount When Using Command-Option-Shift-Delete").

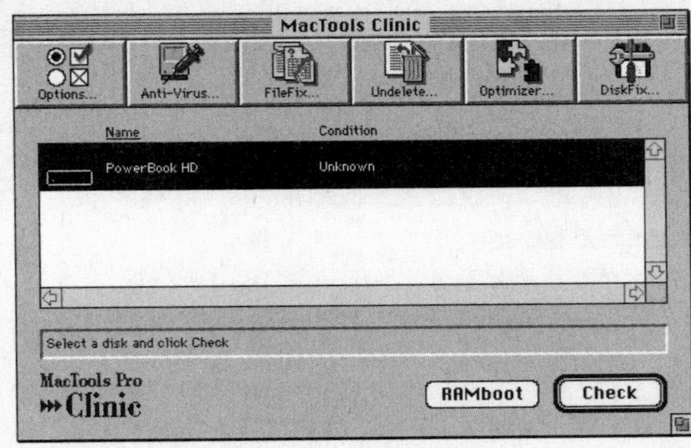

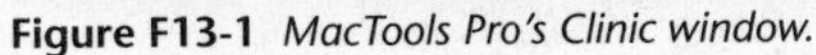
Figure F13-1 *MacTools Pro's Clinic window.*

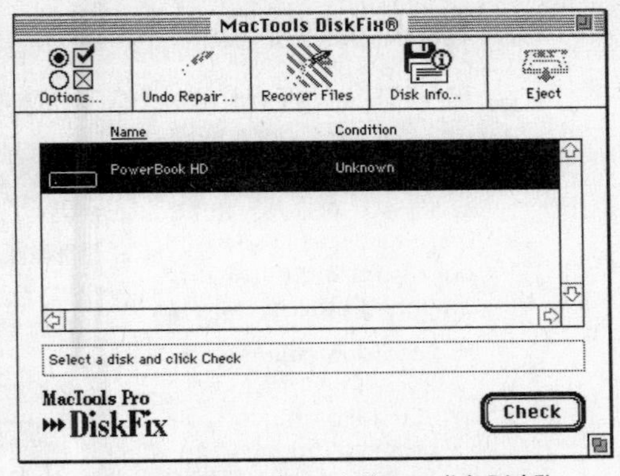

Figure F13-2 *MacTools Pro's floppy disk DiskFix window.*

Make Repairs

1. Launch your repair utility

a. With MacTools Pro, launch MacTools Clinic. A window listing all mounted disks will appear.

Alternatively, you may first be greeted by the MacTools Pro QuickAssist window (offering a list of problems to check for, as appropriate). If you don't want this window to appear automatically in the future, click the More button and then uncheck "Show this dialog at startup." If you want to skip using this window at the moment and instead proceed to the main Clinic window, click Cancel. Otherwise, put a check next to any symptoms you now have and click the Check button (there is no option here to select which mounted disk to check).

If you are using a MacTools emergency floppy disk, it will take you immediately to a special DiskFix window. This window is similar to (but has more limited options than) the window of the full MacTools Clinic application.

b. With Norton Utilities, if the Norton Utilities Main Menu window is displayed, click the Norton Disk Doctor button. Otherwise, from any other area in Norton Utilities, select Norton Disk Doctor from the Utilities menu. A window listing all mounted disks will appear.

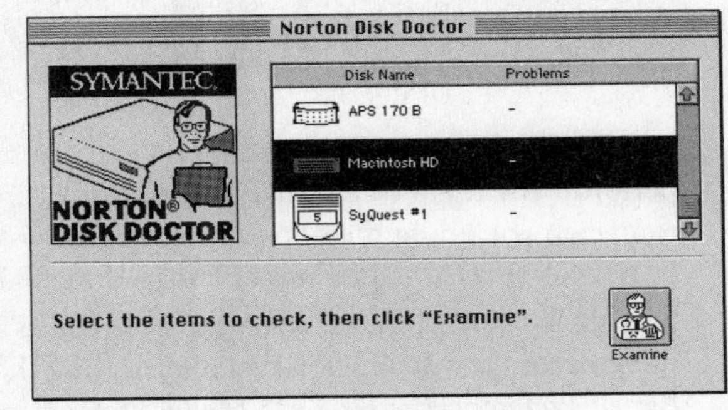

Figure F13-3 *The Norton Disk Doctor window.*

2. Set repair options (in particular, decide whether or not to check for bad blocks)

Do this any time you want to change the default preference settings of these applications. Ideally, you should do it before you check the potentially damaged disk.

a. With MacTools Pro's Clinic, click the Options button from the top row of buttons. From the Options window that appears, click the DiskFix button if it is not already selected (if you are using the floppy disk version of DiskFix, there is no

TECHNICALLY SPEAKING

IF A SCSI DISK'S NAME IS NOT LISTED, OR AN UNKNOWN DISK IS LISTED

If a disk's name is not listed in the utility's main window, and it is a SCSI disk, try to mount it using special SCSI bus rescan and disk mounting procedures.

- MacTools no longer has a rescan command. If you are having a problem mounting an external hard disk, however, try keeping it off until DiskFix launches, and then turn it on. Its name may then appear. If so, when you go to check the disk, MacTools may give you special options to mount the disk's driver (in this case, consult the MacTools Pro manual for more details).

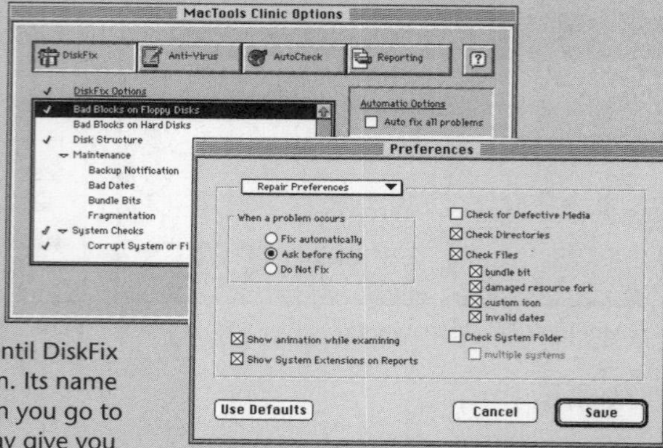

Figure F13-4 *MacTools Pro's DiskFix options (top) and Norton Disk Doctor's Preferences dialog box (bottom).*

- For Norton Disk Doctor, select the "Show Missing Disks" command from Disk Doctor's Disks menu. If even this fails to get the disk's name to appear, select the "Add Custom Disks" command from the same menu. This will result in a new window appearing. Consult the Norton Utilities manual or online help for details on what to do here; this is one case where having a VIF file (see "Take Note: Using MacTools or Norton Utilities to Create Startup Disks") may prove useful.

If none of this gets the disk to mount, it's time to give up on these utilities. Other solutions are discussed elsewhere (such as Chapter 5 and Fix-It #16). Ultimately, you may have to reformat the disk (thereby losing all the data on it) or discard the disk.

If you launch Norton Disk Doctor on a PCI-based Mac and it lists a mysterious otherwise invisible hard drive volume called "unknown," you probably have an Apple HD SC Setup driver installed on your drive. You need to update the driver using Drive Setup; otherwise, still more problems may be reported if you try to analyze this or other drives.

DiskFix button to select). From here, you can select which tests you wish DiskFix to perform. (By the way, a similar set of options are available by clicking the More button when you are in the QuickAssist window.) Most notably, you can decide whether or not to check for bad blocks (damaged media) on floppy disks and/or hard disks.

b. With Norton Utilities, select the Preferences command from Disk Doctor's Edit menu. From the dialog box that appears, use the pop-up menu to select between Repair Preferences and Check Media Preferences. With Repair Preferences, you have the option to select "Check for Defective Media" as part of Norton Disk Doctor's standard checks. The Check Media Preferences selection (not shown) refers to a separate "Check Disk Media" command in Disk Doctor's Tools menu; this command does a more thorough scan of the disk, including making repair attempts as needed.

By the way, you can also check for bad blocks from within the Speed Disk utility (see Fix-It #8) by selecting "Check Media" from Speed Disk's Explore menu.

I singled out bad blocks for special mention here because I would typically keep this option off—it takes a long time to make this check, and it is only rarely the source of a problem (especially for hard disks). You might turn on the option to check for bad blocks if a previous check of an apparently damaged disk did not identify any problems. Otherwise, you are most likely to want to check this when a problem with a specific file suggests that bad blocks are the cause (such as a read or write error when trying to copy a file). What to do in this case is more specifically covered in Fix-It #14 ("Resolve Problems with Bad Blocks").

If bad blocks are located in the critical Directory area of a disk, a repair utility may not even be able to scan the disk successfully. In this case, the only solution is to try to recover files if needed (as described later in this Fix-It) and then reformat the disk. For floppy disks, it is often simpler and safer to discard the disk.

SEE: • **Chapter 2 and Fix-Its #14 and #15 for more background information on bad blocks**

One other option that I would avoid is having the utility repair any damage without first asking if you want the problem repaired (e.g., "Auto fix all problems"). It's always safer to see what the utility intends to do before letting it go ahead. There are times when you may even want to skip a particular repair (which you cannot do if "auto fix" is on).

For help in deciding what other options to turn on or off, consult each utility's manual.

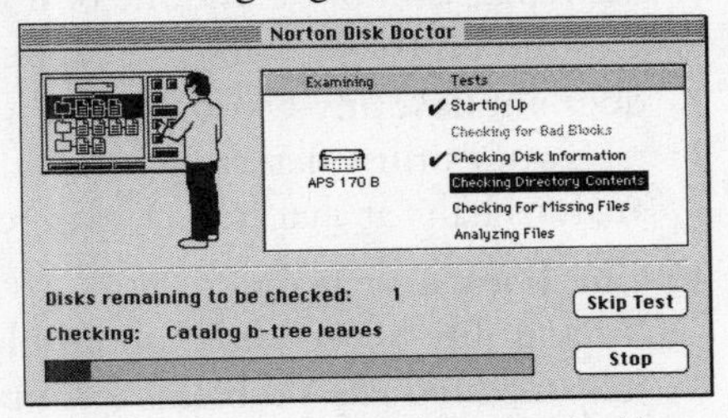

Figure F13-5 *Norton Disk Doctor checking a disk.*

3. Attempt to repair the disk

a. From MacTools Clinic (or DiskFix on the MacTools floppy startup disk), click on the name of the disk you wish to check and click the Check button.

b. With Norton Disk Doctor, click on the name of the disk you wish to check and click the Examine button.

In either case, the program now begins to check the disk. If it discovers a problem, it stops to alert you—under the default options, a window appears that describes the nature of the problem and suggests what to do about it. It usually gives you the choice to repair the problem (if possible) or skip over it (if desired). In general, repair any problem that is detected and can be repaired (though you can ignore minor problems, such as incorrect modification dates, without affecting your ability to use the disk).

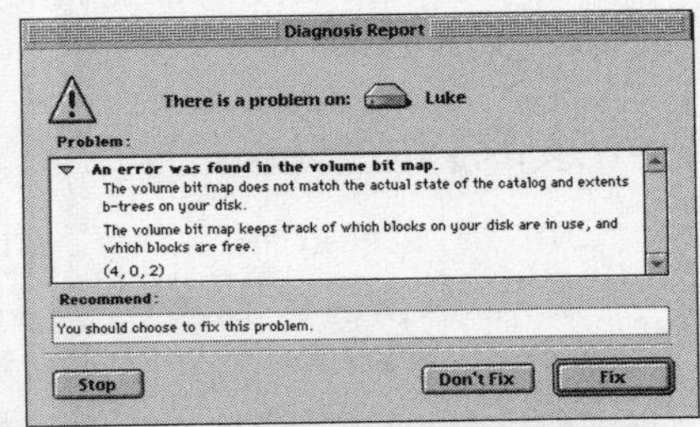

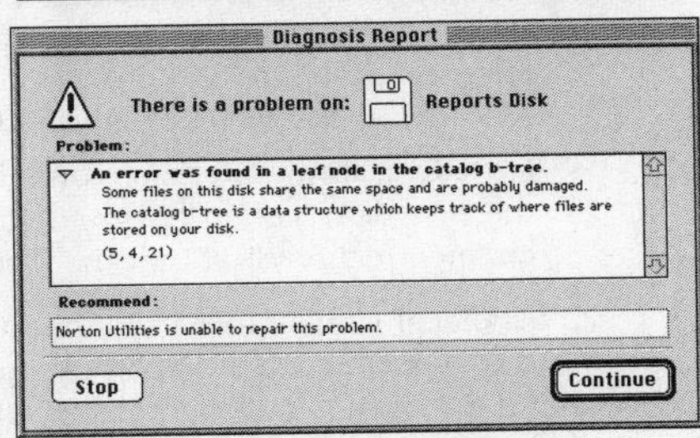

Figure F13-6 *Norton Disk Doctor finds a problem it can fix (top) and one it cannot (bottom).*

BY THE WAY ▶

IF DISK DOCTOR REFUSES TO ANALYZE

If Norton Disk Doctor claims it cannot check your disk because "files are open," even though you have closed all other applications and are running Norton Disk Doctor from a different disk than the one you want to analyze, check if the name of the disk is "Macintosh HD." If it is, change it to any other name, and the problem should disappear. Otherwise, make sure that virtual memory and file sharing are off.

After making your choice, the analysis then proceeds, pausing again as needed until the entire disk is checked. Normally, that's all there is to doing repairs.

If anything happens that you wish to undo, MacTools gives you the option to undo any repairs that it has made (via the "Undo DiskFix Repair" command in the Clinic or DiskFix menu). To use it, however, you must first have selected the "Create a file to undo DiskFix repairs" option, which is accessed by clicking the Custom button from the window that appears when a problem is detected. If the repair cannot be undone or if an Undo file is already present, clicking the Custom button—if one even appears—will not list this option. Norton Utilities does not have any Undo option.

If your utility detects a problem that it cannot repair (and especially if the disk analysis halts at that point), skip to Step 6.

4. **Check the disk again**

   If the utility has reported no problems with the disk, or if it claims to have successfully repaired any problems it found, check the disk again anyway. As with Disk First Aid, problems may be detected on subsequent runs that were not spotted or not fixed on the first run. Ideally, check the disk at least until no problems are detected on two consecutive runs.

TECHNICALLY SPEAKING ▶

UTILITIES REPORT PROBLEMS THAT AREN'T

Sometimes when a utility reports a problem, it is really a false alarm caused by bugs in the software. Here are some examples:

- A flaw in the TrashBack feature of MacTools may cause the utility's AutoCheck to list a problem with the disk, even though there is no problem. It may also cause Disk Express to report problems and prevent it from working. This should no longer be a problem in MacTools Pro, which has substantially revised the way TrashBack works.
- If the QuickDraw GX extension is installed and active, Norton Utilities may report that the extension has a problem, describing it as having either a "Damaged Resource Fork" or "Incorrect Physical Length." This can be ignored; Norton Utilities is wrong.

In general, if a repair utility reports an unusually large number of problems when you are not experiencing any problems using the disk, or if it reports a problem with a specific file that is not giving you any problem, be a little skeptical. It is sad but true that even programs designed to detect problems may have problems of their own!

5. **If repairs are successful**

If your utility detects no further damage on retesting, your problems should be over. Quit the utility, restart the Macintosh, and try using the problem disk. If it now works as expected, you are done.

If the disk seems okay for the moment but the same problem recurs within a few days, you should probably reformat the disk rather than repair it again. In the meantime, make sure your important files are backed up, just in case disaster strikes.

6. **If repairs aren't successful**

A data recovery utility may detect a Directory problem but report that it is unable to repair it. In some cases, a disk is so damaged that the utility either cannot start or cannot complete its analysis of the disk. Rarely, it may wrongly claim to have repaired a problem. For example, you may have *cross-linked files,* which occur when the Directory indicates that two different files are occupying the same sector of a disk. Usually one or both of the files are damaged, with lost data almost a certainty. Although a repair utility may offer to repair the incorrect Directory listing, it can't entirely repair the damaged files.

In some cases where repairing a file is impossible, MacTools may give you the option to copy the damaged file to another disk, salvaging whatever possible. Similarly, if Norton Utilities cannot fix a certain problem, it may directly launch its Volume Recover function (using this is discussed later in this Fix-It). In other cases, it may simply report that it cannot repair the volume.

Figure 13-7 *MacTools Pro suggests trying to recover files from a disk that cannot be repaired.*

Whenever you are unable to repair a damaged disk successfully, try to recover any files that you want to save (for example, any files you have not already recovered or backed up). After completing any recovery, reformat the disk, then restore the data from your backups.

BY THE WAY ▶

SAM SPOTS A DAMAGED DISK

I had an unusual case where SAM (Symantec Antivirus for Macintosh) was able to spot disk damage that was missed by both Norton Utilities and MacTools Pro. A floppy disk caused a system freeze whenever I inserted it (the disk would not mount, and I had to restart to get things working again). Oddly, the disk worked fine if I started up with extensions off. I used this fact to check the disk with Norton and MacTools Pro, but both reported the disk was fine.

I then checked for viruses with SAM. It reported an error for the Desktop file on the disk, adding the message, "This is probably not a valid resource." Although this message does not typically indicate a virus, I took it seriously and reformatted the disk (thereby creating a new Desktop file; if this was critical, using TechTool to rebuild the desktop might have worked also). This fixed the problem! SAM reported the disk as okay on the next check, and the disk mounted fine even with extensions back on.

SEE: • Fix-It #9 on rebuilding the desktop

Using More than One Repair Utility By the way, if you own both MacTools and Norton Utilities, it pays to try them both. If one can't fix a problem, maybe the other one can.

Occasionally, however, one utility may "undo" a repair made by the other, leading to a potentially endless cycle of repairs as you switch back and forth between utilities. For minor problems such as a Bundle bit error, you can probably ignore this and just stop at the end of one utility's analysis. For more serious problems (such as a "B-tree header" problem), though, this situation may result from each utility spotting separate damage to the same area, with neither one able to effect a complete repair (one utility's repair may even allow the other utility to spot damage that it would have otherwise missed). Similar problems can occur between these utilities and Disk First Aid. In these cases, reformatting may again be your only solution.

SEE:
- **"Recover Selected Files from a Damaged Disk," later in this Fix-It**
- **Chapter 2 on restoring from backups**
- **Fix-It #15 on reformatting disks**

BY THE WAY ▶

AUTOMATED CHECKING AND REPAIRS

Both MacTools Pro and Norton Utilities offer options to scan a disk periodically in the background, while the computer is otherwise idle. Norton Utilities does this via FileSaver, while MacTools uses a special AutoCheck extension. With the most recent version of AutoCheck, you can often repair the disk without needing to launch the separate Clinic application.

SEE:
- **Chapter 2, "Protect Against Disk Damage" (in the "Install Protection Utilities" section), for more on setting up these auto-scanning options**

BY THE WAY ▶

DISK DAMAGE AND WEB BROWSERS

Web browsers, such as Netscape Navigator and Internet Explorer, probably write more often to your disk than any other applications you own, mainly due to the frequent updating of their so-called cache files. The result of all of this activity is an increase in the risk of data corruption occurring when running your browser. If you often use a Web browser, check your disk regularly for directory damage with Disk First Aid, MacTools, or Norton Disk Doctor. If your utility frequently reports B-tree or other related errors, your Web browser should be a prime suspect.

SEE:
- **"System Freezes, Crashes, and Directory Damage," in Chapter 14, for more details on how to minimize this risk**

BY THE WAY ▶

DISK DOCTOR "ERASES" A DISK

If you thought you were lucky to get one of the first PCI Macs to roll off the assembly line, think again—there is a chance that running Norton Disk Doctor can appear to erase your entire hard disk. To eliminate any chance of this happening, get and run Disk Spot Check, a free utility available online from Symantec. It tells you whether you have the problem, eradicates it if it is found, and includes instructions on how to recover your data. The problem can potentially occur on 5200, 6200, 7200, and 7500 Power Macs, though it was primarily on the PCI-based Macs that it was noted. Happily, Apple has since altered its manufacturing process so as to eliminate this problem entirely.

Restore a Damaged or Accidentally Erased Disk

You will not often need to restore a disk, maybe never. For irreparable Directory damage or an accidentally erased hard disk, however, this procedure can sometimes save the day (but see "Take Note: Use Backups Instead of Restore or Recover" for some cautions).

MacTools Pro does not have a restore option. To restore a disk, you must use a special feature of FileSaver (a control panel included as part of Norton Utilities, as described more in Chapter 2) that maintains a backup copy of the Directory. This option does not work with floppy disks.

Before Attempting to Restore a Disk

1. **Make sure FileSaver is installed and active prior to the onset of the problem**
   You can only restore a disk if you have installed and activated FileSaver prior to the occurrence of the problem; this Norton Utilities control panel creates and updates the needed invisible files. In particular, make sure the On/Off button in the FileSaver control panel is on, and that the Protected checkbox is checked next to each disk you want to protect. If you have not already done this, the best you can do for an immediate problem is to recover files, as described in the next section ("Recover Selected Files from a Damaged Disk").

   SEE: • **Chapter 2 for more on setting up FileSaver**

2. **Recover recent files that are not already backed up**
   A restore, even if successful, may not return your disk to the exact state it was prior to the crash. In particular, recent changes and additions may not get restored (see "Take Note: Use Backups Instead of Restore or Recover" for details). For this reason, before attempting a restore, you should try to recover files that may have been added, modified, or created since FileSaver's most recent update, unless you know that you already have these files backed up elsewhere. To do this, use methods described in "Recover Selected Files from a Damaged Disk," later in this Fix-It.

When and how often the FileSaver information is updated is set from the FileSaver control panel. If you are unsure when the last update was performed, you will get this information as you carry out the steps in the next section.

TAKE NOTE ▶

USE BACKUPS INSTEAD OF RESTORE OR RECOVER

Older versions of MacTools used to have a control panel, called Mirror, that allowed you to restore a disk much in the same way as you do with FileSaver from Norton Utilities. This feature was dropped from MacTools Pro because the developers believed that it would only rarely, if ever, solve a problem that could not be better handled by the utility's other repair functions. While the overall wisdom of this decision can be debated, the MacTools folks do have a valid point. Consider the limitations of and problems with FileSaver's recover ability:

- If you have not installed and activated FileSaver prior to the crash, the restore function won't work.
- Even with FileSaver active, restoring doesn't always work. For example, if the disk damage involves the FileSaver files, they are rendered useless. Also, FileSaver cannot restore files damaged because of bad blocks.
- Most notably, these protection files cannot necessarily restore a disk to its state at the time of the crash or erasure. This is because the recovery can restore the Directory only to how it was the last time these protection files were updated. Depending on luck and how you configured FileSaver, the last update may have been made just before the problem occurred, or it may have been made several weeks before. Any changes made since the last time the protection file was updated are not restored. In fact, trying to restore a disk with an out-of-date Directory may cause problems of its own (for example, if a file listed in the outdated Directory has since been deleted from the disk).

Thus, unless the last update was made relatively close to the occurrence of the problem (or you have made very few recent changes to the contents of your disk), I would not consider using this restore feature. Neither would I want to depend on a utility's recover feature. Frequent backups (which you should always maintain, whether you use FileSaver or not) remain your best protection against data loss. Backing up also requires regular updating to be effective, of course, and restoring a disk from backups can be time-consuming—but backups are much more reliable than the alternative methods. If you have an up-to-date set of backups, successful recovery is almost guaranteed.

SEE: • Chapter 2 for more on setting up FileSaver and on backing up disks

Restore the Disk

1. **Access Volume Recover from Norton Utilities**
   Launch Norton Utilities. From the main menu, click the Volume Recover button. A window listing all mounted volumes will appear.
2. **Select the disk to be restored**
   Select the volume you wish to restore and click the Recover button. You cannot restore the startup disk or the disk that contains the active copy of Norton Utilities; in these cases, starting up from an alternate disk will be required.

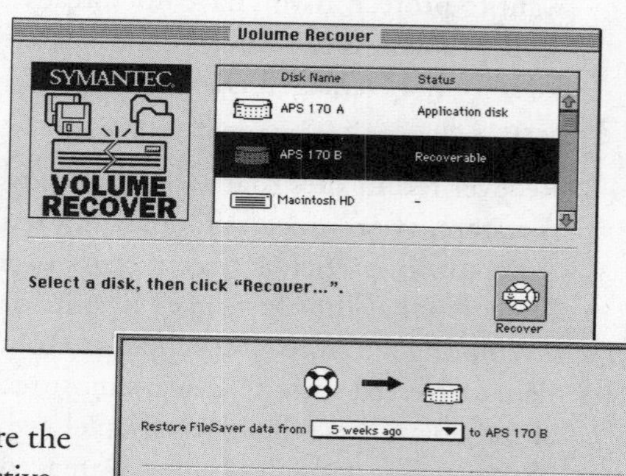

Figure F13-8 *The Volume Recover feature of Norton Utilities restores a disk's Directory—first, select a volume (top), and then start the restore (bottom).*

3. **Attempt to restore the disk**

   After you select Recover, Volume Recover searches for the needed FileSaver data. A dialog box then appears with a pop-up menu listing the dates of all available FileSaver files. Generally, pick the most recent date (unless you suspect the damage occurred prior to that date), then click Restore.

   Note that if the FileSaver file's date is much older than the current date, your restore is unlikely to result in a good match to the current status of your disk (as described in "Take Note: Use Backups Instead of Restore or Recover").

   If no FileSaver data are found, Volume Recover offers to shift to UnErase (described more in the next section) to recover files.

4. **a. If the restore is successful**

   If the restore succeeds, your disk should be returned to normal; congratulations. Return any separately recovered files (as described in "Before Attempting to Restore a Disk," earlier in this section) that were not restored. To be safe, go back and check for repair problems using Disk Doctor (as described in the previous section). Actually, Norton Utilities will prompt you to run Disk Doctor after completing its Volume Recover.

   b. If the restore fails

   If the initial restore attempt fails, you can try to restore again using another FileSaver backup file (if available). Alternatively, you can go to Disk Doctor to see if it can now repair the disk despite the apparently failed restore attempt. Otherwise, recover any files that you have not already backed up or tried to recover (using methods described in the next section), then reformat the disk and restore it from your backups and recovered files.

Recover Selected Files from a Damaged Disk

This section emphasizes the general procedure for using MacTools or Norton Utilities to recover files from a severely damaged disk that could not otherwise be repaired or restored. For more detailed information on this and other ways to recover individual damaged files from any disk, crashed or not, see Fix-It #14.

FIX-IT #13

For Norton Utilities, successful recovery is more likely if you have previously installed FileSaver.

1. **Launch your repair utility**

   a. With MacTools Pro, launch MacTools Clinic; a window listing all mounted disks should appear. If you are first greeted with the QuickAssist window, click Cancel. If you are running from a floppy disk, DiskFix will launch automatically.

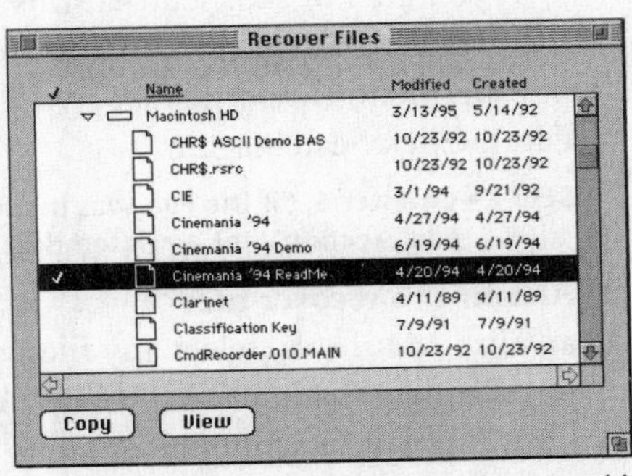

Figure F13-9 *MacTools Pro's list of recoverable files.*

b. With Norton Utilities, simply launch Norton Utilities to get to the Norton Utilities Main Menu window or (if you are using a floppy startup disk) the Disk Doctor window.

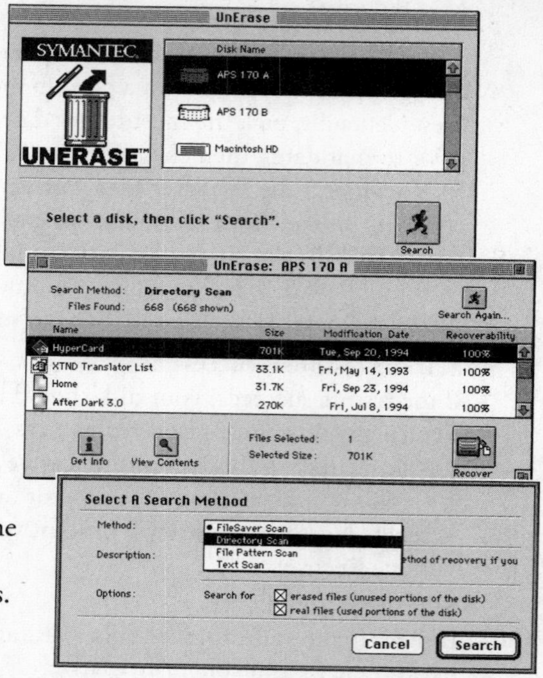

2. **Generate a list of recoverable files**

a. With MacTools Pro's Clinic, select the desired volume, and then select the Recover Files command from the Clinic menu. (If you are using a MacTools emergency floppy disk, select the Recover Files button from the DiskFix window.)

After scanning the disk, you will be presented with a Recover Files window showing the name of the volume. Click the triangle symbol to the left of the volume name to display the list of recoverable files.

b. With Norton Utilities, select UnErase either from the Main Menu window (if present) or the Utilities menu. A window listing all mounted disks will appear. From here, select the name of the desired disk and then click the Search button to perform a search for erased files based on FileSaver data, if available.

Figure F13-10 *The Norton Utilities UnErase main window (top) and Search Again dialog box (bottom).*

When the initial search is complete, a window will appear. From here, click the Search Again button. This will open a dialog box where you will see two checkbox options, one for "erased files" and the other for "real files." To recover files from a damaged disk, you want to check the "real files" option. Click Search once again.

This second search will give you a list of recoverable files. The list may also include partially recoverable and totally irrecoverable files, unless you select the "Hide Unrecoverable Files" command in the Options menu.

If you are not satisfied that this list contains all the files you wish to recover, click the Search Again button once more and select a different option from the Method pop-up menu (in particular, try Directory Scan if you do not have current FileSaver data). Click Search again.

SEE: • **Chapter 6, "If the File Was Inadvertently Deleted" (in the "When You Can't Locate a File" section), for a related description of undeleting files**

3. **Attempt to recover files**

a. With MacTools, select any files you wish to recover (by placing a check mark next to their name) and click the Copy button. For text files, you may first click the View button to see the contents of a file. This may help in your decision as to whether to try to recover it.

b. With the UnErase feature of Norton Utilities, select files and click the Recover button. You can click the View Contents button to see the contents of a file before deciding whether to recover it or not (this is primarily useful for text files).

In either case, be sure to save the files to another disk—*not* the damaged disk—when you are prompted to select a destination disk.

Not all files can be recovered successfully. Some files can only be partially recovered, and each program may have different success in recovering a specific file. So if you own both MacTools and Norton Utilities, it is worth trying to recover with both of them. In any case, this sort of file recovery can be long and tedious, especially if you want to recover many files. As a result, you should try to restrict your recovery efforts to essential files that are not backed up elsewhere (typically, your most recently created files).

4. **Check on success or failure of recovered files**

When the recovery is done, quit the utility; if possible, go to the Finder (restarting the Mac with an appropriate startup disk, if necessary). Recovered files should be on your selected disk, typically in a folder called Recovered Files. Try to open the files—if documents do not directly open from the Finder's desktop, they usually open from within their creating application (see Chapter 6 for more on how to deal with this problem).

With luck, the files are intact or (for text files) only require minor reformatting. Some documents, however, may have only partial contents or will be otherwise unusable. In any case, what you now have is the best you are likely to get by this method.

5. **Repair and/or reformat**

If you have not yet done so, try to repair the damaged disk. If repair attempts fail, any files that are still unrecovered probably cannot be saved. Some disk repair companies, though, specialize in recovering data from disks that you have given up for dead; if you absolutely must get your data back, they're worth a try.

Otherwise, it is time to reformat the disk (for floppy disks, it's safer to discard the disks rather than reformat them). If the hard disk fails to work after reformatting (or if you can't reformat the disk), you have more serious problems. Hardware damage is a likely possibility.

For related information

MacTools and Norton Utilities can repair minor problems unrelated to Directory damage. Such problems are called "minor" because their symptoms typically do not directly interfere with your use of the Macintosh. Checks for these problems can be done as part of the overall repair examination of the disk, as described in this Fix-It; for example, you can check whether files have invalid creation dates or incorrect Bundle bit settings. These utilities can also check for whether your desktop files are corrupted and can rebuild the desktop if needed. These problems, however, are not the focus of this Fix-It and are covered elsewhere.

There are also reasons why a disk may not mount that do not involve Directory damage. These too are covered elsewhere, as listed in the following cross-references.

SEE:
- **Fix-It #9 on rebuilding the desktop**
- **Fix-It #14 on recovering damaged files**
- **Fix-It #15 on reformatting disks and for problems with floppy disks that appear to be damaged but are really not**
- **Fix-It #16 on SCSI-related problems that may prevent a disk from mounting**
- **Fix-It #17 on hardware repairs**
- **Chapter 2 for information on disk damage, backing up your disks, and installing invisible files needed for restore and recovery**
- **Chapter 5 for more details on startup problems and other problems mounting disks**
- **Chapter 6 on undeleting files**
- **Chapter 8 for more on the Directory, Bundle bits, and other file attributes**

Fix-It #14:
Check for Damaged Files: Replace or Recover

QUICK SUMMARY ▶

Replace damaged files from backups, if possible. Otherwise, use utilities (such as Norton Utilities for Macintosh, MacTools Pro, and CanOpener) to repair or recover data from damaged files, especially document files. In all cases, check for and "repair" bad blocks.

When to do it:

- Whenever launching an application consistently results in a system crash, freeze, or other serious malfunction.
- Whenever a program's feature that worked correctly on previous occasions now causes problems or simply does not work.
- Whenever opening a document consistently results in a system crash, freeze, or other serious malfunction.
- Whenever a document opens but displays only part of its content, or unintelligible gibberish rather than its expected data.
- Whenever specific documents will not print but other similar documents print without a problem.
- Whenever the error message "Unable to read from disk" appears when you try to open a file.
- Whenever you cannot successfully copy a file, especially when attempts to do so result in an error message such as "File could not be read [or written, or verified] and was skipped." These messages indicate bad blocks (media damage) on at least one of the disks involved in the copy operation.
- If you are using a floppy disk, a bad block is also indicated by a distinctive and uncharacteristic whining sound that emanates from the drive as it attempts to read from the defective area of the disk.

Why to do it:

If you have a damaged file, you want to replace it or fix it. In Chapter 2, the causes of damaged files were briefly described in the section entitled "Damage Control." Here is a closer look at how these causes apply to solving problems with damaged documents and applications.

Damaged Files Due to Miscopied Information

Many damaged files appear to be normal on the desktop, and they can be moved or copied without any problem. When you try to open the file, however, problems appear. Applications may crash when launched. Documents, if they can be opened at all, display only part of the expected contents or display garbage data. In these cases, the file damage is usually due to some alteration in the data that make up the file; the damage usually originates as an error made when the file is copied, saved, or modified in any way. Since many files, such as the System file, are regularly modified as part of their normal use, this damage can happen to a file without you directly modifying it. This software damage is analogous to a book that has some words misprinted. Technically, you have no problem reading the book—it's just that the words don't always make sense.

Damaged Files Due to Bad Blocks

The other common type of damage is usually referred to as *bad blocks.* As indicated in Chapter 2, bad blocks are usually the result of media damage (that is, physical damage to the disk media) in a given area (block or sector) of a disk. In a strict technical sense, this is not a file-related problem; it is a disk problem. In fact, a bad block can occur in an area of the disk where there is no file at all. Similarly, a bad block can occur in the Directory area of a disk—usually resulting in a crashed disk and almost certainly necessitating reformatting the disk.

SEE: • Fix-It #13 for more on problems with damaged disks

When a bad block occurs in an area where a document or application file exists, however, it is also considered a file problem. In these cases, you have two separate problems to solve.

First, the file is damaged. Even small files are usually several blocks in size, so a single bad block damages only a small part of most files. Still, this damage can render an entire file unusable; the information in the bad block region is most often permanently lost in any case. Usual solutions here are either to replace the file with a backup or, if it is a document file, to try to recover at least some of the data. If the bad block problem is intermittent, which happens occasionally, you may be able to recover the entire file.

Second, regardless of what you do to recover the file, the bad block problem remains and must also be remedied, typically by marking the block so that it will no longer be used. Otherwise, the bad blocks lie in wait, ready to cause problems the next time the Macintosh accesses that area of the disk.

Overall, floppy disks are much more susceptible to bad blocks than hard disks.

Caveats

First, several of the situations described in the "When to Do It" section have other causes besides damaged files. So don't automatically assume that your file is damaged if you have one of these symptoms (see Chapter 6 for a more general discussion of file problems).

Second, this Fix-It assumes that despite any potential damage, you can get to the desktop and locate the damaged files. If this is not the case, you should refer first to Fix-It #13.

TECHNICALLY SPEAKING ▶

WHY ARE MY BLOCKS BAD?

You cannot read any data from a bad block; often, you cannot write (that is, copy or save) any data to one, either. This is why attempts to access these areas of a disk result in error messages that say a file could not be read or written.

Most bad blocks are caused by media damage. This can result from media material flaking off, being scratched, or an assortment of other related possibilities. The probability of such damage increases as a disk ages, even if it is just a floppy disk sitting on a shelf. Other cases of bad blocks are harder to categorize, but they are most often the result of a loss or disruption of the magnetic field needed to store data in the block. For example, exposure to strong magnetic fields can cause such bad blocks to appear.

When you first detect a bad block, there is no way to identify easily what type of bad block it is, and it probably isn't worth trying very hard to do so. Whatever the cause of the bad blocks, the symptoms are the same and the solutions are similar. The different causes, however, can determine what happens to the bad blocks when you try to fix the disk. If the bad blocks are the result of media damage, they cannot be repaired; they can only be marked to prevent their future use. For other causes of bad blocks, reformatting the disk often returns the blocks to normal.

Intermittent Bad Blocks. Occasionally, a bad block problem may be intermittent—that is, the damaged area of the block may "flip" back and forth between its correct and incorrect state, such that sometimes it behaves normally and other times it responds as a bad block. Left alone, the intermittent response usually worsens until the area always responds as a bad block. Data written to an intermittent bad block have a reasonably good chance of recovery; the idea is to read the block over and over again until you catch it on one of the times when it reads correctly.

Third, recall that not all types of "damaged files" are detectable by the utilities described here—in particular, damage due to miscopied information may not always be detected. In these cases, other specialized utilities that may help include TechTool and TechTool Pro (for damage to the main system software files; see Fix-It #5), Conflict Catcher (for damage to startup extensions; see Fix-It #4), and Font Box (for damage to font files; see Chapter 9).

What to do:

This section covers three strategies: replace the damaged file, recover the damaged file, and resolve problems with bad blocks.

FIX-IT #14

Replace the Damaged File

Your first line of defense against damaged files is to replace them, typically from your backup copies.

For Applications

Go to your original backup disks and use them to make a copy of the file(s). If the application came with an Installer utility, use it.

If these newly copied files work properly, delete the suspected damaged files from your disk. Remember to consider that the damage may be to associated files, such as preferences files, rather than the application itself (see especially Fix-Its #2 and #3). In that regard, be aware that preferences files may not get replaced when you reinstall the application; instead, you need to delete the suspected preferences file separately.

If you have no replacement copies, order new copies from the company that makes the software. If you are a registered user, you can typically do this for a small fee. Otherwise, particularly if the damage is caused by an intermittent bad block problem, you may still be able to recover the file (as described in the next major section of this Fix-It). Failing that, your application is hopelessly lost.

For Documents

If you have a backup copy of your document, use it. If it works, delete the damaged file.

Even if you are diligent about making backups, you can find yourself without a backup copy for a given document—for example, the document may get damaged after you have saved it but before you have a chance to back it up. Or you may inadvertently back up an already damaged file, leaving your backup copy damaged. In these cases, proceed to the next section on recovering damaged files.

Recover the Damaged File

In some cases, you may be able to recover a damaged file all the way back to its original condition, but don't count on this happening often. Partial recovery is usually the best you can hope for, because there is usually no way to figure out exactly what the "correct" data in the damaged area of the file should be.

Most of the techniques here emphasize recovery of document files, because document recovery has a better chance of success (even partial recovery can be of some value) and is more likely to be needed (for applications, it is more likely that you have a backup copy).

Make a Copy of the Damaged File

Make a copy of the file, ideally to another disk. There are two reasons for this. First, if your recovery attempts make things worse, you have a duplicate copy with which to try again. Second, sometimes copying a file from the Finder succeeds in recovering it, either fully or partially.

1. From the Finder, copy the file to another disk.
2. Try to open the newly copied file.
3. If the copy works normally, make a new backup copy of the now-recovered file and delete the damaged copy. You are done; skip the following steps and go back to work.
4. If the copy seems just as "damaged" as the original (or if you get only partial recovery), proceed to the next section, "Try to Open the Damaged Document."

5. If, when you try to make a copy, you get a message that says the file could not be read, this indicates that a bad block is the cause of the damaged file. In this case, proceed to "Resolve Problems with Bad Blocks," later in this Fix-It.

Try to Open the Damaged Document

Sometimes, even though a document appears damaged (as indicated by an inability to copy the document from the Finder), you can still open it, although you may find that some data are lost or incorrect when the document is opened.

1. Try to open the document from its creating application. If this does not work, try opening it from another application that reads the damaged file's format (for example, try opening a Word file with ClarisWorks).
2. If you can get the document to open successfully, even if it displays only partial contents or gibberish, use the Save As command to save the contents to a new file. Now open the newly created file to check if the problem symptoms are gone. As with making a copy of the file from the Finder, using Save As sometimes completely repairs a damaged file.
3. If the Save As technique does not work, copy any usable data from the damaged file to the clipboard. Open a new document and paste the data into it, then save the new document.
4. For partially recovered or unrecoverable files, if the damage occurred recently and if you have installed a utility such as NowSave, you may be able to find at least some of the missing data in the special recovery files created by these utilities (see Chapters 2 and 4 for details). Even better, if you have a backup copy of the document, but it is insufficient because it is an older version that does not contain recent modifications to the file, you may be able to combine it with the more recent data recovered from NowSave files to fully reconstruct the current version of the document.

File Recovery Via CanOpener

If all the preceding techniques have failed, you may still be able to use special recovery utilities to extract the text or graphics from the file. For text files, however, even if you succeed in doing this, you will lose all the text's formatting (such as font selections, styles, and margin settings). Still, this is a small price to pay to recover the complete text (or even just part of the text) of a long manuscript.

There are many file recovery utilities on the market. My favorite one is CanOpener, which works with almost any file—damaged or undamaged, document or application. It can extract graphics (of several different formats) as well as text that may be contained within a file; it can even extract sounds and QuickTime movies. Although utilities such as MacTools Pro and Norton Utilities have some similar features (as described next), CanOpener is generally both more effective and easier to use. To use it, follow these steps:

1. Launch CanOpener.
2. Locate the damaged file in CanOpener's scroll box, much as you would use an Open dialog box.

3. Double-click the damaged file's name. This opens a list of what text portions, pictures, sounds, and movies are recoverable from that file, with each one listed as a separate item.
4. Double-click an item to view its contents. You cannot edit the displayed text or graphic in any way, but you can view it to see if it is what you want to recover.
5. Once you have found the desired text or graphic, go to the Item menu and select Save As to save the item. This command saves text to a separate plain text file and graphics to a separate PICT file (see Chapter 8 for more on these file formats).
6. Quit CanOpener and access these saved files, for further editing if needed, in other applications (such as word processors or graphics applications). For example, text files may contain extraneous gibberish text that you want to delete.

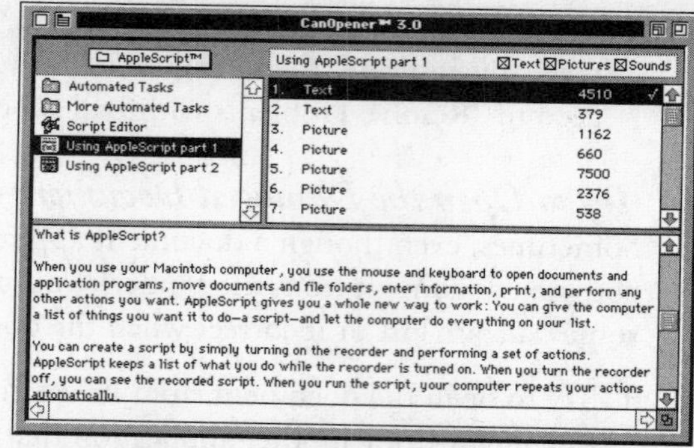

Figure F14-1 *Using CanOpener: double-clicking the name of the file on the left produces the list of text and picture items on the right; double-clicking the highlighted text item opens the text display below.*

If a file contains bad blocks or the disk is severely damaged, CanOpener may not be able to open it, or its name may not even appear in the initial list. If this happens, you have to address the bad blocks problem before you can use CanOpener (see "Resolve Problems with Bad Blocks" later in this Fix-It).

By the way, with version 3.5 or later of CanOpener, you get some additional Internet-related features, including the ability to strip HTML code from a text file, which results in a "clean" text extract.

TECHNICALLY SPEAKING ▶

MAKING REPAIRS WITH RESEDIT

For those of you that use Apple's ResEdit utility, you should know that ResEdit has some built-in repair capabilities. For example, I had a sound file that I could not use (that is, I could not get the sound to play). When I tried to open the file in ResEdit, it reported the file as damaged and offered to fix it. ResEdit was able to resurrect this file well enough that I could recover the sound intact!

File Recovery with MacTools or Norton Utilities

Both MacTools and Norton Utilities have file recovery capabilities (as described in Fix-It #13, "Recover Selected Files from a Damaged Disk"). If utilities such as CanOpener fail to work, these are your last resort. They can also fix minor file problems, such as incorrect Bundle bit settings and incorrect creation and modification dates, that are not addressed by CanOpener. Finally, these utilities have some special file recovery features not mentioned in Fix-It #13, as described below.

Norton Utilities Norton Utilities UnErase is especially good at text recovery. If the text is anywhere on the disk, UnErase is almost certain to find it. An often quicker solution for recovery of a single file, however, is to use the Recover File command from Norton Disk Doctor's Tools menu. In either case, Norton does a good job of saving the file with nonprinting characters and other extraneous gibberish stripped out.

MacTools Pro MacTools Pro includes a utility called FileFix that has special features for fixing damaged Microsoft Excel and Microsoft Word files. It recovers data from these files and then saves the data to a new file; check the MacTools Pro manual for details, if needed. FileFix is also an excellent utility for resolving problems with incorrect file type or creator codes (as explained more in Chapter 8). As this utility is no longer being updated, however, it may not work with current versions of some applications.

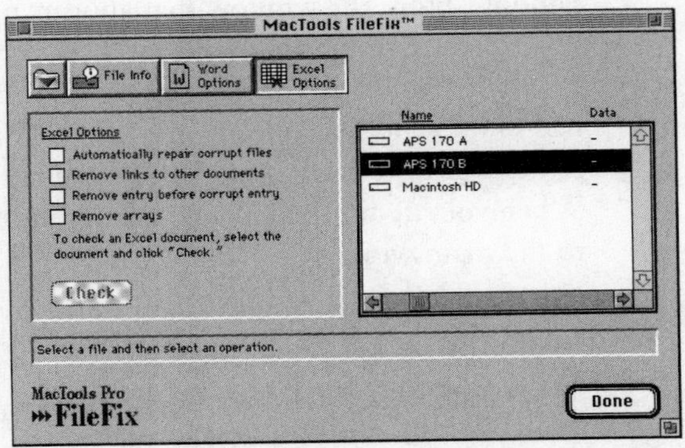

Figure F14-2 *MacTools Pro's FileFix, with special options to repair Excel files displayed.*

Resolve Problems with Bad Blocks

If bad blocks are present in the area of a disk occupied by a file, you typically are unable to open or copy the file—if you try, you get an error message that the file could not be read. A write or verify error when you try to copy a file, also indicates bad blocks, but the file itself is not damaged. Rather, the bad block is in the presently unused destination location for the file copy (though there may also be more bad blocks on this disk, in locations that *are* occupied by files). Fixing bad blocks independently of any specific file problem (such as indicated by a write or verify error) was briefly covered in Fix-It #13. The focus here is on recovering a specific file that is damaged because of bad blocks (as indicated by a read error). In either case, bad block problems need to be resolved before you continue to use the affected disk.

Recover Damaged Files and Repair Bad Blocks

Norton Utilities Norton Utilities does a decent job of checking for and repairing bad blocks, even attempting to fix files that are damaged due to bad blocks. To initiate all of this, select the Check Disk Media command from Norton Disk Doctor's Tools menu. Norton Utilities can also check for bad blocks as part of its more general analysis of the disk.

SEE: • **Fix-It #13, "Set Repair Options (Especially Decide Whether or Not to Check for Bad Blocks)," in "Repair a Damaged Disk," for more details**

MacTools Pro I prefer to use MacTools Pro for dealing with bad blocks problems. The instructions in the steps that follow apply to the DiskFix component of MacTools Clinic. If you are using the DiskFix application from the MacTools startup disk, the options may be somewhat different from what is described here.

1. From the MacTools Clinic window, click the Options button at the top of the main window. From the window that appears next, make sure that either or both of the "Bad Blocks on Floppy Disks" and "Bad Blocks on Hard Disks" options are checked.

   These bad block checking options are off by default. If you want to check only for bad blocks and not bother with the other analysis, uncheck everything else (but remember to recheck them before you later try to do a more thorough analysis). When you are finished, click OK to return to the main window.

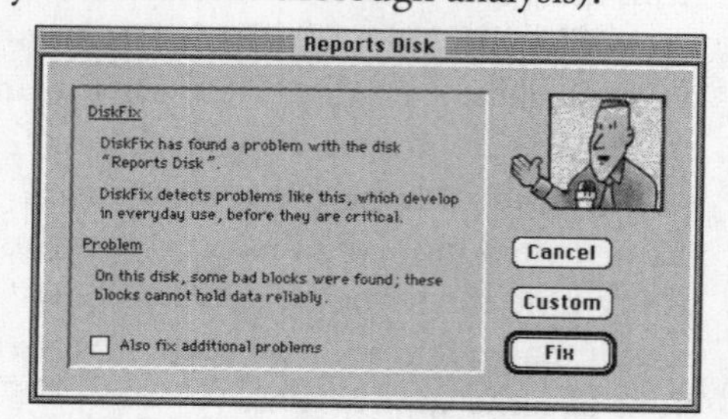

Figure F14-3 *DiskFix reports a bad block problem; click the Custom button to get the dialog box in Figure F14-4.*

2. Click the Check button to begin the analysis of the disk. The analysis can take a while, especially for a large hard disk (which is why this option is unchecked by default). If there are any bad blocks on the disk, DiskFix will report them; you will typically see a dialog box saying that "DiskFix has found a problem with '[name of disk]'."
3. From the dialog box, you can click the Fix button to try immediately to repair the bad block. You will probably be better off, however, if you select Custom instead. Doing this opens up a new dialog box that identifies which files contain bad blocks, as well as indicating bad blocks in unused areas of the disk.
4. DiskFix lists bad blocks in areas of the disk that are currently unused as "Unused bad blocks." To attempt to fix these, select this item and click Repair. What this actually does is to mark the blocks to prevent their future use (see: "Technically Speaking: How Data Recovery Utilities 'Repair' Bad Blocks").

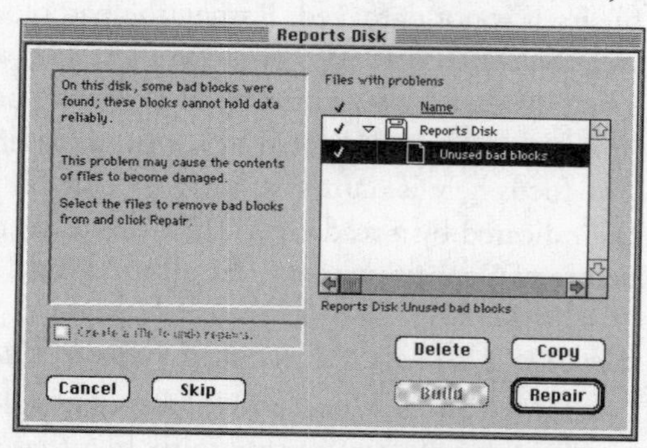

Figure F14-4 *DiskFix reports that bad blocks were found in unused areas of the disk.*

5. For specific files with bad blocks, select the file name(s)—so that a check mark appears before the name—and then click Copy. In this case, DiskFix tries to copy the damaged file to a new location. As DiskFix does this, it reads repeatedly from the bad block area. If the bad block problem is intermittent, one of the repeated attempts may successfully read the block. In this case, you may get a fully recovered copy of the file. When done, if

TECHNICALLY SPEAKING ▶

HOW DATA RECOVERY UTILITIES "REPAIR" BAD BLOCKS

Bad blocks typically cannot be repaired (see "Technically Speaking: Why Are My Blocks Bad?" earlier in this Fix-It). Thus, when a utility such as DiskFix claims to repair a typical bad block, the best it can do is to mark the block to prevent it from being used in the future. As long as not too many blocks are damaged, this should have a negligible effect on your disk capacity.

Bad blocks are marked in one of two ways, depending on what type of disk and what version of what utility you are using. One method is to write a special invisible dummy file over the block that prevents it from being used to store other files. Called sparing the block, this can be done on any type of disk, floppy or hard. The other method, which can be done only on hard disks and other related SCSI devices, is to map out the block by listing it as a bad block in a special area of the Directory. This latter method, which instructs the Macintosh not to use any of these blocks, is more reliable.

DiskFix has not reported that it has already marked the bad blocks to prevent their future use, click Repair.

6. If bad blocks are in the Directory, none of this is likely to work. In this case, refer to Fix-It #13, "Recover Selected Files from a Damaged Disk."

Repairing Bad Blocks: Recovery Utilities versus Reformatting

After you have recovered files from the damaged disk as best as you are able, there is the separate issue of "repairing" the bad blocks on the disk. Although you can use MacTools Pro or Norton Utilities to make these repairs (see "Technically Speaking: How Data Recovery Utilities 'Repair' Bad Blocks"), I usually shun both.

For hard disks, the best and most reliable way to correct bad block problems (and sometimes the only way, if the recovery utility fails) is to reformat the entire disk using a utility such as Apple HD SC Setup or Drive Setup. An added advantage of reformatting is that if the bad blocks are *not* due to media damage, reformatting should allow them to be used again, eliminating the need to map them out. On the downside, because reformatting erases the entire disk, you also need to back up and later restore all undamaged files on the disk, which is considerably more time-consuming than using a utility such as DiskFix to mark the bad block.

At best, though it is a bit riskier, you can try to repair the bad blocks with DiskFix, resorting to reformatting if problems reoccur. Occasionally, if you need to back up the disk before you reformat it, you may find that the bad blocks prevent a normal backup. In this case, do try to mark the bad blocks with a recovery utility, then back up the disk (except for possibly damaged files for which you already have a current backup) and reformat.

For floppy disks with bad blocks, I usually don't even bother with reformatting—I just discard the disk. In any case, to fix bad blocks on floppy disks by reformatting (which can be done only in System 7.*x* anyway), the Macintosh essentially uses the same method as DiskFix or Norton Utilities.

SEE: • Fix-It #15, "Verifying Disks and Media Damage," for related information

Special Case: Recovering Files from Floppy Disks with Bad Blocks

Use Copy Utilities Using a recovery utility to recover files damaged by bad blocks, as described in the previous section, works equally well for floppy disks or hard disks. For floppy disks, however, an alternative method may be even better (or at least simpler). This method doesn't mark or repair the bad blocks in any way—which is of little consequence, since you should discard the damaged disk after recovery—but it is effective at recovering data from damaged files. At its best, it can recover 100 percent of the text from a damaged text file. It is also useful for recovering data from floppy disks with bad blocks in the Directory (as such disks likely cannot be mounted or repaired, as described in Fix-It #13). Here's what to do:

1. Copy the entire disk to a new disk, using a special disk copying utility. For example, use either the Floppier application in Norton Utilities' or MacTools Pro's FastCopy. These programs each have a special feature that copies around bad blocks, so that the bad blocks are not duplicated on the copy.

   With FastCopy, you should turn on the "Skip bad blocks" option, which is accessed by clicking the Options button at the top of the window; with Floppier, this option is always in effect. With either program, you simply identify a source and destination disk by inserting the relevant disks, then click the Copy (with FastCopy) or Start Copy (with Floppier) button. Although these utilities have other option settings, you can ignore them here. Just go with the default settings (except that I would uncheck the "Copy used space only" option in FastCopy).

   Be careful when using other copy utilities. Some may work as well as the ones described here; others may not. For example, with Apple's Disk Copy, I find that it copies too well—it duplicates the disk exactly, bad block data and all. Also, do not depend on the Finder to make copies. After all, an inability to copy the file from the Finder is often how you discovered the problem in the first place.

   By itself, bypassing the bad blocks does not mean that the damaged file is recovered (because the data that were in the bad block area may now be missing), but it's a start. At least you now have a copy of the file that does not contain bad blocks.

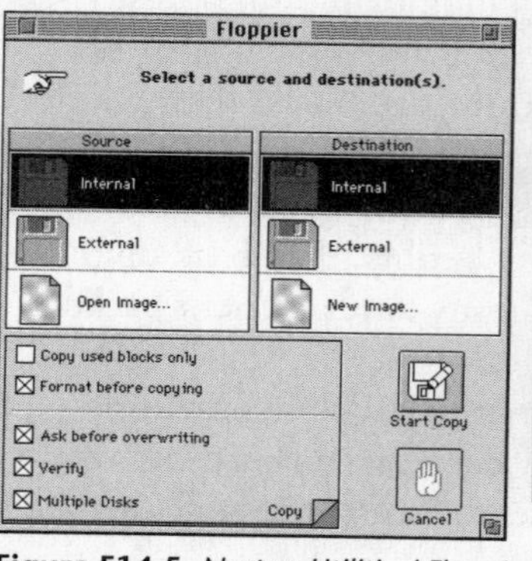

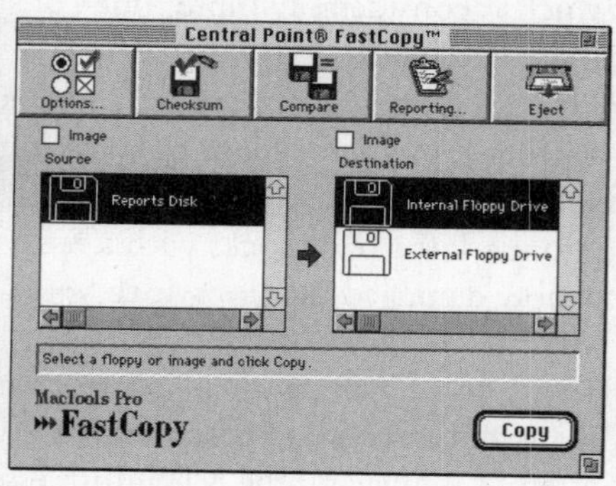

Figure F14-5 *Norton Utilities' Floppier (left) and MacTools Pro's FastCopy (right).*

2. Try to open the newly created copy of the damaged file from within its creating application. If this does not work (and it usually doesn't), next try to open the damaged file using CanOpener or another comparable utility (this usually works, even if CanOpener could not open the original damaged file).
3. If you succeed in opening the file at all, extract data from it using the methods previously described.

SEE: • **"Recover the Damaged File," earlier in this Fix-It**

TAKE NOTE ▶

COPY PROTECTION PROBLEMS

Copy protection is a phrase that describes methods of preventing software from being illegally used or copied (that is, copied for use by someone who did not purchase the program). In one form of copy protection, a program checks on its original floppy disk for a special area that acts like a bad block. If the program does not find this block, the program does not launch. These pseudo-bad blocks are specially designed to defeat the duplication attempts of most, if not all, copy programs.

This onerous method prevents you from successfully copying the program to your hard disk, but don't try to eliminate these phony bad blocks. Doing so does not eliminate the copy protection; it only eliminates your ability to launch the program even from the original disk.

Fortunately, this type of copy protection is almost gone from the Macintosh market, except for a few games. Even game manufacturers have mostly shifted to alternate methods of copy protection that at least allow you to run the game from your hard disk. For example, one popular method requires that you enter a special code every time you want to launch the application; you obtain this code from the documentation that comes with the program. Another type of protection lets you install the game to your hard drive using the game's Installer, but if you make a copy of the game from the Finder, the copy does not work. This can be annoying if you ever try to replace the game (perhaps because it got corrupted) with a backup copy you have made. Because the backup copy likely will not work, you will have to start over with the Installer again.

For related information

SEE:
- **Fix-It #2 for information on corrupted preferences files**
- **Fix-It #4 on startup extension conflicts**
- **Fix-It #5 on replacing damaged system software**
- **Fix-It #13 on damaged disks**
- **Fix-It #15 on reformatting**
- **Chapter 2, "Damage Control," for a general discussion of damage**
- **Chapter 4 on system errors**
- **Chapter 6 for more on problems opening, copying, and saving files**
- **Chapter 8 for more on file types, creators, and Bundle bits**
- **Chapter 9 for problems with corrupted font files**

Fix-It #15: Format, Initialize, and Verify Disks

QUICK SUMMARY ▶

For floppy disks, use the Finder's Erase Disk command to reformat the disk. For hard disks, use a formatting utility (such as Apple HD SC Setup or Drive Setup) to reformat the disk; launch the utility and click its Initialize or Format button, as appropriate.

When to do it:

- Whenever everything else you have tried has failed to fix your problem, especially when your recovery utilities (such as Disk First Aid or Norton Utilities) report damage to a disk that they are unable to repair.
- Whenever you have a problem with bad blocks, especially on a hard disk. This usually becomes apparent when you try to copy a file and get a message such as "File could not be read and was skipped."
- Prior to a complete restoration of your hard disk from your backup files.
- Whenever you want to restore a disk to like-new condition, making sure that virtually all data on it are truly erased.
- Whenever you have an unformatted or incorrectly formatted disk.

Why to do it:

Every disk needs to be formatted before it can be used; otherwise, you cannot even mount the disk. So why cover formatting of disks here, near the end of this book? It would appear that formatting should be one of the first things to do, not one of the last things to consider.

The answer is that *re*formatting of disks is an important problem-solving tool. It is an all-purpose last resort for dealing with many of the problems covered in previous Fix-Its. In particular, if you have a damaged disk that cannot be repaired by utilities such as MacTools or Norton Utilities (as described in Fix-It #13), reformatting usually brings the disk back to life. Reformatting also fixes problems resulting from improper updating of a disk driver (Fix-It #12), and it is the most reliable way to solve a problem with bad blocks on a hard disk (as described primarily in Fix-It #14). Reformatting a disk also rebuilds the desktop (Fix-It #9) and reinstalls the disk driver (Fix-It #12). Finally, when you restore files to a reformatted disk, they are defragmented (Fix-It #8). In other words, in one bold

stroke, reformatting can cure a variety of ills. Reformatting is also advised whenever you want to recycle an old floppy disk, even if you do not suspect any problems with it.

The only real disadvantages of reformatting are that it takes a relatively long time (especially for hard disks) and that it erases everything on the disk (requiring you to back up and subsequently restore your disk's contents in order to get back to where you were before reformatting—thereby adding even more time and hassle to the whole procedure).

The focus of this Fix-It is how and when to reformat problem disks, as well as when *not* to reformat a disk. In particular, there are several situations where the Macintosh incorrectly claims that a perfectly good floppy disk is unreadable; don't reformat these disks, or you will unnecessarily erase them. Finally, this Fix-It briefly covers some problems that may occur when you try to format or reformat any disk.

The common use of the term *format* may actually refer to up to six separate processes, only the first of which is what is technically meant by formatting. (1) *Formatting* affects every block on the disk. It lays down the initial background of data that allows a disk to be recognized as a Macintosh disk. (2) For hard disks, the next step (which is optional) is to *partition* the disk, which means to divide it into separate volumes, each of which then acts as if it were an independent disk. (3) Again just for hard disks, the third step is to *install the disk's driver,* a critical piece of software that allows the Macintosh to communicate with the disk. (4) *Initializing* the disk occurs next; this step primarily consists of creating a new set of Directory files. (5) Another sometimes-optional step is to *verify* the disk, essentially checking that the preceding steps—especially the formatting step—were successfully carried out. A final check for bad blocks may also occur here. (6) *Mounting* the disk, which means causing it to appear on the Finder's desktop, comes last.

In some cases, especially when one is talking about floppy disks, the terms *formatting* and *initializing* are used interchangeably to refer to the entire set of steps. Thus, all of these steps are typically performed in response to a single "Format" or "Initialize" command (although with most hard disk formatting utilities, you can also separately select each step).Verifying a disk can be done separately as a test of an already formatted disk, usually as a way to check for possible media damage.

What to do:

This Fix-It is divided into three topics: floppy disks, hard disks, and verifying disks and media damage.

Floppy Disks

There are three types of floppy disks: 400K (single-sided disks, which are rarely seen these days), 800K (double-sided), and 1.44MB (double-sided high density, or HD). The current SuperDrives can recognize and work with any type of floppy disk: 400K, 800K, or HD. The older 800K drives, however, cannot format and do not recognize HD disks.

SEE: • **Chapter 1 for details on how to identify each type of disk**

BY THE WAY ▶

VARIATIONS IN MESSAGES FOR FORMATTING DISKS

Many dialog/alert boxes asking whether you want to format/initialize a floppy disk have been redesigned for System 7.5 or 7.6. Thus, if you are using an older version of the system software, some of the messages you see will likely look different from what you see in the figures here.

As described in the main text, these dialog boxes may differ yet again if you are using Macintosh PC Exchange.

Formatting an Unformatted Disk

When you insert an unformatted floppy disk into a drive, a message says that "the disk is unreadable" and asks whether you want to initialize it. If you insert an HD disk, the format will be listed as "Macintosh 1.4 MB." If you insert an 800K or a 400K disk, the format will be listed as "Macintosh 800K." If you click the Initialize button, you will next get the alert message that says "Initializing will erase all of the information on this disk." Click the Continue button to begin the formatting process, and the Macintosh does everything else automatically. During this process the Macintosh gives you feedback on its progress with messages such as "Formatting disk…," "Verifying format…," and Creating directory." When it is finished, the newly formatted disk appears on the desktop.

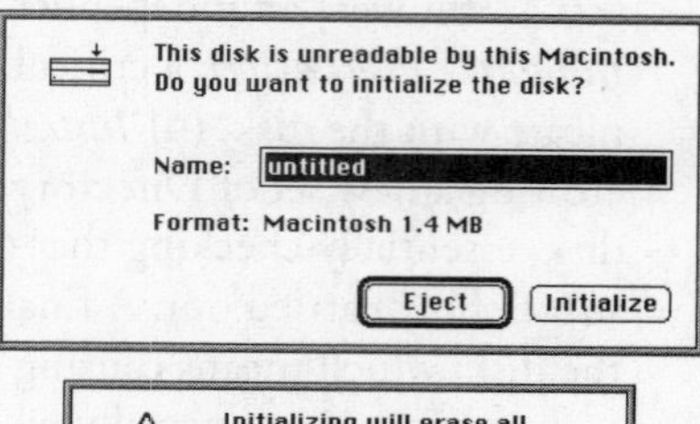

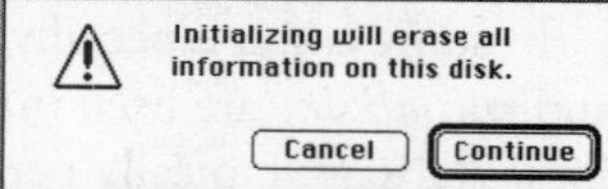

Figure F15-1 *These two messages appear in succession when you format an unformatted floppy disk.*

The initial message box gives you a chance to name the disk (it is named "Untitled" by default). Whatever name you give it, you can always change it later.

Clicking the Cancel or Eject buttons in either of the preceding message boxes prevents the start of a format. The disk then remains unmodified.

HD Disks in 800K Drives (and Vice Versa) If you insert an HD disk into an older 800K drive, rather than a SuperDrive, you are given the chance to format the HD disk as an 800K disk. Do *not* do this; eject the disk instead (for more details, see "Unreadable or Damaged Disks That Really Aren't," later in this section).

Conversely, you may be tempted to figure out a way to get a SuperDrive to format an 800K disk as an HD disk, but don't try. The 800K disks are physically different from the HD disks, and formatting an 800K disk as an HD disk is asking for trouble. Eventually, the Macintosh is likely to treat the disk as damaged, and you may lose data on this disk.

What Happened to the 400K (One-Sided) Format? In System 7.5 or later, you are not given the option to format a disk as a 400K disk. With older versions of the system software, you may get a 400K option, but you should not use it. Not only does an 800K format give you twice as much space, but it is an entirely different and improved format structure.

If you own a bunch of single-sided disks, don't be in too much of a hurry to discard them, because you can still choose to (re)format them as 800K disks. These disks really have two sides, despite their name. Technically, a single-sided disk has only been verified to be without defects on one side, but if it formats successfully, the media is probably okay on both sides. Given how cheap disks are and how important what you put on them is, of course, you may still prefer to throw out these disks.

Figure F15-2 *This message appears when you insert an unformatted 800K or 400K disk into a disk drive with system software prior to version 7.5; a similar message appears if you try to erase an already formatted 800K or 400K disk.*

BY THE WAY

FORMATTING WITH DISK COPYING UTILITIES

Utilities such as MacTools Pro's FastCopy, Norton Utilities' Floppier, and Apple's Disk Copy are mainly used (as their names imply) to make copies of floppy disks. If you decide to make a copy to an unformatted disk, they typically first format the disk (eliminating the need to separately use the Macintosh's built-in format functions, as described in the main text). Disk Copy is unusual in that it makes a copy without first separately formatting the disk; in essence, it copies the format information from the original disk as part of the copy process. This saves time when copying to unformatted disks (though at the risk of copying incorrect data if the original disk is damaged).

You can also use these utilities as efficient floppy disk formatters. For example, for FastCopy, select "Format Copies" from the FastCopy menu. With Floppier, click the turned page corner at the bottom of the window to shift from "Copy" mode (as shown in Fix-It #14) to "Format" mode.

Reformatting an Already Formatted Disk

Erase Disk You can reformat a floppy disk at any time by clicking on the disk and then selecting the Erase Disk command from the Finder's Special menu. A message similar to the Format alert message appears, asking you to confirm that you really want to completely erase the disk; you can also rename the disk here. Click the Erase button and the process begins, formatting the disk in exactly the same way as when it was first formatted. All information currently on the disk is completely erased and forever irretrievable! If you got here by mistake, click Cancel.

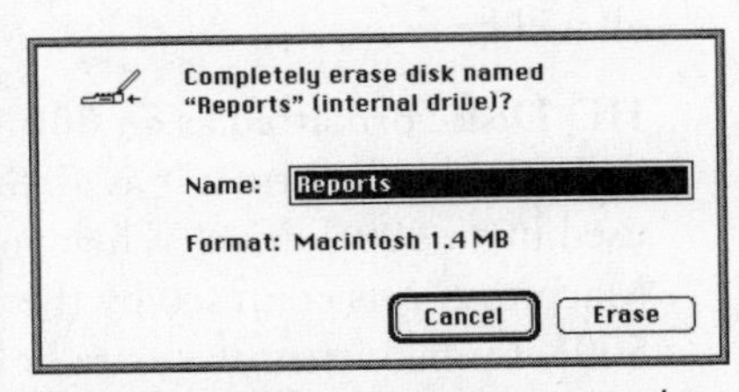

Figure F15-3 *This message appears when you select Erase Disk for an already-formatted 1.4MB disk.*

Command-Option-Tab As a shortcut to initiate reformatting, hold down the Command-Option-Tab keys prior to inserting a disk. Continue to hold down the keys when you insert the disk, until a message such as "Completely erase the disk...." It appears before the disk is mounted.

Completely erase the disk named "Tools" that you just inserted?
Cancel
OK

Figure F15-4 *This message appears when you insert an already-formatted disk while holding down the Command-Option-Tab keys.*

This shortcut is especially useful if there is a problem with the disk that results in a system crash when the Macintosh tries to mount it. By bypassing the mount attempt, you can still reformat the disk.

Reformatting versus Deleting

Reformatting a floppy disk is an effective way to erase all files on the disk. As an alternative, you can delete all files from a disk by dragging them to the Trash and selecting Empty Trash from the Finder's Special menu. Although this is usually faster than reformatting the disk, I don't recommend it. Unlike reformatting, using Empty Trash does not rebuild the desktop, nor does it check for bad blocks. As a result, if there are problems with the disk, deleting the files with Empty Trash does not eliminate them—nor does it really erase the files. It only eliminates the references to the files in the disk's Directory, thus allowing the space occupied by the files to be used for new files as needed. This is why you can use undelete utilities (as described in Chapters 2 and 6) to recover files that have been deleted in the Trash.

Thus, in general, use the Erase Disk command to completely erase floppy disks. Only use Empty Trash if you want to preserve the chance to undelete files or if you want to delete selected files.

Unreadable or Damaged Disks That Really Aren't

HD Disk Inserted into 800K Drive If you insert an already-formatted HD disk into an 800K drive, a message will tell you that the disk is unreadable and ask if you want to initialize it as an 800K disk (just as it would if you inserted an unformatted 800K disk). Clicking OK will format the disk as an 800K disk, but it will also permanently erase any and all data on the disk. Eject the disk and reinsert it into a SuperDrive, and all will be fine.

HD Disk Formatted as an 800K Disk If you insert an HD disk into an 800K drive and mistakenly format it as an 800K disk, it will perform just fine—as long as it is used in an 800K drive. When you insert such a disk into a SuperDrive, though, the Macintosh gets confused by the conflicting signals of an 800K format versus the extra hole in the HD disk (which indicates it should be a 1.44MB formatted disk). The result is that the Mac will display an error message saying that the disk is improperly formatted and ask if you want to initialize it. Do not do this unless you do not care to save the data on the disk!

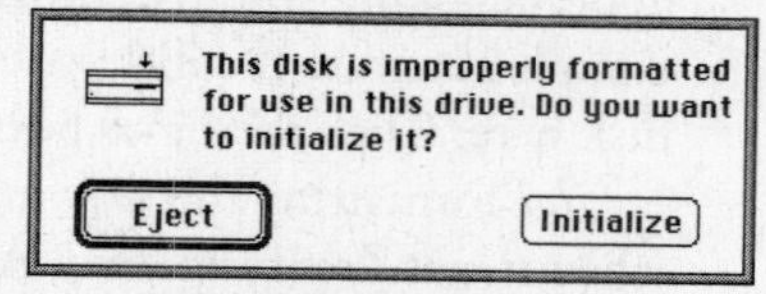

Figure F15-5 *This message appears when you insert an HD disk, formatted as an 800K disk, into a SuperDrive.*

FIX-IT #15

To save the data, eject the disk, put it in an 800K drive, and copy any data from it to a properly formatted disk. Then reinsert the problem disk in a SuperDrive and click Initialize when the message appears; it will now be properly formatted as a 1.44MB disk.

If you do not have an 800K drive available, you can try an alternative—although somewhat riskier—procedure. *Carefully* tape a piece of paper over the hole that the Macintosh uses to recognize it as an HD disk (the one without a tab in the rear of the hole). If you now insert the disk into a SuperDrive, the Macintosh will treat it as an ordinary 800K disk. Be careful that the paper or tape does not dislodge and get caught inside the drive! Once again, transfer the data to another disk, eject the problem disk, remove the tape, and reformat it as an HD disk.

Macintoshes Unable to Recognize 400K Disks Newer Macintosh models (from around the Macintosh Classic onward) no longer format or read 400K disks. If you insert a 400K disk into such a computer, it will not mount. If you need to recover the files from this disk, use a Macintosh model that does recognize 400K disks. Once the disk is mounted, transfer the data from the 400K disk to an 800K or HD disk; then you can discard the 400K disk.

PC-Formatted Disks PC computers (IBM computers and clones) now use the same HD disks as do Macintoshes. Unless you have special software installed (such as Macintosh PC Exchange), if you insert a PC-formatted HD disk into a disk drive, the Macintosh will say that the disk is unreadable and ask if you want to initialize it. Again, do not initialize the disk or you will erase any data on the disk. If you need to mount this disk on a Macintosh, read on.

Macintosh PC Exchange and PC-Formatted Disks

Macintosh PC Exchange is a control panel that allows PC-formatted disks, when inserted into a SuperDrive, to be mounted on the Finder's desktop just as if they were Macintosh-formatted disks. PC Exchange also allows you to format disks in PC-DOS (as well as Apple II's ProDOS) formats, in case you need to create a disk to be used on these other machines. When you insert an unformatted HD disk, a box similar to the common "disk is unreadable" message (as described earlier in this Fix-It) will appear, except that you now have a pop-up menu of choices for how you want the disk to be formatted (you will get a comparable set of options when inserting an 800K disk). You get these same additional pop-up menu options, in yet another alert box, if you select to erase any preformatted disk via the Erase Disk command.

Figure F15-6 *This message appears when you insert an unformatted HD disk into a SuperDrive with Macintosh PC Exchange active.*

Although rarely used for this purpose, PC Exchange can also mount PC-formatted hard disks. If you need to do this, consult the documentation that came with the software or seek other outside help.

By the way, PC Exchange can also be used to help automate the Finder-level opening of PC-formatted documents into Macintosh applications, assuming that the application in question is capable of reading the particular document. This was described briefly in Chapter 6 (in the "When You Can't Open a Document" section).

Damaged Disks

Occasionally, when you insert a disk, you may get a message that says a disk is "unreadable," is "not a Macintosh disk," is "damaged," or "cannot be used," even though you know you have correctly formatted the disk previously. In this case, you probably do have a damaged disk. If you do not need to recover the data on the disk, you can immediately try to reformat it; if it reformats without a problem, it is probably okay (but see "Verifying Disks and Media Damage," later in this Fix-It). Otherwise, discard the disk. Alternatively, if you do need to recover files from the disk, see Fix-It #14. Also, refer to Chapter 5 for a general discussion of problems with floppy disks that do not mount.

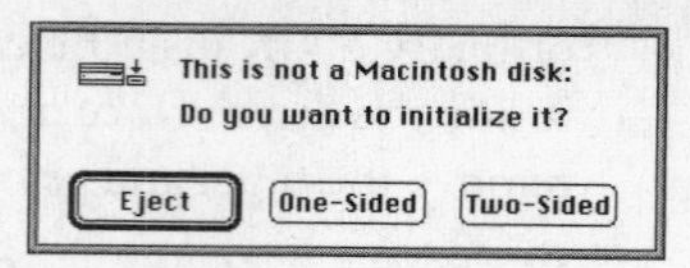

Figure F15-7 *One of several messages that may appear when you try to mount a damaged disk.*

BY THE WAY ▶

POWER MAC FORMAT PATCH SOLVES FLOPPY DISK FORMAT ERRORS

Do you get error messages when you try to initialize or erase floppy disks? Do you have a PCI-based Mac with a 180MHz or faster processor? If so, and you are using System 7.5.3, you need an extension called Power Mac Format Patch (Power Computing clones have a similar patch called Floppy Tuner). The better solution, however, is to update to System 7.5.5 or later. The fix is built into the System file, making the patch no longer necessary.

Hard Disks

Formatting and Reformatting in General

You may be surprised to learn that hard disks need to be formatted just like floppy disks. Because most hard disks come preformatted and, in many cases, never have to be reformatted, many users have no experience with formatting hard disks. As described in the "Why to Do It" section, though, sometimes you want to reformat a hard disk (for example, if a hard disk is damaged in a way that your data recovery utilities cannot remedy).

To format or reformat a hard disk or removable cartridge, you need a special disk formatting utility. Two such utilities are Apple HD SC Setup and Drive Setup; at least one of these should be included with your Macintosh system software. Typically, if you have a third-party hard drive, you should have received a comparable utility when you purchased the drive unit (such as APS PowerTools, which is shipped with all APS drives). Finally, you may separately purchase a universal formatting utility, such as Drive7 or Hard Disk ToolKit; these can be used with virtually any drive you own, including Apple drives. Third-party alternatives tend to offer more options than the rather minimal features of Apple's utilities. Using universal utilities can be especially desirable if you own several hard drives from different sources and you want to use the same formatting utility for all of them (which Apple officially recommends that you do).

Always make sure you are using the latest version of these utilities. At the very least, your version of Apple HD SC Setup should come from the same disks that were used to install the system software on your hard disk.

The major functions of these utilities are the same, no matter which one you use. These include formatting the hard drive, updating the device driver, partitioning the disk, and testing the drive for media damage. Additional functions may include checking the performance of the drive and other special features designed to increase speed (such as disk caches) or assist in troubleshooting.

Ideally, you should have a current backup of the data on your disk (as explained in Chapter 2) before reformatting, unless you no longer care to save the data. If your disk is damaged, however, you may not be able to perform a needed backup (in this case, refer to Fix-Its #13 and #14 for advice).

SEE: • **Fix-It #12, on updating disk device drivers, for a general introduction to these different types of formatting utilities and why you might switch from one to another**

BY THE WAY ▶

DAMAGED REMOVABLE CARTRIDGES

If a removable cartridge (such as a SyQuest or Zip/Jaz cartridge) is damaged, when you next try to mount it, you may get an error message that resembles the message you get when you try to mount a damaged floppy disk. In this case, you may be able to repair the disk with tools such as Disk First Aid or Norton Utilities. It is more likely, though, that you will need to reformat the cartridge.

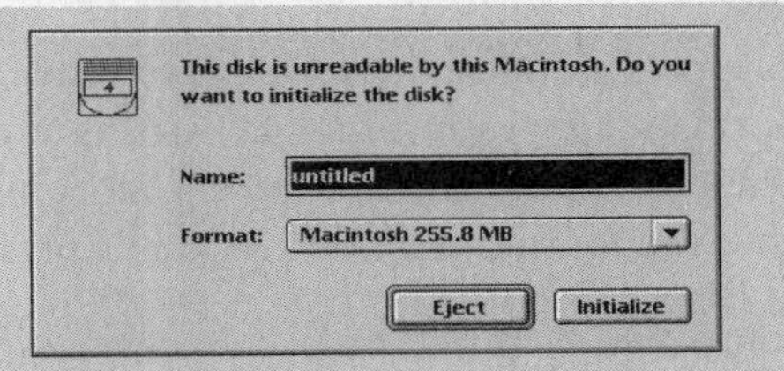

Figure F15-8 *A message that appeared when trying to mount a "damaged" SyQuest removable cartridge.*

Apple HD Setup versus Drive Setup: Which One Do You Use?

Apple now makes two separate disk formatting utilities. Unfortunately, you can't simply choose which one you prefer to use—one utility is designed to work with some Macs, while the other works only with other Mac models. Maybe one day, Apple will resolve this unneeded confusion and settle on just one utility for all its Macs. For now, though, here is the situation in brief:

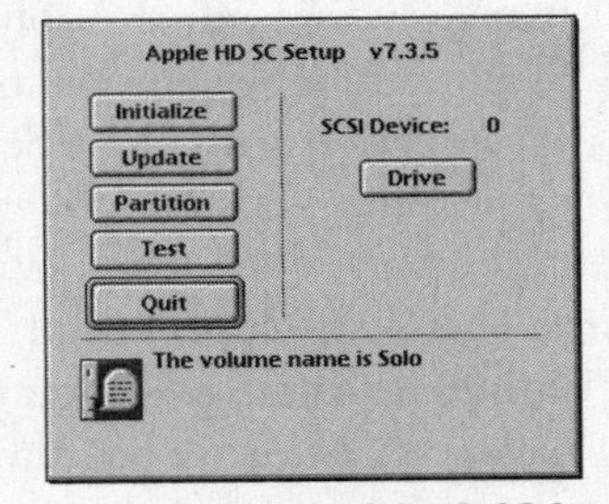

Figure F15-9 *Apple's HD SC Setup.*

First of all, I am assuming that we are talking about using these utilities with an internal Apple-brand drive that came with your Mac. As discussed more in a bit, these utilities will probably not work at all with third-party drives.

Given this assumption, if you have a Power Mac or a Mac with an IDE internal drive, you need to use Drive Setup. Especially if you have a PCI-based Power Mac, it is critical that you use Drive Setup.

For all other Macs, use Apple HD SC Setup.

SEE: • **"Technically Speaking: IDE Drives"**

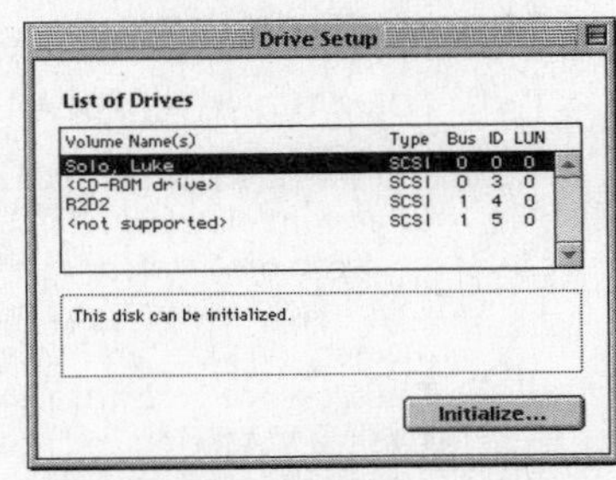

Figure F15-10 *Apple's Drive Setup.*

Unfortunately, there are several exceptions to these general rules. For example, the PowerBook 150 cannot use Drive Setup even though it has an IDE drive. In fact, it cannot even use Apple HD SC Setup; you must use a utility called Internal HD Format that comes with the PowerBook. Drive Setup also does not currently support Macs with a Power Macintosh Processor Upgrade card installed. In an exception to the exception, however, Macs with an IDE drive that use the Upgrade card *can* use Drive

Setup—but you first have to disable the processor with the Upgrade control panel. As this situation keeps changing over time, check the "Read Me" files that come with the formatting software for the latest information. For example, if you have the "unity" version of System 7.5.3 (as described in Chapter 13) or any later reference version of the system software (such as System 7.6), it should come with two Disk Tools disks. One has Apple HD SC Setup on it; the other has Drive Setup. The "Read Me" file describes which Disk Tools disk to use with each Mac model (and thus which of the two formatting utilities to use).

Even if you are using the utility compatible with your Mac, you may still have problems. In particular, Apple HD SC Setup can be used to format or reformat only an Apple-label disk drive (and, even then, only if the disk has not been previously reformatted by some other formatting utility). This is because Apple encodes special instructions onto its hard drives that Apple HD SC Setup checks when it is launched. If it does not find this code, which is present only on Apple drives, it does not list the drive.

Drive Setup has similar restrictions, although it is said to be more "accepting" of non-Apple drives. For example, I have seen reports that an Apple drive reformatted with a third-party driver could still be reformatted again with Drive Setup. Also note that Drive Setup has the ability to update and format removable cartridges (such as those used in SyQuest and Iomega drives), even though these are not Apple drives. Apple HD SC Setup does not have this ability. Be careful, though, because exactly what restrictions Apple applies here are always subject to change.

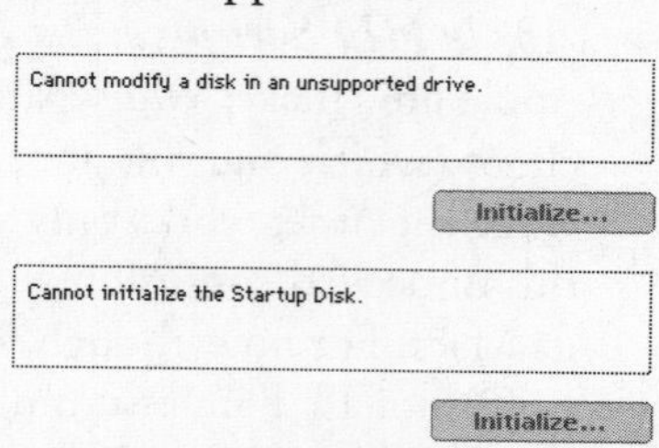

Figure F15-11 *Some error messages that may appear in the Drive Setup window.*

If your Mac cannot use Drive Setup, and you try to use it anyway, you will probably get a message that "Drive Setup cannot be launched on this computer." If your Mac is compatible with Drive Setup but you have a mounted drive that is not supported by it, the drive will still appear in the Drive Setup window. If you select it, however, you will get a message that you "Cannot modify a disk in an unsupported drive." If you get a message that says "Unrecognized driver," you probably have an Apple drive but have used third-party software to reformat it or update its driver.

TECHNICALLY SPEAKING ▶

FORMATTING A DISK AND VIRTUAL MEMORY

You should make sure virtual memory is off before trying to reformat a disk. Ideally, have all extensions disabled.

If you try to reformat a hard disk after starting up with the Apple CD that came with your Mac, however, you may get messages that this cannot be done because virtual memory (VM) is "on" (even though you have not turned it on) or because files are "in use." The apparent problem is that some versions of these CDs set VM to on (and thus place the invisible VM file on your disk, which then leads to the symptoms described). A simple workaround solution is to hold down the Command key when starting up from the CD; this turns virtual memory off for that session.

TECHNICALLY SPEAKING ▶

IDE DRIVES

IDE (Integrated Drive Electronics) hard drives are a lower-cost alternative to SCSI-based drives. They appear in selected models of Macintosh, such as the LC 580, the Macintosh Performas 630 and 640, and the PowerBook 150.

Except for the PowerBook 150 (as mentioned in the main text), Drive Setup can be used for all Apple-brand IDE drives. Some of these Mac models automatically initialize an uninitialized IDE drive at startup, allowing you to use a non-Apple IDE drive as a replacement for Apple's drive. This was important when these drives were first available on Macs, as most third-party formatting utilities did not work with them. Most third-party formatting utilities, however, have now been upgraded to accommodate IDE drives. If you have a third-party drive and/or formatting utility, check with the company that made your utility for specifics.

SEE: • Fix-It #16 for more on SCSI and IDE drives

Reformatting Using Apple HD SC Setup

To reformat a disk with Apple HD SC Setup (assuming you have a Mac and a drive that works with this utility), do the following:

1. Start up with a disk other than the disk you want to reformat. If you intend to reformat your normal startup hard disk, restart with the Disk Tools disk that came with your current system software (or your own customized Emergency Toolkit disk, or any other startup disk that contains Apple HD SC Setup) as the startup disk.
2. Launch Apple HD SC Setup and select the desired drive, using the Drive button.
3. Click Initialize. This selection formats, initializes, and verifies the disk in one step. When it is done, quit Apple HD SC Setup.

   Note: Starting with Apple HD SC Setup version 7.3.5 (included with System 7.5.3), you can create standard partitions on your disk when you reformat it with Apple HD SC Setup (see "Partition the Disk," later in this Fix-It).
4. Most likely, the reformatted disk will not be mounted (that is, it will not yet appear on your desktop). If so, simply restart the Macintosh; the disk should now mount and function normally. If desired, you can instead mount the disk manually prior to restarting by using a utility such as SCSIProbe (as explained in Chapter 5 and Fix-It #16).
5. If the reformatted disk was your normal startup disk, it obviously needs to have the system software reinstalled before it can serve as a startup disk again. To do this, either restore the contents of the disk from your backups (using a startup disk that contains your backup utility) or start fresh with a new set of system software (using the system software's Installer disk as the startup disk, as detailed in Fix-It #5). In either case, restart when finished.

Reformatting Using Drive Setup

To reformat a disk with Drive Setup (assuming you have a Mac and a drive that works with this utility), follow these steps:

1. Start up with a disk other than the disk you want to reformat. If you intend to reformat your normal startup hard disk, restart with the Disk Tools disk that came with your current system software (or your own customized Emergency Toolkit disk or any other startup disk that contains Drive Setup) as the startup disk.
2. Launch Drive Setup and select the desired drive by clicking on its name. If you don't see the name of the disk listed, try selecting the Mount Volumes or Rescan Bus command from the Functions menu.

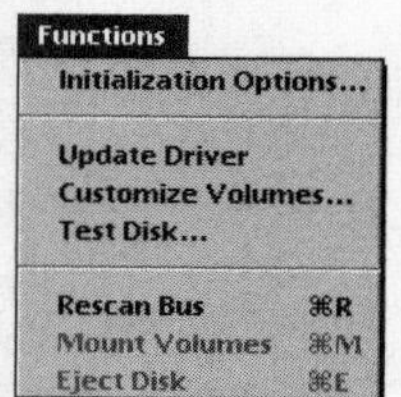

Figure F15-12 *Drive Setup's Functions menu.*

3a. Click Initialize. If another window appears, click the Initialize button in that window as well. If the first Initialize button is dimmed, it means you cannot initialize the disk; typically, the program will give you a message explaining why (such as that you cannot initialize the startup disk).

3b. Instead of just initializing, consider the following options first:

Zero all data Initialization (without "Zero all data" checked) doesn't actually erase all the data on the disk (that is, it is not a "true" reformatting of the disk as is done with Apple HD SC Setup); it essentially just erases and creates new Directory files. In this sense, it is fundamentally similar to what would happen if you selected the "Erase Disk" command from the Finder for a hard disk (as explained in Fix-It #13). This means that with utilities such as Norton Utilities, you might be able to recover data from an initialized disk. If you want to prevent this from happening, typically for security reasons, select Initialization Options from the Functions menu and check the "Zero all data" option, then initialize the disk. This does erase the disk by replacing all data with zeros. It does not truly reformat the disk, however.

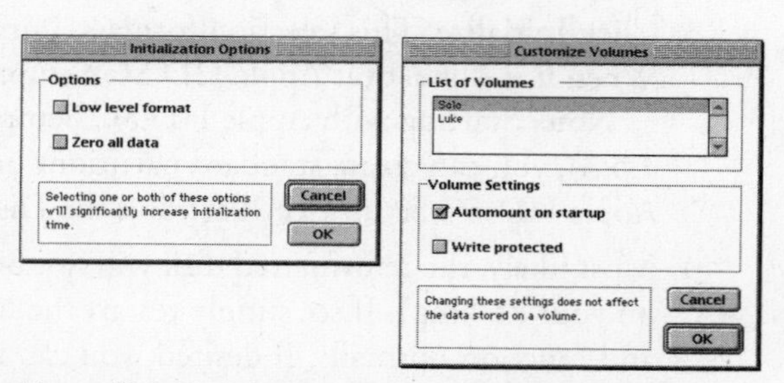

Figure F15-13 *Left: Drive Setup's Initialization Options window (select these prior to initializing the disk for a true low-level format). Right: Drive Setup's Customize Volumes window (typically leave it with its default selections, as shown).*

Low level format The other option available from the Initialization Options window is "Low level format." If you check this prior to Initialization, this does truly erase and reformat the disk. If it works similarly to how low level formatting is done with other utilities it should also zero all data, making this other option redundant. Apple, however, seems a bit ambiguous about this, allowing both options to be checked at once. A low-level format should also check for bad blocks and map out any bad blocks it finds (see Fix-Its #13 and #14), but I could not find any clear statement in any documentation that this is the case.

TAKE NOTE ▶

TROUBLESHOOTING DRIVE SETUP

The following is a collection of miscellaneous problems you may confront when using Drive Setup or that Drive Setup is specifically needed to solve. (Note: Problems that are said to be solved by upgrading Drive Setup from Apple HD SC Setup or from an older version of Drive Setup generally require just updating the disk driver; you do not have to reformat the drive unless specifically stated.)

- **Partitions do not show correct custom icons** With version 1.04 or earlier, if you create partitions with Drive Setup and give each partition a custom icon, you may find that the custom icons are incorrect after you restart. Either both partitions incorrectly have the same custom icon, or the custom icons may be gone altogether.

  What's going on? Here's what Apple says: "This issue is caused by the way the driver interacts with partitions that have the same creation date. Drive Setup is so fast and efficient that it often will create partitions with exactly the same date and time." One solution is to modify the partitions so that they have different creation dates (you'll need a utility such as Snitch or ResEdit to do this), or you can use a utility called IconFixer to correct matters. Happily, this problem has been fixed with Drive Setup 1.0.5. Be aware, however, that simply updating the driver only prevents a future occurrence of this trouble. It will not remedy an existing problem. If you already have the problem, try one of the other fixes just described.

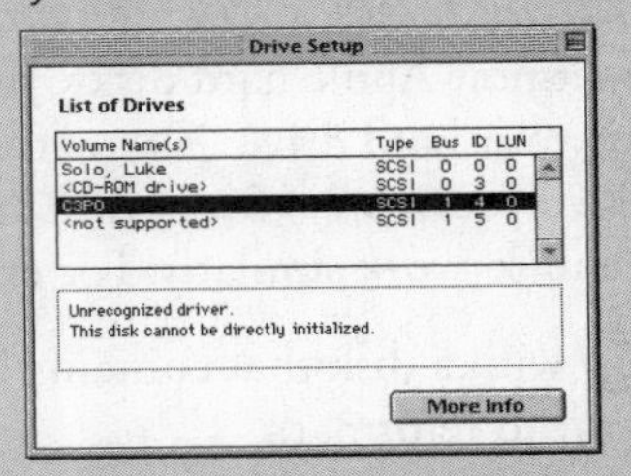

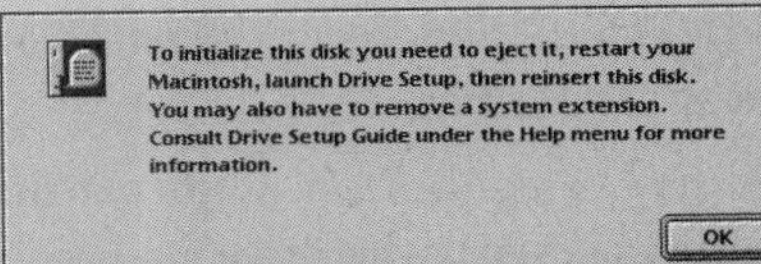

Figure F15-14 *Top: This error message appeared when a SyQuest cartridge was selected. Bottom: The message that appeared after clicking the More Info button. As the message suggested, the solution is to start up with extensions off (notably the APS Power Tools extension, in this case).*

- **Cannot initialize a removable cartridge** If Drive Setup claims it is unable to initialize a removable cartridge that has already been formatted by other third-party software, it may be because an extension included as part of the software that came with your drive is currently in use. For example, for APS drives, you would look for the PowerTools control panel or the APT Extension. In this case, the "Initialize" button will instead read "More Info"; clicking it will inform you of this problem. The solution is to disable the extension (such as by turning it off with an extensions manager) and then restart. Now you should be able to initialize the disk.
- **Miscellaneous other problems** Always use the latest version of Drive Setup, because Apple keeps fixing bugs found in previous versions. For example, Drive Setup 1.0.3 or later (1) corrects a variety of problems specific to IDE drives found in previous versions; (2) fixes a problem with the PowerBook 190, 2300, and 5300 series of computers where, in some cases, the system will freeze after waking from Sleep mode; and (3) corrects a problem with any 200 or 500 series PowerBook updated to a PowerPC that prevents use of the Control Strip's "hard drive spin down" feature. Version 1.2 or later fixes some problems with using external SCSI devices on 6360/64xx/54xx Macintoshes.

If Drive Setup spots a problem with a disk that requires a low-level format to fix, it may inform you that this is required. If so, Drive Setup will perform this format even if this option is not checked.

Apple recommends against selecting "Low level format" for a routine initialization, as it takes much longer to do. Apple recommends using this option only if the disk has never been formatted before (even from the factory) if it was last formatted prior to System 7 being released, or if there is a problem with the disk that initialization alone does not fix. Because my experience suggests that most reformatting is done because of problems that develop, however, I would recommend doing a low level format in almost all cases.

4. Refer to steps 4 and 5 of "Reformatting Using Apple HD SC Setup."

Reformatting Using Other Formatting Utilities

To reformat non-Apple hard disks, you would usually use the formatting utility that came with your hard drive. Alternatively, you can use a universal formatting utility (as described previously) for almost any hard disk, including Apple disks. All of these utilities tend to work similarly. For example, to use Drive7, follow these steps:

1. Start up with a disk that contains Drive7. This disk obviously should not be the one you want to reformat.
2. Launch Drive7 and select the name of the drive you want to format.
3. Click the Format button. Reformatting will also initialize and verify the drive (as is generally the case with any of these utilities).
4. If needed, select "Mount SCSI Devices" from Drive7's Functions menu in order to mount the reformatted drive. You can then quit Drive7.

Figure F15-15 *Drive7's main window.*

5. If the reformatted disk was your normal startup disk, it obviously needs to have the system software reinstalled before it can serve as a startup disk again. To do this, either restore the contents of the disk from your backups (using a startup disk that contains your backup utility) or start fresh with a new set of system software (using the system software's Installer disk as the startup disk, as detailed in Fix-It #5). In either case, restart when finished.

Options for mounting, ejecting, and more

Additionally, depending upon the software you are using, there may be options to select whether you want the drive to function as a startup drive and/or to be mounted auto-

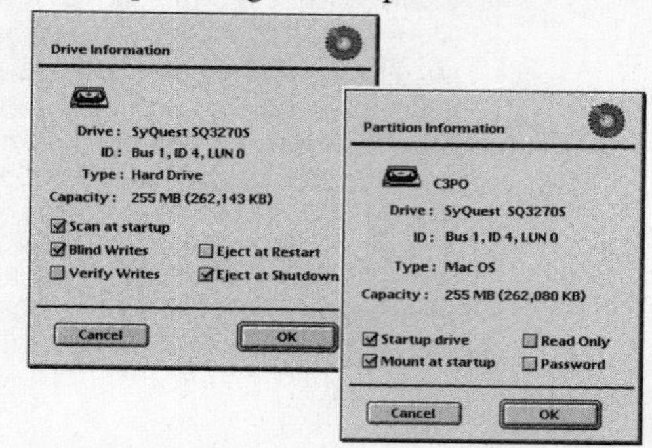

Figure F15-16 *From APS PowerTools, options you can set when formatting (or even just updating a driver for) a drive or removable cartridge.*

matically at startup. Select these options as appropriate. Doing this is especially important for removable cartridges that you want to mount automatically when you insert them after startup is over. For a removable cartridge, there also may be options to select whether you want the cartridge to be automatically ejected at restart and/or at shutdown; again, select these options as desired. Typically, you can change these options at any time without having to reformat the disk.

TECHNICALLY SPEAKING ▶

TROUBLESHOOTING DRIVE7

If you are having problems using Drive7 to format a drive, here are some suggestions. The logic described here also applies to other formatting utilities.

- Start up with extensions off (this advice is not relevant if you are starting up from a floppy disk).
- If a system crash occurs when you are using Drive7 to format a drive that had been previously formatted with a different utility, restart the Macintosh. This time, do not turn on the drive until after you have launched Drive7. To bypass an internal drive at startup, hold down the Command-Option-Shift-Delete keys at startup (see Chapter 5, "Starting with an Alternate Startup Disk," for more on this). After launching Drive7 (and turning on the drive), if the problem driver's name does not appear in the list, select "Rescan SCSI Bus" from the Functions menu. Once the drive is listed, try to format it as usual.
- If Drive7 does not list a drive that has been formatted with a different utility, the drive is probably incompatible with Drive7. In this case, you are out of luck; you cannot reformat this drive with Drive7. Stick to the original utility used to format the drive or try another universal formatting utility.

Drive7 has numerous other options not covered here; consult the Drive7 manual for details.

Reformatting versus Erasing versus Deleting

Never use the Finder's Erase Disk command to format a fixed or removable cartridge hard disk. It does not correctly erase or reformat these disks. Erase Disk is only for floppy disks.

For already formatted hard disks, Erase Disk erases only the Directory, replacing it with an empty one. The net result is that the Macintosh, after checking the Directory, will consider the disk to be empty—just as it would if you selected all the files on the disk, placed them in the Trash, and deleted them using "Empty Trash." This is why recovery utilities can restore a hard disk accidentally erased via the Erase Disk command (as explained in Fix-It #13). Restoring an erased hard disk is functionally similar to using a utility (such as UnErase, from Norton Utilities) to undelete files deleted via Empty Trash (as discussed in Chapters 2 and 6). In both cases, this is possible because the deleted files are still intact, despite the fact that they are not listed in the Directory.

Partition the Disk

A hard drive can be subdivided into separate partitions, which then act as if they are totally separate disks (technically, each partition is referred to as a separate *volume*). Each one mounts separately and has its own icon.

Helpful hint: With most formatting utilities, partitioning a disk requires reformatting the disk and thus erases all data currently on it. Also, reformatting a disk to add new partitions (and then restoring your data to newly named partitions) will typically result in all links between aliases and original files (and other similar types of links) being broken, so be careful.

Why Partition? Partitioning a disk is not required, and many users choose never to partition their drive. Still, there are two main advantages to partitioning larger-capacity drives.

- **Speed** Partitioning can improve disk access speed. For example, a fragmented file (as described in Fix-It #8) always has all of its fragments contained within a single partition. Thus, when trying to open a fragmented file, the Mac will have less "distance" to go to search for fragments if it only has to search within an 500MB partition of a 2GB drive than if it has to search the entire drive. This speed advantage is diminished, however, if you use your partitions in such a way as to require the Mac to frequently traverse partitions. For example, if your application is in one partition and your document is in another, the speed advantage will be less than if both files are in the same partition.
- **File Size** In the current Macintosh operating system, the minimum amount of disk space a file requires gets larger as the size of the drive gets larger. For example, the minimum file size on a 120MB drive is 2K; for a 720MB drive, the minimum is 12K. As a result, a 2K text file would take up only 2K of disk space on a 120MB drive but would require 12K of space on a 720MB drive (wasting 10K).

  For any file, no matter what its size, disk space requirements increase in increments of the minimal file size. Thus a 13K file would require 14K of disk space on a 120MB drive (2K x 7 = 14K) but would require 24K on a 720MB drive (12K x 2 = 24K), again wasting 10K. If you have a large capacity drive with a lot of small files on it, you are therefore probably wasting a significant amount of disk space. The solution to this is to partition the drive—the minimum file size for a partition is based on the size of the partition, not the size of the entire drive.

How to Partition (with Drive Setup) With older versions, Apple HD SC Setup could not create standard Macintosh partitions. Its Partition button was used to create only a special type of partition that (unless you know about and use A/UX, a Unix-based operating system) you would never want to use. Starting with version 7.5.3, however, it appears this utility can create standard Mac OS partitions. Drive Setup (assuming your hardware supports this utility) can easily create standard partitions of any size you choose. For example, to use Drive Setup to create partitions, follow these steps:

1. Start up with a disk that contains Drive Setup. This disk should not be the one you want to partition.
2. Launch Drive Setup and select the name of the drive you want to format/partition.
3. Click the Initialize button.
4. Click Custom Setup from the window that next appears.
5. Select the desired Partitioning Scheme from the pop-up menu (two or three equal-size partitions would be a common choice). You can create unequal-size partitions by dragging the bar handle of the partition box in the graphic depicting the partitions, or by changing the number in the Size box for a selected partition.
6. When you are done, close the window and click the Initialize button.
7. Use the "Customize Volumes" option of the Functions menu to select whether or not to have a volume automatically mount at startup (typically, you would want them all to mount).
8. Quit Drive Setup and restart.

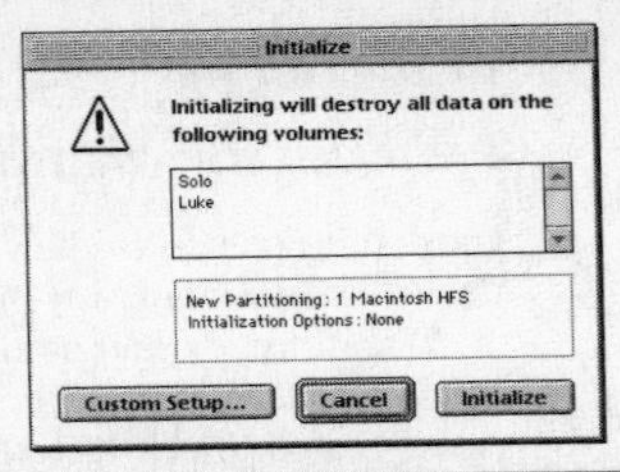

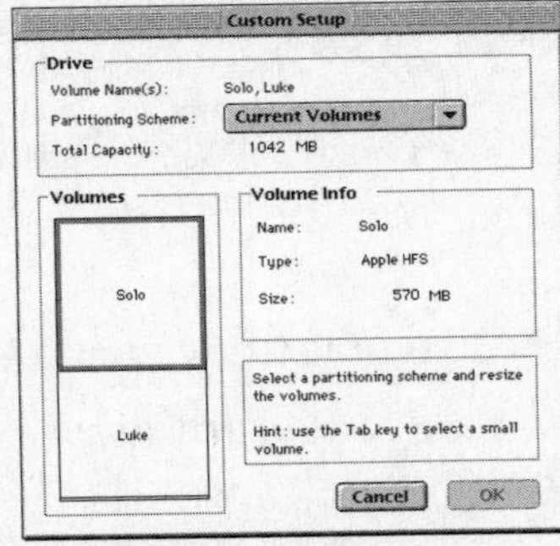

Figure F15-17 *Top: Click Drive Setup's Custom Setup button to get the Partition window. Bottom: Drive Setup's Partition window; use the Partitioning Scheme pop-up menu to select the number of partitions you want.*

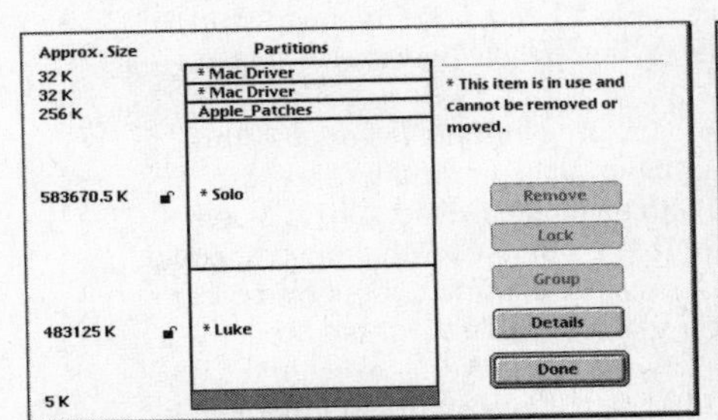

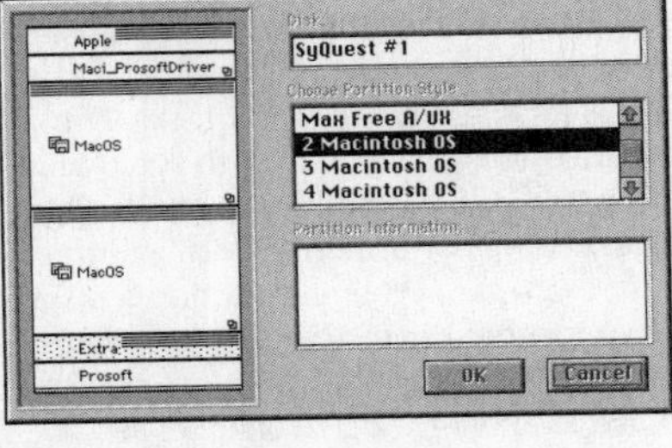

Figure F15-18 *Partition windows of Apple HD SC Setup (left) and Drive7 (right).*

BY THE WAY ▶

THE "EXTRA" PARTITION

When partitioning a disk, you may notice that there is an "Extra" partition (of about 5MB or so) at the bottom of the partition graphic (with Drive Setup, you may need to use the Tab key to see the listing of such a small partition on a large-capacity drive). Apple says the extra partition is used by some duplicating and copying software utilities. It is not essential, however, and it can be deleted or at least reduced to some minimum size (to do this with Drive Setup, for example, you would enlarge another partition to its maximum size and then reformat the disk). Personally, I would not bother doing this merely to reclaim 5MB—with today's large-capacity drives, it is not worth the effort.

Other small partitions contain essential driver-level information. Do not even try to delete them!

BY THE WAY

HARD AND SOFT PARTITIONS

Formatting utilities create what is called a *hard partition*. This process requires reformatting the disk (thereby erasing any data on it) and is thus a true format-level dividing up of the disk.

In contrast, certain partition-making utilities use a *soft partition* method to divide the disk. This does not require reformatting the disk (meaning that you may not have to erase data to create the partitions). These partitions, however, depend on a system extension being present, and so the partitions may "disappear" if the extension is not active. Soft partitions are really a way of fooling the Macintosh into thinking that true partitions have been created, when in fact they have not. In general, I would avoid using soft partitions. In any case, this method is no longer popular, and utilities that use it appear to have largely faded from the scene.

TECHNICALLY SPEAKING

WHAT'S AN INTERLEAVE?

You may have heard that changing something called the *interleave factor* on your hard disk can improve its speed. The basic idea is this: Hard disks are constantly spinning from the moment they are turned on. A drive "reads" requested data from this spinning disk as the relevant portion of the disk passes by the disk's drive head. In some cases, especially with older drives, the drive cannot read data from the disk as quickly as the disk can spin by the drive head. This means the drive has to wait for the next revolution of the disk to read the next sector of data, which can slow things down. Changing the interleave factor alters the way data are written to a disk so that it partially compensates for this problem (essentially, it spaces out data so that the drive does not have to read from contiguous sectors; related sectors are spaced far enough apart so that the drive can read data from them without having to skip over and return to them on subsequent revolutions). The result is that performance speed improves.

The ideal is for the drive to read quickly enough to use an interleave factor of 1 (this means that the drive can keep up with the rate of spinning). All current drives are fast enough to do this, and so they come preformatted with an interleave factor of 1. Slower drives similarly come preformatted with an interleave that is optimal for that drive (it could be 2 or 3, for example). When formatting a disk, most utilities are smart enough to pick the optimal factor for that drive. Thus, in most cases, you should be able to ignore this interleave issue entirely.

If you have an older model of Mac (especially a Mac Plus), however, the transfer rate is slowed down by the Mac itself. In such cases, you may get better performance from a fast drive by changing its interleave factor from 1 to a higher (slower) factor. Even here, though, the drive may use a "cache" to compensate for the slower transfer rate, eliminating the need to change the interleave factor (see Fix-It #6, "By the Way: Driver-Level versus System-Level Disk Caches").

If you have determined that changing the interleave factor is desirable for your hardware, and if you use Apple HD SC Setup, you can do so by typing Command-I. With Drive7, the interleave setting is accessed via the dialog box that appears after selecting "Format Options" from the Options menu.

Changing the interleave factor requires that you reformat the drive.

Verifying Disks and Media Damage

Verifying a disk means checking each sector (block) on the disk to make sure that no media damage exists. Usually, this is done automatically whenever a disk is formatted, although there are ways in which you can choose to do this at other times. Typically, if bad blocks are detected, they are *marked* (this is also referred to as being *mapped out* or *spared)* so that they cannot be used in the future. If successful, this allows the disk to verify despite the bad blocks; otherwise, the verification fails. For more specific details, read on.

For Floppy Disks

Using the Macintosh to Verify When you format a floppy disk, such as with the Finder's Erase Disk command, the Macintosh automatically verifies it.

In System 7, if any media damage is detected during the verification, the disk is verified a second time, during which any bad blocks detected are spared. When this happens, a new message appears during the formatting process. In system software versions prior to System 7.5, the message will say "Reverifying the disk;" in System 7.5 or a later version, the message should read "Updating disk." Reverification takes much longer than the initial verification.

Reverification usually succeeds unless there are too many bad blocks or the damage is in the critical area of the disk needed to store the Directory. In these cases, you will get a message that initialization or erasing the disk "failed," and you should discard the disk. Actually, I take a conservative approach and discard any floppy disk that needs to be reverified, even if it ultimately formats successfully. In my experience, once bad blocks appear on a floppy disk, the probability increases that more will appear soon—why take chances?

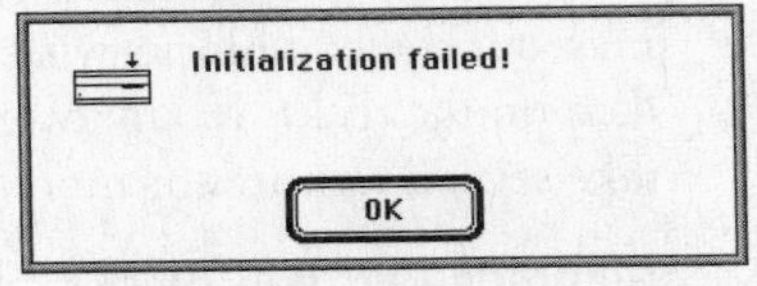

Figure F15-19 *A message such as this appears if the Macintosh is unable to verify a floppy disk that it is attempting to format.*

Occasionally, I have had a disk problem that appeared to be due to bad blocks (such as a write error when copying a file). Yet when I reformatted the disk, it surprised me by formatting successfully without any reverification needed. I am more optimistic about the continued use of such a disk than those that require reverification. The cause, however, may well be an intermittent bad block problem that will inevitably soon return, so be cautious.

If you begin to have problems with many or all disks failing to verify, there is probably a problem with the floppy drive mechanism.

SEE: • **Fix-It #17 for more on hardware repairs**

Using Other Utilities to Verify Floppy disk formatting utilities (such as Norton Utilities' Floppier or MacTools Pro's FastCopy) also verify a disk when formatting it. They typically do not spare bad blocks; if damage is detected, the initialization fails. Floppier, however, has an option to format a disk without verifying it. To do this, unmark the Verify checkbox. Generally, I recommend against doing

Figure F15-20 *Format options for Norton Utilities' Floppier, with the Verify option selected.*

this—it saves time, but it is riskier. Without verifying, you may wind up inadvertently using a damaged disk.

Conversely, with utilities such as MacTools Pro's DiskFix or Norton Utilities' Disk Doctor, you can verify a disk without having to format it. To do this, use the commands for checking the disk media (as described in Fix-It #14, "Resolve Problems with Bad Blocks"). These utilities *can* mark any detected bad blocks, similarly to how System 7's verification works. Still, if bad blocks are detected, I would discard the disk.

For Hard Disks

Testing a Hard Disk Most disk formatting utilities can test a hard disk for bad blocks without having to reformat the disk. To do this with Apple HD SC Setup, click the Test button; for Drive Setup, select "Test Disk" from its Functions menu; and for Drive7, select "Test Drive" from its Functions menu. This feature works most thoroughly if the disk can be unmounted for the test (the startup volume cannot be unmounted, for example).

Recovery utilities, such as MacTools Pro's DiskFix or Norton Utilities' Disk Doctor, can similarly check a disk for bad blocks (as described in Fix-It #14, "Resolve Problems with Bad Blocks"). Recovery utilities can map out any bad blocks that they detect. In contrast, the Test functions of format utilities generally can only identify bad blocks. To map out the bad blocks with a format utility, you must reformat the disk (erasing all data on the disk). In any case, be prepared to wait, because testing for bad blocks can take several minutes or more.

Mapping Out Bad Blocks If media damage is detected with a format utility, you should reformat the disk. Reformatting maps out the damaged areas so that they can no longer be used. When you format a disk with utilities such as Apple HD SC Setup or Drive7, bad blocks are detected and automatically mapped out during the verification stage. Unless an unusually large number of bad blocks exists (which would almost certainly indicate a more serious problem with the disk), the disk will be successfully formatted and verified.

If your hard disk formatting utility has an option to format without verifying (one is usually offered to save time), don't take it. If you have any suggestion of bad blocks, always verify to check for bad blocks when formatting a hard disk. Remember, with Drive Setup, select the "Low level format" option to do this.

Although I recommend discarding floppy disks with bad blocks, even if the disk is ultimately verified, I obviously would not recommend this for hard disks! You would not want to discard an expensive drive unit for a single bad block, especially if the block is successfully mapped out.

A few bad blocks on a hard disk are no cause for concern, once they are mapped out. Actually, many new hard drives come with bad blocks already on them (mapped out before they were ever shipped from the factory); still, if you are careful with the use of your hard drive, you may never have any problems. Bad blocks are much more common with floppy disks. If new bad blocks frequently appear on a hard disk shortly after you have formatted it, however, you probably have a hardware problem. In this case, the disk drive needs to be repaired (if possible) or replaced.

Finally, although recovery utilities can similarly detect and map out bad blocks, reformatting is the most reliable method for permanently preventing these blocks from being used again (see Fix-It #14, "Repairing Bad Blocks: Recovery Utilities versus Reformatting"). After you reformat, restore the disk's contents from your backups.

For related information

SEE:
- **Fix-It #6 on disk caches**
- **Fix-It #12 on using formatting utilities to update the disk driver**
- **Fix-Its #13 and #14 for more on bad blocks and using recovery utilities**
- **Fix-It #16 on SCSI-related problems**
- **Chapter 1 on basic terminology regarding disks**
- **Chapter 5 on problems starting up and mounting drives**

Fix-It #16: Check for Problems with SCSI Devices and Connections

QUICK SUMMARY ▶

Use a utility, such as SCSIProbe, to mount a SCSI device that will not otherwise mount. Check for other possible SCSI-related problems, such as ID conflicts, improper termination, or turning the SCSI device on or off improperly.

When to do it:

- When a SCSI device does not mount or does not function as expected. This includes fixed format disk drives, removable media cartridge drives, and CD-ROM drives.
- When multiple copies of the disk icon of a SCSI disk device appear scattered over the desktop.
- When a system crash or freeze occurs as a result of accessing a SCSI device (for example, when trying to open any or almost any file on an external drive or CD-ROM drive results in a system crash).
- When you cannot start up your Macintosh because a "sad Mac" appears.
- When you cannot start up your Macintosh because a system error occurs, particularly if the error occurs immediately after the "Welcome to Macintosh" message appears.
- When you lose access to all the external SCSI devices connected to your Macintosh.
- Whenever problems develop immediately after you add, remove, or rearrange the order of externally connected SCSI devices.

Why to do it:

Starting with the Macintosh Plus, all models of Macintosh have a port in the rear of the machine called the *SCSI port* or *SCSI bus* (where SCSI stands for Small Computer Systems Interface and is pronounced "scuzzy"). On desktop Macs, it is usually the large 25-pin port in the rear of the machine, under a symbol shaped like a diamond with a horizontal line drawn through one point. On most PowerBooks it is a smaller, squarish, 30-pin port under the same symbol.

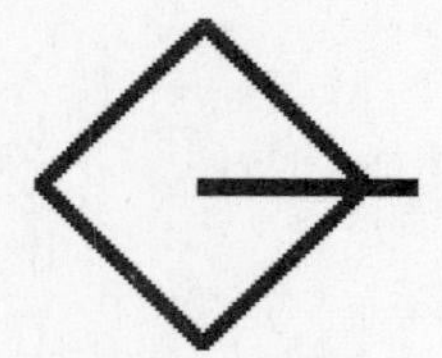

Figure F16-1 *The SCSI symbol.*

You need a SCSI port to connect certain devices to your Macintosh. These *SCSI devices* include external hard drives, CD-ROMs, tape backup devices, scanners, and certain printers. A special SCSI cable is used to connect the device to the Macintosh. Problems involving these devices can often be traced to problems with how these devices are connected, what cables are used, and settings on the SCSI device itself. These are the major subjects of this Fix-It.

Remember, many of the symptoms described here (such as system crashes) have other causes besides SCSI problems. These other causes are covered throughout this book, as appropriate.

What's a SCSI Chain?

Only one device can be connected directly to the SCSI port on the rear of the Macintosh. Each external SCSI device, however, is equipped with two SCSI ports. So if you connect an external hard drive to your Macintosh, for example, this will still leave one SCSI port empty on your external drive. A second SCSI device can be connected to this port. This arrangement can continue, creating a *daisy chain* of SCSI devices. If all devices are connected correctly, the Macintosh will recognize all of them, even though only one device is actually plugged into the Mac.

What's the Problem?

Your Macintosh may be running smoothly right now—but whenever you add or remove a SCSI device, your Mac could come to a halt. The probability of this happening multiplies as you attach more devices. Most of these problems revolve around two important SCSI requirements: unique ID numbers, and proper termination.

SCSI ID Numbers Each SCSI device has an ID number from 0 to 7; the Macintosh uses these numbers to differentiate one SCSI device from another. ID 7 is reserved for the Macintosh (which, despite its number, is technically not part of the SCSI chain), while ID 0 is reserved for internal hard drives (which *are* considered part of the SCSI chain).

Thus you can attach up to seven SCSI devices to one Macintosh (see "Technically Speaking: SCSI-2: Dual SCSI Buses," however, for an important exception to this). With an internal hard drive, you can connect six external SCSI devices, with available ID numbers from 1 to 6.

Some Macintoshes can have more than one internal SCSI device (for instance, both an internal hard drive and a CD-ROM drive). Each device will have its own ID number (internal CD-ROM drives, for example, should have their ID number set to 3).

You assign the ID number to each external device. Usually, you do this by pressing a button located somewhere on the device; each time you press the button, you cycle to another ID number, which should be indicated in a display next to the button. The number currently in the display is the ID number for that device. These ID numbers do not have to be assigned in the order that the devices are connected—for example, the first external device in a chain could have an ID of 4, and the second device could have an ID of 2.

All other things equal, assign ID numbers based on how often you use a device, giving higher ID numbers (where 6 is higher than 5, for example) to those external devices that you use more often. The device with the higher number is given priority when two devices are simultaneously competing for access to the SCSI bus.

The most important rule to remember is that each device must have a different ID number. To repeat: *No two devices can have the same ID number.* Otherwise, problems will certainly result (as detailed in the "What to Do" section).

TECHNICALLY SPEAKING ▶

SCSI MANAGER 4.3

SCSI Manager is the name of the instruction set used by the Macintosh to interact with SCSI devices; a version of it is built into the ROM of all Macintoshes. SCSI Manager 4.3 is the latest version of this instruction set. It is included in the ROM of the Macintosh Quadra 660AV, 840AV, all Power Macs, 500 series PowerBooks, and virtually all other recent Mac models. It adds new features to the SCSI bus, including faster data transfer rates.

Additionally, there is a software SCSI Manager 4.3 extension. Prior to System 7.5.3, there was a good deal of discussion (and confusion!) about whether a given Mac model could use this extension, whether you should install it on a Mac that already had it in ROM, and so forth. Thankfully, the code for this extension (which may update what is in ROM) has been incorporated into the main software (System or Update files) of System 7.5.3 and later. So, if you are using current software, you should no longer need, have, or install this separate extension. The only potential downside here is that if your Mac had problems with SCSI Manager 4.3, you can't get rid of it anymore!

BY THE WAY ▶

A NEW IDE

IDE (Integrated Drive Electronics) is a less-expensive alternative to SCSI that has been used in PC computers for years. Apple has now introduced it into certain Macintoshes. For the moment, Apple contends it will only be used for internal drives in low-end Macs, and even these Macs will still be able to use SCSI drives via the external port. In most ways, this difference will be totally transparent to the user. Almost all applications should run fine, without needing any modification, regardless of the type of drive technology in use. Disk formatting utilities, however, need to be updated to accommodate IDE drives.

SEE: • **Fix-It #15, especially "Apple HD Setup versus Drive Setup: Which One Do You Use?" for details on formatting IDE drives**

SCSI Termination SCSI termination may sound like what you want to do to a drive that has just crashed for the third time this week, but it is nothing of the kind. SCSI termination is a messy topic, though, so let me disentangle it for you.

I am the first to admit that I don't really know the nuts and bolts of what termination is all about. Fortunately, to fix most termination problems, you don't have to know very much.

Essentially, termination tells the Mac where a SCSI bus begins and ends, preventing signals from getting mixed up by reaching the end of a chain and bouncing back again. It is also important for keeping signal strength at an appropriate level and maintaining

TECHNICALLY SPEAKING ▶

SCSI-2: DUAL SCSI BUSES

SCSI-2 is a new SCSI standard for data transfer that should also increase transfer speed. This requires a new SCSI-2 port that is included with many recent Macintosh models, notably PCI-based Macs. Another advantage of SCSI-2 is that Macs with this feature can have more than seven devices attached to a chain, thanks to the presence of two separate SCSI bus ports. To accommodate this wider capacity, a new ID numbering system has been introduced. With SCSI-2, each device has a three-digit ID (called the *long ID);* the old ID numbers are called the *short ID*. For example, short ID 3 is now long ID 0.3.0.

To take full advantage of these new features, assuming your Mac has the appropriate hardware, you may also need to update your disk device driver (see Fix-It #12).

Finally, for those of you that know and care about such matters, here's the technical lowdown (largely adapted from Apple documentation) on the dual SCSI buses found on Apple's PCI-based Power Macs:

- There are two SCSI buses on the Power Macintosh 7500, 7600, 8500, and 9500 (and newer PCI-based Macs): an internal bus (0) and an external bus (1). The internal bus has a maximum transfer rate of 10MB/sec, while the external bus has a maximum transfer rate of 5MB/sec.
- Due to the physical design of these Macs, there is only room for three devices to be attached to the internal bus (typically the internal hard drive and the CD-ROM drive, plus a third optional device). Both buses, however, have the standard full complement of 0–7 ID assignments (with the Mac being assigned ID 7 on both buses). Technically, there is a way to attach an internal device to the external bus, though there would rarely be any reason to do so.
- Some SCSI scanning utilities that have not been updated to list both buses correctly will only list one set of ID numbers; for example, you need APS PowerTools 4.0 or later for a correct listing. With the dual buses, you *can* assign two devices to the same ID number, as long as they are on separate buses.
- Both buses are SCSI-2 compliant: the internal bus is Fast SCSI-2, while the external bus is not. This means (according to Apple) that if you add a second internal hard drive to the internal bus, it *will* be Fast SCSI-2 capable, though I have read other reports to the contrary. ("Fast" and "Wide" are both technologies designed to increase SCSI-2 performance speed. In order to take advantage of this, the hard drive itself must also be designed as a Fast and/or Wide device.) Neither bus is "Wide"; they are both "Narrow" (or 8-bit). If you want SCSI-2 Fast and Wide, you'll need a third-party PCI card to which you attach your SCSI device.
- Due to a problem with Apple's controllers in its SCSI-2 drives, some utilities (such as Hard Disk ToolKit) may report that these drives are SCSI-1 drives. This is mistaken.
- Bus 1 (external) has automatic termination, which means that circuitry on the logic board senses whether or not there are any external SCSI devices attached and adjusts its termination accordingly. Bus 0 (internal) does not have automatic termination, because it is exclusively an internal SCSI bus. If additional devices are added to Bus 0, only the last device should contain termination resistors.
- Note: The Nubus-based Power Macintosh 8100 also has a dual bus architecture, but it is implemented differently. Most notably, the external bus is used for the internal CD-ROM drive.

transmission speed at all locations across your cables. The longer your chain, the more likely it is that termination problems will appear.

That said, *the main thing you need to know is that a typical SCSI chain needs to be terminated at both ends of the chain.* Because most Macintoshes with internal drives are considered terminated at the Macintosh end, all you need to do in those cases is make sure the opposite (external device) end of the chain is terminated. The most common method to do this is to get a special SCSI plug called a *terminator*, which looks like an ordinary SCSI plug with no cable attached. Simply plug it in to the second (empty) port on the last SCSI device in a chain, and you are done.

If you have no external SCSI devices attached, you can skip this whole discussion. If you have two or more external SCSI devices attached, you will likely need to be concerned about termination issues. More details are given in the "What to Do" section of this Fix-It (see "Make Sure All SCSI Devices Are Properly Terminated").

What to do:

This Fix-It addresses two main topics: using a SCSI utility, and SCSI-related problems.

Using a SCSI Utility

A good SCSI utility is nearly essential when working with SCSI devices. I will use an excellent, popular (and free!) such utility, the SCSIProbe control panel, for most of the examples described here. Some hard disk formatting utilities (as described in Fix-It #15) can double as a SCSI utility; they may also include a companion control panel that functions similarly to SCSIProbe. Even Apple's Drive Setup can now handle SCSIProbe's most critical functions.

The primary use of any SCSI utility is to mount SCSI devices. There are two common occasions when you would need to do this: to mount a device turned on after startup is completed, and when a properly connected, mountable SCSI device (turned on at startup, but not the startup disk) does not mount automatically. Here's how to accomplish these tasks with SCSIProbe.

Mounting SCSI Devices with SCSIProbe

1. Make sure the SCSI device you want to mount is turned on and the cables are securely fastened in their respective ports. SCSIProbe can recognize only devices that are turned on.

   If you are having any trouble securing a plug to a SCSI port, check for bent connecting wires on the end of the plug; if you find any, straighten them and try again. If a wire breaks off, you will have to replace the cable. (Only disconnect and connect cables, of course, when the Macintosh is off.)

2. Open SCSIProbe. A window will list every active device connected to your SCSI chain, with each device listed next to its assigned ID number. This will help right away to identify a possible ID number conflict!

Figure F16-2 *SCSIProbe's main window (this is on a Macintosh with dual SCSI buses; Bus 0 is displayed here).*

TAKE NOTE ▶

SCSIPROBE AND SCSI MANAGER 4.3/SCSI-2: VIEWING BOTH BUSES

For Macintosh models that support multiple SCSI buses via SCSI Manager 4.3/SCSI-2, you will need to switch from one bus to the other to see all of your connected devices. To do this with SCSIProbe 4.3 or later, look at the top of the first column of the main SCSIProbe window; you will probably find a "0" there. This means that SCSIProbe is listing those items on Bus 0 (which should be your internal bus). Clicking on the O, however, reveals a pop-up menu with two items. Select the currently unselected item (they will probably both say "Apple Computer") to shift to Bus 1, which will list your externally connected devices (plus the Mac itself again). If no pop-up menu appears when you click ID, your Mac does not support multiple buses.

Note: On older versions of SCSIProbe, the pop-up menu gave a choice of Internal, External, or Both.

Figure F16-3 *Left: SCSI Probe, with the pop-up menu to switch buses displayed. Right: SCSI Probe's main window, with Bus 1 now shown.*

All devices, whether mounted or not, should be listed here. SCSIProbe also lists the type of each device, such as whether it is a hard disk ("disk") or CD-ROM drive ("ROM").

3. If the device you want to mount is not listed, click the Update button. This button forces SCSIProbe to rescan the SCSI bus and locate any devices that it may have missed when it initially opened. Unless your device is damaged or improperly connected (as described in the next section, "SCSI-Related Problems"), it should be listed now.

4. Click the Mount button. Within a few seconds, all SCSI devices in the list that can be mounted should now appear on the desktop.

   By the way, SCSIProbe provides an optional shortcut option for accessing its Mount function. To set this up, first click the Options button. From the dialog box that then appears, select "Install Volume Mounting INIT." You can then designate your desired Mount Key shortcut in the space provided (Command-Space is the default choice). After this, quit SCSIProbe and restart. Now, whenever you press the Mount Key combination, SCSIProbe immediately (without opening the control panel) attempts to mount all available but presently unmounted devices.

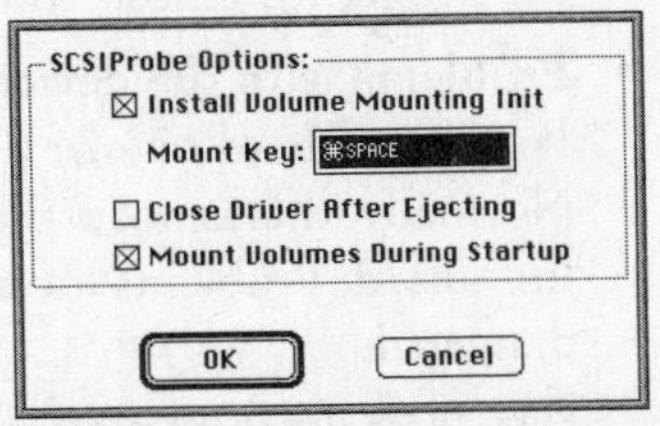

Figure F16-4 *SCSIProbe's Options window.*

5. Close SCSIProbe. You're done.

TECHNICALLY SPEAKING ▶

SCSIPROBE AND PRODUCT LISTINGS

SCSIProbe displays the vendor and product name of each device. These names, though, are not what you might expect to find. For example, Quantum is a popular manufacturer of hard drive devices; its drives are placed in the cases of many different companies that sell hard drives to consumers. Thus, though the outside of your external hard drive may say APS (or whatever other brand you own), the mechanism inside the case may be a Quantum, and Quantum is listed by SCSIProbe as the vendor. Apple's internal drives are often Quantum drives. You may be more surprised to learn that some Apple drives are actually manufactured by IBM!

If SCSIProbe Lists a Device, But Doesn't Mount It

There are two common explanations for why SCSIProbe would list, yet be unable to mount, a SCSI device. These explanations apply to any situation where a SCSI device does not mount as expected, whether you are using SCSIProbe or not.

- **The device isn't supposed to mount**
  Certain SCSI devices, such as scanners and tape backup devices, typically do not mount on the desktop under any circumstances. Clicking SCSIProbe's Mount button does not change this fact. As long as the devices are listed in SCSIProbe's window, they should be okay. In some cases, if SCSIProbe cannot identify the device, it is listed only with the phrase "No Data" for the appropriate ID number line. This does not necessarily indicate any problem.

SCSIProbe — SCSIProbe 3.5

ID	Type	Vendor	Product	Vers...
0	DISK	QUANTUM	P80S 980-80-94xx	A.2
1				
2				
3	DISK	QUANTUM	PD170S	527_
4				
5	•			
6				
7	CPU	APPLE	MACINTOSH IIci	7.1

• No Data — Update — Mount — Options...

Figure F16-5 *SCSIProbe's "No Data" message means it could not properly identify the device.*

  When you launch an application that is designed to work with an unmounted SCSI device, the presence of the device is recognized by the application. Thus, some backup software programs (such as Retrospect) can access an unmounted tape backup device (assuming that the particular brand and model is included among the list of devices compatible with the program). Check your software's manual for details.

- **Problems with the device driver: Hard disks and removable cartridges**
  For a fixed hard disk or a removable cartridge to mount, it needs a disk driver. Normally, this is not a problem, as the driver is typically installed when the disk is initialized. Problems mounting the disk can occur, however, if the driver becomes damaged.

SEE: • **Fix-It #12 for more on disk drivers, including what to do to fix a suspected damaged driver**

For removable media disk cartridges, since different cartridges may use different drivers, you may experience special problems when switching from one cartridge to another.

SEE: • **"Take Note: Mounting Removable Media Cartridges with Different Drivers," for details**

TAKE NOTE

MOUNTING REMOVABLE MEDIA CARTRIDGES WITH DIFFERENT DRIVERS

Removable media cartridges (such as those used with SyQuest and Iomega drives) present a special problem. As with fixed hard disks, each cartridge contains its own device driver, an invisible software file necessary for the Macintosh to interact with the disk (see Fix-It #12 for more on device drivers).

In many cases, there are two sources of this driver: an extension in your startup disk's System Folder, and a "hidden" driver on a cartridge itself. The former source is used if there is no cartridge present at startup; the latter is used if a cartridge is present at startup. The latter case in particular can present some special problems.

When you insert a cartridge into a removable media drive (at startup, and sometimes on other occasions), its driver is copied from the disk and loaded into RAM. It is the RAM copy that is actually used. If you switch cartridges after startup, you may be switching to a cartridge that uses a different driver from the one initially present. This could happen if the cartridges were formatted using different format utilities (see Fix-It #15 for more on formatting utilities), as might especially be the case if you are using a cartridge borrowed from someone else.

The problem here is that when you switch cartridges, the Macintosh may not automatically replace the RAM copy of the initial driver with the driver for the newly inserted cartridge. Thus, a conflict occurs because the Macintosh attempts to use the wrong driver (the one from the previous cartridge) to interact with the current cartridge. This can cause various problems, including an inability to mount the cartridge or a loss of data from the cartridge. The simplest solution to this problem is to make sure that all of your cartridges use the same driver. If this is not possible, consider using a utility such as one of the following:

- **SCSIProbe.** Recent versions of SCSIProbe have an Options dialog box that lists an option called Close Driver After Ejecting. This causes the driver from the ejected cartridge to be removed from memory, forcing a newly inserted cartridge's own driver to be used instead. Note that with some older versions of SCSIProbe, however, the utility may treat an ejected floppy disk as if it were an ejectable cartridge. This can result in the mistaken closing of the driver for a still remaining drive (fixed or removable), leading to a system crash.
- **Drive7/Mount Cache.** Drive7, a disk formatting utility from Casa Blanca Works, provides a control panel called Mount Cache (formerly Drive7rem). It loads a single driver at startup that is compatible with almost all removable media drives. This driver acts as a universal driver, bypassing a cartridge's own unique driver, thereby preventing the potential conflict. To use Mount Cache most effectively, the removable media drive should be on at startup, but without any cartridges inserted until after startup is over (which is possible only if the drive is not used as a startup drive). This prevents a possible conflict between Mount Cache and the cartridge's own driver both trying to load (though, if this happens, Mount Cache is designed to automatically disable itself). Ideally, to prevent conflicts, Mount Cache should load early in the startup sequence. To do this, either create an alias of Mount Cache and place it in the Extensions folder or use a startup management utility to change its loading order (see Fix-It #4).

  To activate Mount Cache, you must first separately select each drive you wish to use it with. You do this by clicking each desired drive from the control panel (which then places a check mark next to its name) and then restarting. This allows you to use Mount Cache with any subset of your SCSI devices that you wish.

The formatting software that came with your hard drive may have similar functions to these two utilities, so check it out. Also note that Iomega's Zip and Jaz drives come with special software that allows you to connect the drive to a Mac that does not have the driver installed. This makes it easy to use the drive as a portable device to be connected to a variety of Macs.

(Continued on next page)

TAKE NOTE

MOUNTING REMOVABLE MEDIA CARTRIDGES WITH DIFFERENT DRIVERS *(Continued)*

Also, a removable cartridge may not automatically mount when inserted after startup, but will mount fine after using a utility such as SCSIProbe. To get it to mount when first inserted, you typically have to set the appropriate driver option for the cartridge. Do this from your disk's formatting software utility (as described in Fix-It #15).

Finally, here's the scoop on a few related problems involving removable cartridge drives:

- **PC-formatted disks and PC Exchange** If you are trying to use PC Exchange to mount a PC-formatted removable media cartridge (or fixed hard drive, for that matter), do not let the disk's driver get installed. Instead, click the Options button from the PC Exchange control panel, select the relevant SCSI device (such as a SyQuest drive) from the list and then restart. This causes the PC Exchange driver to be used in lieu of the disk's PC-based driver.
- **PC-formatted disks and file sharing** Eject DOS-formatted removable cartridges before turning on file sharing (otherwise you can't turn it on) as well as before restarting or shutting down (or you may get a sad Mac when you restart).
- **Drivers as extensions** Years ago, some removable cartridge systems used a startup extension installed in your System Folder as their only disk driver (similar to how CD-ROM drivers work even now), rather than keeping a copy of the driver on the cartridge itself and loading the driver when the cartridge mounted. If you use a cartridge like this, you cannot use a utility such as SCSIProbe to mount the cartridge, since these utilities look for a driver on the cartridge. If you have a recent drive but for some reason still need to work with these older-style cartridges, the best solution—if possible—is to reformat the cartridge, updating it to accommodate the new style of driver.

SEE ALSO: **• Chapter 5, "Special Case: Problems Mounting Removable Media Cartridges," in the "A Hard Disk Won't Mount" section, for more discussion of these problems**

• "By The Way: Removable Cartridge Drives: Drivers And Extensions," in Fix-It #12

- **Problems with the device driver: CD-ROM drives and other devices.** With CD-ROM drives, the device driver is typically a startup extension installed in the Extensions folder of your System Folder; it remains active no matter what CD-ROM disks you eject or insert. The specific driver needed for your drive should have been included on a floppy disk that accompanied the drive. Apple's driver, appropriately called Apple CD-ROM, is also included as standard with System 7.5. Some other drivers, available as a separate software purchase, can be used with a variety of different drive models.

  If the needed extension is not loaded at startup, CD-ROM discs cannot mount. If you find that such a driver extension is missing, install it from the discs that came with your CD-ROM drive and restart (see "Take Note: CD-ROM Drivers and Problems Mounting CD-ROM Discs," for more details).

  Other SCSI devices may similarly use an extension driver. Some SCSI devices, such as scanners, do not require a driver at all; they require only the appropriate application software. Floppy disk drives, which are not a SCSI device anyway, do not require any driver, either.

SEE: • Chapter 5 for more on problems mounting and ejecting CD-ROM discs

If SCSIProbe Doesn't List or Mount the Device

First, check the obvious: make sure the device is turned on and properly connected. Next, if you have a Mac with dual buses (see "Take Note: SCSIProbe and SCSI Manager 4.3/SCSI-2: Viewing Both Buses"), make sure SCSIProbe is displaying the appropriate bus.

Finally, if you cannot mount or even list a connected SCSI device, and SCSIProbe gives a flashing message that says "Bus not terminated," you may indeed have a termination problem. Make sure you have correctly followed all of the preceding procedures; if so, proceed to the section called "SCSI-Related Problems," later in this Fix-It (especially the subsection titled "Make Sure All SCSI Devices Are Properly Terminated").

If you still cannot mount any SCSI devices, you probably have a dead SCSI controller on the Macintosh's logic board. The logic board will need to be replaced.

SEE: • **Fix-It #17 on logic board repairs, if needed**

TAKE NOTE ▶

CD-ROM DRIVERS AND PROBLEMS MOUNTING CD-ROM DISCS

As stated in the main text, CD-ROM drives need a driver extension installed in order for the Macintosh to access the drive. Surprisingly, Apple's CD-ROM driver will not load at startup—even if the extension is correctly installed—unless the CD-ROM drive itself is turned on prior to startup (this is relevant only to external CD-ROM drives). As a result, if you turn on an external CD-ROM drive after startup, any discs inserted in the drive will not mount. Even though SCSIProbe lists the drive in its control panel window, clicking the Mount button will not remedy the problem. To get the CD-ROM drive to work, you must restart after turning on the CD-ROM drive. The same basic problem occurs if you start up with the CD-ROM driver extension disabled. There is a freeware utility called LoadADrive, however, that will load a CD-ROM disc even if the Apple driver was not loaded at startup.

Certain other third-party drivers, such as DriveCD from Casa Blanca Works, can mount CD-ROM discs even if the drive is not turned on until after startup is complete. To do this, you typically first need to mount the drive (for instance, by using the DriveCD control panel, which functions similarly to SCSIProbe). After that, inserted discs will mount.

Also, some nonstandard format CD-ROM discs, such as PhotoCD discs, will not mount unless additional extensions are also installed (such as Apple's Apple Photo Access and Foreign File Access extensions). Check your CD-ROM drive's manual for more details.

If you are having problems with an application that is unable to use files from a CD-ROM disc that is in a nonstandard format, and you have the needed extensions installed, hold down the Option key when you insert the disc and keep it held down until the disc mounts. This should solve the problem.

Finally, as described in Chapter 5, some CD-ROM discs (with system software on them) can act as startup discs. This ability may still strike you as involving a paradox: For a CD-ROM disc to boot at startup, it must load before the supposedly required CD-ROM driver extension has loaded. How can this be? The answer is that in addition to the required System Folder being on the disc, these CD-ROM discs have special instructions, presumably in the boot blocks, that allow the Mac to mount them as startup discs.

Not all system software CD-ROM discs are usable as startup discs, but those that include a System Folder generally are.

Special Case: Disk Drives That Don't Automatically Mount at Startup

If you are using an internal drive as your startup disk, any external drive that is turned on at startup should mount automatically as a secondary drive—that is, when startup is completed, its icon should appear on your desktop. A hard drive, however, needs time to warm up before the Macintosh can detect its presence. If you turn on the external drive too late (such as after the Macintosh is already on and startup has begun), the Macintosh may check for external SCSI devices before the drive is sufficiently warmed up. In this case, the external drive is passed over and does not mount.

Similarly, if the external drive is your default startup disk (as selected by the Startup Disk control panel) but you turn it on too late, the Macintosh will start from its internal drive, instead (assuming there is an internal drive and it has a System Folder on it). Again, in such cases, the external drive may not mount at all. SCSI utilities like SCSIProbe are not essential to solving this type of problem, but they are usually the most convenient solution.

In some cases, especially with most recent versions of the system software, an external disk may mount even if it warms up too late to be recognized by the Macintosh at its first startup check. This is because the Mac makes a second check later in the startup process. The effects of these checks, however, may not be identical. For example, I noted that when mounted via the second check, the custom icon for my disk was absent.

To solve the immediate problem of a disk that does not automatically mount at startup, try one of the following procedures:

- Restart the Macintosh. Assuming they are all turned on, the hard drive(s) will now mount correctly. This is the only solution for an incorrect startup disk selection.
- Mount the disk manually with a utility such as SCSIProbe (as described earlier in this Fix-It). Even if you think the drive had sufficient time to warm up and should have mounted automatically at startup, try using SCSIProbe now; there may have been a one-time glitch. If SCSIProbe mounts the drive, chances are that the next time you restart, the drive will mount automatically as expected. To prevent this problem from recurring, follow either one of the remaining two guidelines.
- Remember to turn the drive on at least several seconds before turning on the Macintosh; this gives the drive enough time to warm up. By the way, if a disk fails to mount even when you gave it sufficient time to warm up, it may be that your disk formatting utility has an option (typically called "auto-mount") to turn automatic mounting of a drive on or off. With this option set to off, the drive will only mount manually after startup is over. The solution is to make sure this option is on. Launch your disk-formatting utility or its companion control panel to check.

- Use a special option available with SCSIProbe called "Mount Volumes During Startup" (selected from SCSIProbe's Options dialog box). You also need to turn on the "Install Volume Mounting INIT" option. When both of these are turned on, SCSIProbe scans the SCSI bus at the time that the Volume Mounting INIT loads, which is significantly later in the startup sequence than when the Macintosh first checks for the presence of SCSI devices. As a result, SCSIProbe recognizes and mounts SCSI devices that are turned on but were skipped over by the Macintosh's initial check. Usually, this is late enough for a hard drive to be detected even if it was not turned on until after the Macintosh was turned on. This option is useful only for mounting drives as secondary drives; it does not switch startup disks.

Various disk formatting utilities have similar options, so check your manual.

BY THE WAY ▶

SWITCHING STARTUP DISKS AT STARTUP

As discussed at several points in this book, if you hold down the Command-Option-Shift-Delete keys at startup, the Macintosh bypasses the internal hard drive and instead uses an external hard drive as the startup disk, assuming one is available. It does this regardless of the setting in the Startup Disk control panel. Although this method is most often used to bypass an internal drive that is crashing at startup, it is also a useful shortcut technique for switching startup disks even if there is no problem with the internal drive. The only inconvenience of this method is that the internal drive may not be mounted during startup; its icon is absent from the desktop when startup is completed. With SCSIProbe installed on your external drive and its Mount Volumes During Startup option selected, however, the bypassed internal drive does mount automatically as a secondary drive at startup.

As another alternative, Now Utilities' Startup Manager, if accessed at startup (this is typically done by holding down a specially defined key, as described in Fix-It #4) has an option to switch the assigned startup disk and immediately restart.

If you have an IDE internal drive (see "By the Way: A New IDE," earlier in this Fix-It), you may find that after using Command-Option-Shift-Delete, the internal drive cannot be mounted. If so, this is because your utility (such as SCSIProbe) is only checking for SCSI devices. In this case, try and get an Apple extension called Mount IDE Drive. When installed, it mounts an internal IDE drive even if you have initially bypassed it at startup. This file is no longer needed if you upgrade to System 7.5.3 or later, however, as the necessary code is built into the system software itself.

TAKE NOTE ▶

THE SCSI ID 5 PROBLEM

There have been sporadic reports that at least on some Macintosh models (especially PCI-based Macs), some SCSI devices (especially array or tape devices) may not always work if they are assigned ID number 5. System freezes may occur as a result, and you may even have problems starting up your Mac.

There is a related ID 5 problem with PowerBook 5300s, where a device connected to ID 5 will not work and SCSIProbe reports it as connected to all ID numbers. Other IDs worked fine.

If any of this happens to you, try reassigning the device to another ID number.

SCSI-Related Problems

This section covers cases when you cannot access one or all SCSI devices, often because system freezes or crashes occur at the time of access. In the worst cases, the system crash occurs at startup. Typically, if SCSI problems are the cause of a startup crash, the crash occurs immediately before or after the "Welcome to Macintosh" message

TAKE NOTE ▶

THE WRITE CACHE PROBLEM AND DATA CORRUPTION

There is a problem that occurs with some brands of hard drives (most notably Quantum Fireballs) in some Power Macs (most notably Macintosh 7500, 8500, and 9500 models) whereby the disk data may occasionally get corrupted at the time of shutdown. This will only happen if the drive is an internal drive stored on bus 0 (which is certainly the bus where your drive will be if you only have one internal drive) and is set to be your startup drive.

The problem is due to what is called a *write cache*. With a write cache, the drive instructs the Mac to hold data in an area of RAM (reserved for the cache) with the intention that it be written to the disk later, presumably at a time when the Mac and the drive are less busy. This results in faster access times for the drive. When you select to shut down your Mac, any data currently in the cache and not yet written to the disk is, of course, written to disk before the Mac actually shuts down—at least, this is what is supposed to happen.

What can mistakenly occur instead is that the Mac fails to recognize the action of the write-cache operation. In this case, the write cache may sometimes still be writing data to the drive from the RAM buffer at the time the Mac shuts off. The result is that some data are only partially written to the drive, and so the data winds up being corrupted. This is most likely to affect your Directory files, which may in turn lead to problems starting up or mounting the drive on your next restart.

Fortunately, drives formatted with Apple formatting utilities (such as Drive Setup) do not have this problem, as Apple's driver makes sure the write cache is flushed before the shut-down occurs. It can, however, affect third-party drives. The ultimate solution here is to have the third parties update their utility software to install a driver that prevents this problem; for example, current versions of APS PowerTools include this fix. A less desirable solution is for the third-party driver to disable write caching, which works but will lead to slower performance. Some utilities allow you to select whether to turn the write cache on, while others simply set this in the driver code.

By the way, to find out if your internal drive is a Quantum Fireball, use a utility such as SCSIProbe. It lists this information in its Product column.

Finally, note that this is only one of a variety of cache-related problems that crop up occasionally. For example, Apple has also described a possible data error problem with its internal 1GB IBM drives that had write cache disabled; in this case, using a driver that *enabled* the write cache fixed the problem. Fortunately, this bug was permanently squashed with System 7.5.3 Revision 2.

appears, prior to any extensions loading. If the crash is accompanied by a bomb alert box, the latter probably says that a bus error has occurred.

As mentioned before, other causes can produce similar symptoms. SCSI causes are most likely if the problems occur immediately after you have made some change to your SCSI chain (such as adding a new device).

Fortunately, if you have a relatively simple setup with no more than one or two external SCSI devices, your chances of confronting these problems are sharply reduced. If you do confront these problems, however, you will find solving them to be among the most difficult and frustrating of all Macintosh troubleshooting tasks. Don't be shy about seeking outside help (as covered in Fix-It #18).

Very helpful hint: Always shut off the Macintosh and all SCSI devices before disconnecting or reconnecting any SCSI devices; otherwise, you could damage your hardware. Restart after each change to test its effect.

Make Sure the SCSI Port Is Functioning

If your problem does not prevent a normal startup, checking the SCSI port is a good starting point. Sometimes the SCSI bus stops transferring data correctly; in such cases, all devices on the SCSI chain—with the possible exception of an internal hard drive—no longer function. A variety of causes could be responsible for this, none of which you can directly prevent. To correct this problem, you need to *reset* the bus. Once again, you can do this with utilities such as SCSIProbe. In particular, follow these steps:

1. Open SCSIProbe, and hold down the Option key. The Update button should change to a Reset button.
2. Click the Reset button.

A corrupted Parameter RAM (PRAM) may also cause this type of problem, so try zapping the PRAM.

SEE: • **Fix-It #11 for details on zapping the parameter RAM**

If the problem persists, continue to the next sections.

Check If All SCSI Devices in the Chain Are Turned On

You may think that you are safe from SCSI problems if all the devices in your chain are turned off, but this is not the case. If anything, the opposite is closer to the truth. Similarly, if you plan to use only one device on your chain, don't assume that you need to turn on only that device. Often, *all* connected devices must be on for the chain to function properly.

Ideally, you should turn on all SCSI devices before turning on your Macintosh. If you have already started up, the safest course of action is to shut down, turn on all your SCSI devices, and immediately restart.

Of course, there are exceptions. I have five external SCSI devices connected to my Macintosh; I can turn any or all of them on or off at any time during a session without any problem. You may not be so lucky.

Be Careful When Turning Off a Non-Startup Drive

Despite the preceding advice, you may decide to turn off a mounted external secondary drive before shutting down. Here's how to do this:

1. Drag the hard disk's icon to the Trash. This unmounts the drive, removing its icon from the desktop. The Finder's Put Away command performs the equivalent action. (At this point, the disk drive is still running. You could remount the drive, using SCSIProbe, if you wanted.)
2. Turn the drive off. If you are as lucky as I have been, this does not cause any problems. If you are unlucky, you cannot do this.

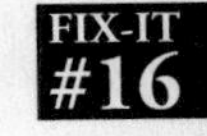

Do not, under any circumstances, turn off a hard drive *before* you drag its icon to the Trash—if you do, *immediately* drag the disk's icon to the Trash. Otherwise, any attempt to use the drive will most often lead to a system freeze or crash!

Similarly, if for any reason the disk icon for a hard disk turns to a shadow icon (similar to what would happen to a floppy disk's icon if you used Command-E to eject the disk), immediately drag the icon to the Trash, then remount it using SCSIProbe.

In general, be careful about turning off any SCSI device (scanner, CD-ROM, or whatever) until after you shut down, because doing so may lead to an immediate system crash.

Disconnect All SCSI Devices

If your problem remains, a logical next diagnostic step is to disconnect the SCSI chain from the Macintosh. To do this, simply shut off all devices, unplug the cord that connects the first device in the chain to the rear of the Macintosh, and restart.

If the problem persists, it is probably not a SCSI problem, so you can reconnect your SCSI chain and look elsewhere. System software problems are likely; check Chapter 5 for a general overview of possible causes.

If the trouble vanishes when the chain is disconnected, a SCSI problem is the probable cause. Although the precise problem may be due to a damaged SCSI device, it is more likely related to how the SCSI devices are connected (cables, ID numbers, or termination). At this point, dealing with SCSI problems becomes something of a black art, but most problems will be solved by checking the steps outlined in the following subsections.

> **TAKE NOTE ▶**
>
> **READ BEFORE YOU CONTINUE WITH THIS FIX-IT**
>
> For the remaining sections of this Fix-It, the solutions apply mainly to situations where you have made a change to the SCSI chain configuration just prior to the onset of your problem. For example, it is unlikely that an ID conflict could be the cause of a new problem if you have not made any recent change to the ID numbers of your devices or added any new devices to your chain (though I suppose you could have accidentally changed the ID number of a device while trying to turn it on or off, or whatever).

Make Sure No Two SCSI Devices Have the Same ID Number

If two or more SCSI devices on the chain have the same ID number, you have an ID conflict. If one of the conflicting devices is a hard drive, a likely symptom is the appearance of multiple copies of the disk icon, scattered across the desktop. System freezes and crashes are likely to follow and loss of data on your disk is a real risk; in other cases, the device simply does not mount. In any case, correct this problem immediately!

1. Turn off your Macintosh and all SCSI devices.
2. Check each device's ID number by examining the location on the device where the number is listed. If you cannot locate it, check the device's manual to learn where its ID number is listed.
3. If you find a conflict, change the ID number to correct it. Remember, all external devices should have numbers between 1 and 6.
4. Reconnect SCSI devices to the Macintosh (if necessary) and restart the Macintosh.

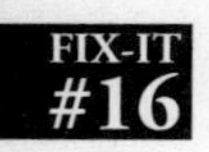

Remember to consider the ID number of any internal SCSI devices, beyond the internal hard drive, that may be present. For example, since an internal CD-ROM drive should have an ID of 3, an external device cannot use the same ID number.

While the Macintosh is on, a utility such as SCSIProbe should be able to tell you what these ID numbers are. Don't rely on it to show an ID conflict, however, as it may get too confused by the conflict to sort things out. Nevertheless, you can use SCSIProbe when you are done with your ID changes to confirm that all is now well. SCSIProbe lists the ID location of each mounted device—if each device has a unique ID number, the conflict is probably resolved.

Another way to see a SCSI device's ID number, if it is a device that mounts on the desktop, is to select the desktop icon for the device and then select Get Info. The Where listing often (though not always) lists the device's ID number.

Make Sure All SCSI Devices Are Properly Terminated

Improper termination may leave you unable to access any of the SCSI devices in your chain, but it does no permanent harm to your hardware. Correctly adjusting the termination should get things working again.

As first explained in the "Why to Do It" section of this Fix-It, the last device in an external SCSI chain should be terminated, and sometimes, the first external device needs to be terminated as well. Generally, no other external SCSI devices should be terminated. If your chain is not set up this way, you should add or remove termination as appropriate (see "Technically Speaking: SCSI Termination Up Close," for details). These rules have exceptions, however, so be prepared to do some experimenting.

TAKE NOTE ▶

HARDWARE HELP FOR SOLVING SCSI PROBLEMS

A technology called Digital Active Termination (DAT) promises to put an end to many SCSI-related nightmares. For example, Allied Peripheral Systems (APS) makes a device called SCSI Sentry that uses DAT. It plugs into your SCSI chain like an external terminator. Drives can also come with DAT built in. In either case, DAT should take care of almost all termination problems, regardless of what other external or internal terminators may or may not be in place. This can mean an end to checking terminators, rearranging device order, switching cables, and other SCSI voodoo. I have not had much cause to test the effectiveness of these DAT devices, but others I have spoken to swear by them.

Some of these DAT devices even allow you to connect or disconnect SCSI devices without having to worry about first shutting the power off.

With more products like this, solving SCSI problems should soon be a lot simpler and quicker to solve.

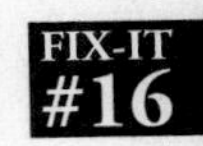

Reconnect and Rearrange the Connection Order of SCSI Devices

If the previous solutions have failed to solve your SCSI problem, it's time to delve still deeper into the black art of SCSI problem solving.

If you have more than one external SCSI device, begin by reconnecting them one at a time. If necessary, remove and reconnect them in various combinations (such as only Device 1 connected, then only Device 2 connected, then both connected).

TECHNICALLY SPEAKING ▶

SCSI TERMINATION UP CLOSE

Most SCSI devices today use external termination. External terminators are plugs that you insert into the unused port of the SCSI device; they can be easily removed and placed on another device if you need to change a termination setup. Some SCSI devices are internally terminated, however, which means the terminator is built into the machine.

Usually there is a way to remove or disable the internal terminator, if necessary. Sometimes it may be as simple as pressing a switch on the rear of the SCSI device. More often, though, it requires accessing the inside of the case in some way and is thus less convenient than removing an external terminator. In the worst cases, there is no way to remove the built-in terminator. This is undesirable, as it typically requires that the internally terminated device be the last device in the chain (which, if you have two internally terminated devices, can become an impossible problem). Refer to the manuals for your SCSI devices to learn if your device is internally terminated and, if so, how to remove the terminator.

Similarly, since exact termination requirements can vary among different models of Macintosh, check with the documentation that came with your Mac for more precise information. Ultimately, you may need to seek outside help here. In the meantime, here is a brief checklist of points to bear in mind:

- Both ends of a SCSI chain should be terminated.
- Macs with an internal drive are typically already terminated. You only need to worry about terminating the far end of the chain.
- If your Macintosh does not have an internal drive (a rare case these days), the Mac may or may not be considered terminated, depending on the particular model. This difference is irrelevant if you are adding only one external SCSI device—just make sure the added device has a terminator. If you add two or more SCSI devices to a Macintosh that is not terminated (and does not have an internal drive), though, both the first and the last device in the chain have to be terminated.
- Most PowerBooks are unusual in that they are not terminated even if they have an internal drive. Thus, even if only one external device is connected, you may need two terminators, one on each end of the device.
- If you have an internally terminated device at the end of a chain, you should not also add an external terminator.
- Typically, there should be no termination in the middle of a chain. Thus, if you have an internally terminated device as a middle device in a chain, you should typically remove the internal terminator. Alternatively, you can move it to be the last device in the chain.
- Most terminator plugs are gray in color. A black terminator plug is only for use with SCSI port on the Macintosh IIfx or the LaserWriter IINTX.

In reality, these rules are often broken. In particular, for short chains (one or two devices with short-length cable), the system may work even without a terminator at the end of the chain (even if your Mac's manual says one is needed); for long chains, a third terminator in the middle of the chain may be required. (Fortunately, in this regard, most external terminators have an outlet on their rear side where another cable can be plugged in, thereby permitting the chain to continue beyond the termination point.) So don't be afraid to experiment—if you are having problems that you think may be solved by adding or removing a terminator, try it. Some people may warn you against this, fearing that turning on an improperly terminated system can permanently harm your hardware, but I have never found that to be the case.

Also rearrange the order in which devices are connected along the chain (such as Device 1 followed by Device 2, and then reverse the order). For obscure reasons, a device may work if it is earlier in the chain than another device but not later in the chain or vice versa. The documentation that came with a given device may offer advice; for example, it may say that the device must be the first in the chain (I hope you don't have two such devices!). Always remember to adjust termination, as needed, when rearranging devices.

If rearranging various devices fails to help, try swapping cables among them. This sometimes works even though the switched cables seem identical. Even shifting ID numbers may help, as long as you make sure that no two devices wind up with the same number. For example, some people claim that it is better to have ID numbers in ascending order as you move to devices further away from the Macintosh.

By the way, the two SCSI ports on your devices are functionally identical. It doesn't matter which port you use as the incoming or outgoing connection.

Overall, explore by trial and error, rearranging until you find a combination that works. There are no hard-and-fast guidelines.

TAKE NOTE ▶

THE LONG AND THE SHORT OF CABLES

Cables that are too long or too short can prevent the normal functioning of the devices connected to a SCSI chain. The standard size for cables is about 18 inches to 3 feet. If you are using other lengths (particularly longer ones) and you are having SCSI problems, try switching to a standard length cable and see if that solves the problem. SCSI problems also become more likely when the combined length of all cables exceeds 19 feet, so try to keep under this length. Inferior-quality cables are another common source of problems. Finally, you may have a defective cable. In any case, if a problem seems specific to a cable, try replacing it.

Confront Cable Connection Confusion

If you start rearranging or disconnecting SCSI devices, or whenever you add a new SCSI device, you may find that you do not have the proper cables to accomplish your goal.

This is because there are two main types of SCSI outlets: a 25-pin outlet (in the back of the Macintosh and on some SCSI devices), and a 50-pin outlet (most common on external SCSI devices). Thus, to attach a typical external drive to a Macintosh, you need a cable with a 25-pin plug on one end and a 50-pin plug on the other end. As you add devices, however, you may find that you need a cable with a 50-pin plug on both ends or a 25-pin plug on both ends.

Even worse, none of these cables will work directly with PowerBooks, which have an altogether differently sized SCSI outlet that requires a special matching cable!

Solving these cable problems typically requires you to purchase the correctly configured SCSI cable. In some cases, you can instead buy an adapter that converts a port from one type to another.

Finally, there is Iomega's Jaz drive, which uses a new 50-pin port that is different from the one used by most other Mac devices. You will need a special adapter and cable to use the Jaz on your Mac, and this may limit your ability to attach other devices to the SCSI chain. Getting a Jaz drive from a vendor other than Iomega (for instance, by purchasing an APS Jaz drive) can avoid this problem, because the vendor can package the Jaz with a standard Mac SCSI port. Alternatively, Iomega makes a PCI card that does support this new port. With the drive connected to the card, rather than to the SCSI chain, you also get faster (Fast SCSI-2) performance.

SEE: • **Chapter 11 for details on connecting SCSI devices to PowerBooks**

Running with Devices Disconnected

Even if you never find a chain combination that works when *all* of your devices are hooked up, you may be able to get your chain working with only some of your SCSI devices connected. Obviously, this is a less than ideal solution, but it may be the best you can do for the moment—and it is probably a lot better than the alternative of having nothing working.

In the meantime, seek outside help, starting with the manufacturers of your SCSI devices. They may be aware of some way to combine components that you have not yet tried, a way that may yet be successful for connecting all of your devices.

Check for Damage

If all of the above suggestions have failed, and the problem seems specific to one SCSI device, the device may be damaged. Take it in to see if it needs to be repaired or replaced. If the problem occurs across all SCSI devices, the Macintosh itself (most likely a component on the logic board) may be damaged. Software damage, however, is also a possible cause. In particular, for hard drives, there may be software damage to the device driver, the Directory, or related "low-level" areas of the disk. These can often be repaired using a disk repair utility such as MacTools or Norton Utilities.

TAKE NOTE ▶

FIREWIRE: THE END OF SCSI?

In 1997, Apple will be introducing a new technology to its Macs. Called FireWire, it is essentially a replacement for SCSI, over which it has numerous advantages: It doesn't require ID numbers or special termination; you can attach almost an unlimited number of devices without having to worry about the cable length; and it is much faster. By 1998, it should be standard on all Macs. With luck, a future edition of *Sad Macs* will no longer need this entire Fix-It on SCSI problems!

For related information

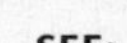

SEE:
- **Fix-It #1 on hardware and software incompatibilities**
- **Fix-It #12 on damaged disk device drivers**
- **Fix-It #13 on fixing damaged disks**
- **Fix-It #17 on hardware repairs**
- **Chapter 5 on startup and disk problems**
- **Chapter 11 on SCSI connections and PowerBooks**

Fix-It #17: Check If Hardware Repairs or Replacements Are Needed

QUICK SUMMARY ▶

Switch problem peripherals to another Macintosh to test for the source of the problem. Make sure cards and memory are properly inserted on the Macintosh's main logic board. Check for possible problems due to defective or incorrectly connected cables. Use specialized software to diagnose your hardware. Try other hardware tests as your skills permit.

When to do it:

- If the Macintosh doesn't turn on at all.
- If the sad-Mac icon appears at startup (especially if there are no F's in the code numbers below the sad Mac). This symptom is most often caused by defective SIMMs.
- If a Macintosh does not play a normal startup tone when you turn it on, and it subsequently refuses to start up. This is again most likely a SIMM-related problem.
- If you get frequent and apparently unrelated system crashes, especially Type 10 or 11 errors. This, too, is most likely a SIMM-related problem.
- If a floppy drive cannot read any disks you insert into it.
- If your monitor display shrinks in size periodically or has a wobbly image. This is often a power supply problem.
- If any peripheral device (monitor, printer, drive, mouse, keyboard, or whatever) is not working as expected (such as a monitor screen that remains constantly dark, or a cursor that does not respond to mouse movements).
- If you have any problem with the Macintosh or a peripheral device and you have exhausted all other possible causes, as described throughout this book.

Why to do it:

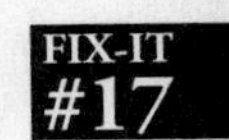

This book is primarily about problems you can solve at your desktop, mostly just by using the information provided here and some appropriate software. This book is definitely *not* about making hardware repairs—when it comes to these problems, I typically advise you to take your Mac to an authorized repair shop.

So what, you may ask, is a Fix-It about hardware problems doing here? The answer is twofold. First, some problems seem like hardware problems when they really aren't, or vice versa. So, at the very least, it's helpful to know how to diagnose a true hardware problem. (Having an accurate diagnosis will also aid in your conversations with a repair technician, should a repair be needed.) The second answer is that some hardware "repairs" are so easy and minimal to do that they are worth knowing no matter what the emphasis of this book may be. Similarly, by clearly identifying whether a problem is or is not hardware related, these techniques can save you hundreds of dollars in unneeded trips to a repair shop. These are the goals of this Fix-It.

TECHNICALLY SPEAKING ▶

WORKING INSIDE THE MACINTOSH

Some hardware checks and simple repairs require opening up the Macintosh's case; these include swapping an internal drive, inserting or removing NuBus cards, and adding or removing SIMMs/DIMMs. No matter what you intend to do once you're inside, always unplug the Macintosh before opening its case.

For a few models (especially the compact Macintoshes), opening the case can be somewhat difficult for an untrained person to do—if you are not careful, it can even be dangerous. In particular, opening up a compact Macintosh exposes the built-in monitor. Some components associated with the monitor maintain a high voltage even when the machine is unplugged, so if you mishandle these components, you risk a serious electrical shock.

At the other extreme, for many models of desktop Macs, opening up the case is quite easy and safe to do; the top of the case simply snaps off (sometimes you must remove a single screw). The latest models of PowerBooks are similarly designed to make access to its inside easier than in previous models. There is no danger to yourself with working inside any of these models. The more real danger (which applies to compact Macs as well), however, is that you could damage the internal components. One common way this could happen is via your own static electricity, so discharge this static electricity by touching a metal object before you start working inside any Macintosh.

This Fix-It gives only rough guidelines for working inside the Macintosh. If you want to add or replace parts, you can usually get the details when you make a relevant purchase. For example, if you purchase memory, they should come with detailed instructions on how to install them. Ask about this before you make your purchase; if these instructions are not sufficient, seek outside help. Otherwise, you can always pay to have a service technician do the installation.

Personally, I consider myself to be totally nonskilled when it comes to making any sort of hardware repair. Yet, over the years, I have replaced memory, swapped internal hard drives, installed an internal modem in a PowerBook, and more. Believe me, if I can do it, so can you.

By the way, a study in contrasts: When Apple came out with its line of PCI-based Macs, the two most popular models were the 7500/7600 and the 8500. In terms of the ease of access to the inside of these machines, they could not be more different. The 7500 is a breeze to access; it was clearly designed by people who wanted to make this as easy to do as possible. The 8500 is a nightmare; just opening it once is enough to convince you never to try it again.

What to do:

This Fix-It is divided into two topics: diagnosing hardware problems, and repairing selected hardware problems.

Diagnose Hardware Problems

Preliminary Checks

If you have reached this Fix-It as a reference from an earlier chapter, you have probably already taken some of the preliminary steps described here—in fact, you have probably taken a host of other steps as well. Generally, unless your symptoms specifically indicate a hardware problem, you should try potential software-based solutions before assuming you have a hardware problem.

Still, a few hardware checks are so simple and basic that it often pays to try them *before* doing anything else, not after you have ruled out all other possibilities. For example, if any or all of your devices seem dead, obvious first things to check include the following:

1. Make sure a device's on/off switch is on.
2. Make sure all cables are plugged in tightly and in their correct port.
3. Make sure devices are connected to an outlet and that, if the outlet is connected to a wall switch, the wall switch is on.
4. If you have a surge suppressor, make sure the fuse is reset.

Use Hardware Diagnostic Utilities

If your symptoms indicate a possible hardware problem, you need not wait for a service technician to confirm your suspicions. Instead, use one of several software utilities designed for the nonexpert that specialize in diagnosing your hardware. These include the following:

- **TechTool Pro, MacEKG, or Peace of Mind**

  These are currently the best available diagnostic utilities. MacEKG and TechTool Pro are both made by MicroMat. MacEKG works as a control panel, checking your Mac each time you start up and comparing its performance to previous checks. TechTool Pro is a separate application that can perform a more extended and potentially more time-consuming set of tasks (don't confuse this program with the freeware TechTool, which has *none* of the hardware checks of TechTool Pro). Peace of Mind is a separate application that you run as needed.

  While these utilities are easy to use, they are likely to give you information whose meaning you will not completely understand. Don't worry about this too much; they can at least help you pinpoint the source of a problem (such as the logic board versus the disk drive), even if the exact cause is not clear. Also, the utility's manual will often provide more details.

Snooper, another excellent diagnostic utility described in the first edition of this book, is unfortunately no longer available. Apple Personal Diagnostics, described in the second edition, is yet another diagnostic utility that has been abandoned.

- **Gauge Series** This collection of freeware utilities from Newer Technology can determine a few obscure but important aspects of your hardware. For example, Cache-22 tells you if you have an L2 RAM cache installed and, if so, what size it is. Clockometer tells you the speed of your CPU (though most model names now include the speed of the CPU, such as 7600/132 for a 132Mz speed, the original CPU may have been upgraded to a faster one; if so, Clockometer will let you know).
- **Other utilities** There are utilities whose sole function is to check for problems with a floppy disk drive. They typically also include a drive cleaning kit that may actually be able to "repair" some floppy drive problems. Two such utilities are DriveTech and MacDrive Probe. Most users do not need a separate utility just to check for floppy drive problems, but if you are subject to persistent hassles with your floppy drive(s), they may be worth a look.

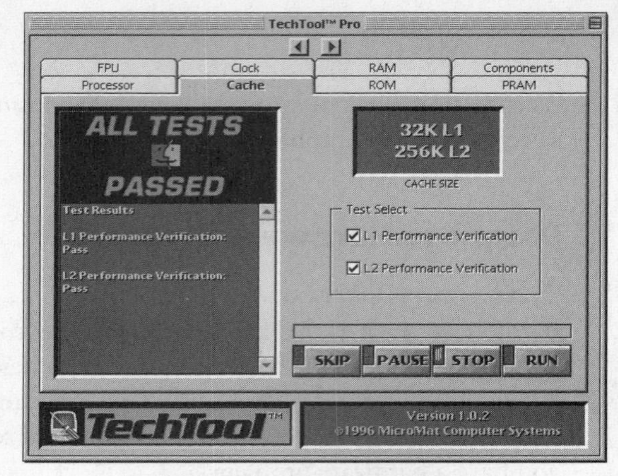

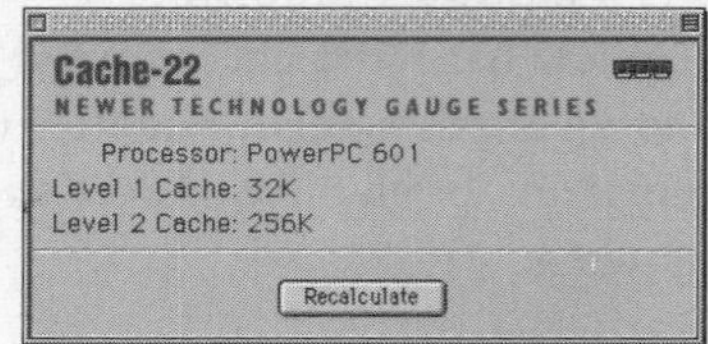

Figure F17-1 *TechTool Pro (top) and Gauge Series' Cache-22, both showing the size of a Mac's L1 and L2 cache (see "Take Note: L2 RAM Cache Modules," later in this Fix-It, for more on what L2 cache is all about).*

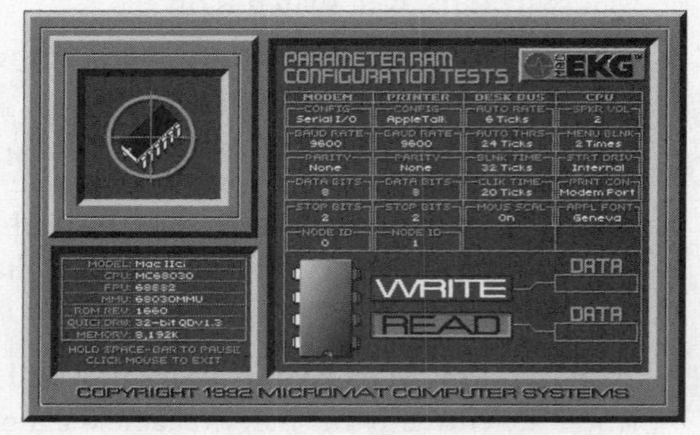

Figure F17-2 *MacEKG, another type of hardware diagnostic utility.*

Some hard drive formatting utilities, especially FWB's Hard Disk ToolKit, include an array of diagnostic options for your hard drive(s) that typically exceed what other diagnostic utilities can do in this area. Another utility like this is MicroNet's DiskWorks.

Norton Utilities can do some diagnostic checking via its System Info module.

Other freeware or shareware utilities also abound. For example, a freeware utility called RAM Check checks for defective memory. Other utilities, such as TimeDrive, can specifically check the performance of your hard drive. MacBench and Speedometer perform a more general set of benchmark tests, primarily checking

performance speed. Profile utilities such as Apple System Profiler (see Fix-It #18) are a quick way to get a profile of system information.

SEE: • **Fix-It #18 for more on using utilities to profile your system**

The main limitation of all of these hardware diagnostic utilities is that using them assumes that you can successfully start up your Macintosh. This can be a real Catch-22. For example, how can you run a utility to check for defective memory if the defective SIMMs/DIMMs are preventing you from starting up your Mac? (You can't.) Second, and not surprisingly, these utilities cannot repair any of the hardware problems they discover.

Still, these utilities can be useful as a preventative measure, or when the problem is not so serious as to prevent using the utility. Often defective hardware initially produces only minor symptoms, as the component continues to function in a "weakened" state. Major symptoms appear later, when the component fails altogether. These programs can help you detect impending disaster, when the symptoms are still so minor that the Mac still appears to be running fine. Other symptoms are intermittent, which means you can check the Mac on those occasions when the symptom is temporarily "on vacation."

Except as described in the next section of the Fix-It, if these programs do spot any hardware problems, my general advice is to take the problem component (or the whole system, if necessary) in for repairs—or at least call the vendor in question, usually Apple, for advice.

BY THE WAY ▶

A DIAGNOSTIC UTILITY FALSE ALARM

Hard drive diagnostic tests may fail on PCI-based Macs, indicating a problem where none really exists. The culprit is the hard drive spin-down feature of the Energy Saver control panel. If the drive spins down during the test, it will indicate a failure. To avoid this, make sure you select "Never" from the Sleep Setup option in the control panel before performing any test.

Repair Selected Hardware Problems

If you have a likely hardware problem, a critical step is to figure out which hardware component is the culprit. Otherwise, for example, you could waste a good deal of time and money bringing your entire Macintosh system in for diagnosis and repair when the problem is just a mouse that needs to be replaced. Similarly, if you are having a printing problem, it helps to know whether the printer or the Macintosh is the source of the problem. Sometimes this may not be easy to distinguish.

Using the previously described hardware diagnostic utilities can sometimes help you make these determinations. Otherwise, disentangling these possibilities requires applying the general strategies outlined in Chapter 3. The most common strategy is to swap peripheral components temporarily with a second Macintosh to assess if the peripheral device or the Mac is the source of the problem; similarly, you should swap cables to check for damaged cables. Specific examples follow.

One important reminder: Turn off the Macintosh and all components before attempting any hardware-related repairs. Better yet, unplug them from the wall outlet. Do not even disconnect or reconnect cables, especially SCSI cables, when the Macintosh and/or peripherals are on; doing this can send a voltage shock to the Macintosh that could damage the machine (though see "Take Note: Hardware Help for Solving SCSI Problems," in Fix-It #16, for a partial exception to this rule).

Hard Drives and Other SCSI Devices

If an external SCSI device refuses to mount or otherwise does not work (and solutions as detailed in Chapter 5 and Fix-It #16 have failed to solve the problem), attach it to another Macintosh. If it exhibits the same symptoms on the second Macintosh, the SCSI device is probably at fault. Take the device in to see if it can be repaired or needs to be replaced. First, though, try swapping SCSI cables between the two machines; sometimes it turns out that just the cable is defective.

For suspected hardware problems with an internal hard drive, swapping drives between two machines requires opening up the Macintosh case. Once the case is open, to remove the drive you will have to unplug the drive's connecting cables and then pry the drive free of its securing brackets. This is a fairly simple operation that usually requires no tools. Still, if you have never done this before, you should probably get some outside help before attempting it.

One particular hard drive problem, described in more detail in Chapter 5, is called *stiction.* In this case, the drive mechanism gets stuck at startup and never starts spinning; as a result, the disk cannot be accessed in any way. A slap to the side of the drive case may get the drive going, but this is a temporary solution, because the symptoms get worse with time. If you succeed in accessing the drive, copy any critical data to other disks, then buy a new drive—your old one is a goner.

Some hard drive repair facilities specialize in recovering data from a crashed disk, even if the disk cannot be repaired. Seek these facilities out if you have important data that is not backed up on a disk that has failed. The best-known and most respected of these repair services is DriveSavers; they can be reached at 415-883-4232.

SEE: • Chapter 5 and Fix-It #16 for more on SCSI devices, including CD-ROM drives

Floppy Drives

If the Macintosh claims that a formatted disk is "unreadable" or "is not a Macintosh disk" (and you have checked other possible causes, as described in Chapter 5 and Fix-It #15), you may have a defective floppy disk drive. To test this out, insert other disks into the drive.

Does the drive refuse to recognize all disks, or just certain ones? If it refuses to recognize all disks, check to see if another floppy disk drive recognizes those same disks. If the disks cause problems with all drives, the disks are the source of the problem. If a second drive properly mounts the disks, however, the original drive may be defective, and so you will need to take it in for repair. A hardware diagnostic utility, especially one specifically designed to check floppy disks (such as DriveTech, as mentioned in the previous section of this Fix-It), can help determine this.

Related points to consider include offspeed and misaligned drives, intermittent mounting problems, cleaning dust from the disk drive, a disk not automatically inserted, and a disk stuck in the drive. These are detailed below.

- **Offspeed and misaligned drives**
  Sometimes, because of minor variations in spinning speed or head alignment among different drives, a floppy drive can read disks that it formatted itself but not those formatted by other drives. Similarly, other drives cannot read disks formatted with the offspeed or misaligned drive. If this seems to be the case, take the drive in for repair.

  In one special case, however, floppy drives in certain models of Macintosh (particularly AV models and Power Macs) may have trouble reading mass-duplicated 800K floppy disks. This problem cannot be repaired. Instead, try one of the following workaround solutions: start up with extensions off, zap the parameter RAM (PRAM), or use another Macintosh to copy the data on the 800K disk to an HD disk.

- **Intermittent mounting problems**
  Sometimes, if you continue to eject and reinsert a disk, the drive may eventually accept and mount the disk correctly. Although the problem may be caused by software damage on the disk, it is also a potential sign of damage to the drive itself (especially if many disks show this symptom). In this case, do not ignore the problem, because it is only likely to get worse. Again, take the drive in for repair.

- **All floppy disks are locked**
  If the Mac indicates that virtually every floppy disk you insert into a floppy drive is locked—even though you know they are not—it is probably a problem with the floppy drive itself. In particular, the pin that goes through the hole of a locked disk is stuck in a way that makes all disks seem locked. You may be able to fix this by opening up the drive and cleaning the gunk out that is making the pin stick, but I'd guess most of you would rather take the drive in for professional servicing.

- **Cleaning dust from the disk drive**
  Because the slot used to insert a disk is uncovered, dirt and dust tend to collect inside a floppy drive. A dirty drive can be the cause of all sorts of unusual symptoms, some of which may seem to have little or nothing to do with the drive.

  To clean the drive, place a portable vacuum cleaner near the disk drive opening, then turn it on briefly to try to draw out the dirt. With luck, this may get things humming again. Disk drive cleaning kits (as mentioned in the previous section on diagnostic utilities) may also help. Otherwise, take the drive to a service technician for cleaning and possible repair.

- **Disk not automatically inserted**
  Older Macintosh floppy disk drives had a feature such that when you inserted a disk part of the way, the drive grabbed it and inserted it the rest of the way. As a cost-saving measure, newer SuperDrives (referred to as "manual inject" drives) no longer do this. All PowerBooks and newer desktop Macs have this type of drive. There is nothing wrong here; you just have to use up an extra half a calorie to get the disk to insert.

- **Disk stuck in the drive**
  Most problems with a disk that will not eject are software related. Possible hardware causes, however, include a disk label that has come loose and is preventing the eject or a disk's shutter slide that is bent. In most of these cases, you can try to eject the disk by inserting a straightened paper clip into the hole next to the drive opening. If even this fails, you will need to take the drive in for repair.

  SEE: • **Chapter 5 for more details on different ways to try to eject a disk**

Keyboard and Mouse/Trackball/TrackPad

If your keyboard seems dead but your mouse functions fine (or vice versa), switch the keyboard (or mouse) with one from another computer. If the second keyboard or mouse works fine on your computer, the original is probably defective. Usually, these items are not repairable and need to be replaced. Some problems may be due to a defective keyboard cable, however, or a problem with the ADB ports on the Macintosh. In particular, check for the following:

- **Keyboard cable okay?**
  Be sure to swap the keyboard cable separately from the keyboard itself; sometimes just the cable is defective. If the problem disappears when you switch cables, replace your original cable.

  For the Macintosh Plus and earlier models, the keyboard is connected to the Macintosh via a cable that resembles the curly cord used with telephones. If you discover that it needs replacement, do not try an ordinary telephone cord—it is not the same.

- **ADB ports okay?**
  The ports that connect the keyboard and mouse to the Macintosh (on all models from the Macintosh SE to the current models) are called Apple Desktop Bus (ADB) ports. Many models of Macintosh have two of these ports. Because only one may be defective, try switching cables to see if a particular port is associated with the problem. If so, you have a defective port, and you need to have it repaired.

  Occasionally, an ADB-related problem may be caused by software (for example, a specific application that somehow conflicts with ADB port communication). Ideally, such applications come with special fixes (usually in the form of an extension, such as one called ADB Fix) that are used to get around this problem. Unfortunately, sometimes the presence of such extensions can be the cause of the problem. In this case, the simple solution is to discard the extension.

- **A false freeze?**
  On many Macintosh models, you can choose to attach your mouse to either the ADB port on the rear of the Macintosh or the one on the side of the keyboard.

  If you attach the mouse to the side of the keyboard, and the keyboard or keyboard cable is defective, then *both* the mouse and the keyboard will cease to function. This may seem to resemble a system freeze (as described in Chapter 4), but it is really a hardware problem. You can usually spot a "false freeze" because, with defective

hardware, the cursor does not respond to the mouse even in the earliest stages of the startup sequence. In general, if the problem recurs no matter what software techniques you try, suspect a false freeze. Again, the simple solution is to replace the defective cable (or keyboard).

- **A false alarm? A beeping occurs whenever you press a key on the keyboard**
  If you hear a beeping sound whenever you hit a key on your keyboard and no character appears on your screen, you have turned on the Slow Keys feature of the Easy Access control panel. This is not a hardware problem; the character will appear if you hold down the key long enough. If the control panel is installed, this feature is turned on by holding down the Return key for more than five seconds. Turning it off will fix the problem—this control panel is designed for people with disabilities. Most other users should simply trash this control panel to avoid this problem in the future.

BY THE WAY ▶

ARE INDIVIDUAL KEYS DEFECTIVE?

Sometimes a problem with a keyboard is limited only to specific keys. A quick way to check for this is to use Apple's Key Caps desk accessory. Press the suspected defective key; if the matching screen image of the key darkens, then the key is okay. Conversely, if there is a key in the Key Caps display that is darkened before you press it, this is a stuck key. Depending on what key is stuck, this can cause a variety of different symptoms (imagine, for example, if the Mac thinks the Command key is always depressed!).

- **Cursor doesn't respond to mouse/trackball movements**
  The inside of the mouse (or trackball), where the rubber ball lies, collects dust and dirt. Eventually, this debris may prevent the rollers inside the mouse/trackball from turning properly, and so the mouse/trackball will respond intermittently, with jerky movements, or not at all. Fortunately, you can easily clean the inside of a mouse or trackball.

  Clean the mouse/trackball. On most mice, you can press on the ring that surrounds the rubber ball and rotate it counterclockwise from its locked to an open position. Turn over the mouse and let the ring and the ball fall out into your other hand. On some mouse models, the ring does not rotate; it slides out and snaps back in. In either case, once the mouse is open, blow briefly and strongly into the mouse to remove any loose dust. Use a cotton swab dipped in isopropyl alcohol to clean the rollers, and use tweezers if necessary to remove stuck-on dirt. Reverse the steps to reassemble the mouse, making sure the ball is dry and free of dirt.

  PowerBooks (other than the newer models that use the TrackPad) have a trackball; as with the mouse, this ball also may need to be cleaned. To do this, turn the ring around the trackball counter clockwise until it pops out, then lift out the ball.

  Black ball? Some mice have inherent problems that prevent them from responding reliably to mouse movement, especially if you use a mouse pad. Mice with a black (rather than gray) ball are particularly known to have this problem. If you have this type of mouse, try not using a mouse pad. Otherwise, see about getting your mouse replaced.

TrackPad unresponsive or erratic For a TrackPad (as found on newer PowerBook models) that is unresponsive, try the following: (1) Put your PowerBook to sleep by closing the display, then wake it up by pressing any key on the keyboard; (2) press the PowerBook's reset button, which is usually on the back of the computer; and (3) zap the PRAM.

If the cursor is jumpy or erratic when you try to move it, make sure you are touching the TrackPad with just your finger (and not also your hand or wrist, for example). Also, wipe off any moisture that may have collected on the TrackPad. For certain PowerBook models (such as the 190 and 1400), installing Apple's TrackPad Climate Control extension will reduce or eliminate these erratic cursor movements.

- **Numeric keypad doesn't work**
  Some applications do not respond to numeric keypad input unless Num Lock is on. To turn it on, on most standard keyboards, press the Num Lock/Clear button on the numeric keypad. The Num Lock light above the keypad should now come on, and you should now be able to use the numeric keypad. Other programs do not respond to numeric keypad input no matter what you do; there is no fix for this.
- **Adjustable keyboard problems**
  Apple's adjustable keyboard does not work properly unless you install special software that is provided on a disk that comes with the keyboard. Even when it is installed properly, some applications—particularly games—may not work with the keyboard. A freeware extension called ADB Keyboard INIT may help solve some of these problems.

BY THE WAY ▶

A DEFECTIVE MOUSE PREVENTS A MAC FROM STARTING UP

As described in Chapter 5, sometimes a disk icon with a question mark inside it will appear at startup. The startup sequence halts at this point. This problem is usually caused by the Mac's failure to find a hard disk with a System Folder on it, or by a damaged hard disk. I am aware of one unusual case, however, where this was caused by a defective mouse. One clue here was that this Mac would not even start up with a startup floppy disk; the disk was just ejected. When a replacement mouse was connected, everything worked fine. Go figure.

Monitor I: No Display or Dimmed Display

If a monitor shows no sign of life or is unusually dim when you turn on your Macintosh, you should determine whether the problem is with the monitor, the connecting cables, the video display card (if one is used), or the Macintosh itself. Diagnosing these problems is generally easier if you have a Mac that uses an external monitor. In any case, check the following:

- **Adjust brightness and contrast**
  If your monitor has brightness and contrast adjustment knobs, buttons, or software controls, make sure that they are not set so low as to prevent you from seeing the image.

- **Check if the monitor is turned on**
  If your monitor has a small light on its face that lights up when the monitor is on, check this light. If it is off, it means the monitor is off. In any case, check the monitor's on/off switch, because most monitors have an on/off switch that is independent of the Macintosh. If it is off, turn it on, and your problems should be over.

- **Check if you are using an Energy Saver extension**
  If you have one of Apple's several different varieties of Energy Saver control panels (different ones are needed for different Mac models), it may be set to automatically turn off the screen display after a specified idle period. If this happens, the monitor is still on, and the display will return a short time after you move the mouse or press a key (you may hear a beeping sound before the display returns).

- **Check if connecting cables are working and correctly connected**
  In most cases, a monitor connects to a Macintosh with two cables: one carries the display image information and the other carries electrical power. Make sure both are connected. As with all peripherals, also check if the cables are defective by swapping them with a matching cable from another Macintosh, if one is available. Replace defective cables.

- **Check the video display card**
  The source of some video problems is inside the Macintosh, not the monitor. For starters, some monitors are connected to the Macintosh via a separate video display card, which is typically located in one of the NuBus or PCI slots on the main logic board of the Macintosh (see "Technically Speaking: Macintosh Slots: NuBus vs. PCI," later in this Fix-It). If you set up your system yourself, you would know if you had used such a card. If you do use a display card, it may be defective or improperly inserted.

  To check this, you need to open up the case of the Macintosh. Once it is open, remove the video card (after disconnecting it from the cable). Check for any bent wires, straightening any that you find. Reinsert the card, making sure it is firmly lodged in its correct slot. If this doesn't work, and if you still believe that the card is the source of your problem, don't immediately assume that the card is defective. Try inserting the card into another slot; sometimes this solves the problem. If so, you may have a defective slot. In this case, even if everything else is working okay and you don't need to use the defective slot, I'd still recommend taking the Macintosh in for repairs.

- **Check more generally for problems with the Macintosh**
  If all of the previous steps have failed to help, find another Macintosh and hook up your monitor to it. If the monitor works, some component inside your Macintosh is the problem, probably the main logic board. Conversely, if the monitor does not work on the second Macintosh, the monitor is the defective component. In either case, take your faulty equipment in for repair.

- **Special case: PowerBook display problems**
  PowerBooks have brightness and/or contrast buttons, as do desktop Macintosh monitors. Check these if your screen is too dim. PowerBooks typically also have a feature called *screen dimming* that does exactly what its name implies; if you are unaware of

this, it may seem like a hardware problem. Also, don't forget that most PowerBooks are set to automatically go to sleep after a specified period of idle activity. Further, on active-matrix screens, spots on your screen may be due to defective pixels. On passive-matrix screens, a disappearing cursor may be due to something called *ghosting*. All of these problems are discussed in more detail in Chapter 11.

- **Special case: The "sync-on-green" problem for AV and Power Macintoshes**
  Sync-on-green is a term used to describe the fact that a special "video synchronization signal" (which is needed for a monitor to work with a Macintosh) is sent to the monitor together with the green color signal. This has been the default method used by almost all color-capable Macintoshes. Recent models of Macintosh handle the sync signal differently, however, including the LC III, AV Macs, and Power Macs. Because of this difference, some older non-Apple monitors cannot work with these newer Macintosh models. There is no solution for this other than to get a different monitor.

  Apple's Basic Color Monitor extension corrects for overly green screen color specific to the Apple Basic Color Monitor (and some non-Apple VGA monitors) when connected to some Quadra and Centris Macs.

  Some Power Computing Macs have a control panel option (such as in the Twin Turbo control panel) to turn sync-on-green off. If your monitor has a green tinge, check to see if this option is on; if it is, turn it off.

  If your monitor includes software that lets you turn off sync-on-green as an option, you should do so.

- **Special case: AppleVision monitors**
  Apple's AppleVision monitors, especially the AppleVision 1710 and 1710AV, have had so many hardware-related problems that I could probably write an entire book just on this topic. Here are three examples: (1) If you have an AppleVision monitor that makes a repeated popping sound when it is in sleep mode, you probably have an early version of the 1710AV. Apple will replace it for you (as long as they still have some in stock), so call 1-800-SOS-APPL. (2) If you have an AppleVision monitor whose screen stays black after recalibration of its color, this may be fixed by special AppleVision Recovery software that Apple may send you. Zapping the PRAM and/or unplugging the monitor may sometimes help. Again, call 800-SOS-APPL if this doesn't help; you again probably have a hardware problem. To minimize the chance of this problem occurring in the first place, do not press any keys nor move the cursor while a recalibration is in progress. (3) Many AppleVision problems are due to incorrect installation of the AppleVision software. Apple has AppleVision Fix software (available online) that is designed to help solve this problem.

  Several other problems may be solved by recalibrating the color of the monitor using the AppleVision software.

SEE:
- **"AppleVision Monitors," in Chapter 12, for many more details on AppleVision troubleshooting**
- **"Technically Speaking: The Cuda Button (and Monitors That Do Not Work)," in Fix-It #11**

TAKE NOTE ▶

SCREEN SAVERS: DO YOU NEED THEM? NO!

Screen savers such as After Dark provide some entertainment benefit, but you don't really need them to protect against damage to the monitor. With some older monitors, there was a chance that if the same image was left on the screen for too long, it would cause a permanent "burn-in" of the screen image that you could see faintly at all times thereafter. This will not happen with any monitors made in the last several years, and it is unlikely even in older monitors.

There is some chance of burn-in on a PowerBook display, but only if you leave it unattended for weeks.

Monitor II: Quality of Display Problems

This category refers to problems with the quality of the display, rather than the absence of a display.

- **Size and form problems**
  A display may shrink in size (horizontally or vertically), or the image may start to flicker. This often indicates a power supply problem—for external monitors, the problem is probably with the monitor's power supply; otherwise, the fault lies with the power supply inside the Macintosh. With compact Macintoshes, the built-in monitor and the computer share the same power supply. In any case, if you have a malfunctioning power supply, it needs to be replaced.
- **Color problems and jittery displays**
  If a color display suddenly shows colored blotches on the screen, it is probably *magnetized.* If your monitor has a *degauss switch,* (check your monitor's manual for where it is located) pressing it should fix this problem. You can often resolve other minor display-size and color problems by adjusting convergence controls, if your monitor has them accessible.

  Other color display problems, especially those limited to certain applications and/or documents, are usually software related. Most solutions center on understanding and using the Monitors or Monitors & Sound control panels; this subject is covered in Chapter 10.

  If you have a PCI-based Mac and have thin, vertical colored lines going down your monitor, your VRAM is probably installed in incorrect slots (if you have only two cards, they should be in the slots labeled "1").
- **Electromagnetic interference**
  Many display anomalies, such as a jittering display, scrolling horizontal lines, or discolorations in the display, can be due to electromagnetic interference (magnets, motors, fluorescent lights, and more). If you have these problems, try moving your monitor to a different location. Larger monitors are affected more by these factors than smaller ones.

- **Multiscan monitor problems and more**
  Many older Macintosh models do not directly support multiscan monitors. In this case, you will probably only be able to select one of the monitor's several possible different resolutions. If in doubt, check with Apple (1-800-SOS-APPL) for specific advice concerning your Mac model. Otherwise, problems getting more than the default resolution (640 x 480, typically) are usually caused by software—extension conflicts, missing display software, or corrupted system software or preferences files.

  Also, if you have a multiscan monitor that has a button on the monitor itself to reset its default settings (it may be a recessed button behind a panel; check with your monitor's documentation for details), this may fix out-of-focus, tilted, or pin-cushioning displays. For some multiscan monitors, such as AppleVision monitors, these controls are in the software (namely, the AppleVision Setup or Monitors & Displays control panels). These controls can also be used to fix a variety of other problems, some of them related more to software than hardware.

SEE: • **Chapter 10 for more on selecting monitor resolutions**
• **"Monitor Problems" and "AppleVision Monitors," in Chapter 12, for more on these issues**

TECHNICALLY SPEAKING

MACINTOSH SLOTS: NUBUS VS. PCI

On the main logic board inside all Macintosh II, Centris, Quadra, and some Power Mac computers, there are special slots called NuBus slots. These are designed to hold (appropriately enough) NuBus cards, which are like mini-logic boards that extend the functionality of the computer. A video display card, various sorts of "accelerators," and a DOS Compatibility card are all common examples of NuBus cards.

On Apple's latest Power Macs, the NuBus slots have been replaced by PCI (Peripheral Component Interconnect) slots. In fact, the Macs that have these slots are officially referred to as "PCI-based Macs" (even though the PCI slots are only one of several significant enhancements that were first introduced in these models). PCI slots/cards are generally faster than NuBus ones; PC computers have been using them for years. Just be careful about mixing and matching, because you can't use a NuBus card in a PCI slot, or vice versa. When you purchase a card or any device that connects via a card, make sure it is the right type for your machine.

Depending on your model of Macintosh, you may have anywhere from one to eight slots, each of which can hold one card. Each card draws power from the Macintosh's power supply. There is a limit on the total combined power that should be used by all cards; if you have several cards, you need to be concerned about exceeding this limit. In rarer cases, even the order in which you fill the slots can be of importance, so check with the documentation that came with your Macintosh and card(s) for more details, if needed. You should also be able to get help from the manufacturer of your card(s). Generally, these issues have been more significant for NuBus cards than PCI cards.

A couple of other types of slots have appeared on Macs over the years. One type is called the processor-direct slot (PDS), found on several lower-end Macintosh models.

Accessing any of these types of slots requires opening up the Macintosh case. The difficulty of doing this varies among different Macintosh models (as described in "Technically Speaking: Working Inside the Macintosh," earlier in this chapter).

SEE: • **"PCI-Based Power Macintoshes," in Chapter 12, for more about these Mac models**

Serial Port Devices: Printers, Modems, and Networks

In the rear of most models of Macintosh are two *serial ports.* These ports are primarily used to connect printers and modems to the Macintosh. A serial port is also used to connect your Macintosh to a network. One port is called the *printer port* and the other is the *modem port* (indicated by a printer and a telephone symbol, respectively, above the ports). Despite their different names, the two ports are quite similar and (except in a few cases) can be used interchangeably.

Notable exceptions are as follows: you should only use the printer port for AppleTalk connections (unless you are using Open Transport, in which case you can use either port as long as you select the desired port from the AppleTalk control panel). Similarly, you should only use the modem port for GeoPort connections. Of course, if you have an internal modem (such as used in PowerBooks), you do not connect it to either port. Finally, some Macintoshes, notably certain models of PowerBooks, have only one serial port; it is a combined printer/modem port.

Common problems with devices attached through the serial ports more often involve software rather than hardware trouble. For example, many printer problems revolve around making the correct selections from the Chooser desk accessory. These and other printing problems are explained in Chapter 7; some problems with modems and with networks (especially as related to file sharing) are covered in Chapters 11 and 14. Otherwise, for many of these problems, you will need to refer to the relevant documentation or seek other outside help.

To check for general hardware problems with devices connected through the serial port, check the serial cables, the serial port, and the serial port peripheral device.

- **Check the serial cables**

  All except the oldest models of Macintosh use round 8-pin serial cables. While all of these serial cables may look identical on the outside, though, they can have quite different wiring inside; for example, a serial cable for non-AppleTalk printers is different from one used for modems. Either cable works correctly with either port, but printer cables may work only with printers, and modem cables may work only with modems.

  The cables used to connect devices on an AppleTalk network (LocalTalk, PhoneNet, etc.) are a third type of cable that connects via the printer serial port. Some newer Macintosh models include a separate Ethernet port, using its own type of cable, for connecting to this type of network.

  If you are having a problem from the first time you connect a serial port device, check to make sure you are using the right cable. If you are in doubt, consult with the place where you purchased your equipment or seek other outside help. As always, if problems persist even though all cable connections appear correct, you may have a damaged cable. Swap cables from another Macintosh, if possible, to check for this.

  SEE: • **"Technically Speaking: Not All Modem Cables Are Created Equal" and "Technically Speaking: The GeoPort and Multimedia Features," for information on yet other cable types**

TECHNICALLY SPEAKING ▶

NOT ALL MODEM CABLES ARE CREATED EQUAL

Even if you are certain that your supposed modem cable is truly a modem cable, your problems may not be over, because there is more than one type of modem cable. In particular, some permit "hardware handshaking" while others (usually older ones, such as those shipped with 2400 bps modems) do not. Hardware handshaking cables are needed to work with the "flow control" setting needed for most high-speed modem connections to the Internet (such as when you make a TCP connection). To put it more simply, if you are having problems using a 14,400 or faster modem, and all your software seems in order, make sure you have a compatible cable (if you have a high-speed modem, it should have come with the correct cable).

SEE: • **"Xon/Xoff Vs. Hardware Handshake (and Using the Correct Cable For Your Modem)," in Chapter 14, for more on this issue**

TECHNICALLY SPEAKING ▶

THE GEOPORT AND MULTIMEDIA FEATURES

On AV and Power Macs, the modem port is technically also referred to as a GeoPort; it has nine holes rather than the eight holes of a regular serial port. If you connect special GeoPort-capable devices (via a cable that has the needed matching nine pins), you can access special functions built into the Macintosh. For example, the GeoPort Telecom Adapter can be used to access a built-in modem capability. The adapter acts to connect the modem feature to your phone line. Unfortunately, the current version of the Telecom software needed to do this does not work on PCI-based Macs that have a LocalTalk device connected to the other serial port. Also note: Use of the Telecom Adapter as a modem requires the Macintosh's processor to do some of the "modem" work. This can lead to significant performance slow-downs at 28.8 bps. Using an ordinary modem avoids this problem. Remember, you can always use the GeoPort as an ordinary serial port for connecting all non-GeoPort serial devices.

The GeoPort is only one of several multimedia features available with the Macintosh. Especially with AV and Power Macs, you can now easily connect a variety of audio/video playback and recording devices (such as microphones, external speakers, and televisions). While this book offers some help for solving problems specific to these features, in many cases you will need to seek outside help.

- **Check the serial port**

  If you are still unable to get a response from a device connected to a serial port, try restarting the Mac. Also, try turning the serial port device off and back on again. These two techniques should solve most serial port problems (for example, it should reset a modem that is not responding and get it working again). If these fail to work, you may have a corrupted PRAM; to fix this, zap the PRAM (as described in Fix-It #11).

  Chapters 11 and 14 cover issues specific to getting "serial port in use" messages when trying to access a port. One suggestion is to use a utility called CommCloser. Otherwise, restarting the Mac is, once again, the most effective solution. Chapter 11 also discusses issues specific to Macs with only one serial port (such as most recent PowerBooks).

Otherwise, one of the two serial ports (assuming your Mac model has two ports; some only have one) may be damaged. To test for this, if your device can work from either serial port, try switching the cable to the other port—to get things to work after switching ports, you will probably also have to readjust Chooser settings (as discussed for printers in Chapter 7). If the device now works, the original port is probably damaged. Take the Macintosh in for repair.

- **Check the serial port peripheral device**
  Finally, the peripheral device may be damaged. If so, indicators on the device often provide additional clues; consult your device's manual for specific details. For example, the different patterns of status lights on Apple LaserWriters indicate different problems. In particular, if both the paper-jam and out-of-paper lights are on at the same time, or are flashing together, a hardware repair is probably needed.

  SEE ALSO: • **"By the Way: Output Too Light, Too Dark, or Streaked?" in Chapter 7**

SEE:
- **Fix-It #1 for more on software/hardware incompatibilities, especially with AV Macs**
- **Fix-It #18, "Take Note: Why a Modem?" for more about modems**
- **Chapter 6, "Technically Speaking: A Few Words About Sound and Sound Files," for more on solving problems using sounds**
- **Chapter 7 for more specific information on printing problems**
- **Chapter 10, "Movies, Video, and More"**
- **Chapter 11 for more on PowerBook-specific serial port problems, including the Express Modem**
- **Chapter 14 for more on modems and the Internet**

The Macintosh

This section deals with the main components of the Macintosh itself: the logic board and the power supply. Problems with memory, which is often considered part of the logic board, are covered separately in the final two sections of this Fix-It.

- **The logic board (and its battery)**
  If you have a hardware problem with the Macintosh itself, this generally means a problem with the circuitry on the main logic board. The symptoms can range from minor (such as a crackling sound from a speaker) to a totally dead Macintosh.

  Logic board Logic board problems almost always require taking the Macintosh in for repair. In fact, Apple's official solution to any logic board problem, no matter how trivial, is to replace the entire board. This can be an expensive repair for what may only be a defective resistor somewhere on the board, but it's still the safest way to go. If you want to risk it, non-authorized dealers may be willing to replace individual components of the board, at a considerable savings of money.

  Battery A dead battery can lead to surprisingly serious symptoms; fortunately, the remedy is simply to replace the battery (rather than the much more expensive logic board replacement). For example, if your Macintosh is one that can be turned on by the keyboard's Power key (not all models use this key), a dead internal battery can actually prevent your Macintosh from starting up. Other symptoms that may mean a dead battery include a sad Mac on startup and a monitor screen that does not come on.

Checking your battery is always a good thing to do before assuming the worst about these problems. According to some reports, if your Mac has a physical on/off switch, turning it on and off rapidly a few times can temporarily revive a Mac with a dead battery problem (letting you get some work done while you wait for a battery replacement).

SEE: • **"Optional: Remove the Battery," and "Technically Speaking: The Cuda Button (and Monitors That Do Not Work)," in Fix-It #11, for related information**

- **Power supply**
  As cited in this Fix-It, problems with distortions in the monitor display are often an early sign of power supply problems. The ultimate sign of a completely failed power supply, of course, is a dead Macintosh. In either case, get the power supply replaced.

TAKE NOTE ▶

APPLE'S REPAIR EXTENSION PROGRAM

In 1996, Apple announced what is essentially a free seven-year extended warranty, called the Repair Extension Program, to fix certain problems with 5200, 5300, 6200, and 6300 series desktop Macs as well as 190 and 5300 series PowerBooks. Needless to say, this recall (especially of the entire 5300 PowerBook line) did not help Apple's marketing efforts. In any case, a variety of symptoms are covered under this program. Among the most notable are the following:

- System freezes caused by specific, known component issues that have been identified by Apple (in other words, not every cause of a system freeze is covered).
- Sudden or intermittent changes in the monitor's color hue on Power Macintosh and Performa 5200 and 5300 series computers (due to a particular cable).
- AC adapter problems (the adapter does not fit, or the Mac takes longer to start up with the AC adapter than with battery power) with PowerBook 190 and 5300 series PowerBooks.

Note: If your PowerBook has an "AA" in the lower right corner of the serial number label, you should be okay. Apple also has freeware utilities, including one called 5XXX/6XXX Tester, that may help determine whether your Mac qualifies under this program. Otherwise, if you own any of these Mac models and have not yet been contacted by Apple, call 1-800-SOS-APPL or 1-800-801-6024 for more details as to whether or not you qualify and what you should do. Repairs may include a free logic board replacement.

Memory I: Adding or Replacing Memory

Memory is added to your computer in the form of modules (or chips) that fit into special slots on your Mac's logic board. These modules look a bit like miniature versions of the NuBus or PCI cards described earlier. The formal names for most of these memory chips are SIMM (for *single inline memory module*) or DIMM (for *dual inline memory module*). Most older Mac models (including all NuBus-based Macs) use SIMMs, while more recent models, notably PCI-based Macs, use DIMMs. DIMMs provide a wider data path than SIMMs, which means they can carry more data and thus allow for faster performance.

Whether you use SIMMs or DIMMS, what you mainly need to know is that they are the hardware components that provide the RAM (memory) for your Macintosh (as first described in Chapter 1). Thus, if someone claims to have "sixteen megs of RAM" in their machine, this means that a total of 16MB of memory modules are installed on the Macintosh's main logic board.

Every Macintosh comes with some memory already installed; if it didn't, it could not work. In a few Mac models, memory is soldered directly to the logic board and cannot be easily removed. More often, it consists of the very same sort of independent, removable modules that you can purchase to add more memory.

In either case, there are almost always some RAM slots that are empty when your Mac arrives; these are used to insert additional RAM. You can also add more RAM by replacing a lower-capacity module with a higher-capacity one. In PowerBooks (and some other models), there is sometimes only one location for adding RAM. A special model-specific memory module is inserted in this location; the amount of RAM on the module can vary. Technically these special modules are not exactly SIMMs nor DIMMs, although they may often be referred to as such.

Exactly how easy it is to add or replace memory yourself depends on which model of Macintosh you have and your own skill levels (see "Technically Speaking: Working Inside the Macintosh," and "Technically Speaking: Memory Modules That Only Seem Defective," elsewhere in this Fix-It). For most modular and PowerBook Macintoshes, you can do it yourself fairly easily with just a screwdriver and a set of instructions.

There are two main reasons to add or replace memory in your Macintosh. These are detailed below.

- **Add memory in order to increase the RAM capacity of your Macintosh**
  If you find that your available RAM is insufficient to meet your needs (as covered in Fix-It #6), adding more memory is the best long-term solution. Minimum recommended memory requirements get larger every year. Experience has shown me that whatever I prescribe as the typical amount of RAM you should have will be out of date by the time you read this. I have recently read, though, that in 1997 Macs will ship with 32MB of RAM; having at least 16MB is almost a necessity right now. As I write this, memory prices are at about their lowest point in history. Assuming that this is still the case when you read this book, it makes sense to get as much RAM as you can possibly afford. There is no such thing as too much RAM.

- **Replace defective memory**
  Memory modules may be defective from the moment they are installed—or, as with any electronic component, they may go bad over time. Defective memory modules cause the most serious types of symptoms; your Macintosh typically will refuse to start up at all, show the sad-Mac icon, and/or sound unusual startup tones (as detailed in Chapter 5, on startup problems). If you do succeed in starting up despite the bad modules, you will likely be plagued with frequent and apparently unrelated system errors.

  In such cases, if you are at all lucky, the Macintosh may remain stable long enough for you to use diagnostic utilities such as TechTool Pro (as described earlier in this Fix-It) to determine if a defective module is the cause. Otherwise, determining which of your several memory modules is the defective one typically requires swapping modules in and out of their slots and testing the Macintosh after each swap to see if the problem goes away.

Depending on what model of Macintosh you have, you may be able to remove a memory module and start up just with what modules remain. If the problem goes away, you know that the module you removed was the source of the problem. In other cases, you may need to replace a potentially defective module with a new one before you can even try to start up. If your Macintosh has soldered-in memory chips and they are the cause of the problem, you will want to take the Mac to a service technician to get them replaced. (I realize that many users will seek out a service technician to replace memory modules, no matter what model they own.) In any case, if you do have a defective memory module, it must be replaced; these modules cannot be repaired.

If you get a sad Mac at startup due to a defective memory module, the sad-Mac error code may help identify which one is the defective module. Various documents are available online that help you interpret these codes (also see Chapter 5 for more on interpreting sad-Mac codes). I believe that at least with PCI-based Macs, however, these codes no longer help in this regard.

TECHNICALLY SPEAKING ▶

MEMORY MODULES THAT ONLY SEEM DEFECTIVE

Sometimes a removable memory module (SIMM or DIMM) that is not properly seated in its slot will mimic the symptoms of a defective module. To check for this, make sure that each module is firmly in its slot and that its wires are unbent.

On some older models of Macintosh, modules are held in place by tabs that clip into holes on the module. When you install a module, make sure that the tabs on the slot click into holes at either end of the module. Removing this type of module requires that you carefully pry back the tab without breaking it off. Because a broken tab can prevent proper seating of the module, with the result that it appears to be defective, be especially careful when removing these modules. An inexpensive tool, sold by many places that sell modules, can assist in this removal task.

On most recent Macs, the slots have a "tang" on one end that, when pressed down, pops up the chip that is installed there. To get a new chip inserted properly, slide it in from the non-tang end first—then, when it is lined up properly, push straight down. This method often requires that you press down on the chip harder than you might otherwise think is needed (or even advisable!). When it is properly seated, though, you should hear a distinct click. If your Mac does not show the additional memory when you are done, check again to make sure you have inserted it properly before assuming you have damaged RAM. If you can pull out the memory chip without opening the slot's "tang," it was not seated properly.

Sometimes (as mentioned in Chapter 4) modules that are merely dirty will behave like defective modules, causing frequent system crashes or startup problems. Using a handheld vacuum cleaner to clean out the inside of your Macintosh may help; otherwise, you may need to remove each module and clean it. In most cases, just blowing dust off of it and wiping it gently with a soft cloth should be enough to clean a module. In really bad cases, you may want to apply a specialized cleaning spray (such as one called DeOxIt). Most users should rarely, if ever, find this necessary. In any case, also remember to take precautions against static electricity damage (see "Technically Speaking: Working Inside the Macintosh" earlier in this Fix-It).

One more symptom that may fool you into thinking you have defective modules is when you cannot use more than 8MB of RAM. Actually, the solution here is simply to turn on 32-bit addressing (as discussed more in Fix-It #6).

TAKE NOTE ▶

L2 RAM CACHE MODULES

What are L2 RAM caches? These days, main memory is not the only type of memory addition you can make. Increasingly popular in current models of Power Macs, especially PCI-based Macs, are Level 2 (L2) RAM cache cards. Some models come with one already installed; in others it is an optional add-on, accomplished much like adding SIMM/DIMM memory.

L2 RAM caches are a special high-speed RAM whose purpose is to increase the speed of your Mac by allowing for more efficient use of your processor. How does it do this? Here's how: The Mac's CPU operates only on data in its "registers." If these registers don't already have the needed information, the Mac it looks for it first on the CPU's on-chip (L1) cache (usually about 32K in size). If the on-chip cache doesn't have it, it then searches the L2 RAM cache, if one is present (these currently run in size from about 256K to 1 MB). If it still can't find the information, only then will it search the slower main RAM (including any disk cache, as described in Fix-It #6). Failing that, it reads the needed information from your hard drive, which is the last resort because it has the slowest access of any of these options.

Thus an L2 RAM cache can give you a speed boost by giving the Mac a faster source of data. On Power Macs, for example, expect to get about a 10 to 15 percent increase in speed if you currently have no cache at all. This benefit, however, primarily affects native code applications. The speed boost is negligible for 680X0 programs run in emulation mode.

For Macs with processors of 150MHz or less, I would not advise getting a cache larger than 256K. The additional speed boost you get from 512K or larger caches is not worth the additional cost (although, over time, as prices drop, these smaller cache sizes will probably disappear from the market). Faster processors (such as the 604e) may benefit from larger L2 caches. As described more in Chapter 12, however, ("Technically Speaking: Speed of Your Power Mac: Beyond Processor MegaHertz"), a L2 cache of any size can paradoxically slow down a very fast processor.

Note that only some Mac models come with a RAM cache slot; if your Mac doesn't have one, you can't get this benefit. Also note that NuBus-based Power Macs use different L2 cache cards than do the PCI-based Power Macs.

Finally, note that as with all RAM, a correctly installed cache card must be firmly inserted into the slot. To check if you have done this, use Newer's Cache-22 utility or MicroMat's TechTool Pro to see if it lists the cache.

Problems with L2 RAM caches (and the "val-4" controversy) There have been reports of L2 RAM cache cards not working on PCI-based Macs. The most likely indicator of a defective RAM cache is an increased frequency of system errors, particularly Type 11 errors, shortly after installing the cache. The immediate cause seems to be the RAM cache itself, rather than some problem with the logic board. Apple's RAM cache is generally immune to this problem. Apple, however, has acknowledged that its 256K caches marked "820-0719-B" may be incompatible with the Power Mac 7500/100, preventing the Mac from starting up. If you have this cache, call Apple about having it replaced. For third-party RAM cache, check with the vendor about any known problems before ordering.

This problem seemed especially virulent on the Power Mac 7500. A lot of rumors concerning this problem revolved around whether Power Mac 7500 logic boards that had the expression "val-4" printed on them (near where the PCI cards go) indicated a pre-production board that was especially likely to have these problems. Apple denies this and claims that the val-4 boards are identical to the other 7500 boards. In fact, reports indicate that Apple restarted stamping "val-4" on all boards after the 7500 was out for awhile. It appears that this problem, whatever the cause, may have disappeared with the arrival of the Power Mac 7600 and newer PCI-based Power Macs. This development has led some to reassert that the problem is somehow due to the logic board after all.

The truth may ultimately never be revealed. It appears, however, that the Apple L2 cache used parts that were made to a "tighter tolerance" than some third-party caches (which also may have used slightly slower chips) and that the 7500—perhaps especially those with the original val-4 motherboards—seemed particularly sensitive to this minor difference.

SEE: • **Chapter 12 on PCI-based Macs for more on this and related issues**

Memory II: Getting the Correct Modules for Your Machine

Purchasing memory modules is yet another area of the Macintosh where the increasing diversity of the hardware has made sweeping generalizations almost impossible. The exact type of module you need (such as whether you need a SIMM or a DIMM, and how many pins the module should have), the maximum amount of RAM you can add, and how it is added, can vary dramatically from one model to another.

In fact, the situation has gotten sufficiently out of hand that Apple has created a freeware Adobe Acrobat document, called the Apple Memory Guide, that describes the exact memory specifications for each Macintosh model. Apple regularly updates this document as new models come out.

As another alternative, Newer Technology has a freeware file called Guide to RAM Upgrades (or GURU) that provides similar information. For issues beyond memory (such as CPU description and ports) don't forget to check out Apple's Apple Spec database file (as described in "Technically Speaking: Learning the Lowdown on Your Hardware," in Fix-It #1).

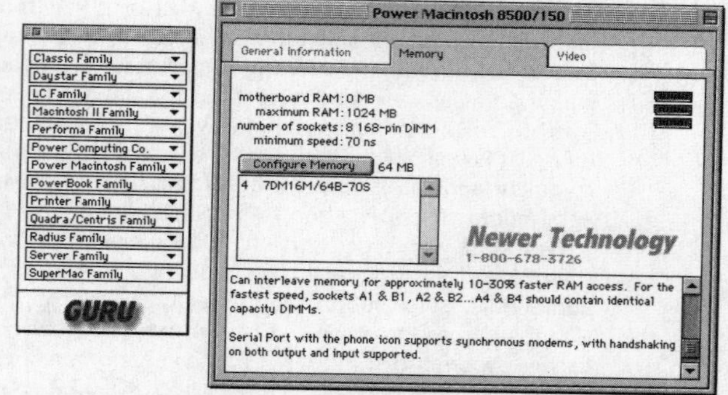

Figure F17-3 *Newer's Guide to RAM Upgrades (GURU).*

If you intend to add to or replace the memory inside your Mac, I definitely advise getting one of these aids. If studying this material seems too daunting, however, don't fret too much. Reputable sellers of memory are knowledgeable about these matters and should be able to advise you.

In any case, what follows is a summary of the major issues you need to be concerned about. The specific examples cited are just a sampling of the variety that exists.

- **The maximum allowable RAM**

  Different Macintosh models have different limits on the maximum amount of RAM that they can use. Older Macs that do not support 32-bit addressing are particularly limited in how much RAM they can use. If you install more than this maximum (assuming this is even possible), at best the Macintosh will not recognize it; at worst, it may lead to sad Macs or system crashes.

  For example, a Macintosh Color Classic can have a maximum of 10MB; the PowerBook 180 can have a maximum of 14MB; a Quadra 660AV can have a maximum of 64MB; and a Power Macintosh 6100 can have a maximum of 72MB.

  Note that if you use virtual memory (as explained in Fix-It #6), the maximum allowable total combined (physical plus virtual) RAM typically exceeds the maximum allowable physical RAM, often by a wide margin. The combined maximum may be as high as 1GB.

- **The size of the memory module**

  The amount of memory on an individual SIMM/DIMM can vary. For example, a single module may hold 1MB or less (no longer seen much these days) or as much as 64MB or more. Thus, if your Macintosh has two memory slots, and you install two 1MB modules, you will have a total of 2MB of RAM. If you install two 64MB modules into the same two slots, however, you will have a total of 128MB.

  Memory module sizes usually double as they increase; typical module sizes are 1, 2, 4, 8, 16, 32, and 64MB. Replacing existing smaller-capacity modules with larger-capacity ones is a way to increase your Mac's RAM when your Mac has no empty memory slots. (Note that "size" in this context does not refer to the physical dimensions of the module, but rather to its MB capacity.)

  Some models of Macintosh have restrictions on what sizes of modules they can use; for example, the 660AV cannot use 1MB, 2MB, or 64MB SIMMs. Using a prohibited size will inevitably cause problems. As usual, either the Apple Memory Guide or GURU will give you the scoop for your particular Mac model.

- **The speed of the memory module**

  Memory module speed is measured in nanoseconds (ns)—the lower the number, the faster the speed. Different Macintosh models require a different minimum speed, with faster machines generally requiring faster memory. Current PCI-based Macs, for example, require at least 70 ns RAM, and 60 ns RAM is already commonly sold. It is okay to add memory that is faster than the minimum needed (you can even combine RAM of different speeds in the same Mac), but faster RAM will just cost you more money without giving you any increase in performance. For example, a Mac that requires 70 ns RAM will not run faster as a result of using 60 ns RAM.

  Still, if you later buy a newer Mac model that requires the faster RAM, you may save some money by being able to transfer your existing RAM to the newer Mac. Some experts also claim that the faster RAM provides a useful "margin of error" in the manufacturing of the RAM, so that even if it is slightly slower than its specs, it is still fast enough not to be below the needed minimum.

  In any case, to avoid problems, do not add RAM that runs slower than the minimum required speed. Otherwise, at the very least, the speed of your Macintosh will decline.

  Several of the 100 series PowerBooks (160, 165, and 180) require a special type of RAM, called "fast RAM," in order to avoid so-called wait states that could slow down the machine if ordinary RAM was used. If you don't use the special fast RAM, performance speed may drop as much as 15 percent. A freeware utility from Newer Technology, called Nightmare on PowerBook Street, tests your Power Book's RAM for this problem.

  Again, to avoid all such problems, stick to reputable and knowledgeable dealers, and take their advice as to what memory to purchase. Personally, I prefer to order RAM from mail-order companies such as TechWorks and Newer rather than retail stores. You'll generally get a better price, and you'll probably speak to a more informed salesperson.

TECHNICALLY SPEAKING

DIMM PLACEMENT AND MAXIMIZING YOUR MAC'S SPEED

Currently, most PCI-based Power Macintoshes (such as the 7500, 7600, and 8500 models) have eights DIMM slots, labeled A1 to A4 and B1 to B4. You have maximum flexibility here—you can put DIMMs in anywhere from one to all eight of these slots, in any location, and the Mac should work fine.

Still, for optimum performance speed, where you put the DIMMs does matter. First off, these Macs support a memory technology called *interleaving*, which improves performance by letting the computer access two DIMMs at the same time in an alternating pattern. Avoiding more details here, this means that you will get better performance if you have DIMMs installed in matching pairs. A matched pair means having DIMMs in both an A and a B slot of the same number (such as A4 and B4); these labels are visible on the motherboard when you open up your Mac. So, for example, having two 8MB DIMMs in slots A4 and B4 will give better performance than one 16MB DIMM in slot A4 or even two 8MB DIMMs in A4 and B1.

A matched pair of DIMMS should be of the same size for interleaving to work. For absolute best performance, these matched DIMMs should also be of the same speed.

With a 604 or faster processor, interleaving can boost speed by as much as 15 percent. With a 601 or slower processor, though, the speed boost will be almost negligible. By the way, the Power Mac 7200 does not support this interleaving feature.

Next, assuming that you are only going to fill up some of your DIMM slots, does it matter which ones you fill up first? Officially, Apple says it should not matter. Many experts, however, have stated that starting with the highest numbered pair (A4/B4) and working your way down to the lowest number pair (A1/B1) is best. One report suggested an exception if you have four DIMMs: in this case, A4, B4, A1 and B1 is the best selection (supposedly this helps to minimize the effects of "noise" across the DIMMs). Other reports say that if you have pairs of DIMMs of different sizes (such as one pair of 16MB DIMMs and another pair of 8MB DIMMs), the higher-capacity DIMMs should preferably go in the highest number slots (that is, A4/B4).

Finally, there have been sporadic reports of 16MB or higher DIMMs working properly in some slots but not in others. So if you suspect a DIMM problem, try rearranging the slot locations of the DIMMs before assuming that you have a defective one.

Worrying about most of this for what may only result in a minimal speed boost may be more than you care to worry about, but Macintosh speed freaks gobble this stuff up like M&Ms.

- **The type of the memory**
  Macs that use DIMMs cannot use SIMMs—and vice versa. Even if two Macintoshes both use the same size and speed of a SIMM or DIMM, there may still be differences in exactly what module each model uses. In particular, as mentioned already, PowerBooks use special memory modules that are different from what desktop Macintoshes use. Also, there are differences in the number of pins on different SIMM modules (for example, 30-pin and 72-pin SIMMs). DIMMs currently have 168 pins.

  Motorola's StarMax clones were the first Macs to use 3.3-volt DIMMs. All previous Macs used 5-volt DIMMs. The expectation is that 3.3-volt DIMMs will soon be used in most Macintosh models. The 3.3v DIMMs use less power and employ a new technology called EDO (Extended Data Out) that allows for faster performance.

  Once again, if you don't get the right type of module, you probably won't even be able to insert it in the slot of your machine—and even if you can, it probably won't work.

- **Other memory restrictions**
  In many older models, all SIMMs in a given Macintosh had to be the same size. Thus, you could not put a 1MB SIMM in one slot and a 4MB SIMM in the next slot. In some cases, the Mac has two separate *banks* of SIMM slots (called A and B); all SIMMs within a bank must typically be of the same size, though each bank can have a different size. Sometimes, the slots in a bank must either be all full or all empty in order for the Mac to work properly. The Macintosh IIci, a classic example of this type of Macintosh, has two banks of 4 slots each.

  With virtually all Macs that use SIMMs, the modules need to be installed in complementary pairs. Thus, in Power Macintosh 6100, 7100, and 8100 modules, both memory slots must both be filled with SIMMs of the same size and speed in order for the Macs to work properly.

  Happily, with Macs that now use DIMMs, almost all of these restrictions are gone. In most cases, each slot can hold a different size DIMM, and there is no restriction on having particular slots filled or empty (see "Technically Speaking: DIMM Placement and Maximizing Your Mac's Speed," though, for some important details).

TECHNICALLY SPEAKING ▶

VIDEO RAM AND PRINTER RAM

Video RAM For a few Macintosh models, the RAM needed to generate the video display is obtained from the same dynamic RAM (DRAM) used for all other RAM-related functions (and the same RAM referred to in the main text of this Fix-It); the basic Power Macintosh 6100 is an example of this. Most recent Mac models, however, include a separate set of video RAM (VRAM) used just for the display screen.

This memory is located in a special area of the logic board, separate from the main memory modules. The amount of VRAM installed determines, among other things, the maximum number of colors that your monitor can display at one time. For example, without enough VRAM, you cannot get 24-bit color (see Chapter 10). Some models of Macintosh allow you to add additional VRAM memory beyond what comes included with the basic configuration. Otherwise, to get more VRAM, you need to add a special video card (NuBus or PCI, as appropriate) that will include its own VRAM and bypass the built-in video altogether. Some Power Macintoshes, taking a hybrid approach, have an option to add a special VRAM Expansion card.

On some PCI-based Power Macs (especially the 7500 or 8500), if you note two vertical lines on your monitor's screen that appear to follow the cursor, this is due to improper installation of VRAM. If you have 2 MB of VRAM, you must install the VRAM DIMMs into the slots labeled 1 (which is the way these models ship if the VRAM is already installed); this will eliminate the problem. Be especially careful about this if you should get a logic board replacement—make sure the VRAM is installed in the same slots that they were located on the original board.

Printer RAM LaserWriters also have their own RAM, and on some models you can add printer RAM. Adding RAM will allow the printer to print faster and to handle complex documents more effectively.

For more details and specifications on VRAM and printer RAM, check out Apple Memory Guide, or otherwise get outside help.

BY THE WAY ▶

BEWARE OF COMPOSITE MEMORY

Some large-capacity SIMMs (or DIMMs) are actually constructed by combining several smaller-capacity SIMMs (or DIMMs) onto one larger card (this is different from the modules used in PowerBooks). These cards are called composite memory. Though they may work fine in many cases, Apple advises you not to use them. As they are usually larger in physical size than a noncomposite memory, there may not be enough room for them to fit alongside other components inside the Macintosh. Even worse, because of technical issues not worth describing here, composite memory may lead to system crashes or a failure to start up.

For related information

SEE:
- **Fix-It #1 on incompatibilities between hardware and software**
- **Fix-It #6 on memory problems**
- **Fix-It #11 on zapping the PRAM**
- **Fix-It #16 on SCSI problems**
- **Chapter 4 on system crashes**
- **Chapter 5 on startup and disk problems**
- **Chapter 7 on printing problems**
- **Chapter 11 on PowerBooks**
- **Chapter 12 on Power Macintoshes and AppleVision monitors**

Fix-It #18: Seek Technical Support or Other Outside Help

QUICK SUMMARY ▶

If you are unable to solve a specific software or hardware problem, contact technical support of the company that makes the product (via a phone call or by checking out their Web page or other online support). Otherwise, seek help from more general online services, user groups, magazines, books, and/or colleagues.

When to do it:

- Whenever symptoms suggest a bug or incompatibility problem.
- Whenever you have searched the relevant manuals for the answer to a question but were unable to find it.
- Whenever you have a problem that you were unable to solve using the advice given in this book.

Why to do it:

Even if you memorize everything in this book, there will still be times when you cannot solve some problem. Perhaps you need some detailed information about your model of Macintosh ("What type of memory does my Mac use?"). Maybe you want some guidance on a particular procedure you have never tried before (such as installing memory). Or maybe you simply can't find the answer to some application- or hardware-specific problem ("How do I import Word documents into this program?" or "Why do I get a system freeze whenever I select Save?"). In all these cases, when you have exhausted your own resources, it's time to seek outside help.

What to do:

This Fix-It divides help into two separate categories: product technical support, and other outside help.

Product Technical Support

At various points throughout this book, I have recommended contacting the technical support staff for a given problem. Here, I will offer more general guidelines for when to do this.

Virtually every computer company maintains some sort of technical support department. Most offer multiple types of support, ranging from a technical support email address to support files on the World Wide Web and telephone technical support. When you have a problem, especially one of crisis proportions, your first thought is usually to grab the telephone. Sometimes this is the best thing to do, but often it is not.

When to Call Technical Support

Telephone support is probably the most frequently used method of getting technical assistance; basically, it is a help line for problems specific to the company's products. The phone number for technical support should be in the manual that came with the product. Arrangements for technical support lines vary, though—some phone numbers are toll-free, others are not. Sometimes you have to pay an annual fee to gain access to a given technical support line.

There are two types of problems that suggest a quick call to technical support. The first is when, having carefully followed the product's installation instructions, a problem still occurs the first time you try to use a product. The other is when a familiar program develops an unknown illness and, after using all the diagnostic skills at your disposal, you are still unable to solve the problem. This means that, before you call, you should at least try common checks, such as checking for extensions conflicts and directory damage. (Otherwise, when you do call, they are almost certainly going to advise you to try them anyway.)

In general, for symptoms that do not clearly point to a likely cause, it pays to call technical support fairly early in the search process. If you are lucky, the staff members there already have the answer to your problem. If so, the phone call can save you from wasting a substantial amount of time and effort looking for a solution on your own.

Still, even here, it might pay to pause for a moment before you grab the phone. I have had more than my share of embarrassing moments as I hastily made a call, only to discover the all-too-obvious solution to the problem while I was talking to the support technician ("Well, what do you know, my surge protector *is* unplugged from the wall outlet.") When this happens, I apologize gracefully and hang up as fast as I can, regretting that they already know my name and are probably adding my conversation to their Stupid Questions Hall of Fame.

In any case, before you call, don't forget to check manuals, "Read Me" files, Apple Guide files, or any other online help that may be available. This is especially true if your problem is more of a "How do I do this?" than an "I think something is wrong" issue.

Technical support is especially helpful for problems due to software bugs and incompatibilities with a company's software. The manufacturer is privy to the latest information, as well as what is being done to resolve such matters. If there is an upgraded version of the program that remedies these problems, you can order it; sometimes you may even get it free of charge. Occasionally, minor bug-fix upgrades are released that are not generally announced to registered users—calling and asking for it (or describing a problem that the upgrade version addresses) is the only way to get it. Otherwise, the manufacturer may suggest some way to work around the problem. Technical support is also a good source of information about the obscure features of a program that are not adequately explained in the documentation.

On the other hand, if the technical support people do not know the answer to your problem, all they can do is suggest the same techniques described in this book. That is why it pays to try the simpler solutions before calling technical support. If these techniques succeed, you have saved yourself a call; if not, you are in a more informed position to make the call.

When to Seek Other Types of Technical Support

Instead of calling a company's technical support phone line right away, you should first consider a company's other support options. Virtually all companies maintain technical support for their products on the World Wide Web, and they may also have support areas on major online information services, such as America Online or CompuServe. This support may include databases of frequently asked questions (FAQs) and their answers, as well as "electronic bulletin boards" or "forums" where you can post a question and get an answer (from the company's technical support staff as well as any other people who visit the forum). The company may also have an email address or a fax line explicitly set up for handling support questions.

The advantage of these services is that they may get you a quicker (and sometimes more accurate or more detailed) response than using the phone. With the phone, you may have to wait on hold for a lengthy period of time before someone answers, or you may even have to leave a message and wait for someone to call you back. And the person who finally responds may have less information about your problem than what is available online.

Typically, the documentation that comes with a product should include a listing of all of a company's support options.

SEE: • **"Seeking Other Outside Help," later in this Fix-It, for more about these services**

Be Prepared Before You Call

Assuming you have decided to call technical support, the key to getting help from technical support is to be prepared. If the technical personnel don't have an immediate answer to your problem, expect them to ask questions about the circumstances surrounding your problem. This information is critical for technical support personnel to successfully diagnose the problem. Here is how you can be prepared to deal effectively with technical support:

- Have your product's registration number ready. Some companies will require this before they help you.
- Have a *specific* description of the problem. Under what circumstances does the problem occur? Is it random or predictable? If an error message appears, what does it say? If you have done any of your own detective work, what did you find?

- Know the details of your hardware and software (such as what Mac model you are using, what version of the system software you are using, how much RAM you have installed, what version of the application you are using, and more).
- Be at your Mac when you call, so that you can try out any suggestions that the support person may make. Also, be prepared to write down what you do so that you can remember it later.

Any attempts you made to solve the problem can pay dividends now, even though they were ultimately unsuccessful. The information you gathered helps to isolate the cause. For example, consider these two differing descriptions of the same problem:

- "I don't know what's going on. I was in the middle of writing my report, and all of a sudden the whole application crashed."
- "The application crashes as soon as I attempt to cut a selection of text, but only if I do it immediately after saving the document. At other times, the Cut command works fine. I know this is not a startup extension conflict, because it happens even when all of my startup extensions are turned off. And it isn't a damaged document, because it happens with any document I use. I tried replacing the application with a backup copy, and that didn't help, either. If you want to know the details of my hardware or system software, I have that available; just ask what you want to know."

Which statement do *you* think is likely to be more helpful to a technical support person?

As an added bonus, the information in the more detailed statement already provides an initial work-around solution: Do not use the Cut command immediately after you save a document—type a few characters first, then cut.

Using Utilities to Help Get Prepared

What if you don't know all the system information you should know before calling technical support? And what if you have no idea where to get this information? Don't worry; any one of several utilities can come to your rescue. They analyze the current state of your System Folder, examine the overall contents of all of your mounted disks, and determine the details of your hardware configuration. When they are finished, they create a report of all this information, which you can then print.

For example, Apple's System Profiler (included with System 7.5.3 and later) can do this; however, it does not work with all Mac models. Another alternative is Now Profile, included as part of Now Utilities. TechTool (described more in Fix-Its #9 and #11) also includes a system information listing.

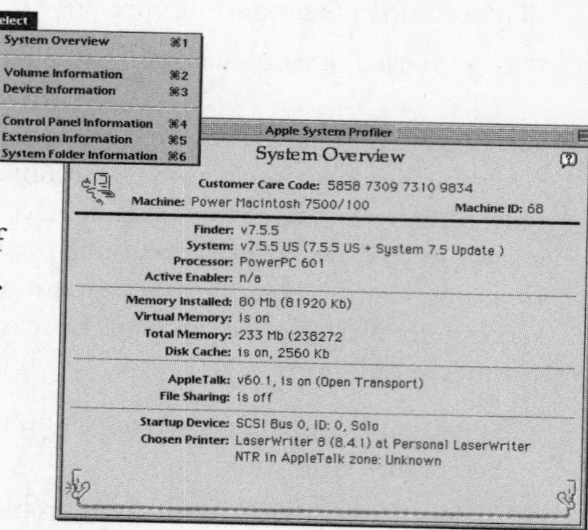

Figure 18-1 *The System Overview window of Apple System Profiler.*

A somewhat different alternative is a program like Help! (first mentioned in "Take Note: Identifying System Software Compatibility Problems and Bugs" in Fix-It #5). In addition to giving system information, Help! identifies various known problems, such as software bugs, startup extension conflicts, and whether a program is compatible with 32-bit addressing. With Help! you may not even need to call technical support to learn the cause of your problem.

TAKE NOTE ▶

REGISTRATION AND UPGRADES

Whenever you purchase a computer product, you almost always find a registration card enclosed. Fill it out and mail it back! You will not regret it. Registering computer products, especially software, is more valuable to you than for almost any other type of product you purchase. Here's why:

- Some companies provide technical support only to registered users. (Otherwise, if you haven't registered, they may require that you tell them the serial number of your software before they help you.)
- Registering your product puts you on the company's mailing list. This means you get the company's newsletter, if any, which often contains useful hints and tips about the product. Similarly, registered owners of anti-virus software are alerted to newly discovered viruses.
- Finally, when an upgrade to the software is released, registered users are given an opportunity to purchase it at a substantially reduced cost. Usually, you will be automatically mailed a notification about the upgrade offer. This is by far the greatest benefit of registering your product—it's like being able to get a new car at a fraction of its normal selling price, simply because you own an older model of the same car. Sometimes, especially if the upgrade is released primarily to fix bugs in the previous version, the upgrade is free and sent to all registered users.

It is true that not all upgrades are worth buying. Some add more style than substance, primarily making the product larger, more RAM-hungry, and slower to use. If you are content with your present version, there may be little to gain by upgrading. More often, however, the upgrade adds significant and valuable new features, fixes bugs, and generally addresses user complaints about the previous version. It also may be the only version compatible with Apple's most recent system software version, which is important if you are staying current with system software.

In most cases, getting an upgrade is worth the cost. Registering the software is always free, however, and at least it gives you the option to decide about the purchase of any upgrades. So register your product!

Make the Call

When calling technical support, make sure you are dialing the technical support number, not the customer service number. The two services are entirely different. The customer service staff deals primarily with sales and generally knows little or nothing about technical problems. Some companies offer only one phone number; in this case, there is usually an automated system for making a choice after the call is answered.

When you get to the technical support location, you will probably be placed on hold. Be patient. Depending on the company's staffing and the popularity of the product, you may be on hold for a minute or for half the day.

TAKE NOTE ▶

GETTING HELP FROM APPLE

Traditionally, Apple has had a poor reputation for providing technical support for its products. Happily, there have been significant improvements in the past few years.

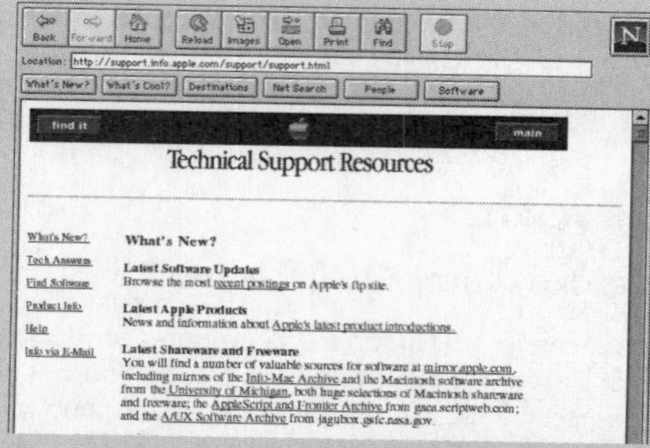

Figure 18-2 *Apple's Technical Support Resources Web page.*

- The most notable improvement is 800-767-2775 (SOS-APPL), your best-bet number to call for Apple technical assistance. This number is especially useful if you are having hardware problems with Apple products, most especially if they are still under warranty. In this case, Apple may actually send someone to your door to pick up the equipment, have it repaired, and return it to you within a few days. Or, especially if just a part replacement is needed, they may simply do the repair on the spot. After being connected to SOS-APPL's automated answering system, however, be prepared to wait a while before a real person answers. Waits of 30 minutes or more are possible.
- Apple maintains a healthy selection of other support options on the World Wide Web:

  Useful starting points include Get Info (*http://www.info.apple.com/),* Welcome to the Mac OS (*http://www.macos.apple.com/),* and Apple Technical Support Resources (*http://support.info.apple.com/support/support.html).* Otherwise, you can simply start from Apple's home page (*http://www.apple.com*) and surf from there. You will likely find many additional useful pages beyond what is listed here.

  For getting the latest Apple free software, try Apple's Software Updates Newest Files (*http://spock.info.apple.com/ftp.newfiles.html).* Another useful starting point for downloading software is Apple's Software Updates Alphabetical Listing (*http://horton.austin.apple.com/wwwalpha.html).*
- Apple currently maintains a daily (Monday-Friday) electronic publication called *Information Alley.* You can get a mailing list subscription to it or download issues from the Info Alley web page (*http://support.info.apple.com/info.alley/info.alley.html*).

  Articles in *Information Alley* are derived from Apple's Technical Information Library (*http://til.info.apple.com/til/til.html).* Check here for a complete listing of thousands of brief technical support articles.
- Apple also maintains a toll-free order center where you can order all updates directly (updates that you could download for free are available here for a nominal charge); the number is 800-293-6617. Of course, it helps to know that an update is available so that you know when to call to ask for it, and this is still a weak link in Apple's support structure. Unlike almost every other computer company, Apple does not reliably notify you of upgrades to its products, even if you are a registered user. Updates are regularly announced, however, in *Information Alley.*
- If you are more technically inclined, you can order a subscription to the same monthly developer's CD-ROM disc that gets sent to Apple developers. It is full of the latest information and software available from Apple. To order it, call the Apple Developer Catalog at 800-282-2732. You can also get other developer-oriented products here.
- Apple sometimes includes a pamphlet, listing many of its customer service phone numbers, as part of the documentation that comes with each Macintosh. If you have a recent copy, it may list still other technical support options. Check it out. As a last resort, try calling 800-538-9696 for help.

When you finally get to speak to someone, be courteous, but be persistent. Restate your question if the initial answer was not helpful. While most technical support people are knowledgeable about their company's product, some may seem like they were just hired yesterday. If the person answering the phone seems unable or unwilling to help, ask to speak to someone else. You should eventually get transferred to someone who knows the product well enough to answer your question.

Seeking Other Outside Help

Product technical support, by definition, is focused on the product the company publishes; it is not prepared to answer questions about more general problems you may have. Occasionally, technical support people may even be unaware of some esoteric problem with their own software. At these times, look elsewhere for help.

Try any or all of the following suggestions, as suits your style for seeking help. The solution you want is almost always available somewhere.

TAKE NOTE ▶

GETTING ONLINE

These days getting online is almost essential to qualify as even an apprentice troubleshooter. There is no better way to stay up-to-date with what's happening.

But before you can get online (whether it be America Online or the World Wide Web or anywhere else), you need to learn how online communications works. This typically means learning how to set up a modem, run the telecommunications software, navigate around the service, leave messages, and download files. While this is all much easier to do than it used to be, it is not yet as easy as it could be. While this book cannot serve as a general introduction to these topics, I do cover a variety of basic online and Internet troubleshooting issues in Chapter 14.

Online Information Services

America Online vs. CompuServe For Macintosh users, the best online services are CompuServe and America Online. If you have never used an online service before, America Online is probably the best service to get. It offers a wide selection of features, with a pleasant graphical interface at a relatively low cost. More experienced users may prefer CompuServe which has the best organized and most comprehensive selection of software and related features.

By the way, Apple's eWorld (covered in the previous edition of *Sad Macs*) has been discontinued. You can also forget about AppleLink; it too is gone. Actually, by the time you read this, CompuServe may have also disappeared (at least in its current form), because it plans to move its operations to the World Wide Web. America Online may also eventually move to the Web—clearly, the Web is the wave of the future.

In the meantime, both CompuServe and America Online provide access to the Internet (including full newsgroup and Web access) as part of their basic service. For many users, these services can be an adequate substitute for a traditional Internet service provider (ISP).

Troubleshooting features Though options vary somewhat from service to service, you can use them for everything from playing games to ordering clothes. For Macintosh problem solving, however, they have two main uses:

- **Bulletin boards**
  Online services maintain electronic *bulletin boards,*where you can post messages for other users to read. Anyone can then reply to your message. If you have a question, leave it as a message on a bulletin board; within a few hours to days, you should get an answer—often several answers—from some of the most knowledgeable Macintosh users in the country. Actually, just by browsing through existing messages, you may find that the answer to your question is already there.

  Many online bulletin boards are independent of any particular product. Software and hardware companies, however, often maintain product-specific message areas where you can leave messages for their technical support staff. If you are having trouble getting past hold on the technical support phone line, this is a good alternative. You should get an answer within 24 to 48 hours.
- **Download libraries**
  Online services maintain libraries of shareware and freeware that you can directly transfer *(*or *download)* to your computer over the phone. This is an alternative to obtaining the same software from user groups. Actually, some of the larger user groups, such as the Berkeley Macintosh User Group (BMUG) maintain their own online library that is free to members (except for the cost of the toll call).

  Again, the major download libraries are independent of any one company. The same areas that contain company-maintained bulletin boards, however, may also have special product-specific software libraries. The software in these libraries typically includes files that can be used to update the company's software to a newer version, as well as other supplementary software that does not come with the purchased product.

The Internet (especially the World Wide Web)

For seeking technical help on the Internet, there are three main places to look:

- **Newsgroups**
  These are the Internet's equivalent of the bulletin boards and forums of online services. They cover every imaginable topic (including some of the most notorious pornographic ones). For Macintosh users, however, a series of newsgroups whose names all begin with "comp.sys.mac" are your best bet for technical support. For general questions, the best of the best is "comp.sys.mac.system." To get to it from the newsreader feature of a Web browser such as Netscape, go to: *news:comp.sys.mac.system.*

  America Online and CompuServe both provide access to these groups. If you have a TCP connection (as described in Chapter 14), you can also get to them from your Web browser or from stand-alone programs such as NewsWatcher.

- **Mailing lists**
  A mailing list is basically an email service that functions like a newsgroup. You post messages as email. Everyone who is subscribed to the list then gets your message (either immediately or as a combined "digest" of all messages received within the last 24 hours); these subscribers may then respond to the message. You subscribe via email (some lists maintain a Web site where you can access subscription information) for free, and you can unsubscribe at any time (by following instructions that are sent to you when you first subscribe).

  Note that some mailing lists do not accept postings; they just send information, typically in the form of electronic magazines or press releases. Apple's Info Alley list (mentioned previously) is one such example. Also, magazines such as *MacUser* and *MacWEEK* have mailing lists that inform you of their latest articles and news.

  You can access email from your Web browser or from stand-alone programs such as Claris Emailer or Eudora.

  For asking troubleshooting questions, my current two favorite mailing lists are as follows:

  - Macintosh PCI Discussion List (subscribe at *http://www.mit.edu/people/rajiv/PCI/*)
    The focus here is limited to questions about PCI-based Macs, but the quality of the material that appears here is great. And all new Macs will be PCI-based Macs anyway.
  - Mac-Wizards (subscribe via email to *Majordomo@cc.gatech.EDU*)
    This list is aimed at more experienced users with questions that standard sources cannot solve. Still, anyone can join and listen in.

BY THE WAY ▶

USING FTP SITES

For the quickest access to the widest selection of ftp sites (used for downloading software over the Internet), use an ftp client program such as Anarchie. Anarchie, in particular, comes preinstalled with a list of dozens of popular ftp sites.

- **The World Wide Web**
  The World Wide Web is the 2000 pound gorilla of the online world—if it isn't already on the Web, it will be. The Web contains such a wealth of information that you can easily become overwhelmed by it. Beyond its massive text content, the Web also features elaborate graphics, sound, animation, and other special effects that cannot be matched anywhere else online. These effects are sometimes criticized as useless glitz, but they definitely add to the Web's appeal. You access Web pages from Web browsers such as Netscape Navigator, Microsoft Internet Explorer, or Cyberdog.

  For Mac troubleshooting, an abundant number of Web pages are worth a visit. Of course, there are all the Web sites maintained by vendors of Macintosh products, starting with Apple itself. But there are also dozens of independently run Mac sites,

from slick e-zines to simple tips pages. Their existence is partly a result of another aspect of the Web's appeal—how simple and inexpensive (relatively speaking) it is to set up your own Web site. Table F18-1 lists my top dozen favorites among these independent Mac Web sites.

Figure F18-3 *The top part of my MacFixIt home page (like everything else in the fast-changing Web environment, it is likely to look different by the time you read this!).*

If you want troubleshooting help or simply want to know about the latest happenings in the Mac world, check these out (and yes, I included my own MacFixIt Web site in this group).

Table F18-1 Best Mac Troubleshooting-Related Web Sites*

Site	Description
MacFixIt *http://www.macfixit.com/*	This is it! This is the site that I maintain as an update to this book and as a general troubleshooting resource. It includes late-breaking news, troubleshooting tips, and a library of troubleshooting utilities that you can download, including all of the freeware/shareware utilities mentioned in this book.
MacInTouch Home Page *http://www.macintouch.com/*	My favorite source for the latest news about new products, updates, and troubleshooting information.
Macintosh Resource Page *http://www.macresource.pair.com/*	Another superb source for news.
MacCentral *http://www.maccentral.com/*	A Macintosh e-zine that provides a useful collection of current news.
MacSense Online *http://www.macsense.com/*	Still another good source for Mac news.
O'Grady's Power Page *http://www.ogrady.com/*	Specializes in PowerBook coverage, but is yet another great source of late-breaking news.
MacSurfer Headline News *http://www.macsurfer.com/news/*	Summarizes the "headlines" from many popular news sources, including all of the ones listed above.
Complete Conflict Compendium *http://www.quillserv.com/www/c3/c3.html*	Probably the most complete listing of conflicts among Macintosh products that you could hope to find.
Mac Pruning Pages *http://www.AmbrosiaSW.com/DEF/*	A great site that explains what all those strange extensions and control panels in your System Folder do.
Version Tracker *http://www.versiontracker.com/*	Lists all the latest updates and new releases for Macintosh software.
CNET's Download.com *http://www.download.com/*	A great searchable database of Mac shareware and freeware.
Recent INFO-MAC Summary *http://hyperarchive.lcs.mit.edu/Recent-Summary.html*	Lists the latest Mac shareware and freeware added to this huge library. You can also search the complete INFO-MAC library from here.

**For more Mac-related Web sites, see: "Take Note: Getting Help from Apple," "User Groups," and "Magazines," elsewhere in this Fix-It.*

User Groups

Macintosh user groups (MUGs) are independent groups formed by and for people who use a Macintosh. You may think that user groups are only for hobbyists and experts—that, by itself, owning a Macintosh is no more reason to join a MUG than simply owning a camera is a reason to join a photography club. If so, you may very well be wrong.

User groups have something for every level of Macintosh user. Besides having regular meetings, many larger groups maintain a telephone help line for answering questions. It's like a super technical support line, not limited to any particular product. Most MUGs also maintain a software library of shareware and freeware programs. Also common is a user group newsletter, with useful tips and advice on Macintosh-related topics.

If you don't have a user group near you, don't worry. The larger groups, such as Berkeley Macintosh User Group (BMUG) (*http://www.bmug.org/*), cater to a national membership. If you join a faraway user group, you won't be attending their meetings, but you can still get the other benefits.

Magazines

Like user groups, Macintosh magazines often have a reputation as being only for the most devoted of Macintosh users. This may be true in certain cases, but the most popular magazines offer something for everyone. Because they publish monthly, or even weekly, magazines are a good place to get relatively late-breaking information about software bugs, upgrades, and new products (although the Web is even better in this regard). Their product reviews are among the best sources of critical information on which products to buy. Finally, regular columns offer help and advice on almost every imaginable topic related to the Macintosh.

MacUser and *Macworld* are the best of the monthly magazines. *MacAddict* is a strong newcomer, geared to a less technical audience, and *Mac Home Journal* is another useful home-user-oriented magazine. They are all available on newsstands. *MacWEEK* is yet another superior publication, though it is more industry-oriented than the others and only available by (a potentially free) subscription. Most of these magazines also have excellent Web sites, as listed below:

- *MacUser: http://www.macuser.com/*
- *MacWEEK: http://www.macweek.com/*
- *Macworld: http://www.macworld.com/*
- *Macworld Daily News: http://www.macworld.com/daily/dailynews.main.shtml*
- *MacAddict: http://www.macaddict.com/*

Books

Since you are reading this book, you presumably already know that there are books on the Macintosh. What you may not know is that Macintosh books are available for virtually every skill level and almost every specialized interest. Some books are devoted to a single popular program, such as Excel or Photoshop. Others are on some specialized topic, such as how to use the Macintosh to create newsletters. Some are for experts who

need help with their programming skills. Still others are a general introduction designed for the first-time user.

Visit a bookstore and check them out. You may find a book on exactly the topic you need.

Other Options

If you have a friend or colleague who is more knowledgeable about the Macintosh than you are, you don't need me to tell you how valuable a resource this can be. Not only can this person usually solve your immediate crisis, but he or she can teach you enough so that the next time the same or a similar problem happens, you can solve it on your own!

If you don't have a friend who is a Macintosh expert, you could hire a consultant or attend special training seminars. These are usually too expensive for an individual user, but they are viable for corporate use. Finally, although their advice is often unreliable, you could ask for help from the sales staff of computer retail stores or mail-order outlets.

For related information

SEE:
- **Chapter 3 on general problem-solving strategies**
- **Chapter 14 for more on using modems and accessing the Internet**
- **Appendix for the phone numbers of all the services and publications cited here, as well as an explanation of exactly what is meant by shareware and freeware**

Appendix

Stocking Your Troubleshooter's Toolkit

Throughout this book, I have described and recommended a variety of troubleshooting software. If you're interested in getting any of these products, but don't know how to obtain them, this appendix will help. The first part explains the different ways that software is distributed—and where best to go to get each different type (including a special offer just for readers of this book). The second section lists the names, vendors, and phone numbers of all the commercial troubleshooting software products mentioned in this book.

Where to Get Software

Commercial Software

Commercial software is the most commonly available and widely used category of software. These products are sold in retail stores and through mail-order outlets. Many of the companies that publish them are probably familiar to you: Claris (ClarisWorks, ClarisDraw), Microsoft (Word, Excel, Works), and Adobe (Illustrator, Photoshop).

Among troubleshooting utilities, Norton Utilities, SAM, Now Utilities, Retrospect, CanOpener, and Drive7 are just a few of the popular commercial products mentioned throughout this book.

For purchasing commercial software, I strongly recommend using mail-order outlets. They almost always have the best prices and the widest selection of products, and they keep current with the latest upgrades. And if they have what you want in stock, your order is delivered overnight. In contrast, most computer stores carry a more limited selection of Macintosh products, often with out-of-date versions on the shelves.

Most recently, I have ordered from three different mail-order firms. I can't speak for any others, but I have been very satisfied with the following:

- The Mac Zone: 800-248-0800 <http://www.maczone.com/>
- MacWarehouse: 800-255-6227 <http://www.warehouse.com/MacWarehouse/>
- Cyberian Outpost <http://www.cybout.com/>

If you work for an educational institution, it may sell products at special discounts that beat even mail-order prices. Check it out.

Shareware and Freeware

Shareware and freeware are usually utilities, games, and other specialized products that do not directly compete with commercial software, such as word processors and spreadsheets. Shareware and freeware are not often even sold in the same outlets that sell commercial software. Although this may make them a bit harder to find, the best ones are well worth the effort. They offer features often not available from any other product at a fraction of what a comparable commercial software program would cost.

SCSIProbe (mentioned in Chapter 5 and Fix-It #16) and Disinfectant (the anti-virus utility cited in Chapter 2 and Fix-It #7), are two popular freeware troubleshooting utilities. Sleeper (described in Chapter 12) and Font Box (mentioned in Chapter 9) are two examples of shareware utilities. Most of the more specialized utilities mentioned in this book, such as TechTool or ShortFinder, are also shareware/freeware.

Freeware and shareware are similar in most ways. The difference is only in how and how much you pay for them. Since it is perfectly legal to make copies of these programs to give to others, one common way to get shareware/freeware is from a friend who already has the program. Alternatively, you can get these programs from any of several services (see "Online Services"). Although there may be a minimal charge involved in obtaining the software from these services, it is important to understand that this payment goes to the service distributing the software, not to the creators of the programs. In this way, shareware and freeware differ.

For shareware, you are obligated to pay an additional fee (usually about $10 to $40) directly to the author of the program. But you need to pay this fee only if you continue to use the program. The idea is that you get to try out the software for a limited time risk-free. It is a sort of honor system: If you use the program, you pay for it; otherwise, you don't. You pay the shareware fee by mailing a check directly to the software developer. The instructions on how to do this are invariably included with the program. After you pay this fee, you may get an immediate bonus in return: a set of printed documentation or a copy of the latest version of the program (in case your version is not the newest one). In some cases, shareware products are distributed in a restricted form. For example, you may need a password to access the full program. To obtain the password, you must pay the shareware fee.

Let me be as clear as possible: The fee to the author is the shareware fee. You are obligated to pay this if you continue to use the program. Otherwise, the author gets no money at all and you are essentially cheating the author.

For freeware, there is no additional fee for continual use. That's why it's called freeware.

Popular sources of shareware/freeware programs include online services, Macintosh user groups, the Internet, and mail-order outlets.

SEE: • Fix-It #18 for more general information on on-line services and user groups

TAKE NOTE ▶

MACFIXIT WEB SITE

Almost all of the freeware and shareware utilities mentioned in *Sad Macs* are available on my *MacFixIt* Web site:<http://www.macfixit.com/>.

SEE: • "On the Web: MacFixIt," in the Preface, for more details

Online Services

If you own a modem and telecommunications software, you can download shareware and freeware products from various online services. The best services (actually about the only remaining services) for Macintosh software include the following:

- America Online: 800-827-6364
- CompuServe: 800-848-8990

Use the phone numbers listed here to get more information about how to sign up for these services; these are not the numbers used to log onto the service with your computer. Most of these services require that you use special communications software, which they supply at a minimal (or no) charge.

Internet and the World Wide Web

All the shareware and freeware mentioned in this book is also available at various ftp and World Wide Web sites on the Internet. My own *MacFixIt* site would be a good first stop. Otherwise check out the Info-Mac software library or CNET's Download.com

You can access any of these offerings from a direct Internet connection (via an Internet Service Provider) or through the online services just described.

SEE: Fix-It #18 (especially Table F18-1) and Chapter 14 for URLs and related information

Macintosh User Groups

Many larger user groups maintain a library of shareware and freeware, with programs available for purchase at a cost of a few dollars per disk (where each disk may contain a dozen or more programs, depending on their size). If you don't live near one of these groups, they will mail your order. Some groups also maintain an online service for downloading software. The best known users group is: Berkeley Macintosh User Group (BMUG); which can be reached at 510-549-2684.

Mail-Order Outlets That Specialize in Shareware/Freeware

Some mail-order companies specialize in selling shareware and freeware products (some may also sell some commercial software). The pricing policy is similar to that of user groups. Typically, they have catalogs from which you order. Two of the better known companies include the following:

- EduCorp: 800-843-9497
- Diskette Gazette: 800-222-6032

Apple's Macintosh Software

The distribution of Macintosh system software doesn't quite fit into either of the two previous categories. Your first set of Macintosh system software comes included with the purchase of your Macintosh. After that, if you want to stay current with each upgrade, you must obtain it on your own.

Depending upon the size and/or significance of the upgrade or new product, Apple may sell it as a commercial product (available through typical retail and mail-order channels as well as from Apple itself) or it may make it available online for free, especially at its own Internet sites (as well as offering it through the mail for no or a minimal charge). Only the commercial products come with printed documentation.

The same general principles hold for Apple's other software, such as Apple Remote Access. These days, distribution of Apple's Macintosh software is actually handled by Claris (which is owned by Apple).

To order Apple products, call one of the following numbers:

- Apple Software Order Center (for end-user software and updates): 800-293-6617
- Apple Developer Catalog (for developer products): 800-282-2732

SEE: • **"Take Note: Getting Help from Apple," in Fix-It #18 for more on calling Apple for assistance**

TAKE NOTE ▶

WHERE TO GET MACINTOSH MAGAZINES

Here are the phone numbers and Web sites of the Macintosh magazines mentioned in Fix-It #18. Call these numbers (or check the Web sites) for subscription information.

MacAddict	415-468-4869	<http://www.macaddict.com/>
Mac Home Journal	800-800-6542	<http://www.machome.com/
MacUser	800-627-2247	<http://www.zdnet.com/macuser/>
MacWEEK	609-461-2100	<http://www.macweek.com/>
Macworld	800-234-1038	<http://www.macworld.com/

Product Directory

The following is a list of the name, vendor, and phone number of almost all of the troubleshooting-related commercial products mentioned in this book (and a few that are not mentioned!). You can use these phone numbers to contact a vendor for more information about a specific program. Shareware and freeware products are not listed here, as they typically do not have a phone number you can call. Apple products (such as Mac OS 7.6 and Apple Remote Access) are not listed here. Refer to the previous section for information about them. Also not listed here are software products mentioned in this book but not directly related to problem solving (such as word processors and graphics programs).

- Adobe Acrobat (Adobe Systems, 800-833-6687)
- Adobe Type Manager (Adobe Systems, 800-833-6687)
- Adobe Type Reunion (Adobe Systems, 800-833-6687)
- APS Power Tools (APS Technologies, 800-233-7550)
- CanOpener (Abbott Systems, 800-552-9157)
- Conflict Catcher (Casady & Greene, 800-359-4920)
- DeBabelizer (Equilibrium Technologies, 415-332-4343)
- Disk Express (ALSoft, Inc., 800-257-6381)
- DiskDoubler Pro (with AutoDoubler and CopyDoubler) (Symantec, 800-441-7234)
- DiskFit Pro (Dantz Development Corp., 800-225-4880)
- DiskTop (PrairieSoft, 515-255-3720)
- DiskWorks (MicroNet Technology, 714-453-6000)
- Drive 7 (Casa Blanca Works, Inc., 415-461-2227)
- DriveTech (MicroMat Computer Systems, 800-829-6227)
- eDisk (Alysis Software Corp., 800-825-9747)
- FONDler (Rascal Software, 805-255-6823)
- Hard Disk ToolKit (FWB, Inc., 415-474-8055)
- Help! (Teknosys, 800-873-3494)
- Last Resort (Working Software, Inc. 800-229-9675)
- MacDrive Probe (Accurite Technologies, 408-433-1980)
- MacEKG (MicroMat Computer Systems, 800-829-6227)
- MacLink Plus (DataViz, 800-733-0030)
- MacTools Pro (Central Point Division of Symantec, 800-964-6896)
- Master Juggler (ALSoft, Inc., 800-257-6381)
- Norton Utilities for the Macintosh (Symantec, 800-441-7234)
- Now Utilities (Now Software, 800-689-9427)
- PartFinder (Kantara Development, 714-515-2130)
- Peace of Mind (DiagSoft, 408-438-8247)
- QuicKeys (CE Software, 800-523-7638)
- RAM Charger (Syncronys Softcorp, 888-777-5600)
- RAM Doubler (Connectix, 800-950-5880)
- Redux (Focus Enhancements, 800-453-7671)
- Retrospect (Dantz Development Corp., 800-225-4880)
- Silverlining (LaCie Ltd., 800-999-0143)

- Speed Doubler (Connectix, 800-950-5880)
- Spring Cleaning (Aladdin Systems, 800-732-8881)
- Stacker (Stac Electronics, 800-522-7822)
- StuffIt Deluxe (with SpaceSaver) (Aladdin Systems, 800-732-8881)
- Suitcase (Symantec, 800-441-7234)
- Symantec Antivirus for Macintosh (SAM) (Symantec, 800-441-7234)
- Tech Tool Pro (MicroMat Computer Systems, 800-829-6227)
- Virex (Datawatch, 919-549-0711)
- VirusScan (McAfee, 408-988-3832)
- Word for Word (Mastersoft, 800-624-6107)

Symptom Index

What follows is an index of all major symptoms and symptom-related alert messages described in this book. Alert messages cited in the text that do not imply any problem (such as *Please name this disk*) are typically *not* listed here. Conversely, a few of the alert messages listed here are not specifically mentioned in the text; in these cases, the page citations refer to the section in the text that describes the problem that would result in the alert message.

Alert/error messages are listed in italics. Other symptoms are listed in plain text. The words *A*, *An*, *The*, or *This*, if they would normally appear as the first word of a message, are typically omitted from this listing.

In general, this index cites only the primary location(s) in the book where a symptom is described and/or where a figure showing the error/alert message is found. Further, if a symptom is discussed over several consecutive pages or as part of a particular section or Fix-It, this index often cites only the first page of that section or Fix-It.

Finally, this index is not exhaustive. If you don't find precisely what you are looking for here, go to the topic that seems most closely related. You may yet find the answer you are seeking!

? disk icon appears at startup and remains indefinitely 140, 773, 858, 886

About This Macintosh/Computer: All memory greater than 8MB is listed as part of System Software rather than available for use by applications 733, 745, 751

About This Macintosh/Computer: Largest Unused Block size is smaller than expected 733–736

About This Macintosh/Computer: Macintosh model name is gone from window 554

About This Macintosh/Computer: Total memory is larger than expected when virtual memory is on (specific to Power Macs) 752

Alias <alias name> could not be opened, because the original item could not be found. 206

Alias broken links 207

Anti-virus utility reports that a virus attack has occurred 756

Apple event errors 242

Apple Guide does not work properly or at all 562

Apple HD SC Setup does not recognize your hard drive 804, 808

Apple menu item not listed in Apple menu 196

Apple Remote Access does not work 498

Apple Video Player, problems launching or using 412

AppleTalk cannot be opened (or *cannot be made active now*) 278

AppleTalk is in use by "File Sharing Extension." 493

AppleVision monitors (and other monitors): the screen goes black and will not reappear 531, 793, 797

AppleVision monitors (and related monitors): general problems with using 530, 888

AppleVision monitors: diagonal lines appear in the display or other unusual display symptoms 531, 535

AppleVision monitors: monitor shows incorrect resolution or color in display 531
AppleVision monitors: no sound from AppleVision speakers 531
AppleVision monitors: no startup sound 536
AppleVision monitors: software does not work properly (such as resolution options that do not appear as expected) 531
AppleVision monitors: software fails to load 533
AppleVision monitors: strange sound emits from the monitor speakers, even when the monitor is asleep or off 531, 536
Application <application name> has unexpectedly quit 106, 204, 729, 737
Application <name of application> could not be opened because an unexpected error occurred. 205
Application could not be found error message 214–216, 303, 309–310, 775
Application does not open at certain color depths 423
Application fails to launch because it detects another copy of the same application 148, 209
Application or control panel does not work as expected; includes problems with dialog boxes and menu commands 238, 665, 671, 678, 708, 827
Application or control panel will not launch 203, 518, 665, 671, 678, 708, 827
Application or control panel will not launch, insufficient memory 518, 559–561, 665
Application requires that the monitor be set to 8 bit color mode... 206
Application's accessory files missing or cannot be located 678
At Ease, problems with using 155–156, 808
Audio CDs, sound problems 525
Background printing, problems with 292
Background processing problems: application does not run in background as expected or background processing does not work in general 240
Bad blocks (media damage) suspected 237, 827, 833, 838, 855–857
Battery power, conserving 446
Battery power, problems with 463
Beep sound occurs whenever you press a key 885
Bitmapped graphics print at inferior quality, as compared to printed text or object-oriented graphics 433
Black Apple in the Apple menu of a color display 396
Blank gray screen persists at startup 140, 858
Breakup of screen display 83
Can't find QuickTimeLib 411
Can't load the Finder! 151
Can't open printer. Use the Chooser command... 275
Cancel printing request does not stop printing from continuing 265
Cannot copy the file 'System' Please delete this file and try again. 551
CD-ROM disc or removable cartridge: won't eject 174
CD-ROM disc: problems using as a startup disc 126, 476
CD-ROM disc: won't mount 172, 858, 866–867

Changing your AppleTalk connection will interrupt current network services and they will have to be reestablished. . . . 499
Chooser Setup button is dimmed . . . 257
Clippings file, contents vanishes from display (or appears outside of open Clippings window) . . . 372
Color matching . . . 431
Color/Grayscale: graphic, when printed, appears distinctly inferior in quality as compared to its on-screen display when printing grayscale or color graphics to a black-and-white printer . . . 426
Color: applications do not open or documents do not display correctly when using particular color depths. Most notably, graphics do not display at 16- or 24-bit color . . . 423
Color: graphic displays on screen correctly but prints in wrong colors or with inferior quality when printed to a color printer (including ImageWriters) . . . 429, 437
Color: graphic documents display in the wrong colors and/or entire display uses incorrect colors . . . 420
Color: thousands (16-bit) or Millions (24-bit) options not listed in Monitors control panel . . . 423, 668, 889
Command could not be completed, because there isn't enough memory available. (or any similar message indicating any other Finder action could not be completed due to insufficient memory) . . . 169, 241, 589, 729
Compatibility problems with system software . . . 709
Computer model name missing from About This Computer window . . . 554
Contents of the RAM Disk volume <disk name> will be lost by shutting down. . . . 454
Control panel <control panel name> cannot be used now. There may not be enough memory available, or the control panel may be damaged . . . 213
Control panel <name of control panel> cannot be used with this Macintosh . . . 208
Control panel cannot be opened because it had not been loaded at startup . . . 208
Control panel settings (such as date or sound level) are not retained when you turn the computer off . . . 793
Control panels need to be stored in the Control Panels folder or they may not work properly. . . . 705
Control Strip vanishes when changing resolutions on monitor . . . 414
Control strip: moving and resizing . . . 445
Copy and/or paste does not work as expected, especially across applications (text or graphics) . . . 369, 414, 418
Copy-protected program will not launch . . . 837
Corrupted data on disk, SCSI write cache as cause . . . 870
Corrupted file is replaced and soon appears damaged again . . . 756
Cursor alternates between a watch cursor and an arrow cursor at startup . . . 154
Cursor movement is erratic . . . 756
Cursor: Animated cursor (such as the watch cursor) remains on screen indefinitely; Macintosh does not respond to input; endless loop . . . 105, 281
Damaged (or corrupted) font file . . . 287, 375
Date of manufacture and hours of use information is incorrect . . . 799
Desk accessory <DA name> could not be opened, because an error occurred . . . 213
Desktop file could not be created. . . . 153
Desktop printer cannot be moved off the desktop because it is busy. . . . 594

Desktop printer cannot be moved off the desktop except to the Trash. 594
Desktop printers: cannot trash and/or move icon 271
Desktop printers: Desktop printer cannot be found 271
Desktop printers: files disappear when saved to the desktop printer "folder" 272
Desktop printers: icons have an "X" over them 271
Desktop printers: insufficient memory to print 272–273
Desktop printers: printing stalls 271, 274
Desktop printers; system crashes associated with desktop printing 272, 273
Desktop printing: multiple unknown desktop printers appear on your desktop 273
Desktop rebuilds every time you start up 783
Diamond symbol in front of application name in Application menu 265
Disk <disk name> cannot be used, because a disk error occurred. 164
Disk <disk name> could not be put away, because it contains items that are in use. . . . 168, 175, 228
Disk <disk name> could not be put away, because it is being shared. 175
Disk <disk name> needs minor repairs. 152, 163, 775, 782
Disk cannot be formatted due to erroneous report of virtual memory being on or files "in use" 846
Disk could not be shared because there is a shared folder inside it. 490
Disk driver; updating attempt fails 801
Disk error occurred. (Read, Write, or Verify errors) 236–237, 790, 810, 827
Disk First Aid lists problem as: *Invalid PEOF* 791
Disk First Aid lists problem as: *Invalid sibling link* 791
Disk is damaged. 154, 164, 790, 810
Disk is full 213, 233, 234
Disk is improperly formatted for this drive. 842
Disk is improperly formatted for use in this drive. 842
Disk is unreadable. or *Disk is unreadable by this Macintosh.* 154, 160, 163, 455, 810, 827, 838, 840–841, 843, 845, 882
Disk must be unlocked in order to perform one-time housekeeping. 153
Display starts up in Black-and-White or Grayscale, even though you have selected Color from the Monitors control panel. 793
Document <document name> could not be opened because the application program that created it could not be found. Do you want to open it using "TeachText/SimpleText"? 215, 303, 305, 309–310, 775
Document <document name> could not be opened, because the application program that created it could not be found. 216, 303, 305, 309–310, 775
Document <document name> could not be printed on <printer name> because AppleTalk is inactive. Use the Chooser to make AppleTalk active and try again. 279
Document <document name> could not be printed on printer <printer name> because of a PostScript error. 284
Document <document name> failed to print…because an unknown error has occurred. 592
Document <document name> failed to print…because the requested printer could not be found. 275, 592
Document <name of document> cannot be opened. The editor <name of editor> is not installed… 570

Document can not be printed at the current time because AppleTalk is inactive. To activate AppleTalk, go to the Chooser 278

Document can not be printed at the current time on the printer <printer name> because the printer is not available on the AppleTalk network. 275

Document cannot be opened (from the Finder or from an application's Open dialog box) 214, 775

Document cannot be printed at the current time because AppleTalk is inactive. 279

Document displays or prints with wrong formatting 357

Document displays the wrong font 350

Document does not import successfully to another application 220

Document opens with wrong application 223, 775

Document opens, but only with partial contents or garbage characters 827

Document prints in a font different from what is displayed on screen 355

Document prints with correct font, but has an occasional incorrect character 357

Document will not launch, insufficient memory 204, 222

Documents do not print at all or garbage characters print instead of the correct output, especially if an error message appears indicating a problem with the serial port 793

DOS files cannot be opened 220

Drive 7, problems using 851

Drive Setup error messages (e.g., *Cannot modify a disk in an unsupported drive.)* . . . 846, 849

Drive Setup, problems using 849

Duos: can't insert Duo or can't eject Duo from a Duo Dock 475

Email messages bounce back 630

Embedded fonts, problems with 293, 381

Emergency floppy startup disk will not start up 814

Endless loop 105, 281

Energy Saver, different versions 524, 557

Error occurred while trying to use the serial port that the modem is plugged into. 625

Error: One-sided disks are not supported. 840

Ethernet, problems with 655

Extension as a cause of a system crash at startup 682, 697

Extension conflicts 682

Extension: does not load at startup or does not work as expected 671, 682, 704

Extension: icon appears at startup with an X over it 682, 706

Extension: loading order and/or renaming problem 700–701

Extension: not enough memory allocated 743

Extension: refuses to be disabled 690

External drive not listed 127

External monitor connected to PowerBook does not display anything 456

Faxing with a fax modem, problems with 623, 626

File <file name> could not be opened, because you do not have enough access privileges. 492

File <file name> could not be read and was skipped (unknown error) 233, 810, 827

File <file name> couldn't be read, because a disk error occurred. 233, 810, 827

File <file name> couldn't be read, because it is in use 236

File <file name> failed to print... 286

File <file name> is damaged and cannot be printed. 286, 810, 827
File <name of file> is newer than what you are about to install 722
File <name of spool file> will be moved to the Trash because no desktop printer exists for this spool file. 271
File adds functionality to your Macintosh... 22
File cannot be copied or saved (*in use* or *illegal access permission* or other error messages) 233
File couldn't be read (or *written* or *verified*) *and was skipped* 810, 827, 838
File inadvertently deleted 200
File is used by system software. It cannot be opened. 222
File or folder cannot be deleted 225, 787, 810
File or folder cannot be located in the Finder and/or in an application's Open dialog box 193, 787
File or folder cannot be renamed 232, 316
File server's connection has unexpectedly closed down 471
File Sharing could not be enabled. 488
File sharing option does not appear in the Sharing Setup window 488
File sharing: problems such as system freezes or crashes 488, 494–495
File sharing: shared disk *could not be opened because it could not be found on the network.* 488, 491
File sharing: shared disk *could not be opened because you do not have enough access privileges.* 488, 492
Files (many or most) are missing from the desktop; possibly erased 182, 756, 775, 787, 810
Files do not open, specific to having very little unused space left on disk 768
Files on a hard disk cannot be accessed or result in a system crash when tried 187
Files take up more space on large capacity hard disks than they do on lower capacity disks 852
Find File reports: *Unable to open <file name> because it is invisible...* 320
Find File reports: *Unexpected error occurred, because the original file could not be found.* 320
Finder commands/settings and/or system-wide operations do not work as expected 708, 810, 827
Finder disappears; all windows, icons, and sometimes even the menubar vanish from screen 108
Flashing icons in the menubar 239
Floppy disk cannot be inserted into disk drive 162
Floppy disk copy is not an exact duplicate 46
Floppy disk drive does not read most or all disks 877, 882
Floppy disk drive makes unusual sounds when reading from or writing to disk 827
Floppy disk will not initialize or erase 526, 844
Floppy disk won't eject 166, 884
Floppy disk won't mount 162, 787, 882
Floppy disks, unlocked disks are listed as locked 883
Folder <name of folder> could not be opened, because it is not in any drive. 171
Font <font name> cannot be put into the System file. 332
Font <font name> will not be available to currently running applications until they have quit. 332

Font file cannot be deleted 375
Font file cannot be removed from suitcase, Fonts folder, or System Folder 375
Font menu does not list font name(s) expected to be there 380
Font menu lists new fonts that you did not install 380
Font menu lists one or more font names dimmed 380, 383
Font menu lists several different variations of the same basic font 383
Font name, 31-character limit 378
Font not found 353
Font suitcase cannot be opened because it is damaged 379
Font suitcase, can't create a new 333
Font type (Bitmapped, TrueType, or PostScript) cannot be identified 337, 345
Font, problem locating 383
Fonts need to be stored in the Fonts folder/System file... 331
Foreign language characters or other unexpected characters appear when you type text 354
Formatting of a paragraph changes unexpectedly during editing 367
Free space on a disk is less than what it should be, based on files listed on disk 775
FreePPP, problems specific to 628
Freeze or hang: Cursor is frozen on screen; Macintosh does not respond to input . . 99, 282, 297, 375, 521, 551, 884, 894, 897

General Controls, problems with 198, 227
GeoPort, problems specific to 892
Get Info comments are lost 782
Ghost monitor problem 522
Graphic cannot be edited as expected 401
Graphic file format shifts when transferred across applications 418
Graphic quality is inferior after being reduced or enlarged 402
Graphic quality is inferior or colors shift after being transferred across applications . 418, 420
Graphics file type, how to identify 407
Graphics objects, such as hairlines, do not print correctly or are missing altogether . 432
Graphics, cannot paste across applications (or problems with placement) 414, 417
Happy Mac icon persists at startup 140
Hard Disk Cable Warning (as appears on PowerBooks) 478
Hard disk (including removable media cartridges) will not mount, at startup or otherwise; its icon does not appear on desktop 157, 773, 787, 793
Hard disk does not make any noise at startup; stiction 161
Hard disk icon becomes a "shadow" dimmed icon; disk is unmounted 177
Hard disk is accidentally erased 810
Hard disk is inexplicably erased 821
HD Target Mode and freeze in PowerBook 500 and 5300 479
Hewlett-Packard printers: slow printing speed 295
Icons: Custom desktop icons are lost, replaced by incorrect or "generic" icons 219, 775, 778–782
Icons: custom icon for hard disk is lost 304, 375
Icons: file displays an icon for an older version of the software rather than the icon for its current version (or other unusual icon) 775, 782

Icons: icons in a Finder window are missing (appear to have moved beyond edges of screen or in distant area of a window) or rearranged 519, 537

Illegal Access Permission 235–236

ImageWriter <ImageWriter name>–The "select" light is off. Please push the select switch, then click Continue. 360

ImageWriter: Draft mode text prints with irregular spacing 436

ImageWriter: graphics print distorted or in poor resolution 436

Importing of a document file does not work; includes file name not listed in application's Open dialog box 220, 418

Infrared connections, problems with 481

Initialization failed! 855

Inserting a Duo in a Duo Dock 443, 475

Installation has been canceled, leaving your disk untouched. 551

Installer cannot update the version of the Macintosh System Software... 721

Installer does not launch successfully. 49

Installing system software, problems with 545, 551, 552, 717, 721, 722

Insufficient memory for Finder operations: such as mount, copy, eject 729

Insufficient memory, specific to Web browsers 643

Insufficient memory: files do not open or are slower than usual 729

Insufficient memory: working with bitmapped graphics 425

Insufficient system heap space 749

Iomega Driver extension could not load 160, 807

Item <file name> could not be deleted because it contains items that are in use. 228–229

Item named <file name> already exists in this location. Do you want to replace it...? . . 230

Items from locked disks cannot be moved to the desktop. 235

Jaggies and anti-aliasing 374, 435

Jaggies appear (text characters have a jagged irregular appearance) 335, 341, 365, 435, 595

Keyboard keys, typing results in incorrect characters 354

Keyboard, problems with 884–886

Kind listing for file in Get Info window is listed only as *document*, rather than with name of creating application 303

LaserWriter 8 Preferences file may be missing or damaged... 277

LaserWriter 8.4.x problems 266

LaserWriter GX document <desktop printer name> could not be opened, because the application program that created it could not be found. 591, 775

Limitcheck error, VM error, and other PostScript errors 290

Mac clones, problems with 528

Mac OS (Macintosh) Easy Open, quirks 216, 783–784

Macintosh appears dead; no response when you turn it on (including special problems with PowerBooks) 131, 468, 797, 877, 893

Macintosh does not start up (see more specific symptoms for other references) . . . 131

Macintosh does not start up; specific to using QuickDraw GX 589

Margin settings or line breaks are incorrect in display and/or printing 357

Memory leak (memory allocated to an application not released even after quitting all open applications) specific to Open Transport 613, 644

Memory leaks and fragmented memory 733–736

Microsoft Word 5.1, memory bug . . . 205
Modem and PPP problems: connection consistently fails or no response after an apparent successful connection or connection is dropped . . . 623, 626
Modem does not seem to be responding. . . . 625
Modem problems: connecting while traveling . . . 628
Modem, general problems using . . . 496, 503, 886
Modification date incorrect . . . 196
Modification date, Finder does not update . . . 39
Monitor display shrinks in size periodically or has a wobbly image . . . 877, 894
Monitor does not work: no display or dimmed display . . . 886
Monitor does not work: screen flickers, size of screen image shrinks, or color blotches appear in display . . . 889
Monitor does not work: specific to when connected to a Power Mac or AV Mac . . . 522–523
Monitor screen does not come on at startup . . . 526, 531, 793, 797
Monitor stays black and will not turn on when waking up from sleep or after recalibrating . . . 534
Monitor: green tint or other monitor discoloration problems . . . 523, 888
Monitors & Sound control panel, problems with . . . 528, 530
Monitors control panel color depth setting incompatible with other application(s) . 206
Mouse/Trackball/TrackPad, problems with . . . 884–886
Multi-session CD-ROM discs do not mount . . . 174
Multiple copies of a disk's icon appear on desktop . . . 187, 858
Multiple master fonts, selecting . . . 385
Multiple System Folders on startup disk . . . 727–728
Multiscan monitors, general problems with . . . 890
Multiscan monitors, resolutions missing from listing . . . 397
Need System 7.1 or later... . . . 558
Need System 7.5.3... . . . 551
Network connection refused by server. . . . 639
No FPU (floating point unit/coprocessor) installed or *No FPU present* . . . 517, 669–670
No reserve battery power remains. (or other similar message indicating you are running low on battery power) . . . 451
Norton Disk Doctor and MacTools error message (btree, extents, nodes, etc.) . . . 817
Norton Disk Doctor fails to work because *files are open.* . . . 818
Norton Disk Doctor lists problem as *Damaged Resource Fork* or *Incorrect Physical Length*; specific to QuickDraw GX extension . . . 818
Nothing can be printed now, because PrinterShare GX could not be found. . . . 593
One or more items could not be shared, because not all items are available for sharing . 492–493
Only a 640 x 480 resolution is available . . . 535
Only one serial port on your Mac; issues regarding . . . 255, 496–497
Open Transport, compatibility problems . . . 617, 621, 622
OpenDoc: editor missing or in wrong location . . . 568, 570
OpenDoc: memory problems . . . 568–570
OpenDoc: orphaned parts . . . 570
Opening binhexed, compressed, disk image or pdf (Acrobat) files, problems with . 220, 634–636, 646, 653, 723

Out of memory... .... 213, 559, 560, 729, 738
or *There is not enough memory to complete this operation.*

Partition: cannot select the desired partition of a hard disk to be the startup partition 128

Password lost (PowerBook or At Ease etc.) 475, 808

Paste command is dimmed after having selected Copy (or otherwise doesn't paste as expected) 369, 414

PCMCIA cards, trouble ejecting 475

Performas, problems with 527, 711

PlainTalk speech does not work 212

Please insert the disk: <disk name> 170

Please make sure that you are connected to an AppleTalk network. 493
or *Please make sure that the AppleTalk network is disconnected.*

PostScript fonts do not print using PostScript 365

PostScript graphics do not print with the quality expected 432

PostScript printer font file is missing 342–345

PostScript printing errors 284, 290

Power Mac: application will not run on a Power Mac or runs significantly slower on a Power Mac 515

Power Mac: Get Info Memory listing does not change for native application when virtual memory is turned on or off 514

PowerBook 1400: *This is not an HFS disk* error message 476

PowerBook appears dead 468, 877, 893

PowerBook battery does not hold a charge 463

PowerBook Repair Extension program, qualifying symptoms on PowerBooks 5300 and 190 .... 472, 894

PowerBook Sleep problems (such as PowerBook not going to sleep as expected) .. 469

PowerBook starts with AC adapter but not on battery power 463

PowerBook, sound problems 474, 793

PowerBook: cursor temporarily disappears when moved 474

PowerBook: defective pixels 472

PowerBook: system error occurs when disk spins up after PowerBook has been "asleep" 469, 472, 801

PowerBook: trouble restarting 95

PPC native applications, how to identify 512–513

Preferences file cannot be opened and/or is damaged... 556

Preferences settings (of an application, Finder, or control panel) are lost or unexpectedly change 671

Printed output too light, too dark, streaked, or smeared 283

Printer <printer name> can't be found on the network. Please check connections... ... 275, 891

Printer can't be found... 275

Printer has been initialized with an incompatible version of the Laser Prep software. ... 288

Printer name not listed in Chooser 275, 891

Printer not responding... .... 275, 891

Printer, can't change name of 252

Printing color/grayscale images to a color printer, problems with 429

Printing graphics printed to a black-and-white printer, problems with 426

Printing halts (or does not begin); no error message appears 281

Printing halts due to a print-related error or system crash 284
Printing PostScript graphics without a PostScript printer 404
PrintMonitor and/or background printing does not work as expected 292
Progress bar (such as seen when copying disks) halts indefinitely . . . . 105 (*see also* freeze or hang...)
Putting the computer to sleep may cause you to lose some network services. 471
QuickDraw GX fonts, how to identify 585
QuickDraw GX will not be active because ColorSync was not installed. 591
QuickDraw GX, paper size selection problems 580
QuickDraw GX: Adobe Type Manager does not work with it 587
QuickDraw GX: applications incompatible with 576
QuickDraw GX: desktop printer icons appear with an X over them 590
QuickDraw GX: displayed font is not the expected one, when using QuickDraw GX or after turning off QuickDraw GX 595
QuickDraw GX: insufficient memory 589
QuickDraw GX: miscellaneous printing related problems 590
QuickDraw GX: printer drivers appear in Chooser 278
QuickDraw GX: problem removing 588
QuickDraw GX: problems with fonts 353
QuickDraw GX: problems with paper size selection 579, 593
QuickDraw GX: programs incompatible with QuickDraw GX 576
QuickDraw GX: Tray Mismatch Alert 593
QuickTime: problems installing and starting up 411
QuickTime: problems playing movies 411, 558
Quit command Command key shortcut (or other shortcuts) do not work 219
Rabbit icons 489
RAM disk cannot be deleted 747
Rebuild of desktop fails 784
Removable media cartridges, problems mounting and/or switching 159, 787, 793, 865–866
Repair utility (Disk First Aid, MacTools, Norton Utilities) does not list name of damaged disk 816
Repair utility (Disk First Aid, MacTools, Norton Utilities) unable to repair disk 790–791, 810, 819
Repeated requests to reinsert a floppy disk 170
Replace existing <file name>? 192
Rescued Items from <disk name> folder appears in Trash 98
Reset button cannot be located 92
Restart command from Finder's File menu does not work 179
Reverifying the disk. 855
Sad Mac icon appears at startup 133, 793, 858, 877, 894–896
Scanning, selecting a scan resolution 429
Screen "blinks" at startup 523, 534
SCSI cables, problems with 875
SCSI device does not mount or does not function as expected, including losing access to all SCSI devices 858, 868–869, 882

SCSI devices: can't access most or all devices on the SCSI chain 793
(see specific SCSI devices for other references)

SCSI Disk mode, freeze while using Norton Utilities 479

SCSI ID 5, special problems with 526, 869

SCSI Manager 4.3, problems with 860

SCSI termination, problems with 874

SCSI utility (such as SCSIProbe), problems with using 862–867

SCSI-2 (Dual SCSI buses), problems with 861, 863

Selecting between Open Transport and MacTCP 610–611

Serial port (or a device attached to it) does not work 891–893

Serial port is in use 284, 287, 497, 498, 793
(usually associated with modem and printer problems)

Serial port slowdown on Performas 527

Shared disk could not be found on the network. 491

Shared library files, missing or other problems with 518, 560

Shut Down command from Finder's File menu does not work 179

Shut Down Items folder items do not run at Shut Down 557

Shut Down warning message appears 91

SimpleText cannot display this kind of document. 594

SimpleText is unable to print this document. Make sure you've selected a printer. 592

SimpleText is unable to setup the page for this document. Make sure you've selected a printer. 592

SimpleText, cannot paste graphics into 312

Sleep and Energy Saver, problems with 524

Slow online response time 623

Some documents could not be opened. Try opening the documents from within the application. 223

Some margins are smaller than the minimum allowed by the printer. Your document may be clipped. 363

Some of the volumes you selected can't be repaired. 788

Sorry, a system error occurred. . . . . . (*see* system error listings)

Sorry, LaserWriter GX cannot be used. 591

Sorry, there is not enough memory available to open <document name>. 222, 424

Sorry, this disk is full or locked or the system is out of memory. 738

Sound file is damaged 210

Sound: alert sound does not play as desired 210

Sound: alert sound/system beep occurs unexpectedly 239

Sound: problems with 210–212, 522, 558

Sound: volume cannot be adjusted as desired or no sound at all 211, 525

Spacing of characters is incorrect 357, 360, 362

Speed of Macintosh is unusually slow (applications take unusually long to open or overall speed is slowed more generally) 183, 768, 775

Spontaneous restart occurs: after selecting Shut Down, at startup, or at any other time 179, 525, 793

Spool file could not be saved because there was not enough disk space. 290

Startup disk will not work on this Macintosh model. Use the latest Installer to update this disk for this model. 147

Startup drive: problems selecting partition as a startup volume 128
Startup floppy disk does not start up 145
Startup page on LaserWriters: how to turn it off 252
Startup time takes unusually long, especially prior to the appearance of the "happy Mac" or the "Mac OS" message 186
Stationery pad does not work 220
Status lights on LaserWriter flash or change from normal 283
Style formatting (such as bold or italics) appears correctly on screen but does not print 342–343, 357
StyleWriters: output is in the wrong color or otherwise distorted 431
StyleWriters: error messages about wrong or no paper 296
StyleWriters: memory problems 297
StyleWriters: PrinterShare does not work 298
StyleWriters: problems installing software 296
StyleWriters: slow printing speed 297
StyleWriters: smeared ink, colors missing, or related problems 297
StyleWriters: system freezes 297
Switching from Printer Port to Remote Only will interrupt any AppleTalk services currently established. 499
System 7.x needs more memory at startup 149
System 7.5 or later, compatibility and memory problems 554
System enabler missing 718
System error (crash or freeze) . . . . 82, 146, 187, 272, 375, 458, 495, 496, 520, 594, 595, 671, 682, 697, 708, 729, 756, 793, 801, 827, 877, 894–897 (*see also* other system error listings)
System error (crash or freeze): frequent and unpredictable 187, 756, 801, 877, 894, 897
System error (crash or freeze): occurs at startup 146, 520, 151, 682, 708, 793
System error (crash or freeze): shortly after ejecting floppy disk 865–866
System error (crash or freeze): specific to accessing a given SCSI device 801, 858
System error (crash or freeze): specific to being online 623
System error (crash or freeze): specific to installing new system software 708
System error (crash or freeze): specific to opening an application or document 827
System error (crash or freeze): specific to PowerBooks 458
System error (crash or freeze): specific to startup 801, 810, 858
System error (crash or freeze): specific to Web browser 642
System error (crash or freeze); specific to Power Macs 520
System error ID type/code: –127 89
System error ID type/code: –192 273
System error ID type/code: –23 278
System error ID type/code: –250 113
System error ID type/code: –34, –39, –43, –97, –108, –127, –192 89

System error ID type/code: –39 . . . . 89, 230
System error ID type/code: –41 151
System error ID type/code: –74 or –620 723
System error ID type/code: –8993 290
System error ID type/code: 01 . . . . 88, 623
System error ID type/code: 01 – 28 88–89
Includes: *bus error, address error, illegal instruction, divide by zero error, line trap error, bad F-line instruction, unimplemented trap error, miscellaneous hardware exception, floating point coprocessor not installed, out of memory,* and *stack ran into heap.*
System error ID type/code: 10 (Bad F-line instruction) 87, 187, 642, 877, 894
System error ID type/code: 11 (hardware exception) 85–87, 187, 520, 623, 642, 793, 877, 894
System error ID type/code: 15 273
System error ID type/code: 84, 87, 88, or 89 errors (WDEF purgeable resource problem) 112
System error ID type/code: Negative number IDs 85, 89
System error ID type/code: No FPU Installed 85–87
System error ID type/code: Positive number IDs 85, 88–89
System error ID type/code: Unimplemented trap 88, 502
System error: on Power Mac when you press the Command key 520
System extension <name of extension> cannot be used, because it is too new 208
System file on the startup disk may be damaged. 153
System file on this startup device does not contain the resources necessary to boot this Macintosh. 153
System Folder icon is missing its mini-Macintosh icon 124–125
System Folder problems, general check 242
System Software 7.x Installer does not recognize this Macintosh 553
System Software version 7.x is required to use this software... 553
System software damaged/corrupted 724
System software features missing after reinstalling system software 708
System software Installers, problems with 717, 721
TeachText/SimpleText document cannot be modified 311–312
Test interrupted because another program is using the disk 790
Text characters in display are spaced too closely together or are otherwise irregularly spaced 357
Text displays in a different font than was selected when document was last saved . . 350
Text document prints with a different font than appears on the screen 355
Text is clipped off at page margins when printed 363
Text turns into bitmapped graphics; no longer editable as text 373
There are people connected to this Macintosh... 494
There is a printing problem. Please choose PrintMonitor from the Application menu or click the PrintMonitor window. . . . 265
There is not a valid printer chosen. 592
There is not enough memory (available) to open <program name>. 729, 732
There is not enough memory to complete this operation. 424

There is not enough memory to load all of your extensions… . . . 149

There is not enough memory to print now nor share a desktop printer. QuickDraw GX will try again when more memory is available. . 589

There is not enough memory to print now. PrintMonitor will attempt to print again when more memory is available. . . . 294

There is not enough memory to print on the <name of printer> printer now. . . . 272

There is not enough memory to show the Clipboard. . . . 741

There is not enough room on the disk…to copy <file name>… . . . 233

There seems to be a problem with your modem. . . . 625

There was no response. Server could be down. . . . 639

Third-party startup extensions, problems with . . . 557

This is not a Macintosh disk… . . . 160, 163, 810, 838, 843, 882

This is probably not a valid resource . . . 819

TIFF translator could not read this file. . . . 416

To temporarily turn off extensions, restart and hold down the shift key. (or other message indicating an extension conflict occurred at startup) . . . 146, 692

Too many files open . . . 209

Trash cannot be emptied…because…items in it are locked. . . . 226

TrashBack problems . . . 58

TV remote does not work . . . 413

TV tuner won't work . . . 413

Unable to read from disk. . . . 810

Undelete utility is unable to recover even recently deleted files . . . 768

Uneditable text in "draw" programs . . . 374

Unexpected error occurred, because an error of type 84 occurred. . . . 112, 238

Unexpected quits or errors . . . 106, 204, 729, 737

Unidentified files and/or folders in your System Folder . . . 52–54

Unusual "nonsense" alert message appears on screen . . . 756

Unusual sounds or system beeps occur at unusual times . . . 756

Unusual tones at startup ("Chimes of Death" or "Chords of Doom") . . . 133, 877, 894

Using Virtual Memory on battery power Macintoshes will reduce your battery life. . . . 450

Vertical alignment of text/columns is incorrect . . . 357, 360

Vertical lines that follow cursor . . . 523

Video programs, such as Avid Cinema, do not work . . . 528

Views control panel cannot be opened . . . 206

Virtual memory, problems with . . . 753, 801

Virus alert warning message appears on screen . . . 756

Virus symptoms, a sampling of . . . 757

Volume control button does not work on Performas . . . 527

Volume or folder cannot be renamed . . . 232

WARNING: This document uses fonts not installed in your System file. . . . 350

Web Browser errors: No DNS Entry; 404 Not found, Server Not Found; Name is illegal, File contains no data, etc. . . . 638–639

Web browser, cache file problems . . . 645

Web browsers: problems with frames . . . 650

Web browsers: problems with loading helper applications or plug-ins . . . 650

Web page authoring, troubleshooting 633
Web pages do not get updated when expected 653
Web pages won't load or load slowly 637
Web pages: display incorrectly (such as incorrect colors or overlapping text) or have features missing (such as no animation) . . . 648
Windows move partially or entirely off screen when changing resolutions 421
Windows refuse to open or close 757
Word 6 documents appear incorrectly as templates 757
X disk icon appears at startup 145
You are now running on reserve power... (and other *reserve power* messages) 451
You cannot change items used by the system while programs other than the Finder are open. 332
You cannot copy <file name> onto this disk...because the disk is locked. 233
You cannot move 'MacTCP' to the folder 'Control Panels,' because an invisible item with the same name already exists in this location. 611
You cannot move <file name> from the folder <folder name>, because the disk is locked. 235
You cannot move <file name>...because you do not have the privileges to make changes 492
You cannot replace the font <font name>, because it is in use. 332, 378
You cannot replace the font suitcase <suitcase name>, because it is in use. 332, 378
You cannot replace the system extension <extension name> because it is in use. 236
You have changed your current printer. 260
You have set the Minimum size below xxxK, which may cause <program name> to crash. 736
Your document will be printed in the background when more memory is available. 294
Your request could not be completed because there are no desktop printers. 592

Common Troubleshooting Keyboard Shortcuts

Here is a listing of the most notable troubleshooting-related keyboard shortcuts cited in *Sad Macs* together with the page number where each one is primarily described. Some commands may not work with all Mac OS machines nor with all versions of the system software.

Keyboard shortcuts that are listed in menus are not listed here. For more shortcuts, check the Shortcuts menu command in the Finder's Apple Guide (Balloon Help) menu.

TO	PRESS	PAGE
Access Find File's additional options	Hold down the Option key while selecting the "Name" popup menu	43
Bypass the internal drive at startup	Command-Option-Shift-Delete at startup	129
Empty the Trash with locked files in it	Option while selecting Empty Trash command	226
Erase a disk automatically when you insert it	Command-Option-Tab	841
Force Quit	Command-Option-Escape	100
Rebuild the desktop	Command-Option at startup or when mounting a non-startup volume	775
Restart (when other methods fail)	Command-Control-Power	92
Restart or shut down	Power key	93
Select to do a clean install of system software	Command-Shift-K when in the Installer (not needed for Mac OS 7.6)	712
Start up with extensions disabled	Shift at startup	682
Startup with a CD-ROM startup disc	C key at startup	126
Zap the PRAM	Command-Option-P-R at startup	793

Index

NOTE: Page numbers in *italics* refer to illustrations or charts.

Symbols & Numbers

24-bit color
  memory allocation, 424
  Monitors control panel, 398
32-bit addressing
  Memory control panel, 745
  reasons for, 751
404 Not Found, browser problems, 638–639
680X0 processors, Power Macs versus, 8, 507–509
? (question-mark icon)
  balloon help, 24–25
  startup problems, 140–144

A

"About This Macintosh," 40–41
  bar graphs, 41
  bar shading, 739
  built-in versus total memory, 752
  Largest Unused Block, 40
  memory management problems (Fix-It #6), 731
  Preferred size option, 40
  quick fixes to oddities, 733
  Total Memory, 40
access privileges, "shared disk could not be opened," 492–493
accessory files
  finding missing (Fix-It #3), 678–681
  memory management problems (Fix-It #6), 737–738
active matrix screens
  defective pixels on PowerBook, 472–473
  passive matrix screens comparison, 473
ADB cables, AppleVision problems, 533
ADB ports
  keyboards and, 132
  repairing hardware problems (Fix-It #17), 884
Additions file, Apple Guide, 563
addresses (Internet), 629–632
  domain names, 629
  dynamic, 634
  e-mail, 630
  static, 634
  URLs, 630–632
  World Wide Web, 630–632
addressing, 32-bit, 745, 751
Adobe
  multiple-master fonts, 385
  Type Manager. *See* ATM
Alert Box messages, 68–69
  error code numbers, 84–87
  rebuilding Desktops (Fix-It #9), 777
alert sound files, 210–211
  accessing, 210
  System file and, 314
  unexpected problems, 239
  volume, 211
aliases
  file sharing and, 484
  launching problems, 206–207
  lost links, 207
  Make Alias command, 24
  startup extension, 701–702
Allow Processor Cycling option, PowerBook battery conservation, 449
America Online
  technical support (Fix-It #18), 909
  via PPP, 621
anti-aliasing
  bitmapped graphics printing problems, 435
  jaggies and, 374
anti-viral utilities, 760–762
  compression, 762
  customizing, 762
  installing, 760–761
  user definitions, 761
Apple events, errors, 242
Apple Guide
  Additions file, 563
  hardware/software incompatibilities (Fix-It #1), 667
  help system, 25–26
  incorrect location of documents, 562–563
  not installed or not enabled, 562
  System 7.5/7.6, 543–544
  System 7.5/7.6 problems, 562–563
Apple HD SC Setup
  disk driver updates (Fix-It #12), 804
  Drive Setup comparison, 845–846
  reformatting hard disks, 847
Apple icons, blackened, 395
Apple Memory Guide, module choices, 898
Apple Menu
  finding files missing from, 196
  Items Folder, 20
  Options control panel, 198, 556
Apple Remote Access (ARA)
  AppleTalk and, 503
  Communication Command Language (CCL) scripts, 501
  file sharing problems, 498–503
  LocalTalk icon, 499
  modem problems, 500, 503
  Network control panel, 499
  Open Transport, 499–500
  OpenTpt Serial Arbitrator, 502
  Remote Only icon, 499, 500
  Serial Port Arbitrator extension, 500–501
  Setup control panel, 500–501
  transferring files via modem, 486–487
Apple Repair Extension Program, 894
Apple Spec document, Macintosh models, 667
Apple technical support, 908
Apple Video Player, 412–414
  Avid Cinema and, 413
  insufficient memory, 412
  launching problems, 413
  MPEG problems, 414
  TV Tuner cards and, 413
AppleScriptLib, System 7.5/7.6 problems, 556
AppleTalk, 251–254
  See also file sharing; network connections; Open Transport
  activating, 251–252
  Apple Remote Access (ARA) and, 503
  control panel and TCP/IP, 616
  described, 480
  file sharing problems, 489
  laser printers, 256
  non-AppleTalk printers, 255–256
  Open Transport comparison, 278, 610–612
  Open Transport problems, 625
  overview, 253
  PowerBook battery conservation, 450
  PowerBook Sleep function problems, 471
  printing with, 279
  printing with extensions off, 278
  turning off problems, 493–494
AppleVision monitors, 529–537
  display errors, 534–535
  multiscan feature, 392, 890
  overview, 529
  repairing hardware problems (Fix-It #17), 888
  software, 530–531
AppleVision problems, 531–537
  ADB cables, 533
  AppleVision Fix utility, 533
  buttons don't work, 537

AppleVision problems *(continued)*
color depth, 535
color recalibration, 534
convergence lack, 535
desktop icons rearranged, 537
diagonal lines in display, 535
display errors, 534–535
Energy Saver feature, 536
installations, 532–533
resolution, 535
screens blinking at startup, 534
Sleep feature, 536
sound, 536–537
application conflicts
background printing and, 293
printing and, 295
application heaps, memory management problems (Fix-It #6), 730
applications
See also software
background processes and unexpected problems, 240
copying and pasting across, 369–373
creator code, 303
defined, 26
embedded fonts in, 381
finding missing accessory files (Fix-It #3), 678–681
launching problems, 203–213
launching wrong from Finder, 223–224
memory management problems (Fix-It #6), 738–741
multiple copies of causing recurring system errors, 116
opening problems, 732–738
QuickDraw GX and, 575–577
replacing damaged files, 829–930
running from RAM disks, 748
sound files, 211
"applications not found," type and creator code problems, 303
"applications in use," opening problems, 223
ARA. *See* Apple Remote Access
archival backups, defined, 51
archival compression utilities, 55
ASCII code, Norton Disk Editor, 322
Assistant Toolbox, PowerBooks and, 448
AT commands and modem initialization strings, 608
At Ease deinstallation, Finder startup problems, 155–156
At Ease for Workgroups, sad-Mac icons, 138
ATM (Adobe Type Manager)
control panel and unexpected problems, 241
fractional character widths and, 362
jaggies and, 366–367
lack of PostScript printers, 343
missing printer font files, 342
PostScript fonts and, 340–343
QuickDraw GX and, 587
substitute fonts, 352
upgrading, 341
WYSIWYG and, 340, 341
attachments, e-mail (MIMEs), 652
attributes. *See* Finder flags
Audio CDs, PCI-based Mac problems, 525
authoring software, World Wide Web, 633
autosave feature, 50
AV Macs
floppy disk mounting problems, 165
GeoPorts, 892
sync-on-green display problem, 523, 888
Avid Cinema, Apple Video Player and, 413

B

background application problems
Shut Down and restart, 180
startup extensions, 690
unexpected, 240
background printing, 258–259
application conflicts, 293
embedded fonts, 293
foreground printing comparison, 266
insufficient memory, 294
Print command, 262
PrintMonitor, 264–267
PrintMonitor Documents folder, 292–293
software reinstalls or upgrades, 293
startup disk free space and, 294
system freezes and, 104
troubleshooting, 282, 292–294
turning off, 293
backups, 50–51
data recovery utilities (Fix-It #13), 822
mirror image, 51
PowerBook problems, 474–475
reinstalling system software from, 725–726
software utilities, 51
strategies, 51
types of, 51
bad blocks
damaged files (Fix-It #14), 828, 829, 833–837
data recovery utilities versus reformatting, 835
how data recovery utilities repair, 835
intermittent, 829
mapping out (verifying hard disks), 856–857
phony (copy protection problems), 837
repairing, 833–835
saving problems, 233
Balloon Help, 24–25
System 7.5/7.6, 543–544
bar graphs, "About This Macintosh," 41
bar shading, "About This Macintosh," 739
batteries
"?" disk icon (startup problems), 144
blown fuses, 468
checking, 466
dead, 132, 797
"intelligent," 467
lithium ion, 466
NiCad, 466
PowerBook problems, 463–468
preserving RAM when replacing, 467
problems with, 893–894
reconditioning, 467
removing and zapping PRAM (Fix-It #11), 796
running out of power and, 451
trickle mode, 464
zapping PRAM, 468
battery conservation (PowerBooks), 446–451
AC outlets, 447
Allow Processor Cycling option, 449
AppleTalk and, 450
brightness, 448
control panel options, 448–450
Custom views, 448–450
Easy view, 448
file sharing, 450
floppy drives, 451
modems, 450
Power Conservation feature, 449
Reduced Processor Speed option, 449
screen dimming, 447, 448
Sleep function, 446, 448
sound volume, 451
Spin Down command, 447, 448
virtual memory and, 450
"white" desktop patterns, 451
battery icons, running out of power, 451
battery module, PowerBook, 445–446
beeping sounds, keyboard repairs, 885
BeOS, future of system software, 597
binary files, downloading with Netscape Navigator, 653
binhex files
appearing as text in browser windows, 652–653
encoded, 634–635
bitmap printing, printing halts and, 289
bitmapped fonts, 334–336
combining fonts, 345–347
described, 334–335

estimating sizes, 335
families, 334–335
jaggies, 335
limiting use of, 347–348
point size, 335
QuickDraw GX, 583
size of, 335–336
bitmapped graphics, 399
editing, 401–402
object-oriented graphics comparison, 401–402
printing problems, 433–435
text turning into, 373–374
blessed System Folders, startup problems, 124, 142
Bomb alert box, system crashes, 82
Bomb Shelter freeware utility, hard disk crash protection, 61
boot blocks
"?" disk icon (startup problems), 142
launching problems, 209
startup disks, 47, 125
viewing invisible files and folders, 321
bounce-backs, e-mail, 630
bps (bits per second), modems, 603–604
brightness, PowerBook battery conservation and, 448
browser problems, 637–655
"404 Not Found," 638–639
cache files, 645–646, 654
cache sizes, 643
color, 649
connections, 639
Directory file damage, 645–646
disk damage, 820
"File Contains No Data," 639
fonts, 649
Force Quit command, 646
frames, 650
incompatible files, 644
insufficient memory, 643–644
long delays before Web pages load, 641
Netscape Defrost, 642
no DNS entry error, 638–639
public betas and, 646
ShrinkWrap, 646
slow downloads, 642
system errors, 647
system freezes and crashes, 642–647
"unable to connect to host," 638
updating cache files, 654
Web pages display incorrectly, 648–649
Web pages load slowly, 639–641
Web pages not updated, 653–654
Web pages won't load, 637–638
browsers
Cyberdog, 655
MIMEs and, 652
multiple uses of, 632
Reload button, 653–654
updating cache files, 654
bugs
applications and unexpected problems, 239–240
clippings file, 372
disk check (defragmenting disks and), 773
Microsoft Word 5.1, 205
printing halts, 285
recurring system errors, 112
software, 30
startup extension problems (Fix-It #4), 693–694
system software problems (Fix-It #5), 709
bulletin boards, technical support (Fix-It #18), 910
Bundle bit
creator code and file type problems, 305
damage and rebuilding Desktops (Fix-It #9), 781
Finder flags, 315–316
bundled icons, 304
bypassing
external drives at startup, 129
hard disks at startup, 131
internal drives at startup, 130
bytes, defined, 9

C

cables
dead Macintoshes and, 132
Ethernet, 656
keyboard, 884
modem, 607, 892
monitor, 887
PowerBook file transfers and, 478
printer, 276–277, 280
printing halts and, 288
SCSI device problems (Fix-It #16), 875–876
serial, 891
StyleWriter, 296
system freezes and, 102
caches
browser problems and, 645–646, 654
L2 RAM, 509, 897
size of and browser problems, 643
slow hard disks and, 185
Cancel command, problem-solving strategies, 75
canceling printing, PrintMonitor, 265
CanOpener utility, file recovery via, 831–832
cards, hardware/software incompatibilities (Fix-It #1), 669
carrier (DCE) versus connect (DTE) speeds, modems, 605
cartridges, removable. *See* removable cartridges
CCL (Communication Command Language) scripts, Apple Remote Access (ARA), 501
CD-ROM discs, 15
ejection problems, 174–177
mounting problems, 172–174, 867
opening with PC formats, 221
sound files and, 212
startup, 48, 126, 522
system software installation problems, 545
CD-ROM drivers
installing, 173
mounting problems and, 867
CD-ROM drives
installation problems with non-Apple, 546–547
SCSIProbe utility and, 866
Chooser, 251–259
AppleTalk and, 251–254
file sharing, 483–484
printer driver icons, 277
printing troubleshooting, 277–280
purpose of, 251
QuickDraw GX drivers, 278, 573–575
Chooser extensions
Extensions folder, 20–21
startup extension problems, 691
Classic AppleTalk
memory management problems (Fix-It #6), 747
Open Transport comparison, 610–612
clean reinstalls, system software, 710–723
Clean Up command, Finder, 196
clipboards
bypassing, 372
copying and pasting across applications, 369–372
memory management problems (Fix-It #6), 732, 739
pasting graphics across applications, 414–415
Show Clipboard command, 415
clippings files
bug, 372
copying and pasting across applications, 371
pasting graphics across applications, 416
clock speed, Power Macs, 508–509
clone problems, 528
Code Fragment Manager
native Power Mac software, 514
Power Mac problems, 519
codependent startup extensions, startup extension problems (Fix-It #4), 704

color
See also color/grayscale; display depth
bit numbers and, 396
browser problems with, 649
monitor problems with, 889
color depth, 422
AppleVision problems, 535
display problems, 423–425
Monitors & Sound control panel, 424
color matching, ColorSync, 430–431
color palettes, display problems and, 421
Color Picker, 422
color printing, 429–432
ImageWriters, 437
Print dialog box, 430
color recalibration, AppleVision
problems, 534
color shifting
display problems, 420–422
higher color depths, 422
color/grayscale
display problems, 420–425
printing to black-and-white printers,
426–429
printing to color printers, 429–432
ColorSync color matching, 430–431
combining fonts, 345–347
Command key crashes, Power Mac
problems, 520–521
Command-Option keys, rebuilding
Desktops (Fix-It #9), 777, 785
Command-Option-Shift-Delete
(COSD) technique, bypassing
internal drives at startup, 130
Command-period
canceling endless loops, 105–106
canceling repeated requests to reinsert
floppy disks, 171
Command-Shift-K, "instant" clean
installs, 712
comments, rebuilding Desktops (Fix-It
#9), 782
commercial software, where to get, 915
Communication Command Language
(CCL) scripts, Apple Remote
Access (ARA), 501
compact Macintoshes, 5
complex documents, printing, 282
composite memory, caveat, 902
compressed files
downloaded files, 635
downloaded system software, 723
launching problems, 207
compression
anti-viral utilities and, 762
modem data, 605
compression utilities, 54–55
archival, 55
slow hard disks and, 185
CompuServe
technical support (Fix-It #18), 909
via PPP, 621
computer systems, defined, 6
Conflict Catcher
linking with, 702
memory management problems
(Fix-It #6), 750
startup extension problems (Fix-It
#4), 687, 696
conflicts
between two extensions, 696–697
font ID number, 350–351, 353–354
software, 31
startup extension problems, 683–684
startup extension problems (Fix-It
#4), 696–697, 699–703
connect (DTE) versus carrier (DCE)
speeds, modems, 605
connection order, SCSI device problems
(Fix-It #16), 873–875
connection types, QuickDraw GX
printing and, 574
connections
browser problems, 639
Open Transport problems, 623–627
PowerBooks to desktop Macs, 483
TCP/IP, 612–621
containers, OpenDoc, 564–565
control panels
See also Control Strip
emulation mode problems, 516
Energy Saver, 94, 557
FreePPP, 617–619, 628
General Controls, 198
hardware/software incompatibilities
(Fix-It #1), 667–668
incompatible settings and launching
problems, 206
INITs and extensions, 302
launching problems, 203–213
MacTCP, 614
Memory. See Memory control panel
Monitors. See Monitors control panel
Monitors & Sounds. See Monitors &
Sound control panel
Network, 499
No INITs bit, 208
NowSave, 61
on/off buttons, 693
Open Transport PPP, 619–621, 623
opening problems with No INITs bit,
208
Options, 198
Pointer Mode, 527
PowerBook, 444–446
Sharing Setup. See Sharing Setup
control panel
Startup Disk, 126–128
startup management utilities, 687
System 7.5/7.6 problems, 555–558
TCP/IP, 614, 615–616
Control Panels folder, System Folder, 21
Control Strip, 445
See also control panels
display depth, 397
module problems, 155
moving and resizing, 445
PowerBooks, *444*, 445–446
convergence, lack of in AppleVision
problems, 535
copy protection problems, phony bad
blocks, 837
copying
damaged files (Fix-It #14), 830–831
entire floppy disks, 46
moving files instead of, 194
copying and pasting across applications,
problems with, 369–373
copying problems, 233–237
bad blocks, 233
Disk Copy utility, 236
disk errors, 233, 236–237
files in use, 235–236
full disks, 234
"illegal access permission," 235–236
locked disks, 234, 235
read errors, 233, 237
verification errors, 234
virtual memory and, 234
write errors, 233, 237
corrupted file types, 304–305
corrupted files
See also damaged files
creator code, 304–305
Preferences file problems (Fix-It #2),
672–673
printing halts and, 285, 286–287
rebuilding Desktops (Fix-It #9), 776
System, 155, 798
system software problems (Fix-It #5),
709–710
corrupted fonts, failed installations, 721
corrupted preferences files, deleting,
674–675
corrupted printer drivers, 280–281
corrupted System files
Finder startup problems, 155
zapping PRAM (Fix-It #11), 798
CPUs, 6–8
clock speed, 508–509
multi-processor PCI-based Power
Macs, 515
multipliers, 508
Power Macs versus 680X0 processors,
8, 507–509
types of, 7
crash protection (hard disk), 59–61
Bomb Shelter freeware utility, 61
NowSave control panel, 61

repairing damaged hard disks, 60
System Error Patch freeware utility, 61
unerasing hard disks, 59–60
crashed disks, mounting problems, 157
crashes. *See* system crashes
creator code, 303–309
"applications not found," 303
Bundle bit problems, 305
corrupted, 304–305
editing, 306–309, 311–315
identifying, 309
missing, 304–305
PICT format, 310–311
Preferences file problems (Fix-It #2), 674–675
searching by, 314–315
TEXT format, 310–311
viewing, 306–309
wrong icons, 304
wrong kinds, 304
cross-linked files, data recovery utilities (Fix-It #13), 819
"Cuda" button
PCI-based Mac problems, 526
zapping PRAM (Fix-It #11), 797
cursor alternates between watch and arrow, Finder startup problems, 154
custom icons, 780
defined, 304
partitions and (Drive Setup), 849
rebuilding Desktops (Fix-It #9), 780–781
Use Custom Icon bit, 316
Custom Install
deciding on, 719–720
System 7.5/7.6, 552–553
Custom views, PowerBook battery conservation, 448–450
customized settings, resetting after zapping PRAM (Fix-It #11), 796–797
Cyberdog browser, 655

D

damage control, 29–31
hardware, 29–30
software, 29, 30–31
damaged disks
checking for. *See* data recovery utilities
Finder startup problems, 153–154
rebuilding Desktops (Fix-It #9), 778
replacing and repairing, 165–166
damaged documents
opening problems, 224
recurring system errors, 114
damaged drivers, disk driver updates (Fix-It #12), 803
damaged files, 29, 30–31
See also corrupted files
deleting problems, 230–231
launching problems, 209–213
mounting problems, 160–161
startup extension problems (Fix-It #4), 702–703
damaged files (Fix-It #14), 827–837
bad blocks, 828, 829, 833–837
CanOpener utility, 831–832
caveats, 828–829
copy protection problems (phony bad blocks), 837
copying, 830–831
FastCopy, 836
floppy disks with bad blocks, 836–837
how data recovery utilities repair bad blocks, 835
MacTools Pro, 832, 833, 834–835
miscopied information, 828
Norton Utilities, 832, 833
opening, 831
reasons for, 827–829
recovering, 830–833
replacing, 829–930
when to check for, 827
damaged floppy disks, 843–844
damaged font files, 375–378
formatting problems, 363
locating, 375–376
printing wrong fonts from display, 355–357
replacing, 377
utilities to check for, 376
damaged font suitcase files, 379
damaged printer drivers, 280–281
damaged sound files, 210
data compression, modem, 605
data recovery utilities, 34–35, 99
recovering unsaved after restarting, 96–99
reformatting comparison, 835
repairing bad blocks, 835
startup disks, 48
data recovery utilities (Fix-It #13), 810–826
automatic scanning, 820
backups instead of restore or recover, 822
cross-linked files, 819
disk damage and web browsers, 820
disk names, 816
emergency disks, 814
false alarms, 818
MacTools Clinic, 815–820, 823–825
multiple repair utilities, 820
Norton Disk Doctor, 815–820
Norton Utilities, 824–825
reasons to use, 810–812
recoverable files, 824
recovering files, 812, 823–825
repairing disks, 811, 812–820
restoring disks, 811, 821–823
when to check for damage, 810
dates, View by Date in Finder, 196
dead batteries, zapping PRAM (Fix-It #11), 797
dead Macintoshes, startup problems, 131–133
defragmenting disks, 62
"?" disk icon (startup problems), 144
defragmenting disks (Fix-It #8), 768–774
disadvantages of, 773–774
disk check bug, 773
disk damage and, 774
free space and, 772
individual file fragmentation, 771–772
MacTools Pro's Optimizer, 771
open files and, 772
optimizing, 769–771
reasons for, 768–769
reformatting and, 773
time required, 773
undeleting files and, 773
utilities, 769
when to, 768
deleting
corrupted preferences files, 674–675
files, 52–53
files accidentally, 200–203
files from System Folder, 52–53
hard disks, 851
multiple System Folders, 724–278
Preferences folder caveat, 676
print documents, 270
spool files, 286
startup extensions, 703
unneeded data and application files, 52
deleting problems, 225–231
damaged files, 230–231
files in use, 228
"folder from hell" problem, 229–230
folders remaining in use, 228–229
last resorts, 231
locked files, 226–227
locked floppy disks, 226
locked folders, 227–228
"desktop file could not be created," Finder startup problems, 153
Desktop files
infected, 766
kinds, 302
Desktop Folder
invisible files and folders, 320
System 7, 200

Desktop icons rearranged, AppleVision problems, 537
Desktop Patterns, insufficient memory, 560
Desktop printer files, QuickDraw GX problems, 594
Desktop printer icons, printing from, 575
Desktop Printers, 249, 267–274
crashes and restarts, 272
creating, 268
deleting print documents, 270
described, 267
disabling, 270
dragging errors, 271
error messages, 271–274
Finder Scripting Extension and, 273–274
icons, *269*, 574
insufficient memory, 272
memory size of, 273
moving, 271
print queue stalls, 274
Printing menu, 269
Save dialog boxes and, 272
selecting default, 268
software, 267
system errors, 273
Trashing, 271
troubleshooting, 270–274
Type 15 errors, 273–274
using, 269–270
window, *269*
"X" icons, 271
Desktop Reset, rebuilding Desktops (Fix-It #9), 786
Desktops
See also Find
files missing from, 182–183
moving files on locked disks to, 235
rebuilding. *See* rebuilding Desktops (Fix-It #9)
startup problems, 151–156
device drivers, updating hard disk. *See* disk driver updates
device independence, outline fonts, 336
diagnostic utilities
false alarms, 881
hardware problems (Fix-It #17), 879–881
dimmed disk icons, unmounted hard disks, 177
dimmed font names, Font Menu problems, 383
dimming screens, PowerBook battery conservation, 447, 448
DIMMs
See also memory
defined, 894
placement and speed maximization, 900
Directory
restart problems and, 181
viewing invisible files and folders, 321
Directory file damage
browsers and, 642–647
checking for. *See* Disk First Aid
recurring system errors, 115
tone errors at startup, 137
disconnected cables, system freezes and, 102–103
disconnecting unexpectedly, file sharing problems, 484–485, 494
disk caches
driver-level versus system-level, 748
Memory control panel, 744
memory management problems (Fix-It #6), 747
slow hard disks, 185
Disk Check bug
"?" disk icon (startup problems), 144
defragmenting disks (Fix-It #8), 773
Disk Copy utility
copying problems, 236
downloaded system software and, 723
disk damage
browsers and, 820
defragmenting disks (Fix-It #8), 774
finding files, 203
Disk Doctor. *See* Norton Disk Doctor
disk driver updates, 143
disk driver updates (Fix-It #12), 801–809
Apple HD SC Setup, 804
caveat, 803
damaged drivers, 803
Drive Setup, 804, 809
driver version numbers, 806
Format button, 809
formatting utilities, 804–805
Initialize button, 809
reasons to update, 801–803
removable media, 805
system software and, 802
updating drivers, 807–809
when to update, 801
disk drives
See also floppy disks; hard disks
not mounting automatically at startup, 868–869
system freezes and, 103
updating, 137
disk errors
mounting floppy disks, 164
saving problems, 233, 236–237
Disk First Aid
files missing from desktop, 183
folder deletion problems, 230
Macintosh tune-ups, 63
ResEdit, 323
system software problems (Fix-It #5), 716
Disk First Aid (Fix-It #10), 787–792
before using, 788–789
Erase Disk command, 791
error messages, 791
latest version of, 789
reasons to use, 787–788
repairing disks, 789–791
verifying disks, 789–791
when to use, 787
disk formatters, system software problems (Fix-It #5), 716
disk icons
dimmed, 177
unmounted hard disks and, 177
disk images
creating with ShrinkWrap, 646
downloaded files and, 636
"disk is damaged," mounting floppy disks, 164
"disk is unreadable"
mounting CD-ROMs, 173
mounting floppy disks, 163
disk names, data recovery utilities (Fix-It #13), 816
"disk needs minor repairs"
Finder startup problems, 152
mounting floppy disks, 163
disk problems, 157–188
ejecting disks, 166–170, 883–884
files missing from desktop, 182–183
frequent crashes, 187–188
mounting CD-ROMs, 172–174
mounting floppy disks, 162–166
mounting hard disks, 157–162
repeated requests to reinsert floppy disk, 170–172
restarts, 179–181
Shut Downs, 179–181
slowness, 183–186
unmounting hard disks, 177–178
Disk Spot Check utility, Norton Disk Doctor, 821
disk storage, 11–14
floppy disks, 11, 13–14
hard disks, 11, 14
measuring capacity of, 11
optical drives, 15
troubleshooting, 12
types of disks and drives, 13–14
Disk Tools startup disks, 45–47
disk-level compression, defined, 54
DiskEdit, MacTools Pro, 308
disks
damaged, 29–30
defragmenting. *See* defragmenting disks
Erase Disk command, 44
floppy. *See* floppy disks
full, 234
hard. *See* hard disks

locked, 234
optimizing. *See* defragmenting disks
startup. *See* startup disks
DiskTop
rebuilding Desktops (Fix-It #9), 786
viewing/editing invisible files and folders, 319
Display control panel, PowerBooks, 445
display depth, 393–397
Control Strip, 397
defined, 393
display problems, 425
dithering and, 394
Monitors control panel, 395–396, 397
overview, 393
pixels, 393
printing and, 394
setting, 395–397
slow hard disks, 185
Sound control panel, 397
Display Enabler, AppleVision software, 531
display problems, 420–425
See also monitors
AppleVision monitors, 534–535
color depth, 422, 423–425
color palettes, 421
color shifting, 420–422
display depth, 425
formatting, 357–363
monitors, 420–425, 886–888
multiscan monitors, 392, 421, 890
wrong fonts, 350–354
dithering
display depth and, 394
graphics printing problems, 428–429
DMA serial ports, modems, 606
documents
See also OpenDoc; SimpleText
applications not found by Finder, 214–219
complex, 282
damaged, 114, 224, 286
defined, 26
displaying wrong fonts, 350–354
graphics and, 417
opening problems. *See* opening documents (problems with)
paragraphs shifting formatting, 367–369
Portable Digital (PDDs), 581–583
replacing damaged files, 830
simplifying to troubleshoot printing, 291
text clipped at margins, 363–364
Documents folder, PrintMonitor, 267
Documents menu, OpenDoc, 568
domain names
Internet addresses, 629
MacTCP control panels, 614
DOS-formatted disks, mounting problems, 163–164
download libraries, technical support (Fix-It #18), 910
downloadable fonts, printing halts and, 289
downloaded files
browser problems, 642
compressed files, 635
compressed system software, 723
disk images, 636
file transfers, 634–636
graphics, 635–636
line break and spacing problems with, 359–360
segmented files, 635
sound, 635–636
video, 635–636
downloading binary files, Netscape Navigator, 653
dpi (dots per inch). *See* resolution
Drag and Drop
copying and pasting across applications, 371
opening files from Finder, 192
pasting graphics across applications, 416
dragging disk icons to Trash, unmounting hard disks, 178
dragging errors, Desktop Printers, 271
draw programs, 403
text turning into bitmapped graphics, 373–374
Drive7
mounting removable cartridges with different drivers, 865
troubleshooting, 851
Drive Setup
Apple HD Setup comparison, 845–846
disk driver updates (Fix-It #12), 804, 809
formatting disks (Fix-It #15), 845–846, 848–850
partitions, 852–853
partitions and custom icons, 849
removable cartridges, 849
troubleshooting, 849
driver descriptor maps, invisible files and folders, 322–323
drivers
CD-ROM, 173
disk updates. *See* disk driver updates
as extensions, 866
LaserWriter printer, 257–258
modem, 497
printer. *See* printer drivers
removable cartridge drives and, 807
selecting printer, 254–255
dropped connections, Open Transport problems, 627
Duo PowerBooks, 443
file transfers, 477–479
problems with, 475
duplicate copies on networks, launching problems, 209
Duplicate Items in folders, 54
duplicates, working only with, 75
duplicating conditions of recurring system errors, 109
dynamic addresses, Internet, 634

E

e-mail
bounce-backs, 630
Internet addresses, 630
MIMEs, 652
Easy Install
deciding on, 719–720
system software, 549
Easy Open utility, opening document problems, 215–216
Easy view, PowerBook battery conservation, 448
Edit menu, OpenDoc, 570
editing
bitmapped graphics, 401–402
creator code and file types, 306–309, 311–315
Finder flags, 317–318
invisible files and folders, 318–323
object-oriented graphics, 401–402
pixel-by-pixel versus object-by-object, 401
TeachText/SimpleText documents, 312
editors
missing OpenDoc, 570–571
OpenDoc, 565–566
ResEdit, 323
Editors folder, OpenDoc, 566–567
EGO (Embedded Graphic Objects), bypassing clipboards, 372
ejecting CD-ROM discs, 174–177
alternative methods, 176
Eject button, 175
file sharing and, 176
Put Away command, 175
virtual memory and, 175
ejecting floppy disks, 166–170
disk error messages and, 164
“files in use,” 168–169, 175
Finder memory problems, 169
Force Quit command, 169
memory problems, 169
nonstandard methods for, 167
with paper clips, 168
PowerBook 500 problem, 170

ejecting floppy disks *(continued)*
problems with, 166–170, 883–884
Put Away command, 166, 167
reinserting disks, 168
repairing hardware problems, 883–884
repeated requests to reinsert floppy disk, 170–172
restarts, 167
shadows, 167
standard methods for, 166–167
ejecting PCMCIA cards, problems with, 475–476
electromagnetic interference, monitors and, 889
embedded fonts
background printing troubleshooting, 293
Font Menu problems, 381
emergency disks, 130–131
See also startup disks
data recovery utilities (Fix-It #13), 814
fitting more utilities on, 313
when you can't start with, 814
Empty Trash command, Finder, 44
emulation mode (Power Macs), native mode comparison, 510–511
emulation mode problems (Power Macs), 516–517
control panels, 516
extensions, 516
math coprocessors (FPU), 517
Modern Memory Manager and applications, 516–517
Enabler files
overview, 718
System 7.5/7.6 problems, 554–555
encoded files, binhex, 634–635
endless loops, 105–106
Command-period, 105
printing troubleshooting, 281
Energy Saver feature
AppleVision problems, 536
monitor problems, 887
overview, 94
PCI-based Mac problems, 524–525
System 7.5/7.6 problems, 557
ENET Compatibility extension, Ethernet problems, 656
enlarging objects, 402
EPS (Encapsulated PostScript) files
graphics file formats, 406
graphics printing problems, 433
Erase Disk command
Disk First Aid (Fix-It #10), 791
Finder, 44
floppy disks, 841
hard disks, 851
error code numbers, 84–85, *86–87*
positive and negative, 85
Type 11, 85, *86*, 88, 89
error codes, sad-Mac, 134–135
error correction, modem, 605
error handling, Print command, 262
error messages
Desktop Printers, 271–274
Disk First Aid (Fix-It #10), 791
printing, 275
printing with QuickDraw GX, 577
PrintMonitor, 265
QuickDraw GX, 577
System 7.5/7.6 problems, 551
errors, system. *See* system errors
errors. *See* preventing problems; problem-solving strategies; troubleshooting
Ethernet, 655–656
cables, 656
ENET Compatibility extension, 656
hardware, 656
Exact Bit Images, Page Setup dialog box, 434
extensions
AppleVision software, 530–531
CD-ROM mounting problems, 173
Color Picker, 422
Desktop Printer software, 267
drivers as, 866
emulation mode problems, 516
Ethernet, 655–656
INITs, 22
INITs and control panels, 302
LaserWriter, 266
memory size increases, 743
printing without, 278
rebuilding Desktops (Fix-It #9), 784–785
removable cartridge drives and, 807
slow hard disks, 184–185
startup. *See* startup extension problems; startup extensions
startup management utilities, 687
System 7.5/7.6 problems, 555–558
Extensions folder, 20–21
Chooser extensions, 20–21
System extensions, 20
Extensions Manager, startup extension problems (Fix-It #4), 687
external hard drives
PowerBook file transfers, 477–479
Startup Disk control panel and, 127
external monitors for PowerBooks, 456–458
activating, 456–457
connecting, 456
disconnecting, 458
video mirroring, 457–458

F

families
bitmapped fonts, 334–335
PostScript fonts, 342–343
FastCopy, recovering files from floppy disks with bad blocks, 836
Faster Bitmap Printing, Page Setup dialog box, 435
fax modems
Performas and memory problems, 527
problems with, 626
fax software
hardware/software incompatibilities (Fix-It #1), 668
Open Transport problems, 625
"fext" files, Network Extension and, 690–691
file formats, problems with shifts across applications, 418–420
file mapping, native Power Mac software, 514
file pattern scan method, undeleting files, 202
file sharing
See also AppleTalk; network connections; Open Transport
accessing, 485–486
aliases and, 484
Chooser and, 483–484
disconnecting, 484–485
file synchronization, 485
infrared connections, 481
intranets and, 480
Make Alias command, 484
memory management problems (Fix-It #6), 746
mounting removable cartridges with different drivers, 866
PowerBook battery conservation, 450
PowerBook file transfers, 479–486
recurring system errors and, 113
setting up, 479–484
Sharing... dialog box, 482
Sharing Setup control panel, 113, *481*, 482
software, 481–482
Timbuktu Pro and, 480
Users & Groups control panel, 483
file sharing problems, 488–495
access privileges and, 492–493
Apple Remote Access (ARA), 498–502
AppleTalk not active, 489
CD-ROM disc ejection, 176
disconnecting unexpectedly, 494
"file sharing could not be enabled," 488–489
modems, 496–497
"shared disk could not be found on network," 491

"shared disk could not be opened," 492–493
Sharing... dialog box, 490
Sharing Setup control panel not accessible, 490
system freezes and crashes, 495
turning off, 493–494
file synchronization, file sharing, 485
file transfers (Internet), 632–637
downloaded files, 634–636
downloading, 632
uploaded files, 636–637
uploading, 632
file transfers (PowerBook), 476–487
cables, 478
external hard drives, 477–479
file sharing, 479–486
infrared connections, 481
modems, 486–487
Norton Utilities problem, 479
passwords, 479
problems with, 488–503
Remote Access Personal program, 487
SCSI ports, 477–479
system freezes, 479
Users & Groups control panel, 487
file types, 302–303
applications not found, 303
Bundle bit problems, 305
changing, 306
corrupted, 304–305
editing, 306–309
editing TeachText/SimpleText documents, 312
missing, 304–305
PICT format, 310–311
problems, 303–309
searching by, 314–315
of SimpleText documents, 582
viewing, 306–309
wrong icons, 304
wrong kinds, 304
file-level compression, defined, 54
files, 189–243
copying problems, 233–237
cross-linked, 819
damaged. *See* damaged files
data recovery utilities (Fix-It #13), 812, 823–825
deleting, 52–53
deleting accidentally, 200–203
deleting problems, 225–231
duplicate copies on networks, 209
finding, 193–203
infected. *See* viruses
invisible. *See* invisible files and folders
kinds, 301–315
launching problems, 203–213
locked, 226–227
missing from desktop, 182–183
moving instead of copying, 194
Open dialog box, 191
opening document, 213–224
opening from Finder, 192
renaming problems, 232
Save & Save As command, 192–193
Save dialog box, 191
saving problems, 233–237
searching for. *See* finding files
searching within text, 197
undeleting, 56–59, 200–203
unexpected problems, 238–243
FileSaver
undeleting files, 56
unerasing hard disks, 59
Find command, 42–44
finding missing accessory files (Fix-It #3), 680
Finder, 18–19, 36–44
About This Macintosh command, 40–41
Clean Up command, 196
closing windows, 196
deleting Preferences files, 676
disappearance troubleshooting, 108–109
Empty Trash command, 44
Erase Disk command, 44
Find command, 42–44
Find File command, 194–196
Force Quit command, 101
Get Info command, 36–39
icon views, 18
kinds, 301–315
launching wrong applications from, 223–224
memory management problems (Fix-It #6), 741–742
memory problems, 169
memory size increases, 742
opening files from, 192
PowerPC Finder Update extension, 512
Preferences file problems (Fix-It #2), 672–673
reopening windows, 196
Restart command, 44
Sharing command, 492–493
Shut Down command, 44
Special menu, 44
startup problems, 151–156
troubleshooting with, 36–44
View by Date, 196
window display modification, 196
window headers, 41–42
Finder flags, 315–318
Bundle bit, 315–316
described, 315
editing, 317–318
Inited bit, 316
Invisible bit box, 315
Name Locked bit, 316–317
No INITs bit, 316
Use Custom Icon bit, 316
viewing, 317–318
Finder Hiding, System 7.5, 198
Finder Preferences file
Finder startup problems, 155
restart problems, 181
zapping PRAM and, 794
Finder Scripting Extension, Desktop Printers and, 273–274
Finder startup problems, 151–156
At Ease deinstallation, 155–156
"Can't load the Finder," 151–152
Control Strip module problems, 155
corrupted Systems and/or Finders, 155
cursor alternates between watch and arrow, 154
damaged disks, 153–154
"desktop file could not be created," 153
"disk needs minor repairs," 152
Finder Preferences file, 155
memory, 154
system errors, 154–156
unreadable disks, 153–154
Finder-less startup disks, 47–48, 313, 314
finding files, 193–203
accidentally deleted files, 200–203
by creator code or file type, 314–315
damaged font files, 375–376
disk damage, 203
Finder, 194–196
missing accessory files (Fix-It #3), 678–681
missing from Apple Menu, 196
moving instead of copying, 194
Open dialog box, 197
saving to unintended locations, 194
finding lost icons, 219, 519
finding missing accessory files (Fix-It #3), 678–681
determining missing, 679
Find command, 680
installations, 679
reinstalling applications, 681
relocating or replacing files, 680–681
firmware (ROMs), modem, 626
Fix-Its, 665–914
damaged files, 827–837
data recovery utilities, 810–826
defragmenting disks, 768–774
disk driver updates, 801–809
Disk First Aid (Fix-It #10), 787–792
extensions problems, 682–707
finding missing accessory files, 678–681

Fix-Its *(continued)*
formatting disks, 838–857
hardware problems, 877–902
hardware/software incompatibilities, 665–670
memory management problems, 729–755
overview, 657–658
parts of, 658
Preferences file problems, 671–677
rebuilding Desktops, 775–786
SCSI device problems, 858–876
system software problems, 708–728
technical support, 903–914
viruses, 756–767
zapping PRAM, 793–800
fixed-size fonts. *See* bitmapped fonts
flags. *See* Finder flags
Flip options with Orientation options, printing halts, 289
Floppier, recovering files from floppy disks with bad blocks, 836
floppy disks, 11, 13–14
copying entire, 46
damaged disks, 843–844
damaged disks that aren't, 842–843
deleting versus reformatting, 842
Disk Copy utility, 236
drive types, 14
ejecting. *See* ejecting floppy disks
Erase Disk command, 841
formats, 163–164
formatting, 839–844
HD disks. *See* HD disks
inserting problems, 162
locked and deleting problems, 226
locking, 37
Macintosh PC Exchange, 843
mounting, 162–166
PC-formatted, 843
PCI-based Mac problems, 526
problems with. *See* disk problems
reformatting, 841–842
reformatting versus deleting, 842
reinitializing to reuse, 783
repairing bad blocks, 836–837
startup disks, 45–49
system software and, 723
types of, 13–14, 839
unmounting. *See* ejecting disks
verifying formatted, 855–856
viruses and, 765
floppy drives
PowerBook battery conservation, 451
repairing hardware problems (Fix-It #17), 882–884
flow control (modem), 607–608
selecting, 608
Xon/Xoff versus hardware handshaking, 607
"folder from hell" problem, deleting problems, 229–230
folders
Deinstalled files, 54
deleting problems, 225–231
Duplicate Items, 54
invisible. *See* invisible files and folders
locked, 227–228
remaining in use (deleting problems), 228–229
renaming problems, 232
Sharing dialog box for, 493
font files
damaged, 375–378
damaged suitcases, 379
described, 330
recurring system errors and, 115
removing from Fonts folders, 378
replacing corrupted, 287
system freezes and, 104
Font Menu problems, 380–385
clutter, 383–384
dimmed font names, 383
embedded fonts in applications, 381
Font/DA management utilities, 381–382
fonts appear or disappear, 380–383
fonts not listed in, 352–352
installer utilities, 381
startup disks, 380
style variant screen fonts, 384
font problems, 350–385
browsers, 649
documents display wrong font, 350–354
formatting problems, 357–363
fractional character widths, 362
jaggies, 365–367
paragraphs shift formatting, 367–369
PostScript fonts do not print with PostScript, 364–365
printing wrong fonts from display, 355–357
QuickDraw GX, 353, 595–596
text clipped at margins, 363–364
text turns into bitmapped graphics, 373–374
font suitcases
creating, 333
damaged, 379
described, 330
Font/DA management utilities, 334
Font Menu problems, 381–382
fonts, 325–385
basics, 330–333
basics summary, *349*
bitmapped, 334–336
checking for installed, 331
choosing formats, 347–349
combining, 345–347
corrupted and failed installations, 721
displaying wrong, 350–354
downloadable and printing halts, 289
embedded, 381
embedded (background printing troubleshooting), 293
fixed-size. *See* bitmapped fonts
formats, 334–349
GX versus non-GX, 585
ID number conflicts, 350–351, 353–354
jaggies, 365–367
Key Caps desk accessory, 331
line break problems due to changing, 359–360
location of, 330–331
monospaced versus proportional, 359
multiple-master, 385
outline, 336–345
printer versus screen, 338–339
QuickDraw GX, 583–588
removing from System Folder, 376
searching for reserved in System 7, 382
substitute ATM (Adobe Type Manager), 352
Substitute Fonts checkbox, 356
System 7 and earlier, 333
System 7.1 and System 7.5, 331–333
System Folder management, 331–333
typefaces of, 330
types of, 334–349
Unlimited Downloadable Fonts checkbox, 356–357
Fonts folders, 332–333
removing font files from, 378
System Folder and, 23
Force Quit command, 100–102
browser problems, 646
ejecting disks, 169
failure of, 102
Finder and, 101
Finder disappearances, 108–109
Restart command and, 101–102
saving and, 101
foreground printing, background printing comparison, 266
Foreign File Access, mounting CD-ROMs, 173
Format button, disk driver updates (Fix-It #12), 809
formats
font, 334–349
graphics, 399–408
mounting floppy disks and, 163–164
shifting across applications, 418–420
sound file, 210
TEXT and PICT, 310–311
video, 409–410

formatting disks (Fix-It #15), 838–857
  See also reformatting
  Drive7, 851
  Drive Setup, 845–846, 848–850
  floppy disks, 839–844, 855
  hard disks, 844–853
  IDE drives, 847
  message variations, 840
  reasons for, 838–839
  verifying, 855–857
  when to, 838
formatting problems, 357–363
  damaged font files, 363
  fractional character widths, 362
  LaserWriter 8 incompatibilities, 361
  line breaks, 358–360
  printer changes, 358–359
  TrueType incompatibility problems, 360–361
  vertical alignment and line lengths, 360
formatting utilities
  disk driver updates (Fix-It #12), 804–805
  switching caveat, 806
FPU (math coprocessors)
  emulation mode problems, 517
  hardware/software incompatibilities (Fix-It #1), 669–670
Fractional Character Widths checkbox
  font problems, 362
  printing halts, 289
fragmented disks. *See* defragmenting disks
fragmented memory, memory management problems (Fix-It #6), 733–734
frames, browser problems, 650
FreePPP control panel
  TCP/IP, 617–619
  troubleshooting, 628
freeware, 916–917
freezes. *See* printer freezes; system freezes
full disks, saving problems, 234

G

Gauge Series utilities, hardware problems (Fix-It #17), 880
General Controls control panel, System 7.5.3, 198
GeoPort Telecom Adapter, Open Transport problems, 625
GeoPorts, multimedia and, 892
Get Info command, 36–39
  Created and Modified data, 37
  Kind data, 36
  Locked check box, 37
  memory management problems (Fix-It #6), 731, 752
  memory options, 38–39
  Memory Requirements, 38
  Minimum size option, 38
  Preferred size option, 38, 39
  System Folder, 23
  Version numbers, 37
Get Info comments, rebuilding Desktops (Fix-It #9), 782
ghost problem
  monitors, 522
  passive matrix screens, 474
global mirror image backups, 51
Global Village extensions, Open Transport problems, 625, 626
graphics, 387–437
  bitmapped, 399
  display depth, 393–397
  documents and, 417
  downloaded files, 635–636
  draw programs, 403
  file formats, 404–408
  memory management problems (Fix-It #6), 741
  movies. *See* video
  object-oriented, 399–400
  paint programs, 402–403
  pasting across applications, 414–417
  PostScript programs, 403, 404
  printing problems, 426–437
  QuickDraw GX and, 588
  QuickDraw versus PostScript, 400
  resolution, 390–393
  in SimpleText documents, 312
  software, 402–404
  types of, 399–403
  utilities, 408
  video, 408–414
graphics accelerators, PCI-based Mac problems, 526–527
graphics file formats, 404–408
  application-specific, 406
  determining type of, 407
  EPS (Encapsulated PostScript) files, 406, 433
  generic, 404–406
  Open dialog box and, 407
  PICT, 310–311, 405
  PNTG (Paint), 405
  Save As command, 407
  TIFF, 405
graphics printing problems, 426–437
  bitmapped graphics, 433–435
  color/grayscale to black-and-white printers, 426–429
  color/grayscale to color printers, 429–432
  dithering, 428–429
  ImageWriters, 436–437
  PostScript graphics, 432–433
graphics transfer problems, 414–420
  file formats shifting across applications, 418–420
  pasting graphics across applications, 414–417
grayscale. *See* color/grayscale; display depth

H

halftones, printing color/grayscale to black-and-white printers, 427, 428
hangs. *See* system freezes
hard disks, 11, 14
  See also disk problems
  alternate startup disks, 128–129
  Apple HD SC Setup, 845–846
  Apple HD SC Setup reformats, 847
  bypassing at startup, 131
  compression utilities, 54–55
  crash protection, 59–61
  defragmenting. *See* defragmenting disks
  deleting, 851
  deleting unneeded data and application files, 52
  Drive Setup reformats, 848–850
  Drive Setup versus Apple HD Setup, 845–846
  drive types, 14
  drivers and recurring system errors, 116
  Erase Disk command, 851
  erasing, 851
  formatting, 844–853
  formatting and virtual memory, 846
  interleave speed, 854, 900
  maintaining, 52–55
  mapping out bad blocks, 856–857
  mounting problem drives, 129
  optimizing. *See* defragmenting disks
  partitions, 128, 852–854
  problems with, 157–188
  protecting against accidental erasure, 59
  reformatting, 161, 844–845, 851
  repairing damaged, 60, 882
  saving space, 54–55
  SCSI ports and external, 14
  SCSIProbe utility, 864
  Spin Down command (PowerBooks), 447, 448, 525
  startup disk protocol, 125
  system crashes, 188
  testing, 856
  unmounting, 177–178
  verifying formatted, 856–857
  virtual memory and formatting, 845–846
hard shutdowns, PowerBook, 459–460

hardware
Apple Spec document, 667
damage control, 29–30
Ethernet, 656
future of, 597–598
handshaking (modem flow control), 607
incompatibilities and recurring system errors, 111
PowerBook Power Manager, 460–462
system freezes and, 103
hardware problems
mounting CD-ROMs, 173–174
mounting hard disks, 161–162
recurring system errors, 116–117
tone errors at startup, 139
hardware problems (Fix-It #17), 877–902
diagnostic utilities, 879–881
Gauge Series utilities, 880
MacEKG, 879, *880*
opening cases, 878
Peace of Mind, 879
preliminary checks, 879
reasons for, 877–878
repairing, 881–901
TechTool Pro, 879, *880*
when to check for, 877
hardware/software incompatibilities (Fix-It #1), 665–670
Apple Guide, 667
cards, 669
control panel settings, 667–668
general strategies, 666–668
insufficient memory, 670
manuals, 666–667
math coprocessors, 669–670
monitors, 668–669
peripheral devices, 669
"Read Me" files, 666–667
reasons for, 665–666
software upgrades, 668
HD disks
damaged disks that aren't, 842–843
floppy disk types, 13–14
formatting floppy disks, 840
problems with reading, 221
HD SC Setup, disk driver updates (Fix-It #12), 804
HD Target mode, SCSI Disk mode as, 478
headers, window, 41–42
heaps
memory management problems (Fix-It #6), 730
size increases after RAM installations, 560
startup extensions and, 684
help systems, 24–26
Apple Guide, 25–26
balloon, 24–25
problem-solving strategies, 71–72
Helper, QuickDraw GX, 576
helper applications (browser problems), 650–653
binhex files appear as text, 652–653
locating, 651–652
obtaining, 651
setting up, 650–651
Hewlett-Packard printers, slow printing, 295
hex code, Norton Disk Editor, 322
hidden features, System 7.5/7.6, 544
HTML (HyperText Markup Language), World Wide Web, 633
http://, World Wide Web addresses, 630–632
hue changes, Power Mac monitor problems, 523
hybrid Macintoshes, 6

I

I-beam cursors, renaming file problems, 232
icon views, Finder, 18
icons
assigning, 304
battery, 451
bundled, 304
custom. *See* custom icons
Desktop Printer, *269*, 574
finding lost, 219, 519
flashing in menu bar, 239
generic problems, 776, 778–781
printer driver, 254–255, 277
rearranged on desktop (AppleVision problems), 537
rebuilding Desktops (Fix-It #9), 776, 778–781
sad-Mac, 133
troubleshooting wrong, 304
Use Custom Icon bit, 316
with "X" (startup extension problems), 706–707
ID numbers
font conflicts, 350–351, 353–354
SCSI device problems (Fix-It #16), 859–860
IDE alternatives, SCSI device problems (Fix-It #16), 860
IDE hard drives
formatting disks (Fix-It #15), 847
PowerBooks and, 143
identifying
PostScript fonts, 345
startup extension problems (Fix-It #4), 693–699
TrueType fonts, 337–338
"illegal access permission," saving problems, 235–236
ImageWriters
color printing, 437
graphics printing problems, 436–437
spacing and, 360
importing files
defined, 417
file formats shifting across applications, 418
graphics, 416–417
opening problems, 220
incremental backups, defined, 51
indicator lights, "?" disk icon (startup problems), 141
infected files. *See* viruses
infrared connections, PowerBook file transfers, 481
Inited bit, Finder flags, 316
initialization strings (modem), 608–609
AT commands and, 608
Initialize button, disk driver updates (Fix-It #12), 809
initializing disks. *See* formatting disks
INITs
control panels and extensions, 302
memory management problems (Fix-It #6), 746
startup extensions comparison, 683
System Folder, 22
inkjet printers. *See* StyleWriters
installation problems, 545–553
AppleVision, 532–533
with non-Apple CD-ROM drives, 546–547
StyleWriters, 296
System 7.5/7.6, 545–553
system software on CD-ROM discs, 545
installation procedures
System 7.5/7.6, 548–551
system software problems (Fix-It #5), 717–723
installations
anti-viral utilities, 760–761
CD-ROM drivers, 173
complete system software, 710–723
Custom Install, 552–553
Easy Install, 549
failure of, 721
finding missing accessory files (Fix-It #3), 679
native Power Mac software, 511–512
OpenDoc, 567
QuickDraw GX, 572
QuickTime video problems, 411
system software, 548–551, 717–723
system software with Mac OS 7.6, 714–715
universal installs, 552
Installer utilities
Font Menu problems, 381

launch troubleshooting, 49
need for, 717
system software problems (Fix-It #5), 716–723
unexpected problems and, 241
insufficient memory
See also memory; memory management problems
Apple Video Player, 412
background printing, 294
browser problems, 643–644
Desktop Patterns, 560
Desktop Printers, 272
hardware/software incompatibilities (Fix-It #1), 670
launching problems, 204–205
opening document problems, 222
Power Mac problems, 518
printing halts, 290, 292
QuickDraw GX problems, 589–590
Scrapbook, 559
System 7.5/7.6 problems, 559–561
"intelligent" batteries, PowerBooks, 467
interleave speed, hard disk, 854, 900
Internet, 629–637
addresses, 629–632
connections. *See* Open Transport; TCP/IP
file transfers, 632–637
mailing lists, 911
newsgroups, 910
shareware and freeware, 917
technical support (Fix-It #18), 910–912
World Wide Web, 911–912
Internet Explorer. *See* browser problems; browsers
Interrupt button, restarts, 91–92
Interrupt command, keyboard, 92–94
intranets, file sharing and, 480
Invisible bit box, Finder flags, 315
invisible files and folders, 318–323
boot blocks, 321
Desktop Folder, 320
driver descriptor maps, 322–323
Norton Utilities, 318–319
partition maps, 322–323
Trash, 320
Iomega drives. *See* removable cartridges
isolating causes, problem-solving strategies, 70–71

J

jaggies, 365–367
anti-aliasing and, 374
bitmapped fonts and, 335
TrueType fonts, 365–366
Jaz drives. *See* removable cartridges

K

Key Caps desk accessory, checking for installed fonts, 331
keyboard shortcuts. *See* shortcuts
keyboards
ADB ports and, 132, 884
beeping sounds, 885
cables, 884
false freezes, 884–885
incorrect text characters, 354
repairing hardware problems (Fix-It #17), 884–886
Reset and Interrupt commands, 92–94
Kind data, Get Info command, 36
kinds, 301–304
creator code, 303
Desktop file, 302
file types, 302–303
overview, 301
wrong, 304

L

L2 RAM caches, 897
clock speed and, 509
laptops. *See* PowerBooks
Largest Unused Block, About This Macintosh command, 40
LaserWriters
See also printers
AppleTalk and, 256
background versus foreground printing, 266
color options, 430
complex documents and, 282
destination option, 263
extensions and, 266
limitcheck errors, 292
Page Setup dialog boxes, 250
PPD files, 257, 258
Preferences files, 277
printer driver versions, 288
printer drivers, 257–258
PrinterLib extension, 266
printing wrong fonts from display, 355–357
status lights, 283
Substitute Fonts checkbox, 356
Unlimited Downloadable Fonts checkbox, 356–357
version 8 incompatibilities, 361
version differences, 248–249
launching problems, 203–213
aliases, 206–207
Apple Video Player, 413
boot blocks, 209
compressed files, 207
damaged files, 209–213
duplicate copies on networks, 209
incompatible control panel settings, 206
insufficient memory, 204–205
memory management problems (Fix-It #6), 732–738
Now Menus, 219
Preferred size option, 205
restarts, 205
ScrapBook, 213
system software incompatibilities, 208
"too many open files," 209
"unable to read from disk," 213
unexpected quits, 204–205
wrong applications, 223–224
leaks, memory, 613, 734–736
libraries
download (technical support), 910
shared (Power Mac problems), 518–519
Libraries folder, OpenDoc, 566
limitcheck errors, printing halts, 292
line breaks, formatting problems, 358–360
line lengths, problems due to font selections, 360
line noise, modems and, 604
linking, startup management utilities, 702
lithium ion batteries, PowerBook, 466
Live Objects. *See* OpenDoc
"load only when needed," Open Transport, 613
loading, startup extension problems, 684–685, 704–707
loading order, startup extension problems (Fix-It #4), 699–702
LocalTalk
See also file sharing
StyleWriters and, 256
LocalTalk icon, Apple Remote Access (ARA), 499
locating files. *See* finding files
Locked check box, Get Info command, 37
locked disks
moving files to desktop, 235
saving problems, 234, 235
locked files, deleting problems, 226–227
locked floppy disks, deleting problems, 226
locked folders, deleting problems, 227–228
locked system files, QuickDraw GX problems, 594
locking floppy disks, 37
logic board problems, 893–894
low-level data, driver descriptor and partition maps, 322–323

M

Mac OS 7.6
- *See also* System #; system software
- installing system software with, 714–715

MacEKG, hardware problems (Fix-It #17), 879, *880*
Macintosh models, Apple Spec document, 667
Macintosh PC Exchange, formatting floppy disks, 843
Macintosh User Groups (MUGs)
- shareware and freeware, 917
- technical support (Fix-It #18), 913

Macintoshes
- battery problems, 893–894
- clone problems, 528
- compact, 5
- CPUs, 6–8
- disk problems, 157–188
- disk storage, 11–144
- help system, 24–26
- hybrid, 6
- Internet and, 602
- locating Reset buttons, 92
- logic board problems, 893–894
- memory. *See* memory; RAM
- models and computer systems, 5–6
- modular, 6
- notebook, 6
- NuBus versus PCI slots, 890
- Performa. *See* Performa Macintoshes
- Power. *See* Power Macs
- power buttons, 93
- power supply problems, 894
- PowerBooks, 439–503
- preventative maintenance, 45–65
- preventing problems, 27–65
- processors. *See* CPUs
- RAM. *See* memory; RAM
- repairing, 893–894
- Reset buttons, 92
- restarts, 90–96
- ROM modules, 6–8
- slots: NuBus versus PCI, 890
- startup problems, 131–156
- system errors, 79–117
- System file, 63–64
- System Folder, 16–26
- tune-ups, 62–64
- turning off and on to restart, 94–95
- user interface, 7
- as Web servers, 634

MacTCP control panels, TCP/IP, 614
MacTCP DNR files, TCP/IP, 617
MacTools Clinic, data recovery utilities (Fix-It #13), 815–820, 823–825
MacTools Pro
- crash protection, 59–61
- data recovery utilities, 34
- DiskEdit, 308
- editing/viewing file types and creator code, 307–308
- editing/viewing Finder flags, 317
- FastCopy, 836
- file recovery via, 832, 833
- folder deletion problems, 230
- Optimizer (defragmenting disks), 771
- repairing bad blocks, 834–835
- startup disks, 813
- undeleting files, 57–59, 201–202
- viewing/editing invisible files and folders, 318–319

magazines, technical support (Fix-It #18), 913
MagicCookie file, Netscape Navigator, 647
mail order, shareware and freeware, 917
mailing lists, technical support (Fix-It #18), 911
Make Alias command, 24
- file sharing, 484

manuals
- hardware/software incompatibilities (Fix-It #1), 666–667
- problem-solving strategies, 72

mapping out bad blocks, verifying hard disks, 856–857
maps, memory, 733
math coprocessors (FPU)
- emulation mode problems, 517
- hardware/software incompatibilities (Fix-It #1), 669–670

media damage
- defined, 30
- recurring system errors, 115

memory, 8–10
- *See also* RAM
- 32–bit addressing, 745, 751
- adding, 754–755, 894–896
- built-in versus total, 752
- composite caveat, 902
- defective false alarms, 896
- DIMM placement and speed maximization, 900
- fragmented, 733–734
- increasing overall availability of, 742–755
- insufficient. *See* insufficient memory
- interleaving, 854, 900
- L2 RAM caches, 509, 897
- maximum allowable, 898
- Minimum sizes, 736–737
- module choices, 898–902
- PostScript printer, 290
- printer, 901
- printing halts and, 290
- replacing, 894–896
- restrictions, 901
- size of modules, 899
- speed of modules, 899
- system freezes and, 104
- types of, 900
- video, 901
- zapping PRAM, 113, 144

memory allocation
- 24-bit color, 424
- recurring system errors, 113

memory bugs, Microsoft Word 5.1, 205
memory chips
- sad-Mac error codes, 134
- tone errors at startup, 139

Memory control panel, 744–745
- 32-bit addressing, 745
- disk caches, 744
- hardware/software incompatibilities (Fix-It #1), 667
- Modern Memory Manager, 745
- RAM disks, 744–745
- virtual memory, 745

"memory effect," NiCad batteries, 466
Memory Guide, module choices, 898
memory leaks, 734–736
- causes of, 735
- defined, 734
- fixing, 735
- Open Transport and, 613
- preventing, 736

memory locations, startup extensions, 684
memory management, OpenDoc, 569
memory management problems (Fix-It #6), 729–755
- *See also* insufficient memory
- About This Macintosh and, 731, 733, 739
- accessory files, 737–738
- applications and, 738–741
- Classic AppleTalk, 747
- clipboards, 732, 739
- Conflict Catcher, 750
- disk caches, 747
- file sharing, 746
- Finder-related, 741–742
- fragmented memory, 733–734
- Get Info, 731, 752
- graphics files, 741
- heaps, 730
- increasing overall memory availability, 742–755
- INITs, 746
- launching problems, 732–738
- Memory control panel, 744–745
- memory leaks, 734–736
- memory maps, 733
- Minimum sizes, 736–737
- Open Transport, 747
- opening applications, 732–738
- physical RAM, 754–755
- plug-ins, 737–738

Power Macs, 752–753
Preferred size decreases, 742–746
Preferred size increases, 740–741
RAM Charger, 745–746
RAM disks, 747–748
RAM Doubler, 753–754
reasons for, 729–730
system heap size increases, 749–750
system software memory size decreases, 746–748
virtual memory, 750–753
when to check for, 729
Memory Manager and applications, emulation mode problems, 516–517
memory maps, memory management problems (Fix-It #6), 733
memory options
About This Macintosh command, 40–41
Get Info command, 38–39
memory problems
ejecting disks, 169
Finder, 169
Finder startup, 154
heap size increases after RAM installations, 560
PCI-based Mac, 528–529
Power Mac, 515–519
QuickDraw GX, 589–590
repairing hardware (Fix-It #17), 894–902
startup extensions, 149–150
startup extensions (Fix-It #4), 703
StyleWriters, 296–297
System 7.5/7.6, 559–561, 743
unexpected, 241
Memory Requirements, Get Info command, 38
memory size
decreasing system software, 746–748
Desktop Printer, 273
increasing extensions, 743
menu bars, icons flashing in, 239
menus, Now Menus, 198
Microsoft Internet Explorer. *See* browser problems; browsers
Microsoft Word 5.1, memory bug, 205
MIMEs, e-mail attachments, 652
Minimum size option, Get Info command, 38
"minor repairs" alert messages, rebuilding Desktops (Fix-It #9), 782–783
mirror image backups, 51
mirroring, video, 457–458
missing file types, 304–305
missing files
creator code, 304–305
system software problems (Fix-It #5), 724–725
modem ports, non-AppleTalk printer options, 255
modems, 603–609
Apple Remote Access (ARA), 500, 503
bps (bits per second), 603–604
cables, 607, 892
carrier (DCE) versus connect (DTE) speeds, 605
connections while traveling, 628
data compression, 605
DMA serial ports, 606
drivers and communication software, 497
error correction, 605
fax, 626
file sharing problems, 496–497
firmware (ROMs), 626
flow control, 607–608
initialization strings, 608–609
line noise, 604
online service connections, 604
Open Transport problems, 623–627
port speeds, 606
PowerBook battery conservation, 450
PowerBook file transfers, 486–487
repairing hardware problems (Fix-It #17), 891–893
"serial port in use" error, 497
speed of, 603–607
Modern Memory Manager
emulation mode problems, 516–517
Memory control panel, 745
modular Macintoshes, 6
monitors
active matrix screens, 472–473
AppleVision, 529–537
cables, 887
color problems, 889
display problems, 420–425, 886–888
electromagnetic interference, 889
Energy Saver extensions, 94, 887
external for PowerBooks, 456–458
ghosting, 522
hardware/software incompatibilities (Fix-It #1), 668–669
hue changes, 523
multiscan, 392, 421, 890
passive matrix screens, 473, 474
Power Mac display problems, 522–523
PowerBook display problems, 887–888
quality of display problems, 889–890
repairing hardware problems (Fix-It #17), 886–890
resolution and, 390–392
screen savers, 889
screen size, 391
sync-on-green problem, 523, 888
vertical lines following cursors, 523
video display cards, 887
Monitors & Sound control panel
AppleVision software, 530
color depth, 424
display depth, 397
functions of, 398
PCI-based Mac problems, 528
Monitors control panel
24-bit color, 398
color depth, 424
display depth, 395–396, 397
external monitors for PowerBooks, 456–457
functions of, 398
hardware/software incompatibilities (Fix-It #1), 668
resolution, 396
Monitors extension, System 7.5/7.6 problems, 556
monospaced fonts versus proportional fonts, 359
MooV video format, 409
motherboards, defined, 6
Mount Cache, mounting removable cartridges with different drivers, 865
mounting CD-ROMs, 172–174
"disk is unreadable," 173
drivers, 173
extensions and, 173
Foreign File Access, 173
hardware-related problems, 173–174
multi-session discs, 174
SCSI-related problems, 173–174
"This is not a Macintosh disk. Do you want to initialize it?," 172
mounting devices with SCSIProbe utility, 862–863
mounting floppy disks, 162–166
AV Macs, 165
"disk error," 164
"disk is damaged," 164
"disk is unreadable," 163
"disk needs minor repairs," 163
ejecting disks, 164
formats, 163–164
inserting problems, 162
"is not a Macintosh disk," 163
PC (DOS)-formatted disks, 163–164
Power Macs, 165
replacing and repairing damaged disks, 165–166
restarting, 165
trashed disks, 162
mounting hard disks, 157–162
crashed disks, 157
damaged files, 160–161
hardware problems, 161–162
manually, 158
power supplies, 161
reformatting option, 161
removable media cartridges, 159–160

mounting hard disks *(continued)*
restarting after, 158
SCSI-related problems, 158
stiction, 161
mouse, repairing, 885
Movie Player, video utility, 409
moving Control Strips, 445
moving files
instead of copying, 194
on locked disks to Desktop, 235
MPEG video format, 409
Apple Video Player problems, 414
MUGs (Macintosh User Groups)
shareware and freeware, 917
technical support (Fix-It #18), 913
multi-homing, PCI-based Macs, 621
multi-processor PCI-based Macs, 515
multi-session CD-ROM discs, mounting problems, 174
multimedia and GeoPorts, 892
multiple copies of applications, recurring system errors and, 116
multiple System Folders, recurring system errors and, 115
multiple-master fonts, 385
multiscan monitors, 392, 421, 890

N

Name Locked bit, Finder flags, 316–317
native mode, Power Macs emulation mode comparison, 510–511
native Power Mac software, 511–514
buying and installing, 511–512
Code Fragment Manager, 514
determining, 512
file mapping, 514
PowerPeek utility, 513
RAM Doubler, 513
upgrading to, 511
virtual memory and, 512–514
Netscape Defrost, browser problems, 642
Netscape extensions, Web pages display incorrectly, 648
Netscape Navigator
See also browser problems; browsers
Cache settings, 654
downloading binary files, 653
MagicCookie file, 647
network connections
See also AppleTalk; file sharing; Open Transport
Ethernet, 655–656
repairing serial port devices, 891–893
startup extension problems, 148
Network control panel, Apple Remote Access (ARA), 499
Network Extension, "fext" files and, 690–691
Network Software Selector (NSS), Open Transport, 611–612
newsgroups, technical support (Fix-It #18), 910
NiCad batteries, "memory effect," 466
"no DNS" entry error, browser problems, 638–639
"No FPU Installed," error code numbers, 85
No INITs bit
control panels, 208
Finder flags, 316
Norton Disk Doctor
data recovery utilities (Fix-It #13), 815–820, 824–825
Disk Spot Check utility, 821
Norton Disk Editor
driver descriptor and partition maps, 322–323
hex/ASCII listings, 322
Norton Utilities
crash protection, 59–61
data recovery utilities, 34
data recovery utilities (Fix-It #13), 824–825
editing/viewing file types and creator code, 307
editing/viewing Finder flags, 317
file recovery via, 832, 833
Floppier, 836
folder deletion problems, 230
PowerBook file transfer problems, 479
rebuilding Desktops (Fix-It #9), 786
repairing bad blocks, 833
startup disks, 813
undeleting files, 56, 201
unerasing hard disks, 59
viewing Directory and boot blocks, 321
viewing/editing invisible files and folders, 318–319
notebooks. *See* PowerBooks
Now Utilities
Now Menus, 198, 219
System 7.5/7.6 problems, 558
system enhancement packages, 35
NowSave control panel, hard disk crash protection, 61
NSS (Network Software Selector), Open Transport, 611–612
NuBus versus PCI slots, 890
numeric keypads, repairing, 886

O

object-oriented graphics, 399–400
bitmapped graphics comparison, 401–402
editing, 401–402
ObjectSupportLib, System 7.5/7.6 problems, 556
on/off buttons
control panel, 693
startup extension problems (Fix-It #4), 706
online connections. *See* Open Transport
online information services
modem connections, 604
shareware and freeware, 917
technical support (Fix-It #18), 909
Open dialog box
finding files, 197
graphics file formats, 407
opening files, 191
open files, defragmenting disks and, 772
Open Transport, 499–500, 609–621
See also AppleTalk; file sharing; network connections; shared libraries
as AppleTalk replacement, 278
Classic AppleTalk comparison, 610–612
files needed by, 610
"load only when needed," 613
Mac models that can use, 610–611
memory leaks and, 613
memory management problems (Fix-It #6), 747
memory requirements, 612
Network Software Selector (NSS), 611–612
PPP control panels, 619–621
reasons for, 609
TCP/IP, 612–621
Open Transport problems, 622–628
AppleTalk and, 625
dropped connections, 627
fax software, 625
Global Village extensions, 625, 626
incompatibilities, 622
modems, 623–627
PPP connections, 623–627
serial port malfunctions, 622
Telecom Adapter, 625
OpenDoc, 564–571
combining parts, 570
containers, 564–565
described, 564
Documents menu, 568
Edit menu, 570
editors, 565–566
Editors folder, 566–567
installing, 567
Libraries folder, 566
location of files, 566–567
memory management, 569
missing editors, 570–571
orphaned parts, 570–571
Size window, 569–570

stationery, 565–566
Stationery folder, 567
summary, 571
system software installation and, 722
viewers, 565–566
opening applications
memory management problems (Fix-It #6), 732–738
problems with. *See* launching problems
opening cases, hardware problems (Fix-It #17), 878
opening damaged files (Fix-It #14), 831
opening documents by default in SimpleText or TeachText, 311–312
opening documents (problems with), 213–224
applications not found by Finder, 214–219
applications in use, 223
damaged documents, 224
Easy Open utility, 215–216
files not intended to be open, 222–223
importing problems, 220
insufficient memory, 222
launching wrong application, 223–224
PC formats, 220–221
preference files, 224
SimpleText, 215
utilities, 216
version incompatibilities, 217–218
opening files from Finder, 192
OpenTpt Serial Arbitrator, Apple Remote Access (ARA), 502
operating systems. *See* System #; system software
optical drives, storage devices, 15
optimizing disks. *See* defragmenting disks
Options control panel, Apple Menu, 198
Orientation options with Flip options, printing halts, 289
orphaned parts, OpenDoc, 570–571
“out of memory”. *See* insufficient memory
outline fonts, 336–345
device independence, 336
PostScript, 338–345
rasterization, 336
TrueType, 337–338

P

Page Setup command, 259–261
changing printer drivers, 260–261
Page Attributes, 259–260
PostScript options, 260
Page Setup dialog box
bitmapped graphics printing problems, 434–435
Exact Bit Images, 434
Faster Bitmap Printing, 435
LaserWriters, 250
paper size selection, 580
Precision Bitmap Alignment, 434, 435
QuickDraw GX, 577–578
Smooth Graphics option, 434
text clipped at margins, 364
paint programs, 402–403
paper clips, ejecting disks with, 168
paper size selection, QuickDraw GX, 580
partition maps, invisible files and folders, 322–323
partitions
“?” disk icon (startup problems), 143
custom icons (Drive Setup), 849
Drive Setup, 852–853
“extra,” 853
hard disk formats, 852–854
hard and soft, 854
reasons for, 852
Startup Disk control panel, 128
passive matrix screens
active matrix screens comparison, 473
ghosting and submarining on, 474
passwords
PowerBook file transfers, 479
PowerBook problems, 475
pasting graphics across applications, 414–417
clipboards, 414–415
clippings files, 416
Drag and Drop, 416
importing graphics, 416–417
Scrapbook, 416
Show Clipboard command, 415
pasting problems. *See* copying and pasting across applications
PC Exchange
formatting floppy disks, 843
mounting removable cartridges with different drivers, 866
PC-formatted disks, 843
mounting problems, 163–164
mounting removable cartridges with different drivers, 866
opening problems, 220–221
PCI versus NuBus slots, 890
PCI-based Mac problems, 523–529
Audio CDs, 525
“Cuda” button, 526
diagnostic utility false alarms, 881
Energy Saver feature, 524–525
floppy disks, 526
graphics accelerators, 526–527
memory, 528–529
Monitors & Sound control panel, 528
Performas, 527
Pointer Mode control panel, 527
screens blinking at startup, 523–524
SCSI ID 5, 526, 869
Sleep feature, 524–525
video, 528
zapping PRAM, 529
PCI-based Macs, 514–515
multi-homing, 621
multi-processor, 515
zapping PRAM (Fix-It #11), 795–796, 800
PCMCIA cards, ejection problems, 475–476
PDDs (Portable Digital Documents), 581–583
SimpleText and, 582, 583
Peace of Mind, hardware problems (Fix-It #17), 879
Performas
problems with, 527
reinstalling system software on, 711
system software and, 17
peripheral devices
hardware/software incompatibilities (Fix-It #1), 669
system freezes and, 103
phone systems, modem connections while traveling, 628
PICT format
avoiding, 433
creator code and file type issues, 310–311
graphics file formats, 310–311, 405
pixels
defective on PowerBook active matrix screens, 472–473
display depth, 393
pixel-by-pixel versus object-by-object editing, 401
PlainTalk speech
Performas and, 527
sound files, 212
plug-ins
memory management problems (Fix-It #6), 737–738
Web pages display problems, 648–649
PNTG (Paint), graphics file formats, 405
point size, bitmapped fonts, 335
Pointer Mode control panel, PCI-based Mac problems, 527
port speeds, modem, 606
Portable Digital Documents (PDDs), 581–583
PostScript
EPS (Encapsulated PostScript) files, 406, 433
graphics printing problems, 432–433
LaserWriters. *See* LaserWriters
options (Page Setup command), 260
programs, 403, 404
QuickDraw GX graphics comparison, 400

PostScript fonts, 338–345
ATM (Adobe Type Manager) and, 340–343
combining fonts, 345–347
described, 338
enabling for QuickDraw GX, 586–587
families, 342–343
identifying, 345
not printing with PostScript, 364–365
PostScript printers and, 343
printer files, 344–345
printer fonts versus screen fonts, 338–339
QuickDraw GX and, 339, 344, 345, 584–587
TrueType fonts comparison, 348
Type 1 Enabler utility, 586–587
type 1 versus type 3, 339
PostScript printers
graphics printing problems, 432–433
memory problems, 290
PostScript graphics without, 404
versus non-PostScript, 346, 349
Power buttons, 93
Power Conservation feature, PowerBook battery conservation, 449
Power Mac problems, 515–523
Code Fragment Manager, 519
Command key crashes, 520–521
emulation mode, 516–517
freezes and PowerPC Interrupt Extension, 521
incompatibilities, 515–519
insufficient memory, 518
memory, 515–519
monitors, 522–523
printing crashes, 521
shared libraries, 518–519
sound, 522
startup crashes, 521
system errors, 520–522
Type 11 system errors, 520
virtual memory, 752–753
Power Macs, 505–529
bus speed and, 508
CD-ROM startup discs and, 522
clock speed, 508–509
emulation mode versus native mode, 510–511
floppy disk mounting problems, 165
GeoPorts, 892
memory management problems (Fix-It #6), 752–753
multipliers, 508
native software, 511–514
PCI-based, 514–515
Repair Extension program, 521
speed of, 507–509
versus 680X0 processors, 8, 507–509
Power Manager, PowerBook resets, 460–462
Power PC Reference Platform (PPRP Macs), future of hardware, 598
power supplies
hard disk mounting problems, 161
problems with, 894
PowerBook 500 problem, ejecting disks, 170
PowerBook problems, 458–476
backups, 474–475
batteries, 463–468
dead appearance, 468–469
defective pixels on active matrix screens, 472–473
Duo PowerBook insertions/ejections, 475
passwords, 475
PCMCIA card ejections, 475–476
Repair Extension program, 472
restarting after system errors, 458–463
Sleep function, 469–472
sound, 474
system errors after restarts, 462–463
version 1400 incompatibilities, 476
PowerBooks, 439–503
active matrix screens. *See* active matrix screens
all-in-one, 443
Assistant Toolbox, 448
batteries and models, 465
battery conservation, 446–451
battery module, 445–446
battery problems, 463–468
blown fuses, 468
connecting to desktop Macs, 483
control panels, 444–446
Control Strip, *444*, 445–446
Display control panel, 445
display problems, 887–888
Duo, 443
external monitors, 456–458
file transfers, 476–487
file transfers via modem, 486–487
hard shutdowns, 459–460
IDE hard drives and, 143
"intelligent" batteries, 467
lithium ion batteries, 466
models, 443–444
models and batteries, 465
modem problems, 496–497
NiCad batteries, 466
overview, 442
passive matrix screens. *See* passive matrix screens
Power Manager resets, 460–462
RAM disks, 452–455
RAM disks and restarts after system crashes, 96
Repair Extension program, 472
Reset button, 459
restarting after system errors, 95–96
reviving "dead," 469
Setup control panel, 444
soft shutdowns, 95
system software installation caveat, 550
transferring files to and from, 476–487
types of, 443–444
variations in models, 444
zapping PRAM, 468
PowerPC Finder Update extension, locating, 512
PowerPC Interrupt Extension, system freezes and, 521
PowerPeek utility, native Power Mac software and, 513
PowerPlug, QuickTime video, 411
PPD files
LaserWriters and, 257, 258
Print command, 262
ppi (pixels per inch). *See* resolution
PPP connections
See also TCP/IP
Open Transport problems, 623–627
PPRP Macs, future of hardware, 598
PRAM zapping. *See* zapping PRAM
Precision Bitmap Alignment, Page Setup dialog box, 434, 435
Preference settings, Web pages display incorrectly, 649
Preferences file problems (Fix-It #2), 671–677
cleaning up unneeded files, 677
corrupted and upgraded, 672–673
creator code, 674–675
deleting corrupted, 674–675
deleting Finder files, 676
deleting system software files, 676
determining which files to delete, 675
Finder, 672–673
Finder startups, 155
finding or replacing customized settings, 673
LaserWriters, 277
loss of customized settings, 672
opening documents, 224
quitting applications, 673
reasons for, 671–673
restart with extensions off, 673
System 7.5 software, 673
Systems 7.5/7.6, 558
Preferences folder
deleting caveat, 676
System Folder and, 23
Preferred size option
About This Macintosh command, 40
decreasing, 742–746
Get Info command, 38, 39

increasing, 740–741
launching problems, 205
slow hard disks, 185
unexpected quits and, 107
preventative maintenance, 45–65
backups, 50–51
hard disk, 52–55
protection utilities, 55–62
saving, 49–50
startup disks, 45–49
tune-ups, 62–64
preventing problems, 27–65
damage control, 29–31
Finder, 36–44
preventative maintenance, 45–65
tools, 29
troubleshooting toolkit, 31–36
viruses (Fix-It #7), 763–764
Prevention checking, SAM SafeZone anti-viral utility, 762
Print command, 261–263
background printing, 262
error handling, 262
PPD files, 262
Print dialog box, 261–262
Save Settings button, 262
Print dialog box
color printing, 430
QuickDraw GX, 578–579
print documents, deleting, 270
Print Later button, 280
Print Preview, QuickDraw GX, 581
Print Queue window, QuickDraw GX, 580–581
Print Time category, QuickDraw GX, 580–581
printer driver icons, 254–255
Chooser and, 277
printer drivers
corrupted, 280–281
LaserWriter, 257–258
LaserWriter versions, 288
Page Setup command, 260–261
printing halts, 288
printing with QuickDraw GX, 573
printer extensions, QuickDraw GX, 578–579
printer font files
missing, 342
PostScript, 344–345
printer fonts, screen fonts comparison, 338–339
printer freezes, StyleWriters and, 296
PrinterLib extension, LaserWriters, 266
printers, 248–263
AppleTalk, 251–254, 256
application conflicts, 295
cables, 276–277, 280
desktop, 249, 267–274
desktop icons, 574
determining RAM in, 290
dialog box variations, 248–250
display depth and, 394
formatting problems from changing, 358–359
Hewlett-Packard, 295
inkjet. *See* StyleWriters
LaserWriters. *See* LaserWriters
Macintosh can't find, 275–281
memory, 901
non-AppleTalk, 255–256
Page Setup command, 259–261
PostScript versus non-PostScript, 346, 349
RAM, 901
reinitializing, 282
repairing hardware problems (Fix-It #17), 891–893
resolution, 392–393
selecting by clicking printer driver icons, 254–255
selecting options, 255–259
software versions and printing halts, 288
startup extension conflicts, 295
StyleWriters with LocalTalk options, 256
toner cartridges, 283
PrinterShare, StyleWriters, 297
PrinterShare GX extension, QuickDraw GX, 576, 593
printing, 245–297
with AppleTalk, 251–254, 279
application conflicts, 295
background, 104, 258–259, 282
bitmap, 289
canceling with PrintMonitor, 265
Chooser and, 251–259
combined fonts, 346
complex documents, 282
Desktop Printers, 249, 267–274
display depth and, 394
endless loops, 281
error messages, 275
extensions off troubleshooting, 278
formatting problems, 357–363
general advice for problems, 274
graphics problems. *See* graphics printing problems
halts, 284–294
halts with no error messages, 281–283
Macintosh can't find printer, 275–281
one page at a time, 291
Page Setup command, 259–261
Print command, 261–263
Print Later button, 280
printer driver versions, 280
printers, 248–263
progress messages, 263
QuickDraw GX problems, 590–594
QuickDraw and QuickDraw GX, 249
resuming, 281
slow with Hewlett-Packard printers, 295
speed of, 283
startup extension conflicts, 295
steps to, 251–267
troubleshooting, 274–297
wrong fonts from display, 355–357
zapping PRAM, 281
printing halts, 281–294
background printing, 292–294
bitmaps and, 289
bugs, 285
cables, 288
causes, 281, 285
corrupted files, 285, 286–287
deleting spool files, 286
disk space and, 290
Document file corruption, 286
downloadable fonts, 289
Flip options with Orientation options, 289
Fractional Character Widths checkbox, 289
free space and, 290
insufficient memory, 290, 292
limitcheck errors, 292
with no error messages, 281–283
Power Mac problems, 521
printer drivers, 288
printer software versions, 288
replacing corrupted files, 286–287
serial ports and, 287
simplifying documents, 291
Split Long Paths option, 291
symptoms, 281, 284
zapping PRAM, 287
Printing menu
Desktop Printers, 269
paper size selection, 580
QuickDraw GX, 579
printing with QuickDraw GX, 573–583
Chooser, 573–575
connection types, 574
desktop printer icons, 574
error messages, 577
Page Setup dialog box, 577–578
PDDs (Portable Digital Documents), 581–583
Print dialog box, 578–579
print methods, 575–577
Print Queue window, 580–581
printer drivers, 573
Printing menu, 579–580
PrintMonitor, 264–267
canceling printing, 265
deleting spool files, 286
Desktop Printer software, 267
Documents folder, 267, 292–293

PrintMonitor *(continued)*
error messages, 265
monitoring printing with, 264
quitting, 265
spool files, 264, 266
window, *264*
problem-solving strategies, 67–75
See also troubleshooting
Alert Box messages, 68–69
avoiding problems, 74–75
Cancel command, 75
fixing problems, 73
getting help, 71–72
isolating causes, 70–71
keyboard shortcuts, 68
manuals, 72
repeatability, 69
risk management, 71
shortcuts, 74
technical support, 72
Undo command, 75
work-arounds, 73
working only with duplicates, 75
problems. *See* preventing problems; problem-solving strategies; troubleshooting
processors. *See* CPUs
product directory, vendor contacts, 918–920
program preferences, recurring system errors and, 115
proportional fonts versus monospaced fonts, 359
protection utilities, 55–62
accidentally-erased hard disks, 59
undeleting files, 56–59
virus detection, 55
public betas, browser problems, 646
purgeable WDEF resources, recurring system errors and, 112
Put Away command
ejecting CD-ROM discs, 175
ejecting disks, 166, 167

Q

question mark (?) disk icon (startup problems), 140–144
battery problems, 144
blessing System Folders, 142
boot block problems, 142
defragmenting disks, 144
Disk Check bug, 144
indicator lights, 141
partition problems, 143
repair utilities, 144
restarting and, 141
SCSI devices and, 141
startup disks, 140
System Folder problems, 141–143
updating disk drivers, 143
zapping PRAM, 144
question mark (?) icon, balloon help, 24–25
QuickDraw 3D, rendering graphics, 410
QuickDraw GX, 572–588
applications and, 575–577
ATM (Adobe Type Manager) and, 587
bitmapped fonts, 583
caveat, 329
Chooser and drivers, 278, 573–575
Custom Remove feature and fonts, 588
enabling PostScript fonts, 586–587
fonts, 583–588
graphics and, 588
Helper, 576
identifying GX versus non-GX fonts, 585
installing, 572
overview, 572
Page Setup dialog box, 577–578
paper size selection, 580
PDDs (Portable Digital Documents), 581–583
PostScript fonts and, 339, 344, 345, 584–587
PostScript graphics comparison, 400
Print dialog box, 578–579
Print Preview, 581
Print Queue window, 580–581
Print Time category, 580–581
printer extensions, 578–579
PrinterShare GX extension, 576, 593
printing, 573–583
Printing menu, 579
printing methods, 575–577
printing software, 249
Remove feature and fonts, 588
system software installation and, 722
TrueType fonts, 583
Type 1 Enabler utility, 586–587
utilities, 588
QuickDraw GX problems, 589–596
desktop printer files, 594
error messages, 577
false alarms, 818
fonts, 353, 595–596
insufficient memory, 589–590
locked system files, 594
printing, 590–594
Tray Mismatch Alert, 593
QuickTime video, 408–412
basic files, 408–409
“Can’t find QuickTimeLib,” 411
installation problems, 411
Movie Player, 409
placing on World Wide Web pages, 409
PowerPlug, 411
QuickTime VR, 410
Sound Manager and, 411
quitting
PrintMonitor, 265
unexpected, 106–108
unexpected problems with, 238

R

RAM, 8–10
See also insufficient memory; memory; memory management problems
adding, 754–755, 894–896
bytes, 9
composite caveat, 902
cost of, 10
defective and false alarms, 896
defined, 8
DIMM placement and speed maximization, 900
heap size increases after installing, 560
L2 caches, 509, 897
maximum allowable, 898
measuring, 9
printer, 901
replacing, 894–896
restrictions, 901
size of modules, 899
speed of, 9, 899
troubleshooting, 10
types of, 900
video, 901
zapping PRAM. *See* zapping PRAM
RAM Charger, memory management problems (Fix-It #6), 745–746
RAM disks, 452–455
Memory control panel, 744–745
memory management problems (Fix-It #6), 747–748
PowerBooks and, 452–455
reasons for, 452
restarts after system crashes and, 96
running applications from, 748
saving contents of, 454–455
ShrinkWrap alternative to, 455
startup disks, 452–453
“unreadable” error, 455
RAM Doubler
memory management problems (Fix-It #6), 753–754
new features of version 2, 754
startup extension problems, 691, 707
unexpected problems and, 241
virtual memory and, 513
rasterization, outline fonts, 336
read errors, saving problems, 233, 237
“Read Me” files
hardware/software incompatibilities (Fix-It #1), 666–667
System 7.5/7.6, 543

rebuilding Desktops, 63
rebuilding Desktops (Fix-It #9), 775–786
  alert boxes, 777
  bloated files, 776
  Bundle bit damage, 781
  Command-Option keys, 777, 785
  comments, 782
  completely, 785–786
  corrupted files, 776
  custom icons, 780–781
  damaged disks and, 778
  Desktop Reset, 786
  DiskTop, 786
  extensions and, 784–785
  generic icon problems, 776, 778–781
  Get Info comments, 782
  minor repairs alert messages, 782–783
  Norton Utilities, 786
  reasons for, 775–776
  reinitializing floppy disks, 783
  TechTool, 782, 785–786
  when to, 775
recalibrating color, AppleVision problems, 534
reconditioning batteries, 467
recording
  sound with SimpleSound, 212
  video, 412
recovering files
  See also data recovery utilities
  damaged files (Fix-It #14), 830–833
  unsaved data after restarting, 96–99
recurring system errors, 99, 109–117
  damaged document files, 114
  Directory file damage, 115
  duplicating conditions of, 109
  file sharing and, 113
  fixing, 111–117
  font files and, 115
  hard disk drivers, 116
  hardware incompatibilities, 111
  hardware problems, 116–117
  media damage, 115
  memory allocation problems, 113
  multiple copies of applications, 116
  multiple System Folders, 115
  program preferences and, 115
  purgeable WDEF resources, 112
  seeking causes of, 109–110
  Sharing Setup control panel and, 113
  software bugs, 112
  software incompatibilities, 111
  startup extension conflicts, 113
  system software and, 114
  System Updates, 112
  unpredictable intervals and situations, 110
  variations in circumstance, 110
  viruses and, 116
  zapping PRAM, 113
recurring system freezes, 102–104
Reduced Processor Speed option, PowerBook battery conservation, 449
reducing objects, 402
reference releases
  system software, 542
  System Updates, 64
  updates comparison, 710
reformatting
  See also formatting disks
  data recovery utilities comparison, 835
  defragmenting disks (Fix-It #8) and, 773
  floppy disks, 841–842
  hard disks, 161, 844–845, 851
reinitializing
  floppy disks, 783
  printers, 282
reinstallations, complete system, 710–723
reinstalling applications, finding missing accessory files (Fix-It #3), 681
reinstalling from backups, system software problems (Fix-It #5), 725–726
Reload button, updating Web pages, 653–654
Remote Access. *See* Apple Remote Access (ARA)
Remote Access Personal program, PowerBook file transfers, 487
Remote Only icon, Apple Remote Access (ARA), 499, 500
removable cartridge drives
  drivers and extensions, 807
  startup disks and, 129
removable cartridges
  disk driver updates (Fix-It #12), 805
  Drive Setup, 849
  ejection alternatives, 177
  ejection problems, 174–177
  mounting with different drivers, 865–866
  mounting problems, 159–160
  SCSIProbe utility, 864
  as startup disks, 176
  as storage devices, 15
renaming
  problems with, 232
  startup extensions, 701
Repair Extension program, 894
  Power Macs, 521
  PowerBooks, 472
repair utilities, "?" disk icon (startup problems), 144
repairing bad blocks, 833–835
repairing disks
  data recovery utilities (Fix-It #13), 811, 812–820
  Disk First Aid (Fix-It #10), 789–791
repairing hardware problems (Fix-It #17), 881–901
  ADB ports, 884
  floppy drives, 882–884
  hard disks, 882
  keyboards, 884–886
  Macintoshes, 893–894
  memory, 894–902
  modems, 891–893
  monitors, 886–890
  mouse, 884–885
  networks, 891–893
  numeric keypads, 886
  printers, 891–893
  Repair Extension Program, 894
  SCSI devices, 882
  serial port devices, 891–893
  Trackballs/Trackpads, 884–886
repeatability, problem-solving strategies, 69
repeated requests to reinsert floppy disks, 170–172
  closing windows, 171
  unmounting disks, 171
Replace option, Save As command, 192
replacing damaged files (Fix-It #14), 829–930
replacing and repairing damaged disks, 165–166
ResEdit, viewing/editing resources, 323
reserved fonts, searching for in System 7, 382
Reset buttons
  locating, 92
  PowerBook, 459
  restarts and, 91, 180
Reset command, keyboard, 92–94
resetting customized settings, zapping PRAM (Fix-It #11), 796–797
resolution, 390–393
  AppleVision problems, 535
  changing "on the fly," 395
  defined, 390
  missing choices, 397
  monitors, 390–392
  Monitors control panel, 396
  printer, 392–393
  scanners and, 429
  setting, 395–397
Restart command
  Finder, 44
  Force Quit command and, 101–102
restart problems, 179–181
  "?" disk icon (startup problems), 141
  causes, 179
  Directory problems, 181
  Finder Preferences file, 181
  floppy disk mounting, 165
  launching applications, 205
  Reset button, 180

restart problems *(continued)*
saving documents, 179
sound errors at startup, 136–137, 138–140
startup extensions, 180
symptoms, 179
system software replacement, 181
restarts, 90–96
alternatives to, 90
"Can't load the Finder," 152
Desktop Printers and, 272
ejecting disks, 167
with extensions off, 673
Interrupt button (physical), 91–92
keyboard Reset and Interrupt commands, 92–94
locating Reset buttons, 92
mounting hard disks, 158
PowerBook, 95–96
PowerBook after system errors, 458–463
RAM disks and, 96
recovering unsaved data after, 96–99
Reset button (physical), 91
Restart button, 90
soft, 458
stopping, 181
System 7.5 and Shut Down warning messages, 91
turning Macintoshes off and on, 94–95
unexpected quits and, 107
waiting before, 459
Restore Mandate feature, TechTool, 799
restoring disks, data recovery utilities (Fix-It #13), 811, 821–823
resuming printing, 281
return characters, paragraphs shifting formatting, 368
Rhapsody, future of system software, 597
risk management, problem-solving strategies, 71
ROM modules, 6–8
user interface and, 7
rotating objects, 402

S

sad-Mac error codes, 134–135
sad-Mac icons
At Ease for Workgroups, 138
author's anecdotes, 139
unusual tones at startup, 133
SAM SafeZone anti-viral utility, 759–767
compression, 762
customizing, 762
eradicating viruses, 764–767
installing, 760–761
preventing viruses from infecting disks, 763–764
Prevention checking, 762
repairing infected files, 767
Scan Preferences window, 762
scanning for and deleting infected files, 765–766
upgrading, 761
user definitions, 761
Save As command, 192–193
graphics file formats, 407
Replace option, 192
Save command, 192–193
Trash and, 235
Save dialog box
Desktop Printers and, 272
saving files, 191
Save Settings button, Print command, 262
saving
autosave, 50
frequency of, 50
preventative maintenance, 49–50
RAM disk contents, 454–455
system freezes and, 100
to protect from system errors, 82
URLs, 631
saving problems, 233–237
bad blocks, 233
causes, 233–234
disk errors, 233, 236–237
documents and restarts, 179
files in use, 235–236
full disks, 234
"illegal access permission," 235–236
locked disks, 234, 235
read errors, 233, 237
symptoms, 233
unintended locations, 194
verification errors, 234
virtual memory and, 234
write errors, 233, 237
Scan Preferences window, SAM SafeZone anti-viral utility, 762
scanners, resolution and, 429
Scrapbook
insufficient memory, 559
opening problems, 213
pasting graphics across applications, 416
screen dimming, PowerBook battery conservation, 447, 448
screen display breakup, system crashes and, 83
screen fonts, printer fonts comparison, 338–339
screen savers, need for, 889
screens blinking at startup
AppleVision problems, 534
PCI-based Mac problems, 523–524
scriptable viruses, 757
scrolling, unexpected problems and, 238
SCSI cables, 875–876
SCSI chains
running with disconnected devices, 876
SCSI device problems (Fix-It #16), 859, 871
SCSI device problems
"?" disk icon (startup problems), 141
mounting CD-ROMs, 173–174
mounting hard disks, 158
repairing hardware problems (Fix-It #17), 882
system freezes, 103
tone errors at startup, 137, 138
SCSI device problems (Fix-It #16), 858–876
cables, 875–876
connection order, 873–875
disconnecting devices, 872
ID numbers, 859–860
IDE alternatives, 860
reasons for, 858–862
running with disconnected devices, 876
SCSI chains, 859, 871
SCSI ID numbers, 869, 872–873
SCSI ports, 858–859, 871
SCSI utilities, 862–869
SCSI-2, 861
SCSIProbe utility, 862–869
termination, 860–862, 873, 874
turning off non-startup devices, 871–872
when to check for, 858
write cache and data corruption, 870
SCSI Disk mode, HD Target mode as, 478
SCSI Manager
SCSI device problems (Fix-It #16), 860
SCSIProbe and, 863
SCSI ports
external hard disks and, 14
PowerBook file transfers, 477–479
SCSI device problems (Fix-It #16), 858–859, 871
SCSIProbe utility, 862–869
CD-ROM drives, 866
devices not listed or mounted, 867
disk drives don't mount automatically at startup, 868–869
hard disks, 864
listed devices don't mount, 864–866
mounting devices with, 862–863
mounting removable cartridges with different drivers, 865
product listings, 864
removable cartridges, 864
SCSI Manager and, 863

searching for
files. *See* finding files
reserved fonts in System 7, 382
text within text files, 197
segmented files, downloaded files, 635
serial cables, checking, 891
Serial Port Arbitrator extension, Apple Remote Access (ARA), 500–501
serial port devices, repairing hardware problems (Fix-It #17), 891–893
"serial port in use" error, modem problems, 497
serial ports
DMA (modems), 606
non-AppleTalk printer options, 255–256
Open Transport problems, 622
Performas and, 527
printing halts and, 287
troubleshooting printing, 276
servers, Macs as, 634
shadow icons, dragging to Trash, 178
shadows, ejecting disk, 167
"shared disk could not be found on network," file sharing problems, 491
"shared disk could not be opened," file sharing problems, 492–493
shared libraries
See also Open Transport
Power Mac problems, 518–519
startup extension problems, 691
System 7.5/7.6 problems, 560
shareware, 916–917
Sharing command, Finder and file sharing problems, 492–493
Sharing... dialog box
file sharing, 482
file sharing problems, 490
sharing files. *See* file sharing
Sharing Setup control panel
file sharing, *481*, 482
file sharing problems, 490
recurring system errors and, 113
shortcuts
Alert Box messages, 68
problem-solving strategies, 74
ShortFinder
fitting more utilities on emergency disks, 313
startup disks, 48
Show Clipboard command, pasting graphics across applications, 415
ShrinkWrap
as alternative to RAM disks, 455
browser problems, 646
creating disk image files with, 646
downloaded system software and, 723
Shut Down command
Finder, 44
hard shutdowns, 459–460
PowerBook Sleep function comparison, 446, 448
soft shutdowns, 95, 458
stopping, 181
Shut Down problems, 179–181
causes, 179
checking for background application problems, 180
saving documents, 179
startup extensions, 180
symptoms, 179
Shut Down warning messages, System 7.5, 91
Shutdown Items folder, System Folder, 22
SIMMs
See also memory
defined, 894
SimpleSound
AppleVision software, 531
recording sound with, 212
SimpleText
See also documents; OpenDoc
editing documents, 312
file types of, 582
graphics in, 312
opening documents by default in, 311–312
opening documents (problems with), 215
PDDs (Portable Digital Documents) and, 582, 583
TeachText comparison, 311
Size window, OpenDoc, 569–570
Sleep function
AppleTalk and, 471
AppleVision problems, 536
PCI-based Mac problems, 524–525
PowerBook battery conservation, 446, 448
problems with, 469–472
slow hard disks, 183–186
causes, 184
compression and, 185
disk caches, 185
display depth, 185
extensions, 184–185
Preferred size option, 185
solutions, 184–186
startup delays, 186
symptoms, 183
virtual memory, 185
slow printing
Hewlett-Packard printers, 295
StyleWriters, 297
Smooth Graphics option, Page Setup dialog box, 434
Snitch
editing/viewing file types and creator code, 308–309
editing/viewing Finder flags, 318
soft restarts, 458
soft shutdowns, 458
PowerBook, 95
software
See also applications; hardware/software incompatibilities
AppleVision monitor, 530–531
backup, 51
bugs. *See* bugs
ColorSync, 430–431
commercial, 915
conflicts, 31
damage control, 30–31
damaged, 29–30
Desktop Printer, 267
file sharing, 481–482
future of, 596–597
graphics, 402–404
incompatibilities, 111
INITs, 22
native Power Mac, 511–514
PostScript, 403, 404
printer versions, 288
QuickDraw and QuickDraw GX, 249
shareware and freeware, 916–917
system. *See* System #; system software
utilities, 31, *32–33*
where to get, 915–918
software upgrades, hardware/software incompatibilities (Fix-It #1), 668
Solve It!
AppleVision problems, 531–537
browser problems, 637–655
color/grayscale displays, 420–425
disk problems, 157–188
display problems, 420–425
file problems, 193–243
file transfer problems, 488–503
font file problems, 375–379
Font Menu problems, 380–385
font problems, 350–374
graphics printing problems, 426–437
graphics transfer problems, 414–420
Open Transport problems, 622–628
PCI-based Mac problems, 523–529
Power Mac problems, 515–523
PowerBook problems, 458–476
printing problems, 274–297
QuickDraw GX problems, 589–596
recurring system errors, 109–117
startup problems, 131–156
System 7.5/7.6 problems, 544–563
system errors, 82–109
video problems, 411–414
Web browser problems, 637–655

sound
AppleVision problems, 536–537
Power Mac problems, 522
PowerBook problems, 474
System 7.5/7.6 problems, 558–559
sound files, 210–212
See also tone errors at startup
alerts, 210–211
application, 211
CD audio, 212
control panels, 210
damaged, 210
downloaded, 635–636
formats, 210
PlainTalk speech, 212
recording with SimpleSound, 212
volume, 211–212
Sound Manager, QuickTime video and, 411
sound volume, PowerBook battery conservation, 451
Special menu, Finder, 44
speech, PlainTalk sound files, 212
speed of
memory, 9, 899, 900
modems, 603–607
Power Macs, 507–509
printing, 283
Spin Down command
PCI-based Macs, 525
PowerBook battery conservation, 447, 448
Split Long Paths option, printing halts, 291
spool files
deleting, 286
Desktop Printer software, 267
PrintMonitor, 264, 266
startup crashes, Power Mac problems, 521
startup delays, slow hard disks, 186
Startup Disk control panel, 126–128
external hard drives and, 127
partitions, 128
System 7.5.3 and, 127
startup disks, 45–49, 124–131
See also emergency disks
"?" disk icon (startup problems), 140
alternate hard disks, 128–129
blessed System Folders, 124
blessing System Folders, 142
boot blocks, 47, 125
bypassing external drives, 129
bypassing hard disks at startup, 131
CD-ROM, 48, 126, 522
control panel, 126–128
creating with MacTools Pro, 813
creating with Norton Utilities, 813
data recovery utilities, 48
determining between two disks, 125
Disk Tools, 45–47
Finder-less, 47–48, 313, 314
Font Menu problems, 380
free space and background printing, 294
mounting problem drives, 129
RAM disks, 452–453
removable cartridge drives and, 129
removable cartridges as, 176
secondary hard drives or partitions as, 49
ShortFinder, 48
starting with alternate, 128–131
switching at startup, 869
system crashes and, 188
System Folders and, 124
tone errors at startup, 136–137
universal, 49
startup extension problems, 148–150
background-only applications, 690
Chooser extensions, 691
conflicts, 683–684
determining, 149
loading, 684–685, 704–707
memory, 149–150
network connections and, 148
Network Extension and "fext" files, 690–691
oddities, 690–692
on/off buttons, 706
printer conflicts, 295
RAM Doubler, 691, 707
recurring system errors, 113
shared libraries, 691
system software and, 150
testing for, 148
"thng" files, 691
unexpected errors, 240–241
zapping PRAM, 150
startup extension problems (Fix-It #4), 682–707
aliases, 701–702
bugs, 693–694
codependent startup extensions, 704
Conflict Catcher, 687, 696
conflicts between two extensions, 696–697
damaged files, 702–703
deleting startup extensions, 703
disabling methods, 685–692
disabling/re-enabling individual extensions, 694–695
Extensions Manager, 687
identifying, 693–699
incompatibilities, 693
loading, 684–685, 704–707
loading order, 699–702
memory, 703
on/off buttons, 706
RAM Doubler, 691, 707
reasons for, 683–685
resolving conflicts, 699–703
Shift key at startup, 686
startup conflicts, 683–684
startup icons with "X," 706–707
startup management utilities, 686–689, 705–706
Startup Manager, 696
system crashes at startup, 697–699
System Folder, 692, 704–705
upgrading, 702
when to check for, 682
startup extensions
aliases, 701–702
codependent, 704
deleting, 703
INITs comparison, 683
loading order, 699–702
loading prior to startup management utilities, 690
memory locations, 684
oddities, 690–692
on/off buttons, 706
renaming, 701
Shut Down and restart problems, 180
system heaps and, 684
upgrading, 702
Startup Items folder, System Folder, 21
startup management utilities, 686–689
See also Conflict Catcher; Startup Manager
control panels and extensions, 687
disabling methods, 688, 689
extensions loading prior to, 690
linking with, 702
loading order, 701
startup extension problems (Fix-It #4), 686–689, 705–706
Startup Manager
linking with, 702
startup extension problems (Fix-It #4), 696
startup problems, 131–156
"?" disk icon, 140–144
dead Macintoshes, 131–133
Finder and desktop, 151–156
system errors prior to or while "Welcome to Macintosh," 146–150
unusual tones. *See* tone errors at startup
"X" disk icon, 145–146
startup sequences, 123–131
normal, 123–124
rebuilding Desktops every time, 783–784
startup disks, 124–131
static addresses, Internet, 634
stationery, OpenDoc, 565–566
Stationery folder, OpenDoc, 567

status lights, LaserWriter, 283
stiction, mounting hard disk problems, 161
storage devices, 11–15
  CD-ROMs, 15
  floppy disks, 13–14
  hard disks, 14
  measuring capacity of, 11
  removable cartridges, 15
strategies, problem-solving, 67–75
style variant screen fonts, Font Menu problems, 384
StyleWriters
  cables, 296
  color options, 430
  color problems, 431–432
  installation problems, 296
  LocalTalk options, 256
  memory problems, 296–297
  PrinterShare, 297
  printing freezes, 296
  printing wrong fonts from display, 355–356
  slow printing, 297
  smeared ink, 297
  toner cartridges, 297
  troubleshooting, 296–297
subfolders, System Folder, 19–23
submarining on passive matrix screens, 474
substitute fonts, ATM (Adobe Type Manager), 352
Substitute Fonts checkbox, LaserWriters, 356
suitcases. *See* font suitcases
sync-on-green monitor problem, 523, 888
synchronization, file, 485
SyQuest drives. *See* removable cartridges
System 7
  Desktop Folder, 200
  fonts, 333
  "instant" clean reinstall of, 712
  searching for reserved fonts in, 382
  zapping PRAM (Fix-It #11), 795
System 7.5/7.6, 542–544
  See also system software
  Apple Guide, 543–544
  Apple Menu Options control panel, 198
  Balloon Help, 543–544
  Custom Install, 552–553
  Easy Install, 549
  Finder Hiding, 198
  fonts, 331–333
  General Controls control panel, 198
  hidden features, 544
  installation procedure, 548–551
  locked files, 227
  "Read Me" files, 543
  release strategy, 542–543
  Shut Down warning messages, 91
  Startup Disk control panel, 127
  universal installs, 552
  update history, 546–547
  WindowShade, 198
System 7.5/7.6 problems, 544–563
  Apple Guide, 562–563
  Apple Menu Options control panel, 556
  AppleScriptLib, 556
  control panels, 555–558
  Enabler files, 554–555
  Energy Saver control panel, 557
  error messages, 551
  extensions, 555–558
  installations, 545–553
  insufficient memory, 559–561
  Macintosh names, 554
  memory, 559–561, 743
  Monitors extension, 556
  Now Utilities, 558
  ObjectSupportLib, 556
  Preferences files, 558
  Preferences files (Fix-It #2), 673
  shared libraries, 560
  sound, 558–559
  System 7.5 Update 2.0 CD, 553
  third-party extensions, 557
  Update files, 554–555
  update history, 546–547
  video, 558–559
System 7.6, overview, 561
system crashes, 82–99
  Bomb alert box, 82
  browser problems, 642–647
  causes, 83
  Desktop Printers and, 272
  error code numbers, 84–87
  file sharing problems, 495
  frequent, 187–188
  hard disk problems, 188
  Power buttons, 93
  restarts, 90–96
  screen display breakup, 83
  startup disks, 188
  symptoms, 82–83
system crashes at startup
  Power Mac problems, 521
  startup extension problems (Fix-It #4), 697–699
system enhancement packages, troubleshooting toolkit, 35
System Error Patch freeware utility, hard disk crash protection, 61
system errors, 79–117
  browser problems, 647
  crashes, 82–99
  Desktop Printers, 273
  endless loops, 105–106
  error code numbers, 84–87
  Finder disappears, 108–109
  Finder startup problems, 154–156
  Power Mac problems, 520–522
  recurring, 99, 109–117
  restarting PowerBooks after, 458–463
  saving to protect from, 82
  solving quickly, 83
  system freezes, 99–104
  unexpected quits, 106–108
  "Welcome to Macintosh" and, 146–150
System extensions, Extensions folder, 20
System files
  alert sound files, 314
  maintaining, 63–64
System Folders, 16–26
  "?" disk icon (startup problems), 141–143
  Apple Menu Items folder, 20
  blessed, 124
  blessing, 142
  Control Panels folder, 21
  defined, 16
  deleting files from, 52–53
  deleting multiple, 727–278
  documents displaying wrong fonts, 350
  Extensions folder, 20–21
  file problems, 242
  Finder, 18–19
  font management, 331–333
  Fonts folder, 23
  Get Info command, 23
  INITs, 22
  minimal, 124
  multiple causing recurring system errors, 115
  Performas and, 17
  placing items in, 19
  PostScript printer font files, 344–345
  Preferences folder, 23
  removing fonts from, 376
  Shutdown Items folder, 22
  startup disks and, 124
  startup extension problems (Fix-It #4), 692, 704–705
  Startup Items folder, 21
  subfolders, 19–23
  System Enabler file, 18
  System file, 17–18
  universal, 718
  versions, 16–17
system freezes, 99–104
  background printing and, 104
  browser problems, 642–647
  causes, 100
  disconnected cables and, 102–103
  disk drives and, 103
  file sharing problems, 495

system freezes *(continued)*
font files and, 104
Force Quit command, 100–102
internal hardware problems as cause of, 103
memory and, 104
peripheral devices and, 103
PowerBook file transfers, 479
PowerPC Interrupt Extension and, 521
recurring, 102–104
saving and, 100
SCSI devices and, 103
symptoms, 99
system software and, 104
system heaps
memory management problems (Fix-It #6), 730
size increases for memory management, 749–750
size of, 730
startup extensions and, 684
system software comparison, 730
system software
See also System 7.5/7.6
Chooser. *See* Chooser
clean reinstalls, 710–723
compressed downloaded, 723
deleting Preferences files, 676
Disk Copy and downloaded, 723
disk driver updates (Fix-It #12), 802
Easy Install, 549
floppy disks and, 723
future of, 596–597
installing, 548–551, 717–723
installing with Mac OS 7.6, 714–715
memory size decreases, 746–748
Performa reinstallations, 711
release strategy, 542–543
ShrinkWrap and downloaded, 723
system freezes and, 104
system heap comparison, 730
updates, 112
upgrade variations, 722
upgrading, 137
version matching, 725
versions, 147–148
where to get, 918
system software problems
clones, 528
launching, 208
"lost" after updating, 713
recurring system errors and, 114
selective install/reinstall/deletion, 724–728
startup extension, 150
tone errors at startup, 138
troubleshooting toolkit, 34
unexpected, 242–243
version matching, 725
system software problems (Fix-It #5), 708–728
backup reinstalls, 725–726
complete installs/reinstalls, 710–723
corrupted files, 709–710
deleting multiple System Folders, 724–278
Disk First Aid, 716
disk formatters, 716
identifying incompatibilities and bugs, 709
installation procedure, 717–723
Installer utilities, 716–723
missing files, 724–725
reasons for, 708–710
selective install/reinstall/deletion, 724–728
version matching, 725
System Updates, 64–65
fixing recurring system errors, 112
overview, 65
reference releases, 64

T

TCP/IP, 612–621
America Online and CompuServe via PPP, 621
AppleTalk control panel, 616
connection alternatives to PPP, 616
control panels, 614, 615–616
FreePPP control panel, 617–619
"load only when needed," 613
MacTCP control panels, 614
MacTCP DNR files, 617
multi-homing, 621
Open Transport PPP control panels, 619–621
TeachText, opening documents by default in, 311–312
technical support, problem-solving strategies, 72
technical support (Fix-It #18), 903–914
alternatives to, 909–914
America Online, 909
Apple, 908
books, 913–914
bulletin boards, 910
calling, 907–909
CompuServe, 909
download libraries, 910
Internet and, 910–912
magazines, 913
mailing lists, 911
newsgroups, 910
online information services, 909
preparing for calls, 905–906
product, 904–909
registration and upgrades, 907
user groups, 913
utilities and, 906–907
Web sites, *912*
when to call for, 904–905
when to seek other types of, 905
when to use, 903
World Wide Web, 911–912
TechTool
rebuilding Desktops (Fix-It #9), 782, 785–786
Restore Mandate feature, 799
zapping PRAM (Fix-It #11), 798–800
TechTool Pro, hardware problems (Fix-It #17), 879, *880*
Telecom Adapter, Open Transport problems, 625
telephone systems, modem connections while traveling, 628
temporary files, recovering unsaved data after restarting, 96–99
termination, SCSI, 860–862, 873, 874
Tex-Edit Plus, graphics in SimpleText documents, 312
text
See also font problems; fonts
bitmapped graphics problem, 373–374
clipped at margins (font problems), 363–364
clippings files, 371, 372
text characters, incorrect keyboards, 354
text files, searching within, 197
TEXT format, creator code and file type issues, 310–311
text scan method, undeleting files, 202
third-party extensions, System 7.5/7.6 problems, 557
"thng" files, startup extension problems, 691
TIFF graphics file format, 405
Timbuktu Pro
file sharing and, 480
file transfers via modem, 486–487
tone errors at startup, 133–140
alternate startup disks, 136–137
causes, 133–134
decoding error codes, 136
Directory file repair, 137
hardware problems, 139
memory chips, 139
restart failure, 138–140
restarting, 136–137
sad-Mac error codes, 134–136
sad-Mac icon, 133
SCSI problems, 137, 138
system software problems, 138
updating disk drives, 137
upgrading system software, 137
toner cartridges
printer, 283
StyleWriter, 297

toolkit, troubleshooting. *See* troubleshooting toolkit
Total Memory, About This Macintosh command, 40
Trackballs/Trackpads, repairing, 885–886
transferring files to and from PowerBooks. *See* file transfers (PowerBook)
transferring files via Internet. *See* file transfers (Internet)
transferring graphics. *See* graphics transfer problems
Trash
  deletion problems, 225–231
  Desktop Printers and, 271
  dragging disk icons and shadow icons to, 178
  Empty Trash command, 44
  invisible files and folders, 320
  Save command and, 235
TrashBack utility (undeleting files), 57–59, 201–202
  false alarms, 818
  invisible folder, 58
traveling, modem connections while on the road, 628
Tray Mismatch Alert, QuickDraw GX problems, 593
trickle mode, PowerBook batteries, 464
Trojan horse viruses, 759
troubleshooting
  See also problem-solving strategies
  background printing, 282, 292–294
  Desktop Printers, 270–274
  disk storage, 12
  Drive7, 851
  Drive Setup, 849
  with Finder, 36–44
  FreePPP control panel, 628
  memory, 10
  preventing problems, 27–65
  printers, 248–263
  printing, 245–297
  RAM, 10
  StyleWriters, 296–297
  system crashes, 82–99
  system errors, 79–117
troubleshooting toolkit, 31–36
  data recovery utilities, 34–35
  system enhancement packages, 35
  system software, 34
  utilities, *32–33*
TrueType fonts
  combining font types, 345–347
  identifying, 337–338
  incompatibility problems, 360–361
  jaggies, 365–366
  PostScript fonts comparison, 348
  QuickDraw GX, 583
tune-ups, 62–64
  defragmenting hard disks, 62
  Disk First Aid, 63
  rebuilding desktops, 63
  System file maintenance, 63–64
  System Updates, 64–65
TV Tuner cards, Apple Video Player and, 413
24-bit color
  memory allocation, 424
  Monitors control panel, 398
Type 1 Enabler utility, PostScript fonts, 586–587
Type 1 errors, Open Transport PPP control panels, 623
Type 1 versus Type 3 PostScript fonts, 339
Type 11 errors
  code numbers, 85, *86*, 88, 89
  Open Transport PPP control panels, 623
  Power Mac problems, 520
Type 15 errors, Desktop Printers, 273–274
typefaces, font, 330
types. *See* file types

U

"Unable to read from disk," launching problems, 213
undeleting files, 56–59, 200–203
  before installing invisible files, 202
  caveats, 203
  defragmenting disks and, 773
  file pattern scan method, 202
  MacTools Pro, 57–59, 201–202
  Norton Utilities, 56, 201
  text scan method, 202
  unplugging Macintosh strategy, 200
Undo command, problem-solving strategies, 75
unexpected problems, 238–243
  alert noises, 239
  ATM control panel, 241
  background processes, 240
  bugs in applications, 239–240
  flashing icons in menu bar, 239
  installer utilities and, 241
  memory and, 241
  RAM Doubler and, 241
  scrolling and, 238
  startup extension conflicts, 240–241
  system software problems, 242–243
unexpected quits, 106–108
  launching problems, 204–205
  Preferred size option and, 107
  restarts and, 107
universal installs, System 7.5/7.6, 552
universal startup disks, 49
universal System Folders, 718
Unlimited Downloadable Fonts checkbox, LaserWriters, 356–357
unmounted hard disks, 177–178
  dimmed disk icons, 177
  dragging disk icons to Trash, 178
  remounting, 178
  removing disk icons, 177
unmounting floppy disks. *See* ejecting disks
unreadable disks
  Finder startup problems, 153–154
  RAM disks, 455
unsaved data, recovering after restarting, 96–99
Update files, System 7.5/7.6 problems, 554–555
updates
  See also System Updates
  disk drive, 137
  disk driver, 143
  overview, 718
  reference releases comparison, 710
  system software, 112, 542
upgrading
  ATM (Adobe Type Manager), 341
  native Power Mac software, 511
  SAM SafeZone anti-viral utility, 761
  software incompatibilities (Fix-It #1), 668
  startup extensions, 702
  system software, 137
  system software variations, 722
uploaded files, 636–637
uploading files, 632
URLs (World Wide Web addresses), 630–632
  saving and using, 631
Use Custom Icon bit, Finder flags, 316
user groups, technical support (Fix-It #18), 913
user interfaces, ROM modules and, 7
Users & Groups control panel
  file sharing, 483
  PowerBook file transfers, 487
utilities
  anti-viral, 760–762
  backup, 51
  compression, 54–55
  damaged font file checking, 376
  data recovery. *See* data recovery utilities
  defined, 31
  defragmenting disks (Fix-It #8), 769
  Disk First Aid. *See* Disk First Aid
  fitting more on emergency disks, 313
  folder deletion problems, 229–230
  font management, 334
  graphics, 408
  hardware diagnostics, 879–881

utilities *(continued)*
opening documents (problems with), 216
protection, 55–62
QuickDraw GX, 588
SCSI, 862–869
technical support and, 906–907
troubleshooting, *32–33*
undeleting files, 56–59

V

vendor product directory, 918–920
verification errors, saving problems, 234
verifying disk formats, 855–857
version incompatibilities, problems with opening documents, 217–218
version matching, system software, 725
version numbers
disk driver updates (Fix-It #12), 806
Get Info command, 37
versions
LaserWriter, 248–249
printer driver, 280
printer software, 288
system software, 16–17
system software and "Welcome to Macintosh," 147–148
vertical alignment, problems due to font selections, 360
vertical lines following cursors on monitors, 523
video, 408–414
downloaded files, 635–636
formats, 409–410
PCI-based Mac problems, 528
QuickTime, 408–412
RAM, 901
System 7.5/7.6 problems, 558–559
video display cards, repairing monitors, 887
video mirroring, external monitors for PowerBooks, 457–458
video problems, 411–414
Apple Video Player, 412–414
installing QuickTime, 411
playing, 411–412
recording, 412
View by Date, Finder, 196
viewers, OpenDoc, 565–566
viewing
creator code and file types, 306–309, 311–315
Finder flags, 317–318
invisible files and folders, 318–323
with ResEdit, 323
views, icon, 18
Views control panel, opening problems, 206
virtual memory
CD-ROM disc ejection problems, 175
formatting hard disks and, 846
Memory control panel, 745
memory management problems (Fix-It #6), 750–753
native Power Mac software and, 512–514
PowerBook battery conservation, 450
RAM Doubler and, 513
saving problems, 234
slow hard disks, 185
viruses
floppy disks and, 765
protection utilities, 55
recurring system errors, 116
viruses (Fix-It #7), 756–767
anti-viral utilities, 760–762
eradicating, 764–767
floppy disks and, 765
hoaxes, 759
infected Desktop files, 766
infection processes, 758
overview, 756–759
preventing, 763–764
repairing infected files, 767
SAM SafeZone, 759–767
samples with symptoms, 757
scriptable, 757
Trojan horses, 759
user definitions, 761
when to check for, 756
voice files, PlainTalk sound, 212
volume control, 211–212
alert sound files, 211
Performas and, 527

W

WDEF resources, purgeable, 112
Web browsers. *See* browsers
Web pages
displaying incorrectly, 648–649
loading slowly, 639–641
long delays before loading, 641
not updating, 653–654
won't load, 637–639
Web servers, Macs as, 634
Web sites
MagicCookie files, 647
technical support (Fix-It #18), *912*
"Welcome to Macintosh," system errors prior to or while, 146–150
"white" desktop patterns, PowerBook battery conservation, 451
window headers, Finder, 41–42
WindowShade, System 7.5, 198
word processing
overview, 329
Word 5.1 memory bug, 205
work files, recovering unsaved data after restarting, 96–99
work-arounds, problem-solving strategies, 73
World Wide Web
See also Internet
addresses, 630–632
authoring software, 633
browsers. *See* browsers
HTML (HyperText Markup Language), 633
shareware and freeware, 917
technical support (Fix-It #18), 911–912
write cache and data corruption, 870
write errors, saving problems, 233, 237
WYSIWYG, ATM (Adobe Type Manager) and, 340, 341

X

"X" icons
Desktop Printers, 271
startup problems, 145–146
Xon/Xoff versus hardware handshaking, modem flow control, 607

Z

zapping PRAM
"?" disk icon (startup problems), 144
Finder Preferences file and, 794
PCI-based Mac problems, 529
PowerBook batteries, 468
printing and data corruption, 281
printing halts, 287
recurring system errors, 113
startup extension problems, 150
zapping PRAM (Fix-It #11), 793–800
battery removal and, 796
corrupted System files, 798
"Cuda" button, 797
dead batteries, 797
how to, 795–798
PCI-based Macs, 795–796, 800
reasons for, 794–795
resetting customized settings, 796–797
System 7, 795
TechTool, 798–800
when to, 793
Zip drives. *See* removable cartridges